Vietnam, Cambodia, Laos
& the Greater Mekong

Nick Ray
Tim Bewer, Andrew Burke,
Thomas Huhti, Siradeth Seng

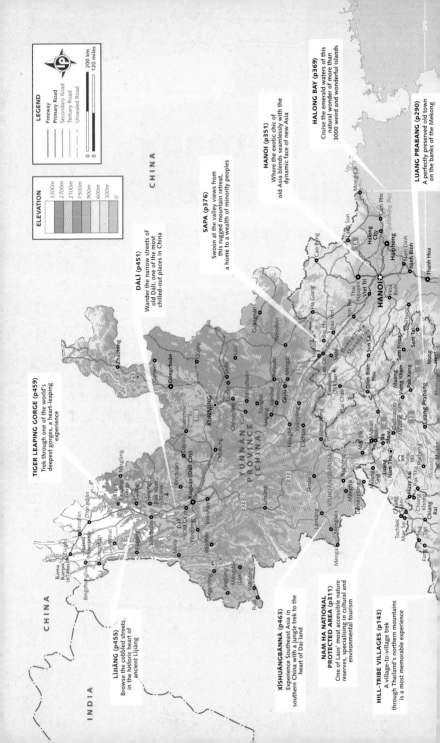

LEGEND

Freeway
Primary Road
Secondary Road
Tertiary Road
Unsealed Road

0   200 km
0   120 miles

ELEVATION

3300m
2700m
2100m
1500m
900m
600m
300m
0

CHINA

INDIA

TIGER LEAPING GORGE (p459)
Trek through one of the world's deepest gorges, a heart-leaping experience

LIJIANG (p455)
Browse the cobbled streets in the historic heart of ancient Lijiang

DALI (p451)
Wander the narrow streets of old Dali, one of the most chilled-out places in China

SAPA (p376)
Swoon at the valley views from this rugged mountain retreat, a home to a wealth of minority peoples

HANOI (p351)
Where the exotic chic of old Asia blends seamlessly with the dynamic face of new Asia

HALONG BAY (p369)
Cruise the emerald waters of this natural wonder of more than 3000 weird and wonderful islands

LUANG PRABANG (p290)
A perfectly preserved old town on the banks of the Mekong

XISHUANGBANNA (p463)
Experience Southeast Asia in southern China with a jungle trek to the heart of Dai land

NAM HA NATIONAL PROTECTED AREA (p311)
One of Laos' most accessible nature reserves, specialising in cultural and environmental tourism

HILL-TRIBE VILLAGES (p143)
A village-to-village trek through Thailand's northern mountains is a most memorable experience

YUNNAN PROVINCE (CHINA)

KUNMING

HANOI

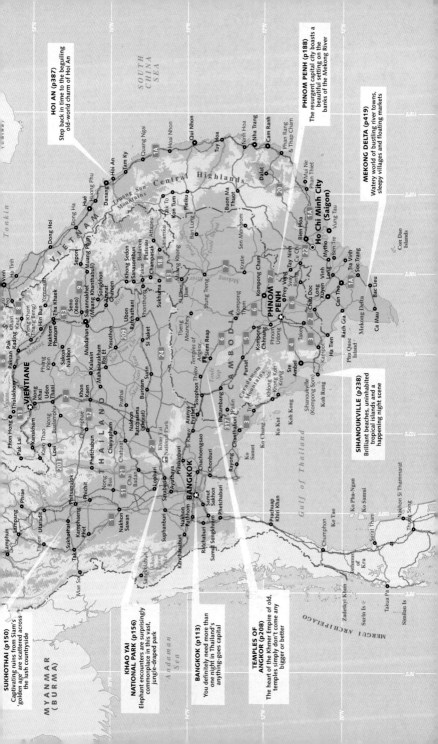

HOI AN (p387)
Step back in time to the beguiling old-world charm of Hoi An

PHNOM PENH (p188)
The resurgent capital city boasts a beautiful setting on the banks of the Mekong River

MEKONG DELTA (p419)
Watery world of bustling river towns, sleepy villages and floating markets

SIHANOUKVILLE (p238)
Brilliant beaches, uninhabited tropical islands and a happening night scene

SUKHOTHAI (p150)
Captivating ruins from Siam's 'golden age' are scattered across the lush countryside

KHAO YAI NATIONAL PARK (p156)
Elephant encounters are surprisingly commonplace in this vast, jungle-draped park

BANGKOK (p113)
You definitely need more than one night in Thailand's anything-goes capital

TEMPLES OF ANGKOR (p208)
The heart of the Khmer Empire of old, temples simply don't come any bigger or better

On the Road

NICK RAY Coordinating Author

When you first set eyes on an ageing Russian Mi-17 helicopter, it looks like the chopper equivalent of the ostrich, a bird just too big to fly. One of the highlights of this trip was finally getting to see majestic Halong Bay from the air. Hold tight, as this is where 'the dragon descends into the sea'.

TIM BEWER

As much as I love Thai art and architecture, acute temple overload is a common occupational hazard since we authors dash through dozens of wats every week. But That Phanom, tucked away in the far end of Isan, is special. It's gleamier and holier than most temples, and you can't help feeling reinvigorated and inspired here. It's like *kaeng phèt* for the mind.

ANDREW BURKE

'We can ride across here, or we have to go 50km around to get to the other side.' Not what I'd anticipated when I'd hired the crappiest bike in Savannakhet. Still, after waiting for locals to lead the way, riding across this river was a highlight, reaffirming that Laos' roads less travelled make the most rewarding travel.

THOMAS HUHTI

My favourite part of researching in China is stumbling into a new place and trying to figure out what's what. A little old dude peers over my shoulder. I grin and say hello. He grins and starts chattering. Seconds later half the village has come out to yak with the crazy foreigner.

SIRADETH SENG

While riding around Kratie we spotted this lady looking utterly exhausted working hard in the morning sun. We thought we'd give her a breather and dived in to help. She was very amused by my efforts; by her calculations I'd probably deprived the villagers of a good few bowls of rice with my dodgy technique.

See full author bios p529

Destination Greater Mekong

The Mekong. It's a name so exotic and evocative that it conjures up images of forbidding tropical jungle, the crumbling ruins of forgotten empires, remote minority tribes in looming mountains and streets steaming after the monsoonal rains.

Winding its way down from the Tibetan Plateau to the South China Sea, the Mekong River binds together the best of Asia. One of the world's great rivers, its dramatic journey southwards includes towering gorges in China, immense waterfalls in Laos, freshwater dolphins in Cambodia and a patchwork of emerald greens in the Mekong Delta.

The river is the gateway to a kaleidoscope of cultures, a bevy of beautiful backwaters and culinary heaven. Experience the splendour of sunrise over Angkor Wat. Be beguiled by historic towns such as Lìjiāng and Luang Prabang. Live life in the fast lane in Ho Chi Minh City. Experiment with fiery flavours at a buzzing market. See tigers and elephants in the wild. Recharge the batteries on a tropical beach. Let's face it, there are few places on earth where so many experiences are there for the taking.

Feel old Asia and new Asia collide. One minute it's Bangkok, riding the Skytrain to a state-of-the-art shopping mall, the next it's an elephant careering through a minority village in Mondulkiri. In the cities, the pace of life runs at a dizzying speed, matched only by the endless rush of motorbikes and cry of commerce. In the countryside, life is timeless, the rural rhythms the same as they have been for centuries, with pyjama-clad peasants tending the fields and monks wandering the streets seeking alms.

Go with the flow and let the spirit of the Mekong course through your veins. Leave the crowds behind and explore the roads less travelled in an older, more authentic Asia.

ANTONY GIBLIN

Highlights

Thailand shows off a splendid example of Angkorian splendour at Phanom Rung (p156)

Damnoen Saduak Floating Market (p129), near Bangkok, is the most famous of Thailand's watery commerical concourses

Trekking (p136) in Chiang Mai, Thailand, can include hitching a ride on an elephant

The glorious terracotta exterior of the National Museum (p192), Phnom Penh, Cambodia, is as much a treasure as the impressive collection of Khmer sculpture housed inside

Royal ballet dancers strike a pose at the Royal Palace (p192), Phnom Penh, Cambodia

Come face-to-face with the mysteries of Ankgor at Bayon temple (p209), Cambodia

TOM COCKREM

Colourful handicrafts are sold at Luang Prabang's night market (p299), Laos

JOHN BANAGAN

Pak Ou caves (p300), Laos, are packed with hundreds of Buddha images

The banks of the Mekong River at Luang Prabang (p290), Laos, are a perfect place to watch the sun set

RYAN FOX

CAROL WILEY

The World Heritage–listed Wat Phu Champasak (p328), Laos, is on many travellers' must-see list

Tat Kuang Si (p300), near Luang Prabang, Laos, is a waterfall worth gushing about

JOHN BORTHWICK

LAWRENCE WORCESTER

The architecture of Vientiane (p266), Laos' laid-back capital, reflects its colonial history

Hoan Kiem Lake (p357), Hanoi, Vietnam, is a tranquil spot for reflection

The charming riverside town of Hoi An (p387), Vietnam

Venture inside the otherworldy caves hidden in the limestone hills of Cat Ba Island (p371), Vietnam

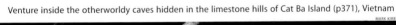

The Royal Tombs (p379) of Hué, Vietnam, are situated in glorious gardens

ANTHONY PLUMMER

SARA-JANE CLELAND

A hill-tribe woman heads to the market at Sapa (p376), Vietnam

The limestone islands of Halong Bay (p369), Vietnam, are simply sublime

MARK DAFFEY

KEREN SU

Your eyes may mist over at the beauty of Yuanyang Rice Terraces (p462), Yúnnán province (China)

The city of Dàlǐ (p451) offers stunning lake and mountain views, Yúnnán province (China)

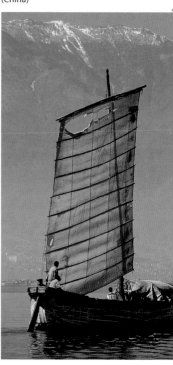

Witness local life on a trek (p467) in Xīshuāngbǎnnà, Yúnnán province (China)

BILL W

Contents

14 CONTENTS

Regional Map Contents

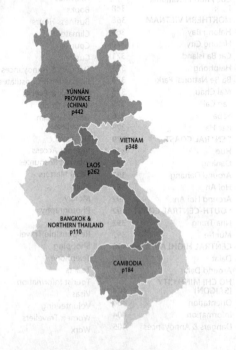

Getting Started

The Mekong is one of the world's most evocative rivers and lining its length are historic cities, blissful backwaters, beautiful landscapes, and friendly locals. Cruise the mother waters from Xīshuāngbǎnnà in Yúnnán Province to the perfect paddies of the Mekong Delta, stopping along the way to see the infamous Golden Triangle, the shimmering temples of Luang Prabang, the real life of Si Phan Don, the river dolphins of Kratie and born-again Phnom Penh. And don't forget some side trips. As well as Bangkok, the region's dynamic gateway, within touching distance of the Mekong lie the majestic temples of Angkor, the outrageous beauty of Halong Bay, pristine national parks such as Khao Yai in Thailand, and beguiling beaches in Cambodia and Vietnam.

The Mekong has all this and more, but it's also raw in places, so pack some flexibility, humour and patience. Come expecting the unexpected, be ready to go with the flow, prepare for an adventure as much as a holiday, and the Mekong region will deliver.

WHEN TO GO

When it comes to weather, it's a tough call, as the region's climate is so diverse. Think frosts and occasional snow in the mountains to the north, and temperatures soaring to 40°C in the dry season further south.

With the exception of northern Yúnnán, the Mekong region lies within the tropics. This means that regardless of when you visit, the weather is likely to be warm or even downright hot. High humidity is also common, with few areas far enough inland to enjoy thoroughly dry weather. Temperatures are much cooler in the mountains.

Cambodia, Laos, Vietnam and the northern and central regions of Thailand have three seasons: hot, hotter and hottest. There is a relatively cool dry season from November to late February, followed by a hot dry season from March to May, and then a humid, rainy season that starts some time in June and peters out in September. Fortunately, even during the rainy season it seldom rains all day and travel is possible over most of the region. The monsoon brings sudden torrential downpours for an hour or so each day, but this can be a real relief from the heat. Further north towards Hanoi and Kūnmíng, the rainy season comes during the summer months (June to August) when the thermometer soars. In contrast the winters can get quite chilly, so pack some warm gear.

See Climate Charts (p485) for more information.

DON'T LEAVE HOME WITHOUT...

Bring as little as possible, as the Mekong region has pretty much anything you can find back home but at lower prices. All the soaps and smellies are cheap and plentiful, and clothing, shoes and backpacks are all manufactured in countries such as Cambodia, Thailand and Vietnam, and available at a snip. Tampons are available in all major towns and cities, but not in more remote areas.

A Swiss army knife or equivalent comes in handy, but you don't need 27 separate functions, just one blade and an opener. A torch (flashlight) and compass are also useful.

Other handy things to bring are business cards, as Asians deal them out like a deck of cards; earplugs to block the ever-present soundtrack; a universal plug adaptor; a rain cover for the backpack; a sweater for the highlands and air-con bus trips; and mosquito repellent to keep the bugs at bay.

Finally, the secret of successful packing: plastic bags, as not only do they keep things separate and clean, but also dry. That means a lot at the end of a long, wet day.

Most of this region lies off the track of tropical cyclones (typhoons). However, typhoons do occasionally strike Vietnam. Peak typhoon season runs from June to early October, which can dampen the spirits of even the most enthusiastic traveller.

The region is pretty crowded from November to March and in July and August. Prices tend to peak over the Christmas and New Year period, and if you don't fancy sharing the sites with the masses, try to avoid these busy times.

Some travellers like to time a visit with Chinese New Year (Tet in Vietnam), which is one of the biggest festivals in the regional calendar and occurs in late January or early February. A nice idea, but not ideal, as the whole region is on the move at this time. Similarly, things get pretty chaotic during the new years of Cambodia, Laos and Thailand, which fall in mid-April. Commerce grinds to a halt and the population turns its attention to staging spectacular water fights or plastering each other with talcum powder.

COSTS & MONEY

The cost of travel in the Mekong region varies from pocket change to the platinum card, depending on your level of taste and comfort. Some countries are slightly more expensive than others, but all are ludicrously cheap compared with Europe or North America. Laos is considered the cheapest country in the region, while China is probably the most expensive. Cambodia, Thailand and Vietnam fall somewhere in between. Generally speaking, budget travellers can live it up on US$20 to US$30 a day. Midrange travellers can have a ball from US$50 to US$100 a day, staying in some style, eating well and travelling comfortably. At the top end, spending US$200 or more a day, anything is possible.

Rooms start from as little as US$3 to US$5 in busy tourist centres. Spending US$10 to US$20 will boost the comforts quickly, and rooms will generally include air-con, satellite TV, fridge and hot water. Make the step up to US$50 and three-star frills are available. At US$100 and above, it's five-star territory. Don't be afraid to negotiate for a discount if it is low season or if numbers are down.

Dining out is where the Mekong region comes into its own. Surfing the street stalls and markets, meals can be found for between US$0.50 and US$1. Local restaurants are more comfortable and you can eat well for US$1 to US$3.50. Then there are the gourmet restaurants and international diners, where you can still only spend around US$10 with drinks; with the right wines you could easily spend US$50. Beer and other alcoholic drinks are pretty reasonable throughout the region, with Laos and Vietnam taking the award for cheapest beer and Cambodia for cheapest wine and spirits.

Bus travel is a real bargain. Buses between major destinations have fixed fares in all the countries, but when travelling by bus in remote areas, overcharging is the rule. Thailand has the best buses, Laos has some of the worst. Trains are a good option in China, Thailand and Vietnam, particularly night sleepers for longer journeys. For maximum flexibility, many prefer to rent a car or 4WD and go exploring with a guide. Costs run from about US$25 around town to as much as US$100 a day upcountry (including the driver's food and lodging). A guide costs from US$20 to US$40, depending on the destination.

Flights around the region vary widely in price. Where budget carriers have entered the market, prices have dropped significantly. Bangkok is the discount flight capital of the region. On other routes, there may only be one or two carriers and prices are artificially high. More and more routes are being developed to link popular tourist centres and a short hop can save considerable time and money, not to mention pain, in the long run. Compare the Luang Prabang to Hanoi run by bus and by plane and you'll soon understand what we mean.

HOW MUCH?

Restaurant meal US$3-10

Hotel room with air-con US$10-20

Internet access per hour US$0.25-2

Bottle of beer US$1-3

Two-kilometre taxi ride US$1-5

Foreigners are frequently overcharged in the region, particularly when buying souvenirs and occasionally in restaurants. Bus and taxi drivers sometimes bump up their rates to several times the local price. China and Vietnam are notorious for overcharging, in Thailand they do it with a smile, in Cambodia they are fast learners, while Laos remains the most honest country. However, don't assume that everyone is trying to rip you off. Despite widespread poverty, many locals will only ask the local price for many goods and services.

Whatever your budget, the Mekong region will deliver. Live it up while it lasts.

TRAVEL LITERATURE

Much ink has spilled in the Mekong region over the years. Seek out some of these titles before taking the plunge.

The classic is Norman Lewis' *A Dragon Apparent* (1951), an account of his 1950 foray into Vietnam, Laos and Cambodia. It offers a good insight into the last days of French rule, an old Indochina that was soon to be sucked into war. The book has been reissued as part of *The Norman Lewis Omnibus* (1995).

To Asia With Love: A Connoisseur's Guide to Cambodia, Laos, Thailand and Vietnam (2004), an anthology edited by Kim Fay, is a delightful introduction to the Mekong region for those looking for some inspiration and adventure, written by writers who know and love their countries.

The Mekong: Turbulent Past, Uncertain Future (2001) by Milton Osborne is a readable history of the great river and the events that have unfolded along its vast length.

Another excellent account of life on the water is *The River's Tale: A Year on the Mekong* (2001) by Edward Gargan. A war-protester-turned-foreign-correspondent, Gargan sees for himself how these countries have brought themselves back from the brink.

'Whatever your budget, the Mekong region will deliver'

Travels in Siam, Cambodia, Laos and Annam by Henri Mouhot has been reprinted in English by White Lotus and gives the inside story of the man credited with 'rediscovering' Angkor.

Jon Swain's *River of Time* (1995) takes the reader back to an old Indochina, partly lost to the madness of war, and includes first-hand accounts of the French embassy stand-off in the first days of the Khmer Rouge takeover.

Tim Page's *Derailed in Uncle Ho's Victory Garden* (1995) covers this infamous photographer's quest for the truth behind the disappearance of photojournalist Sean Flynn (son of Errol) in Cambodia in 1970, and his mission to secure a monument to fallen correspondents on all sides of the Indochina conflict.

An equally legendary news cameraman, Australian Neil Davies, is the subject of Tim Bowden's book *One Crowded Hour* (1990). Davies covered Cambodia and Vietnam for many years, but was tragically killed covering a coup in Bangkok in 1985.

The Indochina Chronicles (2005) by Phil Karber is a lively travelogue taking in adventures and misadventures in Cambodia, Laos and Vietnam.

The ultimate spoof guidebook, *Phaic Tan: Sunstroke on a Shoestring* (2004) is a pastiche of Mekong countries and pokes fun at all of us. No-one is spared, not the locals, not the travellers, not even hallowed guidebook authors. An absolute must for anyone travelling through the Mekong region.

INTERNET RESOURCES

Biking Asia with Mr Pumpy (www.mrpumpy.net) *The* website for cyclists passing through the Mekong region, it is written with candour and humour by Mr Pumpy's best friend Felix Hude.
Golden Triangle Rider (www.GT-rider.com) The motorbiking website for the Mekong region, this is one of the most reliable sources for up-to-date road and border crossing information.

TOP 10

(Burma) Hanoi
LAOS
Vientiane•

MEKONG EXPERIENCES

Travel is not just about visiting, it's about experiencing. You need to get beneath the skin of the region and this can take many shapes or forms. It could be a culinary adventure. It could be a walk on the wild side. It could be a cultural encounter. It could be spiritual enlightenment. At some stage during your journey, the Mekong will enter your soul. Embrace it.

1. Count the number of locals crammed on to one motorbike in the countryside
2. Get the measure of a tailor, the only time you want to be stitched up in the region
3. Haggle with a cyclo driver about price before enjoying the ride
4. Learn to cross the road like a local in a busy city
5. Meet the minorities, a multicoloured mosaic of mountain people
6. Play bottoms up with the locals in a backstreet bar
7. See sunrise over the South China Sea from a beautiful beach
8. Slurp a steaming bowl of noodle soup at a street stall
9. Take some time out in a temple, the spiritual sanctuary for local people
10. Turn down the volume and drift along the Mekong river by boat

MUST-SEE MOVIES

Filmmakers have found a rich vein of material in the turbulent tales of the Mekong region, and both foreign and local directors have tapped it well. There are some moody, atmospheric movies from a time before the madness, a whole host of films dealing with the American experience in Indochina, and some memorable contemporary moments.

1. *Air America* (1990) Director: Roger Spottiswoode
2. *Apocalypse Now* (1979) Director: Francis Ford Coppola
3. *The Beach* (2000) Director: Danny Boyle
4. *Crouching Tiger, Hidden Dragon* (2000) Director: Ang Lee
5. *Iron Ladies* (2000) Director: Yongyoot Thongkongtoon
6. *The Killing Fields* (1984) Director: Roland Joffe
7. *The Last Emperor* (1987) Director: Bernardo Bertolucci
8. *Platoon* (1986) Director: Oliver Stone
9. *The Quiet American* (2002) Director: Phillip Noyce
10. *Two Brothers* (2004) Director: Jean-Jacques Annaud

THE NATIONAL DRINK

The locals in the Mekong region love a tipple and each country has its own flavours. Seize the day and slake your thirst with a selection of drinks as you travel through the region.

1. **Angkor Beer (C)** Angkor is everything to the Khmers, including the national beer
2. **Beer Lao (L)** The best lager in the world (if Carlsberg hadn't used the slogan first)
3. **Bia Hoi (V)** Surely the cheapest beer in the world, it costs about US$0.15 a glass
4. **Dynasty (Y)** One of China's best-known red wines, this goes well with Yunnanese cuisine
5. **Lao Lao (L)** Moonshine made by the minorities in upcountry Laos
6. **Mekhong (T)** Hardly a whisky, but sloshed down it's a fast route to oblivion
7. **Singha (T)** Thailand's national beer, strong enough to make you forget the night before
8. **Snake wine (C,T, L, V, Y)** Infused with the beating heart of a cobra
9. **Wrestler Wine (C)** Like combining sherry and Red Bull, you'll be rolling on the floor
10. **Xeo (V)** Potent rice wine brewed by the minorities of the mountains

Jewels of the Mekong Delta (www.travelmedia.com/mekong) Features travel information and news about countries along the Mekong river.

Lonely Planet (www.lonelyplanet.com) Summaries of countries in the region, the Thorn Tree bulletin board, Haystack accommodation booking site, travel news and useful links to travel resources elsewhere on the web.

Oriental Tales (www.orientaltales.com) Short stories, articles and inspiring photos of travel throughout the Southeast Asia region.

Tales of Asia (www.talesofasia.com) This website has up-to-the-minute information on overland travel in the Mekong region, including the 'Scam Bus' from Bangkok to Siem Reap.

Things Asian (www.thingsasian.com) Bubbling with information on the culture of the Mekong region, this site has everything including architecture, literature and fashion.

Travelfish (www.travelfish.org) Crammed with opinionated articles and reviews about the region, contributed by independent travellers. Plus up-to-date border crossing info.

Responsible Travel (www.responsible-travel.org) A no-nonsense website with common-sense advice on how to travel with a conscience.

Visit Mekong (www.visit-mekong.com) The official travel website for the Mekong, it offers comprehensive information about each country including health, religion, history and maps.

Itineraries
CLASSIC ROUTES

INDOCHINA EXPLORER   Three to Six Weeks

Begin in the graceful Vietnamese capital of **Hanoi** (p351), replete with grand boulevards, peaceful parks and lovely lakes. Take a junk cruise on **Halong Bay** (p369), where myriad karst islands soar from the sea. Head to **Hué** (p379), the old imperial capital and cultural hub of central Vietnam. Take the beautiful coastal road south to the historic trading point of **Hoi An** (p387). Soak up the sun on the sands of **China Beach** (p387) or continue south to the party beach town of **Nha Trang** (p392) or the rolling sand dunes of **Mui Ne** (p397).

Hit **Ho Chi Minh City** (p404), the full-throttle face of new Vietnam, head on. Go underground at the **Cu Chi Tunnels** (p418) and join the faithful at a **Cao Dai Temple** (p418) in Tay Ninh before plunging into the **Mekong Delta** (p419).

Experience the contrasts of **Phnom Penh** (p188), the tragedy of recent decades set against a glorious ancient past. Continue to **Siem Reap** (p201), home to the world's most spectacular collection of temples at **Angkor** (p208).

Board a flight to **Pakse** (p324), gateway to southern Laos, then head north to the Lao capital of **Vientiane** (p266), a world away from the modern metropolis of Bangkok. Finish up in **Luang Prabang** (p290) and see monks at dawn, caves brimming with Buddhas and an old Asia that is increasingly hard to find.

This can be run as a high-speed greatest hits trip in just three weeks, with a fistful of flights to connect the more distant cities. Those with time should slow things down, using some trains in Vietnam to meet more locals and trying the lively local buses in Cambodia and Laos.

MEKONG MEANDERS
Three to Six Weeks

Leave behind the bustle of **Bangkok** (p113) for the **Golden Triangle** (p147), where the borders of Laos, Myanmar and Thailand converge. Step back in time into Laos and take a slow boat down the Mekong from **Huay Xai** (p313), stopping the night in **Pak Beng** (p309), to **Luang Prabang** (p290). Soak up the magic before leaving the river for some relaxation in **Vang Vieng** (p287).

Continue to **Vientiane** (p266) and reunite with the mother river. It's a sleepy place with some great cafés, restaurants and bars, which you won't be encountering for a while. Fly south to **Pakse** (p324) or wind your way down the river through **Tha Khaek** (p317) and **Savannakhet** (p320). Visit the imposing Khmer sanctuary of **Wat Phu** (p328), under the shadow of Lingaparvata Mountain, explore the waterfalls and villages of the **Bolaven Plateau** (p333), or enjoy the laid-back islands of **Si Phan Don** (p329).

Cross into Cambodia and visit the mountains of **Ratanakiri** (p233), home to elephants, hill tribes and pristine nature. Back on the river, call in at **Kratie** (p230) to see the rare Irrawaddy dolphin. Continue south to the revitalised Cambodian capital **Phnom Penh** (p188). Make a diversion up the Tonlé Sap river to the boom town of **Siem Reap** (p201), your base for the majestic **temples of Angkor** (p208).

Next, take a fast boat down the mighty Mekong to **Chau Doc** (p422), gateway to the Mekong Delta. Check out **Cantho** (p421), its commercial heart. Hotfoot it to **Ho Chi Minh City** (p404) for some fun, delve deeper into the delta with a homestay around **Vinh Long** (p420) or make for the tropical retreat of **Phu Quoc Island** (p423), a well-earned reward for following the mother river.

This trip trickles through an older Asia, including some of the hottest spots in the region right now, as well as some of the less-visited backwaters. Move at a slower pace like the great river and soak up the contrasts as you float from country to country.

ROADS LESS TRAVELLED

MINORITY REPORT
Three to Six Weeks

Start in **Chiang Mai** (p133), cultural capital of northern Thailand, and make sure you visit the **Tribal Museum** (p136). Take on the winding road to **Pai** (p142), a mountain retreat that proves the hippy trail is alive and well. Either continue on to **Mae Hong Son** (p143) to take a trek through the villages or head straight up to **Tha Ton** (p145), the entry point for rafting trips down to **Chiang Rai** (p145).

Cross into Laos at **Huay Xai** (p313) and head for **Luang Nam Tha** (p309) and spend a day or two trekking with the award-winning **Nam Ha Ecotourism Project** (p309). Continue to **Muang Sing** (p312), the hub for one of the most diverse minority regions in all Laos.

It's time to take on China to the north. Head up to the Thai region around **Jǐnghóng** (p464), known as **Xīshuāngbǎnnà** (p463), a great area for biking and hiking. Now you've come this far, it would be rude not to visit the highlights of Yúnnán. Chill out in and around **Dàlǐ** (p451) before heading in to the historic of heart of **Lìjiāng** (p455), then it's time to get back on the hill-tribe trail.

Travel via Kūnmíng to the mountains of north Vietnam. **Sapa** (p376) is an old French hill station and the gateway to the minority communities of this region. Consider a side trip to **Bac Ha** (p378), home to the colourful Flower Hmong folk and great walking country. Head south to **Hanoi** (p351), happy in the knowledge that all your ethnic souvenirs were bought direct from the minority people and not in the designer boutiques of the Old Quarter.

This route covers the real Thai land, the mountainous regions of the Mekong where Thai and other tribes have long made a home. Transport is easy in Thailand, but things get a little bumpy in Laos. Up in China, the occasional flight can make life less ordinary, while in Vietnam the night train is a great option to connect Lao Cai (Sapa) and Hanoi.

NATURAL HIGHS

Three to Five Weeks

Leave **Kūnmíng** (p443) for the ancient cobbled streets of old **Lìjiāng** (p455). Further north lies **Tiger Leaping Gorge** (p459), one of the deepest in the world at about 3900m from river to mountain peak. Trek its length for some memorable vistas before heading south to the incredible **Yuanyang rice terraces** (p462), where agriculture becomes art.

Cross the border and continue to **Hanoi** (p351): for adrenaline junkies or nature lovers, Vietnam has plenty to offer. Start out with a visit to **Halong Bay** (p369) for some sea kayaking among the karsts. Experienced climbers with their own gear might leave the water far below, as these limestone outcrops offer some excellent ascents, plus there is some climbing around **Cat Ba Island** (p371).

Further northeast in **Bai Tu Long Bay** (p371), take to the water by local boat to see the 'new' Halong Bay without the tourists. Boating, kayaking, even surfing, are possibilities here and there are some beautiful beaches hidden away.

Heading south to central Vietnam, **Bach Ma National Park** (p382) is well geared up for walkers and has a series of lush trails to secluded waterfalls. Down on the coast below Bach Ma is **China Beach** (p387).

Go under the waves at **Nha Trang** (p392), the dive capital of Vietnam, before heading up towards the hills of the central highlands. Wind up, or down, in **Dalat** (p400), a base for abseiling, cycling or rock climbing. Don't forget two of Vietnam's best-known national parks: the birding hot spot of **Cat Tien** (p402), with a population of rare Javan rhinos, and **Yok Don** (p402), home to elephants, elephants and more elephants.

Adventures take time and there are some major distances to cover in Yúnnán, so consider taking some flights to avoid some travel lows in between the natural highs. Transport in Vietnam is pretty efficient and a combination of bus, train and boat will cover all bases.

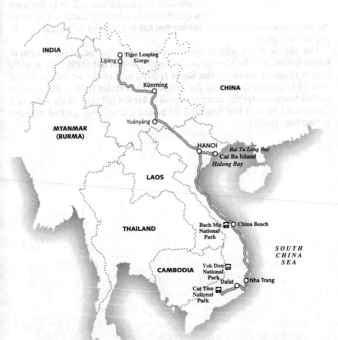

TAILORED TRIP

THE KHMER EMPIRE

Following in the footsteps of the Khmer empire is a relatively straightforward proposition: like the Romans before them, the ancient Khmers built a network of roads connecting the outposts of their empire. First, escape **Bangkok** (p113) for the roads less travelled in Northeast Thailand. Call in on **Ayuthaya** (p130), an outpost of the Khmer empire before it became a glorious Thai capital. Forget the Khmer theme for a day or two with a visit to the lush jungle and lovely waterfalls of **Khao Yai National Park** (p156). Continue east to

the ancient city of **Phimai** (p155), one of the most important regional capitals during the time of Angkor. See the wonderfully restored temple of **Phanom Rung** (p156), set atop an extinct volcano, and the nearby temple of **Meuang Tam** (p157).

Dip your toe into Cambodia by crossing the border to visit the spectacular mountaintop temple of **Preah Vihear** (Khao Praa Vihaan in Thai; p225). Take in the dramatic views as you'll be down below on the plains of Cambodia in a couple more weeks!

Enter Laos and crisscross the Mekong to visit the Khmer sanctuary of **Wat Phu** (p328), one of the oldest sacred sites in the region.

Cross into Cambodia and call in at **Kompong Cham** (p228) before swinging northwest again to the pre-Angkorian capital of **Sambor Prei Kuk** (p226), the first great temple city in the region.

The climax of the pilgrimage is approaching, the incredible **temples of Angkor** (p208). See the Mother of all Temples, **Angkor Wat** (p208), the world's largest religious building; the **Bayon** (p209), one of the world's weirdest with its enigmatic faces; and the jungle-clad **Ta Prohm** (p212). But venture further to encounter the usurper capital of **Koh Ker** (p224) and the River of a Thousand Lingas at **Kbal Spean** (p213) before taking a well-earned massage in **Siem Reap** (p201).

Snapshot

Life for many in the Mekong region has undergone a profound transition in the space of a generation, even if the politics hasn't always come along for the ride. Checking the pulse of democracy along the banks of the Mekong reveals it's just about alive, if not particularly well. China, Laos and Vietnam are one-party states which tolerate no opposition. But communism, the mantra for a generation, has taken a back seat to capitalism and the rush to embrace the market. Following the Chinese road to riches espoused by Deng Xiaoping, Laos and Vietnam have taken the brakes off the economy while keeping a firm hand on the steering wheel. The result is a contradictory blend of ultraliberal economics and ultraconservative politics that has left many inhabitants confused about the country in which they live. Like the Chinese, they have the freedom to make money but not the basic freedom to voice a political opinion. And the more the average person engages with the outside world – through business, tourism, the internet – the harder this paradox is to swallow.

Cambodia and Thailand are the 'democracies' of the region, but even here the diagnosis is depressing. Thailand was long the shining light in the region, but events in recent years have dimmed the torch. First came the CEO–Prime Minister Thaksin Shinawatra and his take-no-prisoners approach to criticism, his shoot-first ask-questions-later war on drugs, and his hard-nosed handling of the separatist south. Then came the coup in September 2006, a throwback to the topsy-turvy politics of an earlier era. Despite the best intentions, a coup is hardly the sign of a healthy democracy. Over the border in Cambodia, the veneer of democracy wears ever thinner. Elections come around every five years, but the Cambodian People's Party continues to control the military, the police, the civil service and the judiciary. There is no separation between party and state and woe betide those who cross the line and criticise the head honchos.

Corruption remains a cancer throughout the Mekong region. Despite the best intentions of a small minority, the worst intentions of many a minister and their underlings continue to cost the Mekong countries hundreds of millions of dollars in lost assets. China and Vietnam have started tackling corruption head on with high-profile executions and prison sentences. Senior party officials have even been put away, but cronyism and nepotism remain alive and well in an undemocratic system. Laos suffers from corruption, but the small size of the economy has kept enrichment to a minimum for now.

In Cambodia, corruption has been elevated to an art form. Democracy has been supplanted by kleptocracy, governance by theft, and millions of dollars have been syphoned away in recent years. National service is dead; it's all about self-service and Cambodian politicians are as self-serving as they come. An anticorruption law has been on the table for more than a decade, but international donors seem to suffer a bout of collective amnesia every time it comes around to signing the cheque books. Thailand has long suffered from corruption, but Thaksin Shinawatra created a new blend by mixing business and politics to turn the country into Shinawatra Plc. Ultimately it backfired and he was overthrown, but it remains to be seen if his successors are serious about tackling this age-old curse.

The Association of Southeast Asian Nations (Asean) includes Cambodia, Laos, Thailand and Vietnam, but is far from unified. Their policy of non-interference in domestic affairs has rendered them toothless when it comes to the Burma question and age-old animosities and suspicions continue to

HOW MUCH?

Thailand
Banana chips 10B

1L bottle of water 15B

Bottle of Singha beer 30B

Souvenir T-shirt 199B

Hotel room with air-con from 300B

Cambodia
Sait ko che-kuh (barbecued beef skewers) 500-4000r

1L bottle of water 1000-4000r

Bottle of Angkor Beer US$1

Souvenir T-shirt US$2

Hotel room with air-con from US$8

Laos
Bowl of fŏe (rice noodles) US$0.60

1L bottle of water US$0.25

660mL bottle of Beerlao US$0.60-1

Souvenir T-shirt US$3

Hotel room with air-con US$6-15

derail integration. As much as they fear, sometimes loathe, each other, many of the members are even more worried about China. Běijīng long sought tribute from the Mekong kingdoms in centuries past and China is once again seeking to stamp its authority on the region through aid and trade. Historically, China has been close to Cambodia, but relations are warming up throughout the region, as Běijīng seeks to outmanoeuvre Japan in the battle for hearts and minds, or more realistically, wallets.

Returning to neighbourly relations for a moment, tensions still boil away under the surface. The Cambodians would be hard pushed to decide who they dislike more, the Thais or the Vietnamese. The Laotians fear the Thais and their cultural pollution, although they don't seem to mind political subservience to Vietnam. The Vietnamese inherited the French theory that they are the natural leaders of Indochina and have long aimed for hegemony over Cambodia and Laos. They still fear the Chinese, who occupied their lands for a thousand years or more and went to war as recently as 1979. The Thais for their part look down on their lowly neighbours of Cambodia and Laos, blissfully ignorant (or wilfully negligent) of the historic cultural debt they owe to the Khmers and the ethnic similarities they share with the Lao. Finally, what of the Chinese? Well, the truth be told, they probably think Southeast Asia is rightfully theirs. But the days of Genghis Khan are long gone and they have to play by the rules. This means engaging rather than invading and they are on good, if unequal, terms with all their little neighbours.

The Mekong River could be the spark for future conflict. The Mekong is the world's 12th-longest river and 10th largest in terms of volume and has long been seen as a potentially lucrative source of hydroelectricity. The power-hungry Chinese have already started damming the river like eager beavers and Laos looks set to follow suit. No-one really knows what impact this will have downstream, although any significant changes to river activity could be disastrous for the Tonlé Sap Lake in Cambodia or the Mekong Delta in Vietnam. The Mekong River Commission is supposed to monitor all developments on the river, but China refuses to join the club. Běijīng is adamant that as long as the river flows through its territory, it has the right to harness its power in any way it sees fit, regardless of the consequences downstream.

But it's not all bad news in the Mekong region. Of course not, as this is one of the most dynamic, creative and vibrant regions of Asia. Democratic credentials aside, life in the Mekong region today has improved immeasurably since the dark days of the 1960s and 1970s when most of these countries were embroiled in brutal civil wars or self-destructive revolutions, often both. These days politics is history for all but the powerful parties in charge. The people are living life, in many cases loving life, for the first time in several generations. Political freedoms may be strictly censored across the region, but economic freedom is proving infectious and slowly but surely seeping into artistic and cultural freedom. It is not only business that is booming, not only tourism that is racing forward, but the arts are also enjoying a renaissance. Traditions are experiencing a rebirth, the classics are fusing with the contemporary, and whether you are in Bangkok, Hanoi or Phnom Penh, you can be sure there will be some unexpected performance playing at a theatre or opera house near you.

Cultural vibrancy, economic expansion and a people keen to embrace new opportunity – this is the new face of the Mekong. The future looks very bright for the next generation. Let's hope the governments of the region seize the chance to drive their countries forward, improving the lives of all their people and not just a small elite in the urban centres. If the regional leadership begins to show half the initiative that the population has shown in surviving the trials and tribulations of life in the turbulent Mekong region, then watch this space. The Mekong is going to be very, very big.

History

This vibrant region has a history as long and dramatic as the Mekong River that cuts through its heart. There have been turbulent moments, there have been calm stretches. Empires have expanded in size only to come crashing down again like the mother river's waters each season. As human habitation has swollen, putting new pressures on this oldest of rivers, so too have the dramas of the region magnified. The Mekong has played host to some of the most brutal wars of the 20th century and the bloodiest revolutions. However, calmer waters lie ahead, as the region is peaceful and stable for the first time in generations. Governments are finally starting to go with the flow, no longer battling against the popular current.

The history of this great region is also the history of two great civilisations colliding. China and India may be making headlines today as the emerging giants of the 21st century, but it's old news. They have long been great powers and have historically overshadowed the Mekong region. The border between Vietnam and Cambodia is as significant a sociocultural border as the Himalaya range is a formidable physical barrier between the great rivals of China and India. It is the divide between Sino-Asia to the east and Indo-Asia to the west, with Vietnam historically under the influence of China, and Cambodia, Laos and Thailand under the influence of India. From art and architecture to language and religion, it manifests itself in many ways. See the Culture chapter (p69) for more on this fascinating phenomenon.

Southeast Asian kingdoms were not states in the modern sense, with fixed frontiers, but varied in extent depending on the power of the centre. Outlying *meuang* (principalities or city-states) might transfer their allegiance elsewhere when the centre was weak. That is why scholars prefer the term mandala, a Sanskrit word meaning 'circle of power'.

THE EARLY YEARS

Modern linguistic theory and archaeological evidence suggest that the first true agriculturalists in the world, perhaps also the first metal workers, spoke an early form of Thai and lived in what we know today as Thailand. The Mekong Valley and Khorat Plateau were inhabited as far back as 10,000 years ago, and rice was grown in northeastern Thailand as early as 4000 BC. China, by contrast, was still growing and consuming millet at the time. The Thais entered the Bronze Age earlier than 3000 BC; the Middle East didn't pass this milestone until 2800 BC and China a thousand years later.

According to Lao legend, the mythical figure Khun Borom cut open a gourd in the vicinity of Dien Bien Phu and out came seven sons who spread the Tai family from east to west. Although previous theory had placed the epicentre of Tai culture in southwestern China, recent evidence suggests it may have been in northern Vietnam and part of the Dongson culture. The Dongson culture is renowned for its elaborate bronze drums and was a powerful trading kingdom, its merchants penetrating as far south as Alor in Indonesia where the people still trade in bronze drums.

The site www.china knowledge.de /History/history.htm has in-depth coverage of China's dynasties and eras, with links to more specific information on everything from the religion to the technology to the economy of each period.

CHINA ENTERS THE RING

In 1899 peasants working in present-day Anyang unearthed pieces of polished bone and turtle shells inscribed with characters. Dating from 1500 BC, these are the earliest examples of the elaborate writing system still used in China today. As successive Chinese dynasties began to expand their territory, they pushed south and westwards towards the Mekong. The first emperor

TIMELINE	100	802
	Indianisation begins, the religions, language and sculpture of India taking root in the region	Jayavarman II proclaims independence from Java, marking the start of the Khmer empire of Angkor

THE CAMBODIAN CREATION MYTH

Cambodia came into being, so the story goes, through the union of an Indian Brahman named Kaundinya and the daughter of a dragon king who ruled over a watery land. One day, as Kaundinya sailed by, the princess paddled out in a boat to greet him. Kaundinya shot an arrow from his magic bow into her boat, causing the fearful princess to agree to marriage. In need of a dowry, her father drank up the waters of his land and presented them to Kaundinya to rule over. The new kingdom was named Kambuja.

Like many legends, this one is historically opaque, but it does say something about the cultural forces that brought Cambodia into existence; in particular its relationship with its great subcontinental neighbour, India. Cambodia's religious, royal and written traditions stemmed from India and began to coalesce as a cultural entity in their own right between the 1st and 5th centuries.

of Qin (Qin Shi Huang, 221 BC) conquered and reigned by the sword. His ruling philosophy was law and punishment and a stark contrast to earlier Confucian teachings (see p79) that emphasised rights and morality. He pursued campaigns as far north as Korea and began linking city defences to create the infamous Great Wall. However, he also attacked and subdued Vietnam, conquering the Red River Delta to usher in 1000 years of Chinese cultural and political domination.

AN EARLY EMPIRE

Much of the Mekong region absorbed Indian culture through contact with seafaring merchants calling at trading settlements along the coast of present-day Thailand, Cambodia and Vietnam. These settlements were ports of call for boats following the trading route from the Bay of Bengal to the southern provinces of China. The largest of these nascent kingdoms was known as Funan by the Chinese, and occupied an area stretching from around present-day Phnom Penh to Oc-Eo in the Mekong Delta in southern Vietnam. Known as Nokor Phnom to the Khmers, this kingdom was centred on the walled city of Angkor Borei, near modern-day Takeo. The Funanese constructed an elaborate system of canals both for transportation and the irrigation of rice. The principal port city of Funan was Oc-Eo in the Mekong Delta and archaeological excavations here tell us of contact between Funan and China, Indonesia, Persia and even the Mediterranean.

Funan was famous for its refined art and architecture, and its kings embraced the worship of Hindu deities Shiva and Vishnu and, at the same time, Buddhism. The *linga* (phallic totem) was the focus of ritual and an emblem of kingly might, a feature that was to evolve further in the Angkorian cult of the god king.

VIETNAM UNDER OCCUPATION

The Chinese introduced Confucianism, Taoism and Mahayana Buddhism to Vietnam, as well as a written character system, while the Indians brought Theravada Buddhism. Monks carried with them the scientific and medical knowledge of these two great civilisations, and Vietnam was soon producing its own great doctors, botanists and scholars.

The early Vietnamese learned much from the Chinese, including the construction of dikes and irrigation works. These innovations helped make rice the 'staff of life', and paddy agriculture remains the foundation of the

Archaeologists conducting excavations at Oc-Eo discovered a Roman medallion dating from AD 152, bearing the likeness of Antoninus Pius.

The Chinese are kicked out of Vietnam after more than a thousand years of occupation

Thanh Long, or City of the Soaring Dragon, known today as Hanoi, becomes Vietnam's capital

Vietnamese way of life to this day. As food became more plentiful the population expanded, forcing the Vietnamese to seek new lands. The ominous Truong Son Mountains prevented westward expansion, so they headed south, bringing them into conflict with first the Chams and later the Khmers.

THE RISE & FALL OF CHAMPA

The Hindu kingdom of Champa emerged around present-day Danang in the late 2nd century AD. Like Funan, it adopted Sanskrit as a sacred language and borrowed heavily from Indian art and culture. By the 8th century Champa had expanded southward to include what is now Nha Trang and Phan Rang. The Cham were a feisty bunch who conducted raids along the entire coast of Indochina, and thus found themselves in a perpetual state of war with the Vietnamese to the north and the Khmers to the south. Ultimately this cost them their kingdom, as they found themselves squeezed between two great powers. Check out some brilliant Cham sculptures in the Museum of Cham Sculpture in Danang (p385) or travel to their former capital at My Son (p392).

THE RISE OF CHENLA

From the 6th century the Funan kingdom's importance as a port of call declined, and Cambodia's population gradually settled along the Mekong and Tonlé Sap Rivers, where the majority remains today.

This era is referred to as the Chenla period. Again, like Funan, it is a Chinese term and there is little to support the idea that Chenla was a unified kingdom that held sway over all Cambodia. Indeed, the Chinese themselves referred to 'water Chenla' (lower) and 'land Chenla' (upper). Water Chenla was located around Angkor Borei and the temple mount of Phnom Da (p246), near the present-day provincial capital of Takeo; and land Chenla in the upper reaches of the Mekong River and east of the Tonlé Sap lake, around Sambor Prei Kuk (p226), one of the first great temple cities of the Mekong region. Upper Chenla included the mountain temple of Wat Phu in southern Laos, beautifully situated under the shadow of Lingaparvata Mountain. Wat Phu had possibly been part of the Cham empire's western reaches. By the time of Chenla, it was under the control of the Khmers, who had begun to pick off western outposts of the Cham empire. Some scholars contend that by the 8th century, Lower Chenla was occupied by the Javanese and was a vassal state of the great Shailindras court based around Jogyakarta.

What is certain is that the people of the lower Mekong were well known to the Chinese, and gradually the region was becoming more cohesive. Before long the fractured kingdoms of Chenla would merge to become the greatest empire in Southeast Asia.

THE KHMER EMPIRE

A popular place of pilgrimage for Khmers today, the sacred mountain of Phnom Kulen (p213), to the northeast of Angkor, is home to an inscription that tells us that in 802 Jayavarman II proclaimed himself a 'universal monarch', or a *devaraja* (god king). It is believed he may have resided in the Buddhist Shailendras' court in Java as a young man. On his return to Cambodia, he set out to bring the country under his control through alliances and conquests. He was the first monarch to rule all of what we call Cambodia today.

For a closer look at China's thousand-year occupation of Vietnam, which was instrumental in shaping the country's outlook and attitude today, try *The Birth of Vietnam* by Keith Weller Taylor.

In AD 679 the Chinese changed the name of Vietnam to Annam, which means the 'Pacified South'. Ever since this era, the collective memory of Chinese domination has played an important role in shaping Vietnamese identity and attitudes towards their northern neighbour.

Founded by King Isanavarman I in the early 7th century, Sambor Prei Kuk was originally known as Isanapura and was the first major temple city to be constructed in Southeast Asia.

1177	1215
The Chams sail up the Tonlé Sap, defeat the Khmers and occupy Angkor for four years	Genghis Khan conquers Běijīng, as the Mongols influence the future of events in the Mekong region

For the fuller flavour of Cambodian history, right from the humble beginnings in the prehistoric period through the glories of Angkor and right up to the present day, grab a copy of *The History of Cambodia* by David Chandler.

Jayavarman II was the first of a long succession of kings who presided over the rise and fall of the Southeast Asian empire that was to leave the stunning legacy of Angkor. The first records of the massive irrigation works that supported the population of Angkor date to the reign of Indravarman I (877–89). His son Yasovarman I (reigned 889–910) moved the royal court to Angkor proper, establishing a temple mountain on the summit of Phnom Bakheng (p213).

The Romans of Asia

Suryavarman I (reigned 1002–49) annexed the Dravati kingdom of Lopburi in Thailand and widened his control of Cambodia, stretching the empire to perhaps its greatest extent. Remnants of the Khmer empire are scattered throughout northeast Thailand and southern Laos, a testament to the might of this powerful empire. Like the Romans in Europe, the Khmers built a sophisticated network of highways to connect the outposts of their empire. Roads fanned out from Angkor connecting the capital with satellite cities such as Ayuthaya and Phimai in Thailand and as far away as Wat Phu in southern Laos.

It was not until 1112, with the accession of Suryavarman II, that the kingdom was again unified. Suryavarman II embarked on another phase of expansion, waging wars against Champa and Vietnam. He is immortalised in Cambodia as the king who, in his devotion to the Hindu deity Vishnu, gave the world the majestic temple of Angkor Wat (p208).

Suryavarman II had brought Champa to heel and reduced it to vassal status. In 1177, the Chams struck back with a naval expedition up the Mekong and into Tonlé Sap lake. They took the city of Angkor by surprise and put King Dharanindravarman II to death. A year later a cousin of Suryavarman II gathered forces about him and defeated the Chams in another naval battle. The new leader was crowned Jayavarman VII in 1181.

There are very few surviving contemporary accounts of Angkor, but Chinese emissary Chou Ta Kuan lived in the ancient Khmer capital for a year in 1296 and his observations have been republished as *The Customs of Cambodia*, a fascinating insight into life during the height of the empire.

Enter Jayavarman VII

A devout follower of Mahayana Buddhism, Jayavarman VII built the city of Angkor Thom (p208) and many other massive monuments. Indeed, many of the monuments visited by tourists around Angkor today were constructed during Jayavarman VII's reign. He is deified by many Cambodians as their greatest leader, a populist who promoted equality, a socially conscious leader who built schools and hospitals for his people. However, there was a darker legacy which sowed the seeds for the eventual collapse of the empire. His programme of temple construction and other public works was carried out in great haste, no doubt bringing enormous hardship to the labourers who provided the muscle, leading to a neglect of the all-important irrigation network upon which Angkor depended. His introduction of a new state religion sparked off several centuries of internecine rivalry and religious conflict, as successive monarchs vacillated between Hinduism and Buddhism.

VIETNAM BOOTS OUT THE CHINESE

In the early 10th century, the Tang dynasty in China collapsed. The Vietnamese seized the initiative and launched a long overdue revolt against Chinese rule in Vietnam. In AD 938, popular patriot Ngo Quyen finally vanquished the Chinese armies at a battle on the Bach Dang River, ending 1000 years of Chinese rule. However, it was not the last time the Vietnamese would tussle with their mighty northern neighbour.

1238	1353
Sukhothai is born, considered the first Thai kingdom	Fa Ngum establishes the Lao kingdom of Lan Xang

From the 11th to 13th centuries, Vietnamese independence was consolidated under the enlightened emperors of the Ly dynasty, founded by Ly Thai To. During the Ly dynasty many enemies, including the Chinese, the Khmer and the Cham, launched attacks on Vietnam, but all were repelled. Meanwhile, the Vietnamese continued their expansion southwards and slowly but surely began to consolidate control of the Cham kingdom.

THE MONGOL HORDES

Genghis Khan (1167–1227) began to flex his muscles in Mongolia at the end of the 12th century. In 1211, he turned his sights on China, penetrated the Great Wall two years later and took Běijīng in 1215. Although these events were unravelling thousands of kilometres from the Mekong, the Mongols were to leave an indelible mark on the peoples of this region due to a major shift in the balance of power. Kublai Khan, grandson of Genghis, reigned over all of China, at the helm of the mightiest empire the world had ever seen. Like the Vikings in Europe, the Mongols were more adept at conquest than consolidation and soon continued their pillaging ways.

For his next trick, Kublai Khan planned to attack Champa and demanded the right to cross Vietnamese territory. The Vietnamese refused, but the Mongol hordes – all 500,000 of them – pushed ahead, seemingly invulnerable. However, they met their match in the legendary general Tran Hung Dao. He defeated them in the battle of Bach Dang River, one of the most celebrated scalps among many the Vietnamese have taken.

THE THAIS MOVE SOUTH

However, Kublai Khan successfully attacked the Thai state of Nan Chao (AD 650–1250), which was located in Xīshuāngbǎnnà in the south of Yúnnán. Thais had already been migrating south for several centuries, settling in parts of Laos and northern Thailand. However, the sacking of their capital provoked a mass exodus and brought the Thais into conflict with a waning Khmer empire. The Mongol empire evaporated into the dust of history, but with the sacking of the Thai capital the die was cast: it was Thailand versus Cambodia, a conflict which has persisted in various shapes and forms through the centuries to the present day. The Mongols had left their mark on the Mekong region without even waging a war.

Thailand: A Short History (1982), by David Wyatt, offers a succinct overview from the early Thai era through to the 1980s.

SUKHOTHAI STANDS UP

Several Thai principalities in the Mekong valley united in the 13th and 14th centuries to create Sukhothai (Rising of Happiness). Thai princes wrested control of the territory from the Khmers, whose all-powerful empire at Angkor was slowly disintegrating. Sukhothai is considered by the Thais to be the first true Thai kingdom. It was annexed by Ayuthaya in 1376, by which time a national identity of sorts had been forged.

At the same time, an allied kingdom emerged in north-central Thailand known as Lan Na Thai (Million Thai Rice Fields), usually referred to as Lanna, and this included the areas of Luang Prabang and Vientiane in modern day Laos. Debate rages as to whether Lanna was essentially Lao or Thai and remains an issue of contention between the two peoples today. There is evidence that both 'Lao' and 'Thai' were used by the people of this kingdom to describe themselves.

In 2006, Thailand's King Bhumibol Adulyadej celebrated 60 years on the throne and is the longest reigning monarch in the world.

1431	1516
The expansionist Thais sack Angkor, carting off most of the royal court to Ayuthaya	Portuguese traders land at Danang, sparking the start of European interest in Vietnam

LAN XANG, THE BIRTH OF LAOS

As the power of Sukhothai grew, the ascendant Thais began to exert more pressure on the Khmer. The Cambodian court looked around for an ally, and found one in the form of an exiled Lao prince who was being educated at Angkor. Forced to flee after he seduced one of his own father's concubines, Fa Ngum was in direct line for the throne.

King Jayavarman VIII married Fa Ngum to a Khmer princess and offered him an army of more than 10,000 troops. He pushed north to wrest the middle Mekong from the control of Sukhothai and Lanna. The reputation of the Khmer armies carried him through the Lao and Thai kingdoms at a rapid rate and by 1353 he declared himself king of Lan Xang Hom Khao, meaning 'a million elephants and the white parasol'. This was really the last hurrah of the declining Khmer empire and quite probably served only to weaken Angkor and antagonise the Thai.

Naga Cities of Mekong
(2006) by Martin Stuart-
Fox provides a narrative
account of the founding
legends and history of
Luang Prabang, Vientiane
and Champasak, and a
guide to their temples.

Within 20 years of its birth, Lan Xang had expanded eastwards to pick off parts of a disintegrating Champa and along the Annamite Mountains in Vietnam. Fa Ngum earned the sobriquet 'The Conqueror' because of his constant preoccupation with warfare. Therevada Buddhism became the state religion in Lan Xang when King Visounarat accepted the Pha Bang, a gold Buddha image from his Khmer sponsors, and Muang Sawa was renamed Luang Phabang.

THE COLLAPSE OF ANGKOR

Some scholars maintain that decline was hovering in the wings at the time Angkor Wat was built, when the Angkorian empire was at the height of its remarkable productivity. There are indications that the irrigation network was overworked and slowly starting to silt up due to the massive deforestation that had taken place in the heavily populated areas to the north and east of Angkor. Following the reign of Jayavarman VII, temple construction effectively ground to a halt, largely because Jayavarman VII's public works quarried local sandstone into oblivion and the population was exhausted. The state religion reverted to Hinduism for a century or more and outbreaks of iconoclasm saw Buddhist sculpture vandalised or altered.

By naming his kingdom
Lan Xang Hom Khao,
Fa Ngum was making
a statement. Elephants
were the battle tanks of
Southeast Asian warfare,
so to claim to be the
kingdom of a million
elephants was to issue a
warning to surrounding
kingdoms: 'Don't mess
with the Lao!'

The Thais grew in strength and made repeated incursions into Angkor, finally sacking the city in 1431 and making off with thousands of intellectuals, artisans and dancers from the royal court. During this period, perhaps drawn by the opportunities for sea trade with China and fearful of the increasingly bellicose Thais, the Khmer elite began to migrate to the Phnom Penh area. Angkor was abandoned to pilgrims, holy men and the elements.

THE GOLDEN AGE OF SIAM

The Thai kings of Ayuthaya grew very powerful in the 14th and 15th centuries, taking over the former Khmer strongholds of U Thong and Lopburi in present-day central Thailand. Even though the Khmers had been their adversaries in battle, the Thai kings of Ayuthaya adopted many facets of Khmer culture, including court customs and rituals, language and culture. The cultural haemorrhage that took place with the sacking of Angkor in 1431 has repercussions even today and continues to strain relations between the two neighbours. The Thais rather ambitiously claim Angkor as their own, while the Khmers bemoan the loss of Khmer kick boxing, classical Khmer dance and Khmer silk to the all-powerful Thai brand.

1767	1864
The Burmese sack the Thai capital of Ayuthaya, forcing its relocation to Thonburi, then to Bangkok	The French force Cambodia into a treaty of protectorate, which prevents it being wiped off the map by Thailand and Vietnam

Angkor's loss was Ayuthaya's gain and it went on to become one of the greatest cities in Asia, a great seaport envied not only by the Burmese, but even the European traders who began to flock here. It has been said that London, at the time, was a mere village in comparison. The kingdom sustained an unbroken monarchical succession through 34 reigns from King U Thong (1350–69) to King Ekathat (1758–67). In 1690, Londoner Engelbert Campfer proclaimed: 'Among the Asian nations, the Kingdom of Siam is the greatest. The magnificence of the Ayuthaya court is incomparable'.

VIETNAMESE EXPANSION

The Chinese seized control of Vietnam once more in the early 15th century, carting off the national archives and some of the country's intellectuals to China – an irreparable loss to Vietnamese civilisation. The Chinese controlled much of the country from 1407, imposing a regime of heavy taxation and slave labour. The poet Nguyen Trai (1380–1442) wrote of this period, 'Were the water of the Eastern Sea to be exhausted, the stain of their ignominy could not be washed away; all the bamboo of the Southern Mountains would not suffice to provide the paper for recording all their crimes'.

In 1418, wealthy philanthropist Le Loi rallied the people against the Chinese. Upon victory in 1428, Le Loi declared himself Emperor Le Thai To, the first in the long line of the Le dynasty. To this day, Le Loi is riding high in the Top Ten of the country's all-time national heroes.

Following Le Loi's victory over the Chinese, Nguyen Trai, a scholar and Le Loi's companion in arms, wrote his infamous *Great Proclamation* (Binh Ngo Dai Cao). Guaranteed to fan the flames of nationalism almost six centuries later, it articulated Vietnam's fierce spirit of independence:

> Our people long ago established Vietnam as an independent nation
> with its own civilisation. We have our own mountains and our own
> rivers, our own customs and traditions, and these are different from
> those of the foreign country to the north…We have sometimes been
> weak and sometimes powerful, but at no time have we suffered from
> a lack of heroes.

Le Loi and his successors launched a campaign to take over Cham lands to the south, wiping the kingdom of Champa from the map, and parts of eastern Laos were forced to kowtow to the might of the Vietnamese.

THE DARK AGES

The glorious years of the Khmer empire and the golden age of Ayuthaya were no guarantee of future success and the 18th century proved a time of turmoil for the region. This was the dark ages when the countries of the Mekong were convulsed by external threats and internal intrigue.

The Continuing Decline of Cambodia

From 1600 until the arrival of the French in 1863, Cambodia was ruled by a series of weak kings who were forced to seek the protection – at a price – of either Thailand or Vietnam. In the 17th century, assistance from the Nguyen lords of southern Vietnam was given on the condition that Vietnamese be allowed to settle in what is now the Mekong Delta region of Vietnam, at

The website www.thai worldview.com/art_hist .htm has thumbnail histories of the various Thai capitals.

1883	1893
The French impose the Treaty of Protectorate on the Vietnamese, marking the start of 70 years of colonial control	France gains sovereignty over all Lao territories east of the Mekong

that time part of Cambodia and today still referred to by the Khmers as Kampuchea Krom (Lower Cambodia).

In the west, the Thais controlled the provinces of Battambang and Siem Reap from 1794; by the late 18th century they had firm control of the Cambodian royal family. That Cambodia survived through the 18th century as a distinct entity is due to the preoccupations of its neighbours: while the Thais were expending their energy and resources in fighting the Burmese, the Vietnamese were wholly absorbed by internal strife.

Saigon began life as humble Prey Nokor in the 16th century, a backwater of a Khmer village in what was then the eastern edge of Cambodia.

The Threat of Burma

Meanwhile, the so-called golden age of Ayuthaya was starting to lose its shine. The Burmese had attacked Ayuthaya on several occasions in the 16th and 17th centuries. In 1765 they laid siege to the city for two years and the capital fell. Everything sacred to the Thais was destroyed, including temples, manuscripts and religious sculpture. The capital was moved first to Thonburi on the Chao Praya River and later across the river to Bangkok. The Thais vented their frustrations on their Lao neighbours. If the 17th century had been Lan Xang's very own golden age, the first Lao unified kingdom began to unravel by the end of the century. The country split into the three kingdoms of Luang Prabang, Wieng Chan (Vientiane) and Champasak. All three were subjected to repeated attacks by the Burmese and Thais, and the Thais had reduced much of Laos to vassal status by the start of the 19th century.

Bang Rajan (2000), by Thanit Jitnukul, is a cine-epic of a doomed Thai rebellion against 18th century Burmese rule.

Civil War in Vietnam

In a dress rehearsal for the tumultuous events of the 20th century, Vietnam found itself divided in half through much of the 17th and 18th centuries. The powerful Trinh Lords were later Le kings who ruled the North. To the south were the Nguyen Lords, who feigned tribute to the kings of the north but carried on like an independent kingdom. The second half of the 18th century saw the Tay Son Rebels carve up the country. It wasn't until the dawn of a new century that they were finally subdued and in 1802, Nguyen Anh proclaimed himself Emperor Gia Long, thus beginning the Nguyen dynasty. When he captured Hanoi, his victory was complete and, for the first time in two centuries, Vietnam was united, with Hué as its new capital city.

THE FRENCH PROTECTORATE

Marco Polo was the first European to cross the Mekong and penetrate the east. In the following centuries many more Europeans followed in his wake, trading in ports as diverse as Ayuthaya and Faifo (Hoi An). However, it was France which was to ultimately claim much of the region as its own.

The concept of 'protectorate' was often employed as a smokescreen by European colonial powers in order to hide their exploitative agenda. However, for the weak and divided kingdoms of Cambodia and Laos, French intervention came not a moment too soon. Both were starting to feel the squeeze as expansionist Thailand and Vietnam carved up their territory. Were it not for the French, it is quite plausible that Cambodia and Laos would have gone the way of Champa, a mere footnote in history, a people without a homeland.

1930	1939
Ho Chi Minh establishes the Indochinese Communist Party	Siam changes its name to Thailand

Vietnam Yields to the French

France's military activity in Vietnam began in 1847, when the French Navy attacked Danang harbour in response to Thieu Tri's suppression of Catholic missionaries. The Catholic Church eventually had a greater impact on Vietnam than on any country in Asia except the Philippines, which was ruled by the Spanish for 400 years. Saigon was seized in early 1859 and, in 1862, Emperor Tu Duc signed a treaty that gave the French the three eastern provinces of Cochinchina. France also went to war against China in 1858 and from 1883 to 1885, finally ending Chinese suzerainty in Indochina, at least for a time.

Cambodia & Laos Join the Fold

Cambodia succumbed to French military might in 1864, when French gunboats intimidated King Norodom I (reigned 1860–1904) into signing a treaty of protectorate. In Laos, the same technique was employed with much success. In 1893 a French warship forced its way up the Chao Phraya River to Bangkok and trained its guns on the palace. Under duress, the Siamese agreed to transfer all territory east of the Mekong to France and Laos became part of Indochina.

In 1883 the French attacked Hué and imposed the Treaty of Protectorate on the imperial court. There then began a tragicomic struggle for royal succession that was notable for its palace coups, mysteriously dead emperors and heavy-handed French diplomacy.

The Indochinese Union proclaimed by the French in 1887 may have ended the existence of an independent Vietnamese state, but active resistance continued in various parts of the country for the duration of French rule.

Territorial Losses, Territorial Gains

The French were able to pressure Thailand into returning the northwest provinces of Battambang, Siem Reap and Sisophon to Cambodia in 1907, in return for concessions of Lao territory to the Thais, returning Angkor to Cambodian control for the first time in more than a century. However, at the same time, they confirmed Vietnam's claims over the Mekong Delta and gifted the island of Koh Tral to Vietnam, known today as the beach paradise of Phu Quoc.

Vietnam was always the most important part of the colonial equation that was French Indochine. Economically it was the most productive and the French relied on the Vietnamese as administrators in both Cambodia and Laos in much the same way the British relied on the Indians in Burma and beyond. Vietnam developed under the French, while Cambodia and Laos languished. This was to set the pattern for power in Indochina for another century and ensured the Vietnamese were the dominant force in the nascent independence movement.

ANGLO-FRENCH RIVALRY

Same old, same old: the English and French have been bickering since the dawn of time. With the British positioned in Burma and the French claiming Indochina, Thailand and Yúnnán became battlegrounds in the struggle for influence.

In 1903 France started to build the railway line from Haiphong and Hanoi to Kūnmíng, a line that would soon become the province's main link to the outside world. By 1911 one million Chinese were riding the train every year.

One of the most illustrious of the early missionaries was the brilliant French Jesuit Alexandre de Rhodes (1591–1660), widely lauded for his work in devising *quoc ngu,* the Latin-based phonetic alphabet in which Vietnamese is written to this day.

The first Frenchman to arrive in Laos was Henri Mouhot, an explorer and naturalist who died of malaria in 1861 near Luang Prabang (where his tomb can still be seen).

1941	1945
Japan enters WWII and sweeps through Southeast Asia	Ho Chi Minh proclaims Vietnamese independence on 2 September, but the French have other ideas

The British crept closer to Yúnnán when they occupied the Kachin state of northern Burma.

The Thais are proud of their independent history and the fact they were never colonised. Successive Thai kings courted the Europeans while maintaining their neutrality. It was an ambiguous relationship, best summed up by King Mongkut: 'Whatever they have invented or done, we should know of and do, we can imitate and learn from them, but do not wholeheartedly believe in them'. In the end, it was less a success story for Thai manoeuvring that kept the country independent, but the realisation on the part of the British and the French that a buffer zone prevented open warfare.

INDEPENDENCE ASPIRATIONS

Throughout the colonial period, a desire for independence simmered under the surface in Vietnam. Seething nationalist aspirations often erupted into open defiance of the French. Ultimately, the most successful of the anti-colonialists were the communists, who were able to tune into the frustrations and aspirations of the population – especially the peasants – and effectively channel their demands for fairer land distribution.

The Birth of Communism in Indochina

The story of communism in Indochina, which in many ways is also the political biography of Ho Chi Minh (see the boxed text, p41), is complicated. Keeping it simple, the first Marxist grouping in Indochina was the Vietnam Revolutionary Youth League, founded by Ho Chi Minh in Canton, China, in 1925. This was succeeded in February 1930 by the Vietnamese Communist Party, part of the Indochinese Communist Party (ICP). In 1941, Ho formed the League for the Independence of Vietnam, much better known as the Viet Minh, which resisted the Japanese and carried out extensive political activities during WWII. Ho was pragmatic, patriotic and populist and understood the need for national unity. Political consciousness was a rarity in Cambodia and Laos at this time and few Cambodians and Laotians rallied to the communist cause until after WWII.

Siam Becomes Thailand

The US Library of Congress maintains a Thailand Studies page (http://countrystudies .us/thailand) that covers history and societal structure.

Meanwhile Siam transformed itself from an absolute monarchy to a constitutional monarchy in a bloodless coup in 1932. Under military leader Phibul Songkhram, the country veered off in a nationalist direction, changing its name to Thailand in 1939 and siding with the Japanese in WWII in order to seize back Cambodian and Lao territory returned to French Indochina in 1907.

CONVULSIONS IN CHINA

China had been through a series of convulsions in the 19th century, as the country was in the grip of the Opium Wars. The 20th century proved just as turbulent as nationalists and communists battled for the hearts and minds of the people. By 1920, the Kuomintang (KMT) had emerged as the dominant political force in China and its main opposition was the Chinese Communist Party (CCP).

In the face of extermination campaigns by nationalist forces, the communists decided to regroup for a counterattack and thus began the Long March, actually a series of gruelling treks across thousands of kilometres

1953	1954
Cambodia and Laos go it alone with independence from France	French forces surrender en masse to Viet Minh fighters at Dien Bien Phu on 7 May, marking the end of colonial rule in Indochina

of inhospitable terrain. Of the 90,000 who set out, only 20,000 made it to Shaanxi. The Japanese took advantage of the power vacuum and invaded Manchuria in 1931, ravaging the rest of China in 1937 in one of the most brutal campaigns of a brutal era for warfare.

WWII

WWII broke out in 1939 and the Japanese entered the conflict in 1941. Japanese forces occupied much of Asia, and Indochina was no exception. However, with many in France collaborating with the occupying Germans, the Japanese were happy to let these French allies control affairs. But with the fall of Paris in 1944 and French policy in disarray, the Japanese were forced to take direct control of the territory by early 1945.

The main forces opposed to both the French and Japanese presence in Indochina were the Viet Minh and this meant Ho Chi Minh received assistance from the US government during this period. As events unfolded in Europe, the French and Japanese fell out and the Viet Minh saw their opportunity to strike.

After WWII, the French returned, making the countries 'autonomous states within the French Union', but retaining de facto control. French general Jacques Philippe Leclerc pompously declared 'We have come to reclaim our inheritance'. The end of the war had brought liberation for France, but not, it seemed, for its colonies.

A FALSE DAWN

By the spring of 1945, the Viet Minh controlled large parts of Vietnam, particularly in the north. On 2 September 1945 Ho Chi Minh declared independence at a rally in Hanoi's Ba Dinh Square. Throughout this period, Ho wrote no fewer than eight letters to US president Harry Truman and the US State Department asking for US aid, but received no replies. Laos also briefly declared independence, but the king promptly repudiated his declaration, in the belief that Laos still needed French protection.

A footnote on the agenda of the Potsdam Conference of 1945 was the disarming of Japanese occupation forces in Indochina. It was decided that the Chinese Kuomintang would accept the Japanese surrender north of the 16th Parallel and that the British would do the same to the south.

In the north, Chinese Kuomintang troops were fleeing the Chinese communists and pillaging their way southward towards Hanoi. Ho tried to placate them, but as the months of Chinese occupation dragged on, he decided 'better the devil you know' and accepted a temporary return of the French. For the Vietnamese, even the French colonisers were better than the Chinese.

WAR WITH THE FRENCH

In the face of determined Vietnamese nationalism, the French proved unable to reassert their control. Despite massive US aid and the existence of significant indigenous anticommunist elements, it was an unwinnable war. As Ho said to the French at the time, 'You can kill 10 of my men for every one I kill of yours, but even at those odds you will lose and I will win'.

The Viet Minh carried the fight to the French in Cambodia and Laos together with a small network of local allies. Most of the fighters in Cambodia

As WWII drew to a close, Japanese rice requisitions, in combination with floods and breaches in the dikes, caused a horrific famine in which two million of northern Vietnam's 10 million people starved to death.

Between 1944 and 1945, the Viet Minh received funding and arms from the US Office of Strategic Services (OSS, the CIA today). When Ho Chi Minh declared independence in 1945, he had OSS agents at his side and borrowed liberally from the American Declaration of Independence. Such irony.

1956	1964
Vietnam remains divided at the 17th Parallel into communist North Vietnam and 'free' South Vietnam	The US begins the secret bombing of Laos; Air America takes off

and Laos were nationalists with little interest in Marxist doctrine, but the Viet Minh slowly began to expand their political influence.

The whole complexion of the First Indochina War changed with the 1949 victory of communism in China. As Chinese weapons flowed to the Viet Minh, the French were forced onto the defensive. After eight years of fighting, the Viet Minh controlled much of Vietnam and neighbouring Laos. On 7 May 1954, after a 57-day siege, more than 10,000 starving French troops surrendered to the Viet Minh at Dien Bien Phu. This was a catastrophic defeat that brought an end to the French colonial adventure in Indochina. The following day, the Geneva Conference opened to negotiate an end to the conflict, but the French had no cards left to bring to the table.

INDEPENDENCE FOR CAMBODIA & LAOS

In 1941 Admiral Jean Decoux placed 19-year-old Prince Norodom Sihanouk on the Cambodian throne, assuming he would be naïve and pliable. As he grew in stature, this proved to be a major miscalculation. In 1953 King Sihanouk embarked on his 'royal crusade': his travelling campaign to drum up international support for his country's independence.

Independence was proclaimed on 9 November 1953 and recognised by the Geneva Conference of May 1954. In 1955 Sihanouk abdicated, afraid of being marginalised amid the pomp of royal ceremony. The 'royal crusader' became 'citizen Sihanouk' and vowed never again to return to the throne.

Laos was granted independence at the same time. The first priority for the Royal Lao Government was to reunify the country. This required a political solution to which the communist Pathet Lao would agree. The tragedy for Laos was that when, after two centuries, an independent Lao state was reborn, it was conceived in the nationalism of WWII, nourished during the agony of the First Indochina War, and born into the Cold War. From its inception, the Lao state was torn by ideological division, which the Lao tried mightily to overcome, but which was surreptitiously stoked by outside interference.

A 'SOLUTION' TO THE INDOCHINA PROBLEM

The Geneva Conference of 1954 was designed to end the conflict in Indochina, but the Vietnamese had done a good job of that with their comprehensive defeat of French forces at Dien Bien Phu. Resolutions included: the temporary division of Vietnam into two zones at the Ben Hai River (near the 17th Parallel); the free passage of people across the 17th Parallel for a period of 300 days; and the holding of nationwide elections on 20 July 1956. Laos and Cambodia were broadly neglected. In Laos two northeastern provinces (Huaphan and Phongsali) were set aside as regroupment areas for Pathet Lao forces. No such territory was set aside in Cambodia, so a group of 1000 Cambodian communists travelled north to Hanoi where they were to remain for the best part of two decades. This group was seen as pro-Vietnamese by the Pol Pot faction of the Khmer Rouge who rose to power in Cambodia and was eliminated in the 1970s.

The 2002 remake of *The Quiet American*, starring Michael Caine, is a must. Beautifully shot, it is a classic introduction to Vietnam in the 1950s, as the French disengaged and the Americans moved in to take their place.

TWO VIETNAMS

After the Geneva Accords were signed and sealed, South Vietnam was ruled by Ngo Dinh Diem, a fiercely anticommunist Catholic. Nationwide elections were never held, as the Americans rightly feared that Ho Chi Minh would

1965	1966
The first US marines wade ashore at Danang, as the Vietnam War hots up	The Cultural Revolution begins in China, spearheaded by the Red Guards

UNCLE OF THE PEOPLE

Ho Chi Minh (Bringer of Light) is the best known of some 50 aliases assumed by Nguyen Tat Thanh (1890–1969) over the course of his long career. He was founder of the Vietnamese Communist Party and president of the Democratic Republic of Vietnam from 1946 until his death. Born the son of a fiercely nationalistic scholar-official of humble means, he was educated at the Quoc Hoc Secondary School in Hué.

In 1911 he signed up as a cook's apprentice on a French ship, sailing the seas to North America, Africa and Europe. He later moved to Paris, where he adopted the name Nguyen Ai Quoc (Nguyen the Patriot). During this period, he mastered a number of languages (including English, French, German and Mandarin) and began to promote the issue of Indochinese independence. During the 1919 Versailles Peace Conference, he tried to present an independence plan for Vietnam to US President Woodrow Wilson.

Ho Chi Minh was a founding member of the French Communist Party, which was established in 1920. In 1923 he was summoned to Moscow for training by Communist International and from there to Guǎngzhōu (Canton), China, where he founded the Revolutionary Youth League of Vietnam.

In 1941 Ho Chi Minh returned to Vietnam for the first time in 30 years. That same year, at the age of 51, he helped found the Viet Minh, the goal of which was the independence of Vietnam from French colonial rule and Japanese occupation. As Japan prepared to surrender in August 1945, Ho Chi Minh led the August Revolution, and his forces took control of much of Vietnam.

The return of the French shortly thereafter forced Ho Chi Minh and the Viet Minh to flee Hanoi and take up armed resistance. Ho spent eight years conducting a guerrilla war until the Viet Minh's victory against the French at Dien Bien Phu in 1954. He led North Vietnam until his death in September 1969 – he never lived to see the North's victory over the South. Ho is affectionately referred to as 'Uncle Ho' (Bac Ho) by his admirers.

The party has worked hard to preserve the image of Bac Ho. His image dominates contemporary Vietnam more than three decades after his death and no town is complete without a statue of Ho, no city complete without a museum in his name. This cult of personality is in stark contrast to the simplicity with which Ho lived his life.

Whatever the Vietnamese may make of communism in private, Ho Chi Minh remains a man for all seasons. Politics aside, he was a nationalist and patriot who delivered Vietnam its independence. Come what may to the party, Ho's place in history as a hero is assured.

win easily. During the first few years of his rule, Diem consolidated power effectively. During Diem's 1957 official visit to the USA, President Eisenhower called him the 'miracle man' of Asia. As time went on Diem became increasingly tyrannical in dealing with dissent. Running the government became a family affair.

In the early 1960s, the South was rocked by anti-Diem unrest led by university students and Buddhist clergy. The US decided he was a liability and threw its support behind a military coup. A group of young generals led the operation in November 1963. Diem was to go into exile, but the generals got overexcited and both Diem and his brother were killed. He was followed by a succession of military rulers who continued his erratic policies and dragged the country deeper into war.

The Geneva Accords allowed the leadership of the Democratic Republic of Vietnam to return to Hanoi. The new government immediately set out to eliminate those elements of the population that threatened its power. Tens

1968	1969
The Viet Cong launches the Tet Offensive, an attack on towns and cities throughout the South that catches the Americans unaware	US President Richard Nixon authorises the secret bombing of Cambodia, which continues to 1973 killing up to 250,000 Cambodians

of thousands of 'landlords', some with only tiny holdings, were denounced to 'security committees' by envious neighbours and arrested. Hasty 'trials' resulted in between 10,000 and 15,000 executions and the imprisonment of thousands more. In 1956 the party, faced with widespread rural unrest, recognised that things had got out of control and began a Campaign for the Rectification of Errors.

THE CULTURAL REVOLUTION

Mao Zedong and the communists had come to power in 1949 and set about creating their utopia. China grew rapidly in the 1950s, but the party embarked on a catastrophic course with its Great Leap Forward. In an effort to boost production, the population was herded into cooperatives and everyone was encouraged to produce steel in their back yards. Agricultural production slumped and by 1960 it is believed as many as 30 million Chinese had died of starvation. It was, in fact, a great leap backwards.

Similarly, there wasn't much culture in the Cultural Revolution. Mao nurtured a personality cult to rehabilitate himself after the failure of the Great Leap Forward. Mao's 'little red book' became the mantra for a young generation of zealous communists and the Red Guards began their rampage. Nothing was sacred. Schools were shut down, manuscripts destroyed, temples ransacked. Old customs, old habits, old culture and old thinking were to be eliminated. Millions died as the party rooted out 'capitalist roaders'. The madness subsided by 1970, but provided a blueprint for the brutality of the Khmer Rouge when they seized power in Phnom Penh in 1975.

> Most of China's middle-aged and elderly population are survivors of the Cultural Revolution; be mindful if discussing this period of history with them as few went untouched by the horrors of the time.

THE WAR IN VIETNAM

The campaign to 'liberate' the South began in 1959 with the birth of the National Liberation Front (NLF), nicknamed the Viet Cong (VC) by the Americans. The Ho Chi Minh Trail, which had been in existence for several years, was expanded. As the communists launched their campaign, the Diem government rapidly lost control of the countryside. In 1964, Hanoi began sending regular North Vietnamese Army (NVA) units down the Ho Chi Minh Trail. By early 1965, the Saigon government was on its last legs. The army was getting ready to evacuate Hué and Danang, and the central highlands seemed about to fall. Vietnam was the frontline in the worldwide struggle against communist expansion. It was the next domino and could not topple. It was clearly time for the Americans to 'clean up the mess'.

> The Private Life of Chairman Mao, by Li Zhisui, is a fascinating and intimate (if somewhat disturbing) look into the world of this historical titan. Li was Mao's personal physician for 22 years and sheds light on everything from Mao's sexual habits to his political philosophy.

The Americans Wade Ashore

For the first years of the conflict, the American military was boldly proclaiming victory upon victory, as the communist body count mounted. However, the Tet Offensive of 1968 brought an alternate reality into the homes of the average American. On the evening of 31 January, as the country celebrated the Lunar New Year, the VC launched a series of strikes in more than 100 cities and towns, including Saigon. As the TV cameras rolled, a VC commando team took over the courtyard of the US embassy in central Saigon. The Tet Offensive killed about 1000 US soldiers and 2000 ARVN troops, but VC losses were more than 10 times higher, at around 32,000 deaths. For the VC the Tet Offensive ultimately proved a success: it made the cost of fighting the war unbearable for the Americans.

1970	1973
Sihanouk is overthrown in a coup and Cambodia's bloody civil war begins	All sides in the Vietnam conflict put pen to paper to sign the Paris Peace Accords on 27 January 1973

Simultaneously, stories began leaking out of Vietnam about atrocities and massacres carried out against unarmed Vietnamese civilians, including the infamous My Lai Massacre. This helped turn the tide and a coalition of the concerned emerged that threatened the establishment. Antiwar demonstrations rocked American university campuses and spilled onto the streets.

Tricky Dicky's Exit Strategy

Richard Nixon was elected president in part because of a promise that he had a 'secret plan' to end the war. The Nixon Doctrine, as it was called, was unveiled in July 1969 and it called on Asian nations to be more 'self-reliant' in defence matters. Nixon's strategy called for 'Vietnamisation', which meant making the South Vietnamese fight the war without US troops.

The 'Christmas bombing' of Hai Phong and Hanoi at the end of 1972 was meant to wrest concessions from North Vietnam at the negotiating table. Eventually, the Paris Peace Accords were signed by the US, North Vietnam, South Vietnam and the VC on 27 January 1973, which provided for a cease-fire, the total withdrawal of US combat forces and the release of 590 US POWs.

In total, 3.14 million Americans served in the US armed forces in Vietnam during the war. Officially, 58,183 Americans were killed in action or are listed as missing in action (MIA). The direct cost of the war was officially put at US$165 billion, though its real cost to the economy was double that or more. A total of 223,748 South Vietnamese soldiers had been killed in action; North Vietnamese and VC fatalities have been estimated at one million. Approximately four million civilians (or 10% of the Vietnamese population) were injured or killed during the war.

The End is Nigh

In January 1975 the North Vietnamese launched a massive ground attack across the 17th Parallel using tanks and heavy artillery. Whole brigades of ARVN soldiers disintegrated and fled southward, joining hundreds of thousands of civilians clogging Hwy 1. The North Vietnamese pushed on to Saigon and on the morning of 30 April 1975 their tanks smashed through the gates of Saigon's Independence Palace (now called Reunification Palace). The long war was over, Vietnam was reunited and Saigon was renamed Ho Chi Minh City. Throughout the entire conflict, the US never actually declared war on North Vietnam.

SIDESHOW: THE CIVIL WAR IN CAMBODIA

The 1950s were seen as Cambodia's golden years and Sihanouk successfully maintained Cambodia's neutrality into the 1960s. However, the American war in Vietnam was raging across the border and Cambodia was being slowly sucked into the vortex.

By 1969 the conflict between the army and leftist rebels had become more serious, as the Vietnamese sought sanctuary deeper in Cambodia. In March 1970 while Sihanouk was on a trip to France, General Lon Nol and Prince Sisowath Sirik Matak, Sihanouk's cousin, deposed him as chief of state. Sihanouk took up residence in Běijīng and formed an alliance with the Cambodian communists, nicknamed the Khmer Rouge, who exploited this partnership to gain new recruits.

For a human perspective on the North Vietnamese experience during the war, read *The Sorrow of War* by Bao Ninh, a poignant tale of love and loss that shows the soldiers from the North had the same fears and desires as most American GIs.

Oliver Stone has never been one to shy away from political point-scoring and in the first of his famous trilogy about Vietnam, *Platoon*, he earns *dix* points. A brutal and cynical look at the conflict through the eyes of rookie Charlie Sheen, with great performances from Tom Berenger and Willem Dafoe.

Hitch a ride with Michael Herr and his seminal work *Dispatches*. A correspondent for *Rolling Stone* magazine, Herr tells it how it is, as some of the darkest events of the American War unfold around him, including the siege of Khe Sanh.

1975	**1976**
Khmer Rouge march into Phnom Penh on 17 April; North Vietnamese take Saigon on 30 April 1975, renaming it Ho Chi Minh City	Mao Zedong, father of Chinese communism, dies aged 83

On 30 April 1970, US and South Vietnamese forces invaded Cambodia in an effort to flush out thousands of Viet Cong and North Vietnamese troops. The Vietnamese communists withdrew deeper into Cambodia, and the ultimate humiliation came in July 1970 when the Vietnamese seized the temples of Angkor.

Neil Sheehan's account of the life of Colonel John Paul Vann, *Bright Shining Lie*, won the Pulitzer Prize and is the portrayal of one man's disenchantment with the war, mirroring America's realisation it could not be won.

The Secret Bombing

In 1969 the US had begun a secret programme of bombing suspected communist base camps in Cambodia. For the next four years, until bombing was halted by the US Congress in August 1973, huge areas of the eastern half of the country were carpet-bombed by US B-52s, killing uncounted thousands of civilians and turning hundreds of thousands more into refugees.

Despite massive US military and economic aid, Lon Nol never succeeded in gaining the initiative against the Khmer Rouge. Large parts of the countryside fell to the rebels and many provincial capitals were cut off from Phnom Penh. Lon Nol fled the country in early April 1975. On 17 April 1975 – two weeks before the fall of Saigon – Phnom Penh surrendered to the Khmer Rouge.

THE LAND OF A MILLION IRRELEVANTS

War correspondents covering the conflict in Indochina soon renamed Lan Xang the land of a million irrelevants. However, the ongoing conflict was very relevant to the Cold War and the great powers were playing out their power struggles on this most obscure of stages. The country remained divided into pro-American and communist groups after independence. The Lao politician with the task of finding a way through both ideological differences and foreign interference was Souvanna Phouma who tried to build a coalition. Successive governments came and went so fast they needed a revolving door in the national assembly.

Author and documentary filmmaker John Pilger was ripping into the establishment long before Michael Moore rode into town. Get to grips with his hard-hitting views on the American War at http://pilger.carlton .com/vietnam.

Upcountry, large areas fell under the control of communist forces. The US sent troops to Thailand, in case communist forces attempted to cross the Mekong, and it looked for a time as if the major commitment of US troops in Southeast Asia would be to Laos rather than Vietnam. Both the North Vietnamese and the Americans were jockeying for strategic advantage, and neither was going to let Lao neutrality get in the way.

A Hmong Army

The Ravens: Pilots of the Secret War of Laos (1988) by Christopher Robbins tells the story of the volunteer American pilots based in Laos who supplied the 'secret army' and identified targets for US Air Force jets.

President John F Kennedy gave the order to recruit a force of 11,000 Hmong under the command of Vang Pao. They were trained by several hundred US and Thai Special Forces advisors and supplied by Air America, all under the supervision of the CIA. The secret war had begun.

In 1964 the US began its air war over Laos. According to official figures, the US dropped 2,093,100 tons of bombs in 580,944 sorties. The total cost was US$7.2 billion, or US$2 million a day for nine years. No-one knows how many people died, but one third of the population of 2.1 million became internal refugees.

But all the bombing was unable to staunch the flow of North Vietnamese forces down the Ho Chi Minh Trail (or trails). More of southern Laos fell to the Pathet Lao. By mid-1972, when serious peace moves got underway, some four-fifths of the country was under communist control. Unlike Cambodia

1978	1979
Vietnam invades Cambodia on Christmas Day, overthrowing the Khmer Rouge government	China invades northern Vietnam in February to 'punish' the Vietnamese for attacking Cambodia

and Vietnam, the communists were eventually able to take power without a fight. City after city was occupied by the Pathet Lao and in August 1975 they marched into Vientiane unopposed.

THE KHMER ROUGE & YEAR ZERO

Upon taking Phnom Penh, the Khmer Rouge implemented one of the most radical and brutal restructurings of a society ever attempted; its goal was to transform Cambodia into a Maoist, peasant-dominated agrarian cooperative. Within days of the Khmer Rouge coming to power the entire population of the capital city and provincial towns, including the sick, elderly and infirm, was forced to march out to the countryside. Disobedience of any sort often brought immediate execution. The advent of Khmer Rouge rule was proclaimed Year Zero. Currency was abolished and postal services were halted. The country was cut off from the outside world.

Counting the Cost of Genocide

It is still not known exactly how many Cambodians died at the hands of the Khmer Rouge during the three years, eight months and 21 days of their rule. Two million or one-third of the population is a realistic estimate.

Hundreds of thousands of people were executed by the Khmer Rouge leadership, while hundreds of thousands more died of famine and disease.

The definitive war movie has to be *Apocalypse Now*. Marlon Brando plays renegade Colonel Kurtz who has gone AWOL, and native, in the wilds of northeast Cambodia. Martin Sheen is sent to bring him back and the psychotic world into which he is drawn is one of the most savage indictments of war ever seen on screen.

THE LAST OF THE GOD KINGS

Norodom Sihanouk has been a constant presence in the topsy-turvy world of Cambodian politics. A colourful character of many enthusiasms and shifting political positions, his amatory exploits dominated his early reputation. Later he became the prince who stage-managed the close of French colonialism, autocratically led an independent Cambodia, was imprisoned by the Khmer Rouge and, from privileged exile, finally returned triumphant as king, only to abdicate dramatically in 2004. He is many things to many people, a political chameleon, but whatever else he may be, he has proved himself a survivor.

Sihanouk, born in 1922, was not an obvious contender for the throne. He was crowned in 1941, at just 19 years old, with his education incomplete. By the mid-1960s Sihanouk had been calling the shots in Cambodia for more than a decade. The conventional wisdom was that 'Sihanouk is Cambodia' – his leadership was unassailable. But as the cinema took more and more of his time, Cambodia was being drawn inexorably into the American war in Vietnam. Government troops battled with a leftist insurgency in the countryside, the economy was in tatters, and Sihanouk came to be regarded as a liability. His involvement in the film industry and his announcements that Cambodia was 'an oasis of peace' suggested a man who had not only abdicated from the throne but also from reality.

On 18 March 1970 the National Assembly voted to remove Sihanouk from office. Sihanouk went into exile in Běijīng and threw in his lot with the communists. Following the Khmer Rouge victory on 17 April 1975, Sihanouk was confined to the Royal Palace as a prisoner of the Khmer Rouge. He remained there until early 1979 when, on the eve of the Vietnamese invasion, he was flown to Běijīng. It was to be more than a decade before Sihanouk finally returned to Cambodia.

Sihanouk never quite gave up wanting to be everything for Cambodia: international statesman, general, president, film director, man of the people. On 24 September 1993 after 38 years in politics, he settled once again for the role of king until his abdication in 2004. It will be a hard act to follow, matching the presence of Sihanouk – the last in a long line of Angkor's god kings.

1989	1991
Vietnamese forces pull out of Cambodia and Vietnam is at peace for the first time in decades	The Paris Peace Accords are signed in which all Cambodian parties agree to participate in free and fair elections supervised by the UN

Disease stalked the work camps, malaria and dysentery striking down whole families, death a relief for many from the horrors of life. Some zones were better than others, some leaders fairer than others, but life for the majority was one of unending misery and suffering. Cambodia had become a 'prison without walls'.

The Khmer Rouge detached the Cambodian people from all they held dear: their families, their food, their fields and their faith. Nobody cared for the Khmer Rouge by 1978, but nobody had an ounce of strength to do anything about it…except the Vietnamese.

The demise of the Khmer Rouge proved to be a false dawn, as the country was gripped by a disastrous famine that killed hundreds of thousands more who had struggled to survive the Khmer Rouge. Caught in the crossfire of Cold War politics, even the relief effort was about political point-scoring and organisations had to choose whether to work with the UN and the 'free world' on the Thai border or the Vietnamese and their Soviet allies in Phnom Penh.

During the 1960s Cambodia was an oasis of peace while wars raged on in neighbouring Vietnam and Laos. By 1970, that had all changed, as Cambodia was sucked into hell. For the full story on how it happened, read *Sideshow: Kissinger, Nixon and the Destruction of Cambodia* by William Shawcross.

THE REUNIFICATION OF VIETNAM

Vietnam may have been united, but it would take a long time to heal the scars of war. Damage from the fighting extended from unmarked minefields to war-focused, dysfunctional economies; from a chemically poisoned countryside to a population who had been physically or mentally battered. Peace may have arrived, but in many ways the war was far from over.

The party decided on a rapid transition to socialism in the South, but it proved disastrous for the economy. Reunification was accompanied by widespread political repression. Despite repeated promises to the contrary, hundreds of thousands of people who had ties to the previous regime had their property confiscated and were rounded up and imprisoned without trial in forced-labour camps, euphemistically known as re-education camps.

BROTHER ENEMY

Relations with China to the north and its Khmer Rouge allies to the west were rapidly deteriorating and war-weary Vietnam seemed beset by enemies. An anticapitalist campaign was launched in March 1978, seizing private property and businesses. Most of the victims were ethnic-Chinese – hundreds of thousands soon became refugees, known to the world as boat people, and relations with China soured further.

Meanwhile, repeated attacks on Vietnamese border villages by the Khmer Rouge forced Vietnam to respond. Vietnamese forces entered Cambodia on Christmas Day 1978. They succeeded in driving the Khmer Rouge from power on 7 January 1979 and set up a pro-Hanoi regime in Phnom Penh. China viewed the attack on the Khmer Rouge as a serious provocation. In February 1979, Chinese forces invaded Vietnam and fought a brief, 17-day war before withdrawing.

Liberation of Cambodia from the Khmer Rouge soon turned to occupation and a long civil war that drained both countries. However, Vietnam had succeeded in stamping its authority on Indochina. Promoted as the masters of the region under the French, the Vietnamese were once more dictating the political destiny of Cambodia and Laos.

The Documentation Centre of Cambodia is an organisation established to document the crimes of the Khmer Rouge as a record for future generations. The excellent website is a mine of information about Cambodia's darkest hour. Take your time to visit www.dccam.org.

1997	1998
The region experiences an economic crisis; Cambodia is convulsed by a coup; Laos joins Asean	Pol Pot passes away on 15th April 1998, forever depriving Cambodians of the chance for justice

REVERSAL OF FORTUNE

The communist cooperatives in Indochina were a miserable failure and caused almost as much suffering as the war that had preceded them. Pragmatic Laos was the first to liberalise in response to the economic stagnation and private farming and enterprise was allowed as early as 1979. However, the changes came too late for the Lao royal family and the last king and queen are believed to have died of malnutrition and disease in a prison camp sometime in the late 1970s. Vietnam was slower to evolve, but the arrival of President Mikhael Gorbachev in the Soviet Union meant *glasnost* (openness) and *perestroika* (restructuring) were in, radical revolution was out. *Doi moi* (economic reforms) were experimented with in Cambodia and introduced to Vietnam. As the USSR scaled back its commitments to the communist world, the far-flung outposts were the first to feel the pinch. The Vietnamese decided to unilaterally withdraw from Cambodia in 1989, as they could no longer afford the occupation. The party in Vietnam was on its own and needed to reform to survive. Cambodia and Laos would follow its lead.

The Killing Fields is the definitive film on the Khmer Rouge period in Cambodia. It tells the incredible story of American journalist Sidney Schanberg and his Cambodian assistant Dith Pran during and after the war.

A NEW BEGINNING

You may be wondering what happened to Thailand in all of this? Well, compared with the earth-shattering events unfolding in Indochina, things were rather dull. Thailand profited handsomely from the suffering of its neighbours, providing air bases and logistical support to the Americans. As the war and revolution consumed a generation in Cambodia, Laos and Vietnam, Thailand's economy prospered and democracy slowly took root, although coups remain common currency right up to the present day. The financial crisis of 1997 shook the country's confidence. More recently, the leadership of billionaire tycoon Thaksin Shinawatra proved very divisive, provoking the military to seize power in 2006. And the south has been gripped by an Islamic insurgency that has claimed hundreds of lives.

Francois Bizot was kidnapped by the Khmer Rouge, interrogated by Comrade Duch and is believed to be the only foreigner to have been released. Later he was holed up in the French embassy in April 1975. Read his harrowing story in *The Gate*.

China reinvented itself during the 1980s, eschewing its radical past for a more pragmatic politics. Economic growth was in and state industries out. Special export zones were established near Hong Kong and Taiwan and the country began to post record growth. However, there was no political liberalisation to accompany the economic flowering. Students demonstrating for greater democracy in China were brutally dispersed from Tiananmen Square in 1989. However, the population seems content as long as there is money to be made: in 1993 Deng Xiaoping proclaimed that 'to get rich is glorious'. This is keeping the communist juggernaut on the road for now.

Cambodia was welcomed back to the world stage in 1991 with the signing of the Paris Peace Accords which set out a UN roadmap to free and fair elections. There have been many hiccups along the way, including coups and a culture of impunity, but Cambodia has come a long way from the dark days of the Khmer Rouge. Democracy is hardly flourishing, corruption most certainly is, but life is better for many than it has been for a long time. Attempts to bring the surviving Khmer Rouge leadership to trial continue to stumble along, but in a politically charged atmosphere that hardly bodes well for a free and fair process.

Several of the current crop of Cambodian leaders were previously members of the Khmer Rouge, including Prime Minister Hun Sen and Head of the Senate Chea Sim, although there is no evidence to implicate them in mass killings.

Vietnam has followed the Chinese road to riches, taking the brakes off the economy while keeping a firm hand on the political steering wheel. With only two million paid-up members of the Communist Party and 80 million

1999	2001
Cambodia finally joins Asean after a two-year delay	Thaksin Shinawatra becomes prime minister of Thailand, setting the country on a divisive course

Vietnamese, it is a road they must follow carefully. However, the economy is booming and Vietnam's rehabilitation was complete when it joined the World Trade Organisation (WTO) in 2006.

And what of Laos? Still irrelevant to most, but that is wonderful news for visitors who are discovering a slice of older Asia. Hydroelectric power is a big industry and looks set to subsidise the economy in the future. On the flip side, illegal logging remains a major problem, as in Cambodia, with demand for timber in China, Thailand and Vietnam driving the destruction. Tourism has good prospects and Laos is carving a niche for itself as the ecotourism destination of Southeast Asia.

The Mekong region is closer than it has been for some time. Most of the countries are at peace and the talk is of cooperation not conflict. Cambodia, Laos, Thailand and Vietnam are members of the Association of Southeast Asian Nations (Asean) and all enjoy close ties with China. All survived the financial crisis of the late 1990s and have bounced back stronger. However, democracy is weaker than ever, with China, Laos and Vietnam one-party states, Cambodia acting like a one-party state and Thailand under the rule of military generals. Like the river that binds them, the countries of the Mekong region have a turbulent past and uncertain future. For more on the present-day politics and society in the region, see Snapshot (p27).

The Politics of Ritual and Remembrance: Laos Since 1975 (1998) by Grant Evans provides a penetrating study of Lao political culture, including attitudes to Buddhism and the 'cult' of communist leader Kaysone.

Environment David Lukas

For nature lovers, the inner heart of Southeast Asia is a mysterious and evocative paradise. Not only do deep unexplored jungles remain home to charismatic creatures like elephants, tigers, rhinos, and some of the most amazing new species discovered anywhere in the world in the past 100 years, but few places in the world remain so unknown to science and so hard to penetrate. Against this exciting backdrop, visitors to the Mekong region can't help but marvel at the fantastic assortment of colourful birds, tropical plants and diverse mammals that abound at every turn. Threading this entire region together is the mighty Mekong River which arises on the high slopes of the Tibetan Plateau and meanders more than 4000km through the gorges and floodplains of five countries.

THE LAND
Geologic Overview

Southeast Asia documents one of the most exciting geologic events in the earth's history – a story that rivets geologists and drives them crazy at the same time. Cloaked in dense forest, remote and inaccessible, and protected by wars and unfriendly regimes, much of the region's geology remains relatively unknown. Piecing the geologic story together is further complicated because the landscape is extremely complex and is fragmented into many diverse pieces by powerful structural forces.

In the simple version, Southeast Asia is a collage of continental fragments mushed together at the confluence of three great plates: Eurasia, IndoAustralia and the Philippine Sea. All of these fragments apparently broke off from a supercontinent called Gondwanaland that lay in the southern hemisphere about 500 million years ago. Over tens of millions of years these fragments rafted their way north, colliding with each other and with the growing landmass we now know as Asia.

Southeast Asia is today formed of two primary components: these rigid fragments that split off from Gondwanaland, and linear belts of rocks folded and uplifted as these fragments collided. On top of this matrix, the Mekong and other rivers flow, cutting pathways along the suture lines and depositing loads of sediment in shallow basins.

Of the major fragments important to Southeast Asia, the northernmost is called the Yangtze Platform and it forms the core of South China. The Yúnnán capital of Kūnmíng sits at the southwestern edge of the billion-year-old Yangtze Platform, while folded mountains and hills rise to the north, west and south.

To the south lies another fragment called the Indochina Block which includes Cambodia, Laos, Vietnam and eastern Thailand. The Red River of northern Vietnam today follows the suture line where Indochina and South China collided about 400 million years ago.

While the Indochina Block is thought to underlie much of Southeast Asia, the ancestral core (or basement rock) is only exposed in central Vietnam where it shapes a 60,000-sq-km feature known as the Kontum Massif.

Other than the Yangtze Platform and the Kontum Massif, both of which have maintained their ancient structure, the rest of Southeast Asia consists largely of old ocean basins that were crumpled into mountains and lifted above sea level by the enormous forces of major blocks and lesser fragments colliding.

The Mekong River is known as Lancang Jiang (Turbulent River) in China; Mae Nam Khong (Mother River of All Things) in Thailand, Myanmar (Burma) and Laos; Tonlé Thom (Great Water) in Cambodia and Cuu Long (Nine Dragons) in Vietnam.

Although India lies a significant distance west of Southeast Asia, it has had a larger role in shaping the region than any other force. After drifting across the ocean for 100 million years, the microcontinent of India ploughed into the southern margin of Asia 50 million years ago with unbelievable force. As a consequence, two-thirds of the entire Asian region has been bent and twisted on a hardly imaginable scale. In the contact zone between India and Asia, the folding is so dramatic that it created the Himalayas and uplifted the Tibetan Plateau – the single most immense feature on the earth's surface.

So powerful is the force of India crushing into Asia that Southeast Asia is essentially squirting out sideways, cracking in long series of faults and rotating clockwise. This is dramatically illustrated in northern Yúnnán, where the east-west line of widely spaced mountains in Tibet take a sudden turn to the south and collapse into a series of high, narrow ridges and deep valleys. The characteristic S-curved mountain ranges and rivers in Vietnam, Cambodia and Laos are further evidence of the incredible torqueing that is taking place.

The release of tension created by this movement typically occurs along faults and is linked to the earthquakes and landslides that plague the region. River courses often follow these same fault lines, and the shifting topography frequently diverts rivers into new channels. The Mekong, for instance, has followed several different channels including one route through central Thailand that terminated at present day Bangkok. The river assumed its current route only 5000 years ago.

Yúnnán

Yúnnán is without a doubt one of the most alluring destinations in China. It's the most geographically varied of China's provinces, with terrain ranging from subtropical forests to snow-capped Tibetan peaks, and with wildlife to match (see p56). It's the place where the broad east-west trending Tibetan Plateau pinches and turns south into a realm of very narrow, parallel mountain ranges with 3000m to 4000m peaks and deep river gorges that offload their waters into a tropical paradise that stretches from Myanmar (Burma) to South China. Included here are three of South Asia's mightiest rivers: the Salween, Mekong and Yangtze.

Much of eastern Yúnnán belongs to the Yúnnán-Guizhou Plateau (the topographic name for the Yangtze Platform), a region of limestone plateaus, gorges, waterfalls and caves which are 1000m to 2000m above sea level. Turning further south and descending in elevation the landscape becomes cloaked in subtropical forests as it nears the border with Laos and Vietnam.

The Mekong River has a special significance in Yúnnán because it follows the fault line between the Sibumasu Block, a recent fragment from Gondwanaland that forms much of western Thailand and Myanmar, and the much older block that formed when South China and Indochina merged.

A major earthquake hit Lijiāng in 1996, killing more than 300 people; another destroyed more than 10,000 homes 100km east of Dàlǐ in January 2000.

Laos

Once the Mekong exits China it enters Laos, a rugged landlocked country with mountains and plateaus covering more than 70% of the land. At 236,000 sq km, Laos is slightly larger than Great Britain. Running about half the length of Laos, parallel to the course of the Mekong River, is the Annamite Chain, a folded mountain range with peaks averaging between 1500m and 2500m in height. All the rivers and tributaries west of the Annamite Chain drain into the Mekong, while waterways east of the Annamites flow into the Gulf of Tonkin off the coast of Vietnam.

Roughly in the centre of the range is the Khammuan Plateau, an area of striking limestone grottoes and gorges. At the southern end of the Annamite Chain stands the 10,000-sq-km Bolaven Plateau, an important area for the cultivation of high-yield mountain rice, coffee, tea and other crops that flourish at higher altitudes.

The larger, northern half of Laos is made up almost entirely of broken, steep-sided mountain ranges that characterise the folded contact zone between the Sibumasu and Indochina blocks. The highest mountains are found in Xieng Khuang Province (p302), including Phu Bia, the country's highest peak at 2820m. Just north of Phu Bia stands the Xieng Khuang Plateau, the country's largest mountain plateau, which rises 1200m above sea level.

The Mekong so dominates Lao topography that, to a large extent, the entire length of the country parallels its course. The flattest and most tropical part of the country lies on the fertile Mekong flood plain between Sainyabuli and Champasak, where virtually all of the domestic rice consumed in Laos is grown. The Mekong and its tributaries are also the source of fish, a primary protein in the Lao diet.

Thailand

Northern Thailand ranges from high mountains in the north to the flat, sea level Chao Phraya Delta near Bangkok. For nearly 100km along the Nan River valley, evidence can be seen of the Nan-Uttaradit suture, a continuation of the important fault line that the Mekong follows through Yúnnán and Laos, which marks the contact zone between the Sibumasu and Indochina blocks.

The mountains of northwestern Thailand represent the southernmost extent of the ranges that tumble down from the Tibetan Plateau and include Doi Inthanon (2576m), the highest peak in Thailand. In contrast the area around Chao Phraya consists of lowland plains, and from the plains the southern fringe of the Khorat Plateau can be seen rising 300m above sea level to the north. This plateau is the dominant feature of eastern and northern

---

UNDERSTANDING KARST

Travellers to the Mekong region can hardly miss the ubiquitous presence of fantastically eroded limestone pillars and caves that characterise many parts of the region. Limestone derives from old sea floor sediments, shells, and corals that have broken down into calcium carbonate and reformed as rock. As this relatively soft sedimentary rock is folded and uplifted by the collision of adjacent land masses, it begins to dissolve slowly in the presence of rain, rivers and waves to create spectacular karst formations. The presence of limestone in Southeast Asia marks a time in the Permian (250 to 300 million years ago) when the region was inundated by seas before the land was uplifted.

Thailand (also stretching into Laos around Vientiane) and is an area known for dry, thin soils and sparse vegetation.

The Mekong runs along a broad floodplain on the northeastern and eastern border of Thailand, making this a valuable region for crops and fishing. The rivers of north and central Thailand drain into the Gulf of Thailand via the Chao Phraya Delta.

Cambodia

At 181,035 sq km, Cambodia is about half the size of Vietnam or Italy. Cambodia is dominated by water, especially the Mekong River and the Tonlé Sap lake (Great Lake). Nourishing sediments deposited during the annual wet-season flooding make for very rich agricultural land in the heart of the country. The Tonlé Sap lake is a remnant of an ancient channel that the Mekong River once followed.

Beyond this vast alluvial plain, there are three main mountainous regions. In the southwest, much of the landmass between the Gulf of Thailand and the Tonlé Sap is covered by the Cardamom Mountains (Chuor Phnom Kravanh) and the Elephant Mountains (Chuor Phnom Damrei). Along Cambodia's northern border with Thailand, the plains abut against a striking sandstone escarpment more than 300km long and 180m to 550m in height that marks the southern limit of the Dangkrek Mountains (Chuor Phnom Dangkrek, p225). In northeastern Cambodia the plains give way to the Eastern Highlands, a remote region of densely forested mountains and high plateaus that extend eastward into Vietnam's central highlands and northward into Laos. As is true elsewhere in Southeast Asia, these mountainous areas represent folds in the earth's crust related to the collision of blocks.

Vietnam

The Mekong ends on the south coast of Vietnam after making a short dash from Cambodia to the sea. Despite this short distance, Vietnam encompasses what is perhaps the most important feature on the entire river, the area of multiple river channels and incredibly productive soils that create one of the largest and most important delta systems in the world.

Vietnam is 329,566 sq km, making it slightly larger than Italy and slightly smaller than Japan. The country possesses 3451km of stunning coastline and 3818km of land borders, including remote, wild regions where new species of plants and animals are still being discovered. The country is S-shaped, broad in the north and south and a mere 50km wide in the centre.

Three-quarters of the country consists of rolling hills and mighty mountains, the highest of which is the 3143m Fansipan (p376) in the far northwest. The Truong Son Mountains, a range of folded hills, runs almost the full length of Vietnam along its border with Laos and Cambodia. The central highland region includes the Kontum Massif, the original Gondwanaland fragment that all of Southeast Asia has coalesced around. The western portion of the highlands, near Buon Ma Thuot and Pleiku, is well known for its incredibly fertile, bright red volcanic soil.

The most striking geological features in Vietnam are the karst formations. Northern Vietnam is a showcase of these features, with stunning examples around Ninh Binh (p367) and the Perfume Pagoda (p366), and at Halong (p369) and Bai Tu Long (p371) Bays where an enormous limestone plateau has steadily sunk into the ocean with its old mountain tops still poking into the sky like bony vertical fingers.

WILDLIFE

The Mekong region is home to one of the richest and most abundant gatherings of animals in the world. Not only is the assortment of species unbelievably diverse and exotic, but the dry forests of Cambodia, Laos and Vietnam are ranked second only to the plains of Africa for numbers of large game animals. Sadly, the region's natural environment and wildlife are under extreme threat and it's not too much of a stretch to say that the vast majority of animals and habitats are highly threatened, many to the brink of extinction.

The region's tremendous biodiversity is partly explained by the fact that Southeast Asia is composed of ancient continental fragments that drifted separately across the ocean for millions of years, with each fragment evolving unique flora and fauna. In addition, species from further north migrated into the northern portions of Southeast Asia, while lowering of sea levels during the Pleistocene 'ice age' connected Southeast Asia to the islands of Java, Sumatra and Borneo and allowed tropical species to expand their range northward. But perhaps the most significant reason for the region's unique species is that the forests of Southeast Asia are about 160 million years old – far older than the forests of the Amazon or equatorial Africa – and evolution has been at work a long time here.

As in all tropical areas, the plants and animals of Southeast Asia have evolved unique strategies for survival. Unlike temperate regions, where 80% of the nutrients are in the soil or at ground level, in tropical forests 80% of the nutrients are contained in the canopy. This requires that every living organism in a tropical forest find ways to access these aerial nutrients, either by living in trees themselves or by competing fiercely for the few nutrients that fall to the ground.

Dipterocarps (which are the dominant and most important group of trees found in Southeast Asia) complicate the equation by producing fruits irregularly. This strategy is called masting, and it means that trees produce no fruits for six to seven years in a row, then in a single season produce massive crops of fruits simultaneously. Masting helps to keep down the number of seed predators and ensures that more seeds survive to grow into trees, but it also has the effect that the jungle's seed-eating animals (many types of insects, birds and mammals) struggle to survive through the nonmasting years.

Biologists have only recently begun to systematically explore and document parts of the Mekong region for the first time. They are realising that this may be one of the richest troves of unknown species in the world. Not only do thousands of plants remain to be discovered but even large mammals are being found for the first time. In 1992, researchers in central Vietnam's Vu Quang Nature Reserve were shocked to run across a 95kg antelope relative that was unknown to science. It was the largest land-dwelling animal discovered

Naturalists will be fascinated to read the well-written *Vietnam: A Natural History* by Eleanor Sterling, Martha Hurley, and Le Duc Minh (2006).

anywhere in the world since 1937 (when the kouprey, another large hoofed mammal, was uncovered in the region). In Vietnam alone, another three deer species, a monkey, a bat, a shrew, a rabbit and seven new birds have been discovered since 1992. This is in addition to three new turtles, 15 lizards, four snakes, 31 frogs and more than 45 fish.

Equally exciting is the fact that species long thought extinct have recently been rediscovered. This includes the finding of a recent skull of a Vietnamese warty pig (Heude's pig) first collected in 1892 and never seen in the wild. The Edwards' pheasant was likewise thought extinct until it was rediscovered in Vietnam. But at the top of the list would be one of the most incredible findings of the past century, the discovery of a remnant population of Javan rhinoceros just 130km northeast of Ho Chi Minh City. Known only from a tiny population of 50 animals in western Java, this is one of the rarest mammals in the world and long feared extinct in Southeast Asia.

Mammals

Wildlife Trade in Laos: The End of the Game (2001), by Hanneke Nooren and Gordon Claridge, is a frightening description of animal poaching in Laos.

Although Southeast Asia is home to an astounding variety of exotic mammals like tigers, leopards, bears, tapirs and elephants, seeing one is the exception rather than the rule. Visitors are far more likely to encounter creatures like monkeys, civets and squirrels (including half a dozen or more types of flying squirrels).

Among the most notable animals are pangolins, 85cm long anteater relatives covered in body armour of overlapping scales that protect the creatures when they curl into protective balls. Pangolins burrow into termite mounds and anthills that dot the Southeast Asian landscape and use their 25cm long sticky tongues to extract insects.

Of several dozen primates, the lanky limbed gibbons are best known for their loud and elaborate bouts of singing that ring through the tropical forests on a daily basis. Macaques are a group of primates known for their brash and gregarious habits, and several of the more common species are ubiquitous pests around tourist traps. Slow lorises weigh a mere 1.2kg but have huge charm with their big round eyes, thick fur and long curious gazes.

Aquatic mammals include otters, and the dugong, one of the last remaining representatives of an ancient group of animals that originated 65 million years ago. Halfway between mermaid and small whale in appearance, these ungainly 300kg mammals graze peacefully on sea plants and live in one of a few protected coastal areas like Vietnam's Con Dao National Park.

Bird-watchers are lucky to have a beautiful resource in *Birds of Southeast Asia* by Craig Robson (2005), which has stunning illustrations of all the region's birds.

One of the region's most endangered mammals is the Irrawaddy dolphin (see the boxed text, p232) that resides in the Mekong upstream of Kratie, Cambodia. Perhaps only a few hundred dolphins remain in this population. Despite their popularity with tourists, they are frequent victims of gill nets used by fishermen.

Birds

More than 1000 species of birds can be found in Southeast Asia, about 10% of the world's birds, making the region a top-notch destination for bird-watchers. Many of these species are found only in Southeast Asia and quite a number are specific to one particular country. Colourful tropical birds include showy barbets, dazzling pheasants and charismatic hornbills. If these birds somehow evade you, then you can always count on seeing the intoxicatingly blue Asian fairy bluebird if you spend time in its forested home.

Serious bird-watchers, however, travel to Southeast Asia to spot one of the many very rare birds. High on this list is the critically endangered Sarus crane, a statuesque wetland bird which is depicted on the bas-relief at Angkor and now found at only a few sites like Vietnam's Tram Chim Nature Reserve. In dense, undisturbed forest, you might find the Siamese fireback, a pheasant with bright yellow back (hence its name) and bright red facial skin. Thailand's Khao Yai National Park (p156) is one of the best places to see this species. The endangered crested argus is a 2m-long pheasant covered in tiny white spots that is one of the most highly sought-after birds in Southeast Asia.

Fish

The Mekong River is second only to the Amazon in terms of fish diversity and is considered the foremost river in the world for giant fish. A record-breaking 293kg giant catfish was netted in 2005 in Thailand. Other contenders for the world's largest freshwater fish in the Mekong include the giant freshwater stingray, dog-eating catfish, arapaima and Chinese paddlefish.

These species, and many other smaller fish, migrate fair distances along the Mekong, moving into tributaries and flooded plains during the rainy season. An increasing number of dams in Southeast Asia have an incalculable impact on these animals even though a vast majority of the people of the Mekong region depend on fish protein every day.

PLANTS

The forest cover of Southeast Asia is mainly a mix of deciduous forest (a forest type that loses its leaves during the dry season) and evergreen forest (commonly, though not always correctly, referred to as 'rainforest'). These forests occur as far north as southern Yúnnán, where they are replaced by northern temperate forests of conifers and rhododendrons on mountain slopes.

What is particularly surprising is how much of the Southeast Asian landscape is comprised of other vegetation types, including the depressingly familiar deforested landscape now planted with crops. Shrublands, grasslands and dry savanna forests are widespread throughout the Mekong region because the monsoon climate supports extensive forest cover through the dry season.

The most important trees in Southeast Asia, both economically and ecologically, are an ancient group of broad-leaved trees called dipterocarps. A fully developed dipterocarp forest is a marvellous sight, a place where tall straight trunks soar 40m or more and disappear into an unbroken forest canopy. The bases of these large trees are often supported by elegantly flaring buttresses that have the appearance of fine cathedral architecture. On high quality sites, a dipterocarp forest supports some of the greatest botanical diversity in the world – up to 200 different tree species per hectare (as compared to 10 different species in the world's best temperate forests).

The most widespread forest type in tropical Southeast Asia is deciduous forest (also known as monsoon forest). Unfortunately, because it grows in lowland areas it is also the forest most readily converted to rice fields. Deciduous forests are shaped by lack of rain in the dry season and by frequent forest fires, and the dipterocarps of these forests tend to be short, gnarled trees loosely scattered among grasslands.

Highly valued teak trees are a characteristic component of these monsoon forests and are harvested everywhere, legally and illegally. In areas of heavy

For more information on issues relating to riverine ecosystems, check with the South East Asia Rivers Network (SEARIN) at www.searin.org/indexE .htm.

logging, bamboo thickets invade the disturbed soils and are now a conspicuous sight in many parts of the region.

Forests with access to water keep their leaves throughout the year and are known as evergreen forests. These forests grow near the equator (the typical 'rainforest'), along rivers and in moist mountain environments, and for these reasons their distribution is patchy in Southeast Asia. Evergreen forests can be recognised by their incredible richness of species and lush vegetation.

Go to www.wwfchina .org/english for details of the WWF's projects for endangered and protected animals in China. You'll also find a kid's page for the budding biologists in the family.

Although strangler figs (Banyan trees) of the rainforest are renowned for their beauty their more important role is as 'keystone' species. Figs are perhaps the single most abundant food source during the years that dipterocarps don't produce crops and many birds, mammals and insects depend on figs for their survival. The fig fruit is actually a hollow capsule with flowers growing on the interior wall that are pollinated by different species of tiny wasps. Fig seeds are spread by animals that eat the fruit, and as a young fig grows it sends out a web of roots that fuse and smother the host tree it lands on, hence the common name strangler fig. Visitors to the Mekong region can see some stupendous ancient fig trees growing on the ruins at Angkor (see p212).

Montane evergreen forests of Southeast Asia are a mix of tropical trees, oaks and pines covered in dense mats of orchids, mosses, ferns and epiphytes at higher elevations. In Yúnnán, these forests are also home to 600 species of rhododendron and 650 of the world's azalea species, in addition to the tantalisingly named dragon spruce.

Conifers may surprise visitors who expect only 'rainforest' trees in Southeast Asia. Vietnam alone has 33 species of conifers and the mountains of southwestern China offer even more species. In 2002 an unusual new conifer called the golden Vietnamese cypress was discovered in the Bat Dai Son Mountains of Vietnam. Its closest relative lives in the Pacific Northwest, and shows the ancient link that existed between East Asia and North America.

Plants growing on limestone karst formations (see the boxed text, p52) tend to be markedly different to those in other forest types. Limestone soils are dry, alkaline and poor in nutrients, creating harsh conditions for survival. Despite these disadvantages, limestone formations have more species per unit area than other plant community and many of these species are endemic, often growing on a single hill and nowhere else in the world.

PARKS

The story of parks and protected areas in the Mekong region is a mixed bag. On one hand the environment is recognised as one of the most biologically diverse in the world, a fact that has not been lost on government authorities who see tremendous scientific and economic value in protecting endangered habitats. But at the same time, even highly touted parks exist as little more than lines on a map and few resources are allocated for wildlife protection or park ranger salaries.

Across much of the Mekong region, local villagers live in close proximity to the natural world, depending on plants and animals for all aspects of their lives. Furthermore, rice is notoriously fickle and nearby forests provide villagers a safety net for food and income – whether the land is protected or not – when rice crops fail.

Yúnnán

Perhaps 12 national parks and 16 national nature reserves have been listed for Yúnnán, many of them in the past 25 years, but this is a rough number because the names and designations for these sites seem nowhere near standardised or adequately documented by visitors and government officials.

Yúnnán's most famous protected areas include the 2070-sq-km Xishuangbanna Nature Reserve on the Laos and Myanmar borders. This reserve area encompasses five separate subreserves that protect about 4% of the total tropical zone in China, as well as several hundred elephants, tigers, leopards and golden-haired monkeys. In the same region is the massive Sanchahe Nature Reserve, site of the popular Banna Wild Elephant Valley, that is home to 40 or so wild elephants.

Further north is the Three Parallel Rivers of Yúnnán Protected Areas, a UN designation for 15 protected areas that encompass the remote forested upper watersheds of the Yangtze, Mekong and Salween Rivers. Many of these protected zones are poorly known and seldom visited, though the Gaoligong Mountain Nature Reserve on the Southern Silk Road is the oldest and best known of these reserves.

Laos

Laos boasts one of the youngest and most comprehensive protected area systems in the world. In 1993 the government set up 18 National Biodiversity Conservation Areas, comprising a total of 24,600 sq km, or just over 10% of the country's land mass. It did this following sound scientific advice rather than creating areas on an ad hoc basis (as most other countries have done). Two more areas were added in 1995, for a total of 20 protected areas covering 14% of Laos. Recently the Lao People's Democratic Republic government renamed these National Protected Areas (NPAs). Another 20 protected areas of varying designations have also been added.

The largest of the NPAs, Nakai-Nam Theun, covers 3710 sq km and is home to one of the two largest elephant populations in the country, as well as several species unknown to the scientific world a decade ago. The

For fuller descriptions of all Laos's National Protected Areas, see the comprehensive website www.ecotourismlaos.com.

WORLD HERITAGE SITES

The true splendour of the Mekong region is well preserved in an extensive variety of World Heritage Sites which protect some of the area's foremost environmental, cultural and historical attractions.

Included on this list is Dong Phaya Yen-Khao Yai Forest Complex of northern Thailand, a cluster of six national parks, the most famous of which is Khao Yai National Park (p156), the first national park in Thailand and home to an incredible diversity of wildlife.

Also in northern Thailand is the Thungyai-Huai Kha Khaeng Wildlife Sanctuaries, a group of protected lands that together constitute the largest conservation area in mainland Southeast Asia. When first established in 1991, it set aside 6222 sq km, but with the addition of other proposed reserves, it is hoped that this sanctuary will grow to 1.2 million hectares and be large enough to protect sizable populations of Southeast Asia's most endangered large mammals. Off limits without special permission, it received only 400 to 500 visitors a year through the 1990s.

Halong Bay (p369) in the Gulf of Tonkin is considered *the* natural wonder of Vietnam. Picture 3000 incredible limestone pillars rising from the emerald waters and you have a vision of greatness. These tiny islands are dotted with isolated beaches and limestone caves that beckon great numbers of tourists.

The 2000-sq-km Phong Nha-Ke Bang National Park was established in 2003 and protects the oldest major karst region in all of Asia. Extending to the border of Laos, the park offers 70km of caves and underground rivers, and dozens of unclimbed peaks and unexplored valleys.

one officially declared national park in Laos, the 2000-sq-km Phu Khao Khuay NPA (p285) situated near Vientiane, has opening hours and an admission fee.

Thailand

The parks of the northern half of Thailand range from Doi Inthanon National Park, which protects Thailand's highest mountain and is home to nearly 400 species of birds, to Khao Yai National Park which is Thailand's oldest and most visited national park and is the crown jewel of the country's national park system. Khao Yai National Park protects one of the largest intact monsoon forests left in Southeast Asia and is home to 200 to 300 elephants.

Thailand's national park system was established in 1961 and has since grown to encompass 112 national parks across the country, plus thousands of 'nonhunting areas', wildlife sanctuaries, forest reserves, botanical gardens and arboretums. Coastal and ocean environments are further protected in a variety of marine parks and preserves.

Cambodia

Before the civil war, Cambodia had six national parks, together covering 22,000 sq km (around 12% of the country). The war effectively destroyed this system and it wasn't reintroduced until 1993 when a royal decree designated 23 national parks, wildlife sanctuaries, protected landscapes and multiple-use areas. Three more protected forests were recently added to the list, bringing the area of protected land in Cambodia to 47,845 sq km (around 26% of the country). In principle this is fantastic news, but in practice authorities don't have the resources or the will to protect these areas on the ground.

Cambodia's most important parks include the 1400-sq-km Bokor National Park (p244), 350-sq-km Kirirom National Park (p201), 150-sq-km Ream National Park (p240) and 3325-sq-km Virachay National Park (p236). Recent additions to the park system include Cambodia's largest protected area, the 4294-sq-km Mondulkiri Protected Forest, which adjoins the 1155-sq-km Yok Don National Park in Vietnam.

Vietnam

Vietnam currently has more than 150 parks, reserves and other protected areas and the Ministry of Agriculture and Rural Development has established a goal of protecting a total area of 20,000 sq km by 2010. The majority of these protected areas are seldom visited by travellers, who tend to get stuck on the 'must-see' tourist trail. Access can be problematic for parks hidden in remote areas, but others are much easier to reach. The 738-sq-km Cat Tien National Park (see the boxed text, p402) is easily reached from Ho Chi Minh City and is very popular with bird-watchers. For those who are willing to undertake the boat ride, the 152-sq-km Cat Ba National Park (p371) preserves beautiful island habitats that are popular with foreign travellers.

ENVIRONMENTAL ISSUES

Behind nearly all environmental issues and crises in Southeast Asia lies the overwhelming fact that the vast majority of the region's people depend directly on the forests and waters for their very survival. When international companies siphon off local resources, it is the people of the nation that suffer. For example, the Mekong provides for the most productive fishery in the world, feeding 73 million people who live along its banks. New dam construc-

Back in the early 1990s, Cambodia had such extensive forest cover compared with its neighbours that some environmentalists were calling for the whole country to be made a protected area.

tion funded by the UN Development Program and the Asia Development Bank has an immediate and incalculable impact on fish populations that migrate along the river and deprives countless people of their daily protein and source of income.

Humans have also had a devastating impact on the region, despite its ruggedness and remoteness. Some conservationists, for instance, consider Vietnam so highly degraded that they write it off as a lost cause. Virtually every inch of usable land has been converted from forest to rice fields, and more forests every year are being cleared for slash-and-burn agriculture. Porous, poorly guarded borders and lax enforcement means that borders are wide open for illegal trade in wildlife and forest products, much of which seems to directly profit local military.

In many areas, cut stumps outnumber living trees and during the peak logging frenzy of 1997, all of Cambodia's unprotected forests had been licensed to logging companies. Thailand banned logging in 1989 after a series of fatal landslides smothered several villages but simply shifted their logging operations to adjacent countries. Under international pressure, Cambodia temporarily froze all logging concessions in 2001. Meanwhile, Chinese companies log without oversight in neighbouring Laos in exchange for building roads, and the issue keeps shifting around the region faster than regulations can keep up.

The United States single-handedly bears a tremendous responsibility for creating some of the most intensive environmental destruction in the region. During the Vietnam-American war, the US military dumped 72 million litres of herbicides over 16% of South Vietnam, defoliating vast stretches of intact forest cover and poisoning the landscape. Another 14 million tons of bombs destroyed villages, hillsides, fields and forests; while massive bulldozers named 'Rome ploughs' were used to rip away the vegetation and topsoil in areas that had been missed. Although there has been nearly miraculous recovery in some of these areas, it is impossible to calculate how many species were thoughtlessly wiped out.

Given the importance of the Mekong, few other topics matter as much as the continued devastation to Southeast Asia's most vital resource. As new roads improve access to markets, local villages are steadily shifting from their ancient subsistence economies to cash economies, resulting in the landscape being stripped of resources as quickly as possible. Fishermen on the river have turned to using gill nets that indiscriminately sweep up nearly every living organism, including the highly endangered Irrawaddy dolphin (see the boxed text, p232). Even in cases where countries have outlawed gill netting, their neighbours on the river continue using this horrific practice and everyone suffers.

It would be impossible to overstate the impact that dams have on the river environment. It's hard to say how many dams are on the table because these plans are guarded secrets, but it's safe to say that quite a few are being discussed and funded by the different countries. Recent dams in southwest China have already cut off an estimated 50% of the upper river's sediment input, and there are apparently plans to dam the entire length of the Mekong in Yúnnán. The majority of the river's fish are migratory to one degree or another and dams prevent them from reaching critical breeding areas, while also dampening the natural flooding cycle that fish depend on.

There are a few positive signs in this gloomy picture. Countless villagers are taking matters into their own hands and creating local management traditions that help protect the landscape. Encouraged by national governments, quite a number of reforestation projects are in the works, including

The giant Mekong catfish may grow up to 3m long and weigh almost 300kg. Due to Chinese blasting of shoals in the Upper Mekong, it now faces extinction in the wild.

the 'Five Million Hectare Program' in Vietnam which has the goal of planting five million hectares of new forest by 2010. International pressure, coupled with amazing discoveries of new species by scientists, has propelled Southeast Asian biodiversity onto front page news and convinced regional governments to get more serious in their conservation efforts. It is too late for some species but we can only hope that the tide is turning in a positive direction for many others.

Ancient Wonders

Marvel at the extravagant beauty of Angkor Wat (p62), the world's largest religious building

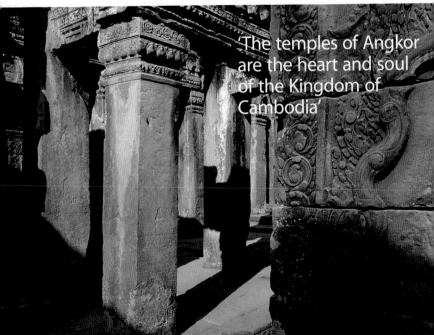

'The temples of Angkor are the heart and soul of the Kingdom of Cambodia'

Explore the maze of vaulted corridors at Preah Khan, one of the biggest temples of Angkor (below)

Ancient Wonders

The Mekong region is littered with the legacy of powerful empires which carved their personality and power into the landscape. Majestic temples, mysterious enigmas and living museums, the Mekong plays host to an abundance of ancient wonders.

THE TEMPLES OF ANGKOR

Prepare for divine inspiration! The temples of Angkor, capital of Cambodia's ancient Khmer empire, are the perfect fusion of creative ambition and spiritual devotion. The Cambodian god kings of old each strove to better their ancestors in size, scale and symmetry, culminating in the world's largest religious building, Angkor Wat (p208), and one of the world's weirdest, the Bayon (p209). The hundreds of temples surviving today are but the sacred skeleton of the vast political, religious and social centre of an empire that stretched from Burma to Vietnam, a city which, at its zenith, boasted a population of one million when London was a scrawny town of 50,000 inhabitants.

The temples of Angkor are the heart and soul of the Kingdom of Cambodia, a source of inspiration and national pride to all Khmers as they struggle to rebuild their lives after years of terror and trauma. Today, they are a point of pilgrimage for all Cambodians and no visitor will want to miss their extravagant beauty when passing through the region.

PRASAT PREAH VIHEAR

The imposing mountain temple of Prasat Preah Vihear (p225) has the most dramatic location of all of the Angkorian monuments, perched atop the cliff face of Cambodia's Dangkrek Mountains. The views from this most mountainous of temple mountains are breathtaking: lowland Cambodia stretching as far as the eye can see, and the holy mountain of Phnom Kulen (p213) looming in the distance. The foundation stones of the temple stretch to the edge of the cliff as it falls precipitously away to the plains below.

Known as Khao Phra Wihan by the Thais, Preah Vihear means 'Sacred Monastery' in Khmer and it was an important place of pilgrimage during the Angkorian period. The 300-year chronology of its construction also offers the visitor an insight into the metamorphosis of carving and sculpture during the Angkor period and there are some impressive touches, including a rendition of the Churning of the Ocean of Milk (p208), later so perfectly mastered at Angkor Wat.

KOH KER

The history of Cambodia is riven with dynastic spats and political intrigue. One of the most memorable came in the 10th century when Jayavarman IV (r 928–42) threw his toys out of the pram, stormed off to the northeast and established the rival capital of Koh Ker (p224). Koh Ker was the capital for just 15 years, but Jayavarman IV was determined to legitimise his rule through a prolific building programme that left a legacy of 30 major temples and some gargantuan sculpture that is on display in the National Museum (p192) in Phnom Penh.

The most striking structure at Koh Ker is Prasat Thom, a seven-storey step pyramid, more Mayan than Khmer, with commanding views over the surrounding forest. Nearby is Prasat Krahom (Red Temple), named after the pinkish Banteay Srei–style stone from which it is built.

Intricate carvings decorate the third *gopura* (entrance pavilion) at Prasat Preah Vihear (above)   JOHN ELK III

LUANG PRABANG

Luscious, lovely and laid back, Luang Prabang (p290) is the place to live a languid life. Dormant for decades, the town survived warfare and communism to emerge as a wonderful living example of a French-colonial town, complete with historic wats and traditional Lao houses. Laos moves at its own pace and seductive Luang Prabang is no exception. Many come for a few days but stay for a few weeks.

The sweeping roof of Wat Xieng Thong (p294) is the most striking of more than 30 ancient temples. Every morning the streets are ablaze with saffron as a stream of monks spills out of the wats seeking alms. The Mekong River is a beautiful backdrop for this World Heritage–listed town and it's the perfect way to reach the Pak Ou Caves (p300), a royal repository for thousands of precious Buddha images. Luang Prabang may not be as ancient as some, but this historic town is an absolute wonder.

PLAIN OF JARS

Among the most enigmatic sights in Laos, the Plain of Jars (p305) is proof that history remains a mystery in some parts of the Mekong region. Scattered across a plain near Phonsavan (p303) are hundreds of stone jars in many shapes and sizes. Archaeologists continue to debate their function, and theories range from sarcophagi to wine fermenters or rice storage jars.

Nobody really knows how old these mysterious jars are or where they came from, but they may be linked to the strange stone megaliths in Sam Neua Province. Locals claim they are 2000 years old and have their own explanation for their origin. In the 6th century, the Lao-Thai hero Khun Jeuam travelled to the area to overthrow the cruel despot Chao

The glittering entrance to Wat Xieng Thong (above), Luang Prabang's most magnificent temple

'Laos moves at its own pace and seductive Luang Prabang is no exception'

Angka. To celebrate his victory, locals believe he had hundred of jars constructed for the fermentation of rice wine. It must have been some party!

HOI AN

Step back in time to the historic heart of Hoi An (p387), a centuries-old Vietnamese trading port that has played home to Chinese, Japanese, Dutch, Portuguese and French merchants. The beautiful blend of architecture reveals the layers of history here, as successive powers struggled to exert their influence. Spared the ravages of war, Hoi An is now a worthy World Heritage Site and is the most popular stop on the Vietnamese coast.

The mysterious Plain of Jars (opposite)
JULIET COOMBE

The Chinese kept their culture alive in the assembly halls and temples that dot the town, reflecting the diverse make-up of the Middle Kingdom. The Japanese bequeathed a classic covered bridge which remains in use today. The French left their graceful architecture, all adding up to Hoi An specialising in fusion long before the gastronomes came to town. Many of the old houses have been preserved to offer a glimpse into the 19th-century life of merchants in old Faifo, as it was once known.

The ancient trading port of Hoi An (above) is set on the Thu Bon River
MARK DAFFEY

MY SON

While the Chams may not have been quite the audacious architects the ancient Khmers were, they certainly knew about beautiful brickwork. Controlling an empire that covered much of south and central Vietnam, the centre of spiritual life was here in My Son (p392) when the political capital was in nearby Tra Kieu (Simhapura). Set under the shadow of Cat's Tooth Mountain, the principal temples suffered greatly at the hands of American attacks, but are slowly being restored to their former glories.

The brickwork is brilliant and was later carved and coated in stucco or plaster. Many of the temples would have been finished in gold leaf and must have been an inspiring and imposing sight for pilgrims of old. Modern pilgrims in the shape of tourists travel here by day. Arrive early in the morning or late in the afternoon for a more reflective experience.

SUKHOTHAI

Thailand's first capital in the 13th century, Sukhothai (p150) symbolises the golden age of Thai civilisation and is a source of national pride. A World Heritage Site, the park includes the remains of 21 temples within the ancient walls of the *meuang kào* (old city), and the art and architecture are considered to be the most classic of Thai styles. The city flourished for 200 years and the first Thai script dates from this period.

The graceful architecture of Sukhothai (meaning Rising of Happiness) is epitomised by the classic lotus bud stupa, but there are shades of Sri Lanka and Srivijaya in some of the stupas. The largest wat is impressive Wat Mahathat (p150), but impressive Khmer temples such at Wat Si Sawai (p150) suggest this was a spiritual centre long before the Thais established their capital here.

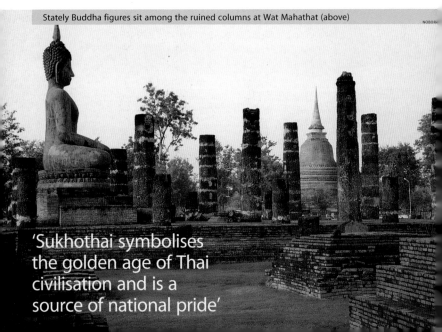

Stately Buddha figures sit among the ruined columns at Wat Mahathat (above)

NOBOR…

'Sukhothai symbolises the golden age of Thai civilisation and is a source of national pride'

The ancient Cham city of My Son (opposite) is a World Heritage Site

PATRICK SYDER

AYUTHAYA

The urban setting might be pretty ordinary in comparison with the Angkors and Sukhothais of the region, but Ayuthaya (p130) is undoubtedly on the historical A-list of the Mekong region. Eclipsing Sukhothai in the 14th century, this was the glittering capital of the Thai kingdom for more than 400 years, until the Burmese managed to finish what they had started centuries earlier and sacked the capital in 1767.

The historical park includes dozens of temples scattered throughout the town of Ayuthaya. Wat Phra Si Sanphet (p130) was once the largest temple here and has an iconic line-up of *chedi* which draw the crowds. The Burmese left little standing at Wat Phra Mahathat (p130), but this is one of the most photographed places in Thailand thanks to an ancient Buddha head caught in the embrace of a tentaclelike tree root.

Buddha head at Wat Phra Mahathat (left)

ANDERS BLOMQVIST

Picturesque Black Dragon Pool Park (below)
TOM COCKREM

top ten

BEST OF THE REST

- Historic Dàlǐ (p451) in Yúnnán
- Cambodia's lost temple of Preah Khan (p213), Preah Vihear province
- Mysterious faces at Banteay Chhmar (p221), Cambodia
- Cambodia's Sambor Prei Kuk (p226), the region's first temple city
- The imposing mountain temple of Wat Phu Champasak (p328) in southern Laos
- Hanoi's bubbling, sizzling, pulsating Old Quarter (p357)
- The golden stupa of Pha That Luang (p270) in Vientiane, Laos
- Bangkok's dazzling Grand Palace (p115) complex
- Beautifully restored Khmer temple architecture at Phanom Rung (p156) in Thailand
- The imperial city of the old emperors, Hué (p379) in Vietnam

LÌJIĀNG

Once upon a time, all of China must have looked like this. Cobbled streets, rickety old wooden buildings and chaotic canals combine to make this the closest thing to an Ang Lee epic that you'll find in Yúnnán. Lìjiāng (p455) was rocked by an earthquake in 1996 that caused widespread damage, although most of the traditional Naxi architecture survived. The government took note of this, and is now committed to replacing cement with cobblestone and wood.

The focus of town, the Old Market Square, was once the haunt of Naxi traders, but these days the souvenir sellers hold court. The Mu Family Mansion (p457) was extensively rebuilt after the 1996 earthquake but is worth a visit for the beautiful grounds alone. Finish up at Black Dragon Pool Park (p457), which offers an incredible view of Yùlóng Xuěshān (Jade Dragon Snow Mountain; p459).

The Culture

The Mekong region is not known as Indochina for nothing. Geographically it is the land in between China and India, and culturally it has absorbed influences from both of these mighty civilisations. This is where two of the world's greatest cultures collide. China has shaped the destiny of Vietnam and Yúnnán and continues to cast a shadow over the Mekong. India exported its great religions, language, culture and sculpture to Cambodia, Laos and Thailand. The border between Vietnam and Cambodia is as significant a sociocultural border as the Himalaya range is a formidable physical barrier between the great rivals of China and India. It is the divide between Sino-Asia to the east and Indo-Asia to the west.

Cambodia was the cultural staging post to the Indianisation of the Mekong region. Indian traders brought Hinduism and Buddhism around the 2nd century and with it came the religious languages of Sanskrit and Pali; Sanskrit forming the root of modern Khmer, Lao and Thai. They also brought their art and architecture, which was redefined so effectively by the ancient Khmers before spreading into Laos and Thailand. Vietnam, meanwhile, was occupied by China for more than a thousand years and, like the Indians, the Chinese brought with them their religion, their philosophy and their culture. Confucianism and Taoism were introduced and still form the backbone of Vietnamese religion, together with Buddhism.

With a millennium or more influence from two of the world's most successful civilisations, it is hardly surprising to find such a dynamic variety of culture in the Mekong region today.

For an in-depth insight into the cultures of the Mekong region, including fashion, film and music, check out www.things asian.com.

PEOPLE

As empires came and went, so too did the populations, and many of the countries in the Mekong region are far less ethnically homogenous than their governments would have you believe. It wasn't only local empire building that had an impact, but colonial meddling, which left a number of people stranded beyond their borders. There are Lao and Khmer in Thailand, Khmer in Vietnam, Thai (Dai) in China and Vietnam, and Chinese everywhere. No self-respecting Mekong town would be complete without a Chinatown and in many of the major cities in the region, Chinese migrants may make up as much as half of the population.

The mountains of the Mekong region provide a home for a mosaic of minority groups, often referred to as hill tribes. Many of these groups migrated from China and Tibet and have settled in areas that lowlanders considered too much of a challenge to cultivate. Colourful costumes and unique traditions draw increasing numbers of visitors to their mountain homes. The most popular areas to visit local hill tribes include Mondulkiri (p236) and Ratanakiri (p233) provinces in Cambodia, Luang Nam Tha (p309) and Muang Sing (p312) in northern Laos, Chiang Mai (p133) and Chiang Rai (p145) in northern Thailand, Sapa (p376) in northern Vietnam and Xīshuāngbǎnnà (p463) in Yúnnán. For more on visiting hill-tribe communities, see p138.

Population growth varies throughout the Mekong region. China's much publicised one-child policy has helped to curb growth in Yúnnán province, while developed Thailand embraced family planning decades ago. Vietnam is coming around to the Chinese way of thinking and starting to promote family planning. Cambodia and Laos have the highest birth rates and large families remain the rule rather than the exception out in the countryside.

Chinese

The Han Chinese make up 92% of the Chinese population, but hav
migrated south to the Mekong lands in search of a better life. The Han
majority in Yúnnán, although this remains the most ethnically diverse p
in China with more than 20 minorities. Coined by some the Jews of Asia
Chinese penetrated the region as merchants, establishing their own neig
hoods and perpetuating their language and customs. Their presenc
the centuries was perhaps more instrumental than the colonial experi
developing the local economies and opening up new opportunities.

Many of the great cities of the Mekong region have significant C
communities and in the case of capitals like Bangkok and Phnom
people of at least some Chinese ancestry may make up half the popu
The Chinese are much more integrated in the Mekong region than in
like Indonesia, and continue to contribute to the economic boom t
investment and initiative. With one eye on history, the Vietnamese ar
suspicious of the Chinese than most.

There could be as many
as 100 million Chinese
in the Mekong region,
concentrated in Yúnnán,
Cambodia, Laos, Thailand
and Vietnam.

Kinh (Vietnamese)

Despite the Chinese view that the Vietnamese are 'the ones that got
the Vietnamese existed in the Red River Delta area long before the firs
of Chinese arrived some 2000 years ago. The Kinh make up about
the population of Vietnam, the rest including hill tribes (or *montagn*
they were known by the French), Cham, Chinese and Khmer. Centur
the Vietnamese began to push southwards in search of cultivable la
swallowed the kingdom of Champa before pushing on into the Mekon
and picking off pieces of a decaying Khmer empire. As well as occupy
coastal regions of Vietnam, the lowland Kinh have begun to move ii
mountains to take advantage of new opportunities in agriculture, ir
and tourism. Like the Chinese, the Vietnamese are incredibly indu
and think nothing of working from dawn until dusk.

There are also significant Vietnamese populations in both Cambo
Laos, although they are not generally as well integrated (read popular
Chinese. There are also sizable Vietnamese communities in countr
Australia and the US, a legacy of the long war.

Most of the Vietnamese population follows the Tam Giao (Trip
gion; p80), a fusion of Buddhism, Confucianism and Taoism. There
a significant proportion of Catholics, the largest in Southeast Asia (
the Philippines.

The Mekong region
is home to around 80
million Kinh, most living
in Vietnam, Cambodia
and Laos.

Khmer (Cambodian)

The Khmer have inhabited Cambodia since the beginning of recorded
around the 2nd century AD, long before the Thais and Vietnamese a
on the scene. During the subsequent centuries, the culture of Cambo
influenced by contact with the civilisations of India and Java. Dur
glory years of Angkor, Hinduism was the predominant religion, but fr
15th century Theravada Buddhism was adopted and most Khmers
devoutly Buddhist today, their faith an important anchor in the stru
rebuild their lives. The Cambodian population went to hell and back
the years of Khmer Rouge rule and it is believed that as much as on
of the population perished as a direct result of their brutal policie
continues to impact on the Khmer psyche today and there has beer
breakdown in trust within society.

Today, government figures suggest that 96% of the population of C
dia is Khmer, but in reality there are probably far larger numbers of C
and Vietnamese than this figure would suggest.

Around 15 million
Khmers live in Cambodia,
Thailand and Vietnam.

There are significant populations of Khmer in both northeast Thailand and the Mekong Delta region of Vietnam. The Mekong Delta was only formally annexed to Vietnam during the French rule in Indochina and there are still about one million or more Khmers living there today, mainly in the districts of Soc Trang and Tra Vinh. In northeast Thailand, the Khmer population lives in provinces near the Cambodian border like Buriram, Surin and Si Saket. There are also significant populations of Khmers in Australia, France and the US, a legacy of war and revolution.

Lao

Laos is often described as less a nation state than a conglomeration of tribes and languages. And depending on who you talk with, that conglomeration consists of between 49 and 132 different ethnic groups. The lower figure is that now used by the government. The Lao traditionally divide themselves into four broad families – Lao Loum, Lao Thai, Lao Thoeng and Lao Soung – roughly defined by the altitude at which they live and their cultural proclivities. The Lao government has an alternative three-way split, in which the Lao Thai are condensed into the Lao Loum group. This triumvirate is represented on the back of every 1000 kip bill, in national costume, from left to right: Lao Soung, Lao Loum and Lao Thoeng.

The dominant ethnic group is the Lao Loum (Lowland Lao), who through superior numbers and living conditions, have for centuries ruled the smaller ethnic groups living in Laos. Their language is the national language; their religion, Buddhism, is the national religion; and many of their customs are interpreted as those of the Lao nation, including the tradition of eating sticky rice.

Although they're closely related to the Lao Loum, the Lao Thai subgroups have resisted absorption into mainstream Lao culture. Like the Lao Loum, they live along river valleys, but the Lao Thai have chosen to reside in upland valleys rather than the Mekong floodplains. The various Lao Thai groups can be identified by the predominant colour of their clothing such as Black Thai (Thai Dam) and White Thai (Thai Khao).

The Lao Thoeng (Upland Lao) are a loose affiliation of mostly Austro-Asiatic peoples who live on midaltitude mountain slopes. The largest group is the Khamu, followed by the Htin, Lamet and other Mon-Khmer groups in the south. The Lao Thoeng are also known by the pejorative term *khàa,* which means 'slave' or 'servant', as they were used as indentured labour by migrating Austro-Thai peoples in earlier centuries.

The Lao Soung (High Lao) include the hill tribes who live at the highest altitudes. They are the most recent immigrants, having come from Myanmar (Burma), Tibet and southern China within the last 150 years. The largest group is the Hmong, also called Miao or Meo, who number more than 300,000 in four main subgroups – the White Hmong, Striped Hmong, Red Hmong and Black Hmong. For years the Hmong's only cash crop was opium, which they grew and manufactured more than any other group in Laos, bringing them into conflict with the central government.

Thai

Thais make up about 75% of the population of Thailand, although this group is commonly broken down into four subgroups: Central Thais or Siamese who inhabit the Chao Praya delta, the Thai Lao of northeastern Thailand, the Thai Pak Thai of southern Thailand, and northern Thais. Each group speaks its own dialect and to a certain extent practises customs unique to its region. Politically and economically, the Central Thais are the dominant group, although they barely outnumber the Thai Lao. This helps explain

There are around 15 million Lao people living across the Mekong region, in Laos, Thailand and Cambodia.

Foreign ethnographers who have carried out field research in Laos have identified anywhere from 49 to 132 different ethnic groups.

what a masterstroke it was changing the name of the country from Siam to
Thailand in 1939. At a stroke, Siamese exclusivity was abolished and everyone
was welcome to be a part of the new Thai family.

As well as the Thais of Thailand, there are Thai tribal peoples throughout the Mekong region. Fanning out from their original homeland in the
Xīshuāngbǎnnà region of Yúnnán, they are now found in north Vietnam
and northern Laos. These groups are usually classified according to their
clothing, such as Black Thai and White Thai.

There are many other minorities living within the borders of Thailand.
According to official estimates, as much as 11% of Thailand's population
may be Chinese, although unofficially it could be even higher still. There
are large numbers of ethnic Khmers in the northeast, not to mention the
fact that Thais are outnumbered by the Lao in this part of the country. In
the far south, there is a significant Malay population of 3.5%. In the far
north, there are a number of hill tribes including the Akha, the Hmong
(below) and the Karen (opposite), as well as Shan refugees from the trou-
bles in Myanmar.

The Mekong region
is home to around 35
million Thais, concen-
trated in Thailand, Laos,
Vietnam and Yúnnán.

Minority Groups

There are many other important minority groups in the region, some rendered stateless by the conflicts of the past, others recent migrants to the
region, including the many hill tribes.

CHAM

The Cham people originally occupied the kingdom of Champa in south-
central Vietnam and their beautiful brick towers dot the landscape from
Danang to Phan Rang. Victims of a historical squeeze between Cambodia
and Vietnam, their territory was eventually annexed by the expansionist
Vietnamese. Originally Hindu, they converted to Islam in the 16th and
17th centuries and many migrated south to Cambodia. Today there are
small numbers of Cham in Vietnam and as many as half a million in Cambodia, all of whom continue to practise a flexible form of Islam. Over the
centuries, there has been considerable intermarriage between Cham and
Malay traders.

HMONG

The Hmong are one of the largest hill tribes in the Mekong region, spread
through much of northern Laos, northern Vietnam, Thailand and Yúnnán.
As some of the last to arrive in the region in the 19th century, Darwinian
selection ensured that they were left with the highest and harshest lands
from which to eke out their existence. They soon made the best of a bad
deal and opted for opium cultivation, which brought them into conflict with
mainstream governments during the 20th century. The CIA worked closely
with the Hmong of Laos during the secret war in the 1960s and 1970s. The
US-backed operation was kept secret from the American public until 1970.
The Hmong were vehemently anticommunist and pockets of resistance
continue today. The Hmong remain marginalised and distrusted by central
government and remain mired in poverty.

To learn more about the
hill tribes of northern
Thailand and how to
conduct yourself in local
villages, take a look at
www.hilltribe.org.

Hmong groups are usually classified by their colourful clothing, including Black Hmong, White Hmong, Red Hmong and so on. The brightest
group is the Flower Hmong of northwest Vietnam, living in villages around
Bac Ha (p378). The Hmong are known for their embroidered indigo-dyed
clothing and their ornate silver jewellery. There may be as many as one
million Hmong in the Mekong region, half of them living in the mountains
of Vietnam.

JARAI

The Jarai are the most populous minority in the Central Highlands of Vietnam, northeast Cambodia and southern Laos. Villages are often named for a nearby river, stream or tribal chief, and a *nha-rong* (communal house) is usually found in the centre. Jarai women typically propose marriage to the men through a matchmaker, who delivers the prospective groom a copper bracelet. Animistic beliefs and rituals still abound, and the Jarai pay respect to their ancestors and nature through a host or *yang* (genie). The Jarai construct elaborate cemeteries for their dead, which include carved effigies of the deceased. These totems can be found in the forests around villages, but sadly many are being snapped up by culturally insensitive collectors.

DZAO

The Dzao (also known as Yao or Dao) are one of the largest and most colourful ethnic groups in Vietnam and are also found in Laos, Thailand and Yúnnán. The Dzao practise ancestor worship of spirits, or *Ban Ho* (no relation to Uncle Ho), and hold elaborate rituals with sacrifices of pigs and chickens. The Dzao are famous for their elaborate dress. Women's clothing typically features intricate weaving and silver-coloured beads and coins – the wealth of a woman is said to be in the weight of the coins she carries. Their long flowing hair, shaved above the forehead, is tied up into a large red or embroidered turban.

KAREN

The Karen are the largest hill tribe in Thailand, numbering more than 300,000. There are four distinct groups, the Skaw Karen (White Karen), Pwo Karen, Pa-O Karen (Black Karen) and Kayah Karen (Red Karen). Unmarried women wear white and kinship remains matrilineal. Most Karen live in lowland valleys and practise crop rotation.

LIFESTYLE

A typical day in the Mekong region starts early. Country folk tend to rise before the sun, woken from their slumber by the cry of cockerels and keen to get the most out of the day before the sun hots up. This habit has spilt over into the towns and cities and many urban dwellers rise at the crack of dawn for a quick jog, a game of badminton or some tai chi moves. Breakfast comes in many flavours, but Chinese *congee* (rice soup) is universally popular throughout the region, as is noodle soup in various flavours. Food is almost as important as family in this part of the world and that is saying something. The family will try to gather for lunch and dinner, but it's not always possible in the dynamic cities, particularly when it can take an hour or more to get from place to place. Long

---

FACE IT

Face, or more importantly the art of not making the locals lose face, is an important concept to come to grips with in Asia. Face is all in Asia, and in the Mekong region it is above all. Having 'big face' is synonymous with prestige, and prestige is particularly important in the Mekong region. All families, even poor ones, are expected to have big wedding parties and throw their money around like it is water in order to gain face. This is often ruinously expensive but far less important than 'losing face'. And it is for this reason that foreigners should never lose their tempers with the locals; this will bring unacceptable 'loss of face' to the individual involved and end any chance of a sensible solution to the dispute. Take a deep breath and keep your cool. If things aren't always going according to plan, remember that in countries like Cambodia and Laos, tourism is a relatively new industry.

TOP 10 TIPS TO EARN THE RESPECT OF THE LOCALS

Take your time to learn a little about the local culture in the Mekong region. Not only will this ensure you don't inadvertently cause offence or, worse, spark an international incident, but it will also ingratiate you to your hosts. Here are a few tips to help you go native. For more country-specific tips, see the individual chapters.

■ Respect local dress standards, particularly at religious sites. Covering the upper arms and upper legs is appropriate, although some monks will be too polite to enforce this. Always remove your shoes before entering a temple, as well as any hat or head covering. Nude sunbathing is considered *totally* inappropriate, even on beaches.

■ Since most temples are maintained from the donations received, please remember to make a contribution when visiting a temple.

■ Learn about the local greeting in each country and use it when introducing yourself to new friends. However, be aware that among men the Western custom of shaking hands has almost completely taken over. When beckoning someone over, always wave with the palm down towards yourself, as fingers raised can be suggestive.

■ Monks are not supposed to touch or be touched by women. If a woman wants to hand something to a monk, the object should be placed within reach of the monk or on the monk's 'receiving cloth'.

■ No matter how high your blood pressure rises, do not raise your voice or show signs of aggression. This will lead to a loss of face (see the boxed text, p73) and cause embarrassment to the locals, ensuring the problem gets worse rather than better.

■ Exchanging business cards is an important part of even the smallest transaction or business contact in the Mekong region. Get some printed before you arrive and hand them out like confetti. Always present them with two hands.

■ Leaving a pair of chopsticks sitting vertically in a rice bowl looks very much like the incense sticks that are burned for the dead. This is a powerful sign and is not appreciated anywhere in Asia.

■ The people of the Mekong region like to keep a clean house and it's customary to remove shoes when entering somebody's home. It's rude to point the bottom of your feet towards other people. Never, ever point your feet towards anything sacred, such as a Buddha image. See how the locals sit and fold your legs to the side with the feet pointing backwards.

■ As a form of respect to elderly or other esteemed people, such as monks, take off your hat and bow your head politely when addressing them. In Asia, the head is the symbolic highest point – never pat or touch an adult on the head.

■ Whilst digging out those stubborn morsels from between your teeth, it is polite to use one hand to perform the extraction and the other hand to cover your mouth so others can't see you do it.

lunch breaks are common (and common sense, as it avoids the hottest part of the day). The working day winds down for some around 5pm, although in the 24-hour world of the cities, some are just getting started at this time. The family will try to come together for dinner and trade tales about their day.

Traditionally, life in the Mekong region has revolved around family, fields and faith, the rhythm of rural existence continuing for centuries at the same pace. For the majority of the population still living in the countryside, these constants have remained unchanged, with several generations sharing the same roof, the same rice and the same religion. But in recent decades these rhythms have been jarred by war and ideology, as the peasants were dragged from all they held dear to fight in civil wars, or were herded into cooperatives as communism tried to assert itself as the moral and social beacon in the ives of the people. Thailand may have had it easier without the great wars and ideological conflicts that ravaged its neighbours, but many rural families have still found it a struggle to adjust to the pace of modern life.

Traditionally rural agrarian societies, the race is on for the move to the cities. Thailand experienced the growing pains first, and now Cambodia, Laos and Vietnam are witnessing a tremendous shift in the balance of population, as increasing numbers of young people desert the fields in search of those mythical streets paved with gold. Until recently, China kept a lid on urban migration by restricting residential permits, but it too has yielded to the inevitable human wave of people seeking a better life. This urban population explosion has the potential to be a social time-bomb if the governments of the region fail to provide opportunities for these new migrants.

Like China and Thailand before them, Cambodia, Laos and Vietnam are experiencing their very own '60s swing, as the younger generation stand up for a different lifestyle to that of their parents. This is creating plenty of feisty friction in the cities, as sons and daughters dress as they like, date who they want and hit the town until all hours. But few live on their own and they still come home to mum and dad at the end of the day, where arguments might arise, particularly when it comes to marriage and settling down.

It is not only the young and old who are living a life apart, but also the urban and rural populations, and the rich and poor. Communism is all but dead in China, Laos and Vietnam; long live the one-party capitalist dictatorship, where survival of the fittest is the name of the game. Some have survived the transition better than others, and this has created strains in the shape of rural revolts and political backlash. One of the great ironies of the revolutions in Asia is they have striven to impose a communist system on a people seemingly born with a commercial gene, a competitive instinct to do business and to do it at any hour of the day or night. To the Chinese and Vietnamese, business, work, commerce – call it what you like – is life.

Extended family is important throughout the Mekong region and that includes second or third cousins, the sort of family that many Westerners may not even realise they have. The extended family comes together during times of trouble and times of joy, celebrating festivals and successes and mourning deaths or disappointments. This is a source of strength for many of the older generation, while for the younger generation it's likely to be friends, girlfriends, boyfriends or gangs who play the role of anchor.

With so many family members under one roof, locals in the Mekong region don't share Western concepts of privacy and personal space. Don't be surprised if people walk into your hotel room without knocking. You may be sitting starkers in your hotel room when the maid unlocks the door and walks in unannounced.

The position of women in the Mekong region is a mixed one, with some countries more enlightened than others. As in many parts of Asia, women in the Mekong region take a lot of pain for little gain, with plenty of hard work to do and little authority at the decision-making level. Thailand is the most progressive society in the region, with women well represented across the spectrum. The communist countries profess an interest in equality, but gender equality hasn't really taken off yet when you do the maths. Generally speaking, the lot of women is fast improving in dynamic urban centres, but remains very difficult in rural areas. Women do get to control the purse strings throughout the region, but that depends on how much of the income the husband 'declares' in the first place. Many men in the Mekong region have 'junior' wives or visit prostitutes and spend much of their time squirrelling away money on extracurricular activities. The sex industry of Thailand needs no introduction, but prostitution is big business in all the

Shadows and Wind by journalist Robert Templer (1999) is a snappily written exploration of contemporary Vietnam, from Ho Chi Minh personality cults to Vietnam's rock-and-roll youth.

IT'S ALL IN THE FENG SHUI

One tradition that remains central to the Chinese and Vietnamese is geomancy, or feng shui as most of us know it today. This is the art (or science) of living in tune with the environment. The orientation of houses, tombs and pagodas is determined by geomancers. The location of an ancestor's grave is an especially serious matter: if the grave is in the wrong spot or facing the wrong way, there's no telling what trouble the spirits might cause. The same goes for the location of the family altar, which can be found in nearly every Chinese or Vietnamese home. Westerners planning to go into business with a local partner will need to budget for a geomancer to ensure the venture is successful.

---

countries of the region. Contrary to the international image, most of the demand is domestic, but it remains a dangerous line of work thanks to the lurking threat of HIV infection.

Most women in the Mekong region consider pale skin to be beautiful. On sunny days, young women can often be seen strolling under the shade of an umbrella in order to keep from tanning. Women who work in the fields will go to great lengths to preserve their pale skin by wrapping their faces in towels and wearing long-sleeved shirts, elbow-length silk gloves and conical hats. To tell an Asian woman that she has white skin is a great compliment; telling her that she has a 'lovely suntan' is a bit of an insult.

SPORT

Football (soccer) is the number one spectator sport in the Mekong region and most people are mad for it. During the World Cup, the European Champions League or other major clashes, people stay up all night to watch live games in different time zones around the world. Sadly, the national teams have not kept pace with this obsession. China is the strongest team in the Mekong region and qualified for the World Cup in 2002. Thailand and Vietnam are two of the stronger teams in Southeast Asia, while Cambodia and Laos remain mere minnows of world football.

Kick boxing has been nationalised as *muay thai* in Bangkok, but in fact it has a history throughout the region and can even be seen on the bas-reliefs of the Bayon (p209) in Cambodia. It is a massively popular spectator sport in Thailand, Cambodia and Laos, and many a bet has been won and lost on the outcome of a match. For the uninitiated, it's pretty violent, with feet entering the fray as well as arms, and legal moves include a knee to the face. Ouch!

Badminton is very popular in all the Mekong countries and locals turn streets and parks throughout the region into public courts to hone their skills. Often they are jostling for space with the legion of tai chi practitioners who are up at the crack of dawn to master their moves.

Tennis has considerable snob appeal these days and rich Asians like to both watch and play. Similarly, golf has taken off as a way to earn brownie points with international investors or local movers and shakers. Golf courses have been developed all over the region, although membership fees ensure it remains a game for the elite.

A legacy of the colonial period, the French game of *pétanque*, or *boules*, is pretty popular in Cambodia, Laos and Vietnam, and it is possible to see games in small towns throughout old Indochina.

RELIGION

The dominant religions of Southeast Asia have absorbed many traditional animistic beliefs of spirits, ancestor worship and the power of the celestial planets in bringing about good fortune. Southeast Asia's spiritual connection

Check out www .muaythai.com for arguably the most comprehensive website on traditional Thai kick boxing, also popular in Cambodia and Laos.

to the realm of magic and miracles commands more respect, even among intellectual circles, than the remnants of paganism in Western Christianity. Locals erect spirit houses in front of their homes, while ethnic Chinese set out daily offerings to their ancestors, and almost everyone visits the fortune teller.

Although the majority of the population has only a vague notion of Buddhist doctrines, they invite monks to participate in life-cycle ceremonies, such as funerals and weddings. Buddhist pagodas are seen by many as a physical and spiritual refuge from an uncertain world.

To find out about the Lao ritual known as the *bąasïi* ceremony, see p298.

Ancestor Worship

Ancestor worship dates from long before the arrival of Confucianism or Buddhism. Ancestor worship is based on the belief that the soul lives on after death and becomes the protector of its descendants. Because of the influence the spirits of one's ancestors exert on the living, it is considered not only shameful for them to be upset or restless, but downright dangerous.

Many of the people in the Mekong region worship and honour the spirits of their ancestors on a regular basis, especially on the anniversary of their death. To request help for success in business or on behalf of a sick child, sacrifices and prayers are offered to the ancestral spirits. Important worship elements are the family altar and a plot of land whose income is set aside for the support of the ancestors.

Animism

Both Hinduism and Buddhism fused with the animist beliefs already present in the Mekong region before Indianisation. Local beliefs didn't simply fade away, but were incorporated into the new religions. Just look at the number of spirit houses throughout the region and you'll soon realise the continuing importance of animism in everyday life.

The purest form of animism is practised among the ethnic minorities or hill tribes of the region. Some have converted to Buddhism or Christianity,

---

THE LUNAR CALENDAR

Astrology has a long history in China and Vietnam, and is intricately linked to religious beliefs. There are 12 zodiacal animals, each of which represents one year in a 12-year cycle. If you want to know your sign, look up your year of birth in the following chart. Don't forget that the Chinese/Vietnamese New Year falls in late January or early February. If your birthday is in the first half of January it will be included in the zodiac year before the calendar year of your birth. To check the Gregorian (solar) date corresponding to a lunar date, pick up any Vietnamese or Chinese calendar.

Rat (generous, social, insecure, idle) 1924, 1936, 1948, 1960, 1972, 1984, 1996, 2008

Cow (stubborn, conservative, patient) 1925, 1937, 1949, 1961, 1973, 1985, 1997, 2009

Tiger (creative, brave, overbearing) 1926, 1938, 1950, 1962, 1974, 1986, 1998, 2010

Rabbit (timid, affectionate, amicable) 1927, 1939, 1951, 1963, 1975, 1987, 1999, 2011

Dragon (egotistical, strong, intelligent); 1928, 1940, 1952, 1964, 1976, 1988, 2000, 2012

Snake (luxury seeking, secretive, friendly) 1929, 1941, 1953, 1965, 1977, 1989, 2001

Horse (emotional, clever, quick thinker) 1930, 1942, 1954, 1966, 1978, 1990, 2002

Goat (charming, good with money, indecisive) 1931, 1943, 1955, 1967, 1979, 1991, 2003

Monkey (confident, humorous, fickle) 1932, 1944, 1956, 1968, 1980, 1992, 2004

Rooster (diligent, imaginative, needs attention) 1933, 1945, 1957, 1969, 1981, 1993, 2005

Dog (humble, responsible, patient) 1934, 1946, 1958, 1970, 1982, 1994, 2006

Pig (materialistic, loyal, honest) 1935, 1947, 1959, 1971, 1983, 1995, 2007

but the majority continue to worship spirits of the earth and skies, and the spirits of their forefathers.

Buddhism

The sedate smile of the Buddhist statues decorating the landscapes and temples summarise the nature of the religion in Southeast Asia. Religious devotion within the Buddhist countries is highly individualistic, omnipresent and nonaggressive, with many daily rituals rooted in the indigenous religions of animism and ancestor worship.

Buddhism, like all great religions, has been through a messy divorce, and arrived in the Mekong region in two flavours. Mahayana Buddhism (northern school) proceeded north into Nepal, Tibet, China, Korea, Mongolia, Vietnam and Japan, while Theravada Buddhism (southern school) took the southern route through India, Sri Lanka, Myanmar and Cambodia.

The Theravada school of Buddhism is an earlier and, according to its followers, less corrupted form of Buddhism than the Mahayana school found around East Asia and the Himalaya regions. As Theravada followers tried to preserve and limit the Buddhist doctrines to only those canons codified in the early Buddhist era, the Mahayana school gave Theravada Buddhism the pejorative name 'Hinayana' (meaning 'Lesser Vehicle'). They considered themselves 'Greater Vehicle' because they built upon the earlier teachings.

Theravada doctrine stresses the three principal aspects of existence: *dukkha* (suffering, unsatisfactoriness, disease), *anicca* (impermanency, transience of all things) and *anatta* (no permanent 'soul'). These concepts, when 'discovered' by Siddhartha Gautama in the 6th century BC, were in direct contrast to the Hindu belief in an eternal, blissful self.

Gautama, an Indian prince turned ascetic, subjected himself to many years of severe austerities to arrive at this vision of the world and was given the title Buddha (the Enlightened or the Awakened). Gautama Buddha spoke of four noble truths, which had the power to liberate any human being who could realise them:

The truth of suffering Existence is suffering.
The truth of the cause of suffering Suffering is caused by desire.
The truth of the cessation of suffering Eliminate the cause of suffering (desire) and suffering will cease to arise.
The truth of the path The eightfold path is the way to eliminate desire/extinguish suffering.

The eightfold path consists of right understanding, right thought, right speech, right bodily conduct, right livelihood, right effort, right attentiveness and right concentration.

The ultimate goal of Theravada Buddhism is nirvana or 'extinction' of all desire and suffering to reach the final stage of reincarnation. By feeding monks, giving donations to temples and performing regular worship at the local wat, Buddhists hope to improve their lot, acquiring enough merit to reduce the number of rebirths.

Every Buddhist male is expected to become a monk for a short period in his life, optimally between the time he finishes school and starts a career or marries. Men or boys under 20 years of age may enter the Sangha (the monkhood or the monastic community) as novices. Nowadays, men may spend less than one month to accrue merit as monks.

Christianity

Catholicism was introduced to the region in the 16th century by missionaries. Vietnam has the highest percentage of Catholics (8% to 10% of the population) in Southeast Asia outside the Philippines.

Mahayana Buddhists believe in Bodhisattvas, which are Buddhas that attain nirvana but postpone their enlightenment to stay on earth to save their fellow beings.

Confucianism

More a philosophy than an organised religion, Confucianism has been an important force in shaping the social system in China and Vietnam, and the lives and beliefs of the people.

Confucius was born in China around 550 BC. He saw people as social beings formed by society yet also capable of shaping their society. He believed that the individual exists in and for society and drew up a code of ethics to guide the individual in social interactions. This code laid down a person's obligations to family, society and the state, and remains the pillar of society in China and Vietnam today.

The extensive Chinese community in the region keeps the spirit of Confucius alive in other regional capitals including Bangkok and Phnom Penh.

Hinduism

Hinduism ruled the spiritual lives of Southeast Asians more than 1500 years ago, and the great Hindu empire of Angkor built grand monuments to their pantheon of gods. The primary representations of the one omnipresent god include Brahma (the creator), Vishnu (the preserver) and Shiva (the destroyer and reproducer). During the time of Angkor, Shiva was the deity most in favour with the royal family, although in the 12th century he was superseded by Vishnu.

The forgotten kingdom of Champa was profoundly influenced by Hinduism and many of the Cham towers, built as Hindu sanctuaries, contain *lingas* that are still worshipped by ethnic Vietnamese and ethnic Chinese alike.

Today some elements of Hinduism are still incorporated into important ceremonies involving birth, marriage and death.

Islam

Southeast Asians converted to Islam to join a brotherhood of spice traders and to escape the inflexible caste system of earlier Hindu empires. The Chams may be Muslims, but in practice they follow a localised adaptation of Islamic theology and law. Though Muslims usually pray five times a day, the Chams pray only on Fridays and celebrate Ramadan (a month of dawn-to-dusk fasting) for only three days. In addition, their Islam-based religious rituals co-exist with animism and the worship of Hindu deities. Circumcision is symbolically performed on boys at age 15, when a religious leader makes the gestures of circumcision with a wooden knife.

Taoism

Taoism originated in China and is based on the philosophy of Laotse (The Old One), who lived in the 6th century BC. Little is known about Laotse and there is some debate as to whether or not he actually existed. He is believed

---

THE RAMAYANA

The literary epic of the *Ramayana* serves as the cultural fodder for traditional art, dance and shadow puppetry throughout the region. In this epic Hindu legend, Prince Rama (an incarnation of the Hindu god Vishnu) falls in love with beautiful Sita and wins her hand in marriage by successfully stringing a magic bow. Before the couple settle down to marital bliss, Rama is banished from his kingdom and his wife is kidnapped by the demon king, Ravana, and taken to the island of Lanka. With the help of the Monkey King, Hanuman, Sita is rescued, but a great battle ensues. Rama and his allies defeat Ravana and restore peace and goodness to the land. The *Ramayana* is known as the *Reamker* in Cambodia or the *Ramakien* in Laos and Thailand.

CAO DAISM

A fascinating fusion of East and West, Cao Daism (Dai Dao Tam Ky Pho Do) is a syncretic religion born in 20th-century Vietnam that contains elements of Buddhism, Confucianism, Taoism, native Vietnamese spiritualism, Christianity and Islam – as well as a dash of secular enlightenment thrown in for good measure. The term Cao Dai (meaning high tower or palace) is a euphemism for God. There are an estimated two to three million followers of Cao Daism worldwide.

Cao Daism was founded by the mystic Ngo Minh Chieu (also known as Ngo Van Chieu; born 1878), who began receiving revelations in which the tenets of Cao Dai were set forth.

All Cao Dai temples observe four daily ceremonies: at 6am, noon, 6pm and midnight. If all this sounds like just what you've been waiting for, you can always join up. Read more on the official Cao Dai site: www.caodai.org. If you just want to visit a Cao Dai temple, head to Tay Ninh (p418), near Ho Chi Minh City.

to have been the custodian of the imperial archives for the Chinese government, and Confucius is supposed to have consulted him.

Understanding Taoism is not easy. The philosophy emphasises contemplation and simplicity. Its ideal is returning to the Tao (the Way, or the essence of which all things are made), and it emphasises the importance of Yin and Yang. Much of Taoist ritualism has been absorbed into Chinese and Vietnamese Buddhism, including, most commonly, the use of dragons and demons to decorate temple rooftops.

Tam Giao

Over the centuries, Confucianism, Taoism and Buddhism have fused with popular Chinese beliefs and ancient Vietnamese animism to create Tam Giao (Triple Religion). When discussing religion, most Vietnamese people are likely to say that they are Buddhist, but when it comes to family or civic duties they are likely to follow the moral and social code of Confucianism, but will turn to Taoist concepts to understand the nature of the cosmos.

ARTS

The Mekong region's most notable artistic endeavours are religious in nature and depict the deities of Hinduism and Buddhism. Artistic and architectural wonders, the temples of Angkor in Cambodia defined much of the region's artistic interpretation of Hinduism and Buddhism. The temples' elaborate sculptured murals pay homage to the Hindu gods Vishnu and Shiva, while also recording historical events and creation myths. Statues of Buddha reflect the individual countries' artistic interpretations of an art form governed by highly symbolic strictures. The Buddha is depicted sitting, standing and reclining – all representations of moments in his life. In Vietnam, representations of the Buddha are more reminiscent of Chinese religious art.

Sadly, many of the region's ancient art treasures have been damaged in times of civil war, destroyed during violent revolution or dispersed by invasion. The riches that remain are a testament to the devotion, creativity and wealth of the ancient Mekong kingdoms.

Architecture

There is some masterful architecture in the Mekong region, blending the best of India and China. No civilisation was more expressive than the ancient Khmers and the architecture of Cambodia reached its peak during the Angkorian era (the 9th to 14th centuries AD). Some of the finest examples of architecture from this period are Angkor Wat (p208) and the structures of Angkor Thom (p208).

The Laos Cultural Profile (www.culturalprofiles .net/Laos) is a new website established by Visiting Arts and the Ministry of Information and Culture of Laos covering a broad range of cultural aspects, from architecture to music. It's an easy entry point to Lao culture.

Temple architecture remains an art form in the Mekong region and each country has its own distinctive style. Wats or Buddhist temples contain a *sim*, where monastic ordinations are held, and a *vihara*, where important Buddha images are stored. Temples in Cambodia, Laos and Thailand have elaborate layered roofs, including the elegant Luang Prabang style, which sweeps almost to the ground beneath. Many temple complexes also include stupas or *chedi*, some of which are said to contain relics (eyelash, hair or something similar) of the Buddha.

China's architectural history stretches back 3000 years, making it one of the longest of any civilisation. It may be the Great Wall that pulls the punters, but Yúnnán is not short of architectural highlights, including the traditional Naxi architecture of Lìjiāng. Buddhist, Taoist and Confucian temples are built on a north–south axis and can be distinguished by their levels of decoration. Taoist temples are usually the brightest, Buddhist temples are a little more understated and Confucian temples are rather plain by comparison.

Many rural houses in Cambodia and Laos are built on high wood pilings and have thatch roofs, walls made of palm mats and floors of woven bamboo strips resting on bamboo joists. The shady space underneath is used for storage and for people to relax at midday. Wealthier families have houses with wooden walls and tiled roofs, but the basic design remains the same. Concrete has already taken over in much of Thailand and is steadily conquering China and Vietnam. However, Thailand has also found a niche developing boutique residences blending the best of traditional and modern lines.

The French left their mark in Indochina in the form of handsome villas and government buildings built in neoclassical style – pillars and all. Some of the best examples are in Hanoi, but most provincial capitals have at least one or two examples of architecture from the colonial period.

Painting

China and Vietnam lead the way in the region in the world of painting. Painting on frame-mounted silk dates from the 13th century and was at one time the preserve of scholar-calligraphers, who painted grand scenes from nature. During the austere communist era, painting became overtly political and most artists dedicated their skills to producing propaganda posters, which have become quite collectable in recent years. Religious murals are an important feature of temples throughout Cambodia, Laos and Thailand, although the modern renditions are fairly garish by comparison with the beautiful 19th-century panels. There is a booming contemporary art scene in China, Thailand and Vietnam, but beware of spending big bucks unless you know what you are doing, as there are a lot of fakes about.

Sculpture

The people of Cambodia produced masterfully sensuous sculpture that was more than a mere copy of the Indian forms from which it drew inspiration. Some scholars maintain that the Cambodian forms are unrivalled in India itself. The earliest surviving Cambodian sculpture dates from the 6th century. The Banteay Srei–style of the late 10th century is commonly regarded as a high point in the evolution of Southeast Asian art. The National Museum (p192) in Phnom Penh has a splendid piece from this period: a sandstone statue of Shiva holding Uma, his wife, on his knee. Anyone passing through Paris should also check out the Musée Guimet, home to the finest Khmer collection beyond Cambodian shores.

The Chams produced spectacular carved sandstone figures for their Hindu and Buddhist sanctuaries. Cham sculpture was profoundly influenced by Indian art, but over the centuries it managed to also incorporate

For a virtual tour of Thai Buddhist architecture around the region, visit www.orientalarchitecture.com/directory.htm.

Vietnamese Painting – From Tradition to Modernity, by Corinne de Ménonville, is a lush look at Vietnamese contemporary painting. For the contribution of women to the art scene, check out *Vietnamese Women Artists* (2004).

For an in-depth look at the beauty of Angkorian-era sculpture and its religious, cultural and social context, seek out a copy of *Sculpture of Angkor and Ancient Cambodia: Millennium of Glory*.

Indonesian and Vietnamese elements. The largest single collection of Cham sculpture in the world is found at the Museum of Cham Sculpture (p385) in Danang.

Thailand's most famous sculptures are its beautiful bronze Buddhas, coveted the world over for their originality and grace. However, the only place you will see them these days is in a temple or a museum. Lao sculpture reached its zenith between the 16th and 18th centuries, the heyday of the kingdom of Lan Xang. The finest examples of Lao sculpture are found in Vientiane's Haw Pha Kaew (p270) and Wat Si Saket (p270) or the Royal Palace Museum (p293) in Luang Prabang.

Chinese sculpture needs no introduction thanks to the Terracotta Warriors of Xian. There is some beautiful Buddhist sculpture in China and this includes some of the temples of Yúnnán. There is also a rich tradition of bronze and jade sculpture.

Textiles

There is a rich tradition of silk weaving in the Mekong region and a beautiful scarf or throw is that much easier to cart home than a large sculpture. Cambodia, Laos and Thailand produce some exceptional hand-woven silk, including both traditional and contemporary designs finished in natural dyes. Check out Carol Cassidy Lao Textiles (p276) in Vientiane, Artisans d'Angkor (p202) in Siem Reap or Jim Thompson House (p122) in Bangkok.

Music

TRADITIONAL

Chinese music has a different scale to Western music. Tone is considered more important than melody. The Chinese once considered music to have a cosmological significance and if a musician played in the wrong tone it could indicate the fall of a dynasty. Popular Chinese instruments include the two-stringed fiddle (*èrhú*), four-stringed banjo (*yuè qín*), horizontal flute (*dízi*), zither (*gǔzhēng*) and ceremonial trumpet (*suǒnà*).

Heavily influenced by the Chinese to the north and Indian-influenced Khmer and Cham musical traditions to the south, Vietnamese music has produced an original style and instrumentation. Traditional music is played on a wide array of indigenous instruments dating back to the ancient *do son* drums. The best-known traditional instrument in use is the *dan bau*, a single-stringed lute that generates an astounding array of tones.

Some of the bas-reliefs at Angkor (p208) show musical instruments that are remarkably similar to those seen in Cambodia today, suggesting a long musical heritage. Most travellers will hear wedding music (*areak ka*) at some stage during their visit, as well as the percussive sounds that accompany classical dance. The *chapaye* is a popular instrument in Cambodia, a sort of two-stringed bass guitar for playing the Cambodian blues.

Cambodia's great musical tradition was almost lost during the darkness of the Khmer Rouge years, but the Cambodian Master Performers Program (www.cambodianmasters.org) is dedicated to reviving the country's musical tradition.

THE INSIDE STORY OF LACQUER

Lacquerware is a popular decorative form in Cambodia, Thailand and Vietnam, as well as Myanmar and China. Lacquer is made from resin extracted from the rhus tree. It is creamy white in raw form, but is darkened with pigments in an iron container for 40 hours. After the object has been treated with glue, the requisite 10 coats of lacquer are applied. Each coat must be dried for a week and then thoroughly sanded with pumice and cuttlebone before the next layer can be applied. A specially refined lacquer is used for the 11th and final coat, which is sanded with a fine coal powder and lime wash before the object is decorated. Designs include engraving in low relief, or inlaying mother-of-pearl, egg shell or precious metals.

Thai music features a dazzling array of textures and subtleties, as a classical orchestra *(pii-phâat)* can feature as many as 20 players. Drums and gongs lend classical Thai music a certain hypnotic quality, as it was originally devised to accompany classical dance. The *pìi* is a common woodwind instrument that features prominently at Thai boxing matches.

Lao classical music was originally developed as court music for royal ceremonies and classical dance-drama during the 19th-century reign of Vientiane's Chao Anou, who had been educated in the Siamese court in Bangkok.

Most ethno-linguistic minorities of the Mekong region have their own musical traditions that often include distinctive costumes and instruments, such as reed flutes, lithophones (similar to xylophones), bamboo whistles, gongs and stringed instruments made from gourds.

The informative *Traditional Music of the Lao*, by Terry Miller (1985), although mainly focused on northeast Thailand, is the only book-length work yet to appear on Lao music.

CONTEMPORARY/POP

China and Thailand lead the way in contemporary music and have exported their stars around the region. However, all the countries of the Mekong region have a lively scene. Thailand has the most developed alternative music with indie rock, hip-hop and jazz.

Hong Kong paved the road for Chinese pop, which started out as starry-eyed love songs. More recently rock and punk bands have taken off, although the only place in the region big enough to have an underground scene in Yúnnán is Kūnmíng.

Cambodia had a thriving pop industry in the 1960s, but the Khmer Rouge destroyed it like the rest of Cambodia, targeting famous artists such as Sin Sisamuth. Cambodian pop music has experienced a resurgence in the past decade and free concerts are often staged in Phnom Penh. Look out for anything by Cambodian-American fusion band, Dengue Fever.

The governments of Laos and Vietnam tended to frown on pop music for a long time, but the liberalisation of recent years has spilt over into the musical arena. Phuong Thanh is the Britney Spears of Vietnam, while Lam Truong takes on the Robbie Williams role. 'Modern' music was virtually outlawed in Laos until 2003 when the government realised foreign music was flooding the country. The first 'star' was Thidavanh Bounxouay, a Lao-Bulgarian singer more popularly known as Alexandra. But it's rap group LOG which has been most successful, including a chart-topping hit over the border in Thailand in 2006.

Speaking of Thailand, *lûuk thûng* is its answer to country and western, while *maw lam* is the northeastern blues. *Phleng phêua chii-wít* (songs for life) emerged in the 1970s in a new wave of politically conscious music, led by local band Caravan. Teen pop is a big industry, nicknamed T-pop, but for something with a bit more bite, check out some *klawng sěhrii* (free drum) or *phleng tâi din* (underground music). Modern Dog was the first Brit pop–style band to make it big.

For insight into China's contemporary rock scene and information on the latest bands go to www.rockinchina.com.

Dance

Indian dance has had a big impact on the Mekong region, the origins of classical dance in Cambodia, Laos and Thailand all found in the subcontinent. In Cambodia, the royal ballet remains a tangible link with the glory of Angkor. Many dancers were killed during the terrible years of the Khmer Rouge, but classical dance has bounced back and it is easy to catch a performance in Phnom Penh (p199) or Siem Reap. Thai classical dance is cut from the same cloth and both have the same stylised hand movements, striking costume, elaborate crowns and feature tales from the *Ramayana* (p79). Masked dance, known as *lákhon*, is also popular in Cambodia and Thailand.

The Conical Hat Dance is one of the most visually stunning dances in Vietnam. A group of women wearing *ao dai* (the national dress of Vietnam) shake their stuff and spin around, whirling their classic conical hats like Fred Astaire with his cane.

Folk dances are popular throughout the region, symbolising the harvest cycle and other scenes from daily life. The ethnic minorities have their own dance traditions that have their roots in spirit worship and it is often possible to catch a performance when experiencing a homestay somewhere in the region.

Theatre & Puppetry

Classical Vietnamese theatre is very formal, employing fixed gestures and scenery similar to classic Chinese opera. There are more than 300 types of opera in China, but Běijīng opera is the medium best known to the western world. Often, the audience has a drum so it can pass judgement on the on-stage action. Red face paint represents courage, loyalty and faithfulness, while traitors and cruel people have white faces. A male character expresses emotions (pensiveness, worry, anger) by fingering his beard in different ways.

The uniquely Vietnamese art form of water puppetry *(roi nuoc)* draws its plots from the same legendary and historical sources as other forms of traditional theatre. It is believed that water puppetry developed when determined puppeteers in the Red River Delta managed to continue performances despite annual flooding. Hanoi (p363) is the best place to see water puppetry performances.

Shadow puppetry is a popular art form in Cambodia and Thailand. Traditionally the light for the performance comes from a bonfire of coconut husks and the leather puppets are set against a giant backdrop.

To learn more about the unique art of water puppetry or 'Punch and Judy in a pool', visit www .thanglongwaterpuppet.org.

Cinema

China dominates the cinema scene in the Mekong region, although Thailand is fast catching up. Cambodia's film industry is slowly getting back on its feet, while in Laos and Vietnam the situation is a little stale due to government interference.

Mainland Chinese cinema was shackled by politics and ideology for many years. After the death of Mao, things slowly warmed up and the 1990s saw a spate of successful films that made a splash in the West, such as *Raise the Red Lantern* (1991) and *To Live* (1994), both starring Gong Li. Hong Kong created its own genre of kung-fu-fighting cop films and several directors have gone on to international fame, including Ang Lee and John Woo. Ang Lee's *Crouching Tiger, Hidden Dragon* (2000) enjoyed far more success overseas than in China.

The Thai film industry experienced a golden age in the 1960s, but by the 1980s it was almost extinct as Hollywood blockbusters flooded the market. Lately, it has experienced a resurgence and critics are talking about a 'new wave'. *Iron Ladies* (2000) tells the tale of a transvestite/transsexual volleyball team from Lampang and became the second most successful film in the history of Thai cinema. *Blissfully Yours* (2002) picked up a commendation in Cannes, completing the rehabilitation of the industry.

For a culture clash of sorts, check out *Tomb Raider*, the action movie starring Angelina Jolie as Lara Croft. The temples of Angkor are culture personified, as for the movie…well there's the clash.

Like Thailand, Cambodia had a golden age of filmmaking in the 1960s, but karaoke and VCDs nearly killed it off. Cinemas have recently reopened throughout the country and a new generation of movie makers is churning out low-budget love stories, horror films and comedies, sometimes unintentionally all in one.

One of Vietnam's earliest cinematic efforts was a newsreel of Ho Chi Minh's Proclamation of Independence in 1945. Propaganda set the tone until the 1990s when a new generation of filmmakers emerged. Tran Anh Hung is Vietnam's best known filmmaker thanks to the touching *Scent of a Green Papaya* (1992) and the gritty underworld violence of *Cyclo* (1995).

Literature

China has a rich literary tradition, but much of it is inaccessible to Western readers as it hasn't been translated into English. Poetry is particularly popular in China and its origins can be traced back as far as the time of Confucius. *The Water Margin* by Shi Nai'an is an epic tale of outlaws fighting against corruption, while *Romance of the Three Kingdoms* by Luo Guanzhong is a lively historical novel about the legendary battles during the latter half of the Han dynasty. More recently, writers have been cautiously exploring the traumatic events of the 20th century. *Wild Swans* by Jung Chang (1991) is the gripping story of three generations of Chinese women struggling to survive war and revolution. It is banned in China.

The *Ramayana* (p79) is the most pervasive and influential story in the Indianised countries of the Mekong region. The Indian epic first came to Cambodia and spread throughout the region via the stone reliefs of the great Khmer temples. Oral and written versions were also likely to have been distributed.

Of the 547 *jataka* tales in the *Pali Tipitaka* (tripartite Buddhist canon) – each chronicling a different past life of the Buddha – most appear in Laos and Thailand almost word-for-word as they were first written down in Sri Lanka. The most popular *jataka* is an old *Pali* original known as the *Mahajati* or *Mahavessandara*, the story of the Buddha's penultimate life. Interior murals in many Lao and Thai wats typically depict this *jataka* as well as others.

There are very few contemporary works from Cambodia, Laos and Vietnam, although translations of anything from Harry Potter to Graham Greene are opening up a whole new world to non-English speakers. Thailand has a lively contemporary literature scene. Piri Sudham writes in English about rural life in *Monsoon Country* and other works.

Sihanouk's CV, as well as including the jobs of king, prime minister and head of state, has also included the title of Cambodia's most prolific filmmaker. For more on the films of Sihanouk, visit the website www .norodomsihanouk.org.

The oldest-surviving printed book in the world is a Chinese Buddhist text dating from AD 868.

Food & Drink Austin Bush

It's amazing what four simple flavours can do. Simply put, sweet, sour, salty and spicy are the parameters that define the cuisines of the Mekong region. From Yúnnán to the Mekong Delta, virtually every dish is a balance of these four tastes. In Laos this might be obtained by a combination of the tartness of lime juice and the saltiness of *paa dàek*, a thick fish paste. In China salty flavours will undoubtedly come from soy sauce, and might be countered by a few dried chillies and strategic splashes of vinegar. Regardless of the methods used, the goal is the same: a favourable balance of four strong, clear flavours.

If there is any other element that is responsible for uniting the cuisines of the region, it is undoubtedly the Mekong River. The Mekong and its tributaries provide fish, by far the region's most essential protein, and water for rice, the area's most important grain. These two staples form the backbone of the region's cooking, and appear in countless forms along the course of the river.

Authored by the confessed 'pimp of Khmer cuisine', Phil Lees, www .phnomenon.com is possibly the only blog on the net to focus exclusively on food and drink in Cambodia.

Along with the Mekong River, the Chinese have probably had the most significant impact on the food of the region, and culinary legacies such as the wok, tea and noodles can be found all the way to the Mekong Delta. China's Yúnnán province, located just south of the Mekong's origin in Tibet, is as diverse in its cuisine as it is in people. And although much of the province's food exhibits strong Han and Sichuanese influences, the cuisines of the various ethnic groups such as the Dai, Bai and Hui are also prevalent. Being one of China's few tropical areas, Yúnnán is also home to a variety of fruit and produce not found elsewhere in the country.

Following the Mekong southwards, the cuisines of northeastern Thailand and Laos are among the most conservative of the region. Earthy grilled dishes, soups and salads rule here, with sticky rice being the preferred carb in both regions. In Laos, wild game and other forms of 'jungle food' make up a large part of the local diet, while Thailand's *isǎan* (northeastern) school of cooking is often associated with simple yet transcendent dishes such as *sôm tam*, a tart 'salad' made from shredded green papaya, fish sauce and lime juice.

For many, Cambodian cuisine is the regional mystery. Often accused of being 'like Thai but less spicy', Khmer cooking has a soul of its own, and makes particularly creative use of the country's freshwater fish and indigenous roots and herbs. Although Cambodian cuisine is often associated with dishes such as deep-fried spiders, much of the protein travellers will

---

TASTES THAT DEFINE A NATION

If there's one thing in each country you shouldn't miss, we suggest:

- Beerlao – the unofficial national beverage of Laos and the best brew in the region.
- *Xuanwei huotui* – this Yunnanese salt-cured ham rivals prosciutto in flavour, and is a whole lot cheaper.
- *Amoc* – a Cambodian dish of fish, coconut and fresh herbs wrapped in banana leaf and steamed or grilled; a perfect introduction to the subtleties of Khmer cooking.
- *Khâo soi* – a curry noodle dish of Shan origin that came to northern Thailand via Muslim traders from Yúnnán; a true example of Southeast Asian fusion cuisine.
- *Banh xeo* – southern Vietnamese stuffed crepes served with copious fresh herbs and a fish sauce–based dipping sauce; Vietnam on a plate.

TRAVEL YOUR TASTEBUDS

No matter what part of the world you come from, if you travel much in the Mekong region you are going to encounter food that might seem unusual. The fiercely omnivorous locals find nothing strange in eating insects, algae, offal or fish bladders. They'll feast on the flesh of dogs, they'll eat a crocodile, or they'll devour a dish of cock's testicles. They'll kill a venomous snake before your eyes, cut out its still-beating heart, feed it to you with a cup of the serpent's blood to wash it down, and say it increases your potency. They'll slay a monkey and then barbecue it at your table.

For Mekong dwellers there is nothing strange about anything that will sustain the body. They'll try anything once, even KFC.

We Dare You! The Top Five

■ crickets   ■ dog   ■ duck embryo   ■ spider   ■ king cobra

come across will be, at most, four-legged – although don't let this stop you from trying!

South Vietnam is the end of the road for the mighty Mekong, and the rich silt left by the river before it flows into the South China Sea has made this area Vietnam's rice basket. As a result, rice and fresh herbs are the hallmark of south Vietnamese cooking, not to mention the famous fish sauce made from anchovies found just offshore. The tropical climate of the Mekong Delta also makes this the only region where coconut milk plays a significant role in the local cuisine.

Add to these elements the culinary remnants of colonialism and foreign influences, such as beer and baguettes, and the Mekong area is without a doubt among the world's most diverse and delicious places to eat.

STAPLES

Like the people who populate the region, the cuisines of the Mekong area are incredibly diverse, but there are certain ingredients that can be found across all borders.

Rice

Rice is so central to Asian culture that the most common term for 'eat' in nearly every regional language translates as 'consume rice'. The grain is thought to have been cultivated here for as many as 7000 years and takes various forms depending on where one is along the Mekong. In Yúnnán, the rice of choice for most people is the long-grained variety that is prepared by being boiled directly in water. As one moves south, the inhabitants of Laos and northeastern Thailand prefer sticky rice, the short stocky grains that are steamed in bamboo baskets. And finally as one nears the Mekong Delta, the people of Vietnam and Cambodia again opt for the lighter long-grained rice that is also boiled.

Noodles

Although strands of rice- or wheat-based dough are probably Chinese in origin, there is hardly a corner of the Mekong region where you won't be able to find noodles. In China, egg noodles are combined with a spicy broth in the Sichuān-influenced soups of Yúnnán. In the rest of the Mekong region rice is the preferred grain, and takes various forms ranging from the flat, translucent noodles of Thailand and Vietnam to the round threads of fermented rice found in Laos and northeastern Thailand.

Perhaps the region's greatest noodle dish is *pho*, the Vietnamese soup usually made with beef and rice noodles (and in the south, copious fresh

Written and photo-graphed by the author of this chapter, RealThai, (http://realthai.blogspot.com/) is one of the few blogs that details food and dining in Thailand.

herbs). Lagging not far behind is *khâo soi,* a curry noodle soup found in northern Thailand that is served with egg noodles and sides of sliced lime, crispy pickled veggies and sliced shallots.

Fish

For the vast majority of the population of the Mekong region, fish represents more than just the occasional catch. Fish is the most common source of protein, and has been so for millennia. Oft-quoted inscriptions from northern Thailand that date back nearly 1000 years declare, 'There are fish in the water and rice in the fields', implying that these are really the only two elements one needed to survive.

Fish means freshwater fish from the region's lakes and rivers. These range from the giant Mekong catfish – among the world's largest freshwater fish – to tiny whitebait that are consumed head and all. One of the most significant sources of piscine protein is Cambodia's Tonlé Sap, an immense lake formed by water from the Mekong River that is considered one of the most productive inland fisheries in the world.

For the residents of southern Cambodia and Vietnam, seafood plays an important role in the local cuisine. In particular, anchovies, which are made into fish sauce (see the boxed text, below), provide a salty condiment for people of the region and, indeed, across all of Southeast Asia.

Meat & Game

In rural areas of the Mekong region, wild animals – especially deer, wild pigs, squirrels, civets, jungle fowl/pheasants, dhole (wild dogs), rats and birds – provide much of the protein in local diets. In part this practice is due to the expense involved in animal husbandry, as well as the Southeast Asian preference for the taste of wild game. During your travels, avoid eating endangered species, as this will only further endanger them.

Other fun forms of protein include the various grubs, larvae and insects that, unfortunately, you'll be hard-pressed to find on the menu of your local Thai joint at home.

Herbs

As Indian cooking is associated with the use of dried spices, Southeast Asian cooking is equally synonymous with the use of fresh herbs. These range from varieties found across the region, such as mint and Thai basil, to more obscure regional herbs such as pennywort or sawtooth coriander. In particular, southern Vietnamese cooking makes good use of fresh herbs, and a platter of several different green leafy things is a typical accompaniment to many dishes.

One of the most highly regarded herbs of the Mekong region is southern Cambodia's pepper which, when combined with the local seafood in the form of stir fries and dips, is one of the region's culinary highlights.

SOMETHING'S FISHY

Westerners might scoff at the all-too-literal name of this condiment, but for many of the cuisines in the Mekong area, fish sauce is more than just another ingredient, it is *the* ingredient.

Fish sauce, essentially the liquid obtained from fermented fish, takes various guises depending on the region. In Laos, Cambodia and northeastern Thailand, discerning diners prefer a thick, pasty mash of fermented freshwater fish and sometimes rice. Elsewhere, where people have access to the sea, fish sauce takes the form of a thin liquid extracted from salted anchovies. In both cases, the result is a highly pungent, but generally salty (rather than fishy) tasting sauce that is used in much the same way as the salt shaker in the West.

MERCI, OBRIGADO, GRACIAS, DANKE

Try to imagine Thai or Yunnanese food without the chillies, Vietnamese cooking without lettuce or peanuts, or Lao papaya salad without the papaya. Many of the ingredients used on a daily basis in the Mekong area are in fact relatively recent introductions courtesy of European traders and missionaries. During the early 16th century, while Spanish and Portuguese explorers were first reaching the shores of Southeast Asia, there was also subsequent expansion and discovery in the Americas. The Portuguese in particular were quick to seize the products coming from the New World and market them in the East, thus introducing modern-day Asian staples such as tomatoes, potatoes, corn, lettuce, cabbage, chillies, papaya, guava, pineapples, pumpkins, sweet potatoes, peanuts and tobacco.

Chillies in particular seem to have struck a chord with the natives of Southeast Asia, and are thought to have first arrived in Thailand via the Portuguese. Before their arrival, the natives of the Mekong region got their heat from bitter-hot herbs and roots such as ginger and pepper.

In more recent times, European colonialism has been responsible for several more introductions to the cuisines of the region, such as baguettes and coffee in former French Indochina, beer in Thailand and China, and in Laos, a thick, meat-based stew served at weddings and festivals known as *lagoo*; that's right, none other than the French ragout.

Fruit

Southeast Asia is a veritable greenhouse and the selection of fruits at even the most basic morning market will make the produce section of your local supermarket back home look pretty shabby. In addition to the standard fruits, many of which actually originate in South America, make an effort to try some of the several varieties native to the Mekong region such as longan, lychee, rambutan, langsat, mangosteen or the infamous durian. The last, a member of the aptly named *Bombacaceae* family, is a heavy, spiked orb that resembles an ancient piece of medieval weaponry. Inside the thick shell lie five sections of plump, buttery and pungent flesh that excite the natives and more often than not, repel the visitors.

Sweets

Although it is difficult to generalise about the vast variety of sweet foods found in the Mekong region, several elements such as coconut milk, palm sugar and sticky rice unite this genre. Many sweets also contain corn, sugar palm kernels, lotus seeds, beans and water chestnuts for added texture and crunch. Due to the region's hot weather, sweets are generally meant to be cooling and are usually taken as snacks (as opposed to postprandial desserts), and are typically served with chipped or shaved ice.

A southern Vietnamese speciality that combines nearly all of the above is *chè*, a glass of sweetened coconut milk or syrup supplemented with beans and, if the weather is hot, ice.

COOKING METHODS

It's not only the ingredients that make the meal. The methods employed in turning a fresh catch into a delicious grilled treat, or handful of greens into a salty stir-fry, are also indicative of the cuisines of the Mekong region.

If you're keen to try your hand at whipping up some local dishes, cooking courses are available in Bangkok (p122), Chiang Mai (p137), Vientiane (p271) and Hanoi (p357). There are also courses offered in Cambodia at Smokin' Pot (p218) in Battambang and ACCB (p208), near Siem Reap.

Grilling

Possibly the oldest cooking method known to man, grilling is still an important cooking method in Southeast Asia. Grilling meat or fish over red-hot

TOP FIVE COOKBOOKS

■ *Thai Food* by David Thompson – the unofficial Bible of Thai food, this massive tome incorporates culture, history, beautiful photos and authentic recipes.

■ *La Cuisine du Cambodge Avec Les Apprentis de Sala Bai* by Joannes Riviere – the most authoritative book on Khmer cooking is unfortunately only available in French.

■ *Traditional Recipes of Laos, Phia Sing* edited by Alan and Jennifer Davidson – one of the few books in English on Lao cooking, this book contains the compiled recipes of Phia Sing, a former cook in the royal palace of Luang Prabang.

■ *Into the Vietnamese Kitchen* by Andrea Nguyen – written by a well-known proponent of Vietnamese cooking in the US, this book just might inspire you to make your first *pho* (noodle soup).

■ *Swallowing Clouds* by A Zee – this book weaves together knowledge on Chinese cooking, culture and language in an insightful, educational and humorous way. You'll find recipes and folk tales and may even come away with the ability to decipher Chinese menus.

coals is particularly prevalent in Laos, where *pîng kai* (grilled chicken) is the unofficial national dish. Another grilled highlight is the street-side grill stalls that pop up every evening in the cities of Yúnnán. Simply point to the skewered ingredients you fancy and they will be brushed with a spicy oil sauce and grilled to perfection before your eyes.

Boiling

Soups, and their thicker, spicier cousins, curries, are essential to Southeast Asian cooking. Particular to the region are the various sour, often fish-based, soups, such as northeastern Thailand's *tôm khlóng* (a spicy/tart soup similar to the central Thai *tôm yam*) and Vietnam's *lau ca* (fish hotpot). Other soupy specialities include the thick bamboo-based stews of northeastern Thailand and Laos, and the root, fruit and herb-laden *samlors* of Cambodia. Due to the relative scarcity of coconut palms in most of the Mekong area, coconut milk–based curries are less of a tradition here, although southern Vietnamese cooking makes keen use of the immense nut.

For expert information on Vietnamese cooking from author Andrea Nguyen, check out Viet World Kitchen (http://vietworldkitchen.com).

Frying

The Chinese art of stir-frying is almost as widespread as noodles, and Laos is the only country in the region where a simple steel or aluminium wok is not part of the kitchen arsenal of every household. Perhaps because it is their invention, the Chinese are particularly adept at taking a few simple ingredients, usually leafy green vegetables, and turning them into a delicious stir-fry. A particularly prevalent stir-fried speciality throughout the region is morning glory, a green aquatic vegetable that stays crispy even after being stir-fried.

Deep-frying food in oil is also widespread and is the preferred method for making savoury snacks such as the legendary spring rolls of southern Vietnam and the infamous deep-fried spiders of rural Cambodia.

Hot & Tangy Salads

Known in various forms as *yam* in Thailand, *làap* in Laos and *nhoam* in Cambodia, these are not 'salads' in the Western sense, but rather main dishes that typically take the form of bite-sized bits of meat or seafood mixed with fresh herbs and a salty and sour (and sometimes sweet and spicy) dressing. In northeastern Thailand and Laos, this typically takes the form of minced pork or fish (either raw or cooked) mixed with chilli and a blast of lime juice and fish sauce. In Yúnnán, the sour element is typically vinegar, and evidence of the Sichuān influence can be seen in the use of bright-red chilli-infused oil.

Perhaps the zenith of this style of cooking is northeastern Thailand's *sôm tam*, a blend of crispy unripe papaya, tomatoes, chillies, garlic, lime juice and *plaa ráa* (thick fish sauce).

DRINKS
Tea & Coffee
Tea, the leaves of which come from a plant native to Yúnnán province, is the most widespread beverage in the Mekong area. The art of brewing and drinking tea has been popular in China since the Tang dynasty (AD 618–907), but probably didn't become widespread in Southeast Asia until as late as the 18th century. Today, an on-the-house pot of weak jasmine or green tea is found in most restaurants across the region. Other than simply being drunk, tea is also grown in the Mekong region, and northern Yúnnán is home to some of China's highest quality teas.

Making inroads to China's beloved tea is coffee. Originally introduced to the Mekong region by the French, coffee is now widely grown (particularly in Vietnam and Laos) and consumed in the region. Although the beans are generally roasted the same way as in the West, the traditional filtering system in Southeast Asia is a narrow cloth bag attached to a steel handle. Hot water is poured through the bag and grounds into a short glass, typically containing a thin layer of sweetened condensed milk.

An old Chinese saying identifies tea as one of the seven basic necessities of life, along with fuel, oil, rice, salt, soy sauce and vinegar. Tea-drinking in China was documented as early as 50 BC.

Fruit Drinks
One of the greatest simple pleasures of the region is the availability of both fresh and blended fruit drinks. Freshly squeezed juices typically include the old standbys of orange and lime, but for pure refreshment there is nothing more thirst-quenching on a hot day than chilled baby coconut or sugar cane juice. The latter is the ultimate pick-me-up in Cambodia, Thailand and Vietnam.

Blended drinks can be made from virtually any fruit and often include a cavity-inducing ladleful of syrup and, in some cases, tinned milk. Visitors to Cambodia wary about consuming raw eggs are forewarned: keep a close eye on juice blenders.

Beer
Perhaps no foreign culinary introduction, bar chillies, has become so widespread in the Mekong area as beer. Modern brewing facilities can be found in every country in the region, and the amber liquid is quickly overtaking the indigenous rice- and toddy-based alcohols as the tipple of choice. Two must-drink brews are Beerlao, in our opinion, the region's finest brew, and Vietnam's equivalent to homebrew, *bia hoi,* by all accounts the cheapest beer in the world.

Rice Whisky
Before beer became the regional booze of choice, an evening out in the Mekong often meant downing powerful shots of typically homemade rice- or sugar-derived alcohols. Rice whisky is still common in many rural areas, and is often associated with ceremony and celebration. For a slightly smoother drink, the most famous commercial brands of rice whisky are the Thai labels Mekong and Sang Som, which are available across the entire region.

WHERE TO EAT & DRINK

For an entertaining and informative view on the 'scoff and swill' scene in Vietnam, check out Englishman Graham Holliday's acclaimed blog at www.noodlepie.com.

It's hard to go hungry anywhere in Southeast Asia as just about everywhere you go there will be myriad food options to suit most budgets. Dining options in the Mekong region range from simple street stalls, complete with minuscule plastic stools and complimentary auto exhaust, to restaurants featuring such modern amenities as air-conditioning and service charges.

Although many visitors rave rhapsodic about street stalls, in our opinion small restaurants are generally a stronger choice for full meals, and offer slightly more refined (and often significantly more sanitary) cuisine. In any case, the best way to find good food is to look for noisy, crowded places; the noisier the better. Such restaurants may not have English menus but it's OK to look at what other people are having and indicate to the wait staff what you want by pointing.

Tourist-friendly restaurants can be found around popular sights and often have English signs and menus. On the downside, the food is usually overpriced and geared towards foreign tastes.

Hotels in larger cities often serve high-end regional dishes and international food, featuring everything from Indian to French cuisine.

Those travelling with children will be delighted by the attention the little ones receive, but may find that feeding kids in this part of the world is something of a challenge. If the spices are a problem, do as the natives do and stick with relatively bland dishes such as rice soup, noodles and breads.

Street Stalls

Because so much of life in Southeast Asia is lived outside the home, street food is an important part of everyday life. The people of the Mekong are inveterate snackers, and can be found at impromptu stalls at any time of the day or night, delving into a range of snacky things such as deep-fried battered bananas or grilled skewers of meat.

Night Markets

One of the most pleasurable venues for dining out in the Mekong region is the night market, which can vary from a small cluster of metal tables and chairs at the side of a road to more elaborate affairs that take up entire city blocks.

In general there are two types of night market. Firstly the evening market, which sets up just before sunset and stays open until around 9pm or 10pm (sometimes later in large cities). Often some of the best regional food is available at these markets, but it is usually only sold to go. If this is the case and you want to 'dine in', we suggest asking your guesthouse/hotel if it's OK to

---

BETEL NUT

One thing you'll undoubtedly see for sale at street stalls in many parts of the Mekong region is betel nut. This is not a food – swallow it and you'll be sorry! The betel nut is the seed of the betel palm (a beautiful tree, by the way) and is meant to be chewed. The seed usually has a slit in it and is mixed with lime and wrapped in a leaf. Like tobacco, it's strong stuff that you can barely tolerate at first, but eventually you'll be hooked.

The first time you bite into a betel nut, your whole face gets hot – chewers say it gives them a buzz. Like chewing tobacco, betel nut causes excessive salivation and betel chewers must constantly spit. The reddish-brown stains you see on footpaths are not blood, but betel-saliva juice. Years of constant chewing causes the user's teeth to become stained progressively browner, eventually becoming nearly black.

DOS & DON'TS

- Do wait for your host to sit first.
- Don't turn down food placed in your bowl by your host.
- Do learn to use chopsticks in China and Vietnam.
- Do tip about 10% in restaurants, as wages are low.
- Don't tip if there is already a service charge on the bill.
- Do drink every time someone offers a toast.

use their dishes in exchange for buying drinks from them. More often than not they'll be happy to oblige.

The second type is the all-night market, which begins doing business around 11pm and keeps going until sunrise. These markets are like informal open-air restaurants, and typically specialise in grilled or fried dishes or noodles. Typical places to look for them include in front of day markets, next to bus or train stations and at busy intersections.

VEGETARIANS & VEGANS

The good news is that there is now more choice than ever before when it comes to vegetarian dining in Southeast Asia. The bad news is that you have not landed in Veg Heaven, for the people of the Mekong area are voracious omnivores. While they love their veggies, they also dearly love anything that crawls on the ground, swims in the water or flies in the air.

China is the only country in the region with a genuine vegetarian tradition, and certain restaurants offer meat-free menus, especially during Buddhist holidays. Another good, though much less common, venue for vegetarian meals in the region are Indian restaurants, which usually feature a vegetarian section on the menu.

Menus at tourist restaurants in larger towns and cities will often have a small list of vegetarian dishes available. Outside of tourist areas, vegetarians and vegans will have to make an effort to speak enough of the local language to convey their culinary needs. And vegetarians should be aware that across the Mekong region, even the most innocuous-looking dishes will probably contain fish sauce, and most stocks, including those used in noodle soup, are often made with meat.

HABITS & CUSTOMS

As odd as it seems to Westerners, eating alone is something that many people in the Mekong region consider unusual. This is due to the fact that in Asia eating is generally a communal activity and meals are usually served 'family-style', from common serving platters. Traditionally, a group orders one of each kind of dish, perhaps a fish, a stir-fry, a salad, a vegetable dish and a soup, taking care to balance cool and hot, sour and sweet, salty and plain.

When ordering from a restaurant menu, don't worry about the proper succession of courses. All dishes are placed in the centre of the table as soon as they are ready. Diners help themselves to whatever appeals to them, regardless of who ordered what. Additionally, most people don't concern themselves with whether dishes are served piping hot, so no one minds if the dishes sit in the kitchen or on the table for a few minutes before anyone digs in.

When serving yourself from a common platter, it's polite to put no more than one spoonful onto your plate at a time. Sometimes serving spoons are provided. If not, you simply dig in with your own spoon or chopsticks.

Ant Egg Soup by Natacha du Pont de Bie (2004) is a well-written account of the author's encounters with food while travelling through Laos, and is garnished with recipes and line drawings.

EAT YOUR WORDS

For pronunciation guidelines see p513.

Useful Words & Phrases

To help make yourself understood in the kitchens and restaurants of the Greater Mekong region, we've put together some essential words and phrases that should smooth the way to dinner.

I'd like ...

Chinese	*Wǒ xiǎng yào ...*	我想要...
Khmer	*sohm ...*	សុំ...
Lao	*khǎw ...*	ຂໍ...
Thai	*khǎw ...*	ขอ...
Vietnamese	*sin jo doy ...*	Xin cho tôi ...

I'm allergic to ...

Chinese	*Wǒ duì ... guòmǐn.*	我对...过敏
Khmer	*kohm dak ...*	កុំដាក់...
Lao	*khàwy phâe ...*	ຂອຍແພ້...
Thai	*phǒm/dì-chǎn pháe ...*	ผม/ดิฉันแพ้...
Vietnamese	*doy bẹe zẹe úhrng ver-eé ...*	Tôi bị dị ứng với ...

I'm a vegetarian.

Chinese	*Wǒ chī sù.*	我吃素
Khmer	*kh'nyohm tawm sait*	ខ្ញុំតមសាច់
Lao	*khàwy kịn tae phák*	ຂອຍກິນແຕ່ຜັກ
Thai	*phǒm/dì-chǎn kin néua sàt mâi dâi*	ผม/ดิฉันกินเนื้อสัตว์ไม่ได้
Vietnamese	*doy uhn jay*	Tôi ăn chay.

I don't eat ...

Chinese	*Wǒ bùchī ...*	我不吃...
Khmer	*kh'nyohm min nham ...*	ខ្ញុំមិនញ៉ាំ...
Lao	*khàwy baw kịn ...*	ຂອຍບໍ່ກິນ...
Thai	*phǒm/dì-chǎn kin ... mâi dâi*	ผม/ดิฉันกิน...ไม่ได้
Vietnamese	*doy kawm duhr-ẹrk uhn ...*	Tôi không được ăn ...

How much is it?

Chinese	*Duōshǎo qián?*	多少钱?
Khmer	*nih th'lay pohnmaan?*	នេះថ្លៃប៉ុន្មាន?
Lao	*thao dại?*	เท่าใด
Thai	*thâo rai?*	เท่าไร
Vietnamese	*bow nyee-oo*	Bao nhiêu?

(Thank you) That was delicious.

Chinese	*Chīde zhēn xiāng!*	吃的真香!

Khmer	*aw kohn, nih ch'ngain nah*	អរគុណ នេះឆ្ងាញ់ណាស់
Lao	*sâep*	ແຊບ
Thai	*aa-hăan níi aràwy*	อาหารนี้อร่อย
Vietnamese	*ğaảm ern, ngon lúhm*	Cám ơn, ngon lắm.

Fried

Chinese	*chǎo*	炒
Khmer	*jien, chaa*	ជៀន, ឆា
Lao	*khùa (phát)*	ຂົ້ວ (ຜັດ)
Thai	*phàt*	ผัด
Vietnamese	*jee-uhn*	chiên

Boiled

Chinese	*zhǔ*	煮
Khmer	*sngor*	ស្ងោរ
Lao	*tôm*	ຕົ້ມ
Thai	*tôm*	ต้ม
Vietnamese	*loo-ụhk*	luộc

Grilled

Chinese	*tiěbǎn kǎo*	铁板烤 (grilled on a hotplate)
Khmer	*ahng*	អាំង
Lao	*pǐing*	ປີ້ງ
Thai	*yâang*	ย่าง
Vietnamese	*nuhr-érng veé*	nướng vl

Steamed

Chinese	*zhēng*	蒸
Khmer	*jamhoi*	ចំហុយ
Lao	*nèung*	ໜຶ່ງ
Thai	*nêung*	นึ่ง
Vietnamese	*húhp*	hấp

Meat

Chinese	*ròu*	肉 (also means 'pork')
Khmer	*sait*	សាច់
Lao	*sǐn*	ຊື້ນ
Thai	*néua sàt*	เนื้อสัตว์
Vietnamese	*tịt*	thịt

Chicken

Chinese	*jīròu*	鸡肉
Khmer	*sait moan*	សាច់មាន់

Lao	*kai*	ໄກ່
Thai	*kài*	ไก่
Vietnamese	*tịt gaà*	thịt gà

Fish

Chinese	*yú*	鱼
Khmer	*trey*	ត្រី
Lao	*pqa*	ປາ
Thai	*plaa*	ปลา
Vietnamese	*ğaá*	cá

Pork

Chinese	*ròu*	肉
Khmer	*sait j'ruuk*	សាច់ជ្រូក
Lao	*sǐn mǔu*	ຊີ້ນໝູ
Thai	*mǔu*	หมู
Vietnamese	*hay-oo*	heo

Beef

Chinese	*niúròu*	牛肉
Khmer	*sait kow*	សាច់គោ
Lao	*sǐn ngúa*	ຊີ້ນງົວ
Thai	*néua*	เนื้อ
Vietnamese	*tịt bò*	thịt bò

Vegetables

Chinese	*shūcài/qīngcài*	蔬菜/青菜 (green, leafy)
Khmer	*buhn lai*	បន្លែ
Lao	*phák*	ຜັກ
Thai	*phàk*	ผัก
Vietnamese	*zoh sáwm*	rau sống

Rice

Chinese	*fàn*	饭
Khmer	*bai*	បាយ
Lao	*khào*	ເຂົ້າ
Thai	*khâo*	ข้าว
Vietnamese	*ğerm*	cơm

Water

Chinese	*(kāi) shuǐ*	(开) 水 (Boiled)
Khmer	*teuk*	ទឹក
Lao	*nâm (tôm/deum)*	ນ້ຳ(ຕົ້ມ/ດື່ມ) water (boiled/drinking)

Thai	*náam dèum*	น้ำดื่ม (drinking water)
Vietnamese	*nuhr-érk*	nước
	nuhr-érk sóo-ee	nước suối (mineral water)

'Must Eat' Regional Specialities

CAMBODIA

aa-mokh	អាម៉ុក	fish in coconut milk curry, wrapped in banana leaves and steamed
lohk-lahk	ឡុកឡាក់	stir-fried, marinated beef served with onions, tomatoes and a fried egg
samlor k'tih ma-noas	សម្លខ្ទិះម្នាស់	pork rib, coconut and pineapple soup
suhm-law muh-joo	សម្លម្ជូរ	sour, tamarind-based soup, generally including chicken or fish, tomato and herbs
kyteow	គុយទាវ	Cambodian noodle soup
baay sait jruuk	បាយសាច់ជ្រូក	rice served with barbecued pork
baw baw	បបរ	Cambodian-style congee, typically served with pork or dried fish
bohk luh-hohng	បុកល្ហុង	Cambodian-style papaya salad
sngao ma-reah	ស្ងោរម្រះ	bitter melon stuffed with minced pork and boiled in pork stock
nom banh chok	នំបញ្ចុក	cold rice noodles served with a yellow fish curry, fresh veggies and herbs

LAOS

khào nĭaw	ເຂົ້າໜຽວ	sticky rice
tąm màak-hung	ຕຳໝາກຫຸ່ງ	spicy green papaya salad
làap pąa	ລາບປາ	a spicy 'salad' of minced fish, roasted rice, lime juice and fresh herbs
pîng kai	ປີ້ງໄກ່	grilled chicken
jąew bąwng	ແຈ່ວບອງ	a chilli-based 'dip' that includes buffalo skin; a speciality of Luang Prabang
khái phâen	ໄຄແຜ່ນ	sheets of deep-fried Mekong River weed; a speciality of Luang Prabang
fŏe	ເຝີ	Vietnamese-style noodle soup
pąa dàek	ປາແດກ	unfiltered, unpasteurised fish sauce; an essential ingredient in Lao cooking
kąa-féh nóm hâwn	ກາເຟນົມຮ້ອນ	Lao-style coffee

NORTHEAST THAILAND

khâo nĭaw	ข้าวเหนียว	sticky rice
sôm tam puu	ส้มตำปู	spicy green papaya salad with salted field crabs
súp nàw mái	ซุปหน่อไม้	a spicy 'salad' of pickled bamboo
tam sùa	ตำสั่ว	papaya salad with the addition of *khànŏm jeen*, fermented rice noodles
lâap mŭu	ลาบหมู	a spicy/sour 'salad' of minced pork

plaa dùk yâang	ปลาดุกย่าง	grilled catfish
khaw mǔu yâang	คอหมูย่าง	grilled pork collar
kaeng laao	แกงลาว	a dark, thick, bamboo-based stew
tôm sâep	ต้มแซบ	a spicy/sour soup similar to tôm yam
plaa ráa	ปลาร้า	unfiltered, unpasteurised fish sauce; an essential seasoning in ìsǎan cooking

VIETNAM

baáng say-òo	Bánh xèo	rice crepes filled with pork, shrimp, bean sprouts, straw mushroom and ground mung bean, and eaten with lettuce and herbs and enjoyed with nước chấm, Vietnam's ubiquitous tangy-savoury-sweet dipping sauce
bò bảy món	Bò bảy món	beef prepared seven ways, from grilled morsels to creamy rice soup
ğaang joo·uh ğaá	Canh chua cá	a sour fish soup with tamarind, pineapple, taro stem, okra and tomato
jaá zò	Chả giò	spring rolls wrapped in lettuce and herbs and enjoyed with nước chấm
ğaá ko dạw	Cá kho tộ	fish simmered in a claypot with a sweet and salty sauce
ğaá nuhr-érng choo-ee	Cá nướng trui	a whole fish (typically snakehead, cá lóc), grilled and served with rice paper, dipping sauce, lettuce and herbs for making hand-rolls
hoỏ dee-oó naam vaang	Hú tiếu nam vang	a noodle soup with sliced pork, pork liver, shrimp, fried shallots, scallions and Chinese celery

YÚNNÁN

rǔbǐng	乳饼	goat milk cheese, a speciality of the Bai minority
bōluò fàn	菠萝饭	pineapple rice, a speciality of the Dai people of Xīshuāngbǎnnà
guòqiáo mǐxiàn	过桥米线	'across-the-bridge' noodles, a do-it-yourself meal of raw ingredients dipped in a boiling broth
pǔ'ěr chá	普洱茶	a highly regarded tea grown in Yúnnán that is sometimes aged as many as 50 years
shípíng dòufu	石屏豆腐	cakes of fermented bean curd that are sometimes smoked
xuānwēi huǒtuǐ	宣威火腿	cured ham produced in the city of Xuanwei that makes its way into countless dishes in Yúnnán
qìguōjī	气锅鸡	chicken steamed with herbs in a specially designed ceramic pot

Border Crossings in the Greater Mekong

During the bad old days of communism and the Cold War, there were pretty much no land borders open to foreigners. Times have changed and there are now more than 20 borders connecting the neighbouring countries of the Mekong region. For a quick visual reference covering the border crossings in the region see the border crossings map (p100).

In this book we give detailed instructions for every crossing open to foreigners. Before making a long-distance trip, be aware of border closing times, visa regulations and any transport scams by referring to the relevant country's Transport section and the specific entries on border towns located in boxed texts in each chapter. Border details change regularly, so ask around or check the **Thorntree** (http://thorntree.lonelyplanet.com).

Visas are available at some borders and not at others. As a general rule of thumb, visas are available at the land borders of Cambodia, Laos and Thailand and are not available at Vietnamese and Chinese border crossings. However, there are a few exceptions in the case of Cambodia and Laos.

There are few legal money-changing facilities at some of the more remote border crossings, so be sure to have some small-denomination US dollars handy. The black market is also an option for local currencies, but remember that black marketeers have a well-deserved reputation for short-changing and outright theft.

Some of the immigration police at land border crossings, especially at the Cambodian and Vietnamese borders, have a bad reputation for petty extortion. Crossing between Cambodia and Thailand can be a pain in the neck, but it's nothing compared with crossing between Laos and Vietnam, which hands down has the most remote borders in the region with terrible transport and little room for leeway. Most travellers find it's much easier to exit overland than it is to enter. Travellers at remote border crossings are occasionally asked for an 'immigration fee' of some kind, although this is less common than it used to be.

For detailed coverage of these border crossings, including transport options, see the individual boxed texts in the destination chapters.

CAMBODIA

Cambodia shares border with Laos, Thailand and Vietnam. Cambodian visas are available at all land borders with Laos and Thailand, but only two of the land borders with Vietnam. They are not currently available at Phnom Den.

From Laos

The only border crossing with Cambodia is at Voen Kham (L), which connects Si Phan Don in southern Laos to Stung Treng (C). Minibuses ply the new road to Stung Treng (Dom Kralor; see p333). There was once a river route (Koh Chheuteal Thom), but Cambodia has closed its border and so the route is no longer possible.

From Thailand

There are now as many as six land crossings between Thailand and Cambodia, but only two are popular with travellers. The border at Aranya Prathet (T) to Poipet (C) is frequently used to travel between Bangkok

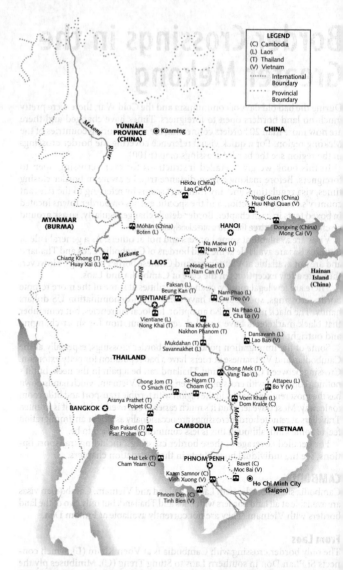

LEGEND
(C) Cambodia
(L) Laos
(T) Thailand
(V) Vietnam
········· International Boundary
········· Provincial Boundary

(T) and Siem Reap (C). See p158 for more information. Try to avoid the 'Scam Bus' (see the boxed text, p219) if possible. Down on the coast, crossings can be made from Hat Lek (T) to Cham Yeam (C) by road (see p158), which connects to Koh Kong (C) and on to Sihanoukville (C) or Phnom Penh (C).

There are also three more remote crossings, which see little traffic. There's a crossing at Chong Jom (T) in Surin Province to O Smach (C), connecting with Samraong (C); see p158. Another crossing is at Choam Sa-Ngam (T) to

MEKONG REGION BORDERS AT A GLANCE

Countries	Border crossing	Connecting towns	Visa on arrival	More details
Cambodia/ Vietnam	Bavet (C)/ Moc Bai (V)	Phnom Penh/ Ho Chi Minh City	Cambodia (Y)/ Vietnam (N)	p227/ p417
Cambodia/ Vietnam	Kaam Samnor (C)/ Vinh Xuong (V)	Phnom Penh/ Chau Doc	Cambodia (Y)/ Vietnam (N)	p228/ p424
Cambodia/ Vietnam	Phnom Den (C)/ Tinh Bien(V)	Takeo/ Chau Doc	Cambodia (N)/ Vietnam (N)	p247/ p424
Cambodia/ Laos	Dom Kralor (C)/ Voen Kham (L)	Stung Treng/ Si Phan Don	Cambodia (Y)/ Laos (N)	p233/ p333
Cambodia/ Thailand	Poipet (C)/ Aranya Prathet (T)	Siem Reap/ Bangkok	Cambodia (Y)/ Thailand (Y)	p222/ p158
Cambodia/ Thailand	Cham Yeam (C)/ Hat Lek (T)	Koh Kong/ Trat	Cambodia (Y)/ Thailand (Y)	p249/ p158
Cambodia/ Thailand	O Smach (C)/ Chong Jom (T)	Samraong/ Surin	Cambodia (Y)/ Thailand (Y)	p222/ p158
Cambodia/ Thailand	Choam (C)/ Choam Sa-Ngam (T)	Anlong Veng/ Sangkha	Cambodia (Y)/ Thailand (Y)	p223
Cambodia/ Thailand	Psar Prohm (C)/ Ban Pakard (T)	Pailin/ Chanthaburi	Cambodia (Y)/ Thailand (Y)	p220
China (Yúnnán)/ Laos	Móhān (Yúnnán)/ Boten (L)	Měnglà/ Luang Nam Tha	China (N)/ Laos (Y)	p470/ p312
China (Yúnnán)/ Vietnam	Hékŏu (Yúnnán)/ Lao Cai (V)	Kūnmíng/ Hanoi	China (N)/ Vietnam (N)	p449/ p376
China/ Vietnam	Youyi Guan (China)/ Huu Nghi Quan (Friendship Pass) (V)	Pingxiang/ Lang Son	China (N)/ Vietnam (N)	p374
China/ Vietnam	Dongxing (China)/ Mong Cai (V)	Dongxing/ Mong Cai	China (N)/ Vietnam (N)	p374
Laos/ Thailand	Vientiane (L)/ Nong Khai (T)	Vientiane/ Nong Khai	Laos (Y)/ Thailand (Y)	p285/ p167
Laos/ Thailand	Paksan (L)/ Beung Kan (T)	Paksan/ Beung Kan	Laos (N)/ Thailand (N)	p317/ p178
Laos/ Thailand	Huay Xai (L)/ Chiang Khong (T)	Huay Xai/ Chiang Rai	Laos (Y)/ Thailand (Y)	p314/ p148
Laos/ Thailand	Tha Khaek (L)/ Nakhon Phanom (T)	Tha Khaek/ Nakhon Phanom	Laos (Y)/ Thailand (Y)	p320/ p165
Laos/ Thailand	Savannakhet (L)/ Mukdahan (T)	Savannakhet/ Mukdahan	Laos (Y)/ Thailand (Y)	p323/ p163
Laos/ Thailand	Vang Tao (L)/ Chong Mek (T)	Pakse/ Ubon Ratchathani	Laos (Y)/ Thailand (Y)	p327/ p162
Laos/ Vietnam	Dansavanh (L)/ Lao Bao (V)	Savannakhet/ Dong Ha	Laos (Y)/ Vietnam (N)	p324/ p384
Laos/ Vietnam	Attapeu (L)/ Bo Y (V)	Attapeu/ Pleiku	Laos (N)/ Vietnam (N)	p334/ p403
Laos/ Vietnam	Na Phao (L)/ Cha Lo (V)	Tha Khaek/ Dong Hoi	Laos (N)/ Vietnam (N)	p321/ p366
Laos/ Vietnam	Nong Haet (L)/ Nam Can (V)	Phonsovan/ Vinh	Laos (maybe)/ Vietnam (N)	p305/ p366
Laos/ Vietnam	Nam Phao (L)/ Cau Treo (V)	Tha Khaek/ Vinh	Laos (Y)/ Vietnam (N)	p318/ p366
Laos/ Vietnam	Na Maew (L)/ Nam Xoi (V)	Sam Neua/ Thanh Hoa	Laos (N)/ Vietnam (N)	p308/ p366

Choam (C), leading to the former Khmer Rouge stronghold of Anlong Veng (C); see p223. The third is at Ban Pakard (T) to Psar Prohm (C) leading to Pailin (C); see p220. Bear in mind that road conditions on the Cambodian side are pretty poor.

There is also a border at Prasat Preah Vihear (C), the stunning Cambodian temple perched atop Phnom Dangkrek mountain range. This is currently just a day crossing for tourists wanting to visit the temple from the Thai side, but may open up as a full international border during the lifetime of this book. See the boxed text, p159, for more information.

From Vietnam

There are three border-crossing options, two by road and a romantic river trip. The most popular option is the road border linking Moc Bai (V) and Bavet (C) for quick passage between Ho Chi Minh City and Phnom Penh (see p417). The most evocative route is the river crossing linking Chau Doc (V) to Phnom Penh (C) via the Mekong border at Vinh Xuong (V) and Kaam Samnor (C); see p424. Finally there is the rarely used option of Tinh Bien (V) to Phnom Den (C) that connects Chau Doc (V) and Takeo (C); see p424.

CHINA

China shares borders with Laos and Vietnam. It is also possible to travel from China to Thailand, through Myanmar (Burma) and Laos, by passenger boat; see p148 for details. China visas are now available on arrival at the Móhān border, but not at any of the borders with Vietnam. Be aware that some travellers, as they enter China, have had their Lonely Planet guides to China confiscated by officials – primarily at the Vietnam–China border. We recommend you copy any essential details before you cross and put a cover on your guide.

From Laos

There is only one international border crossing connecting Boten (L) with Móhān (Yúnnán, China), in a fairly remote region. This crossing links Luang Nam Tha Province in Laos to Yúnnán province in China. From Móhān, on the Chinese side it's a two-hour minibus ride to Měnglà, the nearest large town. See p312 for more information.

From Vietnam

There are currently three border checkpoints where foreigners are permitted to cross between Vietnam and China. Lao Cai (V) to Hékǒu in Yúnnán province is convenient for travellers going between Hanoi (V) and Kūnmíng (Yúnnán); see p376.

The other two borders are outside of Yúnnán province. The Friendship Pass (Huu Nghi Quan on the Vietnamese side, Youyi Guan on the Chinese side), connects Lang Son (V) to Pinxiang in China; see p374. The seldom-used Mong Cai (V) to Dongxing (Yúnnán) is in the far northeast of Vietnam; see p374.

The Vietnam–China border-crossing hours vary a little but are generally between 7am to 5pm (Vietnam time). Set your watch when you cross the border as the time in China is one hour ahead.

LAOS

Laos shares border with all the Mekong region countries. Lao visas are available on arrival at all land borders with Thailand and the land border with China, but not at the border with Cambodia. The border with Vietnam is more complicated; visas are available at Dansavanh and Nam Phao, but not at the other borders.

From Cambodia

Voen Kham (L) is the only international border post with Cambodia; see p233. Dom Kralor (C), on the new road to Stung Treng (C), services Voen Kham and links Cambodia with southern Laos' Si Phan Don area. There used to be a river crossing at Koh Chheuteal Thom (C), but Cambodia has closed its side of the border and so the route is no longer possible.

From China

There is only one international border crossing between Móhān (Yúnnán) and Boten (L), but it's in quite a remote area of both countries; see p470 for more information. It links Yúnnán province in China to Luang Nam Tha Province in Laos. From Boten, it's a two-hour journey to Luang Nam Tha, the nearest large town.

From Thailand

The most popular crossing is from Nong Khai (T) across the Thai–Lao Friendship Bridge to Vientiane (L). See p167 for more information. There is also a river crossing between Beung Kan (T) and Paksan (L), about 120km from Vientiane, but it is rarely used by travellers; see p178.

From northern Thailand, cross the border by boat at Chiang Khong (T) to Huay Xai (L) and continue downriver to Luang Prabang (L); see p148. A new crossing connecting Muang Ngoen (T) and Huay Kon (L), which links Nan Province (T) with Sainyabuli Province (L), may soon be open to foreigners.

MY TOP FIVE BORDER CROSSING EXPERIENCES *Nick Ray*

I've been crossing the borders in this region for more than a decade now. Here are my top five experiences on the overland trail.

- Cambodia–Laos (2001) The new border had just opened up, although even the government didn't seem to realise for a couple of years. Our boat got stuck on a sandbar, we reached the border after dark and the Lao immigration team weren't too impressed by the large motorbike. It led to a negotiated settlement.

- Cambodia–Thailand (1995) The land borders were officially closed, but rumour had it that travellers were making it out via Koh Kong. It was the bad old days and we were nervous, but it was nothing a happy milk shake wouldn't cure. The trip was foggy, but I ended up in Thailand via speedboat and received a tongue-lashing from the Immigration Office in Bangkok.

- China–Laos (1998) We left Kūnmíng 24 hours after Carlos, the Guinea-Bissauan DJ with the 90kg suitcase. After an arduous bus trip of 36 hours we met him at the Boten border. He had got on the wrong bus and gone to the Burmese border at Mong La. Crossing into Laos, he hoped to hit Vientiane in one day, but couldn't fly due to excess baggage charges. We met him in the capital four days later: he'd just arrived!

- China–Vietnam (1995) The bus driver lied to me! There was more than one Friendship Gate and I arrived at a locals-only border in the dark. I hitched a motorbike ride around the mountains to the official border only to be sent back to Pingxiang, as it had closed for the night. Penniless, I met a Vietnamese–Australian trader who arranged me board and lodging for the night.

- Vietnam–Cambodia (1995) There was one rattletrap bus connecting Ho Chi Minh City and Phnom Penh back in the bad old days. It left at some ungodly hour and I had to be on it. Even back then, Saigon rocked and it turned into an all-nighter. How my head hurt the next day, but it got worse as the bus was stripped down at the border to look for contraband. Taxi! Welcome to Phnom Penh – I didn't imagine for a moment it would become my home.

From the northeast, travellers have two options. You can cross the Mekong at Nakhon Phanom (T) to Tha Khaek (L); see p165; or at Mukdahan (T) to Savannakhet (L), where there is a new bridge spanning the river (see p163).

In eastern Thailand, you can cross by land at Chong Mek (T), near Ubon Ratchathani, to Vang Tao (L), an hour west of Pakse (L); see p162.

From Vietnam

The most popular crossing connects Lao Bao (V) to Dansavanh (L), linking the central city of Dong Ha (V) and the southern Lao province of Savannakhet; see p384. Further north there is another land border at Cau Treo (V) to Nam Phao (L); see p366. The nearest Vietnamese city, Vinh, is about 80km from the border and on the Lao side it's about 200km from the border to Tha Khaek, just opposite Nakhon Phanom in Thailand. There is another border in this region at Cha Lo (V) and Na Phao (L), connecting Dong Hoi (V) and Tha Khaek (see p366), but most travellers use Cau Treo (V).

It's also possible to cross at Nam Can (V) to Nong Haet (L), but this is a marathon trek starting in Vinh and aiming for Phonsavan; see p366 for more information. Another northern crossing is open at Nam Xoi (V) to Na Maew (L), connecting Thanh Hoa (V) or Hanoi to Sam Neua in Laos; see p366. However, this is pretty remote and it can take as much as four days to travel between Luang Prabang and Hanoi this way. Finally there is a more southerly border that links Pleiku (V) and Bo Y (V) with Attapeu (L) and Pakse (L); see p403. This crossing has still not been formally been named, as it only opened in mid-2006.

Keep your ears open for news on the border between Tay Trang (V) and Sop Hun (L) near Dien Bien Phu (V) opening up to foreigners. This has been rumoured for years, but it might just happen this time.

LAO–VIETNAM BORDER WOES   Andrew Burke

If we had a Beerlao for every email we've received from travellers who have been scammed while crossing the Lao–Vietnam border, we'd be able to have a very big party. There are several different scams you might encounter, and other lies you'll be told that won't necessarily cost you money but will most certainly piss you off.

Among the most common is the '12-hour' bus between Vientiane and Hanoi, which is in fact a 20- to 24-hour trip including several hours spent waiting for the border to open. Once across the border (mainly at Nam Phao/Cau Treo but also Dansavanh/Lao Bao), another common scam involves the suddenly rising price. You'll know this one when your bus stops and demands an extra, say, US$20 each to continue. Local transport heading further into Vietnam also try this one, especially tourist-oriented minibuses. Annoyingly, there's little you can do to avoid these scams. You just have to expect the worse, but hope your crossing is trouble free, as many are. If trouble strikes, try to keep smiling to get the best result – paying a lower amount.

Alternatively, you could tell the scammers where to go and hope for the best. And as we discovered years ago (these scams have been running forever), sometimes it will pay off. For us, it happened on Rte 8 coming from Vinh to Cau Treo. Our minibus stopped halfway up the Annamite range and the driver demanded more money. We refused, got out and the incredulous driver left. No sooner had we asked ourselves 'What now?' than a truck loaded up with bags of cement lumbered over the hill and stopped. 'To the border?' I asked. 'Yes, yes, no problem,' came the smiling reply, even after I'd shown him we only had 1300d between us. Sitting atop the truck as we wound our way slowly up through the cloudforests was fantastic – and almost as good as the gesture itself, which had restored some of our faith in humanity. We had the last laugh on our greedy driver when we found him at the border trying to rip off a Canadian couple. Our advice: 'Don't, whatever you do, go with that guy.'

THAILAND

Thailand shares borders with Cambodia and Laos in the Mekong region, plus popular borders with Malaysia and Myanmar. Entry stamps are available at all Thailand crossings except for Beung Kan. It's possible to travel from Thailand to China (through Myanmar and Laos) by passenger boat; see p148.

From Cambodia

The border at Poipet (C) to Aranya Prathet (T) is frequently used to access Siem Reap (C) or Bangkok (T); see p222. Don't get scammed by the 'Scam Bus' though (see the boxed text, p219). Along the coast, crossings can be made from Cham Yeam (C) to Hat Lek (T) by road for connections to Trat (T), Bangkok (T) and Koh Chang (T); see p249. There are also three more remote crossings: from the town of Samraong through O Smach (C) to Chong Jom (T) in Surin Province (see p222); from the former Khmer Rouge stronghold of Anlong Veng through Choam (C) to Choam Sa-Ngam (T), see p223; and from the southwest town of Pailin through Psar Prohm (C) to Ban Pakard (T); see p220.

From Laos

The most popular crossing is from Vientiane (L) across the Thai–Lao Friendship Bridge to Nong Khai (T); see p285. There is also a river crossing between Paksan (L) and Beung Kan (T), about 120km from Vientiane, but it's rarely used by travellers; see p317.

Heading to northern Thailand, cross the border by boat at Huay Xai (L) to Chiang Khong (T) from where it is a short hop to the Golden Triangle (T) or Chiang Rai (T); see p314. There is also a new crossing connecting Huay Kon (L) and Muang Ngoen (T), linking Sainyabuli Province (L) with Nan Province (T), which is seldom used by foreigners.

From the south, travellers have the option of crossing the Mekong River at Tha Khaek (L) to Nakhon Phanom (T); see p320; or at Savannakhet (L) to Mukdahan (T); see p323. In the far south, you can cross by land at Vang Tao (L), an hour west of Pakse, to Chong Mek (T), near Ubon Ratchathani; see p327.

From Malaysia

On the west coast, the crossing between Satun (T) to Pulau Langkawi (M) is made by boat. On the east coast, Sungai Kolok (T) to Rantau Panjang (M) is a dusty land crossing for travel between Kota Bharu (M) and Pulau Perhentian (M). The major transit hub in Thailand, Hat Yai, and Penang-Butterworth in Malaysia, receive bus and rail traffic through the borders at Kanger (T) to Padang Besar (M) or Sadao (T) to Bukit Kayu Hitam (M). Betong (T) to Keroh (M) is also a land crossing open to foreigners.

From Myanmar (Burma)

There are two legal crossings: Mae Sai (T) to Tachilek (My) and Ranong (T) to Kawthoung (My). Be sure to have a valid Myanmar visa when exiting and be prepared for unexpected charges from Myanmar officials at the border when crossing into Thailand.

VIETNAM

Vietnam shares borders with Cambodia, China and Laos. Vietnam visas are not currently available at any land crossings, so be sure to arrange a visa in advance.

From Cambodia

There are three border-crossing options for travel between Vietnam and Cambodia: the road border at Bavet (C) to Moc Bai (V) which connects

Phnom Penh and Ho Chi Minh City, see p227; the memorable Mekong River crossing at Kaam Samnor (C) to Vinh Xuong (V) linking Phnom Penh and Chau Doc, see p228; or the remote crossing of Phnom Den (C) to Tinh Bien (V), see p247.

From China

There are currently three border checkpoints where foreigners are permitted to cross between Vietnam and China. The crossing from Hékŏu (Yúnnán) to Lao Cai (V) is convenient for travellers going between Kūnmíng and Hanoi, see p449.

The other two crossings are located outside of Yúnnán province. The Friendship Pass (Huu Nghi Quan on the Vietnamese side, Youyi Guan on the Chinese side) connects Pinxiang (China) to Lang Son (V), see p374. There's also a seldom-used crossing from Dongxing (China) to Mong Cai in Vietnam's far northeast, see p374.

The China–Vietnam border-crossing hours vary a little but are generally between 8am to 6pm (China time). Set your watch when you cross the border as the time in Vietnam is one hour behind.

From Laos

The most popular crossing connects Donsavanh (L) to Lao Bao (V), linking Savannakhet (L) and Dong Ha (V); see p324. Further north there is another border connecting Nam Phao (L) to Cau Treo (V); see p318. From the Lao side it's about 200km to the border from Tha Khaek, while the nearest Vietnamese city, Vinh, is about 80km from the border. There is another border in this region at Na Phao (L) and Cha Lo (V), connecting Tha Khaek (L) and Dong Hoi (V); see p321. However, most travellers use the aforementioned Cau Treo (V). It's also possible to cross from Nong Haet (L) to Nam Can (V), but this is a marathon trek starting in Phonsavan and aiming for Vinh; see p305 for details. Another northern crossing is open from Na Maew (L) to Nam Xoi (V), connecting Sam Neua (L) to Thanh Hoa (V) or Hanoi (V); see p308.

Finally, there is a more southerly border that links Attapeu (L) and Pakse (L) with Pleiku (V) and Bo Y (V); see p334. This crossing has still not been formally been named, as it only opened in mid-2006.

Keep your ears open for news on the border between Sop Hun (L) and Tay Trang (V) near Dien Bien Phu (V) opening up to foreigners. We heard it had finally opened as we went to press, but check this carefully before committing to crossing this way.

Bangkok &
Northern Thailand

MARK ANDREW KIRBY

Bangkok & Northern Thailand

It might be the saffron-robed monk riding the Skytrain, or the sensuous smell of spices wafting up from a curry, or elephants strolling down the street alongside you, but at some point Thailand enters the soul.

All roads lead to Bangkok they say, and this fabled country is the Mekong region's most popular destination by far. In part this is because of all the irresistible attractions – the ancient ruins, the hill-tribe treks, the glorious temples, the golden beaches – but Thailand has also earned this status because of its comfortable balance between East and West, foreign and familiar. Thailand is arguably the world's most accessibly exotic location.

While the rest of the Mekong region suffered various incarnations of war and isolation, Thailand got a head start welcoming visitors, making it the easiest country in the region to travel around. But don't mistake convenience for lack of adventure or diluted culture. True, many visitors get stuck in various backpacker ghettos (often happily so), but the tourist trail still bypasses huge swathes of the country. Yes, Thailand can still facilitate journeys of discovery.

Though Thailand's path through modern history differs greatly from other countries in the Mekong region, its connection is more than just geographical. The ancient ebb and flow of empire spilt myriad cultures across the north of Thailand and took Thai traditions well beyond the nation's current borders. Lao, Khmer and Yunnanese influences remain a vital part of today's Thai tapestry.

Whether Thailand is solely intended as your gateway to the region or you come here with a laundry list of sights to check off, you'll be planning your return before you've even left.

HIGHLIGHTS

- Get back to nature at **Khao Yai National Park** (p156), one of the world's finest parks
- Visit timeless **hill-tribe villages** (p138) as you trek through the northern mountains
- Take time out from the fast lane in soporific **Chiang Khan** (p168)
- Cycle around the awesome ruins of **Sukhothai Historical Park** (p150)
- Explore the gleaming and seamy sides of Thailand's chaotic capital, **Bangkok** (p113)

★ Hill-tribe Villages

★ Chiang Khan

★ Sukhothai Historical Park

Khao Yai National Park ★

★ Bangkok

HISTORY
Rise of Thai Kingdoms

It is believed that the first Thais migrated here from modern-day Yúnnán and Guǎngxī, China, settling into small riverside farming communities that eventually fell under the dominion of the Angkor empire of present-day Cambodia.

By the 13th and 14th centuries, what is considered the first Thai kingdom, Sukhothai, began to chip away at the crumbling Angkor empire. The third Sukhothai king, Ramkhamhaeng, developed a Thai writing system and built Angkor-inspired temples that defined early Thai art. This kingdom is regarded as the cultural and artistic kernel of the modern state.

Sukhothai's intense flame was soon snuffed out by another emerging Thai power, Ayuthaya, which was established by Prince U Thong in 1350. This new centre developed into a cosmopolitan port on the Asian trade route courted by European nations attracted to the region for commodities and potential colonies, though the small nation managed to thwart foreign takeovers. For 400 years Ayuthaya dominated Thailand until the Burmese destroyed the capital in 1767.

The Thais eventually rebuilt their capital in present-day Bangkok, established by the Chakri dynasty, which continues to occupy the throne today. As Western imperialism marched across the globe, King Mongkut (Rama IV, r 1851–68) and his son and successor King Chulalongkorn (Rama V, r 1868–1910) successfully steered Thailand into the modern age without becoming a colonial vassal. Their progressive measures included adopting Western-style education and dress. In return for the country's continued independence, King Chulalongkorn returned huge tracts of Laos and Cambodia to French-controlled Indochina.

A Struggling Democracy

In 1932 a peaceful coup converted Thailand into a constitutional monarchy loosely based on the British model. Nearly half a century of chaos followed. During the mid-20th century, a series of anticommunist military dictators wrestled each other for power, managing little more than the suppression of democratic representation and civil rights. In 1973, student activists staged demonstrations calling for a real constitu-

tion. A brief respite came, with reinstated voting rights and relaxed censorship. But in October 1976, a demonstration on the campus of Thammasat University in Bangkok was brutally quashed by the military, resulting in hundreds of deaths and injuries and the reinstatement of authoritarian rule. Many activists went underground to join armed communist insurgency groups hiding in the northeast.

In the 1980s and 1990s there were slow steps towards democracy, pushed along by massive, and sometimes violently repressed, street protests, but eventually civilian government was restored. Thailand's 16th constitution was enacted in October 1997 by parliamentary vote; Thailand's first charter not written under military order. During these tumultuous times, King Bhumibol Adulyadej (Rama IX, r 1946–) defined a new political role for the monarchy. Although powerless to legislate, the king came to be viewed as a paternal figure who restrained excesses in the interests of all Thais.

Economic & Political Roller Coaster

During the 1990s, Thailand was one of the so-called tiger economies, roaring ahead with one of the world's highest growth rates. But the country's unabated growth imploded in 1997, leading to a nearly three-year recession. Thailand's convalescence progressed remarkably well and it pulled an 'early exit' from the International Monetary Fund's loan package in mid-2003.

The ambitious and charismatic billionaire Thaksin Shinawatra became prime minister in 2001, promising to eliminate corruption, invest in impoverished villages and institute affordable health care. He delivered on

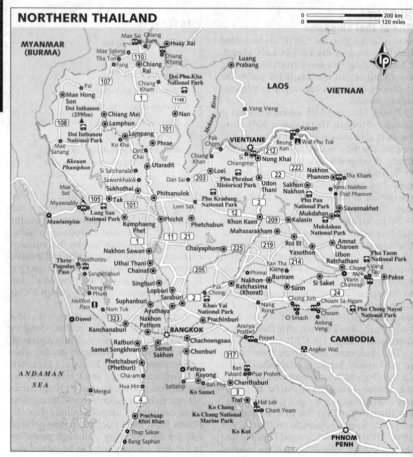

NORTHERN THAILAND

some of these promises, but also showed disdain for the press and civil liberties. His heavy-handed crackdown on the decades-old Muslim insurgency in the far south only flamed separatist and terrorist tendencies. But, thanks to his proactive response to the 2004 tsunami that killed thousands on Thailand's Andaman coast, Thaksin easily kept his job in the February 2005 election. His popularity soon plummeted due to a host of issues including a controversial tax-free US$1.9 billion profit from the sale of his telecom corporation and, in the opinion of many, disrespecting the king.

On 19 September 2006, army chief Sonthi Boonyaratglin led a bloodless military coup. Bangkok citizens were so overjoyed that they showered soldiers with flowers and food. Even go-go dancers staged an outdoor show for the men in uniform. At time of writing elections and a new constitution were due for October 2007.

PEOPLE & THE POPULATION

Thais are master chatters and will have a shopping list of questions: where are you from, are you married, do you have children? Occasionally they get more curious and want to know how much you weigh or how much money you make; these questions to a Thai are matters of public record and aren't considered impolite. They also love to dole out compliments Foreigners who can speak even the most basic Thai are lauded as linguistic geniuses. Why do some foreigners come to Thailand and never

---

NO, THEY'RE NOT TALKING ABOUT FRUIT

Faràng means guava, but it's also the word Thais use for foreigners and can be merely descriptive, mildly derogatory or openly insulting, depending on the situation. While it is almost always the former, you will graduate to the latter by being clueless or disrespectful towards the culture. Here are some tips on avoiding that:

■ Stand when the national anthem is played.

■ Don't lick stamps, which usually bear an image of the king, or your fingers. To the Thais only animals lick things.

■ Keep your feet on the floor, not on a chair, and never step over someone (or some*thing* – there might be a Buddha image in it) sitting on the ground.

■ Don't touch Thais on the head.

■ Dress modestly.

For more tips on earning the respect of locals, see p74.

---

leave? Because Thais know how to make visitors feel like superstars.

The National Psyche

Thais are laid-back, good-natured people who live by a philosophy of *sànùk* (fun), and every task is measured on the *sànùk* meter. Thai-on-Thai culture is tougher to unravel, but the guiding principles are *nâa* (face) and elder-junior hierarchy. Thais believe strongly in the concept of 'saving face', that is, avoiding confrontation and endeavouring not to embarrass themselves or other people (see the boxed text, p73). All relationships follow simple lines of social rank defined by age, wealth, status, and personal and political power. The elder of the table always picks up the tab. The junior in the workplace does the menial chores. The Western mindset is so different in this regard that it becomes something of a handicap in Thai society.

Religion and the monarchy, which is still regarded by many as divine, are the culture's sacred cows. You can turn your nose up at fish sauce or dress like a hippy, but don't insult the king and always behave respectfully in the temples. This applies to pictures of the king, including on Thai currency and stamps.

Population

About 75% of citizens are ethnic Thais, further divided by geography (north, central, south and northeast). Each group speaks its own Thai dialect and to an extent practises regional customs. Politically and economically the central Thais are dominant. People of Chinese ances-

try, many of whom have been in Thailand for generations, make up over 10% of the population. Ethnic Chinese probably enjoy better relations with the majority population here than in any other country in Southeast Asia. Other large minority groups include Vietnamese in the far east, Khmer in the southern side of the northeast and Lao spread throughout the north and east. Smaller non-Thai-speaking groups include the colourful hill tribes living in the northern mountains.

RELIGION

Country, family and daily life are all married to Theravada Buddhism (as opposed to the Mahayana schools found in East Asia and the Himalayas). Every Thai male is expected to become a monk for a short period in his life since a family earns great merit when a son 'takes robe and bowl'. Traditionally the length of time spent in a wat is three months; during the Buddhist lent *(phansǎa)*, which begins around July and coincides with the rainy season, or when an elder in the family dies.

More evident than the philosophical aspects of Buddhism is the everyday fusion with animist rituals. Monks are consulted to determine an auspicious date for a wedding or the likelihood of success for a business. Spirit houses are constructed outside buildings and homes to encourage the spirits to live independently from the family, but to remain comfortable so they bring good fortune to the site. Food, drink and furniture are all offered to the spirits to smooth daily life.

Roughly 95% of the population practises Buddhism, but there is a significant Muslim community, especially in southern Thailand.

ARTS
Music
TRADITIONAL
Classical central Thai music features an incredible array of textures and subtleties, hair-raising tempos and pastoral melodies. Among the more common instruments is the *pìi*, a woodwind instrument with a reed mouthpiece; it is heard prominently at Thai boxing matches. A bowed instrument, similar to examples played in China and Japan, is aptly called the *saw*. The *ránâat èhk*, is a bamboo-keyed percussion instrument resembling the Western xylophone, while the *khlùi* is a wooden flute. This traditional orchestra originated as an accompaniment to classical dance-drama and shadow theatre, but these days it can be heard at temple fairs and concerts.

In the north and northeast there are several popular wind instruments with multiple reed pipes, which function basically like a mouthorgan. Chief among these is the *khaen*, which originated in Laos; when played by an adept musician it sounds like a rhythmic, churning calliope organ.

MODERN
Popular Thai music has borrowed much from the West, particularly its instruments, but retains a distinct flavour. The best example of this is the rock group Carabao. Performing for more than 30 years now, Carabao has crafted an exciting fusion of Thai traditional forms with heavy metal.

Another major influence on Thai pop was a 1970s group called Caravan. They created a modern Thai folk style known as *phleng phêua chii-wít* (songs for life), which features political and environmental topics rather than the usual moonstruck love themes.

The latest pop craze is hip-hop, best epitomised by Thaitanium and Joey Boy.

Sculpture & Architecture
On an international scale, Thailand has probably distinguished itself more in traditional religious sculpture than in any other art form. Thailand's most famous sculptural output has been its bronze Buddha images, coveted the world over for their originality and grace.

Architecture, however, is considered th highest art form in traditional Thai societ Ancient Thai homes consist of a simple tea structure raised on stilts. The space under neath also serves as the living room, kitche garage and barn. Rooflines in Thailand a steeply pitched and often decorated at th corners or along the gables with motifs relate to the naga (mythical sea serpent).

Temple architecture symbolises element of the religion. A steeply pitched roof syster tiled in green, gold and red represents th Buddha (the Teacher), the Dhamma (Dharm in Sanskrit; the Teaching) and the Sangha (th fellowship of followers of the Teaching).

Theatre & Dance
Traditional Thai theatre consists of six dra matic forms: *khôhn*, formal masked dance drama depicting scenes from the Ramakia (the Thai version of India's Ramayana) an originally performed only for the royal court *lákhon*, a general term covering several type of dance-dramas (usually for nonroyal oc casions), as well as Western theatre; *lí-keh* a partly improvised, often bawdy folk pla featuring dancing, comedy, melodrama an music; *mánohraa*, the southern-Thai equiva lent of *lí-keh*, but based on a 2000-year-ol Indian story; *nang*, or shadow plays, limite to southern Thailand; and *lákhon lék* or *hù lŭang* puppet theatre.

ENVIRONMENT
About as large as France, Thailand stretche from dense mountain jungles in the north through flat central plains to southern tropi cal rainforests. Covering most of the country monsoon forests are filled with a sparse can opy of deciduous trees that shed their leave during the dry season to conserve water.

Wildlife
Thailand is particularly rich in bird life, with over 1000 recorded resident and migrating species; approximately 10% of the world' total. Thailand's most revered indigenou mammal, the elephant, is integral to the country's culture; it symbolises wisdom, strength and good fortune. Sadly, elephants, both wild and domesticated, are now endangered, having lost most of their habitat and their traditional role in society. No longer employable in the timber industry, the domesticated elephant and its mahout often wander through

major cities reduced to beggars and sideshows. **Friends of the Asian Elephant** (☎ 0 2945 7124; www.elephant.or.th) and the National Elephant Institute (p149) work to protect them.

Environmental Issues

Like all countries with high population density, there is enormous pressure on Thailand's ecosystems: 50 years ago about 70% of the countryside was forest, it's now 28%. In response to environmental degradation, the Thai government has created a large number of protected areas since the 1970s. Following devastating floods, exacerbated by soil erosion, logging was banned in 1989. Air and water pollution are problems in urban areas, and though things are improving, Bangkok is one of the world's most polluted cities.

Though Thailand has a better record than most of its neighbours at protecting endangered species, corruption hinders the efforts. Roughly 250 animal and plant species in Thailand are on the International Union for Conservation of Nature list of endangered or vulnerable species, with tigers being one of the most threatened because poachers continue to kill the cats for the lucrative Chinese pharmaceutical market.

BANGKOK

pop 7.5 million

Ladies and gentlemen, fasten your seatbelts. You are now entering Bangkok, a city always on the move. Ancient temples in the shadow of space-age shopping malls, soaring skyscrapers towering over tumbledown hovels, ubercool cafés and restaurants surrounded by simple street stalls, Bangkok is the nexus

of Thailand's past, present and future, and a superb subject for any urban connoisseur. In fact, nowhere else is Thailand's *khwaam pen thai* ('Thai-ness') more apparent than when watching people continue their villagelike lives in front of the 21st-century façade

Following the fall of Ayuthaya in 1767, the capital was briefly brought to Thonburi before moving across the river in 1782. But the name Bangkok, baptised by foreigners, actually refers to a small village within the larger beast. The Thais call their capital Krung Thep, or City of Angels, a much shortened version of the very official tongue-twister: *Krungthep mahanakhon amonratanakosin mahintara ayuthaya mahadilok popnopparat ratchathani burirom udomratchaniwet mahasathan amonpiman avatansathit sakkathattiya witsanukamprasit.*

ORIENTATION

Mae Nam Chao Phraya (the Chao Phraya River) divides Bangkok from the older city of Thonburi. Bangkok can be further divided into east and west by the main railway line feeding Hualamphong station. The older part of the city, crowded with historical temples, bustling Chinatown and the popular travellers' centre of Banglamphu (home of the famous Khao San Rd) is sandwiched between the western side of the tracks and the river. East of the railway is the new city, devoted to commerce and its attendant skyscrapers and shopping centres, particularly the Siam Sq, Sukhumvit and Silom districts.

This simple sketch of Bangkok's layout does an injustice to the chaos that the city has acquired through years of unplanned and rapacious development. A good map, such as Lonely Planet's *Bangkok City Map*, will be a big help.

GETTING INTO TOWN

The **Airport Express bus** (150B) runs four convenient routes to/from central Bangkok between 5am and midnight. Typical metered taxi fares from the airport are 200B to 250B to Th Sukhumvit, 250B to 300B to Th Khao San and 500B to Mo Chit bus terminal. Toll charges (paid by the passenger) vary between 20B to 60B. A 50B surcharge, payable to the driver, is added to all fares departing from the airport.

Public buses (around 35B) stop and drop at the public transportation centre, 3km from the terminal via free shuttle. If you're going to Siam Sq, Sukhumvit or Silom, use the On Nut Skytrain station bus (No 552). For Banglamphu, the Victory Monument bus (No 551) will get you pretty close. You can also get buses direct to Aranya Prathet (187B) and Nong Khai (454B) on the Cambodian and Laos borders respectively.

The Airport Train Link to central Bangkok could open by 2008.

INFORMATION

ATMs, banks, currency-exchange kiosks and internet cafés (charging around 30B on Th Khao San) are widespread.

Emergency

Tourist police (☎ 1155; ☿ 24hr) English-speaking officers.

Internet Resources

Bangkok Recorder (www.bangkokrecorder.com) Good nightlife site.

Khao San Road (www.khaosanroad.com) News, reviews and profiles of Bangkok's famous tourist ghetto.

Real Thai (www.realthai.blogspot.com) Local Bangkok foodie takes a bite out of the Big Mango.

Medical Services

The following hospitals offer 24-hour emergency service and English-speaking staff. Prices are high, but so is the quality. Use these numbers to call an ambulance.

BNH (Map pp118-19; ☎ 0 2632 0550; 9 Th Convent)

Bumrungrad Hospital (Map pp118-19; ☎ 0 2667 1000; 33 Soi 3, Th Sukhumvit)

Post

Main post office (Map pp118-19; Th Charoen Krung; ☿ 8am-8pm Mon-Fri, 8am-1pm Sat & Sun)

Tourist Information

Bangkok Tourism Division (Map p121; ☎ 0 2225 7612; www.bangkoktourist.com; 17/1 Th Phra Athit; ☿ 9am-7pm)

TAT main office (Map pp118-19; ☎ 0 2250 5500; ground fl, 1600 Th Petchaburi; ☿ 8.30am-4.30pm)

Travel Agencies

Not all Bangkok travel agencies are trustworthy, especially for cheap airline tickets. Try:

STA Travel (Map pp118-19; ☎ 0 2236 0262; www.sta travel.com; 14th fl, Wall Street Tower, 33/70 Th Surawong)

Vieng Travel (Map p121; ☎ 0 2280 3537; www .viengtravel.com; Trang Hotel, 99/8 Th Wisut Kasat)

DANGERS & ANNOYANCES

Bangkok's most heavily touristed areas (Wat Phra Kaew in particular) are favourite hunting grounds for con artists. Smartly dressed and slick talking (not all are Thai), their usual spiel is that the attraction you want to visit is closed for the day. This is the bait for the infamous gem scam (see boxed text, opposite) or perhaps the resurfaced card game scams – you won't win either so don't play. Also annoying are the túk-túk drivers who hope to make a commission by dragging you to a local silk or jewellery shop, even though you've requested an entirely different destination. Turn down all offers of 'free' or too-cheap-to-be-real sightseeing and shopping deals.

SIGHTS
Ko Ratanakosin Area

Most of Bangkok's must-sees reside in compact, walkable Ko Ratanakosin, the former royal district. Wat Arun is just a short ferry ride across the river in Thonburi.

Wat Phra Kaew (Map pp118-19; ☎ 0 2224 1833; admission 250B; ☿ 8.30am-3.30pm), also known as the Temple of the Emerald Buddha, is an architectural wonder of gleaming gilded stupas, mosaic-encrusted pillars and rich marble pediments. The highly stylised ornamentation is a shrine to the revered Emerald Buddha, which is housed in the main chapel. Actually made of jasper, the 75cm-tall Buddha image endured an epic journey from northern Thailand, where it was hidden inside a layer of stucco, to its

---

THÀNON & SOI

Throughout this book, *thànon* (meaning 'street') is abbreviated as 'Th'. A *soi* is a small street that runs off a larger street. The address of a site located on a *soi* will be written as 33 Soi 3, Th Sukhumvit, meaning off Th Sukhumvit on Soi 3.

Building numbers can be confounding; the string of numbers divided by slashes and dashes (eg 48/3-5 Soi 1, Th Sukhumvit) indicate lot disbursements rather than sequential geography. The number before the slash refers to the original lot number; the numbers following the slash indicate buildings (or entrances to buildings) constructed within that lot. The preslash numbers appear in the order in which they were added to city plans, while the postslash numbers are arbitrarily assigned by developers.

Some Bangkok *soi* have become so large that they can be referred to both as *thànon* and *soi* (eg Soi Sarasin/Th Sarasin and Soi Asoke/Th Asoke). Smaller than a *soi* is a *trok* (sometimes spelt *tràwk*, meaning alleyway).

THE GEM SCAM

If anyone offers you unsolicited advice about a gem store, you can be sure that you will soon find there is a 'sale' or some such nonsense there. They, or another partner, might also explain how you can sell bulk quantities of gems in your country. When you get home you'll find that they are worth far less than you paid, and might not even be real gems.

---

present home. In between it was seized by Lao forces and carried off to Luang Prabang and Vientiane, where it was later recaptured by the Thais. The admission fee includes entrance to Dusit Palace Park (right).

Within the same grounds is the **Grand Palace**, the former royal residence now used only for certain ceremonial occasions; the king's current residence is Chitlada Palace (closed to the public) in the northern part of the city.

Just northeast of Wat Phra Kaew the **Lak Meuang** (City Pillar; Map pp118-19; Th Ratchadamnoen Nai; admission free; 🕙 8.30am-5.30pm), home of Bangkok's city spirit, is generally alive with the spectacle of devotion, including traditional dancers.

Wat Pho (Map pp118-19; Th Sanamchai; admission 50B; 🕙 8am-5pm) sweeps the awards for superlatives: it's the oldest and largest temple in Bangkok, dating from the 16th century. It houses Thailand's largest reclining Buddha and it has the biggest collection of Buddha images in the country. The *big* attraction is the stunning reclining Buddha, 46m long and 15m high. The figure is modelled out of plaster around a brick core and is finished in gold leaf. The affiliated **Wat Pho Thai Traditional Massage School** (Map pp118-19; ☎ 0 2221 3686; www.watpomassage.com Soi Penphat, Th Sanamchai) is the most famous centre of its kind.

The **National Museum** (Map p121; ☎ 0 2224 1402; Th Na Phra That 1; admission 40B; 🕙 9am-3.30pm Wed-Sun), reportedly the largest in Southeast Asia, provides an overview of Thai art and culture, though labelling isn't always illuminating.

Wat Arun (Map pp118-19; admission 20B; 🕙 9am-5pm) is a striking temple named after the Indian god of dawn, Aruna. It looms large on Mae Nam Chao Phraya's west bank, looking as if it were carved from granite; a closer inspection reveals a mosaic made of broken porcelain covering the imposing 82m Khmer-style *praang*

(tower). These broken ceramics are discarded ballast from Chinese merchant ships.

Chinatown

Gleaming gold shops, towering neon signs and shopfronts spilling out on to the sidewalk – welcome to Chinatown, the epicentre of Bangkok's bustling commercial cult. The neighbourhood's energy is at once exhilarating and exhausting; and it's fun to explore at night when it is lit up like a Christmas tree. Slicing through the centre of the district, the famous **Sampeng Lane** (Map pp118-19; Soi Wanit) is jam-packed with the useful and the useless, all at bargain prices. On the corner of Th Yaowarat and Th Chakrawat is **Thieves Market** (Nakhon Kasem; Map pp118-19; cnr Th Yaowarat & Th Chakrawat), so named for the 'hot' items previously sold here.

On the western edge of Chinatown is **Phahurat**, a small Indian district. Th Chakraphet is chock-a-block with Indian restaurants and shops selling Indian sweets.

Wat Traimit (Map pp118-19; Th Yaowarat; admission 20B; 🕙 9am-5pm) shelters a 3m-tall, 5.5-tonne, solid-gold Buddha image that was 'discovered' when it was being moved in the 1960s and the stucco exterior hiding it, presumably during one of Burma's many invasions, cracked. The labyrinthine passageways of **Wat Mangkon Kamalawat** (Neng Noi Yee; Map pp118-19; Th Charoen Krung; 🕙 9am-6pm), locus of Vegetarian Festival activities (see p174), hold Buddhist, Taoist and Confucian shrines.

Other Attractions

Elegant **Dusit Palace Park** (Map pp118-19; ☎ 0 2628 6300; admission 100B; free with Grand Palace ticket; 🕙 9.30am-4pm) is a relaxing destination with multiple museums. The must-see is the 1868 **Vimanmek Teak Mansion** (Map pp118–19), reputedly the world's largest golden teakwood building. In the early 20th century Rama V lived in this graceful 81-room mansion and today it contains a treasure-trove of early Ratanakosin art objects and antiques. Compulsory English-language tours last an hour. Other exhibits in the park include handicraft displays in **Abhisek Dusit Throne Hall** (Map pp118–19) and the **Royal Elephant Museum** (Map pp118–19), which discusses but doesn't house pachyderms. Traditional Thai dances take place at 10.30am and 2pm.

(Continued on page 122)

To Ayuthaya (66km)

Don Muang Airport

BANG KHEN

Khlong Bang Luang

Th Ramintra

Ramindra Expressway

Th Phahonyothin

Th Ratchadaphisek

Th Lat Phrao

Phahonyothin (S)

Chatuchak Park (S)

Mo Chit (S)

Ratchadaphisek (S)

Chatuchak Park (S)

Bang Sue

Kamphoeng Pet. S

Don Muang

Laksi

Viphavadi Rangsit Hwy

Bangkhen

Th Chaeng Wattana

Th Prachachuen

Khlong Bang Talat

Th Ngam Wong Wan

Expressway (2nd Stage)

Scagraga Rd

Th Dechatungkha

PAK KRET

Mae Nam Chao Phraya

Ko Kret

Th Tivanon

NONTHABURI

BANG SEU

BANG SON

Khlong Om

Khlong Bang Kruai

BANG KRUAY

Khlong Maha Sawat

INFORMATION	(pp114–22)
Chinese Embassy..............1 D5	
Lao Embassy...................2 E5	
SIGHTS & ACTIVITIES	(pp114–22)
Baan Dvara Pratep............3 B1	
Manohra Cruises..............4 B7	
World Fellowship of Buddhists...5 D6	
EATING 🍴	(pp124–6)
Vientiane Kitchen.............6 D6	
ENTERTAINMENT 🎭	(pp124–6)
RCA............................7 E5	
SHOPPING 🛍	(p127)
Chatuchak Weekend Market.....8 D4	
TRANSPORT 🚍	
Eastern Bus Terminal..........9 E6	
Northern & Northeastern Bus Terminal........10 D4	
Southern Bus Terminal........11 B5	

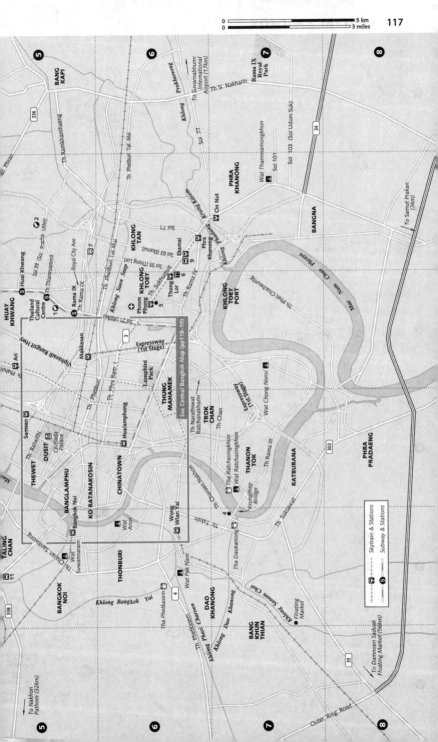

0 _____ 5 km
0 _____ 3 miles

5

BANG
KAPI

336

Th Phra

Th Ramkhamhaeng

To Suvarnabhumi
International
Airport (17km)

Th Phetburi Tat Mai

Prakhanong

6

Khlong

Soi 77

Th Si Nakharin

Rama IX
Royal
Park

7

34

To Samut Prakan
(3km)

8

HUAY
KHWANG

Thailand
Cultural
Centre

Soi 39 (Soc Prachr Uthit)

Royal City Ave

Th Thiamruammit

(S) Huai Khwang

(S) Rama IX
Th Rama IX

Th Phetburi Tat Mai

Th Phetburi

Khlong Saen Saep

Th Phra Ram I

Makkasan

Th Asoke Soi 21

1

(S)

3

Expressway
(1st Stage) (pp118-19)

See Central Bangkok Map (pp118-19)

Vibhavadi Rangsit Hwy

Ari

Th Phaho

Th Phahon

Samsen

THEWET

DUSIT

Chitlada
Palace

Th Ratwithi

Th Phayathai

Th Phra Ram I

Lumphini
Park

Hualamphong

THUNG
MAHAMEK

Th Narathiwat
Ratchanakharin

TROK
CHAN

Th Chan

KLONG
TAN

Soi 55 (Thong Lor)

Soi 63 (Ekamai)

Ekamai

9

Phra
Khanong

Th Sukhumvit

Th Sukhumvit

Soi 71

On Nut

PHRA
KHANONG

Wat Thammamongkhon

Soi 101

Soi 103 (Soi Udom Suk)

Th Arun Amarin

KLONG
TOEY

Phrom
Phong

6

Thong
Lor

5

7

KLONG
TOEY

KLONG
TOEY
PORT

Nam Chao Phraya

Th Phet Chaloeng

BANGNA

PHRA
KHANONG

BANGLAMPHU

Bangkok Noi

KO RATANAKOSIN

CHINATOWN

Wat
Arun

Wong
Wian Yai

Th Chakraphet

Th Charoen Nakhon

Th Chan

Th Narathiwat
Ratchanakharin

Expressway
(1st Stage)

Wat Chong Nonsi

Tha Ratchasingkhon

Wat Ratchasingkhon

THANON
TOK

Th Rama III

Krungthep
Bridge

Th Taksin

RATBURANA

Th Suksawat

303

Nam Chao Phraya

PHRA
PRADAENG

TALING
CHAN

11

Th Chaen Santiphap

Wat
Suwannaram

THONBURI

BANGKOK
NOI

338

Th Phetkasem

Khlong Bangkok Yai

Tha Phetkasem

Wat Pak Nam

Tha Daokanong

DAO
KHANONG

Khlong Dao Khanong

Khlong Phasi Charoen

BANG
KHUN
THIAN

Khlong Sanam Chai

Floating
Market

35

To Nakhon
Pathom (32km)

5

To Nakhon
Pathom

6

To Damnoen Saduak
Floating Market (5ifkm)

7

Outer-Ring-Road

8

Skytrain & Stations

(S) Subway & Stations

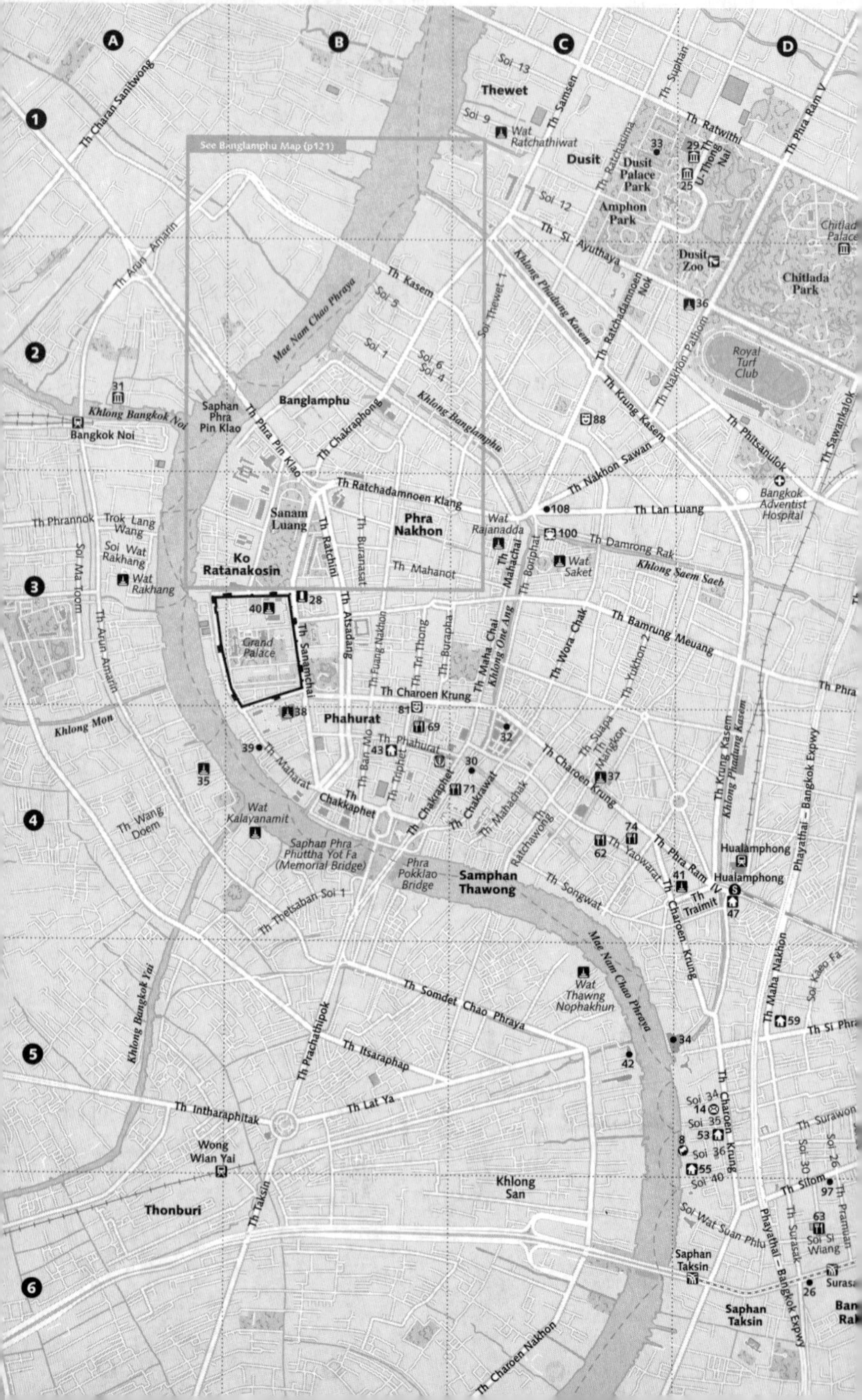

A B C D

1

Thewet
Soi 13
Soi 9
Wat Ratchathiwat

Dusit
Th Ratwithi
33 29
25
Dusit Palace Park
Amphon Park
Th Si Ayuthaya

Th Chaian Santiwong
Th Arun Amarin

Chitlad Palace

Dusit Zoo

Chitlada Park

Th Sawankalok
Th Phitsanulok

2
31
Khlong Bangkok Noi
Bangkok Noi
Th Kasem
Soi 5
Soi 1
Soi 6
Soi 4
Khlong Banglamphu
36

Banglamphu
Th Chakraphong

Saphan Phra Pin Klao
Th Phra Pin Klao

Th Nakhon Sawan
Th Krung Kasem

Royal Turf Club

Bangkok Adventist Hospital

88

Th Phitsanulok

3
Th Phrannok
Trok Lang Wang
Soi Wat Rakhang
Wat Rakhang
Soi Ma Toom

Ko Ratanakosin
Sanam Luang
Th Ratchini
Th Buranasat

Phra Nakhon
Wat Rajanadda
Th Mahanot
Wat Saket

40 28
Grand Palace
Th Sanamchai

108
100
Th Lan Luang
Th Damrong Rak
Khlong Saem Saeb
Th Bamrung Meuang
Th Phra

Th Arun Amarin

4
35
39
Khlong Mon
Th Wang Doem

38
Phahurat
81
43 69
30
71
32
37
74
62

Wat Kalayanamit
Th Maharat
Th Chakkaphet
Saphan Phra Phuttha Yot Fa (Memorial Bridge)
Phra Pokklao Bridge
Th Charoen Krung
Th Charoen Krung
Th Phra Ram

Samphan Thawong
Th Songwat

Hualamphong
41
H
47

5
Khlong Bangkok Yai
Th Prachathipok
Th Itsaraphap
Th Somdet Chao Phraya
Wat Thawng Nophakhun
42
34
59
Th Si Phra

Th Intharaphitak
Th Lat Ya

Wong Wian Yai
Th Taksin

Thonburi
Khlong San

Soi 34
14
Soi 36
53
8
55
Soi 40
Soi 38
97
63
Soi Si Wiang
26
Surasa

Th Charoen Krung
Th Maha Nakhon
Th Silom
Th Surawon

6
Saphan Taksin
Saphan Taksin
Th Charoen Nakhon
Saphan Rat
Ban Rak

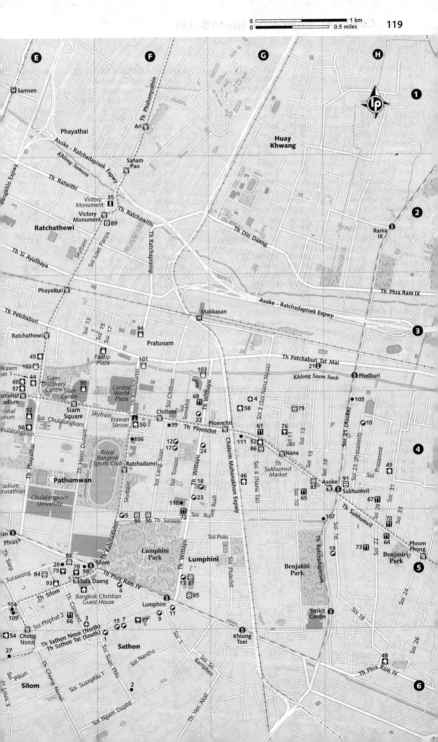

0   1 km
0   0.5 miles

0 _____ 200 m
0 _____ 0.1 mile

INFORMATION
Bangkok Tourist Division...................1 A4
Vieng Travel.....................................2 D3

SIGHTS & ACTIVITIES   (pp114–2)
Jitti's Gym Thai Boxing & Homestay...3 B5
May Kaidee.................................(see 15)
National Museum............................4 A5
Wat Mahathat.................................5 A6

SLEEPING   (pp122–4)
Baan Chantra...................................6 C3
Chai's House....................................7 B4
Donna Guesthouse...........................8 C5
New Siam Guesthouse.......................9 B4
New World Lodge Hotel....................10 C4
Sri Ayuttaya Guest House.................11 D1
Villa Guest House............................12 C3

EATING   (pp124–6)
Arawy..13 D6
Hemlock...14 B4
May Kaidee.....................................15 C5
Roti-Mataba....................................16 B3
Shoshana..17 B4
Ton Pho..18 B4

DRINKING   (p126)
Baghdad Café..................................19 C4
Center Khao San..............................20 C5
Hippie de Bar..................................21 B5

SHOPPING   (p127)
Th Khao San Market.........................22 C5

BANGKOK &
NORTHERN THAILAND

(Continued from page 115)

Wat Benchamabophit (Marble Temple; Map pp118-19; Th Si Ayutthaya; admission 20B; ⏰ 8am-5.30pm), built under Rama V in 1899, is made of white Carrara marble and is a stunning example of modern temple architecture. The real treasure here is a rear courtyard containing a multitude of Buddha images from all periods of Thai Buddhist art.

Jim Thompson House (Map pp118-19; ☎ 0 2216 7368; www.jimthompsonhouse.com; Soi Kasem San 2, Th Phra Ram I; admission 100B; ⏰ 9am-5pm) is the beautiful house of the American entrepreneur Jim Thompson, who successfully promoted Thai silk to Western markets. Atmospherically sited on a small *khlong* (canal), his remarkable house was built from salvaged components of traditional Thai houses. His collection of Thai art and furnishings is equally superb. Compulsory tours in English and French run every 10 minutes.

ACTIVITIES
Spas & Massage
Depending on the neighbourhood, prices for massages tend to stay fixed: around 250B for a foot massage and around 500B for a body massage.

Wat Pho (Map pp118-19; ☎ 0 2221 3686; Th Sanamchai; ⏰ 8am-5pm) runs the nation's premier massage school (p115) and has air-con service there, but the massage pavilions inside the temple itself provide a greater sense of tradition.

Spas are becoming increasingly popular in Thailand, and while **Health Land** (Map pp118-19; ☎ 0 2637 8883; www.healthlandspa.com; 120 Th Sathon Neua; treatments from 750B) is more down-to-earth than most, the pamper factor still soars.

COURSES
Cooking
Run out of a private home, **Silom Thai Cooking School** (Map pp118-19; ☎ 0 4726 5669; 31/11 Soi 13, Th Silom; 1000B) offers an introduction to home-cooking and ordinary Thai life.

May Kaidee (Map p121; ☎ 0 9137 3173; off Soi Damnoen Klang Neua; www.maykaidee.com; 1000B) teaches all-vegetarian cooking. There is a restaurant (p125) here too.

Blue Elephant Thai Cooking School (Map pp118-19; ☎ 0 2673 9353; www.blueelephant.com; Thai Chine Bldg, 233 Th Sathon Tai; 3300B) is considered Bangkok's most gourmet cooking school.

DRESS FOR THE OCCASION
Thai temples are sacred places and visitors should dress and behave appropriately. Wear shirts with sleeves, long pants or skirts past the knees, and closed-toed shoes. Sarongs and baggy pants are available on loan at the entry area for Wat Phra Kaew. Shoes should be removed before entering buildings. When sitting in front of a Buddha image, tuck your feet behind you to avoid the great offence of pointing your feet towards a revered figure.

Meditation
World Fellowship of Buddhists (Map pp116-17; ☎ 0 2661 1284; www.wfb-hq.org; Soi 24, Th Sukhumvit) hosts meditation classes on the first Sunday of every month and can link you up with English-speaking teachers situated across Thailand.

Wat Mahathat (Map p121; ☎ 0 2222 6011) has three daily meditation sessions (7am, 1pm and 6pm) and the International Buddhist Meditation Centre here hosts twice-monthly lectures.

Baan Dvara Prateep (Map pp116-17; ☎ 0 1845 5445; www.baandvaraprateep.com; 53/3 Mu 5, Ko Kret) is more relaxed than the strict temple environment, with the focus on relieving stress.

Muay Thai (Thai Boxing)
Sweating distance from Th Khao San, **Jitti's Gym Thai Boxing & Homestay** (Map p121; ☎ 0 2282 3551; www.jittigym.com; 13 Soi Krasab, Th Chakraphong; training from 300B) specialises in training foreign students of both genders.

FESTIVALS & EVENTS
Bangkok International Film Festival (www.bangkok film.org) Emphasises Asian cinema. Held mid-January.
Royal Ploughing Ceremony The King commences rice-planting season with a royal-religious ceremony at Sanam Luang in early May.

SLEEPING
The following districts offer widely different experiences. It can take quite a long time to get around the city, so choosing your location is as important as choosing your hotel.

Banglamphu & Thewet
Banglamphu, the neighbourhood that includes the backpacker street of Th Khao San, is a well-padded landing zone for jet-lagged travellers. It's getting quite gentrified these days.

At the bottom end, rooms (around 180B) are quite small with thin walls and shared bathrooms. At this price, just show up and start hunting as most cheapies don't take reservations. In the high season (November to February), it's wise to take the first bed you can find. As a rule, you can arrive anytime at night and find a place to crash.

Thewet, the leafy district north of Banglamphu near the National Library, is another travellers' enclave, especially for families and the over-30 crowd.

Chai's House (Map p121; ☎ 0 2281 4901; 49/4-8 Soi Rongmai; s/d 165/275B) This family-run guesthouse, all with shared bathrooms, is a quiet and secure spot that enforces a 1am curfew.

ourpick Villa Guest House (Map p121; ☎ 0 2281 7009; 230 Soi 1, Th Samsen; r 250-500B) This old teak house, tucked away down a small alley, is wrapped in a leafy garden. The atmospheric rooms are furnished in period pieces and antiques, but it's shared bathrooms all the way.

Sri Ayuttaya Guest House (Map p121; ☎ 0 2282 5942; Soi Thewet, Th Si Ayuthaya; d 350-500B; ❄) Sri Ayuttaya has romantic rooms with hardwood floors, exposed brick and other stylish touches.

New World Lodge Hotel (Map p121; ☎ 0 2281 5596; www.newworldlodge.com; Soi 2, Th Samsen; r from 1300B; ❄) New World is large but unassuming. Rooms on the 4th or 5th floors boast terraces overlooking Khlong Banglamphu.

ourpick Baan Chantra (Map p121; ☎ 0 2628 6988; www.baanchantra.com; 120 Th Samsen; d from 2200B; ❄) Unlike many other boutique hotels, Baan Chantra prefers comfortable and roomy over fashionable and pinched. Many of the house's original teak details remain.

Also recommended:

Donna Guesthouse (Map p121; ☎ 0 2281 9374; off Soi Damnoen Klang, Th Ratchadamnoen Klang; d 250-350B; ❄) Clean and quiet with big twin beds. Shared bathrooms.

New Siam Guesthouse (Map p121; ☎ 0 2282 4554; www.newsiam.net; 21 Soi Chana Songkhram, Th Phra Athit; s 290B, d 320-490B; ❄ ❄) Very clean spot with self-accessible lockers. Some facilities are shared.

Chinatown

A stay in this chaotic neighbourhood offers a distinctly anonymous experience from the usual walking-ATM treatment you'll get elsewhere. The downside is that traffic is horrendous.

TT Guest House (Map pp118-19; ☎ 0 2236 2946; 516-518 Soi Sawang, Th Maha Nakhon; r 250-280B) In a

low-key neighbourhood just beyond Chinatown, this family-run guesthouse boasts a shaded courtyard. The shared bathrooms are very clean.

238 Guesthouse (Map pp118-19; ☎ 0 2623 9287; 238 Th Phahurat; r 400-600B; ❄) This converted shophouse within walking distance of Ko Ratanakosin has generous rooms with all the basics.

Bangkok Centre Hotel (Map pp118-19; ☎ 0 2238 4980; www.bangkokcentrehotel.com; 328 Th Phra Ram IV; r from 1400B; ❄ 💻 ❄) You can see your train pull into the station from this hotel tower. It has all the usual midrange amenities.

Siam Square & Pratunam

Siam Sq lies conveniently along both Skytrain lines. A low-key, DIY traveller community bunks down on Soi Kasem San 1.

Pranee Building (Map pp118-19; ☎ 0 2216 3181; 931/12 Soi Kasem San 1; r 450B; ❄) One of the cheapest options on the street, Pranee isn't fancy but the rooms are large with air-con and hot water; the bathrooms are a tad decrepit.

Wendy House (Map pp118-19; ☎ 0 2216 2436; Soi Kasem San 1; d incl breakfast from 1000B; ❄) As professional as they come with genuine Thai-style concern for the guests. Rooms are on the small side though.

Asia Hotel (Map pp118-19; ☎ 0 2215 0808; www.asiahotel.co.th; 296 Th Phayathai; d from 2900B; ❄ ❄) A favourite of ageing backpackers who've moved beyond guesthouses, this huge place has a good location and large rooms. A walkway from the Skytrain is another plus.

Grand Hyatt Erawan (Map pp118-19; ☎ 0 2254 1234; www.bangkok.hyatt.com; Th Ratchadamri; r from US$150; ❄ ❄) Within striking distance of the top shopping malls, the Erawan provides one of Bangkok's most prestigious postcommerce slumbers.

Also recommended:

A-One Inn (Map pp118-19; ☎ 0 2215 3029; www.aoneinn.com; 25/13-15 Soi Kasem San 1; d from 600B; ❄) Simple, but good value.

Pathumwan Princess (Map pp118-19; ☎ 0 2216 3700; www.pprincess.com; 444 Th Payathai; r from 3700B; ❄ ❄) Family favourite connected to MBK shopping centre and Skytrain.

Silom

The city's financial district along Th Silom is not the most charming area of town, but it is conveniently located for nightspots and the Skytrain.

New Road Guesthouse (Map pp118-19; ☎ 0 2237 1094; 1216/1 Th Charoen Krung; d 600-700B; ✖) This friendly cheapie near the river is sandwiched between luxe hotels.

Niagara Hotel (Map pp118-19; ☎ 0 2233 5783; 26 Soi 9/Suksavitthaya, Th Silom; d 700B; ✖) From the outside Niagara looks like just another crummy no-tell motel, but inside is one of the best bargains in Silom. The rooms are immaculate.

our pick La Résidence Hotel (Map pp118-19; ☎ 0 2233 3301; 173/8-9 Th Surawong; d 1200-1500B, ste 2700B; ✖) La Résidence is a boutique inn with playfully and individually decorated rooms. A standard room is very small and fittingly decorated like a child's bedroom. The next size up is more mature and voluptuous.

Oriental Hotel (Map pp118-19; ☎ 0 2659 9000; www .mandarinoriental.com; 48 Soi Oriental/Soi 38, Th Charoen Krung; d US$300; ✖ ☒) While the rest of the city jumps overboard for the new Zen trend, the classic Oriental stays rooted in its Victorian past. It is consistently rated as one of the best hotels in the world and prides itself on personalised service.

Sukhumvit

Th Sukhumvit is the commercial corridor of the newest part of Bangkok; the western side is a busy sex tourist sector. If you're not amused by this, you may want to stay elsewhere, though the sex scene is far from ubiquitous and there are many other charms.

Atlanta (Map pp118-19; ☎ 0 2252 1650; 78 Soi 2, Th Sukhumvit; d from 400B; ✖ ☒) You half expect Humphrey Bogart to trot down the stairs in this perfectly preserved, midcentury lobby. The rooms are skeletal in comparison, but good for the price. Sex tourists are forbidden.

Majestic Suites (Map pp118-19; ☎ 0 2656 8220; www .majesticsuites.com; 110-110/1 Th Sukhumvit; s/d 1160/1500B; ✖) Small and friendly, the hermetically sealed rooms deliver privacy and quiet, even with screaming Sukhumvit right outside. It's positioned between Soi 4 and Soi 6.

Eugenia (Map pp118-19; ☎ 0 2259 9011; www.theeu genia.com; Soi 31, Th Sukhumvit; r from 5800B; ✖ ☒) Colonial manor houses aren't an indigenous legacy in Thailand but this anachronistic 12-guestroom hotel indulges in the anomaly.

Also recommended:

Soi 1 Guesthouse (Map pp118-19; ☎ 0 2655 0604; www.soi1guesthouse.com; 220/7 Soi 1, Th Sukhumvit; dm 250-350B; ✖ ▢) Extraordinarily clean and comfy dorms plus wonderful owners.

Davis (Map pp118-19; ☎ 0 2260 8000; www.davis bangkok.net; Soi 24, Th Sukhumvit; d from 3000B; ✖ ☒) Boutique hotel with stunning, Asian-themed rooms.

EATING

No matter where you go in Bangkok, food is always there. There is so much variety just on the street that you can go days without stepping inside a restaurant. Enacting the modern equivalent of hunter-gatherers, many visitors skip from stall to stall sampling *kŭaytĭaw* (noodles), plates of *râat khâo* (rice and curry) or *mùat phàt* (stir-fries) for 25B to 40B.

When the need comes for a restaurant, Bangkok's best are the décorless mom-and-pop shops that concentrate only on the food; most of these restaurants hover around 60B to 100B for a main dish. Higher prices always bring more ambience, and dining in Bangkok's fashionable or touristy restaurants is sometimes more for show than for flavour. All the great international cuisines, from Mexican to Japanese are available too.

Banglamphu & Thewet

This area near the river is one of the best for cheap Thai eats and because of the traveller presence, Western and vegetarian food are well represented. Prices are lower and the quality higher as you move away from Th Khao San.

Arawy (Alloy; Map p121; 152 Th Din So; mains 35B; ☺ breakfast & lunch) This matron of meatless is one of the best Thai vegetarian restaurants in the city.

our pick Ton Pho (Map p121; ☎ 0 2280 0452; Th Phra Athit; mains 80-100B; ☺ lunch & dinner) This converted floating dock does all the staples with the expertise of a Thai grandmother. The lack of décor inversely matches the strength of the food.

Hemlock (Map p121; ☎ 0 2282 7507; 56 Th Phra Athit; mains 80-200B; ☺ dinner) Living-room-sized restaurants line Th Phra Athit and form a social gathering point for Banglamphu's bohemians. This cosy gem has an eclectic range with many items that don't usually pop up on menus.

Shoshana (Map p121; off Th Chakraphong; mains 100-150B; ☺ lunch & dinner) One of Khao San's longest-running Israeli restaurants, tucked away in an unnamed, almost secret alley beside the petrol station, Shoshana serves gut-filling falafel-and-hummus plates.

Also recommended:

May Kaidee (Map p121; ☎ 0 9137 3173; off Soi Damnoen Klang Neua; mains 50B; ⏲ lunch & dinner) The most popular, but not necessarily the best, of several veggie shops in this area. Cooking classes are also offered (see p122).

Roti-Mataba (Map p121; Th Phra Athit; mains 60-80B; ⏲ lunch & dinner Tue-Sun) This Bangkok legend does a whirlwind business of *kaeng mátsàmàn* (Thai Muslim curry).

Chinatown

When you mention Chinatown, Bangkokians begin dreaming of noodles, usually prepared by street vendors lining Th Yaowarat, near Trok Itsaranuphap (Soi 16), after dark. Of course, the dining is good in the Indian district of Phahurat too.

Old Siam Plaza (Map pp118-19; ground fl, Th Triphet; mains 50-100B; ⏲ lunch) The Thai version of Willy Wonka's factory turns seemingly savoury ingredients like beans and rice into syrupy sweet desserts, like *lûuk chúp* (miniature fruits made of beans) and *tàkôh* (coconut pudding in banana leaves), right before your eyes.

Th Phadungdao Seafood Stalls (Map pp118-19; Th Yaowarat; mains 160-300B; ⏲ dinner) After sunset, this frenetic street sprouts outdoor barbecues, iced seafood trays and sidewalk seating.

Also recommended:

Bà-mìi Hong Kong (Map pp118-19; Th Yaowarat; mains 50B; ⏲ dinner) There is a veritable noodle adventure behind the big red sign.

Royal India (Map pp118-19; ☎ 0 2221 6565; 392/1 Th Chakraphet; mains under 100B; ⏲ lunch & dinner) North Indian cuisine heavily influenced by Persian flavours.

Siam Square & Pratunam

Locals, not wandering *faràng* (Westerners), are the primary target of the food vendors on Soi Kasem San 1, so you know you are getting some quality grub. It's a who's who of Western and Japanese fast-food chains across the rest of Shop-landia.

ourpick Mahboonkrong Food Centre (Map pp118-19; 6th fl, Th Phra Ram I; mains 40-60B; ⏲ lunch & dinner) The typical shopping mall food court in Thailand is similar to Western ones in that the food is cheap. The difference is that it's also fresh and flavourful. Buy coupons from the ticket desk and then cash in whatever you don't spend.

My Collection (Map pp118-19; ☎ 0 2655 7502; 2/10 Th Withayu; mains 250-320B; ⏲ lunch daily, dinner Fri & Sat) Full of pretty things like antique linens, teak furniture and bone China, the ambience is delicate and intimate, everything that Bangkok's fine-dining scene is lacking. The menu is firmly international.

Also worth a try is **Gourmet Paradise** (Map pp118-19; ☎ 0 2610 8000; ground fl, Siam Paragon, Th Phra Ram I; mains 60-250B; ⏲ lunch & dinner), an upmarket international food court.

Silom

Office workers swarm the shanty villages of street vendors for lunch and simple Indian restaurants proliferate towards the western end of Th Silom and Th Surawong, but this area is known for its elegant restaurants preparing international fusion and royal Thai cuisine.

Sara-Jane's (Map pp118-19; ☎ 0 2676 3338; 55/21 Th Narathiwat Ratchanakharin; mains 100-200B; ⏲ lunch & dinner) One of Bangkok's most famous *faràng* has built a small food empire from the marriage of Isan (northeast Thailand) and Italian food.

Eat Me (Map pp118-19; ☎ 0 2238 0931; 1/6 Soi Phiphat 2; mains 200-400B; ⏲ dinner) A little bit of cosmo Sydney has blossomed here off Th Silom. Chic, minimalist décor is accessorised by rotating modern art. And lest we forget, the food is creative and modern, spanning the globe from pumpkin risotto to tuna tartare.

Head to the very popular **Ban Chiang** (Map pp118-19; ☎ 0 2236 7045; 14 Soi Si Wiang, Th Surasak; mains 100-180B; ⏲ lunch & dinner) for northeastern Thai cuisine.

Sukhumvit

This avenue is the communal dining room of most of Bangkok's expat communities, from Italian to Arabic.

Cabbages & Condoms (Map pp118-19; ☎ 0 2229 4611; Soi 12, Th Sukhumvit; mains 150-200B; ⏲ lunch & dinner) This restaurant is the ideal introduction to Thai food for anyone still fine-tuning their chilli radar. Plus all proceeds go towards sex education and AIDS prevention programmes through the Population and Community Development Association (PDA), headquartered next door.

Vientiane Kitchen (Map pp116-17; ☎ 0 2258 6171; 8 Soi 36, Th Sukhumvit; mains 150-220B; ⏲ dinner) *Mǎw lam* (traditional northeastern Thai music) bands play the rollicking tunes of the Isan countryside while the fiery *tôm yam kûng* (hot and sour soup), *lâap mǔu* (minced pork salad) and *kài yâang* (grilled marinated chicken) will give you a bee-stung pout without collagen injections.

GAY & LESBIAN BANGKOK

Bangkok's homosexual community enjoys nearly unprecedented tolerance. **Utopia** (www.utopia-asia .com) and the **Lesbian Guide to Bangkok** (www.bangkoklesbian.com) are good resources.

Patpong Soi 2 and Soi 4 have the highest concentration of gay dance clubs in the city. **DJ Station** (Map pp118-19; ☎ 0 2266 4029; 8/6-8 Soi 2, Th Silom) gets a mixed Thai-*faràng* crowd and has a *kàthoey* (transvestite) cabaret. Old-timer conversation bars, such as **Balcony** (Map pp118-19; ☎ 0 2235 5891; 8/6-8 Soi 4, Th Silom), are over on Soi 4.

Bangkok has just started to develop a lesbian-only nightclub scene with easy-going **Shela** (Map pp118-19; Soi Lang Suan, Th Ploenchit) currently a favourite.

Tamarind Café (Map pp118-19; ☎ 0 2663 7421; 27 Soi 20, Th Sukhumvit; mains 200-250B; ☺ lunch & dinner) Pacific Rim cuisine goes vegetarian at this sleek eatery sharing space with Gallery F-Stop. It's one of the most creative menus in town.

Maha Naga (Map pp118-19; ☎ 0 2662 3060, Soi 29, Th Sukhumvit; mains 300-700B; ☺ lunch & dinner) Its East-meets-West flavours receive mixed reviews, but Maha Naga has a setting to die for: a pan-Asian fantasy of winking candles, Moorish courtyards and Balinese carvings.

Also recommended:

Al Hussain (Map pp118-19; 75/7 Soi 3/1, Th Sukhumvit; mains 150-250B; ☺ lunch & dinner) An open-air café in a winding maze of cramped sublanes known as Little Arabia.

Bourbon St Bar & Restaurant (Map pp118-19; ☎ 0 2259 0328; Soi 22, Th Sukhumvit; mains 150-300B; ☺ breakfast, lunch & dinner) Highly regarded Cajun/ Creole, American and Mexican meals.

Pizzeria Bella Napoli (Map pp118-19; ☎ 0 2259 0405; 3/3 Soi 31, Th Sukhumvit; mains 200-500B; ☺ lunch & dinner) A boisterous crowd gathers in this Little Italy spot.

DRINKING

Center Khao San (Map p121; Th Khao San) offers front-row views of the road's multicultural carnival and bands upstairs, while **Hippie de Bar** (Map p121; Th Khao San) has chill DJs. Low-key **Baghdad Café** (Map p121; Soi 2, Th Samsen), just over Khlong Banglamphu, is a sardine-tight *shishah* (waterpipe) bar that also serves alcohol.

Th Silom and Sukhumvit represent the stock-and-trade of Bangkok bars: English- and Irish-style pubs and yuppie clubs. **O'Reilly's Irish Pub** (Map pp118-19; 62/1-2 Th Silom) and **Cheap Charlie's** (Map pp118-19; Soi 11, Th Sukhumvit; ☺ closed Sun) have wallet-friendly happy-hours for the neighbourhood's wage-slave *faràng*. The **Moon Bar at Vertigo** (Map pp118-19; ☎ 0 2679 1200; Banyan Tree Hotel, 21/100 Th Sathon Tai), outside on the 59th floor, will take your breath away.

ENTERTAINMENT

Bangkok's entertainment scene goes well beyond its naughty side – **Nana Entertainment Plaza** (Map pp118-19; Soi 4, Th Sukhumvit) and **Soi Cowboy** (Map pp118-19; off Th Sukhumvit) lead the way in that scene – but even if you're usually in bed by 9pm, Bangkok still offers interesting postdinner diversions, from flash cinemas to traditional cultural performances.

Dance Clubs

The trick in Bangkok is to catch the right club on the right night. **Bangkok Recorder** (www.bang kokrecorder.com) documents the rotating theme nights and visiting DJ celebs. Cover charges range from 500B to 600B and usually include a drink. Don't even think about showing up before 11pm and always bring ID.

A safe bet, **RCA** (Map pp116-17; Royal City Avenue, Th Phra Ram IX) is a block full of nightclubs offering good times for all kinds. **Lucifer** (Map pp118-19; ☎ 0 2234 6902; 2nd fl, Soi Patpong 1, Th Silom) and its consistently tripped-out techno-rave soundtrack is currently a keystone of Bangkok's dance halls.

Lounge on a row of mattresses at **Bed Superclub** (Map pp118-19; ☎ 0 2651 3537; 26 Soi 11, Sukhumvit), between a meal and a spin on the dance floor.

Live Music

The **Bangkok Gig Guide** (www.bangkokgigguide.com) is a good source of who's on which stage. Of late, Th Khao San has become a hot venue for Thai indie bands.

Bangkok's jazz scene is strong with **Living Room** (Map pp118-19; ☎ 0 2653 0333; Sheraton Grande Sukhumvit, 250 Th Sukhumvit) and **Brown Sugar** (Map pp118-19; ☎ 0 2250 1825; 231/20 Th Sarasin) two sure bets.

Another always enjoyable Bangkok institution is **Saxophone Pub & Restaurant** (Map pp118-19; ☎ 0 2246 5472; 3/8 Th Phayathai) with brilliant acoustics and up-close views of the reggae, rhythm and blues, and jazz acts rocking the house.

Muay Thai (Thai Boxing)

Lumphini Stadium (Map pp118-19; ☎ 0 2251 4303; Th Phra Ram IV; ☢ 6pm Tue, Fri & Sat) and **Ratcha-damnoen Stadium** (Map pp118-19; ☎ 0 2281 4205; Th Ratchadamnoen Nok; ☢ 6pm Mon, Wed & Thu, 5pm Sun) host Thailand's biggest *muay thai* matches. Foreigners pay 1000/1500/2000B for 3rd-class/2nd-class/ringside seats: advance reservations needed for ringside. Don't buy tickets from the hawkers hanging outside the stadium. Lumphini might move, so ask before travelling here.

Traditional Arts Performances

As Thailand's cultural repository, Bangkok offers visitors an array of dance and theatre performances.

The Art Deco **Chalermkrung Royal Theatre** (Map pp118-19; ☎ 0 2222 0434; Th Triphet) provides a striking venue for *khŏhn* (masked dance-drama based on the Ramakian). Don't wear shorts, singlets or sandals when you visit. **Sala Rim Nam** (Map pp118-19; ☎ 0 2437 3080; Soi 38, Th Charoen Krung; 1850B; ☢ 7-10pm), the Oriental Hotel's affiliated dinner theatre, has superb classical dance and mediocre food. Dusit Palace Park (p115) hosts free classical dance performances.

The ancient art of Thai puppetry has been rescued by **Natayasala** (Joe Louis Puppet Theater; Map pp118-19; ☎ 0 2252 9683, www.thaipuppet.com; Suan Lum Night Bazaar, Th Rama IV; 900B; ☢ 7.30pm).

SHOPPING

Bangkok is not the place for recovering shopaholics because the temptation to stray from the path is overwhelming. The best of Bangkok's shopping centres line the Skytrain through Siam Sq. Among your choices are the gleaming **Siam Paragon** (Map pp118-19; ☎ 0 2610 8000; Th Phra Ram I; ☢ 10am-10pm) and **Mahboonkrong** (MBK; Map pp118-19; ☎ 0 2217 9111; Th Phra Ram I; ☢ 10am-10pm), which is just a few air-conditioners and escalators fancier than a street market.

Markets

Don't let the bargaining put you off, it's good fun for seller and buyer.

Chatuchak Weekend Market (Map pp116-17; ☢ 8am-6pm Sat & Sun) The mother of all markets sprawls over a huge area with 15,000 stalls and an estimated 200,000 visitors a day. Everything is sold here, from snakes to handicrafts to aisles and aisles of clothes.

Patpong Night Market (Map pp118-19; Patpong Soi 1 & 2, Th Silom; ☢ 6pm-midnight) More popular than Patpong's Ping-Pong shows; it's full of pirated goods.

Pratunam Market (Map pp118-19; Th Phetburi; ☢ 8am-6pm) The in-town version of Chatuchak.

Th Khao San Market (Map p121; Th Khao San; ☢ 11am-11pm) T-shirts, artwork, souvenirs and traveller ghetto gear.

GETTING THERE & AWAY

Air

All flights use **Suvarnabhumi International Airport** (☎ 0 2723 0000; www.bangkokairportonline.com), pronounced 'soo-wan-na-poom', 30km east of the city. See p177 for specific information about international air services and p178 for a list of domestic airlines.

Bus

Buses using government bus stations are far more reliable and less prone to incidents of theft than those departing from Th Khao San.

The **Northern & Northeastern bus terminal** (Map pp116-17; ☎ 0 2936 2841), commonly called Mo Chit station (*sàthǎanii mǎw chít*), serves almost every destination covered in this book, including unexpectedly, Aranya Prathet. Take the Skytrain to Mo Chit and transfer onto city bus 512, 3, 49 or 77.

Use the **Eastern bus terminal** (Ekamai; Map pp116-17; ☎ 0 2391 2504) – take the Skytrain to Ekamai – if you are headed to Cambodia via Hat Lek and the **Southern bus terminal** (Sai Tai Mai; Map pp116-17; ☎ 0 2435 1200) in Thonburi (take bus 30 from Banglamphu) for Nakhon Pathom.

Train

Bangkok's main train station, **Hualamphong** (Map pp118-19; ☎ 0 2220 4334; Th Phra Ram IV) handles all services to the north and northeast. Ignore all touts here and avoid the travel agencies just outside the train station. **Bangkok Noi** (Map pp118-19; Thonburi) handles services to Nakhon Pathom; it can be reached by river ferry to Tha Rot Fai.

GETTING AROUND

Because of parking hassles and traffic jams, hiring a car for getting around Bangkok is not recommended.

Boat

See the boxed text (p128) for the lowdown on water travel in Bangkok.

BANGKOK & NORTHERN THAILAND

VENICE OF THE EAST

In Bangkok's early days, *khlong* (canals), not roads, transported goods and people, and the mighty Mae Nam Chao Phraya was the superhighway leading to the interior of the country. All life centred on this vast network and Thais considered themselves *jâo náam* (water lords). Most of the canals are gone now, but aqua-transport still flows through Bangkok. It offers a glimpse into the past, and, where the rail lines don't yet run, it's often the swiftest way to get around.

The **Chao Phraya River Express** (www.chaophrayaboat.co.th; tickets 10-32B) has four boat lines on the river – two express (yellow, orange or blue flags), the local (without a flag) and the tourist service that stops at different piers – plus small boats running back and forth across to Thonburi (3B per trip). Services run roughly 6am to 6.30pm.

The quickest option for getting from Banglamphu (use Tha Phan Fah) to points east, such as Siam Sq, are the **khlong taxis** (8-16B; ⊗ 6am-7pm) on Khlong Saen Saep.

The loveliest and leafiest trips are through the remaining canals in Thonburi such as Khlong Bangkok Noi and Khlong Mon, the latter featuring orchid farms. Long-tail boats can be hired from most piers for about 700B per hour.

Dinner Cruises

Combine river transport with dining for a unique Bangkok experience. **Yok Yor Marina & Restaurant** (Map pp118-19; ☎ 0 2863 0565; www.yokyor.co.th; 885 Soi Somdet Chao Phraya 17, Thonburi; adult/child 120/60B plus meal costs; ⊗ 8-10pm) is a favourite among Thais celebrating birthdays.

For a little more entertainment, **Wan Fah Cruises** (Map pp118-19; ☎ 0 2639 0704; River City Shopping Complex; dinner cruise 1200B, ⊗ 7-9pm) operates a wooden boat complete with Thai music and dance. Or for a more regal touch, **Manohra Cruises** (Map pp116-17; ☎ 0 2476 0022; www.manohracruises .com; Bangkok Marriott Resort & Spa, Thonburi; cocktail/dinner cruise 500/1700B, ⊗ 7.30-10pm) runs a fleet of converted teak rice barges. Cocktail cruises run between 6pm and 7pm.

Bus

Bangkok's bus service is frequent and frantic, so a bus map (like *Bangkok Bus Map* by Roadway) is a necessity. Don't expect it to be 100% correct though; routes change regularly.

Fares for ordinary (non-air-con) buses vary from 7B to 8B (red/green buses) to 8.50B (red express). The white-and-blue air-con buses range from 11B up to 19B, depending on the distance travelled. Orange Euro 2 air-con buses start at 12B.

The following bus lines are useful for tourists who are travelling between Banglamphu and Siam Sq:

- **Bus No 73** Huay Khwang to Saphan Phut with stops at MBK (connect to BTS Skytrain), Hualamphong (connect to train or MRT subway), Chinatown and Saphan Phut (connect to River Express).
- **Bus No 15** Tha Phra to Sanam Luang with stops at MBK, Th Ratchadamnoen Klang (accessible to Th Khao San), Sanam Luang (accessible to Wat Phra Kaew).
- **Bus No 47** Khlong Toei Port to Department of Lands with stops along Th Phra Ram IV, MBK, Th Ratchadamnoen and Sanam Luang.

Metro

Bangkok's subway or underground (depending on your nationality) connects Bang Sue train station, near Mo Chit bus terminal, in the north with Hualamphong train station in the centre, stopping in Sukhumvit and Silom along the way. The system will be greatly expanded in coming years, including stops in Chinatown.

Trains operate from 6am to midnight and cost 15B to 39B, depending on distance. Unlimited travel cards cost 120/300B for one/ three days.

Skytrain

The elevated Skytrain (*rót fai fáa*) whisks you through 'new' Bangkok (Silom, Sukhumvit and Siam Sq) in air-conditioned comfort with some interesting bird's-eye views to boot.

The Sukhumvit Line follows its namesake street and swings all the way north to near Chatuchak Weekend Market and Mo Chit bus terminal, while the Silom Line runs from the Siam Sq area to the banks of Mae Nam Chao Phraya. Expansions are planned on both.

Trains run frequently from 6am to midnight and the handy maps in the stations clearly explain the layout. Fares vary from 10B to 40B, and ticket machines only accept coins, but change (plus various discounted passes including the one-day, 120B unlimited ticket) is available at the information booths.

Taxi

Fares for metered taxis are always lower than those for nonmetered taxis. Insist your driver uses the meter; sometimes they 'forget'. Fares generally run from 50B to 80B in central Bangkok and passengers pay freeway tolls. Taxi drivers sometimes seem to know less about the city than you do, so grab your hotel's business card to guarantee getting home.

Motorcycle taxis typically camp out at the beginning of a residential *soi* to transport people the last few kilometres home. *Soi* trips usually cost 10B, but, for about the same price as a túk-túk, they will take you anywhere.

Túk-Túk

Some travellers swear by túk-túk, but most have a hard time bargaining a fair price; patience and a winning smile help. Still, surviving the hassles, the hairpin turns and the suffocating exhaust is part of the Bangkok experience.

If a túk-túk driver offers to take you on a sightseeing tour, walk away – it's a touting scheme designed to pressure you into purchasing overpriced goods.

AROUND BANGKOK & CENTRAL THAILAND

The fertile plains stretching north from the Gulf of Thailand are the cultural heart of the country. The early Thai nation evolved along the 'mother waters' of Mae Nam Chao Phraya and grew to greatness in the former capital of Ayuthaya. Every place featured here is day-trip distance from Bangkok, but Lopburi and Ayuthaya are best as overnighters.

SAMUT PRAKAN

Samut Prakan's main claim to fame is the **Ancient City** (Muang Boran; ☎ 0 2323 9253; www.ancientcity .com; admission 300B; ⏰ 8am-5pm), a 130-hectare outdoor museum with 109 scaled-down replicas of Thailand's most famous historic monuments, including some that no longer survive. Visions of Legoland may spring to mind, but

the Ancient City is architecturally sophisticated and definitely worth the trip.

Ordinary bus 25 (5B) and air-con bus 507, 508 and 511 (16B to 18B) ply regular routes between Bangkok's Southern bus terminal and Samut Prakan. The trip can take up to two hours, depending on traffic. From Samut Prakan's bus station, cross the main road and catch white or red *sǎwngthǎew* 36 (7B) which pass the Ancient City.

NAKHON PATHOM

Nakhon Pathom, 56km west of Bangkok, claims to be the oldest city in Thailand, but the only clue to its longevity is the **Phra Pathom Chedi**, originally erected in the early 6th century. The current bell-shaped structure right in the heart of town was built over the original in the early 11th century by the Khmer king, Suryavarman I. This alteration created the world's tallest Buddhist monument, 127m high. A **museum** (admission by donation; ⏰ 9am-4pm Wed-Sun) has some Dvaravati sculpture.

Other worthwhile stops include **Phra Phutthamonthon**, a 15.8m-tall Sukhothai-style standing Buddha statue, and the lifelike fibreglass sculptures of the **Thai Human Imagery Museum** (☎ 0 3433 2607; admission 250B; ⏰ 9am-5.30pm Mon-Fri, 8.30am-6pm Sat & Sun).

Air-con bus 997 and 83 (41B, one hour) leave frequently to Nakhon Pathom from Bangkok's Southern bus terminal, and they can drop you off at the Thai Human Imagery Museum and near Phra Phutthamonthon. To return to Bangkok, catch a bus on Th Phayaphan, a block from the train station. Bus 78 to Damnoen Saduak leaves from the same stop. Coming by rail, your best bets are the regular runs from Bangkok's Hualamphong station (from 35B, two hours).

DAMNOEN SADUAK FLOATING MARKET

As iconic to Thailand as temples and palm trees, the wooden canoes laden with fruits and vegetables, paddled by women wearing indigo-hued clothes and wide-brimmed straw hats, at **Damnoen Saduak** (⏰ 7am-4pm Sat & Sun) are a sentimental piece of history. This is the most famous and most touristy of Thailand's floating markets, but it's also the most photogenic. Get there before 9am to beat the tour-bus hordes.

Air-con bus 78 and 996 go direct from Bangkok's Southern bus terminal (82B, two hours), starting at 6am. Boat hire along the canals costs about 300B per hour.

AYUTHAYA

pop 90,500

In their race to reach the Gulf of Thailand, three rivers (Chao Phraya, Pa Sak and Lopburi) converge to form the island of Ayuthaya, the former Thai capital. The rivers formed both a natural barrier to invasion and an invitation to trade. From 1350 to 1767, Ayuthaya was the cultural centre of the emerging Thai nation and by the end of the 17th century, the population had reached one million. Many foreign visitors proclaimed it the most illustrious city they had ever seen, but eventually the river defences were unable to repulse the Burmese and after two years of war the capital fell; the royal family fled to Thonburi, near present-day Bangkok, and the Burmese looted the architectural and religious treasures. Today a modern, surprisingly untouristy city has sprung up around the holy ruins and life still largely revolves around the river. The famous Loi Krathong festivities (see p174) take place in Bang Pa-In, 24km south of Ayuthaya.

Information

ATMs and internet cafés are abundant, especially along Th Naresuan.

Ayuthaya Hospital (☎ 0 3524 1446; Th U Thong)

Post office (Th U Thong; ☷ 8.30am-4.30pm Mon-Fri, 9am-noon Sat)

TAT (☎ 0 3524 6076; 108/22 Th Si Sanphet; ☷ 8.30am-4.30pm)

Tourist police (☎ 1155; Th Si Sanphet)

Sights

A Unesco World Heritage Site, Ayuthaya's historic temple ruins are scattered throughout this once magnificent city, and along the encircling rivers. A good way to visit the 'off the island' sites is on a boat tour (from 200B per hour), easily arranged at various guesthouses or at the pier near the night market. Most temples are open 8am to 4pm and many are illuminated between 7pm and 9pm.

ON THE ISLAND

Before hitting the ruins, bone up on their history at the modern and interesting **Ayuthaya Historical Study Centre** (☎ 0 3524 5124; Th Rotchana; admission 100B; ☷ 9am-4.30pm Mon-Fri, to 5pm Sat & Sun). Ayuthaya also has two national museums. The

Chantharakasem National Museum (Th U Thong; admission 30B; ☷ 9am-4pm Wed-Sun) is in a striking 157 palace, but the **Chao Sam Phraya National Museum** (Th Rotchana; admission 30B; ☷ 9am-4pm Wed-Sun) has more impressive collection.

The most distinctive example of Ayuthaya architecture is **Wat Phra Si Sanphet** (admission 30B) where three bell-shaped *chedi* (religious monuments) taper off into descending rings. Built in the late 14th century on the grounds of the royal palace, this was the once the city's largest and most important temple. The adjacent **Wihaan Phra Mongkhon Bophit** houses a huge bronze seated Buddha.

Wat Phra Mahathat (admission 30B) is presumed to be one of the first Khmer-style *praang* built in the capital, but shutterbugs invariably snap more pictures of the Buddha head engulfed by tentacle-like tree roots. The 15th-century *praang* across the street at **Wat Ratburana** (admission 30B) is in better condition. Nearby **Wat Thammikarat**, which probably predates the Ayuthaya period, stands out for the *singh* (guardian lion) sculptures ringing the remains of the central *chedi*.

AYUTHAYA

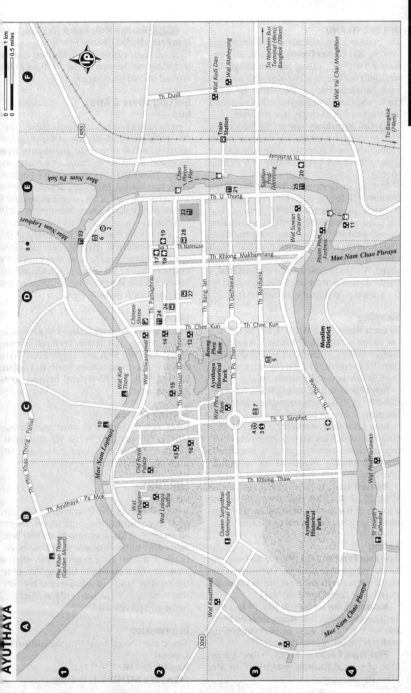

OFF THE ISLAND

The main *wíhǎan* (sanctuary) of the modern-looking **Wat Phanan Choeng** (admission 30B) contains a 19m-high sitting Buddha image. On weekends the temple is crowded with pilgrims from Bangkok who pay for saffron-coloured cloth to be ritually draped over the image and buy bags of fish to empty into the river.

Wat Chai Wattanaram (admission 30B), built in the 17th century and extensively restored in the 1980s, is a good example of Angkor-Khmer style. It's also a premier sunset-watching spot.

Instead of destroying **Wat Na Phra Mehn** (admission 30B) during their 1767 conquest, the Burmese made it their headquarters. The *bòt* (central sanctuary) contains an amazing carved wooden ceiling depicting the Buddhist heavens while the smaller *wíhǎan* has a stone Buddha in a European pose (sitting in a chair). Also to the north is the **elephant kraal**, a restored version of the stockades once used for the annual roundup of wild elephants.

Sleeping

PU Guest House (☎ 0 3525 1213; 20/1 Soi Thaw Kaw Saw; s/d from 200/300B; ⚄ 🖳) Most of Ayuthaya's budget options are clustered around the mini-traveller ghetto of Soi 1, Th Naresuan, including this low-key, well-rounded place.

Tony's Place (☎ 0 3525 2578; 12/18 Soi 1, Th Naresuan; r 200-500B; ⚄) The party atmosphere keeps this longtime favourite packed.

Baan Lotus Guest House (☎ 0 3525 1988; 20 Th Pamaphrao; r 500B) This old teak house overlooking the lotus-covered pond is beautifully restored, smartly appointed and splendidly managed.

Woraburi Hotel (☎ 0 3524 9600; 89 Th Watkluay; r from 1800B; ⚄ 🖳 ⚄) This eight-storey tower has a touch of Bangkok sophistication and most rooms get a bear-hug view of the river.

Eating

Baan Khun Phra (☎ 0 3524 1978; 48/2 Th U Thong; mains 40-80B; ✆ breakfast, lunch & dinner) The intimate riverside terrace restaurant behind its namesake guesthouse serves good nibblers.

Malakor (Th Chee Kun; mains 50-100B; ✆ lunch & dinner) This charming, two-storey wooden house has an incredible view of Wat Ratburana, which is stunning after dark.

Phae Krung Kao (mains 60-200B; ✆ lunch & dinner) One of several floating restaurants on Mae Nam Pa Sak.

our pick **Hua Raw Night Market** (Th U Thong) an **Chao Phrom Market** (Th Naresuan) offer a good va riety of Thai, Chinese and Muslim dishe including *roti sai mai,* a flaky roti wrappe around melted palm sugar.

Getting There & Away

BUS

Ayuthaya has two bus terminals. Buses fror the south, west and east stop at the main bu terminal, which is near the guesthouse are Frequent buses serve Bangkok's Norther bus terminal (63B, 1½ hours) and Lopbu (45B, two hours). Minivans, departing fror Th Naresuan, east of the main bus termina run to Bangkok's Victory Monument (60I two hours).

Long-distance northern buses stop at th **northern terminal** (☎ 0 3533 5304), 5km east of th centre. It has services to most major norther towns, including Sukhothai (216B to 300B, si hours), Chiang Mai (605B to 805B, nine hours and Nan (500B to 800B, eight hours).

TRAIN

Trains to Ayuthaya leave Bangkok's Hualam phong station (15B to 66B, 1½ hours) almos hourly between 6am and 11pm. From Ayu thaya, the train continues north to Lopbu (13B to 57B, one hour) and beyond, or t the northeast.

Getting Around

Bikes can be rented at most guesthouse (30B to 50B per day). A túk-túk trip shoul be about 20B on the island and around 40 from the train station.

LOPBURI

pop 62,800

Founded during the Dvaravati period (6t to 11th centuries), Lopburi serves visitor an interesting juxtaposition of ancient bric ruins and not-so-ancient shophouses an hotels. But most visitors come here, often a a pit-stop on their way to Chiang Mai, to se the resident troop of mischievous monke that make one of Thailand's oldest cities the home and playground.

Information

There are several banks in the old part o Lopburi.

Hospital (☎ 0 3662 1537; Th Ramdecho)
Police (☎ 0 3642 4515; Th Na Phra Kan)

Post office (Th Phra Narai Maharat)

TAT (☎ 0 3642 2768; Th Phraya Kamjat; ◷ 8.30am-4.30pm)

Sights

The former palace of King Narai, **Phra Narai Ratchaniwet** (☎ 0 3641 1458; Th Sorasak; admission 30B; ◷ 7.30am-5.30pm) is a good place to begin a tour of Lopburi. Built between 1665 and 1677, it has an unusual blend of French and Khmer styles. Inside the grounds is the **Lopburi National Museum** (◷ 8.30am-4.30pm Wed-Sun), which houses an excellent collection of Lopburi period sculpture, as well as an assortment of Khmer, Dvaravati, U Thong and Ayuthaya art and traditional tools.

Prang Sam Yot (Th Wichayen; admission 30B; ◷ 8am-6pm) represents classic Khmer-Lopburi style and is a Hindu-turned-Buddhist temple. Originally, the three towers symbolised the Hindu trinity of Shiva, Vishnu and Brahma. Now two of them contain ruined Lopburi-style Buddha images. The monument is lit up at night and constantly crawling with monkeys.

Other Khmer ruins in the old town include **Wat Phra Si Ratana Mahathat** (Th Na Phra Kan; admission 30B; ◷ 7am-5pm) and **Wat Nakhon Kosa** (Th Na Phra Kan), both dating to the 12th century, and **Prang Khaek** (Th Wichayen), Lopburi's oldest monument, which went up sometime in the 11th century.

Two churches for foreigners were founded during the reign of King Narai. A partial brick and stucco tower is all that's left of **Wat San Paolo** (Th Ramdecho) while the *wíhǎan* at **Wat Sao Thong Thong** (Th Wichayen), with its incongruous but intriguing Gothic-style windows, is now a Buddhist temple.

Sleeping & Eating

Nett Hotel (☎ 0 3641 1738; 17/1-2 Th Ratchadamnoen; r 300-350B; ❄) The clean and friendly Nett has newly tiled air-con rooms.

Thepthani Hotel (☎ 0 3641 1029; Th Phra Narai Maharat; r 400B; ❄) Rajabhat University's hotel has spacious rooms with cable TV. Blue buses between old and new town pass here.

White House (Th Phraya Kamjat; mains 60-120B; ◷ dinner) This pleasant little spot opposite the TAT office offers a range of quality Thai-Chinese specialities.

Central Market (off Th Ratchadamnoen & Th Surasongkhram; ◷ 8am-2pm) Just north of the palace, this is a great place to pick up *kài yâang* (fried or roast chicken) with sticky rice, *klûay khàek* (Indian-style fried bananas) and other delights. There's a vegetarian pavilion in the centre.

Getting There & Away

Lopburi's bus station is almost 2km outside the old district. Buses head to Bangkok's Northern bus terminal (air-con 130B, 3½ hours) every 20 minutes.

There are frequent train services throughout the day south to Bangkok's Hualamphong station (local/rapid/express 28/125/170B, 4½/three/three hours). The local train to Ayuthaya (13B) takes about an hour. Lopburi's train station is on the edge of the old town and has luggage storage if you are just making a short stop here.

CHIANG MAI

pop 204,000

To Thais, Chiang Mai is a national treasure; a cultured symbol of nationhood. For visitors, it's a cool place to kick back and soak up some Thai-ness while still having all the comforts of home close at hand. Beyond the city limits, Chiang Mai Province boasts a multitude of mountains and more natural forest cover than any other province in the north, so trekking and other outdoor outings are big business.

The old city of Chiang Mai is a neat square bounded by moats and remnants of a medieval-style wall built 700 years ago to defend against Burmese invaders. A furious stream of traffic flows around the old city, but inside narrow *soi* branch off the clogged arteries into a quiet world of charming guesthouses with leafy gardens.

ORIENTATION

Th Moon Muang, along the east moat, is the main traveller centre. Intersecting with Th Moon Muang, Th Tha Phae runs east from the exterior of the moat towards Mae Nam Ping, changing into Th Charoen Muang across the river where it passes the train station. The trendy Th Nimmanhaemin area is west of the old city.

Navigating Chiang Mai is fairly simple, but a copy of Nancy Chandler's *Map of Chiang Mai* is a good investment. Several free, ad-filled maps are also available.

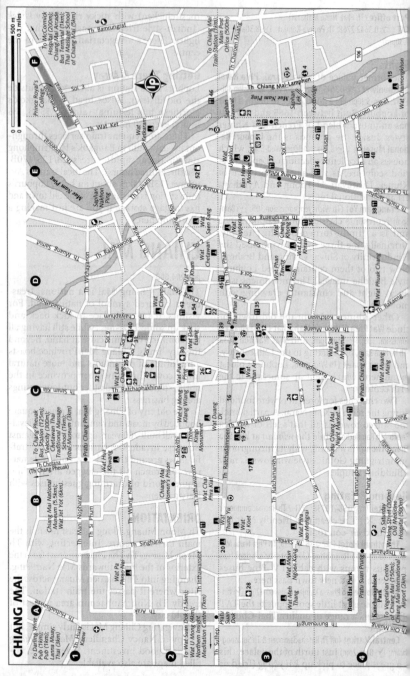

CHIANG MAI

INFORMATION

You will stumble over internet cafés, banks and ATMs on seemingly every street you visit in Chiang Mai.

Emergency

Tourist police (☎ 1155; Th Chiang Mai-Lamphun)

Internet Resources

Chiang Mai Online (www.chiangmai-online.com) Basic information about Chiang Mai and comprehensive accommodation listings.

City Life (www.chiangmainews.com) Posts articles on local events, culture and art, along with current news developments.

Media

Chiangmai Mail Weekly newspaper; good source of local news.

City Life Oriented as much towards residents as tourists, with articles on local culture, politics and people.

Medical Services

Chiang Mai Ram Hospital (☎ 0 5322 4861; 8 Th Bunreuangrit) The most modern hospital in town, with higher-than-average prices.

McCormick Hospital (☎ 0 5326 2200; 133 Th Kaew Nawarat) The best-value place for minor treatment.

Post

Main post office (Th Charoen Muang; ⏰ 8.30am-4.30pm Mon-Fri, 9am-noon Sat & Sun)

Tourist Information

TAT (☎ 0 5324 8607; Th Chiang Mai-Lamphun; ⏰ 8am-4.30pm) Keeps a list of registered trekking guides, plus maps and brochures.

DANGERS & ANNOYANCES

Many travellers report that their belongings (particularly credit cards) stored at Chiang Mai guesthouses have gone walkabout. If you stow your bags while you go trekking, make an itemised list of all belongings, including travellers cheques, and note your credit card balance. See Guest House Blues (p139) for further warnings.

Take care in the unlit backstreets around the Night Bazaar. A few women have been attacked.

SIGHTS
Temples

Chiang Mai has more than 300 temples – almost as many as Bangkok. The temple architecture here is markedly different from other parts of Thailand. Notice the intricate woodcarvings and colourful murals; hallmarks of the Lanna period (13th and 14th centuries). Three-tiered umbrellas adorning the tops of the temples, Singha lions guarding the entrances and high-base *chedi* are all Burmese influences.

A perfect example of Lanna architecture, **Wat Phra Singh** (Th Singarat) is the star of the inner-city's soaring stupas. Established in 1345, this wat contains murals depicting Lanna customs and dress, a scripture repository and the city's most revered Buddha image, Phra Singh (Lion Buddha).

Wat Chiang Man (Th Ratchaphakhinai), the oldest wat within the city walls, was erected by King Mengrai, Chiang Mai's founder, in 1296. Two famous Buddha images (Buddha Sila and the Crystal Buddha) are kept here in the *wíhǎan* to the right of the main *bòt*.

The huge ruined *chedi* at **Wat Chedi Luang** (Th Phra Pokklao) either collapsed during an earthquake in 1545 or from cannon fire in 1775 during the recapture of Chiang Mai from the Burmese. A partial restoration has preserved its 'ruined' look while ensuring it doesn't crumble further.

The large, old teak *wíhǎan* at **Wat Phan Tao** (Th Phra Pokklao) is one of Chiang Mai's unsung treasures.

Modelled somewhat imperfectly on the Mahabodhi Temple in Bodhgaya, India, **Wat Jet Yot** (Hwy 11) was built to host the eighth World Buddhist Council in 1477. The seven spires represent the seven weeks Buddha was supposed to have spent in Bodhgaya after his enlightenment.

Built in a forest grove in 1373, **Wat Suan Dok** (Th Su) contains a 500-year-old bronze Buddha image and colourful *jataka* murals, but the scenic sunsets are the biggest attraction.

The forest temple of **Wat U Mong** (Soi Wat U Mong), dating from Mengrai's rule, has a fine image of the fasting Buddha. Brick-lined tunnels in an unusual looking large, flat-topped hill were supposedly fashioned around 1380 for a clairvoyant monk; some are still open for exploration.

Museums

Lanna history and works of art are documented at the superb **Chiang Mai National Museum** (☎ 0 5322 1308; www.thailandmuseum.com; Hwy 11; admission 30B; ◷ 9am-4pm Wed-Sun) northwest of town.

Chiang Mai's former Provincial Hall, a masterpiece of Thai architecture, has been converted into the **Chiang Mai Arts & Cultural Centre** (☎ 0 5321 7793; www.chiangmaicitymuseum.org; Th Phra Pokklao; admission 90B; ◷ 8.30am-5pm Tue-Sun). There are interesting interactive historical displays, temporary art exhibitions and more in the 15 rooms.

Whether you plan to do a hill-tribe trek or not, the **Tribal Museum** (☎ 0 5321 0872; admission free; ◷ 9am-4pm Mon-Fri), at Ratchamangkhla

Park north of the city, is worth a visit. Video shows run between 10am and 2pm and cost 20B to 50B.

Chiang Mai Night Bazaar

Chiang Mai's leading tourist attraction is the legacy of the original Yunnanese caravans that stopped here along the ancient trade route between Sīmáo (in China) and Mawlamyine (on Myanmar's – Burma's – Indian Ocean coast). Today the **bazaar** (cnr Th Chang Khlan & Th Loi Kroh; ◷ sunset-midnight) sprawls over several blocks with the epicentre at the Th Chang Khlan and Th Loi Kroh junction. Made up of hundreds of street vendors, several different roofed areas and ordinary shops, the market offers a huge variety of handicrafts, as well as designer goods (both fake and licensed) at very low prices, if you bargain well.

Walking Streets

A more chilled-out shopping experience than the Night Bazaar, Chiang Mai's **Sunday Walking Street** (Th Ratchadamnoen; ◷ 4pm-midnight Sun) is very popular. Blocked off to traffic, the street fills with colourful stalls selling wares ranging from food to hill-tribe crafts. Buskers playing down the street add to the atmosphere. Th Wualai, the new **Saturday Walking Street** (◷ 4pm-midnight Sat) isn't as popular.

ACTIVITIES
Ping River Trips

From a small pier behind Wat Chaimongkhon, **Mae Ping River Cruises** (☎ 0 5327 4822; www.maepingrivercruise.com; Th Charoen Prathet; per person 400B; ◷ 8.30am-5pm) offers two-hour daytime cruises in long-tail, roofed boats through the countryside with stops at a small fruit and flower farm.

Rock Climbing

Chiang Mai Rock Climbing Adventures (☎ 0 6911 1470; www.thailandclimbing.com; 55/3 Th Ratchaphakhinai; 1-/3-day course 1800/6600B) leads climbing and caving trips to an impressive set of limestone cliffs known as Crazy Horse Buttress, about 20km east of town. The office offers gear sales and rentals and a partner-finding service.

Trekking

Chiang Mai is one of the most popular places in Thailand to arrange a trek. Many guesthouses and lots of travel agents want a slice of action in this 'competitive' (read: cut-throat) business and it's important to shop around before signing up. Most treks include visits to hill-tribe villages, some jungle action, plus the option of rafting or elephant rides. See the boxed text, p138, for further information.

COURSES

Buddhist Meditation

Northern Insight Meditation Centre (0 5327 8620; www.palikanon.com/vipassana/tapotaram/tapotaram.htm; donation) Offers 10- to 26-day individual intensive courses in Vipassana with English-speaking interpreters available.

Wat Suan Dok (0 5380 8411, ext 114; www.monkchat.net; Th Suthep; retreats/courses free) Wat Suan Dok has a two-night, three-day meditation retreat at the end of each month, as well as an overnight meditation course every Tuesday (2.15pm Tuesday to 1.30pm Wednesday). Informal 'monk chats' are offered 5pm to 7pm Wednesday and Friday.

For a more casual introduction to Buddhism, attend the Sunday afternoon (3pm) lectures at Wat U Mong (opposite) or drop by for 'monk chat' from 1pm to 6pm at Wat Chedi Luang (opposite) where you can ask questions.

Cooking

Cooking classes (usually costing 800B to 1000B per day) are a big hit in Chiang Mai. Try the following:

Baan Thai (0 5335 7339; www.baanthaicookery.com; 11 Soi 5, Th Ratchadamnoen)
Chiang Mai Thai Cookery School (0 5320 6388; www.thaicookeryschool.com; 47/2 Th Moon Muang)
Gap's Thai Culinary Art School (0 5327 8140; www.gaps-house.com; 3 Soi 4, Th Ratchadamnoen)
Thai Farm Cooking School (08 7174 9285; www.thaifarmcooking.com; 2/2 Soi 5, Th Ratchadamnoen)

Muay Thai (Thai Boxing)

Lanna Muay Thai (Kiatbusaba; 0 5389 2102; www.lannamuaythai.com; 64/1 Soi Chiang Khian; day/month 350/7000B) The former training camp of famous kàthoey (transvestite) boxer Parinya Kiatbusaba welcomes foreign students.

Traditional Massage

More visitors learn to pummel bodies the Thai way in Chiang Mai than anywhere else. We've received good reports about the following:
Chetawan Thai Traditional Massage School (0 5341 0360; www.watpomassage.com/map_chiangmaien.html; 7/1-2 Soi Samud Lanna, Th Pracha Uthit; 5-day foot/Thai massage course 5500/7000B) Affiliated with the Wat Pho massage school in Bangkok. Offers tuition in foot and Thai massage.

Lek Chaiya (0 5327 8325; www.nervetouch.com; 25 Th Ratchadamnoen; 5-day course 4000B) Khun Lek, a Thai woman who has been massaging and teaching for more than 40 years, specialises in jàp sên (similar to acupressure) and the use of medicinal herbs.

Old Medicine Hospital (OMH; 0 5327 5085; www.thaimassageschool.ac.th; 78/1 Soi Siwaka Komarat, Th Wualai; 10-day course 4000B) The OMH curriculum is very traditional, with a northern-Thai slant. A two-day foot massage course (2000B) is also offered.

Thai Massage School of Chiang Mai (TMC; 0 5385 4330; www.tmcschool.com; Th Chiang Mai-Mae Jo; 5-day course 5300B) Northeast of town, TMC has a solid, government-licensed massage curriculum. Transport to the school is included.

FESTIVALS & EVENTS

Flower Festival The mother of Chiang Mai festivals features parades of flower-draped floats. Held February.
Loi Krathong This nationwide festival (see p174) is celebrated with gusto in Chiang Mai in October and November.
Winter Fair Held late December to early January, this is a big event on the Chiang Mai calendar, with all sorts of activities and interesting visitors from the hills.

SLEEPING

Most budget lodging guesthouses are clustered on either side of the east moat, and most will arrange free transport from the bus or train station if you call.

Lamchang House (0 5321 0586; Soi 7, Th Moon Muang; r 90-170B) This wooden Thai-style house has lots of character, including some Thai decoration and fresh flowers in the rooms and a small garden restaurant. Bathrooms are shared.

Julie Guesthouse (0 5327 4355; www.julieguesthouse.com; 7 Soi 5, Th Phra Pokklao; dm 60B, r 90-300B) This funky place has a colourful range of rooms, and the covered roof terrace with hammocks and the garden café with a pool table are good places to meet other travellers.

Siri Guesthouse (0 5332 6550; www.siri.gh@hotmail.com; Soi 5, Th Moon Muang; r 300-350B) This new place offers fantastic-value rooms stylishly decorated with dark-wood furniture and some Thai touches.

Chiangmai Gold Star Hotel (0 5323 2492; 53 Th Sitiwong; r 350-750B;) Straddling the budget-midrange divide, this friendly 29-room hotel is a little old fashioned but has character. The large rooms are decorated with ornate Burmese furniture and Thai pictures.

TREKKING TIPS

Thousands of visitors trek into the hills of northern Thailand each year. Most come away with a sense of adventure, but, due to bad guides or incompatible group members, some are disillusioned by the experience.

Do your homework before you sign up for a trek. Ask how many people will be in the group (six to 10 is a good range), find out exactly when the tour begins and ends (some three-day treks last less than 48 hours) and be sure you know exactly what the tour includes so you are not hit with additional expenses.

As for choosing the guide, many work freelance, so there's no way to predict which companies will give the best service, but at least make sure your guide is licensed. The TAT office in Chiang Mai (p135) maintains a list of licensed agencies and is making efforts to regulate trekking companies. Ultimately, the most important thing to do is talk to people who have just returned from a trek.

Also, don't overestimate your level of physical fitness; you'll be crossing mountainous terrain in unpredictable weather. The best time to trek is November to February, when the weather is refreshing, there's little or no rain and wildflowers are in bloom.

Trekking can be arranged in numerous towns, and there are benefits to organising your trek outside Chiang Mai and Chiang Rai. Prices tend to be lower, the companies smaller and friendlier and you usually get into more remote areas. Of course, the downside is that there are fewer companies to choose from and less opportunity to get the low-down from fellow travellers.

Visiting Hill-Tribe Villages

The natural scenery can be stunning, but just about everyone who treks does so to visit villages. The term 'hill tribe' (*chao khǎo*, or 'mountain people', to Thais) refers to ethnic minorities living in mountainous northern and western Thailand. Each hill tribe has its own language, customs, mode of dress and spiritual beliefs. Most are of seminomadic origin, having migrated to Thailand from Tibet, Myanmar (Burma), China and Laos during the past 200 years or so. The Tribal Research Institute in Chiang Mai estimates the total hill-tribe population to be around 550,000.

For the hill-tribe groups of Thailand, tourism is a mixed blessing. Since the Thai government is sensitive about the image it displays to the West, tourism has forced it to improve some of its policies towards hill tribes, but tourism has also contributed to the erosion of traditional customs. Because trekking is big business, some villages have become veritable theme parks with a steady supply of visitors filtering in and out, creating exactly the opposite environment to the one trekkers hope to find. In fact, the only villages that now offer a truly authentic experience are ones you shouldn't be visiting. But that's not to say that sensitive and inquisitive visitors can't have a meaningful experience. Treks do still offer a chance to see how traditional, subsistence-oriented societies function and if you have a good guide you will learn a lot.

It's impossible to leave a community unaffected by your visit, but observing local taboos (which your guide should explain) greatly minimises the impact. The following protocol applies to pretty much all villages.

- Do not hand out candy, pens or other small gifts. These may bring smiles to the children, but it brings shame to their parents and cultivates a tradition of begging. If you want to give a gift, talk to your guide beforehand about materials the local school or health centre may need.

- Dress modestly no matter how hot and sweaty you are.

- Always ask for permission before taking photos, even if you think nobody is looking.

- Show respect for religious symbols and rituals. Don't touch totems at village entrances or any other object of obvious symbolic value without asking permission.

- Set a good example to hill-tribe youngsters by not using drugs. An increasing number of young people in the villages are now hooked on opium, heroin and amphetamines, in part due to the influence of young trekkers.

Sri Pat Guest House (☎ 0 5321 8716; www.sri patguesthouse.com; 16 Soi 7, Th Moon Muang; r 900B; 🔀) Rustic-looking tiles in the bathrooms and rattan furniture give this 17-room guesthouse a chic Thai-modern style. All rooms have a terrace and plenty of extras.

Galare Guest House (☎ 0 5381 8887; www.galare com; 7/1 Soi 2, Th Charoen Prathet; r 1100B; 🔀) Set in an old-style Thai house on the river near the Night Bazaar, this friendly and well-managed guesthouse has spacious rooms with some charm.

Rachamankha (☎ 0 5390 4111; www.rachamankha com; 6 Th Ratchamankha; r 6900-18,000B; 🔀 🔳 🖳) This architect-owned hotel, filled with exquisite Lanna antiques and artworks, feels like the compound of a 16th-century temple built for royalty.

Also recommended:

Daret's House (☎ 0 5323 5440; 4/5 Th Chaiyaphum; 180B) A longtime travellers' fave with well-worn rooms.

Montra House (☎ 0 5341 8658; Soi 5, Th Ratchad-mnoen; r 200B; 🖳) Basic but spotless digs, some with shared bathroom.

CN Court (☎ 0 5341 8280; 35 Soi 7, Th Moon Muang; 300-450B; 🔀 🖳) Well-equipped rooms and lots of extras like a small fitness centre.

Tri Gong Residence (☎ 0 5321 4754; www.trigong com; 8 Soi 1, Th Sribhum; r 600B; 🔀 🖳) Stylish rooms with rattan and teak furniture surrounding a courtyard. Free wi-fi.

Parasol Inn (☎ 0 5381 4011; www.parasolinn.com; 105/1 Th Prah Pokklao; r 1000-1500B; 🔀 🖳) New hotel just off Sunday Walking Street.

GUESTHOUSE BLUES

Beware bus or minivan services from Th Khao San in Bangkok that advertise a free night's accommodation in Chiang Mai. What usually happens on arrival is that the 'free' guesthouse demands you sign up for one of their hill treks immediately; if you don't, the guesthouse is suddenly 'full'. Sometimes they levy a charge for electricity or hot water. The better guesthouses don't play this game.

Many cheaper guesthouses make more money from their restaurants and tour services than room charges, hence you may be pressured to eat and to sign up for a trek; you might even be evicted if you don't. It's always best to ask if it's OK to take a room only.

EATING

You won't lack for variety in Chiang Mai as the city has arguably the best assortment of restaurants outside Bangkok.

Thai

Si Phen Restaurant (☎ 0 5331 5328; 103 Th Inthawarorot; mains 40-80B; 😋 lunch & dinner) Si Phen serves both northern- and northeastern-style dishes, including a variation of *sôm-tam* (spicy papaya salad) made with pomelo fruit.

Aroon (Rai) Restaurant (☎ 0 5327 6947; 45 Th Kotch-asan; mains 40-90B; 😋 breakfast, lunch & dinner) A top spot for Chiang Mai specialities, such as *kaeng awm* and *kaeng khae*, curries which rely on local roots and herbs for their distinctive, bitter-hot flavours. The spacious open-air dining area upstairs catches the night breeze.

Just Khao Soi (☎ 0 5381 8641; 108/2 Th Charoen Prathet; mains 100B; 😋 lunch & dinner) Chiang Mai is famed for its fine *khâo sawy*, a Shan-Yunnanese concoction of chicken (or, less commonly, beef), spicy curried broth and flat, squiggly wheat noodles. This place offers a gourmet version of it, letting you create your own.

Also recommended:

Ratana's Kitchen (☎ 0 5387 4173; 320-322 Th Tha Phae; mains 30-90B; 😋 lunch & dinner) Inexpensive Thai dishes from several regions, and a few *faràng* favs.

Antique House (☎ 0 5327 6810; 71 Th Charoen Prathet; mains 80-160B; 😋 lunch & dinner) Eat northern Thai dishes in an elegant teak house.

Chiang Mai is full of interesting day and night markets serving inexpensive and tasty foods. The buzzing **Anusan Night Market** (Soi Anusan, Th Chang Khlan; 😋 dinner), known mainly for its seafood, is part of the Chiang Mai Night Bazaar (p136). The nearby **Galare Food Centre** (Th Chang Khlan; 😋 breakfast, lunch & dinner) features Thai classical dancing nightly. Also recommended is the **Pratu Chiang Mai Night Market** (Th Bamrung-buri; 😋 dinner) where people tend to make an evening of eating and drinking.

International

Juicy 4U (☎ 0 5327 8715; 5 Th Ratchamanka; mains 50-135B; 😋 breakfast & lunch) Silly name, but serious food. This cute café serves fantastic organic breakfasts, create-your-own sandwiches, salads, smoothies and juices.

Chiangmai Saloon (☎ 08 1930 2212; 80/1 Th Loi Kroh; mains 80-300B; 😋 lunch & dinner) Ignore the ersatz Wild West décor and head straight for the huge steaks and Tex-Mex.

Giorgio Italian Restaurant (☎ 0 5381 8236; 2/6 Th Prachasamphan; mains 100-250B; ✆ lunch Mon-Sat, dinner daily) Chiang Mai's most ambitious, and some say the best, Italian eatery features a full range of pasta and exceptional salads.

House (☎ 0 5341 9011; 199 Th Moon Muang; mains 200-790B, tapas 50-110B; ✆ dinner) This ambitious restaurant occupies a mid-20th-century house that once belonged to an exiled Burmese prince. The menu successfully fuses Thai and European elements, complemented by an excellent wine list.

Also recommended:

Mike's (Th Chaiyaphum; mains 40-115B; ✆ dinner) Damn good hamburgers served until 3am.

Herb Garden (☎ 0 5341 8991; Soi 1, Th Ratchad-amnoen; mains 40-150B; ✆ breakfast, lunch & dinner) Unusually, the Thai food here is as good as the Western.

Riverside Bar & Restaurant (☎ 0 5324 3239; 9-11 Th Charoenrat; mains 75-200B; ✆ lunch & dinner) A river cruise (70B) departs nightly at 8pm.

Vegetarian

Chiang Mai has a huge choice of vegetarian food thanks to its love of all things healthy.

Vegetarian Centre of Chiang Mai (☎ 0 5327 1262; 14 Th Om Muang; mains 15-30B; ✆ breakfast & lunch Mon-Fri) Sponsored by the Asoke Foundation, an ascetically minded Buddhist movement, this cafeteria serves some of the cheapest food in the city.

Whole Earth Restaurant (☎ 0 5328 2463; 88 Th Si Donchai; mains 120-300B) Set in a teak house, with a suitably mellow atmosphere. The food is well-presented Thai and Indian, both vegetarian and nonvegetarian.

DRINKING & ENTERTAINMENT

The ale flows fast and furiously at the strip of bars along Th Moon Muang near the Pratu Tha Phae. It's a familiar sight: lots of sweaty *faràng*, cheap beer and miles of neon. More low-key is the cluster of rustic outdoor bars behind Th Ratchaphakhinai, such as Rasta Café and Heaven Beach, serving cheap beers and cool tunes to travellers and expats.

Riverside Bar & Restaurant (☎ 0 5324 3239; 9-11 Th Charoenrat) In a twinkly setting on Mae Nam Ping, this is one of the longest-running live-music venues in Chiang Mai. Two cover bands play nightly and the food is reliably good.

Pinte Blues Pub (33/6 Th Moon Muang) Another old-timer (open more than 20 years), Pinte serves only espresso and beer.

Darling Wine Pub (☎ 0 5322 7427; 49/21 Th Hua Kaew) Darling serves fine wines by the glas or bottle in a sophisticated but relaxe atmosphere.

Pub (☎ 0 5321 1550; 189 Th Huay Kaew) In an ol Tudor-style cottage set well off the road, thi venerable Chiang Mai institution semisuc cessfully calls up the atmosphere of an Englis country pub.

Bubbles (☎ 0 5327 0099; Th Charoen Prathet) Th Pornping Tower Hotel's disco heaves with mix of locals and *faràng* remembering hov to do rave moves. The 100B entrance ticke exchanges for a drink.

SHOPPING

From modern art to Burmese antiques, yo can buy just about anything in Chiang Ma Even long before tourists began visiting th region, Chiang Mai was an important centr for handcrafted ceramics, silks, umbrellas silverwork and woodcarvings; and toda it's still the country's number-one source c handicrafts.

The city's top shopping stops are the Nigh Bazaar (p136) and the Walking Streets (p136 Other good retail destinations are **Talat Waroro** (off Th Chang Moi; ✆ 5am-6pm), the oldest and mos famous market in Chiang Mai, which has little of everything, and Th Tha Phae with mix of antiques, jewellery, homewares an clothes.

GETTING THERE & AWAY
Air

Regularly scheduled international fligh arrive at **Chiang Mai International Airport** (☎ 5327 0222) from Kuala Lumpur (Malaysia Kūnmíng (China), Singapore, Taipei (Tai wan), Vientiane and Luang Prabang (Laos and Yangon and Mandalay (Myanmar).

Domestic routes include Bangkok, Ma Hong Son, Pai and Sukhothai. Discoun flights to Bangkok can go as low as 899B on way, almost as cheap as a VIP bus.

See p177 for further information on in ternational airlines and p178 for details c domestic carriers.

Bus

There are two bus stations in Chiang Mai: **A cade** (☎ 0 5324 2644), northeast of town, handle Bangkok and most long-distance routes, whi **Chang Pheuak** (☎ 0 5321 1586), north of the centr primarily handles destinations within Chian

BUSES FROM CHIANG MAI

Destination	Bus type	Fare (B)	Duration (hr)
Bangkok	air-con	434	11
Bangkok	VIP	651	10
Chiang Rai	ordinary	100	4
Chiang Rai	air-con	140	3
Chiang Rai	VIP	280	3
Mae Hong Son (via Mae Sariang)	ordinary	187	8
Mae Hong Son (via Mae Sariang)	air-con	337	8
Mae Hong Son (via Pai)	ordinary	142	7
Mae Hong Son (via Pai)	air-con	200	7
Nan	ordinary	158	6
Nan	air-con	221	7
Pai	ordinary	80	4
Pai	air-con	142	4
Sukhothai	ordinary	167	6
Sukhothai	air-con	234	5

Mai Province. From the town centre, a túk-túk or chartered *sǎwngthǎew* to the Arcade bus terminal should cost about 50B to 60B; to Chang Pheuak, get a *sǎwngthǎew* at the normal 20B per person rate.

Train

The **train station** (☎ 0 5324 5364; Th Charoen Muang) is on the eastern edge of town, and many travellers arrive by overnight train from Bangkok. Advance booking is highly advised. There are seven rapid and express trains per day between Chiang Mai and Bangkok with prices starting at 231B for 3rd-class fan seats and running to 1353B for a 1st-class air-con sleeper. The trip takes anywhere from 12 to 15 hours.

GETTING AROUND

Airport taxis cost 120B. Pick up a ticket at the taxi kiosk just outside the baggage-claim area, then present the ticket to the drivers outside arrivals. The airport is about 3km from the city centre. Public bus 4 (red *sǎwngthǎew*, 15B) and 10 (white bus, 10B) run from the airport to Th Tha Pae between 6am and 9pm. You can charter a túk-túk or red *sǎwngthǎew* from the centre of Chiang Mai to the airport for around 65B.

Hordes of red *sǎwngthǎew* circulate the city with fares of 15B to 20B per person, but drivers often try to get you to charter. The *sǎwngthǎew* don't have set routes; you simply flag them down and tell them where you want to go. Túk-túk only do charters at

30B for short trips and 40B to 60B for longer ones. Chiang Mai still has loads of *sǎamláw*, especially in the old city around Talat Warorot. They cost around 20B to 30B for most trips. There are five fledgling fixed-route bus services (the free maps available at TAT show the routes), three with white air-con buses (10B) and two with red *sǎwngthǎew* (15B), but most people still use the regular *sǎwngthǎew*.

There are numerous car-hire agencies in town with reliable cars from 1000B. Two well-regarded agencies are **North Wheels** (☎ 0 5387 4478; www.northwheels.com; 70/4-8 Th Chaiyaphum) and **Alternative Travel** (☎ 08 1784 4856; noree9000@hotmail.com; 56 Mu, 9 Th Mea Faek Mai), the latter specialising in cars with drivers and customised tours.

Traffic is a bit heavy, but Chiang Mai is small enough that everything is accessible by bike. Rentals cost 30B to 50B a day from guesthouses and various places along the east moat. **Contact Travel** (☎ 0 5381 2444; www.activethailand.com; 73/7 Th Charoen Prathet) and **Velocity** (☎ 0 5341 0665; velocity@thaimail.com; 177 Th Chang Pheuak) rent good-quality rides.

NORTHERN THAILAND

The peaks and valleys of northern Thailand are the guardians of an abundance of natural and cultural attractions that make the area a must for most travellers traversing the kingdom. The first true Thai kingdoms arose in the north, endowing this region with a wide range of traditional culture and architecture, which are now the country's most beautiful Thai temple ruins. It's also the home of Thailand's hill tribes. But the scenic beauty of the north has been fairly well preserved: the region boasts more natural forest cover than any other.

Northern Thais (khon meuang) are very proud of their local customs, considering northern ways to be part of Thailand's original culture. Look for symbols frequently displayed by northern Thais to express cultural solidarity – clay water jars placed in front of homes, kàlae (carved wooden 'X' motifs) that decorate house gables, Shan or hill tribe–style shoulder bags and the sêua mâw hâwm (indigo-dyed rice-farmer's shirt) worn on Friday at many banks, universities and other institutions.

PAI

pop 3000

The hippy trail is alive and well in Pai, a cool, moist corner of a mountain-fortressed valley. A solid music, art and New Age scene has settled in with the town's more permanent population of Shan, Thai and Muslim Chinese, though in the high season Pai can feel completely overrun by faràng. The town itself can be explored in a matter of minutes, but the real adventure lies along the paths in the hills beyond.

Sights & Activities

Guesthouses can provide information on local trekking for as little as 700B per day if no rafts or elephants are involved.

Thai Adventure Rafting (☎ 0 5369 9111; www .activethailand.com/rafting; Th Rangsiyanon) has a great reputation (some companies are very lax about safety). Its two-day white-water rafting trips from Pai to Mae Hong Son cost 2400B per person.

Elephant rides through the jungle are just one of the choices at **Thom's Pai Elephant Camp Tours** (☎ 0 5369 9286; www.geocities.com/pai_tours; Th Rangsiyanon; 1-/2hr rides 300/450B). Other options include bamboo-raft trips and hill-tribe village stays.

Across Mae Nam Pai and 8km southeast of town is **Tha Pai Hot Springs** (admission free, soaking 50B), a scenic, well-kept local park. There is a dry-season camp site (30B per pitch) here.

Sleeping

The most atmospheric guesthouses are sprea along the banks of Mae Nam Pai and the number in the dozens.

Good View Guest House (Ban Mae Yen; r 100-250B This sociable place about a kilometre out c town has simple, shared bathroom, A-fram bungalows and rooms with views of th mountains and rice fields. There are lots o thatched communal areas with hammocks and places for campfires.

Shan Guest House (☎ 0 5369 9162; off Th Rang siyanon; r 100-300B) This well-run and well-wor spot is close to Pai's nightlife. A dining an lounging pavilion sits in the middle of a bi pond.

Baan Pai Village (☎ 0 5369 8152; www.baanpai lage.com; Th Wiang Tai; r 500-650B) Beautiful woode bungalows set among winding pathways an a garden give Baan Pai charm.

Pairadise (☎ 0 9838 7521; www.pairadise.com; 98 M 1, Ban Mae Yen; bungalows 650-1000B) Atop the ridge Pairadise features superstylish, spacious an chic bungalows among a pretty garden. Th spring-fed pond is suitable for swimming.

Also recommended:

Pravee's House (☎ 0 5369 9368; Soi Wanchaloem; r 200-600B; 🞇) An attractive house with large rooms and small verandas.

Pai River Corner (☎ 0 5369 9049; www.pairivercorne .com; Th Chaisongkhram; r 3000-6000B; 🞇) Elegant rooms by the river for the design-conscious.

Eating & Drinking

Pai's expat population has generated a larg and varied roster of restaurants.

Cher Xin Jai (Th Ratchadamnoen; mains 20B; 🕑 break fast & lunch) This simple place with low table on rattan mats serves delicious and chea vegan Thai food.

Edible Jazz (Soi Wat Pa Kham; mains 30-90B; 🕑 lunc & dinner) The cushions-on-the-floor atmos phere makes this place a good choice fo a leisurely late-night pasta, sandwiches o Mexican. Jazz CDs play in the backgroun and occasionally the Thai owner breaks ou the guitar.

Baan Benjarong (☎ 0 5369 8010; Th Rangsiyanon mains 40-120B; 🕑 lunch & dinner) It doesn't loo much from outside, but this could be the bes Thai food in Pai, and the tables in the bac have views of the rice paddies.

Taku Art Bar (Th Rangsiyanon) Partially owne by a well-known Thai artist, Taku is the mai centre for visiting Thai hipsters. Both the

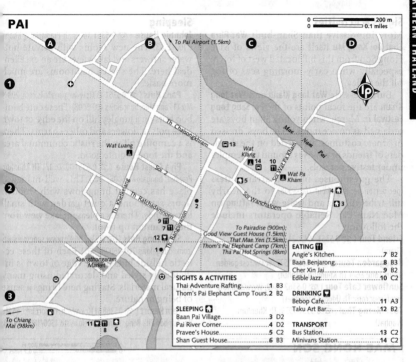

PAI

0 ————— 200 m
0 ————— 0.1 miles

To Pai Airport (1.5km)

Th Chaisongkhram

Wat Luang

Wat Klang

Wat Pa Kham

Soi 2

Th Khettelang

Th Ratchadamnoen

Th Rangsiyanon

Saengthongaram Market

To Paradise (900m);
Good View Guest House (1.5km);
That Mae Yen (1.5km);
Thom's Pai Elephant Camp (7km);
Tha Pai Hot Springs (8km)

To Chiang Mai (98km)

SIGHTS & ACTIVITIES
Thai Adventure Rafting...............1 B3
Thom's Pai Elephant Camp Tours.2 B2

SLEEPING
Baan Pai Village.........................3 D2
Pai River Corner.........................4 D2
Pravee's House...........................5 C2
Shan Guest House.......................6 B3

EATING
Angie's Kitchen..........................7 B2
Baan Benjarong..........................8 B3
Cher Xin Jai...............................9 B2
Edible Jazz................................10 C2

DRINKING
Bebop Cafe...............................11 A3
Taku Art Bar..............................12 B2

TRANSPORT
Bus Station...............................13 C2
Minivans Station........................14 C2

---

music (live and otherwise) and the pop-arty décor are rather funky.

Also recommended:

Angie's Kitchen (☎ 0 5369 9105; Th Rangsiyanon; mains 30-100B; ☯ breakfast, lunch & dinner) All the typical Thai and Western dishes balanced by unusual fruit shake mixes.

Bebop Cafe (Th Rangsiyanon) This old traveller favourite hosts blues, R&B and rock bands nightly.

Getting There & Away
Siam General Aviation (☎ 0 2664 6099; www.sga.aero) has daily Chiang Mai flights (one way 1450B, 35 minutes).

Buses to Chiang Mai (ordinary/air-con 80/142B, four hours) and Mae Hong Son (ordinary/air-con 70/98B, three hours) leave five times daily. Air-con minibuses (150B) to these towns go hourly.

MAE HONG SON
pop 8300

Hemmed in by mountains, Mae Hong Son, Thailand's far northwestern provincial capital, feels like the end of the road, but because of the surrounding beauty and hill-tribe villages,

it's a solid link in the tourist trail. The town's population is predominantly Shan, but the feel is more a Thai town than minority mountain getaway.

Among the province's biggest draws are the 'long-necked' Padaung refugee villages where women wear brass coils to push down the collarbone and rib cage. Opinions vary on whether visiting these villages is constructive (they fled ethnic conflict in Myanmar and survive on tourist dollars) or exploitive (body modification was dying out before tourists started coming, now young girls are getting it).

Information
There are plenty of banks with ATMs and foreign-exchange services on Th Khunlum Praphat. Internet access is widely available.
Post office (Th Khunlum Praphat; ☯ 8.30am-4.30pm Mon-Fri)
Srisangwal Hospital (☎ 0 5361 1378; Th Singhanat Bamrung)
TAT (☎ 0 5362 3016; Th Khumlum Praphat; ☯ 8.30am-4.30pm Mon-Fri)
Tourist police (☎ 1155; Th Singhanat Bamrung)

Sights & Activities

More impressive than Shan-built **Wat Phra That Doi Kong Mu** itself are the views of Mae Hong Son from this hill located west of town; especially when early-morning seas of fog fill the valley.

Burmese-style **Wat Jong Klang** and **Wat Jong Kham** are the focal points of the **Poi Sang Long Festival** in March, when young Shan boys are ordained as novice monks. The boys, dressed in ornate costumes, are carried on the shoulders of friends or relatives around the temples under festive parasols.

The guesthouses in town arrange **treks** (per person per day about 700-800B) to the nearby hill-tribe villages and **white-water rafting** on Mae Nam Pai. Reliable operators include the following:

Friend Tour (☎ 0 5361 1647; 21 Th Pradit Jong Kham)

Rosegarden Tours (☎ 0 5361 1577; www.rosegarden -tours.com; 86/4 Th Khunlum Praphut)

Sunflower Café Tour (☎ 0 5362 0549; www.sunflow ercafétour.com; Th Udom Chaonithet)

Tour Merng Thai (☎ 0 5361 1979; Th Khunlum Praphat)

Sleeping

Johnnie House (☎ 0 5361 1667; Th Pradit Jong Khar r 100-250B) The new rooms with private ho water showers and lake views are an excellen deal here. The shared bathrooms are muc more basic.

Pana Huts (☎ 0 5361 4331; www.panahuts.com; 293 Mu 11 Pang Moo; bungalows 400-500B) These cute bam boo huts on a jungley hill on the edge of tow have pots of flowers and other charms. Ther is a campfire pit in the rustic communal are and the food is quite good.

Piya Guest House (☎ 0 5361 1260; 1/1 Th Khunlur Praphat; bungalows 600B; ✷) This well-manage place has cement bungalows with woode floors set around a quiet garden with smal lotus ponds. There is a pleasant lake view from the restaurant up front.

Sang Tong Huts (☎ 0 5362 0680; www.sangtonghut .com; bungalows 700-1600B; ✷) Each of these ec lectic hillside huts on the edge of town is in dividually styled and decorated using many natural materials. Staying here brings a sense of being in nature.

Fern Resort (☎ 0 5368 6110; www.fernresort.info; 64 M Bo, Tambon Pha Bong; standard/deluxe/ste 1500/1800/2500B

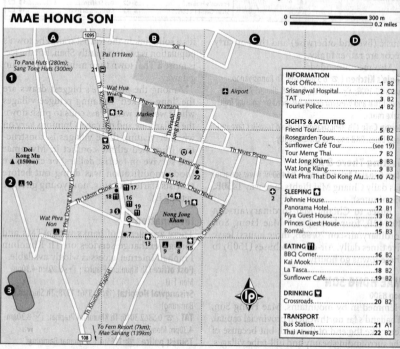

MAE HONG SON

0 ——— 300 m
0 ——— 0.2 miles

To Pana Huts (280m);
Sang Tong Huts (300m)

Pai (111km)

Sol 1

Airport

Wat Hua Wiang

Wattana Market

Doi Kong Mu ▲ (1500m)

Th Singhanat Bamrung

Th Nives Pisarn

Th Udom Chao Nites

Nong Jong Kham

Wat Phra Non

To Fern Resort (7km);
Mae Sariang (139km)

⊠ ⊠) This lush, ecofriendly resort 9km outside town (free transport available) features Shan-style wooden bungalows with stylishly decorated interiors. To encourage community-based tourism, most of the employees come from local villages.

Also recommended:

Princes Guest House (☎ 0 5361 1136; princesguesthouse@gmail.com; Th Pradit Jong Kham; r 150-400B; ⊠ ⊡) Spotless, great-value rooms on the lake.

Romtai (☎ 0 5361 2437; Th Chumnanatit; r 250-600B; ⊠) Spacious, clean rooms and bungalows looking over a garden.

Eating & Drinking

Sunflower Café (☎ 0 5362 0549; Th Udom Chaonithet; mains 40-150B; ☯ breakfast, lunch & dinner) A fine place to while away some time, Sunflower offers freshly baked breads, serious soups and salads, and popular pizzas.

Kai Mook (☎ 0 5361 2092; 23 Th Udom Chaonithet; mains 55-160B; ☯ lunch & dinner) This smart, open-air restaurant has one of the better Thai-Chinese menus in town, with creative specialties like *yam bai kùt* (yam with fern leaves).

Crossroads (Th Singhanat Bamrun; mains 50-200B) This two-storey bar set in a wooden house is a friendly, laid-back place with a pool table and huge cocktail list.

Also recommended:

BBQ Corner (☎ 08 1385 7277; Th Udom Chaonithet; all-you-can-eat 69B; ☯ dinner) Cook your all-you-can-eat meal right at your table.

La Tasca (☎ 0 5361 1344; Th Khunlum Praphat; mains 90-145B; ☯ lunch & dinner) Decent pizzas, pastas and calzones.

Getting There & Away

Thai Airways (☎ 0 5361 2220; www.thaiair.com; Th Singhanat Bamrung; one-way 1270B) and **Nok Air** (☎ 1318; www.nokair.com; one-way 900B) fly to Chiang Mai in 35 minutes. **PB Air** (☎ 0 5361 4369; www.pbair.com; one-way 2370B) flies direct from Bangkok.

There are two bus routes from Chiang Mai: the northern (ordinary/air-con 142/200B, seven hours) is faster by about an hour and has the best scenery, but the southern (ordinary/air-con 187/337B, eight hours) includes more bathroom breaks and smells better (ie fewer motion-sick passengers).

THA TON

In the far northern corner of Chiang Mai Province, little Tha Ton is the launching point for river trips to Chiang Rai, and, to a much

lesser degree, for hill-tribe treks. The relaxing ride down Mae Nam Kok is a big hit with tourists, and the villages along the way are geared up for visitors.

The best places to stay in Tha Ton tend to be on the opposite side of the river from the riverboat dock, including spic-and-span **Thaton Garden Riverside** (☎ 0 5345 9286; r 300-500B; ⊠).

From Chiang Mai's Chang Pheuak terminal you can take a bus (ordinary 90B, four hours, seven daily). Direct or air-con minivans (120B, 3½ hours, half-hourly) depart from behind Chang Pheuak on Soi Sanam Kila for Fang where yellow *săwngthăew* continue to Tha Thon (20B, 40 minutes).

Chiang Rai–bound boats (350B, three to five hours) taking up to 12 passengers leave Tha Ton at 12.30pm. More comfortable six-person charters are available for 2200B. Another alternative are three-day bamboo house-raft rides with stops in the villages along the way. Guesthouses run these trips for 2500B per person, but if you organise it yourself, it could cost around 1900B for a six-person raft.

CHIANG RAI

pop 73,300

Leafy and well groomed, Chiang Rai is more liveable than visitable, lacking any major tourist attractions; though the fact that it's less polluted and more laid-back than Chiang Mai are good enough reasons to come here, plus it's an exceptional spot for arranging hill-tribe treks.

Information

You'll have no problem finding banks and internet access.

Orn's Bookshop (☎ 08 1022 0318; ☯ 8am-8pm) Turn right down the *soi* past Boonbundan Guest House.

Overbrook Hospital (☎ 0 5371 1366; Th Singkhlai)

Post office (Th Utarakit; ☯ 8.30am-4.30pm Mon-Fri, 9am-noon Sat & Sun)

TAT (☎ 0 5374 4674; Th Singkhlai; ☯ 8.30am-4.30pm)

Tourist police (☎ 1115; Th Phahonyothin)

Sights

In the mid-14th century, lightning cracked the *chedi* at **Wat Phra Kaew** revealing the much-honoured Emerald Buddha (now at Bangkok's Wat Phra Kaew, see p114). There is now a near copy of the original sculpture here, and another at nearby **Wat Phra Singh**. **Wat Rong Khun**, 13km south of town, is a unique contemporary take on temple design.

The **Hilltribe Museum & Education Center** (☎ 0 5374 0088; www.pda.or.th/chiangrai; 620/1 Th Thanalai; admission 50B; � 9am-6pm Mon-Fri, 10am-6pm Sat & Sun), run by the nonprofit PDA, is very educational.

Trekking

More than 30 travel agencies, guesthouses and hotels offer trekking trips. Daily rates average 950B per person. Profits from the following agencies go directly to community-development projects.

Akha River House (☎ 08 9997 5505; www.akhahill .com; 423/25 Soi 1, Th Kohloy) Wholly owned and managed by Akha people.

Mirror Art Group (☎ 0 5373 7412; www.mirrorart group.org; 106 Mu 1, Ban Huay Khom, Tambon Mae Yao) One-week homestay programmes are a speciality. Volunteer opportunities available.

Natural Focus (☎ 0 5371 5696; www.naturalfocusecot our.com; 129/1 Soi 4, Th Pa-Ngiw, Rop Wiang) Specialising in nature tours.

PDA Tours & Travel (☎ 0 5374 0088; crpdatour@hot mail.com; Hilltribe Museum & Education Center; 620/1 Th Thanalai) Culturally sensitive tours led by PDA-trained hill-tribe members.

Sleeping

our pick Akha River House (☎ 0 5371 5084; www.akha .info; 423/25 Soi 1, Th Kohloy; s 100-200, d 150-300B; 💻) This Akha-owned guesthouse has comfortable rooms and bungalows in a manicured

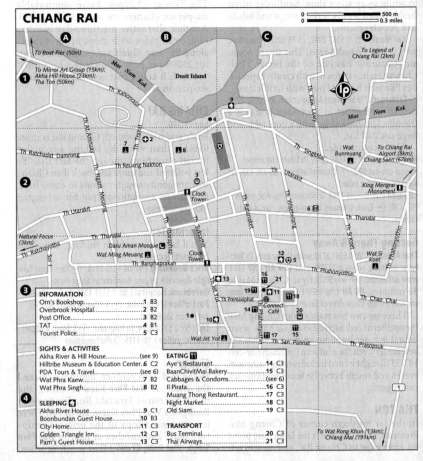

CHIANG RAI

0   500 m
0   0.3 miles

garden, a lounge area along the river and free bikes. Some profits go towards community projects.

City Home (☎ 0 5360 0155; 868 Th Phahonyothin; r 400B; ⊠ 🖵) Down a tiny *soi*, smack in the middle of town, this quiet four-storey hotel offers excellent value.

Golden Triangle Inn (☎ 0 5371 1339/6996; www .goldenchiangrai.com; 590/2 Th Phahonyothin; r incl breakfast 800B; ⊠) Though it has 39 rooms, all with tile or wood floors and stylish furniture but no TVs, this place feels more like a home than a hotel.

Also recommended:

Pam's Guest House (☎ 08 9433 5134; Th Jet Yot; r 150-250B) Plain, but clean and friendly.

Boonbundan Guest House (☎ 0 5375 2413; 1005/13 Th Jet Yot; r 170-500B; ⊠) The old favourite has something to suit every budget.

Legend of Chiang Rai (☎ 0 5391 0400; www .thelegend-chiangrai.com; 124/15 Th Kohloy; studio 3900-5900, villa 8100B; ⊠ 🖵 🐾) Perfect if you want to be pampered.

Eating

Muang Thong Restaurant (☎ 0 5371 1162; Th Phahonyothin; mains 60-100B; ☯ 24hr) Packed nightly for Thai and Chinese dishes such as *kaeng pàa phèt*, a delicious duck curry.

Aye's Restaurant (☎ 0 5375 2535; 869/170 Th Phahonyothin; mains 90-500B; ☯ breakfast, lunch & dinner) Rattan furniture and parasols give this friendly spot a slightly colonial feel, and everything from the steak schnitzel to the curries is tasty and well presented.

Old Siam (☎ 0 5371 4282; 541/2 Th Phahonyothin; mains 105-250B; ☯ breakfast, lunch & dinner) Low lighting and lovely decoration make this teak house a romantic gem. The fish and curry dishes are quite good.

Also recommended:

BaanChivitMai Bakery (☎ 08 1764 7020; Th Prasopsuk; ☯ breakfast, lunch & dinner Mon-Sat, dinner Sun) Profits from this Swedish bakery at the bus station support work with orphans.

Cabbages & Condoms (☎ 0 5395 2314; 620/1 Th Thanalai; mains 35-200B; ☯ breakfast, lunch & dinner) Decent northern Thai food, and all profits to PDA.

Il Pirata (☎ 08 9758 9173; 868/8 Th Phahonyothin; mains 50-200B; ☯ lunch & dinner) A simple Italian-run Italian restaurant.

The night market, off Th Phahonyothin, offers a good collection of food stalls, plus music and dance shows.

Getting There & Away

Chiang Rai Airport (☎ 0 5379 3048), 8km north of town, fields eight daily Bangkok flights. **Air Asia** (☎ 0 5379 3545; www.airasia.com), with prices starting at 1400B, is the cheapest. **One-Two-Go** (☎ 0 5379 3555; www.fly12go.com) and **Thai Airways** (☎ 0 5371 1179; www.thaiair.com; 870 Th Phahonyothin) are the competition.

Chiang Rai is also accessible by a popular boat journey originating from Tha Ton (see p145 for details). Boats head upriver daily at 10.30am.

Chiang Rai's **bus terminal** (☎ 0 5371 1224; Th Prasopsuk) is in the heart of town. Buses head frequently to Bangkok (air-con/VIP 511/900B, 11 hours), Chiang Mai (ordinary/air-con 100/140B, three hours) and Chiang Khong (ordinary 57B, 2½ hours).

GOLDEN TRIANGLE & AROUND

The tri-country border between Thailand, Myanmar and Laos forms the legendary Golden Triangle, a mountainous frontier where the opium poppy was once an easy cash crop for the region's ethnic minorities. As early as the 1600s, opium joined the Asian trade route, along with spices and other natural resources, and the world was soon hooked on opium and its derivatives, morphine and heroin. While Myanmar and Laos remain big players in the drug trade, Thailand has successfully stamped out its cultivation through crop-substitution programmes and aggressive law enforcement. Today the region's sordid past is marketed as a tourist attraction. Sop Ruak, which sits at the junction, has become a tour-bus tourist trap, but other villages in this area are worth a look.

CHIANG SAEN
pop 55,000

Despite steady riverbarge traffic trade with China, Chiang Saen remains a pretty sleepy town. You can while away a day exploring the scattered ruins of the long-extinct Chiang Saen kingdom, visiting the small **Chiang Saen National Museum** (☎ 0 5377 7102; 702 Th Phahonyothin; admission 30B; ☯ 8.30am-4.30pm Wed-Sun) or watching boat traffic.

Simple but good-value rooms and A-frame bungalows, a handy (though slightly noisy) location opposite the river and night market, plus a variety of travel services available on site have made **Chiang Saen Guest House** (☎ 0 5365 0196; s/d with shared bathroom 80/100B,

CROSSING INTO CHINA: CHIANG SAEN TO JǏNGHÓNG

Although it was once possible to travel by cargo ship from Chiang Saen to Jǐnghóng in China, now it's only permitted via passenger boat through **Xishuangbanna Tianda Tourism & Shipping** (☎ 0 5365 1136, 08 9637 1178; one way/return 4000/7000B; ⌚ 8am-5pm). The office is located on the main road opposite the Chiang Saen port (1km south of the ferry pier). The 50-seater speedboat goes through Myanmar and Laos but passengers stay on board. To do this trip you must already have your visa for China (quicker to arrange from Chiang Mai or Bangkok). The people at Chiang Saen Guest House (p147) can book you a ticket and help you get a visa for China. It takes at least four workdays to get the visa.

The trip from Chiang Saen to Jǐnghóng takes 15 hours when conditions are good. During drier months the going is slower, as rocks and shallows can hamper the way. When this is the case a night's stay in Guanlei is included. Boats depart from Chiang Saen on Monday, Wednesday and Saturday at 5am.

s/d 200/250B, bungalows 250B) a longtime favourite with travellers.

Chiang Saen is most easily reached by bus via Chiang Rai (33B, 1½ hours). Blue *sǎwngthǎew* go to Chiang Khong (60B, two hours).

CHIANG KHONG

pop 9000

More remote yet more lively than Chiang Saen, Chiang Khong is an important market town for local hill tribes: several villages inhabited by Mien and White Hmong are nearby. Lots of travellers pass this way between Thailand and Laos. Several banks have branches in town with ATMs and foreign exchange services.

There is no shortage of lodging in town, much of it on the river. **Reuan Thai Sophaphan** (☎ 0 5379 1023; p_durasawang@hotmail.com; 8 Th Sai Klang; r 200-600B; 💻) has spacious rooms in a beautiful teak building while the southern location of **Nomad's Guest House** (☎ 0 5365 5537; 153/4 Mu 3, Baan Sop Som; r 200-500B; 💻) makes it a good place for people who aren't getting on the morning's first bus or ferry.

Buses depart hourly for Chiang Rai (57B, 2½ hours) and daily for Bangkok (air-con/VIP 493/985B, 12 hours). Boats taking up to 10 passengers can be chartered up the Mekong River to Chiang Saen for 2700B.

CROSSING INTO LAOS: CHIANG KHONG TO HUAY XAI

Ferries (20B) make the passage from Chiang Khong to the Lao village of Huay Xai frequently between 8am and 6pm from Tha Reua Bak, a pier situated at the northern end of Chiang Khong. If you're driving, there's the option of a vehicle ferry (US$50). The two-day boat trips to Luang Prabang are a good way to continue on. For information on crossing the border in the other direction, see p314.

NAN

pop 24,300

Nan was a semiautonomous kingdom until 1931, and it still retains something of its former isolation and individuality along with parts of the old city wall.

Information

Internet services and banks with ATMs are easy to find.

Post office (Th Mahawong; ⌚ 8.30am-4.30pm Mon-Fri, 9am-noon Sat & Sun)

Tourist information centre (☎ 0 5471 0216; Th Pha Kong; ⌚ 8am-5pm)

Sights & Activities

Survey the town's distinctive Lanna and Thai Lü–influenced **temples** and take a look at Wat Phumin's **murals**. Visiting the **National Museum** (☎ 0 5477 2777; Th Pha Kong; admission 30B; ⌚ 9am-noon, 1-4pm) helps to pass an unhurried day. Many visitors stop in Nan only long enough to arrange a trek into mountainous **Doi Phu Kha National Park** (☎ 0 5470 1000; admission 400B) and Mabri, Hmong, Mien, Thai Lü and Htin villages.

Ever reliable **Fhu Travel Service** (☎ 0 5471 0636; www.fhutravel.com; 453/4 Th Sumonthewarat) has been leading treks to hill-tribe villages in the surrounding mountains for two decades. Tours start from 800B per person per day. Fhu also offers boat, bike and elephant trips.

Sleeping

Doi Phukha Guest House (☎ 0 5475 1517; 94/5 Soi 1, Th Arayawarat; s/d 100/150B) The helpful English-speaking owner is the best asset at this rambling old house north of the centre.

SP Guest House (☎ 0 5477 489; Soi Tok Huawiang Tai; 250-350B; 🕃) All rooms at this well-situated guesthouse are large and well-equipped, making it the best value in town.

Dhevaraj Hotel (☎ 0 5471 0078; www.dhevarajhotel.com; 466 Th Sumonthewarat; r incl breakfast 700-1200B; 🕃 🖳 🌣) This city-centre hotel is a tad disorganised, but the rooms are clean with the amenities you'd expect at this price.

Eating

Pota Vegetarian Restaurant (Th Mahawong; mains 10-35B; 🕑 breakfast & lunch) The owner here is the friendliest lady in town, and she will not let you walk away hungry.

Da Dario (☎ 08 7184 5436; Th Mahayot; mains 40-160B; 🕑 breakfast, lunch & dinner) This Italian restaurant gets it right in all regards from the homy atmosphere and attentive service to it's mixed Western and Thai menu. Breakfast and lunch are served at the Th Mahayot location and then the action moves around the corner to Th Anantaworarittidet at 5pm.

The night market on Th Anantaworarittidet by the junction with Th Pha Kong, has some tasty food stall offerings.

Getting There & Away

PB Air (☎ 0 5477 1729; www.pbair.com) flies to Bangkok (one way 3160B) once daily.

The government bus station is about 500m southwest of town. Buses travel frequently to Bangkok (air-con/VIP 388/770B, 10 to 11 hours), occasionally to Chiang Mai (ordinary/air-con/VIP 158/221/440B, seven hours) and once daily to Chiang Rai (air-con 150B, seven hours).

LAMPANG & AROUND

Lampang is like a low-key, laid-back little Chiang Mai. Like its larger sibling, Lampang was constructed as a walled rectangle and boasts magnificent temples.

Sights & Activities

TEMPLES & MUSEUMS

Wat Phra Kaew Don Tao is one of the many former homes of the Emerald Buddha, now residing in Bangkok's Wat Phra Kaew (p114). Its **Lanna Museum** (admission by donation) displays

religious paraphernalia and woodwork. Nearby, **Baan Sao Nak** (Many Pillars House; ☎ 0 5422 7653; admission 30B; 🕑 10am-5pm) is a huge teak Lanna-style house supported by 116 teak pillars and furnished with Burmese and Thai antiques. Three rooms display northern Thai crafts.

The wooden *mondòp* (a square, spire-topped shrine room) at **Wat Pongsanuk Tai** is one of the best remaining local examples of original Lanna-style temple architecture, which emphasised open-sided wooden buildings. The old town's other fine structures include **Wat Si Rong Meuang** and **Wat Si Chum**, both built in the late 19th century by Burmese artisans.

In the village of **Ko Kha**, 18km to the southwest of Lampang, lies **Wat Phra That Lampang Luang**, arguably the most beautiful wooden Lanna temple in northern Thailand. It is an amazing structure with walls like a huge medieval castle. Three small museums outside the southern gate display Buddha images, festival paraphernalia and other ethnographic artefacts. To get here, catch an eastbound *sǎwngthǎew* (20B) on Th Rawp Wiang to Ko Kha's *sǎwngthǎew* station where it's a 3km chartered motorcycle taxi ride (30B) to the temple.

NATIONAL ELEPHANT INSTITUTE

The **National Elephant Institute** (☎ 0 5422 8035; www.thaielephant.org; admission 50B; 🕑 elephant bathing 9.45am & 1.15pm) protects elephants by promoting ecotourism, providing medical care and training young elephants. The centre features elephant shows (10am, 11am and 1.30pm) and rides through the surrounding forest. Rides operate between 8am and 3.30pm and cost 100B (10 minutes) to 800B (one hour) depending on duration. There are also a variety of mahout courses including a one-day introduction (2500B) and a three-day (8000B) homestay programme.

Bus and *sǎwngthǎew* (25B) bound for Chiang Mai will drop you off 1.5km away where vans (20B) shuttle visitors to the centre.

HORSE CARRIAGE RIDES

Lampang is known throughout Thailand as Meuang Rot Mah (Horse Cart City) because it's the only town in Thailand where horse-drawn carriages are still used as transport. A 15-minute/one-hour ride around town costs 150/300B.

Sleeping & Eating

Tip Inn Guest House (☎ 0 5422 1821; 143 Th Talat Kao; r 100-160B; ❄ ▨) Friendly hosts, very basic rooms. A renovation is planned.

Riverside Guest House (☎ 0 5422 7005; www.the riversidelampang.com; 286 Th Talat Kao; r 300-600B, ste 800B; ❄) The walls are thin, but this characterful, restored teak building tucked away near the river is still a champ. There is a midnight curfew.

Pin Hotel (☎ 0 5422 1509; 8 Th Suan Dok; r from 450B; ❄) The pristine and quiet Pin feels like a Hyatt or Marriott, only smaller and more intimate.

Heuan Chom Wang (☎ 0 5422 2845; 276 Th Talat Kao; mains 40-120B; ◷ lunch & dinner) This romantic riverside spot in a beautiful old teak building serves northern and central Thai fare.

Riverside Bar & Restaurant (☎ 0 5422 1861; 328 Th Thip Chang; mains 45-225B; ◷ lunch & dinner) Set in a rambling old teak structure on the river, this is *the* place to be in Lampang. There's live music, a full bar and an enormous menu of vegetarian, northern Thai and Western dishes, though pass on the pasta.

Getting There & Away

PB Air (☎ 0 5422 6238; www.pbair.com; one way 1950B) flies daily to Bangkok. Buses to Lampang (ordinary/air-con 51/71B, two hours) leave Chiang Mai's Arcade terminal every half-hour during the day and also from a small bus station near TAT. The **bus terminal** (☎ 0 5427 7410) in Lampang is some way out of town; 15B by shared *săwngthăew*. You can also travel between Lampang and Chiang Mai by train (2nd/3rd class 50/23B, two hours).

SUKHOTHAI

pop 39,800

The Khmer empire extended its influence deep into modern-day Thailand before a formidable rival arose in 1257 to undermine the distant throne's frontier. Naming its capital Sukhothai (Rising Happiness), the emerging Thai nation flourished militarily, claiming lands as far north as Vientiane, and culturally, developing a Thai alphabet and distinctive architecture and art. All this was accomplished in 150 years, before Sukhothai was superseded by Ayuthaya to the south. If you can only digest one 'ancient city', Sukhothai should top the list; the ruins here are better preserved and less urban than those at Ayuthaya. While the old city will charm the pants off anyone, the

modern town of Sukhothai (12km from th ruins) is the embodiment of ordinary.

Information

Post office (Th Nikhon Kasem; ◷ 8.30am-noon Mon-Fri, 1-4.30pm Sat & Sun)

Sukhothai hospital (☎ 0 5561 0280; Th Jarot Withithong)

Tourist police (☎ 1155) At Sukhothai Historical Park.

Sights & Activities

SUKHOTHAI HISTORICAL PARK

The original capital of the first Thai king dom was surrounded by three concentri ramparts and two moats bridged by fou gateways. Today the remains of 21 histori sites lie within the old walls, with another 7 within a 5km radius. The ruins are divide into five zones, and there is a 30B admis sion fee for each zone; the central zone i 40B. A 150B ticket includes entrance to a sites and associated museums. Thailand' **Loi Krathong festival** originated here and i celebrated over five days. In addition to th magical floating lights, there are firework folk-dance performances and a light-and sound production.

The **historical park** (◷ 6am-6pm), known a *meuang kào* (old city), is best reached fror town by frequent *săwngthăew* (15B, 30 min utes) leaving from the south side of Th Jaro Withithong near Mae Nam Yom. Bicycle (20B per day) are the best way of gettin around the park and can be rented near th park entrance. The park operates a tram serv ice through the old city for 20B per person.

Central Zone

Ramkhamhaeng National Museum (☎ 0 5561 216. admission 30B; ◷ 9am-4pm) provides an excel lent introduction to Sukhothai history an culture.

The crown jewel of the old city, **Wat Maha that**, is one of the best examples of Sukhotha architecture, typified by the classic lotus-bu stupa that features a conical spire toppin a square-sided structure on a three-tiere base. This vast assemblage, the largest in th city, once contained 198 *chedi*, as well a various chapels and sanctuaries. Some of th original Buddha images remain, includin a 9m standing Buddha among the broke columns.

Wat Si Sawai, just south of Wat Mahatha has three Khmer-style *praang* and a pictu

:sque moat. **Wat Sa Si** is a classically simple
Sukhothai-style temple set on an island. **Wat
Trapang Thong**, next to the museum, is reached
by the footbridge crossing the large, lotus-
filled pond that surrounds it. It remains in
use today.

Other Zones

In the northwestern corner, **Wat Si Chum**
contains a massive seated Buddha tightly
squeezed into an open, walled *mondòp*.
Somewhat isolated to the north of the city,
Wat Phra Pai Luang is similar in style to Wat Si
Sawai, but the *praang* are larger. The large,
bell-shaped stupa at **Wat Chang Lom**, to the
east, is supported by 36 elephants sculpted
into its base. **Wat Saphaan Hin**, on a hill 4km
west of the old city walls, features a 12.5m-
high standing Buddha image looking back
to Sukhothai.

Sleeping

Most accommodation is in New Sukhothai,
and budget options predominate. The local
taxi mafia is particularly obnoxious here;
don't believe anyone who tells you a guesthouse has closed. Many guesthouses offer free
pick-up from the bus terminal.

Garden House (☎ 0 5561 1395; tuigardenhouse@yahoo
.com; 11/1 Th Prawet Nakhon; r 150B, bungalows 250-350B;
🞱 🖳) This popular and great-value place
has characterful bungalows with large terraces
and well-kept rooms in a wooden house. The
restaurant screens movies nightly.

Ban Thai (☎ 0 5561 0163; banthai_guesthouse@yahoo
.com; 38 Th Prawet Nakhon; r 150B, bungalows 250-450B; 🞱)
As friendly as they come, Ban Thai's excellent
rooms (the cheapest with shared bathrooms)
sit around an intimate garden. This is a great
resource for local information, and it runs a
range of interesting bicycle tours (half-/full
day 400/700B).

Lotus Village (☎ 0 5562 1484; www.lotus-village
.com; 170 Th Ratchathani; r 350-1350B; 🞱 🖳) These
Thai-style houses with tastefully decorated
modern rooms and bungalows sit in a lush
garden among lotus ponds. There's a spa, arty
boutique and communal seating area.

Ruean Thai Hotel (☎ 0 5561 2444; www.rueanthaiho
l.com; 181/20 Soi Pracha Ruammit, Th Jarot Withithong; r 250-
800B; 🞱 🖳 🞱) This antique-filled, two-storey
hotel has heaps of character and prices to
meet everyone's budget. The cheapest rooms
re nothing special, but hit the midrange and
ey are quite nice indeed.

Other recommendations:

Ninety-Nine Guest House (☎ 0 5561 1315; 234/6 Soi
Panitsan; s/d 120/150B) A two-storey teak house surrounded by gardens.

River House (☎ 0 5562 0396; riverhouse_7@
hotmail.com; 7 Soi Watkuhasuwan; r 150-350B)
Simple, tidy rooms in an old teak house overlooking the
river.

Old City Guest House (☎ 0 5569 7515; 28/7 Mu 3;
r 120-600B; 🞱) A range of rooms around an old teak
house close to the Historical Park.

Eating

Kuaytiaw Thai Sukhothai (Th Jarot Withithong; mains
20-30B; 🕑 lunch & dinner) This is a good spot to
try Sukhothai-style *kŭaytĭaw*.

Poo Restaurant (☎ 0 5561 1735; 24/3 Th Jarot Withithong; mains 25-80B; 🕑 breakfast, lunch & dinner) This
simple bar-restaurant in the heart of town
offers great breakfasts, hearty sandwiches
and very tasty Thai dishes – plus delectable
chocolates.

Dream Café (☎ 0 5561 2081; 86/1 Th Singhawat; mains
60-140B; 🕑 lunch & dinner) This compelling café is a
treasure-trove of 19th-century Thai antiques.
The food is no slouch either, with a selection
of sandwiches, pastas, Thai standards and
'stamina drinks'.

The **night market** (Th Jarot Withithong & Th Rat
Uthit), near the bridge has tasty treats and
many vendors have bilingual menus. There
is a collection of food stalls and simple open-
air restaurants near the ticket kiosk in the
historical park.

Getting There & Away

Bangkok Airways (☎ 0 5564 7224; www.bangkokair
.com) operates a daily flight from Bangkok
(1700B, 70 minutes) and Chiang Mai (1440B,
40 minutes). Bangkok Airways charges 120B to
transport passengers between the airport and
Sukhothai; the airport is 27km out of town.

The **bus terminal** (☎ 0 5561 4529) is 4km northwest of the town centre. Options include Bangkok (air-con/VIP 273/407B, seven hours),
Chiang Mai (ordinary/air-con 167/234B, five
hours) and Khon Kaen (ordinary/air-con
179/322B, 6½ hours).

Getting Around

A chartered *săwngthăew* should cost 40B
to any guesthouse from the bus terminal.
Shared rides (10B) run down Th Jarot
Withithong. *Săamláw* and motorbike taxi
rides should cost 30B in town or 80B to the

historical park. Poo Restaurant and several guesthouses hire motorcycles.

SI SATCHANALAI-CHALIANG HISTORICAL PARK

Set amid rolling mountains 56km north of Sukhothai, Si Satchanalai and Chaliang were a later extension of the Sukhothai empire. The 13th- to 15th-century ruins in the **historical park** (☎ 0 5567 9211; admission 40B or free with all-inclusive Sukhothai ticket; ☉ 8.30am-5pm) are in the same basic style as those in Sukhothai Historical Park, but the setting is more peaceful and almost seems untouched. The **information centre** (☉ 8.30am-5pm) distributes free park maps and has a small historical exhibit. Bikes (20B) can be hired around town, or take the tram (20B) site to site.

Wat Chedi Jet Thaew has seven rows of stupas in classic Sukhothai style. **Wat Chang Lom** has a *chedi* surrounded by Buddha statues set in niches and guarded by the fine remains of elephant buttresses. Head along the riverside for 2km to **Wat Phra Si Ratana Mahathat** (admission 10B), a very impressive temple with well-preserved *praang* and a variety of seated and standing Buddhas. Climb to the top of the hill supporting **Wat Khao Phanom Phloeng** for a view over the town and river.

The beautiful pottery of the Si Satchanalai-Sukhothai area was once exported across Asia. Much of it was made in Si Satchanalai, and rejects, buried in the fields, are still being discovered. Several of the old kilns have been carefully excavated and can be viewed along with original pottery samples at the **Si Satchanalai Centre for Study & Preservation of Sangkhalok Kilns** (admission 30B or free with the all-inclusive Sukhothai ticket). There are two groups of kilns that are open to the public: one in Chaliang and the larger outdoor Sawankhalok Kilns site 5km northwest of the Si Satchanalai ruins.

Wang Yom Resort (Sunanthana; ☎ 0 5563 1380; bungalows 600-1000B; ☒) has rustic, worn bungalows in a mature garden just outside the old city. It's nothing special. There are more choices in the nearby town of Sawankhalok, about 20km south of the park.

Si Satchanalai-Chaliang Historical Park is off Rte 101 between Sawankhalok and new Si Satchanalai. From Sukhothai, take a Si Satchanalai bus (38B, 1½ hours) and ask to get off at *meuang kào*. The last bus back leaves around 4.30pm.

KAMPHAENG PHET

pop 27,500

Kamphaeng Phet (Diamond Wall) was once an important front line of defence for th Sukhothai kingdom. It's a nice place to spen a day wandering around the ruins and expe riencing a small northern provincial capita that sees few tourists.

The **Kamphaeng Phet Historical Park** (☎ 0 557 1921; admission 40B; ☉ 8am-5pm) contains a numbe of temple ruins and the very fine remains o a long city wall. The **Kamphaeng Phet Nationa Museum** (☎ 0 5571 1570; admission 30B; ☉ 9am-noon 1-4pm Wed-Sun) has a collection of artefacts fron the Kamphaeng Phet area plus the usual sur vey of Thai art periods, while the **Kamphaen Phet Regional Museum** (☎ 0 5572 2341; admission 10 ☉ 9am-4pm) next door fills a series of centra Thai-style wooden structures on stilts se among nicely landscaped grounds.

Among the many temples outside the cit wall (included in the historical park ticke are **Wat Phra Si Iriyabot**, which features the sha tered remains of standing, sitting, walkin and reclining Buddha images sculpted in th classic Sukhothai style, and **Wat Chang Raw** (Elephant-Encircled Temple), which is jus that, a temple with an elephant-buttresse wall.

Sleeping & Eating

Three J Guest House (☎ 0 5571 3129; threejguest@hotm .com; 79 Th Rachavitee; r 200-500B; ☒ ☐) This pleas ant collection of bungalows, the cheapest wit shared facilities, in a pretty garden has a ver hospitable host. Bicycles and motorcycles ar available for rent.

Phet Hotel (☎ 0 5571 2810; 189 Th Bamrungrat; r 50 800B; ☒ ☐ ☒) This comfortable hotel featur spacious, well-maintained, modern room with views over Kamphaeng Phet.

A small night market sets up every evenin in front of the provincial offices, near the ol city walls, and there are some cheap resta rants near the roundabout. There are also few floating restaurants on the river, inclu ing **Phae Rim Ping** (☎ 0 5571 2767; mains 40-14C ☉ lunch & dinner).

Getting There & Away

The government bus station is across the rive so hop off in town when you arrive. Buses t Bangkok (air-con/VIP 215/274B, five hour and Sukhothai (ordinary/air-con 39/70B, 1 hours) leave throughout the day.

NORTHEAST THAILAND

For most travellers, and even many Thais, the northeast is Thailand's forgotten backyard. In some ways Isan, as the region is called, offers a glimpse of the Thailand of old: rice fields run to the horizon; water buffalo wade in muddy ponds; silk weaving remains a cottage industry; pedal rickshaw drivers pull passengers down city streets; and, even for people who've had to seek work in the city, hearts and minds are still tied to the village.

You'll also find as many differences as similarities to the rest of Thailand. The language, food and culture are more Lao than Thai, with hearty helpings of Khmer and Vietnamese thrown into the melting pot. And though it's Thailand's poorest region by far, based on an official government Well-Being Index the people of the northeast are also the nation's happiest; a fact that is evident if you spend even just a little time here.

And spend time here you should. The scenery along parts of the Mekong is often nothing short of amazing, Angkor temple ruins pepper the region and superb national parks protect some of the wildest corners of the country. Thailand's tourist trail is at its bumpiest here (English is rarely spoken), but the fantastic attractions and daily interactions will likely be highlights of your trip.

NAKHON RATCHASIMA (KHORAT)

pop 215,000

Khorat, the brash gateway to the northeast, is a city you grow to know. Get past the sprawl along Hwy 2 and you'll find a distinctly Isan city with many quiet nooks (inside the east side of the historic moat, for example), where Thai life, largely untouched by the country's booming tourist industry, goes on in its own uncompromising way.

Information

There are banks galore in Khorat, all with ATMs and exchange services.

Net Guru (☎ 0 4425 7441; Th Phoklang; per hr 20B; ☻ 24hr)

Post office (Th Jomsurangyat; ☻ 8.30am-4.30pm Mon-Fri, 9am-noon Sat)

Ratchasima Hospital (☎ 0 4426 2000; Th Mittaphap)

TAT (☎ 0 4421 3666; 2102-2104 Th Mittaphap; ☻ 8.30am-4.30pm) On the western edge of town.

Tourist police (☎ 1155; Th Chang Pheuak) Opposite bus terminal 2.

Sights

In the city centre, the **Thao Suranari Memorial** honours a local heroine who led the inhabitants against Lao invaders during the reign of Rama III (r 1824–51). A holy shrine, the statue receives visitors who offer gifts and prayers or hire singers to perform Khorat folk songs. The steady activities of the devotees make for a lively cultural display. Behind the memorial is **Chumphon Gate**, the only original city gate still standing.

For a dose of Khmer and Ayuthaya art, visit **Maha Wirawong National Museum** (☎ 0 4424 2958; Th Ratchadamnoen; admission 10B; ☻ 9am-4.30pm Wed-Sun), housed in the grounds of Wat Sutchinda.

Sleeping

Doctor's House (☎ 0 4425 5846; 78 Soi 4, Th Seup Siri; r 150-180B) One of the few cheapies where guests bearing rucksacks are the norm, this old wooden home has three shared bathrooms, but it is not for party animals as the gate is locked at 10pm.

Tokyo Hotel Mansion (☎ 0 4424 2873; 331 Th Suranari; r 240-366B; ☻ ☐) Around the corner from the bus terminal, this hotel shows a little more attention to detail than most of Khorat's cheapies.

Srivijaya Hotel (☎ 0 4424 2194; 9-11 Th Buarong; r 480-530B; ☻) The Srivijaya is much too ordinary to deserve its self-appointed 'boutique hotel' label; nevertheless the comfy, spic-and-span rooms guarantee a good night's sleep.

Rachaphruk Grand Hotel (☎ 0 4426 1222; www.rachaphruk.com; 311 Th Mittaphap; r 1200B; ☻ ☐ ☎) 'Grand' is laying it on a little thick, but the only hotel in this class in the city centre is a decent bet if you fancy a few business-style comforts.

Eating

Cabbages & Condoms (☎ 0 4425 3760; 86/1 Th Seup Siri; mains 35-180B; ☻ lunch & dinner) Like the original in Bangkok, this is dining for a cause to help the PDA. It has a leafy terrace to indulge in a carefully crafted menu of Thai and Western favourites.

our pick Rabiang Pa (☎ 0 4424 3137; 284 Th Yommarat; mains 40-220B; ☻ lunch & dinner) The leafiest, loveliest and lowest-key restaurant on this stretch of Th Yommarat has a massive picture menu for risk-free ordering.

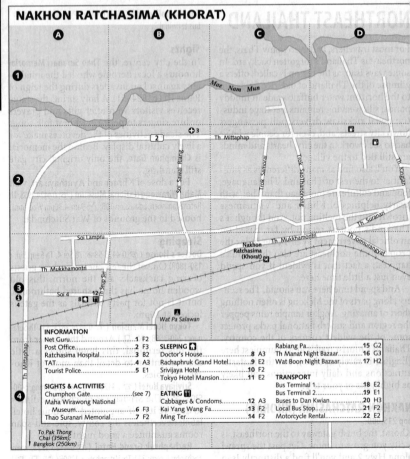

NAKHON RATCHASIMA (KHORAT)

INFORMATION
Net Guru................................**1** F2
Post Office..........................**2** F3
Ratchasima Hospital.............**3** B2
TAT.....................................**4** A3
Tourist Police.....................**5** E1

SIGHTS & ACTIVITIES
Chumphon Gate.................(see 7)
Maha Wirawong National	
Museum..........................**6** F3
Thao Suranari Memorial.......**7** F2

SLEEPING
Doctor's House...................**8** A3
Rachaphruk Grand Hotel........**9** E2
Srivijaya Hotel.....................**10** F2
Tokyo Hotel Mansion............**11** E2

EATING
Cabbages & Condoms...........**12** A3
Kai Yang Wang Fa................**13** F2
Ming Ter............................**14** F2

Rabiang Pa..........................**15** G2
Th Manat Night Bazaar..........**16** G3
Wat Boon Night Bazaar..........**17** H2

TRANSPORT
Bus Terminal 1....................**18** E2
Bus Terminal 2....................**19** E1
Buses to Dan Kwian..............**20** H3
Local Bus Stop....................**21** F2
Motorcycle Rental...............**22** E2

To Pak Thong
Chai (35km);
Bangkok (250km)

Khorat is overflowing with tasty Thai and Chinese restaurants serving cheap meals, particularly along Th Ratchadamnoen near the Thao Suranari Memorial. Two notables are **Ming Ter** (☎ 0 4424 1718; 698 Th Ratchadamnoen; mains 25–60B; ☽ breakfast & lunch), a simple vegetarian affair, and **Kai Yang Wang Fa** (Th Ratchadamnoen; whole chicken 75B; ☽ lunch & dinner) with takeaway grilled chicken. The **Wat Boon Night Bazaar** (Th Chumphon) is the best night market for dining, though **Th Manat Night Bazaar** (Th Manat) is also fun.

Getting There & Away

There are two bus terminals in Khorat. **Terminal 1** (☎ 0 4424 2899; Th Burin) in the city centre serves Bangkok and towns within the province. Other destinations, plus more Bangkok

buses, use **terminal 2** (☎ 0 4425 6006) off Hwy 2. There are frequent departures to Bangkok (air-con 212B, three hours), Ubon Ratchathani (ordinary/air-con 155/279B, seven hours) and Nong Khai (ordinary/air-con 220/338B, six hours).

Eleven trains a day connect Khorat with Bangkok's Hualamphong train station (1st, 2nd/3rd class 460/221/95B), and 10 continue to Ubon Ratchathani (1st/2nd/3rd class 268/133/58B). The fastest trains to Bangkok take 4½ hours.

Getting Around

Săwngthăew (8B) run fixed routes through the city, with most starting at bus terminal 1 and then passing down Th Suranari. *Săwngthăew*

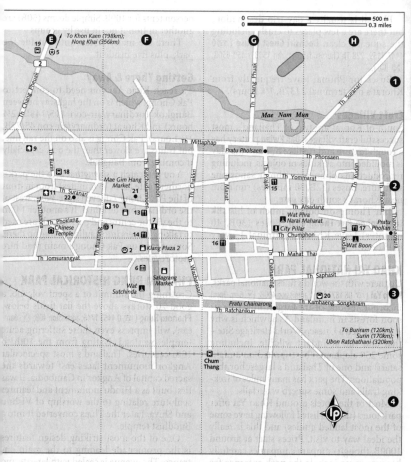

1 takes you past the train station and near Doctor's House and the TAT office, while *săwngthăew* 15 takes a scenic route to bus terminal 2.

Túk-túk and motorcycle taxis cost between 30B and 70B to most places around town. Several shops on Th Suranari near the intersection with Th Buarong hire motorcycles.

AROUND NAKHON RATCHASIMA
Phimai

One of northeastern Thailand's finest surviving Khmer temple complexes sits at the heart of this innocuous little town 60km northeast of Khorat. Originally started by Khmer King Jayavarman V in the late 10th century and finished by King Suryavarman I early in the

11th, **Prasat Phimai** (☎ 0 4447 1568; admission 40B; ⏰ 7.30am-6pm) shares a number of design features with Angkor Wat, including the roof of its 28m-tall main shrine, and may have been its model. Thanks to a superb restoration, Phimai projects a majesty that transcends its modest size. There is a grand sound-and-light show at the ruins the second weekend of November, as part of the **Phimai Festival**, and a smaller version the last Saturday of the month from October to April.

    Phimai National Museum (☎ 0 4447 1167; Th Tha Songkhran; admission 30B; ⏰ 8.30am-4pm), outside the main complex, has a fine collection of Khmer sculpture, including a serene bust of Jayavarman VII, Angkor's most powerful king.

Phimai is usually a day-trip destination, but there are a few places to crash, including the squeaky clean **Boonsiri Guest House** (☎ 0 4447 1159; 228 Th Chomsudasadet; dm 150B, r 450-650B; ⊠ ⊑).

Buses for Phimai leave frequently from Khorat's bus terminal 2 (37B, 1¼ hours).

Craft Villages

South of Khorat are two of Thailand's most successful craft villages. **Dan Kwian** pottery has a rough texture and rustlike hue and the clay is moulded into all kinds of objects, including reproductions of ancient Khmer sandstone sculpture. Buses (12B, 30 minutes) run from near Khorat's south city gate.

Jim Thompson bought much of his silk in **Amphoe Pak Thong Chai**. Buses (30B, 40 minutes) leave Khorat's terminal 1 every half-hour.

KHAO YAI NATIONAL PARK

Up there with the world's finest national parks, **Khao Yai** (☎ 08 1877 3127; admission 400B; ⏱ 6am-9pm) incorporates one of the largest intact monsoon forests in mainland Asia, which is why it was named a Unesco World Heritage Site – that and the abundant wildlife, including some 250 elephants (best spotted on a night safari) and one of Thailand's largest hornbill populations. The park has many miles of trekking trails and some superb waterfalls.

Most of the hotels around Khao Yai offer park tours (the two listed following have some of the most lauded guides) and this is really the ideal way to visit. Prices start at around 1000B, though compare companies carefully because some include the park entrance fee while others do not.

Sleeping & Eating

There are many hotels on the road to the park, but you can also sleep in the park itself.

our pick Greenleaf Guest House (☎ 0 4436 5024; www.greenleaftour.com; Th Thanarat; r 200-300B) This place has some of the few budget rooms outside nearby Pak Chong.

Khao Yai Garden Lodge (☎ 0 4436 5178; www .khaoyai-garden-lodge.com; Th Thanarat, r 350-2500B; ⊠ ⊑ ⊠) The lodge has a good variety of rooms in a lovely garden setting.

There are two campgrounds offering basic two-sleeper bungalows (800B) and fancier three-bedroom villas (3500B). You will pay 30B per person to camp and can rent two-

person tents for 100B. Simple dorms (50B) are another option if not in use by groups.

There are many restaurants outside the park, plus five inside it.

Getting There & Away

To reach Khao Yai you need to connect to Pak Chong, which is on the highway between Bangkok (ordinary/air-con 115/148B, 2¼ hours) and Khorat (ordinary/air-con 45/77B, 1½ hours). Pak Chong is also on the rail line but trains are slower than the bus, especially if coming from Bangkok.

You can catch a *săwngthǎew* to the park's northern gate (25B, 45 minutes) from in front of the Pak Chong 7-Eleven store 300m west of the ordinary bus terminal. It's another 14km to the visitor centre and park guards are used to talking drivers into hauling *faràng* up there. Some shops on Pak Chong's main road hire motorcycles.

PHANOM RUNG HISTORICAL PARK

Crowning the summit of a spent volcano, a good 70 storeys above the flat fields below, **Phanom Rung** (☎ 0 4463 1746; admission 40B; ⏱ 6am-6pm), will impress even those suffering acute temple overload. Dating from the 10th to 13th centuries, Thailand's most spectacular Angkor monument faces east towards the sacred capital of Angkor in Cambodia. It was first built as a Hindu monument and features sculpture relating to the worship of Vishnu and Shiva. Later the Thais converted it into a Buddhist temple.

One of the most striking design features is the promenade leading to the main entrance. The avenue is sealed with laterite and sandstone blocks and flanked by sandstone pillars with lotus-bud tops. The avenue ends at the first and largest of three *naga* (mythical serpent) bridges. The central *prasat* (tower) has a gallery on each of its four sides, and the entrance to each gallery is itself a smaller incarnation of the main tower. The galleries have curvilinear roofs and false-balustrade windows. Once inside the temple walls, check out the galleries and the *gopura* (entrance pavilion), paying particular attention to the lintels over the doors. The craftsmanship at Phanom Rung represents the pinnacle of Khmer artistic achievement, on a par with the bas-reliefs at Angkor Wat.

The rice-growing region around Phanom Rung is peppered with dozens of minor Khmer ruins. Most are little more than jumbled piles of laterite block, but **Prasat Meuang Tam** (Lower City; admission 30B; 6am-6pm), which gets few visitors despite sitting only 7km southeast of Phanom Rung, is in good shape. Though it also has an ancient past, **Wat Khao Angkhan** (daylight hr), some 20km west of Phanom Rung atop another extinct volcano, stands out for its flamboyant nouveau Khmer–style buildings that sort of harken back to the age of empire.

Sleeping

Phanom Rung can be undertaken as a day trip from Khorat, Buriram or Surin, each with a full spread of lodging choices. But the closest place to lay your head is Nang Rong where several places stand out. You can arrange motorcycle and car hire and guides at each.

ourpick Honey Inn (0 4462 2825; www.honeyinn .com; 8/1 Soi Si Kun; r 200-350B;) A longtime travellers' favourite, this welcoming guesthouse manages to be very homey despite the functional design. It's 1km northeast of the bus station.

ourpick P California Inter Hostel (0 4462 2214; Th 59/9 Sangkakrit; california8gh@yahoo.com; r 250-500B;) Newer and cosier than Honey Inn, this hostel is on the far east side of town and is another friendly and helpful choice.

Cabbages & Condoms (0 4465 7145; Hwy 24; r 240-1500B;) This pleasant PDA-run resort (all profits to charity) is ringed by gardens and little lakes west of town, and has a full range of rooms.

Getting There & Away

From Buriram take a Chanthaburi-bound bus to Ban Ta Pek (ordinary/air-con 35/55B, 1½ hours, every 40 minutes) where you'll need to take a motorcycle taxi (150B) or *săwngthăew* (300B for three people) the rest of the way. These rates include waiting times while you tour the ruins.

Buses from Nang Rong to Chanthaburi also pass through Ban Ta Pek (20B, 30 minutes, every 40 minutes), or you can take one of the five daily *săwngthăew* (20B, 45 minutes) from the market on the east end of town that go to the foot of the mountain (where a motorcycle taxi to the top will cost about 30B less).

Those coming by bus from Khorat (air-con 78B, two hours) or Surin (air-con 65B, two hours) should get off at Ban Ta-Ko, a well-marked turn-off about 14km east of Nang Rong. Once in Ban Ta-Ko you can wait for one of the buses or *săwngthăew* from Nang Rong that will pass through Ban Ta Pek (10B) and then continue as previously mentioned, or take a motorcycle taxi all the way to Phanom Rung (300B return).

Motorcycle taxi drivers will add Meuang Tam onto Phanom Rung for about 100B.

SURIN & AROUND
pop 41,200

Quiet Surin doesn't have much to say for itself until November, when the provincial capital explodes into life for the Elephant Roundup when some 300 pachyderms come to town to perform battle re-enactments and other tusker tricks.

Information

Microsys (Th Sirirat; per hr 15B; 24hr) You can access email here.

Post office (Th Tanasan; 8.30am-4.30 Mon-Fri, 9am-noon Sat & Sun)

Ruamphet Hospital (0 445 1392; Th Thesaban 1)

Siam Commercial Bank (Th Sratara; 10.30am-8pm) Has ATM and exchange facilities inside Surin Plaza shopping centre.

Sights

Surin is best enjoyed as a base for day-tripping to nearby attractions.

To see Surin's elephants during the low season, visit the **Elephant Study Centre** (08 1879 2773; donations appreciated; 9am-5pm) in Ban Tha Klang, about 50km north of Surin. Dozens of the performers at the annual festival live here, some in traditional Suay homes sheltering both elephants and humans, and there are one-hour shows (donations expected) daily at 10am and 2pm. The village hosts an Elephant Parade, with all the pachyderms brightly painted, around May's full moon for the new monks' ordination ceremony. Buses from Surin (30B, two hours) run hourly. The village **homestay** (08 1879 2773; per person 250B) programme includes three meals and a little elephant time.

Several renowned craft villages are within easy striking distance of the capital, including **Ban Tha Sawang** where exquisite 'ancient brocade silk' is made on enormous looms worked by four women simultaneously. The village is 8km west of Surin city via Rte 4026, and *săwngthăew* (12B, 20 minutes) run regularly from the market in Surin. Eighteen kilometres north of Surin via Rtes 214 and 3036 are **Ban Khwao Sinarin** and **Ban Chok** known for silk and silver respectively, though you can buy some of both in each village.

Saren Travel (☎ 0 4452 0174; sarentour@yahoo .com; 202/1-4 Th Thesaban 2; ☒ 8am-5pm Mon-Sat) and

Pirom-Aree's House (opposite) lead a wide range of tours to these places, as well as nearby Khmer ruins.

The **Surin National Museum**, about 5km south of town on Rte 214, was built years ago and looked set to open in mid-2007.

CROSSING INTO CAMBODIA: THE POPULAR ROUTES

Thai–Cambodian border crossings are open 7am to 8pm. Cambodian visas cost US$20 (riel and baht are also accepted) at the border and you must bring a passport photo. Officials routinely ask for 'stamp fees' or other such bollocks; refuse, remain polite, and they will usually relent.

Chong Jom to O Smach

Eight *sǎwngthǎew* (40B, 3½ hours) and eight minibuses (60B, two hours) run daily from Surin to Chong Jom. Once on the Cambodian side, there are shared taxis to Siem Reap (US$10, seven to eight hours). This is not the easiest border to access but because so few foreigners use this crossing, it's relatively hassle free.

For information on travelling this route in the reverse direction, see p222.

Aranya Prathet to Poipet

This, the busiest border crossing, is the direct route to Angkor Wat. Frequent daytime buses (ordinary/air-con 118/207B, four to five hours) from the Northern bus terminal and two trains (3rd class 48B, six hours, 5.55am and 1.05pm) per day connect Bangkok with Aranya Prathet. Do not take the direct Siem Reap buses promoted along Th Khao San or you will end up with an extra-long and uncomfortable ride meant to ensure that you arrive so late you will want to stay at the guesthouses the bus operators are in cahoots with.

After running the gauntlet of touts and scammers (ignore them all; you do not need to change money before entering Cambodia or get assistance getting the visa) you'll get to the border and then things get pretty hassle free. Take the free shuttle to the Poipet 'Tourist Lounge' (five to 10 minutes away) which is the bus terminal for Siem Reap (bus 40,000r, taxi US$40 to US$50; five hours), Phnom Penh (bus 60,000r, taxi US$70 to US$80; seven to eight hours) and Battambang (bus 32,000r, taxi US$40, share taxi 10,000r, pick-up inside/outside 16,000/8000r, three hours). The public buses, around the corner, are slightly cheaper than the private.

To travel this route in reverse, see p222.

Hat Lek to Cham Yeam

Buses to Trat (ordinary/air-con 188/257B, 5½ hours) are frequent from both Bangkok's Eastern bus terminal and Northern bus terminal, with those from the latter also stopping at Suvarna-bhumi Airport. The easiest way to Hat Lek from Trat is the air-con minibuses (110B, one hour, every 45 minutes between 6am and 6pm). *Sǎwngthǎew* (50B) also trundle to Hat Lek from the bus station when full.

Motorcycle and automobile taxis will take you across the border for 50B to 80B. Most people take the fast boat to Sihanoukville (US$15, four hours) which leaves at 8am. There are also mini-buses going to Sihanoukville (550B) and Phnom Penh (650B) leaving at 9am from the taxi stand on Ph 3, north of the creek before Ph 12. The journeys take about five and six hours respectively on bad roads. There is accommodation on the island of Koh Kong in Cambodia, but if you leave Trat on the 6am minibus, you can make the boat connection that morning.

Cambodian visas cost 1200B here; dollars and riel are not accepted. The money changers are notorious for short-changing you around 30% to 40%, and even the honest ones offer the lowest rates in the country. The 'Health Quarantine' office on the Cambodian side of the border is a scam, walk right by.

For details on travelling this route in the opposite direction, see p249.

VISITING PREAH VIHEAR TEMPLE IN CAMBODIA

Cambodia's Preah Vihear (p225) ruins, known as Prasat Khao Phra Wihan in Thailand, are all but inaccessible from the south so to see them you've got to go through Thailand. Catch a bus from Ubon Ratchathani to Kantharalak (37B, 1½ hours, half-hourly) and then a sǎwngthǎew to Phum Saron (30B, 40 minutes, half-hourly), which is 10km before the temple. From here you'll have to hire a motorcycle taxi to the park; figure on 200B return with a couple of hours' waiting time. A truck will cost 400B for four people. If you are coming from the west, you can get to Kantharalak from Si Saket (40B, 1½ hours, half-hourly) and continue from there as above.

Sleeping

Sangthong Hotel (☎ 0 4451 2009; 279-281 Th Tanasan; r 80-500B; 🛏) This labyrinthine older property is run with jet-engine precision by smiling staff. The 125 rooms range from some rachitic shared bathroom cheapies on the roof to large and comfy midrangers. Air-con rooms start at 240B.

our pick Pirom-Aree's House (☎ 0 4451 5140; Soi Arunee, Th Thungpo; r 120-200B) The new setting 1km west of the city for this longtime budget favourite can't be beat. Simple wooden rooms (all with shared bathrooms) in two new houses and a shady garden overlook an old flower-filled rice paddy. Pirom knows all about the region.

Surin Majestic Hotel (☎ 0 4471 3980; www.sur inmajestic.net; 99 Th Jit Bamrung; r 800-1800B; ste 3000B; 🛏 🖥 🖵) This shiny new top-ender behind the bus terminal has plenty of extras, such as a fitness centre.

Eating

Petmanee 2 (☎ 0 4451 6024; Th Munrasat; mains 20-80B; 🕐 lunch) This simple spot between Ruamphet Hospital and Wat Salaloi is Surin's most famous purveyor of sôm-tam and kài yâang.

Larn Chang (☎ 0 4451 2869; 199 Th Siphathai Saman; mains 30-180B; 🕐 dinner) This old wooden house, with a garden and a rooftop patio overlooking a surviving stretch of the city moat (now known as Sǔan Rak or Love Park), serves tasty Thai and Isan dishes.

Surin has a good **night bazaar** (Th Krung Si Nai; 🕐 5-10pm) with an excellent selection of Thai and Isan dishes, including, as always, barbecued insects. Two blocks west, vendors fronting the municipal market serve until 2am.

Getting There & Away

Surin's **bus terminal** (☎ 0 4451 1756) connects the city to most others in the region, including Khorat (ordinary/air-con 93/130B, four hours), as well as Chiang Mai (air-con/VIP 690/960B, 14 hours) and Bangkok's northern terminal (ordinary/air-con/VIP 248/342/495B, eight hours).

Surin is on the Bangkok–Ubon train line and there are nearly a dozen services daily to each. A 1st-/3rd-class seat to Ubon (three hours) starts at 140/31B; to Bangkok (eight hours) 1st-/3rd-class prices begin at 346/73B.

UBON RATCHATHANI

pop 115,000

With many interesting temples, frontage along Mae Nam Mun, Thailand's second-longest waterway, and a sluggish character, few Thai cities reward aimless wandering as richly as Ubon.

With the nearby Thai–Lao border crossing at Chong Mek drawing a steady stream of foreigners, Ubon is an increasingly popular destination. The hotel scene is glum, but there are plenty of good restaurants and well-stocked stores offering a chance to stock up on the good life before heading off into rural Laos.

Information

Internet Pirch (382 Th Phrom Rat; per hr 10B; 🕐 9am-11pm)

Post office (Th Si Narong; 🕐 8.30am-4.30pm Mon-Fri, 9am-noon Sat & Sun)

Saphasit Prasong Hospital (☎ 0 4524 0074; Th Saphasit) Has 24-hour casualty.

TAT (☎ 0 4524 3770; 264/1 Th Kheuan Thani; 🕐 8.30am-4.30pm)

Tourist police (☎ 1155; Th Suriyat)

Sights

Housed in a former palace of the Rama VI era, **Ubon National Museum** (☎ 0 4525 5071; Th Kheuan Thani; admission 30B; 🕐 9am-4pm Wed-Sun) is a good place to delve into Ubon's history and culture before exploring the city or province. Just north of the museum is **Thung Si Meuang Park**,

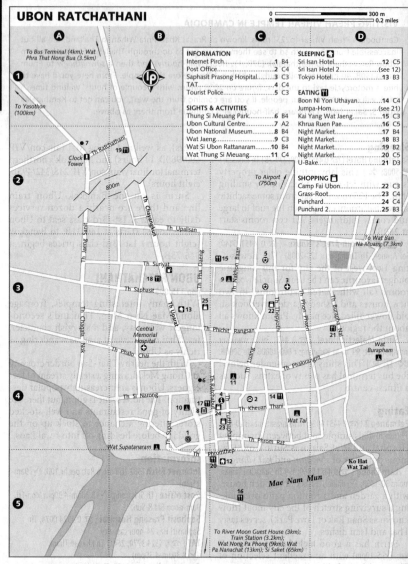

UBON RATCHATHANI

0 _____ 300 m
0 _____ 0.2 miles

INFORMATION
Internet Pirch.........................1 B4
Post Office.............................2 C4
Saphasit Prasong Hospital.....3 C3
TAT.......................................4 C4
Tourist Police.........................5 C3

SIGHTS & ACTIVITIES
Thung Si Meuang Park............6 B4
Ubon Cultural Centre.............7 A2
Ubon National Museum..........8 B4
Wat Jaeng.............................9 C3
Wat Si Ubon Rattanaram.......10 B4
Wat Thung Si Meuang...........11 C4

SLEEPING
Sri Isan Hotel.......................12 C5
Sri Isan Hotel 2..............(see 12)
Tokyo Hotel.........................13 B3

EATING
Boon Ni Yon Uthayan...........14 C4
Jumpa-Hom.................(see 21)
Kai Yang Wat Jaeng.............15 C3
Khrua Ruen Pae...................16 C5
Night Market.......................17 B4
Night Market.......................18 B3
Night Market.......................19 B2
Night Market.......................20 C5
U-Bake................................21 D3

SHOPPING
Camp Fai Ubon....................22 C3
Grass-Root..........................23 C4
Punchard............................24 C4
Punchard 2..........................25 B3

To Bus Terminal (4km); Wat
Phra That Nong Bua (3.5km)

To Yasothon
(100km)

Clock
Tower

Th Ratchathani

To Wat Ban
Na Muang (7.3km)

To Airport
(750m)

Th Upalisan

Th Suriyat

Th Saphasit

Th Jaeng Sanit

Th Chayangkun

Th Pha Daeng

Th Nakhon Baan

Th Phon Phaen

Th Thepyotha

Th Burapha Nai

Wat
Burapham

Central
Memorial
Hospital

Th Uparat

Th Phichit Rangsan

Th Chagtai Nok

Th Phalo Chai

Th Luang

Th Phaloranglit

Wat
Burapham

Th Si Narong

Th Ratchabut

Th Suphat

Th Kheuan Thani

Wat Tai

Wat Supatanaram

Th Phromthep

Th Phrom Rat

Ko Hat
Wat Tai

Mae Nam Mun

To River Moon Guest House (3km);
Train Station (3.2km);
Wat Nong Pa Phong (9km); Wat
Pa Nanachat (13km); Si Saket (65km)

the centrepiece of which is a huge concrete replica of the elaborate votive candles seen during July's **Candle Parade**.

There is more about local culture, plus plenty of wax sculpture, at the museum in the **Ubon Cultural Centre** (☎ 0 4535 2000; Th Jaeng Sanit; admission free; ⏰ 8.30am-4pm) at Rajabhat University.

The main things Thai visitors to Ubon want to see is the 7cm-tall Phra Kaew Busarakham, aka the Topaz Buddha, in the *bòt* at **Wat Si Ubon Rattanaram** (Th Uparat). Binoculars are available. Most *faràng* are more fascinated by **Wat Thung Si Meuang** (Th Luang), which has a photogenic *hǎw trai* (Tripitaka library) on stilts in the middle of a pond, and **Wat Jaeng** (Th Nakhon Baan).

with its adorable little Lan Xang-style *sĭm* (chapel).

The two most interesting temples are just north of the city, and easily reached by *săwngthăew*. The square *chedi* at **Wat Phra That Nong Bua** is richly adorned with *jataka* reliefs and is an almost exact replica of the Maha-bodhi stupa in Bodhgaya, India. The *bòt* at **Wat Ban Na Muang** sits on a boat; a ceramic-encrusted replica of King Rama IX's royal barge **Suphannahong**, complete with a sculpted crew, to be precise. The *wíhăan* also has a boat-shaped base, this time the prince's personal craft, and the temple's entrance gate is an immense statue of Airavata, Hindu God Indra's three-headed elephant mount.

South of the city is **Wat Pa Nanachat** (www.watpahnanachat.org), where English is the primary language. It holds little interest as a tourist destination, but a senior monk is available most days after the 8am meal to answer questions about Buddhism. Any Si Saket–bound bus can drop you on Hwy 226, about 500m from the entrance.

Sleeping

River Moon Guest House (☎ 0 4528 6093; 43 Th Sisaket 2; r 120-150B) This ramshackle place 200m from the train station somehow manages to exude a positive vibe. Facilities are shared.

Sri Isan Hotel 2 (☎ 0 4525 4544; 60 Th Ratchabut; r 160-350B; ✹) This older, dishevelled place, hidden behind its flashier sister sleeper, is, for the price, one of the city's better budget hotels.

Tokyo Hotel (☎ 0 4524 1739; 360 Th Uparat; r 220-500B; ✹) The Tokyo is rather bland, but it's a well-run midranger with some humble budget rooms in the old building.

ourpick Sri Isan Hotel (☎ 0 4526 1011; www.sriisan-hotel.com; 62 Th Ratchabut; r 550-1300B; ✹ 🖳) Natural light swims through the atrium, brightening the lobby of this cheerful place. The rooms, which come with fridge and TV, are small but standards are high.

Eating

Boon Ni Yon Uthayan (☎ 0 4524 0950; Th Si Narong; per plate 15B; ✹ breakfast & lunch) Most of the food for this vegetarian buffet is grown organically just outside the city.

Kai Yang Wat Jaeng (☎ 08 1709 9393; 228 Th Suriyat; mains 20-100B; ✹ lunch) It looks like a tornado whipped through this no-frills spot, but the chefs cook up a storm of their own. This is considered by many to be Ubon's premier

purveyor of *kài yâang, sôm-tam*, sausages and other Isan cuisine.

Khrua Ruen Pae (☎ 0 4532 4342; mains 60-250B; ✹ lunch & dinner) One of two floating restaurants on Mae Nam Mun, Krun Ruen Pae serves up tasty food and a relaxed atmosphere.

Sharing a water- and plant-filled wooden deck are **U-Bake** (☎ 0 4526 5671; 49/3 Th Phichit Rang-san; chocolate cake 40B; ✹ lunch & dinner), which has internet access, and **Jumpa-Hom** (☎ 0 4526 0398; mains 65-1500B; ✹ dinner). Both the bakery and the chichi restaurant serve Thai, Chinese and Western cuisine.

Ubon has many small **night markets** (✹ 4.30pm-midnight) rather than a large one.

Shopping

The speciality of Ubon Province is naturally-dyed, hand-woven cotton and you'll find a fantastic assortment at **Grass-Root** (☎ 0 4524 1272; 87 Th Yutthaphan; ✹ 9am-6pm) and **Camp Fai Ubon** (☎ 0 4524 1821; 189 Th Thepyothi; ✹ 8am-8pm Mon-Sat). **Punchard** (☎ 0 4524 3433; 158 Th Ratchabut; ✹ 8am-8pm Mon-Sat) and **Punchard 2** (☎ 0 4526 5751; 156 Th Pha Daeng; ✹ 9.30am-8.30pm) stock a wider array of handicrafts.

Getting There & Away

Thai Airways (☎ 0 4531 3340; www.thaiair.com) has three daily flights to/from Bangkok (one-way 2700B) while **Air Asia** (☎ 0 2515 9999; www.airasia.com) has one flight (1650B).

Ubon's **bus terminal** (☎ 0 4531 6085) is north of the town centre, just off Th Chayangkun; take *săwngthăew* 2, 3 or 10. Frequent buses link Ubon with Mukdahan (ordinary/air-con 80/144B, three hours) and Bangkok's North-ern bus terminal (air-con/VIP 411/594B, eight hours).

The **train station** (☎ 0 4532 1004) is located in Warin Chamrap, south of central Ubon; take *săwngthăew* 2. There are night trains in both

---

CROSSING INTO LAOS: CHONG MEK TO VANG TAO

Chong Mek is the only place in Thailand where *faràng* can cross into Laos by land (that is, you don't have to cross the Mekong). The border is open from 5am to 6pm daily and you are almost sure to be charged a 'stamping fee' by the Lao immigration officials. Air-con buses direct to Pakse in Laos (200B, three hours) leave Ubon four times daily; they wait for passengers to get their Lao visas. If you got here from somewhere else, you can continue to Pakse by *sǎwngthǎew* (US$0.80, 75 minutes), taxi (US$2 per person or US$10 for whole vehicle, 45 minutes).

For details on travelling in the opposite direction, see p327.

---

directions connecting Ubon and Bangkok. Fares for 1st-class air-con sleeper/2nd-class fan sleeper/2nd-class seat/3rd-class seat are 1080/401/301/175B.

AROUND UBON RATCHATHANI

Deep in Ubon Ratchathani Province are two of Thailand's remotest national parks. Neither can be reached by public transport.

Up the Mekong from Khong Jiam is **Pha Taem National Park** (☎ 0 4526 6333; admission 400B), where its long namesake cliff both provides stunning vistas of the river valley and holds prehistoric rock paintings. Elsewhere in the 340-sq-km park are waterfalls, odd, mushroom-shaped rock formations, and what the park calls Thailand's largest flower field (blooming late October to late December).

Down where Laos, Thailand and Cambodia come together, an area sometimes called the Emerald Triangle, you'll find the 687-sq-km **Phu Chong Nayoi National Park** (☎ 0 4541 1515; admission 400B). Most visitors are here to see Nam Tok Huay Luang, which plunges 40m, plus rangers lead short bamboo raft trips when there is enough water. At the far end of the park there are superb vistas of the surrounding countryside; it looks a lot like the view from Pha Taem cliff, but with jungle instead of the Mekong at the bottom of the valley.

Both parks have camping sites. At Pha Taem, you will pay 30B per tent and can rent a two-person tent for 150B. Bungalows are another option in Pha Taem and will set you back 1200B in a six-bed fan room or 2000B in a four-bed room with air-con. Bunking down in a three-bed bungalow will cost 600B at Phu Chong Nayoi.

MUKDAHAN

pop 34,300

Linked to the Lao city of Savannakhet by the Thai–Lao Friendship Bridge 2, which opened in December 2006, Mukdahan is now a well-

oiled revolving door between the two countries. It's a pleasant, though unexciting town known for its riverfront market (Talat Indojin), which stretches under as well as along the riverfront park.

Sights

One of the most oddly, out-of-place landmarks in all of Thailand, **Ho Kaeo Mukdaha** (☎ 0 4263 3211; Th Samut Sakdarak; admission 20B; ᢓ 8am 6pm) is a 65m-tall tower with a good ethno graphic museum at the base and great view from the top.

Just 15km south of town is hilly **Mukdahan National Park** (☎ 0 4260 1753; admission 400B; ᢓ 5am 6pm) famous for its unusual mushroom-shape rock formations. For accommodation, yo have a choice of camping (30B per person) o bunking down in simple rooms in bungalow (500B) that can sleep seven. Three-perso tents can also be rented for 80B. *Sǎwngthǎew* (15B, 20 minutes) headed to Amphoe Do Tan pass the turn-off to the park entrance, an for an extra 20B the driver will take you th remaining 1.5km to the visitor centre.

If you are travelling under your own stean follow the Mekong River north along Ol Hwy 212 (Nong Ak Na Po Yai) for an un varnished look at traditional Thai life. At th 25km mark, you can kick back at **Kaeng Kabae** a stretch of rocky shore and islets that host several restaurants.

Sleeping & Eating

Huanam Hotel (☎ 0 4261 1137; 36 Th Samut Sakdarak 150-320B; ᢓ ᢓ) Rooms aren't quite as slick a the lobby. They are, nonetheless, good valu in a good location. Mountain bike rentals ar 100B per day.

Submukda Grand Hotel (☎ 0 4263 3444; 72 Th Sam Sakdarak; r 500B; ᢓ) This shiny new tower wa erected in 2006 to cash in on the expected ris in tour-bus business the bridge would brin Rooms are boxy, but they're good.

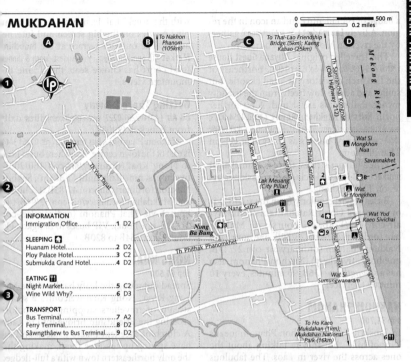

MUKDAHAN

INFORMATION
Immigration Office........................1 D2

SLEEPING
Huanam Hotel...............................2 D2
Ploy Palace Hotel..........................3 C2
Submukda Grand Hotel................4 D2

EATING
Night Market..................................5 C2
Wine Wild Why?............................6 D3

TRANSPORT
Bus Terminal..................................7 A2
Ferry Terminal...............................8 D2
Sǎwngthǎew to Bus Terminal......9 D2

Ploy Palace Hotel (☎ 0 4263 1111; www.ploypalace.com; 40 Th Phitak Phanomkhet; r 1050-3000B; ✸ ▯ ☂)
This executive sleepeasy has plenty of marble and wood for that swanky feel and a decent spread of creature comforts. For something out of the ordinary, ask for the 9th-floor rooms with beehives on the balconies.

Night Market (Th Song Nang Sathit; ✈ 5-10pm) A particularly good spot for eating Isan classics such as *kài yâang*, *sôm-tam*, and deep-fried insects.

our pick **Wine Wild Why?** (☎ 0 4263 3122; 11 Th amron Chaikhongthi; mains 40-130B; ✈ lunch & dinner)
Housed in an atmospheric wooden building right on the river, this romantic little spot serves delicious Thai food and bags of character, though the wine list is history.

Getting There & Away
Mukdahan's **bus terminal** (☎ 0 4261 1421) is on Rte 212, west of town; to get there from the centre, take a yellow *sǎwngthǎew* (8B) from Th Phitak Phanomkhet, near the fountain. There are frequent buses to Nakhon Phanom (ordinary/air-con 52/93B, two hours) going via That Phanom (ordinary/air-con 28/50B,

one hour), Khon Kaen (air-con 155B, 4½ hours), Ubon Ratchathani (ordinary/air-con 80/144B, 3½ hours) and Bangkok's northern terminal (air-con/VIP 364/760B, 11 hours).

THAT PHANOM
This small town might have been forgotten to the world were it not for the looming 57m-tall *chedi* at **Wat Phra That Phanom** (✈ 5am-8pm). It's

CROSSING INTO LAOS VIA THE FRIENDSHIP BRIDGE 2: MUKDAHAN TO SAVANNAKHET

There are 12 daily buses between 7am and 5.30pm crossing the bridge between Mukdahan and Savannakhet, Laos (45B, 40 minutes). Also ferries (50B, 20 to 30 minutes) continue to cross the Mekong from the pier in the heart of town. At our last visit, boat departures were six times between 9.10am and 4pm on weekdays, less often on weekends. Lao immigration is very efficient. See p323 for details on travelling from Laos into Thailand via this border crossing.

a badge of Isan identity and an icon in the region. A lively **Lao market** (☼ 8.30am-noon) gathers by the river on Monday and Thursday.

The traveller original, **Niyana Guest House** (☎ 0 4254 0880; 65/14 Soi 33; r 140B), northeast of the Lao arch of victory, is a tad chaotic, but smiles and advice flow freely from the friendly owner. Bathrooms are shared. A bit further north **Kritsada Rimkhong Resort** (☎ 0 4254 0088; www.kritsadaresort.com; 90-93 Th Rimkhong; r 400-600B; ☒) isn't fancy, but it's as fancy as it gets in That Phanom.

When hunger strikes, there is a small **night market** (☼ 3-9pm) and a clutch of riverside eateries on Th Rimkhong.

Buses depart regularly from the south side of town for Ubon Ratchathani (ordinary/air-con 102/178B, 4½ hours), via Mukdahan (ordinary/air-con 28/50B, one hour) and Nakhon Phanom (ordinary/air-con 27/49B, one hour, five daily). Nakhon Phanom also has a *săwngthǎew* (36B, 90 minutes, every 10 minutes) service.

NAKHON PHANOM
pop 31,700

In Sanskrit-Khmer, Nakhon Phanom means 'city of hills', but they're talking about the ones across the river in Laos. The fabulous views across the Mekong befit this somnolent town, as does the scattering of graceful French colonial buildings. The **TAT** (☎ 0 4251 3490; Th Sunthon Wijit; ☼ 8.30am-4.30pm) office has a map pointing out several of them.

Ho Chi Minh lived and planned his resistance movement here in 1928–29 and **Uncle Ho's House** (donations appreciated; ☼ daylight hr) and the **Friendship Village** (donations appreciated; ☼ 8am-5pm) community centre has displays about his time here. They are about 4km west of town in Ban Na Chok.

Sleeping & Eating

Rarely is a 'Grand' hotel truly grand in provincial Thailand, and Nakhon Phanom's **Grand Hotel** (☎ 0 4251 1526; 210 Th Si Thep; r 190-390B; ☒) is no exception. But it's better than average for the price. The view at **Mae Nam Khong Grand View Hotel** (☎ 0 4251 3564; www.mgvhotel.com; 527 Th Sunthon Wijit; r 700-2600B; ☒ ▢), on the other hand, lives up its label.

There are restaurants along the river, but most of the better eateries are back in the centre of town. **O-Hi-O** (☎ 0 4252 1300; 24 Th Fuang Nakhon; mains 30-220B; ☼ dinner) is an airy bar-eatery

with the usual Thai, Isan and Chinese men plus movies on the big screen and intern access. The outdoor terrace at the **Indochir Market** (Th Sunthon Wijit; ☼ breakfast, lunch & dinne food court has choice seats that frame th mountain views.

Getting There & Away
PB Air (☎ 0 2261 0222; www.pbair.com) flies dai from Bangkok (2905B).

Nakhon Phanom's **bus terminal** (☎ 0 4251344 is east of the town centre. From here buses hea to Nong Khai (ordinary/air-con 160/205B five hours, nine daily until 11.30am), Sakho Nakhon (ordinary/air-con 47/85B, 1½ hours and Mukdahan (ordinary/air-con 52/94B, tw hours), via That Phanom (ordinary/air-co 27/49B, one hour). VIP buses to Bangkok (1 hours) cost 664B to 820B.

NONG KHAI
pop 61,500

Spread out along the leafy banks of the Me kong River, Nong Khai welcomes a stead stream of travellers stopping here befor crossing the Friendship Bridge into Laos A clutch of excellent places to sleep and ea have sprung up to serve them, making thi the only northeastern town with a full-fledge traveller scene; albeit a modest one. But Non Khai's popularity is about more than just it proximity to Vientiane and its bounty of ba nana pancakes. Seduced by its dreamy rive views, sluggish pace of life and surroundin attractions, many who mean to stay a day en up bedding down for many more.

Information
There is no shortage of banks with ATMs an exchange services in town.

Hornbill Bookshop (☎ 0 4246 0272; Th Kaew Worawut; ☼ 10am-7pm) New and used English-languag books, plus internet access.

Immigration Office (☎ 0 4242 0242; ☼ 8.30am-4.30pm Mon-Fri) On the highway bypass that leads to the Friendship Bridge.

Mekong Internet Services (519 Th Rimkhong; per hr 30B; ☼ 10am-10pm)

Nong Khai Hospital (☎ 1669; Th Meechai)

Post office (Th Meechai; ☼ 8.30am-4.30pm Mon-Fri, 9am noon Sat & Sun)

TAT (☎ 0 4242 1326; Hwy 2; ☼ 8.30am-4.30pm Mon-Fri) In the OTOP Center, 1km south of town.

Tourist police (☎ 1155; Hwy 2) In the OTOP Center, 1km south of town.

Sights

Sala Kaew Ku sculpture park (☎ 08 1369 5744; admission 10B; ☽ 7.30am-5.30pm) is a surreal, sculptural journey into the mind of a mystic shaman. This park offers a potpourri of the Hindu and Buddhist pantheon of deities; and the immense statues offer some freaky photo opportunities. While the motivations for its 20-year construction were spiritual, for the casual browser the end result is a masterpiece of mysterious modern art.

The gardens are 5km southeast of town and easily reached by bicycle; Mut Mee Garden Guest House distributes handy maps if you want to take the scenic route. By bus, board a vehicle heading to Phon Phisai or any other eastern destination and ask to get off at Wat Khaek (10B), as the park is also known; it's about a five-minute walk from the highway.

Nong Khai's most famous typical temple is **Wat Pho Chai** (Th Phochai; ☽ 7am-7pm), home of Luang Pu Phra Sai, a Lan Xang–era Buddha, awash with gold, bronze and precious stones.

Sleeping

ourpick **Mut Mee Garden Guest House** (☎ 0 4246 0717; www.mutmee.com; 1111/4 Th Kaew Worawut; dm 90B, 130-600B; ☒) Nong Khai's budget old-timer has a garden so relaxing you may not want to leave. A huge variety of rooms are clustered around a thatched-roof restaurant, Nagarina (right), where the owner, Julian, holds court with his grip of local legend and his passion for all things Isan. There are sometimes cultural performances here.

Sawasdee Guest House (☎ 0 4241 2502; 402 Th Meechai; r 140-420B; ☒) If you could judge a hotel by its cover, this charismatic piece of living history in an old, Franco-Chinese shophouse would come up trumps, though the tidy rooms lack the exterior's old-school veneer.

Nong Khai Grand (☎ 0 4242 0033; www.nongkhai grandhotel.com; Hwy 212; r 1290B, ste 3700B; ☒ 🖳 ☒) This slick, modern place has plenty of sparkle. A big hit with passing suits, 'executive' standards are maintained throughout and swanky suites (usually available at 40% discount) are on offer for those after the Midas touch.

Also recommended:

Ruan Thai Guest House (☎ 0 4241 2519; 1126/2 Th Rimkhong; r 120-400B; ☒) A good variety of high-quality rooms and plenty of garden greenery.

Maekhong Guest House (☎ 0 4246 0689; www.mekongguesthouse.com; 519 Th Rimkhong; dm 150B, r 300-500B; ☒ 🖳) This riverside outfit has little bonuses, like decorative headboards, rarely found at these prices.

Eating

Khrua Sukapap Kwan Im (☎ 0 4246 0184; Soi Wat Nak; mains 20-30B; ☽ breakfast & lunch) The owners of this simple little vegetarian place make a mumsy fuss over *faràng* diners, and serve Thai and Chinese standards that are good enough for carnivores. The juices are excellent too.

Nagarina (☎ 0 4246 0717; mains 35-75B; ☽ lunch & dinner) Mut Mee Garden Guest House (left) tones down its Thai dishes for foreign tongues, but it doesn't spare the spice on its river boat, which is docked just down below. Sunset and night cruises (100B) sail daily.

Rom Luang (☎ 08 7853 7136; 45/10 Th Prajak; mains 40-120B; ☽ dinner) Though the menu is mainly Thai, most of the Yellow Umbrella's best known dishes, like sausages and pork neck, are Isan specialities. The handmade tables and chairs add flair, and the grills stay smoking until 4am.

Café Thasadej (☎ 0 4242 3921; 387/3 Soi Thepbunterng; mains 50-310B; ☽ breakfast, lunch & dinner) Sophistication is in short supply in Nong Khai, but it oozes out of this little restaurant. Both the menu and liquor list, the latter among the best in town, go global. Gyros, weiner schnitzel, pizza and smoked salmon are some of the most popular options.

Also recommended:

Daeng Namnuang (☎ 0 4241 1961; 526 Th Banthoengjit; mains 30-180B; ☽ breakfast, lunch & dinner) This riverside place is an Isan institution thanks to its Vietnamese *năemneuang* (pickled pork spring rolls).

CROSSING INTO LAOS: NAKHON PHANOM TO THA KHAEK

You can catch a ferry (60B) across the Mekong to Tha Khaek in Laos between 8am and 6pm; they run about every hour. Nakhon Phanom's immigration office, where you need to get your exit stamp, is about 250m south of the passenger ferry terminal. In Tha Khaek, Lao immigration *usually* issues 30-day tourist visas on arrival and there's a **foreign exchange bureau** (☽ 8.30am-3pm) at the immigration office. Details for traversing the border in the opposite direction are on p320.

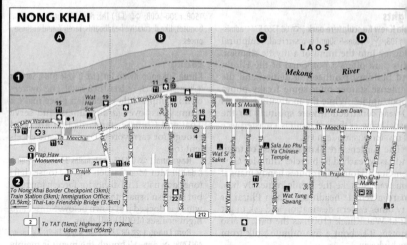

José Ramon's (1128/11 Th Takai; mains 80-140B; ☒ lunch & dinner Mon-Sat) Surprisingly tasty Mexican and Puerto Rican food.

For quick, colourful eats swing by the **Hospital Food Court** (Th Meechai; ☒ breakfast, lunch & dinner) where about a dozen cooks whip up the standards, or visit the **night vendors** (Th Prajak) who set up their stalls each evening between Soi Cheunjit and Th Hai Sok.

Drinking

our pick **Surreal** (☎ 08 1391 3828; 476/4 Th Rimkhong; ☒ noon-1am Nov-Apr, 7pm-1am May-Oct) This little place rises above, both figuratively and literally, the other riverside bars located on this end of Th Rimkhong. It looks out over the river, has a free pool table and book exchange, and the owner Mark nearly never stops smiling.

Coco-Na Coffee (☎ 0 4241 1362; Th Meechai; ☒ 5pm-midnight) This coffeehouse-nightclub hybrid attracts a youthful crowd. Live bands play (November to May) in the terrace out back.

Shopping

In an effort to stem the migration of young women to the bright lights of the big city, **Village Weaver Handicrafts** (☎ 0 4242 2651; www.villageweaver.net; 1020 Th Prajak; ☒ 8am-7pm) established a weaving cooperative making and selling high-quality, moderately priced hand-woven fabrics and ready-made clothing. The *mát-mìi* cotton is particularly good here. Visitors are also welcome in the **workshop** (☎ 0 4241 1236;

1151 Soi Jittapanya; ☒ 9am-4pm Mon-Sat) where som of the products are produced.

The huge **Tha Sadet Market** (Th Rimkhong) offe the usual mix of dried food, electronic item souvenirs and assorted bric-a-brac.

Getting There & Away

Nong Khai's main **bus terminal** (☎ 0 4241 161 is located just off Th Prajak, over 1km fro most of the riverfront guesthouses. Frequer services link Nong Khai to Bangkok (air-cor VIP 482/700B, 11 hours); Udon Thani (or dinary 40B, one hour), a transfer point t other destinations; Khon Kaen (air-cor 148B, 3½ hours); and Loei (ordinary 105I six hours).

The **train station** (☎ 0 4241 1592) is 2km fror town. Nong Khai is at the end of the rail way line that runs from Bangkok throug Khorat, Khon Kaen and Udon Thani. Mos people travelling to or from Bangkok opt fo a sleeper train. There are three night trair out of Bangkok daily and two departing Non Khai. Fares range from 253/388B for 3rd /2nd-class fan seats to 1217B for a first-clas sleeper cabin.

AROUND NONG KHAI

With an early start, these can be day trip from Nong Khai.

Phu Phrabat Historical Park

Steeped in local legend and peppered wit bizarre rock formations daubed with ancier cave paintings, **Phu Phrabat Historical Park** (☎

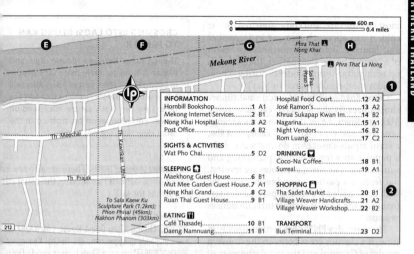

225 1350; admission 30B; 8.30am-4.30pm) is one of the region's highlights, offering great views from the crags of the Phu Phrabat escarpment and plenty of mythical intrigue. Most of the rock formations here feature in an enchanting local legend about two young lovers: there's a short version in the park's museum, but if you're staying at the Mut Mee Garden Guest House (p165) in Nong Khai you can read the complete tale.

To get here, take a bus from Nong Khai to Ban Pheu (35B, two hours), then a *sǎwngthǎew* (8B) to Ban Tiu and then a motorcycle taxi or túk-túk the final 4km to the park itself.

Wat Phu Tok
The soporific atmosphere of **Wat Phu Tok** (6.30am-5pm, closed 10-16 Apr) attracts monks and *mâe chii* (Thai Buddhist nuns) from all over Isan. Monastic *kùti* (meditation huts) and prime meditation places, accessed via a network of rickety staircases, are scattered about an enormous sandstone outcrop.

Ban Kom Kan Phat Tana, the village just outside the wat, runs a **homestay** (08 6086 1221; 200B per person).

To get here without your own wheels, take a bus to Beung Kan (ordinary/air-con 70/110B, two to three hours) where you'll either need to hire a túk-túk (600B for the return journey and a two-hour wait) or take bus 225 from the clocktower to Si Wilai (20B, 45 minutes) where túk-túk drivers charge around 250B to the wat.

LOEI & AROUND
The city of Loei is little more than a brief base from which to prepare for your adventures into the more remote pockets of the mountainous country beyond. **Phu Kradung National Park** (0 4287 1333; admission 400B; trail to summit 7am-2pm Oct-May), about 75km to the south, blankets a high-altitude plateau cut through with trails and peppered with cliffs, waterfalls and wildlife, including elephants. Plan on four hours to climb to the top, where

---

CROSSING INTO LAOS: THE FRIENDSHIP BRIDGE

Nong Khai is the busiest border between Thailand and Laos, and the immigration procedures are straightforward. Take a túk-túk to the border station where you get stamped out of Thailand. From there, catch one of the frequent minibuses that shuttle passengers across the bridge (15B) between 6am and 9.30pm to the Lao immigration checkpoint. Once over the border it's about 20km to Vientiane – there will be plenty of buses ($US0.40), túk-túk and taxis (US$5 to US$7 – bargain hard) waiting for you. If you already have your Lao visa, there are also six direct buses a day to Vientiane from Nong Khai's bus terminal (55B, one hour). To travel across this border from Laos into Thailand, see p285.

most facilities are, and come prepared for the cold, it can approach freezing in December and January. Being the northeast's version of a 'spring break' destination, the park fills up with guitar-toting students during school holidays (especially March to May).

Chiang Khan, still full of traditional timber shophouses, is the archetypical slow-going Mekong town. Several guesthouses arrange boat trips and rent bikes, and **Kaeng Khut Khu**, a set of rapids about 6km downstream, make a popular spot for paddling, picnicking and sunsoaking. The town's temples are modest, but feature a particularly idiosyncratic style with colonnaded fronts and painted shutters that echo the French architectural influences of Laos.

The three-day **Phi Ta Khon Festival**, usually in June, is a curious cross between the drunken revelry of Carnival and the spooky imagery of Halloween. The people of **Dan Sai**, 80km west of Loei, don garish costumes and elaborate masks and dance circles around **Wat Phon Chai**. The small **Dan Sai Folk Museum** (donations appreciated; ⊗ 9am-5pm) on the temple grounds holds some of these costumes. Thirty-metre-tall **Phra That Si Songrak** is the most highly revered stupa in Loei Province (you can't wear shoes or the colour red, or carry food or umbrellas anywhere on temple grounds) while the *jataka* murals at **Wat Neramit Wiphatsana** are superb.

Sleeping & Eating

LOEI

Sugar Guest House (☎ 0 4281 2982; 4/1 Th Wisut Titep Soi 2; r 150-350B; ⊗) The cheapest place in town is also the friendliest. The English-speaking owner arranges trips around the province at reasonable prices and rents motorcycles (200B) if you'd rather get there yourself.

AP Court Hotel (☎ 0 4286 1627; www.apcourthotel .com; 31/29 Th Ruamphattana; r 350-600B; ⊗) The rooms at this newly built property are a bit of a letdown compared with the plant- and art-filled lobby (where you can use wi-fi), but the value is undeniable.

Mobile Steak (☎ 08 5008 8288; Th Chumsai; mains 30-159B; ⊗ lunch & dinner) One of Snow White's dwarves welcomes you to this alfresco eatery that serves tasty Thai, as well as slabs of beef, at wooden tables surrounded by pot plants.

PHU KRADUNG NATIONAL PARK

Atop the mountain there are **camp sites** (per person 30B, 2-person tent rental 150B) and 13 swanky

> **CROSSING INTO LAOS: BEUNG KAN TO PAKSAN**
>
> The crossing between Beung Kan and Paksan is used so rarely that many people in Beung Kan, 136km east of Nong Khai, will tell you that foreigners can't cross to Laos here. They can, but visas are not issued on arrival. For information on crossing in the other direction, see p317.

bungalows (4-sleeper 1600B). There are also sever small open-air eateries serving the usual sti fry dishes for 40B.

CHIANG KHAN

our pick **Chiang Khan Guest House** (☎ 0 4282 169 www.thailandunplugged.com; 282 Th Chai Khong; s/d 200/250/300B) Run by a Dutch tour guide (you never be short of local info) and his affab Thai wife (you'll never stop laughing), th traditional-style place with shared bathroom is built of creaking timber and has bucol views.

our pick **Loogmai Guest House** (☎ 0 4282 2334; 1 Th Chai Khong; r 300-400B) Combining some mir malist modern artistic styling with oodles French-colonial class, this old-school vil offers a handful of sparse but atmospher rooms, an airy terrace with river views and real sense of history.

Mekong Culture & Nature Tours (☎ 0 4282 14 mcn_thailand@hotmail.com; 407 Th Chiang Khan; campi per person 100B, r 800-900B; ▯) Pricey, but seren these six shared-bathroom guestrooms and bungalow sit in the forest 1km upstream fro town. Off-season discounts are available.

The guesthouses and the food vendors Kaeng Khut Khu are generally the best plac to eat.

DAN SAI

Standard lodging consists of flash countrysi resorts and a simple guesthouse, with nothi in between. But the **information centre** (☎ 0 42 1094; Th Kaew Asa; ⊗ 8.30am-4.30pm Mon-Fri) arrang basic homestay accommodation from 15(per person in nearby villages.

Getting There & Around

Nok Air (☎ 1318; www.nokair.com) connects Lo to Bangkok (1750B, 1½ hours), Udon Tha (600B, 35 minutes) and Chiang Mai (2550 2½ hours) on Friday and Sunday.

Săwngthăew (7B) run from the bus station into town about every five minutes, or you can take a túk-túk for 20B. There are several ordinary buses through the morning and early afternoon to Nong Khai (105B, six hours) via the scenic route; it's quicker to go to Udon Thani (ordinary/air-con 60/110B, three hours) and change there. There are also four daily air-con Chiang Mai (438B, 10 hours) departures and many to Bangkok's Northern bus terminal (air-con/VIP 344/685B, 10 hours).

For Phu Kradung National Park, buses on the Loei–Khon Kaen line go to the district town of Phu Kradung (55B, 1½ hours) every half-hour. From there, hop on a *săwngthăew* (20B) to the park visitor centre at the base of the mountain, 10km away.

Chiang Khan has no bus terminal, but all vehicles depart from near the town's main junction. Most Bangkok (air-con/VIP 372/540B, 10 hours) buses depart in the early evening. To Loei, there are frequent *săwngthăew* (30B, 1¼ hours) and nine buses (36B, 45 minutes). Currently the only sure way to get from Chiang Khan to Nong Khai is to take the Loei *săwngthăew* south to Ban Tad (20B, 30 minutes) and catch the bus there.

Buses between Loei and Dan Sai (ordinary/air-con 50/60B, 1½ hours) depart about hourly during the day.

KHON KAEN
pop 145,300

As the site of the northeast's largest university and an important hub for all things commercial and financial, Khon Kaen is youthful, educated and on the move. The city has inherited little of Isan's idiosyncratic appeal, but with fine eateries, swanky hotel rooms and plenty of places to wear holes in your dancing shoes, Khon Kaen is the ideal spot to decompress after humping it through the northeast's quieter corners.

Information

It's hard to walk around Khon Kaen without bumping into an ATM or bank.

Khon Kaen Ram Hospital (☎ 0 4333 3800; Th Si Chan)

Lao consulate (☎ 0 4324 2858; 171 Th Prachasamoson; ☒ 8am-noon & 1-4pm Mon-Fri) Normal turnaround is three days, but for an extra 200B you can get immediate service.

Meeting Net (54/6 Th Klang Meuang; per hr 15B; ☒ 24hr) Check your email here.

Post office (Th Klang Meuang; ☒ 8.30am-4.30pm Mon-Fri, 9.30am-noon Sat & Sun)

TAT (☎ 0 4324 4498; 15/5 Th Prachasamoson; ☒ 8.30am-4.30pm)

Tourist police (☎ 1155; Th Mittaphap) Next to HomePro.

Vietnamese consulate (☎ 0 4324 1586; Th Chatapadung; ☒ 8.30-11.30am & 2-4pm Mon-Fri) Visas ready next day.

Sights

Although it doesn't seem like it at first look, there is more to do in Khon Kaen than revel in the nightlife and shop for souvenirs. First stop should be **Khon Kaen National Museum** (☎ 0 4324 6170; Th Lang Sunratchakan; admission 30B; ☒ 9am-4pm), which has an interesting collection of artefacts from prehistoric times to the present.

For an excellent introduction to Isan culture, swing by the **Khon Kaen City Museum** (Hong Munmung; ☎ 0 4327 1173; Th Rop Buengkaen Nakhon; admission 90B; ☒ 9am-5pm Mon-Sat) which sits at the top of **Beung Kaen Nakhon** (Kaen Nakhon Pond), a 100-hectare lake lined with eateries and walkways. At the lake's south end is **Wat Nong Wang Muang** (Th Robbung) with its gorgeous nine-tier *chedi*. Inside you'll find enlightening murals depicting Khon Kaen history, historical displays and a staircase to the top.

Sleeping

Saen Sumran Hotel (☎ 0 4323 9611; 55-59 Th Klang Meuang; s 150-200, d 250B) The city's oldest hotel is also its most charismatic with the wooden front holding onto its once-upon-a-time glory. The rooms are a little shaky, but scrubbed spotless and the owners are a wealth of knowledge about the area.

Grand Leo Mansion (☎ 0 4332 7745; 62-62/1 Th Si Chan; r 350-450B; ☒) Close to the city's nightlife, this concrete tower is functional and a little frumpy, but the spotless rooms promise a good night's sleep no matter what hour you stumble back at.

Europe Guesthouse (☎ 0 4327 1083; www.europe-khonkaen.com; 23/5 Th Nikorn Samran; r 440-490B; ☒ ☒) This Dutch-owned place is no fancier than the big places in this class, but its six rooms are far cosier. A tiny fan room goes for just 150B, but, like the others it still has TV and fridge.

Kosa Hotel (☎ 0 4332 0320; www.kosahotel.com; 250-252 Th Si Chan; s 1140-1380, d 1260-1500B; ☒ ☒ ☒)

This four-star favourite offers fantastic value with excellent facilities and slick service.

Eating

First Choice (☎ 0 4333 2374; 18/8 Th Phimphaseut; mains 30–180B; ☯ breakfast, lunch & dinner) This plant-ringed, traveller-style eatery has some tasty breakfasts and a good range of Western and Thai dishes, including vegetarian options. It also has some simple rooms upstairs.

ourpick Tawantong (☎ 0 4333 0389; 227/129 Th Lang Sunratchakan; per plate 40B; ☯ breakfast & lunch) This all-veggie health-food restaurant across from the National Museum has one of the best meatless buffets in Thailand.

Bualuang Restaurant (☎ 0 4322 2504; Th Rop Bueng Kaen Nakhon; mains 60–350B; ☯ lunch & dinner) Ask a

local out for dinner and they will probab want to go here. It serves up a great spread Thai, Isan and Chinese dishes on a pier ov Beung Kaen Nakhon.

Also recommended:

Kiwi Café (☎ 0 4322 8858; 311/13 Th Robbung; 50–115B; ☯ dinner Mon-Fri, lunch & dinner Sat & Sun) Coffee, wine, cottage pie and, we swear, the best chocola cake in Isan.

Kao Tom Pae Tee (☎ 0 4324 1932; Th Klang Meuang; mains 50–150B; ☯ dinner) This no-frills local haunt serves up a mean *tôm-yam* until 3am.

Two **night markets** (☯ 5pm-midnight) – a covere one near the air-con bus terminal and a open-air affair on Th Reun Rom – are th life and soul of the budget eating scene.

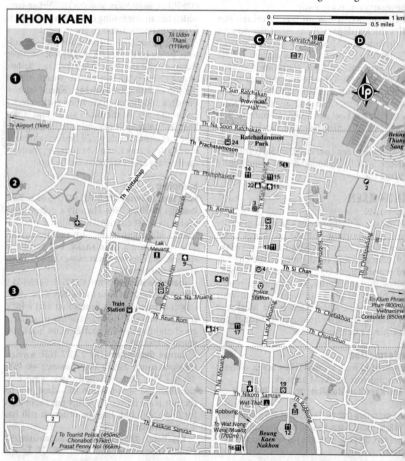

ntertainment

Khon Kaen's exuberant nightlife is centred on Th Prachasumran, sometimes called Disco treet.

Rad Pub (☎ 0 4322 5987; Th Prachasumran) This multifaceted place with two rooms of live music, 'coyote' dancers and an alfresco restaurant and coffee shop satisfies many tastes.

our pick **Iyara** (☎ 0 4332 2855; 43 Th Robbung; mains 5-250B; ☾ dinner) Gorgeously decorated with a Khmer-style art theme, Iyara has a *ponglang* percussion instrument made of short logs) music, dance and comedy show at 7.30pm most nights.

hopping

Khon Kaen is the best place to buy Isan handicrafts. Run by the Handicraft Centre for Northeastern Women's Development, the out of town **Klum Phrae Phan** (☎ 0 4333 7216; 131/193 Th hatapadung; ☾ 9am-6pm Mon-Sat) has a superb selection of natural-dyed, hand-woven silk and cotton produced in nearby villages. **Sueb San** (☎ 0 4334 4072; Th Klang Meuang; ☾ 8am-6.30pm) also stocks natural-dyed fabrics, plus some atypi-

cal Isan souvenirs. Oversized **Prathamakhan Local Goods Center** (☎ 0 4322 4080; 79/2-3 Th Reun Rom; ☾ 9am-8.30pm Thu-Tue) is a great one-stop handicraft shop and has an eclectic museum.

Getting There & Away

The airport (off Hwy 12) is just west of the city centre; a shuttle runs to most hotels for 60B. **Thai Airways** (☎ 0 4322 7701; www.thaiair.com) operates three Bangkok (2305B, 55 minutes) flights daily.

Both the **ordinary bus terminal** (☎ 0 4323 7472; Th Prachasamoson) and the **air-con bus terminal** (☎ 0 4323 9910; Th Klang Meuang) are central and convenient. Buses leave to/from Bangkok's Northern bus terminal (air-con/VIP 329/440B, 6½ hours) frequently. Other air-con destinations include Chiang Mai (542B, 12 hours, 8pm and 9pm), Nakhon Phanom (238B, five hours, four daily) and Nong Khai (148B, 3½ hours, four daily).

Khon Kaen is on the Bangkok–Khorat–Nong Khai railway line, but buses tend to be more convenient. Express trains to Bangkok's Hualamphong station costs (3rd-class/1st-class sleeper 227/1068B) and take about eight hours.

THAILAND DIRECTORY

ACCOMMODATION

Thailand offers the widest and best-priced variety of accommodation in the Mekong region. In Bangkok, the budget range runs up to about 600B and you're looking at about 2500B to move into the top end. In the rest of the country you'll start getting midrange quality at around 400B range and you'll usually start finding true top-end amenities from 1200B.

Rooms under 200B will typically have a shared bathroom and air-con usually kicks in at about the 300B to 400B level. Prices in this guide are high-season rack rates, in US dollars if that's what the hotel uses, but many places offer generous (up to 50%) discounts just for asking. For top-end places, you can usually save money by booking online.

Most national parks have bungalows (typically sleeping six to 10 people and costing between 600B and 2000B) and camp sites (30B per night) for overnight stays. Tents and sleeping bags of varying quality are also usually available for hire. Make reservations through the **National Park Office** (☎ 0 2562 0760; www.dnp .go.th/parkreserve).

ACTIVITIES

Thailand, having a diverse landscape, offers all sorts of athletic escapes from rock climbing to white-water rafting, but most visitors work up a sweat cycling and trekking.

Cycling

Cycling is a wonderful way to see Thailand. In general, drivers are courteous, and most roads are sealed with roomy shoulders. Grades in most parts of the country are moderate, though you'll suffer some lung-chugging climbs in the far north, especially Mae Hong Son and Nan Provinces. Roads running along the Mekong River make ideal touring routes. The 3000-member **Thailand Cycling Club** (www .thaicycling.com) is a good resource.

Guesthouses often hire bicycles for 30B to 50B per day, but check them over carefully; brakes are not necessarily standard equipment. Quality mountain bikes are available in most tourist towns from 100B.

Trekking

Typical trekking programmes in northern Thailand – Chiang Mai and Chiang Rai are the primary base points for organising tours – run for four or five days and feature daily walks through forested mountain areas, coupled with overnight stays in hill-tribe villages to satisfy both ethnotourism and ecotourism urges. These adventures rank high on most travellers' to-do list, but the final verdict is often mixed because of concerns over exploitation and tourism overload in these sensitive communities. See Trekking Tips (p138) for further information.

Other trekking opportunities are available in Thailand's larger national parks, such as Phu Chong Nayoi National Park (p162), where park rangers may be hired as guides and cooks for a few days at a time. Rates are reasonable.

BOOKS

Lonely Planet's *Thailand* guide covers the entire country, or pick up *Thailand's Islands & Beaches* to explore the coast in detail. For more on the capital, try the *Bangkok* city guide or *Bangkok Encounter*.

BUSINESS HOURS

Most government offices are open from 8.30am to 4.30pm weekdays, but often close from noon to 1pm for lunch. Banking hours are typically 8.30am to 3.30pm Monday t Friday, but most department stores have ban branches inside that open 10am to 8pm daily All government offices and banks are close on public holidays. Large shops usually ope from 10am to 9pm while smaller shops usuall open and close earlier. Restaurants generall open 10am until 10pm, though those spe cialising in morning meals usually close b 3pm. By law, bars shut their doors at 1am an nightclubs at 2am, though enforcement wer slack following the coup. The buildings insid Buddhist temples are generally open dawn t dusk; if you find one closed just ask a mon to open it for you.

DANGERS & ANNOYANCES

Thailand is not a dangerous country, but ther are a few things to watch out for.

Thefts are usually a matter of stealth no strength. We receive regular reports of theft from guesthouse rooms on Bangkok's T Khao San, from guesthouse safes in Chian Mai, and on overnight bus and train trips t Chiang Mai. Small locks on bags can help i all of these instances.

Thai friendliness is usually genuine, bu Thais rarely approach foreigners on th street. If someone does this to you in Bang kok, especially around popular attraction there is a good chance it's a prelude to scam. See p114 for more information. An though it's not so common anymore, be sus picious of anyone offering you cigarette drinks or food. Several travellers have re

---

PRACTICALITIES

- *Bangkok Post* and the *Nation* publish national and international news daily.

- There are more than 400AM and FM radio stations; short-wave radios can pick up BBC, VOA, Radio Australia, Deutsche Welle and Radio France International.

- There are five VHF TV networks with Thai programming, plus UBC cable with international programming.

- Thailand uses 220V AC electricity; power outlets usually feature two-prong flat sockets.

- Thailand follows the international metric system.

•orted waking up with a headache and their valuables gone.

A series of bombs exploded in Bangkok on 31 December 2006, and there were two grenade attacks a month later. It's still not certain if this is an escalation of the southern insurgency or postcoup political manoeuvring. This is unlikely to become a future problem, but it would be wise check on this situation.

EMBASSIES & CONSULATES
Thai Embassies & Consulates

Thai diplomatic offices abroad include the following. The Thai Embassy website (www.thaiembassy.org) lists others.

Australia (☎ 02-6273 1149; www.thaiembassy.org.au; 111 Empire Circuit, Yarralumla, Canberra, ACT 2600) Consulates in Adelaide, Brisbane, Melbourne, Sydney and Perth.

Cambodia (☎ 023-726 306; 196 MV Preah Nordom Blvd, Sangkat Tonle Bassa, Khan Chamkar Mon, Phnom Penh)

Canada (☎ 613-722 4444; www.magma.ca/~thaiott/mainpage.htm; 180 Island Park Dr, Ottawa, ON K1Y 0A2) Consulate in Vancouver.

China (☎ 010-6532 1749; www.thaiembbeij.org; 40 Guang Hua Lu, Běijīng) Consulates in Chengdu, Guǎngzhōu, Hong Kong, Kūnmíng, Shànghǎi and Xiamen.

France (☎ 01-56 26 50 50; thaipar@micronet.fr; 8 rue Greuze, 75116 Paris)

Germany (☎ 030-794 810; www.thaiembassy.de; Lepsuisstrasse 64-66, 12163 Berlin) Consulate in Frankfurt.

Israel (☎ 972-3 695 8980; www.thaiembassy.org Telaviv; 21 Shaul Hamelech Blvd, Tel Aviv)

Laos (☎ 21-214581; www.thaiembassy.org/Vientiane; Kaysone Phomvihane Ave, Xaysettha, Vientiane) Consulate in Savannakhet.

Netherlands (☎ 070-345 2088; thaihag@thaihag.demon.nl; Buitenrusweg 1, 2517 KD, The Hague)

New Zealand (☎ 04-476 8616; www.thaiembassynz.org.nz; 2 Cook St, Karori, PO Box 17226, Wellington)

UK (☎ 020-7589 2944; www.thaiembassyuk.org.uk; 29-30 Queen's Gate, London SW7 5JB) Consulates in Birmingham, Cardiff and Liverpool.

USA (☎ 202-944 3608; www.thaiembdc.org/index.htm; 1024 Wisconsin Ave NW, Washington, DC 20007) Consulates in Chicago, New York and Los Angeles.

Vietnam (☎ 04-823 5092; 63-65 Hoang Dieu St, Hanoi) Consulate in Ho Chi Minh City.

Embassies & Consulates in Thailand

Foreign embassies are located in Bangkok; some nations also have consulates in Chiang Mai and Khon Kaen.

Australia (Map pp118-19; ☎ 0 2344 6300; www.austembassy.or.th; 37 Th Sathon Tai)

Cambodia (Map pp118-19; ☎ 0 2254 6630; 185 Th Ratchadamri)

Canada (Map pp118-19; ☎ 0 2636 0540; www.dfait-maeci.gc.ca/bangkok; 15th fl, Abdulrahim Bldg, 990 Th Phra Ram IV)

China Bangkok embassy (Map pp116-17; ☎ 0 2245 7044; www.chinaembassy.or.th/chn; 57 Th Ratchadaphisek); Chiang Mai consulate (Map p134; ☎ 0 5320 0525; 111 Th Chang Lor)

France Bangkok embassy (Map pp118-19; ☎ 0 2657 5100; www.ambafrance-th.org; 35 Soi 36, Th Charoen Krung); Bangkok consulate (Map pp118-19; ☎ 0 2627 2150; 29 Th Sathon Tai)

THAILAND IN WORDS

■ *Monsoon Country* (1990) For a look at rural life in Thailand, the books of Pira Sudham, most famously, are unparalleled. Sudham was born into a poor family in northeastern Thailand and he writes in English in order to reach a worldwide audience.

■ *Sightseeing* (2005) A debut collection of short stories by Rattawut Lapcharoensap that hop from Thai households to tourist cafés. The stories give visitors a 'sightseeing' tour into Thai households and coming-of-age moments.

■ *Thailand: A Short History* (2003) David Wyatt's succinct overview from the early Thai era to the turn of the millennium.

■ *Thailand Confidential* (2005) Ex–*Rolling Stone* correspondent Jerry Hopkins weaves an exposé of everything expats and visitors love about Thailand and much they don't. An excellent read for newcomers.

■ *Very Thai* (2005) A pop-culture encyclopaedia by Philip Cornwel-Smith, it's filled with colourful essays about everyday Thailand from the country's fascination with uniforms to household shrines. As a hardcover, it isn't very portable but it does answer a lot of those first-arrival whys.

Germany (Map pp118-19; ☎ 0 2287 9000; www
.german-embassy.or.th; 9 Th Sathon Tai)

India (Map pp118-19; ☎ 0 2258 0300; www.visa
toindia.com/indian-embassy-in-thailand.html; 46 Soi
Prasanmit/Soi 23, Th Sukhumvit)

Ireland (Map pp118-19; ☎ 0 2677 7500; www.ireland
inthailand.com: 28th fl, Q House, Th Sathon Tai)

Israel (Map pp118-19; ☎ 0 2204 9200; 25th fl, Ocean
Tower 2, 25 Soi 19, Th Sukhumvit)

Japan (Map pp118-19; ☎ 0 2207 8500; www.th.emb
-japan.go.jp; 177 Th Withayu)

Laos Bangkok embassy (Map pp116-17; ☎ 0 2539 6679;
www.bkklaoembassy.com; 502/1-3 Soi Sahakarnpramoon,
Th Pracha Uthit/Soi 39, Th Ramakamhaeng); Bangkok
consulate (Map p170; ☎ 0 4324 2858; 171 Th Prachasamoson, Khon Kaen)

Malaysia (Map pp118-19; ☎ 0 2679 2190; 33-35 Th
Sathon Tai)

Myanmar (Map pp118-19; ☎ 0 2233 2237; www.mofa
.gov.mm; 132 Th Sathon Neua)

Netherlands (Map pp118-19; ☎ 0 2309 5200; www
.netherlandsembassy.in.th; 15 Soi Tonson, Th Ploenchit)

New Zealand (Map pp118-19; ☎ 0 2254 2530; www
.nzembassy.com; 14th fl, M Thai Tower, All Seasons Pl, 87
Th Withayu)

Spain (Map pp118-19; ☎ 0 2661 8284; www.embesp
.or.th; 193 Th Ratchadapisek)

UK Bangkok embassy (Map pp118-19; ☎ 0 2305 8333;
www.britishembassy.gov.uk; 14 Th Withayu); Chiang Mai consulate (Map p134; ☎ 0 5326 3015; 198 Th
Bamrungrat)

US Bangkok embassy (Map pp118-19; ☎ 0 2205 4000;
http://bangkok.usembassy.gov; 120-22 Th Withayu); Chiang Mai consulate (Map p134; ☎ 0 5325 2629; 387 Th
Wichayanon)

Vietnam Bangkok embassy (Map pp118-19; ☎ 0 2251
5836; www.vietnamembassy.or.th; 83/1 Th Withayu); Bangkok consulate (☎ 0 4324 1586; Th Chatapadung,
Khon Kaen)

FESTIVALS & EVENTS

Many Thai festivals are linked to the lunar calendar, so dates change annually. For specific
dates, contact TAT.

Lunar celebrations include the following:

Chinese New Year Celebrated with a week of house-
cleaning, lion dances and fireworks in February/March.

Magha Puja Commemorates Buddha preaching to 1250
enlightened monks who came to hear him 'without prior
summons'. Culminates with a candlelit walk around at
every temple; held February/March.

Visakha Puja Commemorates the date of the Buddha's
birth, enlightenment and passing away. May.

Khao Phansa The beginning of Buddhist 'lent'. July.

Vegetarian Festival For nine days in October, devout

Chinese Buddhists eat only vegetarian food and many
perform acts of devotion. The largest celebrations are in
Bangkok.

Ok Phansa The end of Buddhist 'lent'. Occurs in
October/November.

Loi Krathong Small lotus-shaped boats made of banana
leaves containing candles are floated on rivers, lakes and
canals. Best seen in Ayuthaya, Sukhothai and Chiang Mai.
Held in October/November.

FOOD & DRINK

Welcome to a country where it is cheape
and tastier to eat out than to cook at home
Day and night markets, pushcart vendors
makeshift stalls, open-air restaurants – price
stay low because of few or no overheads, and
cooks become famous in all walks of life fo
a particular dish.

Take a walk through the day markets and
you will see mounds of clay-coloured paste
all lined up like art supplies. These are finel
ground herbs and seasonings that create th
backbone for Thai *kaeng* (curries). The past
is thinned with coconut milk and decorate
with vegetables and meat. Although it is the
consistency of a watery soup, *kaeng* is no
eaten like Western-style soup, but is ladle
on to a plate of rice.

For breakfast and for late-night snacks
Thais nosh on *kŭaytĭaw*, a noodle soup wit
chicken or pork and vegetables. There ar
two major types of noodles you can choos
from: *sên lek* (thin) and *sên yài* (wide and
flat). Before you dig into your steaming bowl
first use the chopsticks (or a spoon) to cu
the noodles into smaller segments so the
are easier to pick up. Then add to taste a few
teaspoonsful of the provided spices: drie
red chilli, sugar, fish sauce and vinegar. Now
you have the true taste of Thailand in fron
of you.

Not sure what to order at some of the pop
ular dinner restaurants? Reliable favourite
are *yam plaa mèuk* (spicy squid salad wit
mint leaves, cilantro and Chinese celery)
tôm yam kûng (coconut soup with prawns
often translated as 'hot and sour soup') or it
sister dish *tôm khàa kài* (coconut soup wit
chicken and galangal).

Thais are social eaters: meals are rarel
taken alone and dishes are meant to be shared
Usually a small army of plates will be place
in the centre of the table, with individua
servings of rice in front of each diner. The
protocol goes like this – ladle a spoonful o

food at a time on to your plate of rice. Dishes aren't passed in Thailand; instead you reach across the table to the different items. Using the spoon like a fork and your fork like a knife, steer the food (with the fork) onto your spoon, which enters your mouth. To the Thais placing a fork in the mouth is just plain weird. When you are full, leave a little rice on your plate (an empty plate is a silent request for more rice) and place your fork so that it is cradled by the spoon in the centre of the plate.

Even when eating with a gang of *faràng*, it is still wise to order 'family style', as dishes are rarely synchronised. Ordering individually will leave one person staring politely at a piping hot plate, and another staring wistfully at the kitchen.

For more on dining out in the Mekong region, see p86.

HOLIDAYS

Businesses typically close and transportation becomes difficult during these public holidays:

New Year's Day 1 January.

Chakri Memorial Day 6 April; celebrates the founder of the current royal dynasty.

Songkran 13-15 April; start of Lunar New Year. Buddha images are 'bathed', and water is splashed on people.

Labour Day 1 May.

Coronation Day 5 May.

Queen's Birthday 12 August.

Chulalongkorn Day 23 October; King Chulalongkorn is honoured.

King's Birthday 5 December.

Constitution Day 10 December.

New Year's Eve 31 December.

INTERNET ACCESS

Internet cafés are very common in Thailand, and connections are usually reliable. The going rate is normally 30B per hour. Wi-fi is becoming common in Bangkok and touristy areas.

INTERNET RESOURCES

Lonely Planet (www.lonelyplanet.com) Country-specific information as well as reader information exchange on the Thorn Tree forum.

Thailand Daily (www.thailanddaily.com) A thorough digest of Thailand-related news in English.

ThaiVisa.com (www.thaivisa.com) More than what the name implies, there is plenty of other travel-related material.

Tourism Authority of Thailand (TAT; www.tourism thailand.org) Thailand's official tourism website is a very handy resource.

LEGAL MATTERS

In general, Thai police don't hassle tourists, unless you are caught holding drugs. If it's a small amount you might be able to get away by paying a 'fine', but traffickers are certain to end up in prison.

If you are arrested for any offence, the police will let you make a phone call to your embassy or consulate, if you have one, or to a friend or relative if not. Thai law does not presume an indicted detainee to be either 'guilty' or 'innocent' but rather a 'suspect', whose guilt or innocence will be decided in court. Trials are usually speedy.

The **tourist police** (☎ 1155) usually speak English, often quite well, and offer a range of assistance from providing road conditions during floods to assistance if you've been ripped-off or robbed.

MONEY

The unit of Thai currency is the baht, which is divided into 100 satang; coins include 25-satang and 50-satang pieces and baht in 1B, 5B and 10B coins. Notes are in 10B (brown), 20B (green), 50B (blue), 100B (red), 500B (purple) and 1000B (beige). Except for top-end hotels, which usually quote rates in dollars (because they don't give the best exchange rate, it's usually cheaper to pay in baht) other currencies are rarely accepted.

ATMs & Credit/Debit Cards

Debit and ATM cards issued by your home bank can be used at ATMs, which are widespread, to withdraw cash (in Thai baht only). Cards can also be used for purchases at many shops, hotels and restaurants. The most commonly accepted cards are Visa and MasterCard, followed by Amex and Japan Card Bureau (JCB).

Changing Money

Banks and private moneychangers (only found in popular tourist destinations) give the best exchange rates and hotels give the worst. Since banks charge commission and duty for each travellers cheque cashed, use large denominations. British pounds and euros are second to the US dollar in general acceptability.

Exchange rates are as follows:

Country	Unit	Baht
Australia	A$1	27.30
Cambodia	100r	0.81
Canada	C$1	29.50
China	Y1	4.30
euro zone	€1	44.40
Japan	¥100	27.30
Laos	1000 kip	3.40
New Zealand	NZ$1	24.20
UK	£1	65.05
USA	US$1	32.80
Vietnam	10,000d	20.50

POST

The Thai postal system is efficient, inexpensive and reliable; though don't send cash or small valuables, just to be on the safe side. Poste restante can be received in any town that has a post office.

RESPONSIBLE TRAVEL

Be aware about having a negative impact on the environment or the local culture. Read the boxed text, p111, for some general guidance on observing social mores. See p122 for advice on what to wear in sacred sites. For trekking tips, see p138 and p484.

Despite Thailand's reputation for sex tourism, prostitution was declared illegal in the 1950s. The government does little to enforce antiprostitution laws in cases of consenting adults; however, anyone caught having sex with a person under 15 years of age could face stiff jail time and a life sentence if the child is under 13. Many Western countries have also instituted extraterritorial legislation where citizens can be charged for child prostitution offences committed abroad. The Thai government encourages people to help eradicate child prostitution by reporting child sexual abuse. **End Child Prostitution & Trafficking International** (Ecpat; ☎ 0 2215 3388; www.ecpat.org) works to stop child prostitution, child pornography and the trafficking of children for sexual purposes.

TELEPHONE

The telephone system in Thailand is quite efficient and offers International Direct Dial universally. You can make international calls on payphones to most countries from about 7B per minute (dial ☎ 001 before the number, though for Laos ☎ 007 and country code 856)

with prepaid phonecards available from 7 Eleven stores, or use the government phone offices at or near main post offices. Hotel and guesthouse phone services are usually considerably more expensive, and internet call vary in quality.

Roaming charges are quite reasonable in Thailand for those with mobile phones. If you buy a SIM card in Thailand for your phone, rates are typically around 3B per minute anywhere in Thailand and between 5B and 7B for international calls.

The ☎ 0 preceding all numbers in this book is only used when dialling domestically.

To accommodate the growth in mobile phone usage, Thailand has introduced an '8' prefix to all mobile numbers; ie ☎ 0 123-5678 is now ☎ 08 1234 5678.

TOURIST INFORMATION

The helpful **Tourist Authority of Thailand** (TAT; www.tourismthailand.org) has more than two dozen offices throughout the country. Most staff speak English. Check TAT's website for a list of overseas offices, plus plenty of tourism information.

VISAS

Citizens of 41 countries (including most European countries, Australia, New Zealand and the USA) can enter Thailand visa-free at no charge. See the website of Thailand's **Ministry of Foreign Affairs** (www.mfa.go.th) for the full story. Sixty-day Tourist Visas (around US$25) and 90-day Non-Immigrant Visas (US$50 for single entry) intended for business, study, retirement and extended family visits are available from Thai embassies or consulates. Officially on arrival, you must prove you have sufficient funds for your stay, but visitors are rarely asked about this.

If you overstay your visa, the penalty is 500B per day, with a 20,000B limit; fines can be paid at any official exit point or the **Bangkok immigration office** (Map pp118-19; ☎ 0 2287 3101; Soi Suan Phlu, Th Sathon Tai; ☑ 9am-noon & 1-4.30pm Mon-Fri, 9am-noon Sat).

You can extend your stay, for the normal fee of 1900B, by visiting any immigration office. The duration is up to the discretion of the immigration officer. You may also leave the county and re-enter in order to receive another 30-day stamp, but the days of unlimited entry stamps is over. Visitors may now not stay more than 90 days in Thailand n any six-month period. Confusingly, some border officials are interpreting this to include only being allowed to enter the country three times; others are not.

VOLUNTEERING

Mirror Art Foundation (☎ 0 5373 7412; www.mirrorartgroup.org) Places English and Thai teachers in Chiang Mai Province's Mae Yao hill-tribe villages.

Open Mind Projects (☎ 0 4241 3578; www.openmindprojects.org) Offers a lengthy list of volunteering options throughout the country.

Starfish Ventures (☎ www.starfishventures.co.uk) Has nursing, English-teaching and other projects in Surin Province plus several environmental projects in the south.

Travel to Teach (☎ 0 8424 60351; www.travel-to-teach.org) Offers flexible volunteering positions from two weeks to six months in schools, English camps or temples teaching monks.

Volunthai (www.volunthai.com) Places teachers at local schools in northeast Thailand with homestay accommodation.

TRANSPORT IN THAILAND

GETTING THERE & AWAY
Air

Almost all international flights use Bangkok's much-maligned (but improving) **Suvarnabhumi Airport** (www.bangkokairportonline.com) – pronounced soo-wan-na-poom'– though there are a handful of flights to and from other cities, including Chiang Mai.

Bangkok is *the* air travel hub for mainland Southeast Asia, and because of the Thai government's loose restrictions on air fares and close competition between airlines and travel agencies, Bangkok is one of the cheapest cities in the world to fly out of. Some of the major carriers:

Air Asia (airline code AK; ☎ 0 2515 9999; www.airasia.com; Suvarnabhumi Airport; hub Kuala Lumpur)

Air China (airline code CA; Map pp118-19; ☎ 0 2634 991; www.fly-airchina.com; Bangkok Union Insurance Bldg, 175-177 Th Surawong; hub Běijīng)

Air France (airline code AF; Map pp118-19; ☎ 0 2635 191; www.airfrance.fr; 20th fl, Vorawat Bldg, 849 Th Silom; hub Paris)

American Airlines (airline code AA; Map pp118-19; ☎ 0 2263 0225; www.aa.com; 11th fl Ploenchit Tower, 898 Th Ploenchit; hub Dallas)

Bangkok Airways (airline code PG; ☎ 0 2265 5555; www.bangkokair.com; hub Bangkok)

British Airways (airline code BA; Map pp118-19; ☎ 0 2627 1701; www.britishairways.com; 21st fl, Charn Issara Tower, 942/160-163 Th Phra Rama IV; hub London)

Cathay Pacific Airways (airline code CX; Map pp118-19; ☎ 0 2263 0606; www.cathaypacific.com; Ploenchit Tower, 898 Th Ploenchit; hub Hong Kong)

KLM-Royal Dutch Airlines (airline code KL; Map pp118-19; ☎ 0 2635 2300; www.klm.com; 20th fl, Vorawat Bldg, 849 Th Silom; hub Amsterdam)

Lao Airlines (airline code QV; Map pp118-19; ☎ 0 2236 9822; www.laoairlines.com; Silom Plaza, Th Silom; hub Vientiane)

Lufthansa Airlines (airline code LH; Map pp118-19; ☎ 0 2264 2400; www.lufthansa.com; 18th fl, Q House, Soi Asoke, Th Sukhumvit; hub Frankfurt)

Northwest Airlines (airline code NW; Map pp118-19; ☎ 0 2254 0789; www.nwa.com; 4th fl, Peninsula Plaza, 153 Th Ratchadamri; hub Minneapolis)

Orient Thai (airline code OX; Map pp118-19; ☎ 0 2229 4260; www.orient-thai.com; 18 Th Rachadaphisek; hub Bangkok)

Qantas Airways (airline code QF; Map pp118-19; ☎ 0 2636 1747; www.qantas.com.au; Tour East, 21st fl, Charn Issara Tower, 942/160-163 Th Phra Ram IV; hub Sydney)

South African Airways (airline code SA; Map pp118-19; ☎ 0 2635 1414; www.flysaa.com; 20th fl, Vorawat Bldg, 849 Th Silom; hub Johannesburg)

Thai Airways International (airline code TG; hub Bangkok; www.thaiair.com) Lan Luang (Map pp118-19; ☎ 0 2356 1111, 6 Th Lan Luang); Silom (Map pp118-19; ☎ 0 2232 8000, 485 Th Silom)

United Airlines (airline code UA; Map pp118-19; ☎ 0 2296 7752; www.ual.com; 14th fl, Sindhorn Bldg, Tower 3, 130 Th Withayu; hub Chicago)

Vietnam Airlines (airline code VN; Map pp118-19; ☎ 0 2656 9056; www.vietnamair.com.vn; Th Sukhumvit; hub Hanoi)

Border Crossings
See p101 for the Mekong region's border crossings at a glance. It's possible to travel from Thailand to China (through Myanmar and Laos) by passenger boat; see p148.

CAMBODIA
Thailand has six border crossings open to Cambodia, but only three are of any practical use. For specific border-crossing info, see p158.

LAOS
There are six gateways from Thailand into Laos. A remote border crossing between Muang Ngoen, in Sainyabuli Province, and

Huay Kon, in Thailand's Nan Province, is seldom used by foreigners. The Beung Kan to Paksan crossing is used so rarely that many people in Beung Kan, 136km east of Nong Khai, will tell you that foreigners can't cross to Laos here. They can, but visas are not issued on arrival.

Most foreigners pay either US$30 or US$35 – though Canadians get socked with a US$42 fee – for 30-day Tourist Visas, which are available at all but the Beung Kan crossing. You are also allowed to pay in baht, but the price works out much higher. Besides the fee, you'll need a passport photo and the name of a hotel you will be staying at in Laos. There is sometimes pressure to pay unofficial 'stamping fees' at some checkpoints. The US$1 (50B) overtime fee charged before 8am, after 4pm and on weekends is obnoxious, but apparently official.

GETTING AROUND
Air
Hopping around the country by air can be quite affordable, and prices can be almost as low as a VIP bus ticket. Most routes originate in Bangkok, either at the new Suvarnabhumi Airport or the old Don Muang Airport. Leading airlines for domestic routes include the following:

Air Asia (☎ 0 2515 9999; www.airasia.com)
Bangkok Airways (☎ 0 2132 0342; www.bangkokair.com)
Nok Air (☎ 1318; www.nokair.co.th)
One-Two-Go (☎ 1126; www.fly12go.com)
PB Air (☎ 0 2261 0220; www.pbair.com)
SilkAir (☎ 0 5327 6459; www.silkair.com)
Thai Airways (☎ 0 2356 1111; www.thaiair.com)

Bicycle
See p172 for information on bicycle touring in Thailand.

Boat
The true Thai river transport is the long-tail boat (reua hǎang yao), so-called because the propeller is mounted at the end of a long driveshaft extending from the engine. Boats are a common (and highly recommended) means of travel in Bangkok and, to a lesser degree, along the Mekong River in the far north.

Bus
Thai bus service is widespread, convenient and phenomenally fast, sometimes nail-bitingly so. You are almost always best off travelling with companies operating out of government bus stations (called 'Baw Khaw Saw') because private companies working through tourist centres like Th Khao San are notoriously corrupt and unreliable, and thefts on the buses are not uncommon.

The cheapest and slowest buses are the fanonly *rót thammádaa* (ordinary buses) that stop in every little town and for every waving hand along the highway, but this class of bus is a dying breed. Most services are in faster and more comfortable air-con buses, usually called *rót ae* (air bus). Longer routes offer 2nd-class and 1st-class air-con services; the latter have toilets. VIP and Super VIP buses have fewer seats so that each reclines more, and hostesses will serve drinks and snacks. On short routes *sǎwngthǎew* (see opposite) operate like buses

Car & Motorcycle
Cars, 4WDs or vans can be rented in most large cities. Agencies, both international and local, tend to congregate around top-end hotels. Always verify (ask to see the dated documents) that the vehicle is insured for liability before signing a contract. If you have an accident while driving an uninsured vehicle, you're in for some major hassles.

An International Driving Permit is necessary to drive vehicles in Thailand, but this is rarely enforced for motorcycle hire.

Thais drive on the left-hand side of the road (most of the time!). Like many places in Asia every two-lane road has an invisible third lane in the middle that all drivers feel free to use at any time and passing on hills and curves is common. The main rule to be aware of is that 'might makes right' and smaller vehicles always yield to bigger ones.

Motorcycle travel is a popular way to get around Thailand. Dozens of places along the guesthouse circuit rent motorbikes for 150B to 300B a day. It's also possible to buy a new or used motorbike and sell it before you leave the country: a good used 125cc bike costs as little as 25,000B. If you've never ridden a motorcycle before, stick to the smaller 100cc step-through bikes with automatic clutches. Motorcycle rental usually requires that you leave your passport, and many provinces require you to wear a helmet.

Local Transport
MOTORCYCLE TAXI
Many cities in Thailand have motorcycle taxi (*mawtoesai ráp jâang*). Rather than cruise the

streets they cluster near busy intersections. Fares tend to run from 10B to 30B.

SǍAMLÁW & TÚK-TÚK

Sǎamláw (also written samlor), meaning 'three wheels', are pedal rickshaws. They are most common in the northeast and are great for short distances. Then there are the motorised *sǎamláw*, called *túk-túk* because of the throaty cough their two-stroke engines make. In tourist centres, Bangkok especially, many (not all, it just sometimes seems that way) túk-túk drivers are unscrupulously greedy, exorbitantly inflating fares or diverting passengers to places that pay commissions.

You must bargain and agree on a fare before accepting a ride, but in many towns there is a de facto fixed fare anywhere in town.

SǍWNGTHǍEW

Sǎwngthǎew (literally, two benches) are small pick-ups with a row of seats down each side. In most towns *sǎwngthǎew* serve as public buses running fixed routes. But in tourist towns you'll also find *sǎwngthǎew* performing the same function as túk-túk, transporting people to and from the bus station or to popular attractions for a bargained fare.

Train

The **State Railway of Thailand** (☎ 1690; www .railway.co.th), has four main lines (northern, southern, northeastern and eastern) branching out from Bangkok. Trains are comfortable, but almost always slower and less frequent than buses; however the sleeper services to/from Chiang Mai and Nong Khai are rightly popular.

Trains are often heavily booked, so it's wise to reserve your place well ahead, especially the Bangkok to Chiang Mai trip. You can make bookings at any train station (English is usually spoken) and, for a small fee, through some Bangkok travel agencies.

Note that English-language timetables rarely list all the available trains.

CLASSES & COSTS

First-, 2nd- and 3rd-class cabins are available on most trains, but each class varies considerably depending on the type of train (rapid, express or ordinary). First class is a private cabin. Second class has individually reclining seats; depending on the train some cabins have air-con. Non-air-conditioned 3rd class is spartan with bench seating.

Ordinary trains often only have 3rd-class cars and they stop at every itsy-bitsy station. Express and rapid are, well, faster making fewer stops; there is a 60B surcharge for rapid trains and an 80B charge for express. Some 2nd- and 3rd-class services are air-con, in which case there is a 120B to 140B surcharge.

Overnight trains have sleeping berths in 1st and 2nd class. The charge for 2nd-class sleeping berths is 100B to 240B depending on whether you take an upper or lower (more headroom) and if there is air-con. All 1st-class cabins come with individually controlled air-con. For a two-bed cabin the surcharge is 400B per person. Single 1st-class cabins are not available, so if you're travelling alone you may be paired with another passenger.

The Thailand Rail Pass, which can be purchased at Hualamphong station in Bangkok, is worthwhile if you will be travelling by train extensively. The cost for 20 days of unlimited 2nd- or 3rd-class train travel is 1500B, or 3000B including all supplementary charges.

Cambodia

RICHARD I'ANSON

Cambodia

CAMBODIA

Drop your jaw at the sight of Angkor, a 12th-century wonder of monumental splendour; it will leave you awestruck and wanting more. Cross the ancient bridges and through the depths of jungle and *more* is what you'll discover; a land strewn with temples engulfed by nature, you'll feel like an explorer in a lucid dream.

Welcome to Cambodia! A heart-shaped country nurtured by the Mekong, it once ruled the delta as a mighty empire. A lost civilisation, cloaked in legends and myths, it has re-emerged as a hot destination on the Asian trail.

Cambodia's landscape is a scenic timeline of erratic history; from the vestiges of mysterious god-kings and the colonial imprints left by the imperialist French, its past spans across never-ending rice plains and small town villages, over mighty rivers and exotic wildlife, past palm trees and tropical beaches to reach the energised cities of present-day mayhem.

A land of contrasts, this is where the islands are deserted but the cities heave, where mountains project from emerald forests but secrets lurk underground. Where hill tribes ride elephants to pounding waterfalls and where everybody is happy to simply be alive. Not surprising given that life was so cruelly stripped away in the 1970s by the despotic Khmer Rouge.

Today the Khmers – with their unbreakable spirit and infectious optimism – are finally clambering back; over the ruins of their temples and the sands of their beaches, they are resurrecting an enigmatic nation: Cambodia, the comeback kid of the new century.

HIGHLIGHTS

- Fall under the spell of the mighty Angkor at the mind-blowing structures of divine spirituality: the **Temples of Angkor** (p208), a heroic feat of ancient civilisation

- Take a tuk-tuk through the chaotic capital and wrap your head around the progressive cacophony that is **Phnom Penh** (p188)

- Plunge into the enormous rock pools hidden by a barrage of giant bamboo before gunning through the mangrove forests at sunset at **Koh Kong** (p247)

- Run for the hills in Cambodia's northeast and steer elephants to cascading waterfalls; drink with the indigenous hill tribes and explore their sacred and primitive burial sites as the sun climbs over pristine forests at **Mondulkiri** (p236) and **Ratanakiri** (p233)

- Make like an Angkor Beer on ice and chill on the beaches of **Sihanoukville** (p238); cruise to neighbouring islands for secluded castaway action and cook fresh fish on the bonfire

HISTORY

Scholars argue about the origin of the Khmers, with some claiming they are a hybrid of migrants from China and India, others that they were travellers who settled from the islands from Southeast Asia (today's Malaysia and Indonesia). Discovery of bones in the eastern parts of Cambodia dating from 1500 BC show a resemblance between prehistoric humans and the Khmers of today.

The Early Years

The first Khmer kingdom arose in the 1st century in what is known as the Funan era. The Funan empire was highly influenced by the culture of India and was a sophisticated civilisation of literacy and arts. Indian traders and scholars had reached Cambodia as early as 100 BC and brought with them Sanskrit, Hinduism and Buddhism. The Khmers adopted this process of Indianisation wholeheartedly and between the 1st and the 6th centuries all royal records were kept in Sanskrit and the deities Shiva and Vishnu were most revered.

The word Funan itself is Chinese, though scholars believe it is derived from the ancient Khmer word *phnom*, meaning mountain.

The Funan empire is believed to have been centred around modern-day Ba Phnom (p228) and northern Vietnam near the Mekong Delta. It is largely considered by academics that Funan was not a united kingdom, but one of many factions which often warred against one another but came to present a unified state when offering tributary goods to the Chinese emperor in order to encourage trade.

Around the 6th century, the mighty Funan declined and in its place rose Chenla. Previously a vassal state to Funan, Chenla achieved independence, grew in power and then conquered the Funan empire. It was to reign supreme until AD 802. Once more this was not a unified kingdom; surviving inscriptions in Sanskrit indicate that there were a number of small kingdoms in Cambodia during this time.

Chinese records describe a Water Chenla and a Land Chenla. Water Chenla is placed around the south of the Mekong River and Land Chenla northeast of Tonlé Sap river.

Rise & Fall of Angkor

In 802 King Jayavarman II gained the throne and declared himself *devaraja* (god-king). In

FAST FACTS

- **Area** 181,035 sq km
- **Capital** Phnom Penh
- **Country Code** ☎ 855
- **Population** 14.071 million
- **Money** US$1 = 4075r (riel)
- **Seasons** wet May-Oct, dry Nov-Apr
- **Phrases** sua s'dei (hello), lia suhn hao-y (goodbye), aw kohn (thank you)

this he began a long line of god-kings spanning centuries and created the kind of devotion that befits a deity.

In the 9th century King Yasovarman I moved the capital to Angkor and a new centre for scholarship, worship and arts emerged. From here on, generations of kings waged wars, alternating between defeat and triumph until, under the rule of King Suryavarman II, Kambuja (as it was then known) grew to encompass Champa (now central Vietnam), Annam (now northern Vietnam) and Siam (now Thailand). In 1130, King Suryavarman II built the temple of Angkor to honour the Hindu god Vishnu.

In 1177, rebellious Chams from Vietnam sacked Angkor and it was not restored to Khmer power until Jayavarman VII, who became the kingdom's most prolific builder and is responsible for many of the archaeological treasures known today. After Jayavarman VII, the kingdom steadily declined. In 1432, the Siam kingdom gained power and captured Angkor, and the Khmers packed up and headed towards Phnom Penh.

The succession of feeble monarchs that followed further weakened Cambodia, until eventually it became a puppet state bowing to its now more powerful neighbours, Siam and Vietnam.

Enter the French

The French arrived in Southeast Asia in 1858, ready to conquer. They set up base in Saigon before setting their sights on Cambodia.

At this time, King Norodom requested French aid against the Siamese and they agreed, forcing him to sign a treaty that made Cambodia a French protectorate. He should have known that nothing came for free, and in 1884 under the threat of cannon fire, was

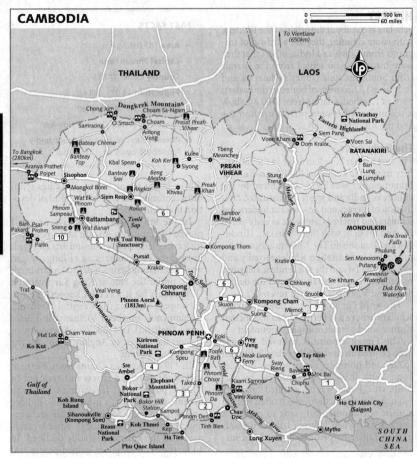

CAMBODIA

'persuaded' to sign another treaty, turning Cambodia into a French colony.

Years of bitter resentment and uprising against French rule followed; Cambodia felt betrayed when after signing the protectorate, the French honoured Siam with their claim for Siem Reap and Battambang.

In 1953, King Norodom's successor, King Norodom Sihanouk, exited his country and demanded the French leave or he would remain in exile. Embarrassed by the international publicity, the French finally withdrew.

Independence

With pressure from the people for an independently elected head of state rather than an absolute rule by monarchy, King Norodom Sihanouk took the genius step of denouncing the throne and formed his own political party. He handed the crown over to his father King Norodom Surmarit and was elected as the new prime minister. When his father died he also became head of state, thus becoming Cambodia's all-powerful one-man political road show.

King Norodom Sihanouk declared Cambodia neutral to international quarrels, but his friendly relations with communist China sparked anger with the US, which at the time was fighting the communist North Vietnamese. Meanwhile, trouble was brewing with the uprising of a US supporter, General Lon Nol, who in 1970 overthrew King Norodom with his party, Khmer Republic.

With the support of the new Lon Nol government, the USA bombarded the Cambodian countryside with bombs in an effort to flush out the Viet Cong. This did not go down well with the countryside dwellers and a bitter army grew. This peasant army, called upon by King Norodom Sihanouk himself to rise and fight against Lon Nol, was gaining in power with one man in particular at the helm. King Sihanouk nicknamed the army the Khmer Rouge, and that man was Pol Pot.

Khmer Rouge Takeover

In April 1975, screaming soldiers armed with AK47s entered government buildings, offices and homes in Phnom Penh and ordered everybody out. They then marched them in a mass exodus to the countryside, where for the next four years they were forced into slave labour to meet Pol Pot's revolutionary dream.

Pol Pot had devised a plan of turning the country into an agrarian utopia through an ultra-Maoist regime. He scratched the calendar and began at year zero. The name of the country under his fanatical rule became the Democratic Kampuchea, viciously ironic.

The poor, uneducated and easily moulded peasants of Cambodia became the 'old people' and their deeply despised city counterparts, the 'new people'. Under this regime, the new people had absolutely no human rights.

Literacy, arts, music and religion were all abolished. Any person deemed educated was instantly executed. It is believed that 1.7 million people died during this time. Families were separated and those who survived were either subjected to starvation and torture or escaped.

On 25 December 1978 the Vietnamese invaded. On 7 January 1979 the Khmer Rouge fell and Pol Pot escaped.

A Sort of Peace

It was not over yet for the people of Cambodia, for those who had survived the blood-soaked regime were now faced with a severe famine. In 1979 and 1980, it is estimated that as many as 625,000 more people died from starvation.

In 1989 Vietnam withdrew all of its troops from Cambodia. In the years that followed a scrabble board of political acronyms formed;

CPP ruled by the current-day prime minister, Hun Sen; Funcinpec led by King Norodom Sihanouk's son, Prince Ranariddh; BLDP, directed by former Lon Nol general, Sak Sutsakhan (just to name a few); and the guerrilla Khmer Rouge who were still controlling the north and west of Cambodia. All were vying for control and fighting for political power. This created even more instability and the UN finally stepped in to help after an agreement was signed in Paris for all parties to participate in free elections supervised by the UN.

In 1992 Untac (UN Transitional Authority in Cambodia) arrived. Its task, along with peacekeeping, was to oversee the overall reconstruction of the country and to supervise the democratic election. Although Funcinpec won, CPP's Hun Sen with his trademark bullying and threats managed to muscle into power – demanding the title of Second Prime Minister. To this Untac agreed and the two parties formed a unique coalition. In 1997, Hun Sen staged a bloody coup, overthrowing the First Prime Minister, Prince Ranariddh.

The fact that Hun Sen is a former Khmer Rouge guerrilla has not been lost on the Khmer people. His strongman tactics more than shadow the ruthless ways of his old comrades and the nation's citizens are well aware that they are living under a thinly guised dictatorship.

End of Khmer Rouge

More than two decades on, the international trial of Khmer Rouge leaders for crimes of genocide is still to take place. The baddest of the KR boys, Pol Pot and Ta Mok, are now dead and the others are ageing rapidly. Though many Cambodians are keen for justice, some new-generation Khmers, who were not present during the regime, believe that the enormous budget allocated to the proposed trial would be better invested in developing Cambodia's future rather than in a past that could never change.

Cambodia Today

The Untac years left a legacy of AIDS when soldiers boosted prostitution activities and Cambodia now has the highest rate of HIV infection in Asia. This can be attributed also to the poor socioeconomic status of the country, where women and children are pushed into prostitution or exploited by the powerful and rich.

The old adage of the rich getting richer and the poor getting poorer couldn't be a more accurate description of Cambodia. Those in power line their pockets in short-term personal gain with no regard to their people or the nation's sustainability.

PEOPLE & THE POPULATION

It is difficult to describe the Khmer people without jumping up and down on a springboard of emotions. Their smiles will lift your spirit and then their stories send you crashing. This is a nation of survivors. From one of the darkest periods of history, they have emerged blinking into the light of hope. They have a fierce pride for their country and are frustrated that throughout history, it has dangled like a marionette, yanked sideways by its neighbours – especially the Thais, whose superior attitude towards Cambodia is loathed.

The Khmers live for today. The idea of short-term gain is not exclusive to corrupt government; the general population cannot see the consequences of burning the country's trees, of overfishing or, in the case of prostitution, submitting to the rich Westerner who will pay for half an hour. The psychological damage caused today will not heal tomorrow, and sometimes in the case of children – they never do.

On the other hand, the Khmers' live-for-the-moment attitude is what makes them so much fun. Walking past a group of Khmers who burst into raucous laughter might make you paranoid that they're making fun of you – they are. Taking the mickey out of others is a national sport, and their wit is as fast as a motorbike speeding through Phnom Penh. They love a good laugh, so make sure to pack your sense of humour.

The estimated population of Cambodia is 14.071 million people, of whom 90% are ethnic Khmers, 5% Vietnamese and 1% Chinese with indigenous hill tribes making up the rest. Life expectancy is 58 years, a stark contrast to the 80 years of life hoped to be enjoyed by Australians and the 78 years expected by Brits.

The official language is Khmer, spoken by 95% of the population; there's also a smattering of French, and a growing number of English speakers.

Lifestyle

Eighty-five per cent of Khmers live off the fat of the land. They are generally farmers, weavers or fishermen, with the majority wet-rice cultivators.

Family is the core and familial bonds are strong. The family unit normally extends far and beyond the immediate members to encompass cousins, second cousins, aunts, great aunts and so on.

Food is incredibly important. Not just because Cambodians know what it's like to be without, but because it acts as a means of connection. In Cambodia, physical displays of affection are awkward and almost nonexistent, except between pals of the same sex. Therefore, a mother will show her adoration for her son through a well-cooked meal: a soup instead of a hug; a well-grilled fish instead of a kiss.

For the older generation, faith is very important and regular trips to shrines to make offerings and to pray are still a part of their regular activities (see below).

The younger generation differ greatly from country to city. The city kids officially want to be doctors, teachers and aid workers, but secretly – like many teenagers – they just want to be pop stars. The country kids just want a way out of poverty.

In any case, this is still very much a traditionalist country. Old customs are practised and values maintained. It helps to keep this in mind when travelling, so as not to offend.

RELIGION

The majority of Khmers (90%) follow the Theravada branch of Buddhism. The main philosophy of this school is to dedicate time and effort to earning merit in this life to gain better karma in the next, until ultimately Nirvana (Nibbana) is achieved. Hinduism is also threaded into the theology, with Hindu symbolism evident in ceremonies and legends.

Other religions found in Cambodia are: Islam, practised by the Cham community; animism, among the hill tribes; and Christianity, which is slowly seeping through the country via missionaries and Christian NGOs.

ARTS

After the Khmer Rouge's attempts to extinguish them, the arts are being revived by a new generation in a bid to preserve Cambodian culture.

Sculpture and carving were traditionally the most practised crafts, and if you take a look at the fine examples at Angkor, you will see that the ancestors had quite a knack for them. Take a walk down Phnom Penh's Ph 178 to see the modern-day artisans at work.

In both style and appearance, the royal dancers of today could have almost stepped off the lintels at Angkor. Their roots lie in India with dances enacting scenes from the Hindu *Ramayana*.

Cambodian folk music is an erratic clanging of instruments smoothed into melody. An orchestra normally includes wood instruments, string instruments, wind instruments, xylophones and drums. The modern stuff seems to be a gross breach of copyright from popular American artists. In fact, everything is copied except the language in which it is sung. Even the video clips are pretty much the same!

Visual artists are now infiltrating Cambodia's art scene and gracing the walls of hip galleries. They usually depict scenes of everyday life with modern styles, borrowing heavily from the West. A group of artists has set up a contemporary arts association, **Saklapel** (www.saklapel.org), which is very active in exposing up-and-coming Khmer artists. Check out Ph 240 in Phnom Penh, where many of the studios and art galleries are concentrated.

The cinema industry isn't about to match Hollywood any time soon, but it is slowly getting off the ground with the majority of films being schlock horrors pinched from Thailand. The most popular film of recent times is *Pos Keng Kong* (The Giant Snake; 2000), the story of a girl who sprang from the union between a human and a snake.

ENVIRONMENT
The Land
Tucked into the arches of its neighbours, Thailand, Laos and Vietnam, Cambodia has a total land area of 181,035 sq km and is cut through the middle by the Mekong River.

At the heart of the country is the great Tonlé Sap lake, one of the most productive fisheries in the world; it provides Khmers with 80% of their protein.

The Dangkrek Mountain range squiggles across the northern border with Thailand and looms over kilometres of grassy plains. In the east, the mountainous expanse takes the form of the Eastern Highlands and in Cambodia's wild west, the Cardamom and Elephant Mountain ranges jut from dense forests.

The lowlands consist of fields of rice, swamps, lakes and mangrove forests. Palm trees are absolutely everywhere and are usually the coconut-dropping variety or sweet sugar palms.

Wildlife
Wildlife numbers have suffered from civil war and illegal poaching in recent years, but Cambodia still boasts a biodiversity of species that inhabit the jungles and mountains, among them elephants, deer, wild boars, sun bears, gibbons, leopards and the elusive tiger. In lower-lying lands, snakes including the king cobra, which hides in the thickest jungle regions, can be found.

Occupying the swamps of Tonlé Sap are crocodiles, and in the lake itself is the biggest diversity of fish species in the world, including

---

TONLÉ SAP: THE WORLD'S GREATEST FLOOD BARRIER

Asia's largest freshwater lake and the world's biggest fish bowl, the Tonlé Sap is an ecological wonder.

It is connected to the Mekong at Phnom Penh by a 100km channel, known as the Tonlé Sap river. In the wet season the level of the Mekong rises and backs up into the river, causing it to flow northwest into the lake, which then swells from 2m deep and 2500 sq km to 10m deep and 13,000 sq km.

In the dry season, when the Mekong level is low, the Tonlé Sap reverses its flow, draining the water back from the lake into the Mekong.

This process produces the perfect breeding grounds for fish, supplying Cambodia with 75% of its annual fish catch and earning it a Unesco biosphere status.

To learn more, visit the Tonlé Sap exhibition at the Krousar Thmey Exhibition Centre (p202), in Siem Reap.

some endemic to Cambodia. The birds of Cambodia include the iridescent kingfisher, jungle fowl, crane, pelican and redheaded vulture. Gliding gracefully through the Mekong are freshwater Irrawaddy dolphins (see the boxed text, p232).

Your best chance of seeing these animals is to visit the sanctuaries: Phnom Tamao Wildlife Sanctuary near Phnom Penh (p201) and the Angkor Centre for Conservation of Biodiversity (ACCB) in Siem Reap (p208).

National Parks

To protect Cambodia's rich flora, fauna and wildlife, 23% of the country has been declared protected areas: Kirirom National Park (p201) in the southwest; Ream National Park (p240) near Sihanoukville, which has lowland evergreen forests and mangrove swamps; Virachay National Park (p236), a massive unexplored territory in the top northwest corner; and the magnificent Bokor National Park (p244), which echoes with the ghosts of French settlers and their now abandoned buildings.

Environmental Issues

Mass-scale deforestation has resulted in the depletion of forest coverage from 70% in the early 1970s to a shocking 30% today.

The deforestation has widespread ecological effects. The extensive logging targets rare and exclusive trees, driving these species into extinction. The degradation has been linked to an increase in the number of floods, which in the past has ruined rice crops and caused

---

DOING YOUR BIT

Cambodia is still largely unaware of environmental issues and measures due to a lack of education.

Lead by example and dispose of your rubbish responsibly. Try not to buy animal products such as ivory or skins or consume exotic meats as this only generates demand from an already threatened wildlife population. Purchasing coral or furniture or carvings made from luxury woods is also fuelling the demise of Cambodia's diminishing forests and reefs.

Lend your support to the various organisations, tours and programmes set up to promote ecotourism in the country.

---

food deficits in already poor and struggling areas. The flood-ruined forests are often cut down, removing the natural habitat for wildlife and degrading their breeding grounds; the wildlife either abandon their homes or simply die.

The damming of the Mekong is also causing grave problems. Dams built in China have led to a 12% decrease in river levels and reduced fish catches by an estimated 20%. Now with plans for Cambodian dams in the pipeline (with funding from the World Bank) the villagers have even more reason to be concerned.

PHNOM PENH

☎ 023 / pop 1.5 million

Phnom Penh is an electric bolt to the senses. In recent history it has been both a glamorous hub under Indochinese rule and a soulless basin, emptied of occupants by the tyrannical Khmer Rouge.

At the heart of 'The Penh' is a buzzing culture of cafés, stylish bars and a multinational vibe that is stamped with the definitive imprint of Khmers. The wats are filled with Buddhists lighting incense and chanting prayers and the markets are piled high with bargains and exotic foods just daring you to try them. While the legendary Boeng Kak moves to its own bohemian rhapsody, artisans can be seen sculpting Cambodia's new treasures along Ph 178, or strolling along the cosmopolitan Sisowath Quay.

ORIENTATION

The eastern edge of Phnom Penh hugs the Tonlé Sap, while the haphazardly numbered streets spread outward in a grid. Generally, odd-numbered streets run north–south, and even-numbered streets run east–west. The largest commercial streets, Monivong Blvd and Norodom Blvd run almost parallel to each other north to south, while Sihanouk Blvd cuts the city near the middle running east–west. The river is traversed via the Chrouy Changvar (Japanese Friendship) Bridge to the northeast with the enormous Boeng Kak lake just a few minutes away.

The riverfront Sisowath Quay is where most travellers hang out, but the points of interests are scattered throughout the entire city and beyond.

GETTING INTO TOWN

From the airport you can catch a moto to your hotel for US$2. Tuk-tuks do the same but charge US$4 and taxis make the run for US$5.

Nearly all buses, taxis and pick-ups drop people off at Psar Thmei (New Market, also known as Central Market) from where it is a short ride into any of the hotels or guest-houses (1000r). Boats arriving from Vietnam dock near Ph 6, where again motos will be waiting.

INFORMATION
Bookshops
With so many tourists pouring in there are literally bookshops everywhere.
D's Books (Map p194; www.ds-books.com; 77 Ph 240) The most reasonably priced and comprehensively stocked, it's popular albeit with tattered titles. There's a second branch near the Foreign Correspondents' Club at 12 Ph 178.

Emergency
Ambulance (☎ 119)
Fire (☎ 118)
Police & Medical (☎ 117)
Tourist police (☎ 724793)

Internet Access
It is not difficult to find somewhere to log on in Phnom Penh. Internet cafés are everywhere and usually charge 4000r per hour. Some bars and cafés also offer free wireless connections for your laptop.

Laundry
Most hotels will include a laundry service, either charging by the kilo (US$1) or item (1000r). As some of their laundry places hand-wash clothes, you may find that underwear will not be touched.

Medical Services
Calmette Hospital (Map pp190-1; ☎ 426948; 3 Monivong Blvd) A reputable hospital in Phnom Penh.
International SOS Medical Centre (Map p194; ☎ 216911; www.internationalsos.com; 161 Ph 51; ⊗ 8am-5.30pm Mon-Fri, 8am-noon Sat, emergency 24hr) International standards for health and teeth.
Naga Clinic (Map p194; ☎ 011-811175; www.nagaclinic.com; 11 Ph 254; ⊗ 24hr) French-run clinic for reliable consultations.

Pharmacie de la Gare (Map p194; ☎ 430205; 81Eo Monivong Blvd) French- and English-speaking pharmacists.
Tropical & Travellers Medical Clinic (Map p194; ☎ 015-912100; 88 Ph 108)

Money
Travellers cheques can be changed at various booths and guesthouses around the city. Below are the banks that offer the widest range of services.
ANZ Royal (Map p194; ☎ 726900) At multiple locations. Cash advances and ATM withdrawal for Visa and MasterCard.
Cambodia Asia Bank (Map p194; ☎ 722105) At multiple locations. Western Union transfers (24-hour) at the Naga Hotel branch.
Canadia Bank (Map p194; ☎ 215286) At multiple locations. Free cash advances on MasterCard and Visa, plus a 24-hour Visa/MasterCard ATM.

Telephone
The cheapest local and domestic calls in Phnom Penh are found at private stalls with the telephone prefixes displayed on them: ☎ 011, ☎ 012 and ☎ 016. Local calls start from 300r a minute.

Many internet cafés offer low-cost international calls via the internet – calls to Europe and North America start from 300r per minute.

Tourist Information
Ministry of Tourism (Map p194; ☎ 426876; www.mot.gov.kh;3 Monivong Blvd) Not your best source unfortunately; guesthouses and other travellers are much more informative.

Travel Agencies
Hanuman Tourism-Voyages (Map p194; ☎ 218396; www.hanumantourism.com; 12 Ph 310) One of the most reliable travel agencies for air tickets and tour services.
Neak Krorhorm Travel & Tours (Map p194; ☎ 219496; 128 Ph 108) Reasonably priced air and bus tickets.
PTM Travel & Tours (Map p194; ☎ 986363; 200Eo Monivong Blvd) A good spot for discount flight tickets.

DANGERS & ANNOYANCES
Phnom Penh is a big bustling city, but in general it is very safe. Be mindful of the traffic rules that seem to only apply to foreigners; get clued up on these from your moto rental place.

lonelyplanet.com

CAMBODIA

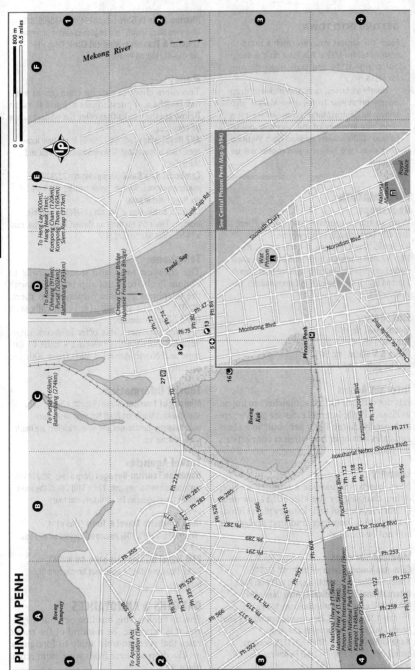

PHNOM PENH

800 m
0.5 miles
0
0

Mekong River

Boeng Pungpuoy

To Apsara Arts
Association (1km)

To Pursat (165km);
Battambang (274km)

To Kompong
Chhnang (91km);
Battambang (293km)

To Heng Lay (500km);
Hang Neak (1km);
Kompong Cham (120km);
Kompong Thom (165km);
Siem Reap (317km)

Chrouy Changvar Bridge
(Japanese Friendship Bridge)

Tonlé Sap

Tonlé Sap Rd.

Royal
Palace

National
Museum

See Central Phnom Penh Map (p194)

Sisowath Quay

Wat
Phnom

Norodom Blvd

Monivong Blvd

Phnom Penh

Quatre de Chulie Blvd

Ph 72
Ph 74
Ph 75
Ph 80
Ph 47
Ph 84
Ph 34

Ph 70

Boeng
Kak

Kampuchea Krom Blvd

Ph 134

Ph 211

Jawaharlal Nehru (Sivutha Blvd)

Pochentong Blvd
Ph 112
Ph 118
Ph 122

Ph 156

Mao Tse Toung Blvd

Ph 253

Ph 273

Ph 281
Ph 283
Ph 285
Ph 528
Ph 566
Ph 614

Ph 287

Ph 289

Ph 291

Ph 392
Ph 608

Ph 355

Ph 339
Ph 337
Ph 335
Ph 528

Ph 566

Ph 317
Ph 315
Ph 313

Ph 592

Ph 257
Ph 259
Ph 261

Ph 122
Ph 132

To National Hwy 3 (1.5km);
National Hwy 1 (15km);
Phnom Penh International Airport (3km);
Kirirom National Park (112km);
Kampot (148km);
Sihanoukville (230km)

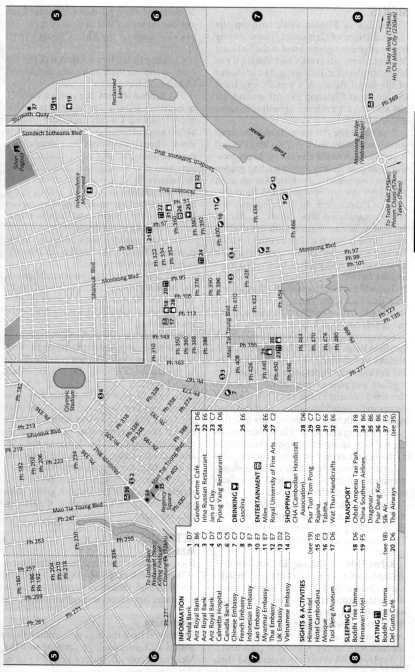

CAMBODIA

INFORMATION	
Acleda Bank........................	1 D7
Anz Royal Bank...................	2 B6
Anz Royal Bank...................	3 C7
Anz Royal Bank...................	4 D7
Calmette Hospital...............	5 C3
Canadia Bank......................	6 C5
Chinese Embassy.................	7 C7
French Embassy...................	8 C2
Indonesian Embassy............	9 E7
Lao Embassy.......................	10 E7
Myanmar Embassy...............	11 E7
Thai Embassy......................	12 E7
UK Embassy........................	13 D2
Vietnamese Embassy...........	14 D7

SIGHTS & ACTIVITIES	
Himawari Hotel..............	(see 19)
Hotel Cambodiana...........	15 F5
Mosque............................	16 C3
Tuol Sleng Museum............	17 D6

SLEEPING	
Boddhi Tree Umma...........	18 D6
Himawari Hotel................	19 F5

EATING	
Boddhi Tree Umma........	(see 18)
Del Gusto Café..............	20 D6

Garden Centre Café............	21 D6
Irina Russian Restaurant......	22 E6
Jars of Clay........................	23 C7
Pyong Yang Restaurant.......	24 D6

DRINKING	
Gasolina............................	25 E6

ENTERTAINMENT	
Miles.................................	26 E6
Royal University of Fine Arts...	27 C2

SHOPPING	
CHA (Cambodian Handicraft	
Association)......................	28 D6
Psar Tuol Tom Pong............	29 C7
Rajana...............................	30 C7
Tabitha..............................	31 E6
Wat Than Handicrafts..........	32 E6

TRANSPORT	
Chbah Ampeau Taxi Park.....	33 F8
China Southern Airlines........	34 B6
Dragonair...........................	35 B6
Psar Dang Kor...................	36 B6
Silk Air.............................	37 F5
Thai Airways...................	(see 35)

To Svay Rieng (125km);
Ho Chi Minh City (230km)

To Tonle Bati (35km);
Phnom Chisor (57km);
Takeo (75km)

Monivong Bridge
(Vietnam Bridge)

Silver
Pagoda

Samdech Sothearos Blvd

Independence
Monument

Reclaimed
Land

Sisowath Quay

Tonlé Bassac

Olympic
Stadium

Sihanouk Blvd

Monivong Blvd

Mao Tse Toung Blvd

Sothearos Blvd

Nordom Blvd

To Lotus Blanc;
Restaurant; Chbah
Killing Fields of
Choeung Ek (12km)

Mao Tse Toung Blvd

Regency
Square

CAMBODIA

SIGHTS

The sights in Phnom Penh sum up the contradictions of Cambodia. The stunning legacy of god-kings exhibited at the National Museum contrasts greatly with the legacy of killers displayed at Tuol Sleng. The grandeur of the Royal Palace is a world away from the gloom at Choeung Ek. All around the city you can see evidence of both splendour and sorrow.

Royal Palace (Map p194; Samdech Sothearos Blvd; admission US$3, camera/video US$2/5; ⏰ 7.30-11am & 2.30-5pm) is outlined across the city sky by its progressive triangular ceiling and cascading golden tiles. It was initiated by King Norodom in 1886 after the capital was moved from Oudong to Phnom Penh. In the palace grounds is the magnificent **Silver Pagoda**, so named because it is constructed with 5000 silver tiles. In the centre is a 17th-century emerald Buddha statue made of Baccarat crystals and all around are lush gardens manicured in an orderly fashion.

You will not be permitted into the grounds with bare shoulders. There is a clever T-shirt stand by the ticket booth that makes a killing out of this common tourist oversight.

Formerly the Tuol Svay Prey High School, **Tuol Sleng Museum** (Map pp190-1; admission US$3; ⏰ 7-11.30am & 2-5.30pm), off Ph 113, was taken over by Pol Pot's security forces and transformed into a prison and zone of unimaginable torment. Renamed Security Prison 21 (S-21), the classrooms were turned into torture chambers and equipped with various instruments to inflict pain, suffering and death. These instruments are still here, along with graphic photographs of the victims as they lay dying. The long corridor is a hallway of ghosts containing photographs of the victims put to death, their faces staring back eerily from the past.

It was the largest incarceration centre in the country, and at the height of its activity, a shocking 100 victims were killed a day. The lives of some are documented in a gallery upstairs.

Killing Fields of Choeung Ek (admission US$2; ⏰ 7am-5.30pm) is where most of the 17,000 detainees held at the S-21 prison were executed. If walking through the now peaceful grounds with their shady trees and butterflies diffuses the impact of what happened here, then the enormous stupa of skulls will send you reeling back with horror. A looming glass tower, it displays 8000 skulls of victims and their discarded clothes; piled into a messy heap just like the bodies that once wore them. See p185 for more on the Khmer Rouge's reign of terror.

Choeung Ek is 14km southwest of Phnom Penh. A trip out there on a moto should cost US$5 round trip.

The **National Museum** (Map p194; admission US$3, camera US$1; ⏰ 8-11am & 2-5pm Tue-Sun) is in a glorious red building. This airy open-door museum houses national treasures – some unfortunately looted – from the country's most historic sites. Built between 1917 and 1920, it contains objects from all of the mighty empires, including the famous 'fighting monkeys' statue. Taken from the temples at Koh Ker (p224), it is a massive 1.94m limestone statue showing two monkey brothers, Sugriva and Valin, in a wrestle grip fighting to the death.

No photography is allowed except in the courtyard. You can hire English- and French-speaking guides from US$2.

Very touristy and not particularly pretty, **Wat Ounalom** (Map p194) is still worth visiting just for the one eyebrow hair of Buddha himself, preciously held in a stupa behind the main building.

Wat Phnom (Map p194; admission US$1), meaning Hill Temple, is appropriately set on the only hill in Phnom Penh. The wat is at the centre of the legend of Phnom Penh and is thus highly revered among the locals. Khmers flock to it to pray for their fortunes. The legend goes that long long ago, in the year 1373, the first temple was built by a lady named Penh to house four Buddha statues that were swept into her home by the Mekong. Penh's statue is in a shrine dedicated to her behind the *vihara* (temple sanctuary). You can also catch sight of Sam Bo here, an elephant who does his day shift giving rides before plodding off home along the river in the evenings.

ACTIVITIES
Massage

Receive massages from trained blind masseurs at **Seeing Hands Massage** (Map p194; ☎ 012-680934; 6 Eo Ph 94; per hr US$4). Helps you to ease those aches and pains, helps them stay self-sufficient.

Swimming

Unless you have the iron-guts immune system of a Khmer, don't go jumping into the Mekong to cool off. Instead head for one of the hotel saviours that offer a swimming pool open to the public:

Himawari Hotel (Map pp190-1; ☎ 214555; 313 Sisowath Quay; US$10)

Hotel Cambodiana (Map pp190-1; ☎ 424888; 313 Sisowath Quay; US$8)

Hotel Le Royal (Map p194; ☎ 981888; Ph 92; US$3)

Boat Tours

There are many companies that offer boat cruises up and down the Mekong. They are stationed along Sisowath Quay and most offer a lunch or dinner cruise for one to two hours for around US$8.

Compagnie Fluviale du Mekong (Map p194; ☎ 012-240859; 30 Ph 240) offers an excellent tour up to Angkor in a beautiful traditional boat with comfy cabins. On the way, it accesses small villages for a truly memorable trip. Tours leave every Monday; contact for bookings and quotes. You can buy tickets from where the boat leaves at Sisowath Quay.

SLEEPING

Budget travellers usually head for Boeng Kak where cheap accommodation lines the lakeside. Those with a more flexible wallet can choose from an array of budget hotels or head for the swankiest of suites. Reservations aren't normally required except when it's peak holiday season.

Boeng Kak Area

Phnom Penh's own budget paradise. Most of the lodgings cluster around this green lake of questionable purity; a murky expanse of water that transforms into a glistening loch of golden shimmers at sunset, a sight worth a thousand mosquito bites and more.

Lake Side 2 Guest House & Restaurant (Map p194; ☎ 012-973811; 3 Ph 93; r US$2-7) For US$2 you'll be sharing the bathroom, but from there on up it's en-suite luxury with the added bonus of hot water. Safety lockers are available for your worldly goods and the atmosphere is suitably chilled.

Floating Island Guest House (Map p194; ☎ 990887; floatingisland_pp@yahoo.com; 11 Ph 93; r US$3-9) Not quite afloat and not quite an island but the upstairs deck could easily win the title of 'best place to view the sunset' and the cleaning lady deserves a pat on the back for spotless rooms.

Number 9 Sister Guest House (Map p194; ☎ 012-424240; 8A Ph 93; r US$3-8) They sure know how to jazz up a walkway here, where the long,

tiled passageway is flanked by pretty orchids, leading onto the lakeside veranda and its magnificent view. A great first impression that actually lasts thanks to clean rooms and an affable atmosphere.

Riverfront Area

Bright Lotus Guest House (Map p194; ☎ 990446; sammy_lotus@hotmail.com; 22 Ph 178; r US$10-18; ✷) Looking a little outdated now compared to the new hotels popping up, but its location just can't be beat. Balconies overlook the action-packed Ph 178 and it is within short walking distance of the Royal Palace, Silver Pagoda, National Museum and river.

Paragon Hotel (Map p194; ☎ 222607; info_paragon hotel@yahoo.com/phannakh@yahoo.com; 219B Sisowath Quay; r US$15-30; ✷) This is the new kid on the riverfront block. Staying in rooms on the 3rd floor and up begins to hurt due to the lack of a lift, but the river views are fabulous.

California 2 Guest House (Map p194; ☎ 982182; 317 Sisowath Quay; r US$20-25; ✷) Rooms are clean and comfortable, the café downstairs is cracking and the staff are informative, fun and friendly.

Bougainvillier Hotel (Map p194; ☎ 220528; www .bougainvillierhotel.com; 277G Sisowath Quay; r US$52-128; ✷ ▣) This charming hotel adds the aah to ooh with contemporary oriental décor. Dry-cleaning and safety deposit boxes mean clean clothes and secure valuables, while the restaurant serves up well-regarded Khmer and French cuisine.

Himawari Hotel (Map pp190-1; ☎ 214555; reservation@himawari.com.kh; 313 Sisowath Quay; ste US$113-306; ✷ ▣ ▣) For some posh pampering, check into one of the large and tastefully decked out Himawari suites. The hotel has every facility imaginable to keep you from leaving: a fitness centre, pool and wi-fi access.

our pick Amanjaya Pancam Hotel (Map p194; ☎ 214747; www.amanjaya.com; 1 Ph 154; r US$155-265; ✷ ▣) Disappear into this stylish and slick hotel with its opulent furnishings and classy service and you could be in any upscale city in the world. But look out the window to the wide Tonlé Sap and distinguished Wat Ounalom and there's no mistaking you're in Phnom Penh – and one of its most superb locations at that.

Also recommended are these two Sisowath Quay favourites with decent rooms and friendly service:

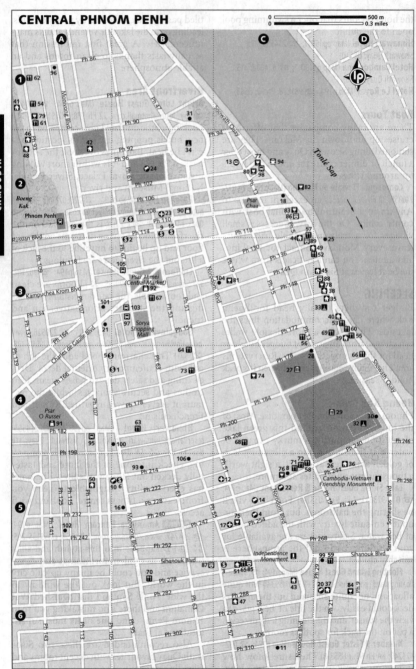

CENTRAL PHNOM PENH

0 — 500 m
0 — 0.3 miles

Indochine Hotel (Map p194; ☎ 724239; indochinehtl@
camnet.com.kh; 251 Sisowath Quay; r US$10-20; 🏵)
Indochine 2 (Map p194; ☎ 211525; 28-30 Ph 130;
r US$10-20)

Around the City

Top Banana (Map p194; ☎ 012-885572; topbanana
_guesthouse@yahoo.com; 9Eo cnr Ph 278 & Ph 51; r US$5;
🏵) The rooms are basic but this is a great
spot for meeting other travellers. The place
is designed for ultimate chill-out: lounges,
cushions, hammocks and the most welcoming of staff.

Spring Guest House (Map p194; ☎ 222155; spring
_guesthouse@yahoo.com; 34 Ph 111; r US$5-10; 🏵) This
unpretentious hotel has a list of valuable and
friendly services that make it a real winner.
Airport transfers are on the house.

ourpick Boddhi Tree Umma (Map p190-1; ☎ 011-
854430; www.boddhitree.com; 50 Ph 113; r US$8-24; 🏵)
Full of charisma. All the timber and stone
rooms come with beds romantically draped
in mosquito nets. The small bathrooms are
tiled with colourful mosaics and leafy plants
graze the windows.

Manor House (Map p194; ☎ 992566; www.manor
housecambodia.com; 8B Ph 288; r US$25-33; 🏵) So clean
it shines, this gay-friendly boutique hotel offers a quieter place to rest. The rooms are
modest but comfortable and breakfast is
included.

Hotel Le Royal (Map p194; ☎ 981888; www.phnom
penh.raffles.com; Ph 92; r US$184-1793; 🏵 🖵 🖲) Like
stepping back in time, this elegant affair is rich
in heritage. It has maintained its old-French
charm, blending it ostentatiously with Royal

Khmer style and modern luxury. It boasts 170 rooms, a spa, gym, pool and some of the most sumptuous restaurants and bars in town.

Also recommended:

Boddhi Tree Del Gusto (Map p194; ☎ 998424; 43 Ph 95; r US$7-24) Equally charming sister hotel to Boddhi Tree Umma.

Boddhi Tree Aram (Map p194; ☎ 998424; 70 Ph 244; r US$13-46; 🐾) Another charming sister hotel to Boddhi Tree Umma.

Hotel Scandinavia (Map p194; ☎ 214498; www .scandanavia-hotel-cambodia.com; 4 Ph 282; r US$30-55; 🐾 🖥 🚗) Trendy boutique hotel with swimming pool.

EATING

For something cheap and colourful, head for the food stalls at the markets, or cross the Japanese Friendship Bridge over to Prek Leap. In the city itself, there is an overwhelming choice, following is just a taster.

Boddhi Tree Umma (Map pp190-1; ☎ 011-854430; www.boddhitree.com; 50 Ph 113; mains US$1-3; 🌙 breakfast, lunch & dinner) Opposite the Tuol Sleng Museum, this is a secret hidey-hole in which to nibble tapas and drink fruit cocktails. The restaurant provides a much needed sanctuary after the ghostly horror of that macabre visit.

Flying Elephant (Map p194; ☎ 012-263332; 3A Ph 93; mains US$1-6; 🌙 breakfast, lunch & dinner) Eclectic and fun, it's what a restaurant might look like if a bunch of uni students turned their living room into a diner. The lounges are comfortable, the staff are energetic and free beer comes with every delicious pizza or burger ordered.

Peking Canteen (Map p194; ☎ 011-909548; 93 Ph 136; mains US$1-8; 🌙 lunch & dinner) Tiny and packed full of chopstick clickin' action and flavour. The noodles and dumplings are fast becoming famous.

Shop Bakery & Delicatessen (Map p194; ☎ 986964; 39 Ph 240; mains US$1.50-5; 🌙 breakfast, lunch & dinner) This tranquil café is a great place to come for a light bite or to grab and go. The freshly baked breads and pastries are excellent, and so is the coffee.

Nature and Sea (Map p194; ☎ 012-879486; cnr Ph 51 & Ph 278; mains US$1.50-5; 🌙 breakfast, lunch & dinner) This relaxed eatery is all about natural and organic foods. The salads are lovely and fresh but it's the French crepes and galettes that are the real draw.

DINING FOR A CAUSE

These fantastic eateries are established as funding vehicles for worthy causes and training centres for young staff.

■ **ourpick Friends** (Map p194; ☎ 012-802072; gustav@friends-international.org; 215 Ph 13; mains US$3-5; 🌙 lunch & dinner) The delightful Friends restaurant is run by the Mith Samlanh Friends NGO. Staffed by street youths training for the hospitality industry, it offers healthy international dishes and delicious fruit cocktails.

■ **Le Café du Centre** (Map p194; ☎ 992432; French Cultural Centre, Ph 184; mains US$1.50-4.40; 🌙 breakfast, lunch & dinner) The third training restaurant of the Mith Samlanh Friends NGO comes in the form of this French café. It serves light meals such as sandwiches and crepes, plus a good selection of ice creams.

■ **Lazy Gecko Café** (Map p194; ☎ 012-619924; 23B Ph 93; mains US$1.50-4.50; 🌙 breakfast, lunch & dinner) This little eatery serves international dishes. Throwing some weighty support behind the Jeannine's Children Association (JCA) Orphanage, it hosts a quiz and raffle night on Thursdays and loads guests and donated goods onto an orphanage-bound minibus on Saturdays, where they can enjoy dinner and a performance by the children.

■ **Lotus Blanc** (☎ 995660; Stung Mean Chey; mains US$3-6; 🌙 noon-2pm Mon-Fri) Fifteen minutes from the city centre, this restaurant acts as a vocational training centre for youths who were found scouring the area's garbage dump for a meagre living. Run by French NGO, PSE–Pour un Sourire d'Enfant (For the smile of a child), it serves Western and Khmer cuisine.

■ **Romdeng** (Map p194; ☎ 092-219565; 21 Ph 278; mains US$4-6.50; 🌙 breakfast, lunch & dinner, closed 2-6pm & Sun) Also under the Mith Samlanh umbrella, the elegant Romdeng specialises in traditional food from the provinces and offers a staggering choice of traditional Khmer fare.

our pick Khmer Borane Restaurant (Map p194; ☎ 012-290092; 389 Sisowath Quay; mains US$1.50-4; ☽ noon-midnight) A charming restaurant that exudes a humble grace reminiscent of the French colonial days of elegant dining. Delicious and authentic Khmer food.

Jars of Clay (Map pp190-1; ☎ 300281; 39B Ph 155; mains US$2-3; ☽ breakfast, lunch & dinner) Scones in Cambodia? Yes, and they aren't half-bad. Just one of the baker's delights to be found in this café near the Russian Market.

Del Gusto (Map pp190-1; ☎ 998424; 43 Ph 95; mains US$2-4; ☽ breakfast, lunch & dinner) Following the same formula as the Umma with a similar Mediterranean/Asian menu, the Del Gusto is set in a creaky old villa that whiffs of the colony. The old French building is perfect for the classical and jazz music that fills its space, adding a relaxed groove to the laid-back ambience.

Cantina (Map p194; ☎ 222502; 347 Sisowath Quay; mains US$2-5; ☽ breakfast, lunch & dinner) A taste of Tijuana riverside. The Mexican food is worth raving about with tortillas and salsa made fresh daily.

Garden Centre Café (Map pp190-1; ☎ 363002; 23 Ph 57; mains US$2.50-11; ☽ breakfast, lunch & dinner, closed Mon) A tropical garden setting and an enormous selection of wholesome and healthy food. The homemade yogurt and muesli will get you started on the right foot and the freshly baked bagels are fabulously filling fare.

Pacharan (Map p194; ☎ 224394; 389 Sisowath Quay; mains US$2.50-18; ☽ 11am-midnight) A fashionable Spanish restaurant with an open kitchen, sleek bar, and stylish interior of Spanish sunburnt colours. The wines are fine and the tapas excellent.

Pyong Yang Restaurant (Map pp190-1; ☎ 993765; 400 Monivong Blvd; mains US$3-15; ☽ lunch & dinner) A quirky North Korean restaurant of singing and dancing waitresses, live music and delicious cold noodles.

Java Café & Gallery (Map p194; ☎ 987420; 56 Sihanouk Blvd; mains US$3-4.75; ☽ breakfast, lunch & dinner) Interesting art exhibitions, wi-fi access, a large airy terrace, and that's before we even get to the menu. Wholesome and filling sandwiches and wraps are the speciality.

Café El Mundo (Map p194; ☎ 012-520775; 219 Sisowath Quay; mains US$3-7; ☽ breakfast, lunch & dinner) If you're on a mission to mellow after a frantic day, sneak inside this café and the madness of Phnom Penh will feel like a world away.

The mezzanine level has wall-to-wall lounges, which makes staying here all day a very tempting prospect. Fruit teas and West-meets-East food.

Foreign Correspondents' Club of Cambodia (FCC; Map p194; ☎ 724014; www.fcccambodia.com; 363 Sisowath Quay; mains US$5-15.50; ☽ breakfast, lunch & dinner) A favoured haunt of local expats, the FCC has big views and a big menu. The food leans heavily to the West and in particular Italy, but there are some Cambodian dishes in there to mix it up.

Irina Russian Restaurant (Map pp190-1; ☎ 012-833524; 15 Ph 352; mains US$3-8; ☽ lunch & dinner) A jovial restaurant where the meals are washed down with vodka. The food is authentically Russian and so heavy, it will leave your jeans happily strained across a stuffed belly.

Tamarind (Map p194; ☎ 012-830139; 31 Ph 240; US$5.50-14; ☽ breakfast, lunch & dinner) A classy and ambient restaurant dishing out a blend of North African and French cuisine. The bar downstairs is happy between 5pm and 7pm with half-price cocktails, but opt to have your shwarma and tajines upstairs on the breezy terrace.

Also recommended:

La Dolce Vita (Map p194; ☎ 012-610015; 78 Ph 93; ☽ breakfast, lunch & dinner) Italian food.

Phò Fortune (Map p194; ☎ 012-871753; 11 Ph 178; ☽ breakfast, lunch & dinner) Vietnamese food.

Garden Bar In The Shade (Map p194; cnr Ph 148 & Sisowath Quay; ☽ breakfast, lunch & dinner) International food.

King's Court Restaurant (Map p194; ☎ 986469; 341Eo Sisowath Quay; ☽ breakfast, lunch & dinner) International food.

When the hunger hits at an ungodly hour, **Midnite Train** (Map p194; Ph 51), a permanently parked truck on Phnom Penh's strip of late-night bars and clubs doles out burgers, kebabs and hot dogs to those just stumbling out, closing its shutters at around 5am, while the weird and wonderful **Walkabout Hotel** (Map p194; ☎ 023-211715; 109 Ph 51; ☽ 24hr) serves standard Western and Khmer food 24 hours.

Self-Catering

Golden Garden (Map p194; ☎ 211534; 23 Ph 240) A range of imported goods from Europe and the USA with fresh produce.

Pencil Supermarket (Map p194; Ph 214; ☽ 7am-9pm) This is a large international supermarket that is generally well stocked.

CAMBODIA

DRINKING

Talkin to a Stranger (Map p194; ☎ 012-798530; talkintoastranger@yahoo.com; 21B Ph 294; ☻ 5pm-late, closed Mon) The strangers here must be very good-humoured as this place is always filled with convivial cheer. A great garden bar that is very popular with local expats, it hosts regular shows and events with live bands sometimes performing.

Elsewhere Bar (Map p194; ☎ 211348; 175 cnr Ph 51 & 254; ☻ 10am-late, closed Tue) Why go Elsewhere? Ambient vibes, lush garden setting, great drinks menu and a beckoning swimming pool, that's why! Happy hour 5pm to 8pm.

Riverhouse Lounge (Map p194; ☎ 220180; 6 Ph 110; ☻ 4pm-2am) Housed in a beautiful colonial building with grand views over the balcony, this richly decorated lounge has regular DJ nights and happy hour 4pm to 8pm.

Magic Sponge (Map p194; ☎ 012-968512; dmriley40@hotmail.com; 12-13 Ph 93; ☻ 6pm-late) The healthy dose of double shots aside, this little bar is a friendly spot for exchanging travel tales and perhaps a game or two of cards.

Pontoon Lounge (Map p194; ☻ 11.30am-late) Floating on the Tonlé Sap at the end of Ph 108, this modish bar with its house and electro DJs is where the beautiful people come. Happy hour 5pm to 8pm.

Blue Chilli (Map p194; ☎ 012-566353; bluechillipub@gmail.com; 36Eo Ph 178; ☻ 7pm-late) Gay-friendly, this contemporary bar is a good place for some banter and boogying. It also has some private booths for those more intimate moments.

Gasolina (Map pp190-1; ☎ 012-373009; 56-58 Ph 57; ☻ 6pm-late, closed Mon) Filled with the sensual sounds of South America, this Latin bar is housed in a simple Spanish-style villa with a large garden. Chilean wines accompany cocktails on the drinks list and salsa lessons are held every Tuesday, Wednesday and Thursday nights.

Monsoon (Map p194; ☎ 016-355867; 17 Ph 104; ☻ 6pm-late) This is a cool little bar with an inviting atmosphere, moody music and a good selection of international drops to get you warmed up. Happy hour 6pm to 8pm.

Also recommended:

California 2 Guesthouse (☎ 982182; 317 Sisowath Quay) Great Mexican food, even better burgers and lively conversation, this bar has long been the watering hole for bikers and adventure travellers. It is also a reliable place for travel information.

Peace Pub (Map p194; ☎ 012-790898; 126 Ph 136; ☻ 4pm-late) A bar with reasonably priced drinks and regular quiz and movie nights, including some arthouse films. Happy hour 4pm to 8pm.

Jungle Bar & Grill (Map p194; ☎ 012-474230; 273 Sisowath Quay; ☻ 7am-2am) An airy and relaxed riverfront bar that has speedy internet access for laptops and serves food until 2am.

Freebird Bar (Map p194; ☎ 224712; 69 Ph 240; ☻ 7am-midnight) An American-style bar also with laptop internet access.

Green Vespa (Map p194; ☎ 012-887228; 95 Sisowath Quay; ☻ 6am-2am) This bar is full of spirit, of both the character and alcohol variety.

ENTERTAINMENT

Entertainment listings can be found in the *Phnom Penh Post, Bayon Pearnik* and *Cambodian Daily.*

HAGGLE ME THIS...

Bargains galore can be found at Phnom Penh's vibrant markets. Navigating the labyrinths of shoes, clothing, bric-a-brac and food is one of the most enjoyable ways to wear your feet out. Markets are open from 6.30am to 5.30pm.

■ **Psar Thmei** (Map p194) Sooner or later you'll see this concrete custard pie. Also known as the New Market or the Central Market, the big yellow building is adjacent to the bus station and houses an array of stalls selling jewellery, clothing, coins and other such curios. The food section is enormous with produce spilling onto the streets.

■ **Psar Tuol Tom Pong** (Map p194) Haggling at this market requires peering over mounds and mounds of clothing and quality *kramas* (chequered silk scarves). It is often referred to as the Russian Market, as back in the 1980s it was the Russians' retail outlet of choice. It is the best place for souvenir T-shirts, CDs, DVDs and miniature carvings.

■ **Psar O Russei** (Map p194) Housed in a sprawling mall-like space, this is the place to come if you want to lose your legion of adoring tuk-tuk fans. It is a complete maze selling everything you can think of.

Live Music

Equinox Bar (Map p194; ☎ 012-586139; 3A Ph 278; ☻ 11.30am-late) Acoustic jam sessions are held every Thursday and Saturday night in this animated bar. Happy hour 5pm to 8pm.

Miles (Map pp190-1; ☎ 011-698470; 17C Ph 370; ☻ 4pm-midnight Tue-Sun) Live jazz Fridays and Sundays in a rooftop bar that offers great views.

Memphis Pub (Map p194; ☎ 012-871263; 3 Ph 118; ☻ 5pm-late) Live rock and blues can be enjoyed most nights but weekends are the best, when it really gets going.

Riverside Bar & Bistro (Map p194; ☎ 213898; cnr Ph 148 & Sisowath Quay; ☻ 7am-1am) A mainstay of the riverfront scene, it often has bands jamming away in the back room at weekends. Happy hour is a liver-threatening noon to 7pm.

Salt Lounge (☎ 012-289905; 217 Ph 136; ☻ 6pm-1am) There are not many full-blown nightclubs in town; this industrial-looking nightclub of steel and strategic lights is probably the best of them. It plays host to regular guest DJs, is gay-friendly and has a decent menu of cocktails and shooters.

Cinemas

Movie Street (Map p194; Sihanouk Blvd) Private viewing booths with big TVs to watch the latest Hollywood and European titles.

French Cultural Centre (Map p194; Ph 184) Frequent weekday movie screenings in French. Ask for the monthly programme.

Peace Pub (Map p194; ☎ 012-790898; 126 Ph 136; ☻ 4pm-late) A drinking spot (see opposite) that has regular film nights, including documentaries and arthouse flicks.

Classical Dance & Arts

The Royal University of Fine Arts and **Apsara Arts Association** (71 Ph 598; ☻ 7.30-10.30am & 2-5pm Mon-Sat) teach students the fine art of Khmer royal ballet. The university dance programme has now moved to a new campus way north of town in Russei Keo district. Alternating performances of classical dance and folk dance are held at Apsara every Saturday at 7pm (admission US$5).

SHOPPING

The national *krama* (chequered silk scarf) is worn around the necks, shoulders and waists of nearly every Khmer – it's almost a uniform. The scarves make superb souvenirs, as do Cambodia's gems, sculptures and handicrafts.

The stores below sell high-quality goods while supporting community organisations. Their aims are to provide the disabled and disenfranchised with valuable training for future employment and business management plus a regular flow of income to improve lives.

CHA (Map pp190-1; 54-56 Ph 113) This well-stocked boutique and workshop sells fine handmade clothing, scarves, toys, bags and photo albums. It is an interesting place to shop as you can poke your head behind the curtain and watch the process.

NCDP Handicrafts (Map p194; 3 Norodom Blvd) Exquisite silk scarves, throws, bags and cushions. Other items: *kramas*, shirts, wallets and purses, notebooks and greeting cards.

Rajana (Map pp190-1; 170 Ph 450) Beautiful selection of cards, some quirky metalware, quality jewellery, bamboo crafts and a range of condiments from Cambodia. It also has a booth in nearby Psar Tuol Tom Pong.

Tabitha (Map pp190-1; cnr Ph 360 & Ph 51) Premium-quality silk with a fantastic collection of bags, tableware, bedroom decorations and children's toys.

Wat Than Handicrafts (Map pp190-1; Norodom Blvd) Similar goods to NCDP. It's set inside Wat Than.

GETTING THERE & AWAY

Air

See p256 for a list of airline offices based in Phnom Penh. See the boxed text, p189, for details on getting to/from the airport.

Boat

During the wet season, boats depart daily at 7am from the tourist boat dock to Siem Reap up the Tonlé Sap river (US$25, five to six hours). Heading to Vietnam, there are daily departures from the same dock at 9am to Chau Doc (US$15, four to five hours).

Bus

Phnom Penh is connected to nearly all of the provincial capitals by bus. There's healthy competition to keep prices down and all the companies are much of a muchness in terms

DEPARTURE TAX

The departure tax for domestic flights is US$6 from Phnom Penh and Siem Reap, and US$5 from Ban Lung.

CAMBODIA

CAMBODIA

CROSSING INTO VIETNAM: DIRECT TO HO CHI MINH CITY

The easiest way to get to Vietnam's Ho Chi Minh City is to catch a Phnom Penh Sorya bus from Psar Thmei (US$12, six hours). They leave every morning at 8am, 9am and 11am and go directly there with no changes at the Bavet–Moc Bai border crossing. For information on crossing this border in the other direction, see p417.

of comfort and price. Their ticket booths are at Psar Thmei, which is also where they depart.

See the relevant sections for individual destinations and details on price and journey times.

Capitol Tour (Map p194; ☎ 217627; 14 Ph 182)
GST (Map p194; ☎ 012-895550; Psar Thmei)
Hour Lean (Map p194; ☎ 012-939905; 97 Sisowath Quay)
Narin Transport (Map p194; ☎ 991995; 50 Ph 125)
Neak Krorhorm (Map p194; ☎ 219496; 127 Ph 108)
Phnom Penh Sorya Transport (Map p194; ☎ 210359; Psar Thmei)

Car & Motorcycle

Guesthouses and travel agencies can arrange a car and driver from US$20 a day, depending on the destination. See right for motorcycle rental details.

Share Taxi, Pick-up & Minibus

Share taxis are an option if you need to travel outside of the bus schedules. Expect to pay US$2.50 for a space at the back and US$5 for a front seat. For Kampot, Krong Koh Kong and Sihanoukville they leave from Psar Dang Kor (Map pp190–1), while minibuses, pick-ups and taxis for most other places leave from near Psar Thmei (Map p194). Vehicles for Svay Rieng and Vietnam leave from Chbah Ampeau taxi park (Map pp190–1).

GETTING AROUND
Bicycle

Bicycles can be hired from most guesthouses and hotels from US$1 a day.

Cyclo & Tuk-tuk

Cyclos aren't so common now that tuk-tuks have invaded the city. Tuk-tuks are a pleasant way to get about town but much slower than

a moto. Cyclos cost 1000r for a short ride. Tuk-tuks are double.

Moto

Motos are everywhere and can be recognised by their baseball caps. The ones near the tourist areas can generally speak a good level of street English. Short rides around the city cost 1000r, and 2000r to venture out a little further towards the market areas. At night these prices double. To charter one for a day expect to pay US$6 to US$8. Night-time prices are double.

Motorcycle

Exploring Phnom Penh and the surrounding areas on a motorbike is a very liberating experience. The following places rent for between US$5 and US$9 per day.

Lucky! Lucky! (Map p194; ☎ 212788; 413 Monivong Blvd)
New! New! (Map p194; ☎ 012-855488; 417 Monivong Blvd)

Taxi

There aren't many metered taxi companies in the city. The most reliable is **Taxi Vantha** (☎ 012-855000), offering taxis 24 hours a day.

AROUND PHNOM PENH

There are several sites close to Phnom Penh that make for interesting excursions. While the significant town of Oudong and the Kirirom National Park each require an entire day on their own, the others are close enough to one another to be realistically combined into one busy day trip.

OUDONG

Before the capital moved to Phnom Penh in 1866, it was based here in Oudong, ruling over the country for more than two centuries from its hilltop location. Now it seems rather abandoned with only a few scattered temples and stupas left standing, some of which contain the royal remnants of King Monivong (1927–41) and King Ang Duong (1845–59). The climb up the hills is steep but offers a great view.

Buses depart from Phnom Penh for Oudong every hour (4500r, one hour). They drop you off at the access road and from there it's another 4000r by moto.

TONLÉ BATI

Locals love to come to this **lake** (admission US$3) for picnics, as along the way they can stop off at the two 12th-century temples: Ta Prohm and Yeay Peau. Ta Prohm is the more interesting of the two; it has some fine carvings still in good nick, depicting scenes of birth, dishonour and damnation.

Buses going to Takeo (5000r) can drop you off here, then it's a quick moto to the temples.

PHNOM CHISOR

This 11th-century structure is a well-preserved laterite **temple** (admission US$3) that runs in a straight line in the direction of Angkor. It has a peaceful locale on the top of the hill, with stunning views of the countryside and the sacred pond, Tonlé Om.

To get here, follow the directions for Tonlé Bati (above), but stay on the bus a little longer.

PHNOM TAMAO WILDLIFE SANCTUARY

The **Phnom Tamao sanctuary** (admission 1000r) for rescued animals is home to gibbons, sun bears, elephants, tigers, deer and a massive bird enclosure. They were all taken from poachers or abusive masters and are kept here for safe keeping and a sustainable breeding programme. All the money raised goes back into protecting Cambodia's frequently preyed upon wildlife.

To get here you will require your own wheels or a moto. A moto should cost around US$8. It is about 45km south of Phnom Penh. Take the NH2 for about 39km then turn right at the sign. From here, head straight down the sandy track and past the side show.

KIRIROM NATIONAL PARK

This is a lush elevated park 112km southwest of Phnom Penh. There are some winding walking trails that lead to cascading waterfalls (in the wet season) or light showers in the dry season. Hiking up the Phnom Dat Chivit (End of the World Mountain) you will arrive cliff side to face an amazing view of the Elephant and Cardamom Mountain ranges.

Kirirom offers a community tourism programme with the proceeds from the educational walks going directly back into the community. For details, contact **Mlup Baitong** (☎ 023-214409; mlup@online.com.kh).

SIEM REAP

☎ 063 / pop 862,500

Before the world's spotlight shone on Siem Reap as home to what some consider the eighth wonder of the world (that's Angkor Wat by the way, not Khmer traffic), it was a sleepy province, somewhere out in the sticks in northwestern Cambodia. Rewind to the 16th century, and the battle between the Siamese and Khmers for control of the area ended with the Khmers as victors and a nose-waving name change; Siem Reap diplomatically means 'Siamese Defeated'.

These days it is a large precinct of sprouting hotels, restaurants and bars, an enviable combination of mind-blowing sights, wildlife activities and a friendly and safe town with a lively nightlife scene.

ORIENTATION

The Stung Siem Reap divides the city into eastern and western blocks that seep out away from the city and into little villages. Most of the action is centred around Psar Chaa, a compact area crammed full of boutiques, eateries and drinking holes. The NH6 leading to the airport is flanked on either side by luxury hotels, and the star attraction, Angkor Wat, is just a few minutes north from the edge of town.

INFORMATION

For up-to-date information on the region, grab a copy of the *Siem Reap Angkor Visitors Guide*.

Emergency
Ambulance (☎ 119)
Fire (☎ 118)
Police (☎ 117)
Tourist police (Map pp210-11; ☎ 012-402424) At the main Angkor ticket checkpoint.

Internet Access
There are internet cafés everywhere. Most of them can be found in the Psar Chaa area and charge between 2000r and 4000r an hour. Laptop users can tap into wi-fi at the Blue Pumpkin (p205).

Medical Services
Naga International Clinic (Map pp210-11; ☎ 964500; 593 NH6; ⏱ 24hr) Best medical facilities in Siem Reap.

CAMBODIA

GETTING INTO TOWN

Airport

Once you have landed, there is a ticket booth just outside the arrivals department selling rides into town. The prices are fixed: moto US$1, taxi US$5 and van US$7. The airport is 8km from town on a pleasant route that is best enjoyed in a tuk-tuk. Tuk-tuks are not allowed in the airport complex, but wait just outside; they cost US$3.

Boat

After pulling into the boat dock at Chong Kneas, there will be a horde of motos waiting for your custom. If you have organised your hotel beforehand then their chariots are normally there waiting for you, otherwise it's US$1 to town.

Bus

Buses drop passengers off at the transport stop about 10 minutes out of town. A moto from here will cost US$1 and you'll pay US$2 for a tuk-tuk. Of course, many will be very insistent on taking you to their guesthouse of choice.

Money

ANZ Royal Bank (Map p204; ☎ 023-726900) In multiple locations. Visa/MasterCard ATMs.

Cambodia Asia Bank (Map p204; ☎ 964741; cnr Ph Sivatha & NH6; ◷ 7.30am-11pm) Cashes travellers cheques. Minimum US$5 charge for credit-card cash advances. Also a booth at the airport.

Canadia Bank (Map p204; ☎ 964808; Psar Chaa) Free credit-card advances and changes travellers cheques. ATM is Visa/MasterCard-compatible.

Union Commercial Bank (Map p204; ☎ 963703; Psar Chaa) Changes travellers cheques and offers free Visa advances.

Post

Main post office (Map p204; Pokambor Ave; ◷ 7am-5.30pm) Make sure your items are franked before you watch them disappear.

Telephone

There are international and domestic phone booths all over the city. Phone cards are sold at the markets and the post office.

Tourist Information

Tourist office (Map p204) Near the Royal Gardens, operates regular opening hours and is quite helpful, though staff are a bit gruff. The Khmer Angkor Tour Guides Association is also based here.

SIGHTS & ACTIVITIES

Giddy-up cowboys! **Happy Ranch** (Map pp210-11; ☎ 012-920002; www.thehappyranch.com; Kraum 4 Svay Dang Kuml; tours US$15-80), a horse ranch situated approximately 1.5km out of town, offers the chance to explore Siem Reap on pure Cambodian horseback. Tours range from one hour to six hours and take you through the surrounding villages and secluded temple spots.

Artisans d'Angkor (Map p204; ☎ 963330) is a centre of arts and ancient crafts with two workshops that you can visit. The Chantiers Écoles branch is the centre of traditional carving and masonry and can be visited from 7.30am to 6.30pm. The Angkor Silk Farm can be visited to see the entire process; from mulberry trees to silk worms and spinning to weaving (8am to 5pm).

Forming part of the NGO, CLMMRF (Cambodian Land Mine Museum Relief Fund), **Cambodia Landmine Museum** (Map pp210-11; ☎ 012-598951; admission free, donations accepted ◷ 7am-6pm) showcases a large collection of mines and artillery with a fascinating documentary of their destructive capabilities and consequences to the land and victims. Check out the garden of hidden mines (deactivated of course!) that visitors are challenged to find.

Krousar Thmey Exhibition Centre (Map pp210-11; ☎ 964694; www.drousar-thmey.org), meaning 'new family', was set up as an education facility for deprived children, including the blind and deaf, and was responsible for creating a Khmer version of Braille and sign language. The permanent exhibition, 'Tonlé Sap, sources of lives', showcases the significance of the Tonlé Sap and all its ecological and cultural glory.

Massages & Spas

With all that traipsing around temples, exhausted limbs and muscles are an inevitability. Thankfully Siem Reap has tapped into the lucrative market of rejuvenation and is crammed with spas and treatment centres. Most of the large resort hotels will have in-house spas that are also open to the public, with the added luxury of swimming pools.

Body Tune (Map p204; ☎ 764141; Psar Chaa area; massage US$16.50) A range of massage styles offered here, including Swedish, Thai and reflexology.

Frangipani (Map p204; ☎ 964391; frangipani_siem reap@yahoo.com; The Alley; massage US$18) Massages are offered alongside body and facial beautifying treatments.

Krousar Thmey (Krousar Thmey Tonlé Sap Exhibition Centre; Map pp210–11; massage US$6) This well-known NGO offers massages by professionally trained blind masseurs in its school behind the exhibition centre.

Seeing Hands Massage (Map p204; ☎ 012-836487; 324 Ph Sivatha; massage US$4) Preformed by the blind with part of the profits going to help the blind in the province.

Visaya Spa & Pool (Map p204; ☎ 760814; FCC Pokambor Ave; massage US$25) The usual spa and massage treatments plus manicures and pedicures and some indulgent aqua therapies.

You can also try the cheerful massage places centred around the Psar Chaa area for a cheap but effective rubdown:

BE VIP Khmer Massage (Map p204; ☎ 012-275051; massage US$6-12)

Khmer Massage (Map p204; ☎ 012-757120; massage US$6-10)

Traditional Khmer Massage (Map p204; ☎ 012-757120; massage US$6-10)

SLEEPING
Psar Chaa Area

Shadow of Angkor Guesthouse Bar & Restaurant (Map p204; ☎ 964774; shadowofangkor@hotmail.com; Pokambor Ave; r US$6-20; 🅇 🖳) This is a smart choice for budget travellers; a colonial building of fine rooms and a brilliant riverside location, plus a balcony restaurant that catches the breeze.

Steung Siemreap Hotel (Map p204; ☎ 965167; www .steungsiemreaphotel.com; Ph 9; r US$70-250; 🅇 🖳) Located in the quiet back streets, this upmarket hotel is a surprising find. It offers all of the trimmings one would expect from a top-end establishment and is just seconds away from all the action.

Phlauv Sivatha Area

Dead Fish Tower Inn (Map p204; ☎ 012-630377; www .deadfishtower.com; r US$5-20; 🅇 🖳) Good, friendly, no-fuss accommodation right next to its famous restaurant (p205).

our pick Hotel de la Paix (Map p204; ☎ 966000; www.hoteldelapaixangkor.com; US$300-750; 🅇 🖳) A highly stylised hotel that is fresh, sumptuous and a touch art nouveau. Its top suite with private swimming pool is the ultimate in luxury.

N6 West

Earthwalkers (Map pp210–11; ☎ 760107; www.earth walkers.no; dm US$4; s/d/tw US$9-17, f US$25; 🅇 🖳) Run by Norwegians in a quiet location. Comfortable rooms, and an intimate bar and restaurant.

Prince Mekong Villa (Map pp210–11; ☎ 012-437972; www.princemekong.com; s/tw/tr US$7/10/11) Happy guests buzz about the range of services provided here; free laundry, breakfast, bicycle and a knowledgeable and helpful manager. The vibe is cordial and communal.

Paul Drubule Hotel & Tourism School (Map pp210–11; ☎ 963673; www.ecolepauldubrule.org; r US$20-35; 🅇) Paul Drubule cofounded the Novotel hotel group, so it's no surprise that his student-run hotel offers high-quality service and well-maintained rooms. Proceeds go back into maintaining this tourism education centre.

East Bank of the River

Golden Banana Boutique Hotel & B&B (Map p204; ☎ 012-885366; www.golden-banana.com; B&B r US$19-25, hotel r US$35-50; 🅇 🖳 🖳) Tranquil pagodas garnished with leafy plants, a swimming pool and wireless internet connection. This boutique hotel packs a lot in and has gained itself a loyal following among regular visitors.

Bopha Angkor Hotel & Restaurant (Map p204; ☎ 964928; www.bopha-angkor.com; r US$38-58; 🅇 🖳 🖳) On the breezy east bank of the river and hiding behind a barrage of plants, this upscale hotel offers tastefully decorated rooms and a comprehensive range of services.

Heritage Suites Hotel (Map p204; ☎ 969100; www .heritage.com.kh; r US$95, ste US$160-225; 🅇 🖳 🖳) Jacuzzi floozies will be impressed with the jet-stream baths in this stylish hotel. With its sleek, oriental-inspired interiors, built-in saunas and private gardens, it has created a zone of glamorous Zen.

CAMBODIA

CAMBODIA

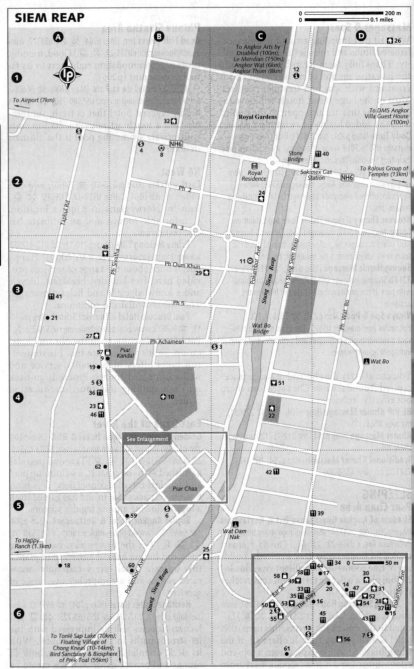

SIEM REAP

To Airport (7km)

To Angkor Arts by Disabled (100m); Le Meridien (150m); Angkor Wat (6km); Angkor Thom (8km)

To DMS Angkor Villa Guest House (100m)

Royal Gardens

Royal Residence

Stone Bridge

Sokimex Gas Station

To Rolous Group of Temples (13km)

Taphul Rd

Ph Sivatha

NH6

Ph 2

Ph 3

Ph Oum Khun

Ph 5

Ph Achamean

Pokambor Ave

Stung Siem Reap

Ph Stung Siem Reap

Ph Wat Bo

Wat Bo Bridge

Wat Bo

Psar Kandal

Psar Chaa

Wat Dam Nak

See Enlargement

To Happy Ranch (1.3km)

To Tonlé Sap Lake (10km); Floating Village of Chong Kneas (10-14km); Bird Sanctuary & Biosphere of Prek Toal (55km)

Bar St

The Alley

Pokambor Ave

Further Afield

DMS Angkor Villa Guest House (☎ 012-531037; svaysavong@gmail.com; s US$5-10, d US$6-12; ❈ ▯) Housing intrepid travellers with a conscience, this ethical accommodation has spotless units with attached bathrooms. A percentage of the profits go to the Savong Language School.

Shinta Mani Hotel & Institute of Hospitality (Map p204; ☎ 761988; www.shintamani.com; r US$80-105; ❈ ▯ ▮) This plush hotel of modern Khmer furnishings and enormous Khmer smiles also offers free hospitality training to high-risk youths. It has an excellent spa offering hot-stone therapy, body wraps, herbal baths and facials.

FCC Angkor (Map p204; ☎ 760280; www.fcccambodia .com; r US$90-330; ❈ ▯ ▮) Reliably sophisticated, the Siem Reap branch of the famous Foreign Correspondents' Club is set in the former governor's mansion. The glamorous hotel has calming rooms and is surrounded by its chic boutiques and gallery.

Victoria Angkor Resort & Spa Hotel (Map p204; ☎ 760428; www.victoriahotels-asia.com; r US$285-440; ❈ ▯ ▮) An enormous resort of 120 consistently luxurious rooms. Book on the net for dramatically reduced rates.

EATING

Taj Mahal Restaurant (Map p204; ☎ 963353; Psar Chaa area; mains US$1.50-4; ❉ breakfast, lunch & dinner) This halal restaurant may not look much from the outside, but while it lacks in design, it packs in flavour. Northern Indian cuisine is the speciality.

Blue Pumpkin (Map p204; ☎ 963574; www.tbpump kin.com; Psar Chaa area; mains US$1.50-5; ❉ breakfast, lunch & dinner; ▯) Climb the stairs of this café and bakery and enter a world of expressionist industrial design and Head Kandi tunes. The wall-to-wall sofa beds incite a gleeful kicking off of dusty flip-flops, while bed-tray refreshments make you feel truly spoilt.

Socheata 2 Restaurant (Map p204; ☎ 761416; socheata_2@yahoo.com; Psar Chaa area; mains US$1.50-12; ❉ breakfast, lunch & dinner) A Khmer restaurant that does not drown everything in oil, it offers a big range of Cambodian salads including banana leaf, pomelo and watergrass.

Viva (Map p204; ☎ 092-209154; Psar Chaa area; mains US$2-5; ❉ lunch & dinner) Mexican food and frozen cocktails are served at this kerbside restaurant, bringing the colour and spirit of Mexico to Siem Reap.

Soup Dragon (Map p204; ☎ 964933; 'Bar St'; mains 3000r-US$4; ❉ breakfast, lunch & dinner) Specialising in Asian breakfasts, including a tasty version of phò (noodle soup), this speedy restaurant also does sandwiches and burgers. Cutlery is hidden in the wooden box.

Dead Fish Tower (Map p204; ☎ 012-630377; Ph Sivatha; mains US$3-19; ❉ breakfast, lunch & dinner) Jungle junk meets tin shed; the radical Dead Fish with its lofty levels, live crocodile pit and appetising

Thai food offers a unique and surreal dining experience.

Amok Restaurant (Map p204; ☎ 012-800309; The Alley; mains US$3.50-6; ☽ dinner) This ambient little restaurant is a consistently excellent provider of authentic Khmer dishes, including of course the famous *amok* (baked fish with coconut and lemongrass in banana leaf).

Les Orientalistes (Map p204; ☎ 012-440627; entenu@online.com.kh; 613 Ph Wat Bo; US$4-12; ☽ lunch & dinner) This bright and exotic restaurant with its voluptuous archways and Turkish rugs channels the souqs of North Africa. It serves an international mix of Khmer, French and Moroccan cuisine.

Le Tigre de Papier (Map p204; ☎ 012-265811; mains US$5.50-9; ☽ breakfast, lunch & dinner) Heaving every night, this restaurant serves everything from Vietnamese *nem* (spring rolls) to Greek moussaka. It also acts as a movie house, used bookstore and is topped off by a lingerie boutique upstairs.

Cambodian BBQ (Map p204; ☎ 965407; cambodian bbq@angkorw.com; The Alley; mains US$8-9; ☽ dinner) This pleasant restaurant has traditional Phnom Pleung stoves to grill up crocodile, snake, ostrich and kangaroo alongside unlimited free noodles and vegetables.

Tell Restaurant (Map p204; ☎ 963289; 374 Ph Sivatha; mains US$1.50-18.50; ☽ lunch & dinner) Enjoy cheese fondue while overlooking the busy street below. This restaurant specialises in German food and beverages, including heavy schnitzels and sausages that will leave you stuffed.

DRINKING

Warehouse (Map p204; Psar Chaa area; ☽ 10.30am-3am) A Western bar where you can hear yourself think and your mates talk. There is also a gallery upstairs that features local arts.

Abacus Garden Restaurant & Bar (☎ 012-644286; Ph Oum Khun; ☽ 11am-late, closed Sun) This is an exceptional bar of alluring grace. A flourishing garden surrounds a traditional villa that serves outstanding food and wine.

Boosters (Map p204; ☎ 012-726758; 'Bar St'; ☽ 6am-late) This casual corner bar blends delicious fruit juices to make an assortment of non-alcoholic cocktails and shakes.

Chili Si-Dang Wine Bar (Map p204; ☎ 012-723488; ☽ 11.30am-late) Riverside and with a balcony to make the most of the location, this is a tranquil bar offering a good selection of international and vintage wines.

Linga Bar (Map p204; ☎ 012-246912; The Alley; ☽ 5pm-late) Madonna hogs the stereo at this gay-friendly bar. Colourful, cool and contemporary, most people are content to sip cocktails on the lounge, but a mirror ball does spin optimistically in the background.

Angkor What? (Map p204; ☎ 012-490755; hasty puddings@yahoo.co.uk; 'Bar St'; ☽ 6pm-late) This Siem Reap institution manages to pack them in

---

DINING FOR A CAUSE

These are some fabulous restaurants that support worthy causes or assist in the training of Cambodia's future hospitality gurus.

- **our pick** **Singing Tree Café** (Map p204; ☎ 965210; info@singingtreecafé.com; mains US$1.50-3; ☽ breakfast, lunch & dinner, closed Mon) Also a community centre, yoga studio and gallery, this garden café of scrumptious muffins, decent coffee and health food dedicates a percentage of profits to worthy sectors of wildlife conservation and street children.

- **Funky Munky Bar & Diner** (Map p204; ☎ 012-1824553; www.funkymunkycambodia.com; ☽ lunch & dinner, closed Mon) There's no 'Royale with cheese' here, but Vincent Vega of *Pulp Fiction* would still enjoy this friendly rock 'n' roll biker bar serving the appealingly named 'Cardiac Arrest' burger with everything needed to clog a good artery. Quiz nights are held every Thursday with proceeds going to a different worthy cause each week.

- **Sala Bai** (Map p204; ☎ 963329; salabai@online.com.kh; set lunch US$5; ☽ noon-2pm Mon-Fri Nov-Jun) This school trains young Khmers in hospitality services. It is run by the NGO, Agir Pour Le Cambodge (To Act for Cambodia), and serves a menu of Western and Cambodian cuisine.

- **Les Jardins des Delices** (Map pp210-11; ☎ 963673; Paul Dubrule Hotel & Tourism School, Airport Rd; set lunch US$7; ☽ noon-1pm) You can have a three-course meal of Asian and Western food, prepared by students training in culinary arts.

every night. The later the night the louder the revelry, with regular drink deals to keep the punters well and truly liquefied.

Laundry Bar (Map p204; ☎ 016-962026; www .laundry-bar.com; ⏰ 6pm-late) One of the few options for late-night grooving. The tunes are cool and the atmosphere is one of passive partying.

ENTERTAINMENT

Nearly all of the major hotels offer nightly *apsara* dances (royal ballet), though they are often touristy and not so authentic. Another alternative is a pleasant evening of classical music. **Beatocello** (Map pp210-11; Jayavarman VII Children's Hospital; admission by donation; ⏰ 7.15pm Sat) has cello concerts featuring original music and Bach compositions. It funds free medical treatment to local children.

SHOPPING

Angkor Arts by Disabled (Map p204; ☎ 012-538059; www.aadcam.org) Stone and marble carvings brought to you by Siem Reap's disabled community. Near Spean Neak or Dragon Bridge.

Colors of Cambodia (Map p204; ☎ 965021; Psar Chaa area) Bright and fun books, cards and works of art by young local painters.

Rajana (Map p204; ☎ 964744; Psar Chaa area) Traditional handicrafts, paintings and clothing can all be found here.

Shenga (Map p204; ☎ 012-260015) A fair-trade boutique of sexy lingerie. Above Le Tigre de Papier restaurant, in Psar Chaa.

Psar Chaa

The old market is a treasure-trove of silks, woven bags, trinkets and souvenirs. Past all the stalls there is an interesting mall just selling jewellery. You will see it blinking in the distance.

Psar Kandal

Just up the road from the old market is Psar Kandal (Central Market). This is a newer, smaller version of the old market selling the same sort of stuff. If it gets too cramped at Psar Chaa, then come here, it's much quieter and the vendors are less in-your-face.

GETTING THERE & AWAY
Air

Siem Reap is now well connected to most neighbouring Asian cities. Prices for a domestic flight to Phnom Penh normally start at

CROSSING INTO THAILAND: SIEM REAP TO BANGKOK

From Siem Reap you can catch a direct bus – with one change over at the Poipet border crossing – to Khao San Rd in Bangkok for US$11. You can arrange tickets through any travel agency. For information on crossing this border in the other direction, see the boxed text, p158.

US$75 (45 minutes). See p256 for a list of airlines in Siem Reap.

Boat

Boats from Battambang to Siem Reap take anywhere from three to eight hours depending on the season. The trip costs US$15 and boats leave from the dock. Travelling in the other direction, boats leave from Chong Kneas.

Bus

The roads from Siem Reap to the major cities are now very much improved. Buses depart from the transport stop.

Buses to Phnom Penh (US$3.50, five to six hours) will normally stop off in Kompong Thom en route so you can hop off there if need be. Buses also travel to Battambang (US$4, four hours) but the boat trip is a far more exciting option. Buses to Poipet (US$4 to US$8, five hours) will normally collect you from the hotel where you are staying. All the major bus companies are represented in Siem Reap, the more reliable ones being Hour Lean, Capitol and GST. Tickets can be purchased at bus company offices prior to departure.

Share Taxi & Pick-up

Taxis leave from the Sokimex gas station (Map p204) near the Stone Bridge. Negotiate before you hop in. See the relevant destination sections for details of prices and journey times.

GETTING AROUND

Siem Reap is easily navigated on foot, but if all that exploring has worn you out then short trips around the town on a moto are 1000r, double that for a tuk-tuk. Motorcycles are not permitted to be driven by foreigners in Siem Reap.

AROUND SIEM REAP

ANGKOR CENTRE FOR CONSERVATION OF BIODIVERSITY (ACCB)

At Kbal Spean, this conservation centre shelters a hundred native animals appearing on the endangered species list. Tours of the centre are free and kick off at 10.30am each day.

It also operates a 'Day in the Life of Tour' where you can take part in rural activities such as roof weaving, rice planting and harvesting, cow cart/tractor driver training and cooking classes. All the proceeds benefit the participating communities.

Currently these tours (paid for by donation) are organised through **Villa Siem Reap Guest House** (Map p204; ☎ 761036; info@thevillasiemreap.com; 153 Taphul Rd).

FLOODED FOREST OF KOMPONG PHHLUK

As part of an Integrated Women Empowerment Project, the young women of Phum T'nout Kombot village take visitors on excursions through the flooded forests of Kompong Phhluk. The money raised supports the conservation of their fisheries. The trips in wooden dugouts weave between the trees and duck beneath the thick foliage. Fantastic fun!

A little further along is Kompong Phhluk's floating centre for ecotourism sponsored by the UNDP, which also houses a small restaurant.

A boat from the town of Roluos costs US$15 to the villages of Kompong Phhluk. A trip in the dugouts is US$2 with all profits going back into the programme.

TEMPLES OF ANGKOR

ANGKOR WAT

Angkor Wat is more than just an astounding architectural feat; it is the national symbol, the source of fierce Khmer pride and the epicentre of their civilisation. At first sight, it is a sumptuous blend of towers and sky, a magnificent spellbinding shrine to Vishnu with its captivating image replicated in the reflective lake below, a feast for unbelieving eyes.

This vision is the creation of King Suryavarman II, the powerful king who, during his reign (1112–52), defeated Champa and extended the empire to northern Thailand, Burma and the northern tips of Malaysia. He built it to serve as a holy capital city and eventually as his funerary temple.

Angkor Wat is surrounded by a wide moat and enclosed by a laterite wall. The centrepieces are the five magnificent towers representing the heavenly peaks of Mt Meru, the tallest of which was the home of Vishnu. The third gallery is famous for its superb bas-reliefs of scenes extracted from the Hindu epics. Among them in the eastern section is the 'Churning of the Ocean of Milk' theme. Carved to dramatic glory, it shows the *asuras* (demons) and *devas* (gods) churning the ocean to produce an elixir of immortality. Also churned from the ocean's waters are the *apsara* (heavenly nymph or angelic dancer) girls; 1876 of the celestial nymphs are carved into the walls and pavilions of Angkor Wat.

Climbing the well-worn steps to the highest point is a vertigo nightmare. Angling at 70 degrees and rising 42m above the base of the upper level, it contains a 27m vertical shaft that once held treasures.

At sunset, Angkor Wat turns into an ancient city of gold. This is the best time to view it in all its glory, but it is also one of the busier times. The quietest is around lunchtime when all of the tour groups return to Siem Reap for lunch.

ANGKOR THOM

The bridge leading to the south gate of Angkor Thom has two incredible balustrades of giants handling *nagas* (mythical serpents, often multiheaded), an incredible first impression made only more dreamlike by the elephants plodding out of the arched entrance topped by the four enormous faces of Avalokiteshvara (the Buddha of Compassion).

Angkor Thom (Grand Angkor) is a walled compound bordered by a 100m-wide moat. It was built by the great King Jayavarman VII (r 1181–1219) as his royal palace. The complex has five gateways, each with double portals. Four of the gateways point to each side of the compass, while the fifth is a Victory Gateway.

Behind the 8m walls lie some of Angkor's most important monuments: the Bayon, the Terrace of Elephants and the Terrace of the Leper King.

EXPLORING THE TEMPLES

One Day

After a morning of exploring Ta Prohm, where the temples have been gripped by the hands of nature, head for Angkor Thom and stare at the serene faces at the Bayon. After lunch stop by Phnom Bakheng before savouring the sunset at Angkor Wat.

Three Days

After the first action-packed day, beat the tourists to the beautiful Banteay Srei with a quick visit to Preah Khan along the way. Then make your way to Kbal Spean to see the carved river bed with a thousand *lingas* (phallic symbols). On the third day, slow it down with a peaceful ride through the tree-lined streets to the Roluos group before visiting the more secluded temples dotted about the area.

One Week

All of Angkor at your own pace plus the long haul out to the abandoned Beng Mealea. Enjoy!

Tickets

The **ticket office** (Map pp210-11; 1-day/3-day/1-week pass US$20/40/60) and checkpoint are on the road to Angkor. One-week passes require a passport photo. You'll be whacked with a US$30 fine if you are found at the temples without a pass.

Sellers

As soon as you dismount your moto/bike/tuk-tuk you will be accosted by hordes of youngsters selling guidebooks, bottles of water and souvenirs. They may form an unwanted gauntlet to the actual temples, but the books are very informative and the bottles of water much needed in the hot sun after some sweaty scrambling over ruins. At least they're not begging.

Eating

Nearly all of the temples have food stalls cluttered about the entrances so you'll never go hungry.

Transport

Motos are the most popular form of transport around the temples, they are zippy and inexpensive (US$6 to US$8 per day). Tuk-tuks take a little longer for those who have the time to savour the experience (US$10 to US$15 per day). Bicycles are great and environmentally friendly, and can be arranged through most hotels for US$2 a day. Hotels can also arrange cars for US$25 to US$30 a day. If you want to travel like the ancient Khmers then leap onto an elephant – they wander around Angkor Thom for US$15.

Those who want to take to the skies can opt for the **hot-air balloon** (☎ 012-814500; helicopter .cam@online.com.kh), attached by a line (US$11), or chopper (around US$140) for 15 minutes.

The Bayon

The Bayon was the King's state temple. It rises from the centre of Angkor Thom's compound in a cluster of conical towers. Smiling in every direction are the four divine faces of Avalokiteshvara, carved with a great likeness to King Jayavarman VII in his state of peaceful meditation. There are 54 towers in total with a staggering 216 faces. Complementing the faces are the intricate bas-reliefs depicting daily life in the king's court and the bloody battles against the Chams.

Terrace of Elephants

East of the Royal Palace is the remarkable Terrace of Elephants. Royal war elephants march along its 350m length topped with hunters and warriors who are seated high enough to avoid the claws of tigers below. At the northern end is a splendid royal horse protected by

TEMPLES OF ANGKOR

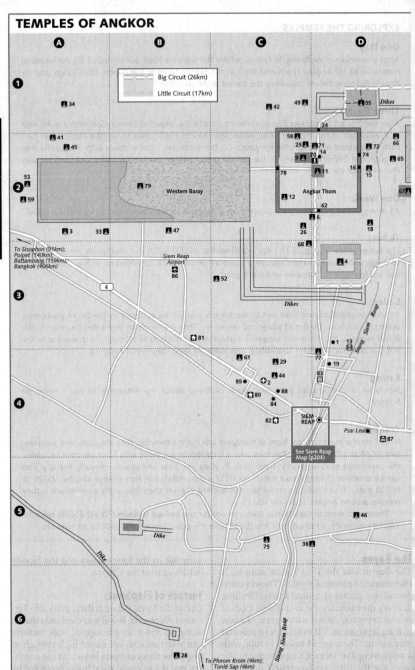

Big Circuit (26km)

Little Circuit (17km)

Western Baray

Angkor Thom

To Sisophon (91km);
Poipet (140km);
Battambang (159km);
Bangkok (406km)

Siem Reap
Airport

Dikes

Dikes

SIEM
REAP

See Siem Reap
Map (p204)

Psar Leu

Dike

Dike

Stung Siem Reap

Stung Siem Reap

To Phnom Krom (4km);
Tonlé Sap (4km)

CAMBODIA

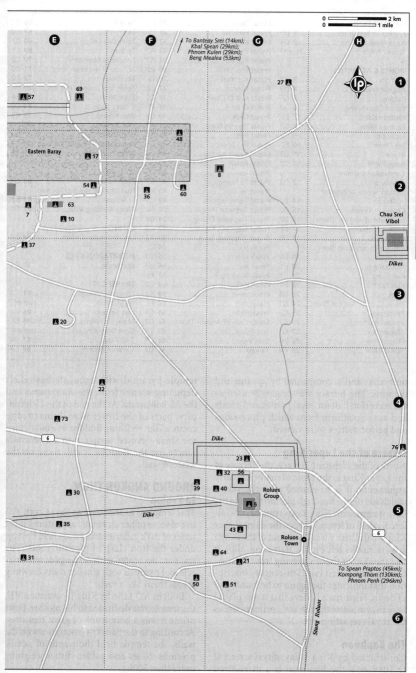

umbrellas and accompanied by *apsaras* and demons. The terrace was originally used as the reception hall for royal parties and guests and as the platform from which processions and performances were viewed.

Terrace of the Leper King

North of the Elephant Terrace, the Terrace of the Leper King is the topic of many scholarly arguments. It is so named after the statue which sits on the 6m-high platform. Some believe it represents King Yasovarman I, who allegedly died of leprosy, hence the name 'Leper King'. This theory was borne out of the lichen growth marks left on the statue, mottling it like the skin of those suffering from leprosy. On the statue itself is a 15th-century inscription that indicates the figure to be Yama, god of death. Historians believe that it was placed here to symbolise the terrace's primary use as the royal cremation site.

The Baphuon

Constructed by King Udayadityavarman II (r 1049–65), the Baphuon is a three-tiered temple-pyramid with exquisite bas-reliefs depicting scenes from the *Ramayana* and the *Mahabharata*. At the end of the 15th century, parts of the tower were dismantled to create a 70m reclining Buddha in a bid to turn the Shiva-devoted temple into a Theravada sanctuary; the Buddha is still there on the western wall.

AROUND ANGKOR THOM
Ta Prohm

This temple is as seductive as Lara Croft. The site of some of her cinematic adventures, it is a series of dark galleries and pillars held hostage under the iron clasp of gigantic roots. The walls are decorated with carvings of sensuous celestial nymphs with smaller roots crawling across them like a rash.

Built in AD 1186 by King Jayavarman VII, the temple was dedicated to his mother. In its prime it was a holy trunk of great treasures. According to the Sanskrit inscriptions on the walls, the temple held thousands of pearls, precious stones and golden dishes weighing more than 500kg.

Phnom Bakheng

When King Yasovarman I (r 889–910) moved the capital to Angkor proper, he built Phnom Bakheng as his capital. The temple, a 65m five-tiered pyramid, is a study of Hindu numerology. At the summit, five towers form a quincunx to echo the five peaks of the heavenly mountain. At its most magnificent, the pyramid was surrounded by 108 towers representing the 27 days of four lunar cycles.

An ascending temple of towers, this is a great place to view the rise and fall of the sun over the distant Angkor Wat. However, a gazillion others try to do the same so it can be rather frustrating to get that money shot.

Preah Khan

Where all faiths collide, this temple is a Buddhist complex with parts dedicated to Vishnu and other sections to Shiva. Part of King Jayavarman VII's impressive portfolio, Preah Khan was dedicated to his father, the multisyllable Dharanindravarman. It was originally a Buddhist complex housing more than 1000 Buddhist teachers. Covering 56 hectares, it is also another compound where temples and trees intertwine, evoking the conquistador feeling of discovering ancient secrets.

Prasat Neak Pean

An island temple, the Prasat Neak Pean is believed to celebrate Buddha's achievement of Nirvana. Sitting pretty in the middle of the Jayatataka reservoir (Northern Baray) it acted as a sacred shrine where pilgrims came to swim in the surrounding waters. The four fountains take four forms: elephant, human, lion and horse sprouted holy water that could cure the pilgrims of their ailments.

Roluos Group

The very first site of the ancient Khmer civilisation was here in Roluos, then known as Hariharalaya. The temples of Roluos were built by King Indravarman I (r 877–89). The first was Preah Ko (Sacred Bull) named after the Nandi statue found on site. Preah Ko has six brick towers each dedicated to his parents, maternal grandparents and to King Jayavarman II and his wife.

Next came Bakong, a terrestrial version of the celestial Mt Meru. It is a five-tiered pyramid-temple and was the inspiration for many of the temples that followed.

FURTHER AFIELD
Banteay Srei

This 'Citadel of Women' dedicated to Shiva is a stunning tour de force of classical art and the most ornate of all of the temples. Though it is relatively tiny in size compared to its mammoth counterparts, it has the most intricate carvings and is believed to be the instigator of the Khmer art movement. The detail is astounding and each doorway, each lintel and every wall is a masterpiece.

Kbal Spean

In the midst of the jungle, cool water rushes over a skilfully carved river bed, known as the 'River of a Thousand Lingas'. The phallic symbols of fertility have been shaped into the rocks along with some deities that recline under a set of rapids. Fifty kilometres northeast of Siem Reap, it takes about 1½ hours to get here from Banteay Srei on a sandy track. From the entrance, it is another 30-minute walk. The trip out here is best combined with a visit to Banteay Srei. Last admission is 3.30pm.

Phnom Kulen

From a lofty height of 20m, the Phnom Kulen waterfall cascades off the mountain where King Jayavarman II announced independence from Java and proclaimed himself god-king. The river here also runs over *lingas* and is an attractive sight for modern-day pilgrims. There is also an 8m-long reclining Buddha and a small temple nearby. It costs US$20 to visit the sight, 60km from Siem Reap. Last admission is 3.30pm.

There is also a little-explored, unnamed set of ruins at the foot of the mountain that is gaining mythical status among locals. Not many know how to get there, though they know of its existence. Would-be explorers are challenged to find it!

Beng Mealea

Visitors to this **temple** (admission US$5) are confronted with a mass of ruins half devoured by a ravenous jungle. Its abandoned stones lie like forgotten jewels swathed in lichen and its temple complex strangled by ivy and vines. Brought to you by the same man who built Angkor Wat, King Suryavarman II, it is similar in style to his later effort but receives only a fraction of the guests.

Beng Mealea is 70km northeast of Siem Reap on a sealed private road. It costs US$40

CAMBODIA

to get there in a chartered taxi. Or you could combine it with a trip around the temples of Angkor for US$65.

NORTHWESTERN CAMBODIA

Throughout history this has been the most war-torn region in Cambodia. Blessed with a luscious wilderness in the mountainous Veal Veng, gem-rich terrain in Pailin and stunning temples in Preah Vihear, it's easy to see why it has been fought over.

KOMPONG CHHNANG PROVINCE

Named after its famous clay pots (*chhnang* means pot), this region has been producing them the traditional way for 5000 years and supplies most of the country. The surrounding area of rich soil benefits the agricultural farmers, who along with the pot makers make up most of the population.

Kompong Chhnang

☎ 026 / pop 44,100

Kompong Chhnang is a city divided. At first sight you would be led to thinking it was a lively port of docking boats and floating villages. Venture into town and a colonial municipality seeping with quiet charm gives way to the Cambodia of intrepid dreams: fields of lush rice paddies, languid oxen and smiley Khmers.

INFORMATION

There is an **Acleda Bank** (☎ 988809) near the market representing Western Union for money transfers. Phone calls can be made at the kiosk next to Sokha Guest House (right) or around the market.

SIGHTS & ACTIVITIES

Clay pot central, Kompong Chhnang is home to gold-specked ceramic pots, made from the earth aggregated from nearby **Phnom Meas** (Gold Mountain). Nearly every dwelling in the village of **Ondong Rossey**, 7km out of town, produces them by hand. If you are curious about their craft, the incredibly cordial people will muck you up with clay and show you how it's done. On your own steam, just head north on the NH5 and turn left at the sign, or hire a moto driver at sunset and travel along the dusty red trail that weaves through tranquil rice fields. Towering sugar palm trees shoot out at regular intervals, punctuating the sky with their tufted silhouettes. With not a tourist in sight, bare-chested Khmers herding cows and chickens will be the only people you will see. If ever there was a reminder of the magic of travel, this simple moto ride is it.

SLEEPING

Holiday Guesthouse (☎ 988802; N5; r US$3-10; 🖾 🖳) 'Bending over backwards' does not half-describe the efforts here: free pick-up, bicycle, and basic Khmer lessons with every room rented over US$5. Internet is available and a restaurant has been recently added on site.

Sokha Guest House (☎ 988622; r US$5-15; 🖾) Great rooms set back from the road in a peaceful garden setting with palm-shaded mat swings and cool verandas. This hotel has a definitive aura of calm.

Sovannphum Hotel (☎ 011-886572; N5; r US$10-15; 🖾) This is the poshest accommodation in town; ornate with carved wooden detailing, lofty ceilings and sun-drenched terraces. The back terrace has a spectacular view of the verdant village and mountain.

Sok Thai San Guesthouse (☎ 012-854595; N5; r US$5-10; 🖾) Another recommended accommodation option.

EATING

Rough-and-ready food stalls are aplenty in both the Psar Krom and Psar Leur markets, and along the river bank.

Restaurant Phnom Meas & 98 (☎ 012-800553; N5; mains 6000-10,000r; 🕒 breakfast, lunch & dinner) A roadside diner out the front, palm-thatched bungalow out the back. The menu is exotic with pig stomach the most heavily featured ingredient.

Monorom Restaurant (☎ 012-785172; N5; mains 6000-20,000r; 🕒 breakfast, lunch & dinner) Only Khmer spoken here, thus a display of pantomime ensues with the *barang* (foreigner) using actions and mime to describe their culinary desire, causing great mirth to the staff who must watch and decipher. The result is generally well-prepared and tasty meals. Prices are not listed, so get them to write it down beforehand.

GETTING THERE & AWAY

From Phnom Penh buses depart from Psar Thmei (8500r, two hours).

Buses bound for Battambang, Sisophon, Pursat, Poipet and Siem Reap will also pick up and drop off in Kompong Chhnang. Just let them know where you are heading along the route so that they charge you accordingly. Prices can go up to US$4 for a two-hour trip to Pursat during festivals.

GETTING AROUND
Motodups charge 500r to 1000r for short spins around town and US$6 for a day.

PURSAT PROVINCE
Encompassing six districts, Pursat is one of Cambodia's largest and most diverse provinces. From the floating villages of Kompong Luong to the jungles afoot the Cardamom Mountains, the region offers a glimpse into the wildly varied Cambodian environment and way of life.

Pursat
☎ 052 / pop 59,850
Pursat is a busy town due to its location smack bang in the middle between Phnom Penh and Battambang. There is not much to do here except catch dust but it is the easiest base for exploring the region's sights.

INFORMATION
Telephone and fax outlets can be found around the market on the west bank of the river. An internet café is next door to the Phnom Pich Hotel.
Acleda Bank (☎ 951434) On the north side of the N5, allows you to transfer money, while moneychangers in the market will convert dollars into riel.
Tourist office (☎ 012-838854; Ph 1) Is very helpful and has a comprehensive brochure on the region.

SLEEPING
New Thansour (☎ 951506, 012-962395; Ph 2; s US$3, d US$5-15; 🎄) The New Thansour (aka Thansour Tmey) is almost identical to the Phnom Pich in comfort and services, except more effort has been thrown into decorating.
Phnom Pich Hotel (☎ 951515; PH 1; r US$6-18; 🎄) Resembling a Hong Kong housing estate, this trusted guesthouse has spacious rooms all with air-con and hot water and a downstairs restaurant. It has a handy internet café next door.

EATING
Mlop Svay (☎ 012-429787; N5; mains 5000-10,000r; 🎄 breakfast & dinner, closed 2-5pm) A small and intimate restaurant oozing ambience. Due to the well-prepared meals, it is very popular

with visiting ministers and NGO personnel – the pretty young waitresses may also be a contributing factor.
Borei Thmei (☎ 951605; N5; mains 5000-20,000r; 🎄 lunch & dinner) Dishes out Khmer, Chinese and Western food. Some of the bungalows come complete with hammocks – that way you can rest easy after the laborious task of stuffing yourself with delicious food.
Sensabymen Restaurant (☎ 012-927036; N5, Ptah Prey village; mains 5000-30,000r; 🎄 breakfast, lunch & dinner, 11am-last customer) Set on a sprawling property a few moto minutes out of town, this modern Khmer restaurant boasts a huge beer garden with bungalows and an unspoilt view of the green fields beyond.

GETTING THERE & AWAY
There are many bus companies serving the Phnom Penh to Battambang–Sisophon–Poipet route that stop at the Pursat bus terminal on the N5. To Phnom Penh costs 10000r to 10400r (two hours) and to Battambang 7000r (one hour).

Around Pursat
KOMPONG LUONG
Wooden planks tied to steel barrels is the ingenious construction method used by over 10,000 people keeping their homes afloat on the Tonlé Sap river. A large community, the majority of whom are ethnic Vietnamese, live, trade, play and pray entirely on water. The floating village is just like any other found in Cambodia, complete with happy children.

Motorboats can be chartered to take you out to the village for US$5 an hour. A friendly wave from a passing tourist is enough to send youngsters into an ecstatic frenzy.

The Vietnamese of the Tonlé Sap have historically been discriminated against throughout time. Most recently at the hands of the Khmer Rouge, the residents, if not killed, were repatriated to Vietnam, only returning after the 1990s when the Khmer Rouge dwindled in numbers and were forced to retreat.

Depending on the season, Kompong Luong can be reached by hired moto from Pursat in 45 minutes to an hour and should cost US$6 for the round trip, US$25 by car.

VEAL VENG
Veal Veng is well and truly out in the sticks. A remote highland district 125km southwest of Pursat, this area forms part of the

Phnom Samkos Wildlife Sanctuary in the Cardamom Mountains. This secluded wilderness of overgrown bamboo, hanging ravines and small waterfalls offers the rare opportunity to view and track jungle animals (elephants, sun bears and, in rare cases, tigers) in their natural habitat.

Local guides with knowledge of animal tracks can take you camping up in the **Phnom Samkos Mountain** and show you what to look for.

Pramoy is the nearest town, set at the base of the Cardamom Mountains. The only decent place to stay is the no-name **guesthouse** (r US$5-7), with no address and no telephone number, but it's a piece of cake to find as everyone knows of it. Referred to as Ptaih Om Bol (Uncle Bol's House), it is made up of quaint log cabins with romantic four-poster beds, no running water but plenty of chickens, cicadas and twittering birds.

To reach the jungles of Veal Veng, you must go to the town of Pramoy from Pursat. Pick-up trucks load up as many people as life-threateningly possible and set off from the main gas station in front of the Pursat market (inside/back of 10,000r/US$5, three hours).

Once there, hire a local moto (two hours to reach Phnom Sam Kos Mountain). The road is rough but spectacularly exhilarating, taking you past isolated jungle villages, wild rice and trickling brooks. Bank on US$4 to US$5 for the outing. Negotiate fees if you plan to camp the night on the mountain and explore deeper into the forest.

BATTAMBANG PROVINCE

Between 1795 and the early 1940s Battambang Province was the object of an entangled-custody battle between the Khmers and the Thais, ping-ponging back and forth between them. After some destructive turbulence at the hands of the Khmer Rouge in the 1990s, Battambang, Cambodia's largest producer of rice and gemstones, has returned to its peaceful state once more.

Battambang

☎ 053 / pop 154,000

Full of old-world charm, Battambang city stretches like a yawning cat – languorously awakening from a historical coma – along both sides of the Sanker River. The residents are friendly and composed and the elegant architecture is a sweet reminder of the colonial days of yore.

ORIENTATION

Split in half by the river, most of the city's commercial activity is centred on the west bank. Though the town is spreading, it is still relatively compact and easy enough to navigate on foot.

INFORMATION

There are phone booths all over town and some internet phones near Psar Nat by the river. There are also a few internet cafés dotted about charging US$1 an hour. The main post office offers international telephone services as well but it is cheaper to go to the internet cafés and phone kiosks.

Conveniently there are a few banks in town that offer money transfers, travellers-cheque services and now finally an ATM at the Canadia Bank.

Acleda Bank (☎ 370122) Money transfers.
Cambodia Commercial Bank (☎ 952267) Cash advances.
Canadia Bank (☎ 952267) The ATM takes Visa and MasterCard.
Tourist office Near the governor's residence.
Union Commercial Bank (☎ 952552) Cash advances.

SIGHTS & ACTIVITIES

You can catch circus shows and dances at **Phare Ponleu Selpak** (☎ 952424; www.phareps.org), a multi-arts centre for disadvantaged children. Phone, or look out for its posters for schedules. Motos can get you to the location out of town.

Battambang Museum (Ph 1; admission US$1; ☼ 8-11am & 2-5pm Mon-Fri) has some fine lintel carvings. The small museum also houses a limited collection of artefacts from around the province.

SLEEPING

Traditionally, accommodation was centred west of the river, but with the town's expansion there has been an upsurge in offerings eastside.

Westside

Chhaya Hotel (☎ 952170; chhaya.best@yahoo.com; Ph 3; r US$4-12; ☒) A free shuttle bus to and from the boat station, helpful staff and some of the best English- and French-speaking guides available have kept the Chhaya popular and well reputed.

Hotel Royal (☎ 016-912034; royalasiahotelbb@yahoo.com; r US$4-20; ☒) Large comfortable rooms

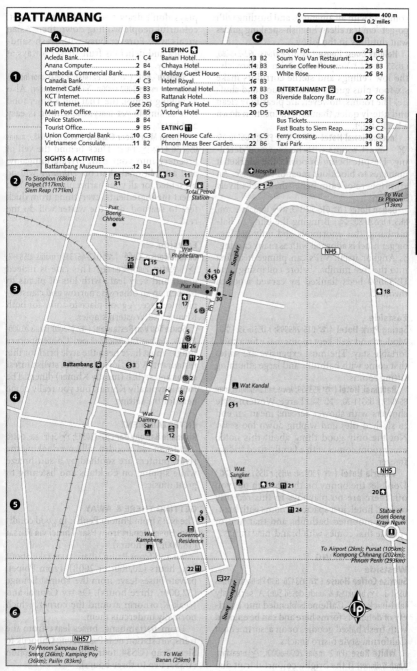

BATTAMBANG

0   400 m
0   0.2 miles

INFORMATION
Acleda Bank	1 C4
Anana Computer	2 B4
Cambodia Commercial Bank	3 B4
Canadia Bank	4 C3
Internet Café	5 B3
KCT Internet	6 B3
KCT Internet	(see 26)
Main Post Office	7 B5
Police Station	8 B4
Tourist Office	9 B5
Union Commercial Bank	10 C3
Vietnamese Consulate	11 B2

SIGHTS & ACTIVITIES
Battambang Museum	12 B4

SLEEPING 🏠
Banan Hotel	13 B2
Chhaya Hotel	14 B3
Holiday Guest House	15 B3
Hotel Royal	16 B3
International Hotel	17 B3
Rattanak Hotel	18 D3
Spring Park Hotel	19 C5
Victoria Hotel	20 D5

EATING 🍴
Green House Café	21 C5
Phnom Meas Beer Garden	22 B6

Smokin' Pot	23 B4
Sourn You Van Restaurant	24 C5
Sunrise Coffee House	25 B3
White Rose	26 B4

ENTERTAINMENT 🎭
Riverside Balcony Bar	27 C6

TRANSPORT
Bus Tickets	28 C3
Fast Boats to Siem Reap	29 C2
Ferry Crossing	30 C3
Taxi Park	31 B2

To Sisophon (68km);
Poipet (117km);
Siem Reap (171km)

Hospital

To Wat
Ek Phnom
(13km)

Total Petrol
Station

Psar
Boeng
Chhoeuk

Wat
Phiphetaram

NH5

Stung Sangker

Psar Nat

Battambang

Wat Kandal

Wat
Damrey
Sar

Wat
Sangker

NH5

Statue of
Dom Boeng
Kraw Ngum

To Airport (2km); Pursat (105km);
Kompong Chhnang (202km);
Phnom Penh (293km)

Wat
Kampheng

Governor's
Residence

Stung Sangker

NH57

To Phnom Sampeau (18km);
Sneng (26km); Kamping Poy
(36km); Pailin (83km)

To Wat
Banan (25km)

CAMBODIA

complete with all amenities and bustling with go-get-'em travellers. English-speaking guides wait dutifully in the lobby.

Holiday Guest House (☎ 012-647648, 092-215880; r US$5-10; ✖) Very 'Being John Malkovich', the low ceilings and sterile corridors make six-foot-plus guests need to stoop and shuffle. The rooms, however, are pleasingly clean and utterly quiet, thanks to its location down a back street.

International Hotel (☎ 953999; Ph 2; r US$10-15; ✖) Smart rooms with heavy wood detailing. Despite being opposite the market it manages to block out most of the noise. An atmosphere of calm belies the hotel's lively location.

Banan Hotel (☎ 016-509349; www.bananhotel.com; NH5; r US$20-80; ✖) Bringing the bling to Battambang, this enormous and only-getting-bigger hotel is adorned with as many carvings as Angkor itself. VIPs can plunge headfirst into the free minibar before collapsing onto US$3000 beds flanked by carved wooden thrones.

Eastside

Spring Park Hotel (☎ 015-789999; r US$6-35; ✖) Modern and well-kept rooms make for a comfortable stay. The most expensive are suites that come with bathtubs and large adjoining sitting rooms.

Rattanak Hotel (☎ 953559; www.rattanakhotel.com; 85 NH5; r US$11-20; ✖ 🖳) Large Western-style showers with shower screens mean an end to sloshed tiles and wiping down loo seats. Not the only good thing about this hotel; every room comes with a family sized fridge-freezer.

Victoria Hotel (☎ 730364; NH5; r US$13-20; ✖) Don't let the bunny on the big sign put you off, there are no playboys in this recently opened hotel, just spacious rooms with luxuriously mounted bathtubs and that hint of sparkle that comes with brand-new things.

EATING & DRINKING
Westside

Sunrise Coffee House (☎ 953426; 630 Ph Royal; mains US$1-3; ✖ breakfast & lunch, closed Sun) A seriously laid-back café. Caffeine is blended into a variety of delicious forms here and can be enjoyed with fresh baked goodies or an assortment of California-style bistro snacks.

White Rose (Ph 2; mains 2000-6000r; ✖ breakfast, lunch & dinner) If the bright, colourful fruit displays don't draw you in, then the bright, colourful people wolfing down their Asian meals will. Forever busy with fresh sandwiches and delicious fruit shakes always at the ready.

Smokin' Pot (☎ 012-821400; vannaksmokinpot@yahoo.com; mains 3000-6000r; ✖ lunch & dinner) Also a cooking school, the Thai and Khmer food here is simple yet tasty; the setting is easy and breezy.

Phnom Meas Beer Garden (☎ 012-510989; mains US$1.50-4.50; ✖ dinner) Duck behind the veil of greenery into your own private bungalow and a traditional charcoal *chhnang* will be presented for all your barbecuing needs. You select the ingredients; everything from duck feet to seafood, and the waiter will do the rest.

Eastside

Green House Café (☎ 012-467313; mains US$1-2; ✖ breakfast, lunch & dinner) This café is indeed green and very leafy with lots of plants to freshen up an otherwise narrow and claustrophobic space. A good place to come for both Khmer and Western staples.

Sourn You Van Restaurant (☎ 952080; mains 20,000-25,000r; ✖ breakfast, lunch & dinner) 'Contemporary Jungle' must have been the style brief for this restaurant. A chic log cabin with stylish forest décor and stylish (mostly Khmer) diners. The food is typically Khmer, but you really come here for the setting.

ENTERTAINMENT
Riverside Balcony Bar (☎ 730313; ✖ 5pm-late, closed Mon) In an old wooden villa overlooking the river, punters are soothed by a soft breeze while sipping on cocktails and listening to great music.

GETTING THERE & AWAY
The NH5 from Phnom Penh is in good condition. Buses depart from Psar Thmei via Pursat (18,000r, six hours).

To and from Pailin, share taxis take about four hours (20,000r or 200B). From Poipet, private buses leave from the Tourist Lounge (32,000r, three hours). Or try Capital and Neak Krorhorm around the corner, which normally undercuts them.

From Battambang, buses leave from the transport station near Psar Boeng Chhoeuk to Siem Reap (US$4, four hours) and Sisophon (US$2, two to three hours).

Tickets can be purchased from booths near Psar Nat. Share taxis also leave from the transport station and depart once full.

Boat

The fascinating boat trip up the Stung Sangker and down the Tonlé Sap to Siem Reap is one of the most picturesque journeys through Cambodia. After chugging through the floating tip of bank-side settlements, the route soon turns into a people- and bird-watcher's paradise. Sailing through wetlands, weaving around water greens and scraping the marshland trees that whip inert heads (or legs depending on the water level) you will see rural Cambodia at its authentic best.

Tickets cost US$15, and boats depart every morning from the dock at 7am. The journey times vary drastically depending on the season; a speedy four hours in the wet and up to eight in the dry.

GETTING AROUND

Motodups around town should cost US$5 a day with that doubling if you take in the provincial sights. Single trips about town should set you back 1000r.

A novel way to cross the river is by remote ferry, pulled by rope. It travels to and from Psar Nat and the east bank for 200r.

The legendary Norry is a bamboo cart (nicknamed bamboo train) powered by motor engine. Travelling along the sporadically used railway tracks is exhilarating fun so long as a train isn't chasing you. Motos can take you for US$10 return to the boarding spot where you climb on for a 30-minute ride (3000r).

Around Battambang

Outside the provincial town lie some picturesque villages of packed-earth boulevards and well-preserved villas. The villagers make their dough by producing banana chips, rice paper and fermented fish paste. Scenic journeys tracing the river can be arranged to see the traditional methods and to sample the goods. Motos will charge US$5 for a trip out from town, and US$10 if you combine it with other sights.

PHNOM SAMPEAU

High on a hill 18km away is the stunning Phnom Sampeau. With its limestone cavities and memories of genocide, it is a sad juxtaposition of beauty and brutality. The eerie

SCAM – CROSSING INTO THAILAND: THE SCENIC ROUTE

There is a bus scam operating from Thailand that takes travellers wishing to cross at Pailin through the rarely accessed crossing at Daun Lem–Ban Laem instead. They do this as the route to Battambang city from here is less straightforward than from Pailin thus dragging out travel time, and making travellers arrive too late to look for their own accommodation. The bus can then take them to their partner guesthouse for a commission. A similar scheme operates through Poipet with buses detouring through O Smach in Samraong or Choam in Anlong Veng (see the boxed text, p222).

caves were used as slaughter chambers by the Khmer Rouge and still contain the skeletal remains of their victims. More than likely these victims were taken from the old temple at the rear, which was used as a makeshift prison.

The hill splits and opens in varying places to a series of grottoes that are decorated with shrines and Buddhas. There is enough of a depression to make for some interesting abseiling and cave exploration. Abseilers need to bring their own equipment and hire a guide.

A stairway to heavenly views can be found near the peak; 700 sweaty steps later, it delivers you to the summit, a golden stupa and a glorious view.

WAT BANAN

'Wat Banana' as it is affectionately known to locals – and the 'mini Angkor Wat' to everyone else, is a 12th-century temple bearing five towers sitting atop a 400m hill. Lying 25km southwest of Battambang, the unpronounceable King Udayadityavarman II is credited for building most of it in the 11th century, but it was that prolific Angkorian property developer, King Jayavarman VII, who finished it off.

WAT EK PHNOM

Built in the 11th century, this **temple** (admission US$2) may not possess the grandeur of Angkor Wat or the drama of Prasat Preah Vihear but it is home to some intact and intricate carvings and the spot is a shady and peaceful place ideal for a lazy picnic.

CROSSING INTO THAILAND: PSAR PROHM TO BAN PAKARD

Catch a moto (100B, one hour) from Pailin to Psar Prohm. In a pick-up this costs 100B to sit in the front and half that to hold on in the back. Cross immigration into Ban Pakard and from there a bus to Bangkok should take four hours. For details of travel between Pailin and Battambang (including the bus scam), see p218.

KAMPING POY

This pretty dam is triumphantly used for recreation and fun; the sort of gaiety its builders, the Khmer Rouge, had not intended it for. As part of a grand irrigation system, the dam was to provide water for the rice fields allowing year-round rice cultivation, which could then be sold to fund the Khmer Rouge's murderous war efforts. However, locals believe it was designed to lure enemies into a watery grave. Whatever the reason, the dam now provides a cool spot to splash about on a hot day. You can also hire a boat for around US$1 an hour. You can incorporate this dam into a day trip with the temples for US$10 by motodup.

Pailin

☎ 053 / pop 23,100

Despite being the gem-mining capital of Cambodia, Pailin's reputation and history lack the sparkle of its precious stones. Once the stronghold of the Khmer Rouge, the majority of its residents are former revolutionaries who struck a deal with the government in 1996 to lay down their guns for an autonomous reign of the region.

Telephone calls can be made at kiosks near the Psar Pailin market. The **Canadia Bank** (☎ 952005) does not cash travellers cheques.

On top of Phnom Yat Hill, **Wat Phnom Yat** is a colourful complex where Buddhists worship; it's enjoyed by all for its hilltop view. The site also contains a century-old stupa and meditation centres. The monks used to be nervous about practising their faith here due to the omnipresent Khmer Rouge population, but with the influx of Khmers from other parts, who are almost all Buddhist, they have relaxed a little.

Twenty kilometres from town, **Phnom Kieu waterfall** is set in pleasant jungle surrounds on

the Phnom Kieu (Blue Mountain). The water runs into pools that are invigoratingly cold, which is great for cooling off after the 5km hike it takes to get here. A moto guide should get you out here for about 100B.

There are quite a few guesthouses in town, but they are normally fronts for festivals of the flesh, and best to avoid. The best of the bunch is **Hang Meas Pailin Hotel** (☎ 012-787554; r US$11-50; 🔊), featuring a restaurant and nightclub. The rooms are smart and clean and have all the amenities like satellite TV, fridge and hot water, and there is a massive selection to suit all budgets.

To and from Battambang, a share taxi should cost 200B for a four-hour journey on a very bad road.

BANTEAY MEANCHEY PROVINCE

Battambang is a little smaller these days, its top half having been lopped off in the 1980s to create Cambodia's newest province Banteay Meanchey. The accents are a little different here and so are the temperaments – with its close proximity to Thailand and a busy overland commercial trade, the inhabitants are all go go go!

Sisophon

☎ 054 / pop 102,900

'Svay' to the locals, Sisophon acts as the refuelling spot for travellers on their way to Poipet and Siem Reap. Though there's nothing much to see and do here, it does make a convenient base to explore the temple of Banteay Chhmar.

Prices are quoted in baht, but riel and dollar are accepted readily. **Acleda Bank** (☎ 958821) acts for Western Union money transfers. Telephone calls can be made at kiosks dotted throughout, and internet is available at the decent price of 2000r an hour at cybercafés around town, though the connection can be frustratingly slow.

The permanently shut-for-something-or-other tourist office is hiding behind the Neak Meas hotel, between the hotel and the NH5. The tourist office staff are hiding too, but we don't know where they are.

Accommodation includes the small, family-run **Roeng Reung Hotel** (☎ 092-260515; s/d US$6/7; 🔊), with snug and tidy chambers. Add $4 to any room and the air shall blow forth strong and cool; in other words you get air-con. At **Phnom Svay Hotel** (☎ 012-656565; NH5; r US$10-12;

⊠) US$12 buys a shabby room, US$10 an even shabbier one. It may not be as well maintained as the others, but nights here are the quietest.

Neak Meas Hotel (☎ 012-555349; r US$12-20; ⊠) is the largest hotel in town, with expansion currently under way. Ears may want to be plugged as the karaoke bar and nightclub swing every night. A great all-rounder, but skip the restaurant; sadly it brings the good team down.

A bustling market doing furious trade provides self-caterers with an interesting shopping and dining experience. Otherwise, the best restaurant is **Phkayproek Banteay Meanchey Restaurant** (☎ 012-838934; NH5; mains US$1.50-5; ⊠ breakfast, lunch & dinner), an enormous and energetic place popular with travellers en route to elsewhere. Khmer, Thai and Western food make up the menu. Diligent and attentive locals make up the staff.

To reach Sisophon, from Poipet you can hail a pick-up either from the market near the roundabout or the Tourist Lounge (one hour). A cabin seat costs 100B, half that to cling on in the back. From Samraong, share taxis leave the transport stop near the market (200B, two to three hours).

Leaving Sisophon, buses and share taxis depart from the transport stop west of the market; to Phnom Penh it's US$4.50, five to six hours, to Battambang it's 8000r, two to three hours.

Single motodup trips around town cost 500r. Venture further out along the NH6 and make it US$1.

Banteay Chhmar

Sixty-one kilometres north of Sisophon are the abandoned ruins of this extravagant symbol of love and gratitude by King Jayavarman VII to his deceased son and the generals who assisted him in his final battle against the Chams. These battles are featured in the bas-relief carvings that depict fierce fighting with the insurgents along with other carvings of *apsara* dancers, and the well-preserved Lokesvara with his 32 arms (that actually represent 1000 arms). The complex of crumbling stones and invading jungle make it a scrambler's delight. It consists of a narrow central sanctuary or fortress, after which it is named (Banteay Chhmar means 'narrow fortress'), a moat, some temples and towers featuring those enigmatic faces (as featured

at the Bayon; p209) and their tight-lipped smiles.

GETTING THERE & AWAY

From Sisophon you can hire a motodup for the day for around US$10 (two hours). On your own steam, head north along NH69 for about 40km until you reach Thmor Puok, and then from there it's about another 20km to the complex.

From Siem Reap, a Camry can be chartered for around US$60 (about four hours).

Poipet

☎ 054 / pop 47,250

As soon as you get here, you should think about getting out. Nothing much to offer except soulless casinos and perhaps soulless scammers, providing the fresh bait from Thailand a less than favourable first impression of Cambodia.

The Cambodian immigration office is near border control (8am to 4pm). Also close by is the **Canadia Bank** (☎ 967101; NH5) for cashing travellers cheques.

Theaksmey Guest House (r 200-400B; ⊠) is charming little guesthouse a stone's throw from the Tourist Lounge. Clean rooms with nicely papered walls are a nice change from the dirt-stained paint-peelers of norm. Ask the guys at the Tourist Lounge and they'll point you in the right direction. Another option is **Orkiday Angkor Hotel** (☎ 967502; oa_tour@online .com.kh; r 400-680B; ⊠), where the bamboo-green marbling creates a cooling effect the minute you step inside. There is a decent restaurant downstairs, while upstairs the rooms are cavernous with all mod cons.

From Thailand, there is a free OSP shuttle bus to the Tourist Lounge. From here coach tickets can be bought to the major cities: Phnom Penh (60,000r, seven to eight hours); Siem Reap (40,000r, five hours); and Battambang (32,000r, 2½ hours). The buses are comfortable, though a little expensive. You can walk around the corner to the Phnom Penh Sorya Transport and Neak Krorhorm offices for cheaper fares.

Private taxis can also be caught from the Tourist Lounge and are priced per car: Siem Reap US$50; Phnom Penh US$70 to US$80; and Battambang US$40.

To climb aboard a pick-up truck, look for the frantic loading of Nissans in front of the market near the central roundabout (50B to Sisophon).

CROSSING INTO THAILAND: POIPET TO ARANYA PRATHET

Once in Poipet, independent travellers not on a direct bus from Siem Reap (p207) need to tell their pick-up drivers or motos to drop them off at *Rong Mool* (roundabout), which is the massive roundabout just in front of the border crossing. From here it is straightforward; pass through immigration and cross to Aranya Prathet, then catch a tuk-tuk 6km to the bus station (50B to 60B) where buses can get you into Bangkok in about four hours. You can also catch the train to Hualamphong station in Bangkok, which will get you there in six hours. For details on the 'scam bus' coming in from the opposite direction see the boxed text, p219. For information on crossing this border in the other direction, see the boxed text, p158.

ODDAR MEANCHEY PROVINCE
Samraong to Anlong Veng
SAMRAONG

This is a transit town west of Anlong Veng. People come here from the O Smach border crossing to pick up connecting transport to elsewhere. There is nowhere to access internet or make telephone calls. **Acleda Bank** (☎ 012-200468), opposite the market, offers the usual Western Union money transfers and cash advances.

There's no reason to stay here, but if you get stuck, the following are your best bets for a bed and food. **Meanchey Hotel** (☎ 011-700099; r US$5-10; ✷), with quality rooms and all the amenities, is fitted out to suit the NGO workers who often stay here; it is all business, no fuss. **Ryk Reak** has no menu (prices on application); just tell them what you feel like and they'll cook it up from whatever ingredients are stocked in the kitchen that day. Opposite Meanchey Hotel, it is very popular with the locals.

To get to most cities from Samraong, a long and bumpy journey along terrible roads is in order. A moto to/from the O Smach border crossing will cost 200B (two hours). There are very few share taxis to O Smach or Anlong Veng.

CROSSING INTO THAILAND: O SMACH TO CHONG JOM

This is not the easiest border crossing to access. From the nearest town of Samraong it is a two-hour bumpy dusty ride to O Smach (see above), but once in O Smach it's easy-peasy – just cross the border into Chong Jom where buses can take you on to Surin (two hours). For information on crossing this border in the other direction, see the boxed text, p158.

A moto to/from Anlong Veng takes around two hours and costs US$10 to US$15 depending on road conditions – usually bad. Cars find it more difficult than a moto due to the trenches.

Share taxis go to Poipet via Sisophon and leave from the taxi station in front of the market around 7am to 8am (200B for a seat, two to three hours).

ANLONG VENG

Anlong Veng is 'up and coming', with money flooding in from the O Smach border crossing and tourists stopping by for a slice of Cambodia's modern and macabre history. It is fast becoming one of the country's most developed destinations.

Information

There is an Acleda Bank on the road to Siem Reap for Western Union money transfers and cash advances. There are a few phone kiosks around town, but no internet access.

Sights

Ta Mok, the ruthless murderer of millions and Pol Pot's right-hand man, died on 21 July 2006. Nicknamed 'The Butcher', he had been awaiting trial on charges of genocide in a Phnom Penh prison. Amid much controversy and protest, his body was permitted to be brought home by his children for a proper funeral and burial. Surrounded by the green Dangkrek Mountains on one side and watched over by monks, his **grave** is a well-tended plot of (some would say) undeserved serenity.

Set as the foreground to the stunning lake he constructed to quell his paranoid fears of attack, Ta Mok's **former residence** now stands empty. The dwelling itself is not much to look at, but the up-close-and-personal views of the lake and wildlife are spectacular. Admission is a cheeky US$2.

In an unkempt field around the corner from the Thailand border crossing is the blink-and-you'll-miss-it **tombstone of Pol Pot**. Nothing more than an unremarkable memorial, it marks the spot of the former Khmer Rouge leader's cremation; reportedly performed by Ta Mok on a disgraceful pile of burning tyres.

Sleeping

Bot Uddom Guest House (☎ 012-779495; r US$5-15; ⊠) The best thing about this guesthouse is that its back yard merges into the pretty lake. Rooms are very clean and upstairs a setup of large wooden tables and chairs is ideal for cards and chinwag sessions.

Monorom Guest House (☎ 012-900726; r US$7-15) There is no hot water here but the staff will boil some up if you need it. Rooms are large and comfortable.

Eating

Pounlok Trorchekchet Restaurant (mains 6000-20,000r; ⊠ breakfast, lunch & dinner) About 500m north of the central roundabout is this shady bungalow-style restaurant. Mostly Khmer food, but Western meals such as fish and chips also make an appearance.

Dara Reah Restaurant (mains 7000-10,200r; ⊠ breakfast, lunch & dinner) Locals come here for the steaming-hot noodles, which come buried under strips of meat and herbs. And also for a drink, as this is the closest thing to a bar the town has; it stocks a varied selection of beer.

Getting There & Away

From the Choam border crossing to Anlong Veng, it is a straightforward ride on a sealed road for US$2 (15km). From Choam to Siem Reap, you can catch share taxis for US$5 for a front seat, US$2.50 to sit in the back.

From Siem Reap, there is a cluster of taxis that waits by the Sokimex station by the Stone Bridge.

For travel between Anlong Veng and Samraong, see opposite. For more details on the challenging route to the Preah Vihear temple, see p225.

Getting Around

The town's centre is tiny and easily navigated on foot. To the nearby sights, a moto can be hired for US$5 to US$6 a day. A single trip to the border crossing should cost US$2.

> ### CROSSING INTO THAILAND: CHOAM TO CHOAM SA NGAM
>
> The border crossing with Thailand is just a few kilometres north of Anlong Veng. Catch a moto (US$2) and hop off en route to see the semiblasted statue of soldiers, placed by Khmer Rouge and destroyed by Khmer soldiers. On the other side, transport is not so frequent. You can catch a taxi to Sisaket, which is the closest town. For details about getting to the major Cambodia cities from Choam, see left.

PREAH VIHEAR PROVINCE

Preah Vihear is a vast and far-reaching province that has had the gloomy job of watching its neighbours prosper while it remained constantly struggling in the background. But now with a commitment to making its treasures – three remarkable Angkorian temples – more accessible with better roads, its future is finally looking up.

Tbeng Meanchey

☎ 064 / pop 23,100

A small and nondescript town, the only thing going for it is its proximity to the temples. Khmers rarely call it Tbeng Meanchey, instead referring to it as Preah Vihear after the province.

INFORMATION

There's a bit of a tourist mafia, whose behaviour exasperates the helpful staff at the **tourist office** (⊠ 7-11am & 2-5pm), who themselves are keen to promote tourism in the area and eager to dissipate the city's bad reputation. The tourist office is located at the southern end of town on the NH64.

Prices are quoted in baht but dollars and riel will never be knocked back. Bring a sizable amount of cash as there is nowhere to cash travellers cheques.

Acleda Bank (☎ 012-289851) Representing Western Union transfers.

SLEEPING

Bakan Guest House (☎ 012-694209; s/d 10,000/10,500r) Tentative steps across the rickety terrace of this quiet Khmer home will lead you to basic but pleasant rooms. Below is a swinging hammock tied to the home's supporting stilts; this is reception.

CAMBODIA

Phnom Meas Guest House (☎ 012-632017; s/d US$5/6) Next door to the Bakan, this place comprises comfortable small units with fans and squat toilets.

Mohasambath Guest House (☎ 012-901844; r 8000-10,500r) An extra couple of thousand riels here is all that it takes to stop others showering in the same bathroom. Clean enough, but hard to distinguish from the others next door.

27 Usaphea (May) Guest House (☎ 011-905472; s US$5-16; 🏠) Small rooms good enough to crash in but not much else. The most expensive come with air-con.

EATING

Mlop Dong Restaurant (mains 2000-5000r; 🕙 breakfast, lunch & dinner) Conveniently near the guesthouses and taxi station, this timber-shed restaurant doles out regular Khmer dishes. Mornings are the most atmospheric as locals on their way to Prasat Preah Vihear fill up the tables to wolf down their breakfast.

Dara Reah Restaurant (☎ 012-556146; mains 8000-15,000r; 🕙 breakfast, lunch & dinner) A large and airy garden restaurant with a standard Khmer menu sprinkled with some Chinese and Thai dishes.

Langeach Sros Restaurant (☎ 012-1879241; mains 10,000-10,200r; 🕙 lunch & dinner) All of your Khmer faves and some Western dishes are served at this breezy eatery. Diners can also request tables to be set up in the upstairs area, good for those wanting a quieter, more secluded meal.

GETTING THERE & AWAY

Share taxis ply the not so bad, but not so good NH64 from Kompong Thom to Tbeng Meanchey (20,000r, four hours).

Phnom Penh is 294km away; pick-ups leave 7am to 8am every day from Psar Thmei (25,000r to 30,000r, eight hours).

Leaving Tbeng Meanchey, share taxis leave from the taxi stand in front of the Bakan and Mohasambath guesthouses.

Preah Khan

Known also as Prasat Bakan, Preah Khan is a 12th-century complex that once served as a Buddhist monastery and for a brief period as the residence of King Jayavarman VII. The largest enclosure of the Angkor period, a mega 5 sq km, it contains numerous temple structures (some dating back to the 9th century), impressive carvings and a 3km-long *baray*

(reservoir). The Prasat Damrei (Elephant Temple) at the east end has fine carvings of deities and stone elephants. In the centre of the *baray* is the island temple of Prasat Preah Thkol and to the west, Prasat Preah Stung, a serene temple with a tower bearing four enormous faces.

Preah Khan is not a well-trodden tourist spot and is therefore a calmer way to experience the grandeur of Angkorian temples.

GETTING THERE & AWAY

From Kompong Thom or Tbeng Meanchey it is a tough five- to six-hour trip. Expect to pay around US$50 for a chartered car, or US$15 to US$20 for a moto. From Siem Reap, bikers can take the rough and romantic Route 66 through Khvau, crossing ancient bridges including the Spean Ta Ong.

Koh Ker

Koh Ker was once the capital of the Angkorian empire under the rule of King Jayavarman IV. Now it plays a subordinate role to the jungle, which has taken over the site of close to 30 structures. The most notable can be found in **Prasat Thom** (admission US$10), a seven-tiered pyramid, which is carpeted in greenery and resembles the Inca formations in Peru. A breathless 40m climb to the top is worth the shin splits for a stunning view. Just beyond is the jungle-immersed Prasat Krahom (Red Temple) that is reached via a causeway of *naga* barriers and made entirely of red blocks. Further still are the outlying temples that are also worth exploring: Prasat Bram for its five towers; Prasat Chen where the 'fighting monkeys' statue was discovered (now in Phnom Penh's National Museum, p192); Prasat Leung with its well-preserved Shiva *linga*; and Prasat Neang Khmau with its fine lintel carvings.

It is possible to stay in the complex in a wooden cabana if you bring your own hammock and food. Otherwise, the nearby town of Siyong (8km southeast of Koh Ker) has one basic guesthouse that offers clean beds, mosquito nets and candles for US$2.50.

To reach Koh Ker, there are two alternatives. The first is to approach from Siem Reap via Beng Mealea on the private toll road. The three-hour journey in a chartered Camry costs US$65 to US$80. From Tbeng Meanchey in the east, the two-hour journey (72km) costs US$10 return by moto.

Prasat Preah Vihear

Perched on the crest of the **Dangkrek Mountains**, the Preah Vihear Temple is divided into four *gopuras* (entrance pavilions) and courtyards. Connected by wide avenues and steep steps, these crumbling relics on the Cambodian side make a sharp ascent to reach its dramatic cliff-top climax and the serene views below.

Occupying the hair-split border between Thailand and Cambodia, Prasat Preah Vihear still remains a knot in the rope in the tug of war between them. Given to Thailand by the generous French in 1954, it was finally handed back after an international ruling in 1962. Despite this, the Thais are still grumbling that the temple belongs to them.

The temple began life in the 9th century and construction spanned the lives of four kings with the final touches added by King Jayavarman VI in the 10th century. It has only become accessible in recent years after the Khmer Rouge, who gained control in the early 1990s, finally waved the white flag in 1998.

SLEEPING

Raksaleap Guest House (☎ 092-224838; Kor Muy Village; r US$5) Situated in the mountain-base village on the way up to the temple is this cosy wooden guesthouse. The rooms here come with a fan and mosquito nets. The bathrooms and toilets are shared and of the squat variety.

GETTING THERE & AWAY

Ignore the locals who tell you there are no share taxis from Tbeng Meanchey to Preah Prasat Vihear. They are the ones who will graciously offer their own car to be chartered for about seven times the price of a seat in a taxi; US$70 is the opportunistic quote.

Pick-ups and share taxis *do* go to the temple and leave from the taxi station at around 9am daily (inside/back of US$2.50/5, entire front cabin US$10, two hours). If you do charter your own vehicle, the official price quoted by the tourist office is US$30 to US$40. From the bottom of the mountain at Kor Muy Village, hire a moto to reach the temple (10,500r up and back).

Starting from Anlong Veng, the moto journey on a horrific road takes about three hours in the dry season, double that in the wet. Cars find it difficult and bog often. Due

> **MINE YOUR STEP**
>
> Stick to well-marked paths as the Khmer Rouge laid landmines around Prasat Preah Vihear like they were going out of fashion.

to the ghastly conditions, expect to pay US$18 for a moto to the base of the mountain. Some may only want to take you to Sa Em Village. From there you will need to hire a moto to get to Kor Muy (US$2).

KOMPONG THOM PROVINCE

The birthplace of Pol Pot and the second-largest province in Cambodia, Kompong Thom bills itself as the 'Province of a Thousand Temples', and the impressive Sambor Prei Kuk contributes a hundred of them to that total. It can also lay claim to some beautiful countryside, which after the destruction of war is well on the way to recovery.

Kompong Thom

☎ 062 / pop 69,300

Kompong Thom is an ungainly city that curves around the Stung Sen to the east and west and is slashed down the middle by the NH6. Unfortunately, there's nothing to see in town. But beyond, the heritage site of Sambor Prei Kuk (p226) lies in a forest waiting to be explored.

INFORMATION

Acleda Bank (☎ 961243) Opposite Mitthapheap Hotel, for money transfers.
Tourist office (☒ 8-11am & 2-5pm) The director is very helpful and it has some good handouts.

SLEEPING

Prasat Prak Guest House (☎ 012-215536; r US$3-5) A cosy new guesthouse, with the warmth of a family home, it has six basic but well-kept rooms that are tucked far enough back from the busy street to be peacefully quiet.

Arunras Hotel (☎ 961294; 39Eo Ph Sereipheap; r US$4-13; ☒) Dominating the accommodation scene in Kompong Thom, this enormous hotel offers something for every wallet, though nothing will send you broke.

Also recommended:
Mitthapheap Hotel (☎ 961213; NH6; r US$5-10; ☒) Part of the big Mittapheap family and looks just like its brothers and sisters, with functional rooms without any fuss.

CAMBODIA

Stung Sen Royal Garden Hotel (☎ 961228; Ph Stung Sen; r US$15-35; ✷) Great big rooms, decked out like a British B&B, it sits next door to its equally sizable restaurant.

EATING & DRINKING

The Arunras and Stung Sen Royal both have large and busy restaurants on their premises catering for the hordes of travellers in transit. But for a more interesting and atmospheric dining experience, head away from the centre.

our pick **Jamnorch Beong** (☎ 011-683752; mains 3000-8000r; ✷ breakfast, lunch & dinner) In a magical lakeside setting where individual bungalows hover delightfully over lilies, diners sit cross-legged around a barbecue stove to grill up their meat or veggies of choice.

Mlop Grawrch (Prey Malech Village; ✷ dinner) Meaning 'orange shade', this outdoor restaurant is appropriately set in a private orchard bearing the citrus fruit. An interesting spot to drown a few whiskeys, it is known locally as 'the soup place'. It does indeed serve soup, and stirring begins from about 4pm.

Jamnorch Prey Malech (☎ 012-637455; Prey Malech Village; mains 10,000r; ✷ lunch & dinner) Dine like a true Khmer, squatting on stilted tables laid with grass mats. A menu does not exist, but ask the matriarchal mamma for your favourite Khmer dish and she'll whip it up in the outdoor kitchen. Get there after 3pm; she won't roll her sleeves up until then.

GETTING THERE & AWAY

From Siem Reap, bus companies leave from the transport stop and head down the easy-peasy NH6 en route to Phnom Penh (US$3, one hour).

Leaving Kompong Thom, share taxis depart from the taxi station, west of the tourist office. It is divided into sides; the south side holds taxis heading south to Phnom Penh (10,000r, 2½ hours) and the north-side taxis head to Tbeng Meanchey (20,000r, four hours).

Around Kompong Thom

SAMBOR PREI KUK

Thirty kilometres out of town, the site of **Sambor Prei Kuk** (admission US$3) spreads through the forest in the same way it did eons ago, when back in the 7th century it served as the capital of Chenla. It was built by King Isnavarman and was originally called Isanapura. The site

consists of hundreds of monuments scattere around four principal complexes: **Norther Group** (Prasat Sambor), **Small Group**, **Centra Group** (Prasat Tao) and **Southern Group** (Prasa Neak Poan). All are dedicated to Shiva wit the Northern Group being dedicated to on of his many incarnations, Gambhireshvar It is an incredible complex, which despit being in a state of ruin and missing its bes (bloody looters!) still emanates an aura c quiet splendour.

In the Northern Group there is a centra tower and others around with carvings tha are still in relatively good condition. Ther were more, but they fell victim to US bomb ing. The Central Group bears the stone lion that typify the Chenla period and some beau tifully carved lintels. The Southern Group i perhaps the most impressive. It contains eigh octagonal towers with relief carvings and i being engulfed by the forest.

To get here from Kompong Thom, a mote can be hired for US$7 for the day. The journe takes about one hour.

PHNOM SONTUK

Phnom Sontuk, the holiest hill in the region is topped by Wat Kiri Chom Chong, a colour ful pagoda with many Buddha images. Some of these images are of the reclining Buddha carved directly into the rocks and have beer there for centuries. Climbing up the punish ing steps to the top (nearly a thousand of them!) will reward you with an incredible view of the flat plains below. The steps are lined with hundreds of statues, men on one side, women on the other and they all appear to be holding *nagas*.

To get here, motos can be hired from Kom pong Thom to travel the 20km to Phnom Sontuk for US$5. If you have your own trans port, take the NH6 bound for Phnom Penh for 18km then take the sandy road on the left that leads to the mountain.

EASTERN CAMBODIA

The most diverse region of the country, you can go from seeing freshwater dolphins and sugar-loaded palm trees one day to bamboo-munching elephants and pine cones the next. If you want a little bit of everything then the east is a veritable smorgasbord of Cambodia's best.

SVAY RIENG PROVINCE

Bordering Vietnam, this is the province that everybody blitzes through on their way to more appealing places. Fortunately, due to its crossroads location, commercial business is starting to seep through and it is beginning to prosper.

Svay Rieng

☎ 044 / pop 22,050

A laid-back town that sits by the Wayko River, there is literally nothing to do here. **Acleda Bank** (☎ 9455545) represents Western Union for money transfers.

If you do get stuck here the best place to stay is **Tonle Waikor Hotel** (☎ 945718; r US$10; ☒), where spacious rooms have all the basic luxuries you need for a quick stopover, including a TV and fridge. **Vimean Monorom Hotel** (☎ 945817; r US$5-10; ☒) offers clean, decent-sized rooms. There are snack stalls along the river and others around the market, otherwise the best of the restaurant bunch is **Boeng Meas Restaurant** (mains US$1-2; ☽ breakfast, lunch & dinner).

Buses leave from Phnom Penh's Psar Thmei (8000r, three hours). To and from the Bavet border crossing, secure a spot in a share taxi for US$2.

PREY VENG PROVINCE

Whether or not the inhabitants know it, they are the subject of nationwide sympathy due to its reputation as one of the most poverty-stricken provinces in the kingdom. But it does boast one gem: the historical Ba Phnom, a 5th-century religious centre and the only reason to come to Prey Veng.

Prey Veng

☎ 043 / pop 57,750

This sleepy little town is a pretty mix of old colonial buildings, tree-lined boulevards and a reflective lake. There's not a great deal to do here, but it does make for a mellow stopover on the way to Kompong Cham.

Acleda Bank (☎ 944555), representing Western Union, will sort out your money transfers.

SLEEPING

Angkor Thom Hotel (☎ 011-773088; r US$5-10; ☒) Spotless, professional and helpful service has made this Chinese-style hotel the most popular place to stay in Prey Veng. Book ahead, as it can fill up quickly.

Chan Kiry Guest House (☎ 011-746014; r US$5-10; ☒) Overlooking the lake, this guesthouse has basic rooms in unit-style lodgings. Top dollar brings air-con, though the breezy location means you don't really need it.

Rong Damrey Hotel (☎ 011-761052; r US$5-10; ☒) A large concrete hotel, lacking in character but in better condition than the others, it recently added a whopping 20 new rooms to its quarters.

EATING

Chan Kiry Restaurant (☎ 011-746014; mains from 2000r; ☽ breakfast, lunch & dinner) This wonky bamboo restaurant sits on stilts above the lake and looks as though it was erected overnight, possibly in the dark, by children. It offers incredible shade, delicious food and a big challenge – no English, no menu. Good luck!

Mitthapeap Restaurant (☎ 011-939213; mains 6000-8000r; ☽ breakfast, lunch & dinner) If you fancy some sparrow, then this restaurant fries them up with rice. A family-run establishment, it also serves the usual Khmer and Chinese dishes that may appeal to a tamer stomach.

GETTING THERE & AWAY

From Phnom Penh, minibuses leave Psar Tmei for Neak Luong (7000r, two hours); once there, disembark and head to the ferry crossing. Here you can pick up a share taxi for 4000r to get you across the bridge and all the way into Prey Veng.

Heading to Kompong Cham, you can squeeze onto a minibus for 4000r or charter a whole car yourself (US$15). The journey only takes 1½ hours on a good road.

Neak Luong

This is the parched, dry interchange that is the first step in the Vietnam–Cambodia overland crossing. To get here from Phnom Penh catch

---

CROSSING INTO VIETNAM: BAVET TO MOC BAI

From Svay Rieng, a share taxi to Bavet takes 45 minutes. Once there, walk through immigration to Moc Bai in Vietnam's Tay Ninh Province, and from here vans and taxis can get you to HCMC in two hours. For details of direct travel from Phnom Penh to HCMC see the boxed text, p200. For info on crossing this border the other way, see p417.

CAMBODIA

CAMBODIA

a bus from Psar Thmei (4500r, 1½ hours) to the drop-off point and then walk a few metres towards the cloud of exhaust fumes. Here you can pay from 4000r up (including the 100r ferry charge) to catch a minibus north to Prey Veng, south to Svay Rieng or all the way to the Kaam Samnor border.

At the time of writing there was still no bridge and the latest news was that it would not be completed until the end of 2007 or the beginning of 2008.

Ba Phnom

Based in the valley between four hills, this 5th-century archaeological site is credited with being the capital of the Funan empire and the birthplace of the Cambodian nation. Ancient documents report that back in its heyday, it produced precious metals such as gold, silver and lead as well as ivory. It is also said to have been the site of human sacrifices up until the 19th century.

Now the compound contains the ruins of **Preah Vihear Chann**, an 11th-century temple. There is also a present-day wat and some small pagodas; a sad lack of sights for such a significant historical spot.

To reach Ba Phnom from Prey Veng, moto-dups can be hired for around US$7 to travel the 45km. If you are in Neak Luong, a moto can be hired for around US$4.

KOMPONG CHAM PROVINCE

Kompong Cham gained its name after the exodus of the Chams from Vietnam into Cambodia in 1720. An ethnic group of Muslims, their origins lay in the Champa kingdom that once controlled the Mekong Delta. Nowadays, they and other non-Cham Khmers work the land, cultivating rice, tobacco and rubber.

Kompong Cham

☎ 042 / pop 48,300

Kompong Cham mills about the Mekong quietly and in no particular hurry. With the rise and rise of Siem Reap and other provincial towns, it seems, at first glance, to be trailing behind. But with the completion of a super bridge across the Mekong and a sexy new esplanade along the west bank, this city is set for cosmopolitan cool.

INFORMATION

Acleda Bank (☎ 941703; Ph Khemerak Phomin) Western Union money transfers.

> ### CROSSING INTO VIETNAM: KAAM SAMNOR TO VINH XUONG
>
> This is the most scenic route from Cambodia to Vietnam. First thing to remember is don't cross the bridge! Instead ask around for ferries to take you down the Mekong to Kaam Samnor (US$2.50, one hour). From here, cross over the border to Vinh Xuong where local Vietnamese transport waits to transfer you to Chau Doc an hour away. For details about travel between Neak Luong and Phnom Penh, see under Neak Luong, p227. For information on crossing this border in the other direction see the boxed text, p424.

Cambodia Asia Bank (☎ 942149) Near the transport stop, this bank offers 24-hour ATM services for Visa and MasterCard.

Canadia Bank (☎ 941361; Preah Monivong Blvd) Cash advances and travellers cheques.

SIGHTS & ACTIVITIES

A pleasant island in the Mekong River, **Koh Paen** is an interesting place for a leisurely bike ride. In the wet season, a local ferry transfers you across, but in the dry, it is connected by a bamboo bridge that is built fresh each year, with locals competing for the honour of constructing it. The island itself is home to some rural Cham communities, who make their living by fishing and silk weaving.

SLEEPING

Phnom Brak Trochak Cheth Guest House (☎ 941507 s/d US$4/5) Ten points if you can say this name after a few. This elaborately titled guesthouse with no air-con and no hot water has been upgraded by its new owners and is now in great condition with spic-and-span rooms.

Phnom Pros Hotel & Restaurant (☎ 941444, 012-757060; r US$5-10; ✷) A 10-minute walk northwest from the market and main cluster of accommodation, this large, fairly modern hotel has a more upmarket feel than its competitors in town. The top end brings hot water and air-con.

Mekong Hotel (☎ 941536; r US$5-20; ✷) Great views of the Mekong if you bag a riverside room. This hotel is of great standard and the gigantic corridors provide a spacious landing strip for tipsy tumbles.

Mittapheap Hotel (☎ 941565; 18 Ph Kosamak Near Roth; r US$5-20; ✷) Subtract the oversized corridors, add a little shabbiness and you have a mini replica of the Mekong Hotel. The US$5 room brings you down to budget with no air-con or hot water, while US$20 makes you a VIP and you get it all.

EATING & DRINKING

The market has some excellent food stalls that sizzle all the way into the night and when the sun goes down along the river, the tables pop up. Impromptu food stalls and mini bars are set up riverfront opposite the Mekong Hotel. Here locals congregate to socialise, look across at the river, up at the stars and out for the town's old monkey that lives in the trees.

Tiger Bar & Restaurant (☎ 012-732379; 25 Vithei Pasteur; mains US$1-3; ☺ breakfast, lunch & dinner) This tiny hole in the wall turns out Khmer and Western meals. Those catching the early bus are welcome to bang on the door for an early breakfast before official opening time; just look for the bright pink walls.

Lazy Mekong Daze (lmdaze@hotmail.com; mains US$1.50-3; ☺ breakfast, lunch & dinner) Run by a British-Khmer couple and bringing a mixture of both into the décor and menu, this restaurant-bar on the river front is a great place to unwind with Mekong views and tasty food. Bicycles are available for rent and a helpful bus timetable is posted up to keep you informed.

Mekong Crossing Restaurant and Pub (☎ 012-432427; 12 Vithei Pasteur; mains US$1.50-4; ☺ lunch & dinner) An old Kompong Cham fave. Khmer and Western staples plus the best Khmer interpretation of spaghetti bolognaise found this end of Cambodia. Travel information is abundant here; just ask for the owner Joe, a longtime resident with extensive knowledge of the hottest spots to visit.

Two Dragons Restaurant (☎ 011-888745; Ph Tuol Sbov; mains US$2-3; ☺ breakfast, lunch & dinner) Incredibly popular with Khmers, this restaurant has exotic dishes with exotic ingredients and an ever-changing specials menu. Try the ginger fried eel, the most popular dish here.

GETTING THERE & AWAY

From Phnom Penh, buses leave from Psar Thmei (10,000r, three hours), and share taxis leave from the southwest corner of the same market (10,000r, two hours).

To and from Kratie, Hour Lean buses depart from their designated stops: near the roundabout in Kompong Cham; and just

south of the boat dock in Kratie (17,000r, three to four hours).

In the wet season, you can catch a boat (from south of the bridge) that goes all the way up to Stung Treng via Kratie (US$15, eight hours).

GETTING AROUND

It'll cost 1000r to get from A to B around town. Motodups for a day will set you back around $10. You can negotiate a cheaper fare if you see fewer sights or travel shorter distances.

There are possibly only two to three tuk-tuks in Kompong Cham, and they are driven by knowledgeable and friendly guides with excellent levels of English and French. Short trips should cost US$1 to US$2.

Bicycles can be hired from Lazy Mekong Daze (left; US$2).

Around Kompong Cham
MAHA LEAP PAGODA COMPLEX

The Maha Leap holds significance for the locals as this is one of the last remaining wooden pagodas left in the country. Over a century old, it was only saved by the temple-burning Khmer Rouge because they found use for it as a hospital. Many of the Khmers who were put to work in the surrounding fields perished here, and 500 bodies were thrown into graves on site, now camouflaged by a tranquil garden.

The pagoda itself is beautiful. The wide columns supporting the structure are complete tree trunks, splendid in gilded patterns and royal blue. The Khmer Rouge had painted over the designs to match their austere philosophies, but the monks have since stripped it back to its original glory. Up above, the ceiling is adorned with colourful frescoes depicting scenes of Buddha and his teachings.

Take socks! You must always remove your shoes to enter a pagoda and this one is carpeted in thick gooey (and fresh) pigeon poop. So unless you want to export some of it between your toes, it is advisable to cover them in something you can dispose of straightaway.

The pagoda is about 40 minutes south of town on the banks of a Mekong tributary. A moto will charge around US$5 for a trip out here, but it is best to pay extra and combine it with the other sites around Kompong Cham. A boat can also get you out here for around US$6 to US$7 per person.

CAMBODIA

PREY CHUNG KRAN WEAVING VILLAGE

This is a tiny village set on the banks of the river where nearly every household has a weaving loom. Under the cool shade provided by their stilted homes, they work deftly to produce the *sampots* (the national sarong-like garments, usually worn at important occasions) and *kramas* of fashion and tradition. The most interesting thing to watch is the dyeing process as the typical diamond and dot tessellations are formed at this stage. The village is a further 20 minutes down river from the Wat Maha Leap and most motos or boats will combine the two in one excursion.

PHNOM PROS & PHNOM SREI

'Man Hill and Woman Hill' are the subjects of a local folklore with many variations, one of which describes a child taken away at infancy and returning as a powerful man to fall in love with the mother he no longer recognised. Disbelieving her proclamations of identity, he demanded her hand in marriage. Desperate to avoid this disaster, the mother cunningly devised a deal; a competition between her team of women and his team of men to build the highest hill by dawn. If the women won, she would not give her hand. As they toiled into the night, the women built a fire with the flames reaching high into the sky. The men mistaking this for the sun lay down their tools and thus the impending marriage was foiled. The versions of this famous story are comparable to zebra stripes – no two are exactly the same. Locals love to relay it, each adding their own herbs and spices as the tale unfolds.

Due to men being stupid and easily manipulated (hey, that's the moral of the story – not our stance!), the Phnom Pros is lower than the Phnom Srei and does not offer the same views. It does, however, have several pagodas and trees full of curious monkeys. Phnom Srei offers great views and a very strokeable Nandi (sacred bull) statue.

The hills are about 7km northwest of town. A moto can get you out here for around US$3.

RUBBER PLANTATIONS

Supplying one of Cambodia's largest industries are the resin tappers working in the large rubber plantations around Kompong Cham. Using an extended scraping instrument, they graze the trunks until the sap appears, drip drip dripping into the open coconut shells

waiting on the ground. In 1921, it was discovered that rich soils from Chub Hill on the left bank of the Mekong were ideal for the cultivation of rubber. From this, the Chub Plantation arose. The plantation is a few minutes from town; its towering trees and their flimsy canopies make for a shady destination to take a leisurely ride.

KRATIE PROVINCE

The upbeat Kratie lies on the banks of the Mekong and is the best place to view Irrawaddy dolphins. During the dry season, the river dries up to reveal sand-bank islands and rocky outcrops, while all around the buzz of activity reverberates from the cheerful people in their patchwork rice fields, hanging from palm trees or in musical ceremonies. If the provinces were Cambodia's children, then Siem Reap would be the pride and Kratie the joy.

Kratie

☎ 072 / pop 82,950

Kratie town wraps around the river to the east and sits under the most dramatic of skies. In the midday heat it burns like a furnace and an escape to the shady villages is required. Once evening comes, the sun melts like hot rubies with streaks of red oozing across the sky.

There's not much to do in town, but there's plenty beyond.

INFORMATION

There's a tourist office but your guesthouse is just as informative. Telephone calls can be made at kiosks around the market and internet is available at the You Hong Guest House.

Acleda Bank (☎ 971707) Offers money transfers.

SLEEPING

You Hong Guest House (☎ 957003; 91 Ph 8; r US$2-5) This guesthouse caters for every need with a bar, restaurant, internet café and good, honest travel advice. The rooms are spotless and the energy is young and vibrant.

Sen Sok Guest House (☎ 012-732185; saratheam@ yahoo.com; r US$3-12; 🅿) A little bit out of the way this laid-back guesthouse offers a quiet and clean alternative to the riverfront lodgings. There is no hot water, but it's a nice spot to be away from the tourists.

Santepheap Hotel (☎ 971537; r US$5-20; 🅿) The reliable Santepheap offers smart, comfortable accommodation, with the front-facing rooms providing a good view of the rather inert riverfront action.

Wat Roka Kandal (☎ 971729; r US$8-15; ❄) A series of wooden stilt constructions makes up these utterly charming rustic capsules of romance with en suite bathrooms, traditional furnishings, hot water and some with air-con.

Also recommended:

Oudom Sambath Hotel (☎ 012-965944; 439 Riverside St; r US$4-15; ❄) Massive rooms with a huge terrace for watching those red sunsets.

Heng Heng II Hotel (☎ 971405; hengheng2hotel@ yahoo.com; r US$5-18; ❄) A longtime favourite among budget travellers. Decent rooms with all amenities.

EATING & DRINKING

Oudom Sambath Hotel (mains 3000-15,000r; ❄ breakfast, lunch & dinner) Basic Khmer and Asiatic food is served in a heavy wood and marble setting. Mostly catering to Khmers but the staff are delighted for the chance to interact with foreigners.

Red Sun Falling (mains 5000-10,000r; ❄ breakfast, lunch & dinner, closed 2-5.30pm & Sun) Run by the town's local larrikin with screaming antics such as high-spirited streaking, this is a congenial restaurant, bar and bookstore of twinkling lights and great Western/Khmer food.

GETTING THERE & AWAY

From Phnom Penh, buses leave from Psar Thmei at 7.30am (18,000r, six to seven hours). Share taxis are faster, though much more cramped (25,000r, five hours). Heading back the other way, Hour Lean buses depart from the riverfront, opposite Red Sun Falling.

From Kompong Cham, you have the option of bus, which departs at 10.30am (17,000r, three hours) or boat, which departs at 7.30am (US$7, three to four hours, July to December).

Heading to Sen Monorom, a bus leaves from outside the Heng Heng II Hotel at 9.45am (US$8, eight hours including the stopover in Snuol). Coming back, however, this journey is cut by half.

GETTING AROUND

Guesthouses can arrange motorcycles for US$5 a day. Motodups, who are often knowledgeable guides, will charge around US$6 to US$10, depending on how far you go.

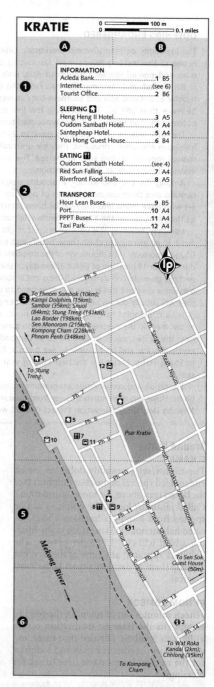

KRATIE

0   100 m
0   0.1 miles

INFORMATION
Acleda Bank.................................1 B5
Internet................................(see 6)
Tourist Office............................2 B6

SLEEPING
Heng Heng II Hotel......................3 A5
Oudom Sambath Hotel.................4 A4
Santepheap Hotel........................5 A4
You Hong Guest House.................6 B4

EATING
Oudom Sambath Hotel.............(see 4)
Red Sun Falling..........................7 A4
Riverfront Food Stalls..................8 A5

TRANSPORT
Hour Lean Buses.........................9 B5
Port...10 A4
PPPT Buses..............................11 A4
Taxi Park..................................12 A4

To Phnom Sombok (10km);
Kampi Dolphins (15km);
Sambor (35km); Snuol
(84km); Stung Treng (141km);
Lao Border (198km);
Sen Monorom (215km);
Kompong Cham (228km);
Phnom Penh (348km)

To Stung Treng

Psar Kratie

Mekong River

To Sen Sok
Guest House
(50m)

To Wat Roka
Kandal (2km);
Chhlong (35km)

To Kompong
Cham

DOLPHINS ENDANGERED

The Irrawaddy dolphin (*Orcaella brevirostris*, called *trey pisaut* in Cambodia, *pqa khaa* in Laos) is one of the Mekong River's most fascinating creatures, and one of its most endangered. It is an endangered species throughout Asia, with shrinking numbers found in isolated pockets in Bangladesh and Myanmar (Burma). From the thousands that populated the Mekong and its tributaries in Cambodia and southern Laos as recently as the 1970s, there are now estimated to be fewer than 100 left. The surviving few live primarily along a 190km stretch of the Mekong between the Lao border and the Cambodian town of Kratie.

The dark blue to grey cetaceans grow to 2.75m long and are recognisable by their bulging foreheads and small dorsal fins. They are unusually adaptable and can live in fresh or salt water, though they are seldom seen in the sea. The only other known populations are thought to be equally, if not more, at risk of extinction.

Among the Lao and Khmer, Irrawaddy dolphins are traditionally considered reincarnated humans and there are many stories of dolphins having saved the lives of fishermen or villagers who have fallen into the river or been attacked by crocodiles. These cultural beliefs mean neither the Lao nor the Khmer intentionally capture dolphins for food or sport.

Ironically, however, this unusual respect might also have contributed to their current predicament. In an attempt to crush these beliefs and to extract oil for their war machinery, the Khmer Rouge reportedly shot thousands of the dolphins in Tonlé Sap, a large lake in northern Cambodia, during their 1970s reign of terror. These days fishermen don't actively target the dolphins, but gill netting, grenade and dynamite fishing in Cambodia have inevitably taken their toll. Gill netting remains a constant threat – as dolphins need to surface and breath every two to three minutes, they will usually drown before the fisherman even knows they are there.

In Laos, dolphins have been seen as far north as Sekong in recent years, but you're most likely to see them in the deep-water conservation zones 10m to 60m deep that have been established near the border, south of Don Khon. In Cambodia, they inhabit stretches of the Mekong River north of Kratie and it's possible to see them at Kampi, about 15km north of Kratie, on the road to Stung Treng. Locals say the best time of year to see the dolphins is at the height of the dry season.

Education and conservation programmes continue, particularly in Cambodia, to save the dolphins. However, their survival is far from guaranteed. For more on this rare creature, visit the Mekong Dolphin Conservation Project (MDCP) website at www.mekongdolphin.org.

Around Kratie

O KAMPI

The freshwater Irrawaddy dolphins are an endangered species of noseless dolphins (see the boxed text, above, for more information). Called *pisaut* by locals, the dolphins can be spotted from Kampi (admission US$2), located half an hour (15km) from town. Sharing a boat will cost US$3 per person. The dolphins appear at any time of the day, but viewing them at dawn or sunset is the most magical.

PHNOM SOMBOK

Fifteen minutes out of town on the road to Kampi sits the tranquil meditation centre at Phnom Sombok. Divided into three levels, it houses meditative huts and lodgings for the monks. Locals come here to ask for blessings.

SAMBOR

Sambor is an active wat complex 35km from Kratie. Tucked in the back are a monastery school and a 19th-century wooden pagoda. Dominating the front is the largest wat in Cambodia. It is known locally as Wat Moi Roi (100) due to the one-hundred–plus columns holding it up – making it the largest wat in Cambodia.

STUNG TRENG PROVINCE

Stung Treng is the overlooked middle child between two luminary siblings: Ratanakiri and Laos. Apart from having the most convenient gateway to Virachay National Park in Siam Pang, it has little else to stop travellers in their tracks on their way to the other two. Hopefully this will all change when people realise the advantages of having so many rivers run through the province and the activities that can be generated from this.

Stung Treng

☎ 074 / pop 25,725

Stung Treng is a relaxed riverside town that is a pleasant place to recuperate before heading off to Ratanakiri, Kratie or Laos.

INFORMATION

The tourist office is among the cluster of cabins making up the government buildings, but seems constantly uninhabited. Money changers, telephone kiosks and internet access can all be found around the bustling market.

Acleda Bank (☎ 973684) For money transfers.

SLEEPING & EATING

Richies Restaurant & Guest House (☎ 012-302017; r US$2) In a rickety wooden house, the rooms are little more than shanties with mossie net-covered beds. The restaurant does a great breakfast and travel information is abundant.

Riverside Restaurant & Guest House (☎ 012-439454; taingpow@yahoo.com; r US$3) The rooms are very basic with attached bathrooms that require squatting action. Good views can be had from the upstairs garden terrace and the restaurant serves a range of tasty Western and Asian food.

Hotel & Restaurant Sekong (☎ 973762; r US$4-16; ❄) This ranch-like hotel offers basic rooms at the bottom end and air-con and hot-water luxury at the top. The long-stretching veranda is a good spot to catch the evening breeze. The restaurant serves Western and Khmer food.

Stung Treng Guest House (☎ 973628; r US$6-18; ❄) Perhaps the best all-round accommodation in town. Sparkling rooms in the same budget-hotel style adopted all over the country: bland but clean.

Kong Ratana Sambath Guest House (☎ 012-964483; r US$7-17; ❄) Almost identical to the Stung Treng, just a little smaller. The service is friendly and the welcome warm.

Ou Dynak Red Guest House (☎ 011-963676; r US$7-25; ❄) The rooms here are lovely and cool even before the air-con kicks in. A touch on the small side but with more character than its competitors.

GETTING THERE & AWAY

All transport leaves from the transport stop, riverfront near the Riverside Guest House.

Minibuses travel to and from the Laos border crossing at Dom Kralor (US$10 to US$15, two hours) along the now decent NH7.

Getting to Stung Treng from Phnom Penh, buses leave from Psar Thmei at 7am (42,000r, 10 hours).

An air-conditioned minivan travels to Ban Lung, Ratanakiri, every morning from around 7.30am. It collects guests from their hotels so make sure to ask yours to book a seat for you the night before (US$7 to US$8, four hours). To and from Kratie is 25,000r (three to four hours).

When the water levels are up (July to November) fast boats can be caught to Stung Treng from Kratie (US$8, six hours) or Kompong Cham (US$15, eight hours).

RATANAKIRI PROVINCE

One of the country's most exciting regions, Ratanakiri is a colourful hotchpotch of natural beauty and cultural diversity. A patchwork of jungle scrub, tribal huts and waterfalls, this is home to many of Cambodia's Chunchiet communities. The Jarai, Tampoun and Kreung are the Khmer Loeu (Upper Khmer) people with their own languages, traditions and customs. Throw in elephants, hikes and the nation's largest national park, and you have an area tailor-made for adventure. The best time to visit is in the dry season (after the wet season's slodge-fest).

Ban Lung

☎ 075 / pop 18,700

No it's not always autumn in the region's capital; the leaves – like everything else – are just forever cloaked in a blanket of red dust. Nicknamed 'dey krahorm' (red earth) after its rust-coloured affliction, Ban Lung provides

---

CROSSING INTO LAOS: DOM KRALOR TO VOEN KHAM

This is it now that the river crossing at Koh Chheuteal Thom has ground to a halt. Catch a minibus from the transport stop in Stung Treng to Dom Kralor then cross over to Voen Kham in Laos' Champasak Province – expect border officials on both sides to ask for more money (US$1 to US$2) in 'stamp fees'. Laos visas are not available on arrival. From here taxis go north to Nakasong, or boats to Don Khone Island. See right for details on getting from Dom Kralor to other Cambodian cities. For information on crossing this border in the other direction, see the boxed text, p333.

a functional base for all of your Ratanakiri romps.

INFORMATION

Bring stacks of cash. The activities here aren't the cheapest and there are no banks in town or anywhere to cash travellers cheques. Cash can be changed at the jewellers in the market.

The post office is on the main road just down from the Tribal Hotel. It offers internet (per hour US$4) and a telephone service but it is cheaper to call from the kiosks around the market.

Guests at Terre Rouges Lodge (right) can use its one computer in reception without charge, but you are sharing it with the receptionist so long emails to Aunty May about what the elephant did next will not be appreciated.

There is a tourist office just for looks; no-one ever seems to be there.

ACTIVITIES

There are no sights or activities in town, but a few quick arrangements will soon have you exploring in the surrounding areas.

If you are unable to make it down to Sen Monorom where the elephant excursions are superior, you can leap onto one here for an **elephant ride**. Guesthouses and hotels will organise them for US$10 an hour.

The jungle terrain and national park are ideal for interesting **treks**, but make it clear to guides before setting off exactly what it is you would like to see and experience. Bank on about US$25 to US$30 per person, less if there's a group. The Terre Rouges Lodge, Star Hotel and Yaklom Hill Lodge are the best places to organise such expeditions. For trekking through Yeak Laom and Virachay National Park, see opposite and p236 respectively.

SLEEPING & EATING

Star Hotel (☎ 012-958322; Village 5, Labanseak Commune; r US$5-10) The rooms aren't the best or brightest but this is all made up with brilliant service. The ever-efficient manager runs a tight ship and ensures guests are wanting for nothing. The hotel's restaurant is excellent.

Lakeside Chheng Lok Hotel (☎ 390063; lakeside -chhenglokhotel@yahoo.com; Village 6, Labanseak Commune; r US$5-20; ⌘) Pristine rooms in the main building and gorgeous brick bungalows by Boeng Kansaign out the back make this address one of the most appealing in Ratanakiri.

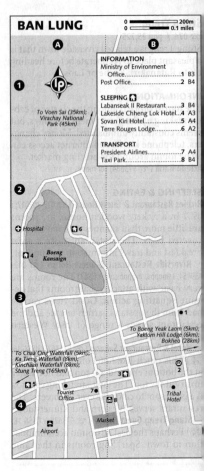

BAN LUNG

0 — 200m
0 — 0.1 miles

INFORMATION
Ministry of Environment
Office 1 B3
Post Office 2 B4

SLEEPING
Labanseak II Restaurant 3 B4
Lakeside Chheng Lok Hotel 4 A3
Sovan Kiri Hotel 5 A4
Terre Rouges Lodge 6 A2

TRANSPORT
President Airlines 7 A4
Taxi Park 8 B4

To Voen Sai (35km);
Virachay National
Park (45km)

Hospital

Boeng
Kansaign

To Boeng Yeak Laom (5km);
Yaklom Hill Lodge (6km);
Bokheo (28km)

To Chaa Ong Waterfall (5km);
Ka Tieng Waterfall (8km);
Kinchaan Waterfall (8km);
Stung Treng (165km)

Tourist
Office

Tribal
Hotel

Market

Airport

Sovan Kiri Hotel (☎ 974001; www.sovannkiri_hote .com; Ph 78; r US$5-30; ⌘) Friendly service and enough driveway space to park every moto in town are the first things to greet you here. Solid wood furnishings in squeaky-clean rooms make up the rest of it.

Yaklom Hill Lodge (☎ 012-644240; www.yaklom. com; r US$10-20) A luxurious garden location and an indigenous stamp on style, the Yaklom consists of a hillside restaurant and wooden cottages with attached bathrooms and terraces. It aims to be ecofriendly and is 10 minutes (6km) east of town.

Terre Rouges Lodge (☎ 974051; www.ratana kiri-lodge.com; r US$30-70; ⌘) Terre Rouges, not Khmer Rouges as sometimes mistakenly understood by a hard-of-hearing motodup, is a sophisticated Chunchiet-style retreat set amid a tropical garden on Boeng Kansaign.

Labanseak II Restaurant (☎ 974165; mains 4000r; ✆ breakfast, lunch & dinner) This restaurant has private garden bungalows frequented by well-heeled Khmers, and the everything-is-fried menu contains very tasty Khmer dishes. Besides the restaurants at the Lakeside Chheng Lok and Star Hotels, this is another good option in town. It also has an impressive list of Johnnie Walker labels – the beverage of status in this country.

GETTING THERE & AWAY

Most people come to Ratanakiri from Stung Treng. There are no buses but a private mini-van service operates the bumpy route (US$8, four hours). It picks you up from your guest-house or hotel. Let them know the night before to secure your seat.

President Airlines (☎ 106-839696; reservations@ presidentairlines.com) flies out of Ban Lung on Mondays and Wednesdays (US$100 one way to Phnom Penh). Alternatively, you can catch a bus from the transport stop near the market (US$15, 11 to 12 hours, once daily) or a share taxi (US$20, 10 to 11 hours).

To Sen Monorom, a mission of a moto ride down the horrendous goat track to Koh Nhek for five hours should only be tackled by the most experienced of riders. Cars can forget about it, as there is no room for the extra two wheels. From Koh Nhek another two hours of travelling is required, this time on a much-improved road to finally reach Sen Monorom.

GETTING AROUND

Single moto trips around town cost 1000r, double that at night. Hiring a motodup for the day starts at US$7 for the nearby sites and climbs the further you go.

Motorbikes can be hired through guesthouses for US$8 to US$10 a day. Jeeps can be hired from the taxi stand near the market for US$50 a day.

Bicycles cost US$1 a day from guesthouses.

Around Ban Lung
BOENG YEAK LAOM

Through the clearing of a dark green forest is the bright blue water of this **volcanic lake** (admission US$1), 5km east of Ban Lung. This picnic, fishing and swimming spot is where Khmers come to plunge into the 50m depths fully clothed – jeans and all. There is a small Cul-

tural Centre housing Tampoun (a Chunchiet minority) artefacts. Donations are required to enter. It also rents out rubber tubes to float around in. For an interesting insight into the community, contact **Yeak Laom Community Based Eco Tourism** (☎ 012-981226), which can organise English-speaking tours.

Motos to the lake cost US$2 return.

WATERFALLS

Chaa Ong (admission 2000r) is the largest of Ratanakiri's waterfalls, dropping some 30m into a rich jungle gorge. Behind the cascade is a rocky ledge that is perfect for some behind-the-falls action. Nearby, the **Ka Tieng** (admission free) has some swinging vines and the **Kinchaan** (admission 2000r) is small but picturesque. A little further out is the **Tuk Chhrou Bram-pul** (admission 2000r); 35km southeast of Ban Lung, it has seven platforms of falling water.

VOEN SAI
pop 3000

On the banks of the Tonlé San, Voen Sai is a bustling little village of Chinese, Lao and Kreung minorities. This is a good place to buy authentic Chunchiet handicrafts for half the price sold in Ban Lung. On the other side of the river is the wealthy Chinese settlement that sits alongside the Lao village. Small ferries can take you across for 1000r return.

To get here on your own, the road from Ban Lung is in poor shape and can take around two to three hours of dusty driving, the distance is approximately 35km but feels much longer. See Chunchiet Villages, below, for tour details.

CHUNCHIET CEMETERIES

From Voen Sai, you can catch a boat (US$15 per boat, one hour) to the Tampoun cemetery at **Kachon** (admission US$1), where amid the jungle foliage, chiselled effigies stand guard over the graves of the deceased. Carved elephant trunks, whittled from wood, are placed to signal the end of mourning, while off in the distance, the call of hunters can be heard, whooping beasts into confusion and ultimately into traps. A slightly primal experience in a very sacred spot.

CHUNCHIET VILLAGES

There are many hill tribes occupying the regions of Ratanakiri that can be visited for a glimpse into the Chunchiet way of life.

Ethnically they are impossible to tell apart from the Khmer Krom (Lower Khmers), especially now that they have traded in their colourful costumes and bright beads for current Khmer dress.

When travelling to the villages, it is best to arrange an accompanying tour guide as the Chunchiet people are rather shy of outsiders. As with polite custom when visiting someone's home, take gifts of pencils or books for the little ones and tobacco or biodegradable goods for the adults. Don't give money; instead trade these gifts with those who want payment for photographs. Avoid plastic-wrapped gifts as they do not have the means to dispose of them in an environmentally friendly way.

Most hotels in Ban Lung will arrange tours for around US$60 per car and usually incorporate visits to the Lao and Chinese villages on the banks of the river.

VIRACHAY NATIONAL PARK

Stretching out in all directions to Laos, Vietnam and Stung Treng, this is the largest protected area in the country with a large diversity of plants and wildlife. For some serious trekking, contact the **Ministry of Environment office** (☎ 974176; virachey@camintel.com) in Ban Lung.

Some of the treks on offer:

Kalang Chhouy A three-day combination excursion, this is one of the easier-going treks.

O'Lapeung Kayaking and Trek A four-day adventure into the forest, over the Ho Chi Minh Trail and down the river in kayaks.

Phnom Veal Thom Wilderness Trek A challenging seven-day affair over mountains and through forests. This is recommended as the best option for seeing wildlife.

LUMPHAT WILDLIFE SANCTUARY

Spanning 250,000 hectares, this sanctuary is home to elephants and an array of bird species including redheaded vultures. It is 35km southwest of Ban Lung.

MONDULKIRI PROVINCE

Mondulkiri is another Cambodian dimension. With not a rice paddy or palm tree in sight, the landscape is a seductive mix of tawny hills and windswept valleys that fade beguilingly into forests of jade green and waterfalls. Sparsely populated, the main inhabitants are the Pnong, an ethnic minority that constitute more than half of the population.

Nights are a little cooler here, so there is no need for air-con, but the thin-skinned among us may need to wear more than just mosquito repellent to bed.

Sen Monorom

☎ 073 / pop 7700

Where the hills stop rolling and come to rest, Sen Monorom sits, a quaint and peaceful town. The buildings, mostly picturesque timber cabins, are spread out with plenty of space to breathe. Your own breathing benefits from the freshness that a high altitude and a surprising pine tree plantation provide, a delightful contrast to the dust-clogged nasal activity of norm.

INFORMATION

There are no banks in town. Everything from food to transport is slightly more expensive here than in the rest of the country, so make sure your wallet's loaded with dollars and riel before you come. Telephone calls can be made from mobile phones around the town.

Arun Reas II Hill Lodge (per hr US$4) Internet access.

Tourist office On the main road to Phnom Penh, is a valuable source of information and can organise tours, treks and local Pnong guides.

SIGHTS & ACTIVITIES

Not much happens in Sen Monorom itself but there's plenty to see and do nearby.

Trips out to the Pnong (minority) villages dotted across the province can be arranged by guesthouses and hotels, including an overnight stay with the community. Each guesthouse has a preferred village to send travellers to, which is a great way to spread the revenue.

Six kilometres northwest of Sen Monorom from the observation deck of **Phnom Bai Chuw** (Raw Rice Mountain), is a jaw-dropping view of the enchanted forest. From here it looks as though you are seeing a vast sea of tree tops hence the locals have named it Samot Cheu (Ocean of Trees).

Elephant Treks

With many of the waterfalls and forests being inaccessible to vehicles, these heavy-hoofed animals are the most effective form of transport. The tourist office and guesthouses can arrange a trek and most quote US$30 for one elephant a day. An elephant sits two people but those who are long of leg may want to splurge and have one to themselves. Overnight sleepovers in the forest can be arranged, just double the price. Take a cushion!

SLEEPING & EATING

Angkor Meas Guest House (☎ 011-696828; Street 69; r US$5-7) Grand rooms with good paint jobs; a small detail but let's face it – yellow-stained walls with cracking paint just don't cut it. The upstairs rooms have more character with wooden panelling and a common veranda to enjoy the evening breeze.

Arun Reah II Hill Lodge and Restaurant (☎ 012-999191; r US$5-10; 🖳) Popular with travellers due to its peaceful valley location and great views, this lodge also offers a great range of services including free bicycles, moto hire and internet.

Long Vibol Guest House and Restaurant (☎ 012-944647; r US$5-15) Rooms climb up the small, gently sloping hill of a large garden locale. A lively mix of international and Khmer guests creates a constant buzz, all ably managed by English-speaking staff who are helpful and knowledgeable about the area.

Pech Kiri Guest House (☎ 012-932102; r US$5-15) If you miss out on the newer spacious bungalows, the older rooms can be rather cramped. The garden surrounds are abundant with blossoms and the restaurant turns out decent Khmer and European dishes.

Sum Dy Guest House (☎ 012-828533; Ospean Village; r US$5-18) The rise and dips of the rolling hills set a picturesque backdrop for this guesthouse. The charming timber huts are clean and cosy and when the spot is bathed in a hazy light of dusk, your breath will be taken away.

our pick **Nature Lodge Café** (☎ 012-230272; naturelodge@gmail.com; mains US$1-3; 🕑 breakfast, lunch & dinner) With an atmosphere as cool and chilled as the hilltop air, this unique café occupies a picturesque setting in the midst of nature. Serving an eclectic menu ranging from Israeli salad to *phàt thai* (Thai dish of stir-fried noodles), it also offers a herbal sauna for weary travel bones, and will soon embark on a worthy collaboration with the International Cooperation Cambodia (ICC) to sell a funky line of local handicrafts.

Middle of Somewhere Bar (☎ 012-1613833; ackhighwood@yahoo.com; 🕑 3pm-late) The only bar in town, it serves beer from as little as US$0.50. Fairy lights twinkling through the back door will lure you into the yard where a delightful beer garden has been set up.

GETTING THERE & AWAY

From Phnom Penh, share taxis depart from the southwest corner of Psar Thmei (70,000r, nine hours).

There is a bus from Sen Monorom to Stung Treng, via Kratie and with a changeover at Snuol that leaves at 7am (50,000r, eight to nine hours). Get your ticket the night before, as it fills up very quickly. It leaves from opposite Pech Kiri Guest House.

From Kratie, the bus officially leaves at 9.45am from outside the Heng Heng II Guesthouse (US$8, eight hours). Change at Snuol.

GETTING AROUND

Single motodup trips across town cost 2000r to 4000r. To hire a motodup for the day, count on US$7 to US$10.

Motorbikes can be hired from the guesthouses around town for US$5 to US$10 a day. Jeeps cost US$40 to US$50 a day, depending on the season and how far you want to go.

Around Sen Monorom

Forty-three kilometres out of town on an unforgiving road, the impressive two-tiered **Bou Sra Waterfall** drops from a dramatic height of 23m from the bottom tier and 10m from the top.

Monorom Falls, also known as Sihanouk Waterfall in honour of the king, is only 5km away from the town centre. It has a swimming pool at the bottom of the 10m drop.

Koh Nhek

For years, only the daring few have managed a Sen Monorom and Ratanakiri back-to-back visit overland. Grand tales of harsh roads, an unforgiving jungle, and the back-breaking battle between nature, humans and motorbike have circulated to earn this route legendary status.

In the centre of these epics is the far-flung town of Koh Nhek, a small village that marks the nearly halfway there point. If you have made it here, then a few locals about town are gracious enough to offer a place to crash and some food for a small fee of 10,000r to 20,000r. Head to the local bar-restaurant and ask around there.

From Sen Monorom, the road has been sealed to cut the travel time to a glorious two to three hours. From there on, the story has not changed and the sandy goat track remains. Count on another four to five hours before reaching Ban Lung in Ratanakiri.

SOUTH COAST

The south coast of Cambodia is an alluring mix of seaside fun and undiscovered nature: clear blue waters, castaway islands and rousing colonial towns. With a growing number of tourists each year, the coastal cities are developing fast, but despite this there is still a great expanse of the less explored and adventure travellers will be just as rewarded as the beach bum in a deckchair.

SIHANOUKVILLE & AROUND
☎ 034

Sandy beaches and a happening bar scene could sum up Sihanoukville (population 170,500) in a sentence, but many more would be required to delve into its nuances. As Cambodia's premier beachside town, many are vying for a stake in its development. The privately owned land has a big military factor, and establishments that set themselves up one day can be muscled off without notice shortly after. But seaside politics aside, the town has come a long way since the fishing village it once was to become a coastal star attraction.

Orientation
Curving around the Gulf of Thailand, Sihanoukville's coast is broken up into four main beaches: Victory, Sokha, Occheuteal and Otres. The city is a boring mass of streets and traffic and has none of the charm of its seaside edge.

Information
Internet access can be found in many of the guesthouses around the beach and in the city. The average rate is 4000r an hour. Telephone calls can be made at booths all over town as well as at the internet cafés and guesthouses.

Acleda Bank (☎ 933723) Representing Western Union for money transfers.

Canadia Bank (☎ 933490; 197 Ph Ekareach) Cash advances and Visa/MasterCard ATM.

Tourist office (Ph Sopheakmongkol; ☯ 9am-6pm) Perhaps the best in the country. Lots of handouts, excellent English spoken, and the staff actually show up to work.

Union Commercial Bank (☎ 933833; cnr Ph Ekareach & Ph Sopheakmongkol) Does cash advances with Visa and changes travellers cheques.

Vietnamese consulate (Ph Ekareach) Turns out the speediest Vietnamese visas (one month US$35); a couple hours is all you'll have to wait at the most.

Dangers & Annoyances
There has been one high-profile case of rap on the beach, so solo women should take cau tion. Some of the lads at certain guesthouse can also be a little too amorous but will no mally back off with a stern warning.

Theft is common on the beach if valuable are left lying about, and motorcycles have bee known to be pinched, so be sure to lock up.

Sights & Activities
BEACHES
The sandy beaches of Sihanoukville are gener ally throbbing with tourists, but it still remain very chilled. **Sokha** beach has been privatise and thus only guests can access it, but ther is a tiny tip that is open to the public and i makes for a nice getaway from the crowd **Occheuteal** is the most popular, with a hig concentration of bungalow bars and restau rants set up on the sand. Its western end is th appropriately named **Serendipity** beach, a fur happy and relaxed section, lacking in sand bu full of easy-going beach babes and bums. **Vic tory** beach is the traditional backpacker hang out, but there is not much of a beach to speal of. And finally **Otres** beach is looking to b the new hot spot as the Occheuteal resident are rumoured to be getting the heave-ho by private hotel company with ambitious plan for a luxury hotel.

ISLANDS
There are quite a few islands dotting the gu within day-trip distance of Sihanoukville.

For snorkelling, **Koh Ta Kiev** and **Koh Khte** are the best. **Bamboo Island** (Koh Russei), **Koh R** and **Koh Rung** all have basic accommodation with boat trips out there encompassing spot of snorkelling along the way. (Though thos who have just arrived from Thailand will b disappointed.)

Bamboo Island is surrounded by clear wa ters and the **bungalows** (r US$8-10) are sweet wit shared bathrooms and breezy terraces. Ther is also a large restaurant. A boat out here cost US$8 return.

Koh Ru has **bungalows** (r US$10) on the beach plus its own restaurant and bar. It's more se cluded than Bamboo Island and costs US$1 for a return boat trip.

SIHANOUKVILLE

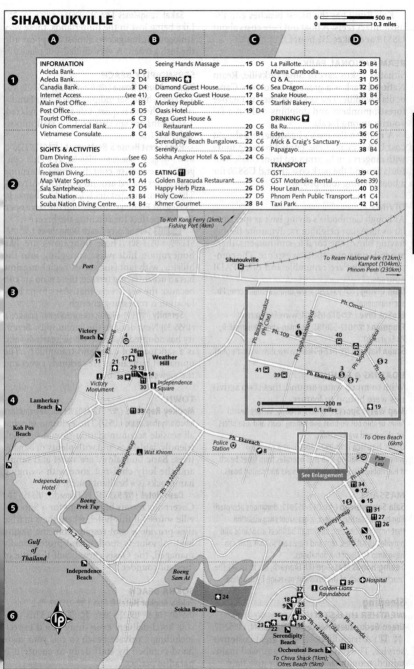

INFORMATION	
Acleda Bank	**1** D5
Acleda Bank	**2** D4
Canadia Bank	**3** D4
Internet Access	(see 41)
Main Post Office	**4** B3
Post Office	**5** D5
Tourist Office	**6** C3
Union Commercial Bank	**7** D4
Vietnamese Consulate	**8** C4

SIGHTS & ACTIVITIES	
Dam Diving	(see 6)
EcoSea Dive	**9** C6
Frogman Diving	**10** D5
Map Water Sports	**11** A4
Sala Santepheap	**12** D5
Scuba Nation	**13** B4
Scuba Nation Diving Centre	**14** B4

Seeing Hands Massage	**15** D5

SLEEPING	
Diamond Guest House	**16** C6
Green Gecko Guest House	**17** B4
Monkey Republic	**18** C6
Oasis Hotel	**19** D4
Rega Guest House & Restaurant	**20** C6
Sakal Bungalows	**21** B4
Serendipity Beach Bungalows	**22** C6
Serenity	**23** C6
Sokha Angkor Hotel & Spa	**24** C6

EATING	
Golden Baracuda Restaurant	**25** C6
Happy Herb Pizza	**26** D5
Holy Cow	**27** D5
Khmer Gourmet	**28** B4

La Paillotte	**29** B4
Mama Cambodia	**30** B4
Q & A	**31** D5
Sea Dragon	**32** D6
Snake House	**33** B4
Starfish Bakery	**34** D5

DRINKING	
Ba Ru	**35** D6
Eden	**36** C6
Mick & Craig's Sanctuary	**37** C6
Papagayo	**38** B4

TRANSPORT	
GST	**39** C4
GST Motorbike Rental	(see 39)
Hour Lean	**40** D3
Phnom Penh Public Transport	**41** C4
Taxi Park	**42** D4

CAMBODIA

0 ————— 500 m
0 ————— 0.3 miles

To Koh Kong Ferry (2km);
Fishing Port (4km)

To Ream National Park (12km);
Kampot (104km);
Phnom Penh (230km)

Port

Sihanoukville

Victory
Beach

Weather
Hill

Victory
Monument

Independence
Square

Lamherkay
Beach

Koh Pos
Beach

Wat Khtom

Police
Station

To Otres Beach
(6km)

Psar
Leu

See Enlargement

Independance
Hotel

Boeng
Prek Tup

Gulf
of
Thailand

Independence
Beach

Boeng
Sam Åt

Sokha Beach

Golden Lions
Roundabout

Hospital

Serendipity
Beach

Occheuteal Beach

To Chiva Shack (1km);
Otres Beach (5km)

Ph Borei Kamakor
(Ph Cite)

Ph 109

Ph Sopheakmongkol

Ph Omui

Ph Sopheakmongkol

Ph Ekareach

Ph 108

0 ————— 200 m
0 ————— 0.1 miles

Koh Rung has the nicest beaches and the most intact reefs. A boat out here costs about US$19 and takes 2½ hours.

REAM NATIONAL PARK

Situated 13km east of Sihanoukville, Ream National Park is a great place to view Cambodia's wildlife. The sandy beaches, mangrove forests, monkeys and dolphins make it a favourite among locals.

A moto to the park's headquarters should cost US$2. From here, guided walking tours with rangers can be arranged from US$5. Boat tours around the park cost around US$20 for a boat holding four people.

DIVING

Although Cambodia's diving isn't as spectacular as its Asian neighbours, dynamite fishing having blown the coral to smithereens, there are still some nice spots to explore. The companies below are reputable and offer PADI courses.

Dam Diving (☎ 934220; www.divingandmore.com; Ph Sopheakmongkol)

EcoSea Dive (☎ 012-654104; www.EcoSea.com)

Frogman (☎ 012-586183; frogman-khmer@hotmail.fr; Ph Ekareach)

Scuba Nation (☎ 012-604680; www.divecambodia.com)

BOATING & FISHING

With so much water around, these two activities were bound to feature.

Map Water Sports (☎ 011-696076; Victory Beach) Takes people out on boat and fishing tours and also offers jet-skiing and water-skiing.

Otres Nautica (☎ 092-230065; otre.nautica@ yahoo.com) A sailing club that operates from Otres beach, it has Hobie Wave catamarans, kayaks and sailing boats.

MASSAGE

Sala Santepheap (☎ 012-952011; donations accepted) Run by the Starfish Project, a grassroots organisation that organises housing and small business assistance and provides all salaries, rent and transport so that staff can hang onto 100% of the donations.

Seeing Hands Massage (Ph Ekareach; per hr US$4) The beachside branch of the excellent massage by the blind.

Sleeping

WEATHER HILL STATION

Green Gecko Guest House (☎ 012-560944; r US$2-12; ⚙ 🖳) A friendly hotel with great customer service. The rooms are clean and well maintained, though lacking in decorative flair.

Sakal Bungalows (☎ 012-806155; r US$6-10; ⚙) Like being lost in the hinterlands, these very atmospheric bungalows almost disappear into the lush garden. A very chilled-out place.

SERENDIPITY BEACH

Diamond Guest House (☎ 016-948929; r US$7-10; ⚙) Tucked behind Serendipity beach, this family-run guesthouse is quiet, safe and very relaxed. The rooms are spotless and the staff impossibly helpful.

Rega Guest House & Restaurant (☎ 012-1758610; www.rega-guesthouse.com; r US$8-16; ⚙) This congenial guesthouse contains some charming bungalows placed around a pretty courtyard. The restaurant upstairs is topnotch thanks to its elegant French manager and the large open space is perfect for catching the breeze.

our pick **Serendipity Beach Bungalows** (☎ 016-513599; r US$5-30) These bungalows are like honeymoon hideaways snuggling into the hillside, with fantastic views. Each bungalow has an ocean-facing terrace; there is no air-con because the sea breeze that soars to its lofty location is refreshing enough.

Serenity (☎ 011-696009; edenserendipity@yahoo.com; r US$5-30) Next door to the Serendipity, Serenity has adopted its name wholeheartedly and is a sanctuary of calm and tranquillity. The upmarket bungalows are seriously sweet and the views are superb.

TOWN

Monkey Republic (☎ 012-490290; monkeyrepubliccambodia@yahoo.co.uk; r US$7) The epitome of what all seaside accommodation should be: cool, friendly, laid-back and with plenty of banana trees. Basic bungalows are sweet and simple and the lofty chill-out zone with swinging hammocks is a brilliant touch.

Oasis Hotel (☎ 933 487; Ph Ekareach; r US$15; ⚙) Cavernous rooms big enough for a Snooky-ville soiree fill this hotel, where their marble tiles provide a cool respite from the baking heat. Absolutely spotless and professionally managed, the Oasis earns itself the title of 'Best all-rounder'.

SOKHA BEACH

Sokha Angkor Hotel & Spa (☎ 935999; Ph 2 Thnou; r US$160-180, ste US$220-1000; ⚙ 🖳 🛎) This five-star hotel delivers everything you'd expect, including a private beach to call your own, hand-combed by staff daily to ensure it is paradise perfect.

Eating

WEATHER HILL STATION

Mama Cambodia (☎ 012-221468; mains US$2-3; ⌚ breakfast, lunch & dinner) 'Mama' is a middle-aged woman with a talent in the kitchen that could make you discard your own. Unlike the bizarre beauty queens laminated into her menus, her traditional Khmer meals are authentic and tasty.

Khmer Gourmet (☎ 012-1799450; ⌚ breakfast, lunch & dinner) Saviours of the sweet tooth, fresh pies, cakes and cookies line the display cabinet of this café, but its *pièce de résistance* is the coffee machine, a proper one, that makes the noise and everything!

Snake House (☎ 012-673805; Ph Soviet; ⌚ breakfast, lunch & dinner) If Tarzan decided to throw in crocodile wrestling to become a restaurateur, then this is what the place would look like. Creatures from the jungle squawk and slither all around the tables while you chow down on hearty servings of European and Russian food.

La Paillote (☎ 012-633247; mains US$6-14; ⌚ lunch & dinner, closed 2-5.30pm) This fine-dining restaurant is a little out of place in the backpacker-Bronx of Sihanoukville, maybe that's why it hides behind a passageway of bamboo in a delightful garden courtyard. It has a great international menu. Try the Balmain bugs in coconut milk and ginger; they're as delectable as they sound.

OCCHEUTEAL BEACH

Sea Dragon (☎ 016-595252; mains US$2-5; ⌚ breakfast, lunch & dinner) This large airy restaurant does tasty Western food, but it's the delicious Khmer that you'd come for.

SERENDIPITY BEACH

Golden Baracuda Restaurant (mains 3000r-US$5.50; ⌚ breakfast, lunch & dinner) A barbecue seafood place that grills up fresh catches from the owner's boat expeditions. Great food, easygoing atmosphere.

TOWN

Q & A (☎ 012-342720; 95 Ph Ekareach; mains US$1.95-2.75; ⌚ breakfast, lunch & dinner) A library, secondhand bookshop and restaurant in one. You can tuck into a meal and a book simultaneously. It serves light Western dishes.

our pick Holy Cow (☎ 012-478510; Ph Ekareach; mains US$2-6; ⌚ breakfast, lunch & dinner) Holy cow, this place is great! A fusion of Asian and West-ern décor and food, the restaurant and bar is overflowing with ambience. The dining and chill-out areas are divided into two levels, each compelling guests to just flop about and relax. It also has a tiny boutique stocking M'lop Tapang products. Profits from M'lop Tapang provide street children with nutrition, counselling, education and medical care.

Happy Herb Pizza (☎ 012-632198; 81 Ph Ekareach; mains US$3-12; ⌚ breakfast, lunch & dinner) This little Italian restaurant serves pasta and pizzas that can make you happy with a few of its additional 'garnishes' from the kitchen.

Starfish Bakery (☎ 012-9522011; ⌚ breakfast & lunch) Freshly baked goods made to order are served in this open-air café. It also does boxed lunches that are perfect for those snorkelling trips out to the islands.

Drinking

Eden (☎ 933585; Serendipity Beach; ⌚ 7am-late) The large rocks jutting from the beach in front of this bar are not ideal for swimming but absolutely perfect for setting the mood. Flickering candle light and breaking waves crashing over the stones make for a very atmospheric venue.

Chiva Shack (☎ 012-360911; Occheuteal Beach; ⌚ 24hr) Full-moon parties, fire throwers, happy pizzas and some delicious cocktails right on the beach keep the punters flowing into this place.

Ba Ru (☎ 012-388860; Golden Lion; ⌚ 8am-late) You can knock them back at this unpretentious bar and perhaps take part in its charity crab races or quiz nights while you're at it. Money raised goes to community organisations based in Sihanoukville.

Mick & Craig's Sanctuary (☎ 012-727740; Golden Lion; ⌚ 7am-late) If you get peckish while hanging about the Monkey Republic, just pop next door into this place; as well as having a fully stocked bar, it does excellent food in a more sophisticated setting.

Papagayo (☎ 012-1928656; Weather Hill Station; ⌚ 8am-late) Don't bother coming here before lunchtime, everyone is still recovering from the night before. This airy bar opens officially at 8am, but doesn't get kicking until very late at night.

Getting There & Away

For information on the southern border crossing into Thailand see the boxed text, p249. See p249 for fast-boat services to and from Sihanoukville.

Several bus companies run to the capital (15,000r, three hours), leaving from the transport station near the market. Tickets can be purchased via guesthouses or at the Hour Lean bus office. To Kampot a share taxi costs 12,000r for a two-hour journey. Charter cars cost between US$18 to US$20. Motorbikes can be hired from most guesthouses and even some restaurants for US$5 a day. Great for exploring nearby Kampot or Kep.

Cramped taxis head to Phnom Penh (10,000r, four hours) and Kampot (8000r, two hours) from the new taxi park in front of the market, but the buses are the better option.

Getting Around

Bicycles can be hired from most guesthouses for US$1 to US$2 a day.

Motos charge 2000r for quick trips around town and 4000r from town to the beaches. From the dock to the beach it's normally US$2.

KAMPOT PROVINCE

An intermingling landscape of oceans and rapids, mountains and caves has proved to be a winning combination for Kampot; there's something for everyone. The Kampot pepper used in fine dining comes from here – the name might have given it away – and the plantations are abundant throughout the south.

Kampot

☎ 033 / pop 34,650

Despite a recent expansion, Kampot has maintained an air of unhurried ease. With the Teuk Chhou River hugging its side and verdant vegetation encircling it, it makes the ideal base in which to unwind after the hi-jinx on Bokor Hill (p244).

INFORMATION

Internet places can be found near the central roundabout for cheap access and at the Bokor Mountain Lodge (opposite). There is a tourist office, but comprehensive information is more readily available from guesthouses.

Acleda Bank (☎ 932880) Represents Western Union for money transfers.

Canadia Bank (☎ 932392) Cash advances and travellers cheques.

SIGHTS & ACTIVITIES

Zero by way of sights, but there are voluntary activities you can become involved in; a couple of these include volunteer teaching or arts

and craft days with the kids. Contact **Epic Arts** (epicarts@camintel.com), the Little Garden Bar or Bodhi Villa to get stuck in.

The very worthy – for them and you – **Seeing Hands Massage** (massage US$4) has a branch near the river and at Bokor Mountain Lodge (opposite).

SLEEPING

our pick **Bodhi Villa** (☎ 012-419140; bodhivilla@mac.com; Ph Teuk Chhou; r US$3-10) Laid-back and friendly, this happy hideaway is tucked behind a luxuriant overgrown garden on the banks of the river. The location provides a good base for the water sports on offer: water-skiing and boat cruising, and some very romantic floating bungalows.

Blissful Guest House (☎ 012-513024; blissfulguesthouse@yahoo.com; r US$4-5) A great place to unwind and relax. The bar-restaurant-shop is a casual meeting place of good food and beverage while the sweet bungalows are humble little hidey-holes in which to get a quiet night's rest.

Orchid Guest House (☎ 932634; orchidguesthousekampot@yahoo.com; r US$4-15; 🗵) A beautiful choice of lodging set in a manicured garden full of (you guessed it): orchids. The more expensive rooms come with hot water and air-con, but the cheapies are still tastefully decorated and spotless.

Utopia (r US$8-10) Like an enormous bird house, surrounded by an emerald forest and unrivalled views, Utopia is a true haven, off Teuk Chhou Rd. The tall stilts dig deep into the silted river bed and it comes complete with floating pontoons. Ambitious plans to upscale are ahead with prices reaching into the top end, but for now travellers can enjoy paradise for a bargain.

Rikitikitavi Riverside Restaurant Bar & Accommodation (☎ 012-235102; rikitikitavi@asia.com; r US$25-40; 🗵) Kampot's poshest residence is a model of stylish refinement. With elegant touches of Khmer décor and a breezy river-bank setting, it has everything for the traveller who wants a little extra, including a great restaurant.

EATING & DRINKING

Little Garden Bar & Guest House (☎ 012-256901; www.littlegardenbar.com; mains 4000-28,000r; 🕑 breakfast, lunch & dinner) The garden may be little but their hearts are big. Supporting and launching community-based projects including a volunteer teaching programme and a drop-in centre for orphans, the staff here do more

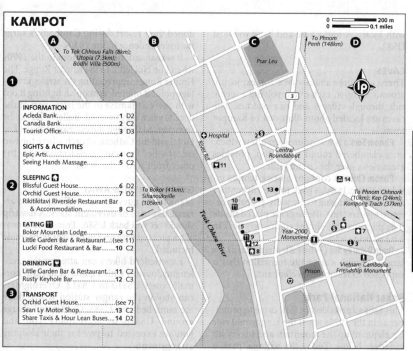

KAMPOT

than just serve up international dishes and cocktails. Has rooms (US$10) also.

Lucki Food Restaurant & Bar (☎ 012-806105; luckifood@yahoo.com; cnr Riverside Rd & Old Market; mains US$2.50-4; ☯ breakfast, lunch & dinner) The restaurant is a fuss-free shell, but the food is anything but standard. Authentic Sri Lankan and Indian dishes are delectable and come with a free drink or snack. The boxed meals are a good idea to take up to Bokor.

Bokor Mountain Lodge (☎ 932314; www.bokorlodge .com; mains US$4-9.50; ☯ breakfast, lunch & dinner; ☒ ⌨) Kiwi owned with an easy-going ambience, this all-in-one establishment boasts a meaty menu including hearty steaks and pies. The drinks selection is wide and varied and includes some Australian wines.

Rusty Keyhole Bar (☎ 012-679607; mains 5000-20,000r; ☯ breakfast, lunch & dinner) A sporty bar with the action screened live, you can come here for happy hour (5pm to 7pm) and enjoy one of the chunky hamburgers.

GETTING THERE & AWAY
From Phnom Penh, share taxis leave from Psar Dang Kor (US$2 to US$3 for a cramped back seat, two hours).

Share taxis leave Sihanoukville from the taxi park in front of the market when they are full (US$3 back space, US$6 front, 2½ hours).

To Kep, a single moto trip costs about US$4 (day trip US$6). Tuk-tuks charge US$7 to US$8.

GETTING AROUND
Around town, single moto trips should cost 1000r. To the nearby caves or zoo, bank on about US$6 to US$8 a day. Beware of some moto drivers who try to charge double, triple or whatever they can get away with.

Motorcycles can be hired from **Sean Ly Motorcycle Shop** (☎ 012-944687). Bikes range from small (US$3) to larger trail bikes (US$5). For advice on tracks and riding, contact the manager at the **Orchid Guest House** (☎ 932634; orchidguesthousekampot@yahoo.com), who used to be a dirt-bike racer and has the trophies to prove it.

Around Kampot
TEK CHHOUU FALLS
A set of rapids a short ride from town, this is a pleasant place to cool off and is very popular

CAMBODIA

with locals. A moto here and back will cost US$2.

CAVES

There are three main caves for exploring around Kampot, each one involving a scenic ride through villages and rice paddies. The caves are located about 8km east of Kampot town.

Phnom Sorsia is a winding formation which, once clambered round to the top, provides great views over the countryside.

Phnom Chhnork contains a brick temple inside the cave. It dates back to the 7th century and has bats clinging to the walls, probably because regular fruit offerings are placed inside it by pilgrims. It is almost completely dark in here so bring a torch.

Rung Damrey Sor (White Elephant Cave) is a large cave with a stalactite formation that is supposed to resemble an elephant.

Bokor National Park

This **national park** (admission US$5) came to prominence in the 1920s when the king would ride his elephant up the mountain and survey his kingdom below. Today the national park is wild and untamed. From the entrance at the foot of the mountain the vehicles climb slowly up. The road is in atrocious condition and those sitting in the back of pick-ups must hang tight and duck fast. Bamboo, trees and flying bugs all take a swing at heads.

The once-stable bridge that led to the **Popokvil Falls** has collapsed entirely. Therefore, a little bit of trekking is required to reach them. From the broken bridge it is about an hour's walk. In the wet season, the falls are an impressive gush down a two-tier drop with a very long platform connecting them. In the dry season there is still enough water for a light shower and the platform becomes a nice paddling pool.

Bokor Hill

The enigmatic and spooky hill is a prairie of wildflowers, howling winds and abandoned buildings.

In the mid-1920s the French created a lavish resort consisting of a hotel, casino, water tower, post office, ranger station and Catholic church. Now all that remains are large shells of what used to be; paneless windows, half doors clinging by creaky hinges and scratched-in graffiti. A real ghost town. The French abandoned their resort during Cambodia's surge for independence in the 1940s.

It was abandoned once more in the 1970s when Lon Nol left it to the Khmer Rouge. The Khmer Rouge, appreciating the strategic vantage point it offered, remained, fighting it out with the Vietnamese in the latter part of the decade when they invaded. Bullet holes can be seen pierced through the exterior of the Bokor Hotel and the Catholic church where the two sides battled for months, each shooting at the other from across the fields.

GETTING THERE & AWAY

Many of the guesthouses in Kampot can arrange day trips or overnight stays. A day trip should set you back US$6. Transport is usually a pick-up with an English-speaking guide included.

Experienced bikers can attempt the challenging journey with a guide. A day trip normally costs US$10 to US$12. Overnighters can stay in the ranger station where there are bunk beds for US$5. Guides will charge around US$20 to accompany you and you are expected to pay for their sleeping arrangements.

Although it may be boiling hot when you set off, the mountain receives a lot of rain, even in the dry season, so pack a mac if you don't want to get wet, and a towel if you don't want to stay wet.

Kep

☎ 036 / pop 4200

Kep *(kape)* is a seaside town still harbouring the remnants of civil war. Though the ocean washes peacefully over the curving beach, the ruinous buildings tell a different story. In the late 1960s, this was the ritzy playground to King Sihanouk and friends, but a decade on glamour turned into gore with the Khmer Rouge taking hold with devastating effects. In the late 1970s, the warring parties took it in turn to obliterate the town, the Khmer Rouge doing most of the legwork before the Vietnamese, in their campaign of 'liberation', pushed them aside to finish the job, looting and dismantling whatever was left.

The Kep of today has put that behind it and is slowly becoming the alluring destination it once was. Smart guesthouses with a character of their own have popped up to provide travellers with a calmer alternative to Sihanoukville.

SIGHTS & ACTIVITIES

There is not much to do but chill out in Kep, but it is a good launching pad for the nearby Koh Tonsay and Koh Pos islands. **Koh Tonsay**, meaning 'rabbit island', is supposed to resemble the furry long-toothed animals – which it kind of does, from far away, if you squint and eat happy pizza.

The island is surrounded on all sides by good beaches. There are seven bungalows available for crashing. All are very basic with just a mattress (per night US$5). There is also a restaurant to save you from spearing your own meal.

Meaning 'snake island', **Koh Pos** has white beaches and good coral for snorkelling.

Boats leave from the tourist office, located near the showers on Kep beach. You must also buy the tickets from here: US$15 return to Koh Tonsay or US$25 to incorporate Koh Pos and another small nearby island, Koh Svay.

SLEEPING & EATING

All the lodgings listed have on-site restaurants open to the public, otherwise some of the freshest seafood in the country can be had in the shacks along the waterfront.

ourpick Veranda Natural Resort (☎ 012-888619; www.veranda-resort.com; Mountain Hillside Rd; r US$18-60; 🏊) A maze of tree-top bungalows connected by wooden boardwalks, this stunning resort has an alluring mix of modern luxury combined with the feeling of being immersed with nature.

Beach House (☎ 012-240090; www.TheBeachHouseKep.com; f US$30-45; 🏊 🖥) A family-orientated hotel that is ideal for large groups, with spacious family-sized rooms. It has a pool and the ocean is straight across the road.

Knai Bang Chatt (☎ 012-349742; www.knaibangchatt.com; r US$350, villas US$750-2200; 🏊) Serious style comes in the form of four modern villas on this private resort. The once-dilapidated ruins have been transformed into a vision of chic architecture and design. The infinity pool, the breathtaking views and the 'wait on hand and foot' staff all reek of luxury and exclusivity. Book well in advance.

GETTING THERE & AWAY

Most people come to Kep from Kampot as it is an easy 24km away. Catch a moto from Kampot for US$4 or do it in a day trip for US$6.

Onwards to Takeo via Kompong Trach, charter taxis can be hired for US$20. Add a little more if you plan to spend some time exploring the Kompong Trach caves (below). Or charter a car, also for US$20.

Kompong Trach

Kompong Trach is an uneventful town between Kep and Phnom Penh and Kep and Takeo. The only reason to stop here is to visit the **Cave of a Thousand Rice Fields**.

This is a difficult-to-reach sight that requires the aid of a guide. From the top of Phnom Kompong Trach, locally known as **Phnom Baikh** (Breaking Mountain) – because every so often a piece breaks off – there is an old ladder that descends into the cave and ultimately to the formations, so named because they resemble the terraced rice paddies of Asia.

Also in Phnom Baikh are a series of caves that lead from the modern Wat Kirisan. Following them around you will come across another shrine and then be led through the hill to the other side, where **Phnom Sor** (White Mountain) and a small lake can be seen.

Children on their breaks from school wait to play guides; they speak good-enough English and are very nimble – so keep up! They ask for small donations.

GETTING THERE & AWAY

From Kep a chartered car can take you to Phnom Penh or Takeo with a stopover in Kompong Trach for around US$20, depending on how long they have to wait.

Bikers can take the NH31 from the south or the scenic NH3.

TAKEO PROVINCE

Takeo (ta-kow) is a district of many lakes and artificial canals dating all the way back to the Funan empire, or the 'Cradle of Khmer Civilisation'. An attractive, sleepy province of swimming buffaloes and more lily pads than a frog could ever dream of, it is also home to some archaeological treasures: Tonlé Bati, Phnom Chisor, Phnom Da and Angkor Borei.

Takeo

☎ 032 / pop 40,950

Apart from the huge **Boeng Takeo** lake and the still handsome colonial buildings, there is not much to see, and as most of the province's sights can be seen in a day trip from the capital, there's no real reason to stay here.

CAMBODIA

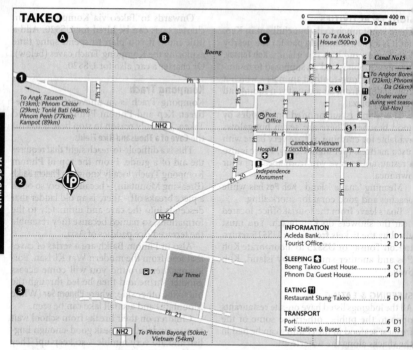

TAKEO

0 — 400 m
0 — 0.2 miles

Boeng

To Ta Mok's
House (500m)

Canal No 15

To Angk Tasaom
(13km); Phnom Chisor
(29km); Tonlé Bati (46km);
Phnom Penh (77km);
Kampot (89km)

To Angkor Borei
(22km); Phnom
Da (26km)

Under water
during wet season
(Jul-Nov)

Post
Office

Hospital

Cambodia-Vietnam
Friendship Monument

Independence
Monument

Psar Thmei

To Phnom Bayong (50km);
Vietnam (54km)

INFORMATION	
Acleda Bank.................................1 D1	
Tourist Office..............................2 D1	
SLEEPING	
Boeng Takeo Guest House............3 C1	
Phnom Da Guest House................4 D1	
EATING	
Restaurant Stung Takeo................5 D1	
TRANSPORT	
Port..6 D1	
Taxi Station & Buses....................7 B3	

There are the usual market money changers, though nowhere to cash travellers cheques. See **Acleda Bank** (☎ 931246) for money transfers. Most likely you won't catch anyone at the **tourist office** (⊗ 7am-5pm) until after 2pm.

For sleeping, **Phnom Da Guest House** (☎ 016-957639; Village 1, Roka Commune; r US$5-10; ❄) is unimaginatively decorated, but has spotless rooms run by an eccentric Khmer family. What **Boeng Takeo Guest House** (☎ 931306; Ph 3-4, Doun Keo District; r US$5-10; ❄) lacks in atmosphere it gains in views; the enormous lake, smothered by water lilies, is directly opposite and always magnificent no matter the season.

At **Stung Takeo Restaurant** (☎ 016-957897; Ph 9; mains 3000-6000r; ⊗ breakfast, lunch & dinner) the drinks are warm, but hey so are the smiles. Perennially popular and built on stilts to survive annual floods, this is the best place to pack in a Cambodian meal while watching lakeside life move slowly by.

Takeo is relatively close to Phnom Penh on the good NH2. Buses leave from Psar Thmei in Phnom Penh and take two hours (5500r). Share taxis are about US$2 for a squishy seat.

Travellers heading to Kampot need to take a moto to Angkor Tasaom and then jump in a share taxi southbound.

Around Takeo
ANGKOR BOREI & PHNOM DA

Thirty scenic minutes by boat in the wet season from Takeo city is the riverside town of Angkor Borei; the once walled-in capital of the pre-Angkorian Chenla civilisation. Artefacts from this period and the Funan era are showcased at the town's small **Chenla museum** (admission $1). Further on, the laterite temple of Phnom Da can be seen perched atop a hill overlooking the often-flooded rice fields that stretch for miles beyond.

KOH KONG PROVINCE

Koh Kong, the untamed province bordering Thailand, is like a rough-cut jewel shimmering in the country's southwest. Wonderful and lustrously wild, the Cardamom Mountains loom over pristine forests on one side, while on the other Robinson Crusoe islands float off the coast like a turtle's back.

CROSSING INTO VIETNAM: PHNOM DEN TO TINH BIEN

This seldom-used crossing is useful if you are already down south. From Takeo catch a share taxi to travel the 60km to Phnom Den (around US$2). Once there just walk across the border to Tinh Bien. From there motos and taxis can take you to Chau Doc where you can continue straight on to HCMC. For information on crossing this border in the other direction, see the boxed text, p424.

Krong Koh Kong

☎ 035 / pop 30,975

Krong Koh Kong is linked to Thailand by a super bridge. Most people zoom over it and out of the city before getting to know that it is a laid-back town full of friendly locals. Casinos dominate the border line and are popular with gambling Thais. The town itself provides a carefree base from which to explore the wilds of Koh Kong.

INFORMATION

Despite what some scammers may tell you at the border, dollars and riel are as readily accepted as baht. Cash can be changed easily at the market. Phone calls can be made from kiosks about town and internet is available at Otto's guesthouse (p248). There is a tourist office near the boat dock but your guesthouse will be more informative.

Acleda Bank (☎ 936693) Representing Western Union for transfers; does not cash travellers cheques.

SIGHTS & ACTIVITIES
Waterfalls

There are some great waterfalls in the region. Sometimes they are completely isolated so you have them entirely to yourself. The most impressive are Kbal Chhay Prek Koh waterfall and the Tatai Waterfalls.

Kbal Chhay Prek Koh, or the Kbal Chhay Kor Poi, as it is sometimes called, is a set of falls that runs over a series of boulders. Situated up a river estuary, this is the most popular with visitors and is only 15 minutes from town.

Tatai Waterfalls is the most spectacular. Surrounded on each side by thick jungle, the water runs off smooth rocks, plunging into a series of pools, some as small as a Jacuzzi and others large enough to do laps.

A moto out here will cost around 400B, the journey taking about an hour. Even if you have your own wheels, you will need a guide as it is difficult to find with no signposts.

Koh Kong Krau

Koh Kong's coast is littered with islands; nearly all of them are completely deserted. The largest is Koh Kong Krau (meaning 'Outside Koh Kong'), a heart-stopping boat ride over turquoise waters and you arrive like the soul survivor of a shipwreck. Kilometres of sandy beaches, fringed with coconut palms and a gently surging ocean, it has the melancholy feeling of a forgotten paradise. For now, it is an exquisitely isolated place to come for a picnic and a swim or to sling your hammock and camp, but there is talk of development on the island and soon the seclusion will be shattered. Enjoy it while you can.

To get here, charter a boat from the jetty (12,000B, one hour). You can incorporate other little islands and a trip through the mangroves along the way.

Mangroves

Around the islands of Koh Kapi and Koh Kong Krau, dense mangroves protrude from the water in long thick lines, forming spectacular corridors of gnarled trees and watery trails that are perfect for boat expeditions. The mangrove forests are nesting sites for hundreds of bird species, crabs and molluscs.

For a thrilling ride through the mangroves, charter a boat from the jetty. A trip out here and back should cost US$20.

SLEEPING

Asean Hotel (☎ 936667; www.aseanhotel.vze.com; r US$10-20; ❄) Unfortunately, views of the river have been blocked from the front rooms by the new Koh Kong City Hotel, but those at the back look out to the stunning palm-fringed lily pond, so ask for one of those. All rooms

---

RUN OUT OF CASH?

There are no ATMs in Koh Kong, but an agreement with border control and the big casinos allows quick crossings, sans visa, for withdrawals from the Thailand-side cash machines, probably arranged so that Thai gamblers need not worry about running out of money to lose.

CAMBODIA

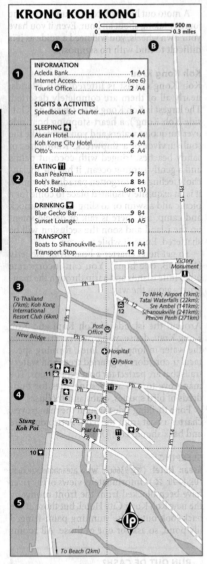

KRONG KOH KONG

0   500 m
0   0.3 miles

INFORMATION
Acleda Bank..............................1 A4
Internet Access....................(see 6)
Tourist Office..........................2 A4

SIGHTS & ACTIVITIES
Speedboats for Charter.............3 A4

SLEEPING
Asean Hotel.............................4 A4
Koh Kong City Hotel................5 A4
Otto's......................................6 A4

EATING
Baan Peakmai...........................7 B4
Bob's Bar.................................8 B4
Food Stalls...........................(see 11)

DRINKING
Blue Gecko Bar........................9 B4
Sunset Lounge........................10 A5

TRANSPORT
Boats to Sihanoukville............11 A4
Transport Stop.......................12 B3

Victory Monument

To Thailand (7km); Koh Kong International Resort Club (6km)

To NH4; Airport (1km); Tatai Waterfalls (22km); Sre Ambel (141km); Sihanoukville (241km); Phnom Penh (271km)

Post Office
New Bridge
Hospital
Police

Stung Koh Poi
Psar Leu

To Beach (2km)

---

little more, and there is a good restaurant attached.

Koh Kong City Hotel (☎ 012-901902; kkct hotel@netkhmer.com; r US$15-30; ❄) Having pinched the views from the Asean, it seems they may have nicked the designer too; the hotels look identical. The big difference is that the Koh Kong City Hotel's Thai and Khmer restaurant sits on stilts above the river and the Asean's doesn't.

Koh Kong International Resort Club (☎ 016-700970; www.kohkonginter.com; r US$25-100; ❄) A sprawling tropical resort and casino, catering to mostly Thai gamblers, it also owns Koh Kong Safari World, an entertainment complex featuring performing orang-utans, crocodiles and dolphins. Not everyone's cup of tea.

EATING & DRINKING

Sunset Lounge (☎ 012-1724909; ⏰ 24hr) A striking bar that creeps all the way out into the river, drinks here can be enjoyed literally above water. The views are undeniably stunning and this is the best place to come for frank and funny travel advice.

Blue Gecko Bar (☎ 016-388075; mains 40-220B; ⏰ breakfast, lunch & dinner) A laid-back, Aussie-run bar, the Blue Gecko serves Western comfort food and also offers some basic lodgings for 150B a room. You can shoot some pool here, too.

Baan Peakmai (☎ 011-788711; mains 60-350B; ⏰ breakfast, lunch & dinner) A nice bit of greenery surrounds this wooden pavilion restaurant. It's Thai, but dishes out some American-style fillings also.

Bob's Bar (☎ 016-326455; mains 70-170B; ⏰ breakfast, lunch & dinner) An easy-going hang-out, Bob's has a foreign menu featuring all-day breakfast, a well-stocked bar and a pool table.

---

are of a great standard, and the staff here are exemplary.

Otto's (☎ 936163; r 100-150B; 🖵) The award for most adorable accommodation goes to Otto's. Like staying in the cubby house that dad built, the rooms are set in a raised traditional house and surrounded by palm trees. Bathroom is shared unless you pitch in a

GETTING THERE & AWAY

Between Phnom Penh and Koh Kong (six to eight hours) is a dusty bounce-fest with occasional moments of pure paved magic. Prepare for a long and arduous journey encompassing four ferry crossings and some breathtaking scenery of rich jungles and dipping valleys. Bridges across the river crossings are were being built and should have been completed by the end of 2007 or start of 2008. This should cut travel time considerably.

The most experienced of riders can attempt the challenging route through the Cardamom Mountains from either Pailin or Veal Veng. An untamed region of remote jungle, the route involves steep inclines, thick jungle, bamboo groves and horrendous ox tracks: dirt-bike enthusiasts will love it.

Share taxis to Koh Kong, normally banged-up minivans, leave Phnom Penh's Psar Dang Kor in the mornings. Afternoon rides will be harder to find due to the distance involved. A cramped seat will cost US$5 or you can charter a whole taxi for around US$20 to US$25. Heading the other way (Koh Kong to Phnom Penh), minibuses leave from the taxi stand north of the creek on Ph 3, just before you reach Ph 12.

The most popular way out of Koh Kong is the fast boat to Sihanoukville. Tickets are US$15 and the journey is a hair-raising, stomach-lurching four hours. Unless you want your valuables saturated in salt water, have the handlers place them inside instead of piled on the roof. Boats leave daily from the dock at 8am.

GETTING AROUND

The fact that Koh Kong is large and vast should be taken into consideration when bartering for transport prices. Chartering a

---

CROSSING INTO THAILAND: CHAM YEAM TO HAT LEK

From Krong Koh Kong, you need to cross the toll bridge (11B for a bike; 44B for a car) to reach Cham Yeam (10 minutes). Take a moto (80B to 100B including toll) or charter a taxi (200B including toll). Once there walk across the border to Hat Lek where there are minibuses and pick-ups waiting on the other side for easy transfers on to Trat or Ko Chang. For information on crossing this border in the other direction, see the boxed text, p158.

---

moto for a whole day of sightseeing, taking in the waterfalls, beaches and city should set you back US$15.

Chartered boats can take you to the islands and costs US$30 to US$40 depending on the size of the boat and how long you wish to spend there.

Your guesthouse can usually organise a bicycle for you to rent (US$2 to US$3 a day).

CAMBODIA DIRECTORY

ACCOMMODATION

Accommodation in rural areas is limited to guesthouses and the further you go the less likely it is you'll have the luxuries of hot or running water or 24-hour electricity.

Guesthouses range from US$2 with shared bathrooms to US$15. Hotels are plentiful and great deals can be had at the midrange and budget places. You will often get attached bathroom, hot water, TV and air-con from as little as US$10.

All rooms reviewed in this chapter have attached bathrooms unless stated otherwise.

ACTIVITIES

Tourism is definitely finding its feet in Cambodia and there is now a wide range of activities. Diving and snorkelling are available off the south coast of Sihanoukville and Kep, with boat trips offered anywhere there is a river.

Dirt biking is very popular; novices can hook up with dirt-bike tour groups such as **Hidden Cambodia Dirt Bike Tours** (www.hiddencambodia.com).

Elephant treks are a novel way to see the eastern provinces of Mondulkiri and Ratanakiri.

BOOKS

Lonely Planet's *Cambodia* is packed with information for extended travel in the country, with wider coverage to help get you off the beaten track. See also the boxed text, p251.

BUSINESS HOURS

Government offices, which are open from Monday to Saturday, theoretically begin the working day at 7.30am, break for a siesta from 11.30am to 2pm, and end the day at 5pm. However, it is a safe bet that few people will be around early in the morning or after 4pm, as their real income is earned elsewhere.

PRACTICALITIES

- The usual voltage is 220V, 50 cycles, but power surges and power cuts are common, particularly in the provinces. Electrical sockets are usually two-prong, flat or round pin.
- Most guesthouses and hotels have cheap laundry services, but check they have a dryer if the weather is bad. There are laundry shops in every town.
- Newspapers to read are *Cambodia Daily* and *Phnom Penh Post*. Magazines include *Bayon Pearnik* and *Cambodia Scene*.
- BBC World Service broadcasts on 100MHz FM. Cambodian radio and TV stations are mainly government-controlled and specialise in karaoke videos and soap operas.
- Cambodians use the metric system for everything except precious metals and gems for which they prefer the Chinese system.

Banking hours vary slightly according to the bank, but most banks keep core hours of 8.30am to 3.30pm Monday to Friday, plus Saturday morning. Tourist attractions such as museums are normally open seven days a week.

Local restaurants are generally open from about 6.30am until 9pm and international restaurants until a little later. Many bars are open all day, but some open only for the night shift, especially if they don't serve food.

Local markets operate seven days a week and usually open and close with the sun, running from 6.30am to 5.30pm. Shops tend to open from about 7am until 7pm, sometimes later.

COURSES

Unfortunately, there aren't any real courses on offer for foreigners. However, travellers can learn the art of Khmer cooking in Battambang with Smokin' Pot (p218) and Siem Reap with ACCB's 'A Day in the Life of Tour' (p208).

CUSTOMS

If Cambodia has customs allowances, it is close-lipped about them. A 'reasonable amount' of duty-free items are allowed into the country. Like any other country, Cambodia does not allow travellers to import weapons, explosives or narcotics – some would say there is enough in the country already. It is illegal to take ancient stone sculptures from the Angkor period out of the country.

DANGERS & ANNOYANCES
Mines, Mortars & Bombs

Never, ever touch any artillery shells or other war material. Cambodia is one of the most heavily mined countries in the world especially in the northern and western regions. Do not stray from well-marked paths under any circumstances.

Theft & Street Crime

Cambodia is now a generally safe place to travel in as long as you exercise common sense. Hold-ups are rare, though petty theft is still rampant in the major cities. Walking or riding alone late at night is strongly advised against, particularly for unaccompanied women.

Stash your cash and passport in a padlocked bag in your hotel room and only carry as much as you think is needed each day.

EMBASSIES & CONSULATES
Embassies & Consulates in Cambodia

The following embassies are found in Phnom Penh:

Australia & Canada (Map p194; ☎ 023-213470; 11 Ph 254)

China (Map pp190–1; ☎ 023-7209920; 156 Mao Tse Toung Blvd)

France (Map pp190–1; ☎ 023-430020; 1 Monivong Blvd)

Germany (Map p194; ☎ 023-216381; 76-78 Ph 214)

Indonesia (Map p194; ☎ 023-217934; 1 Ph 466)

Laos (Map pp190–1; ☎ 023-982632; 15-17 Mao Tse Toung Blvd)

Malaysia (Map p194; ☎ 023-216177; 5 Ph 242)

Myanmar (Map pp190–1; ☎ 023-223761; 181 Norodom Blvd)

Philippines (Map p194; ☎ 023-215145; 33 Ph 294)

Singapore (Map p194; ☎ 023-221875; 92 Norodom Blvd)

Thailand (Map pp190–1; ☎ 023-726306; 196 Norodom Blvd)

UK (Map pp190–1; ☎ 023-427124; 27 Ph 240)

USA (Map p194; ☎ 023-728000; 1 Ph 96)
Vietnam (Map pp190-1; ☎ 023-362531; 436 Monivong Blvd)

There's also a handy Vietnamese consulate in Sihanoukville (p238).

Cambodian Embassies & Consulates Abroad

Australia (☎ 02-6273 1259; 5 Canterbury Cres, Deakin, ACT 2600)
France (☎ 01 45 03 47 20; 4 rue Adolphe Yvon, 75116 Paris)
Germany (☎ 030-48 63 79 01; Arnold Zweing Strasse, 1013189 Berlin)
Japan (☎ 03-5412 8521; 8-6-9 Akasaka, Minato-ku, Tokyo 1070052)
USA (☎ 202-726 7742; 4500 16th St NW, Washington, DC 20011)

For information on Cambodian visas, see p255.

FESTIVALS & EVENTS

Cambodians love a good knees-up and festivals are celebrated with fervour. Dates change according to the lunar calendar.

Chinese New Year Chinese and Khmers alike celebrate in January or early to mid-February with dragon dances, lit lanterns and feasts.

Chaul Chnam A three-day celebration of Khmer New Year, held in mid-April. People file into wats with offerings and prayers for luck and absolutions.

Visakha Puja Celebrated collectively as Buddha's birth, enlightenment and *parinibbana* (passing in nirvana), this festival falls in May or June on the eighth day of the fourth moon and is best observed at Angkor Wat, where you can see candle-lit processions of monks.

P'chum Ben Like a subdued 'Day of the Dead' festival as celebrated in Mexico. Respects and offerings are made at the wats in mid-September and early October.

Bon Om Tuk Celebrates the reversal of the Tonlé Sap river. Boat races take place in early November all over the country and the cities all resemble London's Oxford St during pre-Christmas sales.

FOOD & DRINK

With the Tonlé Sap lake producing tonnes of fish every year, it's not surprising that fish (along with rice) forms the foundations of Cambodia's distinctive and flavoursome diet.

The national dish, *amok*, is almost as synonymous with Cambodia as Angkor Wat. It is fish baked with coconut and lemongrass wrapped in banana leaves. Served piping hot, peeling back the leaves is like unwrapping a gift.

Prahoc is a fermented fish paste with a smell that could make fertiliser step up its game. The salty paste is used to flavour most dishes, with coconut and lemongrass making regular cameos. *Sait ko che-kuh* (barbecued beef skewers) are a favoured snack, a blend of beef infused with lemongrass, sugar and salt, grilled over hot flames and served with pickled salads of papaya and cucumber.

CAMBODIA IN WORDS

■ *Angkor – Heart of an Asian Empire* (1993) The emphasis in this book is more on the discovery and restoration of the ruins of Angkor, but it is lavishly illustrated and dripping with interesting asides. It's a pocket-sized guide by Bruno Dagens.

■ *First They Killed My Father* (2001) A personal memoir of a nation's suffering, in which Luong Ung covers the steady destruction of her family through execution and disease during the time of Democratic Kampuchea. One of best of many survivor accounts.

■ *The Gate* (2003) Francois Bizot was kidnapped by the Khmer Rouge, interrogated by Comrade Duch and is believed to be the only foreigner to have survived this experience. Later he was holed up in the French embassy in April 1975 and became the negotiator between the foreigners inside and the Khmer Rouge outside. This is his harrowing story.

■ *The History of Cambodia* (1994) For the fuller flavour of Cambodian history, from the humble beginnings in the prehistoric period through the glories of Angkor and up to the present day, read David Chandler's account.

■ *When the War Was Over* (1986) Only a few foreigners were allowed to visit Cambodia during the Khmer Rouge period of Democratic Kampuchea. US journalist Elizabeth Becker travelled there in late 1978 and tells the story of her visit in the context of the Cambodian civil war.

The *samlor* (soup) is the cornerstone of nearly every meal. Khmers will either drown their rice with it as the main accompaniment or dribble it sparingly just to flavour. A delicious example is *ko-ko*, a thick broth of chunky cat fish, infused with lemongrass, spices, aubergine and pumpkin.

Try a hearty bowl of *nom banj-chuk*, superfine rice noodles smothered in topping. *Nom banj-chuk curee* is especially wholesome when the noodles are covered by a curry of braised beef or chicken, potatoes, and crowned with a pile of shredded beans and cucumber.

The desserts are particularly divine and like everything else, rice based. The *krolan* is a bamboo flute packed with sticky rice that has been merged together with coconut and black-eyed beans and then set upon hot coals to bake.

Drinking is very popular with Khmers. Generally, rural folk drink palm wine, tapped from the sugar palms that dot the country's landscape. In the city the beers of choice are Angkor and Tiger. Mekong Whiskey is gaining popularity and making its way into shot glasses; it tastes like rice wine. Do not drink tap water or drinks containing ice made from tap water. Bottled water that has gone through a treatment process is the way to go at only 1000r a bottle. Better still, filter your own.

The *tukaluks* (fruit smoothies) are also great thirst quenchers. They are mixed with milk, sugar and sometimes a raw egg. You should also try *tuk-empeau* (sugar cane juice).

For more on dining in the Mekong region, see p86.

GAY & LESBIAN TRAVELLERS

Cambodia is a very tolerant country when it comes to sexual orientation. The scene is slowly coming alive in the major cities. But do keep in mind that this is a conservative country and displays of affection are deemed offensive. **Utopia** (www.utopia-asia.com) features gay travel information and contacts.

HOLIDAYS

Everyone shuts down for public holidays, so plan ahead during these times. Holidays may be rolled over if they fall on a weekend, and some people take a day or two extra during major festivals.

International New Year's Day 1 January
Victory over the Genocide 7 January
International Women's Day 8 March

International Workers' Day 1 May
International Children's Day 1 June
Constitution Day 24 September
Paris Peace Accords 23 October
HM the King's Birthday 30 October to 1 November
Independence Day 9 November
International Human Rights Day 10 December

INSURANCE

Make sure your insurance policy covers emergency evacuation. Limited facilities may mean you have to be airlifted to Bangkok, which will result in hefty bills.

INTERNET ACCESS

Internet access has spread throughout much of Cambodia. Charges range from 2000r per hour in major cities to US$4 an hour in the smaller provincial capitals.

INTERNET RESOURCES

http://andybrouwer.co.uk A great gateway to all things Cambodian, it includes comprehensive links to other sites and regular Cambodian travel articles.

http://angkor.com When it comes to links, this site has them, spreading its cyber-tentacles into all sorts of interesting areas.

www.earthwalkers.no/kft.htm Fun online Khmer tutorial with helpful pictures and phonetics. A great introduction to the language.

www.lonelyplanet.com Summaries on travelling to Cambodia, the Thorn Tree bulletin board and travel news.

www.mrpumpy.net The definitive website for cyclists passing through Cambodia, it's written with candour and humour.

www.talesofasia.com Up-to-the-minute road conditions and other overland Cambodian travel information.

LEGAL MATTERS

All narcotics, including marijuana, are illegal in Cambodia. However, marijuana is traditionally used in food preparation so you may find it sprinkled across a pizza or two.

Paedophilia is a heinous crime and any serious suspicions should be reported immediately to ChildSafe (see opposite). Many Western countries have also enacted much-needed legislation to make offences committed overseas punishable at home.

MAPS

This guidebook has most of the maps you'll need, but if an additional map is required the best all-rounder is Gecko's *Cambodia Road Map* at 1:750,000 scale. In this book, the maps indicate streets as 'Ph', abbreviated from the Khmer word for street *Phlauv*.

MONEY

Cambodia's currency is the riel, abbreviated here by a lower-case r written after the sum. The riel comes in notes with the following values: 50r, 100r, 200r, 500r, 1000r, 2000r, 5000r, 10,000r, 20,000r, 50,000r and 100,000r.

Throughout this chapter, each establishment's prices are in the currency quoted to the average punter. This is usually depicted in US dollars or in riel, but in the west of the region it is often in Thai baht. Currency exchange rates at the time this book went to press:

Country	Unit	Riel
Australia	A$1	3152
Canada	C$1	3453
China	Y1	520
euro zone	€1	5263
Japan	¥100	3352
Laos	10,000 kip	4194
New Zealand	NZ$1	2992
Thailand	10B	1216
UK	UK£1	7984
USA	US$1	4075
Vietnam	10,000d	2539

ATMs

There are now credit-card-compatible ATMs in most major cities (Visa and MasterCard only).

Bargaining

Bargaining is expected when shopping in markets, hiring vehicles and sometimes when taking a room. Hagglers will normally start at triple the price they expect you to pay in the end. So start your bargaining at a third of the initial quote and see how you go. See right for appropriate bargaining etiquette.

Cash

Come armed with loads of cash when travelling overland as there are no ATMs in the border cities. Dollars are accepted everywhere, so do not believe the border touts' claims that you have to change your cash into riel. There are no coins so riel is often used for small change, while dollars are used for larger amounts. The cities bordering Thailand will often quote in baht and therefore a triple currency system is used. Dollars, riel and baht can be changed in

nearly every city at the markets. Those with cash in another major currency can change it in Phnom Penh and Siem Reap.

Credit Cards

Cash advances on credit cards are now available in Phnom Penh, Siem Reap, Sihanoukville, Kampot, Battambang and Kompong Cham. ANZ Royal and Canadia Bank offer the best service with free MasterCard and Visa cash advances.

Travellers Cheques

Travellers cheques aren't much use in Cambodia. Outside the major cities it is difficult to change them. Most banks charge a commission of 2% to cash travellers cheques; you'll be given US dollars, not riel. Some hotels and travel agents will also cash travellers cheques after banking hours.

PHOTOGRAPHY & VIDEO

Film and processing are cheap in Cambodia. A roll of 36 exposures costs about US$2. Processing charges are around US$4 for 36 standard prints. Cheap slide film is widely available in Phnom Penh and Siem Reap, but elsewhere it's hard to find. Many internet cafés in Phnom Penh, Siem Reap, Battambang and Sihanoukville will burn CDs from digital images using card readers or USB connections. The price is about US$2.50 if you need a CD or US$1.50 if you don't.

POST

Post office staff in Cambodia are notorious for pinching packages. Make sure that all of your items are franked before they disappear.

Don't send mail from the provinces, it is best to wait until you get to the big cities. Postcards cost 1500r to 2100r, and a 10g airmail letter 2000r to 2500r. International mail normally takes two to three weeks.

Phnom Penh's main post office has a poste restante service. Although it now checks identification, don't have anything valuable sent there. It costs 200r per item received.

RESPONSIBLE TRAVEL

Cambodia continues to experience unprecedented growth in tourism and this inevitably brings the bad along with the good. Your goal is a simple one: minimise the negatives and maximise the positives. There are simple things like bringing a water filter or tablets to treat tap water instead of buying bottled water, thus minimising the growing problem of plastic waste.

If you witness suspicious behaviour of tourists with Cambodian children, it's your duty to report it. Child exploitation and sexual abuse is now rightly taken very seriously here. Report any suspicions to the **ChildSafe Hotline** (☎ 012-296609). When booking into a hotel or jumping on transport, look out for the Child-Safe **logo** (ChildSafe; www.childsafe-cambodia.org). Each establishment or driver who shows this logo supports the end to child-sex tourism and has undergone child-protection training.

When bargaining for goods or transport, remember the aim is not to get the lowest possible price, but one that's acceptable to both you and the seller. Coming on too strong or arguing over a few hundred riel does nothing to foster Cambodians' positive feelings towards travellers.

Cambodia is an extremely poor country and begging is prevalent in Phnom Penh and Siem Reap. Try not to become numb to the pleas as there's no social security network and no government support. Amputees may also find themselves stigmatised by mainstream society and unable to make ends meet any other way. If you do give, keep the denominations small, so expectations don't grow too big. Many amputees now sell books on the street and buying from them may encourage others to become more self-sufficient. Please don't give money to children as they rarely get to keep the money and it only propagates the problem – giving them some food is preferable.

Looting from Cambodia's ancient temples has been a huge problem. Don't contribute to this cultural rape by buying old stone carvings. Classy reproductions are available in Phnom Penh and Siem Reap, complete with export certificates.

Finally, don't forget what the Cambodians have been through in the protracted years of war, genocide and famine. Support local Cambodian-owned businesses; if anyone deserves to profit from the new-found interest in this wonderful country, it's surely the long-suffering Khmers.

SHOPPING

The shopping here is centred on handicrafts and handmade goods: woven baskets, wood and stone carvings, silver, gems and paintings are among the most popular items to bargain for.

A packed bag heading for home would not be complete without the *krama*, the chequered scarf of a thousand uses. Khmers wear these on every part of the body. They are hand woven to exceptional quality with the best coming from Kompong Cham and Takeo Provinces.

Check out the Shopping sections for Phnom Penh (p199) and Siem Reap (p207) for information on buying craft items produced by Cambodian mine victims and disabled and women's groups.

TELEPHONE & FAX

Private phone booths are found in every city and offer cheap local calls for about 300r a minute. They normally have the numbers 012, 092 or 063 written on them. The cheapest international calls are made on internet phones in cafés and cost 300r to 2000r. International calls (from US$2 a minute) can be made from public phone-card booths, which are found in major cities. Their cards can generally be purchased at the local markets and the post office.

The cheapest fax services are also via the internet and cost around US$1 to US$2 per page for most destinations.

TOILETS

Apart from at road stops and in far-flung places, most toilets are of the Western variety, though some do indicate that you should not flush toilet paper by the telltale waste paper basket on the side; most of Cambodia's plumbing system just can't cope. It is advisable to carry a good stash of your own toilet paper with you at all times.

TOURIST INFORMATION

For the independent traveller, guesthouses, locals and other travellers are a much better source of information than the country's official tourist offices, many of which are either unstaffed or simply useless. Their opening hours are generally 7am to 11am and 2pm to 5pm.

TOURS

Now that ecotourism has begun to take off, there are many interesting community-based tours on offer in the various regions of the country.

The national parks usually have guided tours available, particularly at Bokor, Kirirom and Virachay.

For a grand tour of the country's highlights contact the brilliant **Hands Up Holidays** (www .handsupholidays.com). Promoting ethical holidays to Southeast Asia, it formulates adventure breaks that incorporate activities in AIDS orphanages and deaf and blind schools.

PEPY (Protect the Earth, Protect Yourself; ☎ 023-222804; www.pepyride.org) is a not-for-profit organisation that organises cycling tours to Cambodia's hotspots as well as some of the less explored destinations. Proceeds go towards the building of schools, developing literacy programmes and providing bikes for students who need better access to distant schools. They also run 'voluntours'; noncycling tours for travellers who want to muck in with community initiatives in rural areas.

TRAVELLERS WITH DISABILITIES

Cambodia is not designed for people with mobility impairments. There are very few buildings with elevators and most sidewalks and roads are riddled with potholes. The temples at Angkor Wat are normally accessed via steep steps or crumbling boulders. Transport wise, chartering is the way to go and is a fairly affordable option. Also affordable is hired help if you require it and Khmers are generally very helpful should you need a hand.

VISAS

Visas (US$20) are available on arrival at Phnom Penh and Siem Reap airports and all land border crossings except at the Phnom Den–Tinh Bien Vietnam crossing (see the boxed text, p219, for information about scams.) The visa is a sticker, and it does not cost extra to get this or a stamp, despite what the border police tell you. If you're planning an extended stay, get a one-month business visa for US$25.

Visa extensions are granted in Phnom Penh and Sihanoukville at the tourist and immigration offices. Tourist visas can be extended only once for a month (US$48), whereas business visas can be extended ad infinitum. Extensions cost: one month US$48; three months US$78; six months US$150; and one year US$250. You'll need one passport photo for the extension and you have until three days after the expiry date to extend.

Overstayers are charged US$5 per day at the point of exit.

Visa extensions cannot be granted outside of Cambodia, regardless of what touts tell you at the border.

VOLUNTEERING

Grass-roots organisations are the most appreciative of volunteers. Try the ones below.

Bodhi Villa In Kampot, volunteers can have a go at teaching English or arts to the kids. Contact Bodhi Villa (p242).

DMS Angkor Villa Guest House Arranges voluntary teaching at a community school. In Siem Reap (p205).

Lazy Gecko Café (Map p194; ☎ 012-1912935; 23B Ph 930) In Phnom Penh, contact this café to see how you can help with Jeannie's Orphanage.

Starfish Project (www.starfishcambodia.org) Encourages volunteers, helping to raise funds for local projects. In Sihanoukville.

Check out these websites, which also offer a range of opportunities:

www.volunteerabroad.com Has 53 programmes in Cambodia.

www.volunteerincambodia.org Organises voluntary teaching posts.

WOMEN TRAVELLERS

Women will generally find Cambodia quite a safe country to travel in, though solo females are advised to find a companion when heading to the more remote locations. If you do fall victim to a serious crime such as sexual assault, contact the Women's Rights office of **LICADHO** (☎ 023-330965; contact@licadho.org), where staff speak English and French and will be able to assist you. It has offices in all the major cities.

Khmer women dress fairly conservatively, and it's best to follow suit, particularly when visiting wats. In general, long-sleeved shirts and long trousers or skirts are preferred.

Tampons and sanitary napkins are widely available in major cities and provincial capitals, as is the contraceptive pill.

WORK

Job opportunities are limited. Normally, professional foreigners are recruited overseas. The easiest option is teaching English in Phnom Penh, as experience isn't a prerequisite at the smaller schools. Pay ranges from about US$5 to US$6 per hour (for the inexperienced) to about US$15 to US$20 per hour for those with a TEFL certificate teaching at the better schools.

TRANSPORT IN CAMBODIA

GETTING THERE & AWAY
Air

Cambodia is connected by regular air services to its Southeast Asian neighbours. Prices are always subject to change so contact airline offices for fares.

Bangkok Airways (www.bangkokair.com) Phnom Penh (Map p194; ☎ 023-722545; 61 Ph 214); Siem Reap (Map pp210-11; ☎ 063-380191; NH6) Links Bangkok with both Phnom Penh and Siem Reap.

China Southern Airlines (Map pp190-1; ☎ 023-424588; www.cs-air.com/en/; 168 Ph Monireth A3)

Dragonair (Map pp190-1; ☎ 023-424300; www.dragonair.com; 168 Ph Monireth A4)

Jet Star Asia (www.jetstarasia.com) Phnom Penh (☎ 023-220909; 333B Ph Monivong); Siem Reap (Map pp210-11; ☎ 063-964388; Siem Reap Airport) Offers the cheapest daily flights between Bangkok and Phnom Penh.

Lao Airlines (www.laos-airlines.com) Phnom Penh (Map p194; ☎ 023-216563; 58c Sihanouk Blvd); Siem Reap (Map pp210-11; ☎ 063-963283; www.laos-airlines.com; NH6) Flights to Vientiane.

Malaysia Airlines (www.malaysia-airlines.com) Phnom Penh (Map p194; ☎ 023-218293; Diamond Hotel, 172 Monivong Blvd); Siem Reap (Map pp210-11; ☎ 063-964136; Siem Reap Airport) Daily flights connecting Phnom Penh and Kuala Lumpur.

President Airlines (Map p194; ☎ 023-210388; www.presidentairlines.com; 50 Norodom Blvd)

Siem Reap Airways (www.siemreapairways.com) Phnom Penh (Map p194; ☎ 023-720022; 65 Ph 214); Siem Reap (Map pp210-11; ☎ 063-380191; NH6)

SilkAir (Map pp190-1; ☎ 023-426808; www.silkair.com; 219B Himawari Hotel, 313 Sisowath Quay) Daily flights to Singapore from Phnom Penh and Siem Reap.

Thai Airways (Map pp190-1; ☎ 023-214359; www.thaiair.com; 294 Ph Mao Tse Tuong) Links Bangkok with Phnom Penh.

Vietnam Airlines (www.vietnamairlines.com) Phnom Penh (Map p194; ☎ 023-363396; 41 Ph 214); Siem Reap (Map pp210-11; ☎ 063-964488; NH6) Links Phnom Penh with Vientiane, Ho Chi Minh City and Hanoi. Its daily services also fly from Siem Reap to Ho Chi Minh City and Hanoi.

Border Crossings

Cambodia shares border crossings with Thailand, Vietnam and Laos. For more details on border crossings in the region, see p99. There are now as many as six border crossings with Thailand, but only two are popular with travellers. The 30-day Thai transit visas are available at all border crossings.

There are three border crossings with Vietnam. The crossing from Bavet to Moc Bai links Phnom Penh with Ho Chi Minh City. The Phnom Den to Tinh Bien crossing is not as popular. Vietnamese visas are not available at the border crossings.

There is one border crossing with Laos, from Dom Kralor to Voen Kham, which connects Stung Treng and Si Phan Don. Lao visas are *not* available at this crossing.

OVERCHARGING

Unfortunately, overcharging for visas and nonexistent 'entry/exit fees' is rampant in Cambodia. These 'fees' can be anything from US$1 to 200B. Ask for a receipt with the amount written on it and their name, then make an official complaint to the **Ministry of Tourism** (info@mot.gov.kh), which is trying to clamp down on this behaviour.

GETTING AROUND
Boat

Boats are an interesting way to break up the monotonous road journeys.

The most popular options are the boats between Battambang and Siem Reap and Koh Kong and Sihanoukville. Both of these cost US$15. There is also a boat service running up the Mekong from Kompong Cham to Kratie and in the wet season to Stung Treng.

For short crossings and cruises, a *tonnook* is usually the way to go. These are small motor-powered boats, often made of wood. A ride in one of these costs anywhere from 1000r a passenger to US$15 a boat.

Bus

There are loads of buses travelling great distances with the improvement of roads in the country. Buses to nearly all destinations depart from Psar Thmei in Phnom Penh with reasonable prices. Buses to far-reaching destinations will normally drop off and pick up people along the way.

The biggest companies are Hour Lean and Phnom Penh Sorya Transport. See the individual destination sections for bus links, journey times and prices. Prices range from 4500r for a short trip to US$15 for long hauls.

Car & Motorcycle

With the roads the way they are, self-drive is probably not the best idea. If you do go for this option, guesthouses and hotels can arrange hire cars for you. They cost anywhere from US$20 to US$100 depending on the make and the distance you wish to travel.

Dirt-bike enthusiasts will enjoy Cambodia's challenging roads. Motorcycles (100cc) can be hired for around US$5 a day in the towns, 250cc bikes for around US$7. The big cities have the better deals with some offering bikes for as little as US$3 a day. Siem Reap does not allow foreigners to ride their own motorcycles.

Local Transport

CYCLO & TUK-TUK

The cyclo (pedicab) is a rare sight these days, it has been replaced with the motorised version – the tuk-tuk. They are a relaxing way to get around the city, but perhaps too slow for venturing further. Cyclos cost the same as motos (tip generously as they work hard!) and whatever you pay for them, double it for a tuk-tuk.

MOTO

Motos or motodups (motorcycle plus driver) are the easiest way to travel short distances in Cambodia. A short trip around town usually costs 1000r, double at night. Longer journeys around a municipality cost about a dollar, but trips to other towns will need to be negotiated. It helps if you have a map, often motos don't know where they are going. Settle on a price before you leave to avoid an argument at the end. Chartering a moto for the day costs around US$7 to US$10, more if a greater distance is involved.

REMORQUE MOTO

These trailers pulled by motos are found in the provinces. They are normally wooden carts used for transporting villagers and their goods and are a fun way to get about. They cost the same as a moto.

SHARE TAXI, PICK-UP & MINIBUS

With so many roads in Cambodia still bathing in dust and decorated with potholes, it falls on the smaller vehicles to get you from one place to the next. Share taxis are fastest and usually take the form of a Toyota Camry sedan. There are four seats in this car, but it's considered an eight-passenger vehicle, so unless you are double-jointed (everywhere) or the size of a Hollywood starlet with an eating disorder, buy two spaces for a bearable journey. Minibuses are much the same; they appear to be world-record attempts to see how many people can squeeze into one vehicle.

Pick-ups are an initiation. You haven't travelled in Cambodia until you experience the white-knuckle ride in the back of a beat-up Nissan zooming through the countryside. You are usually required to pile in with half the community and all their possessions, until you loom high above the cabin. Drivers then nonchalantly fly over bumps, and swerve around ditches to reach their destination; not surprisingly, many who have experienced this form of transport claim to have found religion along the way.

Train

When it comes to trains, don't bother. At the time of writing, all official passenger services were suspended, because there were simply not enough train travellers. You can try hitching a ride with a cargo carrier, but their schedules are unreliable and the journeys impossibly slow.

Laos

CHRISTOPHER GROENHOUT

Laos

Laos is different to its neighbours. Where Vietnam and China are intense and entrepreneurial, Laos is the essence of laid-back *c'est la vie*. Where Thailand sweeps away the past in its pursuit of modernity, Laos continues to function from its stock of French-era buildings and ancient Buddhist wat.

For travellers, Laos' apparently serene way of life is a tonic for the soul. It's Southeast Asia's most relaxing destination, somewhere to shift down the gears while at the same time soaking up a heady mix of culture and ecology that's fast disappearing elsewhere.

In both the mountainous north and the dramatic karsts, rivers and plateaus of the south, Laos has a growing reputation for eco- and cultural tourism. These take advantage of vast swathes of pristine wilderness, hundreds of relatively untouched villages populated by scores of ethnic groups and the omnipotent Mekong River that ties it all together. Indeed, getting off the beaten track here is both eminently possible and thoroughly encouraged.

In between is Vientiane, arguably the most laid-back capital on earth with, dollar for dollar, some of its best dining. In Vientiane you'll see the modern face of Laos, where a new urban elite drinks cocktails, races motorbikes and identifies more with Bangkok than Luang Prabang. This, however, is the exception. The rule is just down the road, where subsistence village living is little different from what it was centuries ago.

HIGHLIGHTS

- Decide for yourself whether Unesco-listed **Luang Prabang** (p290) is the most beautiful town in Southeast Asia.

- Meet ethnic villagers and soak up the scenery as you trek through the **Nam Ha NPA** (p311)

- Take a boat through the natural phenomenon that is **Tham Kong Lo** (p316), the astonishing 7km-long limestone cave

- Get thee to **Wat Phu Champasak** (p328) at dawn to feel the mystery and beauty of these Khmer-era temple ruins

- Experience the 'real Laos' – and spend some money where it's needed most – by staying with a family in a village **homestay** (p335)

★ Nam Ha NPA

★ Luang Prabang

Tham Kong Lo ★

Wat Phu Champasak ★

FAST FACTS

▪ **Area** 236,000 sq km

▪ **Capital** Vientiane

▪ **Country Code** ☎ 856

▪ **Population** 5.6 million

▪ **Money** US$1 = 9600 kip

▪ **Seasons** high Dec-Feb & Jul-Aug; dry Nov-Apr, wet May-Oct

▪ **Phrases** *sabqi-dji* (hello), *sábqi-dĭi* (goodbye), *khàwp jqi* (thank you)

HISTORY

From the early Khmer influence around Wat Phu in southern Laos right up to the present day, the peoples living in what we know as Laos have mainly been reacting to the politics and aspirations of more powerful neighbours in Cambodia, Vietnam, Thailand and China. Even its first taste of nationhood, with the rise of the Lan Xang kingdom, was achieved thanks to Khmer military muscle.

Kingdom of Lan Xang

The kingdom of Lan Xang emerged in the mid-14th century when Khmer-backed Lao warlord Fa Ngum conquered Wieng Chan (Vientiane), Xieng Khuang, a chunk of north-eastern Thailand (which is still mainly ethnically Lao), Muang Sawa (Luang Prabang) and eastwards to Champa and the Annamite Mountains.

It was Fa Ngum who gave his kingdom the title still favoured by travel romantics and businesses – Lan Xang, or (Land of a) Million Elephants. He also made Theravada Buddhism the state religion and adopted the symbol of Lao sovereignty that remains in use today, the Pha Bang Buddha image, after which Luang Prabang is named.

Lan Xang waxed and waned under other kings (commemorated today in street names such as Samsenthai and Setthathirat), reaching its peak in the 17th century when it was briefly the dominant force in Southeast Asia. By the 18th century, Lan Xang had crumbled, falling under the control of the Siamese, who coveted much of modern-day Laos as a buffer zone against the expansionist French. Any hope of a restoration of Lao power was savagely crushed in 1827, when the Siamese put down a rebellion led by Lao prince Chao Anou by razing Vientiane to the ground and carting off most of the population.

The French

Soon after taking over Annam and Tonkin (modern-day Vietnam), the French used a mix of sweet talk and gunboat diplomacy to bully Siam into relinquishing all territory east of the Mekong, and Laos was born. France had a fairly dim view of Laos' usefulness and did virtually nothing for the country, except permit opium production to flourish and allow its colonial administrators to become renowned for their 'lotus-eating' lifestyle.

Laos' diverse ethnic make-up and short history as a nation-state meant nationalism was slow to form. The first nationalist movement, the Lao Issara (Free Lao), was created to prevent the country's return to French rule after the invading Japanese left at the end of WWII. The French did come back but departed for good in 1953. Full sovereignty was followed by 20 years of chaos as Laos became a shadowy stage on which the clash of communist ambition and American anxiety over the perceived Southeast Asian 'domino effect' played itself out. Multiple parties with multiple agendas eventually settled into two factions: the communist Pathet Lao supported by the North Vietnamese, Chinese and Soviets, and the right-wing elite backed by the US government, which saw Laos rather disproportionately as the crucial Southeast Asian 'domino'.

War & Revolution

From the early 1960s until 1973 Laos became the theatre for the 'Secret War'. This was a conflict no-one acknowledged but which saw the North Vietnamese funnel massive amounts of war materiel down the Ho Chi Minh Trail in eastern Laos, while the US responded with the largest bombing campaign in history. Despite this, the Pathet Lao and the North Vietnamese slowly won over more of the country, both militarily and through their socialist ideas. The US withdrawal in 1973 saw Laos divided up between Pathet Lao and non–Pathet Lao, but within two years the communists had taken over and the Lao People's Democratic Republic (PDR) was created under the leadership of Kaysone Phomvihan.

Around 10% of Laos' population fled, mostly into Thailand. The remaining opponents of

LAOS

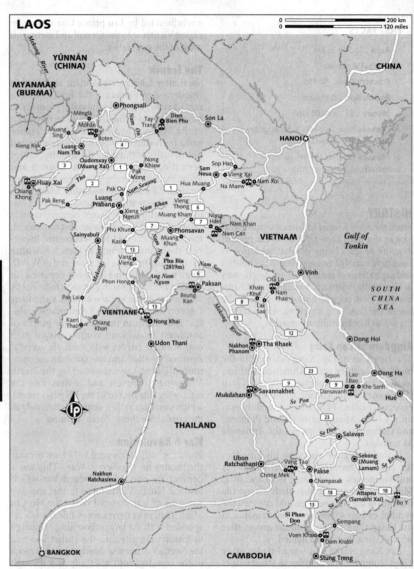

the government – notably tribes of Hmong (highland dwellers) who had fought with and been funded by the Central Intelligence Agency (CIA) – were suppressed, often brutally.

The Lao government quickly recognised the shortcomings of the socialist experiment and since the 1980s socialism has been softened to allow for private enterprise and foreign investment, if not political dissent. Laos entered Asean (Association of Southeast Asian Nations) in 1997, two years after Vietnam.

Laos Today

In 2004 the USA promoted Laos to Normal Trade Relations, cementing the end to a trade embargo in place since 1975. As has been the case since the French arrived, Laos continues to rely on foreign aid to run its economy, though the source of this 'aid' is changing as China commits ever more money to development – mostly for the end benefit of Chinese firms. The rush to increase its capacity to earn foreign exchange has seen Laos agree to a disturbing number of hydroelectric dam projects; expect to hear more about these in coming years.

Politically, the Party remains firmly in control. And with patrons like one-party China and Vietnam, there seems little incentive for Laos to move towards any meaningful form of democracy. The 30-year-long Hmong 'insurgency' seems on its last legs, with thousands of starving, stunted people emerging from the forest in recent years to face a very uncertain future.

PEOPLE & THE POPULATION

The people of Laos hail from dozens of ethnic groups, many of which are also found elsewhere in the region (see Culture, p71). However, the predominant group is the Lao Loum (lowland Lao), and it's their cultural beliefs and way of life that are known as 'Lao culture'.

On the surface at least, nothing seems to faze the Lao and, especially if you're arriving from neighbouring China or Vietnam, the contrasting national psyche is both enchanting and beguiling. *Baw pen nyǎng* (no problem) could be the national motto. Of course, it's not as simple as 'people just smiling all the time because they're happy', as we heard one traveller describe it. The Lao national character is a complex combination of culture, environment and religion.

To a large degree, 'Lao-ness' is defined by Buddhism, specifically Theravada Buddhism, which emphasises the cooling of the human passions. Thus strong emotions are a taboo in Lao society. *Kamma* (karma), more than devotion, prayer or hard work, is believed to determine one's lot in life, so the Lao tend not to get too worked up over the future. It's a trait often perceived by outsiders as a lack of ambition.

Education is not as highly valued as in the West, and avoiding any undue psychological

---

FEELING THE 'REAL LAOS'

A lot of travellers come looking for the 'real Laos', but few know exactly what that is. For about 80% of the population the 'real Laos' is village life, and the best way to really get a feel for how the Lao live is to spend a night or two in a homestay.

A homestay is, as the name suggests, staying with a family in their home, sleeping, eating and living just as they do. So what can you expect? The details vary from place to place, depending on ethnicity, geography and wealth, but the usual experience is described below.

Villages are small, full of kids and, depending on the season, dusty or muddy. You'll be billeted with a family, usually with a maximum of two travellers per family. Toilets will be the squat variety, with scoop flush, in a dark hut at the corner of the block. You'll bathe before dinner, either in a nearby stream or river, or by using a scoop to pour water over yourself from a well, 44-gallon (170L) drum or concrete reservoir in your family's yard. Bathing is usually a public event, hence the sarong. Don't expect a mirror.

Food will be simple fare, usually two dishes and sticky rice. In our experience it's almost always been delicious, but prepare yourself for a sticky rice extravaganza – during a five-day circuit through homestays in southern Laos we ate sticky rice 14 meals out of 15. Even if the food doesn't appeal, you should eat something or your host will lose face. Dinner is usually served on mats on the floor, so prepare to sit lotus-style or with legs tucked under. Don't sit on cushions as that's bad form, and always take off your shoes before entering the house.

Sleeping will probably be under a mosquito net on a mattress on the floor, and might change to 'waking' once the cocks start crowing outside your window.

It might not be luxury but homestay is very much the 'real Laos' and is a thoroughly worthwhile and enjoyable experience. Just remember that for most villagers dealing with *falang* (tourists) is pretty new and they are sensitive to your reactions. Their enthusiasm will remain as long as their guests engage with them and accept them, and their lifestyle, without undue criticism. To get the most out of it, take a phrasebook and photos of your family, and don't forget a torch, flip-flops, a sarong and toilet paper.

stress remains a cultural norm. From the typical Lao perspective, unless an activity – whether work or play – contains an element of *múan* (fun), it will probably lead to stress.

The communist era has had a marked effect on the national consciousness. The government has been at pains to encourage national pride and a 'Lao' identity, despite the fact that more than 30% of the country is made up of non-Lao-speaking non-Buddhist hill tribes with little connection to traditional Lao culture. Government education also ensured that knowledge of the outside world was very limited, though Thai TV is changing that.

Men dominate Lao public life, but you do not have to be in the country long to see who is really running the show. All over Laos you'll see women staffing offices and running businesses. However, they're still expected to organise the family and run the home – often while the husband drinks the ubiquitous *lào láo* (Lao liquor, or rice whisky) with his friends.

In many ways Lao culture is very similar to Thai culture, though more conservative because it's had less exposure to Western influence. Cultural mores are similar (see the Dos & Don'ts boxed text, below), they share many of the same superstitions, and belief in ghosts is almost universal. However, the Lao government goes to great lengths to keep the 'corrupting' influences of modern Thai life at bay, most notably in a strict (superficially, at least) approach to things such as late-night drinking and prostitution.

RELIGION

Most lowland Lao are Theravada Buddhists and many Lao males choose to be ordained temporarily as monks, typically spending any-where from a month to three years at a wat After the 1975 communist victory, Buddhism was suppressed. But it wasn't long before i was back in full swing, with a few alterations Monks are still forbidden to promote *ph* (spirit) worship, which has been officially banned in Laos along with *sâiyasaat* (folk magic).

Despite the ban, *phî* worship remains the dominant non-Buddhist belief system. Ever in Vientiane, Lao citizens openly perform the ceremony called *sukhwǎn* or *bạasîi*, in which the 32 *khwǎn* (guardian spirits of the body) are bound to the guest of honour by white strings tied around the wrists.

Outside the Mekong River Valley, the *ph* cult is particularly strong among tribal Thai but also many other groups. *Mâw* (priests) who are trained to appease and exorcise troublesome spirits preside at important Thai Dam festivals and other ceremonies. The Khamu and Hmong-Mien tribes also practise animism; the latter group combining it with ancestral worship.

ARTS

Lao art and architecture is mostly religious in nature. Distinctively Lao is the Calling for Rain Buddha, a standing image with a rocketlike shape and hands held rigidly at his sides, fingers pointing towards the ground. Wat in Luang Prabang feature *sǐm* (chapels), with steep, low roofs. The typical Lao *thâat* (stupa) is a four-sided, curvilinear, spirelike structure.

Traditional Lao art has a more limited range than its Southeast Asian neighbours, partly because Laos has a more modest history as a nation-state and partly because successive occupiers from China, Vietnam, Thailand, Myanmar (Burma) and France have stolen or burnt it.

Upland crafts include gold- and silver-smithing among the Hmong and Mien tribes, and tribal Thai weaving (especially among the Thai Dam and Thai Lü). Classical music and dance have been all but lost in Laos, although performances are occasionally held in Luang Prabang and Vientiane.

Foot-tapping traditional folk music, usually featuring the *khaen* (Lao panpipe), is still quite popular and inspires many modern Lao tunes. Increasingly, though, soppy heartbreak Thai pop and its Lao imitations are the music of choice.

DOS & DON'TS IN LAOS

- Always ask permission before taking photos.
- Don't prop your feet on chairs or tables while sitting.
- Never touch any part of someone else's body with your foot.
- Refrain from touching people on the head.
- Remove your shoes before entering homes or temple buildings.

ECOTOURISM IN LAOS *Steven Schipani*

With forests covering about half of the country, 20 National Protected Areas (NPAs), 49 ethnic groups, more than 650 types of birds and hundreds of mammals, it's no mystery why Laos is known as having Southeast Asia's healthiest ecosystems and is a haven for travellers looking to get off the beaten path. Nowadays there are many tour companies and local tour guides offering forest trekking, cave exploration, village homestays and river journeys where the roads don't go.

Following the success of the Nam Ha Ecotourism Project in Luang Nam Tha Province, which began in 1999, the Lao Government is actively promoting ecotourism as one way to help reduce poverty and support the protection of the environment and local culture. It is estimated that culture- and nature-based tourism generates more than half of the country's US$150 million in annual tourism revenue.

The Lao National Tourism Administration defines ecotourism as 'Tourism activity in rural and protected areas that minimizes negative impacts and is directed towards the conservation of natural and cultural resources, rural socioeconomic development and visitor understanding of, and appreciation for, the places they are visiting.'

Unfortunately, some uninformed companies label everything 'ecotourism'. Therefore it is important to determine who is the real deal and who is simply greening their pockets. Ask tour operators the following questions to ensure you are on the right track:

- Does my trip financially benefit local people, help to protect biodiversity and support the continuation of traditional culture?

- What will I learn on this trip, and what opportunities will local people have to learn from me?

- Are facilities designed in local style? Do they use local, natural construction materials, and conserve energy and water? Is there local food on the menu?

- Will I be led by a local guide from the area visited?

- Is there a permit, entrance fee or other fee included in the price that is directed towards conservation activities?

- Are there sensible limits in place concerning group size and the frequency of departures to minimize negative impacts?

Supporting businesses that can give clear, positive and believable answers to these questions will most likely result in an enjoyable, educational experience, where you make more than a few local friends along the way. It also raises the profile of sustainable business operators, hopefully encouraging others to follow their example.

www.ecotourismlaos.com

ENVIRONMENT

Laos consists of 236,800 sq km of rugged geography and small population. The sum is the least changed environment in Southeast Asia. Unmanaged vegetation covers about 75% of the country, with 25% of this primary forest.

It's a heady mix in a region that has been so badly savaged for short-term profit, and it's pleasing to report that the Lao government is paying attention to the tourism dollars such rare, pristine environments attract (see the boxed text, above). It's not, however, all safe.

Laos has an impressive 20 National Protected Areas (NPAs) comprising about 14% of the country. But several issues threaten these areas and, more immediately, areas that are not protected. Illegal timber felling, the smuggling of exotic wildlife and a rush to build giant hydroelectric dams – more than 20 are planned or being built – are the main threats.

Laos is rich in wildlife, with wild elephants, jackals, bears, leopards, tigers, deer and the Irrawaddy dolphin among the best known. However, with no full national parks – areas without any human habitation – and hunting still an important source of protein for many Lao families, actually seeing these species isn't easy. Irrawaddy dolphins are the most seriously endangered of Laos' creatures. Their habitat is concentrated in the southern Mekong particularly around Si Phan Don, where you have the best chance of sighting them. There are believed to be fewer than 100 left in the Mekong, so see them soon or, possibly, not at all.

VIENTIANE

☎ 021 / pop 300,000

As Laos opens up to the world, Vientiane is growing, but it can still mount a strong case for being the most relaxed capital city on earth. The combination of tree-lined boulevards and dozens of temples contribute to an atmosphere of timelessness, while the kaleidoscopic architectural styles reflect its historic influences: from classic Lao through Thai, Chinese, French, US and Soviet.

Today it's the stage for the subtle yet dramatic struggle between Laos' communist past and inevitably more capitalist future. You can dance to live music with trendy Lao youth, but the lyrics might have been censored. Or take in the fading glories of the revolution in the Lao National Museum, then pop across the street to another new restaurant in what is becoming one of the best-value eating cities on earth.

Vientiane isn't full of must-see sights, but the 6400 Buddha images at Wat Si Saket, the lotus-inspired lines of Pha That Luang and Patuxai are all worth a look, while the surreal Xieng Khuan (Buddha Park) is, like the city itself, not short of appeal.

HISTORY

Vientiane means Sandalwood City, and is actually pronounced Wieng Chan (the French are responsible for the modern transliteration). Vientiane's peaceful demeanour belies a history in which it's been occupied, looted, razed to the ground and eventually rebuilt by successive Vietnamese, Burmese, Siamese and French conquerors.

The Siamese invasion of 1828, in response to an attack by upstart Lao king Anouvong (Chao Anou), saw virtually every building destroyed. The French rebuilt much of Vientiane when they made it the capital of their protectorate in the early 20th century. During the 1960s and early '70s Vientiane became a den of spies on the front line of the Cold War. It was so debauched that Paul Theroux described it, in his 1975 book *The Great Railway Bazaar*, as a place in which 'The brothels are cleaner than the hotels, marijuana is cheaper

than pipe tobacco and opium easier to find than a cold glass of beer'.

The Pathet Lao soon put an end to that and Vientiane was pretty dull during the 1980s and much of the '90s. Today icons of capitalism – such as multistorey shopping malls and plush hotels – signal its move into the 21st century.

ORIENTATION

The three main streets parallel to the Mekong – Th Fa Ngum, Th Setthathirat and Th Samsenthai – are the central inner city of Vientiane and are where most of the guesthouses, hotels, restaurants and bars are located. Nam Phu is the best inner-city landmark if you're catching a taxi or túk-túk into town. Heading northeast from Th Setthathirat is the wide boulevard of Th Lan Xang, where you'll find the Talat Sao (Morning Market) and Patuxai. Heading further north from Patuxai is Th That Luang, which is home to a number of foreign embassies and is crowned by the magnificent golden Pha That Luang, Laos' most distinctive structure.

INFORMATION

BOOKSHOPS

Kosila Bookshop 1 (Map p272; ☎ 020-224 0964; Th Chanta Khumman; ☉ 9am-5pm)

Monument Books (Map p272; ☎ 243708; 124 Th Nokeo Khumman; ☉ 9am-8pm Mon-Fri, 9am-6pm Sat & Sun) Big range of books on Asia, plus maps, magazines and postcards.

Vientiane Book Center (Map p272; ☎ 212031; laobook@hotmail.com; Th Pangkham; ☉ 8.30am-5.30pm Mon-Fri, 9am-4.30pm Sat)

CULTURAL CENTRES

Centre Culturel et de Coopération Linguistique (Map p272; ☎ 215764; www.ambafrance-laos .org/centre; Th Lan Xang; ☉ 9.30am-6.30pm Mon-Fri, 9.30am-noon Sat) The 'French Centre' has a busy schedule of movies, musical and theatrical performances, a library, French and Lao language classes and a popular café.

GETTING INTO TOWN

Wattay International Airport is about 4km northwest of the city centre. Taxis cost an extortionate US$5 into town. Many passengers simply walk about 500m to the airport gate, where you can get a túk-túk for about US$2, once you've bargained.

EMERGENCY
Ambulance (☎ 195)
Fire (☎ 190)
Police (☎ 191)
Tourist police (Map p272; ☎ 251128; Th Lan Xang)

INTERNET ACCESS
There are several places on Th Setthathirat between Nam Phu and Th Nokeo Khumman, and on Th Nokeo Khumman itself. Rates range from US$0.60 to US$1.20 an hour. Most have international telephone facilities for about US$0.20 a minute.

PlaNet Online (Map p272; Th Setthathirat; ☾ 8.30am-11pm) Sells prepaid internet cards (US$5/10/20) for dial-up access.
Society Internet (Map p272; Th Samsenthai; ☾ 9am-9pm)
Star-Net Internet (Map p272; Th Nokeo Khumman; ☾ 7.30am-11pm)

MEDIA
The government-run *Vientiane Times* (US$0.40) cleaves largely to the party line in its six editions a week. The What's On page and bus-fare table are handy. French speakers should look for the weekly *Le Rénovateur*. The *Bangkok Post, Economist, Newsweek* and *Time* can also be found in minimarts and bookshops.

MEDICAL SERVICES
Vientiane's medical facilities will do for broken bones, tropical diseases and the like, but for anything more serious get thee to Thailand and **Aek Udon International Hospital** (☎ 0066-42-342555; www.aekudon.com), which can dispatch an ambulance to take you to Udon Thani.

In Vientiane try the following:
Australian Embassy Clinic (Map pp268-9; ☎ 413603; ☾ 9am-5pm Mon-Fri) For nationals of Australia, Britain, Canada, PNG and NZ only. This clinic's Australian doctor treats minor problems by appointment; it doesn't have emergency facilities.
International Clinic (Map pp268-9; ☎ 214021/2; Th Fa Ngum; ☾ 24hr) Part of the Mahasot Hospital; probably the best place for not-too-complex emergencies. Some English-speaking doctors.

MONEY
Several banks in Vientiane change cash and travellers cheques and do cash advances against credit cards for a commission. BCEL has an international ATM, but given you can only withdraw about US$70 worth of kip at a time, it's often cheaper to get a cash advance manually.

Licensed moneychanging booths can be found in Talat Sao, among other places, and the unofficial moneychangers near Talat Sao have particularly good rates and keep longish hours.

BCEL (Map p272; ☎ 213200; cnr Th Pangkham & Th Fa Ngum; ☾ 8.30am-7pm Mon-Fri, 8.30am-3pm Sat & Sun) Best rates. Longest hours. Exchange booth on Th Fa Ngum and ATM attached to the main building.
Joint Development Bank (Map p272; ☎ 213535; 75/1-5 Th Lan Xang) Usually charges the lowest commission on cash advances. Also has an ATM.
Siam Commercial Bank (Map p272; ☎ 227306; 117 Th Lan Xang)

POST
Post, Telephone & Telegraph (PTT; Map p272; cnr Th Lan Xang & Th Khu Vieng; ☾ 8am-5pm Mon-Fri, 8am-noon Sat & Sun) Come here for post restante.

TELEPHONE
Lao Telecom Numphu Centre (Map p272; ☎ 214470; Th Setthathirat; ☾ 9am-7pm) International fax and calls for US$0.20 a minute, or US$0.10 for domestic calls.

TOURIST INFORMATION
Lao National Tourism Authority (NTAL; Map p272; ☎ 212251; www.tourismlaos.com, www.ecotourismlaos.com; Th Lan Xang; ☾ 8.30am-4.30pm) Well worth a visit for its descriptions of provincial attractions, helpful English-speaking staff, brochures and regional maps (US$1). Staff can arrange trips to Phu Khao Khuay NPA (p285) for no charge.

TRAVEL AGENCIES
Central Vientiane has plenty of agencies that can book tours, air tickets and in some cases Thai train tickets, including the following:
A-Rasa Tours (Map p272; ☎ 213633; www.laos-info.com; Th Setthathirat; ☾ 8.30am-5pm Mon-Sat) Happy to answer questions; runs some tours.
Green Discovery (Map p272; ☎ 251564, 223022; www.greendiscoverylaos.com; Th Setthathirat) Large range of tours offered as well as normal travel-agent services. Good reputation.

Dangers & Annoyances
Vientiane has a very low crime rate, but readers' reports and local anecdotes suggest petty crime is rising. Be especially careful around the BCEL Bank on the riverfront where bag-snatchers, usually a two-man team with a motorbike, have been known to strike; commonsense should be an adequate defence. Violent crime is rare.

LAOS

VIENTIANE

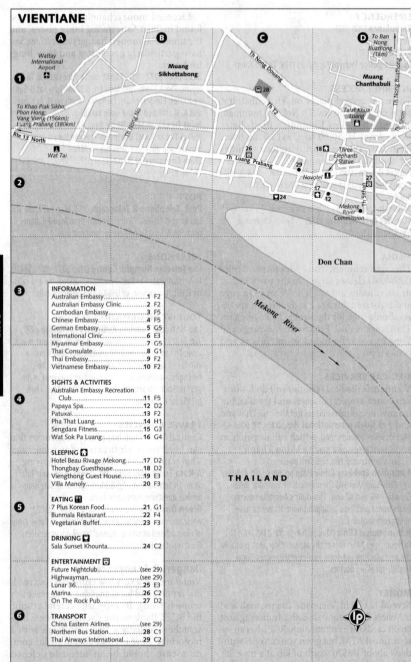

INFORMATION

Australian Embassy	**1** F2
Australian Embassy Clinic	**2** F2
Cambodian Embassy	**3** F5
Chinese Embassy	**4** F5
German Embassy	**5** G5
International Clinic	**6** E3
Myanmar Embassy	**7** G5
Thai Consulate	**8** G1
Thai Embassy	**9** F2
Vietnamese Embassy	**10** F2

SIGHTS & ACTIVITIES

Australian Embassy Recreation Club	**11** F5
Papaya Spa	**12** D2
Patuxai	**13** F2
Pha That Luang	**14** H1
Sengdara Fitness	**15** G3
Wat Sok Pa Luang	**16** G4

SLEEPING

Hotel Beau Rivage Mekong	**17** D2
Thongbay Guesthouse	**18** D2
Viengthong Guest House	**19** E3
Villa Manoly	**20** F3

EATING

7 Plus Korean Food	**21** G1
Bunmala Restaurant	**22** F4
Vegetarian Buffet	**23** F3

DRINKING

Sala Sunset Khounta	**24** C2

ENTERTAINMENT

Future Nightclub	(see 29)
Highwayman	(see 29)
Lunar 36	**25** E3
Marina	**26** C2
On The Rock Pub	**27** D2

TRANSPORT

China Eastern Airlines	(see 29)
Northern Bus Station	**28** C1
Thai Airways International	**29** C2

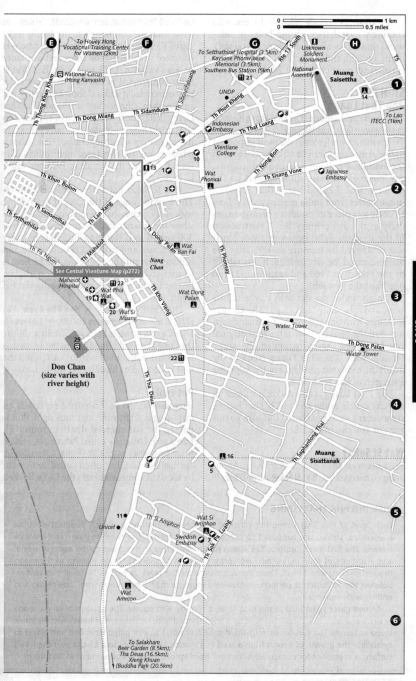

Annoyances include túk-túk drivers, who routinely overcharge; gaping holes in sidewalks that can swallow you whole as you walk home at night; and the fact that most bars and restaurants must close at 11.30pm.

SIGHTS
Pha That Luang
Tall, svelte and golden, **Pha That Luang** (Great Sacred Reliquary or Great Stupa; Map pp268-9; admission US$0.20; 8am-noon & 1-4pm Tue-Sun) is the most important national monument in Laos, a symbol of both the Buddhist religion and Lao sovereignty. An image of the main stupa appears on the national seal. Legend has it that Ashokan missionaries from India erected a *thâat* here to enclose a piece of Buddha's breastbone as early as the 3rd century BC. Construction of the modern *thâat* began in 1566, but it was destroyed by treasure seekers after the Siamese razed the city in 1828. It was rebuilt by the French in 1900 and again in 1931 (no one liked the first job).

A high-walled cloister with tiny windows surrounds the 45m-high stupa. The cloister measures 85m on each side and contains various Buddha images. Two of the four original wat buildings that surrounded the stupa remain, with Wat That Luang Neua to the north the monastic residence of the Supreme Patriarch of Lao Buddhism.

Pha That Luang is about 4km northeast of the city centre at the end of Th That Luang. It's a decent walk, but shared túk-túks go this way, or you can hire a bike.

Wat Si Saket
Built between 1819 and 1824 by King Anouvong (Chao Anou), **Wat Si Saket** (Map p272; cnr Th Lan Xang & Th Setthathirat; admission US$0.50; 8am-noo. & 1-4pm) was the only temple to survive the sack ing of Vientiane in 1828. Chao Anou, who wa. educated in the Bangkok court and was mor or less a vassal of the Siamese state, had Wat S Saket constructed in the early Bangkok style but surrounded it with a cloister similar to – bu smaller than – the one that surrounds Pha Tha Luang (left). The stylistic similarity to their ow wats might have motivated the Siamese to spare this monastery when they crushed Chao Anou': rebellion, even as they razed many others. The French restored the temple in 1924 and again in 1930.

Wat Si Saket has several unique features. The interior walls of the cloister are riddled with small niches that contain more than 200C silver and ceramic Buddha images. More than 300 seated and standing Buddhas of varying age, size and material (wood, stone and bronze) rest on shelves below the niches. A Khmer-style Naga Buddha is also on display brought from a Khmer site at nearby Hat Sai Fong.

Diagonally opposite is **Haw Pha Kaew** (Map p272; Th Setthathirat; admission US$0.50; 8am-noon & 1-4pm), a royal temple built specifically to house the famed Emerald Buddha, but today used as a national museum of religious art; it has the best collection of Buddha images in Laos.

Patuxai
Vientiane's Arc de Triomphe replica is an imposing if slightly incongruous sight, dominating the commercial district around Th Lan Xang. Officially called **Patuxai** (Map pp268-9; Th Lan Xang; admission US$0.30; 8am-4.30pm Mon-Fri, 8am-5pm Sat & Sun), but often called *anusawali* by locals, it commemorates the Lao who died

---

VIEWING PHA THAT LUANG

Each level of Pha That Luang has different architectural features in which Buddhist doctrine is encoded; visitors are supposed to contemplate the meaning of these features as they walk around. The first level supports 323 *siimáa* (ordination stones). It represents the material world, and also features four arched *hǎw wái* (prayer halls) with short stairways leading to them and beyond to the second level. There are 288 *siimáa* on this level, as well as 30 small stupas symbolising the 30 Buddhist perfections (*páalamíi sǎam-síp thâat*), beginning with alms-giving and ending with equanimity.

Arched gates again lead to the next level, a 30m by 30m square. The tall central stupa, made of brick and stucco, is supported here by a bowl-shaped base reminiscent of India's first Buddhist stupa at Sanchi. The curvilinear, four-sided spire resembles an elongated lotus bud and is said to symbolise the growth of a lotus from a seed in a muddy lake bottom to a bloom over the lake's surface, a metaphor for human advancement from ignorance to enlightenment in Buddhism.

in prerevolutionary wars. It was built in 1969 with cement donated by the USA for the construction of an airport; hence it's sometimes called 'the vertical runway'. A stairway leads through two levels stuffed with souvenir T-shirts (seriously, there are thousands) to the top, from where the views are grand. Outside, the park is home to musical fountains that draw families and street vendors most nights.

Lao National Museum

Housed in a well-worn French administrative building built in the 1920s, the **Lao National Museum** (Map p272; ☎ 212461; Th Samsenthai; admission US$1; ⏰ 8am-noon & 1-4pm) was formerly known as the Lao Revolutionary Museum and much of the collection retains an unmistakable revolutionary zeal. Artefacts and photos document the Pathet Lao's lengthy struggle for power, and there's enough historic weaponry to arm all the extras in a Rambo film. None of the exhibits is breathtaking, but the newer rooms emphasising cultural influences, traditional musical instruments, Khmer sandstone sculptures, and historical periods that have nothing to do with the communist victory make an interesting contrast with the 'revolution' rooms. Most exhibits are labelled with at least some English.

Xieng Khuan (Buddha Park)

In a grassy field by the Mekong River, 25km southeast of Vientiane, **Xieng Khuan** (Buddha Park or Suan Phut; admission US$0.50, camera US$0.50; ⏰ 8am-4.30pm, sometimes longer), as the name suggests, is a park full of Buddhist and Hindu sculptures, a monument to one eccentric man's bizarre ambition. Xieng Khuan (which means Spirit City) was designed and built in 1958 by Luang Pu (Venerable Grandfather) Bunleua Sulilat, a yogi-priest-shaman who merged Hindu and Buddhist philosophy, mythology and iconography into a cryptic whole. The concrete sculptures include statues of Shiva, Vishnu, Arjuna, Avalokiteshvara, Buddha and a host of other figures, all supposedly cast by unskilled artists under Luang Pu's direction.

Bus 14 (US$0.40, one hour, 24km) leaves the Talat Sao bus station every 15 or 20 minutes throughout the day and goes all the way to Xieng Khuan. Alternatively, charter a túk-túk (about US$10 return, depending on your bargaining skills) or take a shared jumbo (big túk-túk, US$0.30) to Tha Deua and walk the final 4km to the park. Going by rented motorbike is also popular.

ACTIVITIES
Bowling

Bright lights, Beerlao and boisterous bowlers is what you'll find at the **Lao Bowling Centre** (Map p272; ☎ 218661; Th Khun Bulom; per frame with shoe hire before/after 7pm US$1/1.20; ⏰ 9am-midnight). It is good fun.

Cooking Classes

Courses at **Thongbay Guesthouse** (Map pp268-9; ☎ 242292; www.thongbay-guesthouses.com; Ban Nong Douange; US$10) are organised on demand and start at 10am. A half-day class includes a trip to the market, cooking and feasting on your culinary creations.

Gym & Aerobics

Sengdara Fitness (Map pp268-9; ☎ 414061; 5/77 Th Dong Palan; ⏰ 6am-10pm) is Vientiane's first Western-style mega-gym, with plenty of machines, a sauna, a pool, massage, aerobics and yoga classes. Visitors can buy a US$6 day pass, which includes use of everything plus a one-hour massage – a very good deal. Several upmarket hotels also have modest gyms.

Massage & Herbal Saunas

For a traditional massage experience, head to **Wat Sok Pa Luang** (Map pp268-9; Th Sok Pa Luang; ⏰ 1-7pm). Located in a semirural setting (*wat pàa* means 'forest temple'), the wat is famous for herbal saunas (US$1) and massages (US$3). It's about 3km from the city centre and túk-túk drivers know it well.

Papaya Spa (Map pp268-9; ☎ 216550; www.papaya spa.com; ⏰ 9am-9pm), in an old French villa west of town (follow the signs), is a classy operation offering Lao massage (US$6), Swedish oil massage (US$12), facials, waxing, body scrubs, reflexology and sauna.

Meditation

Foreigners are welcome at a regular Saturday afternoon sitting at Wat Sok Pa Luang (above). The session runs from 4pm until 5.30pm with an opportunity to ask questions afterwards.

Swimming

There are several pools open to the public, including the wonderfully central **Vientiane Swimming Pool** (Map p272; ☎ 020-552 1002; Th Ki Huang;

LAOS

CENTRAL VIENTIANE

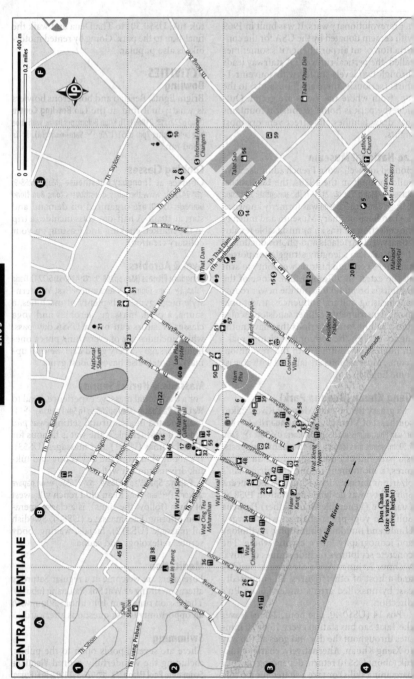

Don Chan
(size varies with
river height)

Mekong River

admission US$1; 🕑 8am-7pm), the **Australian Embassy Recreation Club** (AERC; Map pp268-9; ☎ 314921; Km 3 Th Tha Deua; 🕑 9am-8pm) and, if you fancy laying out with a cocktail, the pool at the **Settha Palace Hotel** (Map p272; ☎ 217581; Th Pangkham; admission US$6).

FESTIVALS & EVENTS

The **That Luang Festival** (Bun Pha That Luang), held in early November, is the largest temple fair in Laos. On the morning of the full moon, hundreds of monks from across the country assemble to receive alms. The festival peaks with a colourful procession between Pha That Luang (p270) and Wat Si Muang. Fireworks cap off festivities and are followed by hours of merriment.

Another huge annual event is **Bun Nam** (River Festival) at the end of Buddhist lent in October, when boat races are held on the Mekong River. Rowing teams from across the country and region compete and, for three nights, the riverbank is lined with food stalls, temporary discos, carnival games and beer gardens.

Vientiane also knows how to celebrate the new year, three times a year. The riverbank is the focus of celebrations on 31 December for the **International New Year**, and again for **Vietnamese Tet-Chinese New Year**, usually in February, then once more in mid-April for **Pii Mai Lao New Year**).

SLEEPING

Vientiane's dozens of guesthouses and hotels range from US$3-a-night cells to opulent colonial-era affairs where no luxury is spared. Most rooms suffer from capital-city syndrome – meaning they cost more than they would elsewhere. Most accommodation is within walking distance of the centre of town, so comparing your options is easy. It's worth booking ahead in high season. December to February and August are the peak tourist times. January, in particular, is very busy.

Mixay Guesthouse (Map p272; ☎ 262210; 39 Th Nokeo Khumman; dm US$2; r US$3-5) This is one of Vientiane's cheapest guesthouses, and while the rooms are clean but basic, the atmosphere is very laid-back. Some rooms have hot-water bathrooms (US$5), but many others have no windows – check a few. Check also the neighbouring RD Guesthouse (☎ 262112).

Soukxana Guesthouse (Map p272; ☎ 264114; soukxana_guest_house@yahoo.com; 13 Th Pangkham; r US$8-15; ❄) Mr Si Mon gives this recently overhauled place, a five-minute walk north of the centre, a relaxed, welcoming feel. Prices depend on the number of people in the room and whether it's air-con or overhead fan.

Thongbay Guesthouse (Map pp268-9; ☎ /fax 242292; www.thongbay-guesthouses.com; r US$10-15; ❄) About 1.5km west of town, the Thongbay is a large, traditional house on a quiet, leafy block.

LAOS

Clean, sizable rooms, English-speaking owners and great food combine to make this a good choice.

our pick **Mali Namphu Guest House** (Map p272; ☎ 215093; 114 Th Pangkham; r with breakfast US$11-17; ✷) Smack bang in the middle of town, the 40-room Mali Namphu is built around a pleasant courtyard and has compact, spotless rooms. Staff are both efficient and eager to please. Great value.

Vayakorn Guest House (Map p272; ☎ 241911; vayakone@laotel.com; 91 Th Nokeo Khumman; s/d US$12/15; ✷) Two blocks west of Nam Phu, Vayakorn's stylish and spacious rooms are a bargain. All have polished floors, satellite TV and spotless bathrooms, though the singles are pretty small. Service is friendly and professional, and rooms are cleaned daily.

Riverside Hotel (Map p272; ☎ 244390; Th Nokeo Khumman; r US$15-16; ✷) At the cheap end of the midrange, this new place offers location and well-equipped rooms, even if it's not going to win prizes for its charisma. The even-numbered rooms on the 4th and 5th floors are best, though there's no lift.

Villa Manoly (Map pp268-9; ☎/fax 218907; manoly 20@hotmail.com; r US$25-40; ✷ ✷) In a quiet street off Th Fa Ngum between Wat Si Muang and the Mekong, the Manoly is a large French-era villa (plus a newer building) fronted by a garden and pool. The house is all hardwood and terrazzo floors, high ceilings and tasteful furnishings (look for the collection of antique typewriters).

our pick **Intercity Hotel** (Map p272; ☎ 242843/4; www.laointerhotel.com; 24-25 Th Fa Ngum; r with breakfast US$30-70; ✷ ▯) The big rooms with high ceilings, polished-wood floors and tasteful Asian décor make the Intercity a great choice. All front rooms have wonderful views of the Mekong, with the suite room 888 (US$70) the standout.

our pick **Hotel Beau Rivage Mekong** (Map pp268-9; ☎ 243375; www.hbrm.com; s US$34, d & tw with breakfast US$43-55; ✷ ▯) Don't be put off by the preponderance of pink, this Australian-owned boutiqueish hotel on the banks of the Mekong is excellent value. All 16 rooms are stylishly laid out, but those at the front are the best, with Mekong views (US$55), terrazzo baths and small balconies.

Settha Palace Hotel (Map p272; ☎ 217581; www.set thapalace.com; 6 Th Pangkham; standard/deluxe US$143/155; ✷ ▯ ✷) Vientiane's classic colonial hotel and probably the best in town, the beautifully restored Settha Palace has 29 tastefully appointed rooms with plenty of French-era style, plus mod-cons such as wireless internet. The poolside bar and Le Belle Epoque restaurant complete the picture.

EATING

When a friend of ours recently described Vientiane eating as 'dollar for dollar the best in the world', we thought he'd had one too many 'happy' pizzas. But the more we ate the more we thought he might be right. The ever-growing number of cafés, street vendors, beer gardens and restaurants now embrace much of the world's cuisine, and it's hard to argue with US$4 or US$5 for a meal that would probably cost five times as much at home. Note that the cafés (opposite) are also good for food.

Lao & Noodles

Noodles of all kinds are popular in Vientiane, especially in the unofficial Chinatown area bounded by Th Heng Boun, Th Chao Anou, Th Khun Bulom and the western end of Th Samsenthai. The basic choice is *fŏe* (rice noodle), *mii* (traditional Chinese egg noodle) and *khào pûn* (very thin wheat noodles with a spicy Lao sauce). *Fŏe* and *mii* can be ordered as soup (eg *fŏe nâm*), fried (eg *khùa fŏe*) or dry-mixed in a bowl (eg *fŏe hàeng*), among other variations.

our pick **Vieng Sawan** (Map p272; ☎ 213990; Th Heng Boun; meals US$1.50-3.50; ⏰ 11am-10pm) In the middle of Chinatown, bustling Vieng Sawan is a real Lao eating experience. It specialises in *nǎem néuang* (barbecued pork meatballs) and many varieties of *yáw* (spring rolls), usually sold in 'sets' (*sut*) with *khào pûn*, fresh lettuce leaves, mint, basil, various sauces for dipping, sliced starfruit and green plantain.

our pick **Ban Anou night market** (Map p272; ⏰ 5-10pm) Setting up on a small street off the north end of Th Chao Anou every afternoon, this market is an encyclopaedia of street food, all freshly prepared and cheap.

Bunmala Restaurant (Map pp268-9; ☎ 313 249; Th Khu Vieng; meals US$2-4; ⏰ 11am-11pm) This open-sided, timber-floored restaurant is archetypal Lao, with all manner of *pîng* (grilled) dishes the specialities. Evenings are best when the full range of *pîng* is on offer and draught beer is US$0.50.

Douang Deuane Restaurant & Wine Bar (Map p272; ☎ 241154; Th François Nginn; meals US$2.50-5; ⏰ 8.30am-

11.30pm Mon-Sat) The tasty Lao, Thai and Vietnamese favourites here are complemented by an attractive traditional setting and a welcoming French host. The upstairs balcony is ideal for couples.

Makphet (Map p272; ☎ 260587; Th Setthathirat; meals US$3-6; ⏰ 11am-4pm Mon-Sat) Run by Friends International (www.friends-international.org), this small restaurant trains homeless youths to cook and wait tables. The modern Lao cuisine is tasty.

Other Asian

PVO (Map p272; ☎ 214444; Th Fa Ngum; meals US$0.70-1.50; ⏰ 7am-9pm) PVO has been selling the best *khào jìi páa-tê* (Vietnamese-style paté baguettes) in town for years, plus Vietnamese spring rolls and assorted soups. It's an excellent breakfast option.

7 Plus Korean Food (Map pp268-9; ☎ 415343; meals US$2-5; ⏰ 10am-11pm) The Korean food here isn't bad, but it's mainly about having a night out Lao-style in a big, noisy beer-garden. It's a young crowd and the atmosphere is always 'up'.

Taj Mahal Restaurant (Map p272; ☎ 020-561 1003; Th Setthathirat; meals US$2-4; ⏰ 10am-10.30pm Mon-Sat, 4-10.30pm Sun) It looks like a garage, but the Taj Mahal serves what we think is the best Indian food in Vientiane. Prices are very reasonable and there are plenty of vegetarian dishes.

YuLaLa (Map p272; ☎ 215214; Th Heng Boun; meals US$2.50-4; ⏰ lunch & dinner Tue-Sun, closed last Sun of month; ✖) Run by a hip young Japanese couple, YuLaLa serves tasty, cheap Japanese fusion cuisine (no sushi or sashimi) in a cool atmosphere.

Western & International

There's a gaggle of long-running French and Italian places around Nam Phu, all of which have good reputations. Elsewhere, French fare is the standout, with plenty of good options around.

Saovaly Restaurant (Map p272; ☎ 214940; Th Manhatulat; meals US$2.50-6; ⏰ lunch & dinner Mon-Sat) Unpretentious little Saovaly serves surprisingly subtle and artistically presented French cuisine, complemented by attentive but not harassing service. Great value.

Le Côte D'Azur Restaurant (Map p272; ☎ 217252; 62-63 Th Fa Ngum; meals US$3-8; ⏰ lunch Mon-Sat, dinner daily; ✖) Le Côte D'Azur is popular with French expats, and when your food arrives you'll understand why. The delicious provençale cuisine, pastas, salads and pizzas are consistently good.

Sticky Fingers Café & Bar (Map p272; ☎ 215972; 10/3 Th François Nginn; meals US$3.50-6; ⏰ 10am-11pm Tue-Sun; ✖) With the atmosphere of a cosmopolitan Sydney café, Sticky Fingers serves a delicious menu of international dishes – we loved Mr Cho's subtly flavoured crispy fish (US$4.90). And the hangover special (US$4) breakfast works wonders.

La Gondola (Map p272; ☎ 264057; 39 Th Chao Anou; meals US$5-8; ⏰ 11.30am-10.30pm Tue-Sun) Reliable Italian fare is served up by the Italian owner in uncluttered surrounds. Warm atmosphere.

Vegetarian

While you can find vegetarian dishes on almost every menu (particularly the Indian restaurants), only a couple of places are marketing themselves directly to vegetarian diners.

Vegetarian Buffet (Map pp268-9; ☎ 020-566 6488; Th Saysetha; lunch buffet US$1.50, meals US$0.50-1.50; ⏰ lunch & dinner Mon-Sat) This place has an excellent, all-you-can-eat vegetarian buffet and an à la carte menu for dinner. Head east along Th Setthathirat to Th Saysetha (a Honda store on the left side marks the street). Turn left and the restaurant is a few doors along with a wooden front.

Just for Fun (Map p272; ☎ 213642; 51/2 Th Pangkham; meals US$1-3; ⏰ 8am-9pm Mon-Sat) Just for Fun has been serving its small but mainly vegetarian menu for years, with offerings inspired by Thai and Lao cuisine, plus Lao coffee and lots of herbal teas.

Self-Catering

The markets are your best bet for fresh food. If there's something Western you're yearning for, check out **Phimphone Market** (Map p272; 94/6 Th Setthathirat; ⏰ 7.30am-9pm), opposite Nam Phu, and visit **Vins de France** (Map p272; ☎ 217700; 354 Th Samsenthai; ⏰ 8.30am-8pm Mon-Sat) for an astonishing range of French wines and a US$6.90 degustation.

DRINKING
Cafés

Trendy cafés are popping up all over the city.

JoMa Bakery Café (Map p272; ☎ 215265; Th Setthathirat; meals US$2-5; ⏰ 7am-9pm Mon-Sat; ✖) Does a brisk trade in delicious pastries, sandwiches, quiche, muesli, fruit, shakes and coffee. Wi-fi is available for US$2.50 an hour.

LAOS

Maison du Café (Map p272; ☎ 214781; 70 Th Pangkham; ☽ 7am-6pm) A few metres north of Nam Phu, this welcoming place brews up a dizzying array of coffees (US$1 to US$2) and serves them with fresh sandwiches or baguettes (US$1.50), plus great shakes. There's plenty to read and the owner offers various tourist services.

Delight House of Fruit Shakes (Map p272; ☎ 212200; Th Samsenthai; ☽ 7am-9pm) One of two places here that make incredible fruit shakes. Understandably popular. It also does laundry.

Bars & Beer Gardens

As the sun goes down over the Mekong River, **riverfront food & drink vendors** (Map p272; ☽ 5-11pm) turn the riverbank into one long beer garden, with tables and chairs set out under the stars and the Full Taste of Happiness (Beerlao) washing down *ping ka* (grilled chicken) and *tạm màak-hung* (green papaya salad).

Sala Sunset Khounta (Map pp268-9; ☎ 251079; ☽ 11am-11pm) At the west end of the dirt road along the riverfront, the 'Sunset Bar' is a Vientiane institution that's been serving Beerlao at sunset for years. The friendly proprietors also offer local food and interesting snacks.

Bor Pen Nyang (Map p272; ☎ 020-787 3965; Th Fa Ngum; ☽ 10am-midnight) If you're on the pull and/ or seeking traveller company, this rooftop bar on the Mekong was the place to be when we were researching.

Chicago Bar (Map p272; ☎ 020-552 6452; Th Nokeo Khumman; ☽ 7pm-late; ⊠) The Chicago Bar is a cocktail-cum-lounge bar with a tendency towards jazz and blues. It's fun, especially as it tends to stay open later than most Vientiane bars. Upstairs is a gallery-cinema with regular events.

Sticky Fingers Café & Bar (p275), Douang Deuane Restaurant & Wine Bar (p274) and 7 Plus Korean Food (p275) are also popular spots for a few drinks.

ENTERTAINMENT

Check the *Vientiane Times* and fliers on shop windows around Nam Phu for info on public one-off events.

Laos Traditional Show (Map p272; ☎ 242978; Th Manthatulat; child/adult US$4/7, still/video camera charge US$1/3) This performance of traditional music and dancing, aimed directly at tourists, plays nightly from about November to March.

Centre Culturel et de Coopération Linguistique (French Cultural Centre; Map p272; ☎ 215764; www.am

bafrance-laos.org/centre; Th Lan Xang; ☽ 9.30am-6.30pm Mon-Fri, 9.30am-noon Sat) The centre runs a year round programme of events such as musical performances and English-subtitled films and documentaries. Check at the centre of the *Vientiane Times* for details.

For live music, check out **On the Rock Pub** (Map pp268-9; ☽ 7.30pm-midnight), down a lane off Th Luang Prabang, which usually has live rock or the similar but more central **Music House** (Map p272; Th Fa Ngum; ☽ 8pm-midnight).

Conveniently, three of Vientiane's better nightclubs are near each other on the airport road, so wander along until you find one you like. First up is **Future Nightclub** (Map pp268-9; Th Luang Prabang; ☽ 8pm-1am) not far past the Novotel, and the nearby **Highwayman** (Map pp268-9; Th Luang Prabang; ☽ 8pm-midnight) has occasional live acts but mainly DJs. A few hundred meters further along, **Marina** (Map pp268-9; ☎ 216978; Th Luang Prabang; ☽ 8pm-1am) is the biggest and most ostentatious club; go bowling if you don't fancy the music. Elsewhere, **Lunar 36** (Map pp268-9; Don Chan Palace Hotel; ☽ 6pm-3am Wed, Fri & Sat), off Th Fa Ngum, was the hottest night in town when we passed through, and opens quite late.

SHOPPING

Talat Sao (Morning Market; Map p272; Th Lan Xang; ☽ 7am-5pm) Vientiane's labyrinthine market sells everything from Lao silks, 'Firkenstocks' and jewellery to white goods, electronics and bedding. At the time of writing, work had begun on the new Talat Sao Shopping Mall, a Malaysian owned shopping complex and multistorey car park that will replace the bustling goods market. It's expected to be completed by 2009.

Numerous handicraft and souvenir boutiques are dotted around the streets radiating from Nam Phu, particularly on Th Pangkham and Th Nokeo Khumman. Among the better places:

Camacrafts (Mulberries; Map p272; ☎ 241217; www .mulberries.org; Th Nokeo Khumman; ☽ 10am-6pm Mon-Sat) A not-for-profit company that sells striking Hmong-inspired textiles and homewares and contributes to villages through training and resource-preservation practices.

Carol Cassidy Lao Textiles (Map p272; ☎ 212123; www.laotextiles.com; 84-86 Th Nokeo Khumman; ☽ 8am-noon & 2-5pm Mon-Fri, 8am-noon Sat, or by appointment) Sells high-end contemporary, original-design textiles inspired by older Lao weaving patterns, motifs and techniques.

(Continued on page 285)

Spicing up your evening at a night market is one of many eating options (p174) in Thailand

JERRY ALEXANDER

Marvel at the craftmanship of statues and mosaics at Wat Arun (p115), Bangkok, Thailand

DENNIS JOHNSON

A túk-túk is waiting to show you around the streets of a city that's always on the move – Bangkok (p113), Thailand

ALAIN EVRARD

DANIEL BOAG

Drink in the scenery at Bokor National Park, (p244),
Cambodia

The crumbling colonial
architecture of Cambodia's
capital, Phnom Penh (p188)

TOM

JULIET COOMBE

Stock up on *kramas*, traditional Khmer scarves, at
Psar Tuol Tom Pong (p198), Phnom Penh, Cambodia

Get wrapped up in Angkor history at jungle-clad Ta Prohm (p212), Cambodia

BILL

Fresh fish is often on the menu in the sleepy riverside town of Kampot (p242), Cambodia

The Royal Palace (p192), Phnom Penh, Cambodia, is a striking structure near the riverfront

Today's peaceful floating villages of Battambang Province (p216), Cambodia, are a world away from the area's turbulent history

Stupendous Pha That Luang (p270), Vientiane, is the most important national monument in Laos

Monks at Wat Xieng Thong (p294),
Luang Prabang, commemorate
Bun Pi Mai (Lao Lunar New Year)

Thirsty work on the streets of Vientiane (p266), Laos

KRAIG LIEB

Visiting Thai Lü villages is a highlight of a trip to remote Luang Nam Tha (p309), Laos

JULIET COOMBE

Colourful celebrations are held during That Luang Festival (p273), Vientiane, Laos

A bridge spans the Nam Song in beautiful Vang Vieng (p287), Laos

JOHN ELK III

GREG ELMS

Tranquil Tam Coc (p367), Vietnam, is nicknamed 'Halong Bay on the Rice Paddies'

Three's not a crowd when travelling by motorcycle on Vietnam's busy city streets

BRENT WINEBRENNER

Step back in time at the Reunification Palace (p405), Ho Chi Minh City, Vietnam, which has been preserved almost as it was on the momentous 1975 day that the Republic of Vietnam fell

STU SMUCKER

JOHN BANAGAN

trip to the market is often fruitful at Nha
rang (p392), Vietnam

The unusual fishing boats will catch your
eye at China Beach (p387), Vietnam

PHIL WEYMOUTH

mong children play in the lush valleys of mountainous Sapa (p376), Vietnam

JULIET COOMBE

284

Traditional Taoist temple music, known as
dòngjīng, is played by the Naxi Orchestra
(p458), Yúnnán province (China)

World Heritage–listed Lìjiāng (p455),
Yúnnán province (China), is an all-round
favourite with travellers

The unusual limestone pillars of Shílín (Stone Forest; p450), Yúnnán province (China)

(Continued from page 276)

GETTING THERE & AWAY
Air
Wattay International Airport is the main air hub for domestic flights, and is also served by five airlines flying internationally (see p342).

Boat
Rare cargo boats head upstream to Luang Prabang (four days to one week) from Kiaw Liaw Pier, 3.5km west of the fork in the road where Rte 13 heads north in Ban Kao Liaw. Go there and speak with the boatmen in advance to see if, when and how far they're running. This is real old-style Lao travel so expect no luxuries.

Bus & Săwngthăew
Buses use three different stations in Vientiane, all with some English-speaking staff. The **Northern Bus Station** (Map pp268-9; ☎ 260255; Th T2), about 2km northwest of the centre, serves all points north of Vang Vieng, including China, and has some buses to Vietnam.

The **Southern Bus Station** (☎ 740521; Rte 13 South), commonly known as Dong Dok Bus Station or just *khíw lot lák kào* (Km 9 Bus Station), is 9km out of town and serves everywhere south. Buses to Vietnam will usually stop here.

The **Talat Sao Bus Station** (Map p272; ☎ 216507) is where desperately slow local buses depart for destinations within Vientiane Province, including Vang Vieng, and some more distant destinations, though for these you're better going to the northern or southern stations. It's also home to the Thai–Lao International Bus; see below.

Our table (p286) gives timetable info.

GETTING AROUND
Central Vientiane is entirely accessible on foot, but for exploring neighbouring districts you'll need transport.

Bicycle & Motorcycle
Bicycles can be rented for between US$0.50 and US$2 per day from loads of tour agencies and guesthouses. Small motorbikes are popular and widely available. The cheapest are from outside the **Douang Deuane Hotel** (Map p272; Th Nokeo Khumman), where 110cc bikes cost US$5.50 a day, but they're notoriously unreliable (we took back four in one day!). Much better Japanese bikes are available from **PVO** (Map p272; ☎ 214444; Th Fa Ngum; per day US$7), which also rents the best 250cc bikes for US$20 a day.

Túk-Túk
Many túk-túks have a laminated list of vastly inflated tourist prices. These guys, usually found in queues outside tourist sights, won't budge for less than the price already agreed upon with the other drivers (starting at US$1). You're better off trying a free-roaming túk-túk (one driving along the street), where negotiation is possible. You can also flag down a shared túk-túk (with passengers already in it); shared túk-túks ply fixed routes and cost about US$0.20 to US$0.50 depending on your destination.

AROUND VIENTIANE

PHU KHAO KHUAY NATIONAL PROTECTED AREA
Covering more than 2000 sq km of mountains and rivers to the east of Vientiane, the underrated **Phu Khao Khuay NPA** (www.trekkingcentrallaos.com) is home to several waterfalls and a herd of wild elephants. Phu Khao Khuay (pronounced poo cow kwai) means 'Buffalo Horn Mountain' and is home to three major rivers flowing off a sandstone mountain range into the Ang Nam Leuk Reservoir.

The main attraction is the wild elephants, which make regular appearances at their

---

CROSSING INTO THAILAND: THE FRIENDSHIP BRIDGE

The Thai–Lao Friendship Bridge is 20km southeast of Vientiane. The border is open between 6am and 10pm, and the easiest way to cross is on the comfortable Thai–Lao International Bus (US$1.50, 90 minutes), which leaves Vientiane's Talat Sao bus station at 7.30am, 9.30am, 12.40pm, 2.30pm, 3.30pm and 6pm. From Nong Khai in Thailand, it leaves at the same times for 55B. Similar buses run to Udon Thani (US$2.20, two hours) six times a day. Visas are issued on arrival in both countries. Alternative means of transport between Vientiane and the bridge include taxi or jumbo (US$5 to US$7 – bargain hard) or regular public buses from Talat Sao (US$0.40) between 6.30am and 5pm. At the bridge, regular shuttle buses ferry passengers between immigration posts. For information on crossing this border in the other direction, see p167.

LEAVING VIENTIANE BY BUS

All services depart daily except where noted. The bus to Huay Xai might not run in the wet season. Note that in Laos buses break down, so it might take longer than advertised. For buses to China, contact the **Tong Li Bus Company** (☎ 242657). For Vietnam, buses leave daily for Hanoi (US$20, 24 hours) via Vinh (US$16, 16 hours); and less often for Hué (US$17), Danang (US$20) and even Ho Chi Minh City (US$45, up to 48 hours).

Destination	Fare normal/ air-con/VIP (US$)	Distance (km)	Duration (hr)	Departures
Talat Sao Bus Station				
Vang Vieng	1.50	153	3½	7am, 9.30am, 10.30am, 11.30am, 1.30pm, 2pm
Northern Bus Station				
Huay Xai	20	869	30-35	5.30pm
Luang Nam Tha	14	676	19	8.30am
Luang Prabang	9/10/11.50	384	11/11/9-10	6.30am (air-con), 7.30am, 8am (VIP), 9am (air-con), 11am, 1.30pm, 4pm, 6pm, 7.30pm (air-con)
Oudomxay	11/12	578	14-17	6.45am, 1.45pm, 4pm (air-con)
Phongsali	15	811	26	7.15am (doesn't leave every day)
Phonsavan	9/10	374	9-11	6.30am, 7.30am (air-con), 3.30pm, 7pm (air-con)
Sainyabuli	10/11.50	485	14-16	4.30pm, 6.30pm
Sam Neua via Phonsavan	15	612	15-17	7am, 9.30am, 12.30pm (7am bus goes via Luang Prabang, and takes up to 30hr)
Southern Bus Station				
Attapeu	11	812	22-24	9.30am, 5pm
Don Khong	11	788	16-19	10.30am
Lak Sao	6	334	7-9	5am, 6am, 7am
Paksan	2.50	143	3-4	take any bus going south, roughly every 30min from 4.30am to 5pm
Pakse	8.5/11/13	677	14-16/9½ (VIP)	normal buses every 30min from 9.30am-5pm; air-con buses at 7pm & 8pm; 4 VIP buses leave at 8.30pm
Salavan	10	774	15-20	4.30pm, 7.30pm
Savannakhet	5.50/7	457	8-10	every 30min 6am until 9am; air-con at 8.30pm; or any normal or air-con bus to Pakse
Tha Khaek	4/5	337	6/4½	5am, 6am, noon, or any bus to Savannakhet or Pakse
Voen Kham	11	818	17-20	11am

favourite salt lick an easy walk from the village of **Ban Na**. Several tour operators in Vientiane work with the local community in running treks that involve staying overnight in the Elephant Observation Tower, which overlooks the salt lick. Travellers who've seen the elephants say it's an awesome experience, but they are wild and the chances of them turning up are only about 50-50, so be prepared for disappointment.

The best way to organise a trek, either to see the elephants or other parts of the NPA, is through the NTAL office in Vientiane (p267), which has loads of information and can do the organising for free (by calling the villagers, who don't speak English). In the case of Ban Na, you could also get a Lao-speaker to call **Mr Bounthanom** (☎ 020-220 8286) direct and arrange it with him. Other treks, including visits to several impressive **waterfalls**, depart from **Ban Hat Khai**. Prices vary depending on the number of trekkers but are reasonable; for example, a three-day trek from Ban Hat Khai is US$37/23 per person in a group of two/eight people. A one-day trip is US$18/13. From Ban Na trekking prices are higher if you stay in the elephant tower, which has a US$10 per person fee that goes to the Elephant Conservation & Research Fund. Prices do not include transport from Vientiane. All moneys go to the village and NPA.

Getting There & Away

Buses from Talat Sao in Vientiane leave regularly for Ban Tha Bok and Paksan. For Ban Na get off near the Km 79 stone near the Tha Baht Phonsan stupa; Ban Na is about 2km north.

For Ban Hat Khai, stay on the bus until a turnoff left (north) at Km 92, just before Ban Tha Bok. Then take any passing săwngthăew the 5km to Ban Huay Leuk. Ban Hat Khai is 2km further. For the various waterfalls, find detailed information at www.trekkingcentral laos.com or the NTAL office (p267) in Vientiane. If you need a bed en route, there are two decent guesthouses in Tha Bok.

VANG VIENG
☎ 023 / pop 30,000
Nestled beside the Nam Song amid stunning limestone-karst terrain, Vang Vieng is one of those destinations everyone has an opinion on. Most travellers enjoy the scenery and the myriad activities – caving, rock climbing, kayaking, rafting and tubing – that take advantage of the convenient supply of dramatic topography and tourists with time and money to spend.

Opinions start varying when you take a closer look at the town itself. The most common complaint is that in earning its stripes as a fully paid-up member of backpacker world, Vang Vieng has lost its soul. The main street of this once-quiet village is now a sort of poor man's Khao San Rd, with backpackers laid out in TV bars watching Hollywood blockbusters and endless reruns of *Friends* while sucking down 'happy' shakes.

But whether this side of Vang Vieng appeals to you or not (if you don't like it, respite is only a short walk away), this is still a truly beautiful part of the world and it's worth stopping here en route between Vientiane and Luang Prabang.

Orientation & Information

Buses stop east of a large patch of tarmac that was the war-era airstrip. Head west into town, then turn right to reach the main concentration of guesthouses, restaurants and bars. Parallel to the main street are a basic provincial hospital and several more restaurants, plus a few newer bungalow-style guesthouses along the river. Internet cafés have popped up almost as fast as the mushrooms in Vang Vieng, most charging 300 kip per minute.

BCEL (☎ 511434; ☽ 8.30am-3.30pm Mon-Sun) Exchanges cash, travellers cheques and handles cash advances on Visa, MasterCard and JCB.

BKC Bookshop (☽ 7am-7pm) Secondhand novels plus guidebooks and maps.

Post office (☎ 511009) Beside the old market.

Provincial Hospital (☎ 511604)) This flash new hospital has X-ray facilities and is fine for broken bones, cuts and malaria.

Dangers & Annoyances

Vang Vieng has its fair share of thefts, many by fellow travellers. Take the usual precautions, and don't leave valuables outside caves. Be aware that there have been several drownings here in recent years, so show the river respect. The other trouble that tends to find travellers is the law. Police are adept at sniffing out spliffs, especially late at night. Getting caught with a stash – be it grass, opium, mushrooms or *yabba* – usually results in the police issuing a US$500 on-the-spot fine. You can try pleading poor (though forget about innocent – if you're carrying, you're guilty), but you'll

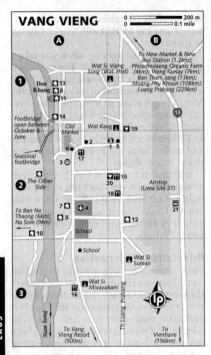

have to pay something – US$200 is usually the minimum. Don't expect a receipt.

Sights & Activities

CAVES

The caves that open out from the surrounding limestone karsts are Vang Vieng's most enduring attractions. Several are open to tourists and have signs to help you find them. Hiring a local guide is a good idea.

The most famous cave, **Tham Jang** (admission US$1), south of town, was used as a hide-out from marauding Yunnanese Chinese in the early 19th century. A set of stairs leads up to the main cavern entrance. There's also a cool spring at the foot of the cave. Follow the signs from the Vang Vieng Resort.

Another popular cave is **Tham Phu Kham** (Blue Lagoon; admission US$0.50). To reach it, cross the **bridge** then walk or pedal 6km along a scenic, unsealed road to Ban Na Thong, from where you have to walk 1km to a hill on the northern side of the village: follow the signs. It's a tough final 200m climb through scrub forest to the cave.

The **Tham Sang Triangle** is a popular half-day trip that's easy to do on your own and takes

in Tham Sang plus three other caves within a short walk of each other. Begin this odyssey by riding a bike or taking a *sǎwngthǎew* 13km north along Rte 13, turning left a few hundred metres beyond the barely readable Km 169 marker. A rough road leads to the river, where a boatman will ferry you across to Ban Tham Sang for a small fee. **Tham Sang** (admission US$0.20), meaning 'Elephant Cave', is a small cavern containing a few Buddha images and a Buddha 'footprint', plus the elephant-shaped stalactite that gives the cave its name. It's best visited in the morning when light enters the cave.

From here a signed path takes you 1km northwest through rice fields to the entrances of **Tham Loup** and **Tham Hoi** (admission US$0.50 for both). Tham Hoi reportedly continues about 3km into the limestone and an underground lake. About 400m south of Tham Hoi, along a well-used path, is the highlight of the trip, **Tham Nam** (admission US$0.50). This cave is about 500m long and a tributary of the Nam Song flows out of its low entrance. In the dry season you can wade into the cave, but when the water is higher you must enter in a tube (available outside). Dragging yourself through the tunnel on the fixed rope is good fun. From Tham Nam an easy 1km walk brings you back to Ban Tham Sang.

KAYAKING & RAFTING

Kayaking is increasingly popular, with day trips (US$8 to US$12 per person) typically taking you down a few rapids and stopping at caves and villages. Longer trips to Vientiane involve paddling for half a day then going the rest of the way by road. Though all guides are supposed to be trained, many are not. Before using a cheap operator, check guides' credentials.

Rafting is less popular but more adventurous, with trips down the Nam Ngum the pick; Green Discovery (below) is the pick of the operators.

ROCK CLIMBING

Green Discovery (☎ 511230; www.greendiscoverylaos .com; Th Luang Prabang) operates guided rock-climbing courses for novices (around US$30 per day) and can lead more experienced climbers up Vang Vieng's dramatic limestone cliffs. It has a good reputation and the number of routes is rising all the time.

TUBING

Tubing down the Nam Song has become a rite of passage on the Indochina backpacking circuit. And it has to be said, it's a lot of fun. The tube renters have formed a cartel that operates from a shed near the old market site; the price is fixed at US$3.50 for the trip, including your tube, life jacket and the túk-túk ride to the launch point 3km north of town. The trip can take two or more hours depending on river conditions and how many of the makeshift bars you stop off at en route! People have died on this trip, so don't go too stupid with the drink and drugs.

Sleeping

Vang Vieng has a dizzying array of guesthouses. Most are cheap and central, so it's easy to compare. Here are some of the better options.

Pan's Place (☎ 511484; neilenolix@hotmail.com; r US$2-6) Expat-run Pan's (named after his wife) has had a makeover but the atmosphere will be more appealing than the basic but clean rooms. The 'backyard' has everything the backpacker could want – a TV sala (open-sided shelter) with big screen, bar, restaurant and kiddie pool – but not a single Lao the night we visited.

Maylyn Guest House (☎ 020-560 4095; jophus _foley@hotmail.com; r US$3-6) On the far side of the Nam Song, the Maylyn's 15 simple rooms and bungalows are set in a lush garden beside a stream. Owner Joe is a good source of local information. The barbecued fish is a highlight.

Vang Vieng Orchid (☎ 020-220 2259; r US$6-10; 🖳) Situated on the banks of the Nam Song opposite Don Khang, this three-storey place has 20 clean, spacious rooms, 12 of which have balconies and wonderful views over Don Khang and the karst peaks beyond. However, the noise from the island can make sleep difficult.

ourpick Elephant Crossing (☎ 511232; d US$25-30, f with breakfast US$45; 🖳) With almost every comfortable room boasting a balcony overlooking the Nam Song and out to the dramatic karsts, it's hard to beat this place in the midrange. Prices fall US$5 in low season. Recommended.

Ban Sabai Bungalows (Xayoh Riverside Bungalows; ☎ 511088; r US$25-30; 🖳) These modern bungalows in a serene riverside setting are a good choice. Some rooms have a bathtub and there are two romantic US$25 'singles' with a double bed and balcony over a pond. There is a riverside bar-restaurant.

A couple of others we like:

Champa Lao (☎ 020-501 8501; www.thelongwander .com; r US$2-3) A real old-style Lao guesthouse in a wooden house with simple rooms, a communal sala and a good feel. There are a couple of others nearby.

Organic Mulberry Farm (☎ 511220; www.laofarm .org; r US$3-5) Known locally as sŭran máwn phúu dìn dqeng (Phoudindaeng Mulberry Farm), this organic farm has simple accommodation and a great restaurant. If you're looking to volunteer, see Mr Thi.

At the north end of town are three small, new places not far from the river that have a refreshing amount of soul. First up is the **Nam Song Garden** (☎ 511544; arnelao@hotmail.com; r US$5), with just five rooms but an atmosphere as serene as owner Arné. A little further is **Champa Lao** (☎ 020-501 8501; www.thelongwander.com; r US$2-3), a real old-style Lao guesthouse in a wooden house with simple rooms, a communal sala and a good feel. Finally the **Sunset Home** (☎ 020-562 3297; r US$4-6) has bungalows with hot-water bathrooms.

Eating

Most of Vang Vieng's restaurants produce a varied selection of cuisines including Lao, Thai, Chinese, Western and Rasta-infusion. Following are a few decent eateries that have so far managed to resist Vang Vieng's *Friends* phenomenon.

ourpick Nokeo (meals US$1-3; 8am-8pm) The last real Lao-style restaurant in Vang Vieng, Nokeo serves consistently good Lao food at low prices. The succulent *pîing pạa* (grilled fish) is excellent, as are the various *làap* (spicy salad of minced meat, poultry or salad). Highly recommended.

ourpick Organic Mulberry Farm Café (511174; meals US$1-3.50) The ever-growing and innovative menu here is one of the best in Vang Vieng, especially for vegetarians. The mulberry shakes (US$0.80) and pancakes (US$1.30) are famous and everything is fairly priced.

Kangaroo Sunset Bar (020-771 4291; meals US$2-4.50) This Australian-run place is a decent sunset and evening drinking hole, with tasty Lao, Thai and fusion-ish food. The fried prawn rolls are delicious.

Erawan Restaurant (511093; Th Luang Prabang; meals US$2-5) The good Asian and European food, lovely owner and chilled ambience refreshingly free of TVs makes Erawan a perennial favourite. Recommended.

Drinking

You can drink in every guesthouse and restaurant in town and you won't need a guidebook to track down the most happening places. In general, they're split into the open-air, anything-goes bars on Don Khang (aka 'the island'), and more familiar-looking places on or just off Th Luang Prabang.

On Don Khang, four bars compete for your business and any one of those could be the most happening place on the night – we trust you to find it. In town, **Jaidee's** (8am-1am) has consistently good music and Supermao (ask him) Jaidee maintains an upbeat vibe. **Sakura** (5-11.30pm) has regular DJs and is the best place to dance, though few people seem to bother.

Getting There & Away

From the airstrip **bus terminal** (511341; Rte 13), which still operates despite the new terminal 2km north of town, buses leave for Luang Prabang (US$7, seven to 11 hours, 168km, several daily), Vientiane (US$2.50, 3½ to 4½ hours, 156km, four times daily) and Phonsavan (US$7.50, six to seven hours, 219km, daily at about 9am). For Vientiane, pick-ups (US$2.50, 3½ to 4½ hours) leave every 20 minutes from 5am until 4pm.

Tickets for minibuses and VIP buses with air-con travelling direct to Vientiane (US$7, three hours) or Luang Prabang (US$9.50, six to eight hours) are sold at guesthouses, tour agencies and internet cafés in town.

Getting Around

The township is small enough to walk around with ease. Bicycles can be rented for around US$1 a day. A few places hire motorbikes for US$8 per day. A túk-túk up to the Organic Farm or the Tham Sang Triangle costs around US$1 per person.

NORTHERN LAOS

Laos' mountainous north is popular with travellers for its spectacular scenery and traditional village life, which remained isolated from the modern world until relatively recently. The hills and valleys are populated by a potpourri of ethnic groups, ranging from the relatively recently arrived Hmong back to the tribal Thai groups who have lived here for millennia. To learn more about the culture and customs of different ethnic groups, a trip to Muang Sing's trekking guide service office (p312) is recommended; you could also opt for a village homestay to see first-hand what the 'real Laos' is for almost 80% of the population. The slow upgrading of roads has made travel in the north less arduous, although you still can't get anywhere very quickly – patience is definite virtue.

LUANG PRABANG

071 / pop 26,000

Luang Prabang is a tonic for the soul. The former royal capital taps into the senses in a way few other cities can. It's thick with the perfume of pearly frangipanis and the enticing flavours of high-quality Asian and European food. The greens of the giant shade trees contrast with the burnt siena robes and bare-foot silence of countless Buddhist monks and novices collecting alms. And the gleaming temples, French-era palace and villas, and the multiethnic peoples who live here give Luang Prabang a romantic and relaxed feel that can captivate even the most jaded travellers.

At the confluence of the Nam Khan (Khan River) and the Mekong River, this ancient royal city retains its colour despite being Laos' foremost tourist showpiece. This is in part

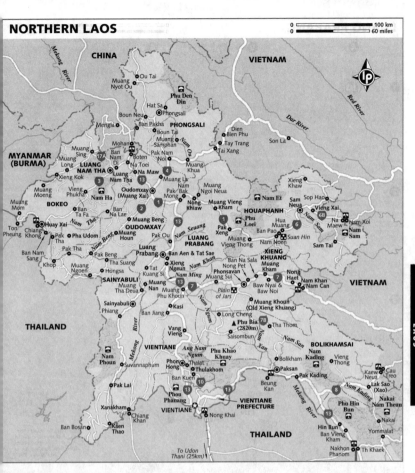

NORTHERN LAOS

because it is Unesco Heritage Listed, which means a blessed ban on buses and trucks, and in part because of the quiet benevolence of its residents, which lulls visitors into somnambulant bliss. Although Luang Prabang teems with travellers, it is not a party destination, and the 11.30pm curfew mercifully maintains its traditional disposition.

Orientation

Most of the tourist sights are in the old quarter, on the peninsula bounded by the Mekong and the Nam Khan. Dominating the centre of town, Phu Si is an unmissable landmark. The majority of restaurants, tour companies and internet cafés line Th Sisavangvong, while accommodation and more eateries dot the surrounding streets. Pedal or pedi power are the best ways to get around.

Information
BOOKSHOPS

L'Etranger Books & Tea (booksinlaos@yahoo.com; Th Kingkitsarat; ☽ 8am-10pm Mon-Sat, 10am-10pm Sun) New and used books about Laos, plus book rental and exchange. There's a tea lounge–cum-gallery on the 2nd floor.

INTERNET ACCESS

For wireless access try Le Café Ban Vat Sene (p297). Internet cafés along Th Sisavangvong charge 300 kip per minute.

Internet email shop (Th Sisavangvong; ☽ 8am-11pm)
Treasure Travel Laos (☎ 245403; Th Sisavangvong; ☽ 7am-11pm)

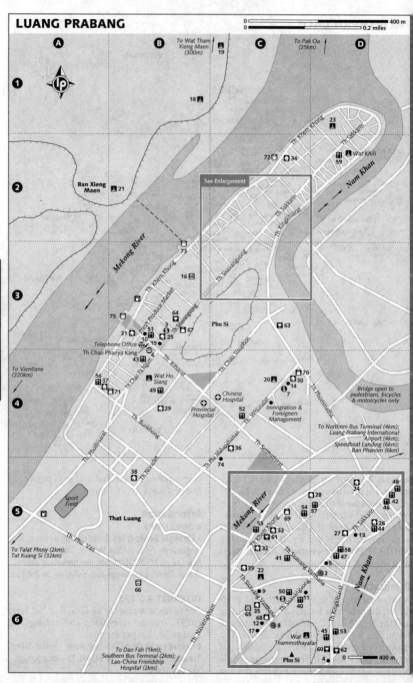

MEDICAL SERVICES

For any serious illness or injury consider travelling to Thailand.

Pharmacie (Th Sakkarin; ⊙ 8.30am-8pm) Stocks basic medicines. On weekends hours are variable.

MONEY

BCEL (Th Sisavangvong; ⊙ 8.30am-3.30pm Mon-Sat) Changes major currencies in cash or travellers cheques, and allows you to makes cash advances against Visa and MasterCard.

Lao Development Bank (65 Th Sisavangvong; ⊙ 8.30am-3.30pm Mon-Sat) Cash only.

POST

Post office (Th Chao Fa Ngum; ⊙ 8.30am-3.30pm Mon-Fri, 8.30am-noon Sat) Phone calls too.

TELEPHONE

Most internet cafés in town have Skype and also offer international calls for 2000 kip per minute.

TOURIST INFORMATION

Provincial Tourism Department (☎ 212487; Th Wisunarat) This office, opposite Wat Wisunarat, stocks a few brochures but is largely useless. Opening hours are erratic.

Unesco World Heritage Information (www .unesco.org; Villa Xiengmouane, Th Sakkarin; ⊙ 9am-6pm Mon-Fri) Siuated in an anteroom of an old French customs house, this office contains information on the Unesco World Heritage project operating in Luang Prabang.

Sights

ROYAL PALACE MUSEUM (HO KHAM)

A good place to start a tour of Luang Prabang is the **Royal Palace Museum** (Ho Kham or Golden Hall; ☎ 212470; Th Sisavangvong; admission US$2; ⊙ 8-11am & 1.30-4pm). The palace was originally constructed in 1904 as a residence for King Sisavangvong and his family. When the king died in 1959, his son Savang Vattana inherited the throne, but shortly after the 1975 revolution he and his family were exiled to northern Laos (never to be heard from again) and the palace was converted into a museum. Various royal religious objects are on display in the large entry hall, as well as rare Buddhist sculptures from India, Cambodia and Laos. The right front corner room of the palace, which opens to the outside, contains the museum's most prized art, including the Pha Bang, the gold standing Buddha after which the town is named. This, however, should

LAOS

have moved to the ornate **Wat Ho Pha Bang** by the time you arrive.

The murals on the walls in the king's former reception room, painted in 1930 by French artist Alix de Fautereau, depict scenes from traditional Lao life. Each wall is meant to be viewed at a different time of day, according to the changing light. Footwear, photography, shorts, T-shirts and sundresses are all forbidden.

PHU SI
The temples on the slopes of 100m-high **Phu Si** (admission US$1; ☾ 8am-6pm) are all of relatively recent construction, but the climb up is well worth it for the superb views – especially near sunset. At the summit is That Chomsi, the starting point for a colourful Pii Mai (Lao New Year) procession. Behind the stupa is a small cave-shrine sometimes referred to as **Wat Tham Phu Si**. Around the northeast flank are the ruins of **Wat Pha Phutthabaht**, which was originally constructed in 1395 during the reign of Phaya Samsenthai on the site of a Buddha footprint.

WAT XIENG THONG
Near the northern tip of the peninsula formed by the Mekong and Nam Khan rivers, **Wat Xieng Thong** (off Th Sakkarin; admission US$1; ☾ 8am-5pm) is Luang Prabang's most magnificent temple. Built by King Setthathirat in 1560, it remained under royal patronage until 1975. Like the royal palace, Wat Xieng Thong was placed within easy reach of the Mekong River. The *sǐm* represents classic Luang Prabang temple architecture, with roofs that sweep low to the ground. The rear wall features an impressive tree-of-life mosaic, and inside richly decorated wooden columns support a ceiling that's vested with *dhammacakka* (dharma wheels). Near the compound's eastern gate stands the royal funeral chapel. Inside are an impressive 12m-high funeral chariot and various funeral urns for each member of the royal family. The exterior of the chapel features gilt panels depicting erotic episodes from the Ramayana.

WAT WISUNALAT (WAT VISOUN)
To the east of the town centre and originally constructed in 1513 (which makes it the oldest continually operating temple in Luang Prabang) is **Wat Wisunarat** (Wat Visoun; Th Wisunarat; admission US$1; ☾ 8am-5pm). After being burnt

down by marauding Haw Chinese in 1887, it was rebuilt in 1898. Inside the high-ceilinged *sǐm* is a collection of wooden Calling for Rain Buddhas and 15th- to 16th-century Luang Prabang *sima* (ordination stones). In front of the *sǐm* is That Pathum (Lotus Stupa), which was built in 1514.

OTHER TEMPLES
In the old quarter, the ceiling of **Wat Xieng Muan** (☾ 8am-5pm) is painted with gold *naga* (mythical serpent-beings) and the elaborate *háang thíen* (candle rail) has *naga* at either end. With backing from Unesco and New Zealand, the monks' quarters have been restored as a classroom for training young novices and monks in the artistic skills needed to maintain and preserve Luang Prabang's temples. Among these skills are woodcarving, painting and Buddha-casting, all of which came to a virtual halt after 1975.

Across the Mekong from central Luang Prabang are several notable temples. The ferry stops near **Wat Long Khun** (admission US$0.50; ☾ 8am-5pm), which features a portico dating from 1937 plus older sections from the 18th century and a few fading *jataka* murals. When the coronation of a Luang Prabang king was pending, it was customary for him to spend three days in retreat here before ascending the throne.

Wat Tham Xieng Maen (admission US$0.50; ☾ 8am-5pm) is in a 100m-deep limestone cave, Tham Sakkarin Savannakuha, a little to the northwest of Wat Long Khun. At the top of a hill peaceful **Wat Chom Phet** (☾ 8am-5pm) offers undisturbed views of the Mekong.

Activities
CYCLING
Cycling is one of the more popular ways to enjoy Luang Prabang. Bicycles can be rented from numerous guesthouses and shops around Th Sisavangvong. The old quarter can be easily covered in half a day, taking in temples and other sights. It doesn't take much effort to get out of town either: head south past Talat Phosy and into the hills (watch out for punctures on rocky roads).

SPA & MASSAGE
Luang Prabang is one of the best places in Southeast Asia to indulge in a herbal sauna or Swedish, Lao or Khamu massage. Prices are generally 30,000 kip for an hour-long body

or foot massage, 40,000 kip for an oil massage, and 10,000 kip for a sauna. Options are abundant, but the following are recommended based on selfless research by the author:

Aroma Spa (☎ 207611255; Th Sisavangvong; ☺ 10am-10pm) Also facials, body scrubs and indulgent combination packages ranging from US$30 to US$50.

Khmu Spa (☎ 212092; Th Sakkarin; ☺ 10am-10pm) Excellent traditional Lao and Khamu massages.

Lao Red Cross (☎ 252856; Th Wisunalat; ☺ massage 9am-9pm, sauna 5-9pm) Housed in a nicely preserved Lao-French building with half-timbered walls. Proceeds go towards the Lao Red Cross, so really, any visit here is an act of pure selflessness. Take your own towel or sarong.

Courses

Luang Prabang is well-known for its quality cooking courses.

Tamarind (www.tamarindlaos.com; Ban Wat Nong) Excellent cooking classes for truly authentic Lao food, including market tours for fresh ingredients and jungle picnics, where you can actually catch your own fish, and more. See p297.

Tamnak Lao Three Elephant Cafe (www.laocooking course.com; Th Sakkarin; per person US$25) Full-day cooking classes including market shopping and a Lao lunch and dinner.

Tum Tum Cheng Restaurant & Cooking School (☎ 253224; tumtumcheng@yahoo.com; 29/2 Th Sakkarin; 1/2/3 days per person US$25/45/60) Well-regarded classes.

Tours

Luang Prabang has plenty of travel agents offering tours from a few hours to several days. Tours to the waterfalls and the Pak Ou Caves (p300) are particularly popular. Many also book domestic and international flights. Prices are similar, but it still pays to shop around and to seek recommendations from other travellers. The following are recommended for good trekking, rafting and cycling excursions:

Action Max Laos (☎ 252417; actionmaxasie@yahoo .fr; cnr Th Ounheuan & Th Khem Khong) Elephant treks and comfortable, small-group tours to surrounding area. Prices around US$30 per person per day.

Green Discovery (☎ 21212093; www.greendiscovery laos.com; Th Sisavangvong) Kayaking, trekking, mountain biking, motorcycling and multiday trips north including motorcycle tours.

Lao Youth Travel (☎ 253340; www.laoyouthtravel .com; 72 Th Sisavangvong) Tour company highly recommended for its focus on community-based ecotourism. Prices around US$35 to US$50 per day, all inclusive.

Tiger Trails (☎ 252655; www.laos-adventures.com; Th Sisavangvong) Single-day and multiday trips involving trekking, rafting, cycling and homestays, but not tigers. Elephant treks and mahout training also offered at an elephant camp. Strong emphasis on conservation and community support. Prices range from US$29 to US$40 per day.

Festivals & Events

The two most important annual events in Luang Prabang are **Pii Mai** (Lao or Lunar New Year) in April, when Luang Prabang gets packed out with locals as well as tourists (book accommodation well in advance), and boat races during **Bun Awk Phansa** (End of the Rains Retreat) in October. See p337 for more.

Sleeping

Luang Prabang is wonderfully compact and you'll need nothing more than your legs to get to and from most of these places. The best area to stay if you want to soak up the Luang Prabang atmosphere is the historical temple district on the peninsula, on and off Th Sisavangvong/Th Sakkarin. Most places in this area are midrange and top-end affairs. If you're looking for a budget room, the old silversmithing district near the Mekong, a neighbourhood known as Ban Wat That (named for nearby Wat Pha Mahathat), and the adjacent Ban Ho Xiang, have become a centre for a cluster of modest guesthouses.

Luang Prabang can get very busy in high season, so it's worth booking ahead, especially for more expensive places. During low season, however, prices might be negotiable.

Oudomphone Guest House (☎ 252419; s/d without bathroom US$4/5, with bathroom US$5/6) Spick-and-span rooms with spring mattresses, fans and small windows greet the weary traveller at this homely guesthouse. Perfect for those looking to escape the tourist glut for a quiet night's sleep.

Koun Savan Guest House (☎ 212297; off Kitsarat Rd; r without bathroom US$4-6, with bathroom US$12; 🅿) In a quiet street Koun Savan spreads around a colourful garden and has compact rooms with outside bathrooms, and spotless doubles with air-con and private bathrooms. The owners are lovely.

Vanvisa Guest House (☎ 212925; vandara1@hotmail .com; 42/2 Ban Wat That; s/d US$8/15) Vanvisa features six rooms at the back of a shop that sells textiles, antiques and handicrafts. The owner, a cultured Lao lady, sometimes makes breakfasts and family-style dinners for guests and can even arrange an informal cooking workshop.

Ammata Guest House (☎ 212175; phetmanyp@yahoo .com.au; Ban Wat Nong; r $15; ☒) One of the best deals in town, this small and popular guesthouse has a low-key ambience and spacious rooms with polished wood interiors and renovated bathrooms. It's midrange quality at small-pocket prices.

Lane Xang Guest House (☎ 212794; villalanexang@ yahoo.com; Th Wisunarat; r & tr incl breakfast US$26-40; ☒) This supremely tasteful villa has just seven big, cool rooms with lofty ceilings and oversized tubs. Its sophisticated blend of colonial and traditional Lao influences is highly recommended.

Xieng Mouane Guest House (☎ /fax 252152; 86/6 Ban Xieng Mouane; r/f US$30/40; ☒) The rooms in this white two-storey colonial house are snug, but stylish. Muted colours, quilted beds, low lighting and high ceilings are matched by ample bathrooms. Many are set in a quadrangle around a flourishing garden at the back.

Sayo River Guest House (☎ 212484; http://sayoguest house.free.fr/cms; Th Khem Khong; r incl breakfast US$30-50; ☒) This new and stylish guesthouse has sizable and tastefully decorated rooms. Cheaper ground-floor rooms have compact bathrooms; others have glossy bathrooms with tubs and/ or balconies with river views.

Ancient Luangprabang Hotel (☎ 212264; www .ancientluangprabang.com; Th Sisavangvong; s/d/tr incl breakfast US$40/45/50; ☒) The boutique-style studio rooms here come with polished teak, local handicrafts and divine timber-clad baths. Some have street views, but triples are a tight squeeze.

Apsara (☎ 212420; www.theapsara.com; Th Kingkitsarat; r incl breakfast US$55-85; ☒) Commonly tagged Luang Prabang's most chic hotel, the Apsara fills its rooms with contemporary Asian décor in bold colours. The cheaper standard rooms are relatively minimalist, but all have huge beds and excellent facilities. Plus, enjoy superb food at the fusion restaurant.

Auberge les 3 Nagas (☎ 253888; www.3nagas.com; Th Sakkarin; r US$105, ste US$140-180; ☒) Straddling both sides of Th Sakkarin in two gloriously restored villas, this hotel has boutique rooms with discreet East-meets-West panache. Suites have private courtyards or balconies, and there's internet access if you have your laptop.

Also recommended:

Thavisouk Guest House (☎ 252022; Th Pha Mahapatsaman; r US$4; ☒ 💻) In a less-inspiring part of town, the laid-back Thavisouk features fatter-than-usual mattresses in clean, sunny rooms.

Thatsaphone Guest House (☎ 020-567 1888; Ban Xieng Mouane; r $8-10) Gorgeous location and airy rooms.

Kongsavath Guesthouse (☎ 212994; khongsavath@hotmail.com; Th Khem Khong; r/ste US$20/30; ☒) Perched on the southern bank of the Mekong, Kongsavath is a cosy place where rooms have large beds, Lao lamps, gleaming bathrooms and shuttered windows. Suites are considerably larger.

Villa Suan Maak (☎ 252775; www.villa-suan-maak -laos.com; Th Noradet; r incl breakfast $20-35; ☒) Gorgeous villa with tastefully decorated rooms, set behind a handsome garden. Owners are endearing and breakfast is served alfresco.

Sala Prabang (☎ 252460; http://salaprabang.salalao .com; 102/6 Th Khem Khong; r incl breakfast US$60-75; ☒) This artistically refurbished, century-old mansion facing the river is joined by a newer wing a few doors up, built in similar style, all painted in earth tones. Boutique and beautiful, rooms come with flowers on the pillows, tiled interiors, gracious French doors and plush sheets and towels. Service is exceptional.

Eating

A bustling set of night food stalls appear on streets running off Th Sisavangvong near the night market. The main congregation is one street north of Th Kitsarat, where you can dine on a whole barbecued pig's head, superb vegetarian dishes and noodles, and just about everything in between. There's even a 'Vegan' stall. All-you-can-fit bowls cost around US$0.50. The baguette and fruit stalls at the corner of Th Sisavangvong and Th Kitsarat are other good budget options, and they're open all day.

Lining the Mekong are numerous **riverside restaurants** (🕑 breakfast, lunch & dinner), often with kitchens in a namesake guesthouse across the street, serving delicious Lao fare at good prices in a wonderfully serene setting.

CAFÉS & BAKERIES

JoMa Bakery Café (☎ 252292; Th Chao Fa Ngum; meals US$1-2; 🕑 breakfast, lunch & dinner) Arguably the best bakery in town, JoMa has a great menu of sandwiches, soups and salads, a large bread and pastry selection and excellent coffee.

Morning Glory Café (☎ 0207774122; Th Sakkarin; meals US$2-3.50; 🕑 breakfast & lunch, closed Tue) Here you'll find jazz, comfy streetside chairs and some of the town's tastiest breakfasts – smoked ham omelettes, fresh muesli, rice soup and fabulous coffee. For lunch tuck into pesto chicken pasta or a fragrant Thai curry.

Le Café Ban Vat Sene (Th Sakkarin; meals US$3.50-5; breakfast, lunch & dinner) This quietly chic café in a restored colonial building serves tapenades and tapas, smoked chicken and feta salads, and roast pork and tarragon-filled baguettes. The tarts and cakes are delicious.

Also recommended:

Phousi Café & Gallery (Th Kingkitsarat; meals US$2-2.50; breakfast, lunch & dinner) Tranquil courtyard café serving set breakfasts, salads, sandwiches and stir fries.

Café des Artes (Th Sisavangvong; meals US$3-10; breakfast, lunch & dinner) Delicious deli fare with plenty of smallgoods, plus French fare, soups, tartines, burgers, brochettes and set menus.

RESTAURANTS

There are plenty of *falang*-oriented restaurants on and around Th Sisavangvong. Several up-market hotels also have top-notch restaurants.

Fruit Shake Restaurant (☎ 5672376; Th Sakkarin; meals US$1; breakfast, lunch & dinner) The effort they didn't spend on the name has all gone into the fine Lao food at this local restaurant. Fried dried beef (Luang Prabang style), fresh chilli pastes and wild deer with basil are up for grabs as well as three-course set menus for US$3.

Somchanh Restaurant (☎ 252021; Th Suvannaban-lang; meals US$1-3; breakfast, lunch & dinner) This simple outdoor place near the guesthouses in Ban Wat That serves a large selection of Lao and Luang Prabang specialities, including the best choice of vegetarian Lao food in town.

Café Toui (☎ 253397; Th Sisavang Vatthana; meals US$3-5; breakfast, lunch & dinner) This cosmopolitan little oasis serves delicious breakfast bagels and mostly European mains, such as grilled buffalo with red wine and tomato sauce.

Tamarind (☎ 020-777 0484; www.tamarindlaos.com; Ban Wat Nong; meals US$2.50-4; breakfast & lunch) Chic little Tamarind has invented its very own make of 'Mod-Lao' cuisine. The à la carte menu boasts delicious sampling platters with bamboo dip, stuffed lemongrass and *meuyang* (DIY parcels of noodles, herbs, fish and chilli pastes, and vegetables).

Lala Café (Th Kingkitsarat; meals US$3.50-6; breakfast, lunch & dinner) Trendy Lala serves refreshingly different Western fare, including Greek dishes, massaman curries and a spicy catfish and mango salad that you won't forget in a hurry.

Restaurant Brasserie L'Elephant (☎ 252482; Ban Wat Nong; meals US$8-16; lunch & dinner) One of Luang Prabang's most elegant eateries features wooden floors, subdued lighting and Lao antiques. The menu is mostly French, but you'll find other treats such as New Zealand rib eye with gorgonzola cheese sauce.

Tum Tum Cheung Restaurant & Cooking School (☎ 252019; Th Sakkarin; meals 10,000-30,000 kip; lunch & dinner) Renowned for its excellent cooking classes (p295), the Lao and Lao-European fusion cuisine here is top notch. It's a short walk north from the centre, in a quieter *bâan* (house) next to Wat Khili. Recommended.

Among the dozens of other eating options are the following:

Nazim Indian Food (☎ 253493; Th Sisavangvong; meals US$1.50-2.50; lunch & dinner) A huge menu of North and South Indian food, though the faux tandoori chicken adorning the walls ain't too appealing.

Paradise Restaurant (☎ 253200; Th Mahapatsaman; meals US$1.50-2; breakfast, lunch & dinner) Quiet, ambient place serving Lao and Luang Prabang specialities, including *ảw lãm* – stewed meat with eggplant and a bitter-spicy root.

Mr Hong's Coffeeshop & Restaurant (71/6 Ban Thongchaleun; meals US$2-2.50; breakfast, lunch & dinner) Fair-priced Lao dishes and potent cocktails make this a traveller favourite.

Lao Lao Garden (Th Kingkitsarat; meals US$3-5; lunch & dinner) Super Thai, Lao and Western fare served in a candle-lit garden. The DIY Lao barbecue is a speciality.

EATING LUANG PRABANG STYLE

Luang Prabang has its own unique cuisine – consider trying some of the local specialities, no matter how unnerving they sound. A local favourite, *jqew bqwng* is a thick condiment made with chillies and dried buffalo skin. *Ảw lãm* is a soup made with dried meat, mushrooms, eggplant and a bitter-spicy root (roots and herbs with bitter-hot effects are a force in Luang Prabang cuisine). The perfect accompaniment to a bottle of Beerlao is *khái pâen*, dried river weed fried in seasoned oil, topped with sesame seeds and served with *jqew bqwng*. Other delicacies include *phák nâm*, a delicious watercress that's unique to Luang Prabang. Salad Luang Prabang is a savoury arrangement of *phák nâm*, sliced boiled eggs, tomatoes and onions with a tasty dressing.

BĄASĬI (BACI)

The *bąasĭi* ceremony is a Lao ritual in which guardian spirits are bound to the guest of honour with strings tied around the wrists. Among Lao it's more commonly called *su khwăn*, meaning 'calling of the soul'.

Lao believe everyone has 32 spirits, known as *kkhwăn*, each of which acts as a guardian over a specific organ or faculty – mental and physical. *Kkhwăn* occasionally wander away from their owner, which is really only a problem when that person is about to embark on a new project or journey away from home, or when they're very ill. Then it's best to perform the *bąasĭi* to ensure that all the *kkhwăn* are present, thus restoring the equilibrium.

The *bąasĭi* ceremony is performed seated around a *pha kkhwăn*, a conical-shaped arrangement of banana leaves, flowers and fruit, from which hang cotton threads. A village elder, known as the *măw phon*, calls in the wandering *kkhwăn* during a long Buddhist mantra. When the chanting is finished, villagers take the thread from the *pha kkhwăn* and begin tying it around the wrists of the guests.

After the ceremony everyone shares a meal. You're supposed to keep the threads on your wrists for three days and then untie, not cut, them.

Drinking

Most of Luang Prabang is sound asleep, or at least nodding off behind a bottle of *khào kam* (pink rice wine), by 10pm, but there are a few bars around. Closing time, by law, is 11.30pm.

LPQ (Th Kingkitsarat) A hint of the South Pacific permeates the interior of this gay-friendly (and straight-friendly, too) bar. The atmosphere is subdued until the after-dinner crowd arrives...

Hive Bar (Th Kingkitsarat) This sultry den has a honeycomb of brick-lined, candlelit rooms and corridors, as well as a cluster of alfresco tables located out the front. The debaucherous mood is offset a tad by the blaring soundtrack, which travels from old-school Pixies to Thai pop. *Lào-láo* cocktails are the house speciality.

Lemongrass (Th Khem Khong) This sleek and sophisticated bar serves classic cocktails and good wine in a chic setting. Unfortunately it's mostly for the benefit of gay travellers, and women might find they get a careless whisper suggesting as much.

Martin's Pub (Th Vatmou-Enna) Martin's is a relaxed English pub à la Laos, with the obligatory curved wooden bar and stools offset by local décor. There's a good range of booze and burgers on the menu and '70s, '80s and '90s classics in the background. Movies are screened nightly at 6pm.

More drinking holes:

Nao's Place (Th Sisavangvong) Central spot with international sports on a big screen.

Lao Lao Garden (Th Kingkitsarat) Two-for-one cocktails, Beerlao and shooters once the dining's done.

Entertainment

Royal Theatre (Th Sisavangvong; admission US$6-15; ⏱ shows 6pm) Inside the Royal Palace Museum compound, local performers put on a show that includes a *bąasĭi* ceremony (see the boxed text, above), traditional dance and folk music. There are traditional dances of Lao ethnic minorities such as the Phoo Noi and Hmong people.

Dao Fah (⏱ 9-11.30pm) A young Lao crowd packs this cavernous club, located off the road to the southern bus terminal. Live bands playing Lao and Thai pop alternate with DJs who spin rap and hip-hop. The bar serves Beerlao and mixers for patrons bringing their own liquor. Dao Fah and Muangsua (following) are the only two places in Luang Prabang where dancing is permitted.

Muangsua Hotel (☎ 212263; Th Phu Vao; ⏱ 9-11.30pm) In a low-ceilinged room behind the hotel, a Lao band plays the usual mix of Lao and Thai pop. Only Beerlao is sold.

There are several minicinemas where you can catch a flick, including the following:

Le Cinema (Ban Xieng Mouane; tickets US$3; ⏱ 6pm-midnight) On a laneway opposite the eastern wing of the Royal Palace, this ingenious spot enables you to hire a room and rent-release DVD for the night. It's fun and cosy.

L'Etranger Books & Tea (booksinlaos@yahoo.com; Th Kingkitsarat; ⏱ 7pm) Screens nightly films, ranging from new blockbusters to old art house.

Shopping

There's some very tempting shopping in Luang Prabang, ranging from cheap but interesting gifts and souvenirs to high-quality and expensive textiles, arts and antiques. Much of it originates in far-off villages and it's possible to buy direct from these producers in the tranquil, no-pressure **handicraft night market** (Hmong night market; Th Sisavangvong; ☺ 5-11pm) that assembles along Th Sisavangvong near the Royal Palace Museum. It's incredibly cheap and because you're injecting currency directly into the local economy you *have* to feel good about splashing cash here.

Shops line Th Sisavangvong and neighbouring streets, and prices and quality are often higher here. Vendors tend to ask more from the well-dressed – so don't be afraid to haggle, but equally don't get upset if you are being asked a fair price.

OckPopTok (Ban Wat Nong (☎ 253219; 73/5 Ban Wat Nong); Ban Xieng Mouane (☎ 254406; Th Sisavangvong) Naturally dyed house-woven Lao silk and cotton is used for bespoke clothing as well as household decorative items. The gallery in Ban Wat Nong is nonprofit and offers weaving classes.

Pathana Boupha Antique House (☎ 212262; 29/4 Ban Visoun) Pathana Boupha carries antique statuary; jewellery; silverwork; Royal Lao government currency and old photos, mostly from the Lao owners' private collection; and high-quality textiles.

Thithpeng Maniphone (Ban Wat That) Thithpeng crafted silverware for Luang Prabang royalty before 1975. He has 15 apprentice silversmiths but still does the most delicate work himself.

Getting There & Away

AIR

Luang Prabang International Airport (☎ 212173) is 4km from the city centre. **Lao Airlines** (☎ 212172; www.laoairlines.com; Th Pha Mahapatsaman) flies from Luang Prabang to Vientiane (one way US$62, daily), Phonsavan (US$40, three times a week) and Pakse (US$135, twice a week). Internationally, flights go to Chiang Mai in Thailand (US$85, Tuesday, Friday, Sunday), Bangkok (US$120) and Hanoi (US$112).

Bangkok Airways (☎ 253334; www.bangkokair.com; Th Sisavangvong) flies from Luang Prabang to Bangkok (US$120). **Siem Reap Airways** (www.siemreapairways.com) goes direct from Luang Prabang to Siem Reap (US$120); bookings are through travel agents.

BOAT

As we went to press there was talk in Laos of banning foreigners from using speedboats. Check the **Thorn Tree** (www.lonelyplanet.com/thorntree) for the latest.

Pak Beng & Huay Xai

Slow boats motor northwest to Huay Xai (US$20), departing at 8am. These boats stand by the Mekong and you can buy tickets direct from them or from a travel agent. The trip takes two days with an overnight stop in Pak Beng (US$10, one day). From Pak Beng it's also possible to take the bus northeast to Oudomxay.

White-knuckle speedboats up the Mekong leave from Ban Don, a 7km, US$1 shared túk-túk ride from the centre. They race to Pak Beng (US$20, three hours) and Huay Xai (US$30, six hours) in half the time…but 10 times the danger.

Nong Khiaw

Although it's quicker by road, many travellers charter a boat for the beautiful trip up the Nam Ou to Nong Khiaw (US$12, four to seven hours). Inquire at the Navigation Office in Luang Prabang or with travel agents in town, where you can add your name to the passenger list of impending departures. With enough passengers, speedboats travel from Luang Prabang to Nong Khiaw (US$16, two hours), though usually from June to January only.

Vientiane

Once in a blue moon slow cargo boats travel between Luang Prabang and Vientiane (US$40, around three days downriver). Check at the Navigation Office for departures. These boats are basically large floating trucks, with all the comforts of trucks – not many – but memorable character.

BUS & SĂWNGTHĂEW

Most interprovincial buses and *săwngthăew* heading north depart from the northern bus terminal (on Rte 13 about 4km north of town), while southbound vehicles use the southern bus terminal, 3km south of town. However, there are exceptions, so double-check if you're buying your ticket in town. On all these routes the durations can vary wildly depending on road and weather conditions. So just remember, this is Laos where arriving late is part of travelling.

Vientiane & Vang Vieng

Several buses leave the southern terminal for Vientiane (ordinary/air-con US$9/10, 10 to 14 hours) between about 6.30am and 9.30am, sometimes later. They stop in Vang Vieng (ordinary/air-con US$7.50/8.50, six to nine hours). Travel agents also sell tickets on minivans (US$18, about eight hours, four daily) and 'VIP' buses (US$12, about 10 hours, two daily). Neither is much more comfortable, but they are faster.

Oudomxay, Luang Nam Tha, Nong Khiaw & Sam Neua

From the northern bus terminal, daily *săwngthăew* and buses go to Oudomxay (US$4.50, five hours, 8am), Luang Nam Tha (US$7, eight hours, 9am and 4.30pm), Nong Khiaw (US$3.20, four hours, two to five daily), and Sam Neua (US$10, 16 hours, 4pm).

Xieng Khuang, Saiyabouli & Huay Xai

From the southern terminal buses leave daily to Phonsavan (US$8.50, 10 hours, 8.30am), Saiyabouli (US$4, five hours, 9am) and Huay Xai (US$14, eight to 11 hours, 5pm), although in the rainy season the Huay Xai bus might not run.

Getting Around

From the airport into town jumbos (big túk-túks) or minitrucks charge a uniform US$5.50 per vehicle, and up to six can share the ride. In the reverse direction you can usually charter an entire jumbo for US$2 to US$4.

Most of the town is accessible on foot. Jumbos charge US$0.40 per kilometre in town, although they usually just ask foreigners for US$1 a ride. Motorcycles can be hired from several shops in the town centre for US$5 a day. Bicycles are widely available for between US$1 and US$3 a day depending on the bike.

AROUND LUANG PRABANG
Pak Ou Caves

About 25km by boat from Luang Prabang up the Mekong River, at the mouth of the Nam Ou, are the famous **Pak Ou caves** (admission US$1). These two caves in the lower part of a limestone cliff are crammed with a variety of Buddha images, a kind of graveyard where unwanted images are placed. Bring a torch (flashlight).

Most boat trips stop at small villages along the way, especially **Ban Xang Hai**. Boatmen call this tourist-dominated place 'Whisky Village', and it's known for its free-flowing *lào-láo*.

You can hire long-tail boats to Pak Ou from Luang Prabang's charter boat landing

at US$15 for one to three people or US$20 for four to five people, including petrol. The trip takes two hours upriver and one hour down, plus stops. Túk-túks make the trip for about half the price.

Tat Kuang Si

This beautiful spot 32km south of town has a wide, many-tiered waterfall tumbling over limestone formations into a series of cool, turquoise pools. The lower level of the falls has been turned into a well-maintained **public park** (parking US$0.25, admission US$2). Near the entrance are enclosures housing a tiger and sun bears rescued from poachers. A trail climbs through the forest to a second tier that is more private (most visitors stay below) and has a pool large enough for swimming and splashing around.

On the way to Kuang Si you'll pass Ban Tat Paen, a scenic Khamu village with a cool stream, rustic dam and several miniature waterfalls. **Vanvisa 2 Guest House** (per person incl breakfast & dinner US$20) is a simple Lao-style wooden guesthouse in this village; with notice they can arrange cooking classes for US$15 per person.

Some visitors come by hired bicycle (for the fit only) or motorcycle, stopping in villages along the way. Freelance guides offer trips by jumbo, or boat and jumbo (both for about US$3 to US$5 per person) – they'll find you.

LUANG PRABANG PROVINCE
Nong Khiaw (Muang Ngoi)
☎ 071

Nestled next to the looming limestone cliffs of Phu Nang Nawn (Sleeping Princess Mountain), Nong Khiaw is a quiet market town on the banks of the Nam Ou. The location is stunning, but most travellers only stop for a short break before catching a boat further north. Those who stay and explore the dramatic surrounds are rewarded with walks to nearby caves and Hmong villages. The friendly guesthouses, on both sides of the river, are markedly less busy than the bungalow huts of Muang Ngoi Neua. Nong Khiaw and Ban Sop Houn have electricity from 6pm to 10pm.

SIGHTS & ACTIVITIES

There are great **trekking** opportunities around Nong Khiaw. You can walk by yourself to **Tham Pha Tok**, a cave where villagers hid out during the Second Indochina War. To get there, walk 2.5km east of the bridge, then look for a clearly visible cave mouth in the limestone cliff to your right (it's about 100m from the road). Longer treks to Hmong and Khamu villages are arranged by the Sunset Guest House for around US$10 per day. You can also try your hand at **traditional river fishing**; ask at Bamboo Paradise.

The **GreenHeart Foundation** (www.wowlao.com) based at Chan-a-Mar Guest House has a gallery and offers sustainable small-group tours with an emphasis on Lao culture.

SLEEPING & EATING

Guesthouses are in Nong Khiaw, near the bridge on the west side of the river, and the more popular Ban Sop Houn, on the east side, where most guesthouses have balconies with panoramic views. Most guesthouses have attached restaurants, and there are several other options that you won't need a compass to find.

Bamboo Paradise Guest House (Ban Sop Houn; r US$2) The friendly owners, decent if basic bungalows (with floor mattresses) and impromptu Lao language lessons make this a good choice.

Sengdao Guest House (r US$8, r with shared bathroom US$3) With the best views from the Nong Khiaw side of the river, this guesthouse has simple huts or pleasant bamboo bungalows with clean private bathrooms.

Sunset Guest House (Ban Sop Houn; s/d without bathroom US$2.50/5, r with bathroom US$12) This Lao-style wooden house has simple rooms or more comfortable bungalows overlooking the river. The shady veranda with reclining cushions, river views and decent food is popular.

Nong Kiau Riverside (Ban Sop Houn; ☎ 254770; www.nongkiau.com; s/d incl breakfast US$12/16) This bargain of a resort has huge bungalows with four-post beds and wide balconies that make you feel like royalty. There's also a good Lao restaurant.

GETTING THERE & AWAY

Boat

In high season boats heading up the Nam Ou to Muang Ngoi Neua (US$1.80, one hour) leave regularly until about 3pm. In low season they're less regular but usually meet buses arriving from Luang Prabang around lunchtime. Tickets are bought at an office at the bus station. Boats sometimes continue to Muang Khua (US$10, seven hours).

Occasional public boats still make the six-hour trip through striking karst scenery south to Luang Prabang, though more likely you'll have to charter one for about US$100. See p299 for information on boat travel from Luang Prabang.

Bus & Săwngthăew

Săwngthăew going to Oudomxay (US$2.50, three hours, three daily) leave from the west end of the bridge. You can also take one of the more frequent *săwngthăew* southwest to Pak Mong (US$1.80, two hours), then change to another *săwngthăew* to Oudomxay (US$2, two to three hours from Pak Mong) and anywhere further west. *Săwngthăew* and buses to Luang Prabang (US$3.20, four to five hours) depart between 8am and 11am; usually the earliest is a public bus.

If you're heading east towards Houaphanh or Xieng Khuang, you can get a bus to Sam Neua (US$7, 12 hours, one daily), or start a *săwngthăew* hop by heading to Muang Vieng Kham and changing there.

Muang Ngoi Neua

After an hour puttering along an almost deserted stretch of the Nam Ou, arriving at Muang Ngoi Neua is a slightly surreal experience. Until a few years ago, this was a small Lao village like many others, dependent on the river for its livelihood and – being inaccessible by road – largely cut off from the outside world. Today it is wall-to-wall guesthouses, and tourism has become the mainstay of the local economy. Despite its undeniable strangeness, Muang Ngoi Neua is a relaxing, scenic place to hang out and a good base for frolicking in the river or trekking into the majestic hills that surround it on all sides. And there are no cars!

INFORMATION

Generators provide electricity from 6pm to 10pm. There are no internet or telephone facilities, but you can exchange US dollars at several guesthouses at unattractive rates. A couple of pharmacies sell basic medicines.

SIGHTS & ACTIVITIES

In town you'll find a sea of signs advertising guides for fishing trips, tubing, kayaking and trekking. Some guides speak decent English, which is imperative if you want to enjoy the cultural aspect of any activity. Treks cost US$5 to US$10 per day and tubing costs around US$1.50 per day.

Recommended English-speaking guides include **Sang Tours** (⊗ 8am-9pm), not far from the boat landing on the main 'street', and **Lao Youth Travel** (www.laoyouthtravel.com; ⊗ 7.30-10.30am & 1.30-6pm) to the left of the boat landing. Run by a former village school teacher, **Muang Ngoi Tour Office** (⊗ 7-8am & 6-7pm) is located behind the main street 300m south of the boat landing – look for the signs. This outfit organises small-group treks to Hmong and Khamu villages for around US$8 per day including food, and **fishing trips**.

Two **caves** can easily be visited in under an hour's walk. At the southern end of the village, turn left (east) in front of Kaikeo Restaurant and follow the path through a large rural schoolyard (don't forget to pay the US$1 admission fee here) and into an area of secondary forest. After a 5km walk along a path passing rice fields, you come to a stream running into **Tham Kang**, a popular spot for spear-fishing. After another five minutes on the same trail you arrive at another cave, **Tham Pha Kaew**. Beyond the caves you can continue on to villages **Huay Bo** (one hour, 3km), **Huay Sen** (1½ hours) and **Ban Na** (another 1km). If you fancy a village stay, try the **Konsavan Guest House** (US$1) in Huay Bo.

SLEEPING

Unless otherwise noted, these guesthouses feature bungalows with river views, shared cold-water bathrooms, squat toilets, hammocks, small restaurants and, often, a local family of friendly rats. This is only a small selection, and as things change fast here, please don't restrict yourself to what we've listed here.

Saylom Guest House (r US$2) This welcoming place on the right of the boat ramp has clean bungalows with decent beds. All have shared bathrooms. The restaurant has delightful river views.

Phetdavanh Guest House (r US$2) This sturdy two-storey building on the main strip is clean and secure. Rooms are rat-free and have crisp sheets and tidy bathrooms, but there are no hammocks or river views.

Lattanavongsa Guest House (r US$5) A step up from the bamboo bungalow brigade, this friendly place to the left of the boat landing has clean rooms with hard beds and tiled bathrooms, but no fans.

Aloune Mai Guest House (r US$5) Off the path and away from the river, this new place is good for a quiet night's sleep and a private bathroom. Look for the signs.

More options:

Kham's Place Bungalows & Restaurant (r US$1) Simple bungalows and cold beer.

Sunset Guest House & Talee 2 (r US$2) At the southern end of the village, it's basic but quiet with a riverfront location.

EATING

Basic Lao and Western food can be found all over town in simple restaurants and at guesthouses; just follow your nose. All are open all day, the following being particularly notable.

Sengdala Bakery (meals US$0.50-1.50) This bakery restaurant serves good rice, noodles, curries, soups and salads but also distinguishes itself with great pancakes and baguettes. Water-bottle refills cost US$0.10 per litre.

Nang Phone Keo Restaurant (meals US$0.50-1.50) The '*falang* roll' of peanut butter, sticky rice and vegies lures ravenous travellers to this restaurant on the main street. The *föe* is good, too.

Lattanavongsa Guest House (meals US$1-2) The restaurant here makes outstanding spring rolls and a hearty noodle soup, served on an ambient open-air deck.

GETTING THERE & AWAY

Boats to Nong Khiaw leave regularly (US$1.80, one hour), the last at about 3pm or 4pm. Heading north, the very occasional public boat (US$8, five hours) goes to Muang Khua, or you can hire one for about US$50. It's a stunning trip. From Muang Khua, take a boat to Hat Sa (another five hours, US$10 or charter US$80 to US$100) or a bus back to Oudomxay (US$6, eight to 12 hours, 8am). From Hat Sa *săwngthăew* take the rough road to Phongsali (US$1.50 per person, US$15 charter). There's a basic guesthouse in Hat Sa.

XIENG KHUANG PROVINCE

Virtually every town and village in Xieng Khuang Province was bombed between 1964 and 1973. Today the awesome beauty of the mountains and valleys of this province is tragically overshadowed by the denuded hills and valleys pockmarked with bomb craters. This remains the province most heavily contaminated with UXO (unexploded ordnance) in Laos; walking off paths is foolish.

UXO IN XIENG KHUANG

Between 1964 and 1973, the USA conducted one of the largest sustained aerial bombardments in history, flying 580,344 missions over Laos and dropping two million tons of bombs, costing US$2.2 million a day. Around 30% of the bombs dropped on Laos failed to detonate, leaving the country littered with unexploded ordnance (UXO). For people all over eastern Laos (the most contaminated provinces are Xieng Khuang, Salavan and Savannakhet), living with this appalling legacy has become an intrinsic part of daily life, and for too many a cause of death. Today about 40% of Xieng Khuang's estimated 30 to 60 casualties per year are children, who continue to play with found UXO. The major problem is the harmless-looking, ball-shaped 'bomb light units' (BLUs, or bombies) left behind by cluster bombs.

Tourists can play a role in reducing the number of UXO and their casualties by visiting the **Mines Advisory Group** (MAG; ⌚ 4-8pm) office in Phonsavan. MAG is a British organisation that has been clearing UXO in conjunction with UXO Lao since 1994. The office has an information display and sells T-shirts and DVDs to fund its operations.

Most visitors come to Xieng Khuang to visit the mysterious Plain of Jars, but there are also several fascinating sites relating to the war that are open to tourists.

Phonsavan

☎ 061 / pop 60,000

A sprawling collection of wide streets and concrete shophouses, Phonsavan (often called Xieng Khuang') has little aesthetic appeal except for the ubiquitous collections of war scrap that decorate guesthouses and restaurants. However, it's a comfortable base for exploring the surrounding area and the locals are known to give foreigners a warm welcome.

Traditionally, the area surrounding Phonsavan and the former capital of Xieng Khuang has been a centre of Phuan language and culture. But these days you'll hear Vietnamese spoken almost as frequently as Lao and Phuan.

INFORMATION

Hot Net (Rte 7; per hr US$3; ⌚ 8am-10pm) Slow internet connections.

Lao Development Bank (☎ 312188) Currency exchange; has two branches.

Lao-Mongolian Friendship Hospital (☎ 312166) Good for minor needs, but medical emergencies will need to be taken to Vientiane.

Post office (⌚ 8am-4pm Mon-Fri, 8am-noon Sat) Has a domestic phone service.

Provincial tourist office (☎ 312217) Useful for simple information if you can find any staff.

Sousath Travel (☎ 312031; www.malyht.laotel.com; Maly Hotel) A reader fave. Trips further afield include Tham Piu, Muang Sui, Sam Neua and Long Cheng (former site

of the CIA's infamous mountain base during the Second Indochina War).

SLEEPING

You should be able to secure a room in Phonsavan at any time of year. Finding character, however, isn't so easy.

KongKeo Guest House (☎ 211354; www.kongkeojar.com; r US$4-5) Hidden off the main street, the popular KongKeo has four spartan rooms with shared bathroom or a scattering of great bungalows with cool interiors and attached bathrooms. The industrious owner can organise tours.

Nice Guest House (r US$6) The clean and generous rooms with firm beds and pretty bathrooms are, well, nice enough. Rooms upstairs share a balcony.

Banna Plain of Jars House (☎ 212484; www.bannagroup.com; r US$10) This polished guesthouse has unadorned but neat rooms upstairs with comfy beds. Some are dark, so ask to see a few. A cheery restaurant downstairs serves breakfast.

Thiengchaleun Guest House (☎ 211774; r US$10-15) This isolated and pleasant guesthouse has sunny rooms with pastel hues, large Western-style bathrooms and ceiling fans. Prices rise with the room size.

Maly Hotel (☎ 312031; www.malyht.laotel.com; r US$8-50; ⌨) The well-run Maly offers 30 comfortable rooms. They vary in size and some have a TV and/or balcony. The US$15 rooms are the best value. The restaurant is among the best in town and the owner speaks good English, German and French.

Duangkeomany Hotel (☎ 020-551 6553; r US$25) The place for fussy travellers, this hotel has spacious rooms with bright interiors, crisp

LAOS

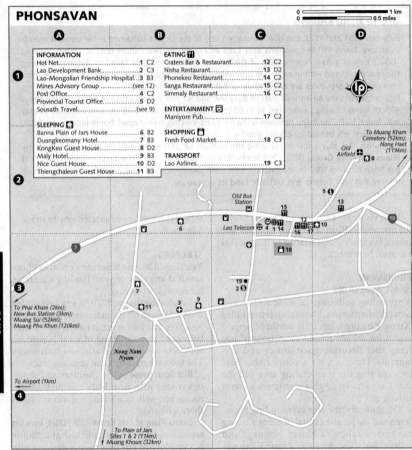

PHONSAVAN

0 _____ 1 km
0 _____ 0.5 miles

INFORMATION
Hot Net...................................1 C2
Lao Development Bank.............2 C3
Lao-Mongolian Friendship Hospital...3 B3
Mines Advisory Group ....(see 12)
Post Office.............................4 C2
Provincial Tourist Office..........5 D2
Sousath Travel....................(see 9)

SLEEPING
Banna Plain of Jars House........6 B2
Duangkeomany Hotel..............7 B3
KongKeo Guest House...............8 D2
Maly Hotel.............................9 B3
Nice Guest House...................10 D2
Thiengchaleun Guest House......11 B3

EATING
Craters Bar & Restaurant.........12 C2
Nisha Restaurant...................13 D2
Phonekeo Restaurant..............14 C2
Sanga Restaurant..................15 C2
Simmaly Restaurant................16 C2

ENTERTAINMENT
Maniyore Pub.......................17 C2

SHOPPING
Fresh Food Market.................18 C3

TRANSPORT
Lao Airlines........................19 C3

To Muang Kham
Cemetery (52km);
Nong Haet
(119km)
Old
Airfield

Old Bus
Station

Lao Telecom

To Muang Kham

Nong Nam
Nyam

To Phai Kham (2km);
New Bus Station (3km);
Muang Sui (52km);
Muang Phu Khun (120km)

To Airport (1km)

To Plain of Jars
Sites 1 & 2 (11km);
Muang Khoun (32km)

---

bedding, TVs, wardrobes and gleaming bathrooms with tubs. Excellent value.

EATING

There are a number of reasonable dining options in Phonsavan, from the daytime-only **fresh food market** (6am-5pm) – with its noodle stands, fresh fruit and other street food – to Indian, Korean, Lao or Western food.

Phonekeo Restaurant (meals US$1; breakfast, lunch & dinner) This friendly noodle shop serves the best *fŏe* in town.

Simmaly Restaurant (211013; meals US$1-1.50; breakfast, lunch & dinner) The welcoming Simmaly has a simple menu that's popular with both locals and tourists. Its fried spicy meats, rice dishes and noodle soups are all done well.

Sanga Restaurant (Sa-Nga; 312318; meals $1-4 lunch & dinner) The clean, well-run Sanga, near the market and post office, offers an extensive menu of Chinese, Thai and Lao food, including good *yám* (a tart, spicy Thai-style salad), *tôm yám* (spicy lemon grass–based soup), *khào khùa* (fried rice) and *fŏe*, plus a few Western items.

Nisha Restaurant (meals US$1-4; breakfast, lunch & dinner) Tuck into delicious *aloo ghobi* (potato and cauliflower), *dosas* (flat bread), tikka masalas and rogan josh at this spacious Indian diner. The list of vegetarian options is long and you can down a whole tandoori chicken for US$4.

Maly Hotel (meals US$1-5) This hotel restaurant has a great selection of Lao and Western food. In the rainy season ask for the delicious *hét wâi* (wild matsutake mushrooms).

Craters Bar & Restaurant (☎ 020-780 5775; meals US$2-4; ☺ breakfast, lunch & dinner) This cosmopolitan eatery has a mostly *falang* menu of club sandwiches, pizzas and even Australian T-bone. There are also Thai and Lao dishes tamed to Western palates.

ENTERTAINMENT

The tourist authority's 'DIY Phonsavan' fact sheet recommends politely crashing a wedding party, provided you're happy to give a monetary gift in a white envelope to the couple. Turning up uninvited is unlikely to offend your hosts, but neglecting to contribute to the gift-giving would be more than a faux pas (and will probably ensure foreigners are no longer welcomed!). If no one's getting married, the Maniyore Pub on the main street serves as a dimly lit nightclub and drinking den, and is well-patronised by locals and travellers.

GETTING THERE & AWAY

Lao Airlines (☎ 212027) flies to/from Vientiane (one way US$53, daily except Tuesday and Thursday) and to/from Luang Prabang (US$40, Wednesday, Friday, Saturday). Jumbos to the airport cost US$1.50 per person.

Most buses now leave from the new bus station, which is about 4km west of town, though some services might still begin in town. Most long-distance buses depart between 7am and 8am – check times the day before. Buses run to Sam Neua (US$7, eight to 10 hours, two daily), Vientiane (ordinary/VIP US$9/10, 11 hours), Vang Vieng (ordinary/VIP US$7.50/10, six hours) and Luang Prabang (ordinary/VIP US$9.50/8.50, 10 hours). There's also a daily bus to Paksan (US$8), but the road is diabolical and trip times vary from long to very long.

There are public buses and *săwngthăew* to Muang Kham (US$2, two hours, four daily),

Muang Sui (US$2, one hour, three daily) and Nong Haet (US$2, four hours, four daily).

Other destinations include Lat Khai (Plain of Jars Site 3; US$1, 30 minutes, one daily) and Muang Khoun (US$2, 30 minutes, six daily). Buses also go all the way through to Vinh in Vietnam (US$11, 11 hours, 6.30am Tuesday, Thursday and Sunday).

Plain of Jars

The Plain of Jars is a large area around Phonsavan where huge jars of unknown origin are scattered in about 20 groupings. Visitors can wander around three main sites, which have been largely cleared of UXO.

Site 1 (Thong Hai Hin; admission US$0.70), the biggest and most accessible site, is 15km southwest of Phonsavan and features 250 jars, most of which weigh from 600kg to 1 tonne each. The largest jar weighs as much as 6 tonnes and is said to have been the victory cup of mythical King Jeuam, and so is called Hai Jeuam.

Two other jar sites are readily accessible by road from Phonsavan. **Site 2** (Hai Hin Phu Salato; admission US$0.70), about 25km south of town, features 90 jars spread across two adjacent hillsides. Vehicles can reach the base of the hills, then it's a short, steep walk to the jars.

More impressive is 150-jar **Site 3** (Hai Hin Lat Khai; admission US$0.70). It's about 10km south of Site 2 (or 35km from Phonsavan) on a scenic hilltop near the charming village of Ban Xieng Di, where there's a small monastery containing the remains of Buddha images damaged in the war. The site is a 2km hike through rice paddies and up a hill.

GETTING THERE & AWAY

It's possible to charter a *săwngthăew* to Site 1 for about US$8 return, including waiting time, for up to six people. All three sites are reachable by bike or motorcycle (per day US$15

CROSSING INTO VIETNAM: NONG HAET TO NAM CAN

The Nong Haet–Nam Can crossing is little used by travellers because it's difficult, potentially expensive if you get ripped off, and not really convenient if you're heading north in Vietnam (you have to go 200km south to grim Vinh first). On the Laos side, Nam Khan is 13km east of Nong Haet via Rte 7. You can get between Nong Haet and Phonsavan by bus (US$2, three to four hours, four daily) or chartered car for about US$30 or US$40. Coming into Laos, do not rely on getting a visa on arrival. There is also a direct bus between Phonsavan and Vinh (US$11, 11 hours, Tuesday, Thursday and Sunday). For information on crossing this border in the other direction, see p366.

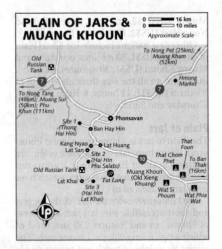

PLAIN OF JARS & MUANG KHOUN

0 — 16 km
0 — 10 miles
Approximate Scale

To Nong Pet (25km);
Muang Kham (52km)

Old Russian Tank

To Nong Tang (48km); Muang Sui (50km); Phu Khun (111km)

Hmong Market

Phonsavan

Site 1 (Thong Hai Hin)   Ban Hay Hin

Kang Nyao   Lat Huang
Lat San   Site 2
(Hai Hin
Phu Salato)   That Foun

Old Russian Tank   That Chom Phet   To Ban Thak (16km)

Muang Khoun (Old Xieng Khuang)

Lat Khai   Tat Lang   Wat Si Phoum   Wat Phia Wat

Site 3 (Hai Hin Lat Khai)

through guesthouses), and Craters Bar & Restaurant (p305) has two bicycles for rent (US$3 per day).

Otherwise, you're on a tour. Guesthouses and a number of travel agents offer tours for US$10 to US$12 per person in a minivan of around eight passengers. **Sousath Travel** (☎ 312031; sousathp@laotel.com), **Phou Kham** (☎ 312121) and **Kong-Keo Guest House** (☎ 020-551 6365; www.kongkeojar.com; off Rte 7) have all received good reports.

Tours are often extended to include other interesting sites, including a crashed US F-105 Thunderchief, a Russian tank, Viet Cong bunkers, the US Lima Site 108 airstrip supposedly used for drug running, and hot springs. Trips can also be arranged to the Tham Piu cave, about 60km east, where 400 local people were killed in a US bombing raid.

HOUAPHANH PROVINCE

Rugged and beautiful, Houaphanh is unlike any other province in Laos. Although home to 22 different ethnic groups, including Yao, Hmong, Khamu, Thai Khao and Thai Neua, the strong Vietnamese influence is evident. The province's high altitude means the climate can be cool – even in the hot season – and forested mountains are shrouded in mist. Road journeys to Houaphanh are memorably scenic, described by one local as 'a journey of a million turns'.

Despite the remote border to Vietnam and Hanoi opening to foreigners, this remains one of the least visited provinces in Laos. Which is a great reason to get off the beaten

track and come; your exploration will be well rewarded.

Sam Neua
☎ 064 / pop 46,800

There is an unmistakable 'frontier' feeling to Sam Neua. Men in military caps and jackets nurse coffees and cigarettes, wrapped up against the morning chill, and pick-up trucks piled high with local villagers, crates of chilli sauce or nylon bags stuffed with goods pass through. It's one of the least touristy provincial centres in Laos. While the town offers little in terms of sights, the riverside market is fascinating – all manner of freshly slaughtered or harvested delicacies, as well as textiles, jewellery and consumer goods are sold here. In mid-December, local ethnic groups take part in all-important courtship games and festivities during a **Hmong Lai Festival**.

INFORMATION

Lao Development Bank (☎ 312171; ☺ 8am-4pm Mon-Fri) On the main road 400m north of the bus station on the left; exchanges cash and travellers cheques.

Post office (☺ 8am-4pm Mon-Fri) In a large building directly opposite the bus station. A telephone office at its rear offers international calls.

Provincial tourist office (☎ 312567; ☺ 8am-noon & 1.30-4pm Mon-Fri) An excellent tourist office with English-speaking staff eager to help.

SLEEPING & EATING

The block between the bus station and the Nam Sam is where the reputable guesthouses and a few restaurants can be found, all within a short walking distance.

Phootong Guest House (☎ 312271; r US$3.50) Simple, cheap and central, this small guesthouse behind a shopfront has basic rooms with ceiling fans, mosquito nets and small cold-water bathrooms. They're a little bit tired but decent value, and the owners are extremely gracious.

Shuliyo Guest House (☎ 312462; r US$5-6) Tucked into an alley near the market, Shuliyo has rudimentary but welcoming rooms with decent bathrooms, hot water, ceiling fans and aged beds. There's a lovely central sitting area with free tea and coffee.

Kheamxam Guest House (☎ 312111; r US$5-7) This pastel-hued, corner hotel next to the bridge is the best value in town. Rooms range from neat and simple affairs with spotless, shared bathrooms to large corner rooms with satellite TV, attached hot-water bathroom and street views.

Dan Nao Restaurant (☎ 314126; meals US$1-1.50; ❤ breakfast, lunch & dinner) At the end of the laneway and a few doors west of Khaemxam, this is probably the best eatery in a town that's not winning any gourmet awards. The basic Lao menu also includes Western-style breakfasts, excellent fried rice, fresh baguettes and tender beef salad.

For cheap *fŏe*, samosas, spring rolls and fried sweet potato, the **market** (❤ 6am-6pm) is the place to go.

GETTING THERE & AWAY

Lao Airlines (☎ 312023; airport) flies three times a week between Vientiane and Sam Neua (one way US$75), though flights are regularly cancelled or delayed because the airport gets shrouded by mist. The airport is 3km from town and a motorcycle taxi costs about US$1.

There are two buses a day from Sam Neua to Phonsavan (US$7, eight to 10 hours, 9am and noon). The bus then continues on to Vientiane (from Sam Neua US$13, 20 to 24 hours), on a winding sealed road.

A daily bus heads southeast along Rte 6 and then Rte 1 to Nong Khiaw (US$7, 12 hours, 8am) and continues on to Luang Prabang (from Sam Neua US$8, 16 hours). If you're heading for Oudomxay, take this bus and change at Pak Mong. The Nam Noen to Nong Khiaw leg runs along winding roads

and past brilliant scenery, passing many Blue Hmong villages along the way.

You can rent a motorcycle (US$6 per day) from a shop between the provincial tourist office and the bus station.

Vieng Xai
☎ 064 / pop 32,800

In a narrow valley of limestone peaks are caves that served as the elaborate homes and shelters of the Pathet Lao leaders and some 23,000 of their followers for more than a decade before their victory in 1975. The caverns are virtually unassailable by land or air, but the area was still heavily pounded by American bombs. Today, the most historically significant caves, named after the leaders who lived in them, are open to tourists. Vieng Xai is a fascinating and peaceful place to spend a day or two in. A wooden board in front of the market features a map of town.

You must report to the **Kaysone Phomvihane Memorial Tour Cave Office** (☎ 314321; ❤ 8am-11.30am & 1-4.30pm), a 2km walk from the bus station, to pay the US$3 fee for entrance and the mandatory guide. It's another US$0.50 for a camera. Two-hour tours leave the office at 9am and 1pm and take in three or four caves. At other times you will need to pay an additional fee of US$5 per tour to cover staff costs.

The leaders' caves feature multiple entrances, bedrooms, offices, and emergency rooms fitted with steel doors and equipped

LAOS

JARS OF THE STONE AGE

The purpose of the Plain of Jars (p305), which are possibly 2000 years old, remains a mystery. And without any organic material – such as bones or food remains – there is no reliable way to date them. Archaeological theories and local myth suggest the enigmatic jars were used for burial purposes – as stone coffins or urns – or maybe for storing *lào-láo* (rice whisky) or rice?

In the 1930s, pioneering French archaeologist Madeline Colani documented the jars in a 600-page monograph *Mégalithes du Haut Laos* (Megaliths of Highland Laos), concluding that they were funerary urns carved by a vanished people. Colani found a human-shaped bronze figure in one of the jars at Site 1, and tiny stone beads nearby. Today the whereabouts of these artefacts is unknown.

The relief of a human figure carved onto Jar 217 at Site 1 – a feature Colani missed – lends weight to the sarcophagi theory. Whether they were used for cremation or in a burial practice where a person is 'distilled', their presence reinforces various theories on the pattern of human migration here over the last two millennia.

Aerial photography suggests a thin 'track' of jars may link the various jar sites in Xieng Khuang, and some researchers hope future excavations will uncover sealed jars whose contents may be relatively intact. Unfortunately, excavations will take some time while UXOs are slowly removed from the area.

---

with large Russian oxygen machines in case of a chemical attack. Many of the caves are now fringed by magnificent gardens, making them look more like holiday grottoes than scenes of war and hardship.

Tham Than Souphanouvong, named after the Red Prince, has a crater from a 230kg bomb near the entrance that has been concreted as a war relic. **Tham Than Kaysone**, named after the former president, has the most to look at, with original beds, clothing, office equipment, books, a portrait of Che Guevara and a politburo meeting room. **Tham Than Khamtay**, where up to 3000 Pathet Lao rank and file would hide out, is the most spectacular of the caves.

SLEEPING & EATING

Naxay Guest House (☎ 314336; r US$2-4) There are five cute twins here that share a homely living room and rudimentary bathrooms, plus one private bungalow with attached bathroom.

Thavisay Hotel (☎ 020-571 2392; r US$4-6) Currently being renovated, this two-storey hotel in a lovely setting promises to be the best place in town, with attached hot-water bathrooms and two double beds with mosquito nets. There's also a restaurant (meals US$2 to US$3, open breakfast, lunch and dinner) overlooking a manmade lake.

GETTING THERE & AWAY

Sǎwngthǎew run regularly between Sam Neua and Vieng Xai (US$0.80, 50 minutes, 29km, 6.20am to 5.20pm), with departures more frequent in the morning.

OUDOMXAY PROVINCE

This rugged province is wedged between Luang Prabang, Phongsali, Luang Nam Tha, Bokeo and Sainyabuli Provinces, with a small section that shares a border with China's Yúnnán province. It is home to 23 ethnic minorities, but the dominant group is increasingly

the Yunnanese working in construction and plantation operations. Most people travelling in northern Laos will pass through Oudomxay, but there are better places to stop.

Oudomxay
☎ 081 / pop 80,000

During the Second Indochina War, the regional capital became the centre for Chinese troops supportive of the Pathet Lao. Today its position at the junction of Rtes 1, 2 and 4 has made it a booming Laos–China trade centre riding on imported Chinese wealth. Despite the enthusiasm of the staff at the tourist office, the town is not particularly exciting.

INFORMATION

BCEL (☎ 211260; Rte 1) Changes US dollars, Thai baht or Chinese yuán into kip.

Oudomxay Internet (Rte 1; per hr US$1.80; ☑ 8am-7pm) Speedy and reliable.

Oudomxay provincial tourism office (☎ 211797; Rte 1; ☑ 8am-noon & 1.30-4pm Oct-Mar, 7.30-11.30am & 1.30-6pm Apr-Sep) Just west of the bridge; information about accommodation, ecotourism tours and transport.

SLEEPING & EATING

Most places are along Rte 1. The **Valving Guest House** (☎ 212503; r US$4) is a good choice for the budget conscious, while the welcoming **Lithavixay Guest House** (☎ /fax 212175; Rte 1; r $7-15; ☒ ☐), east of the bridge, has rooms with private hot-water bathrooms and, for a few dollars more, breakfast, satellite TV and air-con.

The **Sinphet Restaurant** (meals US$0.50-1.50; ☑ breakfast, lunch & dinner), at the base of a basic guesthouse, whips up good Chinese-Lao fusion dishes and a few Western favourites.

GETTING THERE & AWAY

Lao Airlines (☎ 312047; airport) flies to/from Vientiane (one way US$75) every Tuesday, Thursday and Saturday. The Chinese-built bitumen roads that radiate from Oudomxay are in fair condition (except for the road to Pak Beng) and the city is the transport hub of the north. The **bus terminal** (☎ 212218) at the southwestern edge of town has buses to Luang Prabang (ordinary US$4, five hours, three daily; VIP US$5, three hours, two daily), Nong Khiaw (US$3.10, three to five hours, four daily), Pak Beng (US$3.30, five hours, two daily), Luang Nam Tha (US$3.20, four hours, three daily), Muang Khua (US$2.80, four hours, three daily), Boten (US$3, four hours, two daily), Phongsali (US$6, eight to 12 hours, daily) and Vientiane (ordinary US$11, 16 hours, two daily; VIP US$12.10, 14 hours, two daily).

Pak Beng

If you're taking a river boat between Huay Xai and Luang Prabang, there's a good chance you'll spend a night in this rustic town at the junction of the Mekong River and the smaller Nam Beng. Pak Beng isn't nearly as grim as it once was, but it's not that appealing, either. Scams, including overcharging for carrying bags and promising rooms that sound much better than the squalid hovels they are, are common. For electricity most places rely on generators, which run between 6pm and 10pm.

There's little in the way of attractions, but the **Traditional Massage & Sauna** (sauna US$1, massage US$3; ☯ sauna 4-10pm, massage 8am-noon & 2.30-11.30pm) near Bounmee Guest House, is a good way to kill an hour or two.

Several guesthouses populate the riverside road, most with small rooms, hard mattresses, mosquito nets and shared facilities. The **Monsavan Guest House** (☎ 5771935; r US$2-5) isn't bad for budgeteers, while the **Villa Salika** (☎ 212306; r US$5-7) has private bathrooms for a little more. For greater comforts, the **Pak Beng Lodge** (r US$30; ✷) and the eco-friendly **Luang Say Lodge** (☎ 212296; www.mekongcruises.com; r from US$60) should satisfy.

See p314 for details on river travel between Pak Beng, Luang Prabang and Huay Xai. *Săwngthăew* head along potholed Rte 2 towards Oudomxay (US$3.30, five hours, two daily) from a bus station 1.5km from the boat landing.

LUANG NAM THA PROVINCE

With the capital virtually destroyed during the Second Indochina War, Luang Nam Tha has been revived as a commercial node between Thailand, China and Laos, with Chinese plantation operations popping up faster than mushrooms. The success of the Nam Ha Ecotourism Project has seen tourism take off and chances are you'll meet more than one traveller raving about their trekking experience out of Luang Nam Tha or Muang Sing. The new Rte 3 from China to Thailand is set to alter the dynamic of village life here, as Laos reinvents itself as an important crossroads state between two of the world's fastest-growing economies.

Luang Nam Tha

☎ 086 / pop 35,400

Luang Nam Tha is actually two towns set in a wide, flat river valley. The new town, which has the main bus station and the bulk of the guesthouses, restaurants and facilities, lies 7km to the north of the old town – where you find the airport and Nam Tha boat landing. The town itself is not particularly appealing, though a new night market selling textiles, clothing, basketry, paper and other locally produced handicrafts should liven things up a bit. The surrounding mountains and rice fields have a number of Thai Dam, Khamu and Thai Lü villages that are worth visiting by bicycle.

INFORMATION

BCEL (☯ 8.30am-3.30pm Mon-Fri) Changes US-dollar travellers cheques and cash; gives cash advances on credit cards.

Internet Cafe (per hr US$1.80)

KNT Internet (per hr US$1.80; ☯ 8am-10pm) Fast and reliable.

Lao Development Bank (☯ 8.30am-noon & 2-3.30pm Mon-Fri) Exchanges US-dollar travellers cheques and cash.

Lao Telecom Long-distance phone calls.

Luang Nam Tha provincial tourism office (☎ 211534, 312047; ☯ 8am-noon & 2-5pm) Excellent tourist office with English-speaking staff.

Post office (☯ 8am-noon & 1-4pm Mon-Fri)

SIGHTS & ACTIVITIES

The **Luang Nam Tha Museum** (admission US$0.50; ☯ 8.30-11.30am & 1.30-3.30pm Mon-Thu, 8.30-11.30am Fri) contains a collection of local anthropological artefacts, such as ethnic clothing and Khamu bronze drums, Buddha images and a display chronicling the revolution.

However, most people come to Luang Nam Tha for the **trekking**, **kayaking** and **rafting**

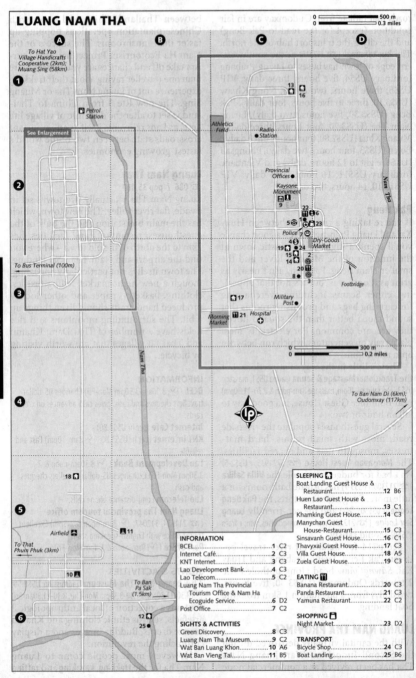

LUANG NAM THA

To Hat Yao
Village Handicrafts
Cooperative (2km);
Muang Sing (58km)

Petrol Station

See Enlargement

To Bus Terminal (100m)

Athletics Field

Radio Station

Provincial Offices

Kaysone Monument

Police

Dry-Goods Market

Footbridge

Military Post

Morning Market

Hospital

To Ban Nam Di (6km);
Oudomxay (117km)

To Ban Nam Di

Nam Tha

Airfield

To That
Phum Phuk (3km)

To Ban
Pa Sak
(1.5km)

0   500 m
0   0.3 miles

0   300 m
0   0.2 miles

INFORMATION
BCEL..1 C2
Internet Café.............................2 C3
KNT Internet..............................3 C3
Lao Development Bank..............4 C3
Lao Telecom.............................5 C2
Luang Nam Tha Provincial
 Tourism Office & Nam Ha
 Ecoguide Service....................6 D2
Post Office................................7 C3

SIGHTS & ACTIVITIES
Green Discovery.........................8 C3
Luang Nam Tha Museum...........9 C2
Wat Ban Luang Khon...............10 A6
Wat Ban Vieng Tai...................11 B5

SLEEPING
Boat Landing Guest House &
 Restaurant...........................12 B6
Huen Lao Guest House &
 Restaurant...........................13 C1
Khamking Guest House............14 C3
Manychan Guest
 House-Restaurant.................15 C3
Sinsavanh Guest House...........16 C1
Thavyxai Guest House.............17 C3
Villa Guest House....................18 A5
Zuela Guest House...................19 C3

EATING
Banana Restaurant...................20 C3
Panda Restaurant....................21 C3
Yamuna Restaurant.................22 C2

SHOPPING
Night Market...........................23 D2

TRANSPORT
Bicycle Shop............................24 C3
Boat Landing...........................25 B6

opportunities in the **Nam Ha NPA**. Many of the tours and treks stop for at least a night in a village; usually Khamu and Lenten to the south and Akha to the north, west and east. Trips follow strict guidelines on group sizes and frequency, limiting the impact of tourism on villages. Profits go back into the local economy, and it's illegal to trek in the Nam Ha NPA with unlicensed guides.

Treks vary in duration and difficulty but most traverse spectacular landscape and involve a decent dose of huffing and puffing. At the time of writing, tours were offered by the **Nam Ha Ecoguide Service** (☎ 211534; ☼ 8am-9pm), a wing of the provincial tourist office, and the privately owned **Green Discovery** (☎ 211484; www .greendiscoverylaos.com; ☼ 8am-9pm). The provincial tourism office has information on trips as well as excellent photocopied brochures on responsible tourism, local flora and fauna, local ethnic minorities, customs and etiquette, and maps. Green Discovery also runs one- to four-day kayaking and rafting trips on the Nam Ha for about US$30 per day, depending on numbers.

Places of interest within easy cycling or motorbiking distance include two 50-year-old wat, **Wat Ban Vieng Tai** and **Wat Ban Luang Khon**, near the airfield; a hilltop stupa, **That Phum Phuk**, about 4km west of the airfield; a small **waterfall** about 3km northeast of town past **Ban Nam Dee**; plus a host of Khmu, Lenten, Thai Dam and Thai Lü villages dotted along dirt roads through rice fields. Pick up a map and brochures at the provincial tourist office before setting off.

Alternatively, join a guided mountain-bike tour with the **Boat Landing Guest House** (☎ 312398; www.theboatlanding.com). Ten percent of profits go to grassroots development projects in the region.

SLEEPING & EATING

Most lodging in Luang Nam Tha is in the newer, northern part of town. Rooms fill up fast during the December-to-March high season, and morning arrivals stand a better chance of finding a bed.

Khamking Guest House (r US$5) Glistening and new, the Khamking has plain but welcoming rooms with large, screened windows, comfy beds, fans and cramped but spotless tiled hot-water bathrooms. Good value.

Manychan Guest House-Restaurant (☎ 312209; r US$5) Central and exceedingly popular, this guesthouse has had a good makeover and contains pleasant fan-cooled rooms with temperamental hot-water showers. The *falang*-oriented restaurant (meals US$1.50 to US$2.50) is also a favourite.

Huen Lao Guest House & Restaurant (☎ 211111; r US$6) Atmospheric rooms are aesthetically appealing and complement the relatively sophisticated open-air restaurant (meals US$1.50 to US$3, open lunch and dinner) upstairs; try the dried pickled bamboo with pork or the tangy chicken.

Thavyxai Guest House (☎ 511 0292; r US$6.50) A great choice close to the bus station, Thavyxai has immaculate rooms that verge on hotel standard. It's run by a friendly family and is relatively quiet.

ourpick **Boat Landing Guest House & Restaurant** (☎ 312398; www.theboatlanding.laopdr.com; r incl breakfast US$32-42) Located 7km south of the new town and about 150m off the main road, this quiet ecolodge near the Nam Tha boat landing has attractive wooden bungalows with river views, and private bathrooms with solar-heated showers. The restaurant (meals US$2 to US$5) serves the most authentic northern Lao cuisine in town, including plenty of vegetarian options (a nightly túk-túk comes from Green Discovery at 6.30pm, returning at 8.45pm, for US$1). Staff can also arrange rafting, tubing, fishing, bird-watching, mountain biking and trekking with English- and French-speaking guides.

Panda Restaurant (☎ 566 3122; meals US$1.50-2.50; ☼ breakfast, lunch & dinner) The phonebook-sized menu at this welcoming open-air restaurant encompasses everything from (divine) pancakes to tasty tofu fry ups and delicious fruit shakes.

Yamuna Restaurant (meals US$1.50-2.50; ☼ breakfast, lunch & dinner) A spread of Indian curries is just what the doctor ordered after days spent in the villages.

Other eating and sleeping options:

Sinsavanh Guest House (☎ 211141; r US$2-4) Bright two-storey wooden house with basic rooms and shared, cold-water bathrooms.

Zuela Guest House (☎ 312183; r US$5) New brick-and-timber house with big, spotlessly clean rooms and hot-water bathrooms.

Villa Guest House (☎ 312425; r incl breakfast US$20) South of town, this colourful place has big, sunny rooms, large beds and an open-air restaurant (meals US$2 to US$4, open for dinner).

Banana Restaurant (☎ 5718026; meals US$1-1.50; ☼ breakfast, lunch & dinner) Cheap and tasty food catering to *falang* palates with Western breakfasts (even cornflakes), stir fries and curries.

GETTING THERE & AWAY

Luang Nam Tha's airport was being turned into an 'international' airport when we passed. When it reopens expect **Lao Airlines** (☎ 312180) to resume flights to/from Luang Prabang (one way US$45) and Vientiane (US$84).

Charter boats make the wonderful trip along the Nam Tha, through truly remote country, to Pak Tha on the Mekong, or all the way to Huay Xai. They leave from the **boat landing** 7km south of town on the Nam Ha, and cost about US$100 to Na Lae, US$170 to Pak Tha, or US$180 to US$200 to Huay Xai. Sign up before your departure to share the charter costs for this two-day trip in an open long-tail boat. In the high season a boat leaves almost every day, depending on passenger numbers. An additional US$4 or so covers food and lodgings in Na Lae, or with the boatman's family. Bring sun protection, plus plenty of water and snacks.

The **bus terminal** (☎ 312164) is opposite the morning market. Buses run to Oudomxay (26,000 kip, three to five hours, four daily) and Boten (US$2, two hours, four daily) on the Laos–China border. One bus runs to Vientiane (US$14, 19 hours) via Luang Prabang (US$7, eight hours, 8.30am); you can't buy tickets the day before, so arrive early.

One *săwngthăew* travels daily to Huay Xai (US$6.50, eight hours), stopping in Vieng Phoukha (US$2.50, four hours); conditions and travel times on this road are improving. About six *săwngthăew* run to Muang Sing daily (US$2, two hours), and one bus goes to Muang Long (US$3.60, five hours).

GETTING AROUND

Jumbos from the main street to the airport, 7km away, cost US$4. Shared pick-ups also ply this route for US$0.30 per person. To the Nam Tha boat landing, or the nearby Boat Landing Guest House, figure on US$5 to charter a jumbo from the bus terminal, or US$0.30 per person on a shared jumbo.

Mountain bikes or garden variety one-speed bikes cost US$0.30/1 per hour/day from the **bicycle shop** (☻ 9am-6pm) on the main street, which also rents motorcycles.

Muang Sing

☎ 081 / pop 29,307

Deep in the legendary 'Golden Triangle', Muang Sing is a cultural melting pot, with the dominant Thai Lü and Thai Neua cultures mixing with Thai Dam, Akha, Hmong, Mien, Lolo and Yunnanese traders. Since the Guide Services Centre was set up to regulate the once exploitative trekking business, trips into the beautiful Nam Ha NPA have improved substantially. If you're keen to visit ethnic minorities on a socially and environmentally responsible tour, this is possibly your best bet in Southeast Asia.

Muang Sing follows a quadratic grid pattern. A map of the old city is on display in the Guide Services Centre. The few services include a **Lao Development Bank** (☻ 8am-noon & 2-3.30pm Mon-Fri), which changes cash only, and a **post office** (☻ 8am-4pm Mon-Fri).

SIGHTS & ACTIVITIES

The crumbling remains of the French colonial presence and a population often wearing colourful traditional dress are charming. And the beautifully restored Lao-French building housing the **Muang Sing Exhibitions Museum** (Tribal Museum; admission US$0.50; ☻ 8.30am-4pm Mon-Fri, 8-11am Sat), displaying traditional textiles, woven baskets, handicrafts, amulets and cymbals, is worth a look. Saturday opening hours vary. But most people come to Muang Sing to trek in the Nam Ha NPA. Treks can only be organised through the **Muang Sing Tourism Information & Trekking Guide Service Center** (☎ 020-239 3534; ☻ 8-11am & 1.30-5pm Mon-Fri, 8-10am & 3-5pm Sat & Sun), which has seven different treks to remote hilltribe villages, ranging from one to three days with homestays. Prices are US$35 per person per day for one person, but drop significantly the more people there are (as little as US$10

CROSSING INTO CHINA: BOTEN TO MÓHĀN

The only crossing between China and Laos that is open to foreigners is between Móhān, in Yúnnán province, and Boten, in the Luang Nam Tha Province. Laos issues 30-day visas on arrival; China does not. The crossing is open from 8am to 4pm on the Lao side and 8am to 5pm in China. In both directions, onward transport is most frequent in the mornings, soon after 8am. In Laos, transport runs to Luang Nam Tha and Oudomxay. If you get stuck in Boten there are a couple of cheap guesthouses. For information on crossing this border in the other direction, see p470.

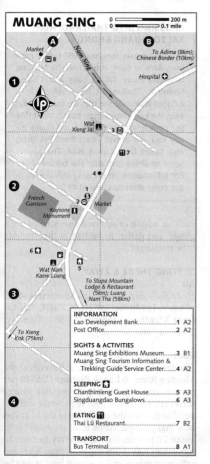

MUANG SING

0 ——————— 200 m
0 ——————— 0.1 mile

Market

A

Nam Sing

B

To Adima (8km);
Chinese Border (10km)

Hospital

Wat
Xieng Jai 3

7

French
Garrison

Kaysone
Monument

Market

Wat Nam
Kaew Luang

To Stupa Mountain
Lodge & Restaurant
(5km); Luang
Nam Tha (58km)

To Xieng
Kok (75km)

INFORMATION
Lao Development Bank......................1 A2
Post Office......................................2 A2

SIGHTS & ACTIVITIES
Muang Sing Exhibitions Museum......3 B1
Muang Sing Tourism Information &
Trekking Guide Service Center......4 A2

SLEEPING
Chanthimieng Guest House..............5 A3
Singduangdao Bungalows................6 A3

EATING
Thai Lü Restaurant........................7 B2

TRANSPORT
Bus Terminal................................8 A1

with seven people). Drug use is banned on these treks. Guides include former farmers, teachers, policemen and agricultural workers. A breakdown of how your money is spent is posted on the wall.

SLEEPING & EATING
Guesthouses in Muang Sing are pretty average. There are a number of large and not overly hospitable options on the main road just north of the old market, with rooms of a similar standard and price. If you're only crashing for one night and have an early trekking departure, these are fine. Check out a few and find the best bed for the night. If you're staying in Muang Sing for a few days, it's worth heading beyond the main street for

better options – and atmosphere. Most of the guesthouses have small dining areas downstairs and the main street is peppered with simple *fŏe* shops selling tasty cheap fare. The large market next to the bus station sells a limited selection of fresh fruit and vegetables.

Chanthimieng Guest House (☎ 212351; r US$4-8) The owners adopt all guests upon entry to this new place, where the beds aren't great but the location and panoramic rice paddy views are idyllic.

Singduangdao Bungalows (r US$5) Choose the roomy timber and bamboo bungalows for good-value access to hot-water showers.

Adima (☎ 212372; r US$5-6) The long-running Adima, in a rice field 8km north of Muang Sing, is within walking distance of several Mien and Akha villages. Call to coordinate with their transport.

Stupa Mountain Lodge & Restaurant (☎ 020-568 6555; stupamtn@laotel.com; r US$10) This sits on a hillside 5km south of 'town' and has some lovely wooden bungalows with hot-water bathrooms and private verandas.

Thai Lü Restaurant (☎ 212375; meals US$1-1.60; ☺ breakfast, lunch & dinner) Muang Sing's top spot for authentic Thai Lü fare such as *nam pik awng* – fermented soy bean paste, or *jeow* (local chilli paste) wafers. There's also Thai, Lao and Western dishes, and the open setting is pleasant.

GETTING THERE & AROUND
Săwngthăew ply back and forth between Muang Sing and Luang Nam Tha (US$2, two hours, about six daily). There are also about four *săwngthăew* a day to Xieng Kok (US$2, three to four hours) on the Burmese border, from where speedboats race down to Huay Xai. Most passenger vehicles depart from the 'new' bus station in the northwest of town, near the Nam Sing. Rent bikes from shops and guesthouses.

BOKEO PROVINCE
Laos' smallest province, wedged between the Mekong River border with Thailand and Luang Nam Tha Province, is a popular entry point for travellers from Thailand. Despite its small size and tiny population, it is home to 34 different ethnic groups, second only to Luang Nam Tha for ethnic diversity.

Huay Xai
☎ 084 / pop 15,500
Huay Xai is a busy riverside town that has existed for centuries as a staging point for

LAOS

trade between Thailand and China. That function remains, though as you walk down the main street (there aren't many streets) you'll soon see that tourism is also a major industry. Many guesthouses have sprung up to cater for tourists waiting to catch the slow boat to Luang Prabang, head north by road or river, or cross to Thailand. Chinese barges still navigate this far, and a couple of passenger ferries come down this stretch of the Mekong from China. However, they only stop on the Thai side.

INFORMATION

Khaenlao Tours (Th Saykhong) Sells boat tickets and tours around Bokeo.

Lao Development Bank (☉ 8am-3.30pm Mon-Fri) Not far from the boat landing.

Phoudoi Travel Co (Th Saykhong) Boat tickets and tours to Lanten and Khamu villages.

Post office (Th Saykhong) Contains a telephone office (open 8am to 10pm).

SLEEPING & EATING

Most hotels and guesthouses in Huay Xai quote their rates in Thai baht. There are loads of open-air rice and noodle stands along Th Saykhong.

Thanormsub Guest House (☎ 211095; Th Saykhong; r US$5) One of the best deals in town, this single-storey guesthouse has fresh rooms with ceiling fans and hot-water showers. It's low-key, immaculate and welcoming.

Arimid Guest House (Alimit; ☎ 211040; Ban Huay Xai Neua; r US$5.50-13; 🕽) This collection of bamboo bungalows, about 200m from the slow boat pier, is run by a husband-and-wife team who speak French and English. Good choice.

BAP Guest House (☎ 211083; Th Saykhong; s/d US$3/6) Turn left coming from the pier, and BAP is 50m up. All rooms come with fan and hot-water shower, and management has information on boats to Luang Nam Tha via Pak Tha or Xieng Kok. There's a good restaurant downstairs.

Keoudomphone Hotel (☎ 211405; Th Saykhong; r US$5-10; 🕽) The big, bright, charming rooms here are the best in town, making it worth the 15-minute walk from the main strip.

Latsuly Restaurant (meals US$1.50-2; 🕒 6.30am-9pm) Overlooking the Mekong beside the slow-boat landing, Latsuly serves noodle and rice dishes, buffalo steaks, a good basil pork and sandwiches to take on the boats.

Muang Neur (Th Saykhong; meals US$1.50-3; 🕒 6.30am-9pm) There's plenty of fragrant Lao cuisine,

---

CROSSING INTO THAILAND: HUAY XAI TO CHIANG KHONG

Long-tail boats (one way US$1, five minutes, 8am to 6pm) run across the Mekong between Huay Xai in Laos and Chiang Khong in Thailand. A huge vehicle ferry (US$50) also does the trip. On the Huay Xai side, the Lao immigration post is alongside the pedestrian ferry landing and issues 30-day visas on arrival. Boats from Pak Beng and buses from Luang Nam Tha always seem to arrive just after the border shuts. For information on crossing this border in the other direction, see p148.

---

such as whole crisp fried fish stuffed with ginger and garlic, to be had at this humble little restaurant.

GETTING THERE & AWAY
Air

Huay Xai's airport lies a few kilometres south of town. **Lao Airlines** (☎ 211026, 211494) flies to/from Vientiane (one way US$84, Tuesday Thursday and Saturday).

Boat

The slow boat down this scenic stretch of the Mekong River to Luang Prabang (US$20 per person, two days) is hugely popular among travellers. However, your experience will depend largely on the condition of the boat and how many people are on it. Boats should hold about 70 people, but captains try to cram in more than 100. If this happens, passengers can refuse en masse and a second boat might be drafted in. Even better, you can get a group together and rent your own boat for US$500 and enjoy the trip with plenty of space.

Boats leave from the boat landing at the north end of town and stop for one night in Pak Beng (US$9.50, six to eight hours) Tickets are available from the boat landing the afternoon before you travel, or from guest houses. It is wise to see the boat in person (not just the photo) before you buy. Some boats are enclosed, with no view out and 80 or more people plus their cargo packed in side, which makes it a cramped, disappointing experience.

For more comfort, consider the *Luang Say*, a steel-hulled boat operated by **Asian Oasis** (☎ 2525533; www.asian-oasis.com; Ban Vat Sene, Luang Pra bang; per person May-Sep/Oct-Apr US$185/270) that runs three times a week in each direction. **Phoudoi Travel Co** (Th Saykhong) also has a comfortable boat (US$60) that makes the trip in one day, twice a week – see www.chiangsaenriverhill .com for details.

Six-passenger speedboats to Pak Beng (US$14, three hours) and Luang Prabang (US$28, six hours) leave from a landing about 2km south of the town centre. This is not the safest transport south, and fatalities are not uncommon. When we passed there was even talk of banning *falang* from these boats.

Slow boats also run to Luang Nam Tha (US$180 to US$200 per boat split between passengers, plus US$4 each for food and accommodation) via Ban Na Lae. However, in the dry season this small river can be so shallow you'll need to wade some of the way. These boats are uncovered, so bring sun protection. Ask at BAP Guest House for more information.

For any journey take plenty of water and food supplies. Keep a sleeping bag or towel separate from your pack as the hard wooden benches lose their novelty value very quickly.

Bus

Buses and large *săwngthăew* ply the road northeast to Vieng Phoukha (US$4.50, five hours, three to four daily), Luang Nam Tha (US$6.50, eight hours, three daily) and Oudomxay (US$10, 11 hours, one daily). There are also daily buses to Luang Prabang (US$13, eight hours) and Vientiane (US$17, 18 hours).

SOUTHERN LAOS

After years of being ignored in favour of the north, southern Laos is starting to attract the travellers it deserves. What they're finding is a contrasting yet incredibly seductive combination of dramatic landscapes, pristine forest areas, sleepy Mekong cities, timeless riverine islands and chilled-out villagers. Most of this vast area remains refreshingly undertouristed, so it's easy to just get on a *săwngthăew* or motorbike and get off the beaten track. And a series of community-based tourism projects has made getting to the seriously remote villages and untouched forests – and getting inside village life Lao-style – easier than ever.

Many travellers still blast straight through from Vientiane to Si Phan Don, but it pays to take your time heading south. The 7km-long cave at Tham Kong Lo, trekking in the Phu Hin Bun NPA, exploring the cooler climes of the Bolaven Plateau and seeing Wat Phu Champasak are just some of the recommended stops before you reach the hammocks of the Four Thousand Islands.

BOLIKHAMSAI & KHAMMUAN PROVINCES

Bolikhamsai and Khammuan straddle the narrow, central 'waist' of the country, climbing from the Mekong valley to the Annamite range via an area of moderately high but often spectacular mountains. Laid-back and well-connected Tha Khaek (p317) is the logical base.

Much of the region is relatively sparsely populated and five large swathes of forest have been declared NPAs. These areas have turned into a battleground for those wishing to exploit Laos' largely untapped hydroelectricity capacity and those wishing to preserve some of the most pristine wilderness areas in Asia. Dam-builders, it seems, are winning.

Paksan

The capital of Bolikhamsai Province, Paksan sits at the confluence of the Nam San (San River) and the Mekong River. There's nothing to see here, but there is a little-used crossing into Thailand (see p317). If you have to stay, the **BK Guesthouse** (☎ 054-212638, 020-561 2348; r US$5-8; ✕) is Paksan's best budget choice; cross the bridge going east then take the first right (south), and it's a few hundred metres along on the right. Alternatively, the new **Paksan Hotel** (☎ 054-791333; fax 791222; Rte 13; r US$10-15; ✕) is more upmarket. All buses going to or from Vientiane stop on Rte 13 outside the Talat Sao (Morning Market).

Route 8 to Lak Sao

Route 8 has been described as like something out of a video game, with its smooth winding road through spectacular forest, hills and limestone karst scenery. The first major stop is **Ban Khoun Kham** (also known as Ban Na Hin), 41km east of Rte 13, in the lush Hin Bun valley. The village is not without charm but it serves mainly as a base from which to visit the extraordinary Tham Kong Lo (p316). While you're there, however, it's worth visiting the twin-cataract

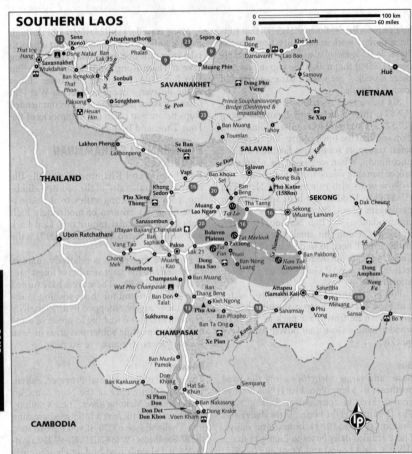

of **Tat Namsanam**, 3km north of town along a sometimes slippery trail. Community-based treks should also be available from the **tourist information centre** (Rte 8) just south of the Tat Namsanam entrance.

The best place to stay is **Mi Thuna Restaurant & Guesthouse** (☎ 020-224 0182; Rte 8; r US$5-9; ✗ 🖳), where the new rooms are surprisingly comfortable and owners Ralph and Mon are, respectively, a great source of local information and Western and Lao food. Mi Thuna is about 800m south of the market on Rte 8, past the Shell station. The best of the basic guesthouses in town is the **Seng Chen Guesthouse** (☎ 051-214399; s/d US$4/6), opposite the market.

All transport along Rte 8 stops at Ban Khoun Kham. Buses for Vientiane (US$4) usually stop between 7am and 9.30am. For Tha Khaek (US$4, three hours, 143km) there are a couple in the morning, while for Lak Sao take any passing bus or *săwngthăew*.

THAM KONG LO

Imagine a river disappearing at the edge of a monolithic limestone mountain and running 7km through a pitch-black, winding cave and you'll start to get an idea of **Tham Kong Lo**, truly one of the natural wonders of Laos. The cave-cum-tunnel is in the **Phu Hin Bun NPA**, a 1580-sq-km wilderness area of turquoise streams, monsoon forests and striking karst topography across central Khammuan. The cave is up to 100m wide in some places and almost as high. It takes a motorised canoe nearly an hour to pass through – be sure to bring a torch (flashlight) and wear rubber sandals as you'll probably need to get out and wade at shallow points.

You can make a long day-trip to Tham Kong Lo from Ban Khoun Kham, but it's more fun to overnight near the cave. At the edge of Phon Nyaeng, about 12km from Tham Kong Lo, **Sala Hin Boun** (☎ 020-561 4016; www.sala lao.com; r with breakfast US$18-23) offers comfortable Lao-style rooms overlooking the mountains and river. Food is available if you order in advance. In Ban Tiou, about 6km closer to Ban Kong Lo, the same outfit runs the simpler **Sala Kong Lor** (www.salalao.com; r US$4-12).

More memorable are the **homestay** (per person incl dinner & breakfast US$5) options in Ban Kong Lo, about 1km downstream from the cave mouth. For more on homestays, see p263.

Getting There & Away

A 50km road from Ban Khoun Kham (Ban Na Hin) to Ban Kong Lo should be finished by mid-2008, when it will be an easy one-hour motorbike or *săwngthăew* trip. Until then, you have to go by boat during the wet season. Go by bike or *săwngthăew* to Ban Na Phuak (US$1 per person, 35 minutes, 14km), from where boats follow the beautiful Nam Hin Bun for about 3½ hours to Ban Kong Lo. It costs US$50 (the price is fixed) a boat for the return trip, with a maximum of four people.

Between about late-October and June you can ride a motorbike to Ban Kong Lo along the road (as far as it's been completed), then through the dry rice paddies – which is like riding a jackhammer. You'll almost certainly get lost, so leave early.

In Ban Kong Lo boatmen charge US$10 per boat for the return trip (about 2½ hours, maximum four people) through the cave, plus there's the US$0.20 entrance fee. For the latest information ask at Mi Thuna Guesthouse.

LAK SAO
☎ 054 / pop 28,000

While the forest, mountain and karst scenery near Lak Sao (Lak Xao; literally, Kilometre 20) is strikingly beautiful, the town itself is a disappointment. If you get stuck here travelling to or from Vietnam (see p318) there is a **Lao Development Bank** (Rte 8B) but no internet café. The **Souriya Hotel** (☎ 341111; Rte 8B; r US$5-8; ✷), is a good choice, with clean rooms and a manager who speaks some French and English, and a good Lao restaurant next door.

Scheduled buses leave from near the market for Vientiane (US$6, six to eight hours, 334km) at 5am, 6am and 8am, stopping at Vieng Kham (Thang Beng, US$3, 1½ to 2½ hours, 100km), while other transport to Vieng Kham leaves throughout the day.

Tha Khaek
☎ 051 / pop 70,000

With Franco-Chinese architecture in varying states of repair, tall trees shading quiet streets and no-one seeming in any particular hurry, Tha Khaek is a charming base from which to explore Khammuan Province. On the banks of the Mekong River, the area has been settled since the Mon-Khmer Funan and Chenla empires, when it was known as Sri Gotapura (Sikhottabong in Lao). The modern city traces its roots to French-colonial construction in 1911–12. Tha Khaek means 'guest landing', believed to be a reference to its role as a boat landing for foreign traders.

The epicentre (if we can call it that) of the old town is the modest Fountain Sq at the western end of Th Kuvoravong near the river. Riverside beer shops near here are a good place for sundowners.

INFORMATION

BCEL (☎ 212686; Th Vientiane) Changes major currencies and travellers cheques, and makes cash advances on Visa.
Lao Development Bank (☎ 212089; Th Kuvoravong) Cash only.
Post office (Th Kuvoravong) Also offers expensive international phone calls.
Tha Khaek Hospital (cnr Th Chou Anou & Th Champasak) Fine for minor ailments or commonly seen problems such as malaria or dengue.

CROSSING INTO THAILAND: PAKSAN TO BEUNG KAN

The Mekong River crossing (open 8am to noon and 1.30pm to 4.30pm) between Paksan and Beung Kan is rarely used and Laos does not issue visas on arrival. The boat (60B, 20 minutes) leaves when five people show up or you charter it (300B). To get there, go west along Rte 13 from Paksan for about 1.5km and turn south – look for the 'Port' sign. Thailand doesn't issue visas on arrival at this border either. For information on crossing this border in the other direction, see p168.

LAOS

CROSSING INTO VIETNAM: NAM PHAO TO CAU TREO

The border at Nam Phao (Laos) and Cau Treo (Vietnam) through the Kaew Nuea Pass is 32km from Lak Sao and is open from 7am to 6pm. *Săwngthăew* (US$1.50, 45 minutes) leave every hour or so from Lak Sao market. Alternatively, direct buses from Lak Sao to Vinh (100,000d or equivalent, three to four hours) leave several times between about noon and 2pm; you might need to change conveyance at the border. You'll need your Vietnamese visa in advance. Laos issues 30-day visas on arrival.

From the border to Lak Sao, jumbos and *săwngthăew* leave when full or cost about US$10 to charter. There's a good chance you'll get ripped off crossing here, particularly on the Vietnamese side; see the boxed text, p104. For info on crossing this border the other way, see p366.

Tha Khek Travel Lodge (☎ 030-530 0145; travell@laotel.com; per hr US$3) Tha Khaek's only internet when we passed.

Tourist information centre (☎ 212512; Th Vientiane; 8am-4pm) Get information on community-based treks and meet the English-speaking guides here. As trek prices vary depending on group size, it's worth calling Mr Somkied (☎ 020-571 1797) to see when other travellers are booked in.

Tourist police (☎ 250610; Fountain Sq)

SIGHTS

Tha Khaek doesn't have much in the way of sights, the main attractions being out of town. The large **Talat Lak Sawng** (Km 2 Market; Th Kuvoravong) is good for an atmospheric lunch or if you want to watch silversmiths at work, but isn't especially notable.

SLEEPING

Tha Khaek has a small range of rooms. These three are reliable and have decent restaurants.

Phoukhanna Guesthouse (☎ 212092; Th Vientiane; r US$3.50-8; 🛠) The English-speaking manager creates an easygoing atmosphere. Rooms out the back are the best value.

our pick Tha Khek Travel Lodge (☎ 030-530 0145; travell@laotel.com; dm US$2.50, r US$5-11; 🛠 🖳) Despite its location away from the river, the Travel Lodge is the clear favourite with travellers for its easy atmosphere, decent food, welcoming staff and clean if slightly more expensive rooms. The travellers' book has feedback from the popular motorbike trip the Loop, and the lodge hires motorbikes (US$10 to US$15 per day).

Mekong Khammouane Hotel (☎ 250777; Th Setthathirat; r US$11; 🛠) You can't miss the blue exterior of this Vietnamese-run, four-storey hotel on the riverfront. The clean, well-equipped if-a-bit-dim rooms are typically good value for a Vietnamese hotel.

EATING & DRINKING

Thakhek Restaurant (Th Vientiane; meals US$1.50-4; 7.30am-10.30pm) This big place has indoor and outdoor seating and a large menu of Lao and Thai dishes, the fish being especially good.

Smile Barge Restaurant (☎ 212150; meals US$3-4.50; noon-1am) One of several floating restaurants set up along the Mekong south of Fountain Sq, the Smile Barge is popular for its karaoke and tasty Lao and seafood. There's also a landlubbing version opposite.

Boua's Place (Th Setthathirat; 3pm-10pm) On the river just south of Fountain Sq, wonderfully camp Boua is a hairdresser-turned–bar owner who serves sundowners with atmosphere and tables overlooking the river; order snacks from nearby restaurants.

Several *khào jìi* (baguette) vendors can be found on or near Fountain Sq in the morning, and the riverfront near here is good for a cheap meal any time. **Duc Restaurant** (meals US$1.50; 6am-10pm) serves delicious *fŏe hàeng* (dry rice noodles served in a bowl with herbs and seasonings but no broth), and **Phavila Restaurant** (Fountain Sq; meals US$1-2; 6am-9pm) serves standard Lao-Chinese rice and noodle dishes.

GETTING THERE & AWAY

Tha Khaek's **bus station** (Rte 13) is about 3.5km from the centre of town and has a sizable market and basic guesthouses. For Vientiane (US$4, six hours, 332km), buses leave every hour or so between 4.30am and midnight, stopping at Vieng Kham (Thang Beng; US$2, 90 minutes, 102km) and Paksan (US$3, three to four hours, 193km).

Southward buses to Savannakhet (US$2, two to three hours, 125km) and Pakse (US$4.50, six to seven hours, 368km) are reasonably frequent between 10.30am and midnight. For Vietnam, buses leave at 8am for Hué (US$8) and

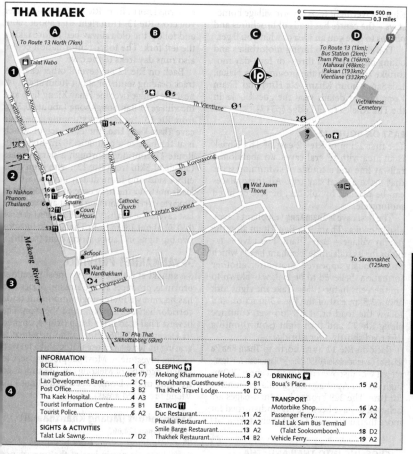

THA KHAEK

INFORMATION
BCEL...1 C1
Immigration.............................(see 17)
Lao Development Bank.................2 C1
Post Office...................................3 B2
Tha Kaek Hospital.......................4 A3
Tourist Information Centre.........5 B1
Tourist Police...............................6 A2

SIGHTS & ACTIVITIES
Talat Lak Sawng..........................7 D2

SLEEPING
Mekong Khammouane Hotel......8 A2
Phoukhanna Guesthouse............9 B1
Tha Khek Travel Lodge...............10 D2

EATING
Duc Restaurant...........................11 A2
Phavilai Restaurant.....................12 A2
Smile Barge Restaurant..............13 A2
Thakhek Restaurant....................14 B2

DRINKING
Boua's Place...............................15 A2

TRANSPORT
Motorbike Shop..........................16 A2
Passenger Ferry..........................17 A2
Talat Lak Sam Bus Terminal
  (Talat Sooksomboon)...............18 D2
Vehicle Ferry..............................19 A2

LAOS

8pm for Danang (US$8) and Hanoi (US$16, 17 hours).

Săwngthăew heading east along Rte 12 depart every hour or so from the Talat Lak Sam Bus Terminal (Sooksomboon Bus Terminal) between 7am and 3pm for Mahaxai (US$1.50, 1½ to 2½ hours, 50km), Nyommalat (US$2, two to three hours, 63km), Nakai (US$2.50, 2½ to 3½ hours, 80km) and Na Phao for the Vietnam border (US$3.50, five to seven hours, 142km).

GETTING AROUND
Chartered jumbos cost about US$1.50 to the bus terminal. The Tha Khek Travel Lodge (opposite) rents Chinese 110cc bikes for US$10 or US$15 a day, and a small river-front **motorbike shop** (Th Setthathirat), just north of Fountain Sq, rents similar bikes for similar prices. The tourist information centre can arrange bicycle hire.

Around Tha Khaek

Apart from the nationally important **Pha That Sikhottabong** (Pha That Muang Ka; admission US$0.30; 8am-6pm) stupa 6km south of town, which is said to date from the 1st-millennium Si Khotabun kingdom, the main reasons for staying in Tha Khaek are the caves along Rte 12 east of the city and the stunning limestone terrain in the nearby **Phu Hin Bun NPA**. Treks into the NPA come in one-, two- and three-day varieties operated by the guides at the **tourist information centre** (212512; Th Vientiane) in Tha

Khaek. Overnight trips involve village home-stays – the centre has loads of brochures and photos to give you an idea of what you'll get.

Travellers are also hiring motorbikes and taking on the **Loop**, a three- or four-day motorbike trip through the province via Nakai, Lak Sao, Khoun Kham (Na Hin) and Tham Kong Lo; for details read the guestbooks in the Tha Khek Travel Lodge (p318).

EAST ON ROUTE 12

The first 22km of Rte 12 east of Tha Khaek is an area with several caves, an abandoned railway line and a couple of swimming spots that make a great day trip. All these places can be reached by túk-túk, bicycle or hired motorcycle.

The first cave is **Tham Xang** (Elephant Cave), also known as Tham Pha Ban Tham after the nearby village – Ban Tham. The cave is famous for its stalagmite 'elephant head', which miraculously appeared soon after another formation, believed to be evil, was blown to smithereens in the 1950s. Take the right fork about 2.5km east of the Rte 13 junction and follow the road or, if it's too wet, continue along Rte 12 and turn right (south) onto a dirt road shortly after a bridge.

Back on Rte 12, turn north to **Tham Pha Pa** (Buddha Cave; admission US$0.20; ⊙ 8am-noon & 1-4pm), which was discovered 15m up a sheer 200m-high cliff in April 2004 by a villager hunting for bats. The 229 bronze Buddha images are believed to have been sitting undisturbed for more than 600 years. To get there, take a lat-erite road north from Rte 12 about 4km afte you cross Rte 13. Turn right after about 500m and follow the old railway bed before taking the left fork. The tourist information centre also runs day treks to the cave.

Back on Rte 12 are several other caves. A track heading south for about 400m at Km 14 near the bridge over the Huay Xieng Liap an the village of Ban Songkhone (about 10.5km from Rte 13), leads to the stunning limeston cave **Tham Xieng Liap**, the entrance of which is at the base of a dramatic 300m-high clif Route 12 continues through a narrow pas (about 11.5km from Rte 13), with high cliff either side, and immediately beyond a track leads north to the holy cave of **Tham Sa Pha I** (Tham Phanya Inh); swimming is not allowed. The last cave is the touristy **Tham Nang Aen** (admissio US$0.50), about 18km from Tha Khaek; look fo two big signs in Lao pointing right (south).

SAVANNAKHET PROVINCE

Savannakhet is the country's most populou province, produces a huge amount of rice and has become an increasingly important trad corridor between Thailand and Vietnam; the newest Thai–Lao Friendship Bridge, opene in December 2006, means the province i gearing up for even more traffic and a fat wad of Thai investment. Most people stop here to experience a bit of Mekong city life and/or g trekking in the Dong Natad and Dong Ph Vieng protected areas.

Savannakhet (Muang Khanthabuli)
☎ 041 / pop 124,000

The crumbling colonial-era buildings of Sa vannakhet are reminders of the importance the French attached to what was their larges trading and administrative centre south of Vi entiane. These days the city's riverside centre re tains a languid ambience, with tall trees shadin French-era buildings that remain appealing de spite their ever-more-forlorn appearance. Out side the centre, Savannakhet (officially calle Muang Khanthabuli but usually known simpl as Savan) is growing fast, with a sharp rise in number of bars particularly notable. The large lively **Talat Savan Xai** (Th Sisavangvong; ⊙ 7am-5pm north of the centre near the bus terminal, is th site of much of the city's commerce.

INFORMATION
BCEL Bank (☎ 212226; Th Ratsavongseuk; ⊙ 8.30am-4pm) Cash exchange and credit-card advances.

CROSSING INTO VIETNAM: NA PHAO TO CHA LO

This border (open 7am to 5pm) is rarely used by *falang* (Westerners) because it's way off the beaten track. Transport on both sides is infrequent; *săwngthăew* from Tha Khaek (US$3.50, five to seven hours, 142km) leave at least daily. Chances are you'll have to wait for transport on the other side. Neither Laos nor Vietnam issues visas here.

On the Vietnam side the nearest sizable city is Dong Hoi. A bus does run directly between Tha Khaek and Dong Hoi (US$13, 10 to 14 hours). It leaves Tha Khaek at 7am on Wednesdays and Sundays and returns from Dong Hoi at 6am on Mondays and Fridays. For information on crossing this border in the other direction, see p366.

Lao Development Bank (☎ 212272; Th Udomsin; ☽ 8.30-11.30am & 1.30-3.30pm) Same services as BCEL.

Police (☎ 212069; Th Ratsaphanith)

Post office (☎ 212205; Th Khanthabuli)

Provincial hospital (☎ 212051; Th Khanthabuli)

Provincial tourism office (☎ 214203; Th Ratsaphanith; ☽ 8am-11.30am & 1.30pm-4.30pm) One of the best-organised tourism offices in Laos. English-speaking staff provides information on and books treks to Dong Natad and Dong Phu Vieng NPAs, plus plenty of other info.

SPS Furniture Shop (Th Khanthabuli; per hr US$0.60; ☽ 10am-10pm) The pick of several internet places.

SIGHTS & ACTIVITIES

Much of the charm of Savannakhet is in just wandering through the quiet streets situated in the centre of town, between the new and old buildings, the laughing children and, along Th Phetsalat near Wat Sainyamungkhun, among the slow-moving, *petang*-playing old men.

The **Savannakhet Provincial Museum** (Th Khanthabuli; admission US$0.50; ☽ 8-11.30am & 1-4pm Mon-Sat) should be the main attraction, but these days it's rarely open, so you'll have to settle for seeing the few rusting artillery pieces and the barely recognisable remains of an American-built plane in the front yard. Not that you're missing much if you don't get in.

It might come as some surprise to learn Savannakhet Province is an exciting place for palaeontologists. In a colonial-era building, the small but well-presented **Dinosaur Museum** (☎ 212597; Th Khanthabuli; admission US$0.50; ☽ 8am-noon & 1-4pm) displays some of the finds from the five sites where dinosaur bones or footprints have been found. The curators are unfailingly enthusiastic and are more than willing to use their limited English or French on you.

The oldest and largest monastery in southern Laos, **Wat Sainyaphum** (Th Tha He) was origi-

nally built in 1542, although most of what stands today is from the last century. The large grounds include some centuries-old trees and a workshop near the river entrance that's a veritable golden-Buddha production line.

SLEEPING

Savannakhet has a reasonable range of budget options but little in the way of luxury. Most places are in the attractive old town, though there are also a couple of cheapies at the bus station.

Saisouk Guesthouse (☎ 212207; Th Phetsalat; r US$2.50-5; ☒) Just south of the centre of town, the atmosphere in this airy wooden house is almost invariably warm and welcoming. Rooms come in several shapes and sizes but are clean and some are quite big – ask to see a few. The husband-and-wife owners speak English. Recommended.

Leena Guesthouse (☎ 212404; 020-564 0697; Th Chaokeen; r US$4-8; ☒) It's a little far from the river, but the 26 smallish rooms here are clean and good value; room with bathrooms with hot water cost US$7 or US$8. You can rent bicycles (US$1.50 per day) and motorbikes (US$8 a day).

Sayamungkhun Guest House (☎ 212426; Th Ratsavongseuk; r US$5-8; ☒) In an attractive colonial-era building, the superfriendly Sayamungkhun has spacious and spotlessly clean rooms and an inviting atmosphere. It's on the main road, so front rooms are a bit noisy.

Phonepaseut Hotel (☎ 212158; fax 212916; Th Santisouk; r US$25-100; ☒) On the far side of town, the Phonepaseut has the best rooms and service, with most rooms boasting English TV, minibar and bathtubs.

EATING & DRINKING

Baguette vendors on the corner of Th Ratsavongseuk and Th Phagnapui sell *khào jìi*

LAOS

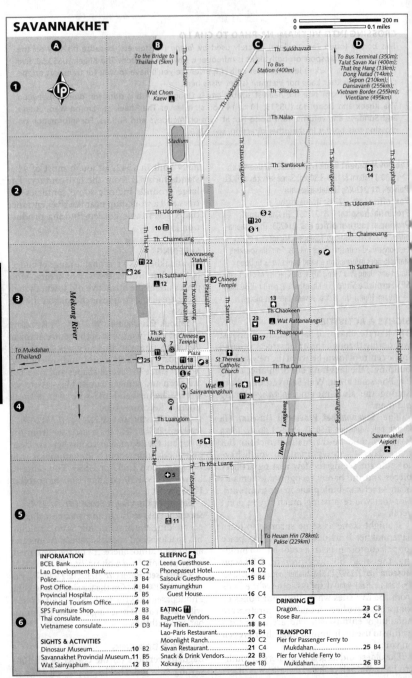

SAVANNAKHET

0 ———— 200 m
0 ———— 0.1 miles

páa-tê (baguette sandwiches) all day and breakfast baguettes filled with scrambled eggs (*khào jîi sai khai*).

Hay Thien (☎ 212754; Th Si Muang; all dishes US$1.50; ☺ 10am-8pm) This modest-looking restaurant in the centre of town specialises in freshly prepared, delicious and cheap Chinese dishes.

Xokxay (☎ 213122; meals US$1-2) A couple of doors up from Hay Thien, this eatery offers up a similar menu.

Lao-Paris Restaurant (☎ 212792; Th Si Muang; US$1.50-4; ☺ 7am-10pm) In an old Chinese shophouse opposite the ferry terminal, the mostly reliable Lao, Vietnamese and French offerings here make this a travellers' favourite. Service is rarely enthusiastic, but the portions are big and prices reasonable.

Savan Restaurant (☎ 214488; Th Mak Havena; meals from US$2; ☺ 6-10pm) In an oddly romantic outdoor setting with private compartments, this place is all about *sîin daat,* Korean-style barbecue. There's no English menu, but it's easy enough to just point and shoot.

Moonlight Ranch (☎ 030-531 5718; Th Ratsavongseuk; meals US$2-8; ☺ 10am-11pm) Run by a quirky Lao-Danish couple, this place has become popular with travellers and expats seeking comfort food. The hamburgers aren't bad.

Opposite Wat Sainyaphum the riverside **snack & drink vendors** (☺ afternoons & evenings) are great for sundowners; look particularly for the friendly family of long-haired ladies. More recognisable drinking establishments include **Dragon** (Th Ratsavongseuk; ☺ 7-11pm), with its young crowd and deafeningly karaoke, and **Rose Bar** (Th Ratsavongseuk; ☺ 6-11pm) with its occasional live music and more spacious feel.

GETTING THERE & AWAY
Savannakhet's **bus terminal** (☎ 212143), usually called the *khíw lot,* is near the Talat Savan Xai at the northern edge of town. Buses leave here for Vientiane (US$5.50, eight to 11 hours, 457km) hourly from 6am to 10pm, stopping at Tha Khaek (US$2.50, 2½ to four hours, 125km). A VIP bus (US$7, six to seven hours) to Vientiane leaves at 9.30pm.

Heading south, loads of buses either start here or pass through from Vientiane for Pakse (US$3, five to six hours, 230km). Buses for Lao Bao (US$3, five to seven hours) leave at 6.30am, 9.30am and noon, stopping at Sepon (US$3, four to six hours). *Săwngthăew* leave more frequently.

GETTING AROUND
A túk-túk to the bus terminal will cost about US$1, or US$0.50 each shared; prices double after dark. Elsewhere you'll probably be able to walk. Several guesthouses and the Lao-Paris Restaurant rent bicycles (between US$1 and US$2 per day) and motorcycles (US$7 to US$10 per day), though usually only for a day at a time.

East on Route 9
If you're heading east towards Vietnam, there are several places worth stopping. The first, and probably the most popular, is **Dong Natad Provincial Protected Area**, just 15km from Savannakhet. The provincial tourism office (p321) runs informative day and overnight treks here, with local guides explaining the myriad uses of the forest, and overnighters staying in a village home. Three-day treks into the remote **Dong Phu Vieng NPA** offer a similar but more extreme experience. Staying in Katang villages, local guides show how they live with the many taboos governing life in their animist community. These treks are relatively expensive, but prices fall as numbers rise, so contact the tourism office before you arrive to see when people are heading out.

Further east is **Sepon**, which has a couple of decent guesthouses. Sepon exists because its predecessor was bombed into the Stone Age during the Second Indochina War – you can see what's left at **Sepon Kao** (Old Sepon), a few kilometres east. About 20km east of Sepon is **Ban Dong**, a sleepy village on what was once an important branch of the Ho Chi

---

CROSSING INTO THAILAND: SAVANNAKHET TO MUKDAHAN

The new Friendship Bridge linking Savannakhet and Mukdahan in Thailand means the days of regular ferries might be numbered. A Thai–Lao International Bus connects the towns' bus stations 12 times a day; check the tourism office for details. Ferries should continue from the boat pier, crossing (US$1.30 or 50B, 30 minutes) the Mekong six times between 9.10am and 4pm on weekdays, less often on weekends. Visas are usually available on arrival in Laos (see p341). For information on crossing this border in the other direction, see p163.

CROSSING INTO VIETNAM: DANSAVANH TO LAO BAO

The busy border (open 7am to 11am, and 1pm to 6pm) at Dansavanh (Laos) and Lao Bao (Vietnam) is regularly used by travellers. Buses leave from Savannakhet (US$3, five to seven hours) at 6.30am, 9.30am and noon, and regularly from Sepon (US$1.40, one hour, 45km). It's a walk between the border posts, but formalities don't take long if you have your Vietnam visa; Laos issues 30-day visas on arrival. Entering Laos, *săwngthăew* to Sepon leave fairly regularly. There is simple accommodation on both sides of the border. Alternatively, a daily 10pm bus runs from Savannakhet to Dong Ha (US$12, about eight hours, 329km), Hué (US$11, about 12 hours, 409km) or Danang (US$14, about 14 hours, 508km). No matter what you are told, you *will* have to change buses at the border. For information on crossing this border in the other direction, see p384.

Minh Trail. Today there are a couple of rusting American-built tanks (kids will direct you) that are among the most accessible war relics in southern Laos.

Buses and *săwngthăew* head in both directions along Rte 9 between Savannakhet and Dansavanh; your best bet is to travel in the morning.

CHAMPASAK PROVINCE
Pakse
☎ 031 / pop 66,000

Founded by the French in 1905 as an administrative outpost, Pakse sits at the confluence of the Mekong River and the Se Don and is the capital of Champasak Province. Its position on the way to Si Phan Don in the far south, the Bolaven Plateau and remote provinces to the east, and Thailand to the west means anyone travelling in the south will almost certainly spend time in Pakse.

The centre of Pakse retains the sort of lowland lethargy found in Savannakhet and Tha Khaek, though with fewer colonial-era buildings and less charm. Some people find Pakse a bit dull (there's little to see here), but its unhurried ambience and relative comforts do draw in others. The vast Talat Dao Heung (New Market) and day or overnight trips to Don Kho, Wat Phu Champasak (p328) and Tat Fan (p333) are highlights.

ORIENTATION
Central Pakse is bound by the Mekong to the south and by the Se Don to the north and west. Route 13 cuts through the northern edge of town. On and below Rte 13 towards the Mekong are most of Pakse's guesthouses, shops and restaurants. Heading west across Se Don takes you to the northern bus terminal. The southern bus terminal and market are 8km in the opposite direction.

INFORMATION
Emergency
Hospital (☎ 212018; cnr Th 10 & Th 46)
Police (☎ 212145; Th 10)

Internet Access
There are several places on Rte 13, or nearby, which have ADSL:
Next Step Internet (Rte 13; per hr US$0.60; ☻ 8am-11pm) Burns CDs and DVDs for US$1.50 each.
SD Internet (Rte 13; per hr US$0.60; ☻ 7am-8pm) Fast connections.

Money
BCEL (☎ 212770; Th 11; ☻ 8.30am-3.30pm Mon-Fri & 8.30-10am Sat) South of Wat Luang, this has the best rates for cash and travellers cheques. Cash advances against Visa and MasterCard.
Lao Development Bank (☎ 212168; Rte 13; ☻ 8am-4pm Mon-Fri, 8am-3pm Sat & Sun) Changes cash and travellers cheques in the smaller exchange office; cash advances (Monday to Friday only) in the main building.

Post
Post office (cnr Th 1 & Th 8; ☻ 8am-noon & 1-5pm)

Tourist Information
Provincial tourism office (☎ 212021; Th 11; ☻ 8am-noon & 1.30-4pm Mon-Fri) Beside the Lao Airlines office; the well-organised English-speaking staff can book you onto community-based treks in Xe Pian NPA and Phu Xieng Thong NPA, and into homestays on Don Kho and Don Daeng. There's no commission. Staff can also help with bus schedules.

Travel Agencies
Most hotels and guesthouses can arrange day trips to the Bolaven Plateau, Wat Phu Champasak and Si Phan Don.
Green Discovery (☎ 252908; www.greendiscoverylaos.com; Rte 13) Operates rafting, kayaking (both US$27 per person for four or more), mountain biking and trekking trips. Well respected.

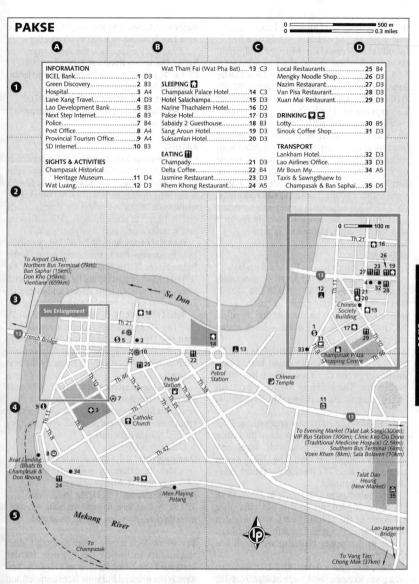

PAKSE

0 ———————— 500 m
0 ———————— 0.3 miles

INFORMATION
BCEL Bank...........................**1** D3
Green Discovery...................**2** B3
Hospital.............................**3** A4
Lane Xang Travel..................**4** D3
Lao Development Bank...........**5** B3
Next Step Internet................**6** B3
Police.................................**7** B4
Post Office..........................**8** A4
Provincial Tourism Office.......**9** A4
SD Internet.........................**10** B3

SIGHTS & ACTIVITIES
Champasak Historical
 Heritage Museum...............**11** D4
Wat Luang..........................**12** D3

Wat Tham Fai (Wat Pha Bat).....**13** C3

SLEEPING 🏠
Champasak Palace Hotel.........**14** C3
Hotel Salachampa..................**15** D3
Narine Thachalern Hotel.........**16** D2
Pakse Hotel..........................**17** D3
Sabaidy 2 Guesthouse............**18** B3
Sang Aroun Hotel..................**19** D3
Suksamlan Hotel....................**20** B3

EATING 🍴
Champady.............................**21** D3
Delta Coffee.........................**22** B4
Jasmine Restaurant................**23** D3
Khem Khong Restaurant..........**24** A5

Local Restaurants...................**25** B4
Mengky Noodle Shop..............**26** D3
Nazim Restaurant...................**27** D3
Van Pisa Restaurant................**28** D3
Xuan Mai Restaurant...............**29** D3

DRINKING 🍷 🍸
Lotty..................................**30** B5
Sinouk Coffee Shop................**31** D3

TRANSPORT
Lankham Hotel.....................**32** D3
Lao Airlines Office.................**33** D3
Mr Boun My........................**34** A5
Taxis & Sawngthaew to
 Champasak & Ban Saphai.....**35** D5

To Airport (3km);
Northern Bus Terminal (7km);
Ban Saphai (15km);
Don Kho (15km);
Vientiane (659km)

Se Don

See Enlargement

French Bridge

Th 21

Chinese
Society
Building

Champasak Plaza
Shopping Centre

Petrol
Station

Petrol
Station

Chinese
Temple

Catholic
Church

To Evening Market (Talat Lak Song)(300m);
VIP Bus Station (300m); Clinic Keo Ou Done
(Traditional Medicine Hospice) (2.5km);
Southern Bus Terminal (6km);
Voen Kham (8km); Sala Bolaven (10km)

Boat Landing
(Boats to
Champasak &
Don Khong)

Talat Dao
Heung
(New Market)

Men Playing
Petang

Mekong River

To
Champasak

Lao-Japanese
Bridge

To Vang Tao;
Chong Mek (37km)

LAOS

Lane Xang Travel (Xplore Asia; www.xplore-asia.com;
Rte 13) Similar trips to Green Discovery, with more trips to
Si Phan Don.

SIGHTS & ACTIVITIES

Pakse's 20 wat are not the most impressive in
Laos. The largest are **Wat Luang** (Th 11), featuring
ornate concrete pillars and carved wooden

doors and murals, and **Wat Tham Fai** (Rte 13),
which has a small Buddha footprint shrine in
its grounds. The monks in both will be happy
to practise their English with you, especially
in the afternoon.

The **Champasak Historical Heritage Museum**
(Rte 13; admission US$0.50; 🕐 8.30-11.30am & 1.30-4pm)
has a small collection of interesting artefacts

including three old Dong Son bronze drums and striking 7th-century sandstone lintels found at Um Tomo (Um Muang). Still, you'll do well to be here longer than 15 minutes.

A massage and sauna at the **Clinic Keo Ou Done** (Traditional Medicine Hospice; ☎ 251895, 020-543 1115; ♥ 4-9pm Mon-Fri & 10am-9pm Sat & Sun) is a real Lao experience. The herbal sauna (US$0.80) usually comes first, with three stints of 15 and eight minutes each, before showering and heading in for a vigorous massage, often with medicated balms (US$3 per hour). Go east on Rte 13, turn right about 100m before the Km 3 marker, and follow the 'Massage Sauna' signs another 800m. The **Champasak Palace Hotel** (♥ 2-10pm) has a compact gym, and it costs just US$0.70 for visitors to use the weight room. It also has massages, sauna and Jacuzzi.

SLEEPING

In peak season rooms in Pakse fill up fast.

Sabaidy 2 Guesthouse (☎ /fax 212992; www.sabaidy 2laos.com; Th 24; dm US$1.90, r US$3.50-5.50; ✿) If you want cheap-but-clean lodgings, good information and to be surrounded by other backpackers, look no further – book ahead in high season.

Suksamlan Hotel (☎ 020-563 2077; Th 14; r US$5.50-6.50; ✿) The central Suksamlan has 24 ageing but large and clean rooms with hot-water bathrooms. The building itself has a certain fading charm and manager Mr Bouphan is helpful.

Pakse Hotel (☎ 212131; www.paksehotel.com; Th 5; r US$12-32; ✿) This six-storey place in the centre of town has smart rooms and professional service at very competitive rates. The US$19 rooms are the best value. The rooftop restaurant-cum-bar is great at sunset.

Hotel Salachampa (☎ 212273; fax 212646; Th 14; r US$13-15; ✿) Rooms in this old villa offer a flavour of the colonial past, with wooden floors, high ceilings and tasteful furnishings. Those in the newer building are much less charismatic.

Champasak Palace Hotel (☎ 212777; www.cham pasak-palace-hotel.com; Rte 13; r with breakfast US$20-150; ✿ ▢) The vast, wedding-cake-style Champasak Palace is a sight in itself. Built as a palace for Chao Boun Oum na Champasak, the last prince of Champasak and the prime minister of Laos between 1960 and 1962, it wasn't finished until the 1990s. Rooms are mostly excellent value, particularly the superior (US$40) and VIP suites (US$50), the latter of which have panoramic views. All rooms superior and above have free broadband internet connections.

Other options include the following:

Narine Thachalern Hotel (☎ 212927; Th 21; s/d US$4/8; ✿) Central, clean and welcoming budget option. Ask to see a few rooms.

Sang Aroun Hotel (☎ 252111; Rte 13; r US$17-20; ✿) New Thai-style place with modern, well-equipped rooms if not much soul.

EATING

Eating with the locals, especially at breakfast and lunch, is the most interesting option in Pakse. The Mengky Noodle Shop on Rte 13 is rightly popular for its duck *fŏe* breakfasts, while each of the nameless local restaurants on Th 46 serves something slightly different; just wander along and take your pick.

Xuan Mai Restaurant (☎ 213245; Th 4; meals US$1-2.50; ♥ 6am-midnight) On the corner opposite the Pakse Hotel, Xuan Mai serves top-notch *fŏe* (US$0.80), *khào pûn* (white flour noodles with sweet-spicy sauce), fruit shakes and even garlic bread. It's the best place for a late feed.

Delta Coffee (☎ 030-534 5895; Rte 13; meals US$1.50-5; ♥ 7am-10pm) Delta serves a vast array of food, with the Thai dishes and most Italian pretty good. Breakfasts are great value and the coffee – from its own plantation – is arguably the best in town.

Khem Khong Restaurant (☎ 213240; Th 11; meals US$2-5; ♥ 11am-10pm) On the banks of the Mekong, this floating restaurant has a well-earned reputation for excellent seafood. The *pîing pạa* (grilled fish) is delicious.

Other good options:

Champady (☎ 020-513 0513; meals US$1.50-4.50; ♥ 6.30am-10pm) Champady serves Thai cuisine and coffee in an attractive streetside location.

Van Pisa Restaurant (☎ 212982; Rte 13; pizzas US$3.50; ♥ 8am-10pm) An Italian-run Italian restaurant where the pizzas, pastas and ice cream are all good.

Travellers flock to two neighbouring Indian restaurants in the centre of town. **Jasmine Restaurant** (☎ 251002; Rte 13; meals US$2-4; ♥ 8am-10pm) is the original but now faces competition from a former partner running **Nazim Restaurant** (☎ 252912; Rte 13; meals US$1.50-3.50; ♥ 5.30am-11.30pm). In both the food, including loads of vegetarian dishes, is cheap and tasty.

DRINKING & ENTERTAINMENT

Sinouk Coffee Shop (☎ 212552; cnr Th 9 & Th 11; coffee US$0.60; ♥ 7am-8pm) The closest thing to a café in Pakse, this renovated French shophouse is good for a brew – bean or beer.

At sunset, both the Champasak Palace Hotel and Pakse Hotel have rooftop bars with panoramic views. For something more local, **Lotty** (Th 11; ☉ 6-11pm) was the favourite nightclub among young Lao looking to drink and dance when we passed through.

SHOPPING

Sala Bolaven (☎ 020-580 0787; Km 12, Rte 16; ☉ 9am-4pm) Sala Bolaven sells Fair Trade produce from the Bolaven Plateau, including jams, tea, Lao Bia (palm beer), local wine and coffee. It's on the road up to the plateau, about 12km slightly uphill from Pakse.

GETTING THERE & AWAY

Air

Lao Airlines (☎ 212252; www.laoairlines.com; Th 11; ☉ 8-11.30am & 1.30-4.30pm Mon-Fri) flies between Pakse and Vientiane daily (one way US$95, 70 minutes), and usually twice a week to Luang Prabang (US$135, one hour 40 minutes). International flights go to Phnom Penh (US$95, one way, 70 minutes) and Siem Reap (US$85, 45 minutes) two or three times a week. Bangkok Airways should be flying from Pakse to Bangkok by the time you read this.

The airport is 3km northwest of town and has a BCEL exchange office. A jumbo to the airport should cost about US$1.

Boat

The public boat from Pakse to Don Khong has more or less stopped, unable to compete with soaring fuel prices and cheaper, faster road transport. We've heard a private boat is now running tourists as far as Champasak (US$5) – ask at the provincial tourism office. Alternatively, get a group together and

find **Mr Boun My** (☎ 020-563 1008; Th 11) at the first barbecue pork stall opposite the Mekong as the road bends left. He rents boats to Champasak (from US$50, one hour) and Don Khong (from US$140, four to five hours).

Bus & Săwngthăew

Pakse has several bus and *săwngthăew* terminals. VIP buses leave the **VIP Bus Station** (Km 2 Bus Station; ☎ 212228), off Rte 13, for Vientiane (US$13, eight to 10 hours, 677km) every evening, though they usually also stop in town. The handy Thai–Lao International Bus also leaves from here; see below for details.

At the **northern bus terminal** (☎ 251508; Rte 13), usually called *khíw lot lák jét* (Km 7 bus terminal), agonisingly slow normal buses (without air-con) rattle north every hour or so between 6.30am and 4.30pm for Savannakhet (US$3, four to five hours, 277km), Tha Khaek (US$5.50, eight to nine hours) and, for those with a masochistic streak, Vientiane (US$8.50, 16 to 18 hours).

For buses or *săwngthăew* anywhere south or east, head to the **southern terminal** (Rte 13), which is usually called *khíw lot lák pǎet* (Km 8 bus terminal). The terminal is 8km south of town and costs US$0.50 on a shared túk-túk. For Si Phan Don, transport departs for Muang Khong (US$3.50 including ferry, three hours, 120km) between 10am and 3pm; and to Ban Nakasang (for Don Det and Don Khon; US$3, three to four hours) between 7.30am and 3pm. A *săwngthăew* runs to Kiet Ngong and Ban Phapho (US$1.50, two to three hours) at 1pm.

To the Bolaven Plateau, transport leaves for Paksong (US$1.50, 90 minutes) hourly between 9am and 1pm, stopping at Tat Fan if you ask. Transport leaves for Salavan (US$2, three to four hours, 115km) five times between 7.30am

---

CROSSING INTO THAILAND: VANG TAO TO CHONG MEK

The crossing at Vang Tao (Laos) and Chong Mek (Thailand) is the busiest in southern Laos and is open from 5am to 6pm. From Pakse, *săwngthăew* (US$0.80, 75 minutes, 44km) and some of the most battered taxis (US$2 per person or US$10 for whole vehicle, 45 minutes) you'll ever see run between Talat Dao Heung (New Market) and Vang Tao. Easier is the Thai–Lao International Bus (200B or equivalent, 2½ to 3 hours, 126km) direct from the VIP Bus Station to Ubon at 7am, 8.30am, 2.30pm and 3.30pm, returning at 7.30am, 9.30am, 2.30pm and 3.30pm. For details on crossing the border in the other direction, see p162.

At the border you have to walk a bit but formalities are straightforward. Laos issues visas on arrival, as do the Thais in their startling new building, which looks vaguely like a plate full of purple nachos minus the guacamole.

LAOS

and 2pm, most going via Tat Lo. Transport also leaves for Sekong (US$2.50, 3½ to 4½ hours, 135km) at 7.30am, 9.30am and 2pm; and for Attapeu (US$3.50, 4½ to six hours, 212km) at 6.30am, 8am and 10.30am.

Regular buses and *săwngthǎew* leave the **Dao Heung Market** for Champasak (US$1.30, one to two hours) and Ban Saphai (for Don Kho; US$0.50, about 40 minutes).

GETTING AROUND

Pakse's main attractions are accessible by foot. Bicycles (10,000 kip per day) and scooters (US$8 to US$10 per day) can be hired from **Sabaidy 2 Guesthouse** (☎ 212992; Th 24) and **Lankham Hotel** (☎ 213314; latchan@laotel.com; Rte 13), which also has some Honda Bajas for US$20 a day.

Champasak

☎ 031

Once the capital of a Lao kingdom, Champasak is now the epitome of the somnolent Lao riverside town. The main road runs parallel to the river before turning inland toward the dramatic mountainside location of Wat Phu Champasak. Most visitors use the town as a base for visiting the ruins, and a lucky few have discovered the idyllic lifestyle of **Don Daeng**, the 8km-long island opposite Champasak, where you can stay in a basic community guesthouse or a homestay – ask at the new **Champasak District visitor information centre** (☎ 020-220 6215; ☺ 8am-4.30pm Mon-Fri) for details. In Champasak itself, activity – such as it is – centres on the ferry wharf and in riverside guesthouses-cum-restaurants.

Champasak cranks it up every year when pilgrims from near and far amass for **Bun Wat Phu Champasak**. During this three-day Buddhist festival (usually held in February) worshippers wind their way up and around Wat Phu Champasak, praying and leaving offerings; bands play traditional and modern music; and Thai boxing, comedy shows and cockfights all add to the entertainment. Stands selling food and drink do a roaring trade along the road from town to Wat Phu and accommodation in town is booked out weeks in advance; camping at Wat Phu is possible, but take care of your gear.

SIGHTS

Overlooking the Mekong valley, **Wat Phu Champasak** (admission US$3; ☺ 8am-4.30pm) is one of the most impressive archaeological sites in Laos. Wat Phu has been worshipped since the mid-5th century, though most of what you see today dates from the late Angkorian period (see p32). It was added to the World Heritage List in 2001.

The site is divided into three main levels linked by a processional causeway. The lower level consists of one large and two smaller *baray* (rectangular water reservoirs). The latter are split by the recently restored processional causeway – the marker posts lining the causeway are now standing for the first time in centuries. The middle level is actually several levels, on which two large pavilions stand, with the Nandi Pavilion just behind the southern pavilion.

The processional causeway, lined with frangipani trees, climbs via a steep stairway with *naga* balustrades to the upper level and the temple sanctuary itself, which once enclosed a large Shiva *linga*. The sanctuary was later converted into a Buddhist temple, but original Hindu sculpture remains in the lintels. Just north of the lingam sanctuary, you'll find the enigmatic elephant and crocodile stones. The upper platform affords spectacular views of the Mekong River Valley below.

Much more history is available in the pamphlet you should receive with your ticket, and in the small but accessible **museum** (admission with Wat Phu ticket; ☺ 8am-4.30pm) near the ticket office. Getting here at dawn is worth it (pay for the ticket when you leave).

SLEEPING & EATING

Champasak has several decent guesthouses strung along its main road, most of which have bedrooms with fans and peaceful riverside restaurants. We like these two, but comparing is easy enough on foot.

Khamphoui Guest House (☎ 252700; r US$2-3) Just south of the circle, the simple rooms and bungalows with cold-/hot-water (US$2/3) bathrooms at this friendly place are recommended.

Souchitra Guesthouse (☎ 920059; r US$3-15; ❄) Souchitra has a touch more style. The rooms are good value if you opt for a fan (US$5), though the same room with air-con is overpriced at US$15. The spacious common veranda, riverside hammocks and restaurant (meals US$1 to US$2.50, open 7am to 10pm) are good places to hang out. Motorbikes can be hired for US$5/10 per half-/full day.

GETTING THERE & AROUND

Regular buses and *săwngthăew* run between Champasak and Pakse from about 6.30am until 3pm (US$1.30, one to two hours); early morning is busiest.

If you're heading south to Ban Nakasang (for Don Det) or Muang Khong (on Don Khong), take a ferry from Ban Phaphin (1.8km north of Champasak) over the Mekong to Ban Muang (US$0.20), then a *săwngthăew* or motorcycle taxi to Ban Lak 30 (on Rte 13), where you can flag down anything going south.

Bicycles (US$1 to US$2 per day) and motorbikes (US$5/10 per half-/full day) can be hired from guesthouses. A túk-túk to Wat Phu costs about US$6 to US$8 return, including waiting time, depending on your bargaining skills.

Si Phan Don

☎ 031

Si Phan Don (Four Thousand Islands), where the Mekong fans out forming an intricate network of channels, rocks, sandbars and islets 14km wide, is one of nature's marvels. At night the Mekong is dotted with the lights of fishermen bobbing in the river, while during the wet season the islands, studded with coconut and betel palms, are alight with fireflies. Water buffalo wade in the shallows, in the morning women wash clothes and children in the river, and steady flows of long-tail boats motor back and forth between the islands and the mainland. Si Phan Don is also home to a couple of impressive waterfalls and the rare Irrawaddy dolphins, which can be seen at the southern tip of Don Khon.

DON KHONG

pop 13,000

The largest and most populous of the islands, Don Khong lacks the magical scenery of its neighbours to the south; however, it's an excellent choice if you're after a more 'authentic' experience. The 32km round-island cycle through rice fields, villages and a small huddle of hills in the north is highly recommended for its absence of traffic and its excellent paved – if often rather exposed – road (thank you, President Khamtai Siphandone, who hails from here). The island boasts a few interesting old temples, 24-hour electricity (coming soon to the islands further south) and virtual silence after nightfall. For visitors, the

guesthouses and life-support services are all in Muang Khong, the district capital.

Information

One road back from the river, 400m south of the distinctive *naga*-protected Buddha at Wat Phuang Kaew, the **Agricultural Promotion Bank** (☾ 8.30am-3.30pm Mon-Fri) exchanges travellers cheques and cash at poor rates. The **telephone office** (☾ 8am-noon & 2-4pm Mon-Fri) is west of the boat landing. The **post office** (☾ 8am-noon & 2-4pm Mon-Fri) is just south of the bridge. **Alpha Internet** (☎ 214117; per hr US$6; ☾ 8am-9pm), 100m north of Pon's River Guest House, has slow internet and international calls at high prices.

Sleeping & Eating

Don Khong has a good collection of guesthouses and rarely gets so busy you can't find a bed. Virtually all are dotted along the riverfront road. Most have attached restaurants.

Souksabay Guesthouse (☎ 214122; r fan/air-con US$5/10; ☒) We like this little place, as much for the genuine welcome as the darkish but clean, fair-value rooms.

Villa Kang Khong (☎ 213539; r US$5-10; ☒) If being laid-back was a palpable thing, you'd be able to feel it here. The traditional teak house a block back from the boat landing is a favourite for its easy, convivial atmosphere, large and clean rooms and shaded communal balcony (that guests actually use). Every room is different.

Pon's River Guest House (☎ 214037, 020-227 0037; r US$6-20; ☒) Located just north of the bridge, English-speaking Mr Pon's busy place reflects his entrepreneurial style. He's generous with information and the 18 clean rooms are fair value, particularly the US$6 fan rooms.

Auberge Sala Done Khong (☎ /fax 212077; www.sala lao.com; s/d with breakfast US$23/28; ☒) About 250m south of the bridge, the setting in two French-era teak mansions is atmospheric but the rooms don't have the same charisma; ask to see several. Prices drop US$5 from May to September.

You'll see all the eating options as you walk along the riverfront. Standards are reasonably good, if not that imaginative. If you fancy something European, walk about 450m south from the bridge to the relatively intimate restaurant at the **Villa Muong Khong Hotel** (meals US$2-6; ☾ 6.30am-10pm).

Getting There & Away

From Don Khong to Pakse, buses (US$3.50 or US$4, 2½ to 3½ hours, 128km) and

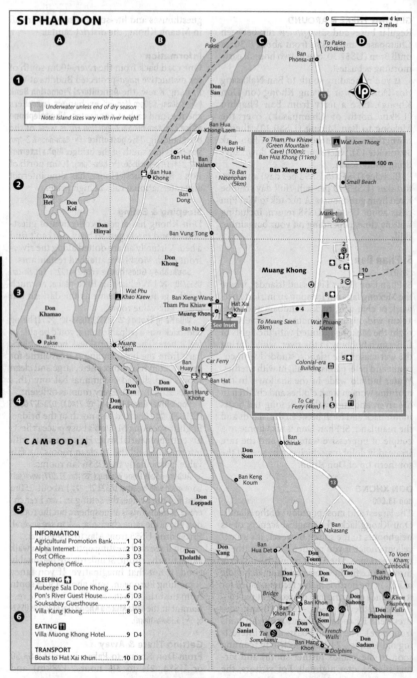

SI PHAN DON

0   4 km
0   2 miles

Underwater unless end of dry season
Note: Island sizes vary with river height

To Pakse

Ban Phonsa-at

To Pakse
(104km)

Inset (Muang Khong / Ban Xieng Wang):

To Tham Phu Khiaw
(Green Mountain
Cave) (100m);
Ban Hua Khong (11km)

Wat Jom Thong

0   100 m

Ban Xieng Wang

Small Beach

Market
School

Muang Khong

Wat Phuang
Kaew

To Muang Saen
(8km)

Colonial-era
Building

To Car
Ferry (4km)

Main map labels:

Don San

Ban Hua
Khong-Laem

Ban Huay Hai

Ban Hat   Ban Nalan   Ban Huay Hai

Ban Hua
Khong

Ban Dong

To Ban
Nasenphan
(5km)

Don
Het   Don
Koi

Don
Hinyai

Ban Vung Tong

Don
Khong

Don
Khamao

Wat Phu
Khao Kaew

Ban Xieng Wang
Tham Phu Khiaw
Muang Khong

Hat Xai
Khun

See Inset

Ban Na

Ban
Pakse

Muang
Saen

Car Ferry

Ban
Huay

Ban Hat

Don
Tan   Don
Phuman   Ban Hang
Khong

Don
Long

CAMBODIA

Ban
Khinak

Don
Som

Ban Keng
Koum

Don
Loppadi

Don
Xang   Ban
Hua Det

Ban
Nakasang

Don
Tholathi

To Voen
Kham;
Cambodia

Ban Thakho

Don
Toum

Don
Det   Don
En   Don
Tao

Bridge

Don
Saniat   Tat
Somphamit   Ban
Khon Tai   Ban Khon   Don
Khon   Don
Som   French
Walls   Don
Sahong   Don
Phapheng

Khon
Phapheng
Falls

Ban Hang
Khon   Dolphins   Don
Sadam

INFORMATION
Agricultural Promotion Bank....... **1** D4
Alpha Internet............................ **2** D3
Post Office................................. **3** D3
Telephone Office........................ **4** C3

SLEEPING
Auberge Sala Done Khong......... **5** D4
Pon's River Guest House............ **6** D3
Souksabay Guesthouse.............. **7** D3
Villa Kang Khong...................... **8** D3

EATING
Villa Muong Khong Hotel.......... **9** D4

TRANSPORT
Boats to Hat Xai Khun............. **10** D3

săwngthăew leave from outside Wat Phuang Kaew between 6am and 8am. After that, head over to Rte 13 and wait for anything going north. Guesthouses also run daily minibuses to Pakse (US$7).

If you're heading south to Cambodia, guesthouses arrange transport to the border, which links with the rare minibuses from the border to Stung Treng, so is recommended. Otherwise, cross the river to Hat Xai Khun, get to Rte 13 and wait for the Pakse–Voen Kham bus, which usually passes about 8.30am or 9am. There are regular boats between Hat Xai Khun and Don Khong; it's US$3 per boat for one to three people, or US$1.50 per person for more. Bargaining is futile.

Boats for Don Det and Don Khon (US$15, 1½ hours) leave whenever you stump up the cash – boatmen hang out under the tree near the bridge. Alternatively, Mr Pon's boat (US$4 per person) leaves daily at 8.30am.

Getting Around
Bicycles (US$1 a day) and motorbikes (US$10 a day) can be hired from guesthouses and elsewhere along the main street. Alternatively, start haggling with a jumbo driver.

DON DET & DON KHON
The beautiful, palm-fringed islands of Don Det and Don Khon, 16km south of Don Khong on the border with Cambodia, have managed to largely retain their chilled-out charm in spite of a veritable flood of tourism in recent years. From a couple of ultrabasic guesthouses and no electricity Ban Hua Det, at the north end of Don Det, has emerged as a sort of traveller tractor beam, with cheap bamboo bungalows and restaurants where you can make any order 'happy' for an extra US$0.50. At this stage that side of life is mainly confined to Ban Hua Det, so getting away from it is easy enough.

Don Det is linked to Don Khon by an attractive arched railway bridge that carried cargo between freighters operating above and below the falls. The line hasn't operated since WWII, though a rusted engine sits just to the south of the bridge. A report in early 2007 said the government was planning to rebuild the railway, but don't hold your breath.

Life on Don Khon is even more laid-back than on Don Det, and marginally more luxurious. It's less active by night, but better if you want to explore by day the narrow and mostly shady paths that cross the islands. Electricity will probably arrive in the next couple of years, but until then generators provide power to some places between about 6pm and 10pm.

Information
A couple of places offer slow internet for high prices. Otherwise, there is no bank, no medical services and not even a post office. **Lane Xang Travel** (www.xplore-asia.com) has an office-cum-bar-cum-internet café in Ban Hua Det. It offers various activities, including kayaking, rafting and sunset pleasure cruises, and can arrange all manner of transport. Bring as much money as you'll need, including plenty of kip.

Sights & Activities
Rare **Irrawaddy dolphins** can sometimes be seen off the southern tip of Don Khon, mainly in the mornings and evenings from December until May. Boats chartered (US$5, maximum three people) from the old French pier at the south end of Don Khon run out to a small island that looks over a deep-water conservation zone.

Don't expect Flipper-style tricks from these dolphins. If they are there at all you'll see a brief flash as they surface to breathe, then they're gone. If they don't show, that's not the boatman's fault, so don't expect a discount. Alternatively, most guesthouses offer tours for about US$5 per person.

Walking or hiring a **bicycle** is the best way to explore the dirt paths that cross the islands. The defunct **railway line** (a little rocky on a bike: don't be shocked if you get a puncture and have to push it home) links the two French loading piers, but it's pretty hot and using alternate shaded paths is more pleasant. Heading east from the bridge on Don Khon, turn south through a wat (past Sala Phae) to see a local village and the French-built **concrete channels** once used to direct logs through the falls. In the other direction, go through Wat Ban Khon and follow the shaded path about 1km to the dramatic **Tat Somphamit** waterfalls, also known as Li Phi Falls, which means 'spirit trap' because locals believe bad spirits are trapped here as they wash downstream. Two travellers have drowned here, so be careful. There's a charge of US$0.90 per day to cross the bridge, including entry to Tat Somphamit.

LAOS

Book accommodation online at lonelyplanet.com

At the muscular **Khon Phapheng Falls** (admission US$0.90), millions of litres of water crash over the rocks and into Cambodia every second at the largest (by volume, not height) waterfall in Southeast Asia. The falls are often included on the itinerary of dolphin-viewing trips.

Tubing, **kayaking** and **rafting** are also possible – you'll see them widely advertised; speak to Lane Xang Travel. See p508 for information on water-borne parasites.

Sleeping & Eating

Seemingly every farmer on Don Det has jumped aboard the bungalow bandwagon and there are now dozens of guesthouses around the edge of the island. Most feature basic stilted wooden- or bamboo-thatched bungalows with mosquito nets, hammocks and shared or basic attached bathrooms. The greatest concentration is squeezed into Ban Hua Det, which is the place to be if you want to socialise into the night. Sunrise Blvd, on the eastern edge, is busier and noisier than the footpath known as Sunset Strip along the northwestern edge. The rest of the accommodation is spread further along Sunrise down to the pleasant southern shore. Don Khon is home to more upmarket places, pleasant eateries on the water and a less-youthful atmosphere. Most places also serve food and drinks.

Most bungalows look the same, but they do differ in subtle but important ways. Thatched roofs are cooler, detached bungalows are more private, two windows are better than one, and almost all have shared bathroom and cold water. Also note, things are changing fast. By the time you arrive, there are bound to be new places, so use this list as a guide only. Boatmen will drop you near your chosen guesthouse – saving you a walk – if you insist. On Don Khon, all the sleeping and eating options are spread along the river either side of the bridge.

These first few are on Don Det:

Santiphab Guesthouse (☎ 030-534 6233; Don Det; bungalow US$1) Beside the north end of the bridge, the long-running Santiphab is a good option if the view and chilled atmosphere is more important than partying. The restaurant (meals US$1 to US$2.50) is a cooler place for sundowners.

Seng Chan's Bungalows (Sunrise Blvd, Don Det; bungalow US$1-2) These thatch-roofed and detached bungalows have two beds and two windows each and sit right on the river. Good choice.

Mr Phao's Sunrise Bungalows (Sunrise Blvd, Don Det; bungalow US$1.50) South of the pier, Mr Phao's has a wonderfully warm, family feel to go with tasty food and bungalows with multiple windows and hammocks. Good option.

Sunset Bar & Guesthouse (Sunset Strip, Don Det; bungalow US$1.50) There's a fun atmosphere here and it's the bar over the river that drives it. Warning: the *lào-láo* mojitos (US$0.50) can become addictive.

River Garden (☎ 020-527 4785; Southern Shore, Don Det; r US$1.50) This three-bungalow place on the southern shore calls itself Don Det's friendliest guesthouse, and the guests agreed. Good value.

Mama Tanon Café Guest House (☎ 020-546 5262; Sunrise Blvd, Don Det; r US$3) If you're partial to a bit of the Bob Marley air freshener, this basic but communal place and vivacious Mama (expect to be slapped for any insolence) should appeal.

Noy's Sunset Bungalows & Restaurant (☎ 030-534 6020; Don Det; bungalow US$3) In a prime sunset location, Noy's was one of the first guesthouses on Don Det and it's still very popular. Noy's Belgian husband has introduced some tasty European food to the restaurant (meals US$1.50 to US$5), which we thought was worth the little extra.

Guesthouse Souksanh (Don Khon; r US$2-3) The cheapest place on Don Khon, about 600m east of the bridge, this has a family feel and small rooms overhanging the river (US$2), or bungalows with bathroom and fan (US$3).

Pan's Guesthouse & Restaurant (☎ 020-563 1434; pkounnavong@yahoo.co.uk; Don Khon; r US$8; 🖳) Not far east of the bridge, Pan's wooden bungalows are a cut above the bamboo places, with soft mattresses, fans, clean bathrooms and plans for solar hot water. Over the track the restaurant isn't bad and information is free-flowing. Internet costs US$6 per hour.

Auberge Sala Don Khone (☎ 020-563 3718; www .salalao.com; Don Khon; s/d with breakfast US$16/21) Romantics will love the three rooms in this converted French-era hospital. There are also sturdy wooden rooms (single US$11, double US$16) with verandas and attached cold-water bathrooms. From May to September prices drop by US$3. A generator runs from 6pm to 10pm.

Seng Ahloune Restaurant (☎ 030-534 5807; Don Khon; meals US$1-4; ⏱ 7am-10pm) The Seng Ahloune serves delicious comfort food, including great fish and chips (US$3), and local dishes in a prime location just downriver from the bridge.

They were also building four rooms (US$10 with breakfast) when we passed.

Also recommended:

Mr Vong's Guest House Hang Det (☎ 020-526 2591; Southern Shore, Don Det; r US$1.50-4) At the south end of Don Det. Has simple bungalows but English-speaking Mr Vong is a great guy.

Souksan Hotel (☎ 030-534 5154; Don Det; r US$5-15) Squeezed onto the north tip of the island. Don Det's best rooms are overpriced and there's not much atmosphere. Electricity runs 6pm to 10pm.

Mr B's Guest House & Bungalows (☎ 030-534 5109; Sunset Strip, Don Det; bungalow US$3-4) English-speaking Mr B's is next door to Noy's; has reasonable bungalows in a quiet position and delicious food. The pumpkin burger (US$2) is legendary.

Getting There & Away

It seems hyperinflation has struck the Si Phan Don boatmen. Prices have tripled for trips between Ban Nakasang and Don Det (US$1.50 per person or US$2 alone) or Don Khon (US$2 per person or US$4 alone). Boats can be hired to go anywhere in the islands for about US$10 an hour.

For Pakse (US$3, 2½ to 3½ hours, 148km), buses or săwngthăew leave Ban Nakasang at 6am, 8am, 9am and 10am. See p327 for buses from Pakse.

Bolaven Plateau

The fertile Bolaven Plateau (Phu Phieng Bolaven in Lao) rises more than 1000m above the Mekong River Valley. It's a beautiful claw-shaped highland fortress of forests, rivers, waterfalls and plantations. The plateau is a centre for several Mon-Khmer ethnic groups, including the Alak, Laven (Bolaven means 'land of the Laven'), Ta-oy, Suay and Katu. The Alak and Katu are known for a water-buffalo sacrifice they perform yearly, usually on a full

moon in March. The area wasn't farmed intensively until the French planted coffee, rubber and bananas here. Today the Laven, Alak and Katu tribes have revived cultivation and it's here that the distinctive Lao coffee is grown.

The plateau has several spectacular waterfalls, including **Tat Fan**, a few kilometres west of **Paksong**, the biggest town on the plateau where there are two modest guesthouses. The **Tad Fane Resort** (☎ 020-553 1400; www.tadfane.com; r with breakfast US$30-40), overlooking the falls, is very nice.

TAT LO
☎ 034

Tat Lo, about 90km from Pakse on Rte 20, is a sort of backpacker retreat with cheap accommodation, an attractive setting and things to do, but not many travellers. Which is much of its charm. Waterfalls are the town's *raison d'être* and they give it a serenity that sees many visitors stay longer than they planned. Soulideth at Tim Guesthouse is great for local information, and has an expensive internet connection (US$6 per hour) too.

There are actually three waterfalls on this stretch of river. The nearest to town is **Tat Hang**, which can be seen from the bridge, while **Tat Lo** itself is about 700m upriver via a path leading through Saise Guesthouse. The spectacular third cascade is **Tat Suong**, about 10km from town and best reached by motorbike or bicycle – get directions from Soulideth. Guides to the falls and local villages are available from Tim Guesthouse or the community guides, office nearby. Trips start at US$4 per person for a four-hour trip. Elephant rides (US$5 per jumbo) can be organised here too.

Sleeping & Eating

The town is a one-street affair, with most accommodation either side of the bridge.

CROSSING INTO CAMBODIA: VOEN KHAM TO DOM KRALOR

This remote but popular border actually has two different crossings, but when we passed only one was really being used. That was the road via Dom Kralor that continues on smooth tar to Stung Treng. Cambodia issues visas on arrival at Dom Kralor for US$20 plus 'processing fee' – have small notes ready; Laos does not issue visas. From the islands, most travellers are taking a traveller minibus at least as far as Stung Treng (US$13, two hours), and given there is barely any other transport on the Cambodian side, this makes sense despite the cost. Minibuses leave in the morning and tickets are available all over the islands. For information on crossing this border in the other direction, see p233.

The second crossing is by boat from Voen Kham, but given Cambodia has closed its border post here and speedboats are hugely expensive and hard to find, it's not recommended.

CROSSING INTO VIETNAM: ATTAPEU TO BO Y

In far southeastern Attapeu Province a new border to Vietnam links to Kon Tum and Pleiku. It's 113km southeast of attractive Attapeu town, where there are several guesthouses. Visas are not issued here (yet). It's a new border, and transport is sketchy, but at least three Vietnamese-run buses were operating each week from Attapeu to Pleiku via Kon Tum (US$10, 12 hours) when we visited. The buses depart Attapeu at 9am Monday, Wednesday and Friday, and come the other way on Tuesday, Thursday and Saturday. Tickets are sold at the Thi Thi Restaurant just west of the bridge. For information on crossing this border in the other direction, see p403.

Budget places are concentrated on the east side of the bridge. **Siphaseth Guest House & Restaurant** (☎ 211890; r US$2-6) is the pick with newish fan-rooms (US$4 to US$6) and more traditional bamboo rooms (US$2) with shared bathroom. The **restaurant** (meals US$1.50-3) is ideal for sundowners. Next door the **Saylomyen Guest House** (r US$2.50) offers simple fan-conditioned huts with balcony and an equally simple shared bathroom.

The cane-and-wood bungalows at **Tim Guesthouse & Restaurant** (☎ 211885; 020-564 8820; soulidet@gmail.com; r US$4-6; 🖳) are not luxurious, but the jazz-fueled atmosphere, English- and French-speaking Soulideth and social restaurant (meals US$1.50 to US$3, open from 6.30am to 10pm) make it a good choice all the same.

More comfort and better views can be found at the riverside **Saise Guest House** (☎ /fax 211886, 020-564 2489; r US$6-60) and the **Tadlo Lodge** (☎ /fax 211889; souriyavincent@yahoo.com; bungalows s/d with breakfast US$20/30), though both these options can involve long walks to dine in their restaurants.

Getting There & Away

Just say 'Tat Lo' at Pakse's southern bus station and you'll be pointed to one of the several morning buses to Salavan that stop at Ban Khoua Set. It's 1.8km to Tat Lo from here. To Paksong, get yourself up to Ban Beng, at the junction, and jump a bus coming through from Salavan.

LAOS DIRECTORY

ACCOMMODATION

There's no shortage of accommodation in Laos, where even the smallest town will have a guesthouse or a village homestay option. Standards are rising across all price ranges but remain modest compared with the other countries in this book. Rates are usually quoted in US dollars or kip, though many also accept payment in Thai baht.

Outside of major centres such as Vientiane, Pakse and Luang Prabang, or tourist magnets such as Vang Vieng, there isn't a huge range to choose from. In those centres you'll find some very stylish top-end rooms and a decent selection of midrange comforts. But in most other places, including many provincial capitals, the best room in town won't be too luxurious. Fortunately, prices are also modest, with a budget air-con room going for less than US$10, or half that with a fan. Accommodation is cheapest in the rural north and far south, where it's still possible to find a US$2 bungalow in backpacker spots such as Muang Ngoi Neua and Si Phan Don, and most expensive in Vientiane and Luang Prabang.

Accommodation prices are high-season prices for rooms with attached bathroom, unless stated otherwise. An icon is included to indicate if air-con is available; otherwise, assume a fan will be provided. In this book, accommodation is listed by price order, starting

PRACTICALITIES

■ Laos uses 220V AC circuitry; power outlets usually feature two-prong round or flat sockets.

■ The *Vientiane Times* (www.vientiane times.org.la), published Monday to Friday, cleaves to the party line in English. Francophones can read the weekly *Le Renovateur*.

■ Lao National Television has two TV channels, but most people watch the more exciting Thai TV and/or karaoke videos. The single radio station, Lao National Radio (LNR), broadcasts sanitised English-language news twice daily.

■ Laos uses the metric system.

at the cheapest. Budget is defined as accommodation costing less than US$15, midrange as US$16 to US$50, and top end as more than US$50.

Homestays

For more then 75% of Laotians the 'real Laos' is life in a village. To get a taste of this families in villages across the country welcome travellers into their homes to experience life, Lao-style. This means sleeping, eating and washing as they do. It's not luxury, and often the mattress will be on the floor and you'll 'shower' by pouring water over yourself from a 44-gallon (170L) drum while standing in the middle of the yard (men and women should take a sarong). But it's exactly this level of immersion that makes a homestay so worthwhile. It's also good to know the US$5 you'll pay for bed, dinner and breakfast is going directly to those who need it most.

If you're up for it, remember to pack a sarong, torch, flip-flops or sandals, a phrasebook and some photos from home.

For more info on homestays, see p263.

ACTIVITIES
Cycling

Laos' relatively peaceful roads are a haven for cyclists, and bringing your own bicycle into the country is easy. Traffic is light and, unlike Thailand and Vietnam, drivers quite considerate. Even better, if you get knackered, you can flag down any passing bus or *săwngthăew*. Laos' main towns all have bicycle-rental shops. In cities be careful about leaving bags in the front basket, as passing motorcyclists have been known to lift them. Several companies offer mountain-bike tours, particularly from Luang Nam Tha (see Boat Landing Guest House & Restuarant, p311) and Luang Prabang (p295).

Kayaking & Rafting

Kayaking and white-water rafting have taken off and Laos has several world-class rapids, as well as lots of beautiful, although less challenging, waterways. Unfortunately, the industry remains dangerously unregulated and you should not go out on rapids during the wet season unless you are completely confident of your guides and equipment. Vang Vieng has the most options. **Green Discovery** (☎ 023-511440; www.greendiscoverylaos.com) has a good reputation, but for really serious expeditions speak with **Wildside** (www.wildside-asia.com).

Rock Climbing

Organised rock-climbing operations are run by **Green Discovery** (☎ 023-511440; www.greendiscoverylaos.com) in the karst cliffs around Vang Vieng and, on a smaller scale, near Luang Prabang. Vang Vieng has the most-established scene, with dozens of climbs ranging from beginner to very tough indeed. Climbers have compared the routes and guides here favourably to the high-profile climbing at Krabi in Thailand. Green Discovery has a very good reputation for safety and equipment; see its website for more details.

Trekking

Laos' large areas of wilderness are a trekker's dream and for many travellers trekking has become one of their primary reasons for visiting Laos. Fortunately, several environmentally and culturally sustainable tours have been developed that allow you to both get into these pristine areas and experience the lives of those who live there, without exploiting them.

These treks are available in several provinces and are detailed on the excellent website www.ecotourismlaos.com. You can plan to trek from Luang Nam Tha, Luang Prabang, Vientiane, Tha Khaek, Savannakhet and Pakse. Treks organised through the provincial tourism offices are the cheapest, while companies such as **Green Discovery** (www.greendiscoverylaos.com) offer more expensive and professional operations.

Tubing

Something of a Lao phenomenon, 'tubing' simply involves inserting yourself into an enormous tractor inner tube and floating down a river. Vang Vieng is the tubing capital with Muang Ngoi Neua and Si Phan Don popular runners-up.

BOOKS

Lonely Planet's *Laos* has all the information you'll need for extended travel in Laos, with more detailed descriptions of sights and wider coverage to help get you off the beaten track. Lonely Planet also publishes the very useful *Lao Phrasebook*. See also p336.

BUSINESS HOURS

Government offices are typically open from 8am to 11.30am or noon, and 1pm to 4pm or 5pm, Monday to Friday. Banking hours are generally 8.30am to 4pm Monday to Friday. Shops have longer hours and are often open on weekends. Most businesses close Sunday, but not restaurants, which typically open early and close by 10pm. Bars stay open until the officially mandated closing time of 11.30pm, sometimes a little later.

CLIMATE

Laos has two distinct seasons, mid-May to mid-November is wet, and at other times it's dry. The coolest time of year is November to January and the hottest is March to May. The lowlands of the Mekong River Valley are the hottest, peaking at around 38°C in March and April and dropping to a minimum of around 15°C in the cool season. Up in the mountains of Xieng Khuang and Sam Neua, cool season night-time temperatures can drop to freezing and even in the hot season it can be pleasant.

The wettest area of the country is southern Laos, where the Annamite mountain peaks get more than 3000mm of rain a year. Luang Prabang and Xieng Khuang receive less than half that amount of rain and Vientiane and Savannakhet get from 1500mm to 2000mm.

CUSTOMS

Customs inspections at ports of entry are very lax as long as you're not bringing in more than a moderate amount of luggage. You're not supposed to enter the country with more than 500 cigarettes or 1L of distilled spirits.

Of course, all the usual prohibitions on drugs weapons and pornography apply.

DANGERS & ANNOYANCES

Urban Laos is generally safe. You should still exercise ordinary precautions at night, but your chances of being robbed, mugged, harassed or assaulted are much lower than in most Western countries. There are significant dangers around the country, however. For the latest travel warnings for Laos, check government travel advisories on the internet.

Shootings have plagued Rte 13 between Vang Vieng and Luang Prabang since the '75 revolution. Route 7 between Phu Khun and Phonsavan has also had a spot of trouble in the past.

In 2003 the security situation deteriorated. Ambushes in and around Sam Neua in Houaphanh Province, bombings in Vientiane and attacks on public transport in southern Laos caused considerable anxiety for travellers and locals alike. While there have been no recent incidents of serious civil unrest that has affected tourists, the population of Laos is not exactly happily and peacefully governed by the current administration, so be sure to stay abreast of the political situation before – and while – travelling in Laos.

In the eastern provinces, particularly Xieng Khuang, Salavan and Savannakhet, UXO is a hazard. Never walk off well-used paths.

LAOS IN WORDS

■ *Another Quiet American* (2003) Brett Dakin's account of two years working at the National Tourism Authority of Laos reveals a lot about what drives – or does not – people working in Laos, both local and *falang* (Western).

■ *One Foot in Laos* (1999) Dervla Murphy's lone bicycle trip through off-the-beaten-track Laos is written with passion for the local people and some stinging assessments of travellers and modern ways.

■ *Shooting at the Moon: The Story of America's Clandestine War in Laos* (1998) Roger Warner's well-respected book exposes the 'Secret War' against the Ho Chi Minh Trail, and the CIA and Hmong role in it.

■ *Stalking the Elephant Kings: In Search of Laos* (1998) and *Bamboo Palace: Discovering the Lost Dynasty of Laos* (2003) Christopher Kremmer's two thoroughly researched and entertaining books detail his pursuit of the truth behind the final demise of the Lao monarchy in the late 1970s; great for history fans.

■ *The Ravens: Pilots of the Secret War of Laos* (1987) Christopher Robbins' page-turning account of the 'Secret War' and the role of American pilots and the Hmong is an excellent read.

EMBASSIES & CONSULATES
Lao Embassies & Consulates
See the relevant chapters for Lao embassies in neighbouring countries.

Australia (☎ 02-6286 4595; lao.embassy@interact.net
.au; 1 Dalman Cres, O'Malley, Canberra, ACT 2606)

China Běijīng (☎ 010-6532 1224; 11 Dongsie Jie, San-litun, Chao Yang, 100600); Kūnmíng (☎ 0871-317 6624;
Rm 3226, Camelia Hotel, 154 E Dong Feng Rd, 650041)

France (☎ 01 45 53 02 98; www.laoparis.com; 74 Ave Raymond Poincaré, 75116 Paris)

Germany (☎ 030-890 60647; hong@laos/botschaft.de;
Bismarckallee 2A, 14193 Berlin)

Japan (☎ 03-5411 2291; 3-3-21 Nishi Azabu, Minato-ku, Tokyo)

Myanmar (Burma; ☎ 01-222482; A1 Diplomatic Headquarters, Tawwin (Fraser) Rd, Yangon)

Sweden (☎ 08-668 5122; Hornsgaten 82-B1 TR 11721, Stockholm)

USA (☎ 202-332 6416; www.laoembassy.com; 2222 South St NW, Washington, DC 20008)

Embassies & Consulates in Laos
Australia (Map pp268-9; ☎ 021-413600; www.laos
.embassy.gov.au; Th Nehru, Ban Phonxai) Also represents nationals of Britain, Canada and New Zealand. The Austral-ian embassy is set to move to Th Tha Deua, just past the Australian Embassy Recreation Club at Km 4, during the life of this book.

Cambodia (Map pp268-9; ☎ 021-314952; fax 021-314951; Km 3, Th Tha Deua, Ban That Khao) Issues visas for US$20.

China (Map pp268-9; ☎ 021-315105; fax 021-315104; Th Wat Nak Nyai, Ban Wat Nak) Issues visas in four working days.

France (Map p272; ☎ 021-215258, 215259; www.amba france-laos.org; Th Setthathirat, Ban Si Saket)

Germany (Map pp268-9; ☎ 021-312111, 312110; Th Sok Pa Luang)

Myanmar (Burma; pp268-9; ☎ 021-314910; Th Sok Pa Luang) Issues tourist visas in three days for US$20.

Thailand Vientiane embassy (Map pp268-9; ☎ 021-900238; www.thaiembassy.org/vientiane; Th Phonkheng; ⏰ 8.30am-noon & 1-3.30pm Mon-Fri); Vientiane consulate (Map pp268-9; Th That Luang; ⏰ 8am-noon & 1-4.30pm); Savannakhet consulate (Map p322; ☎ 041-212373; Th Kuvoravong)

USA (Map p272; ☎ 021-267000; http://vientiane/usem bassy.gov; Th That Dam)

Vietnam Vientiane embassy (Map pp268-9; ☎ 021-413400; Th That Luang); Savannakhet consulate (Map p322; ☎ 041-212418; Th Sisavangvong) The embassy in Vientiane issues tourist visas in three working days for US$50, or in one day for US$55. The consulate in Savanna-khet issues a one-month tourist visa for US$45, one photo, three working days.

FESTIVALS & EVENTS
The Lao Buddhist Era (BE) calendar calculates year one as 638 BC, so AD 2008 is 2646 BE in Laos. Festivals are mostly linked to agricul-tural seasons or historic Buddhist holidays. Dates change with the lunar calendar and even from village to village, but www.tourismlaos .gov.la has more accurate dates for some major festivals, known as *bun* in Lao.

February
Makha Busa (Magha Puja or Bun Khao Chi, Full Moon)
This commemorates a speech given by the Buddha to 1250 enlightened monks who came to hear him without prior summons. Chanting and offerings mark the festival, culminating in candlelit circumambulation of wat through-out the country. Celebrations in Vientiane and at Wat Phu (p328) are most fervent.

Vietnamese Tet & Chinese New Year (Tut Jiin) Cel-ebrated in Vientiane, Pakse and Savannakhet with parties, fireworks and visits to Vietnamese and Chinese temples.

April
Bun Pi Mai (Lao Lunar New Year) Practically the whole country celebrates the Lao new year; held 14 to 16 April. Houses are cleaned, people put on new clothes and Buddha images are washed with lustral water. Later, people douse one another (and sometimes random tourists) with water. This festival is particularly picturesque in Luang Prabang, where it includes elephant processions and lots of tradi-tional costuming. The 14th to 16th are public holidays.

May
Visakha Busa (Visakha Puja, Full Moon) Falling on the 15th day of the sixth lunar month (usually in May), this is considered the day of the Buddha's birth, enlightenment and *parinibbana* (passing into nirvana). Activities are centred on the wat.

Bun Bang Fai (Rocket Festival) One of the wildest festivals in Laos. It's a pre-Buddhist rain ceremony celebrated alongside Visakha Busa, involving huge homemade rockets, music, dance, drunkenness, cross-dressing, large wooden phalluses and the occasional incinerated house...great fun.

July
Bun Khao Phansa (Khao Watsa, Full Moon) Late July is the beginning of the traditional three-month-rains retreat, when Buddhist monks are expected to station themselves in a single monastery.

October
Bun Awk Phansa (Ok Watsa, Full Moon) Celebrating the end of the three-month-rains retreat.

Bun Nam (*Bun suang héua*, Boat Racing Festival) Held the day after Awk Phansaa. Boat races are held in most riverside towns, though in smaller towns they're often postponed until National Day (2 December).

November

Bun Pha That Luang (That Luang Festival, Full Moon) Takes place at Pha That Luang in Vientiane in early November. Hundreds of monks assemble to receive alms and floral votives early on the first day. There is a colourful procession between Pha That Luang and Wat Si Muang. Elsewhere, it's all fireworks, music and drinking.

December

Lao National Day Held on 2 December, this public holiday celebrates the 1975 victory of the proletariat over the Royal Lao with parades and speeches.

FOOD & DRINK
Food

Lao cuisine lacks some of the variety of Thai food, but don't limit yourself to the ubiquitous diet of noodles, fried rice and 'travellers' fare' so common in Southeast Asia (fruit pancakes, muesli, fruit shakes…) There are some excellent Lao dishes to try.

The standard Lao breakfast is *fŏe* (rice noodles), usually served floating in a broth with vegetables and a meat of your choice. The trick is in the seasoning, and Lao people will stir in some fish sauce, lime juice, dried chillies, mint leaves, basil, or one of the wonderful speciality hot chilli sauces that many noodle shops make, testing it along the way, before slurping it down with chopsticks in one hand and a spoon in the other.

Làap is the most distinctively Lao dish, a delicious spicy salad made from minced beef, pork, duck, fish or chicken, mixed with fish sauce, small shallots, mint leaves, lime juice, roasted ground rice and lots and lots of chillies. Another famous Lao speciality is *tạm màak hung* (known as *som tam* in Thailand), a salad of shredded green papaya mixed with garlic, lime juice, fish sauce, sometimes tomatoes, palm sugar, land crab or dried shrimp and, of course, chillies by the handful.

In lowland Lao areas almost every dish is eaten with *khào nǐaw* (sticky rice), which is served in a small basket. Take a small amount of rice and, using one hand, work it into a walnut-sized ball before dipping it into the food. When you've finished eating, replace the lid on the basket. Less often, food is eaten with *khào jâo* (plain white rice), which is eaten with a fork and spoon.

In rural areas, where hunting is more common than raising animals for food, you're likely to encounter exotic meats that apparently make delicious, but not always ecologically sound, meals.

In main centres, French baguettes are a popular breakfast food. Sometimes it is eaten with condensed milk or with *khai* (eggs) in a sandwich that also contains Lao-style pâté and vegetables. When they are fresh, they are superb.

For more on dining in the Mekong region, see p86.

Alcoholic Drinks

Beerlao is ubiquitous, excellent and a source of great pride in a country where international recognition of any kind is scarce. Carlsberg now owns half of the brewer – Lao Brewery Co – and competition from international brands is rising. But Beerlao is still the choice of more than 90% of Lao beer drinkers.

Lào-láo (Lao liquor, or rice whisky) is a popular drink among lowland Lao. Strictly speaking, *lào-láo* is not legal but no-one seems to care. *Lào-láo* is usually taken neat, sometimes with a plain water chaser, and this is what you're most likely to be fed when you bowl up in some remote village. In a Lao home the pouring and drinking of *lào-láo* takes on ritual characteristics – it is first offered to the house spirits, and guests must take at least one offered drink or risk offending the spirits.

In rural provinces, a weaker version of *lào-láo* known as *lào hái* (jar liquor) is fermented by households or villages. *Lào hái* is usually drunk from a communal jar using long reed straws. It's not always safe to drink, since unboiled water is often added to it during and after fermentation.

Nonalcoholic Drinks

Water purified for drinking purposes is simply called *nâam deum* (drinking water), whether it's boiled or filtered. All water offered to customers in restaurants or hotels will be purified, and bottles of purified water are sold everywhere.

Lao coffee is usually served very strong and sweet enough to make your teeth clench. If you don't want sugar or sweetened condensed milk, ask for *kạa-fáe dạm* (black coffee).

Chinese-style green or semicured tea is the usual ingredient in *nâam sáa* or *sáa láo* – the weak, refreshing tea traditionally served free in restaurants. If you want Lipton-style tea, ask for *sáa hâwn* (hot tea).

GAY & LESBIAN TRAVELLERS

Laos has a fairly liberal attitude towards homosexuality, but a very conservative attitude to public displays of affection. Gay couples are unlikely to be given frosty treatment anywhere. Unlike Thailand, Laos does not have an obvious gay scene, but you'll find a greater concentration of gays in Vientiane's late-night clubs. Luang Prabang boasts Laos' first openly gay bar, with the rainbow-coloured gay pride flag flying in a few places around town.

Lesbians won't be bothered, but do expect some strange looks. Lao men, in particular, can't understand why women 'would be lesbians'.

HOLIDAYS

Schools and government offices are closed on these official holidays, and the organs of state move pretty slowly, if at all, during the festivals mentioned previously. Most Chinese- and Vietnamese-run businesses close for three days during Vietnamese Tet and Chinese New Year in February. International Women's Day is a holiday for women only.

International New Year 1 January
Army Day 20 January
International Women's Day 8 March
Lao New Year 14–16 April
International Labour Day 1 May
International Children's Day 1 June
Lao National Day 2 December

INTERNET ACCESS

You can get online in most, but not all, provincial capitals. Generally, if tourists go there in numbers, someone will have established a connection. In places where there's plenty of competition – such as Vientiane and Luang Prabang – rates are usually very low, about US$0.50 to US$1.50 an hour. In towns where there are only one or two places, or where they need to call long-distance to reach the server, rates will be higher – US$3 to US$6 an hour.

INTERNET RESOURCES

Ecotourism Laos (www.ecotourismlaos.com) Excellent site focussing on trekking and other ecotourism activities. Recommended.
Lao National Tourism Authority (www.tourismlaos .gov.la) Mostly up-to-date travel information from the government.

Travelfish (www.travelfish.org) The most consistently updated website for independent travellers in Southeast Asia, including excellent coverage of Lao border crossings.
Vientiane Times (www.vientianetimes.org.la) Website of the country's only English-language newspaper. Operated by the government.

LEGAL MATTERS

There is virtually nothing in the way of legal services in Laos. If you get yourself in legal strife, contact your embassy in Vientiane, though the assistance it can provide may be limited. In most cases you will have actually committed a crime if you're being held. If so, you're going to pay, one way or the other.

It's against the law for foreigners and Lao to have sexual relations unless they're married. Travellers should be aware that a holiday romance could result in being arrested and deported.

MAPS

The best all-purpose country map is GT-Rider .com's *Laos,* a sturdy laminated affair with several city maps. Look for the 2005 or more recent editions. Hobo Maps has produced a series of good, if sometimes unwieldy, maps to Vientiane, Luang Prabang and Vang Vieng, widely available in the relevant destinations.

MONEY

Though not as bad as a few years ago, the Lao kip remains relatively volatile, so prices in this chapter are quoted in US dollars at a rate of 10,000 kip to the dollar. In Laos you'll see prices quoted in kip, dollars and/or Thai baht but it's always worth having a stock of kip for smaller purchases or if you're out of town.

ATMs

Vientiane's lone ATM linked to the international network should soon have some brothers, if only in the capital. You can only withdraw 700,000 kip at a time (about US$70).

Bargaining

The Lao will bargain with you – especially in markets – but it's nothing near as intense as in Thailand or Vietnam, and you shouldn't expect prices to fall too far. A quiet, gentle bargaining technique works much better than arm-waving melodramatics.

Foreigners often pay more than locals, particularly in more heavily touristed areas where the concept of overcharging tourists has caught on. Túk-túk drivers are the worst, but elsewhere price differences are minimal and usually not worth getting angry about.

Cash

The only legal currency is the Lao kip, but three currencies are in everyday use: the kip, US dollar and Thai baht. Most places will accept any of these currencies, or combinations of all three, as payment. Kip come in denominations of 500, 1000, 2000, 5000, 10,000, 20,000 and new 50,000 kip notes, which look deceptively like the 20,000s.

Credit Cards

A limited number of hotels, upmarket restaurants and gift shops in Vientiane and Luang Prabang accept Visa and MasterCard, and to a much lesser extent Amex and JCB – Visa is best. Banque pour le Commerce Extérieur Lao (BCEL) branches in Vientiane, Luang Prabang, Vang Vieng, Savannakhet and Pakse offer cash advances/withdrawals on Visa credit/debit cards for a 3% transaction fee.

Exchanging Money

US dollars and Thai baht can be exchanged all over Laos. Banks in Vientiane and Luang Prabang, and some provinces, change euro, Thai baht, UK pounds, Japanese yen, and Canadian, US and Australian dollars. US-dollar travellers cheques can be exchanged in most provincial capitals and attract a better rate than cash.

The best overall exchange rate is usually offered by BCEL. The only advantage of other moneychangers – often found in gold shops and at markets – is longer opening hours. In rural areas exchange rates can be significantly lower. For the latest rates check www.bcel laos.com; at the time of press, the following exchange rates applied:

Country	Unit	Kip
Australia	A$1	7630
Cambodia	1000r	2600
Canada	C$1	8365
China	Y1	1220
euro zone	€1	12,380
Japan	¥100	7900
New Zealand	NZ$1	7410
Thailand	10B	2750
UK	UK£1	18,000
USA	US$1	9600
Vietnam	10,000d	5930

Travellers Cheques

Banks in most provincial capitals will exchange US-dollar travellers cheques. If you are changing cheques into kip, there is usually no commission, but changing into dollars attracts a minimum 2% charge.

POST

Postal services from Vientiane are generally reliable, the provinces less so. If you have valuable items or presents to post home, there is a **Federal Express** (Map p272; ☎ 021-223278; ☯ 8am-noon & 1-5pm Mon-Fri, 9am-noon Sat) office inside the main post office compound in Vientiane.

RESPONSIBLE TRAVEL

Laos is a poor country and all the usual guidelines for responsible travel apply here. On the environmental front, relatively rapid economic growth has seen traditional packaging, such as banana leaves, replaced by millions of plastic bags. Try to set a positive example by either not accepting a plastic bag in the first place, or at the least putting any bags or other rubbish in a bin.

Begging children seldom keep the money they are given and kids grow up with an expectation that survival depends upon hand-outs; if you want to give something to a child give food. On the other hand, the legless beggars you'll see, mostly victims of the Second Indochina War, have mostly fallen through the sizable gaps in the Lao system and, unable to work, rely almost completely on hand-outs. There is no downside to giving money to these guys. And it's always worth rewarding people who have helped you out as guides or porters.

One of the most appealing aspects of Laos has always been the friendly, open nature of the Lao people. However, many of those who work in the tourism business have become jaded in recent years by what they see as unreasonably aggressive bargaining, usually by travellers who lose a little perspective in their pursuit of the cheapest stay possible. One guesthouse owner told us: 'Some people spend 20 minutes negotiating to get a US$5 room for US$4, then go and drink US$7 of beer, or they spend US$45 on a rafting trip. Is that US$1 so important for them?'

When you stop for a moment and consider what that US$1 would buy you at home – a small fraction of one beer, perhaps – the answer is it's probably not.

By all means try to get the best rate you can – that's part of travelling. But be aware of the cultural context. Generally speaking, the Lao avoid conflict as much as they can and while they are happy to bargain a little, they don't usually buy into protracted negotiations/arguments over price. If the rate seems unfair to you (as opposed to being beyond your budget) by all means make a counter offer. This will usually be accepted straight away, or not at all.

It's also worth understanding that international economic imperatives such as inflation and the price of oil affect inflation in Laos as much as they do prices in your own country. Room rates will probably go up compared with those listed in this book. When that happens remember that this book is called a guidebook for a reason – it's just a guide.

For information on responsible trekking, see p484 and p138.

TELEPHONE

Laos' country code is ☎ 856. To dial out of the country press ☎ 00 first, or ask for the local mobile operator's cheaper code. You will find public phone booths in Laos, but these days they're little better than rusting greenhouses and phonecards are no longer sold. Instead, for long-distance calls use a post office, Telecom Lao centre (rates vary in these, but in Vientiane are very reasonable) or internet cafés.

As a guide, all mobile phone numbers have the prefix ☎ 020 followed by seven digits, while the newer WIN Phones (fixed phones without a landline) begin with ☎ 030.

Mobile Phones

You can use your own GSM mobile phone in Laos, either on roaming (expensive) or by buying a local SIM card for about US$5, then purchasing prepaid minutes. Domestic calls are reasonably cheap. In our experience, Lao Telecom and ETL have the widest network coverage.

TOURIST INFORMATION

The Lao National Tourism Administration (NTAL) and provincial tourism authorities have offices throughout Laos, though standards vary greatly. The offices in Tha Khaek, Savannhket, Pakse, Luang Nam Tha, Sainyabouly, Phongsali and Sam Neua are excellent, with well-trained staff and plenty of brochures. Travel agencies and tour compa-

nies such as Green Discovery and Lane Xang Travel are also worth a look.

NTAL also has three good websites:
Lao National Tourism Administration www
.tourismlaos.gov.la
Lao Ecotourism www.ecotourismlaos.com
Central Laos Trekking www.trekkingcentrallaos.com

VISAS

Laos issues 30-day tourist visas on arrival at several popular airports and borders. They are available at Vientiane, Luang Prabang and Pakse airports. For land borders, see the table, p101. Visas on arrival cost US$30 to US$42 in US dollars or Thai baht cash, depending on what passport you hold, plus two passport photos.

However, regulations and prices change regularly, so it's worth checking online, on the traveller grapevine or with the nearest Lao embassy (but not their websites, which are way out of date), before pitching up to some remote border. See p337. If you want to be doubly sure, or plan to use a border where visas are not issued, consulates and travel agents in Vietnam, China, Cambodia and Thailand all issue/arrange visas.

Visa Extensions

Visa extensions cost US$2 per day from the **Immigration Office** (Map p272; ☎ 021-212250; Th Hatsady; ☑ 8am-4.30pm Mon-Fri), in the Ministry of Public Security building in Vientiane, and give up to a maximum of 30 days. Outside Vientiane, travel agents and guesthouses can usually arrange extensions for US$3 per day. Your passport will be sent to Vientiane, so it can take a few days. If you overstay your visa, you'll have to pay a fine on departure of US$10 for each day over.

VOLUNTEERING

It's not easy to find short-term volunteer work in Laos. The Organic Mulberry Farm in Vang Vieng (p289) needs volunteers occasionally. Otherwise, just ask around the expat community and you might get lucky.

WOMEN TRAVELLERS

Women travellers are more likely to be troubled by aggressive Western 'guru' male travellers, who have unravelled the spiritual mysteries of existence and are willing to share them in exchange for an invitation to your room, than by Lao men. Elsewhere, long-distance buses and guesthouses are where you're most likely to attract unwanted attention. Choosing a guesthouse with female staff and management helps avoid this.

The best way to avoid unwanted attention from Lao men is to refrain from wearing overly revealing clothes. Laos is much more conservative than Thailand and it's highly unusual for most women, even in more modern places such as Vientiane and Vang Vieng, to wear singlet tops or very short skirts or shorts. So when travellers do, people tend to stare. Lao people will almost never confront you about what you're wearing, but that doesn't mean they don't care. As one young woman in Vang Vieng told us: 'I wouldn't say anything, but I'd prefer it if they put on a sarong when they get out of the river. It's not our way to dress like that [a bikini only] and it's embarrassing to see it.' It's good advice – every woman traveller should carry a sarong.

WORK

English teaching is the most common first job for foreigners working in Laos, and schools in Vientiane are often hiring. There is also an inordinate number of development organisations – see www.directoryofngos.org for a full list – where foreigners with technical skills and volunteer experience can look for employment. Ask around.

TRANSPORT IN LAOS

Transport infrastructure in Laos is barely recognisable from what existed a few years ago. Huge, foreign-funded road construction projects have transformed a network of rough dirt tracks into relatively luxurious sealed affairs. The lack of potholes has ushered in a battalion of buses and scheduled services, making domestic transport easy and cheap, if sometimes very slow.

GETTING THERE & AWAY

There are many land and river borders into Laos and they're becoming increasingly popular with travellers. By air, there is a small but growing number of routes and airlines, though prices don't vary that much.

Air

There are no intercontinental flights operating to Laos. You can fly into or out of Laos

at Vientiane (from or to Cambodia, China, Thailand and Vietnam), Luang Prabang (Cambodia, Thailand and Vietnam) or Pakse (Cambodia and Thailand).

The following airlines fly to and from Laos. All fares are one way. See also the regional air fares map, p499.

Bangkok Airways (☎ 071-253334; www.bangkokair .com; 57/6 Th Sisavangvong, Ban Xiengmuan, Luang Prabang)

China Eastern Airlines (Map pp268-9; ☎ 021-212300; www.ce-air.com; Th Luang Prabang, Vientiane)

Lao Airlines (Map p272; ☎ 021-212051; www.laoair lines.com; Th Pangkham, Vientiane)

Thai Airways International (THAI; Map pp268-9; ☎ 021-222527; www.thaiair.com; Th Luang Prabang, Vientiane)

Vietnam Airlines (Map p272; ☎ 021-217562; www .vietnamairlines.com; 1st fl, Lao Plaza Hotel, Th Samsenthai, Vientiane)

CAMBODIA

Between Phnom Penh and Vientiane (US$145, 1½ hours) there are two flights a week with Lao Airlines (stopping in Pakse) and a daily direct flight with Vietnam Airlines. Lao Airlines flies between Siem Reap and Vientiane (US$110, 2½ hours) five times a week, stopping at Pakse (US$70, 50 minutes), and from November to March offers two more flights between Siem Reap and Pakse that continue to Luang Prabang (US$135).

CHINA

Lao Airlines shares three services a week between Kūnmíng and Vientiane (US$120, 2½ hours) with China Eastern Airlines.

THAILAND

Lao Airlines and THAI (Thai International Airways) have regular flights between Bangkok and Vientiane (US$99 to 5000B). Bangkok Airways flies daily between Bangkok and Luang Prabang (5000B, 1¾ hours), and Lao Airlines has three flights a week for US$120. Lao Airlines has five flights a week between Vientiane and Chiang Mai (US$111, 2½ hours) via Luang Prabang (US$85, one hour).

Some people save money by flying from Bangkok to Udon Thani in Thailand, then carrying on by road to Vientiane. Udon Thani is 55km south of Nong Khai and Bangkok–Udon tickets on **Thai Air Asia** (www.airasia.com) start at about 1300B.

Bangkok Airways should have started flights between Bangkok and Pakse by the time you read this.

VIETNAM

Lao Airlines and Vietnam Airlines fly between Vientiane and Hanoi (US$115, one hour, 10 times a week), and Ho Chi Minh City (US$140, three hours) daily; and between Luang Prabang and Hanoi.

Border Crossings

Laos has open land borders with Cambodia, China, Thailand and Vietnam, but not Myanmar. Under current rules, 30-day tourist visas are available on arrival at several (but not all) international checkpoints. These crossings are outlined in the table (p101), and in detail in boxes in the relevant chapters. However, we still recommend checking the **Thorntree** (http://thorntree.lonelyplanet.com/) and checking with other travellers before setting off because things change frequently. Note that most crossings involve changing transport at the border.

Car & Motorcycle

If you have your own car or motorcycle, you can import it for the length of your visa after filling in forms and paying fees at the border; it's much easier if you have a carnet. Motorcyclists planning to ride through Laos should check out the wealth of info at www.gt-rider.com.

GETTING AROUND
Air

Lao Airlines (www.laoairlines.com) handles all domestic flights in Laos. Both the airline's safety record and the reliability of its schedules are better than they were. However, during holiday seasons it can be difficult to get a seat, so book ahead. Prices have been fairly stable recently. Except at Lao Airlines' offices in Vientiane and Luang Prabang, where credit cards are accepted for both international and domestic tickets, you must pay in US dollars cash.

Always reconfirm your flights a day or two before departing as undersubscribed flights may be cancelled, or you could get bumped off the passenger list.

Bicycle

The light and relatively slow traffic in most Lao towns makes for favourable cycling conditions. Bicycles are available for rent in major tourist destinations, costing around 10,000 kip per day for a cheap Thai or Chinese model. For long-distance cyclists, bicycles can be brought into the country usually without any hassle, and if the mountains prove too challenging, you can always jump on a passing bus or *săwngthăew*. Several companies offer cycling tours.

Boat

With the highway-upgrading process almost complete, the days of mass river transport are as good as over. Sadly, most boat services today are geared at tourists, pushing prices up and taking away the fun of travelling with the locals, their produce…and domestic animals.

ON THE BUSES

The buses of Laos probably won't be what you're used to. Depending on your luck, you might get a relatively new bus, moving at something approaching 60km/h, with two seats to yourself and no karaoke. Or you might not…

The bus might be so old and rubbish it makes an otherwise flat road feel like a potholed monster. The music might be deafeningly loud and diabolically bad, and you might be sharing the bus with a menagerie of farmyard animals. While researching this chapter we had several flat tires; a bus without windows driving through a storm; a bus that picked up 5 tonnes of rice from a local mill and stuffed them everywhere flat, including the aisle, seats and roof; and a broken engine that the driver tried (unsuccessfully) to fix with a condom (full marks for improvisation, though).

Our advice is don't look at your watch too much and just soak it up. These sort of trips are actually more fun than they sound. They're inevitably social events and make much better stories than a few uneventful hours on a VIP bus.

The most popular river trip in Laos – the slow boat between Huay Xai (p313) and Luang Prabang – remains a daily event. Other popular journeys – between Pakse and Si Phan Don, or between Nong Khiaw and Luang Prabang – are no longer regular, so you'll probably have to charter a boat.

River ferries are basic affairs and passengers usually sit, eat and sleep on the wooden decks; it's worth bringing some padding. The toilet (if there is one) is an enclosed hole in the deck at the back of the boat.

For shorter river trips, such as Luang Prabang to the Pak Ou caves, you can easily hire a river taxi. The *héua hang nyáo* (long-tail boats), with engines gimbal-mounted on the stern, are the most typical, though for a really short trip (eg crossing a river) a *héua phai* (rowboat) or a small improvised ferry will be used.

Along the upper Mekong River, between Luang Prabang and Huay Xai and between Xieng Kok and Huay Xai, Thai-built *héua wái* (speedboats) are common. These craft are little more than surfboards with car engines mounted on the back, and are both deafeningly loud and painfully uncomfortable. They do, however, cover a distance in six hours that might take a river ferry two days or more. They're not cheap but some ply regular routes, so the cost can be shared among several passengers. For some, a ride on these boats is a major thrill, but for others they're a nightmare that can't end soon enough. They also kill and injure people every year when they disintegrate on contact with floating debris, which is in plentiful supply during the wet season, or flip when they hit a standing wave. Word from Laos is that foreigners might be barred from using these boats in 2007.

Bus & Săwngthăew

Long-distance public transport in Laos is either by bus or *săwngthăew* (literally 'two rows'), which are converted trucks or pickups with benches down either side. Buses are more frequent and go further than ever before, and destinations that were all but inaccessible a few years ago now see regular services. Privately run VIP buses operate on some busier routes, but slow, simple standard buses (occasionally with air-con) remain the norm. Prices are about US$2 per 100km for VIP buses, and US$1.50 per 100km on standard buses.

Săwngthăew usually service shorter routes within a given province. Most decent-sized villages have at least one *săwngthăew*, which will run to the provincial capital daily except Sunday, stopping wherever you want. Given everyone is sitting on top of, or facing each other, they're even more social than the bus.

Car & Motorcycle

Chinese- and Japanese-made 100cc step-through motorbikes can be rented for US$5 to US$15 a day in Vientiane, Vang Vieng, Tha Khaek, Savannakhet, Pakse and Luang Nam Tha. No licence is required, and gallivanting about the countryside by motorcycle has become increasingly popular with travellers. Try to get a Japanese bike if you're travelling any distance out of town. In Vientiane, Pakse and Vang Vieng it's also possible to rent dirt bikes for around US$20 per day. Motorcycle tours of Laos are offered by **Asian Motorcycling Adventures** (www.asianbiketour.com), among others.

Car rental in Laos is a great if relatively costly way of reaching remote places. In Vientiane, **Asia Vehicle Rental** (AVR; Map p272; ☎ 021-217493; www.avr.laopdr.com; Th Samsenthai) has sedans, minibuses, pick-ups and 4WDs, with or without drivers; they're very reliable.

Hitching

Hitching is possible in Laos, if not common. It's never entirely safe and not recommended, especially for women as the act of standing beside a road and waving at cars might be misinterpreted.

Vietnam

MANFRED GOTTSCHALK

Vietnam

Welcome to another world, a world where the colours are more vivid, where the landscapes are bolder, the coastline more dramatic, where the culture is richer, the history more compelling, where the tastes are more divine, where life is lived faster. This is the world of Vietnam, the latest Asian dragon to awake from its slumber.

Nature has blessed Vietnam with a bountiful harvest: with soaring mountains, a killer coastline and radiant rice fields, it is simply stunning. After more than 4000 dramatic kilometres, the mighty Mekong spills into Vietnam, blanketing the landscape in a patchwork of emerald-green rice paddies, timelessly tended by peasant women in conical hats. This is Cuu Long, or the river of nine dragons, a water world of floating markets and bobbing boats.

Vietnam is a nation of determined optimists who have weathered war upon war; survived colonialism, a closed society and communist rule; and come out alive and kicking as an intact culture. Fiercely protective of their independence and sovereignty, the Vietnamese are graciously welcoming of foreigners who come as guests not conquerors.

Don't believe the hype. Or the propagandist party billboards that are as common as statues of 'Uncle Ho'. Believe your senses, as you discover one of the most enriching, enlivening and exotic countries on earth.

HIGHLIGHTS

- Discover a stunningly situated former hill station hemmed in on all sides by rugged mountains at **Sapa** (p376), home to a dizzying mix of minority people

- Explore the captivating capital **Hanoi** (p351), steeped in history, pulsating with life, bubbling with commerce, buzzing with motorbikes and rich in exotic scents

- Experience nature at its outrageous best in **Halong Bay** (p369), where hundreds of limestone peaks tower above the shimmering seas; it's a karst system with a difference

- Fall in love with the old-world atmosphere of **Hoi An** (p387), a place to savour slowly

- Enter the **Mekong Delta** (p419), a world of water, a carpet of dazzling greens in the rice basket of the country, a place for slow boating, markets floating and delicious fish

★ Sapa
Hanoi ★ ★ Halong Bay

Hoi An ★

★ Mekong Delta

HISTORY

Vietnam has a history as rich and evocative as anywhere on earth. Sure, the American War in Vietnam captured the attention of the West, but centuries before that the Vietnamese were scrapping with the Chinese, the Khmers, the Chams and the Mongols. Vietnamese civilisation is as sophisticated as that of its mighty northern neighbour China, from where it drew many of its influences under a thousand-year occupation. Later came the French and the humbling period of colonialism from which Vietnam was not to emerge until the second half of the 20th century. The Americans were simply the last in a long line of invaders who had come and gone through the centuries and, no matter what was required or how long it took, they too would be vanquished. If only the planners in Washington had paid a little more attention to the history of this proud nation, the trauma and tragedy of a brutal war might have been avoided.

Early Vietnam

The sophisticated Indianised kingdom of Funan flourished from the 1st to 6th centuries AD in the Mekong Delta area. Archaeological evidence reveals that Funan's busy trading port of Oc-Eo had contact with China, India, Persia and even the Mediterranean. Between the mid-6th century and the 9th century, the Funan empire was absorbed by the pre-Angkorian kingdom of Chenla.

Around the late 2nd century when the Hindu kingdom of Champa was putting down roots in the Danang area, the Chinese conquered the Red River Delta near Hanoi.

Thus began a thousand-year pattern of the Vietnamese resisting the yoke of Chinese rule, while at the same time adopting many Chinese innovations to evolve into today's rice-growing society. The most famous act of resistance during this period (c 200 BC–AD 938) was the rebellion of the two Trung sisters (Hai Ba Trung), self-declared queens of the Vietnamese state, who drowned themselves rather than surrender to the Chinese.

By the 10th century, Vietnam had declared independence from China and so began almost one thousand years of a dynastic tradition. During this era, the Vietnamese successfully repulsed attacks by foreign invaders, eventually absorbing the kingdom of Champa as they expanded south.

FAST FACTS

- **Area** 329,566 sq km
- **Capital** Hanoi
- **Country Code** ☎ 84
- **Population** 84 million
- **Money** US$1 = 16,035d (dong)
- **Seasons** south hot & wet Apr-Sep, hot & dry Oct-Mar; north hot & dry Apr-Sep, cool & wet Oct-Mar; central coast typhoons Jul-Nov
- **Phrases** *xin chào* (hello), *tam biêt* (goodbye), *cam ơn* (thank you)

Contact with the West

In 1858 a joint military force from France and the Spanish colony of the Philippines stormed Danang after several missionaries were killed. Early the next year, it seized Saigon. By 1883 the French had imposed a Treaty of Protectorate on Vietnam. French rule often proved cruel and arbitrary. Ultimately, the most successful resistance came from the communists, first organised by Ho Chi Minh in 1925.

During WWII, the only group that significantly resisted the Japanese occupation was the communist-dominated Viet Minh. When WWII ended, Ho Chi Minh – whose Viet Minh forces already controlled large parts of the country – declared Vietnam independent. French efforts to reassert control soon led to violent confrontations and full-scale war. In May 1954, Viet Minh forces overran the French garrison at Dien Bien Phu.

The Geneva Accords of mid-1954 provided for a temporary division of Vietnam at the Ben Hai River. When Ngo Dinh Diem, the anticommunist, Catholic leader of the southern zone, refused to hold the 1956 elections, the Ben Hai line became the border between North and South Vietnam.

The American War in Vietnam

Around 1960, the Hanoi government changed its policy of opposition to the Diem regime from one of 'political struggle' to one of 'armed struggle'. The National Liberation Front (NLF), a communist guerrilla group better known as the Viet Cong (VC), was founded to fight against Diem.

A brutal ruler, Diem was assassinated in 1963 by his own troops. After Hanoi ordered

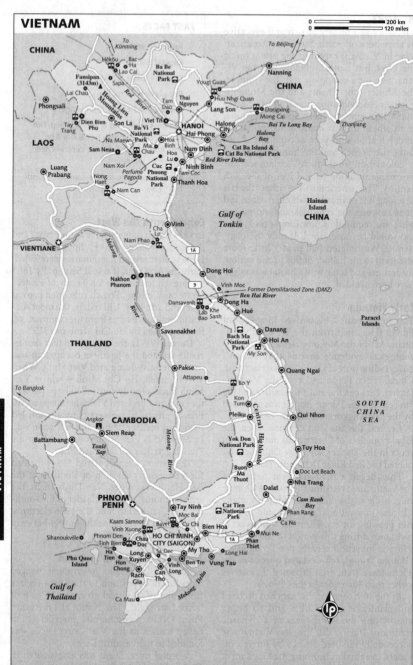

VIETNAM

0 — 200 km
0 — 120 miles

CHINA

To Kūnming

Hékou
Bac Ha
Lao Cai
Fansipan (3143m)
Sapa
Ba Be National Park
Lai Chau
Phongsali
Tay Trang
Dien Bien Phu
Son La
Hoang Lien Mountains
Na Maew
Sam Neua
Mai Chau
Nam Xoi
Nong Haet
Perfume Pagoda
Nam Can
Ba Vi National Park
Hoa Binh
Hoa Lu
Cuc Phuong National Park
Tam Coc

LAOS

Luang Prabang

Tam Dao
Thai Nguyen
Viet Tri
Lang Son
HANOI
Hai Phong
Nam Dinh
Ninh Binh
Thanh Hoa

Yougi Guan
Huu Nghi Quan
Halong City
Dongxing
Mong Cai
Bai Tu Long Bay
Halong Bay
Cat Ba Island & Cat Ba National Park
Red River Delta

Nanning
CHINA

Zhanjiang

Red River

Vinh
Cha Lo
Nam Phao

Gulf of Tonkin

Hainan Island
CHINA

VIENTIANE

Nakhon Phanom
Tha Khaek
Dong Hoi
Vinh Moc
Former Demilitarised Zone (DMZ)
Ben Hai River
Dansavanh
Lao Bao
Khe Sanh
Dong Ha
Hué
Bach Ma National Park
Danang
Hoi An
My Son

Mekong River

Savannakhet

THAILAND

Paracel Islands

Pakse
Attapeu
Bo Y
Quang Ngai

Kon Tum
Pleiku
Central Highlands
Qui Nhon

SOUTH CHINA SEA

To Bangkok

Angkor
Siem Reap
CAMBODIA
Battambang
Tonlé Sap

Yok Don National Park
Buon Ma Thuot
Tuy Hoa
Doc Let Beach
Nha Trang
Dalat
Cam Ranh Bay
Phan Rang
Ca Na

Mekong River

PHNOM PENH

Kaam Samnor
Vinh Xuong
Phnom Den
Tinh Bien
Sihanoukville
Ha Tien
Hon Chong
Phu Quoc Island
Long Xuyen
Rach Gia
Ca Mau
Chau Doc
Sa Dec
Can Tho
Vinh Long

Tay Ninh
Moc Bai
Bavet
Cu Chi
Cat Tien National Park
Bien Hoa
HO CHI MINH CITY (SAIGON)
My Tho
Ben Tre
Vung Tau
Long Hai
Phan Thiet
Mui Ne

Mekong Delta

Gulf of Thailand

VIETNAM

North Vietnamese Army (NVA) units to infiltrate the South in 1964, the situation for the Saigon regime became desperate. In 1965 the USA committed its first combat troops, soon joined by soldiers from South Korea, Australia, Thailand and New Zealand in an effort to bring global legitimacy to the conflict – sound familiar?

As Vietnam celebrated the Lunar New Year in 1968, the VC launched a surprise attack, known as the Tet Offensive, marking a crucial turning point in the war. Many Americans, who had for years believed their government's insistence that the USA was winning, started demanding a negotiated end to the war. The Paris Agreements, signed in 1973, provided for a cease-fire, the total withdrawal of US combat forces and the release of American prisoners of war.

Reunification

Saigon surrendered to the NVA on 30 April 1975. Vietnam's reunification by the communists meant liberation from more than a century of colonial repression, but was soon followed by large-scale internal repression. Hundreds of thousands of southerners fled Vietnam, creating a flood of refugees for the next 15 years.

Vietnam's campaign of repression against the ethnic Chinese, plus its invasion of Cambodia at the end of 1978, prompted China to attack Vietnam in 1979. The war lasted only 17 days, but Chinese-Vietnamese mistrust lasted well over a decade.

Vietnam Today

With the end of the Cold War and the collapse of the Soviet Union in 1991, Vietnam and Western nations sought *rapprochement*. The 1990s brought foreign investment and Association of Southeast Asian Nations (Asean) membership. The USA established diplomatic relations with Vietnam in 1995, and in 2000 Bill Clinton became the first US president to visit northern Vietnam. George W Bush followed suit in 2006, as Vietnam was welcomed into the World Trade Organisation (WTO).

Relations have also improved with the historic enemy China. China still secretly thinks of Vietnam as a renegade province, but Vietnam's economic boom has caught Běijīng's attention.

Vietnam's economy is growing at more than 8% a year and tourists just can't get enough of the place. The future is bright, but ultimate success depends on how well the Vietnamese can follow the Chinese road to development: economic liberalisation without political freedom. With only two million paid-up members of the Communist Party and 80 million Vietnamese, it is a road they must tread carefully.

PEOPLE & THE POPULATION

The Vietnamese are battle-hardened, proud and nationalist, as they have earned their stripes in successive skirmishes with the world's mightiest powers. But that's the older generation, who remember every inch of the territory for which they fought. For the new generation, Vietnam is a place to succeed, a place to ignore the staid structures set in stone by the communists, and a place to go out and have some fun.

As in other parts of Asia, life revolves around the family; there are often several generations living under one roof. Poverty, and the transition from a largely agricultural society to that of a more industrialised nation, sends many people seeking their fortune to the bigger cities and is changing the structure of the modern family unit. Women make up 52% the nation's workforce but are generally not in high positions of power.

Vietnam's population is 84% ethnic Vietnamese (Kinh) and 2% ethnic Chinese; the rest is made up of Khmers, Chams and members of more than 50 ethnolinguistic groups known as Montagnards (French for 'highlanders').

RELIGION

Over the centuries, Confucianism, Taoism and Buddhism have fused with popular Chinese beliefs and ancient Vietnamese animism to form what's collectively known as the Triple Religion (Tam Giao). Most Vietnamese people identify with this belief system, but if asked, they'll usually say they're Buddhist.

Vietnam has a significant percentage of Catholics (8% to 10% of the total population), second in Southeast Asia only to the Philippines.

The unique and colourful Vietnamese sect called Cao Daism was founded in the 1920s. It combines secular and religious philosophies of the East and West, and was based on seance messages revealed to the group's founder, Ngo Minh Chieu.

ARTS
Contemporary Arts

It's sometimes possible to catch modern dance, classical ballet and stage plays in Hanoi and Ho Chi Minh City (HCMC). The work of contemporary painters and photographers covers a wide swathe of styles and gives a glimpse into the modern Vietnamese psyche. Check the *Guide* or *Time Out* for current theatre or dance listings in Hanoi and HCMC.

Traditional Arts
ARCHITECTURE

The Vietnamese were not great builders like their neighbours the Khmer, who erected the Angkor temples in Cambodia. Most early Vietnamese buildings were made of wood and other materials that proved highly vulnerable in the tropical climate. The grand exception is the stunning towers built by Vietnam's ancient Cham culture. These are most numerous in central Vietnam. The Cham ruins at My Son (p392) are a major tourist draw.

SCULPTURE

Vietnamese sculpture has traditionally centred on religious themes and has functioned as an adjunct to architecture, especially that of pagodas, temples and tombs.

The Cham civilisation produced exquisite carved sandstone figures for its Hindu and Buddhist sanctuaries. The largest single collection of Cham sculpture is at the Museum of Cham Sculpture (p385) in Danang.

WATER PUPPETRY

Vietnam's ancient art of *roi nuoc* (water puppetry) originated in northern Vietnam at least 1000 years ago. Developed by rice farmers, the wooden puppets were manipulated by puppeteers using water-flooded rice paddies as their stage. Hanoi is the best place to see water-puppetry performances, which are accompanied by music played on traditional instruments. There are also performances in HCMC.

ENVIRONMENT

Environmental consciousness is low in Vietnam. Rapid industrialisation, deforestation and pollution are major problems facing the country.

Unsustainable logging and farming practices, as well as the USA's extensive spraying of defoliants during the American War, have contributed to deforestation. This has resulted not only in significant loss of biological diversity, but also in a harder existence for many Montagnard groups.

The country's rapid economic and population growth over the last decade – demonstrated by the dramatic increase in motorbike numbers and helter-skelter construction – has put additional pressure on the already-stressed environment.

The Land

Vietnam stretches over 1600km along the east coast of the Indochinese peninsula. The country's land area is 329,566 sq km, making it slightly larger than Italy and a bit smaller than Japan.

As the Vietnamese are quick to point out, it resembles a *don ganh,* or the ubiquitous bamboo pole with a basket of rice slung from each end. The baskets represent the main rice-growing regions of the Red River Delta in the north, and the Mekong Delta in the south.

Of several interesting geological features found in Vietnam, the most striking are the karst formations (limestone regions with caves and underground streams). The northern part of Vietnam has a spectacular assemblage of karst areas, particularly around Halong Bay (p369) and Tam Coc (p367).

THE NORTH–SOUTH DIVIDE

The north–south divide lingers on. The war may be history, but prejudice is alive and well. Ask a southerner what they think of northerners and they'll say they have a 'hard face', that they are too serious and don't know how to have fun. Ask a northerner what they think of southerners and they will say they are too superficial, obsessed by business and, well, bling.

When it comes to the older generation, the South has never forgiven the North for bulldozing their war cemeteries, imposing communism and blackballing whole families. The North has never forgiven the South for siding with the Americans against their own. Luckily for Vietnam, the new generation seems to have less interest in their harrowing history and more interest in making money. Today there is only one Vietnam and its mantra is business.

Wildlife

Because Vietnam has such a wide range of habitats, its fauna is enormously diverse; its forests are estimated to contain 12,000 plant species, only 7000 of which have been identified. Vietnam is home to more than 275 species of mammal, 800 species of bird, 180 species of reptile and 80 species of amphibian. In the 1990s, one species of muntjac (deer) and an ox similar to an oryx were discovered in Vietnam – the only newly identified large mammals in the world in the last 60 years.

Tragically, Vietnam's wildlife is in precipitous decline as forest habitats are destroyed and waterways become polluted. Illegal hunting has also exterminated the local populations of certain animals, in some cases eliminating entire species. Officially, the Vietnamese government recognises 54 mammal species and 60 bird species as endangered.

The trade in wildlife for export and domestic consumption goes largely unregulated by the government, though laws are in place to protect the animals. Poachers continue to profit from meeting the demand for exotic animals for traditional medicinal purposes and as pets.

Animal welfare is not a priority in the Vietnamese culture, evidenced by the appallingly inadequate conditions for caged wildlife throughout Vietnam.

National Parks

The number of national parks in the country has been rapidly expanding and there are now almost 30, about 3% of Vietnam's total territory. The most interesting and accessible are: Cat Ba (p371), Bai Tu Long (see the boxed text, p371), Ba Be (p374) and Cuc Phuong (p368) National Parks in the north; Bach Ma National Park (p382) in the centre; and Yok Don National Park (see the boxed text, p402) in the south.

With the help of NGOs, including the UN Development Programme and the World Wildlife Federation, the Vietnamese government is taking steps to expand national park boundaries, crack down on illegal poaching and educate and employ people living in national park buffer zones.

Flora and Fauna International produces the excellent *Nature Tourism Map of Vietnam*, which includes detailed coverage of all the national parks in Vietnam. All proceeds from sales of the map go towards supporting primate conservation in Vietnam.

HANOI

☎ 04 / pop 3.5 million

Hanoi is where the exotic chic of old Asia blends seamlessly with the dynamic face of new Asia. Where the medieval and modern coexist. It's a city with a quixotic blend of Parisian grace and Asian pace, an architectural museum piece evolving in harmony with its history, rather than bulldozing through it like many of the region's capitals.

A mass of motorbikes swarms through the tangled web of streets that is the Old Quarter, a cauldron of commerce for almost 1000 years and still the best place to check the pulse of this resurgent city. See the bold and beautiful dine at designer restaurants and cut the latest moves on the dance floor. Hanoi has it all, the ancient history, a colonial legacy and a modern outlook. There is no better place to untangle the paradox that is contemporary Vietnam.

Known by many names down the centuries, Thanh Long (City of the Soaring Dragon) is the most evocative, and let there be no doubt that this dragon is on the up once more.

ORIENTATION

Rambling along the banks of the Red River (Song Hong), Hanoi's centre extends out from the edges of Hoan Kiem Lake. Just to the north of this lake is the Old Quarter, characterised by narrow streets whose names change every block or two. Most visitors prefer to base themselves in this part of town.

Along the western periphery of the Old Quarter, the Hanoi Citadel was originally constructed by Emperor Gia Long. It's now a military base. Further west is Ho Chi Minh's mausoleum, in the neighbourhood where most foreign embassies are found, many housed in classical architectural masterpieces from the French-colonial era. Hanoi's largest lake, Ho Tay (West Lake), lies north of the mausoleum.

Street designations in Hanoi are shortened to P for *pho* (abbreviated on maps only) or Đ for *duong* (both meaning street).

There are decent city maps for sale at bookshops in Hanoi for around US$1. There is also an excellent bus map (*Xe Buyt Ha Noi;*

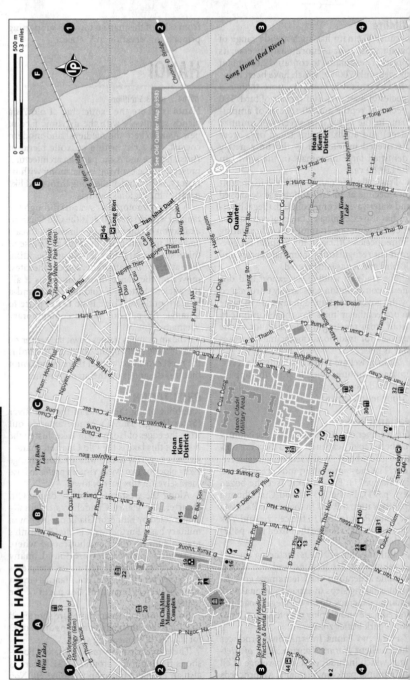

CENTRAL HANOI

0   500 m
0   0.3 miles

Song Hong (Red River)

Ho Tay (West Lake)

Truc Bach Lake

Hoan Kiem Lake

Old Quarter

See Old Quarter Map (p358)

Hoan Kiem District

Hanoi Citadel (Military Area)

Ho Chi Minh Mausoleum Complex

Long Bien Bridge

Chuong D Bridge

Long Bien

To Thang Loi Hotel (1km); Hanoi Water Park (4km)

To Vietnam Museum of Ethnology (6km)

To Hanoi Family Medical Practice & Dental Clinic (1km)

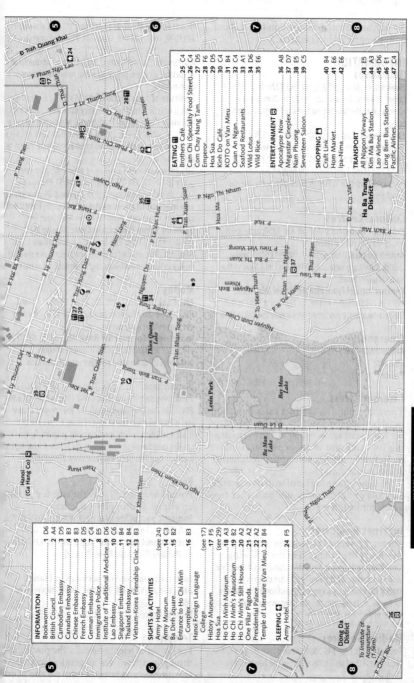

INFORMATION
Bookworm	1 D6
British Council	2 A4
Cambodian Embassy	3 D5
Canadian Embassy	4 B3
Chinese Embassy	5 B3
French Embassy	6 D5
German Embassy	7 C4
Immigration Police	8 E5
Institute of Traditional Medicine	9 D6
Lao Embassy	10 C6
Singapore Embassy	11 B4
Thailand Embassy	12 B4
Vietnam-Korea Friendship Clinic	13 B3

SIGHTS & ACTIVITIES
Army Hotel	(see 24)
Army Museum	14 C3
Ba Dinh Square	15 B2
Entrance to Ho Chi Minh Complex	16 B3
Hanoi Foreign Language College	(see 17)
History Museum	17 F5
Hoa Sua	(see 29)
Ho Chi Minh Museum	18 A3
Ho Chi Minh's Mausoleum	19 B2
Ho Chi Minh's Stilt House	20 A2
One Pillar Pagoda	21 A2
Presidential Palace	22 A2
Temple of Literature (Van Mieu)	23 B4

SLEEPING 🏨
Army Hotel	24 F5

EATING 🍴
Brothers Café	25 C4
Cam Chi (Speciality Food Street)	26 C4
Com Chay Nang Tam	27 D5
Emperor	28 F6
Hoa Sua	29 D5
Kinh Do Café	30 C4
KOTO on Van Mieu	31 B4
Quan An Ngan	32 C4
Seafood Restaurants	33 A1
Wild Lotus	34 D6
Wild Rice	35 E6

ENTERTAINMENT 🎭
Apocalypse Now	36 A8
Megastar Cineplex	37 D7
Nam Phuong	38 E5
Seventeen Saloon	39 C5

SHOPPING 🛍
Craft Link	40 B4
Hom Market	41 E6
Ipa-Nima	42 E6

TRANSPORT
All Nippon Airways	43 E5
Kim Ma Bus Station	44 A3
Lao Airlines	45 D6
Long Bien Bus Station	46 E1
Pacific Airlines	47 C4

VIETNAM

5000d), an essential companion to get about on the improved bus network.

INFORMATION
Bookshops
Bookworm (Map pp352-3; ☎ 943 7226; bookworm@fpt.vn; 15A Pho Ngo Van So; ☺ 10am-7pm Tue-Sun) Hanoi's best selection of new and used English-language books.

Love Planet (Map p358; ☎ 828 4864; 25 Pho Hang Bac) Trade in used books for other secondhand reads.

Thang Long Bookshop (Map p358; ☎ 825 7043; 53-55 Pho Trang Tien) One of the biggest bookshops in town with English and French titles, plus some international press.

Cultural Centres
American Club (Map p358; ☎ 824 1850; amclub@fpt.vn; 19-21 Pho Hai Ba Trung)

British Council (Map pp352-3; ☎ 843 6780; www.britishcouncil.org/vietnam; 40 Pho Cat Linh) Next to the Hanoi Horison Hotel.

Centre Culturel Française de Hanoi (Map p358; ☎ 936 2164; alli@hn.vnn.vn; 24 Pho Trang Tien) In the L'Espace building, a modernist venue near the Opera House.

Emergency
Ambulance (☎ 115)
Fire (☎ 114)
Police (☎ 113)

Internet Access
There are countless internet cafés in Hanoi, notably along Pho Hang Bac in the Old Quarter. Rates start as low as 3000d, but overcharging isn't unheard of in some places. Most budget and midrange hotels offer free internet access as standard.

Wi-fi has come to Hanoi with a vengeance and lots of hotels, cafés and bars offer free access for laptop users.

Internet Resources
There are several good websites to help you get the most out of Hanoi. Try the following:

New Hanoian (www.newhanoian.com) This is the place to get the rub on what Hanoi expats get up to in the city.

Sticky Rice (http://stickyrice.typepad.com) The website for foodies in Hanoi, this has the lowdown on dozens of places to dine and drink in the city.

Medical Services
Dental Clinic (☎ 846 2864; thedental@netnam.vn) The tooth hurts? Deal with it here, part of the Hanoi Family Medical Practice.

Hanoi Family Medical Practice (☎ 24hr emergency 843 0748, 0903-401 919, 0913-234 911; www.vietnammedicalpractice.com; Van Phuc Diplomatic Compound, 298 Pho Kim Ma, Ba Dinh District) Has a team of international physicians; service is pricey, so make sure your insurance is up-to-date.

Institute of Acupuncture (☎ 853 3881; 49 Pho Thai Thinh) Holistic medicine? Well, very small holes anyway.

National Hospital of Traditional Medicine (Map pp352-3; ☎ 826 3616; 29 Pho Nguyen Binh Khiem) Check out some Vietnamese solutions to what might be Vietnamese problems.

SOS International Clinic (Map p358; ☎ 24hr emergency 934 0555, 934 0555; Central Bldg, 31 Pho Hai Ba Trung; initial consultations US$55-65) Has a 24-hour clinic with international physicians speaking English, French and Japanese; house calls available for an additional fee.

Vietnam-Korea Friendship Clinic (Map pp352-3; ☎ 843 7231; 12 Chu Van An; initial consultations US$5) Nonprofit clinic reputed to be the least-expensive medical facility in Hanoi; maintains a high international standard.

Money
ANZ Bank (Map p358; ☎ 825 8190; 14 Pho Le Thai To) Has cash-advance facilities and a 24-hour ATM, churning out four-million dong per hit.

Industrial & Commercial Bank (Map p358; ☎ 825 4276; 37 Pho Hang Bo) Cashes travellers cheques, exchanges US dollars and also gives credit-card cash advances.

Vietcombank Pho Hang Bai (Map p358; ☎ 826 8031; 2 Pho Hang Bai); Pho Tran Quang Khai (Map p358; ☎ 826 8045; 198 Pho Tran Quang Khai) The towering headquarters is located a few blocks east of Hoan Kiem Lake and it has an ATM and offers most currency services. Several smaller branches with ATMs are in the centre, including the handy one on Pho Hang Bai, near Hoan Kiem Lake.

Post
Postal kiosks are all over the city, for picking up stamps or dropping off letters.

Domestic post office (Map p358; ☎ 825 7036; 75 Pho Dinh Tien Hoang; ☺ 7am-8.30pm)

International post office (Map p358; ☎ 825 2030; cnr Pho Dinh Tien Hoang & Pho Dinh Le)

International courier services in Hanoi:

DHL (Map pp352-3; ☎ 733 2086; 49 Pho Nguyen Thai Hoc)

Federal Express (☎ 824 9054; 63 Pho Yen Phu)

Telephone
For domestic telephone calls, the post offices throughout town are as good as anywhere. Guesthouses and internet cafés are also a con-

venient option for local calls within Hanoi. For international telephone calls, the cheapest option is usually guesthouses or internet cafés as they offer cheaper internet services.

Tourist Information

Even though this is the capital, forget anything really useful like a helpful tourism office that dishes out free information. The best source of tourism information in Hanoi is asking around at different guesthouses, travel agencies and bars, and talking to your fellow travellers.

Travel Agencies

Hanoi has heaps of budget travel agencies. It is not advisable to book trips or tickets through guesthouses and hotels. Dealing directly with tour operators gives you a much better idea of what you'll get for your money, and of how many other people you'll be travelling with. Seek out tour operators that stick to small groups, and use their own vehicles and guides.

New travel agencies open all the time and existing places have a tendency to change, so shop around. Successful tour operators often have their names cloned by others looking to trade on their reputations, so check addresses and websites carefully. Consider the following places in the Old Quarter:

ET Pumpkin (Map p358; ☎ 926 0739; www.et-pumpkin.com; 89 Pho Ma May) Tours throughout the north, plus it operates its own private carriage on the night train to Sapa.

Ethnic Travel (Map p358; ☎ 926 1951; www.ethnictravel.com.vn; 35 Pho Hang Giay) A newer company offering an innovative selection of adventures that ensures you meet the real Vietnamese.

Handspan Adventure Travel (Map p358; ☎ 926 2581; www.handspan.com; 80 Pho Ma May) A deservedly popular company offering Halong Bay, Bai Tu Long Bay and jeep tours in the far north. The walk-in office is in the Tamarind Café.

Ocean Tours (Map p358; ☎ 926 1294; www.oceantoursvietnam.com; 7 Pho Dinh Liet) This operator has been earning a good name for itself by specialising in Halong Bay.

ODC Travel (Map p358; ☎ 824 3024; www.odctravel.com; Camellia Hotel, 13 Pho Luong Ngoc Quyen) Formerly Old Darling Café, this is one of the most established names in the business for budget tours.

For a list of nationwide operators, see p437. For more on specialist companies offering motorbike tours of the north, see the boxed text, p369.

DANGERS & ANNOYANCES

The biggest scams in town are inextricably intertwined. The taxi and minibus mafia at the airport shuttle unwitting tourists to the wrong hotel. Invariably, the hotel has appropriated the name of another popular property and will then attempt to appropriate as much of your money as possible. Keep your antennae up. We have heard several substantiated reports of verbal aggression and physical violence towards tourists when deciding against a hotel room or tour. Stay calm and back away slowly or things could quickly flare up.

Western women have reported being hassled by young men around town who follow them home. Women walking alone at night are generally safe in the Old Quarter but should always be aware of their surroundings. Catching a *xe om* (motorbike taxi) is a good idea if it's late and you have a long walk home.

Gay men should beware of a scam going on around Hoan Kiem Lake. Scenario: friendly stranger approaches foreigner, offering to take him out. They end up at a karaoke bar, where they're shown into a private room for a few drinks and songs. When the bill is brought in, it's often upwards of US$100. The situation deteriorates from there, ending in extortion. Exercise caution and follow your instincts.

SIGHTS
Vietnam Museum of Ethnology

The wonderful **Vietnam Museum of Ethnology** (☎ 756 2193; Đ Nguyen Van Huyen; admission 20,000d; ⏰ 8.30am-5.30pm Tue-Sun) should not be missed. Designed with assistance from Musée de l'Homme in Paris, it features a fascinating collection of art and everyday objects gathered from Vietnam and its diverse tribal people. From the making of conical hats to the ritual of a Tay shamanic ceremony, the museum explores Vietnam's cultural diversity. Displays are labelled in Vietnamese, French and English.

The museum is in the Cau Giay District, about 7km from the city centre. The trip takes 30 minutes by bicycle. Other options include *xe om* (20,000d one way) or a metered taxi (40,000d one way). The cheapest way to get here is to take bus 14 (3500d) from Hoan Kiem Lake and get off at the junction

VIETNAM

between Đ Hoang Quoc Viet and Đ Nguyen Van Huyen.

Temple of Literature

Hanoi's peaceful **Van Mieu** (Temple of Literature; Map pp352-3; Pho Quoc Tu Giam; admission 5000d; 8am-5pm) was dedicated to Confucius in 1070 by Emperor Ly Thanh Tong, and later established as a university for the education of mandarins. A well-preserved jewel of traditional Vietnamese architecture in 11th-century style with roofed gateways and low-eaved buildings, this temple is an absolute must.

Five courtyards are enclosed within the grounds. The front gate is inscribed with a request that visitors dismount from their horses before entering. Make sure you do. There's a peaceful reflecting pool in the front courtyard, and the Khue Van Pavilion at the back of the second courtyard.

In 1484, Emperor Le Thang Tong ordered the establishment of stelae honouring the men who had received doctorates in triennial examinations dating back to 1442. Each of the 82 stelae that stands here is set on a stone tortoise.

The Temple of Literature is 2km west of Hoan Kiem Lake.

Ho Chi Minh Mausoleum Complex

This is the holiest of the holies for many Vietnamese. In the tradition of Lenin, Stalin and Mao, the final resting place of Ho Chi Minh is a glass sarcophagus set deep within a monumental edifice. As interesting as the man himself are the crowds coming to pay their respects.

Built contrary to his last will to be cremated, the **Ho Chi Minh Mausoleum Complex** (Map pp352-3; Pho Ngoc Ha & Pho Doi Can; admission free; 8-11am Sat-Thu) was constructed between 1973 and 1975, using native materials gathered from all over Vietnam. Ho Chi Minh's embalmed corpse gets a three-month holiday to Russia for yearly maintenance, so the mausoleum is closed from September through early December. Some sceptics have suggested Madame Tussaud's has the contract these days.

All visitors must register and leave their bags, cameras and mobile phones at a reception hall. You'll be refused admission to the mausoleum if you're wearing shorts, tank tops or other 'indecent' clothing. Hats must be taken off inside the mausoleum building.

Photography is absolutely prohibited inside the building.

After exiting the mausoleum, check out the following nearby sights.

Ho Chi Minh Museum (Bao Tang Ho Chi Minh; Map pp352-3; admission 5000d; 8-11am & 1.30-4.30pm Sat-Thu) Displays each have a message, such as 'peace', 'happiness' or 'freedom'. Find an English-speaking guide, as some of the symbolism is hard to interpret on your own

Ho Chi Minh's Stilt House (Nha San Bac Ho; Map pp352-3; admission 5000d; 8-11am & 2-4pm) Supposedly Ho's official residence, on and off, between 1958 and 1969, its simplicity reinforces his reputation as a man of the people.

One Pillar Pagoda (Chua Mot Cot; Map pp352-3) Built by Emperor Ly Thai Tong (r 1028–54) and designed to represent a lotus blossom, a symbol of purity, rising out of a sea of sorrow.

Presidential Palace (Map pp352-3; admission 5000d; 8-11am & 2-4pm Sat-Thu) In grand contrast to Ho's stilt house, this grand building was constructed in 1906 as the palace of the governor general of Indochina.

Other Museums

The terrific **Women's Museum** (Bao Tang Phu Nu; Map p358; 36 Pho Ly Thuong Kiet; admission 20,000d; 8am-4pm) includes the predictable tribute to women soldiers, balanced by some wonderful exhibits from the international women's movement protesting the American War. The 4th floor displays costumes worn by ethnic-minority groups in Vietnam. Exhibits have Vietnamese, French and English explanations.

Hoa Lo Prison Museum (Map p358; 824 6358; Pho Hoa Lo; admission 5000d; 8-11.30am & 1.30-4.30pm Tue-Sun) is all that remains of the former Hoa Lo Prison, ironically nicknamed the 'Hanoi Hilton' by US POWs during the American War. The bulk of the exhibits focus on the Vietnamese struggle for independence from France. Tools of torture on display include an ominous French guillotine used to behead Vietnamese revolutionaries; some exhibits have explanations in English and French.

One block east of the Opera House, the **History Museum** (Bao Tang Lich Su; Map pp352-3; 1 Pho Pham Ngu Lao; admission 15,000d; 8-11.30am & 1.30-4.30pm Fri-Wed) is one of Hanoi's most stunning structures. Ernest Hebrard was among the first in Vietnam to incorporate design elements from Chinese and French styles in his architecture; this building was completed in 1932. Collections here cover the highs more than the lows of Vietnamese history.

The **Army Museum** (Bao Tang Quan Doi; Map pp352-3; Pho Dien Bien Phu; admission 20,000d; 8-11.30am &

1.30-4.30pm Tue-Sun) displays Soviet and Chinese equipment alongside French- and US-made weapons captured during years of warfare.

Old Quarter

This is the Asia we dreamed of from afar. Steeped in history, pulsating with life, bubbling with commerce, buzzing with motorbikes and rich in exotic scents, the Old Quarter is Hanoi's historic heart. Hawkers pound the streets, sizzling and smoking baskets hiding a cheap meal for the locals. *Pho* (noodle soup) stalls and *bia hoi* (draught beer) dens hug every corner, resonant with the sound of gossip and laughter. Modern yet medieval, there is no better way to spend some time in Hanoi than walking the streets, simply soaking up the sights, sounds and smells.

Hoan Kiem Lake is the liquid heart of the Old Quarter, a good orienting landmark. Legend has it that in the mid-15th century, heaven gave Emperor Ly Thai To (Le Loi) a magical sword that he used to drive the Chinese out of Vietnam. One day after the war, while out boating, he came upon a giant golden tortoise; the creature grabbed the sword and disappeared into the depths of the lake. Since that time, the lake has been known as Ho Hoan Kiem (Lake of the Restored Sword) because the tortoise returned the sword to its divine owners.

Ngoc Son Temple (Jade Mountain Temple; Map p358; admission 2000d; 8am-7pm), which was founded in the 18th century, is on an island in the northern part of Hoan Kiem Lake. It's a meditative spot to relax, but also worth checking out for the embalmed remains of a gigantic tortoise of the species said to still inhabit the lake.

Memorial House (Map p358; 87 Pho Ma May; admission 5000d; 9-11.30am & 2-5pm) is well worth a visit. Thoughtfully restored, this traditional Chinese-style dwelling gives you an insight into how local merchants used to live in the Old Quarter.

Bach Ma Temple (Map p358; cnr Pho Hang Buom & Pho Hang Giay; 8-11.30am & 2.30-5.30pm) is the oldest temple in Hanoi and resides in a shred of Chinatown in the Old Quarter.

Stepping inside **St Joseph Cathedral** (Map p358; Pho Nha Tho; 5-7am & 5-7pm) is like being transported to medieval Europe. The cathedral (inaugurated in 1886) is noteworthy for its square towers, elaborate altar and stained-glass windows. The main gate is open when mass is held.

ACTIVITIES
Massage & Spa

The government has severely restricted the number of places licensed to give massages because of the concern that naughty 'extra services' might be offered (as indeed they are at many places). At present, you can get a good legitimate massage at the **Hoa Binh Palace Hotel** (Map p358; per hr US$8) and the **Sofitel Metropole Hotel** (Map p358; US$32).

QT Salon (Map p358; 928 6116; 28 Pho Le Thai To; 10am-8pm) For a spa splurge on facials or body treatments, head to this place overlooking Hoan Kiem Lake.

SF Salon & Spa (Map p358; 926 2032; 16 Pho Hang Buom; 8.30am-11pm) A newer spa offering Swedish and Thai massage (US$10), plus the full range of spa treatments, including wraps, scrubs and polishes.

Swimming

Feel like a dip? There are several places for swimming in Hanoi and most upmarket hotels let nonguests swim or use the gym for a fee.

Army Hotel (Khach San Quan Doi; Map pp352-3; 825 2896; 33C Pho Pham Ngu Lao; day use US$3.50) Big enough to do laps, the pool is open all year.

Hanoi Water Park (753 2757; admission 30,000-50,000d) Open from 15 April to November, 5km from the city centre; features a variety of pools and slides.

Thang Loi Hotel (Cuban Hotel; 829 4211; thangloihtl@hn.vnn.vn; Đ Yen Phu; 30,000d) Near Ho Tay (West Lake), the pool is open from May to October.

COURSES
Language

Hanoi Foreign Language College (Map pp352-3; 826 2468; 1 Pho Pham Ngu Lao), housed in the History Museum compound, is a branch of Hanoi National University where foreigners can study Vietnamese for about US$7 per lesson.

Cooking

Hoa Sua (Map pp352-3; 824 0448; www .hoasuaschool.com; 28A Pho Ha Hoi) Offers classes for a cause to raise funds for its training programme for disadvantaged youth. Costs vary depending on the dishes cooked.

Highway 4 (Map p358; 926 0639; 5 Pho Hang Tre) This popular restaurant-bar also has cooking classes. Prices range from US$19 to US$32 depending on numbers.

SLEEPING

Most visitors makes for the Old Quarter. There is an excellent range of accommodation within 1km of Hoan Kiem Lake.

VIETNAM

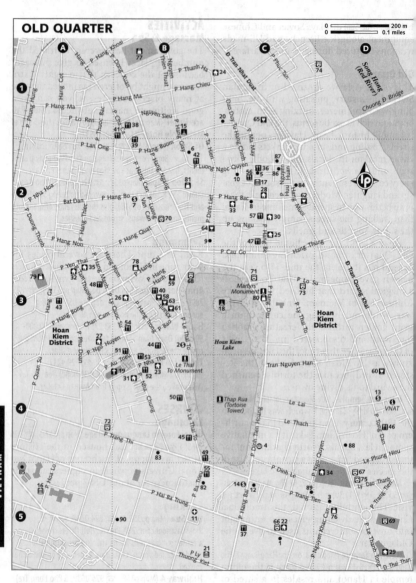

OLD QUARTER

VIETNAM

Budget

our pick **City Gate Hotel** (Map p358; ☎ 828 0817; www
.citygatehotel.com.vn; 10 Pho Thanh Ha; r US$8-18; 🕱 🖳)
Hidden away down a small lane near the old
East Gate, this smart minihotel offers a warm
welcome. Rooms are superclean, bathrooms
include a bath, there's free internet downstairs
and even a lift.

Hanoi Backpackers Hostel (Map p358; ☎ 828 5372;
www.hanoibackpackershostel.com; 48 Pho Ngo Huyen; dm
US$6, r US$20; 🕱 🖳) This Aussie-style backpackers pad offers smart and secure dorms and a
couple of dedicated rooms. There's always
plenty of action on the rooftop bar.

Hotel Thien Trang (Map p358; ☎ 826 9823; thient
ranghotel24@hotmail.com; 24 Pho Nha Chung; r US$10-20;

INFORMATION

American Club........1 C5
ANZ Bank........2 B3
Centre Culturel Française de Hanoi........3 D5
Domestic Post Office........4 C4
ET Pumpkin........5 C2
Ethnic Travel........6 B2
Handspan Adventure Travel....(see 56)
Industrial & Commercial Bank........7 B2
International Post Office........(see 4)
Love Planet........8 C2
Ocean Tours........9 B2
ODC Travel........10 C2
SOS International Clinic........11 B5
Thang Long Bookshop........12 C5
UK Embassy........(see 11)
Vietcombank........13 D4
Vietcombank........14 C5

SIGHTS & ACTIVITIES

Bach Ma Temple........15 B1
Highway 4........(see 62)
Hoa Lo Prison Museum ('Hanoi Hilton')........16 A5
Memorial House........17 C2
Ngoc Son Temple........18 C3
QT Salon........(see 50)
SF Salon & Spa........19 C1
St Joseph Cathedral........20 B4
Women's Museum........21 B5

SLEEPING

Artist Hotel........22 C5
Church Hotel........23 B4
City Gate Hotel........24 C1
Classic Street Hotel........25 C2
Golden Lotus Hotel........26 B3
Hanoi Backpackers Hostel........27 A3
Hanoi Elegance Hotel........28 C2
Hilton Hanoi Opera........29 D5
Hoa Binh Palace Hotel........30 C2
Hotel Thien Trang........31 B4
Manh Dung Guesthouse........32 A3
Queen Hotel........33 C2
Sofitel Metropole Hotel........34 D5
Thu Giang Guesthouse........35 A3

EATING

69 Bar-Restaurant........36 C2
Al Fresco's........37 C5
Baan Thai Restaurant........38 B1
Baguette & Chocolat........39 B2
Café des Arts........40 B3
Cha Ca La Vong........41 B1
Culi Café........42 B2
Cyclo Bar & Restaurant........43 A3
Dakshin........44 B3
Fanny........45 B4
Fivimart........46 D4
Green Tangerine........47 C2
Hanoi Garden........48 A3
Hapro Coffee Kiosk........49 B4
Intimex........50 B4
La Place........51 B3
La Salsa........52 B4
Moca Café........53 B4
Pepperoni's Pizza & Café........54 B3
Pho24........(see 14)
Restaurant Bobby Chinn........55 B5
Tamarind Café........56 C2
Tandoor........57 C2
Thuy Ta Café........(see 68)

DRINKING

Amazon Bar........58 B3
Funky Monkey........59 B3
Gambrinus........60 D4
GC Pub........61 B3
Highway 4........62 C2
Le Pub........(see 30)
Polite Pub........63 B3
Quan Bia Minh........64 B2
Toilet Pub........65 C1

ENTERTAINMENT

Centre Culturel Française de Hanoi........(see 3)
Cinematheque........66 C5
Club Opera........67 D5
Dinh Lang Restaurant........68 B3
Hanoi Opera House........69 D5
Jazz Club By Quyen Van Minh..70 B2
Municipal Water Puppet Theatre........71 C3
New Century........72 A4
R&R Tavern........73 C3
Solace........74 D1
Terrace Bar........75 D5

SHOPPING

Chi Vang........76 D5
Dong Xuan Market........77 B1
Hadong Silk........78 B3
Hang Da Market........79 A3
Shoe Market........80 C3
Vietnamese House........81 B2

TRANSPORT

Air France........82 B5
Airport Minibus........83 B4
Buffalo Tours........84 C2
Cathay Pacific........85 A5
Cuong's Motorbike Adventure..86 C2
Free Wheelin' Tours........87 C2
Malaysia Airlines........88 D4
Singapore Airlines........89 C5
Thai Airways International........90 B5
Vietnam Airlines........(see 83)

) Close enough to the trendy Nha Tho to live the dream, but cheap enough not to break the budget, the spacious rooms are great value given the location.

our pick Artist Hotel (Map p358; ☎ 825 3044; vietcultour@hn.vnn.vn; 22A Pho Hai Ba Trung; s/d US$18/21;) The rooms here might be more appropriate accommodation for the struggling artiste, but they are set around a lovely leafy courtyard. Rooms include satellite TV, but who needs it when there is the Cinematheque (p363) downstairs?

A couple more old favourites include the following:

Thu Giang Guesthouse (Map p358; ☎ 828 5734; www.tgguesthouse.com; 5A Pho Tam Thuong; r US$5-10;) The taste of old Hanoi, a small, friendly, family-run place with cheap yet cheerful rooms.

Manh Dung Guesthouse (Map p358; ☎ 826 7201; tranmanhdungvn@yahoo.com; 2 Pho Tam Thuong; r US$5-10;) Opposite the Thu Giang, the family here really look after their guests.

Midrange

Hanoi Elegance Hotel (Map p358; ☎ 825 3740; www.hanoielegancehotel.com; 8 Pho Hang Bac; r US$18-30;) The friendly staff here make it feel like a home away from home. Rooms are large and each includes a computer for personal internet access.

Classic Street Hotel (Map p358; ☎ 825 2421; www.classicstreet-phocohotel.com; 41 Pho Hang Be; r US$25-30;) Hang Be is one of the liveliest streets in the Old Quarter and this hotel is a stylish base from which to explore it. All rooms have air-con and satellite TV.

Army Hotel (Khach San Quan Doi; Map pp352-3; ☎ 825 2896; armyhotel@fpt.vn; 33C Pho Pham Ngu Lao; r US$30-40;) Owned by the army, operated by the army, but it's a world away from boot camp. The uninspiring décor may be military bland, but it's the cheapest place in town with a pool.

our pick Queen Hotel (Map p358; ☎ 826 0860; www.azqueentravel.com; 65 Pho Hang Bac; r US$35-65;) The Zen lobby sets the standard for one of

Hanoi's most atmospheric properties. The rooms include wooden furnishings, silk lamps and DVD players. Book ahead.

our pick Golden Lotus Hotel (Map p358; ☎ 928 8583; www.goldenlotushotel.com.vn; 32 Pho Hang Trong; r incl breakfast US$40-50; 🔀 🖵) A rich blend of Eastern flavours and Western chic, rooms at the Golden Lotus have wooden floors, silk trim, art aplenty and broadband internet connections.

Church Hotel (Map p358; ☎ 928 8118; churchhotel@vnn .vn; 9 Pho Nha Tho; r US$40-70; 🔀 🖵) Looking for a hotel with a holistic touch? Look no further, the Church has elegant rooms with decorative flair, plus the functional extras such as in-room internet.

Hoa Binh Palace Hotel (Map p358; ☎ 926 3646; www .hoabinhpalacehotel.com.vn; 27 Pho Hang Be; s/d US$50/60; 🔀 🖵) An unlikely intruder in the heart of backpackersville, this smart new property brings new-world comforts to old-world Hanoi.

Top End

Hilton Hanoi Opera (Map p358; ☎ 933 0500; www.hanoi .hilton.com; 1 Le Thanh Tong; r from US$110; 🔀 🖵 📾) Rubbing shoulders with the grand old dame that is Hanoi Opera House, this striking property is an indulgent base to discover the city.

our pick Sofitel Metropole Hotel (Map p358; ☎ 826 6919; sofitelhanoi@hn.vnn.vn; 15 Pho Ngo Quyen; r from US$169; 🔀 🖵 📾) Whispered in the same breath as Raffles in Singapore and the Oriental in Bangkok, this is one of Asia's great luxury hotels. This place has a French motif that just won't quit – close the curtains and you'll think you're in Paris.

EATING

Hanoi is a gourmand's wonderland, full of restaurants serving regional specialities such as *cha ca* (fish braised in broth and served with noodles and fresh dill and peanuts) as well as a broad palette of international cuisine.

The real culinary treasures in Hanoi are its speciality food streets (Map pp352–3). Cam Chi, 500m northeast of Hanoi train station, is an alley crammed full of lively street stalls serving delicious budget-priced food. Đ Thuy Khue, on the south bank of West Lake, features a strip of 30-odd outdoor seafood restaurants with pleasant lakeside seating. Pho To Hien Thanh also specialises in small seafood restaurants, south of the city centre,

east of Bay Mau Lake. Pho Nghi Tam, 10km north of central Hanoi, has 1km of dog-meat restaurants. Dog lover has a whole different meaning in Hanoi!

For some of the tastiest, and certainly cheapest Vietnamese food, stroll up to some of the street stalls around town. The food is as fresh as it comes and the kitchen is right there in front of you. Try *bun cha gio* (rice vermicelli with spring rolls) on a street corner or venture into a tiny shopfront selling *chao vit* (rice porridge with duck). Check out how many locals are chowing down; the more, the merrier, as the food must be good. Overcharging is the norm rather than the exception at many places, so check the price before you order a spread.

Vietnamese

Pho 24 (Map p358; 1 Pho Hang Khay; meals 25,000d) Fast *pho*, Vietnamese-style, this place offers heavenly noodle soups. *Pho* is cheaper on the street, but rarely better.

our pick 69 Bar-Restaurant (Map p358; ☎ 926 0452; 69 Pho Ma May; meals 20,000-60,000d) Set in a beautifully restored old Vietnamese house, the predominantly Vietnamese menu includes succulent tuna steaks and a large vegetarian selection.

our pick Quan An Ngan (Map pp352-3; ☎ 942 8162; 15 Pho Phan Boi Chau; dishes 30,000-60,000d) Fancy that street food experience, but afraid to take the plunge? Build your courage with a meal here, the place that brings street and market food to the middle-class masses.

Hanoi Garden (Map p358; ☎ 824 3402; 36 Pho Hang Manh; mains from 40,000d) This restaurant is very popular with Vietnamese diners, always a positive sign, thanks to its southern Vietnamese and spicy Chinese dishes.

Cha Ca La Vong (Map p358; ☎ 825 3929; 14 Pho Cha Ca; cha ca 70,000d) The *cha ca* capital of the Old Quarter, this place has been family-run for five generations. The succulent fish is all that's on the menu, so it's great for indecisive types.

Vietnamese Gourmet

Wild Rice (Map pp352-3; ☎ 943 8896; 6 Pho Ngo Thi Nham; mains 40,000-120,000d) Deceptively simple from outside, the elegant interior is a fine backdrop for the contemporary Vietnamese cuisine. Start with a spring roll selection, as there is a unique take on this most traditional of foods.

Emperor (Map pp352-3; ☎ 826 8801; 18B Pho Le Thanh Tong; mains 50,000-100,000d) Long considered one of

---

DINING FOR A CAUSE

Combine food for the body with food for the soul at restaurants and cafés that run vocational training programmes for street kids. Good cause, good food, good idea.

■ **KOTO on Van Mieu** (Map pp352-3; ☎ 747 0338; www.streetvoices.com.au; 59 Pho Van Mieu; mains 30,000-50,000d; ♡ breakfast, lunch & dinner, except Mon dinner; 💻) Recently relocated into a larger property, KOTO offers local specialities, home comforts, delicious sandwiches and cakes, real coffees, fruit shakes, plus free wi-fi. KOTO is a not-for-profit grassroots project providing opportunities for former street kids. KOTO stands for 'Know One, Teach One'.

■ **Hoa Sua** (Map pp352-3; ☎ 824 0448; www.hoasuaschool.com; 28A Pho Ha Hoi; Vietnamese/French set lunch 35,000/75,000d; ♡ 11am-10pm) A shady retreat by day, a dignified diner by night, this restaurant offers the perfect blend of East and West. Hoa Sua trains a steady stream of disadvantaged kids for culinary careers. It also offers cooking classes (p357).

■ **Baguette & Chocolat** (Map p358; ☎ 923 1500; 11 Pho Cha Ca; cakes around 10,000d; ♡ 7am-10pm) Another member of the extended Hoa Sua family, this is a bewitching bakery with divine (or devilish) cakes and pastries, depending on your calorie count.

---

the best Vietnamese restaurants in town, try and get a table overlooking the lively courtyard. Experience traditional music (7.30pm to 9.30pm) on Wednesday and Saturday.

ourpick Wild Lotus (Map pp352-3; ☎ 943 9342; 55A Pho Nguyen Du; mains 50,000-150,000d) The ultimate designer restaurant, this is an art gallery as much as an eatery. The seafood is superb, including scallops and king crab.

Brothers Café (Map pp352-3; ☎ 733 3866; 26 Pho Nguyen Thai Hoc; lunch/dinner buffet US$6.50/12) Located in the courtyard of a beautifully restored 250-year-old Buddhist temple, it's buffet only and the lunch is a snip.

International

Café des Arts (Map p358; ☎ 828 7207; 11B Pho Bao Khanh; ♡ lunch & dinner) Head to this casual café for couscous or cassoulet, and other French classics. Modelled on a Parisian brasserie, it lives up to its name with regular art exhibitions.

Pepperoni's Pizza & Café (Map p358; ☎ 928 5246; 29 Pho Ly Quoc Su; mains from 40,000d; ♡ from lunch) A laudable lunch stop, thanks to the US$2 all-you-can-eat weekday lunchtime pasta and salad bar.

La Salsa (Map p358; ☎ 828 9052; 25 Pho Nha Tho; ♡ 10.30am-midnight) Specialising in paella, slabs of steak and tapas, this bar-restaurant has a prime position on the hip strip opposite St Joseph Cathedral.

ourpick Restaurant Bobby Chinn (Map p358; ☎ 934 8577; www.bobbychinn.com; 1 Pho Ba Trieu; mains US$10-20; ♡ 10am-late) Owner-chef Bobby Chinn is part Chinese and part Egyptian, and the fusion is evident in the original menu. For

an apéritif or a coffee, move through the silk drapes to the chill-out cushions at the back where smokers can stoke up a *sheesha* (water pipe).

ourpick Green Tangerine (Map p358; ☎ 825 1286; 48 Pho Hang Be; mains around US$15) A beautifully restored 1928 house is the backdrop for this renowned French restaurant. Salmon steak in tamarind sauce and an impressive wine list.

Also try the following:

Cyclo Bar & Restaurant (Map p358; ☎ 828 6844; 38 Pho Duong Thanh; mains around 60,000d; ♡ lunch & dinner) Hop into one of its converted cyclos and have yourself some casual Vietnamese or French fare.

Al Fresco's (Map p358; ☎ 826 7782; 23L Pho Hai Ba Trung; mains 80,000d; ♡ lunch & dinner) Fantastic ribs, pizzas and salads, all in family-sized portions.

Vegetarian

Com Chay Nang Tam (Map p358; ☎ 826 6140; 79A Pho Tran Hung Dao; meals from 30,000d) It is a mystery how this place can make simple vegetables and pulses look and taste like meat. Yes, it really is down that unlikely looking alley behind those buildings.

ourpick Tamarind Café (Map p358; ☎ 926 0580; 80 Pho Ma May; meals US$2-4; ♡ 6am-midnight) Vegetarian heaven, there are some wonderful creations here blending together Asian and European elements. Impressive shakes and smoothies, plus free wi-fi.

Dakshin (Map p358; ☎ 928 6872; 94 Pho Hang Trong; meals 25,000-60,000d) Under the same ownership as Tandoor (p362), Dakshin is all-vegetarian and enjoys legendary status among the curry crew in Hanoi.

VIETNAM

Other Asian Cuisine

Baan Thai Restaurant (Map p358; ☎ 828 1120; 3B Pho Cha Ca; mains 30,000-100,000đ) An established Thai restaurant with a loyal following among the Thai community. There is a handy photo-illustrated menu of favourites at the door.

Tandoor (Map p358; ☎ 824 5359; 24 Pho Hang Be; mains 40,000-80,000đ) Right in the thick of things in the Old Quarter, this is a place to spice up your life. Not surprisingly, the tandoor is tops here, plus there are good-value thalis.

Cafés

Check out the slightly manic, fun Vietnamese coffee shops along Pho Hang Hanh, and watch the motorbikes come and go from the balconies upstairs.

Kinh Do Café (Map pp352-3; ☎ 825 0216; 252 Pho Hang Bong; pastries 7000đ; ⏲ breakfast & lunch) Where Catherine Deneuve took her morning cuppa during the filming of *Indochine* – don't mistake the flashier bakeries nearby for this unassuming place.

Fanny (Map p358; ☎ 828 5656; 48 Pho Le Thai To; ice cream 10,000đ; ⏲ lunch & dinner) Churns out the yummiest Franco-Vietnamese ice cream in the city. Sample alluring seasonal flavours such as *com* (sticky rice) or *mang cau* (custard apple).

Moca Café (Map p358; ☎ 825 6334; 14-16 Pho Nha Tho; espresso 20,000đ; ⏲ 7.30am-11pm) One of the most popular cafés in Hanoi, this the perfect spot for people-watching while you eat good-value Vietnamese, Western and Indian food.

ourpick La Place (Map p358; ☎ 928 5859; 4 Pho Au Trieu; meals from 30,000đ) Readers have been raving about this place. The menu is small but includes iced shakes with bite and delicious savoury crepes.

Culi Café (Map p358; ☎ 926 2241; 40 Pho Luong Ngoc Quyen; meals around 50,000đ; ⏲ 7.30am-11pm) Sangers, pies, burgers and more, this Australian-run café-bar is a popular stop for tasty tucker. Free wi-fi.

Other good lakeside cafés:

Thuy Ta Café (Map p358; ☎ 828 8148; 1 Pho Le Thai To; pastries 10,000đ; ⏲ 6am-11pm) Thuy Ta's shady garden is right on the northern shore of Hoan Kiem Lake.

Hapro (Map p358; Pho Le Thai Tho) At the opposite end of Hoan Kiem Lake, this café has a prime patio for leisurely drinks.

Self-Catering

Dong Xuan Market (Map p358; P Dong Xuan; ⏲ 6am-10pm) Swing by for fresh fruits and veggies and freshly baked baguettes (see p364).

If you want some comfort food from home, stop by the following supermarkets for imported treats and road-trip munchies:

Fivimart (Map p358; 210 Tran Quang Khai) One of the best-stocked supermarkets in the centre of town.

Intimex (Map p358; Pho Le Thai Tho) On the western side of Hoan Kiem Lake, tucked down a driveway behind the Clinique beauty shop.

DRINKING

There is something for everyone in Hanoi, with sophisticated bars, congenial pubs and grungy clubs. Don't forget to warm up with some quality time drinking *bia hoi*, the world's cheapest beer. Busy Bao Khanh has a cool choice of bars and is a good starting or finishing point for a bar crawl.

ourpick Le Pub (Map p358; ☎ 926 2104; 25 Pho Hang Be) The name says it all: the attitude of a British pub with the atmosphere of a Continental bar. It's a friendly place to drink and draws both expats and tourists.

Quan Bia Minh (Map p358; ☎ 934 5233; 7A Pho Dinh Liet) Bottled beer doesn't come much cheaper than this, a buzzing backpacker favourite with a blissful balcony terrace overlooking Dinh Liet.

ourpick Highway 4 (Map p358; ☎ 926 0639; 5 Pho Hang Tre) Discover the mystical, medicinal, not to mention intoxicating qualities of Vietnamese *xeo* (rice wine) – take it straight, fruity or 'five times a night'. It's a rallying point for members of Hanoi's infamous Minsk Club.

Gambrinus (Map p358; ☎ 935 1114; 198 Pho Tran Quang Khai) Czech beer lovers will be rubbing their hands in glee. It's a vast, impressive *brauhaus* (brewhouse) with shiny vats of freshly brewed Gambrinus beer.

Toilet Pub (Map p358; ☎ 928 7338; 10 Pho Bao Khanh) Spirits are displayed in urinals and toilets are everywhere here. Very trendy, the drinks are expensive (50,000đ a beer).

Amazon Bar (Map p358; ☎ 928 7338; 10 Pho Bao Khanh) Reinforcing Bao Khanh's reputation as a drinkers' den, Amazon has nightly promotions that keep the crowds coming.

Funky Monkey (Map p358; ☎ 928 6113; 15B Pho Hang Hanh) An extension of the Bao Khanh beat, the action regularly spills over onto the dance floor at this hip bar-club.

Other places in the Bao Khanh strip include the following:

Polite Pub (Map p358; ☎ 825 0959; 5 Pho Bao Khanh) There is always a crowd here for big sporting events and drinks are affordable.

GC Pub (Map p358; ☎ 825 0499; 5 Pho Bao Khanh) GC has swung right back into favour with Hanoi residents.

ENTERTAINMENT

Cinemas

Megastar Cineplex (Map pp352-3; ☎ 974 3333; 6th fl, Vincom Tower, 191 Ba Trieu) The international multi-plex arrives in Hanoi. This is a serious cinema, complete with the latest international films.

Cinematheque (Map p358; 22A Hai Ba Trung; ☎ 936 2648) The Cinematheque offers an adventurous choice of films.

Centre Culturel Française de Hanoi (Map p358; ☎ 936 2164; 24 Trang Tien) Set in the sublime L'Espace building near the Opera House, it offers a regular programme of French flicks.

Classical Music

Hanoi Opera House (Nha Hat Lon; Map p358; ☎ 825 4312; Pho Trang Tien) This magnificent 900-seat venue, built in 1911, hosts occasional classical music performances and the atmosphere is incredible.

Clubbing

The shelf life of Hanoi's discos is short, so ask around about what's hot or not during your visit.

Apocalypse Now (Map pp352-3; Pho Pham Ngoc Thach, Dong Da District; ☾ 8pm-late) Although it's now some way from the centre, Apo, as locals call it, continues to pack in the pretty people. There's no cover but the drinks will cost you.

New Century Nightclub (Map p358; ☎ 928 5285; 10 Pho Trang Thi) New places come and go, but the New Century remains the place to see and be seen for young Vietnamese. Dress sharp, as the beautiful people are out in force.

Solace (Map p358; ☎ 932 3244; Red River, Phuc Tan District) Floating in the Red River, many a drinker

---

GAY & LESBIAN HANOI

There's a lively gay scene in Hanoi, with cruising areas such as the cafés on Pho Bao Khanh and around Hoan Kiem Lake. Gay boys should take care not to fall victim to a very organised extortion scam going on around the lake (see p355).

Funky Monkey (opposite) is gay-friendly and has wild Friday and Saturday nights. There's a healthy gay scene at Apocalypse Now (above), but watch for hustlers.

---

has found their night floats by here as well. It doesn't really warm up until after midnight and bobs along until daybreak.

Live Music

Jazz Club By Quyen Van Minh (Cau Lac Bo; Map p358; ☎ 825 7655; 31-33 Pho Luong Van Can; ☾ performances 9-11.30pm) The place in Hanoi to catch live jazz. Owner Minh teaches saxophone at the Hanoi Conservatory and moonlights here.

R&R Tavern (Map p358; ☎ 934 4109; 47 Pho Lo Su) A reliable little venue for live music, the Vietnamese band here know all the counterculture '60s classics.

Seventeen Saloon (Map pp352-3; ☎ 942 6822; 98 Tran Hung Dao) Yee-haa! Welcome to the wild west. Cowboy bars are curiously popular in Asia and this place has live music every night.

Terrace Bar (Press Club; Map p358; ☎ 934 0888; 59A Pho Ly Thai To) A popular place to be on Friday, when half of Hanoi's high-flyers seem to descend here for the happy hour (6pm) and live music.

Traditional Music

Some of the best places to catch live traditional music are upmarket Vietnamese restaurants in central Hanoi, such as **Club Opera** (Map p358; ☎ 824 6950; 59 Pho Ly Thai To), **Dinh Lang Restaurant** (Map p358; ☎ 828 6290; 1 Pho Le Thai Tho) and **Nam Phuong** (Map pp352-3; ☎ 928 5085; 16 Pho Bao Khanh). They might be aimed at tourists, but close your eyes and the music is hauntingly beautiful.

Water Puppetry

Municipal Water Puppet Theatre (Roi Nuoc Thang Long; Map p358; ☎ 825 5450; www.thanglongwaterpuppet.org; 57B Pho Dinh Tien Hoang; admission 20,000-40,000d, still-camera fee 10,000d, video fee 50,000d; ☾ performances at 4pm, 5.15pm, 6.30pm, 8pm & 9.15pm) This fascinating art form originated in northern Vietnam, and Hanoi is the best place to catch a show. The higher admission buys better seats and a cassette of the music; you must pay extra fees to take photos and video.

SHOPPING

The Old Quarter is brimming with temptation; price tags signal set prices. As you wander around you'll find clothes, cosmetics, fake sunglasses, luxury food, T-shirts, musical instruments, plumbing supplies, herbal medicines, jewellery, religious offerings, spices, woven mats and much, much more. And even if you don't need new shoes, take a walk along Pho Hang Dau to gawk at the wondrous shoe market (Map p358). Larger Western sizes are rare, but for petite feet, bargains abound.

Handicrafts

If you don't make it up to Sapa, you can find a selection of ethnic-minority garb and handicrafts in Hanoi; a stroll along Pho Hang Bac or Pho To Tich will turn up a dozen places.

North and northwest of Hoan Kiem Lake around Pho Hang Gai, Pho To Tich, Pho Hang Khai and Pho Cau Go you'll be tripping over shops offering Vietnamese handicrafts (lacquerware, mother-of-pearl inlay, ceramics), as well as watercolours, oil paintings, prints and assorted antiques – real and fake.

Local artists display their paintings at private art galleries, the highest concentration of which is on Pho Trang Tien, between Hoan Kiem Lake and the Opera House (Map p358). The galleries are worth a browse even if you're not buying.

Craft Link (Map pp352-3; ☎ 843 7710; 39-45 Pho Van Mieu) Promote fair trade at Craft Link, across from the Temple of Literature. High-quality tribal handicrafts with profits funding community development initiatives.

Vietnamese House (Map p358; ☎ 826 2455; 92 Pho Hang Bac) This small, attractive shop deals in a hodge-podge of old and new treasures.

Markets

Dong Xuan Market (Map p358; Pho Dong Xuan; ⊙ 6am-10pm) With hundreds of stalls, the three-storey market, 600m north of Hoan Kiem Lake, is a tourist attraction in its own right.

Hom Market (Map pp352-3; Pho Hué) On the northeastern corner of Pho Hué and Pho Tran Xuan Soan, this is a good general-purpose market with lots of imported food items.

Hang Da Market (Map p358; Yen Thai) West of Hoan Kiem Lake, Hang Da is relatively small, but good for imported foods, wine, beer and flowers. The 2nd floor is good for fabric and ready-made clothing.

Silk Products & Clothing

Pho Hang Gai, about 100m northwest of Hoan Kiem Lake, and its continuation, Pho Hang Bong, is a good place to look for embroidery such as tablecloths, T-shirts and wall hangings. This is also the modern-day silk strip, with pricey boutiques offering tailoring services and selling ready-to-wear clothing.

Other fashionable streets include the blocks around St Joseph Cathedral (Map p358): Pho Nha Tho, Pho Ly Quoc Su and Pho Hang Trong. Designer boutiques here sell silk clothing, purses, homewares and antiques.

Check out the following places:

Hadong Silk (Map p358; ☎ 928 5056; 102 Pho Hang Gai) Hillary Clinton shopped here during her visit with Bill in 2000.

Ipa-Nima (Map pp352-3; ☎ 933 4000; www.ipa-nima .com; 34 Pho Han Thuyen) This boutique promises 'smart humour, bright colours, subtle satire'.

Chi Vang (Map p358; ☎ 824 0933; 17 Pho Trang Tien) Exquisite lace creations, including clothing and homeware.

GETTING THERE & AWAY
Air

Hanoi has fewer international flights than HCMC, but with a change of aircraft in Hong Kong or Bangkok you can get anywhere. For more on international flights in and out of Hanoi, see p433.

Vietnam Airlines (Map p358; ☎ 943 9660; www.vietnamair.com.vn; 25 Pho Trang Thi; ⊙ 7am-6.30pm Mon-Fri, 8-11.30am & 1.30-5pm Sat & Sun & holidays) links Hanoi to destinations throughout Vietnam.

Pacific Airlines (Map pp352-3; ☎ 974 5555; 193 Đ Ba Trieu) is rebranding as a budget carrier and currently has flights to Danang and HCMC.

Bus

Hanoi has several main bus stations, each serving a particular area. It's a good idea to arrange your travel the day before you want to leave. The stations are pretty well organised with ticket offices, and printed schedules and prices.

Gia Lam bus station (☎ 827 1569; Đ Ngoc Lam) is the place for buses to points northeast of Hanoi, including Halong Bay (40,000d, 3½ hours), Hai Phong (35,000d, two hours), and Lang Son (50,000d, three hours) and Lao Cai (53,000d, nine hours), both near the Chinese border. The bus station is 2km northeast of the centre – cross the Red River to get there. Cyclos can't cross the bridge, so take a taxi or motorbike. More convenient is the Loung Yen bus station in the southeast of town, serving the same places, plus Cao Bang (80,000d, eight hours) and Ha Giang (76,000d, seven hours).

Kim Ma bus station (Map pp352-3; cnr Pho Nguyen Thai Hoc & Pho Giang Vo) is for buses to the northwest regions, including Dien Bien Phu (120,000d, 16 hours).

Son La bus station (Km 8, Pho Nguyen Trai) is for buses to the northwest, including Son La

(63,000d, 12 to 14 hours) and Dien Bien Phu (120,000d, 16 hours). It's southwest of Hanoi, near Hanoi University.

Giap Bat bus station (☎ 864 1467; Đ Giai Phong) serves points south of Hanoi, including Ninh Binh (28,000d, two hours) and Hué (80,000d, 12 hours). It is 7km south of the Hanoi train station.

My Dinh bus station (☎ 768 5549; Đ Pham Hung) is another option in the west of town, which serves a real range of destinations, including Halong City, Lang Son, Cao Bang, Ha Giang and Dien Bien Phu.

Tourist-style minibuses can be booked through most hotels and cafés. Popular destinations include Halong Bay and Sapa.

Car & Motorcycle

To hire a car or minibus with driver, contact a travel agency or travellers café. The main roads in the northeast are generally OK, but in parts of the northwest they're pretty rough and require a 4WD.

A six-day trip in a 4WD can cost US$250 to US$500 (including 4WD, driver and petrol). You should inquire about who is responsible for the driver's room and board – most hotels have a room set aside for drivers, but work out ahead of time what costs are included.

For reliable Minsk rental, make for **Cuong's Motorbike Adventure** (Map p358; ☎ 926 1534; 1 Pho Luong Ngoc Quyen). Cuong rents out bikes for US$5 a day, including spares and a repair manual.

Train

The main **Hanoi train station** (Ga Hang Co; Map pp352-3; ☎ 825 3949; 120 Đ Le Duan; ⏰ ticket office 7.30-11.30am & 1.30-7.30pm) is at the western end of Pho Tran Hung Dao. Trains from here go to destinations south. It's best to buy tickets at least one day before departure to ensure a seat or sleeper. To the right of the main entrance of the train station is a separate ticket office for northbound trains to Lao Cai (for Sapa) and China (counter 13).

The place you purchase your ticket is not necessarily where the train departs, so be sure to ask exactly *where* you need to catch your train.

Tran Quy Cap station (B station; Map pp352-3; ☎ 825 2628; Pho Tran Qui Cap) is just two blocks behind the main station on Đ Le Duan. Northbound trains leave from here.

Gia Lam station (Nguyen Van Cu, Gia Lam District) has some northbound (Yen Bai, Lao Cai, Lang Son) and eastbound (Hai Phong) trains departing from here, on the eastern side of the Red River.

To make things complicated, some of the same destinations served by Gia Lam can also be reached from **Long Bien station** (Map pp352-3; ☎ 826 8280).

Check with **Vietnam Rail** (www.vr.com.vn) for current timetables and prices.

GETTING AROUND
Bicycle

Pedalling around the city is a great way to cover lots of ground and it immerses you in Vietnamese daily life. Many of the hotels and cafés in the city rent bicycles for about US$1 per day.

Bus

There are now more than 60 public bus lines serving routes in and around Hanoi. The buses are clean and comfortable and the fare is just 3500d. Pick up a copy of the *Xe Buyt Hanoi* or *Hanoi* bus map (5000d) from recommended bookshops (p354).

Cyclo

Cyclos in Hanoi are wider than the Ho Chi Minh City breed, making them big enough for two to share the fare. Around the city centre, most cyclo rides should cost around 5000d to 10,000d. Longer rides – from the Old Quarter to the Ho Chi Minh Mausoleum Complex, for example – would cost double or more again. One common cyclo-driver's ploy when carrying two passengers is to agree on a price and then double it on arrival, saying the price was for one person, not two.

The cyclo drivers in Hanoi are even less likely to speak English than in HCMC, so take a map of the city with you. That said, many are wising up and now have a command of basic English.

Motorcycle

Walk down any major street and you'll be bombarded by offers for *xe om*. They should cost about the same as a cyclo and are advisable for longer distances.

For travellers well versed in the ways of Asian cities, Hanoi is a lot of fun to explore by motorbike. Most guesthouses and hotels can arrange motorbikes for around US$5 a

VIETNAM

day. However, for the uninitiated, it is *not* the easiest place to learn.

Taxi

There are several companies in Hanoi offering metered taxi services. Flag fall is around 10,000d to 15,000d, which takes you 1km or 2km; every kilometre thereafter costs about 8000d. Bear in mind that there are lots of dodgy operators with high-speed meters. Try and use the more reliable companies, including:

Airport Taxi (☎ 873 3333)
Hanoi Taxi (☎ 853 5353)
Mai Linh Taxi (☎ 822 2666)
Taxi CP (☎ 824 1999)

AROUND HANOI

PERFUME PAGODA

North Vietnam's very own Marble Mountains, the **Perfume Pagoda** (Chua Huong; admission incl return boat trip 35,000d) is a striking complex of pagodas and Buddhist shrines built into the karst cliffs of Huong Tich Mountain (Mountain of the Fragrant Traces). This is a domestic drawcard and it is an interesting experience just to see the Vietnamese tourists at play.

If you want to do the highly recommended scenic river trip, travel from Hanoi by car to My Duc (two hours), then take a small

---

CROSSING INTO LAOS: THE ROADS LESS TRAVELLED

All of the border crossings between North and Central Vietnam and Laos have a degree of difficulty. If you've got the time, you're much better to head south and cross at Lao Bao.

Nam Xoi to Na Maew

This is the most remote border in a mountainous area 175km northwest of Thanh Hoa city and 70km east of Xam Neua (Laos). Try to find a bus or take a motorbike from Thanh Hoa. However, we've heard reports of drivers demanding 300,000d for the journey from Thanh Hoa – more than six times the going rate. All in all, expect a 15-hour ordeal if you take this route. For information on crossing this border in the other direction, see p308.

Nam Can to Nong Haet

This crossing links Vinh with Phonsavan. Catch a morning bus from Vinh to Muang Xen (29,000d, seven hours) and grab a motorbike for the spectacular 25km uphill run to the border (50,000d). Local transport on to Nong Haet is about 5000 kip if anything shows up. From Nong Haet, there are several buses a day on to Phonsavan (20,000 kip, four hours). On Tuesday, Thursday and Sunday it's possible to catch a bus at 6am from Vinh to Phonsavan (US$12, 11 hours, bookings Mr Lam ☎ 038-383 5782). For information on crossing this border in the other direction, see p305.

Cau Treo to Nam Phao

This border is 96km west of Vinh and about 30km east of Lak Sao in Laos. There are still lots of horror stories from travellers on this route. Catch a bus from Vinh to Tay Son (formerly Trung Tam; 10,000d). Chronic overcharging and being kicked off in the middle of nowhere are common. From Tay Son, it's 26km to the border. Take a minibus or hire a motorbike to cover the last stretch; both cost 50,000d.

The Vietnamese border guards have been known to close the country for lunch – any time from 11.30am to 1.30pm. From the Vietnamese side it's a short walk to the Laos border. Once in Laos, jumbo (three-wheeled taxis) and *sawngthaew* (pick-up trucks) to Lak Sao leave the border when full or cost about US$10 to charter. For information on crossing this border in the other direction, see p318.

Cha Lo to Na Phao

Bus services link Dong Hoi and Tha Khaek (190,000d, 11 hours, twice weekly, bookings Mr Thang ☎ 828 939). The buses depart Dong Hoi at 6am on Monday and Friday, returning from Tha Khaek at 7am on Wednesday and Sunday. For information on crossing this border in the other direction, see p321.

boat rowed by two women to the foot of the mountain (1½ hours).

The main pagoda area is about a 4km walk up from where the boat lets you off. The good news is that there is now a cable car to the summit, costing 30,000d one way. A smart combination is to use the cable car to go up and then walk down.

Hanoi's travellers cafés (see p355) offer day tours to the pagoda from US$10, inclusive of transport, guide and lunch (drinks excluded). If you're going with a small-group tour, expect to spend around US$15 to US$20. You can also rent a motorbike to get here on your own.

HANDICRAFT VILLAGES

There are numerous villages surrounding Hanoi that specialise in particular cottage industries. Visiting these villages can make a rewarding day trip, though you'll need a good guide to make the journey worthwhile.

Bat Trang is known as the ceramic village. You can watch artisans create superb ceramic vases and other masterpieces in their kilns. Bat Trang is 13km southeast of Hanoi.

So, known for its delicate noodles, mills the yam and cassava flour for noodles. It is in Ha Tay Province, about 25km southwest of Hanoi.

You can see silk cloth being produced on a loom in **Van Phuc**, a silk village 8km southwest of Hanoi in Ha Tay Province. There's also a small produce market every morning.

Dong Ky survives by producing beautiful, traditional furniture inlaid with mother-of-pearl. It is 15km northeast of Hanoi.

The locals in **Le Mat** raise snakes for the upmarket restaurants in Hanoi, and for producing medicinal spirits. Fresh snake cuisine and snake elixir is available at this village; for around 100,000d or so you can try a set meal of snake meat prepared 10 different ways. Le Mat is 7km northeast of central Hanoi.

NINH BINH

☎ 030 / pop 53,000

Ninh Binh has evolved into a popular travel hub in recent years. Its sudden transformation from sleepy backwater to tourist magnet has little to do with Ninh Binh itself, but rather with its proximity to Tam Coc (9km; right), Hoa Lu (12km; p368) and Cuc Phuong National Park (45km; p368). Travel agencies and traveller cafés in Hanoi (p355) offer inexpensive day trips to the region that take in most of the sights.

The surrounding countryside is gorgeous, confirming all the postcard fantasies that Vietnam has to offer – water buffalos, golden-green rice paddies, majestic limestone formations and more.

Information

Internet cafés are spread around town, with a cluster on Ð Luong Van Tuy, west of Ð Tran Hung Dao.

Incombank (☎ 872 675; Ð Tran Hung Dao) Deals with cash, travellers cheques and has an ATM outside.

Main post office (Ð Tran Hung Dao)

Sleeping & Eating

Folks who run guesthouses in Ninh Binh have a reputation for honest, friendly service. All the places listed can arrange tours and hire motorbikes and bicycles.

Xuan Hoa Hotel (☎ 880 970; 31Ð Pho Minh Khai; dm US$3, r US$4-12; 🍴) The kind of guesthouse you wish existed in every town, the charming owners and staff make this is a firm favourite.

Thanhthuy's Guest House & New Hotel (☎ 871 811; tuc@hn.vnn.vn; 128 Ð Le Hong Phong; r guesthouse US$5-8, hotel US$12; 🍴 🖥) The central courtyard is a great place to meet other travellers over a meal or a beer. The New Hotel is set back from the street, while the guesthouse is basic and clean.

Thuy Anh Hotel (☎ 871 602; www.thuyanhhotel.com; 55A Ð Truong Han Sieu; US$7-40; 🍴 🖥) The smartest operation in town, the old wing offers spotless rooms, while the slick new wing, complete with lift, pulls in the tour groups. In addition to a large restaurant, there's a rooftop bar.

Getting There & Away

Ninh Binh is 93km southwest of Hanoi. Regular public buses leave almost hourly from the Giap Bat bus terminal in Hanoi (28,000d, 2½ hours). The bus station in Ninh Binh is across the Van River from the post office.

Ninh Binh is also a hub on the north–south open-tour bus route (see p436). Ninh Binh is a scheduled stop for some *Reunification Express* trains travelling between Hanoi and HCMC, but travelling by road is faster.

AROUND NINH BINH
Tam Coc

Known as 'Halong Bay on the Rice Paddies' for its huge rock formations jutting out of rice paddies, **Tam Coc** (admission 30,000d, boat 40,000d) boasts breathtaking scenery.

The way to see Tam Coc is by rowboat on the Ngo Dong River. The boats row through karst caves on this beautiful trip, and take about three hours, including stops. Tickets are sold at the small booking office by the docks. One boat seats two passengers.

Tam Coc is 9km southwest of Ninh Binh. By car or motorbike, follow National Hwy 1 south and turn west at the Tam Coc turn-off, marked by a pair of tall stone pillars.

Hoa Lu

The scenery here resembles nearby Tam Coc, though Hoa Lu has an interesting historical twist. Hoa Lu was the capital of Vietnam under the Dinh dynasty (968–80) and the Le dynasties (980–1009). The site was a suitable choice for a capital city due to its proximity to China and the natural protection afforded by the region's bizarre landscape.

The **ancient citadel** (admission 10,000d) of Hoa Lu, most of which, sadly, has been destroyed, once covered an area of about 3 sq km.

There is no public transport to Hoa Lu, which is 12km north of Ninh Binh. Most travellers get here by bicycle, motorbike or car.

CUC PHUONG NATIONAL PARK

☎ 030 / elev 150–648m

This **national park** (☎ 848 006; adult/child 40,000/20,000d) is one of Vietnam's most important nature preserves. Ho Chi Minh personally took time off from the war in 1963 to dedicate the area as a national park, Vietnam's first. The hills are laced with many grottoes, and the climate is subtropical at the park's lower elevations.

Excellent trekking opportunities abound in the park, including a trek (8km return) to an enormous 1000-year-old tree (*Tetrameles nudiflora,* for botany geeks), and to a Muong village where you can also go rafting. A guide is mandatory for longer treks.

During the rainy season (July to September) leeches are common in the park; the best time to visit is between December and April. Try to visit during the week, as weekends and Vietnamese school holidays are hectic.

One marvellous organisation based in the park is the **Endangered Primate Rescue Center** (☎ 848 002; www.primatecenter.org; admission free; ⊗ 9-11am & 1-4pm). The centre is home to around 120 rare monkeys bred in captivity or confiscated from illegal traders. These gibbons, langurs and lorises are rehabilitated, studied

and, whenever possible, released back into their native environments or into semiwild protected areas. Seeing them in full swing is quite a sight.

Sleeping & Eating

There are two accommodation areas in the park, with a complicated range of prices and options.

The centre of the park, 18km from the gate, is the best place to be for an early-morning walk or bird-watching. Here there are basic rooms in a **pillar house** (per person US$6), or there's a couple of self-contained **bungalows** (s/d US$15/25). There's also an enormous river-fed swimming pool.

At park headquarters, there are **self-contained bungalows & guesthouse rooms** (s/d US$15/20), as well as rooms in a **pillar house** (per person US$5). You can **camp** (per person US$2) at either location, but need to bring your own gear. **Meals** (10,000-25,000d) are available from reception, including a vegetarian option.

Getting There & Away

Cuc Phuong National Park is 45km from Ninh Binh. There is no public transport on this route, but it's a beautiful drive by car or motorbike. Ask for directions or pick up basic area maps at the hotels in Ninh Binh.

NORTHERN VIETNAM

Welcome to the roof of Vietnam, where the mountains of the Tonkinese Alps soar skyward, delivering some of the most spectacular scenery in the country. Forbidding and unforgiving terrain for lowlanders, the mountains have long provided a haven for an eclectic mix of hill tribes. Dressed in elaborate costumes, living as they have for generations, extending the hand of friendship to strangers, an encounter with the Montagnards is both a humbling and heart-warming experience.

Bizarre but beautiful, Halong Bay is geology gone wild, with hundreds and thousands of limestone pinnacles protruding from the waters. North of Halong Bay is the less-visited Bai Tu Long Bay, where nature's spectacular show continues all the way to the Chinese border. To the south of Halong Bay is Cat Ba Island, a 'lost world' landscape with hiking, biking or just hanging around the order of the day.

HALONG BAY

Majestic and mysterious, inspiring and imperious, words alone cannot do justice to the natural wonder that is Halong Bay, where 3000 or more incredible islands rise from the emerald waters of the Gulf of Tonkin. Halong Bay is pure art, a priceless collection of unfinished sculptures hewn from the hand of nature. A Unesco World Heritage Site, the vegetation-covered islands are dotted with innumerable grottoes created by the wind and the waves. Besides the breathtaking vistas, visitors to Halong Bay come to explore the countless caves.

Ha long means 'where the dragon descends into the sea'. The legend says that the islands of Halong Bay were created by a great dragon that lived in the mountains. As it ran towards the coast, its flailing tail gouged out valleys and crevasses; as it plunged into the sea, the areas dug up by its tail became filled with water, leaving only pockets of high land visible.

From February through until April, the weather is often cold and drizzly, and the ensuing fog can cause low visibility, although the temperature rarely falls below 10°C. Tropical storms are frequent during the summer months.

Halong City is the gateway to Halong Bay but not the ideal introduction to this incredible site. Developers have not been kind to the city and most visitors sensibly opt for tours that include sleeping on a boat in the bay. In short, Halong Bay is the attraction, Halong City is not.

All visitors must purchase a 30,000d entry ticket that covers all the sights in the bay. Tickets are available at the tourist boat dock in Bai Chay, but it is usually included for those on a tour. See the boxed text, p370 for more on organised trips out of Hanoi.

It's hard to do it any cheaper on your own, but if you prefer travelling independently it's simple enough to do so. Take a bus to Halong City from Hanoi (40,000d, 3½ hours) and book a passage on a Cat Ba tourist boat (130,000d including entry ticket, six hours). Chill out on Cat Ba before taking a hydrofoil to Haiphong and a bus to Hanoi. Alternatively, run the route in reverse and try and hook up with a tour boat in Cat Ba.

Halong Bay Management Department (☎ 033-846 592; http://halong.org.vn/; 166 Đ Le Thanh Tong), about 1.5km west of Halong City, regulates pricing for independent cruises on the bay. There is no need to rent a whole boat for yourself as there are plenty of other travellers, Vietnamese and foreign, to share with. The official prices are ridiculously reasonable at 30,000d/40,000d for a four-/six-hour cruise.

If time is an issue, **Northern Airport Flight Service Company** (☎ 04-827 4409; fax 04-827 2780; 173 Pho Truong Chinh, Hanoi) offers a helicopter charter service from Hanoi to Halong Bay on Saturday from 8am, costing US$175 per person.

EXPLORING THE FAR NORTH

Motorcycling in Vietnam's wild northern territory is unforgettable. If you're not confident riding a motorbike yourself, it's possible to hire someone to drive you. Four-wheel drive trips in the north are also highly recommended, though the mobility of travelling on two wheels is unrivalled.

One of the most popular routes is the 'Northwest Loop', which follows Hwy 6 through the heart of the Tonkinese Alps. There are many variations, but the standard route takes in a homestay in the **White Thai villages** around Mai Chau (p375), a stop in **Son La**, a visit to the historic battlefield of **Dien Bien Phu**, before finishing up at Sapa, the queen of the mountains. However, some companies also specialise in taking bikers right off the trail into the far north of **Ha Giang** or the beautiful northeast province of **Cao Bang** and the nearby lakes of Ba Be National Park (p374).

While it's possible to organise a motorcycling trip on your own, hiring a guide will certainly make the trip run smoothly and get you places you'd never discover from a cursory scan of a map.

The 125cc Russian-made Minsk is the best overall cycle for touring the north. The daily hire cost for a Minsk starts from US$5. Foreign guides charge considerably more than local Vietnamese guides, but are worth every dong. Check out these outfits in Hanoi:

Explore Indochina (☎ 0913-524 658; www.exploreindochina.com) Run by Digby, Dan and Thuan, these guys have biked all over the country and can take you to the parts others cannot reach.

Free Wheelin' Tours (☎ 04-747 0545; www.freewheelin-tours.com) Run by Fredo, who speaks French, English and Vietnamese, this company has its own homestays in the northeast, plus 4WD trips.

CRUISING THE KARSTS: TOURS TO HALONG BAY

Don't even think about a day trip to Halong, as the real beauty of the bay is best experienced from the deck of a junk over a gin and tonic, as the sun sinks into the horizon. Halong Bay is hard to explore properly without the services of an experienced tour company.

Budget trips sold out of Hanoi are very reasonably priced, starting from as little as US$15 per person for a dodgy day trip and rising to as much as US$100 for two nights on the bay with a bit of kayaking. Remember, you get what you pay for and the cheaper the tour, the more basic the boat, the meals and the service. Drinks are extra and are generally more expensive than on the mainland.

If you book a tour, there is always a small chance that the boat-trip part may be cancelled due to bad weather. This may actually entitle you to a partial refund, but remember that the boat trip is only a small portion of the cost of the journey.

For a list of reliable operators offering two- and three-day tours of the bay, check out the travel agents listed in the Hanoi section (p355).

Boat Operators

There are hundreds of boats plying the waters these days. The following is just a selection of the most interesting. For more on the government-run boats that are available for charter, see the Halong Bay section (p369).

Emeraude Classic Cruise (☎ 04-934 0888; www.emeraude-cruises.com; s/d US$245/290) A replica paddle steamer that cruises the waters of Halong Bay daily.

Halong Ginger (☎ 04-984 2807; www.cruisehalong.com; d from US$373) A beautiful junk that is well finished throughout.

Huong Hai Junks (☎ 033-845 042; www.halongtravels.com; s/d US$125/220) The leading boat company in Halong Bay, Huong Hai has a fleet of traditional junks.

Tropical Sails (☎ 04-923 2559; www.tropical-sails.com; s/d from US$127/196) The only junks with working sails, allowing the boats to get up a head of steam on a windy day.

HALONG CITY

☎ 033 / pop 149,900

If Halong Bay is heaven, Halong City can be hell. Overdeveloped but underloved, the hideous high-rise hotels come in every shade of pastel and the beaches are definitely not the region's best. This is sin city, with 'massage' promoted at every hotel.

Orientation & Information

Halong is a tale of two cities. The western side is called Bai Chay, where all the tourist life-support systems are found. Across the bay on the eastern side is Hon Gai, a much more Vietnamese entity.

Post office (☎ 840 000; Đ Halong; ☺ 7.30am-5pm) Internet access available.

Vietcombank (Đ Halong) Exchange services and an ATM.

Sleeping & Eating

The heaviest concentration of hotels is in town, in the aptly named 'hotel alley' of Đ Vuon Dao. This is where you'll find more than 50 minihotels, most of them almost identical (a guidebook author's nightmare). Expect to pay something between US$8 and US$12 for a double room with private bathroom and air-con.

Hoang Lan Hotel (☎ 846 504; 17 Đ Vuon Dao; s US$8-12, d US$10-15; ✷) Right in the thick of the action on hotel alley, this family place has a friendly feel.

Halong 1 Hotel (☎ 846 320; fax 846 318; Đ Halong; r US$30-55; ✷ 🖳) Set in a rambling old colonial-era building, splash the extra for the space of a suite. Catherine Deneuve stayed here during the filming of *Indochine*.

Halong Plaza Hotel (☎ 845 810; www.halongplaza.com; 8 Đ Halong; r from US$140; ✷ 🖳 ✺) A huge hotel where the 200 rooms are businesslike, but are packing four stars. Discounts are usually available.

Unsurprisingly, seafood is a serious feature of most menus. There are a couple of seafood strips in the centre of town, just south of the post office along Đ Halong. Aim for the places with fresh seafood in tanks out the front or gravitate to where the locals are dining.

Getting There & Away

Buses from Halong City to Hanoi (40,000d, 3½ hours) leave from **Mien Tay bus station** (Đ Ca Lan) in Bai Chay every 15 minutes, as do buses to Haiphong (25,000d, 1½ hours).

Most buses to northeastern destinations start from Mien Tay bus station before passing through **Hon Gai bus station** (Đ Le Loi). Buses for Mong Cai (42,000d, five hours) and Cai Rong (20,000d, 1½ hours) for Van Don Island (Dao Cai Bau) depart frequently during daylight hours.

From Bai Chay, **Mui Ngoc** (☎ 847 888; Đ Halong) operates hydrofoils to Mong Cai (US$15, three hours), on the Chinese border, leaving at 8am and 1pm; the ticket office is situated almost next door to the Mien Tay bus station. Book ahead, as demand often outstrips supply.

The best way to get to Cat Ba Island is to hop onto the regular tourist boats (one way 100,000d, six hours) from Bai Chay tourist-boat dock, including a leisurely cruise through the most beautiful parts of the bay.

CAT BA ISLAND

☎ 031 / pop 7000

Rugged, craggy and jungle-clad Cat Ba, the largest island around Halong Bay, is straight out of Jurassic Park. Lan Ha Bay, off the eastern side of the island, is especially scenic and offers numerous beaches to explore. While the vast majority of Halong Bay's islands are uninhabited vertical rocks, Cat Ba has a few fishing villages, as well as a fast-growing town.

Much of Cat Ba Island was declared a national park in 1986 in order to protect the island's diverse ecosystems and wildlife, including the endangered golden-headed langur, the world's rarest primate. There are beautiful beaches, numerous lakes, waterfalls and

grottoes in the spectacular limestone hills, the highest of which rises 331m above sea level.

The island's human population is concentrated in the southern part of the island, around the town of Cat Ba. A sleepy fishing village just a decade ago, it is now the Costa del Cat Ba. Since being 'discovered' by Hanoi residents, Cat Ba has turned into a highly popular summer getaway, filling up on weekends and holidays, when prices fluctuate accordingly.

Information

There are no banks in Cat Ba town, but there are a few jewellery stores north of the harbour that exchange dollars. There are now several internet cafés in Cat Ba. Prices are higher than the mainland, at 15,000d an hour or more.

Main post office (Đ 1-4) A one-stop-shop for postal needs and telephone calls.

Tourism Information & Development Centre (☎ 688 215; Đ 1-4) Located opposite the boat pier, the staff here can bring you up to speed on transport options around Cat Ba.

Sights & Activities

Home to various species of monkey, wild boar and hedgehog, **Cat Ba National Park** (☎ 216 350; admission 15,000d, guide fee per day US$5; ☼ dawn-dusk) has plenty of trekking opportunities. Even though a guide is not mandatory, it's definitely recommended.

There's a very challenging 18km trek (five to six hours) through the park that many enjoy. You need a guide, transport to the trailhead and a boat to return, all of which can be arranged in Cat Ba town. If you're planning on doing this trek, equip yourself with proper trekking shoes, rainwear, a generous supply of water, plus some food.

OFF THE BEATEN TRACK: BAI TU LONG BAY

There's more to northeastern Vietnam than Halong Bay. The sinking limestone plateau, which gave birth to the bay's spectacular islands, continues for some 100km to the Chinese border. The area immediately northeast of Halong Bay is part of **Bai Tu Long National Park** (☎ 033-793 365).

Bai Tu Long Bay is every bit as beautiful as its famous neighbour. Indeed, in some ways it's more beautiful, since it has scarcely seen any tourist development. This is good news and bad news. The bay is unpolluted and undeveloped, but there's little tourism infrastructure. Highlights include amazing karst formations, hidden beaches and a few surf breaks off **Quan Lan Island**.

Charter boats can be arranged to Bai Tu Long Bay from Halong Bay (five hours); boats range from 100,000d to 250,000d per hour depending on size and amenities. A cheaper alternative is to travel overland to Cai Rong and visit the remote outlying islands by boat from there.

To reach the national park headquarters at Trung Trang, take a minibus (15,000d, 30 minutes, 17km) from Cat Ba town. All restaurants and hotels should be able to sell you minibus tickets. Another option is to hire a motorbike (one way 30,000d).

Hospital Cave (admission 30,000d) is the intriguing site that was used as a secret hospital during the American War – another amazing example of Vietnamese engineering born of necessity.

The white-sand Cat Co beaches (called simply Cat Co 1, Cat Co 2 and Cat Co 3) are perfect places to lounge around for the day; however, Cat Co 1 and 3 have been taken over by big resorts. Cat Co 2 is the most attractive beach, also offering simple accommodation and camping.

The beaches are about 1km from Cat Ba town and can be reached on foot or by motorbike for about 10,000d.

Sleeping

Most of the island's 40 or so hotels are concentrated along the bayfront in Cat Ba town. Room rates fluctuate greatly between high-season summer months and the slower winter months. The following are low season prices.

Quang Duc Family Hotel (☎ 888 231; fax 888 423; Đ 1-4; r US$10; ﹡) One of the longest-running cheapies in town, this friendly little family hotel has just seven rooms. Satellite TV and hot water come as standard.

Noble House (☎ 888 363; thenoblehousevn@yahoo .com; Đ 1-4; r US$10-30; ﹡) Small in size, big in character, this place has thoughtful decoration and elegant bathrooms. It's worth booking ahead, but bear in mind that prices leap during peak season.

Sun and Sea Hotel (☎ 888 315; sunseahotel@mail.ru; Đ Nui Ngoc; r US$12-15; ﹡) This popular little hotel is a friendly place to rest a weary head. All rooms include satellite TV, fridge and hot water.

Sunrise Resort (☎ 887 366; catba-sunriseresort@vnn .vn; Cat Co 3; s/d from US$79/89; ﹡ ▢ ▨) Occupying a private beach, this is the most sophisticated place on Cat Ba. Rooms are spacious and smart and facilities include a swimming pool and spa.

The small village of Hien Hao offers authentic homestays in local houses. For more

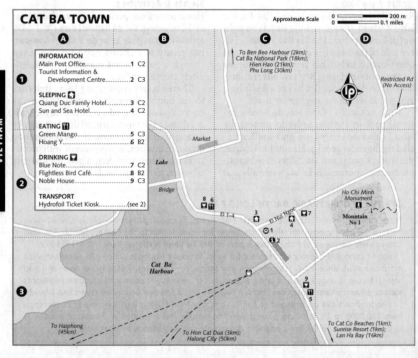

details contact **Mr Tuan** (☎ 888 737). Hien Hao is about 20km from Cat Ba town.

Eating & Drinking

For a memorable dining experience in Cat Ba, try the floating seafood restaurants in Cat Ba or Ben Beo harbours, where you choose your own seafood from pens underneath the restaurant. A rowing boat there and back should cost about 30,000d with waiting time; a feast for two should cost around 100,000d. Overcharging is a possibility, so work out meal prices beforehand.

Hoang Y (mains 15,000-50,000d; ☽ lunch & dinner) For a variety of delicious seafood and vegetarian dishes, check out Hoang Y, at the western end of town. This place is always busy.

Green Mango (☎ 887 151; Đ 1-4; mains 50,000-100,000d) *The* restaurant of choice in Cat Ba, the chef here learnt his tricks at Bobby Chinn's in Hanoi. The braised duck is superb but save some space for the delightful desserts. The interior is all drapes and candles, so customers often linger for cocktails.

As the night wears on, travellers gravitate to the **Flightless Bird Café** (☎ 888 517; ☽ from 6.30pm). Little more than a hole in the wall, this small, welcoming place is a good option for those with their drinking boots on.

Other popular spots:

Noble House (☎ 888 363) As well as a popular restaurant downstairs, this spot has a great 2nd-floor bar.

Blue Note (Đ Nui Ngoc) The after-hours haunt in town, this is karaoke with kudos, including indie anthems from Oasis and Radiohead.

Getting There & Around

Cat Ba Island is 133km from Hanoi, 45km east of Haiphong, and 20km south of Halong City. Hydrofoils link Cat Ba and Haiphong (45 minutes). There are three departures a day in the high summer season and just one a day the rest of the year. **Transtour** (☎ 888 314) runs the *Mekong Express* (100,000d, 2.45pm departure), which is the safest and most comfortable option.

Chartered private boats run trips between Cat Ba and Halong Bay (100,000d, five hours); make inquiries at the pier at either end.

Rented bicycles are a good way to explore the island. Most hotels can provide a cheap Chinese bicycle.

Motorbike rentals (with or without driver) are available from most of the hotels. If you're heading to the beaches or national park, pay the parking fee to ensure the bike isn't stolen or vandalised.

HAIPHONG

☎ 031 / pop 1.67 million

Haiphong is a graceful city that has the flavour of Hanoi a decade ago. Bicycles are as common as motorbikes and the verdant tree-lined boulevards conceal some classic colonial-era structures. Stroll around the centre and soak up the atmosphere.

Despite being one of the country's most important seaports and industrial centres, and officially Vietnam's third-largest city, Haiphong today seems a somnolent place with clean streets and an understated air of prosperity.

Information

There are a couple of internet cafés on Pho Le Dai Hanh near Pho Dien Bien Phu.

Main post office (3 Pho Nguyen Tri Phuong) Easy to spot, standing on a corner in dignified yellow.

Vietcombank (☎ 842 658; 11 Pho Hoang Dieu; ☽ closed Sat) Cashes travellers cheques, does cash advances and has an ATM.

Vietnam-Czech Friendship Hospital (Benh Vien Viet-Tiep; ☎ 700 463; Pho Nha Thuong) In emergencies, seek help here; otherwise, head back to Hanoi.

Sights & Activities

Though there isn't a whole lot to see in Haiphong, its slow-paced appeal is enhanced by the French-colonial architecture lining the streets.

Du Hang Pagoda (Chua Du Hang; 121 Pho Chua Hang; ☽ 7-11am & 1.30-5.50pm), founded three centuries ago and rebuilt several times since, has architectural elements that look Khmer. Equally enjoyable is wandering along the narrow alley to get here, Pho Chua Hang, which is buzzing with Haiphong street life.

Sleeping

Hotel du Commerce (☎ 384 2706; fax 384 2560; 62 Pho Dien Bien Phu; r US$10-18; 🖭) Located in a venerable old building from the French period, this remains a characterful place with high ceilings and gigantic bathrooms. Think atmosphere above amenities.

Monaco Hotel (☎ 374 6468; monacohotel@hn.vnn.vn; 103 Pho Dien Bien Phu; r US$20-40; 🖭) One of the newer hotels in town, the décor here is a cut above the competition. All rooms are well appointed, but US$40 buys an apartment.

Harbour View Hotel (☎ 382 7827; www.harbour viewvietnam.com; 4 Pho Tran Phu; s/d US$70/80; 🅿 🖳 🖩) The leading address in Haiphong, rooms are smart and stylish, while the facilities include a swimming pool, gym and spa. Discounts are often available.

Eating & Drinking

Pho Minh Khai offers a good selection of cheap eateries; and most hotel restaurants dish up variations on the fresh seafood available in Haiphong. Also check out Pho Quang Trung with its many cafés and *bia hoi*.

Com Vietnam (☎ 384 1698; 4 Pho Hoang Van Thu; mains 20,000-60,000d) A blink-and-you'll-miss-it courtyard restaurant, it's consistently popular thanks to affordable local seafood and Vietnamese specialities.

BKK (☎ 382 1018; 22 Pho Minh Khai; mains 30,000-60,000d) The card says 'trendy Thai restaurant' and they're damn right. All the Thai favourites, plus a serious amount of seafood.

La Villa Blanche (Pho Tran Hung Dao) For a one-size-fits-all night stop, head to this old French mansion which has a shady garden housing several bargain *bia hoi* shops.

Getting There & Away

Vietnam Airlines (☎ 9381 0890; www.vietnamair.com .vn; 30 Pho Hoang Van Thu) has flights to HCMC and Danang.

Haiphong is 103km from Hanoi; minibuses for Hanoi (35,000d, two hours) leave from the **Tam Bac bus station** (P Tam Bac), 4km from the waterfront. Buses heading south leave from **Niem Nghia bus station** (Đ Tran Nguyen Han). **Lac Long**

bus station (Pho Cu Chinh Lan) has buses to Halong City (25,000d, 1½ hours), plus Hanoi, convenient for those connecting with the Cat Ba hydrofoil.

A local express train heads to Hanoi (24,000d, two hours) from the **Haiphong train station** (Đ Luong Khanh Thien & Đ Pham Ngu Lao) at 6.10pm daily. From Hanoi, trains leave **Tran Quy Cap station** (B station; Map pp352-3; ☎ 04-825 2628; Pho Tran Qui Cap) at 5.50am; slower trains leave from Long Bien train station several times daily.

BA BE NATIONAL PARK

☎ 0281 / elev 145m

Boasting waterfalls, rivers, deep valleys, lakes and caves, **Ba Be National Park** (☎ 894 014; fax 894 026; person/car 10,000/20,000d) is set amid towering peaks. The surrounding area is home to members of the Tay minority, who live in stilt homes. This region is surrounded by steep mountains up to 1554m high. The park is a tropical rainforest area with more than 400 named plant species. The 300 wildlife species in the forest include bears, monkeys, bats and butterflies and other insects.

Ba Be (Three Bays) is in fact three linked lakes, with a total length of 8km and a width of about 400m. The Nang River is navigable for 23km between a point 4km above Cho Ra and the **Dau Dang Waterfall** (Thac Dau Dang), which is a series of spectacular cascades between sheer walls of rock. The interesting **Puong Cave** (Hang Puong) is about 30m high and 300m long, and passes completely through a mountain. A navigable river flows through the cave.

CROSSING INTO CHINA: THE NORTHEAST BORDERS

There are two borders in northeast Vietnam where foreigners can cross into China.

Huu Nghi Quan to Youyi Guan

This is the most popular border crossing. The border post itself is at Huu Nghi Quan (Friendship Gate), 3km north of Dong Dang. Catch a bus from Hanoi to Lang Son (50,000d, 2½ hours), a small minibus (5000d) to Dong Dang and a *xe om* (20,000d) to the border. On the Chinese side, it's a 20-minute drive from the border to Pingxiang by bus or a shared taxi. Pingxiang is connected by train and bus to Nanning.

Trains from Hanoi to Běijīng via the Friendship Pass depart the capital on Tuesday and Friday at 6.30pm, a 48-hour journey that involves a three-hour stop for border formalities.

Mong Cai to Dongxing

Mong Cai is on the Chinese border in the extreme northeastern corner of Vietnam, but is rarely used by foreigners. See p371 for details of hydrofoils that run here.

Renting a boat is *de rigueur*, and costs from 150,000d per hour. The boats can carry about 12 people (but it's the same price if there are just two), and you should allow at least seven hours to take in most sights. Enjoy the ride: it's lovely despite the noisy engines. An optional guide, worth considering, costs US$10 per day. The boat dock is about 2km from park headquarters.

Sleeping & Eating

Not far from the park headquarters are two accommodation options.

Guesthouse (r 165,000d) Rooms in this newer guesthouse are fine, if a bit pricey. There are also comfy air-con two-room cottages (r 275,000d). There's a reasonable restaurant (dishes 10,000d to 30,000d) – you'll need to place your order an hour or so before you want to eat.

Stilt houses (per person 60,000d) It's possible to stay in these stilt houses at Pac Ngoi village on the lakeshore. The park office can help organise this. Food is available at the homestays, which can include fresh fish from the lake, and prices are reasonable.

Take enough cash for your visit – there are no money-exchange facilities, although there are banks in Bac Kan, the provincial capital en route from Hanoi.

Getting There & Around

Ba Be National Park is in Bac Kan Province not far from the borders of Cao Bang and Tuyen Quang Provinces. The lakes are 240km from Hanoi, 61km from Bac Kan and 18km from Cho Ra.

Most visitors to the national park get there by chartered vehicle from Hanoi. The one-way journey from Hanoi takes about six hours; most travellers allow three days and two nights for the trip.

Reaching the park by public transport is possible, but not easy. Take a bus from Hanoi to Phu Thong (50,000d, five hours) via Thai Nguyen and/or Bac Kan, and from there take another bus to Cho Ra (15,000d, one hour). In Cho Ra arrange a motorbike (about 40,000d) to cover the last 18km.

MAI CHAU

☎ 018 / pop 47,500

Mai Chau is one of the closest places to Hanoi where you can visit a hill-tribe village. The area is a beautiful collection of farms and stilt homes spread out over a large valley. Most of the people here are ethnic White Thai, the majority of whom dress the same as Vietnamese. Traditional weaving is practised here and the beautiful results can be purchased direct from the weaver. Guides can be hired for around US$5 for a 7km to 8km walk.

Sleeping

There are two accommodation centres in Mai Chau: the village of Lac and the village of Pom Coong. Pom Coong is slightly more rural and less developed than Lac, so opt for it if you have the choice.

Thai stilt houses (per person 60,000d) Set just a few hundred metres back from the 'main' roadside, both villages offer a rustic experience in these traditional houses. Villagers will sometimes organise traditional song-and-dance performances in the evenings and anyone is free to join in the fun. A mild word of warning about the showers: the doors sometimes have fairly large gaps between the walls and the occasional opportunist guide or driver has taken the chance to observe proceedings. Use your towel to good effect.

Getting There & Around

Mai Chau is 135km from Hanoi and just 5km south of Tong Dau junction on Hwy 6. There's no direct public transport to Mai Chau from Hanoi; however, buses to nearby Hoa Binh (25,000d, two hours) are plentiful. From Hoa Binh there are several scheduled buses to Mai Chau (20,000d, two hours) daily. Usually these stop at Tong Dau junction; a *xe om* from there to Mai Chau proper will cost about 15,000d.

Theoretically, foreigners must pay a 5000d entry fee to Mai Chau; there's a toll booth at the state-run guesthouse on the 'main' road. More often than not, there is nobody there to collect the fee.

LAO CAI

☎ 020 / pop 100,000

One of the gateways to China, Lao Cai lies at the end of the train line on the Chinese border. The border crossing slammed shut during the 1979 war between China and Vietnam and remained closed until 1993. Lao Cai is now a major hub for travellers journeying between Hanoi, Sapa (38km away) and Kūnmíng.

There is a post office next door to the train station, plus an internet café close by. **BIDV bank** (Đ Thuy Hoa) offers currency exchange and an ATM.

VIETNAM

CROSSING INTO CHINA: LAO CAI TO HÉKǑU

The Lao Cai–Hékǒu crossing (open 7am to 5pm) is popular with travellers making their way between northern Vietnam and Yúnnán. China is separated from Vietnam by a bridge over the Red River that pedestrians pay a 10,000d toll to cross. The border is about 3km from Lao Cai train station; the short motorbike journey costs 10,000d.

The train service running directly from Hanoi to Kūnmíng in China has been suspended indefinitely since 2002. However, it's possible to take a train to Lao Cai, cross the border into China, and catch a midmorning or overnight sleeper bus (US$11, 12 hours) from the Chinese border town of Hékǒu to Kūnmíng. For information on crossing this border in the other direction, see p449.

There is no need to stay the night with Sapa just up the mountain, but **Gia Nga Guest House** (☎ 830 459; Pho Moi) offers showers (20,000d with towel and soap) to freshen up after the night train. **Nhat Linh Restaurant** (☎ 835 346; Pho Nguyen Hué) is a reliable little travellers café outside Lao Cai station with friendly staff and an extensive menu.

Getting There & Around

Minibuses to Sapa (25,000d, 1½ hours) leave regularly until late afternoon. Minibuses to Bac Ha (28,000d, two hours) leave several times daily; the last at 1pm.

Lao Cai is 340km from Hanoi (85,000d, nine hours), but most travellers sensibly prefer the train.

When it comes to life on the rails, tickets to Hanoi (10 hours) start at 79,000d for a hard seat (bad choice!) to 223,000d for an air-conditioned soft sleeper, and rise by about 10% at weekends. There are also several companies operating special private carriages with comfortable sleepers, including the affordable **ET Pumpkin** (www.et-pumpkin.com) and the more expensive **Victoria Express** (www.victoriahotels-asia.com). There are two night trains and one day train in either direction.

The border is 3km from Lao Cai train station; a *xe om* will cost about 10,000d.

SAPA

☎ 020 / pop 36,200

The Queen of the Mountains, Sapa sits regally overlooking a beautiful valley, lofty mountains towering over the town on all sides. The premier destination of northwestern Vietnam, Sapa is a French hill station that was built in 1922. The whole area is spectacular and frequently shrouded in mist. Hill-tribe people from surrounding villages don their most colourful costumes and head to the market on Saturday.

Don't forget your winter woollies – Sapa is known for its cold, foggy winters (down to 0°C). The dry season for Sapa is approximately January to the end of June – afternoon rain showers in the mountains are frequent.

Information

Internet access is available in countless hotels and travel offices around town, usually at 5000d per hour.

BIDV (☎ 872 569; Đ Ngu Chi Son; ☼ 7-11.30am & 1.30-4.30pm) Offers an ATM, plus travellers cheques and cash can be exchanged.

Post office (Đ Ham Rong) Post things from Hanoi, as it is much faster.

Sights & Activities

Surrounding Sapa are the Hoang Lien Mountains, including **Fansipan**, which at 3143m is Vietnam's highest peak. The trek from Sapa to the summit and back can take several days. Treks can be arranged at guesthouses and travel agencies around town, including **Mountain View Hotel** (☎ 871 334; 54A Pho Cau May) and **Auberge Hotel** (☎ 871 243; Pho Cau May). **Topas Travel** (☎ 871 331; www.topas-adventure-vietnam.com; 24 Muong Hoa) is a reliable ecotourism operator which employs many guides from the local area. **Handspan Travel** (☎ /fax 872 110; www.handspan.com; 8 Pho Cau May) is a popular place to arrange treks with homestays and mountain biking in the area.

Some of the better-known sights around Sapa include the epic **Tram Ton Pass; Thac Bac** (Silver Falls); and **Cau May** (Cloud Bridge), which spans the Muong Hoa River.

Sleeping

Lotus Hotel (☎ 871 308; 5 Đ Muong Hoa; r US$4-10) Occupying a strategic corner in the centre of town, this place is enticingly good value. Staff are friendly, the rooms are pretty spacious and all have hot water, TV and a fireplace.

our pick **Mountain View Hotel** (☎ 871 334; fax 871 690; r US$8-18) Location, location, location. This hotel has it, with 180-degree views of the valley below. Invest in the US$18 for doubly dramatic views from corner rooms.

Cat Cat View Hotel (☎ 871 946; www.catcathotel .com; Đ Phan Si; r US$10-30; 🖥) Deservedly popular for its friendly and honest service, this is a sprawling complex draped over the hillside. It's worth the climb, as the views are breathtaking.

Auberge Hotel (☎ 871 243; auberge@fpt.vn; 7 Đ Muong Hoa; r US$15-28; 🖥) A Sapa institution, this place has been around as long as the mist over the valley. Wind your way up through the bonsai garden for clear views. Upper-floor rooms have fireplaces and fine furnishings.

Topas Eco Lodge (☎ 871 331; www.topas-eco-lodge .com; bungalows US$25) Out on its own, with a striking setting overlooking the voluptuous valley below. Solar power, wastewater management and minority staff – let's hope this is the first of many such ventures.

Victoria Sapa Hotel (☎ 871 522; www.victoriaho tels-asia.com; r from US$165; 🖥 🖥 🖥) This is a delightful mountain lodge with stylish service

and smart rooms. The hotel has sweeping views from the restaurant, two bars, a heated indoor swimming pool, a fitness centre and a tennis court.

Eating

our pick **Baguette & Chocolat** (Đ Thac Bac; cakes 6000-15,000d) On a cold and misty morning, this place is a welcome retreat for a warm cocoa and delectable cakes. The menu includes some Asian greatest hits or comfort food from home, with pizzas, salads and baguettes.

Nature Bar & Grill (Pho Cau May; meals 15,000-50,000d) The extensive menu includes some authentic Vietnamese cuisine and a few Western exiles for good measure. Speaking of measures, they also shake up a good cocktail.

Gerbera Restaurant (☎ 871 064; Pho Cau May; mains from 20,000d) This restaurant has an unending menu of Vietnamese favourites. From the upstairs panorama room, there are some great views over the mountains beyond.

Gecko (☎ 871 504; Đ Ham Rong; mains around US$5) The original French restaurant in Sapa – not counting the 1920s of course – this is authentically housed in an old colonial-era property.

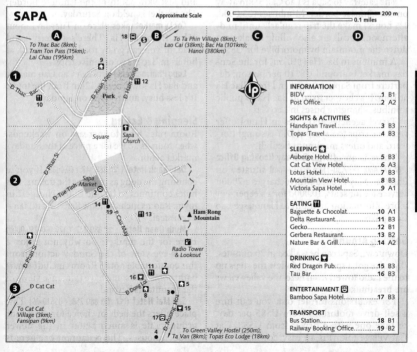

SAPA

Approximate Scale
0 ————— 200 m
0 ————— 0.1 miles

To Thac Bac (8km);
Tram Ton Pass (15km);
Lai Chau (195km)

To Ta Phin Village (8km);
Lao Cai (38km); Bac Ha (101km);
Hanoi (380km)

Đ Thac Bac

Đ Xuan Vien

Đ Ham Rong

Park

Square

Sapa Church

Đ Phan Si

Sapa Market

Đ Tue Tinh

Đ Phan Si

Pho Cau May

Ham Rong Mountain

Radio Tower & Lookout

Đ Cat Cat

Đ Dong Loi

Đ Muong Hoa

To Cat Cat
Village (3km);
Fansipan (9km)

To Green Valley Hostel (250m);
Ta Van (8km); Topas Eco Lodge (18km)

VIETNAM

Delta Restaurant (☎ 871 799; Pho Cau May; mains US$5) The taste of Italy in Sapa, Delta turns out the most authentic pizzas in town. Pastas and home-cooking complete the picture.

Drinking
Red Dragon Pub (☎ 872 085; 23 Pho Muong Hoa) It may look like a quaint tearoom downstairs, but upstairs is a British-style pub that fills up most evenings.

Tau Bar (☎ 871 322; 42 Pho Cau May) As the night warms up, the only place to be is Tau Bar. Claiming to be 'slightly lounge', Tau brings a different kind of cool to the mountains of the north.

Entertainment
Bamboo Sapa Hotel (☎ 871 075; Pho Muong Hoa) Take in free traditional hill-tribe music-and-dance shows here on Friday and Saturday from 8.30pm.

Getting There & Away
Sapa's proximity to the border region makes it a possible first or last stop for travellers crossing between Vietnam and China.

The gateway to Sapa is Lao Cai, 38km away on the Chinese border. Minibuses (25,000d, 1½ hours) make the trip regularly until mid-afternoon. Locals are also willing to take you down the mountain by motorbike for US$5.

A minibus to Bac Ha (110km) for the Sunday market is around US$10 per person; departure from Sapa is at 6am and from Bac Ha at 1pm. It's cheaper to go to Bac Ha by public minibus, changing buses in Lao Cai.

Travel agencies and cafés in Hanoi offer weekend trips to Sapa, but DIY is straightforward and offers maximum flexibility.

There is an official **Railway Booking Office** (☎ 871 480; ◷ 7.30-11am & 1.30-4pm) situated on Pho Cau May in Sapa which charges a 7000d service fee for seats, 10,000d for a sleeper. For more information on trains to Hanoi, see Lao Cai (p376).

Getting Around
Downtown Sapa can be walked in 20 minutes. If you've got a spare hour, follow the steps up to the radio tower; from here, the valley views are breathtaking.

For excursions further out, you can hire a self-drive motorbike from US$5 per day, or take one with a driver from US$8. Cat Cat village (3km) is an easy downhill walk

through green fields and small houses along a winding path.

BAC HA
☎ 020 / pop 70,200
The Sunday market in Bac Ha is the place to stock up on water buffalo, pigs and horses. Once you're all set, you can also browse for bottles of local firewater (made from rice, cassava or corn), or handicrafts made by some of the 10 Montagnard groups living near here – Flower Hmong, Dzao, Giay (Nhang), Han (Hoa), Xa Fang, Lachi, Nung, Phula, Thai and Thulao.

Bac Ha is a less crowded alternative to Sapa, and arriving midweek makes for a relaxing visit. Around 700m above sea level, the highlands around Bac Ha are somewhat warmer than Sapa.

Sights & Activities
Beyond the colourful Sunday Bac Ha market in town, lie several interesting markets nearby, all within about 20km of each other.

Can Cau market, one of Vietnam's most exotic open-air markets, is 20km north of Bac Ha and just 9km south of the Chinese border. The market is held on Saturday.

Coc Ly market takes place on Tuesday, about 35km from Bac Ha. There's a pretty good road, or you can go by road and river; ask at hotels in Bac Ha to organise trips.

Lung Phin market is between Can Cau market and Bac Ha town, about 12km from the town. It's less busy, and is open on Sunday.

Sleeping & Eating
Room rates tend to increase on weekends, when tourists arrive for a piece of the Sunday-market action.

Dai Thanh Hotel (☎ 880 448; r 60,000d) If you're counting the dong as much as the dollars, this hotel continues to be one of the cheapest in town. Rooms include hot water, TV and fan – a real steal.

Minh Quan Hotel (☎ 880 222; r 120,000-150,000d) Here for the market? So why not enjoy a bird's-eye view of the Sunday action from this comfortable hotel? Rooms include smart bathrooms and some have immense views of the mountains beyond.

Sao Mai Hotel (☎/fax 880 288; r US$10-25) This place offers the beds of choice for most tour groups. Life is much better in the newer wooden houses. The restaurant-bar here is one of the leading watering holes in town, plus it holds dance shows for visiting groups.

Cong Phu Restaurant (☎ 880 254; mains 15,000-30,000d) No, the waiters don't look like extras out of a Bruce Lee movie, but they do offer wholesome meals. Just tick the boxes on the photocopy menus and food will arrive.

Getting There & Around

Buses make the 63km trip from Lao Cai to Bac Ha (28,000d, two hours) at 6.30am and 1pm daily. Buses from Bac Ha to Lao Cai leave between 5.30am and 1pm.

Xe om make the Lao Cai–Bac Ha run for US$10, and Sapa–Bac Ha (110km) for around US$15.

Sunday minibus tours from Sapa to Bac Ha cost around US$10, including transport, guide and trekking to a minority village. On the way back to Sapa you can hop off in Lao Cai and catch the night train to Hanoi.

CENTRAL COAST

Home to historical sites, fantastic food and the country's most iconic beach, Central Vietnam deserves to rate as a top priority for travellers. Tourists who want to avoid lengthy bus journeys will find Danang's airport the perfect gateway to a fascinating set of the country's most famous destinations, including three must-see Unesco World Heritage Sites – history-seeped imperial Hué, architecturally impressive Hoi An and the sacred ruins of ancient My Son.

HUÉ

☎ 054 / pop 286,400

Hué is the intellectual, cultural and spiritual heart of Vietnam. Hué served as the political capital from 1802 to 1945 under the 13 emperors of the Nguyen dynasty. Today, Hué's decaying, opulent tombs of the Nguyen emperors and grand, crumbling Citadel comprise a Unesco World Heritage Site. Most of these architectural attractions lie along the northern side of the Song Huong (Perfume River).

For rest and recreation, plus a little refreshment, the south bank is where it's at.

Information

INTERNET ACCESS

There are lots of internet cafés on the tourist strips of Đ Hung Vuong and Đ Le Loi.

MEDICAL SERVICES

Hué Central Hospital (Benh Vien Trung Uong Hué; ☎ 822 325; 16 Đ Le Loi)

MONEY

Industrial & Development Bank (☎ 823 361; 41 Đ Hung Vuong) Same services as Vietcombank, sans ATM.
Vietcombank (54 Đ Hung Vuong) Exchanges travellers cheques, processes cash advances and has an ATM. There's a 24-hour ATM by the Hotel Saigon Morin.

POST

Branch post office (Đ Le Loi) Near the river.
Main post office (14 Đ Ly Thuong Kiet) Has postal and telephone services.

TRAVEL AGENCIES

Café on Thu Wheels (☎ 832 241; minhthuhue@yahoo .com; 10/2 Đ Nguyen Tri Phuong) Immensely popular cycling and motorbiking tours around Hué with a large dose of laughs.
Mandarin Café (☎ 821 281; mandarin@dng.vnn.vn; 3 Đ Hung Vuong) Watched over by the eagle eyes of photographer Mr Cu, this place is great for information, transport and tours.
Sinh Café (☎ 823 309; www.sinhcafevn.com; 7 Đ Nguyen Tri Phuong) Open-tour buses and tickets to Laos.

Sights & Activities

CITADEL

One of Vietnam's decaying treasures is Hué's Citadel (Kinh Thanh), the erstwhile imperial city on the northern bank of the Song Huong. Though it was heavily bombed by the Americans, and much of it now used for agriculture, its scope and beauty still impress.

Construction of the moated Citadel, by Emperor Gia Long, began in 1804. The emperor's official functions were carried out in the **Imperial Enclosure** (Dai Noi, or Hoang Thanh; admission 55,000d; ⏰ 6.30am-5.30pm), a 'citadel within the Citadel'. Inside the 6m-high, 2.5km-long wall is a surreal world of deserted gardens and ceremonial halls.

Within the Imperial Enclosure is the **Forbidden Purple City** (Tu Cam Thanh), which was reserved for the private life of the emperor. The only servants allowed inside were eunuchs, who posed no threat to the royal concubines. Nowadays, all are welcome.

ROYAL TOMBS

Set like royal crowns on the banks of the Song Huong, the **Tombs of the Nguyen Dynasty** (⏰ 8-11.30am & 1.30-5.30pm) are 2km to 16km south of

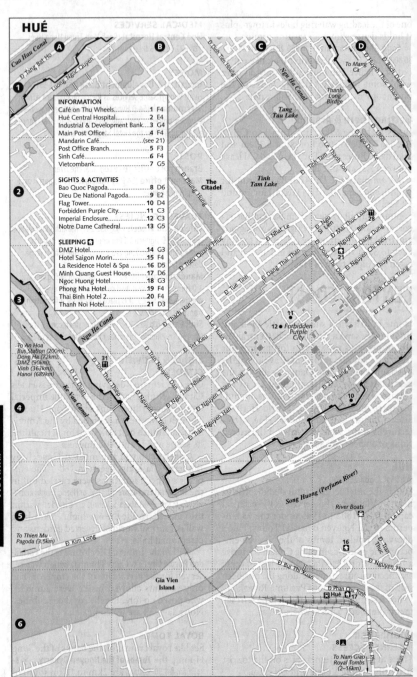

HUÉ

VIETNAM

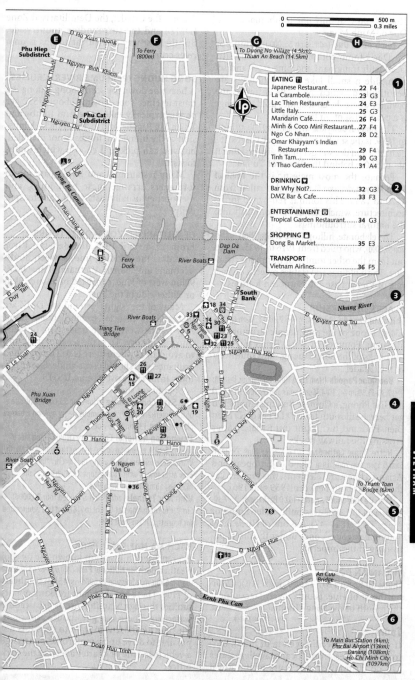

VIETNAM

Hué. If you visit only one tomb, make it Tu Duc or Minh Mang.

Tomb of Tu Duc (admission 55,000d), Emperor Tu Duc's tomb complex, is a majestic site, laced with frangipani and pine trees and set alongside a small lake. The buildings are beautifully designed. Near the entrance, the pavilion where the concubines used to lounge is a peaceful spot on the water.

The **Tomb of Dong Khanh** (admission 22,000d), built in 1889, is the smallest of the Royal Tombs. It's beautiful and doesn't get many visitors; find it about 500m behind the Tomb of Tu Duc.

Perhaps the most majestic is the **Tomb of Minh Mang** (admission 55,000d), who ruled from 1820 to 1840. This tomb is renowned for its architecture, which blends harmoniously into the natural surroundings.

The elaborate, hilltop **Tomb of Khai Dinh** (admission 55,000d), who ruled from 1916 to 1925, stands out from the other tombs for its unique structure. The buildings and statues reflect a distinct mix of Vietnamese and European features.

PLACES OF WORSHIP

Thien Mu Pagoda (Đ Le Duan; 7.30-11.30am & 1.30-5.30pm) is one of the most iconic structures in Vietnam. Founded in 1601, Thien Mu is on the banks of the Song Huong, 4km southwest of the Citadel.

Bao Quoc Pagoda (Ham Long Hill, Phuong Duc District; 7.30-11.30am & 1.30-4.30pm) was founded in 1670 by Giac Phong, a Chinese Buddhist monk. To get here, head south from Đ Le Loi on Đ Dien Bien Phu and turn right immediately after crossing the railway tracks.

Notre Dame Cathedral (80 Đ Nguyen Hue; mass 5am & 5pm, Sun 7pm) is a blend of European and Asian architectural elements; this modern cathedral was built between 1959 and 1962.

Dieu De National Pagoda (102 Đ Bach Dang; 7.30-11.30am & 1.30-4.30pm) was built under Emperor Thieu Tri (r 1841–47). It is one of Hué's three 'national pagodas', once under the direct patronage of the emperor.

THUAN AN BEACH

Thuan An Beach (Bai Tam Thuan An), 15km northeast of Hué, is on a lovely lagoon near the mouth of the Song Huong.

Tours

If you have a specific agenda in mind, motorbike guides from local travellers cafés can do customised day tours of the Royal Tombs, the Citadel, the Demilitarised Zone (DMZ) and the surrounding countryside. But the best way to visit the tombs is on a river cruise.

SONG HUONG (PERFUME RIVER) CRUISES

A boat ride down the scenic Song Huong is a must in Hué. Tours costing about US$2 per person typically take in several tombs and Thien Mu Pagoda, and include lunch. Admission to the individual tombs is not included, but you can pick and choose which tombs to visit.

Many restaurants and hotels catering to foreigners arrange these boat tours, and the journey usually lasts from 8am to 2pm daily.

DEMILITARISED ZONE (DMZ) TOURS

From 1954 until 1975, the Ben Hai River served as the dividing line between South Vietnam and North Vietnam. The DMZ, 90km west of Hué, consisted of an area 5km on either side of the line.

Many of the 'sights' around the DMZ are places where historical events happened, and may not be worthwhile unless you're really into war history. To make sense of it all, and to avoid areas where there is still unexploded ordnance, you should take a guide. Group day tours from Hué cost around US$15.

Significant sites:

Khe Sanh Combat Base (admission 25,000d) The site of the American War's most famous siege, now on a barren plateau about 130km from Hué.

Truong Son National Cemetery (Nghia Trang Liet Si Truong Son) A memorial to the tens of thousands of North Vietnamese soldiers killed along the Ho Chi Minh Trail. Row after row of white tombstones stretch across the hillsides, about 105km from Hué.

Vinh Moc Tunnels (admission & guided tour 20,000d) Similar to the tunnels at Cu Chi (p418), but less adulterated for tourists; 110km from Hué.

BACH MA NATIONAL PARK

A French-era hill station known for its cool weather, **Bach Ma National Park** (054-871330; www.bachma.vnn.vn; admission 10,500d) is 45km southeast of Hué. There are abundant trekking opportunities through beautiful forests to cascading waterfalls. There is a guesthouse and camp site here for those who want to stay. It is not possible to drive up by motorbike, so arrange a vehicle in Hué or charter a jeep at the park office.

Festivals

Festival Hué is a biennial cultural festival, to be next held in June 2008. It lasts about a week and features traditional dance and music from Vietnam and other participating countries. Hotels are jammed during this time, so plan ahead.

Sleeping

Phong Nha Hotel (☎ 827 729; phongnha_hotel@yahoo .com; 10/10 Đ Nguyen Tri Phuong; r US$6-15; ✷ 🖳) The facilities in this spotless minihotel differ from room to room, but what don't change are the good reports we hear about the friendly staff.

DMZ Hotel (☎ 826 831; 1A Đ Pham Ngu Lao; s & d US$9-14; ✷ 🖳) From the people behind the popular tourist bar, this brand-new minihotel has a range of comfortable rooms of different sizes and facilities.

Minh Quang Guest House (☎ 824 152; 16 Đ Phan Chu Trinh; r US$10; ✷) Located near the train station, a long way from the tourist traps, this friendly family offers new, clean rooms with TVs, fridges and bathtubs.

Thai Binh Hotel 2 (☎ 827 561; www.thaibinhhotel -hue.com; 2 Đ Luong The Vinh; r US$12-15; ✷ 🖳) Excellent value for money, the attractive bedrooms have mother-of-pearl inlaid furniture, while the bathrooms have tubs.

Thanh Noi Hotel (Imperial Garden, ☎ 522 478; thanh noi@dng.vnn.vn; 57 Đ Dang Dung; r US$18-45; ✷ 🖳 ☎) Located in a quiet street in the heart of the Citadel, near the Imperial Enclosure, the residential surroundings offer a very different view of Hué. The peaceful tree-shaded compound includes a fair-sized swimming pool.

Ngoc Huong Hotel (☎ 830 111; www.ngochuongho tels.com; 8-10 Đ Chu Van An; r US$30-40, ste US$80; ✷ 🖳) In a popular part of town, this is a smart, friendly hotel. The large rooms include all the creature comforts, plus there's a Jacuzzi and sauna for winding down.

Hotel Saigon Morin (☎ 523 526; www.morinhotel .com.vn; 30 Đ Le Loi; r US$50-500; ✷ 🖳 ☎) Occupying a prime corner opposite the Trang Tien Bridge, this grand hotel exudes historical charm. Along with the four-star comforts of its guest rooms, the hotel has restaurants, bars and a gourd-shaped swimming pool.

La Residence Hotel & Spa (☎ 837 475; www.la -residence-hue.com; 5 Đ Le Loi; r US$95-135, ste US$150-165; ✷ 🖳 ☎) Housed in the former French Governor's residence, this chic boutique hotel has lovely river views, lush gardens and beautiful rooms.

Eating

We have famed fussy-eater Emperor Tu Duc to thank for the culinary variety of Hué. While the elaborate decoration of imperial cuisine may seem excessive, the degustation-style banquets are sublime – well worth the indulgence. The best restaurants aren't necessarily easy to find, and many tourists sadly settle for the Western-oriented eateries of the budget ghettoes.

SOUTH BANK

Mandarin Café (☎ 821 281; mandarin@dng.vnn.vn; 3 Đ Hung Vuong; dishes 5000-40,000d; ☯ breakfast, lunch & dinner) A magnet for travellers, the cheerful owner, Mr Cu, speaks English and French and serves big dollops of travel advice along with *pho*, BLTs, salads and pancakes.

Minh & Coco Mini Restaurant (☎ 821 822; 1 Đ Hung Vuong; mains 10,000-30,000d; ☯ lunch & dinner) Run by two lively sisters, this humble joint is a fun place to get an inexpensive feed.

Tinh Tam (☎ 823 572; 12 Đ Chu Van An; mains from 10,000d; ☯ lunch & dinner) This family place serves excellent and inexpensive vegetarian food. Dishes made with mock meat, such as 'deer' with black pepper and lemon grass, are delish but the noodle soups are also worth trying.

Japanese Restaurant (☎ 834 457; 34 Đ Tran Cao Van; dishes US$1-8; ☯ 11am-2pm & 6.30-9.30pm Mon-Sat) There are no prizes for guessing the cuisine on offer. What's more surprising is that's it's all for a good cause, namely helping street children. The food is excellent and the service exceptionally polite.

La Carambole (☎ 810 491; 19 Đ Pham Ngu Lao; mains 25,000-90,000d; ☯ breakfast, lunch & dinner) Extravagantly decorated, this place has a good range of French dishes. There are also Vietnamese dishes and pizza to keep everyone happy, plus a healthy wine list.

Little Italy (☎ 826 928; littleitalyhue@gmail.com; 2A Đ Vo Thi Sau; mains around 40,000d; ☯ lunch & dinner) Where else do you think you'll find Hué's best Italian food? Pizzas are respectable, pastas are perfectly *al dente*.

A RIGHT ROYAL FOOD CRITIC

Emperor Tu Duc (1848–83) expected 50 dishes to be prepared by 50 cooks to be served by 50 servants at every meal. And his tea had to be made from the dew that accumulated on leaves overnight. Not too demanding then!

Omar Khayyam's Indian Restaurant (☎ 821 616; 10 Đ Nguyen Tri Phuong; curries 30,000-60,000d; ☽ lunch & dinner) This vegetarian-friendly curry house is low on atmosphere, but high on flavour.

NORTH BANK

Lac Thien Restaurant (6 Đ Dinh Tien Hoang; ☽ lunch & dinner) Be deceived not by neighbouring copycats – this is the original deaf-mute restaurant serving up a variety of Hué specialities.

Ngo Co Nhan (☎ 513 399; 47 Đ Nguyen Bieu; dishes 15,000-35,000d; ☽ lunch & dinner) Sitting on stilts in a quiet Citadel street, this open-sided dining platform serves excellent grilled seafood and crates of beer to a local clientele.

Y Thao Garden (☎ 523 018; 3 Đ Thach Han; set-course meal US$8; ☽ lunch & dinner) Tucked in a quiet corner of the Citadel, a seven-course set menu is served among the huge palms on the garden terrace of a traditional Hué home.

Drinking

In the evenings, travellers gather over Huda beers in the cafés along Đ Hung Vuong. If you're looking to party and play a bit of pool, try these spots.

DMZ Bar & Cafe (44 Đ Le Loi) Long the leading late-night spot in town, the beer flows into the night, the tunes match the mood and there is a popular pool table in the middle of things.

Bar Why Not? (☎ 824 793; 21 Đ Vo Thi Sau) Loud rock music, cheap cocktails and a pool table make for a winning formula. Why not, indeed.

Entertainment

Tropical Garden Restaurant (☎ 847 143; 27 Đ Chu Van An; dishes 22,000-85,000d; ☽ from 6.30pm) This popular place offers romantic dining in a lush, leafy garden setting. It's the best place in Hué to

catch a traditional music performance (from 7pm nightly).

Shopping

Hué produces the finest conical hats in Vietnam. The city's speciality is 'poem hats', which, when held up to the light, reveal shadowy scenes of daily life. It's also home to one of the largest and most beautiful selections of rice-paper and silk paintings available in Vietnam, but the prices quoted are usually inflated to about four times the real price.

Dong Ba Market (Đ Tran Hung Dao; ☽ 6.30am-8pm) On the north bank of the Song Huong a few hundred metres north of Trang Tien Bridge, this is Hué's largest market, where anything and everything can be bought.

Getting There & Away

AIR

The main office of **Vietnam Airlines** (☎ 824 709; 23 Đ Nguyen Van Cu; ☽ 7.15-11.15am & 1.30-4.30pm Mon-Sat) handles reservations. Several flights a day connect Hué to both Hanoi and HCMC.

Phu Bai airport is 13km south of the centre and takes about 25 minutes by car. Taxi fares are around US$8, although share taxis cost as little as US$2 – ask at hotels. Vietnam Airlines runs a shuttle (20,000d) from its office to the airport, a couple of hours before flight times.

BUS

The main bus station is 4km to the southeast on the continuation of Đ Hung Vuong (it becomes Đ An Duong Vuong and Đ An Thuy Vuong). The first main stop south is Danang (40,000d, three hours, six daily). **An Hoa bus station** (Hwy 1A), northwest of the Citadel, serves northern destinations, including Dong Ha (25,000d, 1½ hours).

CROSSING INTO LAOS: LAO BAO TO DANSAVANH

The **Lao Bao border** (☽ 7-11am & 1-6pm) is the most popular and least problematic land crossing between Laos and Vietnam. **Sepon Travel** (☎ 855 289; www.sepon.com.vn; 189 Đ Le Duan) in Dong Ha has buses to Savannakhet (US$12, 7½ hours), leaving Dong Ha at 8am every second day and returning the next day. These buses also pass through Hué (US$14 to US$15, add 1½ hours), and can be booked from the Mandarin and Sinh Cafés (see p379).

Travelling independently is possible but hefty overcharging will likely make it more expensive in the long run. Catch a bus to Lao Bao and then a *xe om* (motorbike taxi) to the border (10,000d). Once in Laos, there is only one public bus a day direct to Savannakhet, which leaves when full. *Sawngthaew* (pick-up trucks) leave fairly regularly to Sepon, from where you can get a bus or further *sawngthaew* to Savannakhet. For information on crossing this border in the other direction, see p324.

Hué is also a regular stop on the open-tour bus routes. Mandarin and Sinh Cafés (see p379) can arrange bookings for the bus to Savanna-khet, Laos (see the boxed text, opposite).

TRAIN
Hué train station (Ga Hué; ☎ 822 175; 2 Đ Bui Thi Xuan; ✆ ticket office 7.30am-5pm) is on the south bank of the river, at the southwestern end of Đ Le Loi.

Getting Around
Bicycles (US$1), motorbikes (US$5) and cars (US$25 per day, with driver) can be hired from hotels all over town. **Co Do Taxi** (☎ 830 830) and **Mai Linh** (☎ 898 989) both have air-con vehicles with meters. Cyclos and *xe om* will find you when you need them.

DANANG
☎ 0511 / pop 1.1 million

While most tourists neglect Vietnam's fourth-largest city in favour of nearby Hué and Hoi An, Danang has considerable charm in its own right. The economic powerhouse of central Vietnam, it combines the buzz of a bigger city with beautiful beaches and fine dining. A lot of money has recently been poured into tree-lined boulevards, bridges and beachside resorts.

Information
INTERNET ACCESS
There are internet cafés scattered all over Danang, including several by the river on Đ Bach Dang.

MEDICAL SERVICES
Danang Family Medical Practice (☎ 582 700; 50-52 Đ Nguyen Van Linh) One of Vietnam's most trusted foreign-owned clinics comes to Danang.
Hospital C (Benh Vien C; ☎ 822 480; 35 Đ Hai Phong) The most advanced medical facility in Danang.

MONEY
Vietcombank (140 Đ Le Loi) The only place in town to exchange travellers cheques, it has an ATM.

POST
Danang domestic & international post offices (Đ Bach Dang)

TRAVEL AGENCIES
Dana Tours (☎ 825 653; www.vietnamwelcomes.com; 76 Đ Hung Vuong; ✆ Mon-Sat) Offers car hire, boat trips, visa extensions and treks in nearby Ba Na or Bach Ma.

Sights & Activities
Danang's jewel is the famed **Museum of Cham Sculpture** (Bao Tang Cham; cnr Đ Trung Nu Vuong & Đ Bach Dang; admission 30,000d; ✆ 7am-5pm). This small, breezy building houses the finest collection of Cham sculpture to be found anywhere on earth. These intricately carved sandstone pieces come from Cham sites all over Vietnam, and it's worth the detour to Danang just for this.

Guides hang out at the museum's entrance; should you hire one, agree on a fee beforehand.

Sleeping
Minh Travel Hotel (☎ 812 661; mtjraymond@yahoo .ca; 105 Đ Tran Phu; r US$3-9; ✖) This tiny place is developing a reputation among superbudget travellers for the friendliness and honesty of its owners and its rock-bottom prices.

Bao Ngoc Hotel (☎ 817 711; baongochotel@dng.vnn .vn; 48 Đ Phan Chu Trinh; r US$15-16; ✖ ▢) With an inexplicable kiwi logo and excessively floral sheets, this inner-city hotel offers good-value clean rooms.

Binh Duong (☎ 821 930; fax 827 666; 32-34 Đ Tran Phu; r US$15-25; ✖ ▢) Popular with longer-term stayers, the friendly staff at Binh Duong speaks excellent English and some of the ample rooms have large corner bathtubs.

Bamboo Green Harbourside (☎ 822 722; bamboo green2@dng.vnn.vn; 177 Đ Tran Phu; r US$25-30, ste US$40; ✖ ▢) In a good location opposite Danang Cathedral and near the river, many of the rooms have good views and breakfast is included in the prices.

If you'd like easy access to nearby China Beach, consider one of the following places.
Hoa's Place (☎ 969 216; My An Beach; hoasplace@hotmail.com; r US$6) Small-scale, low-key and laid-back, Hoa and his wife ensure their home is your home. Take the second turning on the left past Furama heading south.
Furama Resort Danang (☎ 847 888; www.furamavi etnam.com; 68 Đ Ho Xuan Huong, My An Beach; s US$207-299, d US$230-322, ste US$575-690; ✖ ▢ ✦) For many years, this was Vietnam's only luxury resort. Perched on a private slice of China Beach, it features a diving facility, golf driving range, gym and two pools.

Eating
Com Chay Chua Tinh Hoi (574 Đ Ong Ich Khiem; dishes from 3000d) Known for the best vegetarian food in town; it's just inside the entrance gate to the Phap Lam Pagoda.

lonelyplanet.com

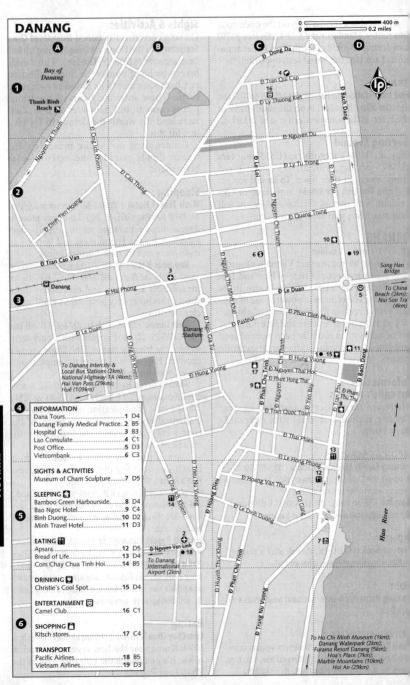

DANANG

0 — 400 m
0 — 0.2 miles

INFORMATION		
Dana Tours	1	D4
Danang Family Medical Practice	2	B5
Hospital C	3	B3
Lao Consulate	4	C1
Post Office	5	D3
Vietcombank	6	C3

SIGHTS & ACTIVITIES		
Museum of Cham Sculpture	7	D5

SLEEPING		
Bamboo Green Harbourside	8	D4
Bao Ngoc Hotel	9	C4
Binh Duong	10	D2
Minh Travel Hotel	11	D3

EATING		
Apsara	12	D5
Bread of Life	13	D4
Com Chay Chua Tinh Hoi	14	B5

DRINKING		
Christie's Cool Spot	15	D4

ENTERTAINMENT		
Camel Club	16	C1

SHOPPING		
Kitsch stores	17	C4

TRANSPORT		
Pacific Airlines	18	B5
Vietnam Airlines	19	D3

Bay of Danang

Thanh Binh Beach

Song Han Bridge

To China Beach (2km); Nui Son Tra (4km)

Danang Stadium

Han River

To Danang Intercity & Local Bus Stations (2km); National Highway 1A (4km); Hai Van Pass (29km); Huế (109km)

To Danang International Airport (2km)

To Ho Chi Minh Museum (1km); Danang Waterpark (2km); Furama Resort Danang (5km); Hoa's Place (7km); Marble Mountains (10km); Hoi An (29km)

VIETNAM

Bread of Life (☎ 893 456; 215 Đ Tran Phu; cakes 10,000d, breakfast 20,000d; ☯ breakfast & lunch Mon-Sat) A great spot for a Western-style breakfast or a coffee and cake, this little café employs deaf staff and gives a percentage of profits to charity.

Apsara (☎ 561 409; www.apsara-danang.com; 222 Đ Tran Phu; meals US$15; ☯ lunch & dinner) The best dining experience in Danang, Apsara has excellent food, great service, a good wine list and an atmospheric setting – with Cham-influenced décor and live traditional music.

Drinking & Entertainment

Christie's Cool Spot (☎ 824 040; 112 Đ Tran Phu) The downstairs bar is the place to meet US war veterans and join their debates about whether the Iraq war is even more pointless than the American War in Vietnam. Christie's also serves Western comfort food.

Camel Club (☎ 887 462; 16 Đ Ly Thuong Kiet; admission 20,000d; ☯ 7pm-1am) This is where Danang's beautiful people come for heavy beats.

Getting There & Away

Danang international airport has connections to Bangkok, Hong Kong and Singapore. **Vietnam Airlines** (☎ 821 130; www.vietnamairlines .com; 35 Đ Tran Phu) has an extensive domestic schedule serving Danang. **Pacific Airlines** (☎ 886 799; www.pacificairlines.com.vn; 6 Đ Le Loi) also has a booking office situated in town. Both **Airport Taxi** (☎ 272 727) and **VN Taxis** (☎ 525 252) provide modern vehicles with air-con and meters. It costs about 20,000d for the trip to the airport.

The **Danang intercity bus station** (Đ Dien Bien Phu; ☯ 7-11am & 1-5pm) is 3km from the city centre. Buses run to Hanoi (87,000d, 16 hours), Hué (22,000d, three hours) and Quy Nhon (65,000d, six hours).

To get to Hoi An, your best bet is to hire a car (around US$10), from a local travel agency, or a friendly neighbourhood *xe om* (around US$6). A stop at the Marble Mountains will cost a little extra. Travel agencies can also arrange passage on open-tour minibuses (US$2) running between Hoi An and Danang.

Danang train station (Ga Da Nang) is about 1.5km from the city centre on Đ Hai Phong at Đ Hoang Hoa Tham. Danang is served by all *Reunification Express* trains. The train ride to Hué is one of the best in the country – worth taking as an excursion in itself.

AROUND DANANG

About 10km south of Danang are the immense **Marble Mountains** (admission 15,000d; ☯ 7am-5pm), consisting of five marble outcrops that were once islands. With natural caves sheltering small Hindu and Buddhist sanctuaries, a picturesque pagoda and scenic landings with stunning views of the ocean and surrounding countryside, it's well worth the climb.

China Beach (Bai Non Nuoc), once an R'n'R hang-out for US soldiers during the American War, is actually a series of beaches stretching 30km north and south of the Marble Mountains. Nearest to central Danang, My Khe Beach is well touristed and accordingly has beachside restaurants and roving vendors. Opposite the Marble Mountains is Non Nuoc Beach, and in between the two are countless spots to explore or spread your beach towel.

For surfers, China Beach's break gets a decent swell from mid-September to December. The best time for swimming is from May to July, when the sea is at its calmest. There's a mean undertow at China Beach, worst in the winter, so take care.

Buses and minibuses running between Danang and Hoi An can drop you off at the entrance to the Marble Mountains and China Beach, and it's easy to find onward transport in either location.

HOI AN

☎ 0510 / pop 75,800

Step back in time and discover the living museum that is Hoi An. Set on the Thu Bon River, Hoi An – or Faifo, as early Western traders knew it – was an international trading port as far back as the 17th century. Influences from Chinese, Japanese and European cultures are well preserved in local architecture and art. Roaming the narrow lanes at night, it's easy to imagine how it might have looked 150 years ago.

Hoi An's charms aren't limited to its exquisite architecture alone; the nearby beach and Cham ruins make excellent expeditions out of town, plus Hoi An is a gastronomic treat.

Information

EMERGENCY

Hoi An Hospital (☎ 861 364; 10 Đ Tran Hung Dao) Serious problems should be addressed in Danang.

Hoi An police station (☎ 861 204; 84 Đ Hoang Dieu)

HOI AN

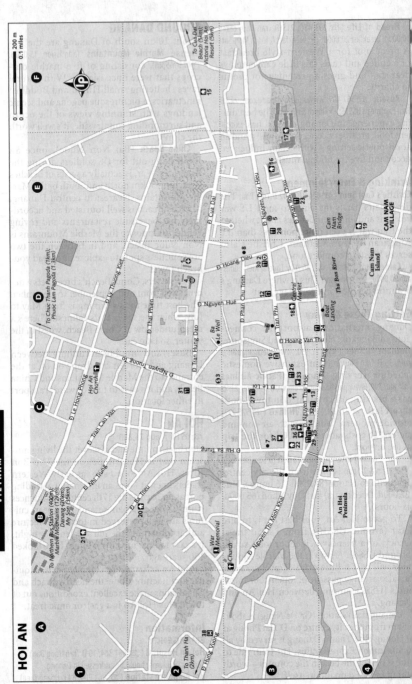

VIETNAM

To Northern Bus Station (400m);
Marble Mountains (12km);
Danang (30km);
My Son (36km)

To Thanh Ha (2km)

To Cua Dai Beach (5km); Victoria Hoi An Resort (5km)

To Chuc Thanh Pagoda (1km); Phuoc Lam Pagoda (1.3km)

To Thanh Ha (2km)

Cam Nam Bridge

CAM NAM VILLAGE

Cam Nam Island

Thu Bon River

An Hoi Peninsula

Boat Landing

Central Market

Hoi An Church

War Memorial

Church

Church

Ba Le Well

INFORMATION			
Hoi An Hospital	**1** D2	Mango Rooms	**29** C3
Hoi An Police Station	**2** D3	Mermaid Restaurant	**30** D3
Incombank	**3** C2	Omar Khayyam's Indian	
Main Post Office	**4** D2	Restaurant	**31** C2
Min's Computer	**5** E3	Restaurant Café 96	**32** C3

SLEEPING 🏠
- Green Field Hotel ... **15** F2
- Ha An Hotel ... **16** E3
- Life Resort Hoi An ... **17** E3
- Minh A Ancient Lodging House ... **18** D3
- Pho Hoi Riverside Resort ... **19** E4
- Thien Nga Hotel ... **20** B2
- Thien Thanh Hotel ... **21** B1
- Vinh Hung 1 Hotel ... **22** C3

SIGHTS & ACTIVITIES
- Assembly Hall of the Fujian Chinese Congregation ... **6** D3
- Hoi An Old Town Booth A ... **7** C3
- Hoi An Old Town Booth B ... **8** D3
- Japanese Covered Bridge ... **9** B3
- Museum of Trading Ceramics ... **10** C3
- Old House at 103 Tran Phu ... **11** C3
- Quan Cong Temple ... **12** D3
- Rainbow Divers ... **13** C3
- Tan Ky House ... **14** C3

EATING 🍴
- Brothers Café ... **23** E3
- Café des Amis ... **24** D4
- Cargo Club ... **25** C3
- Dac San Hoi An ... **26** C3
- Good Morning Vietnam ... **27** C3
- Green Moss ... **28** E3

DRINKING 🍷
- Before & Now ... **33** C3
- Club Salsa ... **34** B4
- Lounge Bar ... **35** C3
- Tam Tam Cafe & Bar ... **36** C3
- Treat's Café ... **37** C3

SHOPPING 🛍
- Reaching Out ... (see 25)

TRANSPORT
- Hoi An Bus Station ... **38** A2

INTERNET ACCESS

Min's Computer (☎ 914 323; 125 Đ Nguyen Duy Hieu; per hr 4000d) Access is slow throughout Hoi An, but this is as good as any.

INTERNET RESOURCES

Hoi An Old Town (www.hoianworldheritage.org) A handy little website on the ins and outs of Hoi An.

MONEY

Incombank (☎ 861 261; 4 Đ Hoang Dieu & 9 Đ Le Loi) These branches change cash and travellers cheques, make credit-card cash advances and have ATMs.

POST

Main post office (48 Đ Tran Hung Dao) At the corner of Đ Ngo Gia Tu.

Dangers & Annoyances

For the most part, Hoi An is very safe at any hour. However, late-night bag-snatchings in the isolated, unlit market are on the rise. By night, avoid walking around this area on your own. There have also been (extremely rare) reports of women being followed to their hotels and assaulted. Lone women should have a friend walk home with them at night.

Sights

HOI AN OLD TOWN

Having been named a Unesco World Heritage Site, **Hoi An Old Town** (admission 75,000d) now charges an admission fee, which goes towards funding the preservation of the town's historic architecture. Buying the ticket gives you a choice of heritage sites to visit, including an 'intangible culture' option, such as a traditional musical concert or stage play. You can also visit these sites, paying as you go, without buying the ticket.

This list of sites is by no means comprehensive; buying a ticket at the Hoi An Old Town booths will also get you an introductory guide to all the sites.

Quan Cong Temple (24 Đ Tran Phu) is dedicated to Quan Cong and has some wonderful papier-mâché and gilt statues, as well as carp-shaped rain spouts on the roof surrounding the courtyard. Shoes should be removed before mounting the platform in front of Quan Cong.

Tan Ky House (☎ 861 474; 101 Đ Nguyen Thai Hoc; ☉ 8am-noon & 2-4.30pm) is a lovingly preserved house from the 19th century, which once belonged to a Vietnamese merchant. Japanese and Chinese influences are evidenced throughout the architecture. The house is a private home, and the owner – whose family has lived here for seven generations – speaks French and English.

The **Japanese Covered Bridge** (Cau Nhat Ban/Lai Vien Kieu; Đ Tran Phu & Đ Nguyen Thi Minh Khai) was constructed in 1593. The bridge has a roof for shelter and a small temple built into its northern side. According to one story, the bridge's construction began in the year of the monkey and finished in the year of the dog; thus one entrance is guarded by monkeys, the other by dogs (neither pair will confirm or deny this story).

The **Assembly Hall of the Fujian Chinese Congregation** (☉ 7.30am-noon & 2-5.30pm) was founded for community meetings; the hall later became a temple to worship Thien Hau, a deity born in Fujian Province in China. Check out the elaborate mural, the unhealthy red or green skin of the statuary, and the replica of a Chinese boat.

VIETNAM

Showcasing a collection of blue-and-white ceramics of the Dai Viet period, the **Museum of Trading Ceramics** (80 Đ Tran Phu; ☺ 8am-noon & 2-4.30pm) is in a simply restored house; it's delightful. In particular, notice the great ceramic mosaic that's set above the pond in the inner courtyard.

The **Old House at 103 Tran Phu** (103 Đ Tran Phu; ☺ 8am-noon & 2-4.30pm) is picturesque with its wooden front and shutters; inside is an eclectic shop where women make silk lanterns.

Chuc Thanh Pagoda (Khu Vuc 7, Tan An; ☺ 8am-6pm) was founded in 1454, making it the oldest pagoda in Hoi An. Among the antique ritual objects still in use are a stone gong, which is two centuries old, and a carp-shaped wooden gong, said to be even older. To get here, go all the way to the end of Đ Nguyen Truong To and turn left. Follow the sandy path for about 500m.

ARTS & CRAFTS VILLAGES

All those neat fake antiques sold in Hoi An's shops are manufactured in nearby villages. Cross the An Hoi footbridge to reach the An Hoi Peninsula, noted for its boat factory and mat-weaving factories. South of the peninsula is Cam Kim Island, where you see many people engaged in the woodcarving and boat-building industries (take a boat from the Đ Hoang Van Thu dock). Cross the Cam Nam bridge to Cam Nam village, a lovely spot also noted for arts and crafts.

Activities

DIVING

Rainbow Divers (☎ 911 123; www.divevietnam.com; 98 Đ Le Loi) has an office in the Old Town, where you can book dives for Cu Lao Cham Marine Park.

Courses

Hoi An is foodie heaven, and budding gourmands who want to take a step further into Vietnamese cuisine will find ample opportunity here. Many of the popular eateries offer cooking classes, and the best part is that you then get to sit down and enjoy the fruits of your labour.

Red Bridge Cooking School (☎ 933 222; www.visit hoian.com) runs a course that starts with a trip to the market, and is followed by a cruise down the river to its relaxing retreat about 4km from Hoi An. The class costs 235,000d per person; it starts at 8.45am and finishes at 1pm.

More informal classes can be found at Restaurant Café 96 (per person 50,000d), Green Moss (choose off the menu and pay a US$2 supplement) and Café des Amis (US$20); see opposite.

Festivals & Events

Hoi An Legendary Night takes place on the 14th day (full moon) of every lunar month from 5.30pm to 10pm. These festive evenings feature traditional food, song and dance, and games along the lantern-lit streets in the town centre.

Sleeping

Little Hoi An is awash with accommodation options after a building boom over the past few years.

Minh A Ancient Lodging House (☎ 861 368; 2 Đ Nguyen Thai Hoc; r US$8-12; 🔀) Brimming with character, this splendid 180-year-old traditional wooden home is a cross between a B&B and a museum. Book ahead, as there are only three rooms.

Thien Nga Hotel (☎ 916 330; thiennga_hotel@pmail .vnn.vn; 52 Đ Ba Trieu; r US$10-20; 🔀 🖭 🖳) An old favourite that keeps getting better, this little place is terrific value, offering clean, comfortable rooms, a swimming pool and free breakfast.

Thien Thanh Hotel (☎ 916 545; www.bluesky-hoian .com; 16 Đ Ba Trieu; r US$15-35; 🔀 🖭 🖳) Most of the rooms have breezy balconies at the back with views over the rice paddies at this smart, laid-back and friendly hotel. Plus wi-fi.

Green Field Hotel (Dong Xanh Hotel; ☎ 863 484; www .greenfieldhotel.com; 423 Đ Cua Dai; dm US$5, r US$15-40; 🔀 🖭 🖳) Painted a lurid rice-paddy green, the rooms here are comfortable and perks include a free 'happy hour' cocktail, free wi-fi, a pool table and a swimming pool.

Vinh Hung 1 Hotel (☎ 861 621; quanghuy.ha@dng .vnn.vn; 143 Đ Tran Phu; r US$15-45; 🔀 🖭) Set in a classic Chinese trading house, the atmospheric rooms are decorated with antiques and beautiful canopy beds. Michael Caine used two of these rooms while filming scenes in *The Quiet American*. If this hotel's full, there are several other branches with swimming pools.

Pho Hoi Riverside Resort (☎ 862 628; www.phohoiri versidehoian.com; T1, Cam Nam Village; r US$15-65, bungalow US$60-70; 🔀 🖭 🖳) This sprawling place on the south bank of the river has the best views in town. The cheaper rooms are in the old block behind, but the majority have a picturesque setting.

Ha An Hotel (☎ 863 126; tohuong@fpt.vn; 6-8 Đ Phan Boi Chau; r US$30-50; 🔀) A French Quarter hotel, with a dose of decorative flair. This strip of buildings is built in Hoi An style (one French, one Chinese and so on), all set in a lush garden.

Victoria Hoi An Resort (☎ 0510-927 040; www.vic toriahotels-asia.com; r US$121-202, ste US$242; 🔀 🖵 🕿) Sitting on a huge slice of beach, this resort boasts all the stylish facilities you'd expect for the price, including a large pool and free wi-fi.

Life Resort Hoi An (☎ 914 555; www.life-resorts.com; 1 Đ Pham Hong Thai; r US$159, ste US$182-308; 🔀 🖵 🕿) The most luxurious option in central Hoi An, Life Resort has a prime French Quarter riverside frontage, lush gardens and a stunning infinity pool.

Eating

Hoi An's restaurants burst with gastronomic delights, three of which are town specialities. Be sure to try *cao lau*, doughy flat noodles mixed with croutons, bean sprouts and greens, topped with pork slices and served in a savoury broth. The real deal is only available in Hoi An, as the water for *cao lau* noodles must come from Ba Le well. The other two culinary specialities are fried wonton, and 'white rose', a petite steamed dumpling stuffed with shrimp.

Dac San Hoi An (☎ 861 533; 89 Đ Tran Phu; dishes 7000-60,000d) True to its name (translating as Hoi An specialities), this place does great *banh xeo* (Vietnamese rice-flour crepe), *cao lau* and 'white rose'. The upstairs balcony has a view of one of Hoi An's nicest streets.

Green Moss (☎ 863 728; 155 Đ Nguyen Duy Hieu; dishes 10,000-30,000d) Housed in a lovely French-colonial-era house, Green Moss serves a tasty mix of Asian dishes with plenty of vegetarian options.

Restaurant Café 96 (☎ 910 441; 96 Đ Bach Dang; dishes 10,000-35,000d) This riverside restaurant has the perfectly decrepit look Western interior designers so crave. The food is sublime – try the grilled fish wrapped in banana leaf.

Mermaid Restaurant (☎ 861 527; 2 Đ Tran Phu; dishes 18,000-68,000d) One of the original Hoi An eateries, this is still a favourite for its fried spring rolls with noodles and herbs, and its excellent 'white rose'.

Cargo Club (☎ 910 489; 107 Đ Nguyen Thai Hoc; dishes 18,000-70,000d) Choose from mouth-watering pastries downstairs and distinguished dining

upstairs, with a balcony terrace overlooking the river. The menu's an eclectic mix of French, Italian, Vietnamese and Thai.

Café des Amis (☎ 861 616; 52 Đ Bach Dang; 5-course set menu 90,000d; ⏱ dinner) This little riverside eatery has earned a loyal following over the past decade. There's no menu. Five-course dinner is whatever the chef, Mr Kim, feels like cooking that day. It's always delicious and there's a vegetarian option.

Mango Rooms (☎ 910 839; 111 Đ Nguyen Thai Hoc; mains 85,000-145,000d) This restaurant's reputation for lively modern Vietnamese cuisine has spread far and wide – with even Mick Jagger seeking culinary satisfaction here. Tropical fruits and fresh herbs feature prominently in the food, as well as in the inventive cocktails.

Brothers Café (☎ 914 150; 27-29 Đ Phan Boi Chau; dishes US$6-12) Looking like a film set, in one of the finest French-colonial buildings in town, the attention to designer detail is perfect. Drop by for a drink in the gorgeous riverside garden.

Other international spots:

Omar Khayyam's Indian Restaurant (☎ 864 538; 24 Đ Tran Hung Dao; dishes 30,000-80,000d) The place for curry connoisseurs, with plenty of vegetarian options.

Good Morning Vietnam (☎ 910 227; 34 Đ Le Loi; mains 38,000-105,000d) Italian owners and chefs, they serve the best pizzas and pastas in town.

Drinking

Tam Tam Cafe & Bar (☎ 862 212; 110 Đ Nguyen Thai Hoc) The mainstay of nightlife in Hoi An is this thoughtfully restored tea warehouse. Hoi An's best margaritas are made here, which you can enjoy over a game of pool or an intimate chat on the balcony.

Lounge Bar (☎ 910 480; 102 Đ Nguyen Thai Hoc) Stylish silk-cushioned seating and a cool upstairs terrace accent this converted ancient house.

Before & Now (☎ 910 599; 51 Đ Le Loi) This swanky bar wouldn't be out of place in London, particularly given the Britpop playlist. The walls are plastered with pop-art portraits of everyone from Marx to Marilyn Monroe.

Treat's Café (☎ 861 125; 158 Đ Tran Phu) The backpacker bar of old Hoi An, this place is regularly full to bursting. The oh-so-happy happy hour between 4pm and 9pm includes two-for-one spirits and bargain beer.

Club Salsa (Pho Nguyen Phuc Chu) As much of Hoi An goes to sleep, Club Salsa awakens, *the* late-night bar in town. Cool cocktails and top tunes ensure this place always draws a lively crowd. An alternative sunrise awaits.

Shopping

Before you even get your bearings in Hoi An, you may find yourself strong-armed with sweetness by a young girl taking you to her 'auntie's' tailor shop, despite periodic clampdowns on touts. Tailor-made clothing is one of Hoi An's best trades, and there are more than 200 tailor shops in town that can whip up a custom-tailored ao dai (traditional Vietnamese tunic and trousers). Other hot items include handmade shoes and silk lanterns.

Hoi An also boasts a growing array of interesting art galleries, especially on the west side of the Japanese Covered Bridge.

Reaching Out (☎ 862 460; 103 Đ Nguyen Thai Hoc; ☻ 7.30am-9.30pm) This is a great place to spend your dong. It's a fair-trade gift shop with profits going towards assisting disabled artisans.

Getting There & Away

The main **Hoi An bus station** (☎ 861 284; 96 Đ Hung Vuong) is 1km west of the centre of town. Buses from here go to Danang (8000d, one hour) and other points north.

A regular stop on the open-bus route, it's easy to pick up a service to or from Hué (US$3, four hours) or Nha Trang (US$6 to US$8, 11 to 12 hours).

The nearest airport and train station are both in Danang.

Getting Around

Metered taxis are available to get to the beach. Motorbike drivers wait to solicit business outside all the tourist hotels. Prices without/with a driver are around US$6/10 per day. Many hotels also offer bicycles for hire for around US$1 per day.

AROUND HOI AN
Cua Dai Beach

This beautiful stretch of sand runs all the way to Danang where it's marketed as the legendary China Beach. Palm-thatch huts give shelter and roaming vendors sell drinks and fresh seafood. Swimming is best between April and October. Weekends can get a little crowded.

To get here, take Đ Cua Dai east out of Hoi An for about 5km.

My Son

The ancient Cham city of **My Son** (☎ 0501-731 309; admission 60,000d; ☻ 6.30am-4pm) is one of the most stunning sights in the area, and another Unesco World Heritage Site. The ruins are nestled in a lush valley surrounded by hills and the massive Hon Quap (Cat's Tooth Mountain). My Son became a religious centre under King Bhadravarman in the late 4th century and was occupied until the 13th century – the longest period of development of any city in the Mekong region.

The ruins are a scenic 35km trip southwest of Hoi An. Day tours to My Son can be arranged in Hoi An for about US$3, not including admission, and there are also trips back to Hoi An by boat. If you want to visit on your own, hire a motorbike, xe om or car. Get here early (preferably predawn) to beat the tour groups, or later in the afternoon.

SOUTH-CENTRAL COAST

Undeniably, the beach is the big attraction in this part of Vietnam. Nha Trang and Mui Ne have become the favoured destinations for those whose idea of paradise is reclining by the water, cocktail in hand, contemplating whether to have a massage or a pedicure before hitting the bars later.

With most visitors not venturing outside of these two main enclaves, the rest of the beautiful coast is wonderfully overlooked – leaving empty beaches to be explored by the more independently minded.

NHA TRANG
☎ 058 / pop 315,200

Nha Trang has a split personality. One half is a bustling Vietnamese city humming with commerce but blessed with access to a beautiful beach. The other is a Western resort town encompassing several blocks of hotels, tourist shops, bars and international restaurants. Entering this sheltered enclave you could be anywhere in the world, if it weren't for the constant hassles from xe om drivers, many of whom seem to moonlight as pimps and dealers.

Nha Trang offers plenty to keep tourists occupied – from island-hopping boat trips and scuba diving, to mud baths and historic sites. But undeniably, the main attraction for most visitors is lounging around on deckchairs at

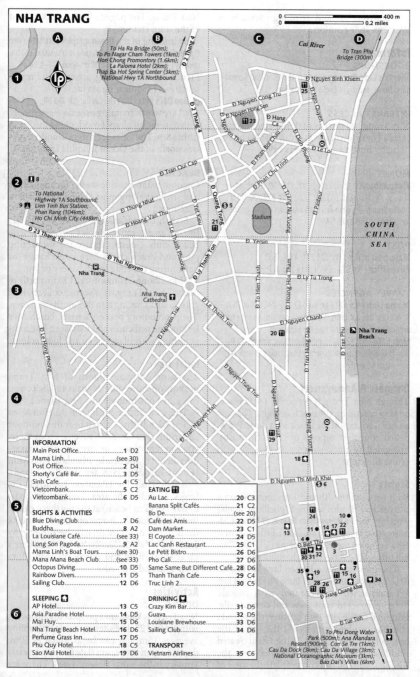

NHA TRANG

0 — 400 m
0 — 0.2 miles

To Ha Ra Bridge (50m);
To Po Nagar Cham Towers (1km);
Hon Chong Promontory (1.6km);
La Paloma Hotel (2km);
Thap Ba Hot Spring Center (3km);
National Hwy 1A Northbound

Cai River

To Tran Phu
Bridge (300m)

To National
Highway 1A Southbound;
Lien Tinh Bus Station;
Phan Rang (104km);
Ho Chi Minh City (448km)

SOUTH
CHINA
SEA

Nha Trang

Nha Trang
Cathedral

Nha Trang
Beach

To Phu Dong Water
Park (500m); Ana Mandara
Resort (900m); Con Se Tre (1km);
Cau Da Dock (3km); Cau Da Village (3km);
National Oceanographic Museum (3km);
Bao Dai's Villas (6km)

VIETNAM

INFORMATION
Main Post Office	1 D2
Mama Linh	(see 30)
Post Office	2 D4
Shorty's Café Bar	3 D5
Sinh Cafe	4 C5
Vietcombank	5 C2
Vietcombank	6 D5

SIGHTS & ACTIVITIES
Blue Diving Club	7 D6
Buddha	8 A2
La Louisiane Café	(see 33)
Long Son Pagoda	9 A2
Mama Linh's Boat Tours	(see 30)
Mana Mana Beach Club	(see 33)
Octopus Diving	10 D5
Rainbow Divers	11 D5
Sailing Club	12 D6

SLEEPING
AP Hotel	13 C5
Asia Paradise Hotel	14 C5
Mai Huy	15 D6
Nha Trang Beach Hotel	16 D6
Perfume Grass Inn	17 D5
Phu Quy Hotel	18 C5
Sao Mai Hotel	19 D6

EATING
Au Lac	20 C3
Banana Split Cafés	21 C2
Bo De	(see 20)
Café des Amis	22 D5
Dam Market	23 C1
El Coyote	24 D5
Lac Canh Restaurant	25 C1
Le Petit Bistro	26 D6
Pho Cali	27 D6
Same Same But Different Café	28 D6
Thanh Thanh Cafe	29 C4
Truc Linh 2	30 C5

DRINKING
Crazy Kim Bar	31 D5
Guava	32 D5
Louisiane Brewhouse	33 D6
Sailing Club	34 D6

TRANSPORT
Vietnam Airlines	35 C6

a beachfront bar and drinking cocktails in Western-style comfort.

Information

BOOKSHOPS

Shorty's Café Bar (☎ 524 057; 1E Đ Biet Thu) Second-hand books, mostly in English, plus a bar.

INTERNET ACCESS

Nha Trang has dozens of designated internet cafés all over town, and you can also get online in many hotels and travellers cafés.

MONEY

Vietcombank Đ Hung Vuong (☎ 524 500; 5 Đ Hung Vuong; ☿ Mon-Fri); Đ Quang Trung (☎ 822 720; 17 Đ Quang Trung; ☿ Mon-Fri) Both branches exchange travellers cheques and have ATMs.

POST

Main post office (☎ 821 271; 4 Đ Le Loi)
Post office (☎ 823 866; 50 Đ Le Thanh Ton)

TRAVEL AGENCIES

Mama Linh (☎ 522 844; fax 522 845; 23C Đ Biet Thu) Known for its boat tours, Mama Linh can also arrange trips around the province and into the highlands.
Sinh Café (☎ 524 329; sinhcafént@dng.vnn.vn; 10 Đ Biet Thu) Offers bargain basement local tours as well as open-tour buses.

Dangers & Annoyances

Though Nha Trang is generally a safe place, be very careful on the beach at night. The best advice is to stay off the beach after dark. We've heard countless reports of rip-offs, mostly instigated by quick-witted working girls who cruise the coast.

Sights

Built between the 7th and 12th centuries on a site used by Hindus for *linga* (phallic symbols) worship, the **Po Nagar Cham Towers** (Đ 2 Thang 4; admission 4500d; ☿ 6am-6pm) are 2km north of central Nha Trang on the left bank of the Cai River. The hill offers blue views of the harbour below.

The impressively adorned **Long Son Pagoda** (Chua Tinh Hoi Khanh Hoa; Đ 23 Thang 10; admission free; ☿ sunrise-sunset) is decorated with mosaic dragons covered with glass and ceramic tile. Founded in the late 19th century, the pagoda still has resident monks. At the top of the hill, behind the pagoda, is the Giant Seated Buddha visible from town. Seated near the Buddha, you too can contemplate the view of

Nha Trang. The pagoda is about 500m west of the train station.

Swimming in the **Oceanographic Institute** (Vien Nghiem Cuu Bien; ☎ 590 036; adult/child 10,000/5000d, English-speaking guide 30,000d; ☿ 7.30am-noon & 1-4.30pm), a French-colonial building, are colourful representatives of squirming sea life.

Bao Dai's Villas (Biet Thu Cau Da; ☎ 590 148; ☿ 8am-10pm) are worth roaming on a slow afternoon, with a scenic lunch spot overlooking the South China Sea. The villas are several hundred metres north of the Oceanographic Institute.

BEACHES

Coconut palms provide shelter for sunbathers and strollers along most of Nha Trang's 6km beachfront.

Stylish **La Louisiane Café** (☎ 812 948; 29 Đ Tran Phu; ☿ 7am-midnight) resembles a Western-style beach club. Guests can use the swimming pool and beach chairs here in exchange for patronising the restaurant, bakery or bar.

Hon Chong Promontory, 1.8km north of central Nha Trang, is a scenic collection of granite rocks jutting into the South China Sea. The promontory borders a rustic beach cove lacking the pedicures and massages, but compensating with island views and local colour.

ISLANDS

The nine outlying islands of Nha Trang beckon offshore. For as little as US$6, you can join a day tour visiting four islands.

There's a working fish farm on Hon Mieu (Mieu Island) that's also a beautiful outdoor aquarium (Ho Ca Tri Nguyen). From there, you can rent canoes, or hire someone to paddle you out to the nearby islands of Hon Mun (Ebony Island) or Hon Yen (Swallow Island).

Idyllic Hon Tre (Bamboo Island) is the largest island in the area. You can get boats to Bai Tru (Tru Beach) at the northern end of the island, but it's also recommended to take the day trips or overnight trips here offered by **Con Se Tre** (☎ /fax 527 522; 100/16 Đ Tran Phu). There's great snorkelling and diving off Hon Mun, Hon Tam and Hon Mot.

Activities

DIVING

Nha Trang is Vietnam's premier diving locale, with around 25 dive sites in the area. Visibility averages 15m, but can be as much as 30m, depending on the season (late October to early January is the worst time of year). There are

SAFETY GUIDELINES FOR DIVING

Before embarking on a scuba-diving, skin-diving or snorkelling trip, carefully consider the following points to ensure a safe and enjoyable experience:

- Get a current diving certification card from a recognised scuba diving instructional agency (if scuba diving).
- Be sure you are healthy and feel comfortable diving.
- Obtain reliable information about physical and environmental conditions at the dive site (eg from a reputable local dive operation).
- Be aware of local laws, regulations and etiquette about marine life and the environment.
- Dive only at sites within your realm of experience; if available, engage the services of a competent, professionally trained dive instructor or dive master.
- Be aware that underwater conditions vary significantly from one region, or even site, to another. Seasonal changes can significantly alter any site and dive conditions. These differences influence the way divers dress for a dive and what diving techniques they use.
- Ask about the environmental characteristics that can affect your diving and how local, trained divers deal with these considerations.

some good drop-offs and small underwater caves to explore, and an amazing variety of corals. Among the colourful reef fish, stingrays are occasionally spotted.

A full-day outing, including two dives and lunch, costs between US$40 and US$70. Dive operators also offer a range of courses, including a 'Discover Diving' programme for uncertified, first-time divers. Consider the following outfits, but shop around:

Blue Diving Club (☎ 527 034; www.vietnam-diving .com; 66 Đ Tran Phu) Owned and operated by French and British divers.

Octopus Diving (☎ 521 629; 62 Đ Tran Phu)

Sailing Club Diving (☎ 522 788; www.sailingclub vietnam.com; 72-74 Đ Tran Phu) This is the same operation, but a separate office, as Octopus Diving.

Rainbow Divers (☎ 524 351; www.divevietnam.com; 90A Hung Vuong) Run by Brit Jeremy Stein, Rainbow Divers sets the standard for diving in Vietnam.

WATER-BASED FUN

Right on the beach front, **Phu Dong Water Park** (Đ Tran Phu; admission 20,000đ; �9am-5pm Sat & Sun) has slides, shallow pools and fountains if salt water is not your thing.

If salt water *is* your thing, check out **Mana Mana Beach Club** (☎ 524 362; www.manamana.com; Louisiane Brewhouse, 29 Đ Tran Phu). Offering windsurfing, sea kayaking, wakeboarding and sailing lessons, Mana Mana uses state-of-the-art equipment.

Perhaps hot muddy water might be your thing? **Thap Ba Hot Springs** (☎ 834 939; 25 Ngoc Son; �8am-8pm) is a fun experiences. To get here, follow the signpost on the second road to the left past the Po Nagar Cham Towers for 2.5km.

Tours

Mama Linh's boats (☎ 522 844; 23C Đ Biet Thu) are the hottest ticket for island-hopping, guzzling fruit wine at the impromptu 'floating bar', and deck-side dancing.

Sleeping

Mai Huy (☎ 527 553; 7H Đ Hung Vuong; r US$5-7; 🅿) Pronounced 'may we' (or 'mais oui!' if you're French) this new family-run minihotel is hidden down a small laneway. At US$5 for a room with a fan, fridge, satellite TV and private bathroom, it's a bargain.

Sao Mai Hotel (☎ 526 412; saomaiht@dng.vnn.vn; 99 Đ Nguyen Thien Thuat; r US$5-8; 🅿) With its pretty rooftop terrace adorned with potted plants, this friendly older place is a solid budget option.

Phu Quy Hotel (☎ 521 609; phuquyhotel@dng.vnn .vn; 54 Đ Hung Vuong; r US$6-20; 🅿 💻) Pronounced Foo-Wee, the highlight of this minihotel is its rooftop terrace – it has awesome views and is great for dining, sunning or hanging around in a hammock. All the rooms are quite comfortable, and for US$10 expect a balcony, bathtub and sea view.

Perfume Grass Inn (☎ 524 286; www.perfume-grass .com; 4A Đ Biet Thu; r US$10-25; 🅿 💻) The best rooms at this inviting inn have wooden floors,

VIETNAM

wood-panelled walls, and bathtubs. Even the US$10 fan rooms have great sea views. Plus free internet access and breakfast.

AP Hotel (☎ 527 544; fax 527 268; 34 Đ Nguyen Thien Thuat; r 200,000-400,000d; ❄ ▯) This wonderful new minihotel has had an expensive fit-out above and beyond the reasonable rates. Pricier rooms have king-size beds, huge bathtubs and balconies with sea glimpses.

Nha Trang Beach Hotel (☎ 524 469; www.nhatrang beachhotel.com.vn; 4 Đ Tran Quang Khai; r US$13-23; ❄ ▯) This multistorey hotel has a cool granite lobby and friendly, efficient staff. Despite its central location, it's refreshingly quiet in the upper floors, where most of the rooms have great views and internet access.

La Paloma Hotel (☎ 831 216; datle@dng.vnn.vn; 1 Đ Hon Chong; r US$15-35; ❄ ▯) This is a commendable little family-run oasis on the northern outskirts of town. Fronting the hotel is a palm garden, where meals (included in the price) are served family-style. Plus free jeep rides into town.

Bao Dai's Villas (☎ 590 148; www.vngold.com/nt /baodai; Cau Da Village; r US$25-80; ❄ ▯) There can't be too many places where the former lodgings of an emperor fall into the midrange category. The only possible reason to stay here is historical interest, or the peace and quiet afforded by the parklike setting.

Asia Paradise Hotel (☎ 524 686; www.asiaparadiseho tel.com.vn; 6 Đ Biet Thu; r US$46-78, ste US$99-124; ❄ ▯ ▮) This new business-style hotel has elegant décor, comfy beds and friendly switched-on staff and is scrupulously clean. Extras include a small rooftop pool, gym and spa centre.

Ana Mandara Resort (☎ 522 522; www.evasonre sorts.com; Đ Tran Phu; villa US$236-438, ste US$450-513; ❄ ▯ ▮) This gorgeous complex of open timber-roofed beach villas is hands-down Nha Trang's classiest accommodation offering. The luxuries here include two excellent restaurants, two swimming pools and a serene spa area.

Eating

Central Nha Trang teems with dining choices too numerous to list here. As always, taking a meal in the market is a culinary adventure, and Dam market on Đ Nguyen Hong Son in the north end of town has lots of local food stalls, including *com chay* (vegetarian food).

Ice-cream fiends will want to make for Nha Trang's own original-versus-copycat rivals, the Banana Split Cafés along the roundabout

where Đ Quang Trung meets Đ Ly Thanh Ton. Banana splits cost 10,000d.

VIETNAMESE

Café des Amis (☎ 521 009; 2D Đ Biet Thu; dishes 7000-40,000d) A popular cheapie focusing on seafood and vegetarian fare, the walls are covered with interesting works by Vietnamese painters.

Pho Cali (☎ 525 885; 7G Đ Hung Vuong; dishes 15,000-25,000d) Meals at this clean, modern eatery are absolutely delicious, and the set menu – comprising soup, rice and a hot pot – is outrageously good value at 20,000d.

Lac Canh Restaurant (☎ 821 391; 44 Đ Nguyen Binh Khiem; dishes 10,000-85,000d) A Nha Trang institution, Lac Canh is one of the busiest local eateries in town. Here beef, squid, giant prawns, lobsters and the like are grilled at your table.

Truc Linh 2 (☎ 521 089; 21 Đ Biet Thu; dishes 15,000-83,000d) With three restaurants dotted around the neighbourhood, popular Truc Linh offers a festive garden setting for diners. In the evening you can choose fresh seafood from a table in front of the restaurant and enjoy a beer while you wait.

Two places serving excellent vegetarian food of the I-can't-believe-it's-not-meat variety are **Au Lac** (☎ 813 946; 28C Đ Hoang Hoa Tham; meals 10,000d) and **Bo De** (☎ 810 116; 28A Đ Hoang Hoa Tham; meals 10,000d), neighbouring restaurants near the corner of Đ Nguyen Chanh.

INTERNATIONAL

Same Same But Different Café (☎ 524 079; 111 Đ Nguyen Thien Thuat; mains 12,000-50,000d; ☯ breakfast, lunch & dinner) A good travellers café, this place serves Vietnamese and Western food at reasonable prices.

Thanh Thanh Cafe (☎ 824 413; 10 Đ Nguyen Thien Thuat; meals 15,000-75,000d) Another travellers café, serving wood-fired pizza, Vietnamese dishes and other standard traveller fare, Thanh Thanh has a pretty terracotta patio surrounded by plants.

El Coyote (☎ 526 320; 76 Đ Hung Vuong; mains 40,000-103,000d) Authentic Tex-Mex food including delicious fajitas served on a sizzling plate. The owner is more fusion than the menu, a mixture of French, Vietnamese, Lao and Cheyenne Indian.

Le Petit Bistro (☎ 527 201; 26D Đ Tran Quang Khai; mains 45,000-180,000d; ☯ lunch & dinner) The best French restaurant in town, Le Petit Bistro has a fantastic wine selection, as well as sourcing quality cheese and *charcuterie* (sausage).

Drinking

Sailing Club (☎ 826 528; 72-74 Đ Tran Phu) The hippest place in town, this open-air beach bar is where most of the party crowd ends up at some point in the evening. Thumping music, wild dancing, flowing shots, pool sharks and general mayhem.

Louisiane Brewhouse (☎ 521 948; 29 Đ Tran Phu; 🍺) This upmarket restaurant cum microbrewery has a swimming pool and beautiful beachfront setting that make this one of the best places to laze the day away.

Crazy Kim Bar (☎ 523 072; crazykimbar.com; 19 Đ Biet Thu) This great party spot is also home base for the commendable 'Hands off the Kids!' campaign, which works to prevent paedophilia. Sign up at the bar if you're interested in volunteering to teach English.

Guava (☎ 524 140; www.clubnhatrang.com; 17 Đ Biet Thu) Cool, clean-lined and atmospheric, this lounge bar is superstylish but never seems particularly busy. Outside is a patio shaded with trees; inside, pillow-laden sofas and a pool table.

Getting There & Away

AIR

Vietnam Airlines (☎ 826 768; www.vietnamairlines.com; 91 Đ Nguyen Thien Thuat) has flights out of Cam Ranh airport (35km south of Nha Trang) to HCMC, Hanoi and Danang. To get to the airport, catch a shuttle bus (25,000d, 40 minutes) from the old Nha Trang airport terminal, two hours before your flight. A taxi should cost about 150,000d, although agree on the price beforehand.

BUS

Minibuses from HCMC to Nha Trang (11 to 12 hours) depart from Mien Dong bus station in HCMC. **Lien Tinh bus station** (Ben Xe Lien Tinh; ☎ 822 192; Đ 23 Thang 10), Nha Trang's main intercity bus terminal, is 500m west of the train station.

Open-tour buses to and from HCMC, Dalat and Hoi An are easy to book at travellers cafés and hotels.

TRAIN

The **Nha Trang train station** (Ga Nha Trang; ☎ 822 113; 🕙 ticket office 7am-2pm) is conveniently located in the middle of town.

Getting Around

Cyclos and *xe oms* can get you to the old airport or the train station for about US$1. Many hotels have bicycle rentals for around US$1 per day.

Nha Trang Taxi (☎ 824 000) and **Khanh Hoa Taxi** (☎ 810 810) have air-con cars with meters.

MUI NE
☎ 062

Far from the madding crowd of HCMC, yet only three hours away, lies an 11km-stretch of beach outside the fishing village of Mui Ne. In the last few years, this out-of-the-way resort strip has quickly transformed from an isolated stretch of beautiful white sand to one long row of resorts.

Mui Ne is developing a reputation as the action capital of the coast. There's no scuba diving, but when Nha Trang and Hoi An get the rains, Mui Ne gets the waves. Surf's up from August to December. Kite-surfing is also very popular.

Orientation & Information

Local addresses are designated by a kilometre mark measuring the distance along Rte 706 from Hwy 1 in Phan Thiet. To mix things up a bit, Rte 706 is also known as Đ Nguyen Dinh Chieu.

A great resource for information on Mui Ne is www.muinebeach.net. Small restaurants along the road offer internet access.

Hanh Café/Ha Phuong Tourist (☎ 847 597; 125A Đ Nguyen Dinh Chieu) Local day tours, open-tour bookings, fast food and internet access.

Incombank (68 Đ Nguyen Dinh Chieu; 🕙 Sun-Fri) At Tropico Resort, this branch can exchange currency and travellers cheques.

Sinh Café (☎ 847 542; 144 Đ Nguyen Dinh Chieu) Operates out of its Mui Ne Resort, booking open-tour buses and offering credit-card cash advances.

Sights

You'll smell Mui Ne as soon as you arrive, and you'll see the pungent source in clay vats along the palm-lined road. This is *nuoc mam* (fish sauce), for which Mui Ne is famous. But Mui Ne is even better known for its enormous sand dunes. Be sure to try the sand-sledding. The Fairy Spring (Suoi Tien) is a stream that flows through a patch of the dunes and rock formations near town. Also nearby are a red stream, market and fishing village. Four-wheel-drive tours of the dunes are popular.

On Rte 706 heading towards Phan Thiet, the small **Po Shanu Cham tower** (Km 5; admission 2000d; 7.30-11.30am & 1.30-4.30pm) occupies a hill with sweeping views of Phan Thiet, the river mouth filled with boats and a cemetery filled with candylike tombstones.

Further afield lies Vietnam's largest reclining Buddha (49m) at Ta Cu Pagoda. Most visitors take the cable car (55,000d return) to the base of the pagoda, from where the Buddha is a short, but steep, hike. Ta Cu Mountain is just off Hwy 1, 28km south of Phan Thiet.

Activities

Jibes (847 405; www.windsurf-vietnam.com; 90 Đ Nguyen Dinh Chieu; 7.30am-6pm) is surfer's heaven, offering lessons and renting state-of-the-art gear such as sailboards, surfboards, kite-surfers and kayaks. Insurance costs extra.

Airwaves (847 440; airwaveskitesurfing.com; 24 Đ Nguyen Dinh Chieu), based at the Sailing Club, is another outfit offering kite-surfing, windsurfing and sailing lessons and equipment rentals.

Sleeping

Kim Ngan Guesthouse (847 046; kimnganvilla@yahoo .com; Km 13; r US$10-15;) The bungalows have tiled balconies jutting over the water, making this friendly family-run place a good choice.

Hiep Hoa Resort (847 262; hiephoatourism@yahoo .net; 80 Đ Nguyen Dinh Chieu; r US$12-16;) This is a great spot with a lovely garden and clean attractive rooms – albeit with few frills such as TVs, fridges and phones.

Sunshine Beach (847 788; www.sunshine-beach .com; 82 Đ Nguyen Dinh Chieu; r US$15-30;) Friendly and welcoming, this hotel has a large open lawn area. The rooms are immaculately clean and comfortable. Free wi-fi.

Indochina Dreams (847 271; fax 08-8322 174; 74 Đ Nguyen Dinh Chieu; r US$20-25;) This dreamy place is on a small scale, but the big stone bungalows are very comfortable. Rooms are cool and well appointed, and there's a good restaurant in front, serving the complimentary breakfast.

Little Mui Ne Cottages (847 550; www.littlemuine .com; 10B Huynh Thuc Khang; r US$50-85;) These comfortable cottages are set in spacious

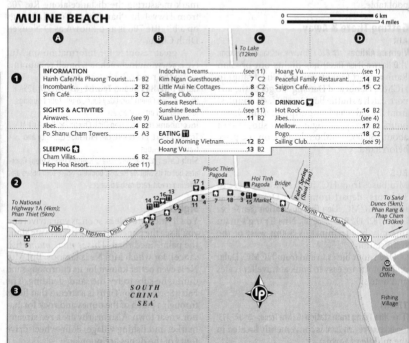

MUI NE BEACH

0 — 6 km
0 — 4 miles

| | | To Lake (12km) | |
| A | B | C | D |

1

INFORMATION		
Hanh Cafe/Ha Phuong Tourist.....**1** B2	Indochina Dreams...................(see 11)	Hoang Vu.................................(see 1)
Incombank.....................................**2** B2	Kim Ngan Guesthouse.................**7** C2	Peaceful Family Restaurant.......**14** B2
Sinh Café.......................................**3** C2	Little Mui Ne Cottages.................**8** C2	Saigon Café...............................**15** C2
	Sailing Club....................................**9** B2	
SIGHTS & ACTIVITIES	Sunsea Resort..............................**10** B2	DRINKING
Airwaves.......................................(see 9)	Sunshine Beach.........................(see 11)	Hot Rock...................................**16** B2
Jibes...**4** B2	Xuan Uyen...................................**11** B2	Jibes...(see 4)
Po Shanu Cham Towers.............**5** A3		Mellow......................................**17** B2
	EATING	Pogo...**18** C2
SLEEPING	Good Morning Vietnam.............**12** B2	Sailing Club..............................(see 9)
Cham Villas...................................**6** B2	Hoang Vu.....................................**13** B2	
Hiep Hoa Resort........................(see 11)		

2

To National Highway 1A (4km); Phan Thiet (5km)

706 Đ Nguyen Dinh Chieu

Phuoc Thien Pagoda

Hoi Tinh Pagoda Bridge

Market

Đ Huynh Thuc Khang

707

To Sand Dunes (5km); Phan Rang & Thap Cham (130km)

Post Office

3

SOUTH CHINA SEA

Fishing Village

VIETNAM

OFF THE BEATEN TRACK: BEAUTIFUL BEACHES

It may be Mui Ne and Nha Trang that are the beach babes of the region, but there are many pristine stretches of sand along this coast, some that see very few tourists. Here's our very own top five from north to south:

- **My Khe** Located near the site of the infamous My Lai Massacre, My Khe (not to be confused with the other My Khe Beach near Danang) is a superb beach, with fine white sand and clear water.

- **Quy Nhon** This major transit town between Hoi An and Nha Trang is fast earning a name as an up-and-coming beach destination. Live cheap at **Barbara's Backpackers** (☎ 056-892 921; nzbarb@yahoo.com; dm 40,000d, r US$6-10) or live it up at **Life Resort** (☎ 056-840 132; www.life-re sorts.com; r US$152-175).

- **Whale Island** Off the coast to the north of Nha Trang, Whale Island is a tiny speck on the map, home to the lovely and secluded **Whale Island Resort** (www.whaleislandresort.com) and a great spot for diving.

- **Doc Let** Within commuting distance of busy Nha Trang, the beachfront is long and wide, with chalk-white sand and shallow water.

- **Ninh Van Bay** This place doesn't really exist – except in an alternate reality populated by European royalty, film stars and the otherwise rich and secretive. Home to the **Evason Hide-away** (www.sixsenses.com).

---

grounds and the pool is big enough to do laps. Free internet access and bicycles.

Sailing Club (☎ 847 440; www.sailingclubvietnam .com; 24 Đ Nguyen Dinh Chieu; r US$55, bungalows US$70-100; ❁ ▯ ▩) Popular for its panoramic bar and restaurant overlooking the sea, the Sailing Club has spacious rooms in a lush garden setting.

Cham Villas (☎ 741 234; www.chamvillas.com; 32 Đ Nguyen Dinh Chieu; r US$95-120; ❁ ▯ ▩) Set in a beautiful tropical garden with an exquisite swimming pool, this luxury boutique resort only has 14 villas, so book ahead.

Other recommendations:

Xuan Uyen (☎ 847 476; 78 Đ Nguyen Dinh Chieu; r US$6-12; ▯) Big on atmosphere, these cute bamboo bungalow rooms are simple and clean.

Sunsea Resort (☎ 847 700; www.sunsearesort-muine .com; 50 Đ Nguyen Dinh Chieu; r US$50-70; ❁ ▯ ▩) The traditionally inspired bungalows are dotted around a beautiful garden and pool.

Eating

Saigon Café (☎ 847 091; 168-170 Đ Nguyen Dinh Chieu; dishes 12,000-45,000d) Great Vietnamese barbe-cue food in a basic setting, with profundities written on the walls in beautiful calligraphy – although we suspect 'It is still very good if you can learn by your mistake to like butter' may have lost something in translation.

Hoang Vu (☎ 847 525; Km 12.2 & 121 Đ Nguyen Dinh Chieu; dishes 25,000-52,000d) Like most successful businesses in Vietnam this one's cloned itself into two restaurants. Staff provide casually

attentive service and delicious, beautifully presented Asian food with a French twist.

Peaceful Family Restaurant (Yen Gia Quan; ☎ 741 019; 53 Đ Nguyen Dinh Chieu; dishes 30,000-70,000d) This friendly family eatery serves wonderful Viet-namese cuisine in a lovely open setting.

Good Morning Vietnam (☎ 847 585; www.good morningviet.com; Km 11.8; mains 60,000-105,000d) This is another in the popular chain of Italian ea-teries. Free hotel pick-ups bridge the distance of the strip.

Drinking

No surfie town would be complete without a smattering of beachside bars and Mui Ne doesn't disappoint. Pretty much all the fol-lowing places have a pool table:

Pogo (138 Đ Nguyen Dinh Chieu) A fun, open-air bar with a big sound system and bean bags.

Mellow (117C Đ Nguyen Dinh Chieu) Popular with the backpacking/kite-surfing fraternity.

Jibes (90 Đ Nguyen Dinh Chieu) Decorated with surf boards, this one's an old favourite.

Hot Rock (12.5km) The Hot Rock also serves good food and plays some excellent music.

Sailing Club (24 Đ Nguyen Dinh Chieu) Not as raucous as its sister in Nha Trang, the Mui Ne incarnation is a stylish place to hang out.

Getting There & Around

Mui Ne is now connected to the main coastal highway to the north as well as the south, making it easier to access. Open ticket buses

VIETNAM

are the best option for Mui Ne, and Sinh Café and Hanh Café (see Orientation & Information, p397) both have daily services to/from HCMC (US$6, four hours), Nha Trang (US$6, five hours) and Dalat (US$7, 5½ hours). The best way to reach the beach from the highway in Phan Thiet is by *xe om* (50,000d).

There are plenty of *xe om* drivers to take you up and down the strip.

CENTRAL HIGHLANDS

The Central Highlands covers the southern part of the Truong Son Mountain Range. This geographical region, home to many Montagnards, is renowned for its cool climate, beautiful mountain scenery and innumerable streams, lakes and waterfalls.

In early 2001 the government forbade travellers from visiting the central highlands because of unrest among the local tribes. In 2004, there was another brief closure of the area, so check the latest situation before heading to the hills.

DALAT
☎ 063 / pop 130,000
Dalat is quite different from anywhere else you'll visit in Vietnam. You would almost be forgiven for thinking you'd stumbled into the French Alps in springtime. This was certainly how the former colonists treated it – escaping to their chalets to enjoy the cooler climate.

Dalat is small enough to remain charming, and the surrounding countryside is blessed with lakes, waterfalls, evergreen forests and gardens; temperate Dalat is nicknamed the City of Eternal Spring. Honeymooners and kitsch-seekers love the place. Days are fine and nights can get cold at an elevation of 1475m.

Information
INTERNET ACCESS
The main post office has fast, cheap connections, plus there are several internet cafés situated along either side of Đ Nguyen Chi Thanh.

MEDICAL SERVICES
Lam Dong Hospital (☎ 822 154; 4 Đ Pham Ngoc Thach)

MONEY
The following downtown banks exchange cash and travellers cheques and offer credit-card cash advances:
Incombank (☎ 822 496; 46-48 Hoa Binh Sq; ☺ closed Sat)
Vietcombank (☎ 510 478; 6 Đ Nguyen Thi Minh Khai) There's a 24-hour ATM here.

POST
Main post office (☎ 822 586; 14 Đ Tran Phu; ☺ 6.30am-9pm) International phone calls and internet access are available here.

TRAVEL AGENCIES
For information on guided tours by motorbike, see Tours, p402.
Dalat Travel Service (☎ 822 125; ttdhhd@hcm.vnn .vn; 7 Đ 3 Thang 2) Offers tours and vehicle rentals.
Groovy Gecko Tours (☎ 836 521; ggtour@yahoo.com; 65 Đ Truong Cong Dinh; ☺ 7.30am-8.30pm) Offers tours, trekking and mountain biking.
Phat Tire Ventures (☎ 829 422; www.phattireven tures.com; 73 Đ Truong Cong Dinh) This ecotourist outfit offers adrenaline activities, plus cycling tours of the Dalat area (US$30 to US$38).
Sinh Café (☎ 822 663; www.sinhcafévn.com; 4A Đ Bui Thi Xuan) Tours and open-tour bus bookings.

Sights
Perhaps there's something in the cool mountain air that fosters the distinctly bohemian vibe and cute kitsch in Dalat. Whatever the reasons, Dalat has attractions you won't find elsewhere in Vietnam.

The **Crémaillère** (☎ 834 409; return 70,000d; ☺ departures 8am, 9.30am, 2pm & 3.30pm) is a cog railway, about 500m east of Xuan Huong Lake that linked Dalat and Thap Cham Phan Rang from 1928 to 1964. The line has now been partially repaired and is a tourist attraction. You can ride 8km down the tracks to Trai Mat village, where you can visit the ornate Linh Phuoc Pagoda.

Bao Dai's **Summer Palace No 3** (Đ Le Hong Phong; admission 5000d; ☺ 7-11am & 1.30-4pm) is a sprawling villa constructed in 1933. The palace is surrounded by landscaped grounds and decked out in the royal colour yellow.

Lam Ty Ni Pagoda (Quan Am Tu; 2 Đ Thien My; ☺ 11.30am & 1-6.30pm) was founded in 1961; this small pagoda is less famous than Mr Thuc, the 'Crazy Monk' who lives here. He's not so much crazy as artistic, and in fact some call him the 'Business Monk' for the brisk sales of his voluminous collection of self-brushed artwork.

Southeast of central Dalat, **Hang Nga Guesthouse & Art Gallery** (☎ 822 070; 3 Đ Huynh Thuc Khang; admission 8000d; ☺ 8am-7pm) is a funky place that's earned the moniker Crazy House from local residents. It's notable for its *Alice in Wonderland* architecture, where you can perch inside a giraffe or get lost in a giant spider web. You can also stay in one of the kooky, slightly spooky rooms (US$19 to US$84), but book in advance.

At the **Valley of Love** (Thung Lung Tinh Yeu; Đ Phu Dong Thien Vuong; adult/child 6000/3000d; ☺ 8am-8pm) you can pose for photos on a pony accompanied by a Vietnamese cowboy. It's about 3km from Xuan Huong Lake, where you can rent a paddleboat shaped like a giant swan.

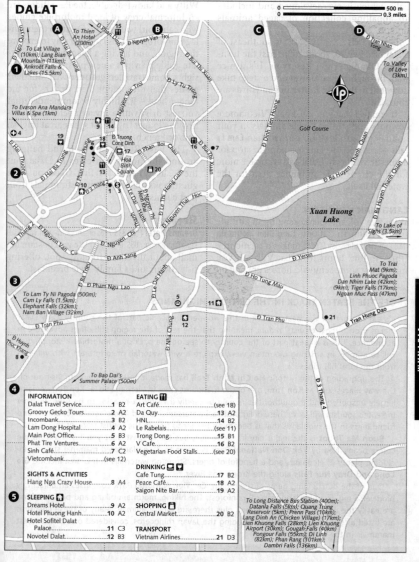

DALAT

0 ____ 500 m
0 ____ 0.3 miles

INFORMATION
Dalat Travel Service	1	B2
Groovy Gecko Tours	2	A2
Incombank	3	B2
Lam Dong Hospital	4	A2
Main Post Office	5	B3
Phat Tire Ventures	6	A2
Sinh Café	7	C2
Vietcombank	(see 12)	

SIGHTS & ACTIVITIES
Hang Nga Crazy House	8	A4

SLEEPING 🏠
Dreams Hotel	9	A2
Hotel Phuong Hanh	10	A2
Hotel Sofitel Dalat Palace	11	C3
Novotel Dalat	12	B3

EATING 🍴
Art Café	(see 18)	
Da Quy	13	A2
HNL	14	B2
Le Rabelais	(see 11)	
Trong Dong	15	B1
V Cafe	16	B2
Vegetarian Food Stalls	(see 20)	

DRINKING 🍷
Cafe Tung	17	B2
Peace Café	18	A2
Saigon Nite Bar	19	A2

SHOPPING 🛍
Central Market	20	B2

TRANSPORT
Vietnam Airlines	21	D3

To Thien An Hotel (200m)
To Lat Village (10km); Lang Bian Mountain (11km); Ankroet Falls & Lakes (15.5km)
To Evason Ana Mandara Villas & Spa (1km)
Golf Course
Xuan Huong Lake
To Lake of Sighs (3.5km)
To Valley of Love (3km)
To Tran Nhan Tong
Hoa Binh Square
To Lam Ty Ni Pagoda (500m); Cam Ly Falls (1.5km); Elephant Falls (32km); Nam Ban Village (32km)
To Trai Mat (9km); Linh Phuoc Pagoda (9km); Dan Nhim Lake (42km); Tiger Falls (17km); Ngoan Muc Pass (47km)
To Bao Dai's Summer Palace (500m)
To Long Distance Bus Station (400m); Datanla Falls (5km); Quang Trung Reservoir (5km); Prenn Pass (10km); Lang Dinh An (Chicken Village) (17km); Lien Khuong Falls (28km); Lien Khuong Airport (30km); Gougah Falls (40km); Pongour Falls (55km); Di Linh (82km); Phan Rang (101km); Dambri Falls (136km)

VIETNAM

Lake of Sighs (Ho Than Tho; admission 5000d) was enlarged by a French-built dam. The sentimentally named natural lake is 6km northeast of Dalat. Hire **horses** (per hr 80,000d) near the restaurants.

WATERFALLS

Dalat's waterfalls are obviously at their gushing best in the rainy season but still flow during the dry season. We advise skipping Prenn Falls, which is overdeveloped and includes an appalling collection of caged animals on-site.

Datanla Falls (admission 5000d) is southeast of Dalat off Hwy 20, about 200m past the turnoff to Quang Trung Reservoir. It's a nice walk through the rainforest and a steep hike downhill to the falls. Butterflies and birds are abundant.

If you feel that you must have Vietnamese cowboys and stuffed jungle animals in your holiday photos, look no further than **Cam Ly Falls** (admission 5000d). This is a popular stop for domestic visitors to Dalat and is notable more for the circus-style ambience than for the waterfall itself.

LANG BIAN MOUNTAIN

With five volcanic peaks ranging in altitude from 2100m to 2400m, **Lang Bian Mountain** (Nui Lam Vien; admission 5000d) makes a scenic trek (three to four hours from Lat Village). You might spot some semiwild horses grazing on the side of the mountain, where rhinoceros and tigers dwelt only half a century ago. Views from the top are tremendous.

The nine hamlets of Lat Village, whose inhabitants are ethnic minorities, are about 12km northwest of Dalat at the base of Lang Bian Mountain.

Tours

Witty and knowledgeable, the Easy Riders are an informal crew of local motorbike guides who can whirl you around Dalat on their vintage motorbikes. This is a great way to explore the region, and having a friendly and articulate guide provides a new perspective on the sights. Some travellers get on so well with their guides that they adopt their drivers for the longer haul – it's highly recommended that you test-drive with a day tour before committing to a longer trip. Most speak great English and/or French.

The Easy Riders can be found hanging around the hotels and cafés in Dalat, but they're likely to find you first. Check out their guestbooks full of glowing testimonials from past clients.

Sleeping

Dreams Hotel (☎ 833 748; dreams@hcm.vnn.vn; 151 Đ Phan Dinh Phung; r US$10-15; 💻) We get constant fan mail about this superfriendly spot, offering tidy rooms and a family-style breakfast.

OFF THE BEATEN TRACK IN THE CENTRAL HIGHLANDS

It's easy to get off the beaten track in this wonderfully scenic part of the country. Only Dalat makes it onto most tourists' radars, meaning that the rest of the region still offers adventure in abundance. This is a great part of the country to see on the back of a motorbike – stopping at will to admire an amazing mountain view, explore a wild waterfall or to interact with villagers from the local hill tribes.

The upgrading of the historic **Ho Chi Minh Trail** has made it easier than ever to visit out-of-the-way places such as **Kon Tum**, one of the friendliest cities in Vietnam. So far Kon Tum remains largely unspoiled and the authorities remain blessedly invisible. It remains to be seen whether increased tourism will leave these delightful backwaters unchanged. There's still an openness and friendliness in the highlands that is becoming harder to find in the tourist traps of the coast.

Buon Ma Thuot is the major city in the region, but the biggest buzz you'll get is from the coffee beans. Nearby **Yok Don National Park** is home to 38 endangered mammal species, including plenty of elephants and a handful of tigers. Stunning waterfalls in this area include **Gia Long** and **Dray Nur Falls** along the Krong Ana River.

One of the outstanding gems of the region, **Cat Tien National Park** comprises an amazingly biodiverse region of lowland tropical rainforest. The hiking, mountain biking and bird-watching are easily the best in southern Vietnam, plus there are lots of animals. Many of these creatures are listed as rare and endangered, including the Javan rhinoceros, considered one of the rarest mammals in the world.

Thien An Hotel (☎ 520 607; thienanhotel@vnn.vn; 272A Đ Phan Dinh Phung; r US$12-15; ▣) Owned by the same family as Dreams, with the same winning formula – great breakfasts, modest rates, sincere friendliness and no hassling for tours. Free bicycles.

Hotel Phuong Hanh (☎ 828 213; fax 838 839; 80-82 Đ 3 Thang 2; r US$7-30) A larger place on the side of a killer hill, the better rooms are spacious and have balconies while the very cheapest are windowless and basic.

Novotel Dalat (☎ 825 777; www.novotel.com; 7 Đ Tran Phu; s US$49-64, d US$55-70, ste US$79-85; ▣) Constructed in 1932 as the Du Parc Hotel, the Novotel retains much of the original French-colonial feel, with an old lift, sombre wooden corridors and period light fittings.

Hotel Sofitel Dalat Palace (☎ 825 444; www.sofitel .com; 12 Đ Tran Phu; s US$148-178, d US$160-190, ste US$258-310; ▣) This grand old place was built between 1916 and 1922. Check out the claw-foot tubs, working fireplaces, 1920s desk lamps and faux period telephones.

Evason Ana Mandara Villas & Spa (☎ 520 558; www .sixsenses.com/evason-dalat/index.php; Đ Le Lai; r US$179-224, ste US$322-460; ▣ ▣) This luxury hillside compound encompasses a collection of unique French villas nestled among the pine trees. Each unique villa has its own butler and kitchen.

Eating

VIETNAMESE

Trong Dong (☎ 821 889; 220 Đ Phan Dinh Phung; mains 24,000-55,000d; ☺ lunch & dinner) Another good place to sample superb Vietnamese food, house specialities include grilled shrimp paste on sugar cane and fish hotpot.

Da Quy (Wild Sunflower; ☎ 510 883; 49 Đ Truong Cong Dinh; dishes 25,000-70,000d) With an upmarket ambience and great service, this newcomer has won lots of fans. The traditional clay pots are excellent.

HNL (☎ 835 505; 94 Đ Phan Dinh Phung; dishes 25,000-75,000d) Painted in pastels and with a classic motorbike as its centrepiece, HNL serves interesting Vietnamese dishes.

Art Café (☎ 510 089; 70 Đ Truong Cong Dinh; dishes 30,000-45,000d) Owned by an artist whose work adorns the walls, the menu features Vietnamese dishes with a twist, including plenty of vegetarian options.

VEGETARIAN

There are vegetarian food stalls in the market area. All serve up delicious 100% vegetarian

> ### CROSSING INTO LAOS: BO Y TO ATTAPEU
>
> This new crossing at Bo Y–Attapeu links Pleiku and Qui Nhon with Attapeu and Pakse. Three Vietnamese-run buses link Attapeu and Pleiku (US$10, 12 hours), departing Attapeu at 9am Monday, Wednesday and Friday, coming the other way Tuesday, Thursday and Saturday. There are direct buses from Qui Nhon to Pakse (250,000d, 12 hours, four per week), but Lao visas are not available at this border. For information on crossing this border in the other direction, see p334.

food, some prepared to resemble and taste like traditional Vietnamese meat dishes.

INTERNATIONAL

Le Rabelais (☎ 825 444; 12 Đ Tran Phu; set dinner US$23-33) For fine French dining, the signature restaurant at the Sofitel cannot be beaten – but bring a wheelbarrow full of dong.

V Cafe (☎ 837 576; 1 Đ Bui Thi Xuan; dishes 25,000-59,000d) A longtime travellers favourite, this cute place serves a mix of Eastern and Western mains, along with a tempting chocolate pie.

CAFÉS

Cafe Tung (6 Hoa Binh Sq) During the 1950s, Cafe Tung was a famous hang-out for Saigonese intellectuals. Old-timers swear that the place remains exactly as it was when they were young.

Drinking

Saigon Nite (☎ 820 007; 11A Đ Hai Ba Trung) The best late-night place to shoot pool and share a drink with expats and visitors.

Peace Café (☎ 822 787; 64 Đ Truong Cong Dinh) A popular gathering point for travellers and Easy Riders, it also serves food.

Shopping

Hoa Binh Sq and the market building adjacent to it are the places to go for purchasing ethnic handicrafts from the nearby Montagnard villages. You can find Lat rush baskets that roll up when empty, as well as gourds for carrying water. Nonhandicraft items at rock-bottom prices include quilted, fake-fur-lined alpine jackets imported from China, and lacquered alligators holding light bulbs in their mouths.

Getting There & Around

Vietnam Airlines (☎ 822 895; www.vietnamairlines.com; 40 Đ Ho Tung Mau) has daily connections with HCMC and Hanoi. Lien Khuong Airport is 30km south of the city. Vietnam Airlines operates a shuttle bus (20,000d, 30 minutes) timed around flights. Private taxis cost about US$10.

Long-distance buses leave from the **station** (Đ 3 Thang 2) about 1km south of the city centre. Services are available to most of the country, including HCMC (60,000d, six to seven hours), Nha Trang (60,000d, seven hours) and Buon Ma Thuot (65,000d, four hours). Open-tour minibuses to Dalat can be booked at travellers cafés in Saigon, Mui Ne and Nha Trang.

Car rental with a driver starts from about US$25 a day. Full-day tours with local motorbike guides are a great way to see the area, as many of the sights lie outside Dalat's centre. Depending on how far you want to go, expect to pay between US$6 and US$10 for a day tour. Many hotels offer bicycle and motorbike hire.

AROUND DALAT

The largest waterfall in the Dalat area, **Pongour Falls** (admission 5000d) is about 55km in the direction of HCMC. The stepped falls are beautiful any time but most spectacular during the rainy season when they form a full semicircle.

Dambri Falls (admission 10,000d), 75km from Dalat, are the tallest falls in the area – walking down to feel the spray from the bottom is divine on a hot day. You can take a lift down and trek back up. There's also a good restaurant with mimosa-framed views near the parking lot.

Waterfalls in the Dalat region are best accessed with your own wheels. Those along long-haul journeys with motorbike drivers can easily detour to the falls on the way to or from Dalat.

HO CHI MINH CITY (SAIGON)

☎ 08 / pop 5.38 million

Boasting an electric, near palpable energy, Ho Chi Minh City (HCMC) is Vietnam's largest metropolis and its undisputed capital of commerce. For the casual visitor, Saigon – as it's still called by all but the city officials

who live here – can seem a chaotic collage of traffic-clogged roads and urban bustle, with nary a green space in sight. Yet thousands of expats and Vietnamese immigrants couldn't imagine living anywhere else. They've long since fallen prey to the hidden charms of one of Southeast Asia's liveliest cities. Stick around this complicated city long enough and you might even find yourself smitten by it, too. HCMC is nonstop, a city full of pilgrims seeking fortune, and open 24 hours a day for the next big thing.

If every town had a symbol, Saigon's would surely be the motorbike. More than three million of them fly along streets once swarming with bicycles. Cruising along boulevards and back alleys astride a *xe om* is the quickest way to sensory overload – daily fare in this tropical town. Teeming markets, sidewalk cafés, acupuncture clinics, centuries-old pagodas and sleek skyscrapers all jockey for attention against the bustling backdrop. Yet the city hasn't forgotten its past. The ghosts live on in the churches, temples, former GI hotels and government buildings that one generation ago witnessed a city in turmoil.

ORIENTATION

A sprawl of 16 urban and five rural *quan* (districts) make up the vast geography of HCMC, though most visitors stick to the centre around the Dong Khoi and Pham Ngu Lao neighbourhoods. Cholon, the city's Chinatown, lies southwest of the centre, and the Saigon River snakes down the eastern side.

Street labels are shortened to Đ for *duong* (street), and ĐL for *dai lo* (boulevard).

INFORMATION
Bookshops

Fahasa Bookshop (☾ 8am-10pm) Dong Khoi (Map p412; ☎ 822 4670; 185 Đ Dong Khoi); ĐL Nguyen Hue (Map p412; ☎ 822 5796; 40 ĐL Nguyen Hue) One of the best government-run bookshops, with good dictionaries, maps and general books in English and French.

Phuong Nam Bookshop (Map p409; ☎ 822 9650; 2A ĐL Le Duan; ☾ 8am-9.30pm) Carries imported books and magazines in English, French and Chinese.

Cultural Centres

British Council (Map p409; ☎ 823 2862; www.british council.org/vietnam; 25 ĐL Le Duan)

Idecaf (Institute of Cultural Exchange with France; Map p412; ☎ 829 5451; 31 Đ Thai Van Lung) French culture, language and arts centre.

Emergency

Ambulance (☎ 115)
Fire (☎ 114)
Information (☎ 1080)
Police (☎ 113)

Internet Access

Hundreds of internet cafés thrive in HCMC – in Pham Ngu Lao (Map p411) you can't swing a dead cat without hitting one. Rates run between 5000d and 15,000d per hour.

Medical Services

Cho Ray Hospital (Map pp406–7; ☎ 855 4137; 201 ĐL Nguyen Chi Thanh, District 5; ☒ 24hr) The largest medical facility in Vietnam, with 24-hour emergency services and excellent, inexpensive care.
HCMC Family Medical Practice (Map p412; ☎ 822 7848, 24hr emergency 0913-234 911; www.vietnammedicalpractice.com; Diamond Plaza, 34 ĐL Le Duan; ☒ 24hr) One of the best international clinics in Vietnam, with prices to match.
International Medical Center (Map p412; ☎ 827 2366, 24hr emergency 865 4025; fac@hcm.vnn.vn; 1 Đ Han Thuyen; ☒ 24hr) This nonprofit organisation may be the least expensive Western healthcare centre in the city. Most doctors are English-speaking French physicians.
International SOS (Map p412; ☎ 829 8424, 24hr emergency 829 8520; 65 Đ Nguyen Du; ☒ 24hr) An international team of docs speaking English, French, Japanese and Vietnamese.

Money

Just inside the airport terminal, there's an exchange counter run by **Sasco** (☎ 848 7142), which gives the official exchange rate. Opening hours are irregular, so carry sufficient US-dollar notes in small denominations in case it's closed.
ANZ Bank (Map p412; ☎ 829 9319; 11 Me Linh Sq) Has a 24-hour ATM.
HSBC (Map p412; ☎ 829 2288; 235 Đ Dong Khoi) Offers a secure 24-hour ATM.
Sacombank (Map p411; ☎ 836 4231; www.sacombank.com; 211 Đ Nguyen Thai Hoc) Conveniently located in the budget-traveller zone, with 24-hour ATM.
Vietcombank (Map p409; ☎ 829 7245; 29 Đ Ben Chuong; ☒ closed Sun & last day of the month) The eastern building is for foreign exchange only, but is also worth a visit just to see the stunningly ornate interior.

Post

Main post office (Buu Dien Thanh Pho Ho Chi Minh; Map p412; 2 Cong Xa Paris) Saigon's striking French-era post office is next to Notre Dame Cathedral.

Tourist Information

Tourist Information Center (Map p412; ☎ 822 6033; www.vntourists.com; 4G Le Loi; ☒ 8am-8pm) This sleek, new information centre distributes city maps and brochures, plus offers advice about goings-on in Saigon.

Travel Agencies

There are lots of travel agents offering tours of the Mekong Delta and other jaunts from HCMC. Some of the better ones include the following:
Delta Adventure Tours (Map p411; ☎ 920 2112; www.deltaadventuretours.com; 267 Đ De Tham) Great Mekong Delta tours.
Handspan Adventure Travel (Map p411; ☎ 925 7605; www.handspan.com; F7, Titan Bldg, 18A Đ Nam Quoc Cang) A new branch brings the high-quality Handspan touch to the south.
Innoviet (Map p411; ☎ 295 8840; www.innoviet.com; 158 Đ Bui Vien)
Sinh Cafe (Map p411; ☎ 836 7338; www.sinhcafévn.com; 246 Đ De Tham; ☒ 6.30am-11pm)
Sinhbalo Adventures (Map p411; ☎ 837 6766, 836 7682; www.sinhbalo.com; 283/20 Đ Pham Ngu Lao) More upmarket, long-running and eminently reliable, Sinhbalo specialises in cycling trips.

DANGERS & ANNOYANCES

Although travellers very rarely face any physical danger in HCMC (besides the traffic), the city has the most determined thieves in the country. Drive-by 'cowboys' on motorbikes can steal bags off your arm and sunglasses off your face, and pickpockets work all crowds. Beware, too, of the cute children crowding around you, wanting to sell postcards and newspapers.

While it's generally safe to take cyclos during the day, it is not always safe at night – take a metered taxi instead.

SIGHTS
Reunification Palace

Built in 1966 to serve as South Vietnam's Presidential Palace is the **Reunification Palace** (Hoi Truong Thong Nhat; Map p409; ☎ 829 4117; 106 Đ Nguyen Du; admission 15,000d; ☒ 7.30-11am & 1-4pm). It was through the gates of this building that the first communist tanks in Saigon crashed on the morning of 30 April 1975, the day Saigon surrendered. The building has been left just as it looked on that momentous day.

Enter on Đ Nam Ky Khoi Nghia, where English- and French-speaking guides are on duty.

VIETNAM

HO CHI MINH CITY

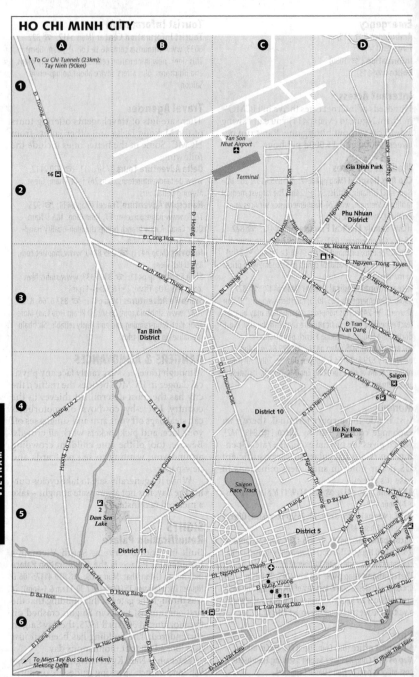

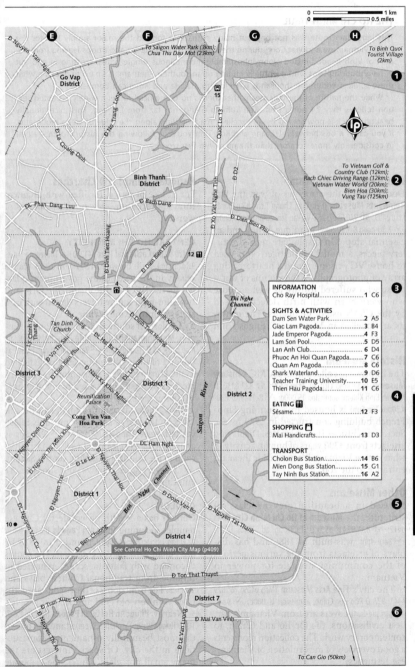

See Central Ho Chi Minh City Map (p409)

INFORMATION
Cho Ray Hospital..........................**1** C6

SIGHTS & ACTIVITIES
Dam Sen Water Park...................**2** A5
Giac Lam Pagoda.......................**3** B4
Jade Emperor Pagoda.................**4** F3
Lam Son Pool.............................**5** D5
Lan Anh Club.............................**6** D4
Phuoc An Hoi Quan Pagoda.......**7** C6
Quan Am Pagoda.......................**8** C6
Shark Waterland........................**9** D6
Teacher Training University......**10** E5
Thien Hau Pagoda....................**11** C6

EATING
Sésame...................................**12** F3

SHOPPING
Mai Handicrafts.......................**13** D3

TRANSPORT
Cholon Bus Station..................**14** B6
Mien Dong Bus Station............**15** G1
Tay Ninh Bus Station...............**16** A2

VIETNAM

THE HO CHI MINH TRAIL

This legendary route was not one but many paths that formed the major supply link for the North Vietnamese and Viet Cong during the American War. Supplies and troops leaving from the port of Vinh headed inland along inhospitable mountainous jungle paths, crossing in and out of neighbouring Laos, and eventually ending up in southern Vietnam. It's hard to imagine what these soldiers endured – thousands were lost to malaria and American bombs.

While the nature of the trail means that there's no one official route, a widely accepted section follows Hwy 14 north from Kon Tum to Giang, not far from Danang. This exceptionally beautiful track is now served by an excellent road winding along the edge of steep mountains. If you catch a bus between Danang and Kon Tum you'll be following this historic path – albeit in considerably more comfort than the men who first trod it.

War Remnants Museum

Documenting the atrocities of war, the **War Remnants Museum** (Bao Tang Chung Tich Chien Tranh; Map p409; ☎ 930 5587; 28 Đ Vo Van Tan; admission 15,000d; ☻ 7.30-noon & 1.30-5pm) is unique, brutal and an essential stop. On display are retired artillery pieces, a model of the tiger cages used to house VC prisoners, and a heartbreaking array of photographs of the victims of war – those who suffered torture as well as those who were born with birth defects caused by the USA's use of defoliants. The exhibits are labelled in Vietnamese, English and Chinese.

History Museum

The impressive collection of HCMC's **History Museum** (Bao Tang Lich Su; Map p409; ☎ 829 8146; Đ Nguyen Binh Khiem; admission 15,000d; ☻ 8-11am & 1.30-4.30pm Tue-Sun) is housed in a stunning Sino-French building constructed in 1929 by the Société des Études Indochinoises. Displaying artefacts from 3300 years of human activity in what is now Vietnam, it's just inside the main entrance to the zoo.

Other Museums

Housed in a beautiful grey neoclassical structure, the **Museum of Ho Chi Minh City** (Map p412; ☎ 829 9741; 65 Đ Ly Tu Trong; admission US$1; ☻ 8am-4pm) was built in 1886 and has displays of artefacts from the various periods of the communist struggle for power in Vietnam.

The city's **Fine Arts Museum** (Map p409; ☎ 829 4441; 97A Đ Pho Duc Chinh; admission 10,000d; ☻ 9am-4.30pm Tue-Sun) covers art from Vietnam's earliest civilisations, the Oc-Eo and Cham, to contemporary work. The collection represents a good overview of the evolution of Vietnamese aesthetics.

Pagodas, Temples & Churches

For a dose of peace, fortified with architectural appreciation, seek out these places of worship.

CENTRAL HO CHI MINH CITY

Notre Dame Cathedral (Map p412; Đ Han Thuyen; ☻ mass 9.30am Sun), built between 1877 and 1883, stands regally in the heart of the government quarter. Its red-brick neo-Romanesque form and two 40m-high square towers tipped with iron spires dominate the skyline.

A splash of southern India's colour in Saigon, **Mariamman Hindu Temple** (Chua Ba Mariamman; Map p409; 45 Đ Truong Dinh; ☻ 7am-7pm) was built at the end of the 19th century and is dedicated to the Hindu goddess Mariamman. The temple is also considered sacred by many ethnic Vietnamese and Chinese.

Constructed by South Indian Muslims in 1935 on the site of an earlier mosque, **Saigon Central Mosque** (Map p412; 66 Đ Dong Du; ☻ 9am-5pm) is an immaculately clean and well-kept island of calm in the middle of bustling central Saigon. As at any mosque, remove your shoes before entering.

CHOLON

Cholon has a wealth of wonderful Chinese temples including **Quan Am Pagoda** (Map pp406-7; 12 Đ Lao Tu; ☻ 8am-4.30pm), founded in 1816 by the Fujian Chinese congregation. The roof is decorated with fantastic scenes, rendered in ceramic, from traditional Chinese plays and stories. The front doors of the pagoda are decorated with very old gold-and-lacquer panels.

Nearby, **Phuoc An Hoi Quan Pagoda** (Map pp406-7; 184 Đ Hung Vuong; ☻ 7am-5.30pm) stands as one of the most beautifully ornamented constructions in the city. Of special interest are the many small porcelain figures, the elaborate brass ritual objects and the fine woodcarvings on the altars, walls and hanging lanterns. This pagoda was built in 1902, also by the Fujian Chinese congregation.

One of the most active in Cholon, **Thien Hau Pagoda** (Ba Mieu or Pho Mieu; Map pp406-7; 710 Đ Nguyen Trai; ⏰ 6am-5.30pm) is dedicated to Thien Hau, the Chinese goddess of the sea. As she protects

fisherfolk, sailors, merchants and any other maritime travellers, you might stop by to ask for a blessing for your Mekong Delta trip.

GREATER HO CHI MINH CITY

Beautiful **Giac Lam Pagoda** (Map pp406-7; 118 Đ Lac Long Quan; ⏰ 6am-9pm) dates from 1744 and is believed to be the city's oldest. The architecture hasn't

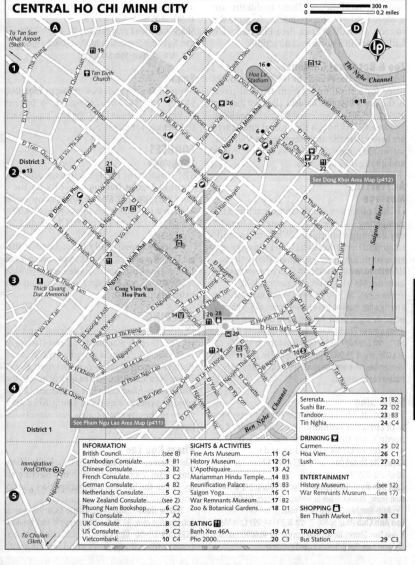

CENTRAL HO CHI MINH CITY

VIETNAM

changed since 1900, and the compound is a meditative place to explore.

Jade Emperor Pagoda (Phuoc Hai Tu or Chua Ngoc Hoang; Map pp406-7; 73 Đ Mai Thi Luu; 7.30am-6pm) is a gem of a Chinese temple, filled with colourful statues of phantasmal divinities and grotesque heroes. Built in 1909 by the Cantonese congregation, it is one of HCMC's most spectacular pagodas. The statues, which represent characters from both the Buddhist and Taoist traditions, are made of reinforced papier-mâché. To get to the pagoda, go to 20 Đ Dien Bien Phu and walk half a block in a northwest direction.

Zoo & Botanical Gardens

Founded by the French in 1864, and a lovely place for a stroll under giant tropical trees, is the **Zoo & Botanical Gardens** (Thao Cam Vien; Map p409; 829 3901; 2 Đ Nguyen Binh Khiem; admission 8000d; 7am-8pm). Although the animal enclosures are better than the usual standard in Vietnam, we would suggest sticking with the gardens and giving the zoo a miss.

ACTIVITIES
Massage

HCMC offers some truly fantastic settings for pampering – the perfect antidote to a frenetic day dodging motorbikes. While many mid-range and upmarket hotels offer massage service, some are more legitimate than others.

L'Apothiquaire (Map p409; 932 5181; www.lapothiquaire.com; 64A Đ Truong Dinh; 1hr massage US$20; 9am-9pm;) The city's most elegant spa is housed in a pretty white mansion tucked down a quiet alley, with body wraps, massages, facials, foot treatments and herbal baths.

Vietnamese Traditional Massage Institute (Map p411; 839 6697; 185 Đ Cong Quynh; per hr 35,000-45,000d, sauna 25,000d; 9am-9pm) This place offers inexpensive, no-nonsense massages performed by well-trained blind masseurs.

Swimming

Most of HCMC's finer hotels have fitness clubs with attractive swimming pools attached. You needn't stay there to swim, but you'll have to pay a fee of US$8 to US$18 per day.

Caravelle Hotel (Map p412; 823 4999; 19 Lam Son Sq; admission US$13)

Lam Son Pool (Map pp406-7; 835 8028; 342 Đ Tran Binh Trong, District 5; per hr 5000d, after 5pm 6000d; 8am-8pm) An Olympic-sized pool.

Lan Anh Club (Map pp406-7; 862 7144; 291 Cach Mang Thang Tam, District 10; admission gym/pool 40,000/25,000d; pool 6am-9pm) There's a good gym here.

Water Parks

Saigon Water Park (897 0456; Đ Kha Van Can, Thu Du District; adult/child 60,000/35,000d; 9am-5pm Mon-Sat 9am-6pm Sun & public holidays) has slides and a wave pool in the suburbia of Thu Duc, north of th centre; shuttle buses (5000d) leave every half hour from Ben Thanh Market station.

Other water parks:

Dam Sen Water Park (Map pp406-7; 858 8418; www.damsenwaterpark.com.vn; 3 Đ Hoa Binh; adult/child 45,000/30,000d; 9am-6pm)

Shark Waterland (Map pp406-7; 853 7867; 600 Đ Ham Tu, District 5; admission 20,000-45,000d; 8am-9pm Mon-Fri, 10am-9pm Sat & Sun)

Yoga

Drop in for yoga classes at **Saigon Yoga** (Map p409; 910 5181; www.saigonyoga.com; 10F Đ Nguye Thi Minh Khai; per session US$12; 8am-7pm). Check the website for class times.

COURSES
Language

The majority of foreign-language students enrol at **Teacher Training University** (Dai Hoc Su Pham; Map pp406-7; 835 5100; ciecer@hcm.vnn.vn; 280 An Duong Vuong, District 5; private/group class US$4.50/3), which is a department of Ho Chi Minh City University.

More informal study is available at **Utopia Café** (Map p412; 824 2487; shop@utopia-café.com; 17/6A Đ Le Thanh Ton, District 1; private lesson per 60/90min 70,000/90,000d; 8.30am-9pm), with one-on-one instruction.

SLEEPING

District 1 is the undisputed lodging capital of HCMC, though whether to go east (fancy) or west (cheap) depends on what you're after. Budget travellers often head straight to the Pham Ngu Lao area, where thrifty hotels and backpacker-filled cafés line the streets. Those seeking upscale digs go to Dong Khoi area, home to the city's best hotels, restaurants and bars.

Pham Ngu Lao

Three streets – Đ Pham Ngu Lao, Đ De Tham and Đ Bui Vien – along with intersecting alleys form the heart of this backpacker ghetto, with more than 100 places to stay.

Yellow House (Map p411; 836 8830; yellowhouse hotel@yahoo.com; 31 Đ Bui Vien; dm/s/d incl breakfast US$5.25/9/12;) One of the cheapest options in town if you don't mind bunking with

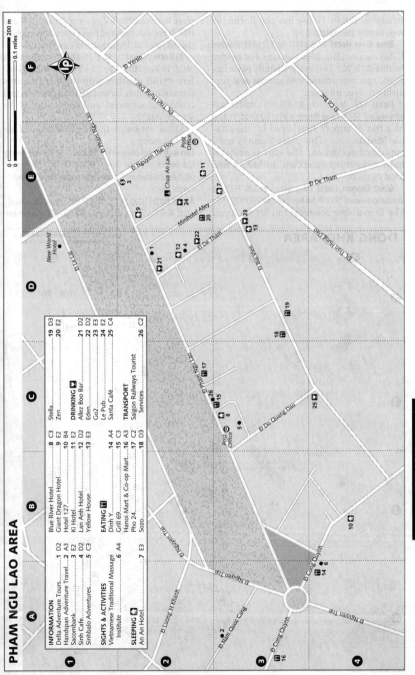

PHAM NGU LAO AREA

INFORMATION
Delta Adventure Tours........................1	D2
Handspan Adventure Travel................2	A3
Sacombank.......................................3	E2
Sinh Cafe...4	D2
Sinhbalo Adventures..........................5	C3

SIGHTS & ACTIVITIES
Vietnamese Traditional Massage Institute..6	A4

SLEEPING
An An Hotel.....................................7	E3
Blue River Hotel................................8	C3
Giant Dragon Hotel...........................9	E2
Hotel 127.......................................10	B4
Ki Hotel..11	E2
Lan Anh Hotel.................................12	D2
Yellow House..................................13	E3

EATING
Dinh Y..14	A4
Grill 69..15	C3
Hanoi Mart & Co-op Mart................16	A3
Pho 24...17	C2
Sozo..18	D3
Stella...19	D3
Zen...20	E2

DRINKING
Allez Boo Bar..................................21	D2
Eden...22	D2
Go2..23	E3
Le Pub...24	E2
Santa Cafe......................................25	C4

TRANSPORT
Saigon Railways Tourist Services..26	C2

VIETNAM

strangers, Yellow House has two dorms, as well as private rooms.

Blue River Hotel (Map p411; ☎ 837 6483; blueriver1126@yahoo.com; 283/2C Đ Pham Ngu Lao; s/d incl breakfast from US$10/12; 🟦) This extra-friendly place has clean, spacious rooms with simple neat furnishings. Free internet.

Hotel 127 (Map p411; ☎ 836 8761; madamcuc@hcm.vnn.vn; 127 Đ Cong Quynh; r US$12-20; 🟦) One of a trio of superb hotels run by the affable Madam Cuc. This place features well-appointed rooms and the staff provides a most welcoming reception, including free local dinners.

Giant Dragon Hotel (Map p411; ☎ 836 1935; gd-hotel@hcm.vnn.vn; 173 Đ Pham Ngu Lao; r/ste US$20/25; 🟦) The immaculate rooms at this lift-equipped

place have satellite TV, international direct dial (IDD) phones, tubs and hair dryers. Superdeluxe rooms have sitting areas and city views.

Ki Hotel (Map p411; ☎ 837 5582; www.tamsonco.com; 28/2 Đ Bui Vien; r US$28-38; 🟦) This new hotel offers stylish quarters with organic elements (bamboo, paper lanterns), thoughtful extras (robe and slippers) and room enough to stretch out.

Other options in this popular area include the following:

Lan Anh Hotel (Map p411; ☎ 836 5197; lan-anh-hotel@hcm.vnn.vn; 252 Đ De Tham; r US$10-18; 🟦) Offering a lift, free breakfast and comfortable rooms, this is a good central choice.

An An Hotel (Map p411; ☎ 837 8087; www.ananhotel.com; 40 Đ Bui Vien; r US$22-35; 🟦 🖥) TV and minibar

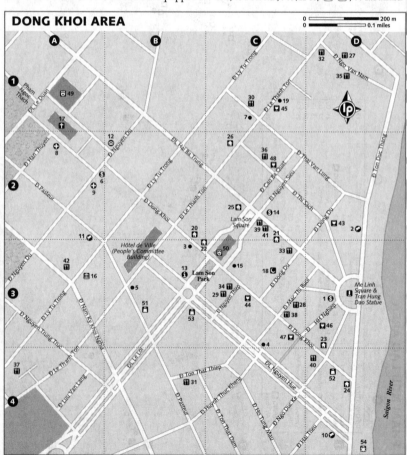

DONG KHOI AREA

0 ——————— 200 m
0 ——————— 0.1 miles

in the clean rooms, plus internet, at this slick, newish place.

Dong Khoi Area

If you want to base yourself in the city centre, you'll find a good number of well-appointed hotels along Đ Dong Khoi or near the Saigon River.

ourpick Spring Hotel (Map p412; ☎ 829 7362; springhotel@hcm.vnn.vn; 44-46 Đ Le Thanh Ton; s/d with breakfast from US$32/40; 🖭) This trim and nicely designed place has a subtle Japanese feel to it. The rooms here are somewhat small and carpeted but are excellent value for the neighbourhood.

Bong Sen Annexe (Map p412; ☎ 823 5818; bongsen2@ hcm.vnn.vn; 61-63 ĐL Hai Ba Trung; s/d with breakfast from US$40/46; 🖭) The BS, as it's affectionately known by business travellers, is an attractive choice, with friendly management and staff. Rooms are good value for the neighbourhood.

Asian Hotel (Map p412; ☎ 829 6979; asianhotel@hcn .fpt.vn; 150 Đ Dong Khoi; s/d with breakfast from US$45/50; 🖭) In the centre of town, this contemporary hotel has well-designed rooms and wi-fi access. Book the superior or deluxe for a balcony and natural light.

Grand Hotel (Map p412; ☎ 823 0163; www.grandhotel .com.vn; 8-24 Đ Dong Khoi; s/d from US$75/85; 🖭 🖵 🖭) Aptly named, the Grand's renovated landmark building is notable for its old-fashioned

lift and spacious suites. There's also an indoor pool and a gym.

Continental Hotel (Map p412; ☎ 829 9252; www .continentalvietnam.com; 132-134 Đ Dong Khoi; r US$75-135; 🖭) One of the city's most historic lodgings, the Continental was the setting for much of the action that occurred in Graham Greene's novel *The Quiet American*. Panelled wood ceilings accent the carpeted, cavernous rooms.

ourpick Majestic Hotel (Map p412; ☎ 829 5517; www.majesticsaigon.com.vn; 1 Đ Dong Khoi; s/d from US$135/150; 🖭 🖭) Dating back to 1925, the Majestic is situated right on the Saigon River. It has a colonial charm and unique atmosphere, setting it apart from more modern behemoths.

Park Hyatt Saigon (Map p412; ☎ 824 1234; saigon .park.hyatt.com; 2 Lam Son Sq; d from US$210; 🖭 🖵 🖭) The Park Hyatt is easily Saigon's finest hotel. Occupying a fine position in the heart of the city, this hotel has an elegant white façade and offers beautifully appointed guest rooms.

EATING

Hanoi may have more lakes and colonial charm, but HCMC is the reigning culinary king of Vietnam. Restaurants here range from dirt-cheap sidewalk stalls to atmospheric villas, each serving a unique interpretation of Vietnamese decadence. Besides brilliant

VIETNAM

regional fare, Saigon offers a smattering of world cuisine, with Indian, Japanese, Thai, French, Italian and East–West fusions well represented.

Good foodie neighbourhoods include the Dong Khoi area, with a high density of top-quality restaurants, as well as nearby District 3. Pham Ngu Lao's eateries, attempting to satisfy every possible culinary whim, are generally less impressive.

Vietnamese

Nam Giao (Map p412; ☎ 825 0261; 136/15 Đ Le Thanh Ton; mains 10,000-15,000đ; ⊗ lunch & dinner) Tucked away in an alley near Ben Thanh Market, Nam Giao serves superb Hué-style mains and is always packed.

ourpick Quan An Ngon (Map p412; ☎ 825 7179; 138 Đ Nam Ky Khoi Nghia; mains 17,000-60,000đ; ⊗ lunch & dinner) Surrounding the garden-style patio is a ring of cooks at individual stations, mixing up softly spiced creations in the open air. An excellent selection of traditional Vietnamese dishes.

Pho Oso (Map p412; ☎ 829 6415; 37 Đ Dong Khoi; mains 18,000-80,000đ; ⊗ lunch & dinner) This tiny noodle shop serves delectable bowls of *pho* in a cosy setting. And remember the Oso mantra: 'no delicious, no pay'.

Banh Xeo 46A (Map p409; ☎ 824 1110; 46A Đ Dinh Cong Trang; mains 20,000-30,000đ; ⊗ breakfast, lunch & dinner) *Banh xeo* has been known to induce swoons of gastronomic delight among certain visitors. Come here to try some of the best *banh xeo* in HCMC.

Pho 24 (Map p411; 271 Đ Pham Ngu Lao; mains 24,000đ; ⊗ breakfast, lunch & dinner) This polished noodle shop serves fantastic bowls of quality *pho* – along with fresh juices and spring rolls. Visit www.pho24.com.vn for other locations throughout Vietnam.

QUIRKY SAIGON

Dam Sen Park (Map pp406-7; ☎ 855 4963; 3 Đ Hoa Binh; admission 10,000đ; ⊗ 9am-9pm) offers a dose of slightly bizarre fun. Giant animals made of coconut shells are outdone only by those made of CDs. Venture inside the park's landscaped gardens embellished with lakes, bridges and pagodas to find an ice-block wonderland inside an enormous freezer-room, cafés and gift shops, and a roller coaster.

Grill 69 (Map p411; ☎ 836 7936; 275H Đ Pham Ngu Lao; mains 35,000-80,000đ; ⊗ lunch & dinner) Sizzling barbecued kangaroo, ostrich and more pedestrian fare (pork, squid, beef) go nicely with the wine selections.

Gourmet Vietnamese

Compared with what you would pay for fine Vietnamese food abroad, HCMC's better Vietnamese restaurants are a bargain. It's possible to eat like royalty in a lavish restaurant for around US$10 for lunch – or US$25 for dinner – per person.

Mandarine (Map p412; ☎ 822 9783; 11A Đ Ngo Van Nam; mains 60,000đ; ⊗ lunch & dinner) The fine selection of traditional dishes on offer draws on all regions. The food is superb, and the traditional music performances make it an all-round good bet.

ourpick Temple Club (Map p412; ☎ 829 9244; 29 Đ Ton That Thiep; mains 70,000-130,000đ; ⊗ lunch & dinner) On the 2nd floor of a beautifully restored colonial villa, Temple Club serves delectable Vietnamese plates such as fish with tamarind or shrimp in coconut milk.

ourpick Sésame (Map pp406-7; ☎ 899 3378; tri angleghvn@hcmc.netnam.vn; 153 Đ Xo Viet Nghe Tinh, Binh Thanh District; set meals 90,000-120,000đ; ⊗ 11.30am-2pm Tue-Fri & 7-10pm Fri & Sat) A hospitality training school for disadvantaged children, French-Vietnamese dishes made with fresh local ingredients are delicious and beautifully presented.

Nam Kha (Map p412; ☎ 828 8309; 46 Đ Dong Khoi; mains around US$10; ⊗ lunch & dinner) The setting here consists of a reflecting pool flanked by gold-leaf-covered pillars, with tables scattered around the outside. Savoury Vietnamese dishes match the surrounds.

Delectable dining is also available at the following places:

Lemon Grass (Map p412; ☎ 822 0496; 4 Đ Nguyen Thiep; mains 50,000-70,000đ; ⊗ lunch & dinner) Despite the simple décor, this is one of the best Vietnamese restaurants in the city centre.

Hoi An (Map p412; ☎ 823 7694; 11 Đ Le Thanh Ton; mains 70,000-120,000đ; ⊗ lunch & dinner) Run by the same team as Mandarine, the speciality here is imperial Hué-style dishes.

International

Mogambo (Map p412; ☎ 825 1311; 20B Đ Thi Sach; mains 30,000-50,000đ; ⊗ lunch & dinner) Noted for its Polynesian décor and juicy burgers, Mogambo is a restaurant, pub and hotel.

Augustin (Map p412; ☎ 829 2941; 10 Đ Nguyen Thiep; mains 60,000đ; ⊗ lunch & dinner Mon-Sat) Many consider Augustin the city's best casual French restaurant. It serves tasty bistro-style food.

Pacharan (Map p412; ☎ 825 6824; 97 Đ Hai Ba Trung; tapas 75,000-90,000d; ☺ lunch & dinner) This colourful Spanish tapas restaurant and wine bar is one of Saigon's trendiest spots to meet up over a drink.

Pomodoro (Map p412; ☎ 823 8998; 79 ĐL Hai Ba Trung; mains 80,000-160,000d; ☺ 10am-10pm) This small Italian restaurant has a cosy setting for good pizzas, pastas and tiramisu.

Camargue (Map p412; ☎ 824 3148; 16 Đ Cao Ba Quat; mains US$15; ☺ lunch & dinner) Housed in a beautiful restored villa, Camargue is also home to trendy Vasco's bar. The menu includes a variety of gourmet dishes complemented by a well-appointed wine list.

Other restaurants to try:

Annie's Pizza (Map p412; ☎ 823 9044; 45 Đ Mac Thi Buoi; pizzas 40,000-70,000d; ☺ lunch & dinner) Great pizzas and free delivery.

Stella (Map p411; ☎ 836 9220; 121 Đ Bui Vien; mains 75,000-125,000d; ☺ lunch & dinner) Stella serves excellent risotto, lasagne and gnocchi in a stylish, Zenlike trattoria.

Other Asian

Indian Canteen (Map p412; ☎ 823 2159; 66 Đ Dong Du; dishes 7000d) For really cheap Indian food, seek out this place behind the Saigon Central Mosque. The fish curry (21,000d) is superb.

Angkor Encore Plus (Map p412; ☎ 829 8814; 28 Đ Ngo Van Nam; mains around 35,000d; ☺ lunch & dinner) Wonderful Khmer cuisine, now cooking in a little haven of pretty décor and authentic flavours.

Chao Thai (Map p412; ☎ 824 1457; 16 Đ Thai Van Lung; mains around 45,000d; ☺ lunch & dinner) Lunch sets are good value, with some of Saigon's best Thai food.

Sushi Bar (Map p409; ☎ 823 8042; shige@hcm.vnn.vn; 2 Đ Le Thanh Ton; sushi 45,000d; ☺ lunch & dinner) Bristling with life, this sushi bar is usually packed with Japanese and has a fun view of a frenzied intersection.

ourpick Tandoor (Map p409; ☎ 930 4839; 103 Đ Vo Van Tan, District 3; set lunch 58,000d; ☺ lunch & dinner) Tandoor serves outstanding North Indian food, and the set lunch is particularly good value.

Vegetarian

Dinh Y (Map p411; ☎ 836 7715; 171B Đ Cong Quynh; mains 7000d; ☺ breakfast, lunch & dinner) Across the road from Thai Binh Market, Dinh Y serves inexpensive and delicious veggie fare, and has an English menu.

ourpick Tin Nghia (Map p409; ☎ 821 2538; 9 ĐL Tran Hung Dao; mains 8000d; ☺ 7am-8.30pm) The owners are strict Buddhists who turn out delicious traditional Vietnamese food, prepared with tofu, mushrooms and other vegetables.

Zen (Map p411; ☎ 837 3713; 185/30 Đ Pham Ngu Lao; mains 10,000-15,000d; ☺ breakfast, lunch & dinner) This casual travellers' favourite serves cheap veggie food in a mellow, family atmosphere.

Cafés

Serenata (Map p409; ☎ 930 7436; 6D Đ Ngo Thoi Nhien; ☺ closed Sun) Tables here are scattered around a lush, pond-filled courtyard and inside a charming villa. Popular with couples after dark with live music some nights.

Sozo (Map p411; ☎ 095-870 6580; 176 Đ Bui Vien; 3 cookies US$1) This lovely café serves coffees, cinnamon rolls, homemade cookies and sandwiches. There's wi-fi access, and more importantly, it trains and employs poor, disadvantaged Vietnamese.

Java Coffee Bar (Map p412; ☎ 823 0187; 38-42 Đ Dong Du) With espresso bar, excellent café fare and even smoothies (35,000d) made with silken tofu, Java is chic and relaxed.

Fanny (Map p412; ☎ 821 1633; 29-31 Đ Ton That Thiep; ice cream scoop 6000-15,000d) Set in an attractive French villa, Fanny creates excellent Franco-Vietnamese ice cream in fruity flavours (dare to try the durian). Has wi-fi.

Food Stalls

Noodle soup is available all day at street stalls everywhere. A large bowl of delicious beef noodle soup usually costs between 8000d and 15,000d. Just look for the signs that say 'pho'.

Pho 2000 (Map p409; ☎ 822 2788; 1-3 Đ Phan Chu Trinh; pho 20,000d) Near the Ben Thanh Market, this is a good place for your first pho – former US president Bill Clinton stopped in for a bowl.

Markets always have a side selection of food items, often on the ground floor or in the basement. Clusters of food stalls can be found in Thai Binh, Ben Thanh and An Dong Markets.

Self-Catering

Simple, dirt-cheap meals can be cobbled together from street stalls and markets with fresh fruits and vegetables, baguettes baked daily and soft French cheese.

Co-op Mart (Map p411; Đ Cong Quynh; ☉ 8am-8pm) A good supermarket west of the traffic circle near Thai Binh Market.

Another good supermarket, just down the street from the Co-Op Mart, is Hanoi Mart.

DRINKING

Wartime Saigon was known for its riotous nightlife. Liberation in 1975 put a real dampener on evening activities, but the bars and clubs have staged a comeback. However, periodic 'crack-down, clean-up' campaigns continue to calm the fun.

Pham Ngu Lao Area

Le Pub (Map p411; ☎ 837 7679; www.lepub.org; 175/22 Đ Pham Ngu Lao) This attractive bar is the new expat fave in the Pham Ngu Lao area. Take a front seat to watch the action in backpacker central.

Allez Boo Bar (Map p411; ☎ 837 2505; 187 Đ Pham Ngu Lao) Watch the world scooter by at this bamboo-decked bar that always packs a (foreign) crowd, with a handful of prostitutes thrown in for good measure.

Eden (Map p411; ☎ 836 8154; 185/22 Đ De Tham; mains 30,000-60,000đ) This multilevel spot has red lanterns over the bar, a cosy, inviting vibe and staff dressed in red *ao dai.*

Santa Café (Map p411; cnr Đ Bui Vien & Đ Do Quang Dau) Divey little place with outdoor seating that's a favourite of the traveller crowd.

Go2 (Map p411; ☎ 836 9575; 187 Đ De Tham) Above an open, airy street-level bar, this popular little club gathers a good mix of expats and Saigon party people. DJs spin the tunes and it's open late.

Dong Khoi Area

These bars are generally a notch or two up in price from other parts of town.

Hoa Vien (Map p409; ☎ 829 0585; www.hoavener.com; 28 Đ Mac Dinh Chi) Notable for being HCMC's only Czech restaurant, the real drawcard is the freshly brewed draught Pilsner Urquell.

Underground (Map p412; ☎ 829 9079; 69 Đ Dong Khoi; ☉ 10am-midnight) Named after the London tube, Underground is a popular gathering spot for expats and travellers alike.

Vasco's (Map p412; ☎ 824 3148; 16 Đ Cao Ba Quat) Much loved by expats, hip Vasco's draws a bigger crowd on weekends when there's live music.

Lush (Map p409; 2 Đ Ly Tu Trong) Lush is an anime-themed bar that gathers an attractive, mixed crowd. The wraparound bar takes centre stage and is great for people-watching.

Carmen (Map p409; ☎ 829 7699; 8 Đ Ly Tu Trong) Carmen has a stone wall exterior and a cosy wine cellarlike interior (duck your head when you enter), with live music nightly.

Q Bar (Map p412; ☎ 823 3479; 7 Lam Son Sq) Attracting a cool clientele for cocktails, Q Bar is where HCMC's fashion-conscious, alternative crowd hangs out.

Other good spots:

Saigon Saigon Bar (Map p412; ☎ 823 3479; 10th fl, Caravelle Hotel, 19 Lam Son Sq) For excellent views over the city centre, stop by Saigon Saigon for a drink around dusk.

Sheridan's Irish House (Map p412; ☎ 823 0973; 17/13 Đ Le Thanh Ton) This traditional Irish pub is beamed in straight from the backstreets of Dublin. Good pub grub.

ENTERTAINMENT

History Museum (Map p409; ☎ 829 8146; Đ Nguyen Binh Khiem; admission 30,000đ; ☉ 8-11.30am & 1-4pm Tue-Sun) This museum hosts water-puppetry performances. Schedules vary, but shows tend to start when about five or more people show up.

Also check out the schedule of performances at the **War Remnants Museum** (Map p409; ☎ 930 5587; 28 Đ Vo Van Tan; admission 30,000đ; ☉ 7.30-11.45am & 1.30-5.15pm Tue-Sun).

Theatre, live music and films around the Dong Khoi area:

Diamond Plaza Cinema (Map p412; ☎ 825 7751; Diamond Plaza, 163 Đ Dong Khoi; tickets 30,000-40,000đ) English-language films.

Idecaf (Map p412; ☎ 829 5451; 31 Đ Thai Van Lung) Screens French-language films.

Municipal Theatre (Nha Hat Thanh Pho; Map p412; ☎ 829 9976; Lam Son Sq) Plays and musical performances.

GAY & LESBIAN HO CHI MINH CITY

Although there are few openly gay venues, Saigon's popular bars and clubs are generally gay-friendly. In Dong Khoi area, Lush (left) attracts a good, mixed crowd with danceable music but no dance floor. Apocalypse Now (opposite) attracts a small gay contingent among an otherwise straight crowd, with solid grooves and a spacious dance floor. **Samsara** (Map p412; ☎ 862 2630; 2nd fl, 131 Đ Dong Khoi), above the Brodard Café, is a mostly gay affair.

Clubbing

Apocalypse Now (Map p412; ☎ 824 1463; 2C Đ Thi Sach)
Dance clubs in Vietnam have a tendency to change with the wind, but 'Apo' is the exception to the rule. It's been around forever and gives a good eyeful of the seamier side of international relations.

Tropical Rainforest Disco (Mua Rung; Map p412; ☎ 825 7783; 5-15 Đ Ho Huan Nghiep; cover US$4) This popular nightspot in the city centre attracts a younger crowd. The cover charge includes one free drink.

SHOPPING

Among the tempting wares to be found in Saigon are embroidered-silk shoes, knock-off Zippo lighters engraved with fake soldier poetry and toy helicopters made from beer cans. Boutiques along Đ Le Thanh Ton and Đ Pasteur sell handmade ready-to-wear fashion. In Pham Ngu Lao, shops sell ethnic-minority fabrics, handicrafts, T-shirts and various appealing accessories.

Ben Thanh Market (Cho Ben Thanh; Map p409) is the best place to start. Part of the market is devoted to normal everyday items, but the lucrative tourist trade also has healthy representation. This means you need to be alert to sticky fingers.

Đ Dong Khoi (Map p412) is one big arts-and-crafts tourist bazaar, but prices can get outrageous – negotiate if no prices are posted.

Russian Market (Map p412; cnr Đ Le Loi & Đ Nguyen Hue) No longer the dowdy but charming cavern of vendors and bargains it was before its face-lift, there are still a few deals here. Worth a look for clothes in Western sizes without the boutique mark-ups.

Check out the following shops around town:

Chi Chi (Map p412; ☎ 824 7812; anhxuanvn@hcm.fpt.vn; 138 Đ Pasteur; ⏰ 8am-8pm) Features well-chosen, lovely fabrics and fine designs; custom tailoring is also offered.

Lotus (Map p412; ☎ 098-908 4449; lotus hochiminh@yahoo.com; 25 Đ Dong Khoi) For vintage propaganda posters (from the 1960s and '70s), this place is a goldmine. Expect to pay upwards of US$85 for an original.

Mai Handicrafts (Map pp406-7; ☎ 844 0988; maivn@hcm.vnn.vn; 298 Đ Nguyen Trong Tuyen, Tan Binh District) Fair-trade shop dealing in ceramics, ethnic fabrics and other gift items, to support poor families and street children.

GETTING THERE & AWAY

Air

Tan Son Nhat Airport was one of the busiest in the world in the late 1960s. For more details on international air travel, see p433.

Most domestic flights are operated by Vietnam Airlines. See the map (p435) for details on routes and schedules.

Boat

Cargo ferries serving the Mekong Delta depart from the **Bach Dang jetty** (Map p412; Đ Ton Duc Thang). Costs for these ferries are negotiable. Also departing from this location are hydrofoils to Vung Tau (US$10, one hour 20 minutes, nine daily). For more information on the services contact **Petro Express** (☎ 821 0650) at the jetty.

Bus

Intercity buses depart from and arrive at several bus stations around HCMC. Local buses (3500d) travelling to the intercity bus stations leave from the station situated opposite Ben Thanh Market (Map p409). There are four useful bus stations located around the city:

Cholon bus station (Map pp406-7; Đ Le Quang Trung) Convenient buses to My Tho and other Mekong Delta towns; the station is located one street north of Binh Tay Market.

Mien Dong bus station (Map pp406-7; ☎ 829 4056) Buses to places north of HCMC; in Binh Thanh District, about 5km from central Saigon on National Hwy 13.

Mien Tay bus station (☎ 825 5955) Even more buses to points south of HCMC, but about 10km southwest of Saigon in An Lac.

Tay Ninh bus station (Map pp406-7; ☎ 849 5935) Buses to Tay Ninh, Cu Chi and points northeast of HCMC, in Tan Binh District.

INTERNATIONAL BUS

There are international bus services connecting HCMC and Phnom Penh touted around the Pham Ngu Lao area. Better are the direct services with **Phnom Penh Sorya Transport** (Map p411; ☎ 920 3624; 309 Pham Ngu Lao). Services depart in either direction five times a day between 6.30am and 1pm, costing US$12. This service avoids a change of bus at the border.

Car & Motorcycle

Hotels and travellers cafés can arrange car rentals from about US$25 per day and up, depending on the destination. Pham Ngu Lao is the neighbourhood to look for motorbike rentals (US$5 to US$10 per day).

VIETNAM

Train

Saigon Railways Tourist Services (Map p411;
☎ 836 7640; 275C Đ Pham Ngu Lao) A convenient place
to purchase tickets.

Saigon train station (Ga Sai Gon; Map pp406-7;
☎ 824 5585; 1 Đ Nguyen Thong; ⊗ 7.15-11am &
1-3pm)

GETTING AROUND
To/From the Airport

Tan Son Nhat Airport is 7km northwest of
central HCMC. Metered taxis are your best
bet and cost around 75,000d (US$5). **Sasco
Taxi** (☎ 844 6448), just beyond the baggage car-
ousels, has a counter where you can prepay
for a taxi.

The driver may try to claim your hotel of
choice is closed, burned down, is dirty and
dangerous, or anything to steer you somewhere else.

A motorbike taxi (50,000d) is an option
for getting to/from the airport, but you're not
saving much for a lot of stress.

Most economical is the air-conditioned
airport bus (3500d), No 152, departing every 15
minutes. It stops at both the international
and domestic terminals before making regular stops along Đ De Tham (Pham Ngu Lao
area) and international hotels along Đ Dong
Khoi.

Bicycle

Bicycles are available for hire from many
budget hotels and cafés, especially around
Pham Ngu Lao.

Car & Motorcycle

If you're brave souls or experienced bikers, it's
a thrill a minute driving here. Motorbikes are
available for hire around Pham Ngu Lao for
US$5 to US$10 per day. Make sure to give it a
test drive first; you'll usually be asked to leave
your passport as collateral.

Cyclo

Cyclos are the most interesting way of getting
around town, but avoid them at night. Overcharging tourists is the norm, so negotiate a
price beforehand and have the exact change.
You can rent a cyclo from 20,000d per hour.

Taxi

Hail taxis on the street. If you don't find one
straight away, ring up and one will be dis-
patched in less time than it takes to say 'Ho

Chi Minh'. Note that faulty meters are much
less common here than in Hanoi.

Try the following:
Ben Thanh Taxi (☎ 842 2422)
Mai Linh Taxi (☎ 822 6666)
Red Taxi (☎ 844 6677)
Saigon Taxi (☎ 842 4242)
Vina Taxi (☎ 811 1111)

Xe Om

Far more prevalent than a traditional taxi is
the *xe om* or moto taxi. The accepted rate is
10,000d to 15,000d for short rides.

AROUND HO CHI MINH CITY

CU CHI TUNNELS

The **tunnel network** (admission 70,000d) at Cu Chi
was the stuff of legend during the 1960s for
its role in facilitating Viet Cong control of a
large rural area only 30km from Saigon. At its
height, the tunnel system stretched from Saigon to the Cambodian border. In the district
of Cu Chi alone, there were more than 200km
of tunnels. After ground operations targeting
the tunnels claimed large numbers of casualties and proved ineffective, the Americans
turned their artillery and bombers on the area,
transforming it into a moonscape.

Parts of this remarkable tunnel network
have been reconstructed and two sites are
open to visitors; one near the village of Ben
Dinh and the other at Ben Duoc. During
guided tours of the tunnel complex, it's possible to actually descend into tunnel entrances
as well as into the tunnels themselves. Although some sections have been widened,
others remain in their original condition. If
you can fit into the narrow passageways, you'll
gain an empathetic, if claustrophobic, awe for
the people who spent weeks underground.

Day tours operated by travellers cafés charge
around US$5 per person (transport only); most
include a stop at the Cao Dai Great Temple in
Tay Ninh. Private tours with a guide are also
available through hotels and travel agencies.

TAY NINH

☎ 066 / pop 41,300
Tay Ninh town, capital of Tay Ninh Province,
serves as the headquarters of one of Vietnam's most interesting indigenous religions

(see the boxed text, p80). The Cao Dai Great Temple was built between 1933 and 1955. Victor Hugo is among the Westerners especially revered by the Cao Dai; look for his likeness at the Great Temple.

Tay Ninh is 96km northwest of HCMC. The Cao Dai Holy See complex is 4km east of Tay Ninh. One-day tours from Saigon, including Tay Ninh and the Cu Chi Tunnels, cost around US$5 and private tours are also available through hotels and travel agencies.

BEACHES AROUND HO CHI MINH CITY

There are several beach resorts within striking distance of downtown Saigon, although most visitors make for Mui Ne (p397). If time is pressing and you want a quick fix, consider Vung Tau or Long Hai.

A short hop from HCMC, **Vung Tau** drones with bass-thumping action on the weekends as Saigonese visitors motor into town. Weekdays, however, are blissfully quiet, with kilometres of empty beaches. The business of oil-drilling here means the azure horizon is marred by oil tankers, and the population flecked with expats. There are stacks of hotels to choose from. Back Beach has the best choice of budget digs, while Front Beach has a row of slick midrange hotels. If you've never been to Rio di Janeiro, Small Mountain (Nui Nho), has a giant **Jesus** (admission free; ☺ 7.30-11.30am & 1.30-5pm) waiting with arms outstretched to embrace the South China Sea.

If you want to escape the mass tourism soullessness of Vung Tau, press on to **Long Hai**, a less-commercialised seaside retreat within a couple of hours' drive (30km) of HCMC. It has a pretty white-sand beach and the area benefits from a microclimate that brings less rain than other parts of the south. Its natural beauty persuaded Bao Đai, the last emperor of Vietnam, to build a holiday residence here (now the Anoasis Beach Resort).

From Mien Dong bus station in HCMC, air-con minibuses (25,000d, two hours) leave for Vung Tau. **Petro Express hydrofoil** (☎ in HCMC 08-821 0650, Vung Tau 816 308) has services to Vung Tau (120,000d, 90 minutes) from Bach Dang jetty in HCMC. Boats leave roughly every two hours from 6.30am. In Vung Tau the boat leaves from Cau Da pier, opposite the Hai Au Hotel.

Long Hai is 124km from HCMC, about a two-hour journey by car. The 30km road between Vung Tau and Long Hai is not served by any public transport; a *xe om* ride should cost around 50,000d.

MEKONG DELTA

Vietnam's 'rice basket', the Mekong Delta is a watery landscape of green fields and sleepy villages, crisscrossed by the chocolaty brown canals and rivulets fed by the mighty Mekong River. Its inhabitants – stereotyped as an extremely friendly and easy-going lot – have long toiled on the life-sustaining river, with their labours marked by the same cycles governing the waterways.

After winding its way from its source in Tibet, the Mekong River meets the sea in southernmost Vietnam. This delta-plain is lush with rice paddies and fish farms. Once part of the Khmer kingdom, the Mekong Delta was the last part of modern-day Vietnam to be annexed and settled by the Vietnamese.

Those seeking an idyllic retreat will find it in Phu Quoc, a forested island dotted with pretty beaches, freshwater springs and empty roads. Good diving and silicon-sand beauty have put it on the map, but it's still possible to find peace along the relatively uncrowded coastline.

By far the easiest and cheapest way to see the Delta is by taking a tour (one to three days) with a travel agency in Ho Chi Minh City (p405). Private tours are available through travel agencies, including driver and guide. It is also possible to travel independently. Although sometimes confusing and time-consuming, this option gives you maximum flexibility.

MY THO

☎ 074 / pop 169, 300

My Tho, the quiet capital city of Tien Giang Province, is the traditional gateway to the delta, owing to its proximity to HCMC. Visitors on a whirlwind Vietnam tour often take a day trip here to catch a glimpse of the famous river. In order to visit floating markets, however, you'll need to continue on to Cantho (p421).

In My Tho, river-boat tours can be booked at the main riverfront office of **Tien Giang Tourist** (Cong Ty Du Lich Tien Giang; ☎ 873 184; 8 Đ 30 Thang 4; ☺ 7am-5pm). Boat tours cruise past picturesque rural villages and are the highlight of a visit to My Tho. Depending on what you book, destinations usually include a coconut-candy workshop, a honey-bee farm and an orchid garden. Getting a group together to hire a boat makes these tours economical; otherwise it's US$25 for two hours on the water.

Sleeping & Eating

Rang Dong Hotel (☎ 874 400; 25 Đ 30 Thang 4; r 130,000-150,000d; 🔀) Privately run, this decent, friendly spot remains popular with budget travellers.

Song Tien Hotel (☎ 872 009; fax 884 745; 101 Đ Trung Trac; r/ste 160,000/260,000d; 🔀) The comfortable rooms here include red-and-white tile floors, TV and fridge. Suites are spacious with polished lacquer furniture. There's also a lift.

Chuong Duong Hotel (☎ 870 875; cdhotelmytho@hcm .vnn.vn; 10 Đ 30 Thang 4; r US$25-35; 🔀) My Tho's most luxurious accommodation, this place boasts a prime riverside location and respectable in-house restaurant. All rooms overlook the Mekong River.

Chi Thanh (☎ 873 756; 279 Đ Tet Mau Than; mains 20,000-40,000d) A tidy spot for delicious Chinese and Vietnamese fare, Chi Thanh has several locations, with menus in English.

My Tho is known for a special vermicelli soup, *hu tieu my tho*, which is richly garnished with fresh and dried seafood, pork, chicken and fresh herbs. Carnivores will enjoy **Hu Tieu 44** (44 Đ Nam Ky Khoi Nghia; soups 7000d), while vegetarians should look for **Hu Tieu Chay 24** (24 Đ Nam Ky Khoi Nghia; soups 4000d).

Getting There & Around

Buses leaving from the Cholon bus station in HCMC drop you right in My Tho (18,000d, two hours). Buses to other Mekong destinations depart from My Tho bus station (Ben Xe Khach Tien Giang), several kilometres west of town. From the city centre, take Đ Ap Bac westward and continue on to National Hwy 1.

Slooow cargo ferries depart from HCMC's Bach Dang jetty. Bring your own food and water and negotiate a price with the ferry captain.

To get to Ben Tre, head west for 1km on Đ 30 Thang 4 – which turns into Đ Le Thi Hong Gam – to the Ben Tre ferry (passengers/motorbikes 1000d/5000d).

My Tho is small and walkable; expeditions out of town can be arranged on a boat or *xe om*.

BEN TRE
☎ 075

Famous for its *keo dua* (coconut candy), Ben Tre is a bucolic 20-minute ferry ride from My Tho. Located away from the main highway, it receives far fewer visitors than My Tho and makes a lovely stop on a Mekong tour.

Ben Tre has a few **internet cafés** (per hr 4000d), including one on Đ Hung Vuong. There's also internet access at the **main post office** (3/1 Đ Dong Khoi; per hr 4000d). Get cash at **Incombank** (☎ 822 507; 42 Đ Nguyen Dinh Chieu).

A few hotels and family-run restaurants face the tiny Truc Giang Lake.

Thao Nhi Guesthouse (☎ 860 009; thaonhitours@yahoo .com; Hamlet 1, Tan Thach Village; r 80,000-250,000d; 🔀) is a friendly, rustic place amid abundant greenery, 11km north of town, and offers a range of comfortable rooms. The in-house restaurant serves excellent elephant-ear fish, plus there's free bike rental. **Dong Khoi Hotel** (☎ 822 501; dongkhoihotelbtre@vmm.vn; 16 Đ Hai Ba Trung; r 196,000-255,000; 🔀) is popular for wedding parties; its lift is the best of the three on the lakefront. It has clean, carpeted rooms, plus there's a decent restaurant (mains 20,000d to 40,000d) on the ground floor.

Nam Son (☎ 822 873; 40 Đ Phan Ngoc Tong; mains 15,000-30,000d) is usually packed with locals feasting on roast chicken and drinking draught beer.

HCMC-bound minibuses leave daily from the petrol station on Đ Dong Khoi, but they don't run on a fixed schedule. Ask at a local hotel for the latest word.

VINH LONG
☎ 070 / pop 130,000

A bit more chaotic than other Mekong towns of its size, Vinh Long has noisy, motorbike-filled streets, though its riverfront makes for a fine escape from the mayhem. Despite the lack of in-town attractions, Vinh Long is the gateway to river islands and some worthwhile sites, including the Cai Be floating market and homestays – which can be a highlight of a Mekong journey.

Cuu Long Tourist (☎ 823 616; cuulongtourist1@hcm .vnn.vn; 1 Đ 1 Thang 5; 🕒 7am-5pm) is one of the more capable state-run tour outfits.

Vietcombank (☎ 823 109; 143 Đ Le Thai To) has two branches in town and can exchange cash and travellers cheques.

What makes a trip to Vinh Long worthwhile are the beautiful islands in the river. Charter a boat through Cuu Long Tourist for around US$10 per person or pay substantially less for a private operator (US$3 to US$4 per hour).

The bustling **river market** (🕒 5am-5pm) is worth including on a boat tour from Vinh

Long. Wholesalers on big boats moor here, each specialising in one or a few types of fruit or vegetable.

Don't stay in town, but opt for a homestay: see the boxed text, below for more.

Thien Tan (☎ 824 001; 56/1 Đ Pham Thai Buong; mains 30,000-50,000d; ☯ lunch & dinner), specialising in barbecued dishes, is the best eatery in town. Recommended is the *ca loc nuong tre* (fish cooked in bamboo) and *ga nuong dat set* (chicken cooked in clay).

Frequent buses go between Vinh Long and HCMC (50,000d, three hours), You can also get to Vinh Long by bus from Can Tho (25,000d), My Tho and other points on the Mekong Delta. Vinh Long's bus station is right in the middle of town.

CANTHO

☎ 071 / pop 330,100

The largest city in the Mekong, Cantho is a buzzing town with a lively waterfront. The political, economic, cultural and transportation heart of the Mekong Delta, Cantho hums with activity. Access to nearby floating markets makes it a major draw for tourists.

Cai Rang is the biggest floating market in the Mekong Delta, 6km from Cantho towards Soc Trang. Though the lively market goes on until around noon daily, show up before 9am for the best photo opportunities. You can hire boats on the river near the Cantho market. Cai Rang is one hour away by boat, or you can drive to Cau Dau Sau boat landing, where

you can get a **rowing boat** (per hr around 50,000d) to the market, 10 minutes away.

Less crowded and less motorised is the **Phong Dien market**, with more stand-up rowboats. It's best between 6am and 8am. Twenty kilometres southwest of Cantho, it's easy to reach by road and you can hire a boat on arrival.

Information

Cantho Tourist (☎ 821 852; fax 822 719; 20 Đ Hai Ba Trung; ☯ 7am-5pm & 6-8pm) Helpful staff speak English and French. Tours available.

Vietcombank (Ngan Hang Ngoai Thuong Viet Nam; ☎ 820 445; fax 820 694; 7 ĐL Hoa Binh) Has foreign-currency exchange and 24-hour ATM.

Sleeping & Eating

Hien Guesthouse (☎ 812 718; hien_gh@yahoo.com; 118/10 Đ Phan Dinh Phung; r with fan/air-con US$5/8; ☷) This friendly, family-run guesthouse is tucked down a narrow alley near the city centre.

Ninh Kieu Hotel (☎ 821 171; 2 Đ Hai Ba Trung; r old wing US$25-30, new wing r US$40-80; ☷) Boasting a terrific location on the riverfront, rooms in the new wing are carpeted and have balconies. Old-wing rooms are clean but dated.

Victoria Can Tho Hotel (☎ 810 111; www.victoria hotels-asia.com; r US$161-282; ☷ ☐ ☲) This lovely place sits right on the riverfront and is Cantho's *crème de la crème*. Lavish rooms have garden or river views and guests have access to the fine restaurant, open-air bar, tennis courts and swimming pool.

A NIGHT ON THE MEKONG

One of the highlights of any Vietnam trip is a homestay with one of the friendly Mekong families. The following places all charge around US$10 per night, which includes a night's sleep, dinner and breakfast the next morning. Vinh Long is the best place to arrange a homestay.

▪ **Nha Co Tran Tuan Kiet** (☎ 073-824 498; 22 Phu Hoa hamlet, Dong Hoa Hip Village, Cai Be District) This traditional wooden house has beautiful ornate details and a history dating back 150 years. The cooking here is excellent. It's in Cai Be, 25km west of My Tho.

▪ **Sau Giao** (☎ 070-859 910; Binh Thuan 2 Hamlet, Hoa Ninh Village, Long Ho District) A few kilometres outside of Vinh Long along the river, Sau Giao is a beautiful traditional wooden house. It serves excellent cuisine. Bicycle hire available (per day US$1).

▪ **Song Tien** (☎ 070-858 487; An Thanh Hamlet, An Binh Village, Long Ho District) Across the Co Chien River from Vinh Long, this friendly place offers accommodation in small bungalows with squat toilets. The owner and his wife, both former Viet Cong soldiers, are known to bust out the mandolin for a bit of traditional singing for their guests.

▪ **Tam Ho** (☎ 070-859 859; info@caygiong.com; Binh Thuan 1 Hamlet, Hoa Ninh Village, Long Ho District) About 1.5km from Vinh Long, Tam Ho is a working orchard run by a friendly, welcoming family – one of the hosts bears a striking resemblance to Ho Chi Minh. Private rooms available.

OFF THE BEATEN TRACK IN THE MEKONG DELTA

It's not hard to get off the beaten track in the Mekong Delta, as most tourists are on hit-and-run day trips from HCMC or passing through the major centres on their way to or from Cambodia. Here are some of the lesser-known gems in the Mekong Delta.

Don't have time to visit Cambodia? Check out some Khmer culture in **Soc Trang**, home to a significant population of Cambodians and their beautiful temples.

Speaking of Cambodia, the Khmer kingdom of Funan once held sway over much of the lower Mekong and the principal port was at **Oc Eo**. Located near Long Xuyen, archaeologists have found ancient Persian and Roman artefacts here.

Birding enthusiasts will want to make a diversion to **Tram Chin Reserve** near Cao Lang, a habitat for the rare eastern sarus crane. These huge birds are depicted on the bas reliefs at Angkor and only found here and in northwest Cambodia.

The small and secluded beach resort of **Hon Chong** has the most scenic stretch of coastline on the Mekong Delta mainland. The big attractions here are Chua Hang Grotto, Duong Beach and Nghe Island.

Restaurant alley (Đ Nam Ky Khoi Nghia) Want to slip away from the tourist scene on the riverfront? Situated in an alley between Đ Dien Bien Phu and Đ Phan Dinh Phung, this alley has about a dozen local restaurants scattered on both sides of the street.

Nam Bo (☎ 823 908; nambo@hcm.vnn.vn; 50 Đ Hai Ba Trung; mains 25,000-50,000d; ☺ lunch & dinner) Housed in a thoughtfully restored, classic French villa, Nam Bo offers excellent European and Vietnamese cuisine in a delightful atmosphere.

Cappuccino (☎ 825 296; 2 Đ Hai Ba Trung; mains 35,000-70,000d; ☺ lunch & dinner) For a break from *pho*, head to this popular Italian restaurant near the riverfront. You'll find a decent selection of pizzas and pastas.

Getting There & Around

Buses and minibuses from HCMC leave the Mien Tay station (65,000d, five hours). The **Cantho bus station** (Đ Nguyen Trai & Đ Tran Phu) is about 1km north of town.

Xe loi (motorbikes with two-seater carriages on the back) cost 5000d or so for rides around town. Most guesthouses also hire out bicycles.

CHAU DOC

☎ 076 / pop 100,000

Perched on the banks of the Bassac River, Chau Doc is a charming town near the Cambodian border with sizable Chinese, Cham and Khmer communities. Thanks to the popular river crossing between Vietnam and Cambodia (see the boxed text, p424), many travellers pass through Chau Doc. Nearby

Sam Mountain is a local beauty spot with terrific views over Cambodia.

War remnants near Chau Doc include Ba Chuc, the site of a Khmer Rouge massacre with a bone pagoda similar to that of Cambodia's Choeung Ek memorial; and Tuc Dup Hill, where an expensive American bombing campaign in 1963 earned it the nickname Two Million Dollar Hill. It's also possible to visit fish farms set up underneath floating houses on the river.

There's **internet access** (per hr 4000d; ☺ 7am-9pm) in the courtyard of Chau Doc's **main post office** (☎ 869 200; 2 Đ Le Loi). Foreign currency can be exchanged at **Incombank** (☎ 866 497; 68-70 Đ Nguyen Huu Canh).

Sleeping & Eating

Vinh Phuoc Hotel (☎ 866 242; 12 Đ Quang Trung; r US$6-15; ☒) A good budget deal, this place is run by an amiable Brit who is an excellent source of local travel info. There's a good restaurant.

Delta Adventure Inn (Nha Khach Long Chau; ☎ 861 249; deltaadventureinn@hotmail.com; r 120,000-240,000d; ☒) This cosy compound sits amid the rice paddies about 4km from Chau Doc. The views of Sam Mountain are lovely from the island café-restaurant on the grounds.

Victoria Chau Doc Hotel (☎ 865 010; www.victoria hotels-asia.com; 32 Đ Le Loi; r US$115-196, internet rates US$92-144; ☒ ▢ ☒) Perched on the riverside, the Victoria is the swishest place in town. All rooms have wooden floors, bathtubs and gorgeous décor. The hotel's Bassac Restaurant is superb.

Good local eateries in Chau Doc include **Bay Bong** (☎ 867 271; 22 Đ Thuong Dang Le; mains from

35,000d) with excellent hotpots and soups, and **Mekong** (☎ 867 381; 41 Đ Le Loi; mains 35,000-45,000d), set in the grounds of a decaying villa opposite the Victoria.

Getting There & Around

Buses to Chau Doc depart HCMC's Mien Tay station (84,000d, six hours). For more on the border crossing to Cambodia, see the boxed text, p424.

RACH GIA

☎ 077 / pop 172,400

Rach Gia's port is perched on a river mouth opening onto the Gulf of Thailand, making it a jumping-off point for Phu Quoc Island. It's a prime smuggling hub, due to its proximity to Cambodia, Thailand and the great wide ocean. The centre of town sits on an islet embraced by the two arms of the Cai Lon River; the north side has your getaway options out of town.

Information

Kien Giang Tourist (Cong Ty Du Lich Kien Giang; ☎ 862 081; 12 Đ Ly Tu Trong) The provincial tourism authority.
Rach Gia Internet Café (152 Đ Nguyen Trung Truc) Has a pretty fast connection.
Vietcombank (☎ 863 178; 2 Đ Mac Cuu) There's a 24-hour ATM here.

Sleeping & Eating

Hong Nam Hotel (☎ 873 090; fax 873 424; Đ Ly Thai To; r 150,000-250,000d; ✷) This minihotel offers sparkly, spacious rooms decked out with all the modern comforts. It's near the Rach Gia Trade Centre. Some have balconies.

Kim Co Hotel (☎ 879 610; fax 879 611; 141 Đ Nguyen Hung Son; r 160,000-200,000d; ✷) This friendly place has colourful rooms (mint walls, orange curtains) and tubs in some bathrooms. Try to get a room with a window.

Hoang Gia 2 Hotel (☎ 920 980; tuananggia@vnn.vn; 31 Đ Le Than Thon; r 180,000-250,000d; ✷) Set with nice wood furnishings and bathtubs, the rooms here are in good shape, but some could use more light. There's a lift.

Ao Dai Moi (☎ 866 295; 26 Đ Ly Tu Trong; soups 8,000d; ✷ breakfast) The name means 'new ao dai' and Ao Dai Moi is run by a local tailor. The simple place has very good pho and wonton soup in the morning.

Tan Hung Phat (☎ 867 599; 118 Đ Nguyen Hung Son; mains 15,000-30,000d; ✷ breakfast, lunch & dinner) This friendly place has a good selection of fish and seafood dishes.

Quan F28 (☎ 867 334; 28 Đ Le Than Thon; mains 30,000-50,000d; ✷ lunch & dinner) With sidewalk seating and a popular night-time buzz, Quan F28 is the place to go for molluscs – crab, shrimp, snails, blood cockles and the like.

Getting There & Away

Vietnam Airlines flies once daily between HCMC and Rach Gia, continuing to Phu Quoc Island. You'll have to catch a *xe om* or *xe loi* from the airport to Rach Gia.

For details on getting to Phu Quoc by hydrofoil, see p425. Stop by the **Rach Gia hydrofoil terminal** (☎ 879 765) the day before, or phone ahead to book a seat.

Buses from HCMC (90,000d, six to seven hours) leave for Rach Gia from Mien Tay bus station in An Lac. Night buses leave Rach Gia between 7pm and 11pm. The **main bus station** (Ben Xe Rach Soi; 78 Đ Nguyen Trung Truc) in Rach Soi, 7km south of Rach Gia, has connections to Cantho and HCMC.

PHU QUOC ISLAND

☎ 077 / pop 52,700

One of Vietnam's star attractions, mountainous and forested Phu Quoc is a splendid tropical getaway set with beautiful white-sand beaches and quaint fishing villages. Adventure comes in many forms here – from motorbiking the empty dirt roads circling the island to sea kayaking its quiet inlets or scuba diving the coral reefs. Plans are afoot to develop the island á la Phuket style.

The tear-shaped island lies in the Gulf of Thailand, 15km south of the coast of Cambodia. Phu Quoc is Vietnam's largest island but is also claimed by Cambodia; its Khmer name is Ko Tral.

The main shipping port is An Thoi at the southern tip of Phu Quoc Island with connections to Rach Gia. Most beachside accommodation options are south of Duong Dong town on the western side of the island. Addresses outside of Duong Dong's centre are designated by the kilometre mark south of town.

Information

The post office is in downtown Duong Dong. There are several internet cafés in town including **Net Café** (5 Đ Nguyen Dinh Chieu; per hr 10,000d; ✷ 7am-10pm). Some of the hotels offer internet access.

VIETNAM

There is a useful ATM at Saigon-Phu Quoc Resort.

Sights & Activities

Deserted white-sand beaches ring the island. Bai Sao and Bai Dam are beautiful beaches on the south end of the island. Long Beach (Bai Truong) is a spectacular stretch of sand from Duong Dong southward along the west coast, almost to An Thoi.

About 90% of Phu Quoc Island is protected forest. The mountainous northern half of the island, where the trees are most dense, has been declared a forest reserve (Khu Rung Nguyen Sinh). You'll need a motorbike to get into the reserve, and as there are no real trekking trails, you'll need a guide anyway. In the centre of the island, just east of the guesthouse coast, are two hot springs, **Suoi Da Ban** (admission 1000d) and **Suoi Tranh**. In the dry season they're more moonscape than waterway.

The **An Thoi Islands** – 15 islands and islets at the southern tip of Phu Quoc – can be visited by chartered boat (US$40 per day), and it's a fine area for swimming, snorkelling and fishing.

Diving and snorkelling in Phu Quoc are just taking off, with few crowds and a more pristine marine environment than along the coast. Stop by the **Rainbow Divers** (☎ 0913-400 964; www.divevietnam.com; Km 1.5) desk at the Saigon-Phu Quoc Resort.

There are several places to rent **kayaks** along Bai Sao beach, and its protected waters make for a smooth ride. Expect to pay around 60,000d per hour.

Sleeping

Lam Ha Eco Resort (☎ 847 369; Long Beach; r/bungalow US$12/15; ❄) Friendly, family-run Lam Ha is excellent value for the money, with trim and tidy rooms and bungalows scattered around a lush garden.

Tropicana Resort (☎ 847 127; www.reservation@tropicanavietnam.com; Long Beach; d US$15, bungalows US$35-70; ❄ ▢ ▣) The pretty Tropicana is the kind of oasis you might need after a rough ferry ride. Attractive, handsomely furnished bungalows, all with veranda, face the garden or the sea.

Nhat Lan (☎ 847 663; Km 1.7; d US$8-12) Another nice family-run place offering comfortable concrete bungalows that come with excellent hammocks.

Beach Club (☎ 980 998; www.beachclubvietnam.com; Long Beach; r/bungalow US$15/20) Run by an English-Vietnamese couple, this laid-back spot provides great value for the money. The owner is a great source of local information.

Mango Bay (☎ 0903-382 207; www.mangobayphuquoc.com; Ong Lan Beach; bungalows US$25-50) This attractive, relaxed resort offers stylish rooms and bungalows, all with terraces. It's eco-friendly, using solar panels and organic and recycled building materials.

CROSSING INTO CAMBODIA: MEKONG DELTA BORDERS

One of the most enjoyable ways of entering Cambodia is via this crossing just west of Chau Doc along the Mekong River. Numerous agencies in Chau Doc sell boat tickets taking you from Chau Doc to Phnom Penh via the Vinh Xuong border. Slow boats for the trip cost around US$8 to US$10 and take eight hours (leaving around 8am and arriving in Phnom Penh at 4pm).

There are several companies offering fast boats. **Hang Chau** (☎ in Phnom Penh 012-883 542) departs Chau Doc at 7am and Phnom Penh at noon and costs US$15. The more upmarket **Blue Cruiser** (☎ in Phnom Penh 023-990 441, in Chau Doc 091-401622) pulls out at 8.30am and at 1.30pm respectively, costing US$35. Both take about four hours including a slow border check. More expensive again is the **Victoria express boat** (www.victoriahotels-asia.com), but at US$75 per person, it tends to be exclusive to Victoria hotel guests.

Some adventurous travellers like to plot their own course. Catch a minibus from Chau Doc to the border at Vinh Xuong (US$1, one hour). Once officially in Cambodia at Kaam Samnor, arrange a speedboat to Neak Luong (US$2.50 per person, US$15 for the boat, one hour). Once in Neak Luong, change to a local bus (4500r, regular departures) to Phnom Penh.

For information on crossing this border in the other direction, see p228.

Also nearby is the little used Tinh Bien–Phnom Den border crossing, which connects Chau Doc to Takeo Province in Cambodia. Cambodian visas are not currently available on arrival. For information on crossing this border in the other direction, see p247.

Saigon-Phu Quoc Resort (☎ 846 510; www.vietnam phuquoc.com; 1 Đ Tran Hung Dao, Long Beach; r US$95-190; 🟦 🖳 🟦) Attractive rooms here are in villa-type houses, with good views overlooking the beach. Book through the website for deals.

Eating & Drinking

Most guesthouses have their own lively cafés or restaurants in-house; wander along the beach until you find somewhere appealing.

Gop Gio (☎ 847 057; 78 Đ Tran Hung Dao; mains 30,000-50,000đ) On the main road into Duong Dong, this casual indoor-outdoor eatery has excellent seafood, with fresh, tasty dishes such as shrimp with mango and steamed grouper with ginger.

Ai Xiem (☎ 990 510; Bai Sao; mains 40,000-60,000đ) Set on the lovely white sands of Bai Sao beach, this is a great, low-key place for fresh seafood. Tables are on the sands, a few metres from lapping waves.

Rainbow Bar (☎ 0903-177 923) The hottest place to hang after dark. It's open-air, with a pool table and good music in a garden setting.

Getting There & Around

Vietnam Airlines has several daily flights (one way US$46) to Phu Quoc from HCMC, plus connections to Rach Gia (one way US$32).

Numerous companies operate speedy hydrofoils sailing between Rach Gia and Phu Quoc. Boats leave the mainland daily between 7am and 8.30am, and return from Phu Quoc between 12.30pm and 1.30pm. Ticket prices for the 2½-hour journey range from 150,000đ to 200,000đ. Hydrofoil companies include **Super Dong** (☎ Rach Gia 077-878 475, Phu Quoc 980 111), **Duong Dong Express** (☎ Rach Gia 077-879 765, Phu Quoc 990 747) and **Hai Au** (☎ Rach Gia 077-879 455, Phu Quoc 990 555).

Xe om rides from An Thoi harbour to Duong Dong cost about 30,000đ. The island's middle road from An Thoi to Duong Dong is paved, but dirt is the colour of the island's other roads. Motorbike rentals are available through guesthouses and hotels for about US$7 per day.

VIETNAM DIRECTORY

ACCOMMODATION

Vietnam has something for everyone – from dives to the divine. Most hotels in Vietnam quote prices in a mix of Vietnamese dong and US dollars. Prices are quoted in dong or dol-

---

PRACTICALITIES

- The usual voltage is 220V, 50 cycles, but sometimes you encounter 110V, also at 50 cycles, just to confuse things. Electrical sockets are usually two-pin.

- Most guesthouses and hotels have cheap laundry services, but check they have a dryer if the weather is bad.

- *Vietnam News* and the *Saigon Times* are popular English-language dailies. Good magazines include the *Vietnam Economic Times,* plus its listings mag, the *Guide,* and the *Vietnam Investment Review.*

- *Voice of Vietnam* hogs the airwaves all day and is pumped through loudspeakers in many smaller towns. There are several TV channels and a steady diet of satellite.

- The Vietnamese use the metric system for everything except precious metals and gems, where they follow the Chinese.

---

lars throughout this chapter based on the preferred currency of the particular property.

Family-run guesthouses are usually the cheapest option; they often have private bathrooms and rates range from around US$5 to US$15. A step up from the guesthouses, minihotels typically come with more amenities: satellite TV, minifridges and IDD phones. Rates often go down the more steps you have to climb; that is, upper floors are cheaper.

When it comes to midrange places, flash a bit more cash and three-star touches are available, such as access to a swimming pool and a hairdryer hidden away somewhere.

At the top end are a host of international-standard hotels and resorts that charge from US$75 a room to US$750 or more a suite. Some of these are fairly faceless business hotels, while others ooze opulence or resonate with history.

Be aware that some budget and midrange hotels apply a 10% sales tax. Check carefully before taking the room to avoid any unpleasant shocks on departure.

Accommodation is at a premium during Tet (late January or early February), when the country is on the move and overseas Vietnamese

VIETNAM

flood back into the country. Prices can rise by 25%. Christmas and New Year represent another high season, but things aren't quite as crazy as at Tet.

Homestays

Homestays are a popular option in parts of Vietnam, but some local governments are more flexible than others about the concept. Homestays were pioneered in the Mekong Delta (see the boxed text, p421). At the opposite end of the map, there are also homestays on the island of Cat Ba (p372).

Many people like to stay with ethnic minority families in the far north of Vietnam. Sapa (p376) is the number-one destination to meet the hill tribes in Vietnam and it is possible to undertake two- or three-day treks with an overnight in a Hmong or Dzao village.

ACTIVITIES

Vietnam's roads and rivers, sea and mountains, provide ample opportunity for active adventures. Travel agencies and travellers cafés all over the country can arrange local trips, from kayaking on Halong Bay to trekking up Fansipan to kite-surfing in Mui Ne.

Cycling

The flatlands and back roads of the Mekong Delta are wonderful to cycle through and observe the vibrant workaday agricultural life. Another spot well away from the insane traffic of National Hwy 1 is Hwy 14, winding through the Central Highlands. Arrange mountain-biking tours in the northern mountains at **Handspan Adventure Travel** (Map p358; ☎ 04-926 0581; www.handspan.com; 78 Pho Ma May, Hanoi); or stop by **Sinhbalo Adventures** (Map p411; ☎ 08-837 6766; www.sinhbalo.com; 283/20 Đ Pham Ngu Lao) in HCMC to meander the Mekong Delta or further afield.

Diving & Snorkelling

Vietnam has several great dive destinations for underwater exploration. Long established, with many dive sites, is the beach resort of Nha Trang (p392). A notable emerging dive destination is Phu Quoc Island (p423), with fewer visitors and a more pristine environment.

Golf

The best golf courses in Vietnam are located in Dalat and Phan Thiet, but there are also plenty of courses in and around Hanoi and HCMC.

Kayaking

For an even closer look at those limestone crags, it's possible to paddle yourself around Halong Bay. Talk to travel agencies in Hanoi to arrange Halong Bay kayaking trips.

Trekking

The most popular region for trekking is the northwest, notably around Sapa (p376), which includes Vietnam's tallest mountain, Fansipan. There's also good trekking in the jungles of Cat Ba (p371) and Cuc Phuong (p368) National Parks. The trekking trails in Bach Ma National Park (p382) are also a good bet.

Water Sports

Mui Ne (p397) is Vietnam's best shoreline for kite-surfing and windsurfing fiends. Nha Trang (p392) is another good locale for windsurfing, sailing or wakeboarding. The area around China Beach (p387), south of Danang, also gets passable surf between September and December.

BOOKS

Lonely Planet's *Vietnam* guide provides the full scoop on the country. If you're interested in cuisine and the culture behind it, sink your teeth into *World Food Vietnam*. The *Vietnamese Phrasebook* is practical and helps pass the time on long bus rides.

BUSINESS HOURS

Offices and other public buildings are usually open from 7am or 8am to 11am or 11.30am and from 1pm or 2pm to 4pm or 5pm. Banks tend to be open during these hours, and until 11.30am on Saturday. Post offices are generally open from 6.30am to 9pm. Government offices are usually open until noon on Saturday and closed Sunday. Most museums are closed on Monday. Temples are usually open all day, every day.

Many small, privately owned shops, restaurants and street stalls stay open seven days a week, often until late at night.

CLIMATE

Vietnam's south is tropical but the north can experience chilly winters – in Hanoi, an overcoat can be necessary in January.

The southwestern monsoon blows from April or May to October, bringing warm, damp weather to the whole country, except those areas sheltered by mountains, namely the central part of the coastal strip and the Red River Delta.

See the Hanoi climate chart (p485).

COURSES
Cooking
Cooking courses are really taking off in Vietnam. Hone your culinary skills in Hanoi, Hoi An or HCMC.

Language
If you want to brush up on your Vietnamese, there are courses offered in HCMC, Hanoi and elsewhere. Lessons usually cost from US$3 to US$10 per hour. Decide whether you want to study in northern or southern Vietnam, because the regional dialects are very different. For more details, see under language courses in Hanoi (p357) and Ho Chi Minh City (p410).

CUSTOMS
Bear in mind that customs may seize suspected antiques or other 'cultural treasures', which cannot legally be taken out of Vietnam. If you do purchase authentic or reproduction antiques, be sure to get a receipt and a customs clearance form from the seller.

DANGERS & ANNOYANCES
Since 1975 many thousands of Vietnamese have been maimed or killed by rockets, artillery shells, mortars, mines and other ordnance left over from the war. *Never* touch any war relics you come across – such objects can remain lethal for decades, and one bomb can ruin your whole day.

Violent crime is still relatively rare in Vietnam, but petty theft is definitely not. Drive-by bag snatchers on motorbikes are not uncommon, and thieves on buses, trains and boats stealthily rifle through bags or haul them off altogether. Skilled pickpockets work the crowds.

One strong suggestion, in particular for HCMC, is to not have anything dangling off your body that you are not ready to part with. This includes cameras and any jewellery. When riding a *xe om,* sling shoulder bags across the front of your body. On public buses, try to stow your bag where you're sitting; on trains, secure it to something if you have to leave it.

EMBASSIES & CONSULATES
Visas can be obtained in your home country through the Vietnamese embassy or consulate. See p432 for more details.

Embassies & Consulates in Vietnam
With the exception of those for Cambodia, China and Laos, the embassies in Hanoi and consulates in HCMC do very little visa business for non-Vietnamese.

Australia (www.ausinvn.com) Hanoi (☎ 04-831 7755; 8 Duong Dao Tan, Ba Dinh District); HCMC (Map p412; ☎ 08-829 6035; 5th fl, 5B Đ Ton Duc Thang)

Cambodia Hanoi (Map pp352-3; ☎ 04-825 3788; 71A Pho Tran Hung Dao); HCMC (Map p409; ☎ 08-827 7696; cambocg@hcm.vnn.vn; 41 Đ Phung Khac Khoan)

VIETNAM IN WORDS

- *Catfish and Mandala* (1999) Part memoir and part travel narrative, this is Andrew X Pham's fascinating account of his escape from the war-torn Vietnam of 1977 and his subsequent return two decades later, equipped with a bicycle and a desire to sort out his mixed-up cultural identity.

- *Dispatches* (1977) For a behind-the-scenes look at the American War, hitch a ride with Michael Herr. A correspondent for *Rolling Stone* magazine, Herr tells it how it is as some of the darkest events of the war unfold around him, including the siege of Khe Sanh.

- *Shadows and Wind* (1999) Journalist Robert Templer explores contemporary Vietnam, from Ho Chi Minh personality cults to Vietnam's rock-and-roll youth.

- *The Sorrow of War* (1996) For a human perspective on the North Vietnamese experience during the war, Bao Ninh's poignant tale of love and loss shows the boys from the North had the same fears and desires as most American GIs.

- *The Quiet American* (1955) Graham Greene's classic novel is the perfect introduction to Vietnam in the 1950s, as the French disengaged and the Americans moved in to take their place. If only the American politicians had shared his foresight.

Canada (www.dfait-maeci.gc.ca/vietnam) Hanoi (Map pp352-3; ☎ 04-823 5500; 31 Pho Hung Vuong); HCMC (Map p412; ☎ 08-827 9899; 10th fl, 235 Ð Dong Khoi)

China Hanoi (Map pp352-3; ☎ 04-845 3736; Pho Hoang Dieu); HCMC (Map p409; ☎ 08-829 2457; chinaconsul _hcm _vn@mfa.gov.cn; 39 Ð Nguyen Thi Minh Khai)

France Hanoi (Map pp352-3; ☎ 04-943 7719; Pho Tran Hung Dao); HCMC (Map p409; ☎ 08-829 7231; 27 Ð Nguyen Thi Minh Khai)

Germany Hanoi (Map pp352-3; ☎ 04-845 3836; 29 Ð Tran Phu); HCMC (Map p409; ☎ 08-822 4385; 126 Ð Nguyen Dinh Chieu)

Japan Hanoi (☎ 04-846 3000; 27 Pho Lieu Giai, Ba Dinh District); HCMC (Map p412; ☎ 08-822 5314; 13-17 ÐL Nguyen Hue)

Laos Danang (16 Ð Tran Qui Cap); Hanoi (Map pp352-3; ☎ 04-825 4576; 22 Pho Tran Binh Trong); HCMC (Map p412; ☎ 08-829 7667; 93 Ð Pasteur)

Netherlands HCMC (Map p409; ☎ 04-823 5932; hcm -ca@minbuza.nl; 29 ÐL Le Duan, HCMC)

New Zealand Hanoi (☎ 04-824 1481; nzembhan@fpt .vn; Level 5, 63 Pho Ly Thai To); HCMC (Map p409; ☎ 08-822 6907; Ste 909, 235 Ð Donh Khoi)

Singapore (Map pp352-3; ☎ 04-823 3965; 41-43 Ð Tran Phu, Hanoi)

Sweden (☎ 04-726 0400; 2 Ð Nui Truc, Hanoi)

Thailand Hanoi (Map pp352-3; ☎ 04-823 5092; 63-65 Pho Hoang Dieu); HCMC (Map p409; ☎ 08-932 7637; 77 Ð Tran Quoc Thao)

UK (www.uk-vietnam.org) Hanoi (Map p358; ☎ 04-936 0500; Central Bldg, 31 Pho Hai Ba Trung); HCMC (Map p409; ☎ 08-829 8433; 25 ÐL Le Duan)

US (http://usembassy.state.gov/vietnam) Hanoi (☎ 04-772 1500; 7 Pho Lang Ha, Ba Dinh District); HCMC (☎ 08-822 9433; 4 ÐL Le Duan)

Vietnamese Embassies & Consulates Abroad

Australia Canberra (☎ 02-6286 6059; www.vietnamem bassy.org.au; 6 Timbarra Cres, O'Malley, ACT 2606); Sydney (☎ 02-9327 2539; tlssyd@auco.net.au; 489 New South Head Rd, Double Bay, NSW 2028)

Cambodia (☎ 023-362531; 436 Monivong Blvd, Phnom Penh)

Canada (☎ 613-236 1398; www.vietnamembassy -canada.ca; 470 Wilbrod St, ON K1N 6M8, Ottawa)

China Běijīng (☎ 010-6532 1125; vnaemba@mailhost .cinet.co.cn; 32 Guanghua Lu, 100600); Guǎngzhōu (☎ 020-8652 7908; Jin Yanf Hotel, 92 Huanshi Western Rd)

France (☎ 01 44 14 6400; 62-66 Rue Boileau, 75016, Paris)

Germany (☎ 030-509 8262; Konigswinter St 28, D-10318, Berlin)

Hong Kong (☎ 22-591 4510; 15th fl, Great Smart Tower, 230 Wan Chai Rd, Wan Chai)

Italy (☎ 06-6616 0726; 156 Via di Bravetta, 00164, Rome)

Japan Osaka (☎ 06-263 1600; 10th fl, Estate Bakurocho Bldg, 1-4-10 Bakurocho, Chuo-ku); Tokyo (☎ 03-3466 3311; 50-11 Moto Yoyogi-Cho, Shibuya-ku, 151)

Laos Savannakhet (☎ 41-212 239; 418 Sisavang Vong); Vientiane (☎ 21-413 409; That Luang Rd)

Thailand (☎ 2-251 7202; 83/1 Wireless Rd, 10500, Bangkok)

UK (☎ 020-7937 1912; www.vietnamembassy.org.uk; 12-14 Victoria Rd, W8 5RD, London)

USA San Francisco (☎ 415-922 1707; www.vietnam consulate-sf.org; 1700 California St, Ste 430, CA 94109); Washington (☎ 202-861 0737; www.vietnamembassy -usa.org; 1233 20th St NW, Ste 400, DC 20036)

FESTIVALS & EVENTS

Vietnam's major festival is Tet – see opposite for details.

Ngay Mot & Ngay Ram Pagodas are packed with Buddhist worshippers on the first and 15th days of the lunar month. Tasty vegetarian meals are served.

Tiet Doan Ngo (Summer Solstice) Human effigies are burnt to satisfy the need for souls to serve in the God of Death's army, on the fifth day of the fifth lunar month.

Trung Nguyen (Wandering Souls Day) On the 15th day of the seventh lunar month, offerings are presented to the ghosts of the forgotten dead.

Mid-Autumn Festival On the night of 15 August, children walk the streets carrying glowing lanterns, and people exchange gifts of mooncakes.

FOOD & DRINK
Food

One of the delights of visiting Vietnam is the cuisine; there are said to be nearly 500 traditional Vietnamese dishes. Generally, food is superbly prepared and excellent value…and you never have to go very far to find it. For more on dining in the Mekong region, see p86.

FRUIT

Aside from the usual delightful Southeast Asian fruits, Vietnam has its own unique *trai thanh long* (green dragon fruit), a bright fuchsia-coloured fruit with green scales. Grown mainly along the coastal region near Nha Trang, it has white flesh flecked with edible black seeds, and tastes something like a mild kiwifruit.

MEALS

Pho is the noodle soup that built a nation and is eaten at all hours of the day, but especially for breakfast. *Com* are rice dishes. You'll see signs saying *pho* and *com* everywhere. Other noodle soups to try are *bun bo Hué* and *hu tieu*.

Spring rolls (*nem* in the north, *cha gio* in the south) are a speciality. These are normally dipped in *nuoc mam* (fish sauce), though many foreigners prefer soy sauce (*xi dau* in the north, *nuoc tuong* in the south).

Because Buddhist monks of the Mahayana tradition are strict vegetarians, *an chay* (vegetarian cooking) is an integral part of Vietnamese cuisine.

SNACKS

Street stalls or roaming vendors are everywhere, selling steamed sweet potatoes, rice porridge and ice-cream bars even in the wee hours. There are also many other Vietnamese nibbles to try:

Bap xao Fresh, stir-fried corn, chillies and tiny shrimp.

Bo bia Nearly microscopic shrimp, fresh lettuce and thin slices of Vietnamese sausage rolled up in rice paper and dipped in a spicy-sweet peanut sauce.

Hot vit lon For the brave. Steamed, fertilised duck egg in varying stages of development (all the way up to recognisable duckling), eaten with coarse salt and bitter herb.

Sinh to Shakes made with milk and sugar or yogurt, and fresh tropical fruit.

SWEETS

Vietnamese people don't usually end meals with dessert, which isn't to say they don't have a sweet tooth. Many sticky confections are made from sticky rice, like *banh it nhan dau,* made with sugar and bean paste and sold wrapped in banana leaf.

Most foreigners prefer *kem* (ice cream) or *yaourt* (yogurt), which is generally of good quality.

Try *che,* a cold, refreshing sweet soup made with sweetened black bean, green bean or corn. It's served in a glass with ice and sweet coconut cream on top.

Drink

ALCOHOLIC DRINKS

Memorise the words *bia hoi,* which mean 'draught beer', probably the cheapest beer in the world. Starting at just 2000d a glass, anyone can afford a round and you can get 'off yer heed' for just US$1! Places that serve *bia hoi* usually also have cheap food.

Several foreign labels brewed in Vietnam under licence include Tiger, Fosters, Carlsberg and Heineken. National and regional brands include Halida and Hanoi in the north, Huda and Larue in the centre, and BGI and 333 *(ba ba ba)* in the south.

> **THERE'S SOMETHING FISHY AROUND HERE...**
>
> *Nuoc mam* (fish sauce) is the one ingredient that is quintessentially Vietnamese and it lends a distinctive character to Vietnamese cooking. The sauce is made by fermenting highly salted fish in large ceramic vats for four to 12 months. Connoisseurs insist the high-grade rocket fuel has a much milder aroma than the cheaper variety. Dissenters insist it is a chemical weapon. It is very often used as a dipping sauce, and takes the place of salt on a Western table.

NONALCOHOLIC DRINKS

Whatever you drink, make sure that it's been boiled or bottled. Ice is generally safe on the tourist trail, but not guaranteed elsewhere.

Vietnamese *cà phê* (coffee) is fine stuff and there is no shortage of cafés in which to sample it. Try seeking out the fairy-lit garden cafés where young couples stake out dark corners for smooch sessions.

Foreign soft drinks are widely available in Vietnam. An excellent local treat is *soda chanh* (carbonated mineral water with lemon and sugar) or *nuoc chanh nong* (hot, sweetened lemon juice).

GAY & LESBIAN TRAVELLERS

Vietnam is pretty hassle-free for gay travellers. There's not much in the way of harassment, nor are there official laws on same-sex relationships (although the government considers homosexuality a 'social evil'). Vietnamese same-sex friends often walk with arms around each other or holding hands, and guesthouse proprietors are unlikely to question the relationship of same-sex travel companions. But be discreet – public displays of affection are not socially acceptable whatever your sexual orientation.

Check out **Utopia** (www.utopia-asia.com) to obtain contacts and useful travel information. Some of the interesting content includes details on the legality of homosexuality in Vietnam and local gay terminology.

HOLIDAYS

The Lunar New Year is Vietnam's most important annual festival. The Tet holiday officially lasts three days, but many Vietnamese take the following week off work, so

---

BEWARE YOUR BLEND

Some consider *chon* to be the highest grade of Vietnamese coffee. It is made of beans fed to a certain species of weasel and later collected from its excrement.

---

hotels, trains and buses are booked solid – and most everything else shuts down. If visiting Vietnam during Tet, memorise this phrase: *Chúc mùng nam mói!* (Happy New Year!). Big smiles and new friends are guaranteed. Vietnamese public holidays include the following:

Tet (Tet Nguyen Dan) 7 February 2008 (Year of the Rat), 26 January 2009 and 14 February 2010.

Liberation Day 30 April, the day the South surrendered to the North in 1975.

International Workers' Day 1 May.

Ho Chi Minh's Birthday 19 May.

National Day 2 September; commemorates the proclamation of the Declaration of Independence of the Democratic Republic of Vietnam by Ho Chi Minh in 1945.

INTERNET ACCESS

Internet access is available throughout Vietnam, even in the most out-of-the-way backwaters. Faster ADSL connections are becoming more widespread.

The cost for internet access ranges from as little as 2000d to 20,000d per minute. Many budget and midrange hotels now offer free internet access, but international hotels charge a hefty fee. Wi-fi access is spreading fast. Hanoi, Ho Chi Minh City and other big towns have plenty of cafés and bars offering free access.

INTERNET RESOURCES

The website www.vietnamadventures.com is full of practical travel information and features monthly adventures and special travel deals.

LEGAL MATTERS

Most Vietnamese never call the police, preferring to settle legal disputes on the spot (either with cash or fists). If you lose something really valuable such as your passport or visa, you'll need to contact the police. Otherwise, it's better not to bother.

The Vietnamese government is seriously cracking down on the burgeoning drug trade. You may face imprisonment and/or large fines for drug offences, and drug trafficking can be punishable by death.

MAPS

A *must* for its detailed road maps of every province is the *Viet Nam Administrative Atlas* (68,000d), published by Ban Do. Basic road maps of major cities such as Hanoi, Saigon, Hué and Nha Trang are readily available. For most other destinations, it's slim pickings.

MONEY

Vietnam's official currency is the dong (d). Banknotes come in denominations of 200d, 500d, 1000d, 2000d, 5000d, 10,000d, 20,000d, 50,000d, 100,000d, 200,000d and 500,000d. Now that Ho Chi Minh has been canonised (against his wishes), his picture is on *every* banknote. There are also small-denomination coins (from 200d to 5000d). US dollars and euros are the easiest currencies to exchange.

ATMs

ATMs can be found in most bigger cities nowadays, with Vietcombank having the widest network. All ATMs dispense cash in dong only. The limit per withdrawal is usually two million dong, but multiple withdrawals are allowed. Most banks charge 20,000d a pop.

Bargaining

For *xe om* and cyclo trips, as well as anywhere that prices aren't posted, bargaining is possible. In tourist hotspots, you may be quoted as much as five times the going price, but not everyone is trying to rip you off. In less-travelled areas, foreigners are often quoted the Vietnamese price but you can still bargain a little bit.

Cash

The US dollar acts as a second local currency. Hotels, airlines and travel agencies all normally quote their prices in dollars, due in part to unwieldy Vietnamese prices (US$100 is around 1.6 million dong). For this reason, we quote some prices in US dollars. For the best deal, pay in dong.

Credit Cards

Visa, MasterCard and Amex are accepted in most cities at top hotels, restaurants and shops. Getting cash advances on credit cards is also possible, but a 3% commission is common.

Exchanging Money

If you need to exchange money after hours, jewellery shops will exchange US dollars at rates comparable to, or even slightly better than, the banks.

Exchange rates are as follows:

Country	Unit	Dong
Australia	A$1	13,360
Cambodia	1000r	4020
Canada	C$1	14,430
China	Y1	2090
euro zone	€1	21,700
Japan	¥100	13,340
Laos	1000 kip	1680
New Zealand	NZ$1	11,820
Thailand	100B	48,877
UK	£1	31,800
USA	US$1	16,035

Tipping

Tipping isn't expected in Vietnam, but it's enormously appreciated. For someone making under US$100 per month, the cost of your drink can equal half a day's wages. Many guests take up a collection for tour guides and drivers, after multiday tours or for outstanding service.

Travellers Cheques

Travellers cheques in US dollars can be exchanged for local dong at certain banks; Vietcombank is usually a safe bet, although it will charge a commission of 0.5% if you exchange cheques for dong. Most hotels and airline offices will not accept travellers cheques.

PHOTOGRAPHY

Vietnam's gorgeous scenery and unique character make prime subject matter for memorable photographs.

Inspiration will surely strike when you see a row of colourfully dressed hill-tribe women walking to market, but remember to maintain an appropriate level of respect for the people and places you visit. Please use common courtesy and ask permission before snapping a photo of someone; if permission is refused, respect that person's wishes.

Photo-processing shops and internet cafés in bigger cities can burn digital photos onto CDs or DVDs, plus memory cards are widely available in big cities. Colour-print film can be found virtually everywhere; slide film is available in HCMC and Hanoi. Processing is fairly cheap, from around US$3 per roll for prints. Process slide film elsewhere.

POST

International postal service from Vietnam is not unreasonably priced when compared with most countries, though parcels mailed from smaller cities and towns may take longer to arrive at their destinations. Be aware that customs inspect the contents before you ship anything other than documents, so don't show up at the post office with a carefully wrapped parcel ready to go. It will be dissected on the table.

Poste restante works in the larger cities but don't count on it elsewhere. There is a small surcharge for picking up poste restante letters. All post offices are marked with the words *buu dien*.

RESPONSIBLE TRAVEL

'When in Rome…' the saying goes, but if Romans are tossing plastic bags into the ocean it doesn't mean you should, too. You can make a difference with your example: pack out your own trash and pick up what you can of others.

Buying coral, limestone or dried sea life encourages harvestation to meet the demand, meanwhile killing the living ecosystems that travellers visit to enjoy. In the same vein, sampling 'exotic' meats such as muntjac, seahorse or bat may seem culinarily adventurous, but many of these species are endangered. Help preserve vulnerable species by not eating them.

Do not remove or buy 'souvenirs' that have been taken from historical sites and natural areas.

When travelling in hill-tribe areas, refrain from giving candy and pens to children, which only encourages a reliance on begging. Instead, donate school supplies to local schools or support the local economy by purchasing goods from the craftspeople themselves.

For more information on responsible trekking, see p484 and p138.

SHOPPING

Vietnam has some fantastic shopping opportunities so it is well worth setting aside half a day or more to properly peruse. Hotspots include Hanoi, Hoi An and HCMC, each of which has a tempting selection of everything from avant-garde art to sumptuous silk suits. Some of the best buys on the block include gorgeous glazed pottery, classic lanterns, 'almost' antiques, embroidered tablecloths, fine furnishings, and lavish silk and linen creations in designer boutiques.

TELEPHONE

Charges for international calls from Vietnam have dropped significantly and cost a flat rate of just US$0.50 per minute to most countries. The service is easy to use from any phone in the country; just dial ☎ 17100, the country code and the number.

International and domestic long-distance calls can be made at hotels, but they're expensive at the smarter places. Many of the cheaper places offer Voice-over Internet Protocol (VoIP) services which are very cheap. Another option is to make these calls from the post office.

Phone numbers in Hanoi, HCMC and Hai Phong have seven digits. Elsewhere around the country phone numbers have six digits.

Useful numbers:

Directory assistance (☎ 116)
General information (☎ 1080)
International operator (☎ 110)
International prefix (☎ 00)
Time (☎ 117)

For mobile phones, Vietnam uses GSM 900/1800, which is compatible with most of Southeast Asia, Europe and Australia but not with North America. If your phone has roaming, it is easy enough, if expensive, to make calls in Vietnam. Another option is to buy a SIM card with a local number to use in Vietnam. Mobile-phone service providers such as VinaPhone and MobiFone sell prepaid phonecards in denominations of 30,000d and up.

Be aware that mobile-phone numbers in Vietnam start with the prefix ☎ 09 and cost more to call than a local number.

TOILETS

Most hotels have the familiar Western-style sit-down toilets, but squat toilets in varying states of refinement exist in some cheap hotels and public places such as restaurants and bus stations. Hotels usually supply a roll, but it's wise to keep a stash of toilet paper while on the road: BYOTP (bring your own toilet paper).

TOURIST INFORMATION

Tourist offices in Vietnam have a different philosophy from the majority of tourist offices worldwide. These government-owned enterprises are really travel agencies whose primary interests are booking tours and turning a profit.

Travel cafés, travel agencies and your fellow travellers are a much better source of information than any of the so-called 'tourist offices'.

VISAS

Tourist visas allow visitors to enter and exit Vietnam at Hanoi, HCMC and Danang airports or at any of its 12 land borders, three each with Cambodia and China, and six with Laos. While Vietnamese bureaucracy is legendary, completing the visa application is pretty painless. You'll need at least one passport-sized photo to accompany the visa application.

It is possible to arrange a visa on arrival through a Vietnamese travel agent. They will need passport details in advance and will send a confirmation for the visa to be issued at your airport of arrival.

Tourist visas are valid for a single 30-day stay and enable you to enter and exit the country via any international border (make sure to specify this when arranging your visa). Depending on where you acquire it, prices for single-entry tourist visas cost around US$30 to US$60. Cambodia is the fastest and cheapest option in the region. Bangkok is another popular place, as many travel agents offer cheap packages including both air ticket and visa.

If you plan to spend more than a month in Vietnam or travel overland between Laos, Vietnam and Cambodia, it's possible to get a three-month multiple-entry visa. These are not available from all Vietnamese embassies, but can be picked up for US$95 in Cambodia.

Business Visas

Business visas are usually valid for three or six months, allow multiple entries and the right to work. Getting a business visa has now become cheap and easy, although prices are about double those of a tourist visa. It is generally easier to apply for a business visa once in Vietnam.

Visa Extensions

If you've got the dollars, they've got the rubber stamp. Visa extensions cost around US$20, but go to a travel agency to get this taken care of – turning up at the immigration police yourself usually doesn't work. The procedure takes one or two days (one photo is needed) and is readily accomplished in major cities such as Hanoi, HCMC, Danang and Hué.

Official policy is that you are permitted one visa extension only, for a maximum of 30 days. Be on the lookout for sudden changes to these regulations.

VOLUNTEERING

15 May School (www.15mayschool.org) A school in HCMC for disadvantaged children, which provides free education and vocational training.

Street Voices (www.streetvoices.com.au) Donate your skills, time or money to help give street children career opportunities. Street Voices' primary project is KOTO restaurant (see the boxed text, p361); check its website to see what you can do to help in Vietnam or Australia.

WOMEN TRAVELLERS

While it always pays to be prudent (avoid dark lonely alleys at night), foreign women have rarely reported problems in Vietnam. Most Vietnamese women do not frequent bars on their own; be aware that you may receive unwanted – though usually harmless – advances if drinking or travelling alone. When travelling on overnight trains it's a good idea to travel with a companion to keep an eye on your bags when you leave to use the toilet, and on each other if you have any overly friendly strangers sharing your compartment.

Some Asian women travelling with Western men have occasionally reported verbal abuse from Vietnamese people who stereotype them as prostitutes. However, with the increase of foreign tourists visiting the country, locals are becoming more accustomed to seeing couples of mixed ethnicity.

WORK

At least 90% of foreign travellers seeking work in Vietnam end up teaching English, though there is some demand for French teachers too. Pay can be as low as US$2 per hour at a university and up to US$15 per hour at a private academy.

Jobs in the booming private sector or with NGOs are usually procured outside of Vietnam before arriving.

It's best to arrange a business visa if you plan to job hunt (see opposite).

TRANSPORT IN VIETNAM

GETTING THERE & AWAY
Entering Vietnam

It's possible to enter Vietnam by train, plane, automobile and other forms of transport. Air is popular for those holidaying in Vietnam, while bus is the most common route for those travelling extensively in the region. Entering from Cambodia, the boat ride down the Mekong from Phnom Penh to Chau Doc is memorable.

Formalities at Vietnam's international airports are generally smoother than at land borders, as the volume of traffic is greater.

Air

Maximise your time and minimise cost and hassle by booking an open-jaw ticket – then you can fly into HCMC and out of Hanoi (or vice versa). These tickets save you from backtracking and are easily arranged in hubs such as Bangkok and Hong Kong.

Keep in mind that international flights purchased in Vietnam are always more expensive than the same tickets purchased outside.

All phone numbers for the following airlines are in Hanoi unless otherwise stated.

Air Asia (airline code AK; www.airasia.com; hub Kuala Lumpur) Daily budget flights connecting Hanoi and HCMC to Kuala Lumpur and Bangkok.

Air France (airline code AF; ☎ 04-825 3484; www.air france.fr; hub Paris) Regular connections from Hanoi and HCMC to Paris via Bangkok.

Asiana Airlines (airline code OZ; ☎ 04-831 5141; www .us.flyasiana.com; hub Seoul) Daily connections from Hanoi and HCMC to Seoul.

Cathay Pacific (airline code CX; ☎ 04-826 7298; www.cathaypacific.com; hub Hong Kong) Has daily connections from both Hanoi and HCMC to Hong Kong.

China Airlines (airline code CI; ☎ 04-824 2688; www .china-airlines.com; hub Taipei) Daily flights from Hanoi and HCMC to Taipei.

China Southern Airlines (airline code CZ; ☎ 04-771 6611; www.cs-air.com; hub Guǎngzhōu) Regular flights from Hanoi and HCMC to Guǎngzhōu.

Japan Airlines (airline code JL; ☎ 04-826 6693; www .jal.co.jp; hub Tokyo) Regular services from Hanoi and HCMC to Tokyo and Osaka.

Jetstar Asia (airline code 3K; www.jetstarasia.com; hub

Singapore) Daily budget flights from Hanoi and HCMC to Singapore.

Lao Airlines (airline code QV; ☎ 04-822 9951; www.laoairlines.com; hub Vientiane) Regular flights from Hanoi and HCMC to Vientiane and Luang Prabang.

Lufthansa (airline code LH; ☎ in HCMC 08-829 8529; www.lufthansa.com; hub Frankfurt) Several flights a week to Frankfurt.

Malaysia Airlines (airline code MY; ☎ 04-826 8820; www.malaysiaairlines.com; hub Kuala Lumpur) Daily connections from Hanoi and HCMC to Kuala Lumpur.

Philippine Airlines (airline code PR; ☎ in HCMC 08-822 2241; www.philippineair.com; hub Manila) Regular flights from HCMC to Manila.

Qantas (airline code QF; ☎ 04-933 3025; www.qantas.com.au; hubs Sydney & Melbourne) Regular connections from Hanoi and HCMC to Sydney, Melbourne and other major cities.

Singapore Airlines (airline code SQ; ☎ 04-826 8888; www.singaporeair.com; hub Singapore) Daily flights linking Hanoi and HCMC with Singapore.

Thai Airways (airline code TG; ☎ 04-826 6893; www.thaiair.com; hub Bangkok) Daily flights connecting Bangkok to Hanoi and HCMC, plus regular services to Danang.

Tiger Airways (airline code TR; www.tigerairways.com; hub Singapore) Budget flights connecting both Hanoi and HCMC to Singapore.

United Airlines (airline code UA; ☎ in HCMC 08-823 1833; www.unitedairlines.com; hub Seattle) Regular flights connecting Hanoi and HCMC with the west coast of the US.

Vietnam Airlines (airline code VN; ☎ 04-943 9660, in HCMC 08-832 0320; www.vietnamair.com.vn; hub HCMC) Global reach including the rest of Asia, Australia, Europe and the US.

Border Crossings

Vietnam shares land border crossings with Cambodia, China and Laos. See the table, p101. Vietnam visas are not currently available at any land borders.

There are currently three crossings with Cambodia, although most people exit Vietnam via Moc Bai or Vinh Xuong, taking the road from HCMC to Phnom Penh or the boat from Chau Doc to the Cambodian capital. The third crossing at Tinh Bien is not so popular, plus there are no visas available on arrival in Cambodia. There are also three crossings into China in the north, all of which are relatively straightforward to use as there are towns on both sides of the border.

There are currently six border crossings with Laos and these borders tend to cause travellers the most headaches, with poor transport links, bad roads, petty corruption and rampant overcharging. The easiest way to exit is via Lao Bao, the most established crossing. Many use Cau Treo when travelling between Hanoi and Vientiane, but it's no picnic: in fact it's a set menu from hell. The other four crossings are in remote areas and rarely used by travellers. Only use these crossings if you are willing to expect the unexpected and are prepared to pay over the odds to do so. Lao visas are not currently available at the more remote borders.

GETTING AROUND
Air

Air travel within Vietnam is dominated by **Vietnam Airlines** (www.vietnamairlines.com), while its newly relaunched budget offshoot **Pacific Airlines** (www.pacificairlines.com.vn) offers limited routes between Ho Chi Minh City, Danang and Hanoi. Reasonably priced domestic flights can trim precious travel time off a busy itinerary.

Bicycle

Long-distance cycling is becoming a popular way to tour Vietnam, most of which is flat or moderately hilly. With the loosening of borders in the Mekong region, more and more people are planning overland trips by bicycle. All you need to know about bicycle travel in Vietnam, Laos and Cambodia is contained in Lonely Planet's *Cycling Vietnam, Laos & Cambodia*.

The main hazard is the traffic, and it's wise to avoid certain areas (notably National Hwy 1). The best cycling is in the northern mountains and the Central Highlands, though you'll have to cope with some big hills. The Mekong Delta is a rewarding option for those who prefer the flat.

Purchasing a good bicycle in Vietnam is hit or miss. It's recommended that you bring one from abroad, along with a good helmet and spare parts.

Bicycles can also be hired locally from guesthouses for US$1 per day, and are a great way to get to know a new city.

INTERNATIONAL DEPARTURE TAX

There is an international departure tax of US$14 from the main airports at Hanoi, HCMC and Danang.

Boat

The extensive network of canals in the Mekong Delta makes getting around by boat feasible in the far south. Travellers to Phu Quoc Island can catch ferries from Rach Gia (p423).

In the country's northeast, hydrofoils connect Haiphong with Cat Ba Island (near Halong Bay), and cruises on Halong Bay are extremely popular. In the south, a trip to the islands off the coast of Nha Trang is popular.

Bus

Vietnam has an extensive network of dirt-cheap buses that reach the far-flung corners of the country. Until recently, few foreign travellers used them because of safety concerns and overcharging, but the situation has improved dramatically with modern buses and fixed-price ticket offices at most bus stations.

Bus drivers rely on the horn as a defensive driving technique. Motorists use the highway like a speedway; accidents, unsurprisingly, are common. On bus journeys, keep a close eye on your bags, never accept drinks from strangers, and consider bringing earplugs.

> ### DOMESTIC DEPARTURE TAX
>
> Domestic departure tax is 25,000d, but is included when you buy the ticket.

LOCAL BUS & MINIBUS

Travelling on the backroads, you'll see local buses of every vintage, packed to the gills. You can travel on these rattletraps, but expect breakdowns, lots of stops and overcrowded conditions. You'll rub shoulders with everyday people, giving you a slice of life many foreigners don't experience.

Most buses pick up passengers along the way until full. It's a good idea to try buying tickets at the station the day before; while not always possible, this reduces your chances of having to bargain with the driver immediately before departure.

The only time we recommend avoiding these buses (and the public ones) is around Tet when drivers are working overtime and routes are dangerously overcrowded.

Generally, buses of all types leave early in the morning, but shorter, more popular

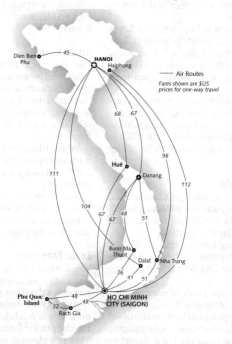

Dien Bien Phu — 45 — HANOI / Haiphong

——— Air Routes
Fares shown are $US prices for one-way travel

68 · 67

98

Hué · 111

Danang · 112

104

67 · 48 · 51

67

Buon Ma Thuot

26 · Dalat · Nha Trang

41 · 51

Phu Quoc Island — 48 —— HO CHI MINH CITY (SAIGON)

32 · 48

Rach Gia

VIETNAM

routes will often leave at intervals throughout the day.

Costs are negligible, though on rural runs foreigners are typically charged anywhere from twice to 10 times the going rate. As a benchmark, a typical 100km ride is between US$2 and US$3.

OPEN-TOUR BUS

For the cost of around US$23, the ubiquitous open ticket can get you from HCMC to Hanoi at your own pace, in air-con comfort. Open-tour tickets entitle you to exit or board the bus at any city along its route, without holding you to a fixed schedule. Confirm your seat the day before departure.

These tickets are inexpensive because they're subsidised by an extensive commission culture. All of the lunch stops and hotel drop-offs give monetary kickbacks to the bus companies. But you're never obligated to stay at the hotel you've been dropped at; if you don't like it, find another.

Although it's convenient and cheap, the open-tour ticket isolates you from experiencing Vietnam. These vehicles rarely see Vietnamese passengers, since they're tailored to foreign travellers.

An alternative to the open-tour ticket is to buy individual, point-to-point tickets along the way; though this will cost more, you have the flexibility to take local buses, trains or flights, or to switch open-tour companies.

All companies offering open-tour tickets have received both glowing commendations and bitter complaints from travellers. As a general guide, Sinh Café still has some of the best buses, closely followed by Hanh Café.

Car & Motorcycle

Self-drive rental cars have yet to make their debut in Vietnam, which is a blessing in disguise given traffic conditions, but cars with drivers are popular and plentiful.

For sightseeing trips around HCMC or Hanoi, a car with driver can be rented by the day. It costs about US$25 to US$50 per day, depending on the car.

For the really bad roads of northwestern Vietnam, the only reasonably safe vehicle is a 4WD. The cheapest (and least comfortable) are Russian made, while more cushy Japanese vehicles are about twice the price. Expect to pay about US$80 to US$100 a day for a decent 4WD in the far north of Vietnam.

Motorbikes can be hired for US$5 to US$10 per day, depending on the make of the cycle and what region you're in. Prices with a driver start at about US$8 for day tours around town. In smaller towns and cities, observe how people drive and go with the flow. In HCMC or Hanoi, consider hiring a driver unless you're used to driving in the region. Fifteen minutes on a bus travelling National Hwy 1 should convince you to leave the long-distance driving to a local.

Hiring a motorbike guide leaves you free to observe the kaleidoscope of daily life and scenery, and guides are experts on their own turf. Many travellers hit it off so well with their guides that they hire them for the long haul. It's a wonderful way to travel, and you'll get an insider's perspective on the country.

DRIVING LICENCE

International driving licences are not valid in Vietnam. If you have a motorcycle licence, you must have the document translated into a Vietnamese equivalent in order for it to be officially recognised. In practice, most foreign residents and visitors drive without a licence.

ROAD RULES

The road rule to remember: size matters and small vehicles get out of the way of big vehicles. Vehicles drive on the right-hand side, but there is an invisible middle lane many like to use. Traffic cops are fastidious and usually require a pay off. Horrendous accidents are frequent.

When driving on Vietnam's highways, helmets are required by law only for motorbikes (and a necessary accessory if you're fond of your skull).

Never leave a motorbike unattended – if you can't park it where you can keep it in constant view, use the guarded parking and don't lose the ticket.

Local Transport

You'll never have to walk in Vietnam if you don't want to; drivers will practically chase you down the street offering rides.

At least once during your visit, take a whirl on a *xich lo* (cyclo), a bicycle rickshaw with the chair at the front, the bicycle at the back. They're a pleasant, nonpolluting way to see a city. Generally, cyclo rides should cost 5000d per kilometre, or US$5 to US$8 for a day tour.

Xe om or *Honda om* (literally, 'Honda hug'; motorcycle taxi) are faster – made up of a motorbike, a driver and you. Short rides around town typically start at 5000d.

Metered taxis are abundant and comfortable, but check the meter before you get in and make sure the driver uses it.

Hiring a bicycle is arguably the most fun way to see any city, and an adventure in itself. Hotels and travellers cafés usually hire them out for about US$1 per day.

Tours

The following are Vietnam-based travel agencies that offer premium tours throughout Vietnam:

Buffalo Tours (Map p358; ☎ 04-828 0702; www .buffalotours.com; 11 Pho Hang Muoi, Hanoi)

Destination Asia (☎ 08-844 8071; www.destination -asia.com; 143 Đ Nguyen Van Troi, Phu Nhuan District, HCMC)

Exotissimo (☎ 04-828 2150; www.exotissimo.com; 26 Tran Nhat Duat, Hanoi)

Phoenix Voyages (☎ 04-716 1956; www.phoenixviet nam.com; 52 Pho Nguyen Khac Hieu, Hanoi)

Tonkin Travel (☎ 08-747 3239; www.tonkintravel .com; 8, 34A Đ Tran Phu, Hanoi)

Train

Vietnam Railways (Duong Sat Viet Nam; ☎ 04-747 0308; www.vr.com.vn) operates the 2600km-long Vietnamese train system that runs along the coast between HCMC and Hanoi, and links the capital with Haiphong and northerly points. Odd-numbered trains travel south; even-numbered trains go north.

The *Reunification Express* chugs along the 1726km journey between Hanoi and HCMC at an average speed of 48km per hour, and takes from 30 to 41 hours. There are five classes of train travel in Vietnam: hard seat, soft seat, hard sleeper, soft sleeper (normal) and soft sleeper (air-con). Conditions in hard seat and soft seat can be rough, even less comfortable than the bus.

Prices change, but at the time of writing, a ticket for an air-con soft sleeper for the 30-hour fast train from Hanoi to Hué was around US$30. Check out the website for the latest fares.

Theft can be a problem, especially on overnight trains. In sleeper cars, the bottom bunk is best because you can stow your pack underneath the berth; otherwise, secure it to something for the duration of the trip. Although trains are sometimes slower than the bus, they're a terrific way to meet local people.

Yúnnán Province (China) 云南

RICHARD I'ANSON

Yúnnán Province (China) 云南

You've won the travel lottery if your Mekong travels take you to Yúnnán, arguably the one province in China to choose if you have time for but one. Strong words, but hyperbole is, remarkably, possibly an understatement here.

China's lengthy segment of the mighty Mekong garners little press compared with the attention given to the river's rolls through its Southeast Asian neighbours. Yet don't overlook it – from the Mekong's source in Tibet to its exit from China in Yúnnán's Xīshuāngbǎnnà Region, China has half the length of the river! With herculean transport infrastructure continuing to be built near the province's borders with Laos (towards Thailand), Vietnam and Myanmar (Burma), within the next half-decade Yúnnán will truly 'belong' to the Southeast Asian neighbourhood.

Along the Mekong's roll southward, majestic, and often sacred, peaks thrust from the Tibetan Plateau to the north; here you'll find some of China's most precious time-locked towns as well as superb trekking. Lush jungle lies a two-day bus ride south in the Xīshuāngbǎnnà Region, where you can search out elephants in extraordinarily dense rainforest, hike (or pedal or paddle) from village to village and eat a hell of a lot of pineapple rice. To the east, away from the Mekong River itself on the route to Vietnam, spreads some of Asia's most drop-jaw-gorgeous rice terraces.

Best of all: Yúnnán province has China's most diverse population. Village-hop in this breathtaking province and be greeted by a new minority group each day, many in time-capsule towns that you'll never forget.

Smacks of PR pulp, no? Well, just be prepared that if you start here, you may never get to another province. It has happened.

HIGHLIGHTS

- Feel your jaw hit your chest at the **Yuanyang Rice Terraces** (p462)
- Trek the jungle and do your anthropologist thing in **Xīshuāngbǎnnà Region** (p463)
- Lose your cares among the canals and cobbled lanes of **Lìjiāng's old town** (p456)
- Stroll the flagstone streets and shop maniacally in **Dàlǐ's old town** (p452)
- Strengthen your legs (and spirit) trekking **Tiger Leaping Gorge** (p459)

FAST FACTS

- **Area** 394,000 sq km
- **Capital** Kūnmíng
- **Country Code** ☎ 86
- **Population** 42.1 million
- **Money** US$1 = Y7.70 (yuán)
- **Seasons** high May-Sep & all national holidays; rainy May-Sep (especially Jun-Aug)
- **Phrases** nǐ hǎo 你好 (hello), zàijiàn 再见 (goodbye), xièxie 谢谢 (thank you)

HISTORY

With its remote location, harsh terrain and diverse ethnic make-up, Yúnnán, China's sixth-largest province, has always proved to be a province eminently troublesome to govern. Thus, for much of its history –including today – the province felt a greater pull toward its Southeast Asian neighbours than any dynasties to the north. Understandable, given that many of Yúnnán's ethnic groups have for centuries been tied directly to Thailand, Laos and Vietnam (and Burma).

Yúnnán's first kingdom, the kingdom of Dian, near present-day Kūnmíng, was established during the Warring States Period (453–221 BC). In the 2nd century BC, Chinese forces conquered the Red River Delta in modern Vietnam, beginning a millennium of Chinese cultural if not political domination. Chief among the Chinese exports were Confucianism, Taoism and Mahanaya Buddhism. While Vietnam gained much from the Chinese, they would struggle to throw off the yoke of its dragon neighbour until finally succeeding after the fall of the Tang dynasty in the 10th century. (China would reclaim Vietnam in the early 15th century, carting away much Vietnamese heritage and doing irreparable harm; only later in the century would they finally overthrow Chinese hegemony for good.)

The Indianised Cambodian kingdom of Funan had cultural and quasi-diplomatic ties with Yúnnán's chieftain leaders from the 1st through 6th centuries AD. Later, Qin Shi Huang (China's 'first' emperor) and subsequent Han emperors held tentative imperial power over the southwest and forged southern Silk Road trade routes to Burma, but by the 7th century the Bai people (among other groups) had established their own powerful kingdom, Nanzhao, south of Dàlǐ. Initially allied with the Chinese against the Tibetans, this kingdom extended its power until, in the middle of the 8th century, it was able to challenge and defeat the Tang armies. It took control of a large slice of the southwest and established itself as a fully independent entity, dominating the trade routes from China to India and Indochina. During the reign of Nanzhao, the Tai (today, Dai) peoples began their migration southward, moving into Laos and Thailand.

The Nanzhao kingdom fell in the 10th century and was replaced by the kingdom of Dàlǐ, an independent state that lasted until it was overrun by the Mongols in the mid-13th century. After 15 centuries of resistance to northern rule, this part of the southwest was finally integrated into the empire as the province of Yúnnán.

Even so, it remained an isolated frontier region, with scattered Chinese garrisons and settlements in the valleys and basins, a mixed aboriginal population in the highlands, and various Dai (Thai) and other minorities along the Mekong River (Láncāng Jiāng). During the Ming dynasty, much infrastructure work began; the famed tea-horse trading routes from Yúnnán to India and Tibet were extended south through Yúnnán's Xīshuāngbǎnnà Region into Laos.

Right up to the 20th century, Yúnnán looked to its southern neighbours Indochina and Burma, as it did to the Chinese emperor. Wracked by ethnic disturbances, including the bloody 1855 Muslim uprising and even bloodier Chinese army put-down, the province was exploited by local warlords, Europeans, and the emperor. During the Republican period, Yúnnán, like the rest of China's southwest, continued its history of breaking ties with the northern government. During China's countless political purges, fallen officials often found themselves here, adding to the province's character.

During WWII, Yúnnán's fortunes strangely improved, at least infrastructure-wise, thanks to herculean works projects by the US and allied Kuomintang government. (Imperious government treatment of locals was another matter.) The Communist takeover was generally smooth – the Yunnanese figured they couldn't be any worse than leaders of the last

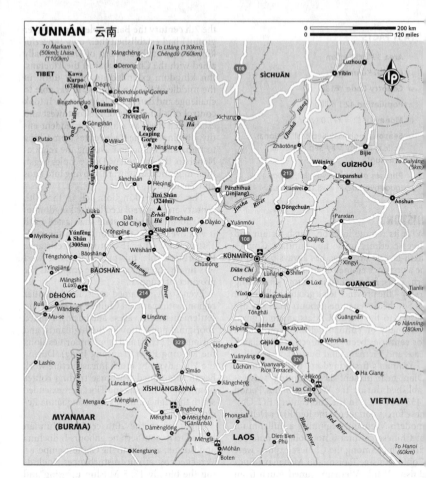

two millennia and appreciated the back-to-the-land ethos espoused by Mao – but suffered a few hiccups when the daunting task of modernising the province halted any real Chinese Communist Party (CCP) actions, not to mention a horribly ill-fated 1979 war (and equally black-eye skirmishes in 1984) with Vietnam, during which Yúnnán was used as a base of operations and suffered cross-border attacks.

Presently, it seems the same as it ever was, historically. While Yúnnán's modernisation has been marvellous when compared with other provinces in China's southwest, it genuinely seems even more interested in going its own way – southward, towards its neighbours, as much as north, towards Běijīng. Not technically part of the Mekong River Commission,

Yúnnán nonetheless is acting as if it is – pouring epic monies into dams (a baker's dozen on the Mekong alone), highways, airports and commercial ventures with its neighbours. (Indeed, Yúnnán's Mekong-based trade with Thailand has more than doubled in some years.) Ultimately, it seems poised to become part of a powerful new Southeast Asian trading group, whether the capital likes it or not.

PEOPLE & THE POPULATION

Home to more than half of all China's 56 ethnic minorities, Yúnnán is nearly 50% non-Han; most populous are the Naxi (near Lìjiāng), the Bai (Dàlǐ), Tibetans (throughout northwestern Yúnnán) and the Dai (Xīshuāngbǎnnà). Yúnnán sees very little surface ethnic hostility

---

KŪNMÍNG IN WWII

Kūnmíng was the eastern terminus of the famous Burma Road, a 1000km haul from Lashio to Kūnmíng. Today, Renmin Xilu marks the tail end of the Burma Road.

In 1942 the Japanese captured Lashio, cutting the supply line. Kūnmíng continued to handle most of the incoming aid from 1942 to 1945, when US planes flew the dangerous mission of crossing the 'Hump', the towering 5000m mountain ranges between India and Kūnmíng's vicinity.

(though utopia it ain't). Problems here are typical of China as a whole: urban growth (migration to the cities), an unbalanced gender ratio (around 117 boys to 100 girls) and a fast-ageing populace (by 2020 nearly 16% of the population will be over 60).

RELIGION

Three major schools of thought – Taoism, Confucianism and Buddhism – commingle with animism. Yúnnán also has one of the highest concentrations – some 600,000 – of China's Hui, a Muslim group distinct from China's dozen or so other Muslim groups; they're found largely in Kūnmíng and in the province's northwest.

ARTS

Kūnmíng's Yunnan Provincial Museum (p446) details the local contributions to China's culture. Yúnnán's ethnic groups have made equally important contributions to China's artistic legacy. Architecturally, comparing the temple styles alone could take up an entire trip. If there is one not-to-be-missed cultural experience in the province, it is the Naxi Orchestra in Lìjiāng (see p458), which performs Taoist temple music (known as *dòngjīng*) that has been lost elsewhere in China.

ENVIRONMENT

Yúnnán's landscape is as diverse as its people: from a low point of 76.4m above sea level in Hékǒu, near Vietnam, to 6740m in the northwest Tibetan Plateau.

Geomorphologically, it's got everything one could want. From the stunning peaks of the northwest, you pass through splendid river valleys as the land moves into subtropics near its southwestern border with Myanmar,

and it finally becomes full-blown rainforest in Xīshuāngbǎnnà, near Laos and Vietnam. Eastern Yúnnán is the province's fertile belt – a cornucopia of agricultural lands featuring some of China's most splendid rice terraces.

Yúnnán's primary environmental issue is deforestation – once 60% covered by forest, it's down to 25%. Logging was banned in the 1980s in northwest Yúnnán, with devastating effects on local economies. Newer environmental rallying cries are massive dam projects on the Nu (near Myanmar and Tibet) and Jinsha (along Tiger Leaping Gorge) Rivers.

CENTRAL YÚNNÁN

KŪNMÍNG 昆明
☎ 0871 / pop 1.01 million

'Yúnnán' means 'South of the Clouds', and Kūnmíng, with the apt moniker 'Spring City', couldn't be a better meteorological metaphor for a place situated far from inclement weather. At an elevation of 1890m, Kūnmíng has a milder climate than most other Chinese cities. Come in from the tropics and take a big gulp of the (relatively) fresh and cool air!

It's not unlike one big park, with tree- and flower-lined boulevards every which way. With a populace that refuses to be anything but laid-back, there is no sense of hurry-up here and the quotient of cell-phone-yapping wannabes is relatively low.

Sure, traffic and smog are worsening by the minute and most of the city's quaint architecture has gone, but in the end you'll likely find yourself quite relaxed here.

Orientation

The centre of the city is the traffic circle at the intersection of Zhengyi Lu and Dongfeng Xilu. To the southwest, down to Jinbi Lu, are a few interesting old alleys.

Situated to the north of the intersection is lovely Green Lake Park (Cuìhú Gōngyuán),

---

GETTING INTO TOWN

Buses 52 and 67 run between the centre of town and the airport (situated 7.5km southeast of town). A taxi averages Y20, depending on where you're going.

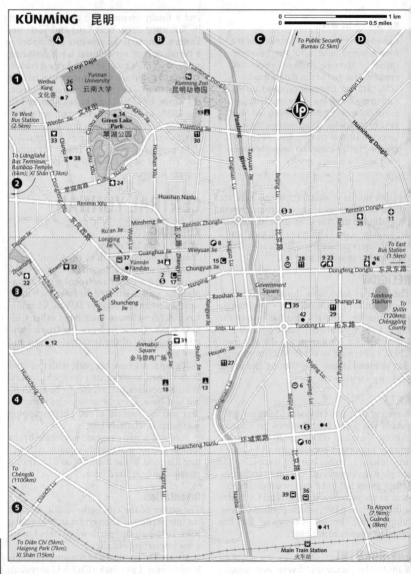

KUNMING 昆明

Yuantong Temple and the Kunming Zoo. East of the intersection is Kūnmíng's major north–south road, Beijing Lu. At the southern end is the main train station and the long-distance bus station. At about the halfway point, Beijing Lu is intersected by Dongfeng Donglu, where the luxurious Kunming Hotel can be found.

MAPS

Get maps near the bus and train stations and in bookshops; those with English lack detail.

Information

BOOKSHOP

Mandarin Books & CDs (☎ 220 6575; West Gate, Yunnan University; ⏰ 9am-10pm) Has a variety of media in English, German, French, Dutch, Italian and Spanish.

INTERNET ACCESS
Kunming Cloudland Youth Hostel (p447) has free access (and is wireless equipped). Rates at Kūnmíng's zillion internet cafes are Y2 to Y3 per hour.

MEDICAL SERVICES
Yanan Hospital (Yán'ān Yīyuàn; ☎ 317 7499, ext 311; 1st fl, Block 6, Renmin Donglu) Has a foreigners' clinic.

MONEY
Bank of China (Zhōngguó Yínháng; 448 Renmin Donglu; ◷ 9am-noon & 2-5pm) Changes travellers cheques and foreign currency and offers cash advances on credit cards. There is an ATM here. There are branches at Dongfeng Xilu and Huancheng Nanlu.

POST & TELEPHONE
China Telecom (Zhōngguó Diànxìn; cnr Beijing Lu & Dongfeng Donglu) You can make international calls here.
International Post Office (Guójì Yóujú; 231 Beijing Lu) The main office has poste restante and parcel service (per letter Y3, ID required) and is the Express Mail Service (EMS) and Western Union agent. There's a branch on Dongfeng Donglu.

PUBLIC SECURITY BUREAU (PSB)
PSB (Gōngānjú; ☎ 571 7030; Jìnxīng Huáyuán, Jìnxīng Lu; ◷ 9-11.30am & 1-5pm daily) The Foreign Affairs

Branch will issue visa extensions in three to five days. The bureau is north of the city centre. The main entrance is off Erhuan Beilu. Bus 3, 25 or 57 will get you within a couple of blocks.

TOURIST INFORMATION
Lodging options can assist with travel queries and make ticket reservations (ranging from free to Y20 per ticket). The Camellia Hotel (p447) has four (at last count) agencies, including Mr Chen's Tours (p447).
China International Travel Service (CITS; Zhōngguó Guójì Lůxíngshè; ☎ 356 6730; 285 Huancheng Nanlu; ◷ 9am-5.30pm) Organises tours but doesn't like to dispense information. French and English spoken.
Tourist Complaint & Consultative Telephone (☎ 316 4961) Where you can complain about or report dodgy tourist operations.

Dangers & Annoyances
Kūnmíng is one of the safest cities in China but take special precaution near the train and long-distance bus stations. The area can get seedy at night and there have been reports of travellers having their bags razored.

Sights & Activities
TANG DYNASTY PAGODAS
To the south of Jinbi Lu are two Tang pagodas ageing gracefully as the neighbourhood gentrifies around them. **West Pagoda** (Xīsì Tǎ; Dongsi Jie;

THE HUI

Of the province's approximately 600,000 Hui (one of China's Muslim groups), Kūnmíng holds the lion's share, though their once-thriving neighbourhoods of shops and restaurants have slowly been dispersed as the wrecking balls moved in.

In the 13th century Mongol forces swooped into the province to outflank the Song dynasty troops and were followed by Muslim traders, builders and craftsmen, whose descendants made extraordinary contributions to Chinese civilisation. Yúnnán-boy-done-good Cheng Ho (Zheng He) was a famed eunuch admiral who opened up the Chinese sea channels to the Middle East and may have visited the Americas.

admission Y2; 9am-6pm) is the more interesting. Attached is a compound that is a popular spot for older people to get together, drink tea and play cards and mah jong (and perhaps get a shave and a haircut).

East Pagoda (Dōngsì Tǎ; Shulin Jie) was, according to Chinese sources, destroyed by an earthquake; Western sources say it was destroyed by the Muslim revolt.

YUANTONG TEMPLE 圆通寺

This **temple** (Yuántōng Sì; Yuantong Jie; admission Y4; 8am-5pm), at the base of Luofeng Hill, is the largest Buddhist complex in Kūnmíng and attracts a fair number of pilgrims. An excellent example of Tang dynasty design, it is about 1200 years old; the highlight is a statue of Sakyamuni, a gift from the king of Thailand.

The fabulous Yuquanzhai Vegetarian Restaurant (opposite) is opposite the main temple entrance.

YUNNAN PROVINCIAL MUSEUM
云南省博物馆

This **museum** (Yúnnán Shěng Bówùguǎn; Wuyi Lu; admission Y10; 9am-5pm Tue-Sun) was just putting the finishing touches on a much-needed face-lift; the previous incarnation was as much tomb as museum.

The Bronze Drums Hall has a collection dating from the Western Han periods. Of 1600 such drums known to exist in the world, China has 1400, 400 of which were found in Yúnnán itself. The Ancient Buddhist Art Hall has examples of the art at Shíbǎoshān, near Dàlǐ, and the murals of Báishā outside Lìjiāng. The Minority Nationality Hall gives an overview of Yúnnán's ethnic diversity.

GREEN LAKE PARK 翠湖公园

This **park** (Cuìhú Gōngyuán; Cuihu Nanlu; 6am-10pm) is a great place to while away a morning or afternoon, especially on Sunday, when half of the city is here. Try to pay a visit for the **Lantern Festival** in late September to early October.

MOSQUES 清真寺

The oldest mosque, or at least located on the site where a mosque has sat the longest, is the 400-year-old **Nancheng Mosque** (Nánchéng Qīngzhēn Gǔsì; 51 Zhengyi Lu). It can be identified by its telltale greenish onion domes, though the lower floors essentially look like the white-tiled offices that they are!

Another **mosque** is nearby, wedged between Huguo Lu and Chongyun Jie; yet another sits at the corner of Jinbi Lu and Dongsi Jie. Both are more historical landmarks than places of active worship.

CHUÀNG KÙ (THE LOFT) 创库艺术主题社区

In a disused factory district now housing several art galleries, **TC/G Nordica** (诺地卡;

OLD KŪNMÍNG

One place to go to still see little old men puttering about in their funky blue Mao suits is **Guāndù** (官度), about 8km south of downtown.

Now, living museum this ain't. 'Old' flagstone alleys are being repaved in 'new' brick and 'old' wooden façades are giving way to new ones (like in the rest of China), and pavilions are draped in dropcloths for a garish paint job.

Yet it's a real kick. When you get off Bus 31 (from the train station all the way to the last stop), follow the donkey carts. They'll take you to a very laid-back and pretty much tourist-free section of town. A handful of temples (admission Y5), pagodas and other historic structures are great to search out.

Nuòdìkǎ; ☎ 411 4692; www.tcgnordica.com/en; 101 Xiba Lu; ⌚ 5-11.30pm Mon, 11.30am-11pm Tue-Sat, noon-4pm Sun), the epicentre of sorts, is best described as a gallery–exhibition hall–cultural centre–Scandinavian restaurant. Most weekends you'll find live entertainment.

Tours

Several tour outfits cover Kūnmíng and its surrounding sights faster than public minibuses would, but be forewarned that many are pricey and include lots of shopping – er, sorry, toilet – stops. Hostels are the best places to find tours.

Mr Chen's Tours (☎ 318 8114; Room 3116, No 3 Bldg, Camellia Hotel, 154 Dongfeng Lu) can organise trips to almost anywhere you want to go.

Sleeping

our pick **Kunming Cloudland Youth Hostel** (Kūnmíng Dàjiāoshí Qīngnián Lǚshè; ☎ 410 3777; www.cloudland2004 .com; 23 Zhuantang Lu; 篆塘路23号; 4-/6-bed dm Y30/20; 🖵) This charming new place has comfy beds, wondrous staff, free internet access and loads of extras. To get here from the train or long-distance bus station take bus 64. Get off at the Yunnan Daily News stop (云南日报社站).

Kunming Youth Hostel (Kūnmíng Guójí Qīngnián Lǚshè; ☎ 517 5395; youthhostel.km@sohu.com; 94 Cuihu Nanlu; 翠湖南路94号; dm Y25, d from Y80) Tucked along a lane beside the Zhengxie Hotel, right by Green Lake Park, dorms here are institutional but staff are friendly and the hostel has been slated for a makeover.

Camellia Hotel (Cháhuā Bīnguǎn; ☎ 316 3000; www .kmcamelliahotel.com; 96 Dongfeng Donglu; 东风东路96号; dm Y30, d Y188-288; 🍴) This landmark budget option has grubby rooms on offer (though toilets and showers are good) and a staff trying not to be weary of budget travellers. But with travel services, bicycle hire, foreign exchange, cheap laundry and a breakfast buffet, it's still a good lodging option.

Yúndà Bīnguǎn (Yunnan University Hotel; ☎ 503 3624; fax 514 8513; d from Y160; 🍴) The university area – laden with foreign student-centric restaurants, coffee shops, bookshops and the like – makes for a nice base, and the standard doubles here are a good choice. Staff practically fall over themselves to help.

Míngdū Dàjiǔdiàn (☎ 624 0666; fax 624 0898; 206 Baita Lu; 白塔路206号; s & d Y388, ste 688; 🍴) A rarity in China – a hotel that seems to have actually taken a shot at a design scheme. Decent amenities and service for the price.

ACROSS-THE-BRIDGE NOODLES

Yúnnán's best-known dish is across-the-bridge noodles (过桥米线; *guòqiáo mǐxiàn*). You are provided with a bowl of very hot soup (stewed with chicken, duck and spare ribs) on which a thin layer of oil is floating, along with a side dish of raw pork slivers (in classier places this might be chicken or fish), vegetables and egg, and a bowl of rice noodles. Diners place all of the ingredients quickly into the soup bowl, where they are cooked by the steamy broth.

Prices generally vary from Y5 to Y15 depending on the side dishes. It's usually worth getting these, because with only one or two condiments it lacks zest.

---

our pick **Kunming Hotel** (Kūnmíng Fàndiàn; ☎ 316 2063; www.kunminghotel.com.cn; 52 Dongfeng Donglu; 东风东路52号; s & d Y780, ste Y1419; 🍴) This place has always received – and still gets – tons of raves. Its laundry list of amenities includes a bar, disco, karaoke hall, outstanding restaurants, tennis court and even a bowling alley on-site.

Eating

Brothers Jiang (Jiāngshì Xiōngdì; Dongfeng Donglu; noodles Y10-60) Yúnnán's speciality – across-the-bridge noodles (see the boxed text, above) – are the hit here at this filled-to-the-sidewalks fave, with branches all over town. The noodles come with eating instructions!

White Pagoda Dai Restaurant (Báitǎ Dǎi Wéitíng; ☎ 317 2932; 127 Shangyi Jie; dishes from Y10; ⌚ 9am-9pm) Dai cuisine makes its way north here, with a slew of fish dishes and the old standby, pineapple sticky rice.

our pick **Yuquanzhai Vegetarian Restaurant** (Yùquánzhāi Cāntíng; Yuantong Jie; dishes from Y10) No meat in the fabulous dishes, but you'll swear there is. The menu – with English – is encyclopaedic, so ask for help!

our pick **1910 La Gare du Sud** (Huǒchē Nánzhàn; ☎ 316 9486; dishes from Y20) Ensconced cosily down an alley south of Jinbi Lu, here you'll find Yúnnán specialities in a classy neocolonial-style setting. Travellers rave about the place.

Drinking

Wenhua Xiang near Yunnan University has quieter options. If you need strobe lights and dancing, Jinmabiji Sq literally thumps

---

ONE-STOP SHOPPING

The **Flower & Bird Market** (Huāniǎo Shìchǎng; Tongdao Jie) has long been one of the more enjoyable and relaxing strolls in the city. It's also known as **Lǎo Jiē** (Old Street). Flowers and birds most certainly aren't the main draw here anymore; it's more endless curios, knick-knacks and doo-dads, some occasionally fine rugs and handmade clothing, and a hell of a lot of weird stuff. (Kurt Cobain or KISS T-shirt? Hmmm.)

For real antiques it's better to look among the privately run shops on Beijing Lu and Dongfeng Donglu.

---

the night away with a dozen places. And for hard-core techno (and outrageous prices), the Kundu Night Market has dozens of discos frequented by the seen-on-the-scene.

Speakeasy (Shuōbā; Dongfeng Xilu; ☺ 8pm-late) A hipster mainstay, it's got a nice mix of expat and local and isn't trying too hard to be cool.

Shopping

Well, Kūnmíng isn't exactly on any shopaholic's itinerary but it ain't a total wash. Yúnnán specialities are marble and batik from Dàlǐ, jade from Ruìlì, minority embroidery, musical instruments and spotted-brass utensils.

Some functional items make good souvenirs: large bamboo water pipes for smoking angel-haired Yúnnán tobacco and local herbal medicines such as Yúnnán Báiyào (Yunnan White Medicine), which is a blend of more than 100 herbs and is highly prized by Chinese throughout the world.

Yunnanese tea is also an excellent buy and comes in several varieties, from bowl-shaped bricks of smoked green tea called *tuóchá*, which has been around since at least Marco Polo's time, to leafy black tea that rivals some of India's best.

One teashop worth checking out is **Tian Fu Famous Teas** (Tiānfù Míngchá; cnr Shangyi Jie & Beijing Lu).

Getting There & Away

AIR

There are international flights to most major Asian cities including Hanoi, Chiang Mai/Bangkok, Rangoon, Vientiane and Siem Reap. For more information on flights and airlines serving Kūnmíng, see p478.

BUS

The long-distance bus station on Beijing Lu is the best place to organise bus tickets to almost anywhere in Yúnnán. Exceptions to this are more local destinations such as Diān Chí or even southeastern Yúnnán.

TRAIN

You can buy train tickets up to 10 days in advance, which is good news because at peak times, especially public holidays, tickets get sold out days ahead of departure.

Trains no longer serve Hékǒu on the border with Vietnam.

Rail options from Kūnmíng (all prices are for hard sleepers) include trains to Běijīng (Y578), Shànghǎi (Y519), Guǎngzhōu (Y353), Xīān (Y258) and Chéngdū (Y222). Several trains run daily to Dàlǐ (Y95).

Getting Around

BICYCLE

Many backpacker hotels and hostels rent bikes for around Y15 per day.

Fat Tyres Bike Shop (☎ 530 1755; 61 Qianju Jie; per day Y20) has a large stock of bicycles including some very good mountain bikes. It also organises Sunday morning bike rides.

KŪNMÍNG BUS TIMETABLES

Destination	Price (Y)	Duration (hr)	Frequency	Departs
Dàlǐ	74-126	5-8	frequent	7.30am-7.30pm
Dàlǐ (sleeper)	95	9	2 daily	9pm, 9.30pm
Lìjiāng	171	9	hourly	7.30-11.30am
Lìjiāng (sleeper)	139	10-12	2 daily	8pm, 8.30pm
Jǐnghóng	185-223	9-10	4 daily	9.30am, 6pm, 7.45pm, 8.30pm
Jǐnghóng (sleeper)	165	10-11	half-hourly	4-8pm
Yuányáng	73-82	6-7	4 daily	10.40am, noon, 7.30pm, 8pm

BUS

Bus 63 runs from the east bus station to the Camellia Hotel and on to the main train station. Bus 23 runs from the north train station south down Beijing Lu to the main train station. Fares range from Y1 to Y4. The main city buses have no conductors and require exact change.

AROUND KŪNMÍNG

There are some fabulous sights within a 15km radius of Kūnmíng, but local transport isn't comprehensive. If you don't have that much time, the Bamboo Temple and Xī Shān are probably the most interesting.

Bamboo Temple 笻竹寺

This **temple** (Qióngzhú Sì; admission Y10; ⊗ 8am-6pm) dates back to the Tang dynasty and is worth a visit for its tremendous 500 life-sized and precisely sculpted *luóhàn* (arhats or noble ones), individually masterpieces but together a *tour de force*. Espying the wall of surfing Buddhas is worth the price of admission.

The temple is about 12km northwest of Kūnmíng. Minibuses (Y10, 30 minutes) leave when full from opposite the Yúnnán Fàndiàn from 7am. Minibuses return regularly to Kūnmíng.

Diān Chí 滇池

The shoreline of Diān Chí (Lake Dian), to the south of Kūnmíng, is dotted with settlements, farms and fishing enterprises; the western side is hilly, while the eastern side is flat country.

Plying the waters are *fānchuán* (pirate-sized junks with bamboo-battened canvas sails). It's mainly for scenic touring and hiking, and there are some fabulous aerial views from the ridges at Dragon Gate in Xī Shān. Buses leave for here from the same minibus stop in Kūnmíng as those going to Bamboo Temple and Xī Shān.

Xī Shān 西山

Spread out across a long wedge of parkland on the western side of Diān Chí, Xī Shān (Western Hills) offers hills for walking, exploring and discovering all the temples and other cultural relics. The path up to the summit passes a series of famous temples – it's a steep approach from the north side. The hike from Gāoyáo bus station, at the foot of the hills, to Dragon Gate takes 2½ hours, though most people take a connecting bus from Gāoyáo to the top section. Alternatively, it is also possible to cycle to the hills from the city centre in about an hour.

At the foot of the climb, about 15km from Kūnmíng, is **Huating Temple** (Huátíng Sì; admission Y4), a country temple of the Nanzhao kingdom.

Sānqīng Gé, near the top of the mountain, was a country villa of a Yuan dynasty prince, and was later turned into a temple dedicated to the three main Taoist deities.

Further up, near the top of the mountain, is **Dragon Gate** (Lóng Mén; admission Y30). This is a group of grottoes, sculptures, corridors and pavilions that were hacked from the cliff between 1781 and 1835 by a Taoist monk and coworkers, who must have been hanging up there by their fingertips.

GETTING THERE & AWAY

Minibuses (one way/return Y10/20, one hour, 7.30am to 2pm) leave when full from opposite the Yúnnán Fàndiàn.

It's more reliable to use local buses: take bus 5 to the terminus at Liǎngjiāhé, and then change to bus 6, which will take you to Gāoyáo bus station.

Chénggòng County 呈贡县

This county (Chénggòng Xiàn) is an orchard region on the eastern side of Diān Chí. Once one of Yúnnán's poorest areas, it now sells literally millions of sprays of flowers each day and is a primary reason Yúnnán has so many nicknames exclaiming its botanical heavenliness.

Many Western varieties of camellia, azalea, orchid and magnolia derive from southwestern Chinese varieties. Azaleas are native to China – of the 800 varieties in the world, 650 are found in Yúnnán.

Flowers bloom year-round but during the **Spring Festival** (January/February and into March) a profusion of blooms can be found in the environs.

Take bus 5 heading east to the terminus at Júhuācūn, and change there for bus 12 to Chénggòng.

SHÍLÍN 石林
☎ 0871

A conglomeration of utterly bizarre karst geology, **Shílín** (Stone Forest; ☎ 771 0316; admission Y140) is a massive collection of grey limestone pillars about 120km southeast of Kūnmíng. Split and eroded by wind and rainwater, the tallest pillar reaches 30m high. Legend has it that the immortals smashed a mountain into a labyrinth for lovers seeking privacy.

It's packed to the gills – oft-bemoaned by travellers – and pricey as hell, but there are idyllic, secluded walks within 2km of the centre and by sunset or moonlight the place becomes otherworldly.

Shílín doesn't have much in the way of accommodation and what it does offer is overpriced.

The **Stone Forest International Youth Hostel** (Shílín Guójì Qīngnián Lǚguǎn; ☎ 771 0768; 4-bed dm Y50, small s & d Y120, big s & d Y140), directly opposite where the buses drop you off, offers the cleanest, best-value accommodation you'll find.

Getting There & Away

Buses to Shílín (Y30 to Y40, two hours, every 30 minutes from 8am to noon) leave from the **bus station** (Beijing Lu, Kūnmíng) opposite the long-distance bus station. Make sure you don't get dragged onto one of the tourist buses. In the afternoon there are minibuses waiting at Shílín's car park, leaving when full (Y20).

XIÀGUĀN 下关
☎ 0872

An important FYI: Xiàguān, the capital of Dàlǐ prefecture, is also referred to as Dàlǐ on buses, maps and tickets. So when you hop off your bus, you're probably not in the 'real' (that is, old) Dàlǐ (Dàlǐ Gǔchéng); this is around 15km north.

There is no reason to stay in Xiàguān and you only need to come here for visa extensions or transport.

To go straight to old Dàlǐ, turn left out of the long-distance bus station and left again at the first intersection. Just up from the corner is the station for local bus 4, which runs to the real Dàlǐ (Y1.50, 30 minutes) until around 8pm.

The regional **Public Security Bureau** (PSB; Gōngānjú; 21 Tianbao Jie; ☒ 8-11am & 2-5pm Mon-Fri), south of town, handles *all* visa extensions for Xiàguān and Dàlǐ (for directions from Dàlǐ, see opposite).

Getting There & Away

AIR

Xiàguān's airport is 15km from town. The Yunnan Airlines ticket office is inconveniently located near the train station. There are no public buses to the airport; taxis cost Y50 from Xiàguān or Y80 from Dàlǐ. There are three flights daily to Kūnmíng (Y430).

BUS

Xiàguān has several bus stations, which throws some travellers. Luckily, the two main ones are both on the same side of the street, approximately two blocks apart. You might get dropped off at either one.

Journeys from Xiàguān's long-distance bus station include Kūnmíng (Y90 to Y126, seven hours, every 40 minutes from 7.50am to 7pm), Lìjiāng (Y41 to Y58, three hours, five daily at 8.30am, 10am, 2pm, 4pm and 7pm) and Jǐnghóng (Y170, 17 hours, three daily at noon, 2pm and 7.30pm).

Minibuses to Lìjiāng also run regularly from Xiàguān.

Tickets for nearly all destinations can be booked in Dàlǐ.

TRAIN

Overnight sleeper trains leave Kūnmíng's main train station between 10pm and 11.30pm, arriving in Xiàguān between 6am and 8.05am. Hard sleepers are Y95. Returning to Kūnmíng, trains leave Xiàguān at 2.34pm, 9pm, 9.40pm, 10.02pm and 10.20pm.

AROUND XIÀGUĀN
Jīzú Shān 鸡足山

Packed with temples and pagodas, **Jīzú Shān** (Chicken-Foot Mountain; admission Y60), is a major attraction for Buddhist pilgrims – both Chinese and Tibetan. Today, it's estimated more than 150,000 tourists and pilgrims clamber up the mountain every year to watch the sun rise. Jīndǐng, the Golden Summit, is at a cool 3240m so make sure to bring warm clothing.

Accommodation is available at the base of the mountain, about halfway up and on the summit. Prices average Y20 to Y30 per bed.

To get here from Xiàguān's north bus station, take a bus to Bīnchuān (Y11, two hours), from where you'll have to change for a bus or minibus to Shāzhǐ at the foot of the mountain (Y10, one hour).

Wēishān

Some 55km or so south of Xiàguān, Wēishān is a funky, small and cheery town with traditional architecture and strollworthy flagstone streets. It's most famous for **Wēibǎo Shān** (admission Y50), about 7km south of town, purportedly the birthplace of the Nanzhao kingdom. During the Ming and Qing dynasties it was the zenith of China's Taoism and you'll find some superb Taoist murals here.

Xiàguān's south bus station has buses (Y12, two hours) to Wēishān from 6am to 6pm. Travelling to the mountain you have to wait for minivans to fill up, which isn't very often outside of summer. Hiring the whole van is only Y40 (for Y50 the guy'll wait for you).

DÀLǏ 大理

☎ 0872 / pop 136,800

Ah, Dàlǐ. Just say the name and watch long-time China travellers grin, thinking of the first of Yúnnán's (nay, China's) backpacker sanctuaries decades ago. Yet today Dàlǐ finds itself getting slagged by quite a few travellers. 'Touristy' has become a cliché in backpacker discussions and online forums.

Yup, expect a *constant* friendly invasion of tourists clambering off tour-group buses, way too many souvenir shops, some misguided renovations to streets and structures, and un-interested guesthouse staff – the usual pitfalls of a town gone famous.

Then again, so what? It's still in a stunning location, sandwiched between mountains and Ěrhǎi Hú (Erhai Lake), and it has a fabulous climate. Just keep wandering the ancient alleys to find your own nook, hike the trails above the town, get on a boat on Ěrhǎi Hú or, better, get your hands on a bike and get the hell out of town.

History

For much of the five centuries in which Yúnnán governed its own affairs, Dàlǐ was the centre of operations. The main inhabitants of the region are the Bai. The Bai people have long-established roots in the Ěrhǎi Hú region, and are thought to have settled the area some 3000 years ago. In the early 8th century they grouped together and succeeded in defeating the Tang imperial army before establishing the Nanzhao kingdom.

The kingdom exerted considerable influence throughout southwest China and even, to a lesser degree, Southeast Asia, since it controlled upper Burma for much of the 9th century. This later established Dàlǐ as an end node on the famed Burma Road.

Orientation

Dàlǐ is a miniature city that has some preserved cobbled streets and traditional stone architecture within its old walls. It takes about half an hour to walk from the South Gate (Nán Mén) across town to the North Gate (Běi Mén).

Huguo Lu is the main strip for cafés – locals call it Yangren Jie (Foreigner's St) – and this is where to turn to for your café latte fix.

Information

All the hotels offer travel advice and can arrange tours and book tickets for onward travel.

Bank of China (Zhōngguó Yínháng; cnr Huguo Lu & Fuxing Lu) Changes cash and travellers cheques. An ATM here accepts all major credit cards.

China Post (Yóujú; cnr Fuxing Lu & Huguo Lu; ☻ 8am-8pm) The best place to make international calls as it has direct dial and doesn't levy a service charge.

China Telecom (cnr Fuxing Lu & Huguo Lu; per hr Y2; ☻ 8am-10pm) For internet access. Most hotels and guesthouses also offer free internet access for guests.

Jim's Tibetan Guesthouse & Peace Café (☎ 267 1822; 63 Boai Lu; 博爱路63号; www.china-travel.nl/) Offers a long list of trips that have been very highly rated by travellers.

Mandarin Books & CDs (Wǔhuá Shūyuán; Fuxing Lu) Has maps, along with a decent selection of guidebooks and novels in Chinese, English and Dutch.

Public Security Bureau (PSB; Gōngānjú; 21 Tianbao Jie, Xiàguān; ☻ 8am-11am & 2-5pm Mon-Fri) The PSB branch in Dàlǐ will *not* issue visa extensions. You need to go to the Xiàguān branch (opposite). To get there, take bus 4 until just after it crosses the river in Xiàguān. The PSB office is a short walk south from here.

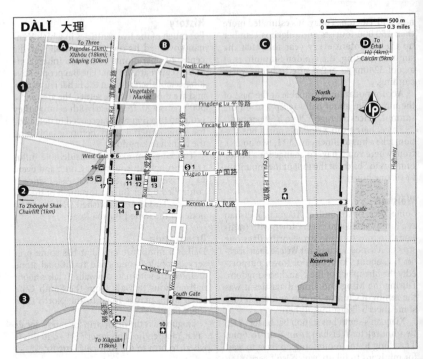

DÀLǏ 大理

Dangers & Annoyances

The hike up to Zhonghe Temple (Zhōnghé Sì) and along the mountain ridges is super, but there have been several reports of robbery of solo walkers. Try to find a partner to go with you.

Be careful on the overnight sleeper buses coming in from Kūnmíng as someone often finds a bag pinched or razored.

Sights

Well, you're going to spend at least a chunk of your time wandering about/getting lost in the old town. Nothing much exists to 'see' other than remanufactured architecture – a bit of the original remains – and a helluva lot of dirt-cheap shopping.

The **Three Pagodas** (三塔寺; Sān Tǎ Sì; admission incl Chongsheng Temple Y121; 8am-7pm) are among the oldest standing structures in southwestern China and are definitely *the* symbol of Dàlǐ. It's a hell of an admission price (especially given that you can't enter the pagodas), but it's fun enough just to watch Chinese tourists tearing about here to take their snaps.

Festivals & Events

Merrymaking during the **Third Moon Fair** (Sānyuè Jiē) begins on the 15th day of the third lunar month (usually April) and ends on the 21st day. The origins of the fair lie in its commemoration of a fabled visit by Guanyin, the Buddhist Goddess of Mercy, to the Nanzhao kingdom.

The **Torch Festival** (Huǒbǎ Jié) is held on the 24th day of the sixth lunar month (normally July). Flaming torches are paraded at night through homes and fields.

Sleeping

Despite heaps of accommodation, during peak summer months brace yourself for a long slog about town in search of a bed.

No 3 Guesthouse (Dìsān Zhāodàisuǒ; ☎ 266 4941; Huguo Lu; 护国路; 6-bed dm Y20; 🖳) A fab staff buzzes about, new wooden furniture fills the rooms with a pleasant pinelike smell, each bunk has a bamboo curtain for privacy and facilities are immaculate.

our pick MCA Guesthouse (☎ 267 3666; mcahouse@ hotmail.com; Wenxian Lu; 文献路; dm Y20, s/d Y100/120; 🖳) Dorms sport lovely touches such as wall art, hardwood floors and furniture that's actually pleasant to look at; the standard rooms have commanding lake views.

Liùhéyuàn Qīngnián Lǚshè (☎ 267 0701; 415 Renmin Lu; 人民路415号; dm Y20, s & d Y100-200; 🖳) Not much like it in town. Along with loads of extras, each room was designed by local artists and it shows – call it funky chic. You'll find a handful of other extras.

our pick **Jim's Peace Hotel** (Jímǔ Hépíng Jiǔdiàn; ☎ 267 7824; www.china-travel.nl; 13 Yuxiu Lu; 玉秀路中段13号; d Y200; 🖳) Newly opened by a Dàlǐ *long*timer, rooms manage to be both sleek and cosy. There's a garden, a rooftop terrace, and restaurant and bar below.

Eating

Ěr kuài (饵块) are flattened and toasted rice 'cakes' with an assortment of toppings (or plain); these are found province-wide. Fish are a mainstay here. Try *shāguō yú* (沙锅鱼), a claypot fish casserole/stew made from salted Ěrhǎi Hú carp – magnolia petals might be added!

Yunnan Café & Bar (Yúnnán Kāfēiguǎn & Jiǔba; Huguo Lu; dishes from Y5) This cosy town stalwart with eminently friendly staff has always been raved about for its pizza, but you pretty much can't go wrong.

Marley's Café (Mǎli Kāfēiguǎn; ☎ 267 6651; 105 Boai Lu; dishes Y5-25) Marley's has always been a cornerstone of the town. Well-done food, great service and helpful advice, all in a just-subdued-enough environment. Check out the Bai banquet on Sunday night (reserve early).

Drinking

Birdbar (Niǎobā; ☎ 266 1843; 22 Renmin Lu) This place is worth trying. It's a low-key off-the-main-drag watering hole with a pool table.

Shopping

Huguo Lu has become a smaller version of Bangkok's Khao San Rd. Dàlǐ is famous for its marble and for blue-and-white batik printed on cotton and silk. A lot of the batik is still made in Dàlǐ and hidden behind many of the shopfronts are vast vats of blue dye. Most of the 'silver' jewellery sold in Dàlǐ is really brass.

Most shopkeepers can also make clothes to your specifications.

Bargain politely but firmly. For those roving sales ladies badgering you incessantly, don't feel bad to pay one-fifth of their asking price – that's what locals advise. For marble from street sellers, 40% to 50% is fair. In shops, two-thirds of the price is average. And don't fall for any 'expert' opinions; go back later on your own and deal.

Getting There & Away

AIR

Xiàguān's airport (p450) is served often by flights from Kūnmíng, possibly by other cities in the near future.

BUS

The golden rule: find out in advance whether your bus is for Dàlǐ or Xiàguān. Coming from Lìjiāng, Xiàguān-bound buses stop at the eastern end of Dàlǐ to let passengers off.

For information on getting to Dàlǐ from Kūnmíng, see p448.

From the bus stop near the west gate in Dàlǐ there are express buses to Kūnmíng (Y106, five hours, 9.30am, 10.30am, 4.30pm and 9pm). A slow bus for Kūnmíng also leaves daily at 8am (Y65). Buses to Lìjiāng (Y30 to Y50, three hours, every 30 minutes from 7.30am to 7.20pm) also leave from here.

A bus also leaves from here for Shāpíng every Monday morning (Y5, one hour, 9.30am) for the market. At all other times, local buses run regularly to Shāpíng, Xīzhōu and other local destinations from opposite the bus station in Dàlǐ.

TRAIN

The overnight sleeper train from Kūnmíng is comfy but the times aren't grand – you arrive pretty early in the morning. For more details, see p450.

Getting Around

From Dàlǐ, a taxi to Xiàguān airport takes 45 minutes and costs around Y80; to Xiàguān's train station it costs Y30.

Bikes are the best way to get around (Y10 to Y15 per day). Most of the guesthouses and several other places on Boai Lu rent bikes.

Bus 4 runs between Dàlǐ and central Xiàguān (Y1.50, 30 minutes) every 15 minutes from 6.30am, which means that unless your bus leaves Xiàguān earlier than 7.30am you won't have to stay the night there.

Bus 8 runs from Dàlǐ to Xiàguān's train station.

AROUND DÀLǏ
Markets

Usually markets follow the lunar calendar, but now there's a regular scheme so that tourists have a market to go to nearly every day of the week. See right for information on the Monday Shāpíng market. Markets also take place in Shuānglláng (Tuesday), Shābā (Wednesday), Yòusuǒ (Friday, the largest in Yúnnán) and Jiāngwěi (Saturday). There's a daily morning market in Xīzhōu and a daily afternoon market in Zhōuchéng.

Wāsè also has a popular market every five days with trading from 9am to 4.30pm.

Most cafés and hotels in Dàlǐ offer tours or can arrange transportation to markets for around Y150 for a half day.

Ěrhǎi Hú 洱海湖

At 1973m above sea level and covering 250 sq km, Ěrhǎi Hú is the seventh-biggest freshwater lake in China. Bike-worthy trails, old villages, temples, islands – you can't *not* find something to like.

The best way to explore is either renting a bike or zipping about on one of the many ferries that crisscross the lake. A great bike trip is from Dàlǐ to Shāpíng and it can be done in a day. The lakeside road may seem the most picturesque, but it's congested; stick to side roads.

From **Cáicūn**, a pleasant little lakeside village east of Dàlǐ (Y2 on minibus 2), there's regular ferries to **Wāsè** (Y3 to Y5) on the other

side of the lake. Plenty of locals take their bikes over.

Ferries crisscross the lake at various points, so there could be some scope for extended touring; timetables are flexible and departures are somewhat unreliable.

Roads now encircle the lake so it is possible to do a loop (or partial loop) of the lake by mountain bike.

Zhonghe Temple 中和寺

This **temple** (Zhōnghé Sì; admission Y2) is a long, steep hike up the mountainside behind Dàlǐ; the delightful slog and the vistas of Ěrhǎi Hú will be treasured memories, even if the temple isn't. To reach the top take the **chairlift** (one way/return Y30/50) up **Zhōnghé Shān** (Zhonghe Mountain). Or hike.

Branching out from either side of the temple is a trail that winds along the face of the mountains, taking you in and out of steep, lush valleys and past streams and waterfalls. From Zhōnghé it's an amazing 11km up-and-down hike south to **Gantong Temple** (Gǎntōng Sì) or **Qingbi Stream**, from where you can continue to the road and pick up a Dàlǐ-bound bus. There's also a new cable car between the two temples (one way/return Y52/82).

Alternatively, you can spend some more time here and stay the night at **Higherland Inn** (☎ 0872-266 1599; www.higherland.com; dm/s/d Y25/30/50) located just above Zhonghe. The hostel has fabulous views and is a true getaway. You can reserve rooms at the booking office on Renmin Lu in Dàlǐ.

Xīzhōu 喜洲

The old town of Xīzhōu is worth a look for its well-preserved Bai architecture. You can catch a local bus from the south gate in Dàlǐ (Y3) to make the 18km trip, but a bicycle trip with an overnight stop (there's accommodation in town) is also a good idea. From here, the equally interesting town of **Zhōuchéng** is 7km north.

Shaping Market 沙坪赶集

Every Monday at Shāpíng, about 30km north of Dàlǐ, there is a colourful Bai **market** (Shāpíng Gǎnjí). The hustle starts at 10am and ends around 2.30pm. Expect to be quoted ridiculously high prices on anything you set your eyes on, so get into a bargaining frame of mind.

Head out on the road to Lìjiāng and flag down anything heading north. By bike it will take about two hours at a good clip.

NORTHWEST YÚNNÁN

LÌJIĀNG 丽江
new town ☎ 08891, old town ☎ 0888 / pop 60,000

Lìjiāng's maze of cobbled streets, rickety old wooden buildings and gushing canals makes it one of the most visited sites in northern Yúnnán. Those same tour buses disgorging the hordes in Dàlǐ also inevitably call here – and they all manage to get snarled up in epic waves of human jams in the town's tiny alleys.

But don't let the crowds or any bitchy travellers discourage a trip. Get up early enough and it will be just you, Lìjiāng and a few bun sellers. Then skedaddle before the onslaught begins around 9am.

In 1996 an earthquake measuring over seven on the Richter scale rocked the Lìjiāng area, killing more than 300 people and injuring 16,000. The Chinese government took note of how the traditional Naxi buildings held up and sank millions of yuán into rebuilding most of Lìjiāng County with traditional Naxi architecture, replacing cement with cobblestone and wood. The UN placed all of Lìjiāng County on its World Heritage Site list in 1999.

Orientation

Lìjiāng is separated into old and new towns that are starkly different. The approximate line of division is Shīzī Shān (Lion Hill), the green hump in the middle of town topped by Looking at the Past Pavilion. Everything west of the hill is the new town, and everything east is the old town. You *will* get lost in the old town; just follow a stream, all of which lead back toward the centre.

Information

Lìjiāng's cafés and backpacker inns are your best source of information on the area. There's a slew of Travel Reception Centres all over the old town but they mostly arrange tours.

Many of the cafés in the old town have International Direct Dial (IDD) lines. Prague Café (p457) has internet access for Y5 per hour.

Bank of China (Zhōngguó Yínháng; Dong Dajie) This branch has an ATM.

China International Travel Service (CITS; Zhōngguó Guójì Lǚxíngshè; ☎ 516 0369; 3rd fl, Lifang Bldg, cnr Fuhui Lu & Shangrila Dadao) Can arrange tours in and around Lìjiāng.

China Post (Yóujú; Minzhu Lu; ☉ 8am-8pm) Offers EMS. Another branch is located in the old town, just north of the Old Market Square.

China Telecom (Minzhu Lu) Next door to China Post; you can make international calls from here.

Eco-tours (☎ 131-7078 0719; www.ecotourchina.com) Run by Zhao Fan at Café Buena Vista (see p459).

Mandarin Books & CDs (Lìjiāng Wǔhuā Shūyuán; Xin Dajie) Has a fantastic choice of English books and maps on Lijiāng and the region. Also German, French and other foreign-language titles.

Public Security Bureau (PSB; Gōngānjú; ☎ 518 8437; Fuhui Lu; ☉ 8.30-11.30am & 2.30-5.30pm Mon-Fri) Reportedly very speedy with visa extensions. So be nice.

Dangers & Annoyances

Pickpockets love the old town's crowds. There's been a handful of reports of solo

---

THE NAXI 纳西

Lìjiāng has been the base of the 286,000-strong Naxi (also spelt Nakhi and Nahi) minority for about the last 1400 years. The Naxi descend from ethnically Tibetan Qiang tribes and lived until recently in matrilineal families. Since local rulers were always male it wasn't truly matriarchal, but women still seem to run the show.

The Naxi matriarchs maintained their hold over the men with flexible arrangements for love affairs. The *azhu* (friend) system allowed a couple to become lovers without setting up joint residence. Linguistically, nouns enlarge their meaning when the word for 'female' is added; conversely, the addition of the word for 'male' will decrease the meaning. For example, 'stone' plus 'female' conveys the idea of a boulder; 'stone' plus 'male' conveys the idea of a pebble.

The Naxi created a written language over 1000 years ago using an extraordinary system of pictographs – the only hieroglyphic language still in use. The most famous Naxi text is the Dongba classic *Creation*, and ancient copies of it and other texts can still be found in Lìjiāng. The Dongba were Naxi shamans who were caretakers of the written language and mediators between the Naxi and the spirit world.

Useful phrases in the Naxi language are: *nuar lala* (hello) and *jiu bai sai* (thank you).

LÌJIĀNG 丽江

women travellers being mugged when walking alone at night in isolated areas of historic Lìjiāng. Also try to avoid going solo to Xiàng Shān in Black Dragon Pool Park (Hēilóngtán Gōngyuán).

Sights

Crisscrossed by canals, bridges and a maze of narrow streets, the **old town** is the reason why people come to Lìjiāng. The town's web of arterylike canals once supplied the city's drinking water.

The focus is the **Old Market Square** (Sìfāng Jiē). Once the haunt of Naxi traders, they've long since made way for tacky souvenir stalls.

Now acting as sentinel of sorts for the town, the **Looking at the Past Pavilion** (Wànggǔ Lóu; admission Y15) was raised for tourists at a cost of over one million yuán. It's famed for a unique design using dozens of four-storey pillars – unfortunately these were culled from northern Yúnnán old-growth forests. Still, from here you get superb eyefuls of the old town's misty mornings.

MU FAMILY MANSION 木氏土司府

The former home of a Naxi chieftain, the **Mu Family Mansion** (Mùshìtú Sīfŭ; admission Y35; ⏰ 8.30am-5.30pm) was heavily renovated (more like built from scratch) after the 1996 earthquake. Poor captioning notwithstanding, many travellers find the beautiful grounds reason enough to visit.

BLACK DRAGON POOL PARK 黑龙潭公园

On the northern edge of town is the **Black Dragon Pool Park** (Hēilóngtán Gōngyuán; Xin Jīe; admission Y30, free after 6pm; ⏰ 7am-7pm). Note the admission price is expected to rise to Y60 soon. Apart from strolling around the pool – its view of Yùlóng Xuěshān (Jade Dragon Snow Mountain) is the most obligatory photo shoot in southwestern China – you can visit the **Dongba Research Institute** (Dōngbā Wénhuà Yánjiūshì).

Trails lead straight up **Xiàng Shān** to a dilapidated gazebo and then across a spiny ridge past a communications centre and back down the other side, making a nice morning hike. Avoid going to this area solo.

The **Museum of Naxi Dongba Culture** (Nàxī Dōngbā Wénhuà Bówùguǎn; admission Y5; ⏰ 8.30am-5.30pm) is at the park's northern entrance.

Festivals & Events

The 13th day of the third moon (late March or early April) is the traditional day to hold a **Fertility Festival**.

July brings the **Torch Festival** (Huǒbǎ Jié), also celebrated by the Bai in the Dàlǐ region and the Yi all over the southwest. The origin of this festival can be traced back to the intrigues of the Nanzhao kingdom, when the wife of a man burned to death by their king eluded the romantic entreaties of the monarch by leaping into a fire.

Sleeping

There is no shortage of charming Naxi-style lodging here. Note that prices can spike in July and August and especially during holidays.

Mama Naxi's Guesthouse (Gǔchéng Xiānggéyún Kèzhàn; ☎ 510 0700; 78 Wenhua La, Wuyi Jie; 五一街文化巷78号; dm Y15, s & d from Y50; 🖥) This place's enormous popularity derives mainly from

Mama's dynamic personality; you'll be glad to have her looking out for you. It's packed, a bit chaotic (though well run and clean) but eminently fun. Midnight curfew.

International Youth Hostel Lijiang (Lìjiāng Lǎoxié Chēmǎdiàn; ☎ 511 6118; 25 Jishan Alley, Xinyi Jie; 新义街, 积善巷25号; dm Y20, s Y40-120, d Y100-140, tr Y150-180) Well-kept rooms of every conceivable variation and nice touches set it apart from the generic hostels in town. Hot water from 6pm to 2am only.

ourpick Carnation Hotel (Kāngnǎixīn Kèzhàn; ☎ 511 1237, 511 7306; ewan_215@yahoo.com.cn; 134 Wenzhi Alley; 文治巷134号; s & d Y50-120, Jul & Aug Y150; 🖥) This relaxing place has solicitous owners – chatty, with some English – and comfy rooms set around a large courtyard. Budget prices, midrange service. The hotel is located just east of town.

Moon Inn (Xīnyuégé Kèzhàn; ☎ 518 0520; mooninn@163.com; 34 Xingren Xiaduan, Wuyi Jie; 五一街, 兴仁下段34号; s & d Y200; 🖥) A casual but mod place, its bright and breezy rooms have wood furniture and fetching colours. The courtyard is lovely and there's a relaxing common room as well.

Zen Garden Hotel (Ruíhé Yuán Jiǔdiàn; ☎ 518 9799; www.zengardenhotel.com; 36 Xingren La, Wuyi Jie; 五一街, 兴仁下段36号; d Y400, 'wedding rooms' Y1400) This sybaritic place, run by a Naxi teacher and decorated with help from her artist brother, is like a sumptuous museum with glittery night views of old Lìjiāng. Amazing attention to detail.

Eating

There are always several 'Naxi' items on the menu, including the famous *bābā* (粑粑), thick flatbreads of wheat, served plain or stuffed with meats, vegetables or sweets. Great pretrekking or biking sustenance.

Prague Café (18 Mishi Xiang; meals from Y15; ⏰ from 7.30am) An old favourite, the Naxi breakfast (Y22), will have you set for Tiger Leaping Gorge. Great atmosphere with a loyal crowd, this café also has a book exchange, magazines and internet (Y5 per hour).

ourpick Petit Lijiang Bookcafé (☎ 511 1255; 50 Chongren Xiang, Qiyi Jie; dishes from Y15) Owners Mei and Olivier (a Chinese-Belgian couple) are inveterate travellers and great sources of travel info. Sublime food, and the bookshop has English-and French-language titles focusing on Yúnnán and elsewhere in China.

Lamu's House of Tibet (Xīzàngwū Xīcāntīng; ☎ 518 9000; 56 Xinyi Jie; dishes from Y10) Away from the main drag, this place serves excellent food from a hugely varied menu. Try the *momo* (Tibetan dumplings), which come with a variety of fillings, but make sure you save room for the desserts – they're massive.

Blue Papaya (Lán Múguà; ☎ 661 2114; 70 Xinyi Jie; dishes from Y30) Serves pasta and fish dishes that are terrific not just against Chinese standards but by any benchmark. Service is outstanding and the menu has creative flourishes such as pineapple or sweet potato ice cream. This is a perfect place to relax and linger over a first-rate meal.

Entertainment

The **Naxi Orchestra** (Nàxī Gǔyuè Huì; ☎ 512 7971; Naxi Music Academy; tickets Y100-140; ☯ performances 8pm) is perhaps the town's most legendary attraction. The 20 to 24 Naxi members play a type of Taoist temple music (known as *dòngjīng*) that has been lost elsewhere in China. The pieces they perform are supposedly faithful renditions of music from the Han, Song and Tang dynasties, and are played on original instruments.

Famed local historian Xuan Ke often speaks – too much, some say – explaining each musical piece and describing the instruments. BTW, don't grouse about the somnolent musicians – they're ancient and it's half the fun!

Getting There & Away

AIR

Lìjiāng's airport is 25km east of town. Tickets can be booked at the **CAAC** (Zhōngguó Mínháng; ☎ 516 1289; cnr Fuhui Lu & Shangrila Dadao; ☯ 8.30am-9pm). Most hotels in the old town also offer an air-ticket booking service.

From Lìjiāng there are oodles of daily flights to Kūnmíng (Y660) and in season to other Chinese cities.

BUS

Lìjiāng has three bus stations: one just north of the old town; the main long-distance bus

station in the south; and an express bus station to Kūnmíng and Xiàguān on Shangrila Dadao in the north of town.

From the express bus station there are daily departures to Kūnmíng (Y171 to Y193, 8am, 9am, 10am, 11am and 12.30pm). Two sleeper buses also leave daily for Kūnmíng at 8.30pm. One terminates at Kūnmíng's west station, the other at its south station. Buses also leave for the 160km trip to Xiàguān (Y41 to Y58, 8am, 11.10am, noon, 2.10pm, 3.50pm and 6.10pm).

Buses from the northern bus station include Kūnmíng (Y119, eight hours, daily at 8pm) and Xiàguān (Y35 to Y37, two hours, 20 a day from 7.30am to 6pm).

Getting Around

Buses to the airport (Y15) leave from outside the CAAC 90 minutes before flight departure times.

Taxis start at Y6 in the new town and are not allowed into the old town (the whole of the old town is pedestrianised).

Bike hire is available at the International Youth Hostel Lijiang (see p457; Y15 per day).

AROUND LÌJIĀNG

It is possible to see most of Lìjiāng's environs on your own, but a few agencies do offer half- or full-day tours, starting from Y150 to Y200 *without* entrance fees.

Monasteries

The monasteries around Lìjiāng are Tibetan in origin and belong to the Karmapa (Red Hat) sect. There's not much monastic activity nowadays though seeing the scenery from a bike saddle is lovely. **Puji Monastery** (普济寺; Pǔjì Sì) is around 5km northwest of Lìjiāng (on a trail that passes the two ponds to the north of town).

LÌJIĀNG BUS TIMETABLES

Buses from the long-distance bus station include the following:

Destination	Price (Y)	Duration (hr)	Frequency	Departs
Kūnmíng	151	12	hourly	8.30-11.30am & 1pm
Kūnmíng (sleeper)	119	8	11 daily	6.30-9pm
Xiàguān	35-50	3½	27 daily	7.10am-6.30pm
Qiáotóu	20	2	daily	1pm

West of Báishā lies the remains of the **Fuguo Monastery** (富国寺; Fùguó Sì), once the largest of Lìjiāng's monasteries. To get there head west from the main intersection in Báishā until you reach a small village. Turn right at the fork in the road and continue for around 500m before taking the next left that you come to. It's 30 minutes uphill from here.

Jade Peak Monastery (玉峰寺; Yùfēng Sì) is on a hillside about 5km past Báishā. The last 3km of the track require a steep climb. At the foot of Yùlóng Xuěshān, the monastery's main attraction is the Camellia Tree of 10,000 Blossoms (Wànduǒ Shānchá). A monk on the grounds risked his life to keep the tree secretly watered during the Cultural Revolution.

BÁISHĀ 白沙

Báishā is a small village on the plain north of Lìjiāng, near several old temples, and is one of the best day trips out of Lìjiāng, especially if you have a bike. Before Kublai Khan made it part of his Yuan empire (1271–1368), Báishā was the capital of the Naxi kingdom and still offers a close-up glimpse of Naxi culture for those willing to spend some time nosing around.

The star attraction of Báishā, Dr Ho (or He), looks like the stereotype of a Taoist physician. Travel writer Bruce Chatwin propelled the good doctor into the limelight when he mythologised Dr Ho as the 'Taoist physician in the Jade Dragon Mountains of Lìjiāng' and Dr Ho, previously an unknown doctor in an unknown town, has achieved worldwide renown.

Almost directly opposite Dr Ho's clinic is **Café Buena Vista** (Nànà Wéisītǎ Jùlèbù; ☎ 131-7078 0719; info@ecotour.com), a lovely little café and gallery run by artist Zhao Fan and his girlfriend. It's

---

FRESCOES

Lìjiāng is famed for its temple frescoes, most of which were painted during the 15th and 16th centuries by Tibetan, Naxi, Bai and Han artists but, of course, were damaged heavily during the Cultural Revolution.

In Báishā the best frescoes can be found in **Dabaoji Palace** (Dàbǎojī Gōng; admission Y15; ⏰ 8.30am-5.30pm). Nearby, **Liuli Temple** (Liúlí Diàn) and **Dading Ge** also have some and frescoes can be found on the interior walls of **Dajue Palace** (Dàjué Gōng), in the neighbouring village of Lóngquán.

---

a fantastic place to get travel information and organise tours.

There are a couple of frescoes worth seeing in town and surrounding the area; see left for details.

Báishā is an easy 20- to 30-minute bike ride from Lìjiāng. Otherwise take a minibus (Y15) from the corner of Minzu Lu and Fuhui Lu. From Báishā minibuses return to Lìjiāng regularly (Y20).

YÙLÓNG XUĚSHĀN 玉龙雪山

Also known as Mt Satseto, **Yùlóng Xuěshān** (adult/student Y80/60, protection fee Y40) soars to some 5500m. Its peak was first climbed in 1963 by a research team from Běijīng and now, at some 35km from Lìjiāng, is mobbed (not an exaggeration at times) by hordes of the Gore-Tex-clad for its superlative scenery.

Dry Sea Meadow (甘海子; Gānhǎizi) is the first stop you come to if travelling by bus from Lìjiāng. A chairlift (Y160) ascends to a large meadow at 3050m which, according to geologists, was actually a lake 2000 years ago. It can often get freezing at this elevation even when warm below: warm coats can be rented for Y30, deposit Y300, and oxygen tanks are Y40.

Cloud Fir Meadow (云杉坪; Yúnshānpíng) is the second stop and a chairlift (Y40) takes you up to 4506m where walkways lead to awesome glacier views. Horses can be hired here for Y80.

Get here early to get a head start on the tour groups, or you'll have an hour wait to get either up or down the mountain.

Around 60km from Lìjiāng, or a 30-minute drive from Dry Sea Meadow, is **Yak Meadow** (牦牛坪; Máoniúpíng), where yet another chairlift (Y60) pulls visitors up to an altitude of 3500m; there are ample hiking opportunities near Xuěhuā Hǎi (Snowflake Lake). Crowds and long waits are almost unheard of here.

Bus 7 (Y15 to Y20) leaves for all three spots from the intersection of Minzu Lu and Fuhui Lu in Lìjiāng and passes by Báishā on the way. Returning to Lìjiāng, buses leave fairly regularly but check with your driver to find out what time the last bus will depart.

If you enter the region from the north (Tiger Leaping Gorge) there's no ticket gate.

TIGER LEAPING GORGE 虎跳峡
☎ 0887

Yúnnán's original trek, Tiger Leaping Gorge (Hǔtiào Xiá) is now considered a traveller's

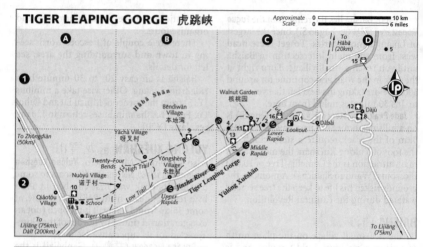

rite of passage. One of the deepest gorges in the world, it measures 16km long and is a giddy 3900m from the waters of Jīnshā Jiāng (Jinsha River) to the snowcapped mountaintops of Hābā Shān (Haba Mountain) to the west and Yùlóng Xuěshān to the east. And it's preternaturally lovely pretty much everywhere. Admission to the gorge is Y50 (you can pay at either ticket office).

Dangers & Annoyances

The gorge trek is not to be taken lightly. Even for those in good physical shape, it's a workout. The path constricts and crumbles; it certainly can wreck the knees. When it's raining (especially in July and August), landslides and swollen waterfalls can block the paths, in particular on the low road. Half a dozen people – including a few foreign travellers – have died in the gorge. A few solo travellers have also been assaulted on the trail.

Check with cafés and lodgings in Lìjiāng for trail and weather updates. Most have fairly detailed gorge maps; just remember the maps are not to scale and occasionally out of date.

Make sure you bring plenty of water on this hike – 2L to 3L is ideal – as well as plenty of sunscreen and lip balm.

Gorge Trek

There are two trails – the higher (the older route, known as the Twenty-Four Bends path), and the lower, the new road, replete with belching tour buses. Only the high trail is worth hiking. Arrows help you avoid getting lost.

The following route commences at Qiáotóu Village.

To get to the high road, after crossing through the gate, cross a small stream and go 150m. Take a left fork, go through the schoolyard's football pitch, and join the tractor road. Continue until the track ends and then follow the yellow arrows to the right. It's six hours to Běndìwān Village or a strenuous eight hours to Walnut Garden. Guesthouses dot the trail.

One option is **Halfway Lodge** (Zhōngtú Kèzhàn; Běndìwān; dm Y15), which was once a simple home to a guy collecting medicinal herbs and his family. It's now a busy-busy – but cosy and well-run – operation.

About 1½ hours from Běndìwān you descend to the road to **Tina's Guest House** (Zhōngxiá Lǚdiàn; dm Y15) – budget more time if you are ascending. A good detour from here leads down 40 minutes to the middle rapids and Tiger Leaping Stone, where a tiger is once said to have leapt across the Yangzi, thus giving the gorge its name. The man who restored the path charges Y10.

From Tina's to Walnut Garden it is a 40-minute walk along the road. A new alternative trail leading to Walnut Garden keeps high where the path descends to Tina's, crosses a stream and a 'bamboo forest', before descending into Walnut Garden.

Sean's Spring Guesthouse (Shānquán Kèzhàn; ☎ 880 6300; www.tigerleapinggorge.com; dm Y15) is one of the original guesthouses on the trail and still the spot for lively evenings and socialising. Sean's has electric blankets and mountain-bike hire (Y10 per hour), and can organise camping, guides and horse trips.

Chateau de Woody (Shānbáilián Lǚguǎn; dm Y15) is the other original and is just fine too.

The next day's walk is slightly shorter at about four to six hours. There are two ferries and so two route options to get to Dàjù. After 45 minutes you'll see a red marker leading down to the new (winter) ferry (xīn dùkǒu; one way Y10); the descent includes one hairy section over planks with a sheer drop below.

Many trekkers call it a day when they reach the bottom and flag down anything heading back Qiáotóu. The road to Dàjù and the village itself are pretty uninteresting so you won't be missing anything if you decide to skip it.

If you do decide to head on to Dàjù, it's a hard climb to the car park where you should register with the Lìjiāng Public Security Bureau (PSB; Gōngānjú). The PSB officer offers a car to take you into Dàjù for Y10, avoiding the dull 1½-hour's walk along the road.

The second, lesser-used option continues along the road from Walnut Garden until it reaches the permanent ferry crossing (Y10). From here paths lead to Dàjù.

If you're doing the walk the other way round and heading for Qiáotóu, walk north through Dàjù, aiming for the white pagoda at the foot of the mountains.

Sleeping & Eating

Lodging options abound but in peak times – particularly late summer – up to 100 people per day can make the trek, so bed space is short. Be prepared to sleep in a back room somewhere. Supplies of bottled water can be chancy.

JOSEPH ROCK

Yúnnán was a hunting ground for famous, foreign plant-hunters such as Kingdon Ward and Joseph Rock. Rock lived near Lìjiāng between 1922 and 1949, becoming the world's leading expert on Naxi culture and local botany. More than his academic pursuits, however, he will be remembered as one of the most enigmatic and eccentric characters to travel in western China.

Born in Austria, he taught himself eight languages – including Sanskrit – and began learning Chinese at 13 years of age. He later convinced the US Department of Agriculture, and later Harvard University, to sponsor his trips to collect flora for medicinal research. After becoming the world's foremost authority on Hawaiian flora, he devoted much of his life to studying Naxi culture, which he feared was being extinguished by the dominant Han culture. He became *National Geographic* magazine's 'man in China' and it was his exploits in northwestern Yúnnán and Sìchuān for the magazine that made him famous.

Rock's caravans stretched for half a mile, and included dozens of servants, including a cook trained in Austrian cuisine, trains of pack horses, and hundreds of mercenaries for protection against bandits, not to mention the gold dinner service and a collapsible bathtub.

Rock lived in Yùhú village (called Nguluko when he was there) outside Lìjiāng. Many of his possessions are now local family heirlooms and his residence is now a museum.

The *Ancient Nakhi Kingdom of Southwest China* (1947) is Joseph Rock's definitive work, along with his Naxi dictionary. For an insight into the man and his work, take a look at *In China's Border Provinces: The Turbulent Career of Joseph Rock, Botanist-Explorer* (1974) by JB Sutton, or Rock's many archived articles for *National Geographic*.

THE END OF THE GORGE?

If only the gorge's annoying new road and its ubiquitous shuttle buses were all. Tiger Leaping Gorge could disappear in a matter of years if plans to build eight dams along 564km of the upper reaches of the Yangzi River go ahead. Once completed, the dams will flood more than 13,000 hectares of prime farmland, force over 100,000 people (some claim up to a million) to relocate, and wash away local culture, history, unique architecture, and indigenous plant and animal life.

Local opposition has been uniform and ferocious (there have been one or two reports of assaults against officials) but even with every environmental group in China and abroad lobbying against it, it's hard to believe that those in charge will take much notice. Chinese media report that preparatory work, including blasting, has already begun and proper construction on the dams is expect to begin by 2008.

QIÁOTÓU VILLAGE

Jane's Guesthouse (☎ 880 6570; janetibetgh@hotmail .com; dm Y15, s & d Y30; 🖳) Jane is one of the gorge's true characters and has all the straight dope on the trek.

Gorged Tiger Café (☎ 880 6300; mains Y50-20) Run by Australian woman Margo, the food gets mixed reviews, but Margo herself gets raves.

DÀJÙ

Snowflake Hotel (Xuěhuā Fàndiàn; r with shared bathroom from Y20) Rooms are spartan and a bit dark but the hotel's friendliness will snag most sweaty TLG trekkers.

Daju Longhu Inn (Dàjú Lónghǔ Kézhán; ☎ 888 532 6040; standard/deluxe d with shared bathroom Y20/50) You may need to stick a smoke into your nostrils in the communal showers and toilets and the budget rooms are nondescript, but the deluxe ones are quite impressively done up.

Getting There & Away

Transport is ever easier. Most people take a Shangri-la-bound bus (Y20, hourly from 7.30am to 5pm) early in the morning, hop off in Qiáotóu, and hike quickly to stay overnight in Walnut Garden.

Returning to Lìjiāng from Qiáotóu, buses start running through from Shangri-la around 9am. The last one rolls through around 7.40pm (Y20). The last bus to Shangri-la passes through at around 7pm.

Buses (Y24, four hours) run in the morning – whenever they feel like it – from just north of the old town in Lìjiāng. From Dàjù to Lìjiāng buses leave at 7.30am and 1.30pm.

If you want to cheat, alight in Qiáotóu and then catch a shuttle bus to the main viewpoint 10km away; bargain to around Y15. You could even take a taxi (Y50) the 23km from Qiáotóu to Walnut Garden and hitchhike back.

SOUTHEAST YÚNNÁN

YUANYANG RICE TERRACES
☎ 0873

These rice terraces, hewn from the rolling topography by the Hani over centuries, cover roughly 12,500 hectares and are another of Yúnnán's – nay, China's – most spectacular sights. At sunrise or sunset these pools are an artist's palette of colours; hiking in the morning mists, you'll honestly swear they're dancing about. An unforgettable experience.

Yúanyáng is actually split into two: Nánshā, the new town, and Xīnjiē, the old town, located an hour's bus ride up a nearby hill. Either can by labelled Yuányáng, depending on which map you use. Xīnjiē is the one you want, so make sure you're getting off at the right one.

Sights & Activities

Dozens of villages, each with its own terrace field, spiral out from Xīnjiē. The terraces around each village have their own special characteristics that vary from season to season. A rule of thumb: follow the everpresent photographers.

Duōyīshū, about 25km from Xīnjiē, has the most spectacular sunrises and is the one you should not miss. For sunsets, **Bádá** and **Lǎohǔzuǐ** can be mesmerising.

Maps are available at all accommodation options in town. Most are bilingual Chinese-English, though some include Japanese, German and French labels as well.

There is a fleet of minibuses by Xīnjiē's Titian Sq that leave when full to whiz around the villages, but you are much better off arranging a car and driver through your accommodation. It's also easy just to hook up with other travellers and split the cost of chartering a minibus for the day (Y400 to Y450).

Sleeping

Yuányáng Chénjiā Fángshé (☎ 562 2342; dm/s/tr Y10/40/60) This open and breezy guesthouse – overseen by four smiling generations of the same family – has spotless rooms with splendid views.

Government Guesthouse (Yuányáng Xiànshāchéng Dàjiŭdiàn; s/d Y150/180) Just off Titian Sq, rooms here are nothing special but the lobby has the best tourist information desk.

Yúntì Dàjiŭdiàn (☎ 562 4858; s/d Y328/258) These are the town's swankest digs, offering clean, modern rooms and a staff used to foreigners.

Getting There & Away

There are three buses daily from Kūnmíng to Yuányáng (Y90, 6½ hours, 10.40am, 7.30pm and 8pm). Buses from Xīnjiē back to Kūnmíng leave at 10.12am, 5pm and 9pm.

From here destinations include Hékŏu (Y37, four hours) or you can take the long way to Xīshuāngbănnà. To get there, take the 7.30am bus to Lŭchūn (Y25, four hours), where you'll have wait to get the Jiāngchéng bus at 4pm (Y31, five hours). By the time you arrive, there'll be no more buses but you can stay at the hotel attached to the bus station which has cheap rooms (dorms Y10, doubles Y60). Buses to Jĭnghóng (Y50, 8½ hours) start running at 6am.

This can be a gruelling route over bumpy dirt roads, but it will take you through magnificent scenery. Buses along this route are frequently stopped for routine police checks.

XĪSHUĀNGBĂNNÀ REGION 西双版纳

Just north of Myanmar and Laos, Xīshuāngbănnà, a Chinese approximation of the original Thai name of Sip Sawng Panna (Twelve Thousand Rice Fields), is better known simply as Bănnà and has become China's own mini-Thailand, attracting tourists looking for sunshine and water-splashing festivals, hikers readying for epic jungle treks and pissed-off

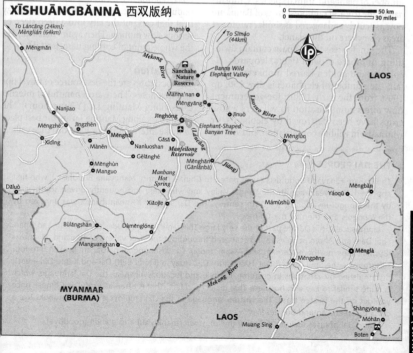

XĪSHUĀNGBĂNNÀ 西双版纳

expats fleeing the congestion (and cold weather) of China's cities.

People

About one-third of the 800,000-strong population of this region are Dai; another third or so are Han Chinese and the rest is made up of a conglomeration of minorities that include the Hani, Lisu and Yao, as well as lesser-known hill tribes such as the Aini (a subgroup of the Hani), Jinuo, Bulang, Lahu and Wa.

Climate

Two seasons: wet and dry. The wet season is between June and August, when it rains ferociously almost every day. From September to February there is less rainfall, but you often experience thick fog.

November to March sees temperatures average about 19°C. The hottest months of the year are from April to September, when you can expect an average of 25°C.

Environment

Xīshuāngbǎnnà is home to an extraordinary number of plant and animal species. Unfortunately, the tropical rainforest areas of Bǎnnà are now as acutely endangered as similar rainforest areas elsewhere on the planet.

The jungle areas that remain contain dwindling numbers of wild tigers, leopards, elephants and golden-haired monkeys. To be fair, the number of elephants is now 250, up 100% from the early 1980s; the government now offers compensation to villagers whose crops have been destroyed by elephants, or who assist in wildlife conservation. In 1998 the government banned the hunting or processing of animals, but poaching is notoriously hard to control.

Festivals & Events

The **Water-Splashing Festival** is held in mid-April and washes away the dirt, sorrow and demons of the old year and brings in the happiness of the new. Jĭnghóng usually celebrates it from the 13th to the 15th. Dates in the surrounding villages vary. The third day features the water-splashing freak-out. Foreigners get special attention so remember, the wetter you get, the more luck you'll receive!

During the **Tanpa Festival** in February, young boys are sent to the local temple for initiation as novice monks. The **Tan Ta Festival** is held during the last 10-day period of October or November, with temple ceremonies, rocket launches from special towers and hot-air balloons.

JĬNGHÓNG 景洪

☎ 0691 / pop 94,150

Jĭnghóng is the capital of Xīshuāngbǎnnà prefecture but with its palm-lined streets and relaxed ambience it can feel like a giant, overpopulated village. Prepare for searing late-day heat that can put the city into a deep sleep or serious slow motion. Then again, that's kind of the whole point of coming here, isn't it?

Information

The local cafés are the best source of travel tips and trek notes. There are a handful of internet cafés along Manting Lu (Y2 per hour). The phone bars along Manting Lu are the best place to make international or long-distance calls.

THE DAI PEOPLE 傣族

The Dai are Hinayana Buddhists (as opposed to China's majority Mahayana Buddhists), who first appeared 2000 years ago in the Yangzi Valley and who were subsequently driven southwards by the Mongol invasion of the 13th century. The Dai state of Xīshuāngbǎnnà was annexed by the Mongols and then by the Chinese.

Linguistically, the Dai are part of the very large Thai family that includes the Siamese, Lao, Shan, Thai Dam and Ahom peoples found scattered throughout the river valleys of Thailand, Myanmar (Burma), Laos, northern Vietnam and Assam (India). The Xīshuāngbǎnnà Dai are broken into four subgroups – the Shui (Water) Dai, Han (Land) Dai, Huayao (Floral Belt) Dai and Kemu Dai – each distinguished by variations in costume, lifestyle and location. All speak the Dai language, which is quite similar to Lao and northern Thai dialects. In fact, Thai is often as useful as Chinese once you get off the beaten track. The written language of the Dai employs a script that looks like a cross between Lao and Burmese.

Some Dai phrases include *doūzaŏ lĭ* (hello), *yíndíi* (thank you) and *goīhán* (goodbye).

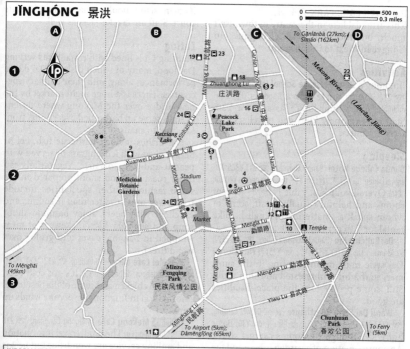

JĬNGHÓNG 景洪

Bank of China (Zhōngguó Yínháng; Xuanwei Dadao)
Changes travellers cheques and foreign currency, and has
an ATM. There's another branch on Ganlan Zhonglu.

China Post (Yóudiàn; cnr Mengle Dadao & Xuanwei Dadao;
⏰ 8am-8.30pm)

Public Security Bureau (PSB; Gōngānjú; Jingde Lu;
⏰ 8-11.30am & 3-5.30pm) Has a fairly speedy visa-
extension service.

Dangers & Annoyances

The Kūnmíng–Jĭnghóng bus trip has had a
couple of reported drug-and-rob instances. Be

careful who your friends are on buses, accept
nothing, and leave nothing unattended.

Sights
TROPICAL FLOWER & PLANTS GARDEN
热带花卉园

This terrific **botanical garden** (Rèdài Huāhuìyuán;
☎ 212 0493; 28 Jinghong Xilu; admission Y40; ⏰ 7am-6pm),
west of the town centre, is one of Jĭnghóng's
better attractions with more than 1000 different types of plant life in a lovely tropical
rainforest setting.

PEACOCK LAKE PARK 孔雀湖公园
This artificial lake in the centre of town isn't much, but the small park (Kǒngquè Hú Gōngyuán) next to it is pleasant.

Activities
Jǐnghóng's **Blind Massage School** (Mángrén Ànmó; ☎ 212 5834; cnr Mengle Dadao & Jingde Lu; ☺ 9am-midnight) offers hour-long massages for Y30. Staff are extremely kind and travellers give terrific reports.

Sleeping
Banna College Hotel (Bǎnnà Xuéyuàn; ☎ 213 8365; Xuanwei Dadao; 宣慰大道; dm Y15, tw/d per person Y40/50; ☒) Overall your best value is here – decent rooms and helpful (usually) staff, some of whom speak a smattering of English. Bike rental for Y15 per day, Y150 deposit.

Dai Building Inn (Dǎijiā Huāyuán Xiǎolóu; ☎ 216 2592; 57 Manting Lu; 曼听路57号; dm Y25) Traditional Dai style must mean sweating in the summer, staff a bit uninterested and thin walls. Still, some people love the place. Facilities are good.

Wanli Dai Style Guesthouse (Wànlǐ Dàiwèi Cāntīng; ☎ 1357 811 2879; Manting Lu; 曼听路; dm Y30) Basic but OK, although the rooms can get stuffy. An approximation of a garden is here and the restaurant is decent.

Tai Garden Hotel (Tàiyuán Jiǔdiàn; ☎ 212 3888; fax 212 6060; 8 Minghang Lu; 民航路8号; d Y640 plus 15% tax; ☒ ☒) The best of the town's innumerable posh options, it has quiet grounds replete with its own island, pool, sauna, gym and tennis court. Staff are crackerjack, as well.

Eating
Manting Lu is lined with restaurants serving Dai food, many of which dish up Dai dance performances along with their culinary specialities. There is a huge night market by the new bridge over the Mekong where dozens of stalls serve up barbecued everything, from sausages to snails.

Dai dishes include barbecue fish, eel or beef cooked with lemongrass or served with peanut-and-tomato sauce. Vegetarians can order roast bamboo shoot prepared in the same fashion. Other specialities include fried river moss (better than it sounds and excellent with beer), spicy bamboo-shoot soup and *shāokǎo* (烧烤; skewers of meat wrapped in banana leaves and grilled over wood fires).

Mei Mei Café (Měiměi Kāfēitīng; ☎ 212 7324; Manting Lu roundabout; dishes from Y5) It's got cold beer, genius Dai chicken and some of the best travel information in Jǐnghóng. Everyone winds up here.

our pick Mekong Café (Méigōng Cānguǎn; ☎ 216 2395; 111 Manting Lu) The food, travel information and smiling service are wondrous but best is the upstairs balcony, which gets you away from the polluted chaos outside.

Entertainment
Měngbālā Nàxī Arts Theatre (Měngbālā Nàxī Yìshùgōng; Ganlan Zhonglu; tickets Y160; ☺ 8.30pm) This theatre has daily song and dance shows.

YES Disco (Mengle Dadao; admission free; ☺ 9pm-late) Discos come and go but YES keeps thumping along; just ask the heavy-lidded café patrons any morning.

Shopping
A fabulous fish and produce market is tucked behind some modern buildings across from the long-distance bus station. The Jade Market is nearby on Zhuanghong Lu, with lots of Burmese and other south Asians hawking their goods alongside locals.

Getting There & Away
AIR
There are several flights a day to Kūnmíng (Y730) but during the Water-Splashing Festival you'll need to book tickets several days in advance to get either in or out.

ETIQUETTE IN DAI TEMPLES
Around Dai temples the same rules apply as elsewhere: dress appropriately (no tank tops or shorts); take off shoes before entering; don't take photos of monks or the inside of temples without permission; leave a donation if you do take any shots and consider a token donation even if you don't – unlike in Thailand, these Buddhists receive no government assistance. It is polite to 'wai' the monks as a greeting and remember to never rub anyone's head, raise yourself higher than a Buddha figure or point your feet at anyone. (This last point applies to secular buildings too. If you stay the night in a Dai household it is good form to sleep with your feet pointing towards the door.)

TREKKING IN XĪSHUĀNGBĂNNÀ

Used to be you'd be invited into a local's home to eat, sleep and drink *báijiŭ* (literally 'white alcohol, a type of face-numbing rice wine). Increasing numbers of visitors have changed this. Don't automatically expect a welcome mat and a free lunch just because you're a foreigner, but don't go changing the local economy by throwing money around either.

If you do get invited into someone's home, establish whether payment is expected. If it's not, leave an offering or modest gifts such as candles, matches, rice etc – even though the family may insist on nothing.

It's a jungle out there, so go prepared, and make sure somebody knows where you are and when you should return. In the rainy season you'll need to be equipped with proper hiking shoes and waterproof gear. At any time you'll need water purification, bottled water or a water bottle able to hold boiling water, as well as snacks and sunscreen.

Seriously consider taking a guide. You won't hear much Mandarin Chinese on the trail, let alone English. And it's an eminently more rewarding experience. Expect to pay about Y250 per day.

Forest Café (☎ 898 5122; www.forest-café.org/; Manting Lu) in Jĭnghóng is a great place to start. Sara, the owner, has years of experience leading treks and comes recommended. The other cafés mentioned in this book also have been recommended and each emphasises different things.

Try the **Xishuangbanna Travel & Study Club** (Xĭshuāngbănnà Lǔxué Júlébù; Mengzhe Lu) for trekking equipment.

For information on responsible trekking, see the boxed text, p484.

In high season there are also two flights daily to Lìjiāng (Y840). You can also fly – usually daily – to Bangkok (Y1630), often via Chiang Mai (Y830), from here.

Tickets to anywhere can be bought at the **CAAC Booking Office** (☎ 212 7040; Jingde Lu; ⏰ 8am-9pm) or at any café.

BUS

The Jĭnghóng long-distance bus station (Minhang Lu) is the most useful for long-distance destinations. If you want to explore Xĭshuāngbănnà, go to the No 2 bus station.

There is supposed to be a daily bus from Jĭnghóng to Luang Prabang in Laos, but it wasn't running when we were there.

Getting Around

There's no shuttle bus or public transport to the airport, 5km south of the city. A taxi will cost around Y20 but expect to be hit up for up to three times that during festivals.

Jĭnghóng is small enough that you can walk to most destinations, but a bike makes life easier and can be rented through most accommodation for Y15 to Y25 a day.

A taxi anywhere in town costs Y5.

AROUND JĬNGHÓNG

First morning? Hop on a bike and strike out around Jĭnghóng. You can't go wrong. Depending on where you go, you'll get lovely dirt paths interspersed with wide concrete runways, then perhaps a few ferries across the Mekong River. Travellers in cafés will have the latest scoop on which village roads haven't been bulldozed yet.

Sanchahe Nature Reserve
三岔河自然保护区

This **nature reserve** (Sānchàhé Zìrán Băohùqū), 48km north of Jĭnghóng, is one of five enormous forest reserves in southern Yúnnán. This

---

DOWNSTREAM TO THAILAND

For a couple of years, travellers were having some luck hitching rides on cargo boats heading south into Laos and Thailand, but in November 2006, authorities put the hammer down on that, giving boat operators serious fines (and revoking licences). New fast ferries leave Jĭnghóng on Monday, Wednesday and Saturday for the seven-hour ride (Y800) to Chiang Saen in Thailand; plans were to ultimately build up facilities to allow for six stops along the way. Get to the dock at 7.30am to start customs proceedings. Also note that this could all change – other ferries have come and gone just as quickly in the past. See the boxed text, p148, for information on travelling in the opposite direction.

JǏNGHÓNG BUS TIMETABLES

Buses from Jǐnghóng long-distance bus station include the following:

Destination	Price (Y)	Duration (hr)	Frequency	Departs
Kūnmíng	156.50	9	2 daily	4pm, 7.30pm
Kūnmíng (sleeper)	145-169	9	20 daily	7.30am-7pm
Xiàguān	152	18	daily	12.30pm

The following bus services depart from the No 2 bus station:

Destination	Price (Y)	Duration	Frequency	Departs
Dàměnglóng	15	3-4hr	every 20min	6.30am-6.30pm
Jǐngzhēn	11	2hr	every 20min	7am-6pm
Měnghǎn	7.5	40min	every 20min	7.15am-10pm
Měnghǎi	11	45min	every 20min	7.30am-1.40pm & 2.20-7pm
Měnghùn	15	90min	every 20min	7am-6pm
Měnglà	33	4-5hr	every 20min	6.30am-6pm
Měnglún	14	2hr	every 20min	7am-6pm
Měngyǎng	7	40min	half-hourly	8am-6pm
Sānchàhé	10-11.50	1½hr	every 20min	6.15am-6.30pm

one has an area of nearly 1.5 million hectares. The part of the park that most tourists visit is **Banna Wild Elephant Valley** (Bǎnnà Yěxiàngǔ; admission Y25, with guide Y50), named after the 40 or so wild elephants that live in the valley; it's worth a visit if you want to see something of the local forest. Avoid the depressing 'wild' elephant performances. A 2km-cable car (one way/return Y40/60) runs over the treetops from the main entrance into the heart of the park.

If you want to stay by the park there's a generic **hotel** (d 200) or stay in a Swiss Family Robinson–type **canopy treehouse** (d Y200); definitely negotiate. A *few* travellers who have slumbered in the trees have reported seeing elephants bathing in the stream beneath them at dawn.

Just about any bus travelling north from Jǐnghóng to Sīmáo will pass this reserve (Y12, one hour). Returning to Jǐnghóng there is a bus that leaves the north entrance daily at 2.30pm (Y10).

Měngyǎng 勐养

The **Elephant-Shaped Banyan Tree** (Xiàngxíng Róngshù) is why most people visit Měngyǎng, a centre for the Hani, Floral-Belt Dai and Lahu.

Měngyǎng is 34km northeast of Jǐnghóng; it's another 19km southeast to **Jīnuò**, the centre of the Jinuo minority.

Měnghǎn 勐罕 (Gǎnlǎnbà 橄榄坝)

Watching this town come alive in the evening after its long afternoon siesta is reason enough to visit. After sundown the streets of Měnghǎn (or Gǎnlǎnbà as it's also known) fill with the smells of cooking, the sounds of gossip and wandering locals trying to escape the indoor heat. It's worth coming by bike (or hiring one in Měnghǎn) as there's plenty of scope for exploration in the neighbourhood.

SIGHTS

The premier 'attraction' is the **Dai Minority Park** (傣族园; Dàizúyuán; ☎ 0691-250 4099; Manting Lu; adult/student Y50/25), which is simply part of the town that's been cordoned off and had a ticket booth stuck at the entrance. Tourists can spend the night in villagers' homes and partake in water-splashing 'festivals' twice a day. Despite this zoolike aspect, travellers who've come say it's been well worth it. If you stay overnight in the park, your ticket is valid for the next day.

Travellers recommend heading to the south of town, crossing the Mekong by ferry (Y2 with a bike), and then heading left (east). The last ferry returns at 7pm.

Beds in a Dai home within the park will cost around Y20 per person. Food is extra. Beds are traditional Dai mats and are usually very comfortable. Most homes will also have showers for you.

GETTING THERE & AWAY
Microbuses to Měnghăn leave from Jǐnghóng's No 2 bus station (Y8, every 20 minutes, 7am to 6pm). Minibuses depart from Měnghăn's bus station for destinations throughout the region including Měnglún (Y10, one hour) and Měnglà (Y29, five hours).

It's possible to cycle from Jǐnghóng to Měnghăn in a brisk two hours or a leisurely three hours, and it's a pleasant ride.

GETTING AROUND
You can rent a mountain bike at the entrance to the Dai Minority Park (Y20 per day).

Měnglún 勐仑
East of Měnghăn, the major attraction in Měnglún is the **Tropical Plant Gardens** (热带植物园; Rèdài Zhíwùyuán; adult/student Y60/40; ☻ 7am-midnight). The gardens are gorgeous and get high marks from visitors; there's also a midrange hotel.

To get here, turn left out of the bus station and walk to the first corner. Walk one block and turn left again. You'll come to market hawkers, and a road leading downhill to the right side. Follow this until you reach a footbridge across the Mekong. The ticket booth is just in front of the bridge.

The **Bus Station Hotel** (车站招待所; Chēzhàn Zhāodàisuǒ; d with shared bathroom Y30) is your best-value option in a city of not-too-good options. There's no air-con, but the shared bathrooms are clean and there's a TV in each room.

The **Friendship Restaurant** (友谊餐厅; Yǒuyì Cāntīng; Main Hwy) has lots of dishes made from strange vegetables, ferns and herbs only found locally.

From Jǐnghóng's No 2 bus station there are buses to Měnglún (Y14, two hours, every 20 minutes from 7am to 6pm). The buses pass through Měnghăn. Some travellers have cycled here from Měnghăn.

From Měnglún, there are buses to Měnglà (Y20 to Y25, 2½ hours, 8.30am to 7.30pm) and Jǐnghóng every 30 minutes.

Měnglà 勐腊
Měnglà is a *grim* town, but if you're crossing into Laos at Móhàn, you'll probably be stuck here for the night.

There is a **Bank of China** (中国银行; Zhōngguó Yínháng; ☻ 8-11.30am & 3-6pm Mon-Fri) in the south-ern half of town that changes cash and travellers cheques but won't give cash advances on credit cards. To change Renminbi back into US dollars, you need your original exchange receipts.

The **Jīnqiáo Dàjiǔdiàn** (金桥大酒店; ☎ 0691-812 4946; d/tr Y50/60; ✗) is a convenient sleeping option for the north bus station just up the hill on the left, but don't expect much else. Don't expect much from any of the other options here either.

Měnglà has two bus stations: the northern long-distance bus station which has buses to Kūnmíng (Y218, hourly from 8.30am to 11.30am) and No 2 bus station in the southern part of town. From Měnglà's No 2 station, destinations include Jǐnghóng (Y30 to Y34, every 20 minutes from 6.20am to 6pm), Měnglún (Y20 to Y24, every 20 minutes from 6.20am to 6pm) and Móhàn (Y14, every 20 minutes from 8am to 6pm).

DÀMĚNGLÓNG 大勐龙
Dàměnglóng (written just 'Měnglóng' on buses), about 70km south of Jǐnghóng and a few kilometres from the Myanmar border, is one of those sleepy places to aim for when you want a respite from the beaten path and a base from which to do some aimless rambling looking for decaying stupas and little villages. You can hire bicycles at Dàměnglóng Zhàodàisuǒ (大勐龙招待所) for Y15 per day.

The border-crossing point with Myanmar has been designated as the entry point for a planned highway linking Thailand, Myanmar and China.

Sights
WHITE BAMBOO SHOOT PAGODA 曼飞龙塔
This **pagoda** (Mànfēilóng Tǎ; admission Y5), built in 1204, was, as the legend says, built on the spot of a hallowed footprint left by Sakyamuni Buddha, who is said to have visited Xīshuāngbǎnnà; look for it in a niche below one of the nine stupas.

To get there walk back along the main road towards Jǐnghóng for 2km until you reach a small village with a temple on your left. From here there's a path up the hill; it's about a 20-minute walk. There's an entry fee, but often there's no-one around.

BLACK PAGODA 黑塔
Just above the centre of town is a Dai monastery with a steep path beside it leading up

THE BULANG PEOPLE 布朗族

The Bulang live mainly in the Bulang Xīdìng and Bada mountains of Xīshuāngbǎnnà. They keep to the hills farming cotton, sugarcane and Pu'er tea, one of Yúnnán's most famous exports.

The men wear collarless jackets, loose black trousers and turbans of black or white cloth. They traditionally tattoo their arms, legs, chests and stomachs. The Bulang women wear simple, bright clothes and vibrant headdresses decorated with flowers. Avid betel-nut chewers, the women believe black teeth are beautiful.

to the **Black Pagoda** (Hēi Tǎ; admission free) – you'll notice it when entering Dàměnglóng. The pagoda itself is actually gold, not black. Take a stroll up, but bear in mind that the real reason for the climb is more for the views of Dàměnglóng and surrounding countryside then the temple itself.

Sleeping

Lai Lai Hotel (Láilái Bīnguǎn; d/tr Y20/30) Simple rooms and a lovely owner meticulous about cleanliness – remember, though, this is China! – has made this hotel the most popular accommodation. You'll see the English sign right next to the bus station.

Getting There & Away

Buses for the bumpy ride to Dàměnglóng (Y15, three to four hours, every 20 minutes, 6.30am to 6.30pm) leave from Jǐnghóng's No 2 bus station. Remember that the 'Da' character won't be painted on the bus window. Buses for the return trip run regularly between 6am and 6pm.

AROUND DÀMĚNGLÓNG
Xiǎojiē 小街

The village of Xiǎojiē, about 15km north of Dàměnglóng, is surrounded by Bulang, Lahu and Hani villages. Lahu women shave their heads; apparently the younger ones aren't happy about this any more and hide their heads beneath caps. The Bulang are possibly descended from the Yi of northern Yúnnán. The women wear black turbans with silver decorations; many of the designs are of shells, fish and marine life.

MĚNGHǍI 勐海

Most come here to head out for markets in the surrounding area. It's also worth visiting the huge daily produce market that attracts members of the hill tribes.

Buses run from Jǐnghóng's No 2 bus station to Měnghǎi (Y11, 45 minutes, every 20 minutes from 7.30am to 1.40pm and 2.20pm to 7pm). Buses return to Jǐnghóng every 20 minutes until 7pm.

AROUND MĚNGHǍI
Měnghùn 勐混

Located about 26km southwest of Měnghǎi, the village of Měnghùn has a colourful **Sunday market**. The town begins buzzing around 7am and the action lingers on through to noon.

There are several guesthouses here, though none is remarkable. Y40 will get you a spartan double with bathroom and TV (but no air-con).

CROSSING INTO LAOS: MÓHÀN TO BOTEN

On-the-spot 30-day visas for Laos can be obtained at the border. The price will depend on your nationality (but generally cost US$30 to US$35). The **Chinese checkpoint** (☎ 0691-812 2684; ⏰ 8am-5pm) is generally not much of an ordeal; see p312 for details on crossing from the Lao side. Don't forget that Laos is an hour behind.

Měnglà has one daily bus at 9am running to Luang Nam Tha in Laos (Y32); it takes 90 minutes to the border, where you wait for around an hour to deal with paperwork, before reboarding for the final two-hour leg.

If you miss that, from Měnglà there are also buses to Móhàn every 20 minutes or so from 8am to 6pm.

No matter what anyone says, there should be no 'charge' to cross. Once your passport is stamped (double-check all stamps), you can jump on a tractor or truck to take you 3km into Laos for around Y5. Whatever you do, go early, in case things wrap up early on either side. There are guesthouses on both sides; people generally change money on the Lao side.

Buses departing from Jǐnghóng for Měnghùn (Y15, 90 minutes, every 20 minutes from 7am to 6pm) run from Jǐnghóng's No 2 bus station.

From Měnghùn, minibuses run regularly to Měnghǎi (Y6), Xīdìng (Y11, 1½ hours, 7.10am and 4pm) and throughout the day to Jǐnghóng.

Unless you have a very good bike with gears, cycling to Měnghǎi and Měnghùn is not a real option.

Xīdìng 西定

This sleepy hillside hamlet comes alive every Thursday for its weekly market. You can either catch one of the two direct buses from Měnghǎi (Y11, 10.40am and 3.30pm) or travel via Měnghùn and change for a bus to Xīdìng. To see the market at its most interesting, you'll really have to get here the night before. The small guesthouse at the bus station has beds for Y20. Buses from Xīdìng leave twice a day (Y11, 7.20am and 1pm) for Měnghùn. If you miss the bus you can always get a ride on a motorbike (Y30), a spectacular if not hair-raising experience, from the only bike shop in town.

YÚNNÁN PROVINCE DIRECTORY

ACCOMMODATION

Yúnnán is one of the cheapest Chinese provinces, with decent youth hostels (青年旅社; *qīngnián lǚshè*; www.hostelchina.cn), guesthouses (招待所, *zhāodàisuǒ*; or 旅馆,

lǚguǎn) and budget hotels galore in all locations included in this chapter. Figure an *average* of Y20 (US$2.90) for a bed in a dorm and from Y30 to Y60 per bed in a twin or double in a budget hotel. Midrange prices are Y200 to Y600 and top end ranges from Y600 to US$300.

Budget hotels are generally decrepit, but safe and not dirty. For midrange and top-end hotels, you should subtract a star from whatever they claim. The former are generally vanilla – in the sense of bland – the latter not all that common (or worth it) in the province.

Discounts & Reservations

Always negotiate prices at hotels. Discounts (*dàzhékòu*) are, outside of holiday periods (the first week of May and October, Chinese New Year and Spring Festival), virtually always available (30% off on average). Travel agencies can often get good deals, as can websites such as www.china-hotelguide.com, www.sinohotel.com, or, once in China, www.english.ctrip.com.

Hostels and cheap guesthouses don't much like to haggle over dorm beds.

ACTIVITIES

By far the most common activity in the province is trekking and the Tiger Leaping Gorge trek (see p460) is one of China's best. The Xīshuāngbǎnnà region is legendary for its jungle trekking from ethnic village to ethnic village (see the boxed text, p467).

Outfits in China itself, such as **Wildchina** (www.wildchina.com), offer a host of dramatic treks in remote parts of China.

PRACTICALITIES

- There are four types of plugs: three-pronged angled pins (as in Australia), three-pronged round pins (as in Hong Kong), two flat pins (US style but without the ground wire) or two narrow round pins (European style). Electricity is 220V, 50 cycles AC.

- The standard English-language newspaper is the *China Daily* (www.chinadaily.com.cn). The *People's Daily* has an English-language edition at www.english.peopledaily.com.cn. Imported English-language media? Try Kūnmíng's top-end hotels.

- Listen to the BBC World Service (www.bbc.co.uk/worldservice/tuning/) or Voice of America (www.voa.gov), although these websites are at times jammed. China Radio International (CRI) is China's overseas radio service and broadcasts in about 40 foreign languages. The national TV outfit, Chinese Central TV (CCTV), has an English-language channel – CCTV9.

- The ancient Chinese weights and measures system features the *liǎng* (tael, 37.5g) and the *jīn* (catty, 0.6kg), which are both commonly used. There are 10 *liǎng* to the *jīn*.

THE HOTEL RITUALS

At check-in you'll need your passport and the registration form will need your visa information; for most people it's type 'L'. Most hotels require a deposit (yājīn), for which you receive a receipt – do NOT lose it – to be returned at checkout, and here you should budget an extra 10 minutes while the clerk rouses from behind the desk and rings the vacant attendant's desk upstairs to see if you've pilfered the stringy towels. It's *maddening*.

Credit cards can still be hard to use, even at three- and even some four-star hotels.

Oh, and expect regular phone calls from prostitutes, who ask whether ànmó (massage) or xiǎojiě (a young lady) is required; unplug your phone, as they can be persistent.

BOOKS

For more on Yúnnán, Lonely Planet's *China's Southwest* covers the province in more detail. Pick up Lonely Planet's *China* guide if you're planning to travel further afield in the country.

BUSINESS HOURS

China has a five-day working week. Banks, offices and government departments are usually open weekdays from 9am to 5pm, with a loooong lunch break; banks may be open on Saturday, but the exchange counters might not be. Note that all of these are shut tight for national holidays.

Department stores and shops are generally open daily from 9am or 10am to 10pm. Standard restaurant hours are 10.30am to around 11pm – they may also shut down for a few hours around 2pm. The Chinese are accustomed to eating lunch around midday and having dinner about 6pm.

CLIMATE

Yúnnán – 76.4m above sea level in Hékǒu to 6740m in the Tibetan Plateau with an average of 2000m – has dozens of microclimates. In summer (June through August) you can still freeze your tail off near Tibet, and in the midst of winter (mid-November to late February) you can get by with a light coat in Kūnmíng, the capital, its mean temperature never fluctuating more than 10°C throughout the year.

The Xīshuāngbǎnnà border with Laos lies on the 21° latitude – meaning steamy subtropics; here the summer months soar to 33°C.

COURSES

It seems everyone and his or her grandmother is studying Mandarin in Kūnmíng these days, especially at Yunnan University. In Dàlǐ and Lìjiāng you can also study Mandarin or even local languages (along with private tutorials in painting, calligraphy and martial arts); your guesthouse or local cafés can help you find a teacher or course.

CUSTOMS

The duty-free allowance is 400 cigarettes, two bottles of wine or spirits and 50g of gold or silver. Fresh fruit and cold cuts are prohibited. You can legally only bring in or out Y6000 in Chinese currency; there are no restrictions on foreign currency (though you should declare any cash exceeding US$5000 or its equivalent currency).

It's rather uncommon for any foreigners to have their bags searched; the officials likely won't even glance at your forms. The exception is Hékǒu, the Yúnnán border town leading to Vietnam. Officials here have a reputation for being particularly testy.

DANGERS & ANNOYANCES

Traffic notwithstanding, China is an amazingly safe country, and Yúnnán overall has an incredibly low crime rate for travellers. But violent crime against foreigners, long almost unheard of in China, does happen, though it's almost always of the snag-your-bag variety.

Just keep your wits about you and don't help out the thieves by practising unsafe habits, and you'll be fine. The number-one rule is to avoid being in remote locations alone.

Train and bus stations are haunts for pickpockets. Overnight trains and sleeper buses are also places where travellers have had bags razored while they slept. A new tactic is to race by you as you pedal on your bike and grab anything you have in your basket.

Hotels are generally safe; some even have attendants on each floor. But you still shouldn't leave your laptop just lying around. Don't assume hostels are perfectly safe either; most will provide at least a locker for each bed.

Carry just as much cash as you need and keep the rest in travellers cheques.

Lǎowài!

Get ready to hear the word *lǎowài* a lot. (Usually followed by a bellowed 'Hullo!' and a Grand Canyon–esque grin.) It means 'foreigner' and don't be offended – virtually every time you hear it, it's due to happy surprise and precious, endless Chinese curiosity.

Loss Reports

Report any thefts to the nearest Foreign Affairs branch of the Public Security Bureau (PSB). Be prepared for a headache – this can at times be the ultimate in through-the-looking-glass bureaucracy.

Pollution & Noise

China has an enormous pollution – air and water most of all – problem, for which you'd best prepare yourself, especially if you have allergies, skin conditions or chest, eye, nose and throat problems.

You'll likely be most annoyed by the noise. Constant. Never. Ending. Racket. Bless the authorities for attempting to ban car horns and sidewalk speakers, but seriously – in a country of a billion people (and cars), what can one expect? To avoid becoming as deaf as everyone else seems to be, take industrial-strength earplugs!

Queues

A smart-aleck might ask, 'What queues?' And they'd be partially right. There is a semblance of lining up in China today. That's about all that can be said at times.

Scams

Con artists have worked out a few scams in which they ostensibly invite a foreigner to 'try' some tea or local delicacies, then hit them up for an ungodly bill.

Most annoying of all for travellers is simply poor – or nonexistent – service from a travel agent or guide service. Ask around before plunking down money on tickets or tours.

Spitting

Well, it isn't as bad as it once was in the cities, but out in the sticks? Hawk and let fly. Even on the bus next to you!

EMBASSIES & CONSULATES
People's Republic of China Embassies & Consulates

For a full list of diplomatic representation abroad, go to the Ministry of Foreign affairs website at www.fmprc.gov.cn/eng/and click on Missions Overseas.

Australia Canberra embassy (☎ 02-6273 4783, 6273 7443; http://au.china-embassy.org; 15 Coronation Dr, Yarralumla, ACT 2600); Melbourne consulate (☎ 03-9822 0604; www.chineseconsulatemel.org); Perth consulate

---

YÚNNÁN IN WORDS

- *The Search for Modern China* (2001) This is one of the best by Jonathan Spence, but all of his books are worth reading. Also try *God's Chinese Son*.

- *South of the Clouds: Tales from Yunnan* (1994) This fascinating anthology of Yúnnán tales, edited by Guo Xu and Lucien Miller, provides a wonderful thumbnail sketch of the cultural ethos(es) of the province and its people.

- *Mr China's Son, A Villager's Life* (2002) You cannot possibly not be moved by this account of a simple man's ordeal during all of China's 20th-century upheavals. He Liyi was unlucky enough to have studied English, a crime for which he later found himself sent to the countryside and otherwise persecuted for much of his life. In the end, he wound up sharing his wondrous outlook on life with foreign travellers in his café (now closed) in Dàlǐ.

- *Soul Mountain* (2001) Nobel Prize winner for literature Gao Xingjian weaves a search for his own 'soul mountain' as he wanders about the countryside of southwest China. Brilliant.

- *Ancient Nakhi Kingdom of Southwest China* (1947) This is Joseph Rock's definitive work. For more on Rock, see the boxed text, p461.

- *The Age of Wild Ghosts: Memory, Violence, and Place in Southwest China* (2001) Erik Mueggler's compelling account of a Tibetan-Burmese minority community on the fringes – literally and figuratively – of the Han empire in the 20th century.

YÚNNÁN PROVINCE (CHINA)

(☎ 08-9222 0302); Sydney consulate (☎ 02-8595 8000; http://sydney.chineseconsulate.org/eng)

Cambodia (☎ 023-427428; 156 Mao Tse Toung Blvd, Phnom Penh)

Canada Ottawa embassy (☎ 613-789 3434; www .chinaembassycanada.org; 515 St Patrick St, Ottawa, Ontario K1N 5H3); Calgary consulate (☎ 403-264 3322); Toronto consulate (☎ 416-964 7260); Vancouver consulate (☎ 604-736 3910)

Denmark (☎ 039-460 889; www.chinaembassy.dk; Oeregarrds Alle 25, 2900 Hellerup, Copenhagen)

France (☎ 01 47 36 02 58; www.amb-chine.fr; 9 Ave V Cresson, 92130 Issy les Moulineaux, Paris)

Indonesia (☎ 021-576 1037; www.chinaembassy -indonesia.or.id; JL Mega Kuningan No 2, Jakarta)

Japan (☎ 03-3403 3389, 3403 3065; www.china -embassy.or.jp; 3-4-33 Moto-Azabu, Minato-ku, Tokyo) Consulates in Fukuoka, Osaka and Sapporo.

Laos (☎ 021-315100; Th Wat Nak, Ban Wat Nak, Vientiane)

Malaysia (☎ 03-242 8495; 229 Jln Ampang, Kuala Lumpur) Consulate in Kuching.

Netherlands (☎ 070-355 1515; Adriaan Goekooplaan 7, The Hague)

New Zealand (☎ 04-472 1382; www.chinaembassy .org.nz; 2-6 Glenmore St, Wellington) Consulate in Auckland.

Singapore (☎ 65-734 3361; 70 Dalvey Rd)

Thailand (☎ 02-245 7032/49; 57 Th Ratchadaphisek, Bangkok)

UK London embassy (☎ 020-7299 4049, 24hr visa information 0891 880 808, visa section 020-7631 1430; www.chinese-embassy.org.uk; 31 Portland Pl); Edinburgh consulate (☎ 0131-337 3220); Manchester consulate (☎ 0161-224 7478)

USA Washington embassy (☎ 202-338 6688; www .china-embassy.org; Room 110, 2201 Wisconsin Ave NW, Washington DC); Chicago consulate (☎ 312-803 0098); Houston consulate (☎ 713-524 4311); Los Angeles consulate (☎ 213-380 2508); New York consulate (☎ 212-330 7410); San Francisco consulate (☎ 415-563 9232)

Vietnam Hanoi (☎ 04-845 3736; eossc@hn.vnn.vn; 46 P Hoang Dieu); HCMC consulate (☎ 08-829 2457; chinacon sul_hcm_vn@mfa.gov.cn; 39 D Nguyen Thi Minh Kai)

Embassies & Consulates in Yúnnán

Laos (Map p444; ☎ 0871-317 6624; Room N120, ground fl, Camellia Hotel, 96 Dongfeng Donglu; ◷ 8.30am-noon & 1.30-4.30pm Mon-Fri)

Myanmar (Map p444; ☎ 0871-360 3477; fax 360 2468; www.mcg-kunming.com; B503, Longyuan Haozhai, 166 Weiyuan Jie; ◷ 8.30am-noon & 1-4.30pm Mon-Fri)

Thailand (Map p444; ☎ 0871-314 9296; fax 316 6891; Ground fl, South Wing, Kunming Hotel, 52 Dongfeng Donglu; ◷ 9-11.30am Mon-Fri)

Vietnam (Map p444; ☎ 0871-352 2669; 2nd fl, Kaihua Plaza, 157 Beijing Lu; ◷ 8am-noon & 2-5.30pm Mon-Fri)

FESTIVALS & EVENTS

Chinese New Year/Spring Festival (Chūn Jié)

This starts on the first day of the first month in the lunar calendar. This is China's biggest holiday and demand for transport/rooms (and prices) skyrocket. Falls on 7 February 2008 and 26 January 2009.

Lantern Festival (Yuánxiāo Jié) Not a public holiday, but very colourful. Falls on the 15th day of the first moon and will be celebrated on 22 February 2008 and 9 February 2009.

Tomb Sweeping Day (Qīng Míng Jié) People visit and clean the graves of their departed relatives, placing flowers on tombs and burning ghost money. Generally falls close to Easter, on 5 April in most years or 4 April in leap years.

Water-Splashing Festival (PōShuǐ Jié) Held in the Xīshuāngbǎnnà Region of Yúnnán, this is held in mid-April (usually 13 to 15 April). Wash away the dirt, sorrow and demons of the old year – and get each other utterly soaked.

Torch Festival (Huǒbǎ Jié) Celebrated by the Naxi in Lìjiāng and the Bai in Dàlǐ, it's generally held in July, on the 24th day of the sixth moon and commemorates a woman who immolated herself rather than be taken by a king who had killed her husband.

Mid-Autumn Festival (Zhōngqiū Jié) This is also known as the Moon Festival, when you gaze at the moon and eat yuè bǐng (moon cakes); it's also the de facto day for lovers. Takes place on the 15th day of the eight moon, and will be celebrated on 25 September 2007, 14 September 2008, and 3 October 2009.

FOOD & DRINK

Yúnnán has a fabulous array of provincial specialities, including qìguōjī (汽锅鸡; herb-infused chicken cooked in an earthenware steam pot), xuānwēi huǒtuǐ (宣威火腿; Yúnnán ham), guòqiáo mìxiàn (过侨米线; across-the-bridge noodles; see the boxed text, p447), rǔbǐng (乳饼; goats' cheese) and various Muslim beef and mutton dishes. Qìguōjī is served in dark-brown casserole pots and is imbued with medicinal properties – chóngcǎo (虫草; caterpillar fungus, or pseudoginseng) is one such property.

Do treat yourself to mógū (蘑菇; mushrooms) here. Yúnnán is blessed with infinite varieties, many rare and pricey in other provinces but delightfully common and dirt-cheap here, especially cháshùgū (茶树菇; tea tree mushrooms), which grow only in proximity to tea trees and which are infused deliriously with their essence.

A meal for one at any budget eatery should cost under Y30, midrange between Y30 and Y100 and top-end choices (not many in Yúnnán) up to Y800 or more.

For more on dining in the Mekong region, see p86.

GAY & LESBIAN TRAVELLERS

The Chinese Psychiatric Association no longer classifies homosexuality as a mental disorder. The large cities are more tolerant than rural areas, yet even in moderately hip Kūnmíng it is not recommended that gays and lesbians be too open about their sexual orientation in public, though you will see Chinese same-sex friends holding hands or putting their arms around each other in public. The situation is slowly changing as more prominent Chinese are 'outed', but the police periodically crack down on gay meeting places.

Check www.utopia-asia.com/tipschin.htm for tips for gay and lesbian travellers.

HOLIDAYS

China has nine national holidays:

New Year's Day 1 January
Chinese New Year (Spring Festival) usually February
International Women's Day 8 March
International Labour Day 1 May
Youth Day 4 May
International Children's Day 1 June
Birthday of the Chinese Communist Party 1 July
Anniversary of the Founding of the People's Liberation Army 1 August
National Day 1 October

Many of these are nominal holidays and do not result in leave. The 1 May, 1 October and Chinese New Year holidays are week-long fests – this means transport is tough to get, hotels (if you can get a room) cost stratospherically more and you'll get nothing bureaucratic done.

INTERNET ACCESS

Be prepared for glacial connection speeds (if you're accessing foreign sites) or, occasionally, some sites (CNN, BBC) being blocked by censors. Higher-end hotels have in-room broadband access but it can be a pain (unreliable and staff don't always know how to set it up); even a few hostels do too now. Broadband wi-fi access is creeping into Yúnnán's cafés and guesthouses, especially in Kūnmíng, Dàlǐ and Lìjiāng; for more information on travel-

---

GETTING ONLINE

Memorise the characters for internet café: 网吧 (wǎngbā). All cities in this chapter have loads of them, with rates usually ranging from Y1.50 to Y3 per hour. You are rarely required to show ID though it's possible in some areas of China; a deposit of Y10 or so is more common. Note that on weekends – especially Sundays – every kid in China is packed into these place and getting a spot can be tough – go early!

---

ling with your portable computer, check www .teleadapt.com.

LEGAL MATTERS

Anyone under the age of 18 is considered a minor, and the minimum age at which you can drive is also 18. There is no minimum age for consumption of alcohol or use of cigarettes.

The Chinese legal system does not presume innocence and no fair trial is guaranteed. If arrested, most foreign citizens have the right to contact their embassy. Do not expect preferential treatment from police anywhere just because you are a foreigner.

Do not mess with drugs in China. Penalties are harsh. Foreign nationals have been executed for drug trafficking (China conducts more judicial executions than the rest of the world combined).

MAPS

Maps are available at all train and bus stations and bookshops; these are usually fairly good but only in Chinese. If you find one in English, it'll be limited in its detail. These generally cost Y3 to Y6.

MONEY

Chinese currency is the Renminbi (RMB), or 'People's Money'. The basic unit is the yuán (Y), which is divided into 10 jiǎo, and again divided into 10 fēn. Colloquially, the yuán is referred to as kuài and jiǎo as máo. You'll most likely encounter bills in denominations of one, five, 10, 20, 50 and 100 yuán; coins come in denominations of one yuán, five jiǎo, one jiǎo and the useless five fēn.

Everyone will tell you to be very wary of counterfeit bills; the problem is, it's pretty tough for a novice to tell the difference.

Virtually everyone in China will check to see if a Y50 or Y100 bill is real before accepting it, though few of them really can tell either.

ATMs & Credit Cards

ATMs exist but not many accept foreign cards and you may have to do some slogging to find an ATM that accepts yours (check www .international.visa.com/ps or www.master card.com/cardholderservices/atm). Bank of China and Industrial & Commercial Bank of China branches are the best places to start. You can generally get cash advances at the Bank of China, but the service comes with a 4% commission.

Otherwise, credit cards are of very, very limited use in China, especially Yúnnán.

Exchanging Money

Always carry enough cash; this must be stressed. You can get Renminbi in most Southeast Asian countries and especially Hong Kong but not generally in countries outside the region. Not all banks in China can/will change cash and/or especially travellers cheques; this is a major pain at times. Good news: in all of this chapter's locations exchanging is fairly easy.

Country	Unit	Yuán
Australia	A$1	6.40
Cambodia	1000r	1.90
Canada	C$1	6.90
euro zone	€1	10.40
Japan	¥100	6.40
Laos	1000 kip	1.90
New Zealand	NZ$1	5.70
Thailand	100B	23.40
UK	£1	15.20
USA	US$1	7.70
Vietnam	10,000d	4.80

Tipping

Tipping isn't expected, so restrain yourself. Any tips will be included in midrange or top-end restaurants or hotels.

Travellers Cheques

Bring travellers cheques with you. They're safer and you get a better rate than for cash (around 2% higher). Outside of the areas detailed in this chapter they're of little use. Note that many banks won't cash travellers cheques on weekends.

POST

International and domestic post is amazingly efficient. International letters and cards arrive in a week to 10 days for most destinations.

Then again, it ain't cheap. Postcards to international destinations cost Y4.50; airmail letters up to 20g cost Y5 to Y7.

Larger China Post branches operate an Express Mail Service (EMS) that's reliable and safe; rates vary by country but it's about Y160 to Y200 for parcels up to 500g. If you mail parcels home, take them *unpacked* with you to the post office to be inspected and an appropriate box or envelope will be found for you.

There are fairly reliable poste restante (*cúnjú hòulíng*) services in Kūnmíng, Dàlǐ and Lìjiāng; expect to pay Y1 to Y2.50 per item.

RESPONSIBLE TRAVEL

China will undoubtedly lead the world in tourism numbers in the future. This can be a good thing or a bad thing. We wish to emphasise the good.

Most of all, keep your cool, whether questioning a cost – get prices beforehand to avoid this – or bargaining for a souvenir. You, after all, are an ambassador (one that is seen as phenomenally wealthy, no matter what you think).

Environmentally, take the bus or train instead of flying. China has mountains of empty plastic bottles everywhere, so carry a water bottle and top it up; many places have communal water bottles to refill from, or you can purify.

Yúnnán has some of China's most serious drug-use problems. Don't contribute to it. Not only is it just perpetuating a problem, it's a crime and the authorities do NOT care about your nationality when they close the prison door.

For information on responsible trekking, see p484 and p138.

SHOPPING

Dàlǐ and Lìjiāng are absolute shoppers' paradises. You can do your birthday/Christmas shopping for five years in these cities, snapping up everything from hand-painted souvenir T-shirts to lovely batik and ethnic clothing. Let the haggling begin.

Bargaining

You can bargain in small shops and markets (but not department stores). Always be polite (duh). Aim for Chinese price – tough to do, but if you can, you should feel pleased.

TELEPHONE

The easiest way to call domestically or internationally is to find a private 'phone bar' (话吧; *huàbā*), usually just an open-air place with phones along the walls. Most of these use internet phone systems and can be dirt cheap, even for international calls. Luckily, in Jǐnghóng, Dàlǐ and Lìjiāng, these are ubiquitous; in Kūnmíng, your guesthouse or hotel will know the nearest one.

Otherwise, you can buy a phonecard, of which there are IC (Integrated Circuit) and IP (Internet Phone) cards. The latter (IP 卡; IP *kǎ*) are much cheaper, with rates of around Y1.80 per minute to the USA or Canada and Y3.20 to other international destinations. Local long-distance calls are around Y0.30 per minute.

Note however that infinite varieties of IC and IP cards exist and not all can be used everywhere. Definitely ask at your guesthouse or a fave café for help.

Mobile phones are ubiquitous but tricky to buy if you don't speak Mandarin; you can buy SIM cards here but it's also a hassle figuring out how to install it in your phone.

TOILETS

Public toilets (look for 'WC') are everywhere but can be downright putrid. You just pay the attendant whatever the cost is, usually around Y0.20. Always – and this is key – carry your own toilet paper, though in public toilets for Y0.50 you can get a tiny packet of tissues. Put the toilet paper in the wastebasket next to the toilet (which, incidentally, will probably be of the squat variety).

Always remember:

Men   男
Women   女

TOURIST INFORMATION

The **Chinese National Tourism Association** (www.cnta .gov.cn) has branch offices around the world; also check www.travelchinaguide.com, one of the few very useful sites.

Once in Yúnnán, you're pretty much out of luck. By far the best sources of information are the hostels, guesthouses and foreign-centric cafés. Most cities and towns have a branch of the **China International Travel Service** (CITS; 中国国际旅行社; *Zhōngguó Guójì Lǚxíngshè*). There is usually a member of staff who can speak English who may be able to answer questions and offer some travel advice, but the main purpose of CITS is to get you onto a tour.

VISAS

For most travellers, the type of visa issued is an L, from the Chinese word for travel (*lǚyóu*). This letter is stamped right on the visa. The L visa can be either a multiple- or single-entry visa. Visas are readily available from Chinese embassies and consulates in most Western and many other countries. A standard 30-day, single-entry visa from most Chinese embassies abroad can be issued in three to five working days. Prices have risen steadily over recent years, and express visas cost twice the usual fee.

You can obtain applications online from www.fmprc.gov.cn/eng. A visa mailed to you will take up to three weeks. You can also make arrangements at certain travel agencies. Visa applications require at least one photo (normally 51mm by 51mm). Try to list standard tourist destinations such as Kūnmíng and Dàlǐ (not Tibet or western Xīnjiāng); the list you give is not binding.

A 30-day visa is activated on the date you enter China, and must be used within three months of date of issue. Sixty-day and 90-day travel visas are no longer issued outside China. You need to extend your visa in China if you want to stay longer. A Chinese visa covers virtually all of China, although some restricted areas still exist that will require an additional permit from the PSB, at a cost. In addition to a visa, permits are also required for travel to Tibet.

At the time of writing, Chinese embassies in the USA were no longer accepting mailed visa applications, so this may mean you will have to mail your passport to a visa service agency. Many people use the **China Visa Service Center** (☎ 1-800 799 6560; www.mychinavisa.com), which offers impeccable service. Expect it to take 10 to 14 days.

Political events can suddenly make visas more difficult to procure. When you check into a hotel, there is a question on the registration form asking what type of visa you hold, as follows:

Type	Description	Chinese name
L	travel	*lǚxíng*
F	business or student	*fǎngwèn*
D	resident	*dìngjū*
G	transit	*guòjìng*
X	long-term student	*liúxué*
Z	working	*rènzhí*
J	journalist	*jìzhě*
C	flight attendant	*chéngwù*

Visa Extensions

The Foreign Affairs Branch of the local PSB (公安局; Gōngānjú) – the police force – handles visa extensions. A first-time extension of another 30 days is easy to obtain on a single-entry tourist visa, but further extensions are harder to get and may only give you a further week. Offices outside of Kūnmíng may be more lenient and more willing to offer further extensions, but don't bank on it. Extensions to single-entry visas vary in price. American travellers pay Y185, Canadians Y165, UK citizens Y160 and Australians Y100; prices can go up or down. Expect to wait up to five days. If you have used up all your options, popping into Hong Kong for a new one is common. The penalty for overstaying your visa in China is up to Y500 per day.

Visas for Countries in the Region

LAOS

It is now possible to get a visa for Laos at the border (p470), or visit the Lao consulate (p474) in Kūnmíng for a 15-day tourist visa. For those from Western European countries, Australia and New Zealand, visas cost Y270 and for American, Japanese and German nationals the cost is Y320. You must bring one passport photo with your application. Visas take three working days to process or you can pay a surcharge for next-day service.

THAILAND

Travellers from most countries won't need a Thai visa unless they plan to stay in the country more than 30 days. The Thai consulate (p474) in Kūnmíng can issue a 60-day tourist visa for Y200. Visas take two days to process.

VIETNAM

Kūnmíng has a Vietnam consulate (p474) where you can pick up a 30-day tourist visa (Y400). Visas take three working days to process or you can pay an extra Y200 for the express service. You must bring along a passport photo with your application.

VOLUNTEERING

There are endless opportunities for volunteer work in Yúnnán; just have a look at guesthouse notice boards to get a start. Websites to consult include www.volunteerchina.org and www.volunteerinchina.org.

WOMEN TRAVELLERS

Principles of decorum and respect for women are deeply ingrained in Chinese culture. Despite the Confucianist sense of superiority accorded to men, Chinese women often call the shots and wield considerable clout (especially within marriage). Nonetheless, in its institutions, China is a patriarchal and highly conservative country. In general, foreign women are unlikely to suffer serious sexual harassment.

Solo travellers are at risk of crime. Try to stick to hotels in the centre, rather than the fringes of town. Taking a whistle or alarm with you would offer a measure of defence in any unpleasant encounter. As with anywhere else, you will be taking a risk if you travel alone. If you have to travel alone, consider arming yourself with some self-defence techniques.

Tampons (卫生棉条; wèishēng miántiáo) can be found almost everywhere, especially in big supermarkets. It's best to take plentiful supplies of the pill (避孕药;bìyùnyào) unless you are travelling to the big cities where brands like Marvelon are available from local pharmacies, as are morning-after pills (紧急避孕药; jǐnjí bìyùnyào). Condoms (避孕套; bì'yùntào) are widely available.

WORK

Teaching English can be particularly lucrative, and there are opportunities for acting, modelling work, editing, proofreading, freelance writing and IT work. Large numbers of Westerners work in China through international development charities such as VSO (www.vso.org.uk). Those with Chinese-language skills will find it much easier to source work. Useful places to start looking for positions include Chinajob.com (www.chinajob.com).

TRANSPORT IN YÚNNÁN PROVINCE

GETTING THERE & AWAY

Air

Kūnmíng is served by all Chinese airlines and has daily flights to most cities in the country. International destinations via innumerable airlines include – but are not limited to – Hanoi (Y1480 to Y2230, daily), Chiang Mai/Bangkok (Y1580), Rangoon (Y1710), Vientiane (Y900) and Siem Reap (Y1700). Most of these have daily flights. Jǐnghóng,

Xīshuāngbǎnnà's air link, has direct flights to Bangkok (Y1400) via Chiang Mai in Thailand throughout the year.

Yunnan Airlines/CAAC (Map p444; ☎ 0871-316 4270, 313 8562; Tuodong Lu; ⏰ 24hr) in Kūnmíng issues tickets for any Chinese airline but the office only offers discounts on Yunnan Airlines flights.

Foreign airline offices in Kūnmíng:

Dragonair (Map p444; ☎ 0871-356 1208, 356 1209; 2/F Kaīhuá Guǎngchǎng, 157 Beijing Lu)

Lao Aviation (Map p444; Camellia Hotel, 154 Dongfeng Donglu)

Thai Airways (Map p444; ☎ 0871-351 1515; 68 Beijing Lu) Next to the King World Hotel.

Boat

In November 2006 a new high-speed passenger boat began running from Jǐnghóng to Chiang Saen in Thailand; see p467.

Border Crossings

Yúnnán province has border crossings with Laos and Vietnam. See the table, p101. The crossing from Hékǒu to Lao Cai in Vietnam is convenient for travellers going between Kūnmíng and Hanoi. There are two other border crossings between Vietnam and China, located outside of Yúnnán (see p374).

Train

Yúnnán's capital, Kūnmíng, is linked comprehensively to the rest of China. Book early for trains to popular destinations, especially Guǎngxī province, which borders Vietnam.

Yúnnán once had a funky old narrow-gauge rail system linking Kūnmíng with Hékǒu on the border with Vietnam. The provincial government has announced plans to completely redevelop the rail system, along with other Association of Southeast Asia (Asean) nations.

GETTING AROUND
Air

Within Yúnnán province daily flights to/from Kūnmíng connect with Jǐnghóng (Y780), Lìjiāng (Y660) and Xiàguān/Dàlǐ (Y520).

During the high season it's possible to fly from these centres to other Chinese cities as well.

Bicycle

It's a grand Chinese tradition to hire a bicycle (自行车; *zìxíngchē*) and tool around. Renting them is quite easy and the bikes nowadays are not too bad, though always check the conditions first and never use your passport as a deposit. Traffic is sheer madness. Only park in designated bicycle parking areas (it costs a pittance); thieves will steal the bike if you don't.

Bus

Roadwise, Yúnnán has a comprehensive and smooth bus network to all major destinations. Expect a few curlicue ribbons but no tailbone smashing. Expressways link Kūnmíng with Dàlǐ (and soon Lìjiāng), south to Jǐnghóng and southeast towards (but not to, yet) Hékǒu.

These expressway networks link Kūnmíng with neighbouring provinces and, by the time this book is printed, further on to Laos (and ultimately Thailand).

Car & Motorcycle

Forget about it. Only rarely is it possible for a tourist to drive a car in China, and then only in large eastern cities. This is mostly because the authorities think you'd be mad – rightfully so – to want to attempt driving here. That said, recently a few shops in Jǐnghóng in the Xīshuāngbǎnnà Region have been hiring out motorbikes to tourists who were looking to spend a pleasant day buzzing about the jungles.

Train

Rail travel within Yúnnán is not so easy. A rail line exists to gotta-go-there Dàlǐ (a further extension from Dàlǐ to Lìjiāng was reportedly half-completed at the time of writing).

Regional Directory

CONTENTS

This chapter includes general information about the Mekong region. Specific information for each country is listed in the Directory section at the back of each country chapter.

ACCOMMODATION

The Mekong has something for everyone – from fleapits to five-star resorts – and we cover them all. Prices are quoted in the local currency or US dollars throughout this book based on the preferred currency of the particular property. Accommodation prices listed are high-season prices for rooms with attached bathroom, unless stated otherwise. An icon is included if air-con is available; otherwise, assume that a fan will be provided.

Accommodation costs vary slightly across the region, but prices are consistently cheap compared with those found in Europe or North America. Check the Directory sections in individual chapters for the budget breakdowns used within that chapter.

Across the region when it comes to budget, we are generally talking about family-run guesthouses or minihotels where the majority of rooms cost less than US$20. Budget rooms generally come well equipped for the money, so don't be surprised to find air-con, hot water and a TV for as little as US$10.

Moving on to midrange, we are referring to rooms from about US$20, which buys some pretty tasty extras in this region. At the lower end of this bracket, many of the hotels are similar to budget hotels but with bigger rooms or balconies. Splash a bit more cash and three-star touches are available, such as access to a swimming pool and a hairdryer hidden away somewhere.

At the upper end are a host of international-standard hotels and resorts that charge from US$75 a room to US$750 a suite. These are mostly restricted to big cities and major tourist centres. Some of these are fairly faceless business hotels, while others ooze opulence or resonate with history. There are some real bargains when compared with the Hong Kongs and Singapores of this world, so if you fancy indulging yourself, the Mekong region is a good place to do so. Most hotels at the top end levy a tax of 10% and a service charge of 5%, displayed as ++ (plus plus) on the bill.

BOOK ACCOMMODATION ONLINE

For more accommodation reviews and recommendations by Lonely Planet authors, check out the online booking service at www.lonelyplanet.com. You'll find the true, insider lowdown on the best places to stay. Reviews are thorough and independent. Best of all, you can book online.

Peak tourist demand for hotel rooms in the region comes at Christmas and New Year, when prices may rise by as much as 25%. There is also a surge in many cities during Chinese New Year (Tet in Vietnam), when half the population is on the move. Try to make a reservation at these times so as not to get caught out.

Camping

With the exception of the national parks in Thailand, the opportunities for camping are pretty limited.

Guesthouses & Hotels

There is an excellent range of guesthouses and hotels in the Mekong region, no matter what your budget. As tourism is a relatively recent phenomenon in Cambodia, Laos and Vietnam, there are lots of newly built places that are excellent value for money.

There is some confusion over the terms 'singles', 'doubles', 'double occupancy' and 'twins', so let's set the record straight here. A single contains one bed, even if two people sleep in it. If there are two beds in the room, that is a twin, even if only one person occupies it. If two people stay in the same room, that is double occupancy. In some hotels 'doubles' means twin beds, while in others it means double occupancy.

While many of the newer hotels have lifts, older hotels often don't and the cheapest rooms are at the end of several flights of stairs. It's a win-win-win situation: cheaper rooms, a bit of exercise and better views! Bear in mind that power outages are possible in some towns and this can mean 10 flights of stairs just to get to your room.

Many hotels post a small sign warning guests not to leave cameras, passports and other valuables in the room. Most places have a safety deposit system of some kind, but if leaving cash (not recommended) or travellers cheques, be sure to seal the loot in an envelope and have it countersigned by staff.

Homestays

Homestays are a popular option in parts of the Mekong region, but some countries are more flexible than others about the concept. Homestays are well-established in parts of Thailand, Vietnam and Yúnnán, and many treks through minority areas in the far north include a night with a local family to learn

about their lifestyle. Homestays are just starting up in Cambodia and Laos. Cambodia is quite DIY and many visitors end up staying with local families when motorbiking in remote areas. Politics mean the DIY approach is more problematic in China and Laos. Communist countries are not the sort of places where you can just drop-in and hope things work out, as there are strict rules about registering foreigners who stay overnight with a local family. For more on Laos homestays, see the boxed text, p263.

ACTIVITIES

There are plenty of activities to keep visitors busy in the Mekong region. Go on the water, go under the water, crank up the revs on a motorbike or cruise down a slope on a mountain bike, the possibilities abound. Thailand is the adventure capital of the region, with Vietnam fast catching up, but every country has something to offer.

Boat Trips

With the Mekong cutting a swathe through the heart of the region, it is hardly surprising to find boat trips are a major drawcard here. There are opportunities to explore small jungled tributaries leading to remote minority villages in Cambodia and Laos. It is possible to explore cave systems by boat in Vietnam, as well as experience the bustle of a floating market in the Mekong Delta. Whole villages float on the waters of the Tonlé Sap lake in Cambodia. Cruising the waters of Halong Bay on a junk is one of the most iconic boat trips in the region (see the boxed text, p370).

It is also possible to make some functional boat trips that offer some beautiful scenery. The two-day boat trip from Huay Xai and the Golden Triangle down to Luang Prabang includes a stunning stretch of the Mekong. Travelling by boat from Chau Doc in the Mekong Delta to Phnom Penh offers a tantalising glimpse of rural life, or go one better with a boat cruise from Ho Chi Minh City to Siem Reap.

In time you should even be able to take the proverbial slow boat to China, as river cruise companies enter the market to connect Luang Prabang and Jínghóng.

Cycling

The Mekong region is steadily establishing itself as a cycling destination. Thailand has long been the most popular place for cycling tourists, but Vietnam is fast catching up. Even Cambodia and Laos see their share of cyclists these days. For hardcore cyclists, the mountains of northern Vietnam, northern Laos and Yúnnán are the ultimate destination. For those who like a more gentle workout, meandering along Mekong villages is memorable, particularly in the Mekong Delta in Vietnam. Biking around Angkor is a great way to get around, and Thailand's northeast can be rewarding thanks to good roads and light traffic.

For some laughs, as well as the lowdown on cycling in the Mekong region, visit the website www.mrpumpy.net.

Diving & Snorkelling

Compared with the rest of Southeast Asia, diving and snorkelling opportunities are limited. However, Vietnam, and to a lesser extent Cambodia, have up-and-coming dive industries. The most popular place to dive in Vietnam is Nha Trang (p394), but the island of Phu Quoc (p424) is a rising star. In Cambodia, Sihanoukville (p240) is the only place really geared up for diving and snorkelling, but the best diving is further afield and requires an overnight on a boat.

Kayaking

Kayaking has taken off around Halong Bay (see the boxed text, p370) in the past few years, following in the footsteps of Krabi in Thailand. There are also kayaking trips on many rivers in Laos (particularly from Vang Vieng; see p289) and Thailand, although some of the white water is for experienced paddlers only.

Motorbiking

For those with a thirst for adventure, motorbike trips into remote areas of Cambodia, Laos and Vietnam are unforgettable. The mobility of two wheels is unrivalled. Motorbikes can traverse trails that even the hardiest 4WD cannot follow. Just remember to watch the road when the scenery is sublime! If you are not confident riding a motorbike, it's comparatively cheap to hire someone to drive it for you.

Rock Climbing

When it comes to organised climbing, Thailand has the most on offer (see p136 for info on Chiang Mai), but the region is liberally peppered with karst, so there is huge potential in the future. Bring your own gear and

---

RESPONSIBLE DIVING

Please consider the following tips when diving and help preserve the ecology and beauty of reefs:

- Never use anchors on the reef and take care not to ground boats on coral.

- Avoid touching or standing on living marine organisms or dragging equipment across the reef. Polyps can be damaged by even the gentlest contact. If you must hold on to the reef, only touch exposed rock or dead coral.

- Be conscious of your fins. Even without contact, the surge from fin strokes near the reef can damage delicate organisms. Take care not to kick up clouds of sand, which can smother organisms.

- Practise and maintain proper buoyancy control. Major damage can be done by divers descending too fast and colliding with the reef.

- Take great care in underwater caves. Spend as little time within them as possible as your air bubbles may be caught within the roof and thereby leave organisms high and dry. Take turns to inspect the interior of a small cave.

- Resist the temptation to collect or buy coral or shells or to loot marine archaeological sites (mainly shipwrecks).

- Ensure that you take home all your rubbish and any litter you may find as well. Plastics in particular are a serious threat to marine life.

- Do not feed fish.

- Minimise your disturbance of marine animals. *Never* ride on the backs of turtles.

anything is possible from Halong Bay to Vang Vieng (see p289).

Surfing

Most serious surfers head further south to Indonesia, but there is some surf in Vietnam. Check out China Beach (p387) for some of the biggest waves or try kite-surfing at Mui Ne (p398).

Trekking

Trekking in the Mekong region isn't quite as high and mighty as in Nepal, but the more demure peaks are home to many minority hill-tribe villages, which host overnight trekking parties. The northern Thai cities of Chiang Mai (p136), Mae Hong Son (p144) and Chiang Rai (p146) are very popular for treks, often in combination with white-water rafting and elephant rides. For trekking tips, see p138.

Muang Sing (p312) in Laos has developed an award-winning ecotourism project for visits to local ethnic-minority villages. The mountain village of Sapa (p376) in Vietnam is another base for organised hill-tribe journeys. Trekking in northeast Cambodia is beginning to take off in the provinces of Mondulkiri (p236) and Ratanakiri (p234), and the Cardamom Mountains (see Veal Vang, p215) have huge potential for the future.

In Yúnnán, the trek at Tiger Leaping Gorge (p459) remains one of the most popular hikes in China and Xīshuāngbǎnnà (see the boxed text, p467) is a great area to explore Dai (Thai) minority villages.

BOOKS

See the Directory of each country chapter for recommended reading (fiction and nonfiction), and p19 for books covering the whole region's history and culture. There are also lots of recommended books tucked away in the sidebars of the History, Culture, Environment and Food & Drink chapters at the front of the book.

For more detailed information on a specific area or country, refer to the large range of travel guidebooks produced by Lonely Planet. Titles to look for include *China*, *Cambodia*, *Laos*, *China's Southwest*, *Thailand*, *Thailand's Islands & Beaches* and *Vietnam*. Travellers wanting to really dig beneath a city's surface should keep an eye out for *Bangkok*.

Also of interest to travellers who like to learn some of the local lingo are Lonely Planet's phrasebooks, which include the *Hill Tribes Phrasebook*, *Lao Phrasebook*, *Southeast Asia Phrasebook*, *Thai Phrasebook* and *Vietnamese Phrasebook*.

BUSINESS HOURS

Business hours are reasonably standard across the region. Most government offices, embassies and businesses open between 8am and 9am and close around 4pm to 5pm. Government offices and some businesses break for lunch, usually just one hour in China and Thailand, often two hours in Cambodia, Laos and Vietnam. Banks often keep shorter hours until about 3.30pm but don't close for lunch. Banks are also open on Saturday morning.

Small businesses such as shops may keep much longer hours – from 7am to 7pm or later – and don't close at weekends. Markets are usually open from dawn until dusk, although most cities have at least one night market that rumbles on all night.

Local restaurants open and close early, serving breakfast from 6am and winding down dinner before 9pm. Fancy restaurants usually stay open until about 11pm. Opening hours for bars vary dramatically depending on the country in question and the mood of the government that month. It is usually possible to drink or dance into the wee hours, although places in Laos tend to close before midnight, while places in Cambodia stagger on all night.

CHILDREN

Children can live it up in the Mekong region, as they are always the centre of attention and almost everybody wants to play with them. However, this attention can sometimes be overwhelming, particularly for blond-haired, blue-eyed babes. Cheek pinching, or worse still (if rare), groin grabbing, are distinct possibilities, so keep close. For the full picture on surviving and thriving on the road, check out Lonely Planet's *Travel with Children* by Cathy Lanigan, with a rundown on health precautions for kids and advice on travel during pregnancy.

Practicalities

When it comes to feeding and caring for babies, pretty much everything is available in the major centres, but supplies dry up quickly elsewhere.

REGIONAL DIRECTORY

RESPONSIBLE TREKKING

To help preserve the ecology and beauty of the Mekong region, consider the following tips when trekking.

Rubbish

- Carry out *all* your rubbish. Don't overlook easily forgotten items, such as silver paper, orange peel, cigarette butts and plastic wrappers. Empty packaging should be stored in a dedicated rubbish bag. Make an effort to carry out rubbish left by others.

- Never bury your rubbish: Digging disturbs soil and ground cover and encourages erosion. Buried rubbish will likely be dug up by animals, who may be injured or poisoned by it. It may also take years to decompose.

- Minimise waste by taking minimal packaging and no more food than you will need. Take reusable containers or stuff sacks.

- Sanitary napkins, tampons, condoms and toilet paper should be carried out despite the inconvenience. They burn and decompose poorly.

Human Waste Disposal

- Contamination of water sources by human faeces can lead to the transmission of all sorts of nasties. Where there is a toilet, please use it. Where there is none, bury your waste. Dig a small hole 15cm (6in) deep and at least 100m (320ft) from any watercourse. Cover the waste with soil and a rock. In snow, dig down to the soil.

- Ensure that these guidelines are applied to a portable toilet tent if one is being used by a large trekking party. Encourage all party members, including porters, to use the site.

Washing

- Don't use detergents or toothpaste in or near watercourses, even if the products are biodegradable.

- For personal washing, use biodegradable soap and a water container (or even a lightweight, portable basin) at least 50m (160ft) away from the watercourse. Disperse the waste water widely to allow the soil to filter it fully.

- Wash cooking utensils 50m (160ft) from watercourses using a scourer, sand or snow instead of detergent.

Erosion

- Hillsides and mountain slopes, especially at high altitudes, are prone to erosion. Stick to existing trails and avoid short cuts.

- If a well-used trail passes through a mud patch, walk through the mud so as not to increase the size of the patch.

- Avoid removing the plant life that keeps topsoils in place.

Fires & Low-Impact Cooking

- Don't depend on open fires for cooking. The cutting of wood for fires in popular trekking areas can cause rapid deforestation. Cook on a light-weight kerosene, alcohol or Shellite (white gas) stove and avoid those powered by disposable butane gas canisters.

- If you are trekking with a guide and porters, supply stoves for the whole team. In alpine areas, ensure that all members are outfitted with enough clothing so that fires are not a necessity for warmth.

- If you patronise local accommodation, select those places that do not use wood fires to heat water or cook food.

- Fires may be acceptable below the tree line in areas that get very few visitors. If you light a fire, use an existing fireplace. Don't surround fires with rocks. Use only dead, fallen wood. Remember the adage 'the bigger the fool, the bigger the fire'. Use minimal wood, just what you need for cooking. In huts, leave wood for the next person.

Wildlife Conservation

- Don't buy items made from endangered species.

- Don't attempt to exterminate animals in huts. In wild places, they are likely to be protected native animals.

- Discourage the presence of wildlife by not leaving food scraps behind you. Place gear out of reach and tie packs to rafters or trees.

- Do not feed the wildlife as this can lead to animals becoming dependent on handouts, to unbalanced populations and to diseases.

Cot beds are available in international-standard midrange and top-end hotels, but not elsewhere. Apart from in Thailand, there are rarely safety seats in rented cars or taxis, but some restaurants can supply a high chair when it comes to eating.

Breastfeeding in public is quite common, so there is no need to worry about crossing a cultural boundary. But there are few facilities for changing babies other than the usual bathrooms. Pack a baby bag everywhere you go. For kiddies who are too young to handle chopsticks, most restaurants also have cutlery.

The main worry throughout the region is keeping an eye on what strange things infants are putting in their mouths. Their natural curiosity can be a lot more costly in countries where dysentery, typhoid and hepatitis are commonplace. Keeping their hydration levels up and insisting they use sunscreen, despite their protests, is also important. For more on health, see p503.

On a similar note, encourage children to take a cautious approach to animals in the region, as rabies is present. Monkeys are some of the biggest offenders when it comes to bites, so be extra vigilant when they are around.

Most urban areas are pretty straightforward these days, although be very aware of the chaotic traffic conditions – better to restrict your child's movements than have them wander into danger. Parts of rural Cambodia, Laos and Vietnam are not such good travel destinations for children, as there are land mines and unexploded ordnance (UXO) littering the countryside. No matter how many warnings a child is given, can you be certain they won't stray from the path?

CLIMATE CHARTS

For more details on the climate in the region and best time to travel, see p17.

COURSES

There are a variety of courses available throughout the Mekong region, from language, meditation and massage to *muay thai* (Thai boxing) and cooking, and from formal programmes sponsored by international agencies to informal classrooms run in homes. The **Council on International Educational Exchange** (☎ 888-268-6245; www.ciee.org/study) arranges study-abroad programmes in language, art and culture in Thailand and Vietnam,

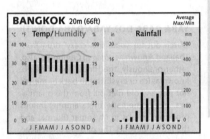

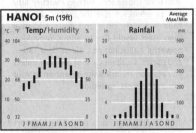

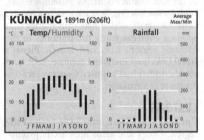

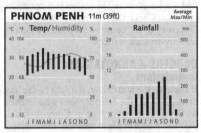

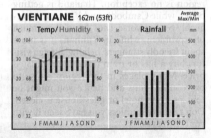

YABA DABA DO? YABA DABA DON'T!

Watch out for *yaba*, the 'crazy' drug from Thailand, known as *yama* in Cambodia, also, rather ominously, the Hindu god of death. Known as ice or crystal meth back home, it's not just any old diet pill from the pharmacist, but homemade meta-amphetamines produced in labs in Myanmar (Burma) and the region beyond. The pills are often laced with toxic substances, such as mercury, lithium or whatever else the maker can find. *Yaba* is a dirty drug and more addictive than users would like to admit, provoking powerful hallucinations, sleep deprivation and psychosis. Steer clear of the stuff unless you plan on an indefinite extension to your trip in the Mekong region.

hosted in local universities. The University of Texas at Austin maintains a useful website, **Study Abroad Asia** (http://asnic.utexas.edu/asnic/stdyabrd/StdyabrdAsia.html), which lists universities that sponsor overseas study programmes in the Mekong region. Also visit Lonely Planet's **Travel Links** (www.lonelyplanet.com/travel_links), and see the individual country Courses sections for more information.

CUSTOMS

Customs regulations vary little around the region. Drugs and arms are strictly prohibited – a lengthy stay in prison is a common sentence. Check the Customs sections in the Directory of the country chapters for details on duty-free allowances.

DANGERS & ANNOYANCES
Commissions

It could be the taxi driver, it might be the bus driver or even the friendly tout who latches on to you at the train station. Commission is part and parcel of life in Asia and the Mekong region is no exception. Thailand is getting better, while Cambodia and Vietnam are arguably getting worse. Laos doesn't have much of a problem, while in Yúnnán, it is more about friendly strangers 'helping' foreign visitors buy a bus or train ticket at an inflated price. Many places in the region refuse to pay commissions and hence you might be told a certain hotel or guesthouse is closed. Don't believe it unless you have seen it with your own eyes.

Drugs

The risks associated with recreational drug use and distribution have grown to the point where all visitors should exercise extreme caution even in places with illicit reputations. A spell in a local prison is true Third World torture. With heightened airline security after the 11 September 2001 attacks in the USA, customs officials are zealous in their screening of both luggage and passengers. See the boxed text, left, for the dangers of *yaba*.

Pollution & Noise

Pollution is a growing problem in the major cities of the region. Bangkok has long been famous as a place to chew the air rather than inhale. However, Ho Chi Minh City, Kūnmíng and Phnom Penh also have problems of their own. Laos remains blissfully pollution-free for the most part.

Remember Spinal Tap? The soundtrack of the cities in this region is permanently cranked up to 11! Not just any noise, but a whole lot of noises that just never seem to stop. At night there is most often a competing cacophony from motorbikes, discos, cafés, video arcades, karaoke lounges and restaurants; if your hotel is near any or all of these, it may be difficult to sleep. Fortunately most noise subsides around 10pm or 11pm, as few places stay open much later than that. Unfortunately, however, locals are up and about from around 5am onwards.

One last thing… Don't forget the earplugs!

Queues

What queues? Most locals in the Mekong region don't queue, they mass in a rugby

YOU WANT MASSAGE?

Karaoke clubs and massage parlours are ubiquitous throughout the region. Sometimes this may mean an 'orchestra without instruments', or a healthy massage to ease a stiff body. However, more often than not, both of these terms are euphemisms for some sort of prostitution. There may be some singing or a bit of shoulder tweaking going on, but ultimately it is just a polite introduction to something naughtier. Legitimate karaoke and legitimate massage do exist in the bigger cities, but as a general rule of thumb, if the place looks sleazy, it probably is.

scrum, pushing towards the counter. When in Rome… This is first-seen, first-served, so take a deep breath, muscle your way to the front and wave your passport, papers or whatever as close to the counter as you can.

Scams

Every year we get hundreds of letters and emails from hapless travellers reporting that they've been scammed in this region. In almost all cases there are two culprits involved: a shrewd scam artist and the traveller's own greed.

Two perennial scams involve card games and gemstones. If someone asks you to join a card game be extremely wary. If the game involves money, walk away – it's almost certainly rigged. As for gemstones, if there really were vast amounts of money to be made by selling gems back home, more savvy businesspeople than yourself would have a monopoly on the market already. Don't believe the people who say that they support their global wanderings by re-selling gemstones; in reality they support themselves by tricking unsuspecting foreigners.

Other common scams include losing money on black market exchange deals, having your rented bicycle or motorbike 'stolen' by someone with a duplicate key and dodgy drug deals that involve police extortion. There are many more so it pays to keep your antennae up during a trip through the Mekong region.

See Dangers & Annoyances in the individual country chapters for local scams.

Theft

Theft in this part of the world is usually by stealth rather than by force. Keep your money and valuables in a money belt worn underneath your clothes. Be alert to the possible presence of snatch thieves, who will whisk a camera or a bag off your shoulder. Don't store valuables in easily accessible places such as packs that are stored in the luggage compartment of buses, or the front pocket of daypacks.

Violent theft is very rare but occurs from time to time – usually late at night and after the victim has been drinking. Be careful walking alone late at night and don't fall asleep in taxis.

Always be diplomatically suspicious of overfriendly locals. Don't accept gifts of food

---

> **HAPPINESS IS A STATE OF MIND**
>
> 'Don't worry, be happy' could be the motto for the Mekong region, but in some backpacker centres the term 'happy' has taken on a wholly different connotation. Seeing the word 'happy' in front of 'shake', 'pizza' or anything else does not, as one traveller was told, mean it comes with extra pineapple. The extra is usually marijuana, added in whatever quantity the shake-maker deems fit. For many travellers 'happy' is a well-understood alias, but there are others who innocently quaff down their shake or pizza only to spend the next 24 hours floating in a world of their own.

---

or drinks from someone you don't know. In Thailand, thieves have been known to drug travellers for easier pickings.

Finally, don't let paranoia ruin your trip. With just a few sensible precautions most travellers make their way across the region without incident.

Unexploded Ordnance & Landmines

The legacy of war lingers on in Cambodia, Laos and Vietnam. Laos suffers the fate of being the most heavily bombed country per capita in the world, while all three countries were on the receiving end of more bombs than were dropped by all sides during WWII. There are still many undetonated bombs and explosives out there, so be careful walking off the trail in areas near the Laos–Vietnam border or around the Demilitarised Zone (DMZ). Cambodia suffers the additional affliction of land mines, some four to six million of them according to surveys. Many of these are located in border areas with Thailand in the north and west of the country, but it pays to stick to marked paths anywhere in Cambodia.

Violence

Violence against foreigners is pretty rare and is not something you should waste much time worrying about, but if you do get into a flare up with some locals, swallow your pride and back down. You are the outsider. You don't know how many friends they have nearby, how many weapons they are carrying or how many years they have studied kick boxing.

TRAVEL ADVISORY WEBSITES

Travel advisories are government-run websites that update nationals on the latest security situation in any given country, including the countries of the Mekong region. They are useful to check out for dangerous countries or dangerous times, but they tend to be pretty conservative, stressing dangers where they don't always exist...otherwise known as covering your back or 'I told you so'.

Australia (www.dfat.gov.au/travel)
Canada (www.voyage.gc.ca/dest/index.asp)
New Zealand (www.mft.govt.nz/travel/)
UK (www.fco.gov.uk/travel)
USA (www.travel.state.gov)

DISCOUNT CARDS

The International Student Identity Card (ISIC) is the official student card, but is of limited use in the Mekong region. Some domestic and international airlines provide discounts to ISIC cardholders, but because knock-offs are so readily available the cards carry little bargaining power.

ELECTRICITY

Most countries work on a voltage of 220V to 240V at 50Hz (cycles); note that 240V appliances will happily run on 220V. You should be able to pick up adaptors in electrical shops in most of the main towns and cities.

EMBASSIES & CONSULATES

It's important to realise what your own embassy – the embassy of the country of which you are a citizen – can and can't do to help you if you get into trouble.

Generally speaking, it won't be much help in emergencies if the trouble you're in is remotely your own fault. Remember that you are bound by the laws of the country you are in. Your embassy will not be sympathetic if you end up in jail after committing a crime locally, even if such actions are legal in your own country.

In genuine emergencies you might get some assistance, but only if other channels have been exhausted. For example, if you need to get home urgently, a free ticket home is exceedingly unlikely – the embassy would expect you to have insurance. If you have all your money and documents stolen, it might

assist with getting a new passport, but a loan for onward travel is out of the question.

Most travellers should have no need to contact their embassy while in the Mekong region, although if you're really going off the trail, it may be worth letting your embassy know. However, be sure to let them know when you return. In this way valuable time, effort and money won't be wasted looking for you while you're relaxing on the beach somewhere in a different country.

For details of embassies in the Mekong region see the Directory sections in the individual country chapters.

FESTIVALS & EVENTS

Most holidays in the region revolve around religious events and typically provide an excellent display of the country's culture, food and music. Businesses are usually closed and travelling is difficult, so plan ahead.

Chinese New Year & Vietnamese Tet Probably one of the loudest festivals on the planet; it is celebrated countrywide in Vietnam and in Chinese communities throughout the region in late January or February, with fireworks, temple visits and all-night drumming.

Thai, Lao & Cambodian New Year The lunar New Year begins in mid-April, and in addition to religious devotion, locals take to the streets dousing one another with water, particularly in Thailand.

Buddhist Lent At the start of the monsoonal rains in June or July, the Buddhist monks retreat into monasteries in Cambodia, Laos and Thailand. This is the traditional time for young men to visit the monasteries.

Ramadan Observed in southern Thailand and the Cham areas of Cambodia and Vietnam during October, November or December, the Muslim fasting month requires that Muslims abstain from food, drink, cigarettes and sex between sunrise and sunset.

Christmas This holiday needs no introduction and is celebrated by Vietnamese Catholics, but has also been adopted as an honorary holiday throughout the region.

FOOD & DRINK

This is arguably the best region in the world when it comes to sampling the local cuisine. The food of China, Thailand and Vietnam needs no introduction, but Laotian and Khmer cuisine is also a rewarding experience. See the Food & Drink chapter (p86) for the full story and check out the signature dishes in the boxed text, opposite. For drinkers, there is plenty to get excited about from divine fruit shakes and coffee with a kick to microbrewed beers and homemade hooch.

THE NATIONAL DISH

If there's just one dish you try, make it one of these. These are the dishes that capture the cuisine of the country in a single serving. Enjoy.

Cambodia *Amoc* (baked fish in a banana leaf)
Laos *Laap* (spicy salad with meat or fish)
Thailand *tôm yam kûng* (hot and sour soup with shrimp)
Vietnam *Pho bo* (rice noodle soup with beef)
Yúnnán *Guoqiao mixian* (across-the-bridge noodles)

Food is fantastic value throughout the region. Street snacks start from as little as US$0.25, meals in local restaurants start from US$1 to US$2 and even a serious spread at a decent restaurant will only be in the US$5 to US$10 range.

GAY & LESBIAN TRAVELLERS

Cambodia, Thailand and Laos have the most progressive attitudes towards homosexuality. While same-sex displays of affection are part of most Asian cultures, be discreet and respectful of the local culture. Extra vigilance should be practised in Vietnam, where authorities have arrested people on charges of suspected homosexual activities. In 2001, the Chinese Psychiatric Association stopped classifying homosexuality as a mental disorder, but it pays to be discreet in more conservative parts of Yúnnán. There is not usually a problem with same-sex couples checking into rooms throughout the region, as it is so common among travellers.

Check out **Utopia Asian Gay & Lesbian Resources** (www.utopia-asia.com) for more information on gay and lesbian travel in Asia. Other links with useful pointers for gay travellers include www.gayguide.net and www.outandabout.com.

HOLIDAYS

For full details on public holidays in each of the Mekong-region countries, see the individual country Directory sections. Allegedly, Cambodia has the most public holidays in the world. Chinese New Year (or Tet in Vietnam) is the one holiday common to all countries and can have a big impact on travel plans, as businesses close and all forms of transport are booked out.

INSURANCE

A travel insurance policy to cover theft, loss and medical problems is essential. There's a wide variety of policies available, so check the small print. For more information about the ins and outs of travel insurance, contact a travel agent or travel insurer.

Some policies specifically exclude 'dangerous activities', which can include scuba diving, motorcycling and even trekking. A locally acquired motorcycle licence is not valid under some policies. Check that the policy covers ambulance rides, emergency flights home and repatriation of a body.

Also see p503 for further information on health insurance and p501 for more information on car and motorcycle insurance.

INTERNET ACCESS

You can access email and internet services in all countries of the region. Access points in the Mekong region vary from internet cafés to post offices and hotels. The cost is generally low and the connection speeds pretty reasonable. Wi-fi access is increasingly common in major cities and is often free in cafés and bars. Many hotels in urban Vietnam now offer free internet access as standard. See the Internet Access sections in the country chapters for further details.

LEGAL MATTERS

Be sure to know the national laws before unwittingly committing a crime. In all of the Mekong-region countries, using or trafficking drugs carries stiff punishments that are enforced, even if you're a foreigner. See p486 for more on the risks associated with drugs in the region.

INSURANCE ALERT!

Do not visit the Mekong region without medical insurance. Hospitals are often basic, particularly in remote areas. Anyone who has a serious injury or illness may require emergency evacuation to Bangkok or Hong Kong. With an insurance policy costing no more than the equivalent of a bottle of beer a day, this evacuation is free. Without an insurance policy, it will cost US$10,000 to US$20,000. Don't gamble with your health in the Mekong region or you may end up another statistic!

If you are the victim of a crime, contact the tourist police, if available; they are usually better trained to deal with foreigners and foreign languages than the regular police force.

MAPS

Country-specific maps are usually sold in English bookstores in capital cities. Local tourist offices and guesthouses can also provide maps of smaller cities and towns. There aren't many maps that cover the Mekong region as a whole. There are some good maps of Indochina that include Bangkok and Northeast Thailand: check out Nelles *Vietnam, Laos & Cambodia* map at a scale of 1:1,500,000.

MONEY

Most experienced travellers will carry their money in a combination of travellers cheques, credit/bank cards and cash. You'll always find situations in which one of these cannot be used, so it pays to carry all three. For information on bargaining, see p492.

ATMs

In most large cities ATMs are widespread, but before banking on this option review the individual country's Money section for specifics; Laos is still almost ATM-free.

Some banks back home charge for withdrawals overseas, others don't. Consider shopping around for an account that offers free withdrawals. Similarly, some local banks in the region charge for withdrawals, particularly in Vietnam, although the sums are small.

Black Market

There is still something of a black market in money changing in Laos and Yúnnán. However, given the tiny differences and rates and the huge chance that you'll be ripped off, it is not really worth pursuing this path.

Credit Cards

Credit cards are quite widely accepted in the region. Thailand leads the way, where almost anything can be paid for with plastic. However, things dry up beyond major tourist centres or bigger towns, so don't rely exclusively on credit cards. It is quite common for the business to pass on the credit card commission (usually 3%) to the customer in Cambodia, Laos and Vietnam, so check if there is an additional charge before putting it on the plastic.

Exchanging Money

The US dollar is the currency of choice in the Mekong region. It is widely accepted as cash in Cambodia, Laos and Vietnam, and can be easily exchanged in Thailand and Yúnnán. Other major currencies are also widely accepted by banks and exchange bureaus, but the rates get worse the further you get from a major city. The Thai baht is also accepted throughout Laos and in parts of western Cambodia.

Tipping

Tipping is not a standard practice but is greatly appreciated, particularly in the poorer countries of the region where salaries remain low. Locals often don't tip, but tourism has introduced the concept to hotels and restaurants, as well as to tour guides and drivers.

Travellers Cheques

Travelling with a stash of travellers cheques can help if you hit an ATM-free zone, like most of Laos. Get your cheques in US dollars and in large denominations, say US$100 or US$50, to avoid heavy per-cheque commission fees. Keep careful records of which cheques you've cashed and keep this information separate from your money, so you can file a claim if any cheques are lost or stolen.

PHOTOGRAPHY
Airport Security

X-ray machines that claim to be film-safe generally are. You are advised to have very sensitive film (1000 ISO and above) checked by hand. *Never* put your film in your checked baggage – the X-ray machines used to check this luggage will fog your film.

Film & Equipment

Print film is readily available in cities and larger towns throughout the region. The best places to buy camera equipment or have repairs done are Bangkok, Ho Chi Minh City, Kūnmíng or Phnom Penh.

For those travelling with a digital camera, most internet cafés in well-developed areas let customers transfer images from the camera to an online email account or storage site. Flash memory is also widely available and most internet cafés can burn shots on to a DVD if you are running out of storage space. Before leaving home, find out if your battery charger will require a power adapter by visiting the website of the **World Electric Guide** (www.kropla.com/electric.htm).

If you're after some tips, check out Lonely Planet's *Travel Photography: A Guide to Taking Better Pictures,* written by travel photographer, Richard I'Anson.

Photographing People

You should always ask permission before taking a person's photograph. Many hill-tribe villagers seriously object to being photographed, or they may ask for money in exchange; if you want the photo, you should honour the price.

POST

Postal services are generally reliable across the region. Of course, it's always better to leave important mail and parcels for the big centres such as Bangkok, Kūnmíng or Hanoi.

There's always an element of risk in sending parcels home by sea, though as a rule they eventually reach their destination. If it's something of value, it's worth considering air freight – better still, register the parcel or send it by courier. Don't send cash or valuables through government-run postal systems.

Poste restante is widely available throughout the region and is the best way of receiving mail. When getting people to write to you, ask them to leave plenty of time for mail to arrive and to print your name very clearly.

RESPONSIBLE TRAVEL

The Mekong region continues to experience unprecedented growth in tourism and this inevitably brings the bad along with the good. With a little bit of thought, visitors can help to minimise the negatives and maximise the positives.

Child-sex tourism and the abuse of minors remains a problem in the Mekong region. For more on this ugly phenomenon, see the boxed text, below.

Many parts of the region remain mired in poverty. Support local businesses by buying locally made products. Eat in local restaurants when possible and dine in villages rather than taking picnics from town. Use local guides for remote regions, including indigenous minority peoples. Consider the option of homestays where they are available and support national park programmes by visiting one of the many protected areas in the region.

When bargaining for goods or transport, remember the aim is not to get the lowest possible price, but one that's acceptable to both you and the seller. Coming on too strong or arguing over a few cents does nothing to foster positive feelings towards foreign visitors.

Begging is common in many countries of the region and the tug on the shirtsleeve can become tiresome for visitors after a time. However, try to remember that many of these countries have little in the way of a social-security net to catch the fallen. It is best to keep denominations small to avoid foreigners becoming even more of a target than they already are. Avoid giving money to children, as it is likely going straight to a 'begging pimp' or family member. Food is an option, but better still is to make a donation to one of the many local organisations trying to assist in the battle against poverty.

THE ABUSE OF INNOCENCE

The sexual abuse of children by foreign paedophiles is a serious problem in some parts of the Mekong region, particularly Cambodia and Vietnam. Many child prostitutes are actually sold into the business by relatives. These sex slaves are either trafficked overseas or forced to cater to domestic demand and local sex-tourism operators.

Fear of contracting HIV/AIDS from mature sex workers has led to increasing exploitation of (supposedly as yet uninfected) children. Unicef estimates that there are close to one million child prostitutes in Asia – one of the highest figures in the world.

Paedophiles are treated as criminals in the region and several have served or are serving jail sentences as a result. Many Western countries have introduced much-needed legislation that sees nationals prosecuted in their home country for having underage sex abroad. Visitors can do their bit to fight this menace by keeping an eye out for suspicious behaviour on the part of foreigners. Don't ignore it. Try to pass on any relevant information such as the name and nationality of the individual to the embassy concerned. **End Child Prostitution & Trafficking** (Ecpat; www.ecpat.org) is a global network aimed at stopping child prostitution, child pornography and the trafficking of children for sexual purposes, and has affiliates in most Western countries.

For information on responsible trekking, see p484 and p138. For advice on responsible diving, see p482. Also check each country's Directory for more information of responsible travel.

SHOPPING

Recovering shopaholics beware…the Mekong region offers some incredible opportunities to shop 'til you drop. Bangkok is the gateway to the region and also one of the world's best-known shopping destinations. Everything that is produced in the Mekong region, from textiles to handicrafts, state-of-the-art electronics to suspect antiques, ends up in Bangkok's malls and markets. Browse Chatuchak Weekend Market (p127) for the best range in the region.

Cambodia is famous for its superb silk, as are Laos and Thailand. There is good quality silver throughout the region, but purity can be a problem. There are fine handicrafts, including excellent woodcarving, intricate lacquerware and striking stone carving, in all the countries of the region. The ethnic minorities of the region are also in on the act and produce a range of handicrafts and colourful clothing that make popular keepsakes. Art is increasingly popular, with Thailand, Vietnam and Yúnnán leading the way. Antiques are a popular purchase, but be aware that there are a lot of fakes about. If the price seems too good to be true, it probably is. Precious stones is another area where it's almost always too good to be true. Bangkok is the gem scam capital of Asia, but buying precious stones anywhere in the region is a risk unless you really know what you are doing.

There are some great clothing and electronic stores in the region. Bangkok is the fashion capital of the Mekong region, offering everything from Prada to Kevin Clein (yes there are lots of fakes!). Cambodia and Vietnam both produce a lot of textiles for export, so it's easy to pick up high-street names for a fraction of the price back home. Most of China's production is geared for export, but the stores in Kūnmíng are brimming with the latest trends. When it comes to electronics, Bangkok is the most reliable place, but Cambodia is sometimes a cheaper option thanks to a lack of tax and duty.

Bargaining

Most of the countries in the Mekong region have inherited the art of bargaining from ancient Indian traders and Chinese émigrés. Remember that it is an art not a test of wills, and the trick is to find a price that keeps everyone happy. Bargaining is acceptable in markets and souvenir shops, where fixed prices aren't displayed. Ask the price and then ask if the seller can offer a discount. If the discounted price isn't acceptable give a counter offer but be willing to accept something in the middle. Once you counter you can't name a lower price. Don't ask the price unless you're interested in actually buying it. If you become angry or visibly frustrated then you've lost the bargaining game.

TELEPHONE

Phone systems vary widely across the Mekong region. For international calls, most countries have calling centres (usually in post offices) or public phone booths that accept international phonecards. Each country's system is different, so check the Telephone sections in each country's Directory before making a call.

These days, the cheapest and most popular option is to use an internet-based phone system to make calls. Anyone with a Skype or Messenger account can simply sign in and start talking to friends if there's a headset available. Many of the internet cafés in Cambodia, Thailand, Vietnam and Yúnnán have headsets and webcams, but this is not so common in Laos. Otherwise you can pay a small charge to make a call, often as little as US$0.10 a minute to countries in the West. Many of the budget and midrange hotels in Vietnam have switched over to internetbased telephone systems for their guests and it seems the rest of the region will soon follow. Cheap calls, good news for everyone!

You can take your mobile phone on the road with you and get respectable coverage in major population centres. Not all mobile phones, especially those from the USA, are outfitted for international use. Check with your service provider for global-roaming fees and other particulars. Double-check the rates before you start calling, or even texting away, as prices can be prohibitively high. Consider buying a local sim card for a local network if you plan to make a lot of local telephone calls. Some phones are 'locked' by the issuing company back home, but most telephone shops in the Mekong region can 'unlock' them in seconds for a small charge.

Fax services are available in most countries across the region. Try to avoid the business centres in upmarket hotels – tariffs of 30% and upwards are often levied on faxes and international calls.

TIME

Cambodia, Laos, Thailand and Vietnam are seven hours ahead of Greenwich Mean Time or Universal Time Coordinated (GMT/UTC). When it is midday in Bangkok or Hanoi, it is 10pm the previous evening in San Francisco, 1am in New York, 5am in London, 6am in Paris and 3pm in Sydney. Yúnnán operates on Běijīng time, which is one hour ahead of Cambodia, Laos, Thailand and Vietnam, eight hours ahead of GMT/UTC. See also the World Time Zones map (pp546–7).

TOILETS

As tourism continues to grow in the region, sit-down toilets are increasingly common. Apart from the very cheapest guesthouses, most rooms include a sit-down toilet, as do restaurants and other businesses catering to foreigners. However, in rural areas, it is another story and squat toilets are common.

Even in places where sit-down toilets are installed, the plumbing may not be designed to take toilet paper. In such cases, the usual washing bucket will be standing nearby or there will be a waste basket in which you place used toilet paper.

Public toilets are common in department stores, bus and train stations and large hotels. Elsewhere you'll have to make do; while on the road between towns and villages it's acceptable to go discreetly behind a tree or bush. In land mine– and UXO-affected countries such as Cambodia and Laos, stay on the roadside and do the deed, or grin and bear it until the next town.

TOURIST INFORMATION

All the countries in the Mekong region have government-funded tourist offices with varying degrees of usefulness. Thailand offers by far the most efficient tourism information service. When it comes to the rest, better information is often available from dedicated internet sites, guesthouses and travel cafés, or your fellow travellers, rather than through the state-run tourist offices. See the Tourist Information section in each country's Directory for more information.

TRAVELLERS WITH DISABILITIES

Travellers with serious disabilities will likely find the Mekong region a challenging place to travel. Even the more modern cities are very difficult to navigate for the mobility- or vision-impaired. In general, care of a person with a disability is left to close family members throughout the region and it's unrealistic to expect much in the way of public amenities.

International organisations that can provide information on mobility-impaired travel include the following:

Mobility International USA (☎ 541-343-1284; www .miusa.org; PO Box 10767, Eugene, OR 97440, USA)

Royal Association for Disability & Rehabilitation (Radar; ☎ 020-7250 3222; www.radar.org.uk; 12 City Forum, 250 City Rd, London EC1V 8AF, UK)

Society for Accessible Travel & Hospitality (SATH; ☎ 212-447-7284; www.sath.org; 347 Fifth Ave, Suite 610, New York, NY 10016, USA)

VISAS

Visas are available to people of most nationalities on arrival in most countries of the Mekong region, but rules vary depending on the point of entry. Many nationalities do not require a visa for Thailand and are given 30 days on arrival. For Cambodia and Laos, a visa is required, but is issued on arrival at airports and most land borders. For China and Vietnam, it is necessary to arrange a visa in advance. For more details, see the Visas section in each country's Directory.

Get your visas as you go rather than all at once before you leave home; they are often easier and cheaper to get in neighbouring countries and visas are only valid within a certain time period, which could interfere with an extended trip.

Procedures for extending a visa vary from country to country. In some cases, extensions are quite complicated, in others they're a mere formality. See the Visas section in each country's Directory for further information. And remember the most important rule: treat visits to embassies, consulates and borders as formal occasions and look smart for them.

In some countries in the Mekong region, you are required to have an onward ticket out of the country before you can obtain a visa to enter. In practice, however, as long as you look fairly respectable, it's unlikely that your tickets will be checked.

VOLUNTEERING

There are fewer opportunities for volunteering than one might imagine there would be in a region that remains predominantly poor. This is partly due to the sheer number of professional development-workers based here, and development is a pretty lucrative industry these days. For details on local volunteer projects in the region, see the Directory of individual country chapters.

The other avenue is professional volunteering through an organisation back home that offers one- or two-year placements in the region. One of the largest is **Voluntary Service Overseas** (VSO; www.vso.org.uk) in the UK, but other countries have their own organisations, including the **US Peace Corps** (☎ 800-424-8580; www .peacecorps.gov), **VSO Canada** (☎ 613-234 1364; www .vsocan.org), **Australian Volunteers International** (AVI; www.australianvolunteers.com) and **Volunteer Service Abroad** (VSA; www.vsa.org.nz). The UN also operates its own volunteer programme; details are available at www.unv.org. Other general volunteer sites with links all over the place include www.worldvolunteerweb.com and www.volunteerabroad.com.

WOMEN TRAVELLERS

While travel in the Mekong region for women is generally safe, there are several things visitors can do to make it safer still.

Keep in mind that modesty in dress is culturally important across all Southeast Asia. Causes for commotion include wearing the ever-popular midriff T-shirts that inadvertently send the message that you're a prostitute. At the beach, save the topless sunbathing for home rather than this conservative region of the world. This is particularly important when travelling from Thailand to Cambodia or Laos. Thailand may be very Westernised with an 'anything goes' atmosphere, but Cambodia and Laos are much more traditional. Walking around Angkor dressed like you are going to a full moon party won't impress the locals.

Solo women should be on guard especially when returning home late at night or arriving in a new town at night. While physical assault is rare, local men often consider foreign women as being exempt from their own society's rules of conduct regarding members of the opposite sex.

Use common sense about venturing into dangerous-looking areas, particularly alone or at night. If you do find yourself in a tricky situation, try to extricate yourself as quickly as possible – hopping into a taxi or entering a business establishment and asking them to call a cab is often the best solution.

Treat overly friendly strangers, both male and female, with a good deal of caution.

Many travellers have reported small peepholes in the walls and doors of cheap hotels, some of which operate as boarding houses or brothels (often identified by their advertising 'day use' rates). If you can, move to another hotel or guesthouse.

WORK

The range of jobs available in the region is quite staggering, but many of the better jobs such as working with the UN or for international corporations are appointments from overseas or from a pool of well-qualified locals. The main opportunities for people passing through the region are teaching English (or another European language), landing a job in tourism or starting a small business such as a bar or restaurant.

Teaching English is the easiest way to support yourself in the Mekong region. For short-term gigs, the large cities such as Bangkok, Ho Chi Minh City, Kūnmíng and Phnom Penh have a lot of language schools and a high turnover. **Payaway** (www.payaway.co.uk) provides a handy online list of language schools and volunteer groups looking for recruits for its regional programmes.

With tourism booming, there are plenty of jobs in tourism. Most of these deservedly go to locals, but there are opportunities for wannabe guesthouse or hotel managers, bartenders, chefs and so on. This can be a pretty memorable way to pass a few months in a different culture.

Starting up a business is a possibility, but tread with caution. Many a foreigner has been burned in the region. Sometimes it's an unscrupulous partner, other times it's the local girlfriend, or boyfriend, who changes their mind and goes it alone. Sometimes the owners burn out themselves, drinking the profits of the bar or dabbling in drugs. Do your homework regarding ownership laws and legal recourse in the event of a dispute. That said, there are many success stories in the region, where people came for a holiday and built an empire.

Transitions Abroad (www.transitionsabroad.com) and its namesake magazine covers all aspects of overseas life, including landing a job in a variety of fields. The website also provides links to other useful sites and publications for those living abroad.

Transport in the Region

CONTENTS

This chapter gives an overview of the transport options for getting to the Mekong region, and getting around once you're there. For more specific information about getting to (and around) each country, see the relevant Transport sections in each chapter. For general details of the region's border crossings, see p99.

Flights, tours and rail tickets can be booked online at www.lonelyplanet.com /travel_services.

GETTING THERE & AWAY

ENTERING THE REGION

All the countries in the region have international airports, but Bangkok is by far and away the most important hub. There are long-haul flights linking Hanoi and Ho Chi Minh City to Europe and North America, but Kūnmíng, Phnom Penh and Vientiane are only accessible via a regional gateway such as Bangkok, Hong Kong or Singapore.

When it comes to land borders, Thailand is linked to Malaysia for those visiting more of Southeast Asia. Myanmar (Burma) looks a tantalising option for overland travel to India, but this is not currently permitted. China is

> **THINGS CHANGE...**
>
> The information in this chapter is particularly vulnerable to change. Check directly with the airline or a travel agent to make sure you understand how a fare (and ticket you may buy) works and be aware of the security requirements for international travel. Shop carefully. The details given in this chapter should be regarded as pointers and are not a substitute for your own careful, up-to-date research.

connected to a host of countries, including North Korea, Russia, Mongolia, India, Nepal, Bhutan and several of the Central Asian republics, such as Kazakhstan and Kyrgyzstan. However, it's a major undertaking to do an overland journey from Europe to the Mekong region unless you opt for the *Trans-Manchurian* or *Trans-Mongolian Express*.

Passport

To enter the Mekong region countries, your passport must be valid for at least six months from your date of entry, even if you're only staying for a few days. You may be refused entry if your passport doesn't have enough blank pages available for a visa. When checking into hotels in Vietnam, staff will request a copy of your passport. In China, it is necessary to carry your passport with you at all times.

AIR

For specific information on airports and airlines operating to (and around) each country in the Mekong region, see the Transport section of the relevant chapter.

Tickets

The major Asian gateways for cheap flights are Bangkok, Hong Kong and Singapore. Bangkok is the best place to shop for onward tickets and tickets around the region.

To research and buy a ticket on the internet, try these services:

Cheapflights (www.cheapflights.com) No-frills website with a number of locations.

Lonely Planet (www.lonelyplanet.com) Use the Trip-Planner service to book multistop trips.

OneTravel (www.onetravel.com) Another with a number of locations.

Travel.com (www.travel.com.au) There is also a New Zealand version at www.travel.co.nz.

ROUND-THE-WORLD & CIRCLE ASIA TICKETS

Bucket shops, consolidators and online search engines offer cheap tickets to the region. If Asia is one of many stops on a global tour, consider a round-the-world (RTW) ticket, which allows a certain number of stops within a set time period as long as you don't backtrack; for more information, talk to a travel agent.

Circle Asia fares are offered by various airline alliances for a circular route originating in the USA, Europe or Australia and travelling to two destinations in Asia, including Southeast and east Asia. Prices usually start around US$2000. Before committing, check out the fares offered by the budget regional carriers to see if the circle pass provides enough of a saving. Contact individual airlines or a travel agent for more info.

Asia

Bangkok is easily the best-connected city in the region, with flights to the Indian subcontinent, the Far East, Central Asia and the

Middle East. Japan is well connected to the region, with flights to many of the larger cities, as is South Korea.

Reliable travel agents in Hong Kong:

Four Seas Tours (☎ 2200 7760; www.fourseastravel.com)

STA Travel (☎ 2736 1618; www.statravel.com.hk)

Recommended travel agents in Japan:

No 1 Travel (☎ 03-3205 6073; www.no1-travel.com)

STA Travel (☎ 03-5391 2922; www.statravel.co.jp)

Australia

The best place to look for cheap fares is in the travel sections of weekend newspapers, such as the *Age* in Melbourne and the *Sydney Morning Herald*. There are good connections between major Australian cities and both Thailand and Vietnam. Elsewhere, you'll need to connect through a regional hub.

Two well-known agencies for cheap fares:

Flight Centre (☎ 133 133; www.flightcentre.com.au) Dozens of offices throughout Australia.

STA Travel (☎ 1300 733 035; www.statravel.com.au) Has offices in all major cities and on many university campuses.

Canada

It is cheaper to fly from the west coast than it is to fly from the east coast. Canadian air fares tend to be higher than those sold in the USA. The *Globe & Mail*, the *Toronto*

CLIMATE CHANGE & TRAVEL

Climate change is a serious threat to the ecosystems that humans rely upon, and air travel is the fastest-growing contributor to the problem. Lonely Planet regards travel, overall, as a global benefit, but believes we all have a responsibility to limit our personal impact on global warming.

Flying & Climate Change

Pretty much every form of motor travel generates CO_2 (the main cause of human-induced climate change) but planes are far and away the worst offenders, not just because of the sheer distances they allow us to travel, but because they release greenhouse gases high into the atmosphere. The statistics are frightening: two people taking a return flight between Europe and the US will contribute as much to climate change as an average household's gas and electricity consumption over a whole year.

Carbon Offset Schemes

Climatecare.org and other websites use 'carbon calculators' that allow jetsetters to offset the greenhouse gases they are responsible for with contributions to energy-saving projects and other climate-friendly initiatives in the developing world – including projects in India, Honduras, Kazakhstan and Uganda.

Lonely Planet, together with Rough Guides and other concerned partners in the travel industry, supports the carbon offset scheme run by climatecare.org. Lonely Planet offsets all of its staff and author travel.

For more information check out our website: www.lonelyplanet.com.

Star, the *Montreal Gazette* and the *Vancouver Sun* carry travel-agency ads and are good places to look for good-value fares. **Travel CUTS** (www.travelcuts.com) is Canada's national student travel agency and has offices in all major cities.

Continental Europe

Although London is considered the discount travel capital of Europe, the major airlines and big travel agents will usually have offers available from all of the major cities on the continent.

FRANCE

Nouvelles Frontières (☎ 08 25 00 07 47; www.nouvelles-frontieres.fr)

OTU Voyages (www.otu.fr) This agency specialises in student and youth travel.

Voyageurs du Monde (☎ 01 40 15 11 15; www.vdm.com)

GERMANY

Just Travel (☎ 089-747 33 30; www.justtravel.de)

STA Travel (☎ 0180-545 64 22; www.statravel.de)

ITALY

CTS Viaggi (☎ 064 62 04 31; www.cts.it)

NETHERLANDS

Airfair (☎ 0206-20 51 21; www.airfair.nl)

NBBS Reizen (☎ 0900 1020 300; www.nbbs.nl)

SPAIN

Barcelo Viajes (☎ 902 11 62 26; www.barceloviajes.com)

Nouvelles Frontières (☎ 902 17 09 79; www.nouvelles-frontieres.es)

SWITZERLAND

SSR Voyages (☎ 058 450 4020; www.ssr.ch)

New Zealand

The *New Zealand Herald* has a helpful travel section. **Flight Centre** (☎ 0800 243 544; www.flightcentre.co.nz) has a large central office in Auckland and many branches throughout the country. **STA Travel** (☎ 0508 782 872; www.statravel.co.nz) has offices in Auckland and other major centres.

UK

Advertisements for many travel agencies appear in the travel pages of the weekend broadsheets, such as the *Independent* and the *Sunday Times*.

Popular travel agencies in the UK:

Flightbookers (☎ 087-0010 7000; www.ebookers.com)

North-South Travel (☎ 01245-608291; www.northsouthtravel.co.uk) North-South Travel donates part of its profit to projects in the developing world.

STA Travel (☎ 087-0160 0599; www.statravel.co.uk)

Trailfinders (☎ 084-5050 5891; www.trailfinders.co.uk)

Travel Bag (☎ 087-0890 1456; www.travelbag.co.uk)

USA

Ticket promotions frequently connect Asia to San Francisco and Los Angeles, New York and other big cities. The *New York Times*, the *Los Angeles Times*, the *Chicago Tribune* and the *San Francisco Examiner* all produce weekly travel sections in which you will find a number of travel-agency ads and fare promos.

Useful online options in the USA:

www.cheaptickets.com

www.itn.net

www.lowestfare.com

www.sta.com

www.travelocity.com

LAND

The land borders between the Mekong region and the rest of Asia include the Yunnanese provincial boundary with the rest of China and the frontier that Thailand shares with Malaysia and Myanmar. China itself shares borders with, take a deep breath, Myanmar, India, Bhutan, Nepal, Pakistan, Afghanistan, Tajikistan, Kyrgyzstan, Kazakhstan, Russia, Mongolia, and North Korea.

See p99 for general details of the region's border crossings.

SEA

Apart from a few cruises that call at ports in Thailand, Vietnam and occasionally Cambodia, there are no real options for travelling to the Mekong region by sea.

TOURS

Tours through the Mekong region are offered by travel agencies worldwide. Tours come in every shape and size from budget trips to ultimate indulgences. Tours are not bad value when you tally everything up (flights, hotels, transport), but then again it's a cheap region in which to travel.

It's easy enough to fly into Bangkok or another major city in the region and make travel arrangements from there. See individual country chapters for recommended local travel agents. The main saving through booking before arrival is time, and if time is more precious than money, a prebooked tour is probably right for you.

For a rewarding trip through the Mekong region, consider contacting the following.

Australia
Adventure World (☎ 02-8913 0755; www .adventureworld.com.au) Adventure tours throughout the region.
Intrepid Travel (☎ 1300 360 667; www.intrepidtravel .com.au) Small-group tours for all budgets with an environmental, social and cultural edge.
Peregrine (☎ 02-9290 2770, www.peregrine.net.au) Small-group and tailor-made tours supporting responsible tourism.

France
Compagnie des Indes & Orients (☎ 01 53 63 33 40; www.compagniesdumonde.com)
Intermedes (☎ 01 45 61 90 90; www.intermedes.com)
La Route des Indes (☎ 01 42 60 60 90; www .laroutedesindes.com)

New Zealand
Adventure World (☎ 09-524 5118; www.adventure world.co.nz) A wide range of adventure tours covering the region.
Pacific Cycle Tours (☎ 03-972 9913; www.bike -nz.com) Mountain-bike tours through Vietnam, Laos and Cambodia, plus hiking trips to off-the-beaten-path destinations.

UK
Audley Travel (☎ 01604-234855; www.audleytravel .com) Popular tailor-made specialist covering all of Vietnam.
Cox & Kings (☎ 020-7873 5000; www.coxandkings .co.uk) Well-established high-end company, strong on cultural tours.
Exodus (☎ 020-8675 5550; www.exodus.co.uk) Popular adventure company with affordable overland trips.
Hands Up Holidays (☎ 0776-501 3631; www.handsu pholidays.com) A new company bringing guests closer to the people of the Mekong through its responsible holidays with a spot of volunteering.
Mekong Travel (☎ 01494-674456; www.mekong -travel.com) A name to inspire confidence in the Mekong region.
Selective Asia (☎ 0845-370 3344; www.selectiveasia .com) New company that cherry-picks the best trips from leading local agents.

Symbiosis (☎ 020-7924 5906; www.symbiosis-travel .com) Small travel company with an emphasis on cycling and diving.
Wild Frontiers (☎ 020-7376 3968; www.wildfrontiers .co.uk) Adventure specialist with themed tours and innovative adventures.

USA
Asia Transpacific Journeys (☎ 800-642 2742; www .asiatranspacific.com) Group tours and tailor-made trips across the Asia-Pacific region.
Distant Horizons (☎ 800-333 1240; www.distanthori zons.com) Educational tours for discerning travellers.
Geographic Expeditions (☎ 800-777 8183; www .geoex.com) Well-established high-end adventure-travel company.
Global Adrenaline (☎ 800-825 1680) Luxury adventures for the experienced traveller.

GETTING AROUND

See p99 for general details of the region's border crossings.

AIR

Air travel is a mixed bag in the Mekong region. Some routes are now a real bargain, as no-frills regional carriers such as **Air Asia** (www .airasia.com) offer heavily discounted fares out of Bangkok. However, on many other routes, there may only be one carrier and prices are artificially high.

One of the best airlines in the region is **Bangkok Airways** (www.bangkokairways.com), billing itself Asia's boutique airline. It links some of the most popular places in the Mekong region and offers a high level of service. At the other end of the spectrum, there are several no-frills budget carriers operating out of Thailand, such as Air Asia. Among the national carriers, **Thai Airways** (www.thaiair.com) has the best reputation, but **Vietnam Airlines** (www.viet namairlines.com.vn) has upped the level of its game in recent years.

For a quick look at the most popular routes in the region, see the Mekong Region Air Routes map (p499). More detailed air routes are listed in the Transport sections of each country chapter.

A little caution is necessary when buying tickets from travel agents. Carefully check the tickets to make sure that the dates meet your specifications and confirm with the airline as soon as possible.

MEKONG REGION AIR ROUTES

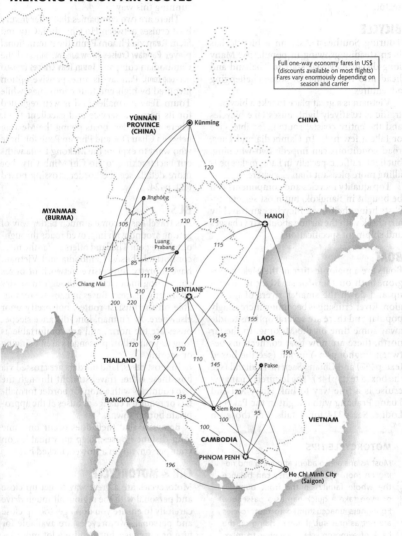

Full one-way economy fares in US$
(discounts available on most flights)
Fares vary enormously depending on
season and carrier

Most airports in Southeast Asia charge a departure tax, so make sure you keep some local currency in reserve.

Air Passes

The national airlines of Southeast Asian countries frequently run promotional deals from select Western cities or for regional travel.

Airtimetable.com (www.airtimetable.com) posts seasonal passes and promotions.

An ongoing deal is the Asean Air Pass, offered through cooperating airlines for travel in Southeast Asia; coupons cost US$130. Check with Thai Airways for more details. An even better deal is the Bangkok Airways Discovery pass which offers domestic coupons for US$60 and international coupons from US$90 per sector.

BICYCLE

Touring Southeast Asia on a bicycle has been steadily growing in popularity. Many long-distance cyclists start in Thailand and head into Indochina for some challenging adventures.

Vietnam is a great place to take a bicycle – traffic is relatively light, buses take bicycles and the entire coastal route is feasible, give or take a few hills. In Cambodia and Laos, road conditions can impede two-wheeling, but light traffic, especially in Laos, makes pedalling more pleasant than elsewhere.

Top-quality bicycles and components can be bought in Bangkok, but most serious cyclists bring their own. Bicycles can travel by air; check with the airline about extra charges and shipment specifications.

BOAT

Boats are a major feature of the Mekong region, both on the Mother River itself and up and down the smaller rivers of the region. River cruising is becoming increasingly popular and there are several options to idle away some time on the Mekong. In the far north, there are now boat connections between Jĭnghóng in Yúnnán (see the boxed text, p467) and Chiang Saen in Thailand (see the boxed text, p148). The leisurely Luangsay cruise is a fine way to link Huay Xai and Luang Prabang with a night in the Pakbeng Lodge. See p314 for details. For those on

MOTORCYCLE TIPS

Most Asians are so adept at driving and riding on motorcycles that they can balance the whole family on the front bumper, or even take a quick nap as a passenger. Foreigners unaccustomed to motorcycles are not as graceful. If you're riding on the back of a motorcycle remember to relax. For balance hold on to the back bar, not the driver's waist. Tall people should keep their long legs tucked in as most drivers are used to shorter passengers. Women (or men) wearing skirts should always ride side-saddle and collect longer skirts so that they don't catch in the wheel or drive chain. Enjoy the ride.

a budget, there are plenty of public boats running this way.

There are two companies that offer luxury boat cruises between Ho Chi Minh City and Siem Reap via Phnom Penh: the international player **Pandaw Cruises** (www.pandaw.com) and the Cambodian company **Toum Teav Cruises** (www.cf-mekong.com). Pandaw is an expensive option favoured by high-end tour companies, while Toum Teav is smaller and is well regarded for its personal service and excellent food. There are also fast boats plying the Mekong between Chau Doc and Phnom Penh for those who want to explore the Mekong Delta without backtracking to Ho Chi Minh City. For more details see the border crossing boxed text, p424.

BUS

Bus travel has become a much better way of getting around with improved roads throughout the region. Thailand offers by far the most comfortable buses. Cambodia and Vietnam have a pretty impressive network of buses connecting major cities, although these dry up in remote areas. Buses in Laos are reasonable on the busiest routes, but pretty poor elsewhere. In Yúnnán, long-distance sleeper buses are the norm, and are comfortable as long as your fellow passengers aren't singing or snoring.

In most cases, land borders are crossed via bus; these either travel straight through the two countries with a stop for border formalities or require a change of buses at the appropriate border towns.

Be aware that theft does occur on some long-distance buses; keep all valuables on your person, not in a stowed, locked bag.

CAR & MOTORCYCLE

Motorcycles are a great way to get up close and personal with the region, although drive carefully to ensure you don't get too up close and personal. Motorcycles are available for hire or purchase, but require a lot more investment and safety precautions than many visitors realise.

It is advisable to hire a car or motorcycle in a certain locality rather than depend upon it for regional travel. You could cover Thailand by car pretty easily and enjoy well-signposted, well-paved roads. Vietnam has decent roads these days, but self-drive is not possible. Road conditions in Laos and Cambodia vary, although sealed roads are slowly becoming the norm. Both countries offer brilliant motorbiking for experienced riders. In Yúnnán, the distances are just too great to really opt for driving.

Driving Licence

Self-drive car hire is only really possible in Thailand. If you are planning to do any driving, get an International Driving Permit (IDP) from your local automobile association before you leave your home country; IDPs are inexpensive and valid for one year. There are some fantastic motorbiking opportunities in the region, but it is usually a case of no licence required.

Hire

Thailand is the only place with Western car-hire chains and self-drive. However, vehicles with driver are available at very reasonable rates in the other countries of the region. For rural areas of Cambodia, Laos and Vietnam, 4WDs are necessary. Guesthouses and families rent motorcycles cheaply throughout the region, usually for around US$5 a day. In Cambodia and Laos, 250cc dirt bikes are available and are a lot of fun if you know how to handle them. In Thailand, motorbikes of every shape and size are available, but to rent a bigger bike you will need to show a licence.

Insurance

Get insurance with a motorcycle if at all possible. The more reputable motorcycle-hire places insure all their motorcycles; some will do it for an extra charge. Without insurance you're responsible for anything that happens to the bike. To be absolutely clear about your liability, ask for a written estimate of the replacement cost for a similar bike.

Insurance for a hired car is also necessary. Be sure to ask the car-hire agent about liability and damage coverage.

Motorcycle Tours

Specialised motorbike tours through Indochina are growing in popularity. It is a great way to get off the trail and explore remote regions. Two wheels can reach the parts that four wheels sometimes can't, traversing small trails and traffic-free backroads.

For specialised companies in each country, see the individual country chapters. One company that runs adventurous trips covering all

> ### SURVIVING THE STREETS
>
> Wherever you roam in the region, you'll have to cross some busy streets eventually, so go armed with this survival tip: step into the street and walk *slowly* across so that drivers can see you and drive around you. If you lack the nerve, look for locals crossing the street and walk alongside.

three countries is **Explore Indochina** (☎ 0913-524 658; www.exploreindochina.com).

Road Rules

Basically, there aren't many, arguably any. Drive cautiously. An incredible number of lives are lost on roads in this region every year, particularly around major holidays. Size matters and the biggest vehicle wins by default, regardless of circumstances – might makes right on the road. The middle of the road is typically used as an invisible third lane, even if there is oncoming traffic. And the horn is used to notify other vehicles that you intend to pass them. Be particularly careful about children on the road. It's common to find kids playing hopscotch in the middle of a major highway. Livestock on the road is also a menace; hit a cow on a motorbike and you'll both be hamburger.

Safety

Always check a vehicle thoroughly before you take it out. Look at the tyres for treads, check for oil leaks, test the brakes. You may be held liable for any problems that weren't duly noted before your departure. When driving a motorcycle, wear protective clothing and a helmet. Long trousers, long-sleeved shirts and shoes are highly recommended as protection against sunburn and as a second skin if you fall. If your helmet doesn't have a visor, then wear goggles, glasses or sunglasses to keep bugs, dust and other debris out of your eyes.

HITCHING

Hitching is never entirely safe in any country in the world and is not recommended. Travellers who decide to hitch should understand that they are taking a small but potentially serious risk. People who do choose to hitch will be safer if they travel in pairs and let someone know where they are planning to go.

Locals do flag down private and public vehicles for a lift, but some sort of payment is usually expected.

LOCAL TRANSPORT

Beyond Thailand, personal ownership of cars in the region is not that common, so local transport in towns and cities is a roaring trade. Anything motorised is often modified to carry passengers – from Thailand's obnoxious three-wheeled chariots, known as túk-túk, to the Cambodian motorbike and trailer *(remorque-moto)*. Metered taxis are now common in Thailand, Vietnam and Yúnnán, but are still few and far between in Cambodia and Laos. Motorcycle taxis are another popular way to get around, but watch out for the hot exhaust – many a visitor has returned from the region with a souvenir burn on their leg.

In large cities, extensive public bus systems either travel fixed routes or do informal loops around the city picking up passengers along the way. Bangkok, Hanoi, Ho Chi Minh City and Kūnmíng have efficient bus networks, but there is no such thing in Phnom Penh or Vientiane.

Bangkok boasts a state-of-the-art light-rail and underground system that make zipping around town feel like time travel. At the other end of the scale, the bicycle rickshaw still survives in the region, assuming such aliases as *săamláw* in Laos and Thailand and cyclo in Cambodia and Vietnam.

TRAIN

China, Thailand and Vietnam have efficient railway networks, including the option of comfortable air-con sleeper berths. Cambodia's railways are in a severely dilapidated state and passenger services have been suspended, while poor old Laos has no railways at all. Partly due to these missing links, there aren't many international trains in the region. Thai trains serve the Thai border towns of Nong Khai (for crossing into Laos) and Aranya Prathet (for crossing into Cambodia). In Vietnam, there are local trains to the Chinese border towns of Lang Son and Lao Cai. There is also a twice-weekly international service between Hanoi and Běijīng. There is a rail line connecting Hanoi and Kūnmíng, but there are no services currently operating.

Health   Dr Trish Batchelor

CONTENTS

Health issues and quality of medical facilities vary enormously depending on where and how you travel in the Mekong region. Many major cities are now very well developed, although travel to rural areas can expose you to a variety of health risks and inadequate medical care.

Travellers tend to worry about contracting infectious diseases when in the tropics, but infections are a rare cause of serious illness or death in travellers. Pre-existing medical conditions such as heart disease, and accidental injury (especially traffic accidents), account for most life-threatening problems. Becoming ill in some way, however, is relatively common. Fortunately, most common illnesses can either be prevented with some common-sense behaviour or be treated easily with a well-stocked traveller's medical kit.

The following advice is a general guide and does not replace the advice of a doctor trained in travel medicine.

BEFORE YOU GO

Pack medications in their original, clearly labelled, containers. A signed, dated letter from your physician describing your medical conditions and medications, including generic names, is a good idea. If carrying syringes or needles, be sure to have a physician's letter stating their medical necessity. If you have a heart condition, bring a copy of your ECG taken just before travelling.

If you take any regular medication, bring a double supply in case of loss or theft. In most Mekong region countries, you can buy many medications over the counter without a doctor's prescription, but it can be difficult to find some of the newer drugs, particularly the latest antidepressants, blood-pressure medications and contraceptive pills.

INSURANCE

Even if you are fit and healthy, don't travel without health insurance – accidents do happen. Declare any existing medical conditions you have – the insurance company *will* check if your problem is pre-existing and will not cover you if it is undeclared. You may require extra cover for adventure activities such as rock climbing. If your health insurance doesn't cover you for medical expenses abroad, consider getting extra insurance. If you're uninsured, emergency evacuation is expensive – bills of more than US$100,000 are not uncommon.

Find out in advance if your insurance plan will make payments directly to providers or reimburse you later for overseas health expenditures. (In many countries doctors expect payment in cash.) Some policies offer a range of medical-expense options; the higher ones are chiefly for countries that have extremely high medical costs, such as the USA. You may prefer a policy that pays doctors or hospitals directly rather than you having to pay on the spot and claim later. If you have to claim later, make sure you keep all documentation. Some policies ask you to call (reverse charges) a centre in your home country, where an immediate assessment of your problem is made.

VACCINATIONS

Specialised travel-medicine clinics are your best source of information; they stock all available vaccines and will be able to give specific recommendations for you and your trip. The doctors will take into account factors such as past vaccination history, the length of your trip, activities you may be undertaking and underlying medical conditions, such as pregnancy.

Most vaccines don't produce immunity until at least two weeks after they're given, so visit a doctor four to eight weeks before departure. Ask your doctor for an International Certificate of Vaccination (otherwise known as the yellow booklet), which will list all the vaccinations you've received.

Recommended Vaccinations

The World Health Organization (WHO) recommends the following vaccinations for travellers to the Mekong region:

Adult diphtheria and tetanus Single booster recommended if you haven't had one in the previous 10 years. Side effects include a sore arm and fever.

Hepatitis A Provides almost 100% protection for up to a year; a booster after 12 months provides at least another 20 years' protection. Mild side effects such as headache and a sore arm occur in 5% to 10% of people.

Hepatitis B Now considered routine for most travellers. Given as three shots over six months. A rapid schedule is also available, as is a combined vaccination with Hepatitis A. Side effects are mild and uncommon, usually headache and a sore arm. Lifetime protection occurs in 95% of people.

Measles, mumps and rubella (MMR) Two doses of MMR are required unless you have had the diseases. Occasionally a rash and flulike illness can develop a week after receiving the vaccine. Many young adults require a booster.

Polio In 2002, no countries in the Mekong region reported a single case of polio. Only one booster is required as an adult for lifetime protection. Inactivated polio vaccine is safe during pregnancy.

Typhoid Recommended unless your trip is less than a week long and only to developed cities. The vaccine offers around 70% protection, lasts for two to three years and comes as a single shot. Tablets are also available, but the injection is usually recommended as it has fewer side effects. A sore arm and fever may occur.

Varicella If you haven't had chickenpox, discuss this vaccination with your doctor.

The following immunisations are recommended for long-term travellers (more than one month) or those at special risk:

Japanese B Encephalitis Three injections in all. A booster is recommended after two years. A sore arm and headache are the most common side effects. A rare allergic reaction comprising hives and swelling can occur up to 10 days after any of the three doses.

Meningitis Single injection. There are two types of vaccination: the quadrivalent vaccine gives two to three years' protection; the meningitis group C vaccine gives around 10 years' protection. Recommended for long-term travellers aged under 25.

Rabies Three injections in all. A booster after one year will then provide 10 years' protection. Side effects are rare – occasionally a headache and a sore arm.

Tuberculosis (TB) A complex issue. Long-term adult travellers are usually recommended to have a TB skin test before and after travel, rather than vaccination. Only one vaccine is given in a lifetime.

Required Vaccinations

The only vaccine required by international regulations is for yellow fever. Proof of vaccination will only be required if you have visited a country in the yellow-fever zone within the six days before entering the Mekong region. If you are travelling to the Mekong region from Africa or South America you should check to see if you require proof of vaccination.

MEDICAL CHECKLIST

Recommended items for a personal medical kit:

- antibacterial cream, eg Muciprocin
- antibiotic for skin infections, eg amoxicillin/Clavulanate or Cephalexin
- antibiotics for diarrhoea, such as Norfloxacin or Ciprofloxacin; for bacterial diarrhoea Azithromycin; for giardiasis or amoebic dysentery Tinidazole
- antifungal cream, eg Clotrimazole
- antihistamine – there are many options, eg Cetrizine for daytime and Promethazine for night
- anti-inflammatory such as Ibuprofen
- antiseptic, eg Betadine
- antispasmodic for stomach cramps, eg Buscopan
- contraceptives
- decongestant, eg Pseudoephedrine
- DEET-based insect repellent
- diarrhoea treatment – consider an oral rehydration solution (eg Gastrolyte), diarrhoea 'stopper' (eg Loperamide) and anti-nausea medication (eg Prochlorperazine)
- first-aid items such as scissors, plasters, bandages, gauze, thermometer (but not one with mercury), sterile needles and syringes, safety pins and tweezers
- indigestion medication, eg Quickeze or Mylanta

- iodine tablets (unless you are pregnant or have a thyroid problem) to purify water
- laxative, eg Coloxyl
- migraine medication – sufferers should take personal medicine
- paracetamol
- Permethrin to impregnate clothing and mosquito nets
- steroid cream for allergic or itchy rashes, eg 1% to 2% hydrocortisone
- sunscreen and hat
- throat lozenges
- thrush (vaginal yeast infection) treatment, eg Clotrimazole pessaries or Diflucan tablet
- Ural or equivalent if you're prone to urine infections

ONLINE RESOURCES

There is a wealth of travel health advice on the internet. For further information, **Lonely Planet** (www.lonelyplanet.com) is a good place to start. The **World Health Organization** (www.who.int/ith) publishes a superb book called *International Travel & Health*, which is revised annually and is available online at no cost. Another website of general interest is **MD Travel Health** (www.mdtravelhealth.com), which provides complete travel health recommendations for every country and is updated daily. The **Centers for Disease Control & Prevention** (CDC; www.cdc.gov) website also has good general information.

FURTHER READING

Lonely Planet's *Healthy Travel – Asia & India* is a handy pocket-size book that is packed with useful information, including pretrip planning, emergency first aid, immunisation and disease information, and what to do if you get sick on the road. Other recommended references include *Traveller's Health* by Dr Richard Dawood and *Travelling Well* by Dr Deborah Mills – check out www.travelling well.com.au.

IN TRANSIT

DEEP VEIN THROMBOSIS (DVT)

Deep vein thrombosis (DVT) occurs when blood clots form in the legs during plane flights, chiefly because of prolonged immobility. The longer the flight, the greater the risk. Although most blood clots are reabsorbed uneventfully, some may break off and travel through the blood vessels to the lungs, where they may cause life-threatening complications.

The chief symptom of DVT is swelling or pain of the foot, ankle or calf, usually but not always on just one side. When a blood clot travels to the lungs, it may cause chest pain and difficulty in breathing. Travellers with any of these symptoms should immediately seek medical attention.

To prevent the development of DVT on long flights you should walk about the cabin, perform isometric compressions of the leg muscles (ie contract the leg muscles while sitting), drink plenty of fluids and avoid alcohol and tobacco.

JET LAG & MOTION SICKNESS

Jet lag is common when crossing more than five time zones; it causes insomnia, fatigue, malaise or nausea. To avoid jet lag try drinking plenty of (nonalcoholic) fluids and eating light meals. Upon arrival, seek exposure to natural sunlight and readjust your schedule (for meals, sleep etc) as soon as possible.

Antihistamines such as dimenhydrinate (Dramamine) and meclizine (Antivert or Bonine) are usually the first choice for treating motion sickness. The main side effect of antihistamines is drowsiness. A herbal alternative is ginger, which works like a charm for some people.

IN THE MEKONG REGION

AVAILABILITY OF HEALTH CARE

Most capital cities in the Mekong region now have clinics that cater specifically to travellers and expats. These clinics are usually more expensive than local medical facilities, but are worth utilising, as they will offer a superior standard of care. Additionally, they understand the local system and are aware of the safest local hospitals and best specialists. They can also liaise with insurance companies should you require evacuation. Recommended clinics are listed under Information in the capital city sections of country chapters in this book.

It is difficult to find medical care in rural areas. Your embassy and insurance company are good contacts.

Self-treatment may be appropriate if your problem is minor (eg traveller's diarrhoea), you are carrying the appropriate medication and you cannot attend a recommended clinic. If you think you may have a serious disease, especially malaria, do not waste time – travel to the nearest quality facility to receive attention. It is always better to be assessed by a doctor than to rely on self-treatment.

Buying medication over the counter is not recommended, as fake medications and poorly stored or out-of-date drugs are common.

The standard of care in the Mekong region varies from country to country:

Cambodia There are a couple of international clinics in Phnom Penh, and one in Siem Reap, that provide primary care and emergency stabilisation.

Laos There are no good facilities in Laos; the nearest acceptable facilities are in northern Thailand. The Australian Embassy Clinic treats citizens of Commonwealth countries.

Thailand There are some very good facilities in Thailand, particularly in Bangkok. This is the city of choice for expats living in the Mekong region who require specialised care.

Vietnam Government hospitals are overcrowded and basic. In order to treat foreigners, a facility needs to obtain a special licence, and so far only a few have been provided. The private clinics in Hanoi and Ho Chi Minh City should be your first port of call. They are familiar with the local resources and can organise evacuations if necessary.

Yúnnán (China) Kūnmíng has international-standard facilities, but elsewhere options are more limited. Smaller cities have good clinics, but limited options in the event of a serious problem.

INFECTIOUS DISEASES
Cutaneous Larva Migrans
Risk All countries.

This disease, caused by dog hookworm, is common on the beaches of Thailand. The rash starts as a small lump, then slowly spreads in a linear fashion. It is intensely itchy, especially at night. It is easily treated with medications and should not be cut out or frozen.

Dengue
Risk All countries.

This mosquito-borne disease is becoming increasingly problematic throughout the Mekong region, especially in the cities. As there is no vaccine available it can only be prevented by avoiding mosquito bites. The mosquito that carries dengue bites day and night, so use insect-avoidance measures at all times. Symptoms include high fever, severe headache and body ache (dengue used to be known as breakbone fever). Some people develop a rash and experience diarrhoea. There is no specific treatment, just rest and paracetamol – do not take aspirin as it increases the likelihood of haemorrhaging. See a doctor to be diagnosed and monitored.

Filariasis
Risk All countries.

This mosquito-borne disease is very common in the local population, yet very rare in travellers. Mosquito-avoidance measures are the best way to prevent this disease.

Hepatitis A
Risk All countries.

A problem throughout the region, this food- and water-borne virus infects the liver, causing jaundice (yellow skin and eyes), nausea and lethargy. There is no specific treatment for hepatitis A; you just need to allow time for the liver to heal. All travellers to the Mekong region should be vaccinated against hepatitis A.

Hepatitis B
Risk All countries.

The only sexually transmitted disease that can be prevented by vaccination, hepatitis B is spread by body fluids, including sexual contact. In some parts of the Mekong region, up to 20% of the population carry hepatitis B, and usually are unaware of this. The long-term consequences can include liver cancer and cirrhosis.

Hepatitis E
Risk All countries.

Hepatitis E is transmitted through contaminated food and water and has similar symptoms to hepatitis A, but is far less common. It is a severe problem in pregnant women and can result in the death of both mother and baby. There is currently no vaccine, and prevention is by following safe eating and drinking guidelines.

HIV
Risk All countries.

HIV is now one of the most common causes of death in people under the age of 50 in Thailand. The country in the region with the worst and most rapidly increasing HIV problem is Vietnam, plus Yúnnán province. Heterosexual sex is now the main method of transmission in these countries.

Influenza

Risk All countries.

Present year-round in the tropics, influenza (flu) symptoms include high fever, muscle aches, runny nose, cough and sore throat. It can be very severe in people over the age of 65 or in those with underlying medical conditions such as heart disease or diabetes; vaccination is recommended for these individuals. There is no specific treatment, just rest and paracetamol.

Japanese B Encephalitis

Risk All countries.

While rare in travellers, this viral disease, transmitted by mosquitoes, infects at least 50,000 locals each year. Most cases occur in rural areas and vaccination is recommended for travellers spending more than one month outside of cities. There is no treatment, and a third of infected people will die while another third will suffer permanent brain damage. Highest-risk areas include Thailand and Vietnam.

Malaria

Risk All countries.

For such a serious and potentially deadly disease, there is an enormous amount of misinformation concerning malaria. You must get expert advice about whether your trip will actually put you at risk. Many parts of the Mekong region, particularly city and resort areas, have minimal to no risk of malaria, and the risk of side effects from the prevention tablets may outweigh the risk of actually getting the disease. For most rural areas in the region, however, the risk of contracting the disease far outweighs the risk of any tablet side effects. Remember that malaria can be fatal. Before you travel, seek medical advice on the right medication and dosage for you.

Malaria is caused by a parasite transmitted by the bite of an infected mosquito. The most important symptom of malaria is fever, but general symptoms such as headache, diarrhoea, cough or chills may also occur. Diagnosis can only be made by taking a blood sample.

Two strategies should be combined to prevent malaria – mosquito avoidance and antimalarial medications. Most people who catch malaria are taking inadequate or no antimalarial medication.

Travellers are advised to prevent mosquito bites by taking the following steps:

- Use a DEET-containing insect repellent on exposed skin. Wash this off at night, as long as you are sleeping under a mosquito net. Natural repellents such as citronella can be effective, but must be applied more frequently than products containing DEET.
- Sleep under a mosquito net that is impregnated with Permethrin.
- Choose accommodation with screens and fans (if not air-conditioned).
- Impregnate clothing with Permethrin in high-risk areas.
- Wear long sleeves and trousers in light colours.
- Use mosquito coils.
- Spray your room with insect repellent before going out for your evening meal.

There are a variety of medications available. Derivatives of Artesunate are not suitable as a preventive medication. They are useful treatments under medical supervision.

The effectiveness of the Chloroquine and Paludrine combination is now limited in most of the Mekong region. Common side effects include nausea (40% of people) and mouth ulcers. Generally not recommended.

SCORCHED OUEF POLICY

There have been periodic outbreaks of avian influenza (bird flu) in the Mekong region in the past few years. Dozens of people have died and the threat of human-to-human transmission remains very real. Now the H5-N1 strain has gone global, Asia is no longer in the spotlight, but this remains a region with the greatest concentration of cases. When outbreaks occur, eggs and poultry are usually banished from the menu in hotels and restaurants in parts of Thailand and Vietnam. Even where eggs are available, we recommend a 'scorched ouef' policy. Ensure they are well cooked in whatever shape or form they come. No runny omelettes, no sunny side up. Don't take risks or you might end up with egg on your face.

The daily Doxycycline tablet is a broad-spectrum antibiotic that has the added benefit of helping to prevent a variety of tropical diseases, including leptospirosis, tick-borne disease, typhus and meliodosis. The potential side effects include photosensitivity (a tendency to sunburn), thrush in women, indigestion, heartburn, nausea and interference with the contraceptive pill. More serious side effects include ulceration of the oesophagus – you can help prevent this by taking your tablet with a meal and a large glass of water, and never lying down within half an hour of taking it. It must be taken for four weeks after leaving the risk area.

Lariam (Mefloquine) has received much bad press, some of it justified, some not. This weekly tablet suits many people. Serious side effects are rare but include depression, anxiety, psychosis and seizures. Anyone with a history of depression, anxiety, other psychological disorders, or epilepsy should not take Lariam. It is considered safe in the second and third trimesters of pregnancy. It is around 90% effective in most parts of the Mekong region, but there is significant resistance in parts of northern Thailand, Laos and Cambodia. Tablets must be taken for four weeks after leaving the risk area.

Malarone is a combination of Atovaquone and Proguanil. Side effects are uncommon and mild, most commonly nausea and headache. It is the best tablet for scuba divers and for those on short trips to high-risk areas. It must be taken for one week after leaving the risk area.

A final option is to take no preventive medication but to have a supply of emergency medication should you develop the symptoms of malaria. This is less than ideal, and you'll need to get to a good medical facility within 24 hours of developing a fever. If you choose this option the most effective and safest treatment is Malarone (four tablets once daily for three days). Other options include Mefloquine and Quinine, but the side effects of these drugs at treatment doses make them less desirable. Fansidar is no longer recommended.

Measles

Risk All countries.

Measles remains a problem in some parts of the Mekong region. This highly contagious bacterial infection is spread via coughing and sneezing. Most people born before 1966 are immune as they had the disease in childhood. Measles starts with a high fever and rash and can be complicated by pneumonia and brain disease. There is no specific treatment.

Meliodosis

Risk Cambodia, Laos and Thailand.

This infection is contracted by skin contact with soil. It is rare in travellers, but in some parts of northeast Thailand up to 30% of the local population is infected. The symptoms are very similar to those experienced by tuberculosis sufferers. There is no vaccine but it can be treated with medications.

Rabies

Risk All countries.

Still a common problem in most parts of the Mekong region, this uniformly fatal disease is spread by the bite or lick of an infected animal – most commonly a dog or monkey. You should seek medical advice immediately after any animal bite and commence postexposure treatment. Having pretravel vaccination means the postbite treatment is greatly simplified. If an animal bites you, gently wash the wound with soap and water, and apply iodine-based antiseptic. If you are not prevaccinated you will need to receive rabies immunoglobulin as soon as possible.

Schistosomiasis

Risk All countries.

Schistosomiasis is a tiny parasite that enters your skin after you've been swimming in contaminated water – travellers usually only get a light infection and hence have no symptoms. If you are concerned, you can be tested three months after exposure. On rare occasions, travellers may develop 'Katayama fever'. This occurs some weeks after exposure, as the parasite passes through the lungs and causes an allergic reaction – symptoms are coughing and fever. Schistosomiasis is easily treated with medications.

Sexually Transmitted Diseases (STDS)

Risk All countries.

Sexually transmitted diseases (STDs) most common in the Mekong region include herpes, warts, syphilis, gonorrhoea and chlamydia. People carrying these diseases often have no signs of infection. Condoms will prevent gonorrhoea and chlamydia but not warts or herpes. If after a sexual encounter you develop any rash, lumps, discharge, or pain when passing urine, seek immediate medical attention. If you have been sexually active during your travels, have an STD check on your return home.

Strongyloides
Risk Cambodia, Laos and Thailand.

This parasite, transmitted by skin contact with soil, is common in travellers but rarely affects them. It is characterised by an unusual skin rash called *larva currens* – a linear rash on the trunk that comes and goes. Most people don't have other symptoms until their immune system becomes severely suppressed, when the parasite can cause an overwhelming infection. It can be treated with medications.

Tuberculosis
Risk All countries.

While rare in travellers, medical and aid workers and long-term travellers who have significant contact with the local population should take precautions. Vaccination is usually only given to children under the age of five, but adults at risk are recommended to have pre- and post-travel TB testing. The main symptoms are fever, cough, weight loss, night sweats and tiredness.

Typhoid
Risk All countries.

This serious bacterial infection is spread via food and water. It gives a high and slowly progressive fever, headache and may be accompanied by a dry cough and stomach pain. Typhoid is diagnosed by blood tests and treated with antibiotics. Vaccination is recommended for all travellers spending more than one week in the Mekong region, or travelling outside of the major cities. Be aware that vaccination is not 100% effective so you must still be careful with what you eat and drink.

Typhus
Risk All countries.

Murine typhus is spread by the bite of a flea, whereas scrub typhus is spread via a mite. These diseases are rare in travellers. Symptoms include fever, muscle pains and a rash. You can avoid these diseases by following general insect-avoidance measures. Doxycycline will also prevent them.

TRAVELLER'S DIARRHOEA
Traveller's diarrhoea is by far the most common problem that affects travellers – between 30% and 50% of people will suffer from it within two weeks of starting their trip. In over 80% of cases, traveller's diarrhoea is caused by bacteria (there are numerous potential culprits), and therefore responds promptly to treatment with antibiotics. Treatment will depend on your situation – how sick you are, how quickly you need to get better, where you are etc.

Traveller's diarrhoea is defined as the passage of more than three watery bowel-actions within 24 hours, plus at least one other symptom such as fever, cramps, nausea, vomiting or feeling generally unwell.

Treatment consists of staying well hydrated; rehydration solutions such as Gastrolyte are the best for this. Antibiotics such as Norfloxacin, Ciprofloxacin or Azithromycin will kill the bacteria quickly.

Loperamide is just a 'stopper' and doesn't get to the cause of the problem. It can be helpful, for example, if you have to go on a long bus ride. Don't take Loperamide if you have a fever, or blood in your stools. Seek medical attention quickly if you do not respond to an appropriate antibiotic.

Amoebic Dysentery
Amoebic dysentery is very rare in travellers but is often misdiagnosed by poor quality labs in the Mekong region. Symptoms are similar to bacterial diarrhoea, ie fever, bloody diarrhoea and generally feeling unwell. You should always seek reliable medical care if you have blood in your diarrhoea. Treatment involves two drugs: Tinidazole or Metronidazole to kill the parasite in your gut and then a second drug to kill the cysts. If left untreated, complications such as liver or gut abscesses can occur.

Giardiasis
Giardia lamblia is a relatively common parasite in travellers. Symptoms include nausea, bloating, excess gas, fatigue and intermittent diarrhoea. 'Eggy' burps are often attributed solely to giardiasis, but work in Nepal has shown that they are not specific to this infection. The parasite will eventually go away if left untreated but this can take months. The treatment of choice is Tinidazole, with Metronidazole being a second option.

ENVIRONMENTAL HAZARDS
Air Pollution

Air pollution, particularly vehicle pollution, is an increasing problem in most of the Mekong region's major cities. If you have severe respiratory problems speak with your doctor before travelling to any heavily polluted urban centres. This pollution also causes minor respiratory problems such as sinusitis, dry throat and irritated eyes. If troubled by the pollution, leave the city for a few days and get some fresh air.

Diving

Divers and surfers should seek specialised advice before they travel, to ensure their medical kit contains treatment for coral cuts and tropical ear infections, as well as the standard problems. Divers should ensure their insurance covers them for decompression illness – get specialised dive insurance through an organisation such as **Divers Alert Network** (DAN; www.danseap.org). Have a dive medical before you leave your home country; there are certain medical conditions that are incompatible with diving, and economic considerations may override health considerations for some dive operators in Cambodia and Vietnam.

Food

Eating in restaurants is the biggest risk factor for contracting traveller's diarrhoea. Ways to avoid diarrhoea include eating only freshly cooked food, and avoiding shellfish and food that has been sitting around in buffets. Peel all fruit, cook vegetables and soak salads in iodine water for at least 20 minutes. Eat in busy restaurants where there is a high turnover of customers.

Heat

Many parts of the Mekong region are hot and humid throughout the year. For most people it takes at least two weeks to adapt to the hot climate. Swelling of the feet and ankles is common, as are muscle cramps caused by excessive sweating. Prevent these by avoiding dehydration and excessive activity in the heat. Take it easy when you first arrive. Don't eat salt tablets (they aggravate the gut), but drinking rehydration solution or eating salty food helps. Treat cramps by stopping activity, resting, rehydrating with double-strength rehydration solution and gently stretching.

DRINKING WATER

- Never drink tap water.
- Bottled water is generally safe – check the seal is intact at purchase.
- Avoid fresh juices – they may have been watered down.
- Boiling water is the most efficient method of purifying it.
- The best chemical purifier is iodine. It should not be used by pregnant women or those people who suffer with thyroid problems.
- Water filters should filter out viruses. Ensure your filter has a chemical barrier such as iodine and a small pore size, ie less than four microns.

Dehydration is the main contributor to heat exhaustion. Symptoms include weakness, headache, irritability, nausea or vomiting, sweaty skin, a fast, weak pulse, and a normal or slightly elevated body temperature. Treatment involves getting out of the heat and/or sun, fanning the person and applying cool wet cloths to the skin, laying the person flat with their legs raised, and rehydrating them with water containing a quarter of a teaspoon of salt per litre. Recovery is usually rapid and it is common to feel weak for some days afterwards.

Heat stroke is a serious medical emergency. Symptoms come on suddenly and include weakness, nausea, a hot, dry body with a body temperature of more than 41°C, dizziness, confusion, loss of coordination, seizures and eventually collapse and loss of consciousness. Seek medical help and commence cooling by getting the person out of the heat, removing their clothes, fanning them and applying cool, wet cloths or ice to their body, especially to the groin and armpits.

Prickly heat is a common skin rash in the tropics, caused by sweat being trapped under the skin. The result is an itchy rash of tiny lumps. Treat by moving out of the heat and into an air-conditioned area for a few hours and by having cool showers. Creams and ointments clog the skin so they should be avoided. Locally bought prickly-heat powder can be helpful.

Tropical fatigue is common in long-term expats based in the tropics. It's rarely due to disease and is caused by the climate, inadequate mental rest, excessive alcohol intake and the demands of daily work in a different culture.

Insect Bites & Stings

Bedbugs don't carry disease but their bites are very itchy. They live in the cracks of furniture and walls and then migrate to the bed at night to feed on you. You can treat the itch with an antihistamine.

Lice inhabit various parts of your body but most commonly your head and pubic area. Transmission is via close contact with an infected person. Lice can be difficult to treat and you may need numerous applications of an antilice shampoo such as Permethrin. Pubic lice are usually contracted from sexual contact.

Ticks are contracted after walking in rural areas. They are commonly found behind the ears, on the belly and in armpits. If you have had a tick bite and experience symptoms such as a rash at the site of the bite or elsewhere, or fever or muscle aches, you should see a doctor. Doxycycline prevents tick-borne diseases.

Leeches are found in humid rainforest areas. They do not transmit any disease but their bites are often intensely itchy for weeks afterwards and can easily become infected. Apply an iodine-based antiseptic to any leech bite to help prevent infection.

Bee and wasp stings mainly cause problems for people who are allergic to them. Anyone with a serious bee or wasp allergy should carry an injection of adrenaline (eg an Epipen) for emergency treatment. For others, pain is the main problem – apply ice to the sting and take painkillers.

Most jellyfish in the waters of Cambodia and Vietnam are not dangerous, just irritating. First aid for jellyfish stings involves pouring vinegar onto the affected area to neutralise the poison. Do not rub sand or water onto the stings. Take painkillers, and if you feel ill in any way after being stung seek medical advice. Take local advice if there are dangerous jellyfish around and keep out of the water.

Parasites

Numerous parasites are common in local populations in the Mekong region; however, most of these are rare in travellers. The two rules for avoiding parasitic infections are to wear shoes and to avoid eating raw food, especially fish, pork and vegetables. A number of parasites are transmitted via the skin by walking barefoot, including strongyloides, hookworm and cutaneous *larva migrans*.

Skin Problems

Fungal rashes are common in humid climates. There are two common fungal rashes that affect travellers. The first occurs in moist areas that get less air, such as the groin, armpits and between the toes. It starts as a red patch that slowly spreads and is usually itchy. Treatment involves keeping the skin dry, avoiding chafing and using an antifungal cream such as Clotrimazole or Lamisil. *Tinea versicolor* is also common – this fungus causes small, light-coloured patches, most commonly on the back, chest and shoulders. Consult a doctor.

Cuts and scratches become easily infected in humid climates. Take meticulous care of any cuts and scratches to prevent complications such as abscesses. Immediately wash all wounds in clean water and apply antiseptic. If you develop signs of infection (increasing pain and redness), see a doctor. Divers and snorkellers should be particularly careful with coral cuts as they can be easily infected.

Snakes

The Mekong region is home to many species of both poisonous and harmless snakes. Assume that all snakes are poisonous and never try to catch one. Always wear boots and long pants if walking in an area that may have snakes. First aid in the event of a snakebite involves pressure immobilisation via an elastic bandage firmly wrapped around the affected limb, starting at the bite site and working up towards the chest. The bandage should not be so tight that the circulation is cut off, and the fingers or toes should be kept free so the circulation can be checked. Immobilise the limb with a splint and carry the victim to medical attention. Do not use tourniquets or try to suck the venom out. Antivenin is available for most species.

Sunburn

Even on a cloudy day sunburn can occur rapidly. Always use a strong sunscreen (at least factor 30), making sure to reapply after a swim, and always wear a wide-brimmed hat and sunglasses outdoors. Avoid lying in the sun during the hottest part of the day (10am to 2pm). If you become sunburnt, stay out of the sun until you have recovered, apply cool compresses and take painkillers for the discomfort. One percent hydrocortisone cream applied twice daily is also helpful.

WOMEN'S HEALTH

Pregnant women should receive specialised advice before travelling. The ideal time to travel is in the second trimester (between 16 and 28 weeks), when the risk of pregnancy-related problems is at its lowest and pregnant women generally feel at their best. During the first trimester there is a risk of miscarriage and in the third trimester complications such as premature labour and high blood pressure are possible. It's wise to travel with a companion. Always carry a list of quality medical facilities available at your destination and ensure you continue your standard antenatal care at these facilities. Avoid rural travel in areas with poor transportation and medical facilities. Most of all, ensure travel insurance covers all pregnancy-related possibilities, including premature labour.

Malaria is a high-risk disease during pregnancy. WHO recommends that pregnant women do *not* travel to areas where there is Chloroquine-resistant malaria. None of the more effective antimalarial drugs is completely safe in pregnancy.

Traveller's diarrhoea can quickly lead to dehydration and result in inadequate blood flow to the placenta. Many of the drugs used to treat various diarrhoea bugs are not recommended in pregnancy. Azithromycin is considered safe.

In the urban areas of the Mekong region, supplies of sanitary products are readily available. Birth control options may be limited so bring adequate supplies of your own form of contraception. Heat, humidity and antibiotics can all contribute to thrush. Treatment is with antifungal creams and pessaries such as Clotrimazole. A practical alternative is a single tablet of Fluconazole (Diflucan). Urinary tract infections can be precipitated by dehydration or long bus journeys without toilet stops; bring suitable antibiotics.

TRADITIONAL MEDICINE

Throughout the Mekong region, the traditional medical systems are widely practised. There is a big difference between these traditional healing systems and 'folk' medicine. Folk remedies should be avoided, as they often involve rather dubious procedures with potential complications. In contrast, traditional healing systems such as traditional Chinese medicine are well respected, and aspects of them are being increasingly utilised by Western medical practitioners.

All traditional Asian medical systems identify a vital life force, and see blockage or imbalance as causing disease. Techniques such as herbal medicines, massage and acupuncture are used to bring this vital force back into balance, or to maintain balance. These therapies are best used for treating chronic disease such as chronic fatigue, arthritis, irritable bowel syndrome and some chronic skin conditions. Traditional medicines should be avoided for treating serious acute infections such as malaria.

Be aware that 'natural' doesn't always mean 'safe', and there can be drug interactions between herbal medicines and Western medicines. If you are using both systems ensure you inform each practitioner what the other has prescribed.

Language

CONTENTS

This language guide offers useful words and phrases for basic communication in the five main languages spoken in the regions covered by this book. For more comprehensive coverage of these languages we recommend Lonely Planet phrasebooks: the *Southeast Asia Phrasebook* for Khmer, Lao, Thai and Vietnamese, and the *Mandarin Phrasebook* for Chinese.

KHMER

PRONUNCIATION

The pronunciation guide below covers the trickier parts of the transliteration system used in this chapter. It uses the Roman alphabet to give the closest equivalent to the sounds of the Khmer language. The best way to improve your pronunciation is to listen carefully to native speakers.

Vowels

Vowels and diphthongs with an **h** at the end should be pronounced hard and aspirated (with a puff of air).

aa	as the 'a' in 'father'
a, **ah**	shorter and harder than **aa**
i	as in 'kit'
uh	as the 'u' in 'but'
ii	as the 'ee' in 'feet'
ei	a combination of **uh** and **ii** above
eu	like saying 'oo' while keeping the lips spread flat rather than rounded
euh	as **eu** above; pronounced short and hard
oh	as the 'o' in 'hose'; pronounced short and hard
ow	as in 'glow'
u	as the 'u' in 'flute'; pronounced short and hard
uu	as the 'oo' in 'zoo'
ua	as the 'ou' in 'tour'
uah	as **ua** above; pronounced short and hard
aa-œ	a tricky one that has no English equivalent; like a combination of **aa** and **œ**
œ	as 'er' in 'her', but more open
eua	combination of **eu** and **a**
ia	as 'ee-ya'; like the 'ee' in 'beer' without the 'r'
e	as in 'they'
ai	as in 'aisle'
ae	as the 'a' in 'cat'
ay	as **ai** above, but slightly more nasal
ey	as in 'prey'
ao	as the 'ow' in 'cow'
av	no English equivalent; sounds like a very nasal **ao**. The final 'v' is not pronounced.
euv	no English equivalent; sounds like a very nasal **eu**. The final 'v' is not pronounced.
ohm	as the 'ome' in 'home'
am	as the 'um' in 'glum'
oam	a combination of 'o' and 'am'
eah	combination of 'e' and 'ah'; pronounced short and hard
ih	as the 'ee' in 'teeth'; pronounced short and hard
eh	as the 'a' in 'date'; pronounced short and hard
awh	as the 'aw' in 'jaw'; pronounced short and hard
oah	a combination of 'o' and 'ah'; pronounced short and hard
aw	as the 'aw' in 'jaw'

Consonants

Khmer uses some consonant combinations that may sound rather bizarre to Western ears and be equally difficult for Western tongues, eg 'j-r' in *j'rook* (pig), or 'ch-ng' in *ch'ngain* (delicious). For ease of pronunciation, in this guide these types of consonants are separated with an apostrophe.

k	as the 'g' in 'go'
kh	as the 'k' in 'kind'
ng	as the 'ng' in 'sing'; a difficult sound for Westerners to emulate. Practise by repeating 'singing-nging-nging-nging' until you can say 'nging' clearly.
j	as in 'jump'
ch	as in 'cheese'
ny	as in 'canyon'
t	a hard, unaspirated 't' sound with no direct equivalent in English. Similar to the 't' in 'stand'.
th	as the 't' in 'two', never as the 'th' in 'thanks'

p	a hard, unaspirated 'p' sound, as the final 'p' in 'puppy'
ph	as the 'p' in 'pond', never as 'f'
r	as in 'rum', but hard and rolling, with the tongue flapping against the palate. In rapid conversation it is often omitted entirely.
w	as in 'would'. Contrary to the common transliteration system, there is no equivalent to the English 'v' sound in Khmer.

ACCOMMODATION

Where is a (cheap) hotel?
sahnthaakia/ohtail (thaok) neuv ai naa?
សណ្ឋាគារ/អូតែល(ថោក)នៅឯណា?

Do you have a room?
niak mian bantohp tohmne te?
អ្នកមានបន្ទប់ទំនេរទេ?

How much is it per day?
damlay muy th'ngay pohnmaan?
តំលៃមួយថ្ងៃប៉ុន្មាន?

I'd like a room ...
kh'nyohm sohm bantohp ...
ខ្ញុំសុំបន្ទប់ ...

  for one person
  samruhp muy niak
  សំរាប់មួយនាក់

  for two people
  samruhp pii niak
  សំរាប់ពីរនាក់

  with a bathroom
  dail mian bantohp tuhk
  ដែលមានបន្ទប់ទឹក

  with a fan
  dail mian dawnghahl
  ដែលមានកង្ហារ

  with a window
  dail mian bawng-uit
  ដែលមានបង្អួច

CONVERSATION & ESSENTIALS
Forms of Address

The Khmer language reflects the social standing of the speaker and subject through various personal pronouns and 'politeness words'. These range from the simple *baat* for men and *jaa* for women, placed at the end of a sentence, meaning 'yes' or 'I agree', to the very formal and archaic *Reachasahp* or 'Royal language', a separate vocabulary reserved for addressing the King and very high officials. Many of the pronouns are determined on the basis of the subject's age and sex in relation to the speaker. Foreigners are not expected to know all of these forms. The easiest and most general personal pronoun is *niak* (you), which may be used in most situations, with either sex. Men of your age or older may be called *lowk* (Mister). Women of your age or older can be called *bawng srei* (older sister) or for more formal situations, *lowk srei* (Madam). *Bawng* is a good informal, neutral pronoun for men or women who are (or appear to be) older than you. For third person, male or female, singular or plural, the respectful form is *koat* and the common form is *ke*.

Hello.
johm riab sua/sua s'dei　ជំរាបសួរ/សួស្តី

Goodbye.
lia suhn hao-y　លាសិនហើយ

See you later.
juab kh'nia th'ngay krao-y　ជួបគ្នាថ្ងៃក្រោយ

Yes.
baat (used by men)　បាទ
jaa (used by women)　ចាស

No.
te　ទេ

Please.
sohm　សូម

Thank you.
aw kohn　អរគុណ

Excuse me/I'm sorry.
sohm toh　សុំទោស

Hi. How are you?
niak sohk sabaay te?　អ្នកសុខសប្បាយទេ?

I'm fine.
kh'nyohm sohk sabaay　ខ្ញុំសុខសប្បាយ

Where are you going?
niak teuv naa?　អ្នកទៅណា? (a very common question used when meeting people, even strangers; an exact answer isn't necessary)

Does any one here speak English?
tii nih mian niak jeh phiasaa awngle te?
ទីនេះមានអ្នកចេះភាសាអង់គ្លេសទេ?

I don't understand.
kh'nyohm muhn yuhl te/kh'nyohm s'dap muhn baan te
ខ្ញុំមិនយល់ទេ/ខ្ញុំស្តាប់មិនបានទេ

DIRECTIONS

How can I get to ...?
phleuv naa teuv ..?　ផ្លូវណាទៅ ...?

Is it far?
wia neuv ch'ngaay te?　វានៅឆ្ងាយទេ?

Is it near here?
wia neuv juht nih te?　វានៅជិតនេះទេ?

Go straight ahead.
teuv trawng　ទៅត្រង់

Turn left.
bawt ch'weng　បត់ឆ្វេង

Turn right.
bawt s'dam　បត់ស្តាំ

EMERGENCIES – KHMER

Help!
juay kh'nyohm phawng! ជួយខ្ញុំផង!
Call a doctor!
juay hav kruu paet mao! ជួយហៅគ្រូពេទ្យមក!
Call the police!
juay hav polih mao! ជួយហៅប៉ូលីសមក!
Where are the toilets?
bawngkohn neuv ai naa? បង្គន់នៅឯណា?

NUMBERS & AMOUNTS

Khmers count in increments of five. Thus, after reaching the number five (*bram*), the cycle begins again with the addition of one, ie 'five-one' (*bram muy*), 'five-two' (*bram pii*) and so on to 10, which begins a new cycle. This system is a bit awkward at first (for example, 18, which has three parts: 10, five and three) but with practice it can be mastered.

You may be confused by a colloquial form of counting that reverses the word order for numbers between 10 and 20 and separates the two words with *duhn: pii duhn dawp* for 12, *bei duhn dawp* for 13, *bram buan duhn dawp* for 19 and so on. This form is often used in markets, so listen keenly.

1	muy	មួយ
2	pii	ពីរ
3	bei	បី
4	buan	បួន
5	bram	ប្រាំ
6	bram muy	ប្រាំមួយ
7	bram pii/puhl	ប្រាំពីរ
8	bram bei	ប្រាំបី
9	bram buan	ប្រាំបួន
10	dawp	ដប់
11	dawp muy	ដប់មួយ
12	dawp pii	ដប់ពីរ
16	dawp bram muy	ដប់ប្រាំមួយ
20	m'phei	ម្ភៃ
21	m'phei muy	ម្ភៃមួយ
30	saamsuhp	សាមសិប
40	saisuhp	សែសិប
100	muy roy	មួយរយ
1000	muy poan	មួយពាន់
1,000,000	muy lian	មួយលាន

SHOPPING & SERVICES

I'm looking for the ...
kh'nyohm rohk ... ខ្ញុំរក ...
Where is a/the ...
... neuv ai naa? ... នៅឯណា?
bank
th'niakia ធនាគារ
hospital
mohntii paet មន្ទីរពេទ្យ
market
p'saa ផ្សារ
police station
poh polih/ ប៉ុស្តិ៍ប៉ូលីស/
s'thaanii nohkohbaal ស្ថានីយនគរបាល
post office
praisuhnii ប្រៃសណីយ
public telephone
turasahp saathiaranah ទូរស័ព្ទសាធារណៈ
public toilet
bawngkohn saathiaranah បង្គន់សាធារណៈ

How much is it?
nih th'lay pohnmaan? នេះថ្លៃប៉ុន្មាន?
That's too much.
th'lay pek ថ្លៃពេក

TIME & DAYS

What time is it?
eileuv nih maong pohnmaan? ពេលនេះម៉ោងប៉ុន្មាន?
today
th'ngay nih ថ្ងៃនេះ
tomorrow
th'ngay s'aik ថ្ងៃស្អែក

Monday
th'ngay jahn ថ្ងៃចន្ទ
Tuesday
th'ngay ahngkia ថ្ងៃអង្គារ
Wednesday
th'ngay poht ថ្ងៃពុធ
Thursday
th'ngay prohoah ថ្ងៃព្រហស្បតិ៍
Friday
th'ngay sohk ថ្ងៃសុក្រ
Saturday
th'ngay sav ថ្ងៃសៅរ៍
Sunday
th'ngay aatuht ថ្ងៃអាទិត្យ

LANGUAGE

TRANSPORT

What time does the ... leave?

... jein maong pohnmaan? ... ចេញម៉ោងប៉ុន្មាន?

boat
duk ទូក

bus
laan ch'nual ឡានឈ្នួល

train
roht plœng រថភ្លើង

plane
yohn hawh/k'pal hawh យន្តហោះ/កប៉ាល់ហោះ

airport
wial yohn hawh វាលយន្តហោះ

bus station
kuhnlaing laan ch'nual កន្លែងឡានឈ្នួល

bus stop
jamnawt laan ch'nual ចំណតឡានឈ្នួល

train station
s'thaanii roht plœng ស្ថានីយរថភ្លើង

LAO

PRONUNCIATION
Vowels

i	as in 'it'
ii	as in 'feet' or 'tea'
ai	as in 'aisle'
aa	long 'a' as in 'father'
a	half as long as **aa** above
ae	as the 'a' in 'bad' or 'tab'
eh	as the 'a' in 'hate'
oe	as the 'u' in 'fur'
eu	as the 'i' in 'sir'
u	as in 'flute'
uu	as in 'food'
aai	as the 'a' in 'father' + the 'i' in 'pipe'
ao	as in 'now' or 'cow'
aw	as in 'jaw'
o	as in 'phone'
oh	as in 'toe'
eua	diphthong of 'eu' and 'a'
ia	as the 'i-a' sound in 'Ian'
ua	as the 'u-a' sound in 'tour'
uay	'u-ay-ee'
iu	'i-oo' (as in 'yew')
iaw	a triphthong of 'ee-a-oo'
aew	as the 'a' in 'bad' + 'w'
ehw	as the 'a' in 'care' + 'w'
ew	same as **ehw** above, but shorter (not as in 'yew')
oei	'oe-i'
awy	as the 'oy' in 'boy'
ohy	'oh-i'

Consonants

Transliterated consonants are mostly pronounced as per their English counterparts (the exceptions are listed below). An 'aspirated' consonant is produced with no audible puff of air. An 'unvoiced' or 'voiceless' consonant is produced with no vibration in the vocal chords.

k	as the 'k' in 'skin'; similar to the 'g' in 'good', but unaspirated and unvoiced
kh	as the 'k' in 'kite'
ng	as in 'sing'; used as an initial consonant in Lao
j	similar to 'j' in 'join' or more closely, the second 't' in 'stature' or 'literature' (unaspirated and unvoiced)
ny	as in 'canyon'; used as an initial consonant in Lao
t	a hard 't', unaspirated and unvoiced – a bit like 'd'
th	as in 'tip'
p	a hard 'p' (unaspirated and unvoiced)
ph	'p' as in 'put', never as 'f'

Tones

Lao is a tonal language, whereby many identical phonemes are differentiated only by tone (changes in the pitch of a speaker's voice). The word *sao*, for example, can mean 'girl', 'morning', 'pillar' or 'twenty', depending on the tone. Pitch variations are relative to the speaker's natural vocal range, so that one person's low tone isn't necessarily the same pitch as another person's.

dji (good) – low tone; produced at the relative bottom of your conversational tonal range – usually flat level

het (do) – mid tone; flat like the low tone, but spoken at the relative middle of the speaker's vocal range. No tone mark is used

heúa (boat) – high tone; flat again, but at the relative top of your vocal range

sǎam (three) – rising tone; begins a bit below the mid tone and rises to just at or above the high tone

sâo (morning) – high falling tone; begins at or above the high tone and falls to the mid level

khào (rice) – low falling tone; begins at about the mid level and falls to the level of the low tone

ACCOMMODATION

Where's a ...?

... yùu sǎi? ... ຢູ່ໃສ?

camping ground
born dâng kêm ບ່ອນຕັ້ງແຄ້ມ

guesthouse
heú-an pak ເຮືອນພັກ

hotel
hóhng háem ໂຮງແຮມ

EMERGENCIES – LAO

Help!
  suay dae!   ຊ່ວຍແດ່!
Go away!
  pai dôe!   ໄປເດີ້!
I'm lost.
  khàwy lŏng tháang   ຂ້ອຍຫລົງທາງ
Where are the toilets?
  hàwng sùam yuu săi?   ຫ້ອງສ້ວມຢູ່ໃສ?

Call a doctor!
  suay tqam hăa măw hài dae!
  ຊ່ວຍຕາມຫາໝໍ ໃຫ້ແດ່!
Call the police!
  suay ôen tam-lùat dae!
  ຊ່ວຍເອີ້ນຕຳຫລວດແດ່!

Do you have a ...?
  jôw mìi ... wâhng baw?   ເຈົ້າມີ ... ຫວ່າງບໍ່?
double room
  hàwng náwn tĭang khuu   ຫ້ອງນອນຕຽງຄູ່
single room
  hàwng náwn tĭang diaw   ຫ້ອງນອນຕຽງດ່ຽວ

How much is it per ...?
  ... thao dqi?   ... ເທົ່າໃດ?
night
  khéun-la   ຄືນລະ
person
  khón-la   ຄົນລະ

bathroom
  hàwng nâm   ຫ້ອງນ້ຳ
toilet
  sùam   ສ້ວມ

CONVERSATION & ESSENTIALS

Greetings/Hello.
  sábqai-dĭi   ສະບາຍດີ
Goodbye. (general farewell)
  sábqai-dĭi   ສະບາຍດີ
Goodbye. (person leaving)
  láa kawn pqi kawn   ລາກ່ອນໄປກ່ອນ
Goodbye. (person staying)
  sŏhk dĭi (lit: good luck)   ໂຊກດີ
See you later.
  phop kqn mai   ພົບກັນໃໝ່
Thank you.
  khàwp jqi   ຂອບໃຈ
Thank you very much.
  khàwp jqi lăi lăi   ຂອບໃຈຫລາຍໆ
Excuse me.
  khăw thôht   ຂໍໂທດ

How are you?
  sábqai-dĭi baw?   ສະບາຍດີບໍ?
I'm fine.
  sábqai-dĭi   ສະບາຍດີ
And you?
  jâo dêh?   ເຈົ້າເດ?
Can you speak English?
  jâo pàak pháasăa qngkít
  dâi baw?   ເຈົ້າປາກພາສາອັງກິດໄດ້ບໍ່?
I don't understand.
  baw khào jqi   ບໍ່ເຂົ້າໃຈ

NUMBERS

0	*sŭun*	ສູນ
1	*neung*	ນຶ່ງ
2	*săwng*	ສອງ
3	*săam*	ສາມ
4	*sii*	ສີ່
5	*hàa*	ຫ້າ
6	*hók*	ຫົກ
7	*jét*	ເຈັດ
8	*pàet*	ແປດ
9	*kâo*	ເກົ້າ
10	*síp*	ສິບ
11	*síp-ét*	ສິບເອັດ
12	*síp-săwng*	ສິບສອງ
20	*sáo*	ຊາວ
21	*sáo-ét*	ຊາວເອັດ
22	*sáo-săwng*	ຊາວສອງ
30	*săam-síp*	ສາມສິບ
40	*sii-síp*	ສີ່ສິບ
50	*hàa-síp*	ຫ້າສິບ
60	*hók-síp*	ຫົກສິບ
70	*jét-síp*	ເຈັດສິບ
80	*pàet-síp*	ແປດສິບ
90	*kâo-síp*	ເກົ້າສິບ
100	*hâwy*	ຮ້ອຍ
200	*săwng hâwy*	ສອງຮ້ອຍ
1000	*phán*	ພັນ
10,000	*meun (síp-phán)*	ໝື່ນ(ສິບພັນ)
100,000	*săen (hâwy phán)*	ແສນ(ຮ້ອຍພັນ)

SHOPPING & SERVICES

Where is the ...?
  ... yùu săi?   ... ຢູ່ໃສ?

I'm looking for (the) ...
khàwy sâwk hǎa ...   ຂ້ອຍຊອກຫາ ...
bank
thanáakháan   ທະນາຄານ
hospital
hóhng mǎw   ໂຮງໝໍ
pharmacy
hâan khǎi yqa   ຮ້ານຂາຍຢາ
post office
pqi-sá-nǐi (hóhng sǎi)   ໄປສະນີ (ໂຮງສາຍ)
public toilet
hòrng nâm sǎ-ta-là-nà   ຫ້ອງນ້ຳສາທາລະນະ
telephone
thóhlasáp   ໂທລະສັບ

How much (for) ...?
... thao dqi?   ... ເທົ່າໃດ?
The price is very high.
láakháa pháeng lǎi   ລາຄາແພງຫລາຍ

TIME & DATES
What time is it?
wáir-láh ják móhng   ເວລາຈັກໂມງ?
At what time?
dorn ják móhng   ຕອນຈັກໂມງ?
At ...
dorn ...   ຕອນ ...
today
mêu nǐi   ມື້ນີ້
tomorrow
mêu eun   ມື້ອື່ນ

Monday
wán jqn   ວັນຈັນ
Tuesday
wán qngkháan   ວັນອັງຄານ
Wednesday
wán phut   ວັນພຸດ
Thursday
wán phahát   ວັນພະຫັດ
Friday
wán súk   ວັນສຸກ
Saturday
wán sǎo   ວັນເສົາ
Sunday
wán qathit   ວັນອາທິດ

TRANSPORT
What time will the ... leave?
... já àwk ják móhng?   ... ຈະອອກຈັກໂມງ
boat
héua   ເຮືອ
bus
lot   ລົດ

minivan
lot tûu   ລົດຕູ້
plane
héua bǐn   ເຮືອບິນ

What time (do we, does it, etc) arrive there?
já pai hâwt phǔn ják móhng?   ຈະໄປຮອດພຸ້ນຈັກໂມງ?

Where is the ...?
... yùu sǎi?   ... ຢູ່ໃສ?
airport
doen bǐn   ເດີ່ນບິນ
bus station
sathǎanii lot pájqm tháang   ສະຖານີລົດປະຈຳທາງ
bus stop
bawn jàwt lot pájqm tháang   ບ່ອນຈອດລົດປະຈຳທາງ

Directions
I want to go to ...
khàwy yàak pqi ...   ຂ້ອຍຢາກໄປ ...
Go straight ahead.
pqi seu-seu   ໄປຊື່ໆ
How far?
kqi thao dqi?   ໄກເທົ່າໃດ?
near/not near
kǎi/baw kǎi   ໃກ້/ບໍ່ໃກ້
far/not far
kqi/baw kqi   ໄກ/ບໍ່ໄກ

Turn ...
líaw ...   ລ້ຽວ ...
left
sǎai   ຊ້າຍ
right
khwǎa   ຂວາ

MANDARIN CHINESE

PRONUNCIATION
Vowels
ian	as the word 'yen'
ie	as the English word 'yeah'
o	as in 'or', with no 'r' sound
ou	as the 'oa' in 'boat'
u	as in 'flute'
ui	as the word 'way'
uo	like a 'w' followed by 'o'
yu/ü	like 'ee' with lips pursed

Consonants
c	as the 'ts' in 'bits'
ch	as in 'chip', but with the tongue curled up and back

q	as the 'ch' in 'cheese'
r	as the 's' in 'pleasure'
sh	as in 'ship', but with the tongue curled up and back
x	as in 'ship'
z	as the 'dz' in 'suds'
zh	as the 'j' in 'judge', but with the tongue curled up and back

Tones

Mandarin has four tones – high, rising, falling-rising and falling, plus a fifth 'neutral' tone which you can all but ignore. To illustrate the importance of getting tones right, look at the word *ma*, which has four different meanings according to tone:

mā (mother) – high tone
má (hemp, numb) – rising tone
mǎ (horse) – falling-rising tone
mà (scold, swear) – falling tone

ACCOMMODATION

I'm looking for a ...
Wǒ yào zhǎo ...　　我要找. . .
　camping ground
　lùyìngdì　　露营地
　guesthouse
　bīnguǎn　　宾馆
　hostel
　zhāodàisuǒ/lǚshè　　招待所/旅社
　hotel
　lǚguǎn　　旅馆
　tourist hotel
　bīnguǎn/fàndiàn/jiǔdiàn　　宾馆/饭店/酒店
　youth hostel
　qīngnián lǚshè　　青年旅舍

I'd like (a) ...
Wǒ xiǎng yào ...　　我想要. . .
　bed
　yí ge chuángwèi　　一个床位
　single room
　yìjiān dānrénfáng　　一间单人房
　bed for two
　shuāngrén chuáng　　双人床
　room with two beds
　shuāngrénfáng　　双人房

How much is it ...?
... duōshǎo qián?　　. . . 多少钱?
　per night
　měitiān wǎnshàng　　每天晚上
　per person
　měigerén　　每个人

EMERGENCIES – MANDARIN

Help!
　Jiùmìng a!　　救命啊!
I'm lost.
　Wǒ mílùle.　　我迷路了
Leave me alone!
　Bié fán wǒ!　　别烦我!
Where are the toilets?
　Cèsuǒ zài nǎr?　　厕所在哪儿?

Call ... !
　Qǐng jiào ...!　　请叫. . . !
　　a doctor
　　yīshēng　　医生
　　the police
　　jǐngchá　　警察

CONVERSATION & ESSENTIALS

Hello.	*Nǐ hǎo.*	你好
	Nín hǎo. (pol)	您好
Goodbye.	*Zàijiàn.*	再见
Please.	*Qǐng.*	请
Thank you.	*Xièxie.*	谢谢
Many thanks.	*Duōxiè.*	多谢
You're welcome.	*Búkèqi.*	不客气
Excuse me, ...	*Qǐng wèn, ...*	请问, . . .
I'm sorry.	*Duìbùqǐ.*	对不起

Do you speak English?
　Nǐ huì shuō yīngyǔ ma?　　你会说英语吗?
I don't understand.
　Wǒ tīngbudǒng.　　我听不懂
Please write it down.
　Qǐng xiěxiàlai.　　请写下来

Yes & No

There are no specific words in Mandarin that specifically mean 'yes' and 'no' when used in isolation. When a question is asked, the verb is repeated to indicate the affirmative. A response in the negative is formed by using the word *bù* (meaning 'no') before the verb.

Are you going to Shanghai?
　Nǐ qù shànghǎi ma?　　你去上海吗?
Yes.
　Qù. ('go')　　去
No.
　Bú qù. ('no go')　　不去
No.
　Méi yǒu. ('not have')　　没有
No.
　Búshì. ('not so')　　不是

LANGUAGE

NUMBERS

0	líng	零
1	yī, yāo	一, 幺
2	èr, liǎng	二, 两
3	sān	三
4	sì	四
5	wǔ	五
6	liù	六
7	qī	七
8	bā	八
9	jiǔ	九
10	shí	十
11	shíyī	十一
12	shí'èr	十二
20	èrshí	二十
21	èrshíyī	二十一
22	èrshí'èr	二十二
30	sānshí	三十
40	sìshí	四十
50	wǔshí	五十
60	liùshí	六十
70	qīshí	七十
80	bāshí	八十
90	jiǔshí	九十
100	yìbǎi	一百
1000	yìqiān	一千
2000	liǎngqiān	两千

SHOPPING & SERVICES

I'm looking for a/the ...
Wǒ zài zhǎo ... 我在找...

bank
yínháng 银行
chemist/pharmacy
yàodiàn 药店
hospital
yīyuàn 医院
market
shìchǎng 市场
police
jǐngchá 警察
post office
yóujú 邮局
public toilet
gōnggòng cèsuǒ 公共厕所

How much is it?
Duōshǎo qián? 多少钱?
That's too expensive.
Tài guìle. 太贵了

TIME & DATES

What's the time?
Jǐ diǎn? 几点?
When?
Shénme shíhòu? 什么时候?

... hour	*... diǎn*	... 点
... minute	*... fēn*	... 分
now	*xiànzài*	现在
today	*jīntiān*	今天
tomorrow	*míngtiān*	明天
Monday	*xīngqīyī*	星期一
Tuesday	*xīngqī'èr*	星期二
Wednesday	*xīngqīsān*	星期三
Thursday	*xīngqīsì*	星期四
Friday	*xīngqīwǔ*	星期五
Saturday	*xīngqīliù*	星期六
Sunday	*xīngqītiān*	星期天

TRANSPORT

What time does ... leave/arrive?
... jǐdiǎn kāi/dào? ... 几点开/到?

boat
chuán 船
intercity bus/coach
chángtú qìchē 长途汽车
local/city bus
gōnggòng qìchē 公共汽车
plane
fēijī 飞机
train
huǒchē 火车

airport
fēijīchǎng 飞机场
long-distance bus station
chángtú qìchē zhàn 长途汽车站
train station
huǒchē zhàn 火车站

Directions
Where is (the) ...?
... zài nǎr? ... 在哪儿?
I want to go to ...
Wǒ yào qù ... 我要去...
Go straight ahead.
Yìzhí zǒu. 一直走
Turn left.
Zuǒ zhuǎn. 左转
Turn right.
Yòu zhuǎn. 右转
near
jìn 近
far
yuǎn 远

Could you show me (on the map)?
Nǐ néng bùnéng (zài dìtú shang) zhǐ gěi wǒ kàn?
你能不能(在地图上)指给我看?

THAI

PRONUNCIATION

The 'ph' in a Thai word is always pronounced like an English 'p', not as an 'f'.

Tones

Thai is a tonal language, where changes in pitch can affect meaning. The range of all five tones is relative to each speaker's vocal range, so there's no fixed 'pitch' intrinsic to the language. The five tones of Thai:

bàat (baht – the Thai currency) – low tone; a flat pitch pronounced at the relative bottom of the vocal range

dii (good) – level or mid tone; pronounced flat, at the relative middle of the vocal range, no tone mark is used

mâi (no/not) – falling tone; pronounced as if emphasising a word, or calling someone's name from afar

máa (horse) – high tone; pronounced near the relative top of the vocal range, as level as possible

sǎam (three) – rising tone; sounds like the inflection used by English speakers to imply a question

ACCOMMODATION

I'm looking for a ...
phǒm/dì·chǎn kam·lang hǎa ...
ผม/ดิฉันกำลังหา...

guesthouse
bâan phák/   บ้านพัก/
  kèt háo ('guest house')   เกสต์เฮาส์
hotel
rohng raem   โรงแรม
youth hostel
bâan yao·wá·chon   บ้านเยาวชน

Do you have any rooms available?
mii hâwng wâang mǎi?   มีห้องว่างไหม?

I'd like (a) ...
tâwng kaan ...
ต้องการ...

bed
tiang nawn   เตียงนอน
single room
hâwng dìaw   ห้องเดี่ยว
room with two beds
hâwng thîi mii tiang   ห้องที่มีเตียง
  sǎwng tua   สองตัว
ordinary room (with fan)
hâwng tham·má·   ห้องธรรมดา
  daa (mii pát lom)   (มีพัดลม)

EMERGENCIES – THAI

Help!
  chûay dûay!   ช่วยด้วย
I'm lost.
  chǎn lǒng thaang   ฉันหลงทาง
Go away!
  pai sí!   ไปชิ

Call ...!
  rîak ... nàwy   เรียก...หน่อย
  a doctor   mǎw   หมอ
  the police   tam·rùat   ตำรวจ

How much is it ...? ... thâo rai?   ...เท่าไร?
  per night   kheun lá   คืนละ
  per person   khon lá   คนละ

CONVERSATION & ESSENTIALS

When being polite, a male speaker ends his sentence with khráp and a female speaker says khâ; it's also the common way to answer 'yes' to a question or show agreement.

Hello.
  sà·wàt·dii (khráp/khâ)   สวัสดี(ครับ/ค่ะ)
Goodbye.
  laa kàwn   ลาก่อน
Yes.
  châi   ใช่
No.
  mâi châi   ไม่ใช่
Please.
  kà·rú·naa   กรุณา
Thank you.
  khàwp khun   ขอบคุณ
Excuse me.
  khǎw à·phai   ขออภัย
Sorry. (forgive me)
  khǎw thôht   ขอโทษ
How are you?
  sa·bai dii rěu?   สบายดีหรือ?
I'm fine, thanks.
  sa·bai dii   สบายดี

NUMBERS

0	sǔun	ศูนย์
1	nèung	หนึ่ง
2	sǎwng	สอง
3	sǎam	สาม
4	sìi	สี่
5	hâa	ห้า

LANGUAGE

6	hòk	หก
7	jèt	เจ็ด
8	pàet	แปด
9	kâo	เก้า
10	sìp	สิบ
11	sìp-èt	สิบเอ็ด
12	sìp-sǎwng	สิบสอง
13	sìp-sǎam	สิบสาม
14	sìp-sìi	สิบสี่
15	sìp-hâa	สิบห้า
16	sìp-hòk	สิบหก
17	sìp-jèt	สิบเจ็ด
18	sìp-pàet	สิบแปด
19	sìp-kâo	สิบเก้า
20	yîi-sìp	ยี่สิบ
21	yîi-sìp-èt	ยี่สิบเอ็ด
22	yîi-sìp-sǎwng	ยี่สิบสอง
30	sǎam-sìp	สามสิบ
40	sìi-sìp	สี่สิบ
50	hâa-sìp	ห้าสิบ
60	hòk-sìp	หกสิบ
70	jèt-sìp	เจ็ดสิบ
80	pàet-sìp	แปดสิบ
90	kâo-sìp	เก้าสิบ
100	nèung ráwy	หนึ่งร้อย
200	sǎwng ráwy	สองร้อย
300	sǎam ráwy	สามร้อย
1000	nèung phan	หนึ่งพัน
2000	sǎwng phan	สองพัน
10,000	nèung mèun	หนึ่งหมื่น
100,000	nèung sǎen	หนึ่งแสน

SHOPPING & SERVICES
I'm looking for ...
phǒm/dì-chǎn hǎa ... ผม/ดิฉันหา...
  a bank
  thá-naa-khaan ธนาคาร
  the market
  ta-làat ตลาด
  the post office
  prai-sà-nii ไปรษณีย์
  a public toilet
  hâwng nám ห้องน้ำสาธารณะ
  sǎa-thaa-rá-ná
  the telephone centre
  sǔun thoh-rá-sàp ศูนย์โทรศัพท์

the tourist office
sǎm-nák ngaan สำนักงานท่องเที่ยว
  thâwng thîaw

I'd like to buy ...
yàak jà séu ... อยากจะซื้อ...
How much is it?
thâo rai? เท่าไร?
It's too expensive.
phaeng koen pai แพงเกินไป

TIME & DAYS
What time is it?
kìi mohng láew? กี่โมงแล้ว?
It's (8 o'clock).
pàet mohng láew แปดโมงแล้ว

today	wan níi	วันนี้
tomorrow	phrûng níi	พรุ่งนี้
Monday	wan jan	วันจันทร์
Tuesday	wan ang-khaan	วันอังคาร
Wednesday	wan phút	วันพุธ
Thursday	wan phá-réu-hàt	วันพฤหัสฯ
Friday	wan sùk	วันศุกร์
Saturday	wan sǎo	วันเสาร์
Sunday	wan aa-thít	วันอาทิตย์

TRANSPORT
What time does the ... leave?
... jà àwk kìi mohng? ...จะออกกี่โมง?
What time does the ... arrive?
... jà thěung kìi mohng? ...จะถึงกี่โมง?

boat	reua	เรือ
bus (city)	rót meh	รถเมล์
bus (intercity)	rót thua	รถทัวร์
plane	khrêuang bin	เครื่องบิน
train	rót fai	รถไฟ

airport
sa-nǎam bin สนามบิน
bus station
sa-thǎa-nii khǒn sòng สถานีขนส่ง
bus stop
pâai rót meh ป้ายรถเมล์
train station
sa-thǎa-nii rót fai สถานีรถไฟ

Directions

Where is (the)...?

... *yùu thīi nǎi?*	...อยู่ที่ไหน?	

Can you show me (on the map)?

hâi duu (nai phǎen thīi	ให้ดู(ในแผนที่)	
dâi mǎi?	ได้ไหม?	

(Go) Straight ahead.

trong pai	ตรงไป

Turn left.

líaw sáai	เลี้ยวซ้าย

Turn right.

líaw khwǎa	เลี้ยวขวา

far

klai	ไกล

near/not far

klâi/mâi klai	ใกล้/ไม่ไกล

VIETNAMESE

There are differences between the Vietnamese of the north and the Vietnamese of the south; where different forms are used in this guide, they are indicated by 'N' for the north and 'S' for the south.

TONES & PRONUNCIATION

To help you make sense of what is (for non-Vietnamese) a very tricky writing system, the words and phrases in this language guide include pronunciations that use a written form more familiar to English speakers. The symbols used for marking the tones are the same as those used in standard written Vietnamese.

SYMBOL & PRONUNCIATION

c, k	ğ	an unaspirated 'k'
đ	đ	(with crossbar) as in 'do'
d	z/y	(without crossbar) as the 'z' in 'zoo' (N); as the 'y' in 'yes' (S)
gi-	z/y	as a 'z' (N); as a 'y' (S)
kh-	ch	as the 'ch' in German *buch*
ng-	ng	as the '-nga-' sound in 'long ago'
nh-	ny	as the 'ny' in 'canyon'
ph-	f	as in 'farm'
r	z/r	as 'z' (N); as 'r' (S)
s	s/sh	as 's' (N); as 'sh' (S)
tr-	ch/tr	as 'ch' (N); as 'tr' (S)
th-	t	a strongly aspirated 't'
x	s	like an 's'
-ch	k	like a 'k'
-ng	ng	as the 'ng' in 'long' but with the lips closed; sounds like English 'm'
-nh	ng	as in 'singing'

There are six tones in spoken Vietnamese. Thus, every syllable in Vietnamese can be pronounced six different ways. For example, depending on the tones, the word *ma* can be read to mean 'phantom', 'but', 'mother', 'rice seedling', 'tomb' or 'horse'. The six tones are represented by five diacritical marks in the written language (the first tone is left unmarked).

ma (ghost) – middle of the vocal range
mà (which) – begins low and falls lower
mả (tomb) – begins low, dips and then rises to higher pitch
mã (horse) – begins high, dips slightly, then rises sharply
mạ (rice seedling) – begins low, falls to a lower level, then stops
má (mother) – begins high and rises sharply

ACCOMMODATION

Where is there a (cheap) ...?

Đâu có ... (rẻ tiền)?	*đoh ğoó ... (zả đee·ùhn)?*	
camping ground		
nơi cắm trại	*ner·ee ğúhm chại*	
guesthouse		
nhà khách	*nyaà kaák*	
hotel		
khách sạn	*kaák saạn*	
air-conditioning		
máy lạnh	*máy laạng*	
bathroom		
phòng tắm	*fòm dúhm*	
hot water		
nước nóng	*nuhr·érk nóm*	
toilet		
nhà vệ sinh	*nyaà vẹ sing*	

LANGUAGE

I'd like (a) ...

Tôi muốn ...   *doy moo·úhn ...*

  single room

  phòng đơn   *fòm dern*

  double-bed

  giường đôi   *zuhr·èrng doy*

  room with two beds

  phòng gồm hai   *fòm gàwm hai*

   giường ngủ   *zuhr·èrng ngoó*

How much is it ...?

Giá bao nhiêu ...?   *zaá bow nyee·oo ...?*

  per night

  một đêm   *mạwt đem*

  per person

  một người   *mạwt nguhr·eè*

CONVERSATION & ESSENTIALS

There are many different forms of address in Vietnamese. The safest way to address people is: *ông* (to a man of any status), *anh* (to a young man), *bà* (to a middle-aged or older woman), *cô* (to a young woman) and *em* (to a child).

Hello.

  Xin chào.   *sin jòw*

Goodbye.

  Tạm biệt.   *dụm bee·ẹt*

Please.

  Làm ơn.   *làm ern*

Thank you.

  Cảm ơn.   *kảm ern*

Excuse me.

  Xin lỗi.   *sin lõ·ee*

Yes.

  Vâng. (N)   *vang*

  Dạ. (S)   *yạ*

No.

  Không.   *kom*

How are you?

  Có khỏe không?   *káw kwảir kom?*

Fine, thank you.

  Khỏe, cảm ơn.   *kwảir kảm ern*

Do you speak English?

  Bạn có nói được tiếng   *Bạan ğó nóy đuhr·ẹrk díng*

   Anh không?   *aang kawm?*

I (don't) understand.

  Tôi (không) hiểu.   *doy (kawm) heé·oo*

NUMBERS

1	một	*mạwt*
2	hai	*hai*
3	ba	*baa*
4	bốn	*báwn*
5	năm	*nuhm*
6	sáu	*sóh*
7	bảy	*bảy*
8	tám	*dúhm*
9	chín	*jín*
10	mười	*muhr·eè*
11	mười một	*muhr·eè mọt*
19	mười chín	*muhr·eè jín*
20	hai mươi	*hai muhr·ee*
21	hai mươi mốt	*hai muhr·ee máwt*
22	hai mươi hai	*hai muhr·ee hai*
30	ba mươi	*ba muhr·ee*
90	chín mươi	*jín muhr·ee*
100	một trăm	*mạwt chuhm*
200	hai trăm	*hai chuhm*
900	chín trăm	*jín chuhm*
1000	một nghìn (N)	*mạwt ngyìn*
	một ngàn (S)	*mọt ngaàn*
10,000	mười nghìn (N)	*muhr·eè ngyìn*
	mười ngàn (S)	*muhr·eè ngaàn*

SHOPPING & SERVICES

I'm looking for ...

Tôi tìm ...   *doy dìm ...*

  a bank

  ngân hàng   *nguhn haàng*

  the hospital

  nhà thương   *nyaà tuhr·erng*

  the market

  chợ   *jer*

  the post office

  bưu điện   *buhr·oo đee·ụhn*

  a public phone

  phòng điện thoại   *fòm đee·ụhn twại*

  a public toilet

  phòng vệ sinh   *fòm vẹ sing*

  tourist office

  văn phòng hướng   *vuhn fòm huhr·érng*

   dẫn du lịch   *zũhn zoo lịk*

How much is this?

  Cái này giá bao nhiêu?   *ğaí này zaá bow nyee·oo?*

It's too expensive.

  Cái này quá mắc.   *ğaí này gwaá múhk*

TIME & DAYS

What time is it?

  Mấy giờ rồi?   *máy zèr zòy?*

It's ... o'clock.

  Bây giờ là ... giờ.   *bay zèr laà ... zèr*

now

  bây giờ   *bay zèr*

today
  hôm nay   *hawm nay*
tomorrow
  ngày mai   *ngày mai*

Monday
  thứ hai   *túhr hai*
Tuesday
  thứ ba   *túhr baa*
Wednesday
  thứ tư   *túhr duhr*
Thursday
  thứ năm   *túhr nuhm*
Friday
  thứ sáu   *túhr sóh*
Saturday
  thứ bảy   *túhr bảy*
Sunday
  chủ nhật   *jỏo nhụht*

TRANSPORT
What time does the (first)... leave/arrive?
Chuyến ... (sớm nhất) chạy lúc mấy giờ?
jwee·úhn ... (sérm nyúht) jạy lúp máy zèr?
  boat
  tàu/thuyền   *dòw/twee·ùhn*
  bus
  xe buýt   *sa beét*

plane
  máy bay   *máy bay*
train
  xe lửa   *sa lúhr·uh*

Directions
Where is ...?
  ở đâu ...?   *ér đoh ...?*
I want to go to ...
  Tôi muốn đi ...   *doy moo·úhn đee ...*
Go straight ahead.
  Thẳng tới trước.   *túhng der·eé chuhr·érk*
Can you show me (on the map)?
  Xin chỉ giùm (trên   *sin jeé zùm (chen*
    bản đồ này)?   *baản đàw này)?*

Turn left.
  Sang trái.   *saang chaí*
Turn right.
  Sang phải.   *saang faỉ*
at the corner
  ở góc đường   *ér góp đuhr·èrng*
at the traffic lights
  tại đèn giao *tawm*   *dại đèn zow thông*
far
  xa   *saa*
near (to)
  gần   *gùhn*

Also available from Lonely Planet:
Southeast Asia and *Mandarin Phrasebooks*

LANGUAGE

Glossary

For food and drink terms, see Eat Your Words, p94.

ABBREVIATIONS

C – Cambodia
L – Laos
T – Thailand
V – Vietnam
Y – Yúnnán province (China)

American War (V) – Vietnamese name for what is also known as the 'Vietnam War'
ao dai (V) – traditional Vietnamese tunic and trousers
APEC – Asia-Pacific Economic Cooperation
apsara (C) – heavenly nymphs or angelic dancers
Asean – Association of Southeast Asian Nations
asura (C) – demon

bâan (T) – house, village; also written as 'ban'
bàasii (L) – sometimes written as 'basi' or 'baci'; a ceremony in which the 32 *khwǎn* are symbolically bound to the participant for health and safety
baht (T) – the Thai unit of currency
báijiǔ (Y) – literally 'white alcohol', a type of face-numbing rice wine
barang (C) – foreigner
baray (C) – ancient reservoir
BCEL (L) – Banque pour le Commerce Extérieur Lao; in English, Lao Foreign Trade Bank
BE (L, T) – Buddhist Era
boeng (C) – lake
bówùguǎn (Y) – museum
Brahman – pertaining to Brahmanism, an ancient religious tradition in India and the predecessor of Hinduism; not to be confused with 'Brahmin', the priestly class in India's caste system
BTS (T) – Bangkok Transit System (Skytrain); Thai: *rót fai fáa*
bun (L) – festival
buu dien (V) – post office

cānting (Y) – restaurant
Cao Daism (V) – Vietnamese religious sect
Cham (C, V) – ethnic minority descended from the people of Champa, a Hindu kingdom dating from the 2nd century BC
chedi (T) – see *stupa*
Chenla (C, L, V) – Pre-Angkorian *Khmer* kingdom covering parts of Cambodia, Laos and Vietnam

chnnang (C) – pot
Chunchiet (C) – ethnolinguistic minority
CITS (Y) – China International Travel Service; deals with foreign tourists in China
CPP (C) – Cambodian People's Party
cūn (Y) – village
cyclo (C, V) – pedicab

deva (C) – god
devaraja (C) – god king
DMZ (V) – the misnamed Demilitarised Zone, a strip of land that once separated North and South Vietnam
doi moi (V) – economic restructuring or reform
dong (V) – the Vietnamese unit of currency
duong (V) – road, street; abbreviated as 'Đ'

Ecpat – End Child Prostitution & Trafficking

falang (L) – Western, Westerner; foreigner
fānchuán (Y) – pirate-sized junks with bamboo-battened canvas sails
faràng (T) – Western, Westerner; foreigner
feng shui – literally, 'wind water'; used to describe geomancy
Funan (C, V) – first *Khmer* kingdom, located in Mekong Delta area
Funcinpec (C) – National United Front for an Independent, Neutral, Peaceful & Cooperative Cambodia

gōng (Y) – temple
gōngyuán (Y) – park
gopura (C) – entrance pavilion in traditional Hindu architecture

háang thíen (L) – candle rail
Han (Y) – China's main ethnic group
hǎw wái (L) – prayer hall
HCMC (V) – Ho Chi Minh City
héua hang nyáo (L) – long-tail boat
héua phai (L) – rowboat
héua wái (L) – speedboat
Hinayana – literally, Lesser Vehicle; the school of Buddhism correctly known as *Theravada*
Ho Chi Minh Trail (V) – route used by the North Vietnamese to move supplies to guerrillas in the South
Hoa (V) – ethnic Chinese, the largest single minority group in Vietnam
Honda om (V) – motorbike taxi
hú (Y) – lake

IDP – International Driving Permit

Indochina – Vietnam, Cambodia and Laos, the French colony of Indochine; the name derives from Indian and Chinese influences

Isan (T) – general term used for northeastern Thailand

jataka (C, L, T) – stories of the Buddha's past lives, often enacted in dance-drama

jumbo (L) – a motorised three-wheeled taxi, sometimes called a *túk-túk*

karst – limestone peaks with caves, underground streams and potholes

káthoey (T) – transvestite, transsexual

khaen (L) – panpipe

khao (T) – hill, mountain

khlong (T) – canal

Khmer (C) – ethnic Cambodians; Cambodian language

Khmer Rouge (C) – literally Red *Khmers,* the commonly used name for the Cambodian communist movement responsible for genocide in the 1970s

khwăn (L) – guardian spirits of the body

Kinh (V) – the Vietnamese language

kip (L) – the Lao unit of currency

ko (T) – island

koh (C) – island

krama (C) – chequered scarf

Kuomintang (Y) – Nationalist Party, also known as KMT; the KMT controlled China between 1925 and 1949 until defeated by the communists

lákhon (C, T) – classical Thai dance-drama

lăowài (Y) – foreigners

liăng (Y) – see *tael*

lí-keh (T) – Thai folk dance-drama

linga (C, L, T, V) – phallic symbol

luóhàn (Y) – arhat or noble one

mâe chii (T) – Buddhist nun

mae nam (L, T) – river

mah jong (Y) – popular Chinese card game for four people, played with engraved tiles

Mahayana – literally, Great Vehicle; a school of Buddhism that extended the early Buddhist teachings; see also *Theravada*

mát-mìi (T) – cloth made of tie-dyed silk or cotton thread; also written as 'mat-mii'

meuang (L, T) – city

MIA (C, L, V) – missing in action, usually referring to US personnel

mondòp (T) – small square, spired building in a *wat*

Montagnards (V) – highlanders, mountain people; specifically the ethnic minorities inhabiting remote areas of Vietnam

moto (C) – motorcycle taxi

Mt Meru – the mythical dwelling place of the Hindu gods, symbolised by the Himalayas

múan (L) – fun, which the Lao believe should be present in all activities

muay thai (T) – Thai boxing

nâa (T) – face

nâam (L, T) – water, river

naga (C, L, T) – mythical serpent-being

nákhon (T) – city

năng (T) – shadow play

nha-rong (C, T, V) – Jarai communal house

NPA (L) – National Protected Area

NTAL (L) – Lao National Tourism Administration

NVA (V) – North Vietnamese Army

Pali – ancient Indian language that, along with *Sanskrit,* is the root of *Khmer,* Lao and Thai

Pathet Lao (L) – literally, 'Country of Laos'; both a general term for the country and the common name for the Lao communist military during the civil war

PDA (T) – Population & Community Development Association

Ph (C) – abbreviation for *phlauv*

phansăa (T) – Buddhist lent

phlauv (C) – road, street; abbreviated as '*Ph*'

phleng phêua chii-wít (T) – songs for life, modern Thai folk songs

phnom (C) – mountain

phu (L) – hill or mountain

Pinyin (Y) – the official system for transliterating Chinese script into Roman characters

ponglang (T) – northeastern Thai marimba (percussion instrument) made of short logs

POW – prisoner of war

praang (C, T) – *Khmer*-style tower structure, found in temples; see also *stupa*

prasat (C, T) – tower, temple

PRC (Y) – People's Republic of China

psar (C) – market

PSB (Y) – Public Security Bureau

quan (V) – urban district

quoc ngu (V) – Vietnamese alphabet

Ramakian (T) – Thai version of the *Ramayana*

Ramayana – Indian epic story of Rama's battle with demons

Reamker (C) – *Khmer* version of the *Ramayana*

remorque-moto (C) – motorcycle-pulled trailer

riel (C) – the Cambodian unit of currency

roi nuoc (V) – water puppetry

rót fai fáa (T) – Skytrain; *BTS*

săamláw (T) – three-wheeled pedicab; also written as 'samlor'

sâiyasaat (L) – folk magic, officially banned in Laos

sampot (C) – the national saronglike garment, usually worn at important occasions

Sanskrit – ancient Hindu language that, along with *Pali*, is the root of *Khmer*, Lao and Thai

sànùk (T) – fun

săwngthăew (L, T) – small pick-up truck with two benches in the back; also written as 'songthaew'

shăn (Y) – mountain

sĭm (L) – chapel

sima (L) – ordination stones

soi (L, T) – lane, small street

song (L, V) – river

Songkran (T) – Thai New Year, held in mid-April

SRV (V) – Socialist Republic of Vietnam (Vietnam's official name)

stung (C) – small river

stupa – religious monument, often containing Buddha relics

tael (Y) – unit of weight; one *tael (liăng)* equals 37.5g; used throughout the Mekong for weighing gold and precious stones

talat (L) – market

Tam Giao (V) – literally, 'triple religion'; Confucianism, Taoism and Buddhism fused over time with popular Chinese beliefs and ancient Vietnamese animism

Tao (V) – the Way; the essence of which all things are made

TAT (T) – Tourism Authority of Thailand

tat (L) – waterfall

Tet (V) – lunar New Year

Th (L, T) – abbreviation for *thànŏn*

thâat (L) – Buddhist *stupa*, reliquary; also written as 'that'

thànŏn (L, T) – road, street, avenue; abbreviated as 'Th'

Theravada – a school of Buddhism found in Cambodia, Laos and Thailand; this school confined itself to the early Buddhist teachings unlike *Mahayana*

tonlé (C) – major river

tripitaka (T) – Buddhist scriptures

túk-túk (L, T) – motorised *săamláw;* written as 'tuk-tuk' in Cambodia

tuóchá (Y) – smoked green tea

UNDP – UN Development Programme

UXO (C, L) – unexploded ordnance

VC (V) – Viet Cong or Vietnamese Communists

vihara (C) – temple sanctuary

vipassana (L, T) – insight awareness meditation

wâi (L, T) – palms-together greeting

wat (C, L, T) – Buddhist temple-monastery

wíhăan (T) – sanctuary, hall, dwelling

xe om (V) – see *Honda om*

yuán (Y) – the Chinese unit of currency

The Authors

NICK RAY
Coordinating author, Vietnam

A Londoner of sorts, Nick comes from Watford, the sort of town that makes you want to travel. He has been floating around the Mekong region for more than a decade now, first as a traveller, later leading people astray as a tour leader for adventure travel companies and more recently as a location scout for film and TV. Living in Phnom Penh, the Mekong is his backyard of sorts and he has written several editions of the *Cambodia* book for Lonely Planet, as well as coauthoring the *Vietnam* book and *Cycling Vietnam, Laos & Cambodia*. Nick has covered almost every corner of the Mekong region, including taking dips in the mother river in Laos and Cambodia. He chickened out in the heavily populated (polluted?) Mekong Delta.

TIM BEWER
Bangkok & Northern Thailand

While growing up, Tim didn't travel much except for the obligatory pilgrimage to Disney World and an annual summer week at the lake. He's spent most of his adult life making up for this, and has since visited over 50 countries, including most in Southeast Asia. He has made multiple trips to Thailand for work and pleasure. When not shouldering a backpack, he lives in Minneapolis, USA.

ANDREW BURKE
Laos

Andrew has lived in Asia since 2001 and in that time he's spent more than six months travelling around Laos. It's the laid-back, simple approach to life that repeatedly draws him back, but he finds the thousands of kilometres of roads less travelled and fascinating photographic subjects just as appealing. This is Andrew's 11th book for Lonely Planet, with titles including *The Asia Book, China* and *Hong Kong Citiescape*. When he's not travelling, Andrew works as a journalist and photographer and calls Bangkok home.

LONELY PLANET AUTHORS

Why is our travel information the best in the world? It's simple: our authors are independent, dedicated travellers. They don't research using just the internet or phone, and they don't take freebies in exchange for positive coverage. They travel widely, to all the popular spots and off the beaten track. They personally visit thousands of hotels, restaurants, cafés, bars, galleries, palaces, museums and more – and they take pride in getting all the details right, and telling it how it is. Think you can do it? Find out how at lonelyplanet.com.

THE AUTHORS

THOMAS HUHTI
Yúnnán province (China)

Thomas hails from Wisconsin, USA, and still calls it home when not barrelling around the world with a backpack. A linguistics major at university, he happily chanced upon Mandarin while fleeing the pesky grammar of Indo-European languages. A semester abroad was followed by two years in Taiwan and the PRC on a study and research (and, naturally, travel) fellowship. Among other books, Thomas has completed five tours of duty on Lonely Planet's *China*. He would always rather be playing ice hockey or hiking the forests of Wisconsin with his better half Yuki and bigheaded lab Bobo.

SIRADETH SENG
Cambodia

After catching the travel bug and then eloping with it seven years ago, Siradeth is still drifting with no permanent address – where she spills her backpack is home. Born in Cambodia but raised in Australia, she jumped at the chance to return to dig up her roots, which she did, along with half the countryside every time she skidded off a moto. Now with London calling, Paris beckoning and Asia luring her back, she has no choice but to keep floating around the world.

CONTRIBUTING AUTHORS

Dr Trish Batchelor wrote the Health chapter (p503). Trish is a general practitioner and travel medicine specialist who works at the CIWEC Clinic in Kathmandu, Nepal, as well as being a Medical Advisor to the Travel Doctor New Zealand clinics. Trish teaches travel medicine through the University of Otago, and is interested in underwater and high-altitude medicine, and in the impact of tourism on host countries. She has travelled extensively through Southeast and East Asia and particularly loves high-altitude trekking in the Himalayas.

Austin Bush wrote the Food & Drink chapter (p86). After graduating from the University of Oregon with a degree in linguistics, Austin received a scholarship to study Thai at Chiang Mai University, and has remained in Thailand ever since. After working several years at a stable job, he made the questionable decision to pursue a career as a freelance photographer/writer. This choice has since taken him as far as northern Pakistan, and as near as Bangkok's Or Tor Kor Market. He enjoys writing about and taking photos of food most of all, because it's a great way to connect with people.

David Lukas wrote the Environment chapter (p49). David is a professional naturalist whose many adventures afield include a year spent studying the tropical rainforests of Borneo. He has contributed environment chapters to more than a dozen Lonely Planet titles ranging from the Dominican Republic to Nova Scotia.

Steven Schipani wrote the Ecotourism in Laos boxed text (p265). Steven was born in New York City and raised on the Atlantic coast of Long Island, New York. He first went to Asia as a United States Peace Corps volunteer, serving in Thailand from 1994 to 1996. He has worked as a professional guide, fisherman, and Thai and Lao language interpreter, and has travelled extensively in Southeast Asia. Since 1999 Steven has been employed by Unesco, the Asian Development Bank, and a number of other international organisations advising on sustainable ecotourism development and heritage management in Laos. His interests include fishing, forest trekking, indigenous knowledge and Lao food. He has one son named Michael.

Behind the Scenes

THIS BOOK

This is the 1st edition of *Vietnam, Cambodia, Laos & the Greater Mekong*. Nick Ray was the coordinating author, skilfully assisted by Tim Bewer, Andrew Burke, Thomas Huhti and Siradeth Seng. Austin Bush wrote the Food & Drink chapter and David Lukas wrote the Environment chapter. This guidebook was commissioned in Lonely Planet's Melbourne office, and produced by the following:

Commissioning Editor Kalya Ryan
Coordinating Editor Sasha Baskett
Coordinating Cartographer Jacqueline Nguyen
Coordinating Layout Designer Paul Iacono
Managing Editor Bruce Evans
Managing Cartographers David Connolly, Julie Sheridan
Assisting Editors Anne Mulvaney, Carly Hall, Simon Williamson, Brooke Lyons, Gennifer Ciavarra, Kate Evans, Diana Saad
Assisting Cartographer Jessica Deane

Assisting Layout Designers Wibowo Rusli, Katie Thuy Bui, Carlos Solarte
Cover Designer Marika Kozak
Language Content Coordinator Quentin Frayne
Project Manager Chris Love

Thanks to Carolyn Boicos, Glenn van der Knijff, Sally Darmody, Celia Wood, Dora Chai, LPI, Mark Germanchis, Jacqueline McLeod

THANKS
NICK RAY

As always, so many people have been instrumental in helping to put this book together. First thanks to my wonderful wife, Kulikar Sotho, who has joined me on many a trip through the Mekong region, sharing boats and bikes the length and breadth of the river. Thanks also to our wonderful young son Mr J (aka Julian Ang Ray) for joining in the softer adventures along the way. Thanks to Mum

LONELY PLANET: TRAVEL WIDELY, TREAD LIGHTLY, GIVE SUSTAINABLY

The Lonely Planet Story
The story begins with a classic travel adventure: Tony and Maureen Wheeler's 1972 journey across Europe and Asia to Australia. There was no useful information about the overland trail then, so Tony and Maureen published the first Lonely Planet guidebook to meet a growing need.

From a kitchen table, Lonely Planet has grown to become the largest independent travel publisher in the world, with offices in Melbourne (Australia), Oakland (USA) and London (UK). Today Lonely Planet guidebooks cover the globe. There is an ever-growing list of books and information in a variety of media. Some things haven't changed. The main aim is still to make it possible for adventurous individuals to get out there – to explore and better understand the world.

The Lonely Planet Foundation
The Lonely Planet Foundation proudly supports nimble nonprofit institutions working for change in the world. Each year the foundation donates 5% of Lonely Planet company profits to projects selected by staff and authors. Our partners range from Kabissa, which provides small nonprofits across Africa with access to technology, to the Foundation for Developing Cambodian Orphans, which supports girls at risk of falling victim to sex traffickers.

Our nonprofit partners are linked by a grass-roots approach to the areas of health, education or sustainable tourism. Many projects we support – such as one with BaAka (Pygmy) children in the forested areas of Central African Republic – choose to focus on women and children as one of the most effective ways to support the whole community.

Sometimes foundation assistance is as simple as helping to preserve a local ruin like the Minaret of Jam in Afghanistan; this incredible monument now draws intrepid tourists to the area and its restoration has greatly improved options for local people.

Just as travel is often about learning to see with new eyes, so many of the groups we work with aim to change the way people see themselves and the future for their children and communities.

and Dad for the support and encouragement that carried me to faraway lands from a young age. And thanks to my extended Cambodian family for understanding my Mekong meanders.

It's a hideous cliché, but there really are too many people to thank on a book like this that covers such an incredible selection of countries. To those of you that have helped, my heartfelt thanks and I extend an open invitation for a sunset drink on the shores of the Mekong.

Thanks to my coauthors for all their work in other parts of the Mekong region, including my old friend and coconspirator Andrew Burke. And a big thanks to the in-house team at Lonely Planet who carried this from conception to reality. Finally, thanks to all the readers who have written in, you're all part of the big picture.

TIM BEWER

A hearty *khàwp khun mâak khráp* to the perpetually friendly people of Thailand who never hesitated to answer my endless questions. I owe an extra special thanks to Tommy Manophaiboon, June Niampan, Veena Puntace, Yata Saengpromsri and Julian Wright, who all helped well beyond the call of duty. Also Bulan Boonphan, Noppadol Khayanngan, Akekapob Polsamart, Kejsiri Pongkietkong, Nuan Sarnsorn and Panleka Suebma, who

---

SEND US YOUR FEEDBACK

We love to hear from travellers – your comments keep us on our toes and help make our books better. Our well-travelled team reads every word on what you loved or loathed about this book. Although we cannot reply individually to postal submissions, we always guarantee that your feedback goes straight to the appropriate authors, in time for the next edition. Each person who sends us information is thanked in the next edition – and the most useful submissions are rewarded with a free book.

To send us your updates – and find out about Lonely Planet events, newsletters and travel news – visit our award-winning website: **www.lonelyplanet.com/contact**.

Note: we may edit, reproduce and incorporate your comments in Lonely Planet products such as guidebooks, websites and digital products, so let us know if you don't want your comments reproduced or your name acknowledged. For a copy of our privacy policy visit www.lonelyplanet.com/privacy.

---

all provided good help and good company. Finally, a big thanks to my fellow authors on this, and the *Thailand* book.

ANDREW BURKE

There are many whom I owe a *khàwp jai lǎi lǎi* for their help in making this book possible. In Laos, Paul Eshoo in particular was a huge help and his dedication to village tourism is inspiring. Others who selflessly offered their friendship and expertise include Steven Schipani, Martin Rathie, Grace Nicholas and Tom Greenwood, Tom Morgan, Bridget McIntosh, Virginia Addison and Annette Monreal in Vientiane; Rachel and Joe Murphy in Vang Vieng; Jan Burrows, Suthep and Somkiad in Tha Khaek; 'Uncle Lee' in Ban Kheun Kham; Oudomxay Thongsavath and Khaisy Vongphoumy in Savannakhet; Craig and Natasha in Salavan; Buali, Emma Townsend-Gault, Phu Vong, Alan and Sririporn and Alex Azis in Pakse; Patrizia Zolese in Champasak; Eric Meusch and Mr Yai in Attapeu; and Bill Robichaud and Jim Johnstone in the middle of nowhere. And to all those guys who appeared from nowhere to fix my bike when the throttle cable snapped, a big thank you!

Several travelling companions made the journey more fun, particular thanks to Andrew Williamson, Frank Zeller, Paul and Simon, Stewart and Ingrid and Jon and Penny.

A special thanks to Justine Vaisutis for sharing my passion for Laos and going the extra miles in the name of research, and to Joe Cummings for the accumulated knowledge we have inherited. Thanks to Kalya Ryan and the various editors and cartographers at LPHQ who put up with me. Last but not least, the biggest thanks of all to my lovely wife, Anne.

THOMAS HUHTI

The following have accumulated boatloads of karma as helpers and/or good-humoured travel mates: Jiang Yingyu, Yang Chunlin and Duan Binbin (Jianchuan); Abe and Kyra (Kūnmíng); Sinon, Lao Zhang and the rest at my wondrous Kūnmíng HQ; Billy Zhao, Sim, Maki and urchins (Chéngdū); the inimitable Nan Qing (Menglian); Liu Jing (Luoping).

And to the people of China in general a huge smile, nod of the head and deep thank you. Your curiosity, eagerness to help, and especially willingness to smile made memorable what can be such a slog.

Thanks to all readers who take the time to write in and, especially, help other travellers on the Thorn Tree.

Bless Amy, Carlos, Dan and the rest of my Madison second family for letting me get away with it all yet again (and their support); and of course my family for their unvanquishable support and bottomless patience.

None of it would be possible mentally without the durability of personal stereos, not to mention the artistry of Chris Whitley, Patty Griffin and Xuan Wei, and the words of Kevin Brockmeier and James Agee.

Most of all, thanks to Yuki and Bighead, for being there, even when so far away.

SIRADETH SENG

Thanks Cambodia for being hilarious and unique. Thanks Mr Keo Serey Utha from Pursat, Mr OK from Battambang, Mrs 'Om' Bol from Veal Veng, Miss Dary from Kratie – the best moto guide in Cambodia! Jim from C2 and Jos from Kampot. Thank you Kalya Ryan for being unintimidating and patient and Nick Ray for all the advice. A million thanks to Mum (Chanda), Dad (Lim), Soc, Nina and Molica for all of your help, much appreciated! Thanks Fin and Callum for letting me go, Zach, Claire and Jonny for always cheering me on and Troy for absolutely everything!

ACKNOWLEDGMENTS

Many thanks to the following for the use of their content:

Globe on title page ©Mountain High Maps 1993 Digital Wisdom, Inc.

Index

INDEX

INDEX

INDEX

000 Map pages
000 Photograph pages

INDEX

INDEX

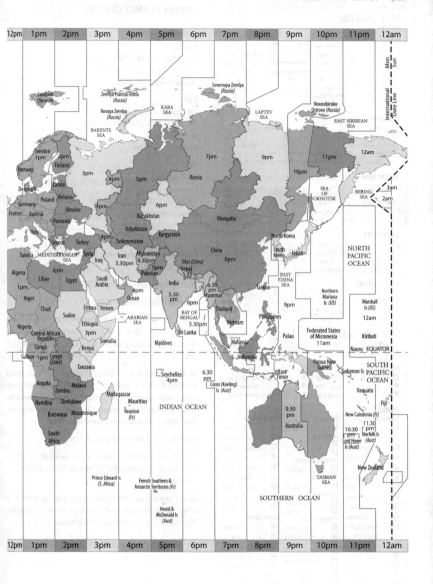

International Date Line

Mon
Sun

Svalbard
(Norway)

Zemlya Frantsa-Iosifa
(Russia)

Severnaya Zemlya
(Russia)

Novaya Zemlya
(Russia)

KARA
SEA

LAPTEV
SEA

Novosibirskie
Ostrovo (Russia)

EAST SIBERIAN
SEA

BARENTS
SEA

Sweden
1pm   2pm
Finland

7pm

9pm

11pm

12am

Norway
3pm

Denmark   4pm   5pm
Latvia

Russia

SEA
OF
OKHOTSK

3am

BERING
SEA   2am

Germany   Poland   Belarus
Austria   Ukraine
France

4pm

6pm

10pm

Italy   Romania

Greece   Turkey   4pm
Uzbekistan   Kyrgyzstan

Kazakhstan

Mongolia

North Korea

Tunisia   MEDITERRANEAN   Syria
SEA   Iraq   Turkmenistan

Iran   Afghanistan
3.30pm   4.30pm

China

8pm

South
Korea   Japan

NORTH
PACIFIC
OCEAN

Algeria   2pm
Libya   Egypt
Saudi
Arabia

Nepal
5.45
pm
Pakistan

Tibet (China)

EAST
CHINA
SEA

Taiwan

Northern
Mariana
Is (US)

Marshall
Is (US)

1pm

Niger   Chad   Sudan
Oman   4pm
India

6.30
pm
Myanmar

9pm

12am

Eritrea   Yemen
ARABIAN
SEA

5.30
pm

6pm
5.30pm

Thailand

Philippines

Federated States
of Micronesia
11am

Kiribati

Nigeria
Central African
Republic
Ethiopia   3pm

BAY OF
BENGAL

Vietnam

Palau

Nauru   EQUATOR

Congo   Somalia
Gabon   1pm   Kenya
Congo
(Zaire)

Sri Lanka

Maldives

Malaysia

SOUTH
PACIFIC
OCEAN

Tanzania

Seychelles
4pm

6.30
pm
Cocos (Keeling)
Is (Aust)

Indonesia

East
Timor

Papua New
Guinea

Solomon Is

Vanuatu

Angola   Malawi
Zambia
Namibia   Zimbabwe
Botswana   Mozambique

Madagascar
Mauritius

Reunion
(Fr)

INDIAN OCEAN

9.30
pm

Australia

New Caledonia (Fr)

Fiji

11.30
pm
10.30   Norfolk Is
pm   (Aust)
Lord Howe
Is (Aust)

South
Africa

Prince Edward Is
(S. Africa)

French Southern &
Antarctic Territories (Fr)
3w

TASMAN
SEA

New Zealand

Heard &
McDonald Is
(Aust)

SOUTHERN OCEAN

MAP LEGEND

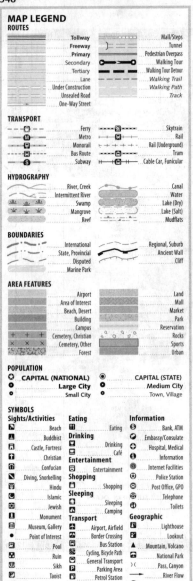

ROUTES

Tollway	Mall/Steps
Freeway	Tunnel
Primary	Pedestrian Overpass
Secondary	Walking Tour
Tertiary	Walking Tour Detour
Lane	Walking Trail
Under Construction	Walking Path
Unsealed Road	Track
One-Way Street	

TRANSPORT

Ferry	Skytrain
Metro	Rail
Monorail	Rail (Underground)
Bus Route	Tram
Subway	Cable Car, Funicular

HYDROGRAPHY

River, Creek	Canal
Intermittent River	Water
Swamp	Lake (Dry)
Mangrove	Lake (Salt)
Reef	Mudflats

BOUNDARIES

International	Regional, Suburb
State, Provincial	Ancient Wall
Disputed	Cliff
Marine Park	

AREA FEATURES

Airport	Land
Area of Interest	Mall
Beach, Desert	Market
Building	Park
Campus	Reservation
Cemetery, Christian	Rocks
Cemetery, Other	Sports
Forest	Urban

POPULATION

CAPITAL (NATIONAL)	CAPITAL (STATE)
Large City	Medium City
Small City	Town, Village

SYMBOLS

Sights/Activities
Beach
Buddhist
Castle, Fortress
Christian
Confucian
Diving, Snorkelling
Hindu
Islamic
Jewish
Monument
Museum, Gallery
Point of Interest
Pool
Ruin
Sikh
Taoist
Zoo, Bird Sanctuary

Eating
Eating

Drinking
Drinking
Café

Entertainment
Entertainment

Shopping
Shopping

Sleeping
Sleeping
Camping

Transport
Airport, Airfield
Border Crossing
Bus Station
Cycling, Bicycle Path
General Transport
Parking Area
Petrol Station
Taxi Rank

Information
Bank, ATM
Embassy/Consulate
Hospital, Medical
Information
Internet Facilities
Police Station
Post Office, GPO
Telephone
Toilets

Geographic
Lighthouse
Lookout
Mountain, Volcano
National Park
Pass, Canyon
River Flow
Waterfall

LONELY PLANET OFFICES

Australia
Head Office
Locked Bag 1, Footscray, Victoria 3011
☎ 03 8379 8000, fax 03 8379 8111
talk2us@lonelyplanet.com.au

USA
150 Linden St, Oakland, CA 94607
☎ 510 893 8555, toll free 800 275 8555
fax 510 893 8572
info@lonelyplanet.com

UK
72–82 Rosebery Ave,
Clerkenwell, London EC1R 4RW
☎ 020 7841 9000, fax 020 7841 9001
go@lonelyplanet.co.uk

Published by Lonely Planet Publications Pty Ltd
ABN 36 005 607 983

© Lonely Planet Publications Pty Ltd 2007

© photographers as indicated 2007

Cover photograph: Rowboats at dusk, Mekong Delta, Vietnam, Stuart Dee/Getty Images. Many of the images in this guide are available for licensing from Lonely Planet Images: www.lonelyplanetimages.com.